Standard Book Numbering:
  No. 8715 2011 7
Library of Congress Catalogue Number: 61-60771

This volume, "Heads of Families, First Census of the United States, 1790 — State of North Carolina", is one of a 12-volume set covering all the available records of the original Census.

Other States on which the 1790 Census are available include: South Carolina, Virginia, Pennsylvania, New Hampshire, Maryland, Rhode Island, Maine, Vermont, Connecticut, Massachusetts and New York.

The Reprint Company is specializing in Colonial and Revolutiona₁y period history in two distinct divisons: (1) Basic material on the Settlement and Colonial periods and (2) Major Battles and Campaigns of the Revolution.

Basic histories available include: Georgia—Author, Jones; Maryland—Authors, McSherry, McMahon, Bozman; New York—Authors, O'Callaghan and Lossing; North Carolina—Authors, Hawks, Creecy; New Jersey—Authors, Smith, Barber & Howe; Pennsylvania—Authors, Proud, Gordon; South Carolina—Authors, Hewatt, Ramsay, Logan, Gregg, Landrum; Virginia — Authors, Stith, Campbell.

Revolutionary period volumes include: Draper's King's Mountain; Stryker's Trenton and Princeton; Tarleton's Campaigns in Southern Provinces (N.C., S. C., Va.); Schenck's Campaigns and Battles in North Carolina, South Carolina and Virginia, Landrum's Battles in Upper South Carolina; French and Murdock's Concord, Lexington, Bunker Hill and Siege of Boston.

Reprint Company also has completed and has available a six-volume set on Women of Colonial and Revolutionary Times. These volumes are: "Martha Washington" and "Dolly Madison" of Virginia; "Eliza Pinckney" of South Carolina; "Catherine Schuyler" of New York; "Margaret Winthrop" and "Mercy Warren" of Massachusetts.

Volumes on Colonial America and the Revolutionary Battles and Campaigns are constantly being added to our list of reprints.

The Reprint Company
154 W. Cleveland Park Drive
Spartanburg, S. C., 29303

First Printing — January, 1961.
Second Printing — November, 1964.
Third Printing—November, 1966.
Fourth Printing — October, 1968.

FIRST CENSUS
OF THE UNITED STATES
1790

❧

NORTH CAROLINA

DEPARTMENT OF COMMERCE AND LABOR

BUREAU OF THE CENSUS

S. N. D. NORTH, DIRECTOR

——

HEADS OF FAMILIES

AT THE FIRST CENSUS OF THE

UNITED STATES TAKEN

IN THE YEAR

1790

NORTH CAROLINA

WASHINGTON

GOVERNMENT PRINTING OFFICE

1908

HEADS OF FAMILIES AT THE FIRST CENSUS
1790

INTRODUCTION.

The First Census of the United States (1790) comprised an enumeration of the inhabitants of the present states of Connecticut, Delaware, Georgia, Kentucky, Maine, Maryland, Massachusetts, New Hampshire, New Jersey, New York, North Carolina, Pennsylvania, Rhode Island, South Carolina, Tennessee, Vermont, and Virginia.

A complete set of the schedules for each state, with a summary for the counties, and in many cases for towns, was filed in the State Department, but unfortunately they are not now complete, the returns for the states of Delaware, Georgia, Kentucky, New Jersey, Tennessee, and Virginia having been destroyed when the British burned the Capitol at Washington during the War of 1812. For several of the states for which schedules are lacking it is probable that the Director of the Census could obtain lists which would present the names of most of the heads of families at the date of the First Census. In Virginia, state enumerations were made in 1782, 1783, 1784, and 1785, but the lists on file in the State Library include the names for only 39 of the 78 counties into which the state was divided.

The schedules of 1790 form a unique inheritance for the Nation, since they represent for each of the states concerned a complete list of the heads of families in the United States at the time of the adoption of the Constitution. The framers were the statesmen and leaders of thought, but those whose names appear upon the schedules of the First Census were in general the plain citizens who by their conduct in war and peace made the Constitution possible and by their intelligence and self-restraint put it into successful operation.

The total population of the United States in 1790, exclusive of slaves, as derived from the schedules was 3,231,533. The only names appearing upon the schedules, however, were those of heads of families, and as at that period the families averaged 6 persons, the total number was approximately 540,000, or slightly more than half a million. The number of names which is now lacking because of the destruction of the schedules is approximately 140,000, thus leaving schedules containing about 400,000 names.

The information contained in the published report of the First Census of the United States, a small volume of 56 pages, was not uniform for the several states and territories. For New England and one or two of the other states the population was presented by counties and towns; that of New Jersey appeared partly by counties and towns and partly by counties only; in other cases the returns were given by counties only. Thus the complete transcript of the names of heads of families, with accompanying information, presents for the first time detailed information as to the number of inhabitants—males, females, etc.—for each minor civil division in all those states for which such information was not originally published.

In response to repeated requests from patriotic societies and persons interested in genealogy, or desirous of studying the early history of the United States, Congress added to the sundry civil appropriation bill for the fiscal year 1907 the following paragraph:

The Director of the Census is hereby authorized and directed to publish, in a permanent form, by counties and minor civil divisions, the names of the heads of families returned at the First Census of the United States in seventeen hundred and ninety; and the Director of the Census is authorized, in his discretion, to sell said publications, the proceeds thereof to be covered into the Treasury of the United States, to be deposited to the credit of miscellaneous receipts on account of "Proceeds of sales of Government property:"

Provided, That no expense shall be incurred hereunder additional to appropriations for the Census Office for printing therefor made for the fiscal year nineteen hundred and seven; and the Director of the Census is hereby directed to report to Congress at its next session the cost incurred hereunder and the price fixed for said publications and the total received therefor.

The amount of money appropriated by Congress for the Census printing for the fiscal year mentioned was unfortunately not sufficient to meet the current requirement of the Office and to publish the transcription of the First Census, and no provision was made in the sundry civil appropriation bill for 1908 for the continuance of authority to publish these important records. Resources, however, were available for printing a small section of the work, and the schedules of New Hampshire, Vermont, and Maryland accordingly were published.

The urgent deficiency bill, approved February 15, 1908, contained the following provision:

That the Director of the Census is hereby authorized and directed to expend so much of the appropriation for printing for the Department of Commerce and Labor allotted by law to the Census Office for the fiscal year ending June thirtieth, nineteen hundred and eight, as may be necessary to continue and complete the publication of the names of the heads of families returned at the First Census of the United States, as authorized by the sundry civil appropriation act approved June thirtieth, nineteen hundred and six.

In accordance with the authority given in the paragraph quoted above, the names returned at the First Census in the states of Connecticut, Maine, Massachusetts, New York, North Carolina, Pennsylvania, Rhode Island, and South Carolina have been published, thus completing the roster of the heads of families in 1790 so far as they can be shown from the records of the Census Office. As the Federal census schedules of the state of Virginia for 1790 are missing, the lists of the state enumerations made in 1782, 1783, 1784, and 1785 have been substituted and, while not complete, they will, undoubtedly, prove of great value.

THE FIRST CENSUS.

The First Census act was passed at the second session of the First Congress, and was signed by President Washington on March 1, 1790. The task of making the first enumeration of inhabitants was placed upon the President. Under this law the marshals of the several judicial districts were required to ascertain the number of inhabitants within their respective districts, omitting Indians not taxed, and distinguishing free persons (including those bound to service for a term of years) from all others; the sex and color of free persons; and the number of free males 16 years of age and over.

The object of the inquiry last mentioned was, undoubtedly, to obtain definite knowledge as to the military and industrial strength of the country. This fact possesses special interest, because the Constitution directs merely an enumeration of inhabitants. Thus the demand for increasingly extensive information, which has been so marked a characteristic of census legislation, began with the First Congress that dealt with the subject.

The method followed by the President in putting into operation the First Census law, although the object of extended investigation, is not definitely known. It is supposed that the President or the Secretary of State dispatched copies of the law, and perhaps of instructions also, to the marshals. There is, however, some ground for disputing this conclusion. At least one of the reports in the census volume of 1790 was furnished by a governor. This, together with the fact that there is no record of correspondence with the marshals on the subject of the census, but that there is a record of such correspondence with the governors, makes very strong the inference that the marshals received their instructions through the governors of the states. This inference is strengthened by the fact that in 1790 the state of Massachusetts furnished the printed blanks, and also by the fact that the law relating to the Second Census specifically charged the Secretary of State to superintend the enumeration and to communicate directly with the marshals.

By the terms of the First Census law nine months were allowed in which to complete the enumeration. The census taking was supervised by the marshals of the several judicial districts, who employed assistant marshals to act as enumerators. There were 17 marshals. The records showing the number of assistant marshals employed in 1790, 1800, and 1810 were destroyed by fire, but the number employed in 1790 has been estimated at 650.

The schedules which these officials prepared consist of lists of names of heads of families; each name appears in a stub, or first column, which is followed by five columns, giving details of the family. These columns are headed as follows:

Free white males of 16 years and upward, including heads of families.
Free white males under 16 years.
Free white females, including heads of families.
All other free persons.
Slaves.

The assistant marshals made two copies of the returns; in accordance with the law one copy was posted in the immediate neighborhood for the information of the public, and the other was transmitted to the marshal in charge, to be forwarded to the President. The schedules were turned over by the President to the Secretary of State. Little or no tabulation was required, and the report of the First Census, as also the reports of the Second, Third, and Fourth, was produced without the employment of any clerical force, the summaries being transmitted directly to the printer. The total population as returned in 1790 was 3,929,214, and the entire cost of the census was $44,377.

A summary of the results of the First Census, not including the returns for South Carolina, was transmitted to Congress by President Washington on October 27, 1791. The legal period for enumeration, nine months, had been extended, the longest time consumed being eighteen months in South Carolina. The report of October 27 was printed in full, and published in what is now a very rare little volume; afterwards the report for South Carolina was "tipped in." To contain the results of the Twelfth Census, ten large quarto volumes, comprising in all 10,400 pages, were required. No illustration of the expansion of census inquiry can be more striking.

The original schedules of the First Census are now contained in 26 bound volumes, preserved in the Census Office. For the most part the headings of the schedules were written in by hand. Indeed, up to and including 1820, the assistant marshals generally used for the schedules such paper as they happened to have, ruling it, writing in the headings, and binding the sheets together themselves. In some cases merchants' account paper was used, and now and then the schedules were bound in wall paper.

As a consequence of requiring marshals to supply their own blanks, the volumes containing the schedules vary in size from about 7 inches long, 3 inches wide, and ½ inch thick to 21 inches long, 14 inches wide, and 6 inches thick. Some of the sheets in these volumes are only 4 inches long, but a few are 3 feet in length, necessitating several folds. In some cases leaves burned at the edges have been covered with transparent silk to preserve them.

THE UNITED STATES IN 1790.

In March, 1790, the Union consisted of twelve states—Rhode Island, the last of the original thirteen to enter the Union, being admitted May 29 of the same year. Vermont, the first addition, was admitted in the following year, before the results of the First Census were announced. Maine was a part of Massachusetts, Kentucky was a part of Virginia, and the present states of Alabama and Mississippi were parts of Georgia. The present states of Ohio, Indiana, Illinois, Michigan, and Wisconsin, with part of Minnesota, were known as the Northwest Territory, and the present state of Tennessee, then a part of North Carolina, was soon to be organized as the Southwest Territory.

The United States was bounded on the west by the Mississippi river, beyond which stretched that vast and unexplored wilderness belonging to the Spanish King, which was afterwards ceded to the United States by France as the Louisiana Purchase, and now comprises the great and populous states of South Dakota, Iowa. Nebraska, Missouri, Kansas, Arkansas, and Oklahoma, and portions of Minnesota, North Dakota, Montana, Wyoming, Colorado, New Mexico, Texas, and Louisiana. The Louisiana Purchase was not consummated for more than a decade after the First Census was taken. On the south was another Spanish colony known as the Floridas. The greater part of Texas, then a part of the colony of Mexico, belonged to Spain; and California, Nevada, Utah, Arizona, and a portion of New Mexico, also the property of Spain, although penetrated here and there by venturesome explorers and missionaries, were, for the most part, an undiscovered wilderness.

The gross area of the United States was 827,844 square miles, but the settled area was only 239,935 square miles, or about 29 per cent of the total. Though the area covered by the enumeration in 1790 seems very small when compared with the present area of the United States, the difficulties which confronted the census taker were vastly greater than in 1900. In many localities there were no roads, and where these did exist they were poor and frequently impassable; bridges were almost unknown. Transportation was entirely by horseback, stage, or private coach. A journey as long as that from New York to Washington was a serious undertaking, requiring eight days under the most favorable conditions. Western New York was a wilderness, Elmira and Binghamton being but detached hamlets. The territory west of the Allegheny mountains, with the exception of a portion of Kentucky, was unsettled and scarcely penetrated. Detroit and Vincennes were too small and isolated to merit consideration. Philadelphia was the capital of the United States. Washington was a mere Government project, not even named, but known as the Federal City. Indeed, by the spring of 1793, only one wall of the White House had been constructed, and the site for the Capitol had been merely surveyed. New York city in 1790 possessed a population of only 33,131, although it was the largest city in the United States; Philadelphia was second, with 28,522; and Boston third, with 18,320. Mails were transported in very irregular fashion, and correspondence was expensive and uncertain.

There were, moreover, other difficulties which were of serious moment in 1790, but which long ago ceased to be problems in census taking. The inhabitants, having no experience with census taking, imagined that some scheme for increasing taxation was involved, and were inclined to be cautious lest they should reveal too much of their own affairs. There was also opposition to enumeration on religious grounds, a count of inhabitants being regarded by many as a cause for divine displeasure. The boundaries of towns and other minor divisions, and even those of counties, were in many cases unknown or not defined at all. The hitherto semi-independent states had been under the control of the Federal Government for so short a time that the different sections had not yet been welded into an harmonious nationality in which the Federal authority should be unquestioned and instructions promptly and fully obeyed.

AN ACT PROVIDING FOR THE ENUMERATION OF THE INHABITANTS OF THE UNITED STATES

APPROVED MARCH 1, 1790

SECTION 1. Be it enacted by the Senate and House of Representatives of the United States of America in Congress assembled, That the marshals of the several districts of the United States shall be, and they are hereby authorized and required to cause the number of the inhabitants within their respective districts to be taken; omitting in such enumeration Indians not taxed, and distinguishing free persons, including those bound to service for a term of years, from all others; distinguishing also the sexes and colours of free persons, and the free males of sixteen years and upwards from those under that age; for effecting which purpose the marshals shall have power to appoint as many assistants within their respective districts as to them shall appear necessary; assigning to each assistant a certain division of his district, which division shall consist of one or more counties, cities, towns, townships, hundreds or parishes, or of a territory plainly and distinctly bounded by water courses, mountains, or public roads. The marshals and their assistants shall respectively take an oath or affirmation, before some judge or justice of the peace, resident within their respective districts, previous to their entering on the discharge of the duties by this act required. The oath or affirmation of the marshal shall be, "I, A. B., Marshal of the district of ———, do solemnly swear (or affirm) that I will well and truly cause to be made a just and perfect enumeration and description of all persons resident within my district, and return the same to the President of the United States, agreeably to the directions of an act of Congress, intituled 'An act providing for the enumeration of the inhabitants of the United States,' according to the best of my ability." The oath or affirmation of an assistant shall be "I, A. B., do solemnly swear (or affirm) that I will make a just and perfect enumeration and description of all persons resident within the division assigned to me by the marshal of the district of ———, and make due return thereof to the said marshal, agreeably to the directions of an act of Congress, intituled 'An act providing for the enumeration of the inhabitants of the United States,' according to the best of my ability." The enumeration shall commence on the first Monday in August next, and shall close within nine calendar months thereafter. The several assistants shall, within the said nine months, transmit to the marshals by whom they shall be respectively appointed, accurate returns of all persons, except Indians not taxed, within their respective divisions, which returns shall be made in a schedule, distinguishing the several families by the names of their master, mistress, steward, overseer, or other principal person therein, in manner following, that is to say:

The number of persons within my division, consisting of ———, appears in a schedule hereto annexed, subscribed by me this ——— day of ———, 179-. A. B. *Assistant to the marshal of* ———.

Schedule of the whole number of persons within the division allotted to A. B.

Names of heads of families.	Free white males of 16 years and upwards, including heads of families.	Free white males under 16 years.	Free white females, including heads of families.	All other free persons.	Slaves.

SECTION 2. And be it further enacted, That every assistant failing to make return, or making a false return of the enumeration to the marshal, within the time by this act limited, shall forfeit the sum of two hundred dollars.

SECTION 3. And be it further enacted, That the marshals shall file the several returns aforesaid, with the clerks of their respective district courts, who are hereby directed to receive and carefully preserve the same: And the marshals respectively shall, on or before the first day of September, one thousand seven hundred and ninety-one, transmit to the President of the United States, the aggregate amount of each description of persons within their respective districts. And every marshal failing to file the returns of his assistants, or any of them, with the clerks of their respective district courts, or failing to return the aggregate amount of each description of persons in their respective districts, as the same shall appear from said returns, to the President of the United States within the time limited by this act, shall, for every such offense, forfeit the sum of eight hundred dollars; all which forfeitures shall be recoverable in the courts of the districts where the offenses shall be committed, or in the circuit courts to be held within the same, by action of debt, information or indictment; the one-half thereof to the use of the United States, and the other half to the informer; but where the prosecution shall be first instituted on the behalf of the United States, the whole shall accrue to their use. And for the more effectual discovery of offenses, the judges of the several district courts, at their next sessions, to be held after the expiration of the time allowed for making the returns of the enumeration hereby directed, to the President of the United States, shall give this act in charge to the grand juries, in their respective courts, and shall cause the returns of the several assistants to be laid before them for their inspection.

SECTION 4. And be it further enacted, That every assistant shall receive at the rate of one dollar for every one hundred and fifty persons by him returned, where such persons reside in the country; and where such persons reside in a city, or town, containing more than five thousand persons, such assistants shall receive at the rate of one dollar for every three hundred persons; but where, from the dispersed situation of the inhabitants in some divisions, one dollar for every one hundred and fifty persons shall be insufficient, the marshals, with the approbation of the judges of their respective districts, may make such further allowance to the assistants in such divisions as shall be deemed an adequate compensation, provided the same does not exceed one dollar for every fifty persons by them returned. The several marshals shall receive as follows: The marshal of the district of Maine, two hundred dollars; the marshal of the district of New Hampshire, two hundred dollars; the marshal of the district of Massachusetts, three hundred dollars; the marshal of the district of Connecticut, two hundred dollars; the marshal of the district of New York, three hundred dollars; the marshal of the district of New Jersey, two hundred dollars; the marshal of the district of Pennsylvania, three hundred dollars; the marshal of the district of Delaware, one hundred dollars; the marshal of the district of Maryland, three hundred dollars; the marshal of the district of Virginia, five hundred dollars; the marshal of the district of Kentucky, two hundred and fifty dollars; the marshal of the district of North Carolina, three hundred and fifty dollars; the marshal of the district of South Carolina, three hundred dollars; the marshal of the district of Georgia, two hundred and fifty dollars. And to obviate all doubts which may arise respecting the persons to be returned, and the manner of making the returns.

SECTION 5. Be it enacted, That every person whose usual place of abode shall be in any family on the aforesaid first Monday in August next, shall be returned as of such family; the name of every person, who shall be an inhabitant of any district, but without a settled place of residence, shall be inserted in the column of the aforesaid schedule, which is allotted for the heads of families, in that division where he or she shall be on the said first Monday in August next, and every person occasionally absent at the time of the enumeration, as belonging to that place in which he usually resides in the United States.

SECTION 6. And be it further enacted, That each and every person more than 16 years of age, whether heads of families or not, belonging to any family within any division of a district made or established within the United States, shall be, and hereby is, obliged to render to such assistant of the division, a true account, if required, to the best of his or her knowledge, of all and every person belonging to such family, respectively, according to the several descriptions aforesaid, on pain of forfeiting twenty dollars, to be sued for and recovered by such assistant, the one-half for his own use, and the other half for the use of the United States.

SECTION 7. And be it further enacted, That each assistant shall, previous to making his return to the marshal, cause a correct copy, signed by himself, of the schedule containing the number of inhabitants within his division, to be set up at two of the most public places within the same, there to remain for the inspection of all concerned; for each of which copies the said assistant shall be entitled to receive two dollars, provided proof of a copy of the schedule having been so set up and suffered to remain, shall be transmitted to the marshal, with the return of the number of persons; and in case any assistant shall fail to make such proof to the marshal, he shall forfeit the compensation by this act allowed him.

Approved March 1, 1790.

Population of the United States as returned at the First Census, by states: 1790.

DISTRICT.	Free white males of 16 years and upward, including heads of families.	Free white males under 16 years.	Free white females, including heads of families	All other free persons.	Slaves.	Total.
Vermont	22,435	22,328	40,505	255	[1] 16	[2] 85,539
New Hampshire	36,086	34,851	70,160	630	158	141,885
Maine	24,384	24,748	46,870	538	None.	96,540
Massachusetts	95,453	87,289	190,582	5,463	None.	378,787
Rhode Island	16,019	15,799	32,652	3,407	948	68,825
Connecticut	60,523	54,403	117,448	2,808	2,764	237,946
New York	83,700	78,122	152,320	4,654	21,324	340,120
New Jersey	45,251	41,416	83,287	2,762	11,423	184,139
Pennsylvania	110,788	106,948	206,363	6,537	3,737	434,373
Delaware	11,783	12,143	22,384	3,899	8,887	[3] 59,094
Maryland	55,915	51,339	101,395	8,043	103,036	319,728
Virginia	110,936	116,135	215,046	12,866	292,627	747,610
Kentucky	15,154	17,057	28,922	114	12,430	73,677
North Carolina	69,988	77,506	140,710	4,975	100,572	393,751
South Carolina	35,576	37,722	66,880	1,801	107,094	249,073
Georgia	13,103	14,044	25,739	398	29,264	82,548
Total number of inhabitants of the United States exclusive of S. Western and N. territory	807,094	791,850	1,541,263	59,150	694,280	3,893,635

	Free white males of 21 years and upward.	Free males under 21 years of age.	Free white females.	All other persons.	Slaves.	Total.
S. W. territory	6,271	10,277	15,365	361	3,417	35,691
N. "						

[1] The census of 1790, published in 1791, reports 16 slaves in Vermont. Subsequently, and up to 1860, the number is given as 17. An examination of the original manuscript returns shows that there never were any slaves in Vermont. The original error occurred in preparing the results for publication, when 16 persons, returned as "Free colored," were classified as "Slave."

[2] Corrected figures are 85,425, or 114 less than figures published in 1790, due to an error of addition in the returns for each of the towns of Fairfield, Milton, Shelburne, and Williston, in the county of Chittenden; Brookfield, Newbury, Randolph, and Strafford, in the county of Orange; Castleton, Clarendon, Hubbardton, Poultney, Rutland, Shrewsbury, and Wallingford, in the county of Rutland; Dummerston, Guilford, Halifax, and Westminster, in the county of Windham; and Woodstock, in the county of Windsor.

[3] Corrected figures are 59,096, or 2 more than figures published in 1790, due to error in addition.

Summary of population, by districts and counties: 1790.

EDENTON DISTRICT.

COUNTY.	Number of heads of families.	Free white males of 16 years and upward, including heads of families.	Free white males under 16 years.	Free white females, including heads of families.	All other free persons.	Slaves.	Total.
Bertie	1,430	1,762	1,841	3,514	348	5,141	12,606
Camden	583	727	759	1,477	30	1,040	4,033
Chowan, excluding Edenton town	376	460	446	876	7	1,647	3,436
Edenton town	180	181	113	306	34	941	1,575
Currituck	794	1,017	1,024	1,960	115	1,103	5,219
Gates	629	790	775	1,515	93	2,219	5,392
Hertford	653	814	823	1,533	216	2,442	5,828
Pasquotank	799	951	1,034	1,810	79	1,623	5,497
Perquimans	709	885	923	1,717	37	1,878	5,440
Tyrrell	705	807	959	1,777	35	1,166	4,744
Total	6,858	8,394	8,697	16,485	994	19,200	53,770

FAYETTE DISTRICT.

COUNTY.	Number of heads of families.	Free white males of 16 years and upward, including heads of families.	Free white males under 16 years.	Free white females, including heads of families.	All other free persons.	Slaves.	Total.
Anson	790	1,034	1,183	2,047	41	828	5,133
Cumberland, excluding Fayetteville town	1,067	1,397	1,362	2,661	49	1,666	7,135
Fayetteville town	281	394	195	398	34	515	1,536
Moore	639	849	968	1,570	12	371	3,770
Richmond	830	1,096	1,205	2,116	55	583	5,055
Robeson	869	1,131	1,141	2,244	277	533	5,326
Sampson	935	1,145	1,281	2,316	140	1,183	6,065
Total	5,411	7,046	7,335	13,352	608	5,679	34,020

HALIFAX DISTRICT.

COUNTY.	Number of heads of families.	Free white males of 16 years and upward, including heads of families.	Free white males under 16 years.	Free white females, including heads of families.	All other free persons.	Slaves.	Total.
Edgecombe	1,260	1,659	1,879	3,495	70	3,152	10,255
Franklin	804	1,089	1,400	2,316	37	2,717	7,559
Halifax, including Halifax town	1,442	1,835	1,778	3,403	443	6,506	13,965
Martin	798	1,064	1,009	2,022	96	1,889	6,080
Nash	853	1,143	1,426	2,627	188	2,009	7,393
Northampton	1,113	1,334	1,273	2,503	462	4,409	9,981
Warren	800	1,070	1,319	2,220	68	4,720	9,397
Total	7,070	9,194	10,084	18,586	1,364	25,402	64,630

HILLSBOROUGH DISTRICT.

COUNTY.	Number of heads of families.	Free white males of 16 years and upward, including heads of families.	Free white males under 16 years.	Free white females, including heads of families.	All other free persons.	Slaves.	Total.
Caswell[1]	1,412	1,801	2,110	3,377	72	2,736	10,096
Caswell district	201						
Gloucester district	211						
Nash district	118						
Richmond district	253						
St. Davids district	166						
St. James district	111						
St. Lawrence district	215						
St. Lukes district	137						
Chatham	1,270	1,756	2,160	3,664	9	1,632	9,221
Granville[1]	966	1,581	1,873	3,050	315	4,163	10,982
Abraham's Plains district	62						
Beaver Dam district	80						
Dutch district	76						
Epping Forest district	65					74	
Fishing Creek district	59						
Fort Creek district	70						
Goshen district	67						
Henderson district	60						
Island Creek district	107						
Granville—Continued.							
Knap of Leeds district	77						
Oxford district	65					182	
Ragland district	58						
Tabb's Creek district	57						
Tar River district	63						
Orange[1]	1,534	2,433	2,709	4,913	101	2,060	12,216
Caswell district	200						
Chatham district	166						
Hillsboro district	187						
Hillsboro town	40						
Orange district	228						
St. Asaph's district	199						
St. Mark's district	138						
St. Mary's district	237						
St. Thomas' district	139						
Randolph	1,160	1,582	1,952	3,266	24	452	7,276
Wake	1,290	1,772	2,089	3,688	180	2,463	10,192
Total	7,632	10,925	12,893	21,958	701	13,506	59,983

MORGAN DISTRICT.

COUNTY.	Number of heads of families.	Free white males of 16 years and upward, including heads of families.	Free white males under 16 years.	Free white females, including heads of families.	All other free persons.	Slaves.	Total.
Burke	1,255	1,706	2,115	3,683	11	595	8,110
First company	114	170	219	357		92	838
Second company	80	90	148	263		24	525
Third company	84	120	156	248	7	76	607
Fourth company	80	99	129	203		10	441
Fifth company	85	124	146	275		51	596
Sixth company	98	141	169	306	2	59	677
Seventh company	99	124	152	268		87	631
Eighth company	113	150	183	324		28	685
Ninth company	114	147	187	317		26	677
Tenth company	74	99	126	213		21	459
Eleventh company	88	133	119	269		38	559
Twelfth company	73	94	155	217		15	481
Thirteenth company	153	215	226	423	2	68	934
Lincoln	1,409	2,053	2,294	4,037		935	9,319
First company	69	110	124	215		43	492
Second company	80	114	127	229		39	509
Third company	85	118	146	221		18	503
Fourth company	113	166	180	349		38	733
Fifth company	98	130	167	289		16	602
Sixth company	187	250	261	494		94	1,099
Seventh company	95	170	174	279		110	733
Eighth company	104	148	184	303		18	653
Ninth company	215	315	309	608		188	1,420
Tenth company	112	145	189	333		51	718
Eleventh company	125	201	227	351		230	1,009
Twelfth company	126	186	206	366		90	848
Rutherford	1,181	1,577	2,121	3,502	2	609	7,811
First company	76	105	110	218		140	573
Second company	84	110	147	244		80	581
Third company	54	70	110	150		60	390
Rutherford—Continued.							
Fourth company	54	71	101	169		24	365
Fifth company	100	97	139	235		22	493
Sixth company	103	151	216	379		50	796
Seventh company	73	111	138	230		35	514
Eighth company	75	103	154	248	2	20	527
Ninth company	98	119	167	287		11	584
Tenth company	85	114	165	259		60	598
Eleventh company	142	186	287	430		51	954
Twelfth company	105	139	209	305		39	692
Thirteenth company	62	93	93	163		9	358
Fourteenth company	70	108	85	185		8	386
Wilkes	1,277	1,615	2,251	3,739	2	549	8,156
First company	81	111	132	237		55	535
Second company	90	101	164	268		76	609
Third company	78	100	131	233	2	38	504
Fourth company	84	106	157	265		13	541
Fifth company	75	88	146	222		11	467
Sixth company	105	121	169	291		20	601
Seventh company	55	76	100	162		54	392
Eighth company	55	76	105	133		5	319
Ninth company	94	118	150	297		66	631
Tenth company	76	109	132	224		23	488
Eleventh company	85	109	149	246		96	600
Twelfth company	68	88	122	199		34	443
Thirteenth company	121	152	205	332		33	722
Fourteenth company	60	75	96	188		18	377
Fifteenth company	63	78	114	173		4	369
Sixteenth company	87	107	179	269		3	558
Total	10,244	13,902	17,562	29,922	30	5,376	66,792

[1] Names taken from county tax lists.

Summary of population, by districts and counties: 1790—Continued.

NEWBERN DISTRICT.

COUNTY	Number of heads of families.	Free white males of 16 years and upward, including heads of families.	Free white males under 16 years.	Free white females, including heads of families.	All other free persons.	Slaves.	Total.	COUNTY.	Number of heads of families.	Free white males of 16 years and upward, including heads of families.	Free white males under 16 years.	Free white females, including heads of families.	All other free persons.	Slaves.	Total.
Beaufort	780	951	926	1,824	129	1,632	5,462	Johnston	776	1,039	1,119	2,083	64	1,329	5,634
Carteret	578	718	707	1,502	92	713	3,732	Jones	583	736	794	1,541	70	1,681	4,822
Craven, including Newbern town	1,440	1,709	1,538	3,227	337	3,658	10,469	Pitt	1,095	1,461	1,507	2,915	25	2,367	8,275
Dobbs	915	1,162	1,293	2,478	45	1,915	6,893	Wayne	804	1,064	1,219	2,256	37	1,557	6,133
Hyde	625	795	718	1,522	37	1,048	4,120	Total	7,596	9,635	9,821	19,348	836	15,900	55,540

SALISBURY DISTRICT.

COUNTY	Number of heads of families.	Free white males of 16 years and upward, including heads of families.	Free white males under 16 years.	Free white females, including heads of families.	All other free persons.	Slaves.	Total.	COUNTY.	Number of heads of families.	Free white males of 16 years and upward, including heads of families.	Free white males under 16 years.	Free white females, including heads of families.	All other free persons.	Slaves.	Total.
Guilford	1,096	1,607	1,799	3,242	27	516	7,191	Stokes	1,329	1,846	2,104	3,778	13	787	8,528
Iredell	769	1,118	1,217	2,239	3	858	5,435	Surry	1,074	1,531	1,762	3,183	17	698	7,191
Mecklenburg	1,742	2,378	2,573	4,771	70	1,603	11,395	Total	9,988	13,908	15,826	28,366	242	8,138	66,480
Montgomery	703	967	1,121	1,798	5	834	4,725								
Rockingham	842	1,173	1,413	2,491	10	1,100	6,187								
Rowan, including Salisbury town	2,433	3,288	3,837	6,864	97	1,742	15,828								

WILMINGTON DISTRICT.

COUNTY	Number of heads of families.	Free white males of 16 years and upward, including heads of families.	Free white males under 16 years.	Free white females, including heads of families.	All other free persons.	Slaves.	Total.	COUNTY.	Number of heads of families.	Free white males of 16 years and upward, including heads of families.	Free white males under 16 years.	Free white females, including heads of families.	All other free persons.	Slaves.	Total.
Bladen	635	837	830	1,683	58	1,676	5,084	Onslow	721	828	939	1,788	84	1,748	3,639
Brunswick	320	380	398	779	3	1,511	3,071	Total	3,028	3,914	4,049	7,801	215	10,056	26,035
Duplin	724	1,035	1,187	2,054	3	1,383	5,662								
New Hanover, including Wilmington town	628	834	695	1,497	67	3,738	6,831								

Assistant marshals for the state: 1790.

DISTRICT.	NAME.	DISTRICT.	NAME.
Edenton district (part of) Bertie county.	Thomas Lee Harrimond.	Hillsborough district (part of) Chatham, Randolph, and Wake counties.	Ellick Sanders.
Edenton district (part of) Camden, Chowan (including Edenton town), Currituck, Pasquotank, and Perquimans counties.	Edmund Blount.	Hillsborough district (part of) Caswell, Granville, and Orange counties (missing).	
Edenton district (part of) Gates county.	James Walton.	Morgan district Burke, Lincoln, Rutherford, and Wilkes counties.	Joseph McDowell.
Edenton district (part of) Hertford county.	Amos Rayner.	Newbern district Beaufort, Carteret, Craven (including Newbern town), Dobbs, Hyde, Johnston, Jones, Pitt, and Wayne counties.	Edw. Pasteur.
Edenton district (part of) Tyrrell county.	Levi Blounts.	Salisbury district (part of) Guilford, Rockingham, Stokes, and Surry counties.	Tho. Henderson.
Fayette district Anson, Cumberland (including Fayetteville town), Moore, Richmond, Robeson, and Sampson counties.	Guilford Dudley.	Salisbury district (part of) Iredell, Mecklenburg, Montgomery, and Rowan (including Salisbury town) counties.	Lᵉ Beard.
Halifax district (part of) Edgecombe, Halifax (including Halifax town), and Martin counties.	Hance Bond.	Wilmington district Bladen, Brunswick, Duplin, New Hanover (including Wilmington town), and Onslow counties.	James Kenan.
Halifax district (part of) Franklin, Nash, and Warren counties.	Benjamin Moss.		
Halifax district (part of) Northampton county.	Rich. W. Freear.		

EDENTON DISTRICT, BERTIE COUNTY.[1]

NAME OF HEAD OF FAMILY.	Free white males of 16 years and upward, including heads of families.	Free white males under 16 years.	Free white females, including heads of families.	All other free persons.	Slaves.
Armistead, Anthony	1		1		13
Ashburn, William	3	2	5	2	12
Ashburn, Benjᵃ	3		1	7	
Asben, James	3	2	4		
Arnold, Richᵈ	3	2	4		8
Archebᵈ, James	3	2	4		
Aulsshart, Alexʳ	1	2	5		
Armistead, William	4	1	4	4	33
Askew, Thomas	1	1			
Askew, James	1	1	3		2
Asbald, James	2	2	4		
Askew, Ann	1		1		
Askew, William	1	1	1		
Askew, John	1		1		2
Avis, Abraham	1	1	2		7
Asbald, Aaron	1	3	4		1
Adkins, Metehill	1	4	2		1
Acru, John	1	1	3		2
Acru, William	1		1	2	12
Acru, Edwᵈ	1	5	2		8
Acru, Leonard	1				2
Acru, John	2	1	5	2	2
Andrews, John	1	4	4		3
Abbington, Littleberry	1	1			16
Ashe, James			1	6	
Andrw, Stephen	1		2		7
Andrw, John	1				3
Andrws, William	2		4		8
Askew, John	1		1	1	1
Asbald, Joseph	1	1	5	1	
Askew, Aaron	1		2		24
Askew, David	3	3	4		17
Allen, John	1	2	2		10
Anthony, John	2		4		32
Appleton, Mary		1	3		
Andrws, William	1				
Adkinson, Mary	1		2		
Allen, John	1	2	5		10
Bailey, Sarah			1	1	
Boyce, Robert	1	3	4		1
Brimage, Elizabeth	1		4		14
Burn, John	1		4		29
Billups, Richᵈ	1	1	3		
Bryan, Edward	2		2		15
Brown, Hardy	2	1	2		
Byrd, John	1	3	2	1	3
Baker, Thomas	1	1	5	1	5
Billups, William	1		2		6
Britt, Jessee	1				
Brantly, Darby					4
Billups, Thomas	1	1	2		
Barber, Charles	1	3	3		
Barber, Prudence	1		3		
Barber, Elizabeth			3		
Byrom, David	1	2	2		
Barns, Thomas	1				
Bond, Thomas	3		4		25
Baker, Edward	1		4		
Butler, Tobias	1	4	3		25
Bryant, Jessee	1	1	4		
Bryant, Michˡ	2		2		
Bryant, Elizᵃ		1	5		1
Boyce, Jessee	1	2	3		
Ditto for S. Williams					26
Barns, Cader	2	3	4		
Bryant, William	2	1	6	1	12
Bridges, Robᵗ	2	1	3		2
Bridges, Robᵗ Junʳ	1	1	2		2
Beazy, Pharoby		1	1		
Barley, Joseph	1	1	2		
Brogdon, William	1	2	2		
Brogdon, John	1	2	1		
Bently, John	2	1	2		1
Blacton, Henry	2		2		1
Bond, John	2		1		12
Barber, Elizᵃ	1		4		
Booth, Mary			3		
Blackledge, Richᵈ	3	1		1	15
Britt, Thomas	1	1	4		4
Bolton, Aaron	2		4	5	
Burn, Levy	2				9
Bond, Thomas	1		1		7
Bond, Mary		3	2		18
Britt, Joel	1	4	6		
Brogdon, John	1		2		1
Bass, Thomas	1		2		
Barber, David	1		2		
Bently, William	1	2	3		
Bently, John	1		5		
Broadwell, David	1		4		
Ditto for Cullen Pollock					14
Bently, John	1				
Bazemore, James	1	5	2		1
Bench, Frederick	1	3	3		1
Bunch, William	2	3	2		
Barrett, Jennett			3		
Bazemore, Malichia	1	2	3		1
Birch, Micajah	1	2	2	3	
Bunch, Zadok	1	1	2		4
Butler, John	1	2	3	3	
Baker, Jonaᵃ	1	3	3		
Britt, Joel	1	2	2		
Bazemore, Jessee	3	2	3		13
Bazemore, John	1	2	6		2
Boyce, John	2	2	2		
Barns, Henry	1	2	5		
Barns, Solomon	1	2	3		
Barns, Thomas	1	4	3		6
Baker, John	1		1		4
Barns, John	1	3	3		4
Brown, Jessee	1	2	3	1	4
Bunch, Nehemᵇ	2	3	4		
Bazmore, John	1	3	3	2	9
Byron, John	2	1	4		1
Bass, William	2				5
Belote, Noah	1				1
Bass, Jacob	2	2	4		1
Bass, John	2	2	2		1
Byrsell, Joseph	1				
Bazemore, James	1	5	2		1
Butler, Isaac	1		3	4	
Burns, John	1	1	3		8
Burry, Jeremiah	3	5	3		3
Bowen, Benjᵃ	2	3	3		
Barrett, John	2	1	3		
Buck, Stephen	4	3	5		
Boswell, Thomas	3	4	4		1
Billips, Ramsom	2	2	8		
Boswell, Charles	1		3		
Baker, James	1	2	1		
Bowin, Hardy	1	1	2		
Byrd, Jacob	1	2	3		
Boswell, William	1				
Butler, Jeremiah	1				
Britt, Jessee	1				
Barber, David	1	2	1		
Boswill, John	1		2		
Bryant, Luis	1	1	1		
Barnecaster, Richᵈ	1	1	1		
Brown, John	1	2	6		3
Bridges, Thomas	1	1	2		
Bates, Sarah			1	4	
Benton, John	1		3	1	
Bridges, James	1			3	
Buice, Jeremiah	1	3	6		
Baker, Blake	2	3	5		9
Baker, Zedckᵇ	1	2	2		
Bently, John	2	2	3		
Baker, Mary		2	5		
Bardell, William					2
Bardell, Joseph	1				3
Bardell, James	1	1			4
Baker, Levi	2		4		2
Boyce, John	3	3	2		1
Baker, Mary		2	5		
Boyce, Hardy	1	1	1		
Burn, James	1	2	3		18
Bailey, Sarah		2	1		1
Bogen, Robert	1	3	4		
Brimage, Elizᵃ	4	2	4	1	16
Burns, John	1		4		20
Billups, Richᵈ	1	1	3		
Bryan, Edward	2		2		15
Bowen, Hardy	2	1	2		
Byrd, John	1	3	2		3
Baker, Thomas	1	1	5	1	5
Billups, William	1		2		6
Britt, Jessee	1				
Bromley, Darby					4
Billups, Thomas	1	1	2		
Barber, Charles	1	3	3		
Barber, Prudence			3		
Barber, Elizᵃ	1		3		
Baker, Elias	1		2		
Berry, John	2	3	4		
Berry, Wright	2	2	3		
Berry, John	1	1	1		
Barker, Demcey	1		2		
Baker, Soˡ	1		2		
Belch, Miles	1		1		
Bryan, William	1		1		
Berry, Miles	1		1		
Butler, Arther	1		1		
Boyce, Demsey	1	1	2		
Barns, William	1	6	4		
Barrett, John	1	1	3		
Brown, Benjᵃ	1		3		
Briton, John	1	1	3		3
Bay, James	3		3		
Byrd, Richᵈ	1	2	2		
Butler, John	1	1	8		
Brown, William	4		9		
Briton, Michˡ	1				
Briton, John	2	1	6		3
Brantly, Mathew	1	4	4		
Belote, John	2	2	6		10
Butler, Joseph	2	4	4		4
Barry, Thomas	2				4
Bass, Jacob	1	2	4		4
Bass, Cader	1	1	2		1
Britt, Joel	1	2	2		4
Bunch, Jeremᵇ	3	6	2		
Bunch, John	1				3
Butler, Isaac	1	2	6		
Beazley, Ambrose	1	3	2		
Butler, William	1	1	1		
Burt, William	1				
Butler, Thomas R	1				
Brantly, Mathew	2	3	4		
Bass, Augᵃ			3		5
Butler, William	1	1	1		
Butler, John	1	1	2		
Belote, Henry	1	1	3		4
Bently, James	1	1	2		2
Byron, James	1				
Boyce, Luis	1				
Bently, James	1				2
Belote, Noah	1				2
Bartlett, Hall				4	
Belote, Peleg	1				
Brogdon, Peter	1	5	1		
Bates, Henry	1	2	2		1
Burkett, William	1	1	5		
Brogdon, John	1	2	1		
Brogdon, William	2		2		
Brinkly, Elia	1		2		
Bates, Sarah		1	4		5
Byrom, John	1	2	5		
Billups, Richᵈ	1		1		
Brogdon, Thomas	1				
Brogdon, Timothy	1				
Bently, Henry	1	1	2		
Burkett, William	1	2	3		
Belote, Thoˢ	1	1	1		
Boyce, Hardy	1	1	1		
Byrom, Abner	1	1	1		
Bond, Thomas	1		2	1	8
Brogdon, John	1	2	2		1
Brinkly, Elijah	1	2	4		5
Brown, Jessee	1				6
Brown, Joel	3	2	2	1	3
Bishop, Moses	1	1	3		3
Brown, James	1				3
Brown, Arther	1				5
Bishop, Mason	2	4	3		6
Barnacaster, Sarᵇ					9
Byrd, Elisha	1				
Barry, Miles	1				
Chery, Solomon	1	1	5		14
Collins, David	1	1	3		
Curry, James	5		2		1
Curry, Jacob	1	1	2		
Collins, Josiah	1	3	3		2
Cherry, Thomas	1	3	3		
Cook, Joel	1	3	2		
Cherry, John	1				
Cowen, John	1	1	8		
Cowen, William	1		5		
Cowen, William	2	3	1		
Cralet, Geo	1				
Cory, Benjᵃ	3	2	2		4
Carter, Joseph	1	2	1		1
Cherry, William	1	3	4		3
Chavis, Cezar				1	
Curry, Marry			2		
Castelow, James			2		
Cob, Henry	1	2	5		2
Cob, Nichoˢ	2		3		
Cook, Samˡ	3	1	4		
Calloway, Thoˢ	2	6	3		3
Castelow, Jnᵒ	1	1	3		
Cowen, John	1	2	2		
Cowen, Willᵐ	1	2	3		
Cob, Edwᵈ	1				
Castelow, James	1	3	4		1
Carter, Joseph	1	2	1		
Collins, Luke	4	2	1		20
Charton, Jesper	1		1		22
Christᵃ, Clark	4	2	4		26
Cullifer, Elizᵃ	3		2		
Clements, Geo	1	1	1		3
Collins, Thoˢ	2		2		13
Cooper, Cadey	1	4	5		1
Caphart, John	1	1	2		4
Cob, James	2	3	6		
Caphart, William	3		2		9
Caphart, Geo	1				

[1] No attempt has been made in this publication to correct mistakes in spelling made by the assistant marshals, and the names have been reproduced as they appear upon the census schedule.

EDENTON DISTRICT, BERTIE COUNTY—Continued.

NAME OF HEAD OF FAMILY.	Free white males of 16 years and upward, including heads of families.	Free white males under 16 years.	Free white females, including heads of families.	All other free persons.	Slaves.
Cob, John	1	1	6		1
Cofield, Jethro	1	2	1		2
Culifer, Nath¹	1		2		
Culfer, Thomas	1				
Cook, Jnº	1	2	4		2
Culifer, James	2	1	4		
Cook, Winifred		3	2		4
Culifer, Nath¹	2	2	6		
Craft, Moses	2	3	2		
Carney, Absolom	3		4		13
Clark, Thomas		1	2		
Castelow, John	2	5	3	1	3
Craft, Moses	1	2	1		
Campbell, John	1	2			1
Campbell, James	3	2	5		41
Curry, David	2	6	4		12
Cole, Rebecca		3	1		
Cole, Cudby	1	3	4		8
Cole, John	1	1	3	1	6
Cokron, Thomas	1	3	3		5
Cokhilgo, William	1		4		
Cokron, Thomas	1	4	6	2	8
Cittrell, John	4		3		31
Cowen, Geo					1
Cowen, William	1	3	1		
Cob, Eleaner			1		
Cole, Sarah			4		
Cob, Dolley		2	1		
Cherry, Aaron	1				
Cherry, Jnº	1	1	1		
Cherry, Joshua	1		3		
Cooper, Blunt	1				
Cofield, Josiah	1	2	3		
Curry, Jacob	1				
Cooper, Jessee	1	4	3		
Curry, Jacob	1	2	2		
Colten, Sam¹	1	1	1		
Cartey, Joseph	1	2	2		1
Callis, Zedekiah	1				9
Callum, David	1	1	3		
Colten, Jessee	2	1	3		14
Callum, Willis	3	2	2		18
Cambell, Elizª			2		
Cox, Benjⁿ	4	2	2		
Collins, Joseph	1	1	2		
Clifton, Ann		2	4		9
Curry, Mary			2	1	
Collins, Joseph	3	1	1	1	8
Collins, Henry	1				
Chevat, Cezer				7	
Collins, Josiah	3	2	4		2
Curry, James	1				
Cooper, Jonª	1				
Curry, Ebenezʳ	1				
Cooper, Jnº	1	1			
Canady, Alis		2	6		
Cowen, Geo			1		1
Curry, Jeames	2		1		
Curry, Jacob	1				
Cox, William	1	1	4		
Conner, Wright	1				
Cox, Benjⁿ	1	3	3		
Cofield, David	1	2	2	1	
Conner, Thomas	1				
Cox, Jnº	1				4
Clark, Thomas	2	1	3		4
Cittrell, Demsey	3	3	3		6
Carney, Josiah	1	1	1		4
Conner, William	1		3		
Cook, James	1	1	2		
Cook, Jnº	1		4		
Cook, Reuben	3	1	5		7
Cole, Job	1		3		
Cole, Christian		1	1		
Cook, Demsey	2	3	3		2
Cob, Nathan	2	2	4		1
Churchwill, Henry	1	3			
Codwell, William	1	1	1	1	1
Cofield, David	1	2	2		1
Channell, Tempey			1		
Chamberlain, Malc	1	3	2	2	2
Churchwill, Ann	1	2	5		
Cartior, Sam¹	1	2	4		
Cone, Thomas	1				
Ditto for W. Williams					21
Collins, Frederick	1	1			1
Cole, Peggy	1		3		
Conner, Edwᵈ	1				
Demsey, Melvin	1	3	2		
Demsey, Shadrack	1	1	5		
Damont, Charles	1	3	4		4
Duning, Shadrack	1	1	5		
Davis, Geo	1	4	6		
Deville, McSteven	3	1	5		2
Davidson, Amos	1	4	3		
Davis, James	2	1	4		
Darnes, Jacob	1				
Darnell, Uriah	1	1	2		
Davison, Amos	1	4	3		3
Dukes, Abraham	1				
Duffin, Salley			4		
Duffin, James	1				
Duning, Jeremiah	3	5	4		
Dotry, Patry	1		4		
Debun, Dennis	1				3
Doore, James	2		1		
Dawson, Richard	5		4	1	9
Darlett, Anthⁱ	1	2	2		10
Dawson, William	1		4		5
Devenport, Joseph	1		1	1	
Doore, John	2	1	4		
Demsey, Melvin	1	4	6		
Davis, Smith	1		2		
Davis, David	1		2		
Davidson, David	1	2	1		
Davis, Geo	1	2	1		
Deane, Sam¹	1	2	1		
Deane, Solo	1	3	1		
Davidson, William	1	1	3		
Dunning, John	1		2		
Dunning, Sam¹	1		3		9
Dunning, Charles	1	2	3		2
Davis, Mary		4	6		
Davis, Nathaniel	1	1	4		
Ditto for Sam¹ Johnston					11
Dunning, Jeremiah	2	4	4		
Deane, Samuel	1		2		
Dunning, Jeremiah	1	1	3	2	
Davis, Thomas	1	2	3		
Dryden, Isaac	1		5		
Darby, Joseph				4	
Dunark, Michel	2	5	7	4	1
Dunston, Edmond	2	2	5		12
Durgan, Ann			2		9
Dyer, Thomas	2				
Demsey, Thowegood					7
Demsey, George					9
Demsey, Joshua					9
Dawson, William	1				
Eason, Abner	3		1		20
Edwards, Nathan	1	3	3	2	
Eason, Joseph	1	1	1	1	5
Edward, Nathan	1	3	6	2	
Eason, Abner	1	4	3		10
Eleaner, Williams	1	3	5		
Engs, Mathew	1		3		
Evarts, Luther	1		1		1
Epperson, Mary		1	3		
Evins, William	1	4	5		1
Evins, Etherald	1				
Evins, Joshua	1	3	2		
Evins, Robert	1		1		
Everite, Luther	1		1		
Edward, John	2	1	2	2	
Everite, John	1		1		12
Edward, David	1				
Engs, Mathew	1		1		
Early, John	1		4		2
Early, Asa	1	1	2		1
Edward, James	1		5		8
Early, Benjⁿ	1	2	7		6
Early, Shadrack	1		2		3
Everite, Henry	1	3	2	2	13
Everite, Jessee			3		21
Everite, Amelia			3		10
Fryar, Willis	1	2	3		
Farmer, James	1	4	8	2	
Freeman, King	2	2	1		8
Ferguson, Alexʳ	1	2	2		4
Fleetwood, Edmond	1	3	4		6
Felps, Henry	1	1	3		
Fleetwood, Hardy	1	3	1		3
Fleetwood, William	2	1	5		1
Freeman, Aaron	1	2	2	2	
Freeman, Charles	1		5		8
Freeman, Hardy	1				1
Freeman, William	1				
Freeman, Joshua	4	1	4	1	30
Freeman, Jeremiah	1				
Freeman, Joshua	1				
Freeman, John	1	2	2		19
Fryer, Sian	1				
Fryar, Willis	1	1	2		
Ford, Alexʳ	1				
Floyd, John		3	4		
Fanner, William	1	2	3		
Frain, John	1	1	3		
Farmer, Joseph	2	4	6		
Freman, Moses	1	5	4		12
Fenner, James	1	2	3		
Freeman, Martha	1	1	8		11
Folk, Thomas	3	3	3		3
Felps, John	1	3	6		2
Felps, Frederick	1	2	4		2
Felps, Cudworth	1	4	7	1	3
Felps, Mary		2	4		
Frazier, Alexʳ	2		2		
Goff, Joney				1	
Gardner, Martin	1				1
Griffin, Abraham	1				
Gardener, Everite	1	1	4		6
Gardener, Bryom	2	2	3	2	6
Gardner, Everite	1	1	1	1	4
Gill, Richard	1	4	4		6
Green, Solo	1	2	3		
Griffin, William	1	1	6		
Griffin, William, Junʳ	2		5		8
Griffin, Creacy	2		3		
Griffin, Lucretia		1	3		
Goff, Rachell		1	3		
Gardener, Mary	1	2	4		7
Gardener, Salley	3		3	8	9
Gardener, Nancy		2	3	3	1
Glisten, Ann		1	5	1	
Godfrey, Ann		1	2		
Gains, Rebeca			3	1	
Gains, Sarah			3	4	
Glawhorn, Willm	1	2	3	2	1
Gardener, William	2	1	3		
Gardener, Isaac	1	2	2		1
Gardener, Thos	1	1	2		
Gaskins, Thos	1	1	3		
Garrett, David	1	2	3		16
Green, George	1	2	2		
Gillum, Moses	1		1		22
Gray, William	1	4	2	5	53
Gardner, Nath¹	1				
Grandbury, John	3		1	1	10
Grover, Sir James	3		1	4	5
Glisten, Edward	1				
Gummery, Ann		2	3		
Garrett, Frederick	1		2	3	
Gains, Rebecca			2		1
Groudy, McHenry	1				
Gardener, John	1	2	5	3	
Gardener, Jean		4	2	3	1
Gardner, Penelope	3		3		
Glisten, Henry	1				
Grimes, Elizª			1		
Garrett, Jacob	1	4	1		8
Garrett, Jessee	2	3	5		20
Green, Malichi	1	1	3		
Green, Elizª	1	1	3		
Green, Malichi	2	1	4		
Harman, Abraham	1	3	4		4
Harman, Stephen	1	1	1		
Holder, Elijah	1	3	1		
Holder, Elzabeth		2	3		
Harmon, Nichos	1	3	6		
Hollum, Joel	1	2	3		10
Hendrickson, Isaac	1	2	2		
Howard, Elijah	1	4	4		
Howard, Benjⁿ	1	1	4		1
Hale, Jessee	1	3	4		
Hunter, William	1	3	2	1	4
Harramond, Henry	2	1	7		19
Harramond, Thomas	1	2	2		22
Harrald, David	1	2	1		
Hyman, Hugh	3		2		14
Hodder, John	1	1	2		
Hawkins, Thomas	1	2	3		
Harden, Thomas	1	4	3		1
Harrill, Davis	1	2	2		
Harris, Amos	1	1	5		8
Harramond, Margt	1	1	4		9
Hawkins, William	1		3		
Hopkins, Alex	1				
Hale, John	1	1	3		
Hexstall, John	1	2	3	2	2
Hardy, Sarah	2	1	3		12
Hopkins, Joseph	2	1	4		2
Holley, Prudence	1				
Hill, Mary		1	3		
Harrill, Noah	2				7
Harrill, John	1		2		1
Hays, Sarah			6		
Higgs, John	2	2	2		5
House, Bailess	1	3	1		6
Horten, Frederick	1		2		
Harrill, Guin	1		1	2	4
Harrill, William	3	3			5
Holland, Frederick	1	1			7
Hinton, Noah	1				28
Hinton, John	1				25
Higgs, John	2	4	3		6
House, James			4		14
Hodges, Mathew	4	1	2	3	3

EDENTON DISTRICT, BERTIE COUNTY—Continued.

NAME OF HEAD OF FAMILY.	Free white males of 16 years and upward, including heads of families.	Free white males under 16 years.	Free white females, including heads of families.	All other free persons.	Slaves.
Hill, Whitnall					130
Hile, Henry	2	5	2	1	37
Harrill, William	3	3			
Harmon, Nicholas	3	3	4		
Hibbls^h, Pithsia	1				
Hays, James	1	2	5	1	
Harrald, Nancy	3	2	5		1
Hays, Joshua	1		9		2
Howell, Thomas	2	2		1	
House, Thomas	3	1	7	3	26
Harrill, William	1	3	1		5
Hawkins, Thomas	1	2	3		7
Hyman, John	1	1	3		7
Hyman, Eliz^a		2	4		
Holten, Sarah			6		
Hardy, William	2		1		
Hardy, Joseph	1	1	4		
Hanes, Edwd	1				12
Hare, Penelope			1		6
How, Mary	1	1	3		16
Hubbord, Bird	2	1	7		7
Hyman, John	1	1	3		10
Hyman, Thomas	1				
Hardy, William	1	1	3		
Hunter, John	1				11
Harte, Samuel	1	4	2		
Harrill, John	1	2	5		
Harrill, Joseph	2	2	4		
Harrill, John	1		5		
Harrill, Isaac	3	2	5		
Harrill, Isaac	1				
Hunsford, Jenkins	1	1	2		
Hendry, William	1				
Hendry, Robert	2	3	2		2
Hunter, Timothy	1				
Hunter, Hardy	1	1	4		16
Harrill, Job	1				
Harris, John	1				
Harrill, Hughs	1				
Hallum, Judah	1	4	1		
Huggins, Humphry	1				
Holland, Chris^a	1	3	3		5
Hughs, Geo	1	3	3		1
Hugh, Sol^e	1	4	4		
Horsen, Reuben	1		1		
Hughs, William	1		5		
Hughs, Josiah	1				
Hughs, James	1	4	3		
Hughs, Thomas	1	1	3		
Horson, Geo	1	2	2		
Hughs, David	1	4	3		
Hughs, Geo	1		1		
Horson, King	1	1	3		
Hughs, George	1	3	3		
Hale, Jonas	1	5	4		
Horten, William	1	5	2		
Horson, Ann			1		
Hughs, Thomas	1	1	3		
Hughs, Geo	1	2	3		
Howly, James	1	5	4		8
Hawley, James		1	4		
Hunter, Timothy	1	3	4		19
Hodder, William	1		1	1	
Harrill, Allen	1				
Howard, Jacob	1				
Hunter, William	1	3	2	1	4
Hudson, Sarah			3		
Hudson, Sarah		2	4		
Hollaway, Arther	2				3
Hays, Joshua	1		7	1	4
Harrill, John W	1				1
Harrill, John	1				
Hollowell, Asa	2		4		1
Howell, Josiah	1	1	2		4
Harrill, Elijah	1				
Harrill, Demsey	1	5	1	1	
Harrill, Luis	2	3	4		2
Harrill, Demsey	2	4	2	1	13
Hollowell, William	1		2		
Harrill, Amos	1	1	3		5
Hollowell, Asa	2				1
Hambleton, Pharober		2	4		
Hollowell, Noah	1		3		2
Higgs, John	1	2	2		5
Holden, Elijah	3	1	3		
Hogart, William	3	3	3		
Hix, John	1	1	2		
Hubbord, Rachall			4		
Hunter, Robert	1				
Huff, Corn^a	1				
Holder, Thomas	1	3	1		
Hardy, Humphrey	3	2	4		18
Horten, William	1	4	1		
Hyman, William	1	2	6		4
Hodder, John	1	2	6		5
Hardy, John	1				
Hopkins, John	2	3	2		1

NAME OF HEAD OF FAMILY.	Free white males of 16 years and upward, including heads of families.	Free white males under 16 years.	Free white females, including heads of families.	All other free persons.	Slaves.
Hawkins, Thomas	2	1	1		
Hardy, Elz^a	1	1	3		
Hardy, Lemuel	1	1	1		
Harlowe, John	1	1	4		6
Holley, James	1	5	4		8
Hays, James	1	2	5	1	
Holland, Lewel	1	1	9		
Harrill, Arther	1		4		4
Hodges, Mathew	1	1	3		1
Higgs, Judith			2		3
Horn, Joseph	1	4	2	1	3
Harrill, Rachell			1		
Harrill, Eliz^a			4		
Harrill, Jacob		4			
Holland, John	1	1	4		
Harrill, David	1	1	2		1
Harrill, James	2	3	5		
Harrill, Henry	2	2	3		
Holland, John	1				
Hays, James	1	3	4		
Hays, Sam	1	3	4		
Hodges, William	1				2
Higgs, Reuben	1	1	6		
Hodges, John	1				
Harrill, Josiah	1				
Hiat, Elisha	1	1	6		
Higgs, William	1	4	3		6
Harrill, Benj	1	3	5		12
Harrill, Christ^a	1		1		
Harrill, Hodges	1				
Harrill, Nancy		4	5		1
Harte, Saml	1	4	2		
Hogard, Patrick	3	1	4		
Hogard, John	1	1	4		
Hays, Susanna		2	1		
Hawley, Prudence			2		
Homes, Shadrack	1	2	3	1	1
Jinkins, Geo	1				
Jordan, James	1				
James, Frederick					9
Johnson, Thomas	3	1	3		
Jenkins, Cader	3	1	3		3
Johnson, John	1	1	6		
Jenkins, Moore	1	3	8	4	5
Jacob, Saml	1		2		1
Jenkins, Luis	1		5		5
James, Andrew				4	
Jordan, Hannah		1	4		26
James, Nancy				3	
Jones, William			9	6	
Jordan, Joseph	1		1		10
Johnson, John	1	2	5		
Johnson, Thomas	1	1	2		
Jordan, Mary	2	2	5		13
Johnson, John	1	1	1		7
Jacocks, Jon^a	2		2		25
Jacocks, Charles	1				10
Johnson, Levy		3	3		
Jordan, James B	3	2	3		24
Jonakin, Jessee	1	1	3		
Barker, Thos, Dec^d					80
Jonathan, James	1		2		
James, Emmanuel	1	1	2		
Jonakin, Arther	2		3		18
Jonakin, Benj^a	1				6
Johnson, Byrrell	2	1	4		
Jenkins, Luis	2		1	5	7
Jones, Mary			5	1	
Jenkins, Nathan	1	1	5		1
Jenkins, Charles	1				
Johnson, Byrrell	3	2	3		
Johnson, Snoden	1		4		
Johnson, James	1				
Jones, Friddle	1		3		
Johnston, James	1				
Johnson, Jacob	3			2	3
Johnson, William	1	1	7		
James, Frederick				5	
James, John				8	
Job, Saml	1		2		
Jenkins, King	1				
Jones, Sol^e	2	2	5		
Jones, Thomas	1				6
Jones, David	1		4	2	4
Jenkins, Isum	1				
Jenkins, James	1		3		2
Jenkins, Jeames	1		2		15
Jenkins, Luis	2	1	5		7
Jonakin, Saml	1		3		4
Jenkins, Godfrey	1	1	3		
Jenkins, Abraham	1	2	4		
Jeames, Mary				3	
Jones, Mary	1		2		
Jones, Jessee	1	1	2		
Jones, William	2		3		
King, Charles	1	3	3		4
Knott, Joseph	1				4

NAME OF HEAD OF FAMILY.	Free white males of 16 years and upward, including heads of families.	Free white males under 16 years.	Free white females, including heads of families.	All other free persons.	Slaves.
Kinnigan, Jacob	1				
King, Henry	1	2	3		5
King, Charles	3	3	2		11
King, Charles	1	3	3		4
King, Michael	1		2		23
King, William	1	2	3		12
Knott, Mary	1		3		
Knight, Reuben	1		1		
Kail, Josiah	1		3		4
Keaton, William	1		2		
King, Cader	1	2	1		
King, James	1				
King, Charles	1		1	1	7
King, Cader	3	2	1		
Kennady, James	1				
King, Charles	1	1	2		
King, James	1				
King, John H	1	1	2		3
Keen, Moses	1	3	5		
Kennedy, Ellis		2	4		
Knott, Thomas	1				
Kinnehorn, Jacob	1				
Lawrence, Abner	1	2	4		
Liscomb, Wilson	2	3	3		11
Lawrence, John	1		3		
Langly, Tho^a	1	2	1		4
Lawrence, Prudence		1	2		
Lawrence, Robt	1	1	4		2
Lawrence, Abner	1	3	4		2
Lawrence, Willi^m	1	2	3		4
Lee, Isaac	1		3		
Lassiter, Mary			3		
Luth, Lydia		3	1		
Liggett, Jeremiah	2	2	2		7
Lockhart, Mary	1	1	5		28
Lawrence, Fred^k	1	2	4	3	13
Lawrence, Reuben	1	3	4		4
Lackey, Thomas	1	1	2		
Liddenham, Jno	1	1	1		
Lazy, Salley			2		
Liggett, Thomas	3	4	6		10
Liggett, Jeremiah	2	2	2		8
Liggett, Alex^r	1	1	3		5
Liggett, Rachell	1		4		5
Liggett, Eliz^a			2		1
Lester, John	1		1		
Lester, John	1	1	1		
Lockhart, James	1	1	2		24
Lane, John	1				
Lassiter, Mary	1	3	4		
Lawrence, Joseph	1	1	2		
Lane, David	1				
Lane, James	3	1	5		
McLallen, Geo	2				
McLallen, Jno	1	1			
Letke, John	1	1	2		
McLane, Drury	1	2	4		7
Lully, William	1	2	4		7
Lattin, William	1				
Lattern, James	1	1	6		1
Lenox, James	1		3		91
Lee, Abraham	1	3	2		
Liggett, Thomas	2	1	2		10
Liggett, Rachell	1	1	6		9
Lee, Isaac	1		2		
Lloyd, James	1	1	2		
Lloyd, Jessee	1	1	1	3	
Lloyd, Josiah	1	2	2		
Lee, Stephen	1		2		
Lee, John	1	2	2		
Low, James	1				
Lassiter, Mary			6		
Long, Joel			2		
Latin, Saml	1	1	3		
Lawrence, John			2		
Lucust, Nancy	1	2	3		
Lucust, Jno	2	3	4		
Lee, Jno	1	2	2		
Lee, Henry	2	1	2		7
Lee, Joshua	1		2		2
Liggett, James	1	2	6		6
Morriss, William	1	2	4	2	5
Milburn, Henry	2	2	2	1	
Moon, John	2	3	3		4
Morriss, James	1	2	6		
Michel, Joseph	1	4	3		3
Mezell, John	1	3	4		
Mais, Saml	1		1		5
Mahone, James	1	3	1		
Meredith, Davis	1	1	1		
McGlawhorn, Jno	1	2	3		9
Morgan, John	1	2	2	1	
McGlawhorn, Wm	1	2	4	1	1
Miller, John	3	5	3		
Morriss, William	1	3	3		
Martin, John	1	3	7		3
Morriss, John			2		

EDENTON DISTRICT, BERTIE COUNTY—Continued.

NAME OF HEAD OF FAMILY.	Free white males of 16 years and upward, including heads of families.	Free white males under 16 years.	Free white females, including heads of families.	All other free persons.	Slaves.
Morriss, John	1		1		
Minard, Meniah		3	2		
Michl, Thomas	1	3	3		1
Manly, Moses				3	
Moore, Titus	1				17
Ditto for L. Collins					2
Moore, Moses	3		8		20
Michel, Jeremiah	1	1	1		9
Mear, Jno	1	2	4		1
Montgomery, Auga	1	1	3		
Minton, Benja	1				
Mitchell, Jerry	1				6
McClone, Hepsiber			4		7
Mahone, James	1	1	2		
Morgan, John	1	2	4		
Monk, Nottingm	1	1	1		
Monk, Nottingh	1	3	3		11
Monk, Letice	4		1		
Miller, John	1	2	2		13
McCate, —				4	
Mitchell, Sarah		1	1		
Murden, Sarah	1	4	6	3	4
Manning, Luke	1	1	3		
Madry, James	2	4	1		1
Meredith, David				20	
Megill, John	1	1	4		
Moore, John	1	1	3		9
Megill, Cader	1	3	3		
Michel, Willim	1	2	3		
Miller, Jonathan	1	3	3		
Megil, Thomas	1	2	4		
Miller, Solomon	1	3	2		
Megill, Henry	1	4	3		2
Megill, Joshua	1	1	3		
Megill, John	1		1		
Megill, Moses	1				
Megill, Aaron	1	2	2		
Morriss, Joseph	1	1	3		
Morriss, Zedekih	1				
Murfrey, Geo	1	1	1		
Meagill, Timothy	1		5		
Mires, Benja	2	3	7		5
Moore, Agness	2		1		
Madry, John		1	3		
Mahone, John	2	2	6		6
Miller, Nathl	1	2	2		
Manly, Moses	1	1	1		6
Mason, Willim	1	1	1		
Mahon, John	1	2	5		
Mahon, Josiah	1	3	4		
Megill, James	1	2	3		
Madry, Thos	1	1	2		
Madry, John	1	1	3		
Morriss, Thomas	1				
Madry, Joseph	1		2		
Moore, John	1				
Morriss, Willi	1		1		
Moore, Joseph	1		1		
Moore, Saml	2	2	1	2	
Morriss, James	1	2	3		
Mullins, Mother			1		
Megill, James	1	2	6		
Megill, John	1		1		1
Magee, James	1				
Minton, Thomas	1	2	3		
Morriss, William	1		1		
Madry, John	1		1		
Mason, John	2	1	5		
Moore, Moses	1	2	7		24
Moore, Joseph	1	1	2		
Madry, Joseph	1		2		5
Michill, Cader	1	5	3		2
Michill, Mathew	3	1	3		1
Morriss, Abrahm	1	1	3		
Morriss, John	1		2		
Michell, Ephm	1	6	4		1
Martin, Miles	1	3	1		
Michell, Jeames	4	1	4		
Michl, Nathan	3	6	3		
Michell, William	1		4		2
Minet, Grime		3	2		
Mitchell, John	2		1		
Newben, Thos	1	1	4		2
Newben, Geo	1	3	4	1	5
Nichols, John	3		4		1
Nichols, John	2	1	3		9
Nichols, Peter	1		1		
Noel, Edgard			2		
Norflett, James	1				3
Norflett, Reuben	1	2	3		48
Northam, Geo	1	2	2		
Neal, John	1				
Norflett, James					1
Northam, George	1	2	2		
Northam, Geo	1	2	2		
North, Joseph	2	2	3		7
Outlaw, James	1				

NAME OF HEAD OF FAMILY.	Free white males of 16 years and upward, including heads of families.	Free white males under 16 years.	Free white females, including heads of families.	All other free persons.	Slaves.
Outhouse, Isarel	1	2	4		
Outlaw Martha	1	1	5		2
Oxley, John	2	2	5		4
Outlaw, Jacob	1		3		4
Outlaw, Geo	2	1	1		21
Outlaw, Aaron	2	3	5		7
Outlaw, Luis	2	1	5		6
Outlaw, James	1				5
Overton, Churton	1		2		
Outlaw, James	1				
Outlaw, Edwd	1	1	3		14
Outlaw, Thomas	1	2	4		
Oldham, George	1				
Owens, Elsi			6		
Outerbridge, Stephen	1	1	1	1	1
Outhouse, Isarel	1	2	4		
Outlaw, Edward	2		3		10
Overton, Andrew	3	4	2		21
Overton, John	3	2	3		21
Overton, John	1	1	3		
Outlaw, Amos	1	1	3		6
Overton, Asa	1		2		
Outlaw, George	1	2	6		18
Owens, Penelope		3	5		
Pierce, Willim	1	1	2		
Perry, Elthred	1				
Peal, William	1	3	3		
Perry, John	1	3	1		
Pierce, Zedekh	1				
Pierce, Reder	1	1	1		
Pierce, John	2		2		2
Pender, Patune	1	2	1		8
Perry, Isaac	1		2		
Perry, James	2	2	2		
Perry, Joshua	2	3	5		16
Powers, Susan	2		3		5
Powers, Samson	1	1	4		4
Parker, Joseph	1				
Ditto for M. King					5
Pierce, Jerry	2	1	2	2	2
Page, James				2	
Pugh, Thos	2	2	4	1	18
Price, James	1	1	2		
Pierce, Jereh	2	1	2		2
Page, Joshua	2	2	1		
Page, Thomas	1	1	1		
Page, Nathan	2	2	1		
Peal, Joshua	1		1		1
Page, Sarah			1		
Page, Catherine		1	3		
Pugh, Francis	3	3	4		30
Prudon, David	1	1	2		
Prudon, Abm	1				
Penay, James	2	1	3		
Purvey, William	1				
Parker, Elisha	1				
Purvis, Cullin	1				
Parker, Isaac	4	3	2		
Parker, Luke	1				
Parker, James	1		3		
Parker, Isaac	1		2		
Purvis, Jean		1	2		16
Peal, Josiah	2	3	5		
Parker, Joseph	1				6
Pugh, Thos	1				45
Ditto for P. Barker	1	1	2		33
Pugh, William	3	7	1		33
Powel, Cader	2	4	7		15
Page, Nathan	4	2	1		
Page, Solo	1	1	1		4
Perry, James	1				
Purvis, Allen	3		2	3	8
Pierce, Thomas	2		1		
Purvis, James					5
Pugh, John	1				
Powell, Willis	1	3	1	1	6
Passmore, Thos	1	1	2		
Pierce, Jeremiah	2	1	2		2
Page, Catherine		1	3		
Parker, Isaac	3	2	3		
Parnell, Joseph	1		3		
Pender, John	2				
Pender, Patience	1	2	3		10
Pierce, John	1		3		2
Pace, Saml	1	5	1		
Pender, William	2	2	1		3
Pierce, John	2		2		2
Pender, William	1	2	4		6
Parnell, Joseph	1	1	1		
Parks, John	1				
Parks, Young	1	3	7	2	3
Prichard, Chris	2				
Pugh, W. Thos	1	1	6		35
Prichard, James	1	1	1		
Prichard, Jona	2		4		
Parker, Joseph	3	2	3		15

NAME OF HEAD OF FAMILY.	Free white males of 16 years and upward, including heads of families.	Free white males under 16 years.	Free white females, including heads of families.	All other free persons.	Slaves.
Perry, Thomas	1		2		9
Parker, Richd	1	4	2		6
Perry, Geo	1		3		2
Parker, Rich'd	1		3		6
Perry, Doctor	1	1	4		3
Pridden, David	1		1		
Pridden, Abm	1				1
Rhodes, Henry	1		2		7
Rhodes, John	1				3
Rice, William	1				
Rhodes, Isaac	1	1	4		
Rhodes, Isaac, Junr	1	4	4		
Rhodes, James	2	4	5	2	3
Rhodes, Henry	1	4	3		
Rhodes, James	2	5	5		2
Rhodes, William	1	1	3		14
Rhodes, James	1				
Ralls, Rebecca			3		
Reed, Christian	3	2	5		23
Ryan, Thomas	2				
Rascoe, Thomas	1	1	2		9
Razor, Josiah	1		3		7
Ridditt, Constant	1		1		
Ridditt, Lodwick	1				
Ryan, Cornelius	4	1	4		38
Razor, Eliza	1	2	6		12
Rhodes, Mary		2	2		
Rogers, Minet	3		2		
Rowlands, Robert	1	2	2		1
Relch, Luis	2	4	3		
Roberson, John	2	4	3		4
Runner, Eliza	1		2		
Roberson, David	1				
Rants, Samuel	3	4	3		6
Runner, William	1				3
Ray, William	1				
Runner, Joshua	1				
Runner, John		1	3		
Ramsey, John	1	2	4		1
Rhodes, Thomas	2	1	7		1
Rhodes, Eliza	1		2		
Rhodes, Henry	3	3	2		18
Rhodes, Jacob	1				
Rhodes, James	1				
Rhodes, William	1	1	2		12
Rutland, John	1	2	3	3	6
Rhodes, Henry	1	2	5		6
Rhobbinson, Eliza		1	2		
Raba, Hester	1	3	3		3
Rhodes, Thomas	3	1	7		12
Rhodes, Elza		1	5		
Rutland, John	1	5	3		6
Raby, Jerutha		1	3		
Rice, James	1	2	3		2
Ridditt, Job	1	2	2		
Ralls, Jonas	1	2	2		
Ralls, Josiah	1	4	4		1
Ralls, Job	1				
Ralls, Henry	1	2	4		
Ralls, Jonas	1				
Rhodes, Robert	1				
Rutland, James	1	1	5		
Ralls, Philip	1		4		
Rhodes, Robert	1	4	3		
Rascoe, Arther	1	2	4	1	2
Ralls, Levy	1		3		
Rauns, Else		3	7		
Ralls, Rebecca		3	7		
Rhodes, Ephraim	1	2	2		1
Raby, Bleak	1				
Ditto for Thos Barkr					74
Rascoe, William	3	5	4	1	3
Ruffin, William	3	5	3		15
Robinson, Eliza	1		2		
Rodgers, Thomas	1	3	4		1
Robinson, John	1	3	5	2	
Rollins, Isaac	1				
Rigging, Thomas (for Cullen Pollock)					83
Rascoe, Thomas	1	1	2		9
Rascoe, James	3	1	4		16
Rascoe, Arther	1	1	4	1	2
Rascoe, Peter	2	1	1		2
Rhodes, Mary		2	2		
Rogers, Minett	2		4		
Rhodes, Henry	1				
Rhodes, Mary		2	3		
Rodah, John	3	2	5		1
Sowel, Charles	1	2	5	1	6
Shehan, Thomas	1	1	2		1
Simons, Joseph	2		6		4
Skiles, William	1	2	4		
Sowell, Francis	1		2		
Standley, Jona	3	1	6		14
Simon, Steven	1	2	3		
Sparkman, R. Willim	1		1		5

EDENTON DISTRICT, BERTIE COUNTY—Continued.

NAME OF HEAD OF FAMILY.	Free white males of 16 years and upward, including heads of families.	Free white males under 16 years.	Free white females, including heads of families.	All other free persons.	Slaves.
Sumner, Jacob	1	1	2		
Shoulders, John	1	1	1		5
Standley, Edmond	3	1	5		12
Shoulder, John	2	1	1		
Shoulder, Hare	1	1	1		5
Shoulder, James	1	2	5		
Shoulder, Benjª	3	3	2		
Stone, Zedkʰ	5	2			25
Sutton, Thomas	1		2		19
Sutton, William	2				1
Smithwick, John	2	1	1		5
Speller, Henry	3	1	2		9
Sutton, Joshua	3	1	1		5
Stue, William	1				
Smith, Stephen	2		1		6
Sparkman, William	1	1	3		
Seal, Thomas	1		1		
Smithwick, Jnᵒ	1	5	1		1
Stone, William	1	2	2		
Sorrell, Nancy		1	2	1	2
Sorrell, Benjª	1		2		
Stone, Solᵒ	1	6	2		
Sorrell, Luis	1	3	1		5
Stoughton, John	1	1	1		
Stone, Sparkman	1				
South, Andrew	1	2	4		
Sparkman, Redwᵐ	1	1	2		2
Spivy, Jonathan	1	1	5		1
Sparkman, James	1				
Sparkman, Edward	1	3	3		
Sparkman, George	1	1	2		1
Slaughter, Thomas	1		3		5
Sylivan, Martha	2		1		
Siles, John	1	3	1		
Spivy, Joshua	1				
Stanby, John	1				
Sylivan, William	2	4	4		
Smith, Josiah	1	2	2		
Sylivan, William	1				
Stanley, Jonathan	1				3
Spivy, Aaron	1	2	2		10
Sylivan, John	2	3	5		
Stanley, William	1		1		1
Shyles, William (for Cullen Pollock)					43
Stanley, William	1		4		4
Shoulder, Thomas	1		1		
Ditto for Blake B. Wiggins					15
Shyles, John	1	2	2		
Stanby, David	2	1	4		23
Spivy, Jonathan	1				
Shyles, Benjamin	1				
Sheton, Mary		1	1		
Spence, John	1	1	2		4
Seay, James	1		6		
Spivy, Aaron	2	4	2		13
Sherlock, Thoˢ	4	5	2		4
Sowel, Frances	3	1	3		2
Sumlin, Noah	1	1	3		
Simons, George	1	1	1		1
Simons, Joseph	1	2	6		
Sowel, James	1				
Sumlin, Jacob	1	1	2		
Simons, James	1	1	3		
Simons, George	1	1	1		1
Simpson, John	1				
Sowel, John	1		3		
Slade, John	1	1	1		4
Spivy, John	1	1	5		2
Stall, John	1	5	4		
Swain, Richᵈ	3	1	2		3
Stallions, John	1		2		2
Smith, William	1		3		
Stallions, Mary	1	4	4		
Sorrel, Matthew	1		1		
Spivy, Easter	3		2		14
Sowel, Josiah	1				
Stallions, Mary	1				
Smith, Silas	1	5	4		2
Staten, Stephen	1		5		1
Stall, John	1		2		
Shoulder, John	1	1	2		
Stall, John	1	4	4		
Smith, Arthur	1				1
Smith, Sally		1	2		5
Sullivan, John	2	3	5		
Shaw, Nancy	2		2		
Stanton, Andrew	2	2	4		3
Swinson, Richard	2	2	4		1
Shiles, John	1	3	2		
Swain, Henrietta		1	4		4
Swain, Elisabeth	1	2	4		12
Todd, Moses	2	5	2		
Todd, Samuel	1		3		
Todd, Jesse	1		4		
Todd, Joshua	1				
Turner, David	3	3	2		12
Todd, Hardy	1				
Todd, William	1	3	5		
Trumble, Jethro					12
Thomas, Amos	1	2	3		
Theston, John	3	2	4		
Taylor, David	3	1	5		5
Turner, Simon	1	3	3		28
Thompson, James	1	1	3		
Thompson, John	3		2		
Turner, William	1	4	3		
Todd, Thomas	2	4	4		
Tibner, Perry	2				5
Tannison, Matthew	1	1	3		
Taylor, John	1				
Thompson, Charles	1		2		
Thompson, William	1	3	2		
Thomas, Jordon	1		2		
Turner, Amos	1	1			7
Thomson, Zedekiah	1				
Thomson, John	3	3	5		
Tarrinton, Benjamin	1	2	2		
Taylor, James	1	3	5		
Taylor, David	4	1	4		5
Turner, James	1	4	5		5
Thomas, Josiah	4		2		4
Talton, Benjamin	1				
Tall, James	1				
Trotman, Thoˢ	1	1	2		4
Tart, Nathan	1	1	2		1
Tart, Thomas	1	2	4		1
Tart, Nathan	4		1	1	3
Taylor, Abraham	2	3	1		3
Thomas, Jonathan	1		5		
Thompson, Noah	1	2	3		35
Thompson, William	1				10
Turner, Matthew			1		7
Thompson, Zedekiah	3		2	1	21
Thompson, Lewis	3		3		20
Trotman, Thomas	1	1	1		1
Turner, James	1	4	2		5
Turner, James	1	2	2		20
Tony, Anthony				4	
Thomas, Ezakiah	1	1	4		5
Thomas, James	1	1	2		
Thompson, James	1	1	2		
Vanpelt, Peter	1	2	3		
Vanpelt, James	1				
Vanson, Thomas	2	4	2		
Ventris, Moses	2		2	1	
Ventris, Moses	1	1	3		
Vale, Thomas	3	2	7	6	5
Virgin, William	1				
William, Allen	1				
Wilkinson, Joshua	1		2		
Willson, William	1	1	3		
Willson, Edward	1	4	5		
Whiteaker, Whitmill	1	1	2		
Willifred, P. Wright	1	1	4		
Williams, William	1				
Willfred, Archibald	1	1	3		
Weston, Willᵐ	1	5	4		
Weston, Ephraim	1	1	1		4
Weston, John	1	1	3	1	3
Weston, Ephraim	2		3		4
Weston, Solomon	1	3	5		
Williams, Joab	1	3	1		5
Wimbelly, Willᵐ	1		2		
West, Penelope	1	2	2		
Winant, Winants	1	1	4		1
White, Joshua	2		1		14
Wolfin, John	1		2	1	12
Williams, Benjamin	3	2	8		26
Wharburton, Luke	2	2			13
William, Moses	1		3		1
Williams, William	2				
Whitefield, Elisabeth			1		4
Worley, Daniel	2	1	3		10
Winslow, Rebecca		2	3		
Wells, Sarah			2		
Whitefield, Benjamin	1	3	6		14
Ward, Mary					6
Warren, James	1	1	2		
Watson, Sarah			3		2
Warwick, Jane		2	8	1	1
Wimbely, Mary		3	4		
Whitefield, Elisabeth			1		3
Ward, Mary			1		5
White, Peter	2	2	1		3
White, Luke	1	6	2		
White, William	1	2	3		4
Whitefield, Elizabeth			1		3
Williams, Benjamin	1		3		
Williams, Sarah			4		1
White, George	1	1	2		
White, Joel	1		2		
White, Luke	1	2	5		1
Wharburton, John				4	
Watford, Jonathan	1	2	1		5
White, William	1	4	3		
White, Jesse	1	3	3		
Wyns, Jesse	2	1	3		5
Wards, Joshua	1				
Ward, Thomas	1		4		16
Williams, John	1	3	3		
Wyns, John	1	3	4		1
Ward, Samuel	1	2	3		
Watford, Joseph	1		2		13
Walter, Timothy	1	3	1	1	8
Ward, Michael	1	2	1	1	3
Ward, James	1	1	2	1	4
Weeler, John	1				
Willson, Isaac	1	1	2		
Wilkins, Joshua	1		2		
Wiggins, Michael				4	
Watson, John	1		6		14
Willson, William	1	1	2		
Watson, John	1	3	5	1	10
Wiggins, Samuel				13	
Wilks, James	1	2	1		5
Willifred, Sarah				14	
Wimbely, Benjamin	1		2	1	
White, Noah	1	2	4		
White, Reuben	1				
Weston, Amos	1		2		
Willson, Edward	2	2	2		
Willfred, Isom	1				
Warren, James	1	1	2		
Whitefield, Elisabeth			3	1	2
Whitehouse, Lydia		1	1		
Watson, William	1	2	5		5
Williams, Elizabeth		3	2	2	7
Walker, Edward	1	1			
Williams, John	1				
Weston, Ephraim	1	1	1		4
West, Robert	1			1	15
Ward, Samuel	1		1		
White, Reuben	1				
Western, Amos	1	3	2		
Wilford, Archibald	1		3		
Williams, John	1				
Weston, William	1	5	2		
Wilks, James	1	3	2	2	
Wilks, Micajah	1		1		2
Wimbely, William	1	5	5		
Wimbely, William					
Wilks, James	1	1	1		6
Wiggins, Anthony	1				
Willson, William	1	2	2		
Wimbely, Willᵐ	1		2		7
Wimbely, John	2	2	4		9
Wimbely, Benjamin	2		3	1	3
Ward, Patsy		1	4	2	
White, Willᵐ	2	1	3	2	
Ditto for Samuel Johnston	2				61
Ware, Jarret	1	3	5		1
Wood, Jones	1	2	2		11
Wimbely, Frederick	1	4	5		5
Wimbely, Ezekiel	2	2	6		5
Wimbely, Lewis	1	2	2	1	8
Wimbely, Levy	1	1	3		
Willson, Edward	1		3		
Williams, James	1	1	6		2
White, Thomas (for John Granbury)					21
White, Thomas	1	1	2		2
Young, John	1	1	2		5
Yeats, William	1	1	2		
Yeats, Thomas	2	2	3		1
Yeats, Peter	1		2		2
Yeats, Elizabeth			4	1	3
Yeats, Ismay	1				
Yeats, Edward	1				
Young, John	1	1	2	1	5
Umplit, Job	1	1	2		
Umplit, Benjamin	1		2		
Ure, Tomfry	1		3		
Urvin, Mary	1	3	2		1
Zilano, George	3	1	2		2

EDENTON DISTRICT, CAMDEN COUNTY.

NAME OF HEAD OF FAMILY.	Free white males of 16 years and upward, including heads of families.	Free white males under 16 years.	Free white females, including heads of families.	All other free persons.	Slaves.	NAME OF HEAD OF FAMILY.	Free white males of 16 years and upward, including heads of families.	Free white males under 16 years.	Free white females, including heads of families.	All other free persons.	Slaves.	NAME OF HEAD OF FAMILY.	Free white males of 16 years and upward, including heads of families.	Free white males under 16 years.	Free white females, including heads of families.	All other free persons.	Slaves.
Mercer, Coy	3		3			Wilroy, William	3	2	4		2	Spence, Grieves	1		3		
Mercer, John	1	2	3			Sawyer, Asa	1	2	2		6	Spence, Mark	1		4		
Sanderlin, Elizabeth	1		4			Winn, Letetia			2			McCoy, Mary	1	1	2		
Sanderlin, Levi	1	1	4			Johnson, Molly			3			Riggs, Isaac, Junr	1		1		
Sanderlin, Jacob	1	2	2			Overton, Garshum	2	2	4			Riggs, Noah	1	1	4		
Upton, Christian		1	3			Sikes, Elizabeth		2	4			Spence, John	1		2		
Shanning, Lovey		3	3			Rifle, Rebecca			5			Rhodes, Newton	2	3	3		
Mercer, Coy, Junr	1		2			Will (a free negro)				2		Bright, Malachi	2	4	5		
Morrissett, Peter	2	1	1		1	Ferrell, Benjamin	1	2	2			Chamberlin, Sally		1	6		
Gregory, Noah	1	1	3		3	Evans, David	2		4			Bright, Hezekiah	1	2			
Lockwood, Holland	1					Etheridge, David	1					Overton, Anthony	1	1	1		
Williams, Leonard	1	1	1		3	Sawyer, Job	1	5	3			Chamberlin, Joshua	1	3	3		1
Gregory, David	1	2	2			Etheridge, Joshua	2	1	3		1	Powers, Caleb	1		1		
Bernard, Prissila		1	2			Sawyer, Jeremiah	2		2		5	Overton, Richard	2	4	3		
Terrel, Mary	1		3		6	Cooper, Seth	2	2	1			Overton, Eli	1	3	2		
Gregory, Judith			4			Taylor, William	1	7	2			Bright, Jeremiah	1		3		1
Greenman, Elizabeth		2	3			Overton, Lazarus	1	1	2			McFarson, Aby	1	1	2		
Oakley, Elizabeth			3			Ketor, William	1	2	1			McFarson, Matthew	2	1	1		
Spelman, Lydia				4		Overton, James	2	1	2			Overton, David	1	2	2		
Whitehouse, Sarah	1		4			Overton, Joseph	2	3	5			Jones, Edward	1	3	3		
Lamb, Abner	1		2		11	Scaff, David	1		2			McFarshon, Demsey	1	1	4		1
Kemp, Ann	2	2	4			Overton, Francis	1	2	4			Brite, Charles	1				
Morrissett, Jonathan	1		1			McCoy, Nancy		1	2		1	Linton, Lemuel	1				
Forbes, Isaac, Junr	1	1	4			Upton, Hilliry	1	2	2		3	Chamberlin, Joshua, Junr	1				
Snow, Dinah			2			Sawyer, Zale	1	1	1			Chamberlin, Jeremiah	1	1	2		
Overton, John	1		1			Robertson, Benjamin B.	1	1	1			McCoy, Joshua	1	3	4		
Bell, William	2	1	2			Robertson, Fanny		1	2			Chamberlin, Elizabeth			1		
Smith, Elizabeth		1	2			Overton, Joshua	2		2			Overton, Aby		3	2		
Forbes, Suthy	1	1	2			McFarson, Sally		3	2			Davis, Francis	1	2	1		2
Forbes, Elib	1	1	5			Culpepper, Daniel	1	2	1			Taylor, William	1	4	4		2
Garrott, Jacob	1		1			McCoy, John	1	2	1		1	Whitehouse, Gedeon	1		3		
Sanderlin, Joseph	1					McCoy, Nathan	1	1	1			Whitehouse, Amy	1	1	2		
Gregory, Samson	1	2	5			McCoy, Kesiah			2			Conner, Asa	2	1	3		
Sawyer, Benjamin	3	3	6			Snowden, Benjamin	1		3			Prichard, Thomas	2				
Lambert, John	1	2	2			Ketor, John	2	2	2			Weavour, John	2		1		
Gregory, James	1	2	3		1	McCoy, Joel	1	1	2			Prichard, Mary	1	2	4		2
Morgan, Macke	3	1	6		1	McFarson, John	1	4	2			Grandy, Ann			2		7
Wilroy, Abraham	2	1	3		6	Harrison, Demsey	2	1	2			Barcoe, Willis	1	1	2		
Sawyer, Jacob	4	2	3			McCoy, Malachi	1	2	1			Sawyer, Enoch	2		4	1	10
Empson, Caleb	1		2		9	Hearring, Jonathan	3	1	3		23	Rhodes, Samuel	1		2	3	
Grandy, Thomas, Junr	1		2		9	Milford, Matthew	1		5		1	Jones, Benjamin	4		2	4	36
O'Daniel, Elizabeth		2	5			McCoy, William	1		4			Milford, Matthew	1	2	2		
Gregory, John	2	1	3			McCoy, Bridget		3	2			Kenady, John	1				
Humphries, John	1					Pritchard, David	2	1	5		3	Sawyer, Mary	1	1	3		
Gregory, Isaac	1	1	1			Linton, Thomas	1	3	6			Hastings, Devotion	1	1	2		
Gregory, Aby			2			McCoy, James	2	2	2			Hastings, Carter	1		4		
Gregory, Matthias	1	2	4			McFarson, Jessie	1		2			Taylor, John	1	1	2		
Spilman, Timothy				1		Kenady, Robert	1	2	3			Herrington, Matthew	1	1	1		
Sikes, William	1	3	2			Taylor, Thomas	1	1	2			Spence, Thomas	1				
Ackland, John	2		2			Kite, William	1	5	2			Jones, Joseph	3	2	5		15
Bell, Joseph	1	2	3		2	Ketor, Solomon	1	1	3			Burges, Thomas	1	2	3		
Bell, Thomas	1					Taylor, Esdars	1	1	1			Grandy, Charles	1	1	4		23
Spence, Thomas, Junr	1		1			Ketor, Elisha	1	1	1			Pugh, James	1	3	1		
Williams, Benjamin	1	3	5			Smith, Daniel	1	2	2			Norton, John	1	1	1		
Williams, Joseph	2		1			Smith, Hannah			1		2	Cartwright, Jesse	1				
Dauge, Caleb	1	1	5		1	Whitehouse, John	1	1				Bray, Samuel	1	4	3		
Sawyer, Demsey	1		2			Overton, Richard	1		1			Needham, Joseph	1		2		7
Grandy, Sarah		2	2		4	Chamberlin, Nathan	1					Willson, Caleb	2		3		
Jackson, Thomas	1					Spence, John	1	2	1			Needham, Thomas	2	3	5		1
Mansfield, John	3	1				Grandy, Caleb	2	3	5		9	Brown, Dinah			1		1
Sawyer, Caleb, Junr	1					Smith, Elizabeth		2	3			Beels, Jesse	1				
Hulett, Abraham	1	1	2			Barcoe, Coston	1	2	1		1	Jones, Britton	1				
Hulett, Isaac	1	1	2			Burges, John	2	2	4			Squires, Elizabeth	1	1	6		
Hulett, Nelly	2	3	1			Burges, Zephaniah	1	1	4		4	Read, Robert	1				
Sawyer, Evan	1	1	8			Forbes, Surthy	1	1	1			White, Elias	1	3	3		
Noble, Thamer			4			Gregory, William	1		3			Snow, William	1		3		
Rifle, Elizabeth		1	1			Gallop, Luke	2	1	3			Godfrey, John	2	4	3		
Dauge, James	2		1		1	Toskey, Caleb	1	1	1			Laughinghouse, John	1	1	8		4
Dauge, Meriam		2	5			Griffin, John	2	3	3			Neval, William	1		6		
Empson, John	2	2	2			Sanderlin, Eli	1	1				Dauge, Willis	1		3		
Jones, Joseph, Junr	1	2	1			Spelman, Aaron				1		Griffin, Elizabeth		3	2		
Cartwright, Robert	2	1	2			Williams, William	1	1	3			Lurry, Thomas	2	1	5		12
Spence, David	1	2	1		1	Jones, Caleb	1		2			Barcoe, William	3	1	4		2
Sawyer, Shadrach	1		4			Jones, John, Junr	1		1		1	Jones, John	2	3	6		
Sawyer, Hilliry	1		4			Kennady, John	1	2				Sanderlin, James	3	1	2		
Smith, James	1	2	3		1	Rhodes, Samuel	1	1	3			Forbes, Aaron	2		1		
Mason, John	10	4	7		10	Payne, Nathaniel	3					Sanderlin, Robert	2	4	4		
Smith, Darcas			2		3	Goodlin, Richard	1		1			Gallop, Joshua	1	2	4		
Dill, Balser	3		2			Dowdy, Dinah			3			Dauge, Peter	2		3		12
Taylor, Lydia	1	1	2			Cartwright, Samuel	1	1	1		2	Bray, Isaac	1	4	4		
Hall, David			1	2		Chamberlin, Henry	1		3			Faircloth, Edward	1		5		
Jones, Joseph (son of Evan)	1	2	5			Overton, Amos	1	2	3			White, Cornelius	2	1	1		
Taylor, Jacob	2	2	3			Overton, Polly		1	4			Gray, Laban	1	2	3		
Edny, Newton	5	2	4		10	Gray, John (R. B.)	1	2	3		1	Harrison, John W	2	1	3		
Cartwright, Daniel	1	1	1		2	Burnham, Ann	3	1	1		2	Wright, Thamer	1	1	2		5
McFarson, Joseph	3	2	1			Edny, Newton (son of S.)	1		2		2	Harrison, Elizabeth	2		3		5
Sawyer, Pharoah	2	1	4			Sawyer, William	1	3	2			Wright, Mary		2	3		
David, Elisha	1		1		4	Riggs, Isaac	2	1				Gregory, Abi	1		2		
Abbott, Mary			2			Sawyer, John	1		1			Garlington, James	1	2	2		
Burnham, David	1	2	4		7	Overton, Asa	1		1			Williams, John	1	5	5		
Etheridge, Willis	2	2	2		3	Cartwright, Jabez	1	1	5			Kite, Zachariah	3		2		
Richardson, Sarah		1	6			Overton, Henry	1	1	2		1	McDowel, Ann		1	1		
Jones, William	1	4	1			Overton, Joshua	1	1	1			Seamore, Benjamin	1	1	3		
White, Benjamin	1					Overton, Peter	2	2	3			Seamore, Adam	1	1	1		
Campbell, Josiah	1	3	3		12	Rhodes, Leven	1	2	2			Burgess, Ann		3	3		
Pritchard, Benjamin	1	1	4		2	Sawyer, Joel	4	1	5			Beals, Julian	2	1	3		
Jones, John	2	1	4		10	Chamberlin, James	1	2	3			Toxey, Sarah		3	3		
Deal, John	1	5	2			Spence, Noah	1	2	2			Cartwright, Edy		1	1		

EDENTON DISTRICT, CAMDEN COUNTY—Continued.

Column headers (applies to each of the three panels below):
- **A** = Free white males of 16 years and upward, including heads of families.
- **B** = Free white males under 16 years.
- **C** = Free white females, including heads of families.
- **D** = All other free persons.
- **E** = Slaves.

NAME OF HEAD OF FAMILY	A	B	C	D	E
Mitchell, Kesiah	1		5		
Smith, William	1	1	1		1
Burgess, Hezekiah	1	5	2		
Burris, John	1		1		
Needham, Thomas Junr	1	2	2		
Gray, Joshua	1	2	3		
Bray, Daniel	1	1	1		
Wright, Barny	1	2	2		4
Beals, Micajah	2	3	3		
Oggs, Charles				4	
Seamore, David	1	1	2		
Mitchell, Mary		2	2		
Burges, Thomas	1	1	3		
Cartwright, Moses	1	2	2		
Cartwright, Elijah	1		1		
Faircloth, Isaac	1		1		
Seamore, Jarvis	3		1		1
Sharborough, Christopher	1	1	1		1
Burges, John (D. R.)	1	2	3		1
Johnston, Ann		1	4		
Cartwright, Tulle	1	1	2		
Cox, Jesse	1		1		
Burges, Zebedee			4		
Canady, Alexander	1				
Bell, Josiah	2	1	3		
Canady, John	1				
Poyner, John	1	3	4		5
Beals, Zephaniah	1	1	2		
Godfrey, Isaac	1		2		
Smith, Thomas	1	1	2		
Seamore, Abel	1		1		1
Mitchell, Richard	1	1	1		
Beals, Jacob	1	1	3		
Cartwright, John	1		4		
Cartwright, Ann		1	2		
Baum, Peter	1	2	3		6
Seamore, Abraham	1		2		1
Curling, Josiah	2	1	3		
Jones, Willoby	1	3	2		
Beals, Asa	1	2	5		
Seamore, John	2	2	3		
Riggs, Isaac	1		3		
Mercer, William	1		6		2
Needham, Gideon	1	3	3		
Dowdy, James	1	4	2		
Miller, Stephen	1	3	4		9
Cartwright, Hosea	1				
Mitchell, William	1	2			
Sandertin, Griffith	1		1		1
Cooper, Benjamin	2	1	4		
Gray, William	2	1	2		
Morrisett, Cason	1	5	1		
Hayvard, Thomas	3	1	3		
Burges, Demsey	1	2	3		30
Divers, Francis	1	2	1		
Gail, Sarah	1	3	4		5
Gregory, Lemuel	1	1	3		
Standley, Evan	1	3	2		
Mercer, Jesse	1		2		
Lewis, William	1	1	1		1
Gregory, Caleb	2	2	3		
Nichols, Thomas	1	1	1		9
Abbott, Henry	1		1		6
Mercer, Thomas	2	3	4		2
Dayley, Thomas	1		2		
Coats, Malchia	2	1	2		9
Lewis, Ralph	1	1	4		10
Wright, Elizabeth			3		1
Taylor, John	1	1	3		
Bell, Nathan	1	1	4		
Sexton, Jeremiah	1		2	2	
Upton, William	1	1	1		3
Snowden, William	2		2		6
Nash, Sally	1	5	2		
Philips, Daniel	1	5	2		3
Riggs, David	1	1	2		
Williams, Lodewick	1	1	4		1
Williams, John (N. R.)	2	4	5		
Linton, Abel	1		2		
Abbott, Joseph	1		3		
Sanderlin, Devotion	2	2	2		8
Watkins, Sarah	1	1	2		6
Grandy, William	1	1	3		18
Hughs, William Junr	1		1		1
Barnard, Lavina		4	3		2
Barclift, Blake	1	5	1		3
Mercer, Peter	4	1	1		
Sawyer, Stephen	1	1	4		
Grandy, Thomas	1	1	4		9
Snowden, Nathan	1	1	4		14
Etheridge, Davis	1		1		
Etheridge, Grandy	4	2	4		6
Sawyer, Willis	2	1	2		5
Gray, John	1		2		13
Sawyer, Griffith	3		2		7
Sawyer, John	1	1	5		18
Godfrey, Jesse	1	3	2		
Fennel, Michael	1				1

NAME OF HEAD OF FAMILY	A	B	C	D	E
Mercer, William	1	1	3		
Sawyer, Elisha	4	1	5		2
Freshwater, William A.	3	1	3		1
Snowden, John	1		3		4
Perkins, John	2		1		
Linton, Isaac	2	2	4		1
Etheridge, Willis	2	3	2		2
Burges, William	1	1	2	2	2
Harney, Silby	1	7	3	1	4
Forbes, Malchia	2	3	2		1
Berry, John	1	2	3		5
Berry, Solomon	1	3	2		
Dunlap, James	2	2	3		1
Bell, Samuel	1	1	2		10
Roberts, Jonathan	1	2	4		3
Nash, Thomas, Junr	1			2	
McBride, Elisha	1	2	6		10
Sawyer, Levi	1	2	4		2
Dicks, Charles	2		2		
Sawyer, Thomas	1		1		
Harrison, Isaac	2	3	5		1
Wright, John	1	1	3		10
Swills, Seth	3	1	7		3
Etheridge, Grace			2		
Wright, Capt William	3	1	5		
Parker, James	2	1	3		
Smithson, John	1		1		2
Lerry, Evan	2	4	3		3
Sawyer, Thomas (up River)	1	1	3		2
Dailey, Enoch	2	3	2		2
Barnard, Edward	1	1	2		2
Brockett, Joel	1		3		4
Squires, John	1	3	4		
Spence, James	1		2		
Toxey, Meriam	1	2	6		
Love, William	2	4	4		
Kerby, James	1	1	1		3
Sawyer, Jacob	3	3	3		2
Riggs, Abraham	1	5	2		2
Jones, Evan	1	1	2		11
Forehand, Lowis		2	3		
Richardson, Hugh	1	3	5		2
Willson, Willis	1	5	2		6
Jalot, Thomas	1	2			
Toxey, Elliott	1	1	1		
Sawyer, Tulle	1	3	4		3
Jerrell, Mary		1	1		
Jerrell, Tabitha		1	2		
Williams, James	1	1	4		
Macoy, William	4	2	4		1
Nash, Thomas	1	4	4		3
Whithurst, William	3	3	4		4
Grandy, Absalom	1		3		14
Gregory, Abner	1	2	4		
Brite, Nathan	4	3	3		
Jones, John	1		3		2
Towner, Richard	1	1	3		
Wright, William	2	1	2		18
Grandy, Noah	1	1	4		1
Casey, Demsey	2	1	1		1
Emson, John	2		1		
Cotter, Timothy	2	2	2		8
Sawyer, Elistra (B.S.)	4	3	4		
Dauge, John	2	2	8		8
Gregory, Nathan	2	1	7		
Humphries, Isaac	1		9		
Ferrell, Samuel	1	1	6		2
Homer, John	1		3		1
Willson, Benjamin	2	1	6		6
Webster, William	1	1	2		2
Humphries, Adam	1		2		
Forbes, Matthias	1	1	2		
Cartwright, Caleb	1	3	3		3
Sawyer, David	1	2	2		
Hatch, Lizar	1				
Kelly, Meriam	2	2	3		7
Sawyer, James	1	2	1		3
Cartwright, Robert	1	1	2		5
Cartwright, James	1	3	3		1
Snowden, Edmund	1		1		10
Bray, Henry	1	2	4		2
Bray, Daniel	1		3		
Cartwright, Isaac	1	1	2		
Aydlott, Henry	1		2		
Dauge, Isaac	1		2		7
Sawyer, Lucy	1		5		
Sawyer, David	2	1			
Pretman, Elijah	1		2		
Gregory, Cornelius	2	2	5		6
Sikes, John	1		1		
Herrington, Jonathan	1	3	1		
Gregory, Richard	1		2		2
Sanderlin, Ezekiel	4	2	2		6
Toxey, Joseph	1		1		9
Edny, Robert	2				1
Forbes, Henry	2	2	3		7
Sanderlin, Nancy			3		6

NAME OF HEAD OF FAMILY	A	B	C	D	E
Davis, Samuel	1	1	2		1
Ferrell, James	1	3	3		1
Bell, William	1	2	3		
Brown, Benjamin	1	3	3		
Morgan, Claudias	1	2	6		
Walkup, Samuel	1		1		
Etheridge, Thomas	1		2		4
Dunkin, David	2	4	6		
Cartwright, Jacob	2	1	3		
Forbes, Caleb	3	1	3		1
Brockett, John	1	4	2		9
Parr, Jesse	1	3	2		
Griffith, Joseph	1				3
Forbes, Adam	1	3	3		
Williams, Lodewick, Senr	1	2	5		1
Barco, Tabitha	1	1	1		
Williams, Urias	1	3	1		1
Jones, Timothy	1	3	4		2
Sawyer, Richard	1	2	4		
Gray, Cornelius	1	1	1		11
Dauge, Evan	1		1		1
Upton, Edward	2	1	5		
Coats, James	1		5		
Coats, Caleb	1		1		
Lamb, Luke	3	2	5		12
Gilford, Isaac	1	2	2		15
Gregory, James	1	1	2		
Gregory, Asael	2	1	2		
Gregory, Judy (up R.)	1	1	2		
Whithurst, Sarah (up R.)	1		4		
Harrison, Robert	4		4		
Harrison, Peter	1	1	4		
Harrison, Caleb	1	1	4		
Harrison, John	1		3		
Sanderlin, Isaac	1		2		
Bray, Christopher	1	2	4		
Tumlin, Susannah	1		4		
Kite, Zachariah	1				
Burges, Mary	1		3		
Perry, Elizabeth	1	2	4		
Upton, Willis	3	1	4		4
Gail, John	1		2		8
Sawyer, Edmund	1				11
Bright, Willis	2		2		13
McPherson, Joshua	2	2	6		9
Cartwright, Morgan	1	1	1		5
Sawyer, Mary	1		1		4
Bell, Robert	1	3	1		2
Herrington, Isaac	1	1			3
Williams, Robert	1	3	3		
Sanderlin, Benjamin	1	1	2		
Barco, Adron	1	1	3		
Garrott, William	1	1	2		
Garrott, James	3	2	3		
Kite, Malchia	1		2		
Mercer, Joshua	1	3	3		
Sanderlin, Thomas	1	1	3		
Barco, Evan	1				
Gregory, Silvia	1		2		2
Walston, Thomas	1	1	2		
Walston, Mary	1		2		
Staples, Thomas	1		2		
Jerroll, James	1		1		
Skilton, Christopher	1	3	4		
Forbes, James	2		3		
Forbes, Jacob	1	1	3		
Sheppard, John	1	1	1		
Adkins, Thomas	1	1	1		
Williams, Shadrach	1	1	1		
Forbes, Joshua, Senr	1	2	3		
Forbes, Sarah	1	1	3		
Forbes, Thomas	3		4		1
Forbes, Isaac, Senr	1	3	2		2
Bray, Thomas	1	2	3		
White, James	1	1	3		
Forbes, Aaron	1		1		
Forbes, Isabella			1		
Barclift, John	2	1	3		
Morris, Benjamin	1	1	1		
Gregory, James (N. River)	1	1	2		
Gray, Lodewick	1		5		
Gallop, Isaac	1	1	3		
Gregory, Genl Isaac	2				23
Gregory, Isaac, Junr	1	1	2		6
Sawyer, Demsey	1	3	5	1	18
Ballance, Joseph					
Bray, Henry (S. N.)	3	1	6		
Griffith, John (M. R.)	1	1	3		15
Gardner, Debby			3		7
Gregory, Abi					
Gregory, Caleb (N. R.)	1	2	2		
Gregory, Arthur	1	2	4		
Gregory, Malchia (N. R.)	1	3	4		2
Mercer, John, Senr	1	1	2		

EDENTON DISTRICT, CHOWAN COUNTY (EXCLUDING EDENTON TOWN).

NAME OF HEAD OF FAMILY.	Free white males of 16 years and upward, including heads of families.	Free white males under 16 years.	Free white females, including heads of families.	All other free persons.	Slaves.
Ashley, William	2	2	3		
Ashley, Meade	1	3	3		
Ashley, Jeremiah	1	1	3		
Ashley, Joseph	1	1	1		
Ashley, William, Junr	3	2	3		
Ashley, Peggy			2		
Avery, John	1		4		1
Bartle, Anthony	4	2	4		2
Bains, George	4	5	4		
Burkett, Thomas	1				
Blount, Ann		2	2		6
Beasley, Martha		1	2		7
Beasley, Elizabeth	1	1	3		20
Barrow, John	1	1	2		5
Benbury, Richard, Esqr	1		4		15
Beasley, John	2		1		8
Beasley, George	1		6		4
Beasley, Robert	2				4
Benbury, Thomas, Esqr	2				88
Benbury, Joseph	1				14
Blount, John	1	2	1		14
Beasley, James	1	1	3		4
Boulton, Jonathan	1		4		12
Bunch, James	1				2
Bunch, Mary	1	2	3		11
Bunch, Joseph	1				1
Bonner, Henry	1	3	4		13
Bond, John, Esqr	1	4	4		9
Benbury, Ruth			5		10
Beasley, Francis	1		1		2
Bennett, William, Esqr	1	4	6		49
Boyd, Meriam			3		6
Badham, Mary	1	1	2		5
Bonner, Thomas	1				
Bains, George, Junr	1	1	4		17
Bond, Elizabeth		2	4		20
Blount, Edmund	4	2	6	2	34
Brinn, James	1	2	1		1
Bunch, Solomon	1	1	1		1
Bunch, Sarah			1		
Bunch, William	1		3		1
Bunch, Ishmael	1	1	3		
Bacchus, John	1				
Bunch, Prissilla		4	5		6
Bunch, Cullin	1	3	2		1
Boyce, Leah	1		2		
Bond, James	1				
Buckley, Richard	2	1	3		3
Bacchus, Thomas	2	2	3		
Byrum, Joel	2	2	4		
Blanchard, Micajah	1	2			6
Bufkin, Sarah			1		
Byrum, Isaac	2	3	3		
Byrum, Isaac, Junr	1	1	1		
Bufkin, William	1				
Byrum, Lavina		2	1		
Bowen, George	1				
Bosworth, Obediah	1				
Crucy, Mary			2		5
Crucy, Lemuel, Esqr	1	2	1		29
Crucy, Nathan	1	1	2		6
Crucy, Frederick	1	2	3		18
Chessire, Willson	1		2		2
Charlton, Thomas	1	2	1		11
Clements, John	1	1	2		
Charlton, John	1	1	3		3
Charlton, Job	1		1		
Cox, John	1		1		2
Chew, Mary			4		
Coffield, Edward	2	1	3	1	12
Coffield, Benjamin	2		1	1	19
Coffield, John	1	3	1		19
Cox, Elisha	1		1		3
Champion, Joseph	3	3	2		1
Chambers, Thomas	1	2	3	2	
Cabarrus, Stephen, Esqr	2		1	1	73
Collins, William	1				8
Cannon, Jeremiah		1	2		1
Coffield, Jeremiah	1	1	2	1	
Coffield, Michal			3		4
Chappell, Micajah	1	1			
Chappell, Josiah	1		1		
Caruthers, William	1	1	1		
Cullen, William	1	2	1		5
Chappell, James	1		1		
Copeland, Josiah, Esqr	3		4		21
Copeland, Josiah, Junr	1	2	2		
Copeland, Joseph	3		2		
Coffield, Job	1		2		2
Cleyland, Rebecca			2		
Donaldson, Robert	2	1	1		2
Deshon, Jacob	1		1		
Deshon, Augustine	2	1	4		3
Deshon, Lewis	1	1	2		1
Deal, William	1		1		
Deal, Malachi	2	3	1		

NAME OF HEAD OF FAMILY.	Free white males of 16 years and upward, including heads of families.	Free white males under 16 years.	Free white females, including heads of families.	All other free persons.	Slaves.
Delany, John	1				
Elliott, Stephen	1		3		4
Evans, James	2	1	2		
Eliff, John	1	2	4		3
Elliott, Miles	1	4	3		6
Eccleston, John	2		3		1
Earl, Charity		1	2		10
Earl, Ann		1	1		26
Evans, John	1	1	5		
Ellis, Thomas	2		6		
Gregory, William	1	2	2		7
Gregory, Luke	1	1	4		7
Garrott, Richard	1	1	5		3
Farrow, Tinch	1				
Fife, John	1	1	2		
Fallow, William	1	1	3		1
Fullerton, John	1				
Farrow, John	1	1	1		
Ford, William	1	1	2		
Floyd, John	2	1	4		
Felton, William	2		1		6
Felton, Shadrack	1	2	1		11
Felton, Ann		1	2		2
Felton, John	1				1
Floyd, William	1	1	5		
Garrott, Everard	3	1	1		2
Garrott, George	1				
Godwin, Caleb	1	1	2		6
Goodwin, William	1	2	5		1
Garrott, James	1	1	1		3
Griffin, Willis	3	2	1		
Goodwin, Thomas	2		5		1
Goodwin, Joseph	1		1		
Goodwin, Lewis	1	1	2		
Gregory, Henry	1		1		7
Gregory, Benjamin	1	3	1	1	1
Hobbs, Moses	1		1		1
Haughton, Jonathan	3	4	4		8
Haughton, William	3	1	3		
Haughton, Jeremiah	1				4
Haughton, Edward	1		4		7
Haughton, Charles	1	3	3		22
Haughton, Richard	1	3	4		15
Holmes, William	1	1	3		4
Hall, Judith			2		3
Horniblow, John, Esqr	2	4	4		27
Hassell, Jesse	3	3	3		4
Hallsey, Henry	1		3		
Hoskins, Sarah		2	4		8
Howent, Nathaniel	1		1		10
Hall, Clement	2		3		5
Hinesley, Martha	1		3		
Hoskins, Samuel	2		2		10
Hoskins, Richard, Esqr	3	1	7		20
Holmes, Mary		1	1		3
Hoskins, John, Junr	1				
Hicks, William	1	1	2		
Hicks, Job	1	3			
Hicks, Patrick	1				
Hurdle, Josiah	1	1	4		5
Hallsey, William	1	3	4		
Hallsey, Daniel	1	3	8		
Hallsey, Malachi	2	2	4		
Hallsey, Cullen	2	2	1		1
Hallsey, Harris	1				
Hoskins, John	1		2		4
Harrell, William	1		4		
Hurdle, Martin	1	2	3		
Hollowell, Luke	1	3	3		
Hurdle, Henry	1	2	2		1
Hurdle, Harmon	1		2		8
Humphries, Richard	1	4	4		
Hobbs, Thomas	1	4	4		
Hurdle, Benjamin	1	1	3		5
Hobbs, John	1				
Hollowell, Abana	2	2	3		6
Harris, Abraham	2	2	1		
Humphries, William	1				
Johnston, Samuel, Esqr	2		3		96
Johnson, Charles, Esqr	2	2			35
Johnson, Joshua	1		1		
James, Edward	1	2	2		3
Jones, James	1	5	4		11
Jones, Thomas	6	2	4		7
Jones, William	2		5		22
Joiner, Humphry	1				
Jordan, Jacob, Esqr	2		2		11
Jordan, Demny	1		2		
Jordan, William	1		2		1
Jordan, Ichabod	1				
Jordan, Hance	1	2	1		
Jordan, Charles	2	2	6		
Jordan, Nicholas	1		3		
Jackson, Mary			1		2
Jackson, William	2	1	7		19
Jones, Josiah	1		3		

NAME OF HEAD OF FAMILY.	Free white males of 16 years and upward, including heads of families.	Free white males under 16 years.	Free white females, including heads of families.	All other free persons.	Slaves.
Jordan, Joseph	1	3	4		2
Jordan, Jacob	1	2	3		
Jordan, Caleb	1		1		1
Jordan, Nathan	1	1	2		
Jameson, Bond	1		3		2
Johnson, Joseph	1	1	3		
Johnson, Bersheba			4		
Jordan, Josiah	1	1	4		
Keal, James	3	1	4		
Kirby, William	1		2		
Leary, John	1		2		8
Luten, Henderson	1	2	3		3
Liles, William	2	2	2		9
Leary, Job	1		3		10
Lane, Samuel	1	1	1		
Lane, Abraham	1	3	5		
Lane, James	1	2	2		
Lane, Miles	1		2		
Mixon, Hannah			2		
Ming, Thomas, Junr	1		2		2
Moran, John		1	2		
Middleton, John	2	3	2		3
McNider, Thomas	2		2		
Ming, Richard	1	1	2		2
Ming, James	1		1		4
Ming, John	1	1	4		1
Ming, Joseph	1	1	2		5
McGuire, Philip, Junr	1	2	2		5
Miller, Ephraim	3				2
Miller, Mason	1	4	2		
Miller, Malachi	1	3	2		4
Miller, Mary		1	1		
Matthias, Thomas	1		3	1	3
Muns, Thomas	1	1	4		
Muns, William	2	2	5		
Muns, William, Junr	2		2		
Mitchel, John	2	6	4		
McGuire, John	2		6	5	
McGuire, Samuel	1		1		2
Meridith, John	1	2	2		
Mansfield, Zebulon	1	2	4		
Moore, Robert	1				
Moore, William	1		4		
Ming, Thomas	2	1	4		10
Martin, William	1	3	2		
McClenny, Ruth		1	4		
McGuire, Philip	1	3	2		26
Norcom, John	3	2	3		26
Norcom, Frederick	3	3	1		15
Newbern, Nicholas	1	1	3		
Newbern, William	1				5
Newbern, Willson	1	2	1		
Norflet, Abraham	1	1	2		4
O'Neil, Peter	1	1	3		
Pettyjoh, Abraham	1	3	1		3
Pittyjohn, John	1	2	3		3
Procter, John	2				4
Procter, Ruben	1		4		1
Perkins, Robert			4		
Price, James	2		2		6
Price, Thomas	2	2	7		9
Price, Noah	1				14
Parker, Seth	1	1			2
Parker, Isaac			3		3
Parker, Willis	1		1		15
Padgett, John	1		3		
Poppleston, John	1		2		
Pettyjohn, Job	1				
Privet, Elizabeth	2		2		
Parrish, James	1				
Parrish, John	3	4	3		2
Parker, Nathan	1		1		2
Parker, Elisha	1	2	3		
Philips, John	1				
Powell, Charles	3	3	2		8
Perry, Samuel	1	3	4		
Parker, Samuel	1	1	5		
Perry, Amos			1		
Paddin, Patsey			3		1
Parker, Peter	1	3	3		
Parker, Job	2	2	8		
Parker, Enoch	1	2	4		
Roberts, Thomas	1	3	1		20
Righton, William	1	3	3		
Rea, Samuel	1		2		
Rea, Thomas	1	2	3		3
Roberts, Willis	1	2	1		5
Robinson, John	1		4		
Roberts, Charles	1	2	3		13
Roberts, William, Esqr	2		3		21
Rodith, Mary			2		
Rodith, John	1	2	7		5
Rogers, Joseph	2		2		26
Roberts, James, Esqr	2	1	3		7
Simons, Argyle	2		2		
Simons, Joshua	1				

EDENTON DISTRICT, CHOWAN COUNTY (EXCLUDING EDENTON TOWN)—Continued.

NAME OF HEAD OF FAMILY.	Free white males of 16 years and upward, including heads of families.	Free white males under 16 years.	Free white females, including heads of families.	All other free persons.	Slaves.
Simons, John	1	2	3		2
Simons, Jacob	1	2	2		23
Simons, Charlton	1				9
Simons, William	1		1		2
Simons, Thomas	1	2	2		2
Simson, Samuel	1	4	3		2
Simson, Benjamin	1		2		
Smith, Rebecca			2		2
Swann, Rebecca			1		2
Sutton, James	1	2	3		8
Small, Benjamin	3	4	5		8
Standin, John	1	2	1	1	
Small, Josiah	3	1	5		5
Sterns, James	1		4		
Sumner, Abraham	1	2	3		7
Standin, Joseph	1		3		15
Sowell, Mary		1	4		
Stewart, Mary	1		3		1
Skinner, Evan	2		1		9
Skinner, Samuel	1	2	4		1
Skinner, William	1	3	1		2
Simson, Evan	1	2	2		
Simson, John	2		1		2
Simson, Mary	1	1	2		1
Simson, William	4	3	3		9
Simson, John, Junr	2	5	3		1
Stacey, Nathaniel	1		1		
Small, Joseph	1	1	2		3
Smith, John	1	1	4		
Stallings, Nathan	1	1	1		
Stallings, Miles	1				
Stallings, Nicholas	2	2	6		1
Stallings, Elias	1	1	3		
Scott, Joseph	2		3		
Taylor, John	1	2	3		1
Taylor, Thomas	1		2		
Taylor, John, Junr	1				
Thack, Gregory	1		1		
Thomson, Thomas W	1	2	2		12
Toppin, Samuel	1	2	5		
Trotman, Amos	1		1		7
Thurston, William	1	1	1		
Underhill, Sarah			3		16
Vail, Thomas	1	4	2		18
Whiteman, Matthew	1	2	2		2
Webb, William	1	1	3		
Wilkins, William	1		1		11
Wyatt, Joshua	1	2	2		2
Walton, Holladay	1		3		2
Wilden, John	1				2
Ward, Thomas (Yeopin)	1	3	3		
Webb, John	3	2	3		
Wedburn, Joseph	1				
Wilden, Francis	1		2		2
White, James	1				2
Woodward, Edward	1	3	4		1
Ward, John	1		2		
Ward, Solomon	1	1	2		
White, Silas	2	3	3		
White, Charles	1	1			
Woodward, Richard	1	2	2		3
Walton, John	1	2	4		3
Welch, Edward	1	6	3		
Ward, Lowderick	1	1	4		
Ward, Thomas	3	1	4		
Ward, Humphrey	1		1		1
Ward, Ephraim	1	1	2		
Ward, Frederick	1				
Woodward, James	1		3		
Wood, Seth	1	2	3		
Ward, William, Junr	1	1	2		
Welch, Isaac	1		3		
Welch, Margaret	1	3	3		
Ward, Jeremiah	1				
Woodward, Jane			4		
Ward, Hardy	1		4		
Wood, Judith			1		
Ward, Thomas (son of Willm)	1	1	2		
Winslow, William	1	1	2		1
Ward, Denby	1		1		1
Ward, Nathan	1		1		
Ward, Aaron	1				
White, Thomas	1		2		9
Ward, Nathan, Junr	1		1		
White, George	1	3	2		
Ward, Elizabeth	1		4		
Ward, Lewis	1	1	5		
Winslow, Job	1	2	1		1

EDENTON DISTRICT, EDENTON TOWN.

NAME OF HEAD OF FAMILY.	Free white males of 16 years and upward, including heads of families.	Free white males under 16 years.	Free white females, including heads of families.	All other free persons.	Slaves.
Allen, Jemima			1		2
Allen, Nathaniel, Esqr	4		5		17
Askens, Elizabeth			1		
Barker, Penelope			1		
Borritz, William, Esqr	2	1	2	1	17
Blair, William	1				2
Blount, Joseph, Esqr	1	2	5		33
Butler, Samuel	1		1		12
Bond, Henry	1	2	3		5
Bent, Thomas	1	1	2		3
Brinkley, Mary		3	3		1
Bissell, Thomas	3	4	1		3
Black, Alexander	1	1	2		6
Bennett, Sarah			4	3	1
Bruster, Lott	1				2
Burdick, Josiah	1		1		
Brown, James	1				
Brown, John	1				
Blount, Jacob	1		2		16
Bateman, Thomas	2	1	2		2
Brown, Ann			2		
Beasley, John	1			2	2
Barr, David	1				
Banks, Jane				2	
Cumming, William, Esqr	1	1			2
Carter, William	1	2	3		3
Collagan, William	1	1	1		
Cameron, John	2		3		3
Cooley, Penelope			1		1
Carpenter, Stephen	1	1	2		6
Chesshire, Henry	2		1		1
Carter, Leah		1	1		
Cunningham, James	1		2		1
Cotten, James	1		3		1
Cox, Thomas	1	1	5		5
Collins, Josiah	3		1		30
Collins, Allen, and Dickenson	3				113
Clark, John	1				
Clark, Abraham					1
Dickenson, Samuel, Esqr	(*)	(*)	(*)	(*)	19
Decamp, James	(*)	(*)	(*)	(*)	7
Dunscomb, James	(*)	(*)	(*)	(*)	2
Dalling, Mary	(*)	(*)	(*)	(*)	(*)
Dear, Ann					
Demsey, Peggy				2	
Eelbeck, Joseph H.	1				8
Engs, Madett	3		3		13
Egan, Robert	2		2		17
Eberton, John	2	2	5	1	4
Eelbeck, Henry	1				3
Frazel, John	1	1	2		3
Farlow, Happy			1		
Forrow, James	1	1	1		2
Ferrybought, Henry	1		3		1
French, Robert	1	2	2		1
Flury, Henry	2	1	1	1	1
Felps, Sarah			1		
Finch, James	1	1	1		2
Gordon, Mary	1	1	1		
Gallop, Jeremiah	2		1		3
Gantz, Frederick	1	1	2		2
Gardner, Henry	1		2		1
Hardy, Robert	1				1
Hardy, Margaret			1		5
Hardy, Rachael			1		
Hopkins, Joseph	1		2		5
Hayse, Kitty			1		
Culver, Ann			1		5
Churton, Joe				1	
Hines, Robert	1	1	2		
Hodge & Wills	3				
Hathaway, James	2		4		3
Hamilton, John	1	1			6
Hamilton, Alexander	1				
Hankins, Thomas	3	3	1		2
Hartford, John	1	1	2		3
Hughs, Charles	1				4
Henderson, Mary			1		
Jameson, Samuel			1		
Iredell, Thomas	1				
Janders, Charles	1				
Imes, Denten	1		1		
Jackson, Samuel	1				
Joseph, Anthony	1		1		
James, Mary					2
Kock, Hans I.	1	3	2		2
Kennedy, Henry	2	1	6		5
Kennedy, Hannah			2		
Lattemore, Samuel	1	3	4		
Litt—*, William	3	3	6		62
Ly——*, Ann			3		
——*, Charles	1	2	2	1	2
——*, Hen——*	1	2	1		1
——*, Absa——*	1	2	1		
——*, King	1	1	2		5
Lit——*, John	1	5	3		17
Leming, John	1		4		2
Linch, Charles	1				
Miller, Robert	1	1	2		2
McKeal, Michael	1	3			1
Mitchel, Nathaniel	1		1		2
Morgan, George	3	3	3		1
McDonald, William	1	1	3		16
McDonald, John	1				
Mare, John, Esqr	2		3	1	22
Miles, Jane			4		5
Montgomery, Sarah			1		2
Murray, Dominigue	1	2	4		1
Murray, William	1	2	1		2
Morris, John	1	1	3		1
Meridith, David	1		2		6
Norflet, Elisha	4	2	3		4
Neil, Honour	1	1			2
Neil, James	1		1		
O'Malley, Matthew	1				4
O'Malley, Miles	1	1	2		12
Overton, Jonathan	1				5
Overin, Samuel	1				
Payne, Michael, Esqr	2		3		25
Powell, Stephen	1	1	1		
Pollock, Cullen, Esqr	1	1	1		204
Purdy, Ivy	1	1	2		6
Parker, Thomas	1		1		
Pollidore, Phebe				1	
Person, William	1				
Pambrune, Elizabeth			1		
Philips, Fanny	1	2	3		
Pierson, John	1	1	1		
Prentice, James	1				
Rumbough, William	2	1	4		8
Reiley, Edward	1		1		
Ramsay, Allen	1		1		3
Ramcker, Frederick	2	1	4	2	12
Rondett, Francis	1	1	5		1
Rodney, Henry	1		1		
Reeves, Richard	1		3		2
Rud, Mary			4		
Stanton, Barbary	(*)	(*)	(*)	(*)	(*)
Swinne, Sarah	(*)	(*)	(*)	(*)	1
Spooner, John	(*)	(*)	(*)	(*)	2
Smith, James	(*)	(*)	(*)	(*)	2
Squires, Roger	(*)	(*)	(*)	(*)	2
Satterfield, James	(*)	(*)	(*)	(*)	(*)
Small, John	1	2	2		1
Satterfield, William	1		1		3
Satterfield, Thomas	1		1		1
Sinkler, Elizabeth	1	1	4		
Standin, Lemuel	2	1	3		7
Spencer, James	1				
Sinkler, Ann		1	4		1
Seaman, Thomas	1		1		3
Starr, Henry	1		1		
Shaw, William	1		2		1
Udell, William	1				
Vernice, Jeremiah	1	1	5		1
Wilkenson, George	1	1	2		
Wynant, Penelope			3		1
Williamson, Rebecca			2		
Webb, Zachariah	1	3	2		1
Watkins, Deborah		1	1		
Waff, Thomas	3	1	2		5
Waff, William	1				
Wallace, Mary			1		1
White, Theresa	1	1	2		1
Whidbee, Joseph	1	1	1		4
Willson, Robert	2	1	4		5
Willson, Rebecca					
Williams, John A.	1		3		
Webb, James	1	2	2		
Waters, Catharine	2		2		
Gelletly, Catharine		2	1		1
Mann, John	1	1	1		
Yeomans, James	1		3		1
Mustapher, Mary				2	
Mustapher, Debby				1	1
Mustapher, Patty				1	

* Illegible.

EDENTON DISTRICT, CURRITUCK COUNTY.

NAME OF HEAD OF FAMILY.	Free white males of 16 years and upward, including heads of families.	Free white males under 16 years.	Free white females, including heads of families.	All other free persons.	Slaves.
Ferebee, Samuel	4	2	2		10
Allcock, Solomon	1	2	1		
Etheridge, Timothy	2	2	5		2
Berry, Samuel	1	3	3		
Parr, Daniel	1		2	2	1
Gregory, Rachael		2	3		
Gregory, Mary		1	2		
Hutchins, Anice		1	3		
Midgett, William	7	6	6		4
Midgett, Samuel, Esqr	1		1		9
Midgett, Thomas	1	1	3		4
Ashby, Solomon	1	1	5		7
Beasley, Jacob	1		5		
Owings, Nathaniel	1				
Fletcher, Stephen	1				
McKinsey, Thomas	1				
Coams, Thomas	1				
Carter, William	1				
Hunt, Charles				6	
Midgett, Samuel	1	3	5		3
Midgett, Joseph	2		2		
Linton, Lazarus	1		1		8
Midgett, Maurice	1	2	2		
Daugh, Samson	2	3	4		5
Daugh, Thomas	1	2	3		
Wescutt, Stephen	5		3		6
Wescutt, John	1	4	3		
Savage, George	1		3		
Ashby, Abel	1	3	4		10
Mann, John	3	2	7		4
Etheridge, Adam	1		4		3
Etheridge, Jesse, Junr	1		1		
Brickhouse, Caleb	4	2	2		
Twifoot, Levin	1		2		
Baum, Abraham	3	4	4		7
Humphry, James	2	4	2		2
Dolby, Absalom	3		3		
Baum, Maurice	4	2	4		6
Etheridge, Jesse	1	2	6		
Etheridge, William	1	5	1		
Etheridge, Tart	1	3	5		
Etheridge, James	2	4	4		
Beasley, William	1	1	4		
Beasley, Ann	3	2	3		
Montigue, Ann	1	2	2		
Etheridge, Ruben	1				
Mann, Edward	2	3	2		7
Savage, Southy	3	1	2		
Midgett, Samuel, Junr	1	2	5		
Hassell, Joseph	1	1			
Beasley, Stephen	1	1	1		
Daniel, Belcher	1	6	3		12
Daniel, William	2	3	6		1
Daniel, Gidion	2	1	2		2
Cudworth, John	1	1	1		
Daniel, David	1	2	2		
Boswell, James				8	
Bryan, Sarah				4	
Daniel, Joseph	2	5	6		2
Daniel, John	1		1		
Daniel, Samuel, Junr	2	4	3		
Daniel, William, Junr	2	1	5		
Brinston, Adam	1		3		
Brickhouse, George	1		3		
Rogers, Harding	1	1	2		
Midgett, Joseph, Junr	1	2	2		
Williams, John (Banks)	2	1	5		
Lurk, Elizabeth		3	2		
Tillitt, Thomas	4		3		4
Fountain, William	1		2		
Beacham, John	1		4		
Jones, Thomas	1	1	3		
Merchant, Caleb	1	1	3		
Guard, Joshua	2		3		
Johnston, Randolph	1		2		
Patterson, William	2		3		
Paddrick, Hannh	1	3	2		
Paddrick, John	1	3	2		
Caps, Lewis	1		1		
Paddrick, Ann			1		
Toaler, Mary	1	3	2		
Beacham, Mary		1	5		
Beacham, Thomas	1	2	2		
Garrott, Thomas	2	3	3		
Parker, James	1	1	2		
Caps, Selenian	1		5		
Gamewell, James	1	2	2		
Best, William	1	2	3		
Franklin, Thomas	1		3		
Williams, Absalom	1	1	2		
Caps, Moses, Junr	1	2	5		
Daugh, John	1		2		
Tillett, Isaac	1		1		
Gallop, Shadrach	1	2	3		
Merrett, Isaac	2	1	3		
Tillett, Lemuel	1	2	5		
Sikes, Henry	3	1	3		
Gallop, Demsey	1	1	2		
Humphries, Joseph	1	1	3		
Perry, John	1	2	3		
Best, Mary	2		3		
Lenark, John	2	1	3		
Best, Thomas, Senr	1	3	2		
Hayman, Daniel	1	1	3		
Best, Thomas	1		1		
Gamewell, Benjamin	1	1	2		
Hill, Joshua	2	1	3		
Gamewell, John, Senr	1				
Gallop, Jonas	1	5	3		
Austin, Daniel	1	2	2		
Austin, Thomas, Junr	1		2		1
Austin, William	1	1	2		
Austin, Thomas	1	2	4		
Stow, Joseph	4		1		
O'Neal, Sarah	1		1		
Ballance, Thomas	1		3		
Ballance, William	4	4	3		
Ballance, John	1		3		
Stow, Samuel	2	2	5		
Quidley, William	1	1	3		1
Dunkin, Thomas	1			1	4
Barcham, John	1		4		
Burris, John	2	2	5		1
Payne, Thomas	2		2		7
Payne, John	1		3		
Midgett, Richard	3		1		1
Midgett, Christopher	1	3	5		1
Midgett, Jesse	1		1		
Midgett, Daniel	1	3	5		3
Midgett, Banister	1	1	2		2
Neal, Christopher	2	6	6		1
Clark, William	1		3		
Neal, William	2	3	5		
Badley, Frankey		2	4		
Lory, Joab	2	3	3		
Stewart, Darby	1		2		
Merchant, Catharine			6		22
Merchant, Thomas	1		1		8
Monden, Stephen	1		4		
Turton, Mary		1	3		5
Doughty, Edward	4		1		9
Pew, Perthena	1	3	2		1
Dohatoon, William	1	1			2
Duglas, Anthony	1	1	2		
Payne, Thomas, Junr	1	4	2		1
Pugh, William	4	4	2		
Flowers, John	1	4	2		
Midgett, John	1	1	2		
Midgett, Christian	1		4		
Meekins, Roger	1	4	5		4
Peal, Francis	1	1	3		
Peal, John	1	1	2		
Peal, Christopher	1		4		
Gray, William	4	1	2		
Gray, Joseph	1	1	1		
Williams, Keziah	1		4		
Price, Henry	1	1	1		
Scarborough, George, Junr					
Scarborough, Edward	2		2		
Scarborough, Ignatius	1	1	4		
Meekins, William	2	4	4		
Williams, Comfort	1		2		
Hooper, Ezekiel	2	3	2		
Williams, Joseph	1	1	5		
Williams, Jacob	1	2	6		
Miller, William	1	3	3		
Farrow, Isaac	2	1	2		1
How, William	1	1	1		
Gray, Thomas	1		4		
Midgett, Thomas	4	3	3		
Midgett, Timothy	1				
Farrow, Francis	2		6		5
Farrow, Francis, Junr	1		3		
Farrow, Thomas	1	3	2		3
Scarborough, Austin	2		3		2
Scarborough, George	1	1	2		
Braydy, Thomas	2		2		
Farrow, Hezekiah, Junr	1	1	3		
Robison, Francis	2	1	3		
Jinnett, Joseph	1	2	4		
Jinnett, Jesse	1	1	4		
Farrow, Hezekiah	3	2	3		
Farrow, John	2		1		
Wahab, James	2		2		
Smith, John	1	2	2		10
Adkins, William	1		2		
Dring, Price				4	
Clark, Henry	3		1		
Clark, Bathiah		1	2		
Clark, Major	2	2	2		
Midgett, Matthew	1		2		
Midgett, William, Junr	1		3		
Neal, Thomas	3	1	2		
Wedby, Elizabeth		1	1		
Midgett, Christopher	1	1	4		
Neal, Christopher, Junr	1	1	3		
Scarborough, Mary		3	3		
Taylor, Caleb	1	1	3		
Holt, Taylor	1	1	2		
Scarborough, William	2	1	4		
Basnett, Mary				4	
Basnett, Robert		1		8	
Farrow, Jacob	1		2		
Farrow, Christopher	1				
Robinson, Christopher	1	2	3		
Burrows, Robert	3		4		1
Robinson, William	1	2	4		
Robinson, Elizabeth		1	1		
Scarborough, Ruth		2	1		
Tolson, Daniel	1	2	2		
Robinson, Christopher, Junr	1		1		
Quidley, Thomas	1	4	3		
Dauge, Griffith	1	6	2		2
Backster, John	2	3	6		
Backster, Joseph	1		1		
Chittam, Benjamin	1	2	4		1
Sawyer, John	1	1	2		
Bell, Brickhouse	2	1	3		10
Collins, Noah	2	1	2		
Simmons, Anthony	1	2	2		
Crab, James	1		2		
Hanners, Lydia	2		3		
Robertson, John	1		4		5
Anderson, William	1		3		1
Simmons, Jiles	2	5	4		1
Turton, Mary		1	2		5
White, Amey	1	2	1		8
Younghusband, Thomas	1	2	1		17
Jarvis, Thomas, Junr	1		2		4
Bates, Andrew	1		2		5
Beasley, William	1	3	3		1
Kennett, Brickhouse	1	2	1		
Neal, Samuel	1	2	1		1
Baxter, Joseph	1	4	4		
Simmons, Hilliry	2		1		7
Lee, Asa	3	1	2		6
O'Neal, Nathan	1	1	3		1
Allen, Jarvis	1		2		
Jones, Malachi	1	1	1		1
Jones, Sarah	2		2		6
Chandler, William	1	2	1	1	1
Brite, Henry	1	2	4		4
Nichols, Josiah	1	4	3		10
Whitehead, Elizabeth	1		6		
Williamson, Jonathan	2	2	3		1
Cox, Thomas	2	4	2		3
Forker, George	2	3	1		
Perkins, Jacob	1	1	4		4
Ferebee, Thomas	1		2		2
Cruf, Gideon	1	1	3		2
Harris, William	1	2	4		
Heath, John	1	1	5		
Sanderson, Thomas	1		2		14
Ward, Jonathan	2	4	4		
Barns, Jonathan	2	3	3		3
Lindsey, Jonathan	1		1		2
Beasley, Mordecai	1	1	2		1
Beasley, Cornelius	1	2	4		1
Gray, John	1		3		7
Holstead, Jesse	1	4	3		1
Etheridge, Samuel	1	1	2		
Etheridge, James	1	2	4		4
Parker, Thomas, Senr	2		4		
Wilber, James	1	1	4		
Beasley, Bridget	2	1	1		
Stevens, John	1		1		
Wilson, Lemuel	1		1		11
Dauge, Enoch	2		2		6
Hughs, James	1				1
Dauge, Dory	1		1		
Grimstead, John	2	3	3		
Phillips, James	1	2	6		4
Williams, Holloway	1	4	2		9
Ferebee, Joseph	1	2	7		8
Butt, Arthur	4	2	1		2
Bray, James	1	3	2		5
Burnal, Edward	1	1	6		
Moncrief, Thomas	1	1	4		3
Morse, Zachariah	1	2	4		1
Poyner, Nathaniel	1	2	4		2
Morse, Francis	1	3	2		
Lurry, William	1		4		9
Simmons, Jesse	1	4	4		3
Gregory, Caleb, Senr	1		1		1
Hall Nathaniel	1	1	2		4
Ballance, Willis	2	1	3		4
Poyner, William	1		1		
Barnard, Thomas	1		1		5

EDENTON DISTRICT, CURRITUCK COUNTY—Continued.

NAME OF HEAD OF FAMILY.	Free white males of 16 years and upward, including heads of families.	Free white males under 16 years.	Free white females, including heads of families.	All other free persons.	Slaves.
Sanders, John Senr	1	1	3		7
Williamson, Williamson	2		3		
McClannan, John	2	4	3		
Taylor, William	2		1		
Lindsey, Daniel	1		2		2
Simmons, John	2		2		4
Gray, Joseph	1	2	5		20
Moncrief, William	1	4	4		1
Perkins, Jeremiah	1	3	2		
Evans, Henry	1		1		
Jarvis, William	1	1	1		
Taylor, Joshua	2	2	4		
Taylor, Thomas	1	1	3		
Bray, John	1		1		
Doxey, John	3	3	5		
Moncrief, William, Junr	1	2	2		
Parker, James, Junr	1		3		
Taylor, Ebenezer, Junr	1	1	1		
Bell, Horey	1	2	2		5
Edy, Samuel	1		1		
Burton, John	1	2	3	1	
White, Thomas	2	2	2		3
Gibson, Henry	2	4	5		
Ball, Ruben	1	4	4		
Brunt, James	1	3	2		
Fisher, George	2		3		
Simmons, William	1	1	5		3
Moss, Caleb	2	1	1		
Taylor, Ebenezer	1	1	2		
Dauge, James	1	3	2		4
Williams, Dorastus	1	1	3		
Miller, Thomas	1	5	4		
Ball, Joshua	1				
Poyner, Peter	1		2		
McClannan, James	1	2	2		1
Jarvis, Foster	1	1	6		
Dauge, Mitchell	1	1	3		4
Hutchings, Nathaniel	1	4	5		3
Gibson, John	1	3	6		
Wilson, Taton	1		5		23
Laton, William	1	2	3		
Taylor, Joseph, Junr	1	1	1		1
Tatom, William	2	3	1		1
Lee, Letetia	1	2	1		
Whutly, John	1	1	1		
Tatom, John	2	3	5		
Mercer, Jeremiah, Junr	1	3	2		5
Barrott, John	1	2	4		
Hall, John	1	1	1		
Hollaway, William	2	3	5		
Holstead, Jolliff	1	2	3		
Tatom, Benjamin	1	2			
Ballantine, Henry	3		2		7
Slaughter, John	3		3		2
Calm, Theophelus	1	3	3		
Lee, Daniel	1	1	3		1
Caps, John	1	3	3		
Gibson, James	2	3	4		
Taylor, Jonathan	1	4	3		
Walker, Caleb	4	2	2		
Campbell, Keziah		1	3		
Poiner, Joel	1		4		
Smith, William	2		2		
Jones, John	1		2		
Gregory, Enoch	1	1	2		
Turner, Sylvanus	1	2	3		2
Whutly, William	1		3		
Berry, John	1	2	3		3
Bell, John	2	1	3		
Hinnings, Zachariah	2		2		
Thomas, James				8	
Case, Jonathan				4	
Hunt, Hyram				2	
Smith, Isaac	1	2	1		
Hunt, Demsey				2	
Holstead, Lydia	1	1	1		6
Purlington, Zachariah	1	1	1		2
Gregory, Griffith	2	1	3		
May, Joseph	1		4		
Simmons, Lemuel	1		2		
Smith, Laban	1	3	4		1
Taylor, Joseph	1	1	4		
Postwood, Benjamin	3		2		
Whitehouse, Godfrey	1		1		
Caves, John	2		3		
Stewart, Affiah		1	3		
Simmons, Meriam	1	2	4		
Tatom, David	1	1	1		7
Nicholls, James	1		4		
Simmons, Elizabeth			1		
Dauge, Philip	2				5
White, Willoughby	2	2	4		
Mercer, Thomas	1		3		
Thomson, Nathan	1	1	1		1
Pell, Joseph	1				
White, James	1	5	4		5
Ives, Thomas	1	4	2		

NAME OF HEAD OF FAMILY.	Free white males of 16 years and upward, including heads of families.	Free white males under 16 years.	Free white females, including heads of families.	All other free persons.	Slaves.
Poyner, Adam	2		5		
Holstead, John	3	2	6		
Dauge, Tulle	3	3	4		16
Burnal, Emely	2		1		
Simmons, Samuel	1	2	8		2
Sheregold, Telamaceus	1	1	2		1
Snowden, Francis	1	3	2		
Miller, Evan	2	3	2		
Stevens, William	3	1	3		
Snoden, William	1	2	2		
Poyner, Thomas	2		2		2
Poyner, Ann	2		2		5
Panderson, Ann			2		5
Poyner, Peter	1	1			
Brite, Hanson	1		3		
Dauge, Peter	1	2	3		3
Howard, George	1				
Gregory, Jacob	1	1	2		
Walker, Willis	2	4	2		
Thomson, Mary	1		6		
Thomson, John	1	3	5		
Mills, Thomas	1		3		
Glasgo, William	1	3	4		
Williams, John	6		6		6
Katon, James	1		2		1
Standly, Thomas	2	4	4		
Lufman, Jonathan	1	2	3		
Thomson, Malachi	1				
Case, Joseph	1	2	3		
Bunnett, Thomas	1	2	3		
Barnard, Robert	2	2			12
Barnard, Luke	1				
Banks, James	1	4	1		
Chittam, John	1				
Mercer, Thomas, Senr	2	2	3		4
Heath, Thomas	1	3	4		5
Nicholson, Griffith	1	2	1		
Morrice, Willoughby	1		2		
Ballance, Jervan	1	1	2		
Ballance, William	1		2		2
Chittim, James	1		3		1
Holstead, Levina	1	1	1		6
Dauge, Elias	1		5		1
Perkins, John	2	1	4		4
Williams, Christopher	1				
Williams, Elizabeth			3		6
Williams, Thomas Pool	3	1	2		12
Gail, William	1	1	1		
Ellis, Matthew	1		2		
Linch, Rilah	1				
Dauge, Richard	1	2	3		
Fulford, Daniel	1	3	4		
Heath, James	1	2	4		
Wheatly, Robert	1	1	4		
Ellis, Thomas	2	1	2		
Fanshaw, Henry	1	1	3		
Griffin, William	1	1	2		
Matthias, Simon	1	2	2		2
Jarvis, Mary		2	3		
Piner, Joseph	1		2		
Etheridge, Amos	2	1			5
Jervis, Solomon	4	1	2		
Glasgo, Cornelius	1				
Simmons, John	1	1	3		1
Gray, Josiah	1	1	4		
Merchant, Gideon	1				5
Gibson, Thomas	1				1
Dill, Michael	1		1		
Williams, James	1	1	1		2
Williams, Samuel	1	1	2		1
Dauge, Rachael			4		
Mercer, Jeremiah	1	1	2		2
Parr, Josiah	1	1	7		1
Jarvis, Willis	1		3		
Whitehouse, Samuel	2	3	4		2
Lee, Thomas	1		2		
Hutchings, James	2	2	2		
Bell, Edy	1		2		4
Leach, Edward	1	2	4		
Avery, Frederick	1	3	2		
Parr, Richard	1	1	3		
Hutchings, Richard	1				
Parr, William	2		2		
Parr, Caleb	1	2	4		
Poiner, Robert	1		1		10
Poiner, James	1		1		1
Poiner, John	1		2		1
Williamson, William	1				
Poiner, Lemuel	1	1	3		
Poiner, Benjamin	1		3		
Poiner, Benjn, Junr	1		3		7
Salyer, Samuel, Junr	3	1	6		8
Salyer, Samuel, Senr	2	1	3		
Walker, Edward	1	1			
Brown, Letia	1		3		7
Thomson, Mason			1		
Taylor, Benjamin, Senr	1	2	6		7

NAME OF HEAD OF FAMILY.	Free white males of 16 years and upward, including heads of families.	Free white males under 16 years.	Free white females, including heads of families.	All other free persons.	Slaves.
Duke, Andrew	2		3		7
Hall, Spence, Junr	2		1		2
Taylor, Ruben	2	3	3		4
Perry, Jesse	1		3		3
Barrot, Richard	1	2	1		
Adderson, Elisha	1	2	1		
Parker, Peter	1	3	3		
Grigs, Charles	1	2	3		
Jarvis, Thomas (B. S.)	1	1	4		3
Sanderson, Jesse	2	2	6		20
Whitehall, Alexander	3	3	4		6
Smith, Sarah	1		4		
Rolands, Sarah	1		4		
Baits, Asa	1	3	1		1
Taylor, Joseph, Junr	1	1	1		1
Burnett, Elizabeth	2		4		
Burnett, Lidia			2		
Woodhouse, Hezekiah	1	1	2		6
Dowdy, Joseph	3	1	2		
Dowdy, Josiah	2		4		
Dowdy, Jacob	1		3		
Ruin, Jeremiah	1		1		
Dowdy, John	1	1	2		
Long, Bathiah	1		2		
Kenly, Lydia	1		2		
Overton, Maryann	1	2	1		
Vever, William				4	
Boswood, Thomas	1	3	2		
Baker, Samuel	1	3	2		
Hall, Spence	1	1			8
Toaler, Matthias	3		3	1	6
Nelson, William	3	2	3		1
Lindsay, John	2		1		8
Evans, Malchia	1	3			
Walker, Thomas	1	3	5		
Simmons, John	1	2	2		
Aydetoll, John	1	2			
Walker, Samuel	1		1		
Walker, O'Neal	3	2	3		
Walker, Adley	1	2	2		
Evans, John	1	2	1		
Woodhouse, Adley	3	3	3		1
Evans, Benjamin	2		2		2
Walker, Michael	2		2		
Evans, Sarah			2		2
Evans, Jane		1	2		
Chaplin, James	2	4	2		4
Forbes, William	1	4	4		1
Wright, Gamial	1	2	3		2
McCoy, William	1	1	2	1	1
McCoy, John	1	1	3		
Padrick, Peter	1	3	2		
Cooke, Cullin	1	2	3		
Walker, John	1		1		
Greaves, David	1		1		
Lindsay, David	1	1	3	1	1
Evans, Joseph	1	2	2		
Lietchfield, Abraham	4	1	5		
Greaves, Matthew	1	2	2		
Adams, John	1	2	3		
Aydetoll, Caleb	1	2	2		
Dewe, Sarah	1		2		
Harrison, Zorobabel	1	1	2		1
Gregory, Thomas	1	1	2		
Duke, Jonathan	2		2		
Harrison, Josiah	2		1		
Aydetoll, William	1		2		
Etheridge, Samson	3	1	6		1
Etheridge, Asa	2		3		
Dowdy, Caleb	1	4	3		
Dowdy, John	1		2		
Gamewell, Joseph	1	2	2		
Grunt, John	2	3	2		
Gregory, Samuel	1		2		
Greaves, Absalom	1	2	2		
Etheridge, Samson, Senr	1		1		
Toaler, Caleb	2		3		
Saunders, Lucy		3	1		
Fuller, Edom	1			1	
Daugh, Richard	2	6	5		4
Daugh, Gideon	1		2		1
Barrott, Thomas	1	2	2		
Sikes, Benjamin	1	2	2		
Jarvis, Thomas, Senr	3	1	3	3	8
Gilbert, John	1	1	2		
Fountain, Jonathan	1		3		
Brown, Nancy		2	3		
Hitom, Elizabeth				5	
Majo, Duke	2	1	1		
Thomas, Laban	1	1	1		
Gordan, Peter				10	
Toaler, James	2		3		2
Garrott, Thomas	3	3	4		
Sikes, Mary		1	1		
Harris, Thomas	2	1	3		
Coffee, Jacob	1				

EDENTON DISTRICT, CURRITUCK COUNTY—Continued.

NAME OF HEAD OF FAMILY.	Free white males of 16 years and upward, including heads of families.	Free white males under 16 years.	Free white females, including heads of families.	All other free persons.	Slaves.
Mann, Thomas	1	1	3		
Harris, Elias		1	2		
Dunton, William	2	2	5		
Burges, George	1	1	2		
Burgess, Peter	1	1	2		
Williams, Rachael	1	2	4		
Gallop, James	2	3	2		
Caps, Moses	1	1	1		
Coffee, George	1	2	1		
Gallop, John	1	2	1		
Hill, Clement	1	2	3		
Hill, James	1	1	4		
Gregory, Jesse	2	2	5		
Gregory, Isaac (N. R.)	1		3		
Lutts, William	1	1	1		
Ferrebee, Elizabeth	2		3		10
Ferrebee, William	1	1	6		17
Spann, Thomas	1		1		
Standly, Richard	1	2	1		1
Humphries, John	7	7	10		23
Mann, William	1		1		4
Killegrew, John	1	1	2		
Wamsley, John	2		1		
Smith, Sarah			1		
Dissiness, Benjamin	1		1		4
Church, Caleb	1	2	1		6
Lindsy, Elizabeth		2	1		
Read, Malachi	1	1	1		2
Caves, Cornelius	2		2		
West, Joshua	1	1	3		
Seers, Caleb	1	1	1		
Rogers, John	1				
Dauge, Milbry		5	2		1
West, Obediah	1	1	1		
West, Edward	2	1	5		
Dauge, Willis	1	2	4		
Mulder, Ann		3	2		
Morse, Archelaus	1		3		2
Mulder, Kedar	3	5	3		5
Payn, Enoch	1	2	1		
Parsons, Ann			2		
Berry, Mallachi	1	3	1		
Lory, Kedar	1	2	2		1
Duglas, Charles				7	
Turner, Bellar				5	
Turner, Samson				6	
West, Mary		2	3		
Merchant, Kedar	1	1			1
Merchant, John	1		2		
Hutchings, Sinney	1	3	4		
Creckmer, Samuel	1	2	2		
Dauge, Willoughby	2	3	4		16
Gregory, Richard	1	4	2		
Gregory, Cornelius	1	2	2		1
Jarvis, John	1	2	3		
Fisher, John	1	2	6		
Gray, Griffith	1	2	2		
Matthias, Robert	1		2		
Evans, Caleb	1		1		
Mackey, John	1		1		8
White, Henry, Junr	1		6		3
White, Patrick	1	1	2		
Mitchell, Elizabeth			2		
Ansell, James	2	1	4		2
White, Solomon			2		6
Harvey, Thomas	1	1	3		
Wisher, Lovey		2	1		
Humphries, Sarah	1		5		
White, Henry, Senr	1	2	4		12
Austin, William	1	2	6		
Capps, Caleb, Senr	2	3	5		1
Capps, Junr	1	1	5		
Miller, Solomon	1		1		
Miller, Willis	1	1	3		
Bryan, John	2	1	3		
Rogers, William, Senr	1		4		
Wicher, Willis	3		4		
Martin, Moses	1	1	3		
Capps, Dennis	2				
Bonney, Jonathan	2	3	2		5
Williams, Jacob	1		1		
Heath, John	1	2	2		
Dunton, Daniel	2		1		3
Williams, Elias	1	3	5		4
Simson, John	1	2	3		3
Smith, Eli	1	2	2		
Capps, Malchia	1	2	2		
Dudley, William	2	1	3		
Jasper, Samuel	3		5		5
White, Winson	2	1	3		1
Waterfield, William	1		3		
Capps, William	1		5		
Waterfield, Abraham	3		3		
Guin, William	1	3	4		
Waterfield, John	1	3	2		
Leitchfield, John	1	2	4		1
Waterfield, Benjamin	1	1	4		
Rogers, William, Junr	1		1		
Waterfield, Michael, Senr	1	1	2		5
Holly, William	1		1		
Gordon, John	1	3	2		
Waterfield, Michael, Junr	1	6	3		
Williams, Capt John	1	2	3		3
Etheridge, Samuel	1	3	3		1
Williams, Thomas	1		2		6
Jasper, Darcas			3		5
Chappel, George	1	2	3		6
Jones, Evan	1	1	6		5
Jemmison, John	1		2		4
Hill, John	1	3	5		
Grigs, George	1	1	1		
Burkett, Caleb	2	1	1		
Simmons, Caleb	3	2	4		
Hill, Luke	1		3		
Jacobs, David	1	1	3		
Morse, Ruben	1		3		1
Morse, Arthur	1	1	1		
Morse, Arche	3	1	2		
Hewett, Benjamin	1	1	1		
Dyer, Sarah	1		1		
Wildlear, James	1	1	3		
Cox, Jonathan	1	1	1		
Simpson, Joshua	1	1	2		
Lugg, Kesiah	2		1		
Leitchfield, Comfort		1	1		
Leitchfield, Jacob	1	1	2		
Swindell, Parker	1	2	2		
Sexton, William	1	2	2		
Cherry, Josiah	1	1	2		
Etheridge, Richard	2				
Etheridge, Richard, Junr	2	1	2		
Hayman, Isabel		1	6		
Jones, Abi				3	
Fruman, William	1		1		
Bright, Courtney			1		
Hayman, John	1	1	1		
Miller, William	1	3	2		
Garrott, Elizabeth			2		
Fruman, Moses	1		2		2
Mekins, Margaret				3	
Bright, Charles	2	2	4		2
Etheridge, Josiah	1		3		
Williamson, Henry	3	2	1		2
Butt, John	2		2		
Etheridge, Abel	2	4	3		
Wormington, John	3	3	3		
Williamson, William	3	1			2
Fruman, Moses	1		2		2
Bennett, Carter	2		2		
Ballentine, James	1				
Brite, Jonathan	1				
Brite, Willis	2	2	3		
Mekins, Richard				3	
Borin, Maximilion	1	3	2		
Brite, Jesse	2		2		2
Grannis, John	3		2		2
Ballance, Daniel	1	1	2		
Cox, Marmeduke	1		2		2
Etheridge, Henry	1	3	2		
Etheridge, Emsley	1		2		
Cason, Hillary	1	2	3		
Etheridge, Mattnias	1		2		
Etheridge, Caleb, Senr	1	3	2		
Powers, Caleb	1	2	3		
Cox, Lewis	1	1	1	1	1
Powers, Willis	1	1	1		
McPharson, Daniel	2	3	3		
Etheridge, Caleb, Junr	2	2	1		
Cox, Solomon, Junr	1	2	4		
Etheridge, Jesse (Moyok)	2	1	2		
Ives, Jesse	2	2	2		
Culpepper, Peter	2	3	4		
Lee, Linton	1	3	4		
Powers, Samuel	1		2		
Brite, Aaron	1	3	1		2
Bennett, Jessu	1		4		
Davis, Cornelius	1				
Powers, George	1	3	5		1
Linton, Benjamin	1		3		
Hubert, Isaac	1		4		
Powers, William	1		1		
Etheridge, Peter	1				
Powers, William, Junr	1		1		
Cherry, Willis	1	3	3		
Bathouse, Mary				2	
Etheridge, Nathan	1	3	2		
Etheridge, Henry	1				
Etheridge, Richd	1				
Northern, John	3	2	3		2
Northern, Charity	1	3	4		5
McPharson, Hewes	1		2		
Cox, Javan	1		1		
Spence, Malchia	1	1			
Spence, Cary	1		2		
Cox, Caleb	1	2	4		2
Powers, Cunett	1				
Burnham, Samuel			4	4	
Ballentine, Joseph	1		4	1	4
Ballentine, Peter	1	2	3		1
Brite, Silas	1	1	2		10
Northen, William	1	2	2		2
Ballentine, Henry	3		3		9
Powers, John	1		1		
May, Joseph	1		4		
Cox, Solomon, Senr	1		1		
Ballentine, Mary		3	4		
Boran, Sarah	1	4	4		
Walker, Prissilla		3	3		5
Glasgo, Elizabeth		3	3		
Standley, Ufan		1	2		
Wist, Willoby	2		2		
Simmons, Mary	2	3	4		6
Thomson, Sarah			2		
Curl, Rachel		2	4		
Palmer, Malchia	1	2	4		

EDENTON DISTRICT, GATES COUNTY.

NAME OF HEAD OF FAMILY.	Free white males of 16 years and upward, including heads of families.	Free white males under 16 years.	Free white females, including heads of families.	All other free persons.	Slaves.
Blanshard, Americas	1	1	4		1
Hobbs, Aaron	1	2	4		4
Hill, Aaron	1	2	3		5
Walton, Ann		1	5	1	1
Barrot, Alse			2		
Matthews, Andrew, Senr	1	1	2		1
Harrell, Asa	1	1	2		1
Matthews, Anthoney, Junr	1	3	2		
Harrell, Aaron, Senr	1		2		
Pierce, Abraham	1		2		
Green, Abraham	1	5	2		1
Harrell, Abraham	3	3	3		7
Hurdle, Abraham	1	1	3		5
Cason, Abraham	1	2	2		8
Spivey, Abraham	1	2	3		1
Matthews, Anthoney, Senr	1	5	1		
Lasitor, Abisha	2	4	3		
Blanshard, Abner	1		2		7
Blanshard, Aaron	1	3	2		
Smith, Amos	2		3		
Lasitor, Aaron, Junr	2	1	2		
Pierce, Abner	1	1	1		
Lasitor, Amos	2	3			
Riddick, Abraham	2		4		
Spight, Ann		1	4		1
Lassitor, Aaron	2	1	5		1
Powell, Ann	1	1	1		4
Parker, Amos	1	4	4		1
Rude, Abraham				1	
Cason, Alexander	1	2	2		2
Parker, Ann		1	2		2
Holland, Arthur	2		2		
Morgan, Abraham	2	2	1		9
Ellis, Aaron			2		
Cross, Abel	3		8		19
Bethey, Ann		1	2		7
Goodman, Ann	2	1	5	1	
Carter, Ann			1		2
Harrall, Aaron	1	2	2		1
Piland, Ann			1		1
Harrell, Ann	1		2		2
Ellis, Ann		1	2		
Jones, Burben	1				
Minehew, Bond	1	4	3		12
Williams, Benjamin	1				
Robbins, Bashford			2	2	
Gordan, Benjamin	2	1	4		22
Jones, Belson	1	2	2		1
Warren, Bray	1	2	1		6
Barnes, Benjamin	2	1	2		6
parker, Benjamin	1	3	4		1
Euri, Blake	1		3		
Euri, Benjamin	1	3	4		
Rude, Benjamin				3	
Smith, Charles	1	1	2		1
Morriss, Charity			3		
Bennet, Christian		1	5		
perry, Chrismas	1	1	3		

EDENTON DISTRICT, GATES COUNTY—Continued.

NAME OF HEAD OF FAMILY.	Free white males of 16 years and upward, including heads of families.	Free white males under 16 years.	Free white females, including heads of families.	All other free persons.	Slaves.
Riddick, Christopher	2	2	5		12
Pierce, Christopher	1		4		
parker, Catherine		2	4		2
Costen, Christian	1	4	3		7
Jones, Charles	1				
Polson, Caleb	1		2		1
Cross, Cyprean	1	3	5		10
Saunders, Charity	2		2		4
Ellis, Charity			2		
Gale, Christopher	2	4	4		8
Euri, Charles	2	3	4		7
Carter, Charles		1	1		
Osten, Claborn	1		2		3
phelps, Demsey	1	1	1		
Small, David	1	4	4		
Hill, David	1		1		
Harrel, David	1	1	2		7
Jones, Demsey	1	2	3		11
powell, Daniel	1		1		
Hays, Daniel	1				
parker, Demsey	1		4		1
piland, David	1				
Trotman, Demsey	1				8
Blanshard, Demsey	1	2	5		1
Jones, Demsey, Junr	2	2	2		2
Jones, Demsey, Senr	2	1	2		
Jones, David, Senr	1		1		10
Jones, David, Junr	1	1	2		
Quinn, Daniel	1		3		
Rue, David	1	1	1		11
Adam, Demsey	3	1	3		11
Williams, Demsey	1	3	3		8
Sumner, Demsey	3	2	2	1	
Watson, David	2		1		4
Cross, David	1	1	2		5
Barnes, Demsey	2		7		7
Williams, Demsey	2	4	3		
Sumner, Demsey (of Virgia)					6
Rooks, Demsey	1	1	1		
Lewis, David	1	1	3		4
Euri, Daniel	2		3		
Umflet, David	3	1	5		
Langston, Demsey	2		3		
Ellis, Daniel	1		2		
Vann, Dorcas	1		1		1
Nobbs, Edmund	1				
Godwin, Exum	1	2	4		4
Briscoe, Edward	1	4	2	1	
Morris, Ephraim	1	3	2		
Piland, Edward	1	3	2		
Piland, Edward	1	1	1		2
Graham, Ebenezar	1				1
Matthews, Easter		1	1		
Beriman, Edward	2		2		1
Harrell, Emelia		1	2		3
Blanshard, Elizabeth	1	1	3		
Sivils, Elizabeth			2		
Harriss, Elisha	1	4	3		
Trotman, Ezekiel	3	4	2		11
Spivey, Elijah	1	1	7		
Rice, Elizabeth			2		2
Jones, Even	2		1		
parker, Elizabeth		2	3		4
Norflet, Elizabeth		1	4		
Norflet, Elisha	1				7
Jones, Edith			3		
Benton, Elisha	1				
Brinkley, Elisha	1				
Daughter, Edward	3		1		6
parker, Elisha	2	1	4		8
Sumner, Edwin	1				10
Rogers, Enos	1	3	2		5
Cross, Elisha	2	5	3		6
potson, Edward	1				
Brinkley, Elisha	2		4		2
Sears, Eborn	1	1	4		1
Harrell, Elisha	1	2	1		1
Harrell, Demsey	1	3	3		
Ellis, Elisha	1	4	4		1
parker, Elisha				4	
parker, Edith			2		
Eason, Frederick	1				4
Brinkley, Francies		1	1		1
parker, Francies	1	2	7		1
Spight, Francies	1	2	3		19
Farrow, Frederick	1	1	3		
Eason, George	2		2		1
Outlaw, George	1	2	5		20
Bennet, George				1	
Allen, George	1	3	4		1
Williams, George	2	3	5		2
piland, George	1		3		1
Williams, George	1	1	4		
Lassitor, George	2		3		5
Eason, George	2		2		7
Martin, Gabril	1	1	4		

NAME OF HEAD OF FAMILY.	Free white males of 16 years and upward, including heads of families.	Free white males under 16 years.	Free white females, including heads of families.	All other free persons.	Slaves.
Russell, George	1	3	5		1
Gatlin, George	1		1		3
Hargroves, George	1	3	1		1
Hobbs, Henry	1	3	4		1
Hill, Henry	2		4		
Hill, Hemrick	1		2		
Forrest, Henry	1	2	6		14
Robins, Hardy				1	
Alphin, Hezekiah	1	2	1		1
Hudgins, Humphey	1	4	2		9
Watton, Henry	2	2	5		9
Jones, Hezekiah	2		3		1
Rude, Hardy				8	
Maroney, Henry	2		2		
Griffin, Henry	1	3	5		1
Willey, Hillory	2		1		1
Wills, Hardy	1		1		
Cross, Hardy (Virginia)					6
Spight, Henry	1	2	1		8
Lee, Henry	4	1	5		10
Saunders, Henry	3		2		9
Dilday, Henry	2		1		3
Goodman, Henry	1	3	2		15
Copeland, Henry	1	1			7
Howard, Hardy	1	3	1	1	1
Brown, Hardy	1	1	4		1
Jones, Hezekiah	1	2	2		
Spivey, Jessey	1	3	3		3
White, John	1	1	3		
White, Joshua	1	2	2		
Freeman, James	3	2	3		9
Hobs, Jacob	2	2			
Ward, Jesse	1		3		
Roberts, John	1	3	3		
Cullan, Jacob	1	1	3		2
Miltear, Jethro	2	2	4	2	3
Roberts, Jonathan	2	2	5		18
Walton, James	1	1	2		4
Outlaw, James	1	1	1		8
Trevathan, James	2		1		
Robins, James			1	15	
Bennet, Joseph				1	
Thomas, Jacob	1	2	3		
Rountree, John	1	1	2		9
Eason, Jacob	1		2		10
Brinkley, Joseph	1	2	3		14
Steptoe, John	1	2	2		
Wilkeson, Joseph	1	1	1		
parker, Josiah	1	1	2		
Bauos, James	2	2	1		
Dirdon, John	1				1
Martin, Jesse	1		1		1
parker, Isaac	3		3		
Sumner, James B.	1		1		19
Figg, Joseph	2	1	4		3
Figg, James	1				
Tugwell, James	1				
Smith, James	1		1		
Smith, Jonathan	1		2		1
piland, James	2	2	2		
Norflet, Joseph	1				
Garret, Joseph	1	2			
Slavin, Jethro	1			3	
Spight, Jeremiah	2	3	9		17
Cuff, John				9	
Rice, John	2	1	2		6
Fillon, John	1	3	2		
Brown, James	1	2	5		2
Shepard, John	3	3	2		3
piland, John	1		2		
Brown, James	1				
Miller, Isaac	2	2	2		4
Baker, John	1	2	4		32
Dukes, John	2		2		1
Slavin, John	2	1	2		
Jonston, John	1	2	2		
pierce, Isaac	1		6		
Nichols, Jonathan	1		1		
Hurdle, Joseph	1	1	2		10
parnall, John	1	1	2		
Jones, James	1	3	7		
pierce, Jacob	1	2	5		1
Holland, Jacob	1	2	1		
Wills, John	1	1	3		
Hays, Jacob	3	1	5		
Alphin, Joseph	1		5		
Foster, Joel	1	1	2		2
Hays, James	2	1	2		9
Wallon, John B.	1	2	1		10
Hunter, Isaac	1	2	2		10
Lassitor, James	2		3	1	
Lassitor, Josiah	2	3	5		
Robbins, John	2		5		1
Briggs, John	3	1	1		
Costen, Isaac	1				6
Costen, James	1		3		12
Riddick, Jobe	1	3	5		27

NAME OF HEAD OF FAMILY.	Free white males of 16 years and upward, including heads of families.	Free white males under 16 years.	Free white females, including heads of families.	All other free persons.	Slaves.
Hunter, John	1		3		1
Eason, Isaac	1		2		4
Hoffler, John	1	1	2		2
Lassitor, Jonathan	2	3	5		5
Gordan, Jacob	3	3	6		8
Baker, James	2		1		3
Hare, John	1	2	3		
Riddick, Joseph	2	1	4		15
Lassitor, Jeremiah	1	1	4		
Jordan, Jeremiah	1	3	2		1
Robbins, John, Junr	1	1	3		
Granbery, Josiah	4	4	2		30
Harrell, Isaac	1	1	2		13
Jones, James (of David)	3	2	5		5
Davis, James	1		3		2
Davis, John	2		3		
Jones, Josiah	1		1		
Brinkley, John	1		2		3
powell, James	1	1	2		8
Jones, John (of Jo)	1		3		1
powell, John	3	1	8		17
Ellis, James	1		2		
Morgan, John	1		3		
Benton, Isaac	3	1	4		
Ellis, John	1	2	2		
Jones, James, Senr	1	1	4		3
Riddick, John	1	1	6		9
Hare, Joseph	1	1	3		1
Brinkley, Josiah	1		2		
Rude, Isaac	1		1	4	
Knight, James	1	2	4		6
Sumner, Jethro	1	1	3		20
Benton, Jethro	1	1	3	1	3
Small, John	1	1	1		4
powell, John, Junr	1		1		
Small, James	1				9
Small, Joshua	1			1	
Sumner, Joseph J.	1				9
Jones, John (of Lewis)	1				
Ballard, Jethro	1	1	6		25
Cowper, John	1	1	1		15
Duke, John	2	3	7		1
Norflet, James	1		5		24
Darden, John	1		1		9
Lamb, Isaac	3	1	3		
Walters, Isaac	1	1	8		3
Dilday, Joseph	1	4	3		4
Garlock, John G.	1				
Benton, Jeremiah	1				
Rogers, Jonathan	2		1		6
Daughter, John	1				
parker, John	1				2
Brady, James	1	3	4		4
Arline, James	1	1	3		4
Arline, John			2		2
Williams, Jonathan	1	5	5		2
Benton, Josiah	1	3	3		2
parker, James	1	2	2		2
Arnold, John	1	1	4		3
Saunders, John	1	1	4		
Benton, Jesse	1		1		2
Matthews, James	1	1	1		1
prenden, James	2	4	3		
phelps, James	3	2	2		4
Bristow, James	2		3		3
potson, John	1		5		
peal, Joseph	1	2	2		
Skinner, James	1		2		
parker, Jonathan	1	2	2		
Weaver, James				6	
Sumner, Jethro (N.)					14
Adam, John (Son of Wm)	1				
Varnal, John	3	1	2		1
Walters, Jacob	2	3	3		1
Goodman, Joel	1	1	2		11
Rooks, Joseph	1		3		3
Lang, James	2		3		1
Gregory, James	1	1	6		29
Gordan, John	2		2		15
Curle, John	1	2	3		
Vann, John	1	5	2		2
Jones, James	1	4	2		
Odam, John	1	3	2		18
platt, Joseph	1	2	2		
Brady, Joseph	1	2	3		2
Hiat, Jesse	2		2		
Gatling, John	3	2	2		20
Lewis, John	2		2		7
pipkin, Isaac	3		5		34
Boon, James				1	
Landing, John	1				1
Ransom, James	1		2		16
bann, Jesse	2	1	5		6
Jones, James	1	2	2		1
parker, John	2		2		3
Saunders, Jesse	3	3	4		21

EDENTON DISTRICT, GATES COUNTY—Continued.

NAME OF HEAD OF FAMILY.	Free white males of 16 years and upward, including heads of families.	Free white males under 16 years.	Free white females, including heads of families.	All other free persons.	Slaves.
Brady, James	1	1	2		17
Bethey, John	2		4		5
Crafford, James	1	1	2		
Weatherly, John	1	3	1		5
Valintine, Joseph	1		3		8
Burges, John	1		2		1
Warren, John	1				9
Wills, James	1	1	3		
Spight, Joseph	1	3	2		25
Durden, Isaac	1		2	2	2
Langston, Jesse	1		2		1
Carter, Isaac	1	3	3		2
Thomas, James	1	2	1		
Carter, James	1	3	2		1
Stallings, John	1	1	1		
Landing, James	3	2	3		
parker, John	1	4	3		1
Langston, Isaac	1	1	3		1
Euri, John	1	1	2		
Green, Isaac	1		2		
Crellings, Jonathan	2		6		
Burman, Joval	2	3	4		1
Harrell, Josiah	1	1	3		
Stallings, Josiah	2	2	4		
Fryer, Isaac	1		2		
Carter, John	1		3		1
Euri, James	1	5	2		
Harrell, Jesse	1	2	3		
Taylor, Jesse	1	1	2		
Worrel, Jesse	2	1	6		
Stallings, Jesse	1				
Odam, Kadar	1	2	2		4
Herston, Kader	2	3	3		5
Benton, Kadar	1		3		
Ballard, Kadar	1	2	2		20
phelps, Kadar	1		1		
parker, Kadar	1	2	2		
Outlaw, Lewis	1	1	1		5
Eason, Levi	1	2	4		2
Taylor, Lamuel	2	1	4		
Walters, Lewis	2	1	4		
Baker, Lawrence	2	3	5	3	29
Brooks, Lodowick	1	1	4		1
Riddick, Leah		1	4		14
Spivey, Lidia	1	1	3		4
Dure, Levin	1		2		1
Jones, Lewis	1	4	4		2
Sumner, Luke	1		5		17
Collings, Lamuel	1	3	2		
Lewis, Luten	1	1			2
Sparkman, Lewis	2	1	5		1
Keen, Lamuel	1	1	1		
Lee, Levi	2	4	4		
Hill, Moses	1	1	6		10
Rountree, Miles	1				4
Rountree, Mary		1	2		7
perry, Mordicae	1	1	4		7
Blanshard, Moses	1				
Carter, Monc	1	1	4		1
Williams, Moses	1		2		
Reade, Micajah					4
Lawrence, Michael	1	1	3		
Boyce, Miles	1		1		
Smith, Mary	1		4		
Riddick, Micajah, Junr	2		1		10
Spivey, Moses	2		3		
parker, Mary		1	2		
Briggs, Moses	2		2		2
Lasitor, Michael	1	1	3		1
Spight, Moses, Senr	3		3		
Spight, Moses, Junr	1	3	3		
Davis, Moses	1	2	5		1
Binton, Moses	4	4	3		2
Ellis, Mills	3		3		
Taylor, Mary	1		2		
Boyce, Moses	3	1	3		1
Benton, Mary	2		3		4
Hines, Moses	2		3		
Odam, Mills	1		5		
Riddick, Micajah, Senr	3	1	3		8
parker, Mills	1	2	1		
phelps, Micajah	1		3		
Morgan, Matthias	1	2	3		
parker, Miles	1	1	3		2
parker, Mary			1		2
Kittrits, Moses	1	3	5		7
Mitchell, Meney				2	
Sumner, Mourning	1	1	2		10
Hare, Moses, Junr	1	2	2		
Hare, Moses, Senr	2		2		7
Benton, Miles	1		3		40
phillips, Major	1	3	1		
Rogers, Milley		1	1		
Lewis, Mills	1				

NAME OF HEAD OF FAMILY.	Free white males of 16 years and upward, including heads of families.	Free white males under 16 years.	Free white females, including heads of families.	All other free persons.	Slaves.
Thomas, Matthew	1	1			
Jones, Moses, Senr	2		3		
Harrell, Milley	2	1	4		2
Euri, Mills	1	2	3		
Jones, Moses	1				
Taylor, Nathaniel	1	1	2		
Harrell, Noah	1		3		6
Riddick, Nathaniel	1		2		7
Fitton, Noah	3		3		4
Nixon, Osten	4	3	6		
Hobbs, Patience		2	2		1
Onley, Penelope	1	1	2		
Rogers, Philip	1	5	3		
parker, Peter	1	4	4		5
Hagrity, Patrick	1	1	3		1
Lewis, Phillip	3		2		11
Dunford, Phillip	2	2	3		
Harrell, Peter	2		7		1
Mitchell, Richard	1	1	1		12
Bond, Richard	2	1	2		6
Taylor, Robert	2	1	2		1
Hobbs, Ruben	1	3	3		
Bond, Richard, Senr	2		1		10
Ward, Robert	1	4	3		
parker, Robert, Senr	1	5	4		3
parker, Robert, Junr	1				
Green, Richard	2	1	5		
Baker, Richard	2		2		6
Fitton, Richard	1		1		
Moore, Robert	1		2		
Rude, Rachel					2
Lassitor, Ruben	1		2		
Riddick, Ruben	1	2	1	1	2
Miller, Rachel		2	1		1
Riddick, Robert	2				2
Briggs, Richard	1	1	1		2
Vann, Rachel	2	3	1		4
Osten, Richard	1	1	2		2
parker, Robert	1	3	3		2
Lasitor, Ruben	1	1	2		
Hiatt, Rebekah			1		
Sparkman, Ruben	1	1	6		1
Rountree, Seth	1	1	3		12
Hinton, Seasbrook	1			2	
Stallings, Simon	1	2	4		15
Trotman, Sarah		2	2		12
Stallings, Seth	1		3		1
Hurdle, Sarah			4		1
Ross, Solomon	1				
Williams, Samuel	2	3	2		
Harrell, Stephen	1	2	3		
Smith, Samuel	3	2	3		3
Euri, Samuel	1	2	4		
Fitton, Sarah	1	1	3		1
polson, Sarah			2		
Wilson, Seasbrook	1				
piland, Sarah				3	
parmile, Salmon	1				
Green, Samuel	1	3	3		1
Harrell, Samuel	4	3	5		6
Eason, Seth	1	2	3		12
Brown, Samuel	1		3		
Briggs, Solomon	3	1	3		
Brinkley, Simeon	1		2		7
Langston, Sarah			2		
Williams, Samuel	1		3		
Baker, Samuel	2	4	3		9
King, Solomon	1		3		15
Watters, Stephen	1		1		
philips, Swin	1		2		
Thomas, Samuel	2	1	2		
Harrell, Samuel	1	2	2		1
Ellis, Shadrick	1				
piland, Stephen	1	3	4		
Green, Samuel	2		4		
Taylor, Samuel	2	2	4		3
Euri, Stephen	1		2		9
Hoffler, Thomas	1	3	2		7
Marshall, Thomas	1	2	2		5
Trotmon, Thomas	3	3	4		18
White, Thomas	1	4	4		2
Freeman, Timothy	1		1		
Langston, Thomas	1	3	5		
Smith, Thomas	3	4	4		17
Robertson, Thomas	1	1	1		
Fitton, Thomas	1		1		
Fryer, Thomas	1	4	4		
Finney, Thomas	1	3	2		7
Green, Thomas	1		1		8
piland, Thomas	1	1	1		
Hurdle, Thomas	2	3	4		4
Lasitor, Timothy	1	3	2		18
Hunter, Thomas	3	2	3		33
Williams, Thomas	1				

NAME OF HEAD OF FAMILY.	Free white males of 16 years and upward, including heads of families.	Free white males under 16 years.	Free white females, including heads of families.	All other free persons.	Slaves.
Travis, Thomas	1	2	2		1
parker, Thomas	1	2	9		4
Ellis, Thomas	1		3		
Hiatt, Thomas	1	3	2		
Barnes, Thomas	1	2	3		7
Vann, Thomas	2	3	4		8
Rogers, Timothy	1		1		
Smith, Thomas	1	1	2		
piland, Thomas	1		2		
Harrell, Thomas	2		3		
Horriss, Thomas	1	3	2		
piland, Thomas	1				1
Odam, Uriah	1				
Euri, Uriah	2	1	2		
Kelley, William	2	2	4		
Freeman, William	1	2	5		11
Beriman, William	1	1	2		3
Robertson, William	1	2	2		1
Hurdle, William	2	5	3		6
Henlove, William	1	3	4	2	12
King, William	2	3	4		2
Cleaves, William	1	3	3		5
Draper, William	1	2	2		
Hays, Write	1	5	1		4
Brown, William	1		1		
Brown, Willis	2	1	3		5
Brooks, William	1		3		6
Williams, William	1	2	4		
Spight, William	1				
Harriss, William			2		31
Boyce, William	1	2	2		
More, Willis	1	1	1		
Hays, William	1		2		1
parker, William	1				
Gren, William	2		1		
Baker, William	1	2	5		35
parker, Willis	1	2	5		
polson, William	1		1		1
Vallintine, William	1	3	3		9
pierce, William	1	3	2		
Hunten, William	2		5		3
Bond, William	1		1		1
Lewis, William	2	1	4		2
Gordan, William	1		3		2
Bristow, William	2	2	4		
Booth, William	1	1	3		3
Hintou, William	1	3	3		26
phelps, William	2		3		
parker, William	1				
Carter, William	1				
Taylor, William	1	1	2	1	7
Matthews, William	1	5	1		
Wiggins, Willis	4	3	2		
Arnold, William	1	1	2		5
Ellis, William	2	3	4		6
Ellis, Wright	1	1	2		
Daughter, William	3	2	5		6
Matthews, William	3	3	3		
Barr, William	1	1	2		3
Guinn, William	1	1	3		
Cralters, William	1		2		11
Jenkins, William				1	1
Howell, Watson	1	1	3		
Odam, William	2	2	2		7
March, William	1	2	2		1
Warren, William	1	3			
Walters, William	1	2	2		
Gatling, William	2		2		20
Gatling, William, Senr	1		3		9
Warren, William	1		2		4
Goodman, William	1	1	3		15
Collings, William	1	3	2		
Dilday, William	1				
Rutter, William	2	1	2		
Fryer, William	1	2	4		1
Hews, Willis	1	1	1		2
Sparkman, Willis	1	1	2		
Umflet, William	1		2		
Ellis, William	3				3
Crafford, William	1	4	1		
Brown, William (of S.)	1		1		
Morriss, William	2	2	2		
Sparkman, Willis	1				
Wiggins, Willis	1		3		2
Hinton, Zadock	1		3		2
Minchen, Zacheriah	1	2	1		
parker, Zacheriah	1	2	1		
Davis, David	1	1	1		
Lassitor, Jonathan	1		1		
Garret, Richard	1	1	2		
Fanney, John	1	1	1		
Blanshard, Keziah		1	5		
Smith, Mary			1		
Tomson, Nathan	1				

EDENTON DISTRICT, HERTFORD COUNTY.

NAME OF HEAD OF FAMILY.	Free white males of 16 years and upward, including heads of families.	Free white males under 16 years.	Free white females, including heads of families.	All other free persons.	Slaves.
McFarlane, Walter	1	2	6		
Hannell, Mary		1	3		11
Hannell, William	1				7
Jones, William	1				6
Evans, Benjamin	3	3	5		5
Brickell, Aron	1	1	7		29
Winborn, Josiah	1				3
Penney, Abner	1		4		10
Moore, James	4	5	2		39
Benthal, Joseph	1	3	4		9
Moore, James	1	3	4		23
Hill, Charles	1	1	1		4
Brown, James	1		2		
Long, John	1	1	2		
Cornelios, Mancha		1	2		
Hooks, Elisha			1		
Darden, Willis	1	3	3		5
Darden, John	2	3	2	2	5
Battle, John	1		2		3
Battle, Martha	1	2	4		9
Goodman, David	2				3
Bolton, Thomas	2		3		
Wilkins, James	1	2			4
Williams, Charles	3		2		
Weakes, Arthur	1				1
Bell, James	1				
Willey, James	2	2	4		
Muller, William	4	4	6		10
Gatling, James	1	2	3		2
Daughtry, Elizabeth	2	1	2		10
Darden, Elisha	1	1	4		4
Williams, Richard	2	1	1		2
Darden, David	4		1	4	8
Barnes, William	1				
Steickey, John	2	2	4		
Muller, James	1	1	3		7
Boone, Arther				6	
Weakes, William	1	1	1		
Cretchelon, Prudence		1	5		
Whitley, Ann	1	3	4		
Baley, William			1	6	
Wilkins, William	1	2	1		
Wilkins, Richard	1		4		
Carr, Robert	3	4	4		14
Wiggans, William	1	4	3		2
Halomon, Hanche	2	1	3		
Beamon, Cullen	1		1		
Darden, Elisha	1	3	6		9
Darden, Allen	1				
Hobbs, William	1				
Porter, Abram	1	4	3		18
Darden, Henry	1	1	2	2	1
Hobbs, William	1		1		2
Hobbs, Jacob	2	2	3		
Weakes, Julin	2	2	3		23
Hill, Henry	2				23
Carr, Matthew	3		4		11
Vasser, Jessee	1				7
Barnes, Randolph	3	1	3		
Carr, Laurence	2	1	2		4
Haine, Joseph	1	4	4		5
Whitley, James	3		3		
Porter, Hubbird	1		3		2
Porter, Henry	1		1	1	
Driver, Samuel	1	1	2		8
Jiggits, Edward	1	1	3		7
Magott, John	1	2	5		17
Johnson, Ben	1	2	3		
Calf, James	1	5	3		7
Mullen, John	1	2			1
Williams, William	1		2		6
Hobbs, Abram	1	1	1		
Drew, Richard	1				8
Britt, James	1	3	4		10
Britt, Abram	1	2	2		1
Christia, James	1		1		
Sandifer, James	1	2	1		1
Hutchins, William	2	1	3	1	3
Britt, Ben	1	3	2		
Story, John	1	1	4		
Sandifer, John	1	1	5		3
Cook, Charles	1	1	2		
Cooke, Ben	1	1	1		
Heart, John	1				7
Britt, Martain	1	4	3		
Boone, Niclis	1	2	3	1	4
Barden, William	2	1	2		1
Hutchins, James	2	1	3		1
Land, Bird	2		1		9
Barden, James	1	1	1		
Williams, Warren	1	2	1		
Jacson, Isaac	1	3	2		
Britt, Silas	1	2	2	1	
Grantham, James	2	1	6		
Britt, Arther	1				
Matthews, Farmer	1				
Foster, James	1		1	1	5
Wernell, Richard	1	1			1

NAME OF HEAD OF FAMILY.	Free white males of 16 years and upward, including heads of families.	Free white males under 16 years.	Free white females, including heads of families.	All other free persons.	Slaves.
Gay, James	1	1	5	2	
Chetulow, Elizabeth		1	5		10
Fulton, Elisha	2	4	2		16
Carter, Lewis	1	3	4		6
Brown, Elizabeth	2		2		12
Howard, Luke	2	3	2		7
Teyler, Helen	1	5	2		14
Carter, Isaac	2	1	1		28
Powell, Shadrick	2				5
Nichols, William	1	3	2		1
Perrey, Simeon	2	3	4		8
White, Henderson	4	1	3		12
Mash, George	1	4	4		
Hancock, Nehemiah	1	3	3		
Howard, Mosses	2		3		3
Beley, Benjamin	1	1	5	2	
Bruse, Abram	1		2		1
Williams, Nathan	1		2		2
Williams, Gilstrap	1	1	1		
Sanders, John P	1	3	3		
Read, Hamilton	2	1			3
Caneday, John	1	1	4		
Bruse, Bennet	1	3	2		1
Davis, Luke	1		2		
Weaver, Ned				7	
Teften, John B	1	1	3		
Nichols, John	2	3	4		
Smith, James				6	
Webb, Ben	3	4	2		2
Duning, Samuel	1	2	1		1
Williford, John	3	4	2		8
Flowed, Randolph	2		2		
Perney, Ezekel	2	1	3		10
Thomas, Isaac	1		1		
Thomas, Josiah	1		2		
Horton, Hugh	2	6	3		7
Humphry, William	2	3	5	1	1
Howard, Elisha	1	2	4		
Harnell, Elijah	3		2		
Moore, Morrice	1	2	1		4
Horton, Matthew	3		5		
Moore, Willis	2	2	4		8
Driver, Martha	1		1		7
Rynals, Thomas	1				
Powell, Anna			1	1	2
Powell, Dempsey	1	1	6		4
Smith, Abram	1	1	3		
Smith, John	1	1	2		
Hipton, William	1	3	1		
Cotten, Godwin	1		6		9
Sumner, William	1	4	8		15
Spires, Elisha	1				1
Spires, Absalom	2	2	1		2
Askew, James	1	2	2	1	6
Irven, Samuel	2	3	3		1
Horton, Elizabeth	1		3		
Hutchens, Aaron	1		1		
Burton, John	1				
Brickell, Thomas N	1	1	3		3
Scull, Edward	1	2	3		
Lee, James	1	1	1		
Blake, Elizabeth		1	3		
Jones, Sarah			3		
Cotten, William	2	3	3		2
Kelley, Delphia		1	2		
Brickell, Mat	2	1	3		11
Askew, Mabell		2	4		8
Brickell, William	1		2		8
Moore, Aron	3		3		13
Haine, Marmaduke	2				5
Turner, William	1	5	1		1
Rawles, William	1	2	3		12
Baker, Blake	2	2	7		3
Brantley, Ben	2	2	2		5
Weston, Jorden	1	1	2		9
Jones, James	1		2		7
Jones, Amilesent			1		2
Wiggans, Sarah		4	3		
Rivets, Mary			4		4
Brown, Fredrick	1		2		3
Rabey, Joel	1	3	2		
Peal, Edward	2	3	3		
McGlauhn, Elisha	1		2		
McGlauhn, George	1		2		1
McGlauhn, James	1		2		
Rhods, Abram	3	1	6		6
Ward, Isaac Hill	1	1	3		9
Newson, Joel	1		4		2
Jornagan, Needham	1	3	2		7
Cherry, James	1	1	2		5
Peal, Dempsey	1	4	1		
Godwin, James	1		4		1
Rasbery, William	1		2		
Outlaw, Thomas		3	5		4
Peal, Ann		3	2		
Brickell, Jonathan	1	1	2		
Bird, Robt	1	1	2		
Horton, Williford	2		3		4

NAME OF HEAD OF FAMILY.	Free white males of 16 years and upward, including heads of families.	Free white males under 16 years.	Free white females, including heads of families.	All other free persons.	Slaves.
Peal, Thomas	1	3	3		1
Pinnen, Rachel	1	1	3		1
Sessoms, Ann	2	3	2		14
Harison, James	1	2	2		3
Askew, Cullen	1	1	4		1
Holomon, Malichi	1	4	6		1
Driver, John	2	3	3		13
Holomon, Samuel	2	2	2		
Outlaw, William	3	4	3		19
Pearce, Daniel	1	7	4		7
Holomon, Silvia	2		2		
Holomon, Aaron	3		6		
Holomon, David	1	4	4		1
Newsom, Charles	1		3		5
Rawles, Moriah	1		3		
Sumner, Moses	2	5	4		28
Williams, Ben	1		1	2	2
Archer, Armstrong				4	
Archer, Evans				3	
Rowals, Jessee				11	
Outlaw, Lewis	1	1	2		1
Brown, Lewis	1	1	3		1
Newsom, Heosia	4	2	7		14
Hill, Handay	1	4	1		
Hill, Michal	2		3		
Brown, Richard	1		2		2
Brown, Sarah			2		1
Brown, Stephen	1	2	4		
Breton, Benjamin	1	1	1		3
Modlin, Dempsey	1	3			
Newsom, John	1		1		1
Rasbery, Marget	2		3		
Denton, Polley		1	1		2
Weston, Jessee	2		3		
Ellis, Oszel	2		5		
Sanders, Nathan	1		3		
Northcutt, John	1		2		
Lewis, Eden	1		2		
Overton, James	1	1	2		
Overton, Nat	1	3	5		
Northcutt, John	2	1	4	1	
Odom, Jacob	1		2	1	1
Russell, Thomas	1		1		3
Brown, Sophiah		3	2		
Spivy, Daniel	1	2	1		
Lewis, Isaac	2		2		
Simons, Joshua	2	1	3		13
Williams, George	1	2	3		
Kail, Jeremiah	1	3	1		
Host, John	1	2	2		
Green, Joseph	2	2	2		
Hays, Ezekel	1		1		3
Fainless, Handay	2	2	4		
Sowell, Dempsey	1	1			2
Williams, Whit	2	1	3	1	8
Luton, Samuel	2		3		2
Luton, Thomas	2	2	3		2
Bayer, John	2	2	3		2
Scull, John	1	1	6		3
Blanchard, Miles	1		4		7
Baker, Zadoc	1		4		3
Roscoe, Alexander	1		1		
Brown, Benjamin	3		2		10
Morgan, Willis	1	2	3		
Holland, Thos	1	2	1		21
Sharp, Jemima	1	1	4		16
Scull, Elisha	1		4		11
Dowing, William	2	3	4		3
Bilch, Elisha	1	1	4		
Evans, Cornelias	2	3	2		3
Evans, William	2	1	3		3
Sessoms, Rachel	2		2		6
Sheephed, Providence	1	2	5		
Wynns, John A	1	1	4		11
Thomas, Ben	1		1		
Cotten, Samuel	1		3		7
Cotten, Noah	1		2		2
Sea, William	2		3		8
Rooks, Dempsey	1	2	3		
Rooks, Joseph	1	1	2		1
Manley, Gabriel				2	
Fley, John	1	1	3	1	7
Deanes, Daniel	3	2	4	1	7
Porter, William	1	2	4		10
Porter, John	1				4
Winson, William	2	3	4		
Vaughn, William	1	2	3		
Gay, John	1	2	3		
Mashborn, William	1	3	3		
Winson, James	1	1	5		2
Gatling, William	1				
Winson, Peter	1	2	2		
Vaughn, William	1				
Figeuns, John	1		1		
Figeuns, William	1	3	6		11
Knight, William	1	2	3		2
Langston, Luke	1	2	4		2
Watson, Micajah	1				

EDENTON DISTRICT, HERTFORD COUNTY—Continued.

NAME OF HEAD OF FAMILY.	Free white males of 16 years and upward, including heads of families.	Free white males under 16 years.	Free white females, including heads of families.	All other free persons.	Slaves.
Yeats, Sarah	1		1		6
Banks, Benjamin	1	3	2		9
Banks, Alexander	3		2		11
Cuyer, James	1		1		
Munfree, William	2		1		20
Michel, William	1	2	2		
Fitt, Thos	4	2	1		13
Masongill, Daniel	3	4	5		3
Miller, John	2	2	2		1
Jiggets, William	1	4	1		
Benson, Ezekel	1	3			3
Denis, Litleton	2				
Christen, David	1				
Trader, Rachel		1	3		
Harison, Thomas	1	3	3		
Greyham, Chancey	1	2	3		2
Warren, Obediah	1	1	3		
Garvy, Patrick	5		2		6
Byrn, John	2		2		3
Frasure, John	2				2
Hichborn, John	4				2
Munfree, Handay	5	3	5		45
Rea, William	1				1
Blak, Ellis Gray	1				
Hall, Mantain	1				
West, James	1				
Cross, Stephen	1				
Tuyler, Samuel	1		8		1
Brewer, Jessee	1	1	3		
Skinner, James	1	2	3		35
Baley, William	2	2		1	
Stricling, Drew	1		4		1
Jacson, Low	1	2	1		1
Sandefer, Nancy	1	1	5		2
Joiner, Charles	1	2	3		
Wernell, Rhodah		1	1		1
Gatling, Edward	1				
Willison, Matthew	2	4	4		21
Boone, Allen	1	3	3		2
Britt, Thomas	2	4	3		4
Britt, Joseph	4		2	1	
Darden, Jethro	1	1	1		11
Darden, Jet	1	1			3
Goodmon, David	1	1	1		7
Manney, James	1	1	3		39
Thannie, Peggey		2	2		7
Glover, William	2	4	5		9
Vasser, Robert	1	1	1		7
Little, George	3		2		36
Figeurs, Thomas	1	1			19
Ridley, Timothy	2				11
Basset, Elizabeth		3	1		11
Morgan, Elizabeth		1	1		
Holoman, Christopher	2	2	5		2
Rawls, Jessee	1	3	2		
Hill, Whitmill	1	1	3		
Holomon, John	1	2	4		3
Pinner, Milley		1	1		1
Archer, William			1	5	
Archer, Peggey				2	
Harnell, Jesse	1	3	3		
Perrey, William	1		2		4
Haine, Ben	1	1	2		17
Moore, William	1	1	1		17
Winborne, Thomas	1		2		2
Peal, Daniel	1	2	1		1
Rindal, Joseph	1	1	2		1
Rutland, William	1		3		4
Wiggans, Wright	2		2	2	
Eley, Michal	1		4		9
Eley, Edward	1	1	1		13
Perrey, James	1	3	2		7
Deanes, James	1		3		7
Walker, Patsey		1	5		11
Riley, William	1	1	1		
Jordan, William					
Best, Henry	1	1	1		
Deanes, William	1	2	1		4
Holoman, Cornelius	1	1	1		1
Cotten, James	1		1		2
Bremagen, John	1	3	5		
Best, Thomas	1	1	2	1	
Best, Mary			3		3
Parker, Samuel	2	2	3		
Cotten, Thomas	1	4	1		3
Wright, Henry	1	1	5		11
Benthal, Daniel	2		5		4
Bass, Willis				4	
Garner, Anthony				2	
Weaver, Jessee				6	
Archer, Caleb				5	
Bowser, Thomas				5	
Nickens, Malichi				5	
Orange, Henry				3	
Shewenaft, William				8	
Read, Shadrick				6	
Haine, Jessee	1				7
Carter, Isaac	3	3	3		23
Williams, Sarah	3			3	
Lewis, Luke	1	1	8		3
West, John	1	2			3
Norvell, Dempsey	2	2	3		1
Lawed, Mauget			4		
White, Absalah	1		2		1
Haine, William	2	2	5		
Fainless, Robert	1	2	1		
Morgan, Handay	1	2	1		
Lassitor, Jeason	1		3		1
Norvell, Ben	1		5		2
Hobbs, Sarah	1	2	3		
Norvell, Mary	1	1	1		
Daws, Ann			2		
Wirtherington Arcada		1	5		1
Vanpelt, John	1		3		1
Henson, Shadrick	2	2	5		1
Wirthington, Sarah	2	1	3		1
Sears, John	1				8
Jinkens, Charles	1	1	4		9
Best, David R.	1	2	3		5
Copland, Mary	3	1			4
Copland, Thos	1	1	1		1
Copland, John	1	4	2		1
Copland, Halowell	1	2			
Copland, Eley	1	1	5		2
Thomson, Elizabeth			4		1
Askew, William	1	1	2		3
Askew, Mary	1		2		1
Pearce, Jobe	1	1	3		
Bridgen, Joseph	3	1	4		5
Jenkins, Webb	1	1	5		2
Yeorley, George	1	3	4		4
Askew, Zachariah	1	5	3		2
Chalk, Stephen	1	1	1		1
Askew, Persillea	1	1	3		2
Perney, Celia	1	1	2		21
Doughtee, Jethoro	2		1		
Askew, Shadrick	1		1		17
Vanpelt, Sarah	1		2		
Brown, Rhodrick	1		2	2	3
Daws, Mary		1	2		
Bezelle, Solomon					11
Dildea, John	1	4	4		
Clarke, Kerney	1		1		
Godwin, Barney	1		2		
Godwin, John	1		2		
Overton, James	1	1	2		
Willibea, John	3	1	7		
Pearce, Jobe	1	3	2		1
Colemon, Thomas	1	3	2		
Archer, Thomas				5	
Manley, Sarah				3	
Evans, Peter	1	2	3		
Rawles, Absalom	2	1	2		6
Evans, Robert	2	2	4		
Boone, Mary	1	2	2		3
Pearce, Richard	1	5	4		
Clark, William	2	1	2		
Barrow, John	2	2	4		
Northcutt, Anthony	1	1	2	1	1
Brown, Francis	1	2	2		3
Parker, Abigale			2		
Beaman, John	2		2		1
Wiggans, Sarah					8
Alexander, Tebbs	1	1	5		
Manley, Moses					11
Harrison, William	2	1	1		
Moore, Laurence	2	3	1		10
Winborn, James	1		2		1
Powell, Charles	3	3	1		20
Evret, James	1		2		6
Lintal, Joseph	1	2	2		
Doughte, James	1		4		
Doughte, William	1		4		
Harton, William	1	3	4		2
Freeman, Josiah	1		2		
Daniel, Joseph	3		2	2	
Gliston, Daniel	2	1			2
Mayne, Robert	2	2	5		4
Pender, Jethro	1	2	1		
Copland, Thomas	2		2		7
Copland, James	2				
Johnson, Anna	1		3		
Beamon, Morning		1	3		1
Brown, Jeremiah	2		4		23
Nicholes, Na	1	1	4		
Rhods, William	1		4		7
Yeats, Jessee	1	1	4		5
Askew, Charnady	1	5		1	5
Copland, Stephen	1			1	2
Jenkins William	2		2		1
Fells, Edward	1	2	2		
Hale, Fereby	1		1	1	
Howell, John	1		2		
Evans, William	1		2		5
Parker, William	1	2	2		2
Dunn, George	1	1	2		12
Spines, Thomas	3	1	3		
Rogers, Jonathan	1	2	3		15
Wiggans, Joshua	2	3	4		2
Macone, William	3	4	2		
Mashborn, Matthew	1	1	6		1
Warren, Jorden	1	1	1		
Parker, William	2		4		3
Gatling, Harday	1	6	6		
Griffith, John	1	4	2		4
Parker, John	1	4	3		8
Jinkens, Dempsey	1	1	2		4
Parker, Silas	2	2	6	1	
Rivel, Matthew	2	1	3		
Best, William	1	1	3		
Cook, Daniel	2		3		2
Carter, Martha	1		2		
Macoone, Ephraim	1		1		
Rivel, Silis	1	1	2		
Sanders, David	1	1	2		
Archer, Jacob				8	
Brown, Thomas	2		3		1
Wynn, Matthew	1		3		2
Jinkens, Samuel	1	1	1		2
Gatling, Arther	2	1	4		5
Winson, Drury	1		2		1
Parker, Peter	3	4	5		2
Langston, John	1	3	3		
Carter, James	1	1	2		
Sanders, William	1		2		
Parker, Ephraim	1	1	3		1
Brown, John	1		2		1
Ezell, Benjamin	2	3	5		
Winborn, John	1		2	1	5
Tayler, Michal	1	2	4		
Matthews, Edmond	1		2		1
Bolton, John	1	2	1		
Fawn, Ann		1	3		4
Shewenaft, William	1	1	3		
Moore, Edward	1	3	3		21
Matthews, Richard	2	1	1		
Langston, Martha	1		3		12
Bushap, John	1		2		8
Hill, Joseph	2	1	4		10
Deanes, Thomas	1		1		4
Larrence, Axum	2	3	2		4
Jenkins, Winborn	1	5	4		5
Jenkins, Henry	2	1	3		17
Livermon, Edimon	1	1	4		
Bushop, Jessie	1	3	3		
Gatling, Edward	1	3	4		
Davis, Samuel	1	2	5		10
Winson, Elisha	1	4	4		
Parker, Daniel	1	1	3		
Denton, James	3		3		3
Vaughn, John	1		2		
Jinkens, Benjamin	1	2	2		3
Dickerson, John	1	2	6		
Nox, James	1		4	1	
Shewenaft, Abram	2		3		
Slade, Thomas	3		3		2
Griffith, Bunnell	1		3		
Griffith, Hirtwell	1		1		1
Knight, William	1		1	2	
Matthews, Giles	1	4	2		
Knight, Dempsey	1	3	4		
Sumter, Elizabeth	1		2		
Mashbonn, Charitey		4	2		
Gatling, Rachel				1	
Williams, Constant				4	
Manley, Letisha			2		1
Gatling, David	2		2		1
Davis, Blake	1	1	2		1
Morgan, James	1	3	3		
Brasure, Abram	1			5	
Manley, William			3		14
Wright, Jane	1		3		
Botton, Jane	2		3		2
Porter, Edward					43
Winborn, Henry	2				1
Tayler, Winiford	1	4			
Perrey, Elisha	1	3	4		
Phelps, Dempsey	1	1	2		4
Hays, James	1	1	2		
Hays, William	1				3
Perry, William	1	2	2		
Lassitor, Zadoc					34
Green, Randolph	1	2	3		
Livermon, Sarah		3	4		34
Wynns, George	4		4		
Stephens, Ann		5	2		1
Montgomery, Elinder	3	1	4		
Sowell, William	1		4		
Simons, Obediah	1		3		
Rider, Nancey			1		10
Pearce, Jaidah (for John Brikele, ded)	1	1	3		3
Bell, Frances	1	1	3		33

EDENTON DISTRICT, HERTFORD COUNTY—Continued.

NAME OF HEAD OF FAMILY.	Free white males of 16 years and upward, including heads of families.	Free white males under 16 years.	Free white females, including heads of families.	All other free persons.	Slaves.
Hall, Mary				6	
Wirtherington, Mary	1		3		2
Brown, Samuel	2		1		4
Boutwell, Adam	1	1	2		11
Manley, Martha			2		
Ronals, Patience			6		
Bacon, James	1	4	3	1	5
Williams, Elizabeth		3	8		2
Sorrell, James					8
Bird, Molley		1	4		
Rogers, James	2	2	7		
Evans, Frances	2	3	5		
Moore, William	1				2
Valintine, Paul	1	1	2		
Valintine, Isaac	1		1		
Valintine, David	2	2	3		2
Boroughs, Handay	1	1	1		
Boroughs, Sarah	3		2		
Morgan, James	1	2	2		
Valintine, Alexander	2	1	4		1
Baker, Ben	2	2	2		
Wiles, Joshu	1		3		26
Howard, Stephen	1		2		
Sander, Nat	1	1	2		
Fainless, William	2	1	2		
Fauney, William	1		3		
Bouroughs, Samuel	1	2	2		
Fainless, William	1	1	2		
Fainless, Ben	1	1	3		
Evans, Thomas	1	1	3		
Lowell, Richard	1	1	2		
Harnell, Nathan	1	2	3		11
Ditto for J. Sharp					5
Ditto for S. Sharp					5
Fainless, Zadoc	1				
Tayler, Boaz	1	1	1		
Keele, Jacob	2	1	5		
Byram, John	2	1	2		
Byram, Thomas	1	1	2		
Morgan, Jacob	1				
Lassetor, William	1			1	18
Quimley, Jessee	2	3	3		7
Rawles, Jessee	1	5	4		2
King, Jessee	1				2
Scott, John	1	2	4		18
Smith, Thomas	1	3	6		
Sorrell, William	1	2	5		
Brown, Lewis	1	3	5	5	6
Crow, Elizabeth				1	
Holland, Keziah		4	2		
Wynns, William	2	1	5		29
Jordan, Elezeth	1	1	4		15
Mountgomery, Robt	1	2	5		17
Holomon, Samuel	1	3	5		2
Godwin, Kenney	3	1	5		10
Godwin, Barney	3		3		
Nickens, James				3	
Merideth, Lewis	3	1	2		19
Ireland, Grafton	2	1	1		4
Roberts, William	1	2	1		5
Hill, John	1				13
Andrews, Richard	1	1	4		
Gatling, Jethro	2	1	2		3
Benberry, Bryan	1		4		11
Rayner, Amos	3			5	
Edes, Stephen	3	1			
Brown, Patrick	1				

EDENTON DISTRICT, PASQUOTANK COUNTY.

NAME OF HEAD OF FAMILY.	Free white males of 16 years and upward, including heads of families.	Free white males under 16 years.	Free white females, including heads of families.	All other free persons.	Slaves.
Arnold, Joshua	2		6		1
Armour, Willis	1				
Ackis, Thomas	2	2	5		6
Albertson, Elias	1	2	3		3
Allen, Benjamin	1				
Albright, William	1		3		1
Albertson, Albert	1				
Allison, Henry	1		3		1
Allison, John	1	1	2		
Albertson, Samuel	1		2		
Banks, Thomas	1	2	3		19
Brosher, John	1				5
Brosher, Thomas	1				
Bundy, Demsey	1				
Blackburn, James	1				
Bailey, John, Junr	1	2	1		
Barns, Thomas	1		1		17
Bundy, John	1	2			
Bundy, David	1	1	2		1
Bundy, Ruth		1	3		
Bailey, Robert	1	1	1		13
Berry, John	1	3	2		2
Banks, Joseph	1	1	2		4
Barns, James	2	2	1		7
Boyd, William	1	2	1		3
Boyd, Roger	2				4
Bell, John	1		1		
Bright, Mary	2	1	2		
Bundy, John	1	1	3		
Benton, John	2	1	2		
Bailey, Patrick	1	4	2		
Bailey, Thomas	1				
Bailey, Benjamin	1				
Bailey, Jane			3		
Bailey, Ann	1	2	1		
Boswell, Joseph	4		5		
Bailey, John	1	1			12
Boswell, Abraham	2	2	3		1
Bundy, Josiah	1	2	3		
Bundy, Joseph	1	1	2		
Bundy, Caleb	1		4		
Bailey, David	1				15
Brothers, Levi	2				3
Brothers, Joseph	2	4	7		1
Brothers, Joshua	1				
Bailey, David, Jur	1	2	2		
Benton, Elkana	1		5		1
Brothers, Richard	3	3	3		
Bundy, Benjamin	1	1	2		
Bundy, Jeremiah	1				
Bright, Ann	2	1	3		
Brown, John					2
Bundy, James	1				
Brown, Mary			1		2
Brewer, William	1	2	1		4
Brownrig, Thomas	3		1		15
Bailey, Sarah		1	2		
Brothers, Jonathan	1	1	3		
Bowe, Robert			5		
Bowe, Tulle			3		
Brothers, John	1		5		
Brothers, Thomas, Jur	1	2	5		
Bundy, Jonathan	2	2	2		4
Bowls, David	1	4	1		
Brothers, William	1	2	3		
Brothers, Andrew	5	3	3		6
Brothers, Job	1	2	3		
Brothers, Lewis	1	1	2		
Barrow, William	2		3		1
Boswell, Isaac	1	1	1		
Burges, John	1	2	2		
Brothers, Malachi	2	3	5		
Bright, Jesse	1	1	3		
Bright, Asa	1		1		
Benton, Devotion	1				
Bright, Willis	1	3	2		
Bright, Ephraim	1	2	4		
Brothers, David	1		1		
Burnham, John	1	2	2		
Blount, James	2	5	2		
Burnham, Ivy	1	1	4		
Burnham, Isaac	1	2	4		2
Beeks, Elizabeth		1	4		
Burnham, Timothy	2	1	3		
Best, Charles	1		5		
Bidwell, James	2	1	1		1
Benton, John	1	1	4		
Bailey, Gabriel	3	2	2		
Brooks, Jonathan	1				
Brothers, Joseph, Jur		1			
Bundy, Meriam	1	1	2		
Bundy, Jebu	1	2	5		
Bailey, Joseph	1	2	2		
Bailey, Joseph, Jur	1		4		
Brothers, Thomas	1	1	6		
Cartwright, Hezekiah	1	1			
Cartwright, Caleb	1	4	3		10
Cartwright, Darius	1	1	2		2
Cartwright, Robert	1		2		
Cory, Davidson	1	4	2		
Cox, John	1	3	2		
Cox, Jacob	1		4		
Chalk, William	1	1	4		4
Coppersmith, Micajah	1		2		
Commander, Thomas	1	1	3		3
Cartwright, Clement	1	1	1		9
Commander, John	2	2	3		2
Commander, Tukes	1				
Clary, William	1	2	3		2
Call, Charles	1	2	5		
Carman, Charity		2	2		
Cooper, Darcas		1	5		
Cartwright, Hezekiah	2				
Cartwright, Benjamin	1		1		
Cartwright, Isaac	1	2	1		
Cammeron, Mary		1	1		
Collins, John, Jur	1				
Charles, Susannah		1	1		
Caruthers, George	1		1		
Cooper, Lucretia			1		
Delon, Charles	2	2	3		1
Davis, William	1	2	1		
Denby, Nathan	1	2	1		
Davis, Levi	1	1	1		
Denby, Benjamin	1				
Davis, Devotion, Esqr	4	1			6
Davis, Robert	1	2	3		1
Davis, David	1	3	1		2
Delon, Mark	1	5	4		
Davis, Reuben	1	4	1		6
Davis, Thomas	1	4	2		4
Duffee, Hugh	1	4	3		
Davis, Benjamin	1				
Davis, Thomas, Jur	1		1		18
Duglass, Hannah		1	4		1
Davis, Elizabeth			1		5
Davis, Thomas, Ser	2	3	1		
Davis, Devotion, Jur	1	1	2		8
Davis, Frederick	1	1	2		6
Dameron, Onisephorus (Living in Virginia)				8	
Davis, Archibald	1	4	2		3
Davis, Jesse	1	1	3		
Davis, Reuben, Senr	1	2	3		
Davis, John	1	3	2		
Davis, Thomas	1	2	2		
Dailey, Jesse	1	1	5		
Davis, Shadrack	1	2	4		1
Davis, Thomas, Jur	1		4		
Davis, Reuben, Jur	1				
Davis, Benjamin	2	1	5		
Davis, Sandford	1	4	2		
Davis, Dedrick	1	1	3		
Davis, Arthur	1	1	3		3
Davis, Willis	1	5	2		
Davis, Robert			1		
Davis, Anthony	2		3		1
Dresser, Joseph	1	1	4		1
Dunscomb, Edward	1	1	5		
Done, Nathan	2	3	5		3
Davis, Devotion (the youngr)	1	2	1		
Deshon, Christopher	1				
Dailey, John	1	1	3		
Duglas, John	1				
Darnell, William	1	3	2		
Davis, Thamer	1	3	3		
Davis, Mary			1		
Davis, Elizabeth (widow)	2	1	2		
Davis, Joseph	1	1	4		
Dammeron, Thomas	1				
Davis, Rebecca			1		
Dick (a free negro)				1	
Evoregan, Edward	1				27
Evans, Grace	1	2	3		
Elliott, Nathan	1	1	2		1
Elliott, Cornelius	1		1		4
Earl, Elizabeth			1		3
Emmerson, James	1		4		1
Easman, Benjamin	2		1		1
Evans, Robert	2		2		
Early, Mary		1	4		
Commander, Joseph	1	1	4		
Commander, Joseph, Jur	2	1	2		
Commander, Elsburg	1				4
Coppersmith, Thomas	1				
Cartwright, Jesse	1	4	1		
Cosant, Gabriel	2	3	2		2
Cook, Isaac	2	1	2		1
Crookham, John	1		1		1
Crawford, Joseph	2				
Carver, Job	1	4	3		13
Cartwright, Jehu	1	3	4		
Crocker, John	2	1	2		5
Chancy, Micajah	1	3	2		
Clark, Martha		1	1		3
Cartwright, Martha			1		3
Clark, Isaac	1	1	4		
Cook, Josiah		2	4		
Casey, Prudence		2	2		
Cartwright, James	1	4	2		1
Cartwright, Thomas, Jur	1	1	1		
Cartwright, John	1	2	4		1
Cartwright, James	2	1	3		
Casey, John	2		1		4

EDENTON DISTRICT, PASQUOTANK COUNTY—Continued.

NAME OF HEAD OF FAMILY.	Free white males of 16 years and upward, including heads of families.	Free white males under 16 years.	Free white females, including heads of families.	All other free persons.	Slaves.
Casey, Arthur	1		1		
Clark, Cornelius	1		1		
Clark, James	2	1	5		
Clark, Benjamin	1				
Cartwright, Ahaz	1	6	2		
Clark, Goshen	1	1	3		
Casey, Willis	1	4	3		1
Cartwright, Elizabeth			1		1
Cook, John	1	4	4		
Cannady, John	1	4	1		
Cooper, Joel	1				
Cartwright, John	1	4	4		
Cartwright, Simon	1	1	4		
Cartwright, Thomas	1		3		
Coppersmith, Thomas	3	3	2		1
Coin, Mary		3	3		2
Clarkson, Elizabeth	1	1	2		
Conner, Demsey, Esquire	1	3	4		53
Evans, Evan	1	2	3		
Elliott, Gabriel	1				2
Everton, Susannah			2		
Freswaters, Thaddeus	2	2	6		21
Fox, Joseph	1	1	3		5
Fox, William	1	1	1		2
Fletcher, Francis	2	2	4		3
Fentress, William	1	3	4		
Foster, William	1		2		
Foster, Andrew	1		2		1
Faringe, William	1				
Fennell, John	1	3	2		
Foster, John	1	3	4		
Fentress, Lemuel	1		1		
Frew, John	1	6	4		
Forbes, Peter	1	2	1		1
Forehand, David	4	4	3		
Forehand, Elizabeth	1	1	1		
Forehand, Jordan	1	1	1		
Forehand, Joseph	1				
Forehand, Lemuel	2	1	4		1
Gordan, William	1				
Gordan, Joseph	2	2	4		
Gardner, Demsey	1	2	4		
Gavin, Samuel	1		3		
George, David	1	2	4		15
Gaskins, Thomas	2		8		17
Gilbirt, Josiah	1				
Grieves, Rhoda		2	4		10
Guy, William	1	1	4		
Griffin, Joseph	2	3	6		
Gilbert, Jeremiah	2	3	3		
Griffin, James	1	2	2		1
Gordon, Abraham, Jur	1				5
Glassgow, Caleb	1	1	3		
Glassgow, Lemuel	1	1	2		
Grieves, Lydia		2	5		
Goldsmith, William	1		4		1
Gray, Joseph	1		1		
Gray, Nathaniel	1				
Gray, Robert	1		1		2
Gray, Anthony	2	2	6		
Gordon, Abraham	1	1	1		7
Gibson, Elizabeth		2	4		
Grice, Charles	2	3	1		2
Gibson, Elizabeth		3	3		
Guyer, Joseph	1		2		
Grindy, Joshua	1				
Henly, Joseph	1	4	5		6
Hall, Lemuel	1				
Howett, Rowan	1	4	1		17
Hosea, Abraham	1				
Hosea, Seth	1		1		4
Hosea, John	1	1	1		1
Harvey, Thomas, Esqr	1	4			34
Hosmer, Sylvester	1		2		13
Hollowell, Samuel	1	4	2		
Harris, Hezekiah	1		5		
Harris, Joseph	2	4	4		
Harris, Joseph, Jur	2		1		
Harris, Josiah	1	1	2		
Harris, John	2	3	1		
Henry, Rolen	1	1	3		
Holstead, John	3	3	6		10
Holstead, Edward	2	2	1		
Holstead, Jarvis	1				
Harrison, Joseph	1				
Harrison, Thomas	1	3	4		
Hankins, John	1	3	2		
Hall, Elisha	1	1	2		
Harris, John, Jur	1				
Hunt, Charles					5
Hastings, Richard	2		1		
Jennings, John	2	2	3		
Jennings, Joseph	2		2		11
Jennings, Demsey	2	4	3		9
Jennings, Lemuel, Jur	2	1	4		1
Jempson, John	1		1		

NAME OF HEAD OF FAMILY.	Free white males of 16 years and upward, including heads of families.	Free white males under 16 years.	Free white females, including heads of families.	All other free persons.	Slaves.
Jempson, James	1		1		2
Jackson, Zachariah	4	8	5		1
Jordan, Isaac	1	3	6		
James, Solomon				1	
Jackson, Joshua	2	1	3		14
Jackson, David	1	4	3		
Jones, Henry	2		5		
Jordan, William	1	1	3		13
Jackson, Zachariah	1	1	5		
Jackson, Jehu	1	1	1		
Jordan, Thomas	2	2	5		
Jackson, Joab	1	1	2		1
Johnston, John	1		3		
Jackson, Daniel	1				
Jackson, Jesse	1	3	2		
Jackson, Mordica	1	7	4		
Jackson, Lemuel	1	2	2		
Jackson, Moses	1	1	1		
Jackson, Bailey	3		4		
Jackson, Demsey	3	3	4		1
Jennings, Isaac, Jur	1	2	2		
Jennings, Zachariah	1	1	4		
Jennings, Arthur	2	1	5		
Jennings, David	1	1	1		
Jennings, Thomas	1	3	4		
Jennings, Lemuel	2	1	4		3
Jennings, Benjamin	1	3	3		
Jennings, Hannah		3	2		
Jennings, Jessee	1	1	1		
Jennings, John, Jur	1	2	1		6
Jones, Isaac			1		
Jones, James	1	1	3		1
Jones, Javis	4	4	4	8	2
Jones, Joseph	1				
Jones, John	1	1	3		
Jackson, Miles	1		5		
Joes, Rhoda		1	2		
Jackson, Courtney		1	1		
James, William	2		1		
Jordan, Isaac	1	4	4		
Jones, Ruth		2	3		
Jackson, Asa	1	4	1		
Jennings, John	1				
Jennings, Elenezer	1				
Jackson, Sarah	2	1	3		
Jackson, Samuel	1	3	2		
Jackson, Lewis	1		2		
James, William, Ser	1	1	2		
Jennings, Jarvis	1		2		
Keel, Charles	1	1	5		
Keaton, Henry	1	1	5		1
Keaton, William	1	5	1		5
Keaton, John	1	3	3		
Keaton, Stephen	1				
Keaton, Ruben	1				1
Keaton, Joseph	2	4	4		17
Keaton, Patrick	1		3		
Keaton, Dorothy		2	4		
Knight, Thomas	1	1	1		3
Knox, Ambros, Esqr	3	3	2		17
Knox, Hugh	1				
Kerby, Abraham	1		3		10
Koin, John	3		3		
Keely, Abraham	1		3		12
Kinyon, John	1	1	2		
Kinyon, Joseph	4		2		4
Lassell, Othniel	2	4	4		5
Luton, Constantine	1	3	2		1
Lowry, Mary	1	2	5		
Lowry, John	1		2		10
Lowry, Robert	1	1	3		10
Lowry, Benjamin	1				5
Lowry, William	1				7
Luffman, William	2	1	3		3
Lowe, Thomas	1				
Lowe, John	1	3	3		3
Lowe, Aaron	1	4	3		
Lowe, Barnabee	1	1	3		
Lowe, Hannah			2		
Lister, Daniel				1	
Lester, Jacob	1	2	1		2
Lancaster, Henry	3		1		8
Lester, Elisha	2	2	4		2
Lowry, Noah	1	2	3		
Lane, John, Esquire	1		6		5
Leonard, Benjamin	1	2	4		6
Lowe, John, Jur	1	1	2		2
Lacey, Peter	1	1	3		1
Lacey, Josiah	1				
Leonard, James	1		1		6
Lancaster, Mary			1		2
Levory, Simon	1	1	2		6
Luther, Ingram	1				
Leake, Isaac	1		3		2
Leake, Thomas	1	2	2		
Linn, Aron	1	3	5		
Lane, William, Esquire	2	4	3		4

NAME OF HEAD OF FAMILY.	Free white males of 16 years and upward, including heads of families.	Free white males under 16 years.	Free white females, including heads of families.	All other free persons.	Slaves.
Markham, Charles	1	2	4		1
Markham, Thomas	1	3	4		
Markham, Lowry	1				
Markham, Joshua	1		3		3
Madux, Alexander	1	2	1		
Madux, Benjamin	1				
Madux, William	1		1		
Moore, Arthur	1				
Moore, Jesse	2	1	3		
Mudes, Thomas	1	1	2		1
Meads, Timothy	1				
McKinney, Neval	1				
Morriss, Aaron	2	1	6		10
Morriss, Mordica	1	7	3		4
Morriss, Joseph, Senr	2	1	7		
Morriss, Anthony	1	2	3		12
Moon, Hulda		2	5		5
Morriss, John	2	2	3		
Morriss, Aaron, Jur	2	3	5		18
Morris, Thomas	1				
McKeel, John	2	1	2		1
Morriss, Nathan	1	5	3		
Mundin, Simon	1	2	2		
Morgan, Seth	1	4	3		
Morgan, James	2	1	5		
Meredith, William	1		1		
Moss, Benjamin	1	1	3		
Mundin, Ruben	1				
Morriss, Aaron, Senr	4	6	6		
Morgan, Charles	3	1	5		
Morriss, Benjamin	1		3		
Morris, Melissent		3	3		
Morris, John, Jur	1		4		
Mitcalf, George	1				
Mundin, John	1	1	3		
McDonald, John	3		2		5
McMorine, Robert	3	1	1		5
Miller, Andrew	1		1		
Mundin, William	1	3	4		
Mann, Thomas	1		2		4
Martin, Zachariah	1		2		5
Moseley, Emperor	1	2	5		10
Morriss, William	1	2	1		
Madrin, John	2	2	3		
Madrin, Nathan	1	1	3		
Morriss, Thomas	1	3	2		
Madrin, Matthias	2	1	2		1
Murdin, Jeremiah	1	3	3		6
McDanil, John	1	3	4		
Morgan, Asa	1	1	5		1
Madrin, Ruben	1	4	3		
McDonald, Caleb	1		2		
McPhason, Jesse	1	1	4		
Milby, Zadock	1				
Mullen, John	1				4
Morriss, Joseph, Jur	1		2		
Miller, John	1	1	2		
Madrin, Sarah			2		
Mackey, Rebecca		2	1		
McMorine, Charles	1				
McNeal, Jane		3	2		
Meads, Benjamin	1				
McPhason, Joseph	1		3		
McDanil, Rachael			2		1
McCoy, Malachi	1	4	5		
Mires, John	1	4	4		
Mundin, Thomas	1	4	3		
Molbern, Malachi	1		3		
Madkins, William	1				
Mundin, Robert	1	1	1		
Mitchell, Rachael					9
Morriss, Will (free negro)					3
Nicholson, Thomas	1				
Nicholson, John	1		1		1
Nicholson, Christopher	1				
Nixon, James	1				6
Newby, John	1		3		
Newby, James	1	1	3		
Needham, John	3	2	3	1	
Nash, Demsey	1	2	5		7
Nichols, Joseph	1	1	4		2
Nicholls, Joseph, Jur	1		2		3
Nicholls, Willibee	1		1		
Nichols, Anthony	2				1
Nicholls, Willis	1	2	3		
Nicholls, William	1	1	1		
Nicholls, Benjamin	1				
Nicholls, James	1				
Norriss, Thomas	1		3		2
Norriss, Malachi	1	3	3		5
Norman, Patience			1		
Overman, Othnial	1	1	1		
Overman, Ohias	1		1		
Overman, Ozias	1				
Overman, Thomas	1	1	2		1
Overman, Nathan	1	3	2		4

EDENTON DISTRICT, PASQUOTANK COUNTY—Continued.

NAME OF HEAD OF FAMILY.	Free white males of 16 years and upward, including heads of families.	Free white males under 16 years.	Free white females, including heads of families.	All other free persons.	Slaves.
Overman, James	2	3	5		1
Overman, William	1	2	5		8
Overman, Sarah		1	4		
Overman, James, Jur	1		4		2
Overman, Joseph	2	1	5		
Overman, Charles	2	5	3		2
Overman, Thomas, Jur	1				
Overman, John	1		4		
Overman, Enoch	1	1	3		4
Overman, Robert	1	1	1		
Overman, Benjamin	1	1	2		2
Overman, Nathan, Jur	1	2	1		1
Overman, Charity		3	2		2
Overman, Samuel	1	2	4		1
Overman, Ephraim	3	2	4		4
Overman, Charles, Jur	1	1	2		
Overman, Isaac	1				
Overton, James	1		2		
Overton, Samuel				3	
O'Bryan, Eustace	1	2	3		
Pettigrew, Charles	2	2			16
Pool, James	2	3	3		1
Palmer, Demsey	1		1		
Palmer, Joseph	1	3	4		1
Palmer, Thomas	2	2	4		
Pendleton, Lemuel	1	3	4		1
Palmer, William	1	1	1		
Pendleton, John F	1		1		1
Pool, Robert	1	3	3		1
Palmer, David	1	1	1		1
Pendleton, Robert	3	3	4		10
Pendleton, Thomas	2	1	2		
Pendleton, Caleb	2	2	2		8
Peirson, Nathan	2		3	3	
Pendleton, Joseph	2	2	3		2
Parr, Noah	1	4	1		2
Pool, Ann		1	4		1
Pritchard, Matthew	1		2		
Pendleton, Joseph, Jur	1	1	5		7
Pendleton, Joshua	1		2		
Pendleton, Zachariah	1	1	1		
Pendleton, Frederick	1	1	2		5
Pendleton, Jesse	1				
Pool, Joshua	2	2	3		4
Pritchard, Thomas	3		3		28
Pendleton, Thomas, Jur	1	1	2		
Pendleton, Ann		1	2		3
Pool, John	1		3		1
Perry, Josiah, Esquire	1	4	3		5
Price, Jonath	3		3		1
Pool, Patrick (son Patk)	1	1	3		3
Pike, John	1	4	4		
Price, Benjamin	1				
Pool, Solomon, Senr	1		1		8
Pool, Thomas	1				
Pool, Patrick (son of Jo)	1	4	4		1
Price, John	2	2	4		2
Pruno, Joshua	2	1	3		
Pritchard, Benjamin	1	5	3		2
Pritchard, Benjamin, Jur	1	1	1		3
Palmer, Willis	1	2	5		
Palin, Thomas	2		5		17
Pool, Solomon, Jur	1	4	1		
Pendleton, John	2	1	3		7
Pritchard, James	1	1	3		14
Pritchard, Samuel	1	1	3		
Pritchard, Thomas, Jur	1	4	6		
Pritchard, Bathiah		1	2		
Proby, William	1	3	5		4
Pritchard, Richard	1				
Pritchard, John	2		4		
Pritchard, John, Jur	1	1	3		
Pritchard, David	2	4	3		4
Price, Samuel	1	1	3		
Pritchard, Joseph	1	1	3		
Pritchard, Elisha	3	2	2		
Pritchard, Elisha, Jur	1		3		
Purdy, William	1		1		
Pendleton, Timothy	1	1	1		
Pendleton, Peleg	1		1		
Pool, Henry	1				
Perkins, Noah	1	2	3		
Relse, Enoch, Esqr	3	2	2		21
Raper, Cornelius	1	3	4		
Rankhoon, Joshua	1	4	3		
Raper, John	1	3	1		1
Robinson, John	2	2	2		1
Redding, Joseph, Esqr	3	2	3		23
Redding, Thomas, Esqr	3	3	4	1	17
Russell, Thomas	1	1	3		5
Relse, Joseph	1	1	1		2
Relse, Darcas	1	1	3		10
Redding, William	1				
Rowe, Samuel	1		3		
Relse, Benjamin	1				
Ripley, Ann		1	4		6
Richardson, William	3	1	3		5
Ratclift, John	1	1	1		
Richardson, Daniel	1	2	2		
Richardson, Labias	1	1	2		
Richardson, John	2	3	6		4
Rud, John	1	1	3		1
Richardson, Richard	1	4	3		
Richardson, Stephen	1	3	3		3
Richardson, Thomas	1		3		4
Richardson, Joseph, Esqr	2	3	5	1	3
Russell, James	1				
Ross, William	1		1		1
Jacob, Richardson	1		4		8
Reding, Samuel	1				2
Spence, Samuel	4	2	2		1
Saunders, Joseph	1	3	3		6
Saunders, Evan	1		3		
Saunders, Richard	1				
Samson, Joshua				1	
Stewart, Samuel	1		1		5
Sanders, Lovey		1	2		8
Sawyer, Frederick	3		3		12
Simons, Matthew	1		1		1
Simons, Elizabeth		1	4		
Simons, Ann		1	3		
Simons, Abraham	1				
Simons, Abraham, Jur	1				
Stevenson, John	1	1	3		16
Simons, John, Jur	1	2	2		
Stamp, Richard	1	1	3		
Small, Nathan	1		3		
Small, John	1	1	1		
Simons, Jesse	2	7	4	2	2
Symons, Jeremiah	1				5
Small, Samuel	2	2	2		1
Small, Joseph	1				
Symons, Absala		2	2		
Shakespear, Samuel	3	2	1		1
Stanton, Andrew	1		1		2
Shipperd, Smith	1				17
Simson, Elizabeth		5	4		
Scott, William	1	4	4		4
Simson, Thomas	3	1	6		
Scott, Joseph	1	2	4		16
Sawyer, Jane	2	1	3		
Scott, Joseph, Jur	1		2		23
Stafford, Samuel	1	3	1		
Simson, William	3	2	5		
Smithson, John, Jur	2	1	5		13
Sproat, John	1	2	2		
Swann, John, Esquire	1		4		60
Sikes, Levi	2	4	3		
Simson, Joab	1	3	2		
Scott, Stephen	4	3	3		
Scott, Samuel, Jur	1		2		
Scott Robert	1	1	2		
Scott, John	1				
Simson, Josiah	1	1	1		
Stafford, John	1	1	4		
Scott, Samuel, Senr	2		3		2
Scott, Simson	1	1	2		
Scott, Marmaduke	1		2		6
Simson, William, Jur	2	2	2		
Sawyer, Prissilla	1	1	5		
Smithson, John	4	1	3		
Sharborough, Luke	2	1	1		
Stafford, Stephen	2	2	4		
Scott, Abraham	1	1	2		
Sharborough, Joseph	1		2		
Sharborough, Jehu	2		2		
Smithson, Matthias	1	2	4		
Smithson, Ruben	1	3	2	1	
Smithson, Isaac	1	1	3		
Sixton, Malachi	1	2	3		
Smithson, Seth	1	2	1		
Smith, Davis	1		2		
Spence, David	1		2		
Sawyer, Ebenezer	2	2	4		2
Sawyer, John	1	1	4		2
Sawyer, James	1		1		
Spence, Samuel	1	1	3		
Sawyer, Isaac, Jur	1		3		
Sawyer, Isaac	1		3		
Stoakley, Joseph	1	2	2		12
Sawyer, Lott	1	2	3		
Spence, Lemuel	1	2	3		1
Smith, Mordica	3	1	3		5
Spence, Marke	2	1	2		1
Sexton, Mark	1		2		
Spence, Rencher	2	5	4		
Sawyer, Solomon	1				
Spence, Samuel	1		4		
Smith, Thomas	1	2	4		
Scott, Thomas	1	1	3		
Sexton, Willis	3	1	6		
Sawyer, John	1	1	5		
Sylvester, Thomas				4	
Shannonhouse, Susannah	1	1	2		2
Stafford, William	1				
Sawyer, Lemuel	1	1	1		
Stafford, Joseph	1				
Spence, Isaac	1		3		
Simons, Sarah		2	6		8
Stafford, Josiah	1	2	2		7
Symons, John	1	2	5		
Sawyer, Matthias	1				
Stone, Lemuel	2	4	2		
Thackery, Oliver	1		2		
Trubloor, Samuel	1	1	2		3
Taylor, John	3		4		
Taylor, Shadrack	1		1		
Taylor, James	1		6		2
Trueblood, Caleb	2	4	3		3
Trubloor, Thomas	1	2	3		10
Trubloor, Timothy	2	1			2
Turner, Sylvanus (free negro)				4	
Turner, Charles				4	
Turner, Demsey				4	
Tatlock, Edward	2	5	4		
Trubloor, Joseph	1	3	2		
Trubloor, Daniel	2		2		18
Trubloor, John	2	2	4		
Trubloor, Jesse	1				
Trubloor, Abell	3	1	5		
Trubloor, Josiah	3	2	4		4
Trubloor, Caleb, Jur	1	1	2		
Trubloor, Aaron	1	4	1		
Tatlock, John	1	2	5		
Trubloor, Joshua	1		1		
Tooley, Adam	1		1		
Trubloor, Caleb	2	1	2		
Tatlock, James	1	1	7		1
Temple, James	1	1	2		3
Temple, Joseph	2	3	5		5
Temple, Thomas	2	1	4		7
Taylor, James	2		5		
Taylor, David	1	2			
Trubloor, Thomas	1		1		
Tuckness, Henry	1	2	1		
Turner, Joseph	2	2	4		2
Tuttle, Joseph	2	3	1		
Trubloor, Fisher	1	3	2		
Taylor, Daniel	1	2	1		
Varden, Elizabeth	1		2		
Varden, Tulle	1		3		
Varden, Moses	1	4	2		
Wootten, Charles	1		1		
Woodley, Hezekiah	1	3	1		
West, Charles	1	1	1		
Wootten, Samuel	1		2		
Willson, John	1		3		
Williams, Asa	3	1	2		1
White, James	2	1	4		
Tummigan, William	2	1	2		2
White, Anthony	1				
White, John	2	1	3		
White, James	1	4	3		1
Warner, Samuel	1	1	1		7
White, Thomas	1	1	2		1
White, Saml, Jur	1	1	4		2
White, Devotion	1	1	2		1
Wood, Thomas	1	2	5		
White, Nathan	1	2	2		2
Wood, Joseph	1		3		
White, Joshua (son of B.)	1	1	1	2	
White, Benja (s. of Z.)	1		2		3
White, Charles	1		2		6
White, John	1		2		
White, Arnold	1		1		
White, James	3		1		
White, Francis	1	1	4	1	1
White, Benja (son Josh)	2	1	2		5
White, Rachael		2	5		
White, Benja, Jur	1		2		
White, Jordan	2	3	2		
Willson, John	1		2		
White, Abraham	1	3	2		
Williamson, Malachi	1		2		
Whorton, Willis	1	3	5		
White, Thomas	1	1	2		
Wood, Evan			2		1
White, Thomas, Jur	1				
Winson, John	1				
Wiggins, Seth			2		
Williams, Rufus	1				
Whidbee, Samuel	1				6
Wayman, Thomas	1	1	4		
Walden, Thomas	1	1	2		1
Wharton, Robert	1	1	3		
Wayman, Corban	1	3	2		

EDENTON DISTRICT, PASQUOTANK COUNTY—Continued.

NAME OF HEAD OF FAMILY.	Free white males of 16 years and upward, including heads of families.	Free white males under 16 years.	Free white females, including heads of families.	All other free persons.	Slaves.
Wormington, Wm	1	3	1		
Wimbery, Winifred				7	
Wood, John	2	2	2		1
Williams, Daniel	1				3
Williams, David	1	2	3		5
Williams, Lauderick	1	1	1		
Williams, Owen	1	4	2		2
Williams, Zebedee	1		3		1
White, Robert	1				
Whidbee, Elizabeth	1	3	3		
Willocks, Winifred	1	2	4		
Walls, John	1				
White, Samuel, Jur	1	1	1		
Williams, Thamer	1	3	4		7
White, Zachariah	1	1	3		2
Wood, Margarett			2		1
White, Elizabeth	1		3		
White, Joseph	2		4		
White, Nehemiah	1				
Willson, Joseph	1	2	3		5

EDENTON DISTRICT, PERQUIMANS COUNTY.

NAME OF HEAD OF FAMILY.	Free white males of 16 years and upward, including heads of families.	Free white males under 16 years.	Free white females, including heads of families.	All other free persons.	Slaves.
Avery, Robert	1		1		
Avery, Ruth			2		
Albertson, Joshua	1		1		
Arrington, Richard	1	2	4		
Arrington, Ezekiel	1	6	2		3
Arrington, William	2	1	4		4
Arrington, William, Junr	1	2	2		4
Asbell, John	1	2	5		
Albertson, Benjamin	3	4	5		1
Albertson, Chaulkley	3	5	3		2
Albertson, Benjamin, Junr	2	3	3		
Albertson, Jesse	1		2		
Anderson, Samuel	1		2		
Anderson, John	2		3		1
Albertson, William	1	1	1		
Anderson, Joseph	1	3	5		
Albertson, Josiah	1	5	4		1
Albertson, Jane	1		3		3
Arnold, William	1	2	2		2
Arkell, William	1	1	8		4
Arrington, Robert	1				
Albertson, Mary	1		3		
Ashburn, Winefred				5	
Bedgood, Joseph	1	1	6		1
Bagley, Joshua	1	1			
Bunch, Jesse	2				
Bunch, Joshua	1	2	4		
Bunch, Nazereth	2	5	2		2
Branch, Issachar	3	2	5		4
Brinkley, James	3	1	2		11
Braughton, Benjamin	1	1	1		
Braughton, Nathaniel	2	4	3		
Brinkley, Eleazer	1				5
Bateman, Jonathan	1		3		
Blaxton, Thomas	1	1	3		
Barrow, Eri	1	1	1		15
Butler, Margaret		2	3		3
Branch, Job	1		4		
Burnham, Caleb	1	1	4		1
Barrow, John	3	1			6
Boush, James	1		2		3
Barrow, Joseph	1	3	3		
Barclift, William	1	3	3		
Bateman, Thomas	1	1	2		3
Bedgood, Benjamin	1	2	2		
Barclift, Joseph	1	3	3		19
Bagley, Elisha	1	1	2		
Briggs, Charles	1		1		
Boyce, Joseph	3	6	6		
Burke, Arnold S.	1		1		4
Barber, Isaac	1				10
Bagley, Thomas	2	2	1		
Brown, Alexander	1	6	2		
Bundy, Josiah	3	3	6		
Bundy, Caleb	1	1	2		
Bagley, Ephraim	1		4		1
Bagley, Nathan	1	2	6		
Boswell, George	1	1	2		
Boswell, William	1				
Boswell, Joshua	1				
Bagley, Samuel	1	1	6		2
Boyce, Joseph	2	3	4		
Boyce, John	1	2	1		
Boyce, Moses	2	2	3		
Bond, William	1	3	1		
Bond, Pritlow	1		1		1
Bagley, John	1	1	6		4
Bunch, Joannah		1	5		
Bundy, Abraham	2	2	5		
Boyce, William	1	2	6		
Barker, William	1	2	3		
Bond, Job	1	2	2		5
Barber, Moses	1				
Barber, Joel	2	1			
Butt, David	1		2		
Bogue, Ann	1	1	3		
Boyce, Mourning		1	2		
Bailey, Henry	1	1	1		
Bond, Abigail		4	3		
Boyce, Benjamin	1	1	3		
Barns, Stephen	1		1	1	
Bateman, Joseph	1	6	4		
Bateman, John	1	2	6		1
Barclift, Marwood			1		3
Berryman, Sarah	1	1	4		
Banks, Richard	1	1	2		
Barber, Sarah			5		
Barker, John	2	2	3		
Crucy, William, Esqr	1	1	3		14
Cale, Timothy	2	1	4		
Collins, Christopher	1	2	3		
Cale, Richard	1	2	5		
Cale, John, Junr	1				
Crucy, Levi	2	2			
Collins, Jeremiah	1		2		1
Copeland, Charles	1		1		
Carter, John	1	3	4	1	7
Clayton, William	1	3	3		10
Crucy, Eleazer	1				7
Cale, Joseph	1		5		
Clements, William	2	3	1		7
Crucy, Thomas	1	2	4		4
Coppage, William	1		2		
Cale, Robert	1	2	5		
Church, Thomas	1	1	3		
Chappell, Jemima		1	2		1
Cox, Joseph	1				
Caruthers, James	1	1	3		
Cosand, Aaron	2	3	8		
Cosand, John	1				
Chappell, Job	2	4	6		
Chappell, John, Junr	1	2	4		
Chappell, Joseph	1	1	2		
Chappell, Robert	1	1	3		
Clary, John	2				3
Chappell, Mark	1		3		
Chappell, Isaac	1		3		
Clyvester, James	1		1		
Clary, Charles	1	2	3		
Chappell, John	1	2	3		1
Chappell, Samuel	1		2		
Champion, Henry	2	2	2		
Cornwall, Ann		1	1		
Caruthers, George	1		3		
Dough, Jeremiah	1		3		
Deal, John	1	3	2		1
Deal, William	1	3	1		
Deerow, Sarah			3		9
Donaldson, Andrew	2	1	3		7
Deal, Elizabeth	3		2		
Draper, Thomas	1	1	2		
Draper, Joseph	1	3	2		
Draper, Silas	1	7	2		
Draper, Josiah	1		1		
Davis, John	1	2	2	1	4
Donaldson, John	1		3		4
Davis, Caleb	2	2	2		
Davis, Elizabeth	2	3	2		
Duglas, David	1		2		
Duglas, Frances			2	5	
Duglas, Elizabeth	1		2		
Edwards, Sanford	1	3	4	1	1
Evans, Joseph	1		2		
Elliott, Ephraim	2	2	1		9
Elliott, Pritlow	1		1		
Elliott, Mary	1	2	2		1
Elliott, Exum, Junr	1				
Elliott, Caleb	1	3	2		7
Elliott, Winslow	1	1	3		1
Elliott, Josiah	1	4	3		6
Elliott, Seth	1	3	1		
Elliott, Exum	1				
Elliott, Meriam	1	4	3		12
Evans, Thomas	1				
Elliott, Samuel	1	1	3		
Evans, Robert	4		1		1
Evans, John	5		1		1
Elliott, Nixon	2		2		3
Edwards, James	1		2		
Elliott, Joseph	1	2	5		
Elliott, Demsey	1		2		
Elliott, Mordecai	1	3	2		1
Elliott, Hannah	1	3	2		
Elliott, Thomas	1	2	2		
Elliott, Joshua	1				
Elliott, Elizabeth	3	1	7		
Elliott, Abraham	1	2	4		1
Elliott, William	1	3			
Elliott, Hushai	1		1		
Elliott, Obediah	1				
Elliott, Job	1				
Foster, Francis	1	4	5		2
Fletcher, Joshua	1	1	1		11
Forbes, Bailey	3	2	2		3
Forehand, Benjamin	1		4		
Foster, Mary		1	2		6
Foster, James	1	1	2		1
Foulon, John B.	1		1		
Fletcher, Jesse	1	1	1		13
Fiveash, John	1	1	2		
Forehand, Cornelius	2	1	2		
Godfrey, Joseph	1	4	5		4
Greer, Bartley	1				
Gilbert, Joseph	1	1	1		
Gray, Isaac	1	1	2		
Gordon, Nathaniel	1	1	3		5
Gilbert, William	1	1	2		1
Griffin, Eliab	1	4	5		2
Griffin, Amos	2	3	3		
Godfrey, Francis	1				
Griffin, William	1		3		
Griffin, James	1		2		
Griffin, Josiah	1	2	3		
Griffin, Josiah, Junr	1				
Gregory, Hosea	1	2	3		1
Guyer, John	2	3	4		
Guyer, Meriam	2	2	4		
Griffin, Jesse	1	1	2		
Goodwin, John	2	2	5		6
Goodwin, Richard	2		3		
Goodwin, Nathan	2	1	2		
Goodwin, Jacob	1		4		6
Gilliam, Hinchea	3	3	2		
Godfrey, Tulle	1	1	4		5
Gurley, Frederick	1	2	2		
Hollaway, Hannah	2	2	3		8
Harvey, John	4	3	5		38
Harvey, Joseph, Esqr	1	1	3		25
Harvey, Benjamin, Esqr	1	4	2		31
Hall, Rachael	5		3		4
Hatfield, John	1				
Hollowell, Ezekiel	2	1	5		2
Howett, Abraham	1		4		14
Hinton, Noah	2	2	2		
Humphries, William	2	2	4		5
Hines, Ann			2		1
Hallsey, Edmund		1	3		
Hatfield, Richard	2	2	2		2
Hodges, Ann		2	4		
Harmon, Thomas	3		2		1
Hall, Edward, Esqr	1	3	5		9
Hallsey, Frederick	1	6	1		4
Hopkins, George	1				
Hollaway, Upharasha			1		6
Hollaway, Thomas	1	1	3		
Hopkins, William	1	1	3		6
Hobdey, Thomas	1	1	2		1
Hodges, John	2	1	4		1
Hinton, Jonas	1	1	2		2
Harrell, Demsey	3	1	3		
Harrell, Samuel	1		2		
Haskett, Silas	2	5	3		
Hatfield, Richard, Junr	1		3		1
Harvey, Mary		2	4		21
Hollowell, James	1		1		
Henby, Thomas	1	4	5		
Haskett, Silas, Junr	1	4	3		
Hollowell, Henry	2	3	4		2
Hall, Isaiah	1	2	2		
Haskett, Thomas	1	2	1		5
Hinton, Demsey	1	2	2		2
Haskett, Joseph	1	2	2		
Henby, Sylvanus	1		2		
Haskett, Joshua	1	1	1		
Hosea, Thomas	1	4	4		
Hendrick, Nathan	1		2		
Haskett, John	2	3	5		2
Haskett, Jesse	1	3	1		3
Haskett, Alice	1		1		
Hall, James	1	2	2		3
Hollowell, William	1	2	4		1
Hendrick, Job	1	1	3		
Hendrick, Joseph	2	1	3		
Hendrick, Nathan, Junr	1		2		

EDENTON DISTRICT, PERQUIMANS COUNTY—Continued.

NAME OF HEAD OF FAMILY.	Free white males of 16 years and upward, including heads of families.	Free white males under 16 years.	Free white females, including heads of families.	All other free persons.	Slaves.
Hollowell, Thomas	2	1	4		
Hollowell, Thomas, Junr	2	1	3		
Hollowell, Joel	1		3		
Hurdle, Christian	1	2	3		4
Hurdle, Martin	1	2	3		
Hudson, Uriah	1		4		6
Hudson, Joseph	1	1	3		
Harmon, Elizabeth		1	2		
Hendrick, Solomon	1		3		
Hartmus, John Peter	1		3		4
Hollowell, Meriam	1	5	2		1
Hosea, William	1	4	4		
Harrell, Abner	1	2	4		
Hendrick, Seth	1		4		
Hackney, Richard	1	1	3		
Jones, Margaret	1		3		
Johnson, James	1	2	1		
Ivy, Lemuel	1		2		3
Johnson, John	1	1	2		
Jackson, Moses, Junr	1		4		
Jones, William	2	2	5		3
Jones, William, Junr	1		3		
Joiner, William Jones	1	2	1		
Jackson, William	1	2	3		
Jones, Joseph	1	3	5		
Jacocks, Elizabeth		1	2		13
Ives, Joshua	1	4	3		1
Jackson, Samuel	1	3	3		2
Jackson, Joseph	2		1	3	1
Jemston, Richard	1				1
Jessop, Thomas	2		1		
Jordan, Elizabeth		2	3		
Jordan, Joseph	4		3		
Johnson, Willis	1				
Jackson, Rachael			1		
Jackson, William, Junr	1				
Johnson, William	1				
Jackson, Moses	1	2	1	3	2
Johnson, Mary			2		
Jordan, Thomas	1				
Kenyon, Benjamin	1				
Kelly, Jethro	1	1	2		
Knowles, William	1	1	4		5
Knowles, Abner	1	1	3		2
Kenyon, Joab	2	2	5		2
Kenyon, Levi	1				
Kenyon, John	1		3		
Lamb, John	1	1	1		1
Lilly, Ruben	1	1	1		
Long, Joshua	1	1	3		2
Long, William	1		3		8
Long, Lemuel	1	2	2		5
Leary, John	2		1		
Lamb, Joseph	1		1		1
Long, Ruben	1	1	3		
Layden, Thomas	2	2	2		4
Lane, Benjamin	1	3	3		
Long, Thomas	1	6	4		
Long, Simeon	1		5		
Long, Nathan	1	1	3		1
Lane, Sitterson	1		1		
Layden, William	1				
Lamb, Phinehas	1	3	4		1
Lacey, John	1		1		
Lunisford, John	1	2	3		
Lawton, Peleg	2				19
Lilly, Sarah		2	3		
Layden, Francis	1	2	3		11
Lacey, William	1		2		
Luten, Frederick	2	2	4		2
Leigh, Gilbert	3	3	1		12
Lane, Jacob	1	1	2		
Lane, William	1	2			
Lane, Moses	2		3		
Lemmon, Joseph	1				
Lane, John	1	2	5		
Lamb, Zachariah	1		3		
Lilly, William	2				3
Lacey, James	1	1	2		
Lacey, Joseph	1	2	4		
Moore, Charles	3	2	3		15
Murdaugh, Josiah	3	3	4		35
Moore, Zebulon	1				7
McClenny, James	1		1		
Matthias, Joseph	1	3	4		
Mullen, William	1				
Mullen, James	2		2		1
Matthias, Isaiah	1		3		
McNider, John	1	1	1		
Morris, Joseph	1		3		
Mullen, Joseph	3		2		
Mullen, Joseph	3	2	2		32
Mullen, Joseph, Junr	1	1	2		
Moore, Charles, Junr	1		2		1
Maudlin, John	2	5	3		
Mullen, Isaac	1		5		8
Mullen, Zadock	1	2	5		1
Morgan, Lemuel	1	1	3		
Morgan, Job	1	1	5		
Morris, Jonathan	1	4	1		
Macke, Joseph	1		1		1
Moore, Joshua	3	1	2		5
Maudlin, Thomas	1	2	3		
Mundin, William	1	1	3		1
Mundin, Elisha	1				
McClanahan, Mary		1	3		7
Maudlin, Joseph	1	2	3		
Morgan, John	1	5	4		
Mundin, Nathan	1				
Mundin, Levi	1	5	4		
Moore, William	1				
Moore, Samuel	2	1	3		
Moore, Thomas	1	1	2		
Miller, Charles	1				
Mullen, Richard	1	1	2		
Maudlin, Nathan	3		4		
Moore, Karonhappuck	1		1		2
McAamd, Joseph	2		3		5
Meridith, Meriam			2		
McCulloch, Robert H	2		2		2
Mitchell, Walter	1	1	4		
Mundin, Elisha	1		2		
Newby, Francis, Esqr	1	1	4		28
Newby, Thomas	2	1	1		2
Newby, Exum	1	1	5		5
Newby, Francis, Junr	1	2	2		1
Nixon, Samuel	1		2		3
Nixon, John	1	1	1		
Nixon, Delight	1	2	3		7
Norcom, Joseph	1				5
Nicholson, Nicholas	2	3	4		3
Nixon, Hannah			3		2
Nixon, Zachariah	3	4	4		18
Nixon, John	2		6		1
Newby, Enoch	1		1		
Nicholson, Samuel	1				
Newby, Robert	1	1	1		4
Newby, Jonathan	3	1	2		3
Newby, Zachariah	1	4			4
Newby, Thomas, Junr	1	3	3		1
Newby, Joseph, Junr	1	4	3		1
Nicholson, Robert	1				1
Newbould, Samuel	1	1			1
Newby, Gabriel	1	3	1		1
Newby, Elizabeth	1		1		6
Newby, Joseph	1	2	5		2
Newbould, William	1		1		
Newby, Gideon	1	1	1		
Newby, William	1		2		
Newby, Jesse	1		1		1
Newby, Thomas (son of Nathan)	2	2	4		5
Newby, Mike	1				2
Newby, William	2				
Newby, Benjamin	1	4	1		
Overton, Thomas	1	1	2		
Overton, John	1	2	2		
Overton, Malachi	1	1	4		
Overton, Elijah	1	1	1		
Overton, Perthena					10
Overton, Rachael					7
Overton, Lemuel					2
Overton, Samuel					1
Overman, Morgan	4	1	6		
Overman, John	1	3	5		
Parks, Daniel	1	2	5		
Pierce, Nathan	2	1			1
Perry, Joseph	1				8
Pierson, Nathan	1	1	2		
Perry, Dwelly	1	2	2		
Perry, Miles	1	3	3		1
Perry, Mary			5		14
Perry, Lawrence	1		2		2
Perry, Rewben	2	2	2		
Perry, Benjamin, Esqr	1	1	3		15
Perry, Jacob	1		1		
Perry, Philip	3	2	5		4
Parrimore, Thomas	3				
Penrice, Samuel	1		3		15
Penrice, Thomas	1				
Pratt, Zebulon	1				7
Portlock, Catharine			4		
Parks, Humphrey	2	1	3		1
Parks, Nathan	1		2		
Pierce, John	1	1	2		
Pointer, Henry	4	3	4	1	10
Pierce, Thomas	1				
Pearson, Eleazor	1		4		
Pierce, David	1		3		
Pearson, William	1	1	6		
Pierce, James	1				
Perry, William					6
Parker, John	1	2	2		
Peed, James	1	2	5		
Perry, Israel	1	2	2		4
Pierce, Joseph	2	4	2		11
Pritlow, Keziah	3		3		12
Perry, Jesse, Esqr	3	4	4		5
Perisho, Joseph	1	4	2		1
Peed, Lemuel	1		2		
Perry, John	1				1
Penrice, Clark		2	5		
Perry, Seth	1		2		
Pierce, Abner	1	1	2		1
Pratt, Mary			2		
Pierce, Miles	1	4	3		
Parker, Elisha	1		1		
Perry, Nathan	1	2	1		
Reddick, Robert, Esqr	1	1	2		13
Reddick, Josiah	1	2	5		
Reddick, Ruth			2		7
Reddick, Solomon	1	2	1		2
Reddick, Seth	1	4	4		2
Reddick, Jacob	2	1	4		3
Rountree, Jesse	1		4		5
Robinson, Thomas	1	1	4		2
Rogerson, Josiah	2	3	3		13
Rogerson, Jesse	1		2		4
Rogerson, John	1		4		
Robins, William	3	2	2		6
Raper, Elizabeth	1	1	3		
Roberts, John	1	4	1		
Russell, Nicholas	1	2	3		
Reed, Benjamin	1	1	3		21
Raper, Robinson	1		2		
Reed, William, Esqr		2	2		29
Reed, George	1	3	2		7
Roberts, William	1	4	1		3
Robins, John	1	1	2		9
Raper, Henry	1	1	3		1
Raper, Luke	1		2		1
Raper, Robert	1	2	4		1
Roberts, William, Junr	1				
Ray, Thomas	1	2	1		
Roberts, Benjamin	2		3		
Roe, Robert	2	1	2		2
Robins, Joseph	1				
Robinson, Josiah	1				
Rowan, John	1				
Roberts, John, Junr	2		4		1
Rogerson, Elizabeth			4		2
Ratclift, Thomas	1	4	3		
Raper, John	1	1	4		1
Raper, Joseph	1	2	1		1
Rogerson, Mary	4	2	4		6
Richards, William	2	2	3		1
Sanderson, Richardson	2		2		10
Skinner, William, Esqr	1		5		47
Skinner, Joshua, Esqr	2	3	7		20
Skinner, John, Esqr	1	1	2		38
Skillings, Sarah			3		8
Scott, Severn	1				
Stakes, Thomas	3	3	3		1
Stacey, Thomas	3	6	2		
Stevenson, Thomas, Junr	1	2	3		
Stepney, William	2	3	5		3
Smith, John	2	1	3		4
Sutton, Francis	1				
Skinner, Richard	2	2	5		5
Stevenson, Thomas	1	3	2		12
Sutton, Jeremiah	1	3	2		
Stone, Elisha	1	1	2		
Skinner, Nathan	1	1	2		
Standin, William	1	2	5		11
Simmons, Thomas	1	3	1		
Saunders, John	1	3	4		
Skinner, Joseph	1	1	1		
Skinner, Ann			3		2
Sutton, Ashbury, Esqr	1	3	6		25
Sitterson, Isaac	1	1	5		
Sitterson, Thomas	1	3	2		
Stanton, John, Junr	1		4		
Sitterson, Samuel	1		2		4
Skinner, Stephen	1		1		
Saunders, James	4		3		
Sutton, George	1	1	5		11
Stafford, Alexander	1	1	2		4
Stafford, Lemuel	1	2	4		
Saunders, Josiah	1	1	1		
Smith, Job	1		5		
Smith, Leah	1		4		4
Saunders, William	1		3		
Saunders, Benjamin	1	2	3		9
Saunders, Joshua	1				
Saunders, Joseph	1				
Smith, Benjamin	2		2		1
Small, Miles	1				
Saunders, Mary	3	1	3		8
Saunders, Stephen	3	1	3		2
Saunders, Richard	2	4	2		3
Sutton, Greenbury	1		2		7
Saint, Daniel	2		3		1
Saint, Thomas	2	1	3		3
Small, William	1	1	4		

EDENTON DISTRICT, PERQUIMANS COUNTY—Continued.

NAME OF HEAD OF FAMILY.	Free white males of 16 years and upward, including heads of families.	Free white males under 16 years.	Free white females, including heads of families.	All other free persons.	Slaves.
Stanton, Thomas	2		4		1
Sutton, Thomas	1	1	5		
Sutton, Thomas, Junr	1		2		
Small, David	1				
Smith, Samuel	1	1	4		
Sumner, James	2		3		26
Sumner, James (for Thomas Sumner)					16
Sutton, Samuel	1	2	4		9
Sawyer, William	3	1	2		
Stafford, Thomas	1		2		
Stafford, William	1		3		
Stafford, Thomas, Junr	1	2	4		
Stevenson, Hugh, Esqr	1	1	4		13
Sitterson, Joseph	1	1	5		
Stanton, John	2		2		
Swann, Henry	1		2		2
Swann, Willson	1		3		
Stone, Moses	1		2		3
Stone, Moses, Junr	1	1	4		
Sutton, Joseph	1	1	1		14
Stallings, Reuben	1	2	4		2
Stallings, Solomon	1				
Stallings, Henry	1	1	1		
Stallings, John	1	1	3		
Stallings, Daniel	3	3	2		7
Smith, James	1		2		
Stallings, Jesse	2		2		3
Stallings, Luke	2		2		3
Stone, Florilla		1	2		
Saunders, John	1		4		4
Scott, James	1	2	1		
Saunders, Benjamin	1	2	5		2
Snowden, Zebulon	2	1	3		
Smith, John, Junr	1	1	3		
Stone, Cornelius	1	1	3		
Smith, Jane	2	2	2		
Scarborough, Benjamin	2	2	2		
Thatch, Levan	1		4		
Thatch, Joseph	1	3	2		
Thatch, Thomas	1	1	1		
Turner, John	1	1	2		
Tow, William	1		2		4
Thatch, Spencer	1	2	1		1
Tucker, John	1	2	2		1
Turner, Joseph	2	1	2		
Turner, Joseph, Junr	2	3	6		11
Turner, Joseph (the younger)	1	1	2		2
Turner, George	1	1	2		
Turner, Joshua	1		2		
Turner, Elsbury	1	2	1		
Turner, Thomas	1		2		3
Turner, Benjamin	2	2	2		
Turner, Miles	1	4	2		3
Jones, Martha		2	1		16
Thornton, Joseph	1	1	1		1
Townsend, Elizabeth		3	3		2
Tuiddy, Aaron	2	3	3		
Toms, John	2	3	5		12
Toms, John, Junr	j				
Toms, Gosby	1	7	4		52
Toms, Foster	1	2	1		18
Talton, Joshua	1	2	3		
Tow, Joseph	2	4	3		2
Taylor, John, Junr	1		2		
Twine, Jesse	2		1		2
Twine, Abraham	1		3		6
Twine, Thomas	1	2	6		8
Taylor, John	2	1	3		
Tow, Deborah		1	2		
Upton, John	1	1	5		2
Versey, Joannah		1	1		1
White, William	2	1			1
White, Sarah	1	2	4		32
Whidbee, Thomas	2	5	5		19
Webb, John	1	1	1		
Weston, Elizabeth		2	1		
Willson, Ann	1		3		
White, Luke	2	1	4		6
White, Isaac	1	1	3		10
Whidbee, Mary			2		4
White, James	1	1	4		11
Wingate, Edward	3	2	3		
White, Joseph	1	1			1
Wood, Edmund	1	2	3		
Wells, Joseph	1	1	5		5
White, Robert	1	1	2		
Williams, Spencer	1	2	2		
Williams, Isaac	1	1	2		
White, Henry	1	3	3		
Winslow, Jesse	1	1	6		
Willson, Christopher	1	1	2		1
Wingate, Ephraim	1	1	2		
Woodley, John	1		3		3
Whitehead, David	1	2	1		
White, Gabriel	2	1	2		
White, Caleb	4	3	4		2
White, Francis	1		2		
Williams, William	1				
Williams, Mary	1	3	4		1
Wheaton, William	1				
Willson, Jacob	2		2		6
Willson, Ruben	3	2	4		1
Willson, Abraham	1		1		
Willson, Jonathan	1				
Williams, Nathaniel	1				1
Williams, Lockhart	1	1	3		2
Whidbee, James	1	1	4		10
White, John	3	1	3		6
Weeks, Willson	1		1		11
Whidbee, Thomas, Junr	1	2	2		7
Whidbee, Seth	1	1	2		4
Whidbee, William	2	1	4		14
Weeks, Thomas, Junr	1	2	3		1
Weeks, Lemuel	1	1	2		
Wardsworth, Caleb	1	1	3		
Weeks, Samuel	2	2	2		1
Weeks, Thomas	1	2	4		4
Wright, John	1	1	1		
Wright, William	1	1	1		
Whidbee, John	1	4	3		3
Winslow, John, Junr	1	2	2		
White, Josiah	1	7	3		2
White, Joshua	1		3		3
White, John, Junr	1	1	1		
White, Edmund	2	1	2		6
Winslow, Jacob	2		3		3
White, Thomas	3		4		4
White, Benjamin	3	4	3		1
Winslow, Caleb	1	3	3		7
Wood, Joseph	2	2	4		
Woollard, Martin	3		8		
Winslow, Benjamin	3	2	2		1
Willson, Lidia	1	2	5		
Williamson, John	1	1	2		1
White, William	2	1	2		8
White, William, Junr	1				
White, Jesse	1	2	2		
Winslow, John	1	1	3		
Winslow, Samuel	2	1	5		1
White, Jacob	1	4	2		1
White, John	1	1	1		2
White, Samuel	1		2		
White, Mary	1	2	3		2
Willson, Ann		1	3		5
White, Benjamin, Junr	2		2		
Winslow, Jesse, Junr	1	1			10
Willson, Isaac	2	4	5		
White, Mary, Junr	1		3		1
Wyall, William	2				1
Willson, Elizabeth			3		
White, Benjamin	1		2		
Whidbee, Robert	1		2		
Weeks, Shadrach	1	1	2		
White, Thomas, Junr	1				1
White, Arnold	1	1	1		
Willcocks, Prissilla			2		
Welch, Comfort			4		
Walls, Absalom	1		3		
Willson, Benjamin	1		2		
Willson, Mary			3		
Willson, Christopher, Junr	1	1	1		

EDENTON DISTRICT, TYRRELL COUNTY.

NAME OF HEAD OF FAMILY.	Free white males of 16 years and upward, including heads of families.	Free white males under 16 years.	Free white females, including heads of families.	All other free persons.	Slaves.
Clifton, John		1	4	1	
Davenport, Jacob	1	2			
Ambrus, James	1	2	3		
Clifton, Robert	3	1	5		
Tarkenton, Benja	1	2	4		
Phelps, Josiah	4	1	3		2
Phelps, James	1	1	3		
Phelps, Rosanna		2	3		
Barnes, Isaac	1		3		
Barnes, Reuben	1	4	3		
Jethro, Thomas	1	2	2		
Tarkenton, Joseph	1	1	3		
Davis, Zephaniah	2	2	7		2
Spruil, Miles	1	2	1		
Bateman, Solomon	1	1	4		1
Phelps, Josiah	1	1	2		2
Smith, Thomas	1	2	3		
Powers, Joshua	1	1	5		
Alexander, Anthony	1	2	3		
Alexander, John	1	1	2		
Oliver, Alexander	1	2	2		
Oliver, Joseph	1		4		
Hassell, Levi	1		8		
Hill, Asa	1	2	1		
Spruil, John	1	1	6		
Skittletharpe, Charles	1	4	3		
Ambrus, Micajah	1	1	1		
Ferlaw, John	2	3	1		
McClary, Keziah		1	3		
Ambrus, Jesse	1	3	1		
Long, James	1	3	1		
Caswell, Samuel	1	2	3		
Oliver, Andrew	1	3	2		1
Ansley, Edward	1		4		
powers, Isaac	1	1	4		
Ansley, Solomon	1		3		1
Bateman, Stephen	1	3	4		
Ansley, Joseph, Junr	1		2		
Hagman, Henry	2		2		
Weatherly, Thomas	1	2	1		
Tellit, Avery	1	1	2		
White, Jonathan	2	3	4		
Simmons, James	1		2		
Simmons, John	1	2	1		
Alcock, William	1				
Cahoon, Joseph	1				
Cahoon, Benjamin	1		1		
Alcock, Sarah	3	2	3		
Simmons, Willis	1				
Sawyer, Jonathan	1	5	1		
Sawyer, Bartlet	1		1		
Richason, Hannah		4	1		
Hutson, Anthony	1	2	2		
Hutson, Elijah	1	3	1		
Howard, Willm, Senr	1	1	1		
Howard, William, Junr	1		1		
Norriss, William	1	3	1		
Howard, Thomas	1	2	2		
Cahoon, John	1	3	3		
Cahoon, James	1	1	5		
Smith, John	1	1	1		
McGown, William	1		1		
McGown, John	1	1	2		
Ronsom, Elizabeth			2		
Liverman, John, Junr	1	1	3		
Mekins, John	1		2		
Gibson, John	1	1	4		5
Smith, Zebedee	1	2	1		
Gibson, Samuel	1		3		
Jarman, John	1	3	3		
Jones, Corbin	1	3	4		
Cullifer, Henry	1		2		
Cullifer, James	1		3		
Liverman, Willm	2	2	5		15
Liverman, Thomas	1	5	3		3
Liverman, John	1		4		
Hoskins, Thomas	2	3	5		37
Mekins, Isaac	1	6	4		
Cahoon, Ezekiel	1	3	5		
Bodwell, Solomon	1	1	1		
Francis, Thos	2	1	2		
Hassell, Solomon	1		4		
Hassell, Solomon, Junr	1		2		
Johnston, Joshua	1				
Hassell, Joshua	1	2	2		
Hassell, John (son of Solomon)	1	1	2		
Riggins, Jemimiah			2		
Armstrong, John	2	2	3		
Phelps, Edward	3	2	6		
Tarkenton, Benjamin	1	3	5		
Banks, Henry	1		1		
Warrington, John	1	1	4		6
Woodland, Samuel	2		2		1
Powers, Josiah	1	2	3		
Davenport, Jacob	1	1	4		1
Patrick, Isaac	1	4	3		
Goddin, John	1	3	2		
Phelps, Jonathan	1	1	2		
Lewark, Anne	1	2	2		
Oliver, John	1	1	2		
Alexander, Ezekiel	1	1	2		
Craddack, Joseph	1	1	1		
Hassell, William	1	3	3		
Goddin, Ezekiel	1	1	4		
Hassell, Zebedee	2	1	2		6
Hopkins, Thomas	2		3		7
Morriss, Cornelius	2	2	3		
Alexander, Henry	2	4	2		
Alexander, Joseph	1		2		
Alexander, John	1	1	2		1

EDENTON DISTRICT, TYRRELL COUNTY—Continued.

NAME OF HEAD OF FAMILY.	Free white males of 16 years and upward, including heads of families.	Free white males under 16 years.	Free white females, including heads of families.	All other free persons.	Slaves.
Alexander, John, Senr	2	2	5		3
McClease, John	1	3	3		
Meades, Benjamin	1		2		
Trueblood, Asa	1	1	4		
Davenport, Hezekiah	1		4		
Duvol, John	1	3	3		
Steatman, Jeremiah	1	3	3		
Barnett, William	1	2	3		
Caroon, John	1	5	4		12
Caroon, Joseph	1		1		1
Midgett, John	1	2	3		4
Mann, Solomon	1	1	3		2
Oneal, Richard	1	2	3		
Brown, Samuel	1	1	1		
Mann, Samuel	2	1	4		3
Popperwill, George	1	2	5		
Barnett, Stephen	2	3	7		
Coffee, William	1	3	5		
Hill, David	1	1	1		
Hill, David, Senr	1		1		
Williams, James	1	2	2		
Psalter, William	1		1		1
Rascow, Daniel	2	1	5		
Payne, John	2	4	3		1
Mann, Thomas	2	2	3		1
McGlocklin, Mitchel	1		1		
Alexander, Zilpha	1	1	7		6
Warrington, Thomas	1		2		3
pierce, Miles	1	4	3		
Davenport, John	1	2	2		
phelps, Seth	3	2	4		5
Saunders, John	1		2		
Hassell, John, Senr	4	1	7		15
Tarkenton, Joseph	1	2	1		2
Brown, William	1	2	4		
Spruil, Sarah	1		2		
Dukes, Hezekiah	1	2	6		
Powers, John	1		2		
Powers, Ephraim	1	2	2		
Hassell, Stephen	1	2	3		
Vollovay, Joseph	5	2	5		
Brim, Richard	1	1	6		
Armstrong, Russell	3	4	2		4
Cullifer, John	1		2		
Cahoon, Catherine			2		8
Clayton, John	1	3	4		8
Hill, Celia		3	3		
Baker, Benjamin	2	2	4		
Jones, Robert	1	2	1		
Foster, Silas	1		4		
Russ, William	1	1	2		
Williams, Josiah	1	4	2		
Sikes, John	1	2	4		
Spence, Anne	1	2	4		
Spence, Robert	1		3		
Sawyer, Robert	1	2	2		
Sawyer, Isaac	1	2	2		
Sawyer, James	1	5	2		
Jannett, Joseph	1	1	1		
Sawyer, Peter	1	4	2		
Smith, Jabith	1	1	3		
Sawyer, Joab	1	3	1		
Sawyer, Leven	1		2		
Sawyer, Keziah			2		
Best, Betsy		2	3		
Belanger, Elisha, Senr	1	1	3		
Belanger, Elisha	1	1	1		
Belanger, Abel	1		1		
Smith, Jesse	1		3		
Smith, John	1	2	4		
Ward, Anthony	1	1	5		
Simmons, Josiah	1				
McDewil, Mary			1		
Liverman, John, Senr	1	2	5		3
Liverman, Hezekiah	1	1	5		
Liverman, John	1		4		
Smith, Rachael		2	1		
Sawyer, Dennis	1		1		2
Brown, Abram	1		3		
Owens, Thomas	1	2	4		4
Owens, Peter	1		3		
Pledger, Joseph	1	4	6		9
Holloway, Moses	2	1	5		
Rhoades, Leven	2	2	3		
Hancock, William	3	1	4		
Howett, William	2	3	3		9
Chapman, Joseph	1	5	3		
Hopkins, John	1	2	3		
Brickhouse, Major	3	2	7		
Spruil, Hezekiah, Esq	2		5		12
Parsons, Asa	2	1	2		
Hopkins, Elizabeth		1	3		
Hopkins, Philip	1				
Ansley, John	2	2	7		7
Ansley, Joseph	1	1	2		1
Arnold, Joseph	3	3	6		1
Ambrus, Shimie	1		2		

NAME OF HEAD OF FAMILY.	Free white males of 16 years and upward, including heads of families.	Free white males under 16 years.	Free white females, including heads of families.	All other free persons.	Slaves.
Alexander, Joseph, Junr	2	3	3		3
Airs, Isaac	2	3	5		
Alexander, Sarah			2		
Alexander, Joshua	1	1	1		
Alexander, Joseph	1	4	3		3
Armistead, John	1	1	2		8
Airs, John	1		1		
Adams, Isaac	1	2	3		2
Adams, Thomas	1		2		
Allen, Henry	1	4	2		
Bateman, Jeremiah	2		2		2
Bateman, Nathan, Senr	2	3	5		3
Bateman, John	1				2
Bateman, Levi	1	1	1		1
Blount, Stevens	1	4	1		
Barnes, John	1		1		
Bateman, Godfrey	1	1	1		
Bateman, Stephen	1	2	2		
Blount, Hannah	1		3		
Brown, James	1		1		
Bateman, Simeon	1		1		
Bates, Thomas	1				
Bateman, Jesse	1	1	3		
Bateman, Pethiah	1	3	2		
Bernbridge, Sarah		1	2		
Blount, Jacob	2		4		3
Blount, Levi	1	1	3		23
Bernbridge, Caleb	3	3	3		5
Blount, John	1		1		
Burns, Anne	1		1		2
Blount, William	1	4	3		22
Blount, Edmund, Junr	2	2	3		13
Bateman, Andrew	1	3	4		5
Bateman, Jonathan	3	5	2		4
Bateman, Isaac	1	3	6		1
Bateman, Solomon	1	2	2		
Blount, Benjamin	1	2	3		5
Bozman, John	1	2	3		
Byrd, R. Martin	1				2
Boyman, Leven	2		1		3
Bozman, Joseph	1	1	1		1
Blount, Nathan	1	1	2		
Chesson, Samuel	1	1	5		8
Cutter, Ebbin	1				
Chesson, John	1		1	1	1
Chesson, William	2	3	2		5
Canady, Richard	1				
Canady, Frederick	1				
Chesson, Joshua	1	1	1		
Canady, John, Senr	2		3		
Cullifer, Isaac	1	3	5		
Collins, Caleb	1	2	1		
Court, John	3	3	2		
Clifton, Mary	1	4			
Canady, John	1		3		
Chesson, Joseph	2	2	2		
Cotrell, Francis		1	2		3
Camel, John	1	2	2		
Crooke, Clement	1	1	5		7
Camel, Rebecca		2	2		
Corprew, Joshua	2	3	2		5
Corprew, Thomas	1	3	2		2
Corprew, Jonathan	3		2		7
Condry, William	1	3	5		
Blount, Edmund, Senr	3	3	5		3
Davenport, Mosses	1	2	3		
Dillin, John	1	3	1		
Davis, Richard	1	1	2		4
Davenport, Daniel	1		3		5
Davenport, Joseph, Junr	1	3	2		
Davenport, Frederick	1	1	2		1
Davenport, Doctr John	2	2	3		
Davis, John	1	3	3		
Davenport, Ephraim	1	3	6		
Davis, Thomas	2	4	2		
Dunston, Abram	1		4		
Davenport, James	1	2	2		3
Davenport, David	1	1	3		
Davenport, John	1	2	2		
Dillin, James	1	4	4		1
Davenport, Joseph, Senr	2	6	2		
Davenport, Joanne	3		6		2
Davenport, Isaac	3	2	4		
Davison, Robert	1	3	4		5
Draper, Richard	2		1	1	
Davis, John, Senr	2	3	3		3
Davis, Arthur	1		1		
Davis, William	1				
Davis, Matilda		1	2		
Airs, David	2	2	1		
Airs, Nathan	1		1		
Collins, Ferubah	2	1	3		
Corprew, Esther			5		
Corprew, John	1	1	3		
Adams, Martha		2	2		

NAME OF HEAD OF FAMILY.	Free white males of 16 years and upward, including heads of families.	Free white males under 16 years.	Free white females, including heads of families.	All other free persons.	Slaves.
Etheridge, Ephraim	2	2	6		1
Earl, William	1		1		10
Everitt, Joseph	1	6	5		
Everitt, Jeresiah	2	3	5		2
Ezekiel, Caleb	1	1	1		
Everitt, Thomas	2	2	4		5
Everitt, Nathaniel	1	3	1		1
Freeman, William	1		2		
Freeman, James	1		2		
Frasier, Richard	1		2		2
Ferlaw, William	1				
Frasier, Jeremiah	2	5	8		6
Floyd, Solomon	1		4		
Fagan, Thomas	1				
Fagan, Frederick	1				
Fagan, Enoch	1				
Fagan, Shadrach	1	1	2		1
Fagan, Richard	2	3	5		
Fagan, William	1	3	3		3
Freeman, Thomas	1		2		1
Goddin, Aaron	1	1	1		
Gilbert, James	1	4	4		
Girkin, Joshua	1				
Girkin, John	1		1		
Girkin, Anne			4		
Gray, Godfrey	1	3	4		
Gray, Henry	3		5		
Gilbert, Nicholas, Senr	1	1	2		
Gilbert, Nicholas, Junr	1		1		
George, Isaac	1		2		1
Griffin, Zilpha		2	4		
Gillikin, George Anson	1	1	1		1
Garrett, James, Junr	1	1	1		
Garrett, Thomas	1		1		
Garrett, Daniel	1	1	1		
Garrett, John, Junr	1	1	2		2
Garrett, Thomas, Junr	1		3		
Garrett, John, Senr	2	1	3		11
Cunningham, Timothy	1	1	1		
Garrett, Samuel	1	1	1		
Garrett, James, Senr	2		1		4
Hooker, Nathan	2	1	2		
Hare, James	1	4	3		9
Hatfield, Jesse	3	1	3		1
Harrisson, John	1	2	2		
Harrisson, Edmund	3	3	3		
Hassell, Benjamin	2	1	2		
Hays, Robert	1		4		
Howet, Edmund	1				
Hassell, Edward, Jun	1		4		
Hawkins, Thomas	2	1	4		
Hassell, Anne	1		4		
Hassell, Mary			3		
Harrisson, Joshua	1	3	1		
Hill, Jesse	1	1	2		
Hardison, Benjamin	2		2		2
Harrisson, William	2		4		3
Hollis, Arnit	2	1	4		
Howard, Sarah	1	1	3		1
Harrisson, Benjamin, Junr	1	3	3		
Harrisson, Thomas, Junr	2	2	3		3
Harrisson, Thomas, Senr	2	2	3		6
Hardison, Mary	1	2	3		8
Hardison, Jasper	1	3	2		2
Hamilton, James	1		2		
Hollis, James	1	2	5		
Harrisson, Frank	1		3		
Harrisson, Susannah	1		2		
Hoff, Richard	2	1	2		3
Jones, Jones	1	3	4		
Giles, John	2	3			
Jones, Joshua	1		2		
Jones, James, Senr	1	2	1		1
Jannett, Abraham	3	1	3		2
Jones, Frileg	2	2	7		11
Jones, Margaret		1	2		
Jones, Joseph, Junr	1		2		
Jones, Joseph, Senr	1		1		
Joy, George	1	1	2		
Jerard, Henry	1	1	1		
Lasher, John	2		1		
Leary, Joshua	1	2	2		7
Long, James (son of Andrew)	1				2
Long, John (son of Cole Long)	1	1	2		11
Long, John, Junr	1		2		4
Langley, James	1		1		
Long, William	1		1		2
Long, Isaac	2	2	1		
Long, James (son of Giles)	1		3		6
Long, Rebecca	4	2	4		
Leary, John	1		1		
Leary, Enoch	1		1		

EDENTON DISTRICT, TYRRELL COUNTY—Continued.

NAME OF HEAD OF FAMILY.	Free white males of 16 years and upward, including heads of families.	Free white males under 16 years.	Free white females, including heads of families.	All other free persons.	Slaves.
Leary, Cornelius	2	2	4		12
Long, Col° James	2		1		18
Lee, Thomas	2	2	1		18
Lewis, Jesse	2	3	2		
Leggett, Daniel	1	1	5		
Leggett, Luke	1		2		
Dwight, William	1	1	2		
Jordan, John	1	1	4		2
Mariner, John, Sen°	1				
Middleton, Josiah	1		2		
Mires, Thomas	1	3	3		9
Mariner, John	1	1	3		
Mariner, Peter	1		1		
M°Dewil, Frederick	1		2		
Mackey, William	1	2	3		15
Mills, Penelope		1	2		
Mariner, Rixom	2	2	4		
Mashaw, Matthew	1	1	3		4
M°Donough, Andrew	1	2	3		1
Moss, Mary			1		
Matthews, George	1				
Norman, Henry	2	1	1		8
Newberry, John	1	1	2		
Norman, Hezekiah	1	2	2		1
Norman, James	1		4		
Norman, Simeon	1	1	3		
Norman, Joseph, Sen°	3		2		
Norman, Joseph, Jun°	1				
Norman, Isaac	1	2	2		
Norman, John, Se°	1	2	5		
Norman, Rachael	1	2	3		6
Norman, Thomas	3		2		
Nevins, John	1	2	1		1
Dauson, George (for estate of Harrymond)					15
Overton, Edward	1		4		
Oliver, George	1				
Orsborn, Philip	1	1	2		
Oliver, Edward	1				
Martin, Charles	1	1	2		
Phelps, John	4	1	1		
Phelps, Joseph	4	1	3		
Phelps, Urijah	1				
Phelps, Benjamin	1	2	1		
Phelps, John, Sen°	1	4	3		2
Phelps, Joseph, Sen°	1	4	2		7
Phelps, James, Sen°	1	1	4		
Pratt, Lott	3	1	5		
Phelps, Godfrey	3	2	4		
Phelps, Joseph, Jun°	1				
Phelps, Anne	2	1	5		
Padgett, Jesse	1				
Phelps, Zadock	1		2		
Phelps, Joshua	1	3	3		
Phelps, Edward	1	1	4		
Phelps, Capt. James	2		2		
Phelps, Asa	1	2	1		
Pettegrew, Charles	2	2	1		16
Patrick, Thomas	1	4	3		
Rowe, Levi	1	3	3		1
Rankhorn, Joseph	1	1	4		
Russell, Thomas	1				
Robason, Peter			2		3
Raby, James	4				
Rogers, Airs	1	1	3		
Rogers, Nathan	1	1	2		
Rogers, Anne	1		4		
Patterson, Mary		1	1		4
Spruil, William	1	3	2		
Spruil, Benjamin	2	1	4		20
Stubbs, Thomas, Jun°	2	1	4		5
Spruil, Samuel, Sen°	3	3	3		
Snell, Roger	2	4	3		
Swain, Stephen	2	2	2		
Swain, John	1	3	3		1
Spruil, Charles	2	1	1		3
Spruil, Col° Joseph	2	1	1		2
Slade, Joshua	1	1	2		6
Skinner, Evan	1	2	3		
Swift, Joseph	1		2		7
Smith, Abram	1	5	6		
Snell, James	1	3	3		
Spruil, Godfrey	1		2		
Spruil, Jesse	1		4		1
Sutton, Lemuel	1	1	3		
Spruil, William	1	1	3		
Spruil, Samuel	1	2	3		
Snell, Sarah	1	2	6		
Swain, Cornelius	1	2	3		1
Spruil, Jose	1	3	1		
Spruil, Tho° Hawkins	1	3	1		
Spruil, James	1	2	3		
Spruil, Simeon	2	1	4		9
Snell, Abijah	1		1		
Snell, Jesse	1		1		
Stealy, Elizabeth	1	2	2		
Spruil, William, Sen°	1		5		
Spruil, Thomas	2	2	6		
Spruil, Joseph	1		3		
Spruil, Miles	1	2	1		
Swain, Eleazer	1	3	4	2	
Stealy, Jeremiah	1		1		
Sutton, William	3		3		
Stealy, Edmund	1				
Stealy, Frederick	1		1		
Smiley, William	1		2		
Stubbs, James	1	2	3		
Stubbs, Aaron	1		1		1
Stubbs, Everard	1	1	4		4
Stewart, Thomas	1		1		4
Stubbs, Samuel	2	1	4		
Stouffer, George	1	1	1		
Stubbs, Levi	1	1	3		
Stubbs, John	1		2		4
Sevinson, John	1	1	1		4
Sexton, Dempsey	1	1	2		
Padgett, John	2	1	3		
Peacock, George	1	2	4		
Stubbs, Thomas, Sen°	1		1		4
Stubbs, Micajah	1		3		2
Stubbs, Richard	1	2	3		4
Stubbs, William	1				1
Snell, John	1		2		
Spruil, Josiah	1	2	3		
Spruil, Sammy	1	2	4		
Spruil, Evan	1	3	4		
Smith, Francis	1	4	1		
Spruil, John	1				
Tarkenton, William	2	2	7		4
Tarkenton, Isaac	3				
Tarkenton, Joseph	1		2		5
Turner, Arthur	1	2	4		7
Tetterton, William	1		2		
Tarkenton, John	1	1	3		10
Tarkenton, Zebulon	2	1	7		1
Tod, John	1	2	5		
Trotter, Thomas (for the Lake Compy)	3				113
Thomas, Elizabeth		1	2		
Tarkenton, Joseph, Jun°	1	2	2		1
Tetterton, Ephraim	1	2	1		
Tyrrell, Justice	1				
Ramsey, William	1		2		
Phelps, Cuthbert	1		2		
Vandal, Isaac	1		1		
Wyatt, Joseph	3		2		7
Wynne, Jesse	3				1
Wynne, Benjamin	2	2	3		
Wood, James	4	4	5		5
Wiley, Stephen	1	2	2		
Walker, John	1	2	3		
Wiley, Thomas	1	2	4		3
Wiley, James	1	1	3		
Wynne, Robert	1	1	3		3
Woodland, John	1		1		
Wynne, Andrew	1	4	2		
Walker, Thomas	2	1	6		13
Webb, Harmon, Jun	1	1	1		1
Williams, Thomas	1	3	6		
Walker, Stewart	1	5	1		
Ward, William	1				1
Webb, Harmon, Sen°	2	2	3		17
Willett, Elizabeth			1		2
Woollard, Joseph	2	1	2		
White, William	1	2	2		
White, Thomas	1		1		
Rhoades, Nathan	1	2	3		
Vandycke, Joseph	1	2	2		
Young, Zilpha			2		6
Swain, Joshua	2	2	4		
Walker, Edward	2	2	4	1	
Simons, Margarett			2		
Revel, Eleven	1	6	2		
Buncombe, Thomas	1				31
Stubbs, Jesse	1	1	3		1
Mackey, Col° Thomas	1	3	1		25
Foster, John	1	1	3		9
Jones, David	1		1		
Hardy, Lewis (for Estate of Humphry Hardy)	1	1	4		23
Gunning, John	1	1	3		
Simpson, Reddin (free colored)	1		3		
Simpson, Jacob (free colored)	1	1	1		
Will, Elizabeth (free colored)		1	2		
Williams, Jack (free colored)	1				
Foster, William (free colored)	1	4	2		
Dempsey, John (free colored)	1				
Biffins, Philip (free colored)	1				
Vollovay, Jane (free colored)	1				
Bryan, Bridgett (free colored)				1	
Pierce, Israel (free colored)	1	2	3		
Pierce, Thomas (free colored)	1	3	4		
Alexander, John	1	4	4		
M°Callister, Robert	1	1	3		
Perisher, Rufus	1	1	5		
Crane, Joseph	1		3		
Twiddy, Benjamin	1	1	2		
Twiddy, David	1	1	1		
Rowton, Daniel	1		1		1
Rowton, Rich°	1	1	4		
Johnston, Jonathan	1	2	3		
Johnston, Randal	1	1	2		
Perisher, Devotion	1	1	2		
Rowton, Edward	1		4		1
Basnett, Jacob	1	2	5		
Jackson, Thomas	1		2		
Orum, George	1	2	1		
Sawyer, Griffin	1	2	4		
Bray, Isaac	1	3	4		
Hassell, Anne	2		2		5
Thorogood, Paul	1	2	1		
Demeritt, Jesse	1	2	2		
Davenport, Ezra	1	2	2		
Mann, Benjamin	1	2	2		
Twiddy, John	2		1		
Twiddy, Devotion	1		2		
Brickhouse, John	1		2		
Alexander, John	1	2	4		1
Alexander, William	1	1	1		1
Alexander, Joseph	1	1	4		
Craddack, Eleazer	1		4		
Chapman, Rich°	2	3	2		
Swain, Natha°	1	3	2		1
Swain, Jeremy	1	1	4		
Alexander, Benj°	1	4	3		3
Alexander, Will°	1		1		
West, William	1	4	7		
Volloway, Elisha	1				
Swain, James	1	1	3		3
Swain, Eliakim	1	3	2		
Swain, Abram	1	3	3		
Swain, Jeremiah	1	6	3		
Smith, Ebenezer	1	2	2		2
Rhoades, Henry	1	1	2		
Armstrong, Andrew	1	1	2		
Horton, William	1	1	1		2
Powers, Samuel	1	3	2		
Hassell, Edward	1	3	2		
Alexander, Edward	1	3	3		
patrick, John	1	3	3		
Tarkenton, John	1		4		
Davis, Elisha	1	3	1		
Alexander, John	1		3		
Tarkenton, John, Sen°	1	1	4		4
Phelps, Amos	2	3	3		
Barnett, Justice	1		1		
Cornel, Ezra	1				
Wynne, Joseph	1	1	5		1
Hassell, Zebulon	1	2	2		
Wynne, George	1	2	3		
Hassell, Joseph	1				
Massey, Adkins	1		1		1
Timmons, Elisha	1	2	4		
Hassell, John	1	1	5		
Hassell, Abram	1	1	3		6
Tarkenton, Joshua	1	2	2		
Tarkinton, Jesse	1				
Perisher, James	1	4	2		
Alexander, Joshua	3		1		3
Hooker, John	1	1	2		
Battin, George	1		1		
Twifoot, William	2	1	6		4
Cowel, William	1	1	3		10
Smith, John	2				
Basnett, William	2	3	5		
Owens, Zachariah	1	1	3		
Basnett, Joseph	1	1	6		
Hooker, William	1				
Twiddy, Samuel	1		2		
Hooker, Nathan	1				
Hooker, Stephen	2	5	3		
Edwards, Jacob	1	2	1		
Owens, Isaac	1				
Owens, John	1				
Basnett, James	3	1	2		
Sawyer, Rich°	1	2	1		
Crank, Levi	1	3	3		
Johnston, Joshua	1				
Alexander, Isaac	1	2	3		

EDENTON DISTRICT, TYRRELL COUNTY—Continued.

NAME OF HEAD OF FAMILY.	Free white males of 16 years and upward, including heads of families.	Free white males under 16 years.	Free white females, including heads of families.	All other free persons.	Slaves.
Alexander, Abram	1		2		
Alexander, Mary			1		4
Jarvis, Foster	1	1	2		
Cooper, Willis	1	2	2		
Ludford, Enoch	1	1	2		2
Creed, Jonathan	1	2	2		
Alexander, Abner	1	3	3		7
Snell, John	5	2	5		2
Wynne, Capt John	2	2	5		9
Hunnings, Zachariah	3	1	2		13
Jones, Bartlet	2	1	4		2
Cahoon, James	1	4	5		3
Neal, William	1	4	5		1
Kelly, William	1				
Spruil, Nehemiah	4	1	3		11
Banks, William	1	1	4		
Holmes, Henry	2	2	2		3
Spruil, Ebenezer	1	1	5		
Phelps, James	1	2	4		
Phelps, Enoch	1	1	5		
Hopkins, Samuel	1	2	3		1
Hassell, Joseph, Senr	4	1	2		2
Rhoades, Henry	1		2		
McDaniel, William	1	2	3		2
Goddin, Joseph	1		1		
Davenport, Isaac, Junr	1	3	7		
Pool, John	1		3		3
Hunnings, Philip	1		1		5
Ethridge, Nathan	1				
Hooker, Anne			2		
Brin, Richd	1	1	3		
Brown, Sarah	1	1	6		
Owens, Lucretia	1	3	2		
Howet, Richd	1	1	4		10
Claghorn, Shubal	1	2	2		

FAYETTE DISTRICT, ANSON COUNTY.

NAME OF HEAD OF FAMILY.	Free white males of 16 years and upward, including heads of families.	Free white males under 16 years.	Free white females, including heads of families.	All other free persons.	Slaves.
Lampden, Robert	1		3		
Arthur, John	1	3	3		
Searcy, William	2		2		
Wood, William	1	3	2		
Denson, Shadrack	1				
Denson, Jesse	1				
Nayes & Porter, Messrs	6				2
Ponsey, Godfrey	1		1		
Barnwell, Joseph	1				
Gilbert, Jesse	2	2	5		6
Yarborough, Humphrey	1	1	1		
Yarborough, William	1				
Allman, James	3	3	6		
Williams, John	2	2	5		
Treddiway, Daniel	1	3	4		
Bloodworth, John	4	2	3		
Bass, Frederick	3	2	3		
Lee, William	1	2	2		
Dudney, John	1	2	4		
Bylue, Henry	1	3	5		
Soward, Nancy		1	4		
Stinson, Mary	1	2	4		
Proctor, Linney		2	6		
Jones, Honor		2	2		
Odom, Richard	1		2		9
Ricketts, John	2	3	3		
Scott, Drury				4	
Scott, Francis				1	
Newton, John	2	1	2		
Bailey, Jacob	1		1		
Murphy, John	3	2	3		
Benton, James	1	1	5		
Johnston, John	1	6	4		
Wade, Thomas	5	1	2		17
Wright, John, Jr	1	1	1		8
Bailey, Mathew	1	3	3		
Bailey, Thomas	1	2	5		
Arrington, James	2	5	2		
Johnston, John, Jr	1	3	1		
Ingram, John	1	5	5		
McRae, Daniel	1	3	4		
Bylue, Abraham	1		2		
Duglas, James	1	1	1		8
German, Robert	2	2	2		
Hall, Robert	1				
Stanill, Sampson	1	1	3		
Dabbs, Josiah	1		3		
May, William	2	4	5		7
Threadgill, Randal	1	3	1		
Sasser, Joseph	2	2	5		
Childs, Elizabeth	1		2		5
Rogers, Job	3	1	3		
Hilldreath, David	1	3	3		
Gould, Daniel	1	2	3		4
Dejarnet, Mumford (minors)		2			5
Kirby, William	1	2	3		7
Hinson, John	3	3	5		3
Boggan, Patrick	1	2	8		7
Lanier, William	1	1	2		10
Covington, Simon	1	1	1		
Johnston, William	3	6	6		
Duncan, John	2	2	3		
Gordon, Frederick	2	2	2		1
May, Lewis	1	1	1		3
Taylor, Charles	2	1	4		
Lindsey, George	2	2	4		1
Caudell, Elizabeth	1		1		
Clinton, Thomas	1		1		5
Tarlton, Thomas	1	2	2		
Pace, Stephen	2	3	5		8
Threadgill, John	1	5	4		
Lanier, Isaac	1		1		7
Gathings, Philip	3	3	3		1
Farr, Richard, jr	1		1		
Rushing, William	1	4	1		9
Hammonds, George	1	4	2		9
Crawford, Michael	2	4	4		12
May, William (carpenter)	1	3	2		8
May, William, Jr	1	1	2		28
Lanier, Burwell	2	1	5		28
McClendon, Ezekiel	1	4	3		
Trull, Stephen	1				
Williams, Josiah	1		1		
Bailey, Lydia	2	2	1		
Isgett, Joseph	1	5	3		
McAskill, Daniel	2		2		
Franklin, Lawrence, Jr	1		1		
Lisles, James	1	4	3		1
Gulledge, William	1	2	4		
Bennet, Neavel	1		1		2
Morris, William	1	1	2		2
Smith, Edward	3	2	4		
Diggs, Marshal	5	4	3		1
Kindred, Elisha	1	1	2		2
Ryal, John	1				1
Colson, Joseph	1	1	2		5
West, John	2	3	2		
Wynn, Zachariah					1
Garrot, James	1				
Lewis, Jeremiah	1		1		
Booth, John	1	1	4		
Bird, John	1	3	5		6
Richeson, William	1	5	3		2
Dabbs, Nathaniel	2	3	3		1
Lewis, Thomas	1	4	7		3
Osborne, Nathan	1		3		
Davis, Arthur	1	4	6		
Birmingham, Joshua	1	2	5		
Birmingham, Charles	2		1		
Ellis, Thomas	1		4		
McClendon, Benjamin	1				
Knotts, John, Jr	1	1	2		
Franklin, Laurence, Sr	1		2		
Wright, John	1		2		
Smith, John, Jr	1	1	2		
Demery, Allen				7	
Grissard, Hardy	1	4	4		1
Smith, John, Sr	2	4	2		
White, Joseph	3		1		5
Burres, Joshua	1	4	4		3
Davis, Joshua	1	3	1		
Brown, Morgan	4	1	2	1	5
Tarlton, Britton	1		1		
Tarlton, John	1	1	1		
Knotts, John, Sr	1	1	3		
Lambden, Bixley, Jno	2	1	2		
Nash, Michael	2	1	3		
Franklin, Esom	1	2	2		
White, Henry	1	2	1		
May, William (2nd)	1		1		1
Lowe, William	1	1	2		
White, George	1	1	2		
Hill, John	1	4	1		
Baylor, John	1	3	1		
Ingram, Jesse	1				
Ingram, John, Jr	1	1	4		
Stanfill, John	1	1	3		
White, John	1		2		
Dixon, John	1	1	2		
Rushing, Robert	2	4	4		
Beachum, Jesse	1		2		
Kirby, John	1		5		17
Jackson, Isaac	1	1	3		2
Jackson, John	1		2		1
Hough, Hezekiah	5		5		6
Adams, Zadock	1				
White, Joseph	1	4	2		6
Colson, Mary		3	6		17
Howlet, Mary	2		5		
Ross, Hugh	3		4		1
Ledbetter, Zedekiah	1	2	5		6
Ratliff, James	1	1	2		
Ratliff, Robt C.	1				
Bylue, John	1				
Long, Nancy			1		
Bass, Frederick, Jr					3
Ratliff, Zacharius	1				
Jackson, Agnes	1		5		
Hinson, Benjamin	2	4	6		2
Weatherford, Charles	1	5	4		
German, William	1	1	1		
Lee, Robert	3	1	3		1
Ganade, Martin	1	2	1		
Threadgill, William	1	1	2		7
Pursley, Anthony	1	3	1		
Atkins, Lewis	1	1	5		
Lowry, John	1	3	4		1
Diggs, Pleasant	1	1	1		
Bittle, John	1				
Tatum, Jesse	1		1		
Plant, Williamson	1	1	3		
Temple, Frederick	2	3	2		
Mooreman, Benjamin	1	3	1		1
Hinson, Charles	1		1		1
Yarborough, James	1	1	3		
Mills, John	1	2	5		
Boggan, James, Sr	5	4	5		3
May, Starling	1	2	2		
Nichols, Isaac	1		3		
Lambden, John	1	2	4		
Harrell, James	1	1	1		
Davidson, Daniel	3	2	4		
Ryal, James	1	3	1		
House, Thomas	1				
Brewer, John	1		3		
Pound, Samuel	1				
Baker, James	1	2	2		
Falkner, Archd	1		2		
Culpepper, John	1	1	3		
Dabbs, John	1	2	2		
Cox, William	1	2	2		
Vivion, Charles	1		2		9
Wadkins, Christo	3	1	2		1
Boggan, James, Jr	1		1		1
Wisdom, William	2	3	5		
Breler, Elisha	1	1	2		
Rushing, Abraham	3	2	3		3
Sparks, Charles	3	1	1		3
Watts, Malachia	1	1	5		6
Colson, John	1		1		9
Whitlow, Henry	1		1		
White, John	1				
Mullis, John	1	1	1		
Winfield, Peter	1	1	4		4
Nash, Griffin	1				
Presley, Elias	1	3	1		
Rushing, Philip	1	3	3		
Harrel, Zachariah	1				
Hamer, Mary	3	1	4		5
Leonard, Jonas	1		4		
Loyd, Edward	1		4		
Griffin, David	2	4	4		
Williams, Roland	1	4	5		3
Hamer, Frances	1	2	3		9
Melton, Jesse	1				
Melton, John	1		5		
Huntly, Thomas, Sr	2		7		
Rushing, Philip, Jr	1	2	2		
Medows, Thomas	3	4	4		
Jackson, David	1	2	1		
Wilson, Samuel	2	2			3
Tison, Jehu	1	6	2		2
Gaddy, Thomas	1	4	4		
Dale, John	1				
Ferrell, Charles	1	1	5		
Hellems, Betty					
Hellems, William	1	2	4		
Hellems, John	1		2		
Hellems, Tillman	1	3	2		
Hellems, David	1				
Hellems, Jacob	1	2	5		
Head, Olive	1		1		
Beachum, William	2	1	3		1
Beachum, Susanah	1		2		
Tomkins, Thomas	1		1		
Price, John	1		1		
Curtis, Elijah	1	2	3		2
Madcalf, William	1	3	3		1

FAYETTE DISTRICT, ANSON COUNTY—Continued.

NAME OF HEAD OF FAMILY.	Free white males of 16 years and upward, including heads of families.	Free white males under 16 years.	Free white females, including heads of families.	All other free persons.	Slaves.
Clark, Cornelius	1		4		
Carter, Benjamin	2	2	4		
Gatewood, Griffin	1		1		
Gatewood, Thomas	1				
Wells, Barnaby	3	2	3		
Green, Joseph	2	2	4		
Curtis, Samuel	1	4	2		
Morris, Jesse	1		2		
Short, Daniel, Sr	1	3	5		
Lowry, Peter	1	2	6		
Griffin, John	1	1	2		
Lisles, James, Sr	3	4	1		
Evans, John	2				
Rushing, Richard	1	4	4		2
Self, Vincent	3	2	5		2
Lanier, Lewis	1		6		13
Pemberton, Richard	1	2	3		3
Johnston, Grisset	3	1	7		
Falkner, Francis	3	1	4		
Loyd, Edward	1		3		
Craft, Frederick	1	2	4		
Turner, John	1		3		
Jones, Thomas	1	3	3		
Smith, William	2	2	4		
Dabbs, Nathl, Jr	1		1		
Phillips, Rueben	1	1	3		
Hinson, Elijah	1		1		
Dotey, Isaac	1	3	5		
Reddish, Willimuth	2	1	4		
Lisles, Rebecca	2		4		
Ingram, Isam	3	5	5		
Hinson, William	1	1	2		1
Hinson, John	1	2	3		
Hinson, Henry	1		1		
Barnes, James	3	4	4		
Barnes, Samuel	1	1	1		
English, James	1	3	2		
May, John	3		4		8
Mallaugh, Sallay		1	1		
Frederick, Phillip	1	5	3		
Wallis, John	1	1	2		
Yarborough, Richard	4		2		
Ingram, Joseph	1	5	2		16
Wallis, Nelly	1		2		
Swearingen, Vann	1	2	5		
Ford, Richard	3	3	3		
Fallent, Moses	2	1	5		
Bass, Frederick			1	2	
Reed, Burlingham, Sr	1	1	3		
Wade, Holden	3		3		10
Vining, Thomas	1	1	5		6
Wade, Jane			3		10
Prout, Joshua	1	1	2		9
King, John	2	2	3		
Jamieson, James	1	3	1		1
Morris, Nathan	1		2		
Short, John	1	1	4		
Nance, Buckner			3		
Laine, James	1		2		
Shepherd, William	3	2	2		2
Thomas, Edmund	1		1		
Spencer, Honble Samuel	1	1	2		18
Everat, Thomas	1		3		
Bylue, Katy	2	3	3		5
Ratliff, Richard	1	4	3		
Ratliff, Thomas	1	3	2		
Bailey, Thomas, Sr	3	1	4		1
Briley, Joseph	1	2	1		
Bermingham, Caleb	1	3	3		
Hand, John	1		4		
Hand, Isaac	1		1		
Lindsey, Edward	3	3	1		
Dickson, Thomas	3		2		
Howell, Lewis	1		3		
Briley, George	1	4	3		
Threadgill, Thomas	1	4	3		9
Vanderford, William	2	2	3		
Tallent, Aron	3	2	3		
Gray, Benjamin	1	1	3		
Stinson, Mary	1	2	4		
Denson, Nathaniel	2	2	3		
May, John	2	2	4		9
Burr, William	1	1	2		
Diggs, Judy	2		2		
Martin, Thomas	1	1	2		
Phillips, Samuel	2	5	2		
Smith, Richard	1		3		6
Hilldreath, William	1	2	6		
Ingram, Joseph, Jr	1	1	3		1
Lee, William	1	2	2		
Wells, George	2	1	5		3
Smith, Francis	1	3	2		15
Williams, Joshua	1	3	6		
Boush, Richard	1	1	2		
Jones, William	1	1	2		
Thomas, Stephen	3	2	3		
Smith, Robert	1	2	9		
Martin, John	1		2		
Phillips, Benja	2	5	2		
Turner, William	3	1	2		8
Ashcraft, John	3	2	5		
Ashcraft, Thomas	2	3	3		
Elliott, John	1	1	3		
Young, Daniel	1	4	4		1
Rogers, William	1		1		1
Meadows, Job	1	1	5		
Howell, Stephen	1	2	4		
Meadows, Lewis	2	3	3		
Slay, Daniel	1	2	1		
Flake, Samuel	2	3	2		1
Hutcheson, William	1	2	1		
Tarlton, Thomas	2		2		
Falkner, Asa		3	3		
Davidson, Daniel	3	2	4		
Snugs, Richard	1	1	2		
Lindsey, William	1	2	5		
Tallent, Richard	1		1		
Smith, William	1	2	4		
Howell, Hardy	1	3	3		
Howell, Joseph	1	1	2		
Baxley, Mary		4	1		
Hamlet, John	1	1	3		
McClendon, Dennis	1	2	1		
Tison, Jacob	1	4	1		1
Haney, Timothy	1	3	2		
May, William	1	1	1		
Vandeford, James	1		3		
Vandeford, James, Sr	2	2	3		
Vickers, Ralph	2	1	2		
Trull, James	1	1	3		
Griffin, Jesse	1	1	2		
Austin, Michael	1	2	4		
Auld, Susanah			4		3
Lindsey, William, Jr	1	1	2		
Phillips, Samuel	3	2	5		
Porter, Charles	2	1	2		2
Benton, William	1		2		2
Brewer, George	1	2	7		
Forehand, Nehemiah	1		2		
Dunham, Joseph	1		1		1
Gordan, John	2	1			
Lacy, Thomas	3	2	4		3
Farmer, James	1	1	4		
Huntly, Thomas	1	1	4		
Bennet, William	2	1	3		1
Falkner, Elizabeth		2	2		
Arrington, Thomas	1	2	2		
Smith, Robert	2	1	2		
Howell, Joseph	1	1	2		
German, John	2	1	3		1
Turner, Mathew	1	1	3		
Hyde, Stephen	1	2	3		11
Tatum, Edward	1	2	2		
Cock, Odom	1	2	7		
Kelley, Thomas	1		5		
Sides, Henry	1	7	5		
Beverley, John	3	3	1		
Pratt, William	3	2	3		1
Ross, Walter	1		1		
Huntley, Robert	1	2	4		
Gulledge, William	3	3	4		5
Rushing, Mathew	1	2	2		
Baker, John, Jr	2		7		
Courtney, John	2	2	4		
May, Pleasant	2	2	3		2
Spencer, Joseph			1		2
Campbell, Charles	1	3			
Faircloth, James	1				
Booth, David	2	2	2		
Booth, John	1		2		
Austin, John	1				
Hemby, Dennis	1		2		
Ricketts, William	1	2	4		
Morris, William	2	2	2		4
Davenport, William	1	2	5		
Rushing, Solomon	1	4	4		
Rainey, David	1	3	6		
Jennings, John	1	1	4		6
Brumbelow, Isaac	2	3	3		
Brumbelow, Edward	3	3	4		
Bennett, James	1	3	5		1
Brumbelow, Isaac, Jr	1		1		
Curlee, William	1	3	4		
Davis, John	1		1		
Falkner, Nathan	2	5	4		
Davis, Isam	1		1		1
Griffin, Thomas	1	5	3		
Parker, John	1	3	3		
Stewart, William	1	3	3		
Hinson, John	1	2	2		
Hinson, William	1				1
Hinson, Daniel	1				
Barnes, James	5		4		
Martin, Kinchen	1	2	1		1
Moses, Samuel	1	1	2		
Moses, Joshua	1	1	4		
Tallent, Thomas	1	1	3		
King, John	2	2	4		
Henry, William	2	2	2		4
Booth, David	1	2	3		
Ducksworth, Joseph	2	2	2		
Martin, Abraham	1				
Short, Daniel, Jr	1	2	2		
Thomas, Joseph	1				
Adams, William	1		1		
Gaddy, Thomas	2	3	5		
Murphy, Daniel	1	1	6		
Bailey, Jacob	1				
Cooper, Benjamin	2	2	6		
Bradley, Hobbs	1		3		
Everat, Henry	2	1	1		1
Watts, Alice		2	3		
Bylew, Henry	1	4	4		
Wiggins, Betty		3	4		
Hudson, William	1		2		
Mullis, Solomon	1	3	1		
McMillen, Amon	1	3	4		
Watson, William, Jr	2	1	3		
Polk, Charles	1	2	2		4
McGehee, Thomas, Jr	1	4	3		
McGehee, James	1	6	3		
McGehee, Thomas, Sr	2		3		
Shelby, Jacob	1		2		
Watson, William, Sr	1	3	3		
Leaird, James	1	1	1		
Godwin, John	2	2	6		
Shelton, Beverly	1		6		
Langley, Noah	1				
Child, John	1				
Strong, Lewis	1	1	1		
Caudell, Absalom	1		3		
Barber, Abraham	1	3	4		
Baker, John, Sr	2		1		
Baker, William	1	3	4		
Manus, Richard	2	3	4		
Manus, John	1	1	2		
Yarborough, Davis	1	3	4		1
Robbins, John	1	1	3		
Croswell, Richmond	1		1		
Hudson, Joseph	1		7		
Alston, Drury	1		4		
Costillo, Michael	2	1	4		
Collins, William	1	1	5		
Yarborough, Jonathan	1	4	6		
High, Gardner	1	2	3		
Yarborough, Humphrey	3	2	5		
Johnston, Solomon	1	3	2		
McHenry, Jesse	2		2		
Broadway, Gracy	3		7		
Plunket, James	1	4	3		
Biven, John	1	1	1		
Bevin, Nathaniel	3	3	3		3
Martin, John H.	2	2	3		
Winfield, Edward	1	1	1		
Meadows, Jason	1	1	1		
Meadows, Edward	1				
Rorey, Sally		1	4		9
Robertson, Drury	1		2		
Meadows, Thomas	1	1	1		
McDonald, Elizabeth	1	2	2		
Meanly, Richard	2	2	2		9
Smith, Jeremiah	2	5	5		
Ramsey, John	3	1	2		
Honey, Elias	1		1		
Raines, Stephen	1				
Lowe, Patty		1	5		
Jackson, Samuel	1	1	5		
Lewes, Jeremiah	1	5	1		
Downer, John	1	3	6		
Murphy, John	1				
Benson, Elizabeth			2		
Harry, John	1	2	5		
Curtis, Thomas	1	2	4		1
Short, James	1	2	1		
Rorey, William	2	1	5		7
Ottery, John	1	1	2		
Lissenby, John	2		4		
Rorey, Sarah			1	4	
Rorey, James			1	1	
May, John, Jr	1		1		6
Cheek, John	1	5	4		
Willoughby, John	1	3	4		
Hendrick, Gustavus	3		4		7
Green, Gideon	2	6	4		1
Shivers, William	2	3	3		
Green, Jacob	1	2	4		
Hinson, John	1	2	3		
White, John	1	3	4		2
Lowry, Robert	2	1	3		6
Jackson, Stephen	3	1	2		3
Grice, Joyner	1	2	1		

FAYETTE DISTRICT, ANSON COUNTY—Continued.

Name of head of family	Free white males of 16 years and upward, including heads of families	Free white males under 16 years	Free white females, including heads of families	All other free persons	Slaves
Presley, John	1		1		
Rushing, Noah	2	1	3		2
Carlisle, William	1		4		
Scott, Nathl	2		1		2
Stokes, Jones	1		1		
Givin, Hardy	1	2	5		
Rushing, Abraham, Jr	1		3		
Harrington, Charles	1	2	5		5
Bennet, Joseph	4	1	3		
Woods, Frame	1	4	3		5
Marshall, James	3	1	8		20
Jones, William	1	1	2		
Honey, Thomas	1		1		
German, John	2	1	3		1
Robertson, Booth	1		2		
Thomas, Evan	1	4	1		
Robertson, Drury	1		2		9
Presley, Thomas	1	2	2		
Presley, Richard	1		4		
Rushing, Jacob	1	1	3		
Presley, Thomas, Sr	1		5		
Rushing, Rowland	2		3		
Halcomb, William	1		2		
Johnston, Charles	1	1	2		
Stuckey, Lucy	2		2		
Exum, William	1		2		
Hair, Elkeny	1				
Austin, John	3	1	1		
Harrel, John	1	1	3		1
Harrel, Mills	1	1	1		
Auld, John	1	4	2		23
Lytle, James	3	2	4		
White, Josiah	1		1		1
Stewart, William	1	3	3		
Cone, John	1	2	2		
Rosser, Joseph	2	3	3		4
Rushing, Mark	2	2	3		
Rushing, Sibrina		3	4		
Yoe, William	2	1	3		
Bass, Frederick, Sr					9
Wimberly, James	1		1		
Howell, Hopkin	1	1	3		
Hogan, James	3	1	3		10
Willoughby, John	1	1	5		
Thomas, Benjamin	1	5	3		
Girley, Jacob	1	4	3		
McClendon, Dennis, Sr	1	1			
McClendon, Frederick	1				
Johnston, Timothy	1	3	3		
Scarbrough, Rebecca		1	2		
Pearce, Wright	1	4	2		
Smith, Robert	2	1	3		
Horton, Robert	1	2	2		
Mercer, Jeremiah	1	1	3		
Smith, Arthur	1	5	3		1
White, John	1				
Presley, John, Sr	1	5	5		
Presley, John, Jr	1		1		
Kimbrell, Buckner	3	3	6		1
Magby, Vardray	1	4	2		
Collins, William	2	1	5		
Gurley, William	2	1	4		3
Sykes, Arthur	1		1		
Wright, Stephen	1				
Richeson, John	1		3		
Boggan, William, Jr	2		1		
Boggan, William, Sr	1		2		
Moses, Joshua	1	1	4		
Moor, Ransom	1				
Abercromby, Isaac	1	3	2		
Hickman, Jesse	1				
Dabbs, William	1				
Bird, Thomas	1		1		
Bird, William	1	2	5		
Creel, Thomas	2		2		
Worley, Joseph Jno	1	4	4		
Melton, Michael	1				
Rushing, William, Jr	1		2		
White, Joseph	1		1		4
Phillips, Jacob	1				
Beachum, William	2	1	3		1
Gaddy, William	1		2		
Dickerson, Leonard	1	2	2		
Vaughn, William	1	1	6		1
Reed, Burlingham, Jr	1		1		
Conner, Ruth	1		3		
Falkner, Francis	3	1	4		

Name of head of family	Free white males of 16 years and upward, including heads of families	Free white males under 16 years	Free white females, including heads of families	All other free persons	Slaves
Milton, Isam	2	2	5		
Ricketts, John	1	2	3		
Ricketts, Moses	1	2	2		
Hews, Saml	1		3		
Elliott, Robert	1	2	2		
Grimes, Charles	2	2	2		
Howell, William	2	1	6		
Thomas, Josiah	1				
Hicks, Charles	2		1		6
Wadkins, Christopher	3	1	2		1
Evans, John	3	3	4		
Magby, Rachael			1		
Finney, Thomas	1		4		
Lee, Richard	2		3		1
Bell, William	2	4	5		
Ferrell, Sarah		1	3		
Medford, John	1	1	1		
Jamieson, David	1	3	3		6
Mullis, Margaret		1	3		
Stroud, William	2		2		
Taylor, John	1	3	3		
Burrows, Joshua	2	3	4		3
Allen, John	1				
Miller, Abraham	1	1	2		
Howard, James	1	3	2		
Tomkins, Stephen	1	5	2		8
Watts, Ealsy		2	3		
Sibly, Benjamin	1				
Tomkins, Stephen, Jr	1		1		1
Churning, Bartholomew	2	1	3		1
Bayles, Ferebe	2	3	4		
Bailey, Lydia	2	3	1		
Bailey, Mary		2	2		
Cruize, Armsby	1	3	3		
Prescot, Rachael		1	2		
Howell, John	1	1	1		
Paul, Sarah	2	2	2		
Perret, John	1		2		
Wagers, Drury	1	2	3		
Packer, George	1	1	2		
Stanfield, John	1		2		
Ross, Gustavus	1	3	4		
Paul, Philip	1	1	1		
Bluford, Henry	1	3	5		
Blackford, Rachael			2		
Jones, Elizabeth		2	4		
Martin, William	2	4	4		3
Purdue, Richard	1	4	1		1
Gray, David	1				
Ross, Andrew	1	3	1		
Long, Margaret		1	1		
Williams, Josiah	1		2		
Ross, Walter	1	1	3		
Mask, Mary			4		
Davidson, John	1		2		
Moore, James	2				
McDonald, Hugh	1	1	1		
Martin, Calvine	1	2	4		3
Ratliff, Richard	1	4	3		
Come, John	1	2	1		
Hooker, Hardy	1		3		
Booth, John, Jr	1	1	3		
Tallent, Joshua	1				
Yoe, Nathan	1				
Lindsey, William, Jr	1	1	1		
Scago, Joseph	1	1	2		
Tallent, Aron, Jr	1	2	1		
Lowe, Daniel	1				
Gordon, Thomas	2		1		
Lisles, Joseph	1	2	1		
Lindsey, George	3	2	2		1
Parsons, Francis	1	3	7		
Tudor, Owen	1	3	4		
Jordan, Charles	2	4	5		
Akin, John, Jr	2		1		
Akin, John	1		4		3
Everat, Thomas	1		2		
Phillips, Robert	1		3		
Phillips, Mary	1		3		
Collier, Drury	2	3	2		8
Lynch, Philip	1	2	2		
Ramsey, John	2	2	2		
Herrin, Anna		2	4		
Robinson, Jeremiah	1	5	3		
Dickson, Thomas	2				
Howell, Lewis	1	1	3		
Melton, John	1	1	3		

Name of head of family	Free white males of 16 years and upward, including heads of families	Free white males under 16 years	Free white females, including heads of families	All other free persons	Slaves
White, Elinor		1	2		
Pearce, William	1	3	4		
Pearce, Desey		1	3		
Redfern, John	1	3	2		
Renfrow, Joel	1	2	5		
Hough, Amos	1	3	3		
Deason, Enoch	1	2	6		
Causley, Michael, Sr	3		2		
Taylor, Frederick	1	2	3		
Thomas, Jacob	1	1	3		
Pearce, Moses	1	2	5		
Adams, Joseph	1	2	3		
Arlige, Caleb	1	2	2		
Price, Monsier	1	2	2		
Price, Isaac	1	3	1		
Wingate, William	1	1	4		
Wingate, Rueben	2	2	1		
Pagett, Ephraim	1		5		
Shepherd, David	3	1	2		2
Cook, Charles	1	2	1		
Causley, Edward	1	1	4		
Smith, Abraham	1		2		
Adams, Elizabeth		1	2		
Medcalf, John	1		2		
Medcalf, William, Jr	1	2			
Evans, Anna			1		
Thomas, John	2	3	4		
Tomerlinson, Moses	1	4	2		
Gillen, Rebecca		1	1		
Shelby, Thomas	1	2	3		
Harris, Rebecca		2	1		
Johnston, Elizabeth			2		
Dees, Nancy			2		
Griffin, David	2	5	5		
Lee, Richard, Sr	1	1	4		
Medford, John	1		2		
Hutson, Joakin	1		4		
Stokes, William	2	4	2		
Bennet, Joseph	4	1	4		
Hamlet, John	1	1	4		
Parnell, Mary			4		
Poll, Arthur	2	1	4		
Pool, Mary			2		
Baker, Samuel	1	3	1		
Austin, John	3				
Packer, Nicholas	1		3		
Wright, Josias	2	3	2		
Gray, John	2				
Meanly, Richard	2	2	2		6
Arnett, John	1		2		
Buse, John	1		3		
McHenry, Milley		1	1		
Jackson, Samauel	1	1	5		
Hewlet, Mary	1	2	4		
Causly, Michael, Jr	1		4		
Thomas, Thomas	2	2	4		
Jones, Abraham					9
Phillips, John	1		2		
Dabbs, Richard	1		1		
White, Moses	1	1	3		
Temples, Frederick	2	3	2		
Moses, David	1				
Roberds, William	1		3		8
Clark, Joseph	1			4	4
Clark, Francis	1	1	1		3
Clark, Robert	1		3		2
Pickett, James	2	3	2		12
Long, Josiah	1	2			
Moore, John	2	1	7		
Blewit, William	2	3	3		
Rogers, Humphrey	4		5		2
Rogers, Richard	1	1	1		
Rogers, William	1		1		1
Martin, Thomas	1		1		
Tallent, Aron, Jr	1	1	1		
Long, Rueben	1				
Clark, Beverley	1	2	3		1
Ross, Andrew	1	3	3		
Williams, William	1		2		
Leek, Walter	1	1	3		16
Martin, William	1	4	3		
Griffin, Richard	1	4	3		
Ponyman, Melton	1				
Fare, Richard, Senr	1		2		11
Fields, Smith	2		5		
Leggett, James	1	2	2		

FAYETTE DISTRICT, CUMBERLAND COUNTY (EXCLUDING FAYETTEVILLE TOWN).

NAME OF HEAD OF FAMILY.	Free white males of 16 years and upward, including heads of families.	Free white males under 16 years.	Free white females, including heads of families.	All other free persons.	Slaves.
Atkins, Ica	4	2			17
Avera, Alexr	4	2	6		11
Avera, Thomas	1		2		
Armstrong, Thomas	3	2	4	1	18
Anderson, William	1	3	2		
Avera, Henry	1	3	1		
Avera, William	1	4	4		3
Adams, John	3		3		
Andrews, Alfred	1	2	5		
Anderson, William	1	3	3		
Atkins, Lewis	1	2	5		10
Anderson, William	1				
Anderson, John	1		2		
Atkinson, Henry	1		1		
Anderson, James	1				
Atkinson, Charlton	2	1	1		1
Anderson, Stephen	1				
Alford, Jacob	1	2	1		
Armour, Andrew	1		2		
Arville, Duke	1				
Anderson, George	2	2	3		
Akin, Barbara		1	4		4
Armstrong, George	1	3	4		2
Anderson, Camell			3		
Allsobrook, John	1		2		1
Anderson, William	1	3	6		
Andrews, Andrew	1	3	6		
Barge, Lewis	2	4	3		17
Buchanan, Hector	1	1	1		7
Bethune, Farquhard	1	1	4		
Blocker, John	1		1		8
Barnes, Amos	1	4	1		
Bolling, William	2		1		1
Black, John	1	2	1		
Blocker, George	3		2	1	8
Blew, John	1	2	1		
Brice, Capt Duncan	4		2		
Booker, Samuel	2	2	4		
Buchanan, John	3	4	3		
Blew, Daniel	1	2	7		1
Bray, Bryant	1	1	2		
Beaton, Martin	3	2	4		
Bullard, James	2	1	6		
Ballard, Katy			6		1
Butler, Mary	2	2	2		
Beard, John	3	2	2		6
Boush, John	2		5		
Bristow, James	1				
Burnsides, Thomas	1	1	2		
Brice, John	3	4	4		1
Bagget, Drury	1		2		
Brewer, William	1	1	4		
Brice, Niel	2		1		
Blew, Duncan	2	1	2		2
Burt, Joseph	1		1		
Baine, Hugh	1		1		
Beaton, Archd	1		1	1	
Brown, Josiah	1	5	2		
Brown, Benjamin	1	3	1		
Battle, Randolph	1				
Battle, James	2		3		17
Burt, Young	1	2	2		6
Black, Niel	1	2	2		1
Bedsole, John	1	2	2		
Breachley, James	1				
Butler, Zachariah	1		2		2
Bohan, David	1	3	2		
Black, Duncan	1		2		
Blew, James	1				
Baker, Archd	1	6	5		
Bristow, George, Jr	1	2	1		
Brice, Daniel	3	1	4		
Blew, Malcolm	1				
Baker, Archd	2				
Bateman, William	1				
Baker, Daniel	1				
Brown, Duncan	1				
Brasswell, Benjamin	1	1	3		
Brice, Archd	1		2		
Black, Dugal	1				
Brice, Niel	2	2	4		
Blew, Malcolm	2		1		
Black, Duncan	1		3		
Brice, Duncan	1		2		13
Bullock, James	1	2	3		
Black, Hugh	1		1		3
Bethune, Collin	1	1	5		1
Blaylock, Hardy	1		2		
Beard, James	1	2	6		4
Bullard, Henry	1				
Baine, Hugh	3	2	3		2
Brice, Gilbert	3	3	2		7
Black, Peggy	1		2		
Brooks, Philip	1				
Brown, John	1	1	4		
Best, Harmon	1	2	4		
Brantley, James	3		2		

NAME OF HEAD OF FAMILY.	Free white males of 16 years and upward, including heads of families.	Free white males under 16 years.	Free white females, including heads of families.	All other free persons.	Slaves.
Byrum, Jacob	1		3		
Brice, Malcom	1				2
Brice, Archd (Piper)	1		2		2
Brice, Archd (Gum Swamp)	3	1	4		
Cook, William	1	1	1		
Carver, Jesse	1		4		9
Champion, William	2	3	4		
Campbell, Farquhard	2	3	3		50
Cox, George	3		4		
Campbell, James	2		4	3	2
Campbell, John (son Robert)	2		6		1
Clark, Daniel	1				1
Clark, Gilbert	4		2		6
Campbell, John (surveyor)	1	4	5		4
Campbell, Daniel	1		1		
Carraway, John, Sr	1		2		14
Carraway, John, Jr	1	2	2		
Curry, John	1				
Clark, Archd	2				
Campbell, Collin	1		3		
Clark, Archd	2				
Coates, Joseph	2	3	3		
Calvin, William	3		2		12
Calvin, James	2	5	2		
Cutts, Paul	1	2	3		
Carraway, William	1	2	3		
Cutts, William	1		6		
Campbell, Edward	1	2	2		
Campbell, Dugal	1	1	6		
Clark, Malcolm	1	3	5		3
Carver, Sampson	1	3	3		7
Carter, Jesse	2	2	5		
Campbell, Duncan	1		1		3
Colbraith, Niel	1		1		4
Clark, David	1		2		2
Clark, John	2	3	2		6
Campbell, Dugal	1	2	1		
Campbell, Alex	1		2		
Clark, Malcolm	1	4	3		1
Carroth, Robert	2	1	4		
Colquhoon, Laughlan	1	2	4		
Colquhoon, Duncan	1		1		
Chasin, Benjamin	1				
Carter, Abraham	1	2	4	1	
Colbraith, John	1				
Cox, Lewis	1				
Champion, John	1	1	4		
Conley, Niel	2		5		
Cameron, Absalom	1	2	2		
Clark, James	2		4		4
Cameron, Allen	1	2	2		
Colbraith, Peter	2	2	3		1
Clark, William	1	2	2		3
Cole, John	1				
Colbraith, John	1				
Clark, John	1				
Cameron, John	4	2	5		4
Colbraith, Daniel	1	2	2		
Colbraith, Daniel	2	2	4		1
Carmichael, Daniel	2	2	4		
Cotton, Jesse	1		4		
Caisey, Abraham	1				
Campbell, Alex	1	1	2		
Cremon, John	1	2	3		
Clark, John (Saylor)	3		3		
Cade, Elizabeth		1	3		1
Colbraith, Archd	2		1		1
Creed, Cornelius	1				
Chavers, Isam				8	
Campbell, Duncan	1		3		6
Carraway, Thomas	2				
Cutts, Sherod	1		2		
Clark, John (Taylor)	2	4	2		9
Campbell, Niel	1		1		
Campbell, Katy			4		1
Campbell, John (Rock Fish)	2	1	3		
Campbell, Alexr (Rock Fish)	2	1	2		
Clark, Archd	2	2	4		9
Cameron, Allen	1	4	2		
Cameron, Kennith	1	2	3		
Campbell, Laughlan	3	3	4		
Cameron, Daniel	4	2	4		4
Cox, Davenport	1		2		
Coleburn, Revil	1		4		
Clements, Rueben	1	3	3		1
Clark, Alexr	1		2		
Colquhoon, Malcolm	1	1	3		
Colquhoon, John	1		1		
Colquhoon, Archd	1		3		
Campbell, Mary	1		1		
Colquhoon, Mrs			2		
Colbraith, Margaret	2		3		

NAME OF HEAD OF FAMILY.	Free white males of 16 years and upward, including heads of families.	Free white males under 16 years.	Free white females, including heads of families.	All other free persons.	Slaves.
Campbell, William	2		3		
Campbell, Daniel	2		3		
Carver, Elizabeth		3	5		11
Carver, William	1	4	5		10
Corbet, Abel	1		1		1
Carver, Robert	1		7		13
Chason, Joseph	2	2	2		
Cook, Ephrim	1				
Clark, Luke	1		3		6
Booker, Isaac	1	1	3		
Broome, Luke	1	3	3		
Blaylock, Charles	1	3	5		
Braser, Elijah	2	1	5		3
Brown, Barnaby	1		3		
Blaylock, Richard	1		1		4
Brice, Hector	1				
Brice, Archd	1				
Blanchet, Edward	3		1		
Bristow, George, Sr	1				
Brown, Archd	2		6		
Brown, Anguish	1		3		
Brown, Niel	1	1			
Baker, John	2	4	3		
Brayford, Mary	2	1	4		
Beard, Daniel	1	2	1		3
Bone, Archd	1	3	4		
Burges, Malachai	1	1	3		2
Duglas, Kezia	1		2		
Draughan, Robert	4	3	2		11
Dyer, James	2	2	2	1	1
Driver, John	2	3	3		
Draughan, Hardy	1				
Dickerson, Thomas M	1	1	6		
Dye, Avera	1	2	1		
Denton, William	1		2		
Duffil, James	1	2	2		
Danock, Malcolm	1				
Dukemineer, Rachael	2		2		
Dunfield, Edward	1				1
Davis, Thomas	1				4
Dobbins, James	2		3		
Dunfield, James	3				
Draughan, John	1	1	3		
Denton, William	1	1	2		
Dawry, John	1	3	2		
Durden, John	1	1	1		
Dukes, John	1	1	2		
Elliott, George	2	1	8		35
Evans, David	1	1			7
Evans, Benjamin	1	2	3		
Evans, John	1		1		
Evans, Mary			1		
Eccles, Gilbert	3	2	3		7
Elkings, John	2	1	1		
Elkings, Owen	1	1	2		
Elkings, John	1	2	4		
Evans, William	1	2	5		
Everat, Demey	1		1		
Evans, Theophilus	1	5	2		9
Evans, Josiah	1	1	1		
Edwards, Susanah	1		3		3
Edwards, Joel	2	5	4		2
Evans, George	1	1	4		
Elwell, John	1	1	5		6
Elwell, Elizabeth					
Folsome, Israel	2		4		7
Folsome, Nathl	5		2		9
Falkner, John	1				
Ferguson, Anguish	1	2	4		
Faircloth, Caleb	2	2	1		1
Falkner, Charles	2	1	3		
Falkner, Caleb	1				
Freelove, Timothy	1	4	4		
Failops, Mary	2		1		
Fox, Thomas	1				
Ferguson, John	1		1		
Fennis, John	1	2	2		
Faircloth, Robert	1		2		
Falkner, Ephraim	1	3	5		
Frazier, Daniel	1				
Forster, William	3		2		
Forster, David	2		3		
Finleyson, John	1		6		
Faircloth, Caleb	1	2	5		
Ferguson, John, Jr	1	3	5		
Fenner, Joseph	1	2	2		
Fort, Sherod	1		2		
Gellespie, David	1		1		2
Gross, James	1				5
Gibson, William	1		1	1	3
Gardner, John	1		4		4
Grimes, Alexr	4	2	2		4
Grimes, Archd	1		2		
Grimes, John	1		4		4
Grimes, Daniel	1	3	5		
Grimes, Daniel	1		3		
Grimes, Alexr	2	1	4		

FAYETTE DISTRICT, CUMBERLAND COUNTY (EXCLUDING FAYETTEVILLE TOWN)—Continued.

NAME OF HEAD OF FAMILY.	Free white males of 16 years and upward, including heads of families.	Free white males under 16 years.	Free white females, including heads of families.	All other free persons.	Slaves.
Gordon, William	2	1	6	...	17
Griffin, John	1	4	4	...	3
Garrick, John	1	...	4		
Garner, John	1	1	4		
Gillies, John	1	2	2		
Graham, John	1				
Graham, Robert	1				
Graham, Walter	1				
Graham, Niel	1				
Gordon, Robert	1	4	1		
Gregory, Alex	2		1	...	11
Godfrey, William	2		3		
Graham, Daniel	1		7	1	
Graham, Alex	2	3	6		
Greer, Robert	2		1	4	
Green, John	1	1	8		
Graham, Edward	1		1		
Graham, Daniel	1	3	5		
Gilmour, Stephen	2	3	4	...	5
Guest, Christopher	1		2	...	3
Gray, William	1	2	4		
Galbraith, Niel	1	5	2	...	8
Gaddy, James	1	3	5		
Germany, Emery	1	1	1		
Griffin, Joseph	2	1	1		
Gurley, Sarah	2		2		
Grimes, Michael	1		3		
Guest, Joseph	2	1	5	1	
Grizzard, Ambrose	1	1	3	...	5
Galbraith, John	1				
Grimes, John	2		3		
Garner, Joseph	4	1	4		
Galbraith, Tarquil	1		3	...	4
Galbraith, Nevin	3	1	7	1	
Galbraith, Duncan	1	2	2		
Graham, Arthur	4		3		
Gillies, Archd	1	3	3		
Hodge, Philemon	1	1	3	...	9
Howard, Edward, Sr	2	2	2	...	14
Hollingsworth, Samuel	7	2	3	...	10
Holton, Abel	1	3	3	...	2
Howard, Edward, Jr	2		1	...	2
Hadley, John	1	1	2	...	9
Harrisson, James	1	1	1		
Henderson, John	1		1		
Harwell, James	1	4	2	...	3
Harrisson, John	1	2	1		
Howell, Barton	1	2	5		
Hadly, Thomas	1		1	...	7
Hadly, Simon	2	3	3	...	12
Hazard, Thomas	1		4		
Homes, Hamer	2		3		
Horsun, Isaac	1	2	2		
Holt, Frederick	2	1	3	...	8
Hicks, Howell	1				
Howell, Thomas	1	4	3		
Hughes, Walter	1	2	1		
Honey, Abner	1	3	4		
Holmes, David	1	3	2		
Hollingsworth, Stephen	3		5	1	
Horn, Sihon	4	4	6		
Hammonds, Ratia	2	1	4		
Howie, Samuel	1	3	2	...	2
Hair, William	1		2		
Hadly, Jesse	1			...	11
Hodge, Joseph	2	1	2	...	1
Herring, Catharine			3		
Holmes, Archd	2	2	4	...	5
Holton, Samuel	1		4		
Holton, Nathaniel	1	2	7		
Hayle, Joel	2		3	...	5
Hayle, Daniel	1	1	2	...	1
Hayle, Hosey	1	1	2	...	1
Hayle, James	2	4	9		
Hailey, Hansel	1	2	1		
Hust, Jesse	1	1	5		
Hust, Hezekiah	3	1	5		
Hadly, Benjamin	1	1	2	...	4
Hayle, James	2		9		
Hair, Ann	1	5	2		
Haney, Lewis	2		3		
Hadly, Hannah		1	3		
Jessop, Isaac	4	2	3		
Jones, Thomas	1	1	4		
Johnston, Archd	1	5	4		
Jolly, James	1				
Johnston, Alex	1	2	3		
Johnston, Clary	1	3	3		
Johnston, Willis	1	1	4		
Johnston, Thomas	1				
Johnston, Archd	1		1		
Johnston, Zilla		1	5	...	2
Johnston, Benjamin	1	2	5		
Johnston, Barnaby	1	4	3		
Johnston, Tapley	1	1	3	...	2
Johnston, Archd	1				
Jones, Solomon	1	3	2		

NAME OF HEAD OF FAMILY.	Free white males of 16 years and upward, including heads of families.	Free white males under 16 years.	Free white females, including heads of families.	All other free persons.	Slaves.
Johnston, Randal	1		3	...	2
Johnston, Samuel	4	3	5	...	1
Johnston, John	2	4	2		
Jordan, Mead	1	2	8		
Jackson, James	3	1	5	...	16
Jones, Joshua	1				
Johnston, Daniel	4	2	1		
Ingram, Simon	1				
Ingram, Alex	1				
Ingram, Jesse	1	2	2		
Jacobs, James	1				
Johnston, George	1		2		
Innis, Raymond	1		1		
Johnston, Arthur	1	2	5	...	1
Johnston, Philip	1				
Johnston, John	1		1		
Johnston, Jacob	1	1	3		
Jones, Marshall	1	1	2		
Knight, John	4	2	6	...	4
Kirven, Thomas	1	1	4		
Kirven, Thomas	3	1	3		
Killen, Thomas	4		3	...	10
Kirven, Kaid	1		3		
Killen, Adam	1		1	...	2
King, Nathan	1	1	1	...	7
Knight, William	1				
Knight, William P	1				
Kelly, Daniel	1		1		
Kelly, Ananias	2		3		
Kerby, John	1				
Kennedy, John	1	3	1		
Kirkpatrick, William	1	1	5	...	8
Kennedy, William	2		2	...	1
Killen, William	1	4	1		
Kile, Daniel	1	1	1		
King, Joseph	1		1		
King, Henry	1		1	...	1
Kemp, John	1	1	1		
Leslie, Hugh	1				
Layton, William	2	3	2		
Lawhorn, Lewis	1	1	7		
Lock, Leonard	2	1	2	...	9
Lawhorn, Norvill	1		3		
Leslie, John	1	2	4		
Leach, Niel	1				
Lee, Elizabeth			3		
Leslie, Coll			3		
Leslie, Duncan	1	3	2		
Leslie, Daniel	1				
Leach, Daniel	3		2		
Lord, William	1		2	...	14
Lamon, Niel	1	2	3		
Livingston, Robert	1	1	1	...	7
Leach, Niel	1		2		
Love, Roger	1	2	5		
Lanier, James	1	1			
Leavens, Richmond	1		1	...	1
Lawhorn, John	1	3	3		
Maloy, John	2		2	...	4
Murchison, Kennith (S.)	1	3	2		
Martinleer, George	1		2		
Murphy, John	2	4	4		
Maloy, Angus	1	3	2		
Mathews, William	1	2	3		
Moore, Abel	1	3	1		
Martinleer, John	1		3		
Moore, Mathew	2	5	3		
Moore, Jordan	1	2	4		
Morgan, Jesse	1				
Morrisson, Roger	1	1	2		
Mathews, Jacob	2	3	3	...	3
Mitchell, James	2		2		
Mathews, Arthur	1	3	6		
Morrisson, Rodorick	1		4		
Mun, Alex	1	1	2		
Monro, Arabell	2	1	2	...	3
Mun, Angus	2	3	3		
Mathews, Jacob	1	3	4	...	2
Morrison, Norman	2		2		
Morgan, Mathew	2	4	2	...	1
Mathews, Hardy	2	2	2		
Murray, James	1		4		
Mathews, David	1	2	2	...	1
Marsh, James	2	4	4		
Massey, Jordan	1		2		
Morrisson, Hugh	2		2		
Maloy, Duncan	1		3		
Montgomery, Robert	1				
Morrisson, Daniel	2		2		
Morrison, John	1		4		
Mason, John	3	3	7		
Morrisson, Daniel	1		2		
Moore, Mary		1	3		
Mitchell, Sarah			3		
Murray, Katy	1		4		
Monro, Patrick	3	4	4	...	1
Morrisson, Cain	1	2	3		

NAME OF HEAD OF FAMILY.	Free white males of 16 years and upward, including heads of families.	Free white males under 16 years.	Free white females, including heads of families.	All other free persons.	Slaves.
Moore, William	1		1		1
Monro, John	1	1	3		
Moore, John	1	1	3		
Murphy, John	1		3	...	1
Martin, Alex	1		4		
Moody, Thomas	1		1		1
Mun, Daniel	1		3		
Morrisson, Daniel	1	1	2		
Monro, Niel	1	5	3		5
Moore, Aron	1	2	5		1
Morrisson, Daniel	2		2		
Morrisson, Kean	1	2	2		
Miller, John	1	1	2		
Murchison, Alex	1	1	3		
Maine, Mary	1		3		
Mun, Niel	1				
Martin, Alex (Rock Fish)	1	5	1		
Murphy, James	1	2	2		
Meachum, Mark	1		2		
Massey, John	2	1	3		
Melton, Charles	1		1		
Moore, Thomas	1	2	4		
Murray, Leonard	1	2	4		
Mitchell, Randal	1	1			1
Monro, Patrick	1	3	4		1
Murphy, Thomas	2	4	4		5
Maloy, Daniel	2	2	3		
Mun, Malcolm	1	2	1		
Mathews, Anthony	1	3	4		
Morrisson, Norman	2	1	3		
Morrisson, Daniel	1	3	3		
McKeathen, John	1	3	3		6
McNiel, Malcolm	3	2	4		6
McMurtry, James	1	1	1		
McKay, John	3	2	4		9
McLeod, Daniel	1	3	4		
McNiel, Archd	1				
McArthur, Peter	1	1	2		
McArthur, Daniel	4		5		
McAllester, Coll	3	3	4		15
McPherson, Collin	2				1
McNiel, John (Bluff)	1				8
McRae, Farquhard	2	3	2		
McNiel, Daniel (Black River)	1	2	1		8
McNiel, Niel	1	3	2		1
McRainey, Niel	2	2	3		
McLerran, John, Sr	2	1	2		
McAllester, Alexr	5	1	7		40
McNiel, John (son Archd)	1	1	2		14
McNiel, Niel	1	3	2		3
McLeod, John	4	2	1		
McRae, Christr	1	3	5		
McNiel, Laughlan	2				6
McLerran, John, Jr	1	1	5		1
McDugal, Daniel	1		7		
McDugal, John	1	2	2		
McDugal, John (E.)	1	2	1		
McDugal, Alexr	1				
McDugal, Daniel	1				
McKay, Hugh	1				
McNiel, Elizabeth	1	2	5		
McSwaine, Anguish	1		3		
McRae, John	1	2	4		
McPherson, Jonathan	1	4	7		
McLellan, Daniel	1	1	2		
McQueen, Norman	2		2		
McAllister, Ann		3	2		2
McLaine, Archd	3	3	2		2
McDugal, Anguish	1				1
McPherson, William	1	4	4		
McPhail, Malcolm	1	1	2		
McAllister, Alexr	3				1
McRae, Daniel	1		3		
McNiel, Henry	1	2	3		3
McKay, Alexr	2		3		1
McDonald, John	1				
McDuffie, Archd	3	2	4		13
McPherson, Mary	1		2		
McNiel, Sarah		2	2		
McNiel, Nancy		1	2		
McNicoll, Christian			3		
McFarland, Jennett					
McGregory, Alexr	1		1		9
McLeod, Malcolm	1	3	3		
McLaine, Nancy		1	2		
McKinney, Daniel	2	1	2		
McLaine, Daniel	1	1	2		
McNiel, Malcolm	1	5	3		6
McDonald, Archd	1	1	1		
McDonald, Angus	1		1		1
McKinnen, Hector	1	3	2		2
McKinney, Mathew	2	3	4		14
McNiel, John	1	4	4		...
McMillen, Gilbert	3		3		

FAYETTE DISTRICT, CUMBERLAND COUNTY (EXCLUDING FAYETTEVILLE TOWN)—Continued.

NAME OF HEAD OF FAMILY.	Free white males of 16 years and upward, including heads of families.	Free white males under 16 years.	Free white females, including heads of families.	All other free persons.	Slaves.
McLeod, Alexr	1	5	4		
McNiel, Niel	1	1	3		2
McLeod, William	1	1	5		
McDugal, Katy			2		
McKeathen, Niel	1	6	4		
McLaine, Daniel	1		2		
McKellar, John	3	1	3		
McMillen, James	1	1	3		
McLaine, John (Dobbins Creek)	1	2	5		
McLaine, Alexr	3		2		
McLaine, Daniel	1	1	4		
McDugal, John	2		4		
McNatt, Robert	3	2	4		
McCreman, Peter	1	1	3		
McSwaine, Angus	1	1	2		
McMillen, Niel	1	3	2		
McRae, Daniel	1	2	3		
McNabb, James	3	2	1		
McIntire, Duncan	1	3	1		
McIntire, Nicholas	1	1	1		
McNicoll, James	1				2
McDugal, Hugh	1				
McIntire, Duncan	2		2		
McLeod, Rodorick	2		1		
McIntosh, Daniel	2	1	4		
McAuley, Auley	2		2		
McAuley, James	1	2	3		
McRae, Philip	1		1		
McRae, Collin	2	1	1		
McDuffie, Duncan	1		1		7
McAlpin, Niel	1	1	1		3
McDuffee, George	1		1		2
McMillen, Edward	1	5	5		
McLeod, Roderick	1	1	2		
McNiel, Laughlan	1	1	5		
McNiel, Niel	1	2	5		
McNiel, Hector	1	1	6		1
McGregor, Hector	1	1	5		
McIntire, John	1				
McColl, Daniel	1	2	3		
McKinnen, Angus	1	2	3		
McPherson, Alexr	1	1	2		1
McCaller, Archd	1	4	3		
McLeod, Niel	1				
McDonald, Randal	1				
McLeod, John	1	2	1		
McDonald, Niel	2	5	2		
McAllum, Duncan	1	3	5		
McMillen, John	4	1	2		
McLeod, Norman	2		3		1
McIntire, Duncan	1	1	3		
McKinnen, Daniel	1				
McIntire, Daniel	2	5	3		
McKellar, John	1	5	1		
McKellar, Malcolm	1				
McDuffee, Alphia			2		
McAlpin, John	1	2	4		
McRae, Malcolm	1	1	2		
McLeod, Norman	1	1	1		
McLaine, John (M.)	2	4	3		14
McLaine, Archd	3	3	2		2
McLaine, Hector	1	3	4		8
McLeod, Murdock	1				
McNiel, Laughlan	1	4	3	2	
McLeod, John	1		2		
McLeod, Norman	1		3		
McKinnen, John	2		1		
McLeod, John	1	1	2		
McLaine, Daniel	1	1	2		1
McPhail, John	2	1	4		
McKay, Duncan	1	1	4		
McRae, John	1	2	4		
McRae, Rodorick	2	1	1		
McNiel, Niel	1	2	2		
McRae, Peggy			2		
McPherson, Alexr	1		2		7
McKay, Malcolm	1				9
McKay, Niel	1				6
McKay, Archd, Sr	2	3	5		19
McGugan, Archd	1		3		
McAuley, Murdock	2		2		
McKellar, Nelly	1	2	4		
McLaine, Hugh	1				1
McLaine, Murdock	1	2	4		1
McKellar, Nelly		3	3		
McPherson, John	1	2	5		1
McIntosh, Duncan	1	2	3		
McLaine, Daniel	1	1	4		1
McIntire, John	1		3		
McMillen, Mary			2		
McKeathen, Malcolm	1		4		1
McNiel, Daniel (Little R.)	1	5	2		10
McInnis, John	1	3	2		
McKellar, Duncan	3	1	3		
McNiel, Hector (son Archd)	1	2	2		6
McNiel, John (Skeablin)	2	3	4		
McNiel, Archd, Sr. (L. R.)	1		1		30
McDugal, Duncan	3	2	3		
McDugal, John	1	1	2		
McColl, Niel	1		2		
McKenzie, Duncan	1	1	1		
McLeod, John	1		2		
McLeod, Malcolm	1	1	1		
McSwaine, Rorey	1	2	1		
McCremon, Sarah	1	2	3		
McDaniel, Rorey	1		3		
McLaine, John	1	1	3		
McLaine, Christian	1	2	3		
McFall, Flora	1	2	3		
McLeod, Christian	1		5		
McLaine, Murdock	2	2	2		2
McDonald, Duncan	2	5	3		
McMillen, Archd	1	1	5		
McQueen, Timothy	2		1		
McMillen, Archd	1	4	4		
McKewing, Alexr	1	1	3		
McDaniel, David	1	4	2		
McAlpin, Angus	2	2	2		2
McIntire, Charles	1				
McNatt, James	1	1	4		
McKeathen, Niel	1	1	2		
McDugal, Angus (Weaver)	2				
McLeod, Roderick	1	1	2		
McLain, Daniel, Jr	1	1	3		
McLaine, John (Indian S.)	2	1	3		
McNiel, Malcolm	1	1	3		
McRae, Alexr	1	1	4		
McNiel, Niel (ShoeM)	1	3	5		
McDugal, Daniel	1				
McDaniel, Katy	2	4	3		
McLaine, Archd	1	5	2		
McSwaine, John	1		1		
McKinney, Niel	1				
McQueen, Daniel	1	1	2		
McDugal, Daniel, Sr	1	4	3		2
McDugal, Daniel, Jr	1		5		
McGee, Duncan	1				
McKeathen, Niel	1	1	2		
McDugal, Anguish	1				
McDugal, Alexr	2		5		
McKay, Archd	2		2		1
McDuffee, Malcolm	1				
McGill, Margaret	1	2	4		
McDuffee, Niel	1	2	1		
McPhail, John (Black R.)	1	2	1		1
McDaniel, Nancy	1	2	3		
McPhail, Dugal, Sr	2		2		
McQueen, Daniel	2		2		1
McLerran, Niel	1		2		
McLerran, Archd	1	1	2		
McKeathen, Daniel	1	1	4		
McKeathen, James, Jr	1	1	3		
McKeathen, James, Sr	1		1		2
McIntire, Gilbert	4	2	2		
McLeod, Daniel	2		2		
McArthur, James	1	1	1		
McLellen, John	3		3		
McGugan, John	2		2		
McLerran, Duncan, Sr	4		3		2
McPhail, Dugal, Jr	1	1	1		
McIntire, Archd	2	1	6		
McNiel, Duncan, esqr	2	2	3	5	7
McDaniel, William Gray	1	3	1		4
McDaniel, John	1	1	2		3
McPhadging, Stephen	1	1	3	1	
McDaniel, Archd	1	1	2		
McGugan, Archd	1		3		
McPherson, Niel	1	1	2		
McSwaine, Daniel	1	1	2		
McMillen, Alexr	1	3	7		1
McColl, Dugal	1	2	5		
McDuffee, Archd	1	3	6		
Nunnery, Amos	1	2	1		
Newberry, Jesse	1	2			17
Newberry, John	1	1	4		4
Northington, John	1		1		11
Nicolson, Niel	2	1	5		
Newberry, John, Sr	1		2		
Northington, Samuel, Jr	1	2	3		12
Newsome, Hartwell	1				
Northington, Samuel, Sr	2	2	1		6
Northington, Jesse	1	4	2		7
Needson, Angus	1	6	2		
Overton, Titus					11
Ocheltree, Hugh	1	1	3		6
Osborn, William	1	1	1		
Patterson, Daniel, Jr	1	3	3		5
Pearle, James	1	2	2		2
Porch, Solomon	2	1	3		7
Phares, John	4	5	5		
Pettiford, Philip				9	
Patterson, Malcolm	1	3	4		2
Perry, Robert	1		1		
Peyton, Thomas	3		1		3
Phillips, William	4		2	4	
Parker, Jacob	1	4	3		7
Parker, David	1	1	5		
Patterson, Niel	1	1	1		
Patterson, Daniel	1	3	6		
Patterson, Duncan	1		1		
Patterson, John	1	3	3		
Patterson, Daniel	1	1	4		5
Plomer, Richard	1		1		
Parker, John	3	3	5		1
Price, Gideon	1				
Pickett, Thomas	1		1		7
Pegram, Richardson	1				4
Pegram, William	1	2	4		1
Patterson, John	2	1	3		
Phares, Samuel	1	4	2		
Phares, John, Sr	1	1	4		
Patterson, Barbara			1		1
Powell, Margaret		1	3		
Po, Elizabeth	1	2	3		
Peterson, John	2	2	3		
Phillips, Margaret	1	3	3		
Purcell, Niel	2	3	2		
Purcell, Daniel	1	3	4		
Porter, Philip	1		2		
Parker, William	3	3	6		
Prince, Nathan	4	4	8		6
Prince, John	1				
Pope, John	5	2	3		
Parsons, Harrison	1				
Prescot, Simon	1				
Philips, Duncan, Sr	1		3		
Patterson, Daniel	1	1	3		
Reeves, Nathaniel	1	2	2		5
Reeves, John D	1	1	1		
Reeves, Darling	1	2	2		3
Ringstaff, Adam	1		3		
Ray, John	2	2	4		4
Russell, Mark	2	2	2		7
Roberts, Philip	1	1	4		
Ray, John	1	4	1		
Reese, Jarrott	1	1	3		
Ryal, Richard	1	1	6		
Roberson, Edward	3	2	3		1
Reeves, Jesse	1				
Rover, James	1		1		
Readen, Robert	1				
Roberts, Philip	1				
Roper, Jesse	3	2	7		
Ray, John	1	3	2		
Ray, Duncan	1	2	8		2
Rogers, Shadrack	1	3	2		
Ray, Malcolm	2		1		
Richards, Morris	1				
Rowan, Robert	2	1	4		11
Ray, Anguish	1				
Ray, Anguish	1	2			5
Raines, Anthony	1	3	5		
Rayford, Robert	1	2	3		9
Ray, John	2		3		3
Raines, Christo	1		1		
Ritcheson, Elizabeth		1	4		
Rand, William	2		4		21
Redding, Timothy	2	1	3		1
Redding, William	2	3	3		2
Roberts, John	1	2	2		
Robertson, Joel	2	5	4		
Roberson, John	1		4		
Ray, Hugh	2	3	4		
Russell, Robert	1	1	2		1
Roberson, Philip	1	3	5		9
Roberson, Mark	1	2	3		1
Redding, Nathan	1	1	2		
Reeves, George	2	1	3		
Ray, Niel	2		4		
Shaw, Daniel	2	5	4		1
Shaw, Collin	2	2	4		2
Shaw, Niel	1		2		
Shaw, Murdock	2	3	4		
Smith, Niel	2				
Stainbeck, Francis	1		1		7
Smith, David	2	5	4		42
Stansell, Peter	2		2		
Strickland, Jesse	3		8		
Shaw, Malcolm	3	1	2		
Smith, William	3	1	5		
Smith, Morris	1		4		
Starling, Robert	1	2	4		
Smith, Archd (Capt)	1	3	2		
Sorrell, John	1	2	6		
Sorrell, Edward	1		5		
Smith, Flora		2	3		1

FAYETTE DISTRICT, CUMBERLAND COUNTY (EXCLUDING FAYETTEVILLE TOWN)—Continued.

NAME OF HEAD OF FAMILY.	Free white males of 16 years and upward, including heads of families.	Free white males under 16 years.	Free white females, including heads of families.	All other free persons.	Slaves.
Sutton, John	2		2		
Smith, Nathan	1		2		
Strahorn, Sarah	1		1		
Shaw, Dusee	3	4	4		4
Stephenson, Henry	1	1	2		1
Smith, Stephen	2	3	3		
Shaw, Norman	1	2	1		
Shaw, Sarah	1	2	1		
Smiley, James	2		3		
Smith, Enus	1		1		
Shaw, Daniel	2		2		6
Smiley, Jacob	1	2	2		4
Stephens, Solomon	1				
Stewart, George	1	1	1		1
Screws, Benjamin	1				
Smith, David	1		2		
Smith, Joab	1	1	3		
Smith, Drury	1	5	2		
Small, John	1		1		
Stewart, Alexr	2	1	1		
Stewart, John	2	4	4		
Smith, John	1		1		3
Sims, Isaac	1		1		
Sims, William	1	4	5		
Smith, John	1	3	4		
Smith, Lewis	1				
Smith, David	1	2	2		
Smith, William	1	3	4		
Smith, James	1				
Sims, James	1				
Sypress, Francis	1	3	2		
Stephens, William	1	1	1		6
Smith, Alexr	1		1		
Smith, John	1				
Smith, William	1	3	4		
Smith, Archd	2		3		
Smith, Hugh	1	1	3		
Stewart, Robert	2	3	1		5
Smith, Edward	1		9		1
Smith, Archd	1	1	2		
Smith, John	3	1	2		
Smith, Duncan	1		1		4
Sullivant, William	1	2	4		
Shaw, Patrick	1	4	2		
Shaw, John	1		2		
Stewart, Daniel	1	3	2		1
Smith, Daniel	1	1	2		
Smith, William	1		1		
Stewart, Norman	3	4	4		
Shaw, Murdock (R. F.)	1	3	4		
Smith, Peter	1				
Smith, Margaret	2		3		
Sentor, William	1	1	3		
Sentor, Stephen	1	1	2		
Sorrell, Lewis	1	2	7		
Scoggins, Sarah		2	3		
Smith, Daniel	1	1	2		
Smith, Hugh	1	1	3		
Shaw, Duncan	1		5		
Stewart, John	1	4	4		
Stewart, Joseph	1	2	1		
Stewart, Charles	1	1	2		1
Stewart, George	1		2		
Smith, John	1	1	6		
Shaw, Angus	1	2	1		
Sikes, Lamuel	1		5		
Spiva, James	1	1			
Smith, Philip	1	3	5		
Shaw, Niel, Sr	3	4	4		5
Smith, John (Black S.)	3	2	6		
Shaw, Nancy	1	1	2		
Sims, Isaac	1		2		
Starling, Robert, Jr	1		2		
Sikes, William	1	2	2		
Sawyer, Thomas	1				
Sanders, Richard	1				
Stewart, Alexr (B. River)	1		2		
Stewart, Daniel (E.)	1	1	2		
Smith, Patrick	2		2		
Smith, Alexr	1	1	1		
Stone, Elias	1	1	2		
Sims, Isaac (Willis's Creek)	1	2	5		2
Sims, Benjamin	2	2	5		2
Trapnell, William	1		2		1
Taylor, John	2	1	4		
Tyler, Aron	2	3	6		
Torry, David	1	4	2		2
Thompson, Peter	3	1	5		2
Turner, James	2		5		5
Tully, John	3	1	1		
Trent, Simon	2	1	4		
Tedder, Jesse	1		2		
Thompson, Malcolm	5	2			3
Tommy, Jonathan	1		8		11
Theams, William	1	4	4		
Tedder, William	1	2	3		
Thegod, George	1		2		
Taylor, Thomas	1	1	2		1
Thomas, John	1	1	2		
Torry, James	1	5	2		1
Torry, John	1		2		
Turner, William	1	1	2		
Townsend, Thomas	1	2	4		
Torry, George	1	1	4		1
Terrell, Micajah	2	4	5		4
Thompson, Niel	2	1	1		
Todd, Joseph	1	1	2		
Thomas, Philip	3	2	3		
Teel, Sampson	1				3
Thomas, Barnaby	1				
Tucker, George	1	4	2		
Thompson, Benjamin	1	1	1		
Tully, Allen	1				
Tully, John, Jr	1				
Tedder, Thomas	2	3	6		
Taylor, Niel	1	2	2		
Taylor, Catherine			1	1	1
Thomas, William	4	1	5		
Theams, Thomas	1	2	3		
Theams, Jesse	1	2	4		1
Theams, Joseph	1	2	3		27
Vaughn, Susanah					6
Vreeland, Henry	1				
Vennagam, John	1				
Vaughn, Anna	2		2		
Urquhart, Norman	1	3	5		
Urquhart, Henry	2	3	5		
Utley, William	1	2	6		
Willson, Robert	1	1	4		4
Washburn, James	1				
Watson, William	4		1		
Walker, Benjamin	3	2	4		9
Wilkerson, Niel	2	6	2		
Williams, Isaac	1	4	1		27
Watson, John	1	3	2		5
Williams, Joel	1				21
Williams, Isaac	1	2	5		
Walker, William L	2	4	6		
Williams, Amos	1	1	3		
Watson, James	1		2		
Williams, Thomas	1	1	2		
Watson, David	3		2		
White, William	1		2		
Willson, Samuel	1		1		
Williams, Rowland	1	1			
Warner, John	1	3	4		1
Warner, Edward	1		1		
Walker, John	1	1	2		
Walker, Solomon	1	1	2		
Warner, Hardin	1	1	3		
West, Onesiphorus	3		1		
Wilder, John	1	1	4	1	
Withersby, Joab	1				
Ward, Mary		2	2		
White, William	1		2		
Watson, Henry D	1				
Williams, Samuel	1	1	2		19
Wright, Katy	1	1	5		
Wright, Duncan	1	2	5		
Williams, William	1		1		
Williamson, Frederick	1				
Williamson, Thomas	1	3	4		
Williford, John	1	1	4		
Walker, Francis	2	1	8		
Williford, Richard	1	1	2		
Wammock, Benjamin	2	2	4		7
Wilson, John	1	1	2		4
White, Henry	1	1	2		
Willis, Sarah	1	1	3		1
Willis, Agerton	1		3		2
Willis, Jeremiah	1	2	5		1
Willis, Benjamin	1		3		1
Young, Thomas	4	2	6		
Yarborough, Joseph	1	2	4		1
Zachary, Jonathan	1	1	1		4
Calvert, William	1		1		
Stewart, John (Tweed-side)	1		1		4
Mullony, Jeremiah	1				
Cameron, John	1	2	3		
Holliway, David	2	2	4		2
Johnston, Simon	1	2	5		
Murchison, Philip	1	3	2		
McLeod, John	1	3	5		
Roberts, Thomas	4	2	6		
Campbell, Malcolm	1	1	2		
Johnston, Duncan	1	1	2		1
Kelley, Angus	2		3		
Leach, Dugal	1		2		
McDuffee, Allen	1				
McNiel, John (Sand Hills)	2	3	5		12
McKinnen, Kennith	1	2	3		
McKeathen, John	1				
McLaine, Niel	1	2	3		
Smith, Robert	4		4		
Smith, Daniel (Capt)	1	1	3		
Priest, Mrs		2			
Melton, John	1		1		
McNiel, Mary			4		7
Ocheltree, Flora			1	1	1
McPherson, John	2		1		
McNaughton, Alexr	1		2		
Moore, Alexr	1		2		
Hope, William	1		2		
Vaughn, Elizabeth		3	4		

FAYETTE DISTRICT, FAYETTEVILLE TOWN.

NAME OF HEAD OF FAMILY.	Free white males of 16 years and upward, including heads of families.	Free white males under 16 years.	Free white females, including heads of families.	All other free persons.	Slaves.
Porterfield, James	4		2		28
McLaine, Daniel	1	2	1		
Bowell, Lewis	7	3	3		
McDugal, Angus	2				
Moore, James	4	2	6		15
Rayford, Philip	2				11
Bloodworth, James	3	5	3		18
Cook, William (& Edwards)	4	4	4		15
McLennen, Collin	1	1	4		
Carmichael, John	2	3	2		
Mitchell, Robert	1	5	2		1
Twigg, Daniel	2	2	3		
Meadows, Ann		1	1		
Doud, Thomas	1		1		
McMillen, Alpha		1	1		
Tannasee, Michael	1	1			
Hero, Mrs	1		1		2
Morfitts, Henry P	2		1		5
Parish, John	1	1	2		
Ward, Nathan & Co	3				
McFarlane, Robert	3				2
Baker, James	3				1
Clark & McLeran	3				
Black, Daniel	4	1	3		
Ritchie, James	4				1
Campbell, Dugal	1				
Miles, William	2		2		1
Eccles, John	3				11
Winslow, John	2		4		2
Howie, Samuel	1				
Duke, Mark	1		2		3
Staunton, Augustine	2	2	1		2
Stiert, Sebastian	2	1			2
Leonard, James	1		2		3
Anderson, David	2				1
Fullar, Samuel	4				1
Stedman, Elisha	2				3
Meng, William	2				
McRae, Findley	1	1	1		
Ellington, Joel	1	1	1		
Trevathen, Lewis	1	1	4		
Ferguson, Alexr	1				
Norris, Robert & William	3				4
Perry & Tarbe	3				2
Young, Alexr	2	1	2		2
Bachop & Patterson	2				1
Fenno, Samuel	2	3	2		3
Dubrutz, Gabriel	2				4
Wheaton, Daniel	1				
Sissions, Isaac	1				
Lutterloh, Henry E	1				2
Malbone, Saunders	1				1
Murchison, Kinnith	3	1	2		1
McLeod, John	1				
Carrol, James	1				
McMurphy, Daniel	1	2	4		3
Burklow, Isaac	5	5	5		4
Strong, Peter	2	1			2
England, William	2	2	7		25
McFedran, John	1		2		1
Rearden, John	1		1		2

FAYETTE DISTRICT, FAYETTEVILLE TOWN—Continued.

NAME OF HEAD OF FAMILY.	Free white males of 16 years and upward, including heads of families.	Free white males under 16 years.	Free white females, including heads of families.	All other free persons.	Slaves.
M'Rae, Duncan	2	1	4		
Murley, Samuel	1				
Gee, James	3	2	4		3
Burnsides, James	1		1		
Lowry, John	2	2	1		
Howat, James	3				1
Powell & Faux	5	1	1		1
Dugan, Joseph	2				
Bebee, Asa	1				
Bland, Joseph	1	1	2		
Adam, Robert	4		3		6
Riley, William	1	2	3		
Gillespie, William	1	1	1		1
Ray, Daniel	1	2	4		
Peacock, Jesse	1	3	3		4
Simpson, John	2				3
Gerry, John	1		2		1
Cant, James	2	1	1	1	
Armour, James	1	2	1		
Walker, George	2	3	3		
Morrisson, Allen	1				
Bethune, Murdock	1	1	3		
Stradford, Sally		1	2		
Golden, Richard	1	3	3		
Lasseter, James	1	1	1		
Hammonds, Isaac				5	
Oliver, William	3		2		
Bane, Hugh	1	1	1		
Story, Patrick	1	1	6		
Belile, Mary			3		
Roling, Nancy		1	1		
Roling, Anna	1	2	1		
M'Leod, Daniel	1		3		
Walsh, John	3	1	5		
M'Millen, Daniel	1		6		
Henderson, Catharine			2		
Murchison, Alexr	2	1	3		4
M'Pherson, John	1				
Johnston, Ann			2		
Richards, Morriss	1		3		
Richey, John	1	2	5		
M'Donald, Hugh	1		1		
Pevee, James				1	
Cole, Mark	2	3	2		1
Osborne, James	1	1	3		
Lockhart, James	1				
M'Donald, Philip	1				
Campbell, Charles	1	1	1		
Fletcher, Rebecca		1	2		7
Kenan, Lawrence	1	1	2		
Smith, Joseph	2				
Biggam, Alexr	1				2
Hawley, Isaac	9	1	1		
Owens, Francis	1				
M'Auslan, Duncan	4				3
Mabry, Jordan	1				
Armstrong, William	1	3	5		4
Newman, Benjamin	1				
M'Arthur, Peter	1	3	4		
Osgood, Christo	1				
Hallet, Richard	2				
Stewart, Archd	1	1	1		
Lamon, John	2		4		
Morrisson, James	2	1	1		2
Greenlees, Robert	1				
Alves, Andrew	1	1	3		
Ellis, John	1	2	2		2
Walker, Mary				1	
Hylan, Michael	1				
Prindle, David	3				
Prindle, Joseph	1				
Walker, Elizabeth			1		
Williamson, John (doctr)	1		1		1
Dick, James	4	3	4	2	1
Bryant, Kedar					4
Martin, Margaret		1	1		
Sutherland, Ann		2	3		4
Hicks, Robert	4		1		
Chisolm, Findley	1	1	3		
Chavers, Mary				1	
Murphy, Thomas C	1		3		
Boyd, Sarah		1	2		
Clide, Robert	1				
Wilson, John (constable)	2	2	3		2
Mears, James	3	3	4		
Mumford, Robeson	1	1	4		6
Wilson, John	2	1	2		5
Swarthlander, Philip	1				
Crawford, Dennis	1				
Kiddia, The Revd Mr	1	1	1		
Thackston, James	1				9
Cutlar, Roger	3	1			
Simpson, Jane			2		13
Ingram, John	1				10
Bolitho, Benjamin	1				
Dekeyser, Lee	3		6		7
Carrol, William	1				
Branton, Thomas	2	1	2		25
English, William	1				
Cochran, Richard	4		1		25
Emmet, Margaret		1	2		7
Willis, John	2		4		14
Shaw, John	1	2	3		
Lumsden, John	2	1	1		1
Elting, James & Edward	2				
Hawkins, Abraham				1	
Bowen, Luke	1	1			2
Winslow, Mary			1		5
Grove, William B	1				17
Currants, Rachael			3	3	3
Sibly, John	7	2	1	1	1
Crawford, William	1		2		2
M'Millen, Jennet			2		
M'Kinnen, Laxy			2		
Grimes, Aphia			1		
Craig, Adam	1	2	1		1
Ranter, Minis	1	1	1		
Dye, Mary		1	2		
Van, William	2	1	7		4
Craine, Anthony	1	1	1		
Bass, William	1		1	5	
Keys, William	1		4		
Moon, Peter	1		1		
Sullivant, Dennis	1	2	1		
Taylor, Jacob	1		2		
Lundy, James	1	2	3		
Ciccaty, Holly		1	7		
Jarrott, Richard	1	5	1		
Jacobs, William					1
White, Thomas	1		3	2	5
Glass, Thomas	1				
Almady, Joseph	1		2		2
Carman, Joshua	1			1	13
Rainey, John	1				
Lachman, Frederick	1				
M'Iver, Alexr	2	3	1		6
Colbraith, Niel	1				
M'Murtry, James	2	1	1		
Walker, James	1	2	5		
Hay, John	1	1	3		10
Brenan, James	2				
Kelly, John	1				
Basset, Cornelius	1				
Turner, Benjamin	1		1		1
Lee, Henry	1				
M'Guire, Edward	1				
Kennedy, John	1				6
Donaldson, Robert & Co	3				1
Pyne, Joseph	3		2		2
Pierce, Oliver & Nathan	2				
Jordan & Burke	2			1	
Taylor, John Louis	1				1
Oniel, Patrick	1				
Jackson, William	1	1	2		
Green, John	1				
Naylor, John	3	2	1		3
Dudley, Guilford	2	2	4		6
Thompson, George	1	1	4		
Read, Lucy					
Barge, George	1	1	3		
Hargan, David	1	1	2		
Saltonstall, Gurdon F	1	1	2		1
Peale, John	1				
Campbell, Archd	2		2		
Young, James	1	1	2		
Smith, George	1	1	2		
Campbell, Duncan	1		1		3
Mott, Joseph	1	1	3		3
Shepherd, David	3	1	5		1
Johnston, Priscilla			1		2
White, James	2	2	3		
Potts, Jesse	1		2		9
M'Naughton, Walter	1				1
Hall, Peter	1		2		1
Langton, John	1		3		2
Work, John	1				
Charles, John	1	1			1
Davis, Dolphin	2	1	3		13
Campbell, Alexr	1		5		1
Newell, Ann		1	2	1	
Young, John	1	2	1		
M'Racking, James	2	3	2		1
Warson, Thomas	1		1		2
Cook, Edmund	3		1		
Smith, John	1				
Fabre, Peter	1				
Hogg, James (of Hillsborough)					2
Campbell, Polly			2		
Spiller, Margaret			1		5
M'Leod, Norman (S. Carpr)	1	1	2		
M'Phail, John	1	2	1		
M'Phail, Peggy			3		
M'Coll, Hugh	1				
Thompson, Daniel	1				
Meeks, James	1				
Tatham, Charles	1				
M'Intire, Peter	1		2		
Tibathan, Elizabeth			3	4	
M'Arthur, Alexr	1				
Fretts, John	1				
Bittle, John	1		2		
Russell, William	1		2		7
Lamon, Jacob	1	1	1		
M'Cants, William	2				1
M'Naughton, John	1	2	3		
Toney, John				5	
Arintz, James	2				1
Coffey, Thomas	2	1	1		
Steeley, William	1				
Callender & Dean	2				
M'Call, Archd	1				
Kerr, The Revd Mr	3	2	2		3

FAYETTE DISTRICT, MOORE COUNTY.

NAME OF HEAD OF FAMILY.	Free white males of 16 years and upward, including heads of families.	Free white males under 16 years.	Free white females, including heads of families.	All other free persons.	Slaves.
Campbell, John	1	1	2		
Mathews, Thomas	7	2	3		7
M'Bride, Archd	1		4		
Watts, Mary			4		
Teague, William	1	2	4		
Glascock, John Melton	1	2	2		
Caddell, James	4		2		
Fry, Nathan	1		2		
Kenney, John	2	2	4		
Glascock, Patty	3	1	6		5
Tison, Cornelius	2		2		
Tison, Benjamin	1	1	3		
Doud, Mary		3	5		3
Tison, Aron	3	3	4		
Sutton, James	1		3		
Temples, Neeham	2	1	1		
Petty, Hubbard	1	5	6		
Petty, John	1	1	6		
M'Daniel, Milley	3		4		
Clark, Jabas	1	1	2		
Barret, William	1	2	3		1
Quimby, John	1		4		
Overton, Thomas	1		4		14
Brown, Joseph	1	1	2		
Jones, Lucy			3		
Fagan, Richardson	1	4	4		1
Wadsworth, Jason	3	1	2		
Bettis, Elijah	2	3	5		3
Grimes, Thomas	3		3		
Grimes, Robert	2	1	3		
Caddell, Jonathan	1		4		1
M'Intosh, Alexr	1	1	2		
Monro, Margaret			4		
M'Rae, Mary		2	4		
M'Kenzie, John	1	2	4		
Murchison, Kenneth	1	4	4		
Hill, James	3		5		
Richeson, William	1	2	1		
M'Intosh, Alexr	1	1	3		
Richeson, Drury	1	1	3		
M'Intosh, Duncan	1	1	2		
Milton, Nathl	1	3	1		
M'Lennan, Mary	2	2	1		
Chapman, Abner	2		4		17
M'Intosh, John	1	3	2		
M'Intosh, Daniel	1	1	2		
Sinclair, John	1	4	4		
Davis, Ralph	2				
Bean, Richard	1	2	5		
Humphry, William	1	1	1		
Morris, Stephen	1		2		
Muse, Jesse	1	3	1		
Muse, Charity		1	5		2
Bullock, John	5		2		
Upton, Edward	1		1		
Upton, John	1	2	4		
Bullock, Francis	1		3		

FAYETTE DISTRICT, MOORE COUNTY—Continued.

NAME OF HEAD OF FAMILY.	Free white males of 16 years and upward, including heads of families.	Free white males under 16 years.	Free white females, including heads of families.	All other free persons.	Slaves.
Seale, William	1	3	4		1
Dun, William	1	2	1		1
Shepherd, John	2	1	3		3
Carrol, John	2	4	3		
Coupland, William	1		3	1	
Bean, Elijah	1		1	2	
Harrington, Sion	1				
Hews, John	1	4	2		
Buie, Gilbert	1				2
Morris, Frederick	2			1	
Bettis, Elijah	3	3	4		2
Carmichael, Graziel		3	3		
Cheek, Robert	3		3		
Caddell, William	1		2		
Baker, John	1	2	4		3
Eggleton, Thomas	3	2	4		
Johnston, Philip	1	1	4		4
McIntosh, Duncan	1	1	2		
Murchison, Duncan	1	1	3		
Campbell, Duncan	1	2	3		
Ottery, Absalom	1	5	2		
McDonald, Alexr	1		1		
Ottery, Mary	1	3	5		
Ottery, James	1	1	3		
Fry, Benjn	1	4	2		
Pitman, Demcy	1	4	7		
Cox, William	1	3	1		
Wadsworth, John	1	4	3		
Oliver, Willis	2	1	2		
Black, Archd	2	1	2		1
Mears, William	1		2		4
Danelly, William	1		4		
McIntosh, Daniel	1		1		
Watson, Hugh	1	3	1		
Watson, Robert	2	3	2		
Davis, Vincent	1		2		
McAuley, William	1	4	1		
Cook, William	2	4	5		
Smith, Everat	2	3	3		
Tidwell, Jeany			2		
Cagle, David	1		2		
Cagle, Leonard	1	7	3		
Boals, Robert	2	2	1		
Goings, William				10	
Yow, Christopher	2	5	4		
Tidwell, Samuel	1		3		
Campbell, Duncan	1	2	3		
Melton, James	1		2		
McKenzie, William	1	1	3		
Garner, Peter	1	3	2		
Love, Daniel	1	2	6		
McIntosh, Murdock	1	1	2		
McIver, Rorey	5		2		
Campbell, Mathew	2		6		
McIver, John	1	1	7		
Cagle, Henry	3	4	4		
Cockman, Joseph	4	1	3		
Moore, Edward, Jr	1		2		
Cagle, Christian	1	1	1		
Patterson, Duncan	1	3	1		
Manus, William	4	3	9		
Ballard, James	2	2	4		
Smotherman, Thomas	2	4	1		
McDonald, Hugh	2	4	3		
McLaine, John	1		2		
Underwood, George	1	4	5		
Blew, Peter	1	3	4		2
Murchison, Murdock	1				
Grimes, Daniel	2	1	1		
McIver, Duncan	1	1	2		
Blew, Duncan	1	2	3		1
Morrison, Maurice	1	1	2		
Overton, John, Sr	1		1		23
Fry, Joseph	2	2	6		
Ritter, Jesse	2	2	5		
Cagle, John	2	2	3		
Stubbs, Jacob	1		1		
Ray, Archd	1		1		
McNiel, Hector	3	1	3		10
Williamson, William	1	4	4		1
Manus, James	1				
Ray, James	2		4		
Murchison, Barbara	1	2	2		
McSwaine, Nancy		1	3		
Smith, Zachariah	2	5	1		
Stubbs, Jacob	3	1	2		
McRae, Murdock	1	2	3		
Hannon, Thomas, Jr	1		2		
Davis, William	2	3	4		6
Smith, Thomas	2	1	2		
Wallace, Everat	1		2		
McDaniel, John	1		2		
Blew, John	1	1	2		
McNiel, John	1	2	3		
McLaine, Niel	1		5		
Patterson, Daniel	1		3		2
Baker, John	2	1	2		
McLeod, Alexr	2	1	5		

NAME OF HEAD OF FAMILY.	Free white males of 16 years and upward, including heads of families.	Free white males under 16 years.	Free white females, including heads of families.	All other free persons.	Slaves.
McDonald, John	4		2		
Cagle, Roger	1	1	2		
Cagle, George	1		2		
Collins, Thomas, Jr	2	3	4		
Thompson, Thomas	1	5	2		
Read, William	1	2	4		
McIntosh, John	1		1		
Manus, Daniel	1	3	2		
Williamson, John	1	2	3		
Ramage, Darius	1		1		
Bethune, John	1	2	8		
Bean, Jesse	1		3		
McCaskill, Angus	3	1	2		
Oliver, Willis	1	4	2		
Schamburger, Peter	2	3	6		1
Teague, William	2	4	5		
Griffin, Jesse	1		4		1
Davis, Robert	2		4		1
Cheek, Richard	1	2	3		
McLeod, Norman	1	2	3		
Fry, George	1	2	8		
Robeson, Daniel	1	6	4		
Records, John	1		2		9
Parsons, Samuel	1		1		6
Brady, James	1	3	5		
Furrow, Leonard	1	4	2		
Dickinson, Willis	2	2	5		
Dun, Hezekiah	1	4	3		
Dun, Richard	1	2	3		
Keys, Thomas	2	7	3		
Eddins, Theophilus	1		3		
Munro, Daniel	3		1		6
Patterson, John	3		2		5
Murchison, Kennith	1	3	4		
Patterson, Robert	1	3	4		
Bethune, Christo	1		1		
Thomas, Keziah			1		
Tolman, Nancy		1	2		
Campbell, Alexr	2	3	5		
Caddell, John	1	2	1		
Morgan, William	1		2		
Dickinson, Robert	1	5	4		
Smith, Nathan	1		1		
Brown, Ambrose	1	2	2		
McDuffie, John	3	1	3		
McDonald, Flora	1	2	3		
Ritter, Thomas	1	1	2		
Muse, James	1	4	2		
Hargrove, John	1		6		
Hannon, Thomas, Sr	1	1	3		
Murray, Duncan	1	1	3		
Richeson, David	1		5		
Morgan, John	2	4	4		
Smith, William	1	1	4		
Ritter, John	1	2	2		
Coggin, Mathew	1	2	5		
Keys, John	3	2	5		
McDonald, John	1	3	2		
McDonald, William	1		2		
Newton, William		1	2		
Monk, Daniel	1	2	2		
Carrender, George	3	3	4		1
Ottery, Elijah	1	3	2		
McIver, Angus	1	3	1		
McCremon, Malcolm	1	3	4		
McCremon, Norman	1	1	2		
Allen, Joseph	1	3	1		
McNiel, John	2	3	2		
Cooper, Benjamin	2	3	2		
Street, Anthony	3	3	3		1
King, William	1	2	1		
Sewell, John	1	2	2		
McIver, Alexr	2	2	2		
Wordsworth, Archd	1				
Hews, William	1		3		
King, Stephen	2	1	4		
McKenzie, Murdock	1	1	3		
Fry, Thomas	1	2	5		
Hodges, Edmund	1		4		
McLeod, John	1		2		
Johnston, Duncan	1	4	3		
Collins, James	1	2	3		2
Maples, Burwell	1	1	2		
Collins, Stephen	1		2		
Smith, William	1	1	4		
Hair, John	1	3	2		
Cox, Henry	1	1	3		
Hair, Peter	1		4		
Worthy, John	1	1	2		
Riddle, James	1	3	6		1
Jackson, Nelson	1		4		
Cox, Moses	1	1	2		
Jackson, Christian	1		2	1	2
Jackson, Nancy		3	2		3
Jackson, Margaret			2	4	
Gilmour, Thomas	1	1	2		
McAuley, John, Sr	2		2		
Wicker, Jonathan	1	1	1		

NAME OF HEAD OF FAMILY.	Free white males of 16 years and upward, including heads of families.	Free white males under 16 years.	Free white females, including heads of families.	All other free persons.	Slaves.
Kennedy, David	1	2	1		
Kennedy, Alexr	2	6	3		
Bryant, Michael	1		2		
Wicker, Benjamin	1		4		
Richeson, Stephen	1	1	4		
Copher, William	1	4	4		
Hurley, Edmund	3	3	3		
Cole, Thomas	1	2	2		
Brown, Jesse	1		4		
Johnston, John	1		3		
Martin, Martin	2	1	2		
Dun, Bartholomew, Jr	1	1	1		
Dun, William	1	3	6		
Campbell, James	1	1	1		
Dun, Thomas	1	1	3		
Williams, George	1	4	2		
Buchannan, John	2	2	2		
Dun, Bartholomew, Sr	1		2		
Manus, Ambrose	1	4	3		
Cagle, George	1	2	2		
McNiel, Hector	1	1	4		
Cox, Edward	1		3		
Morgan, William	1	1	7		
Sewell, Mary	1	3	3		
Nall, Nicholas	2	1	3		8
Davis, Hardy	1	3	4		
Davis, Thomas	1	2	1		
Garner, John	1	1	2		13
Garner, Lewis	1	1	3		2
Garner, Bradley	1	1	3		1
Dun, Samuel	1		3		
McQueen, Donald	1	1	4		
McKenzie, Murdock	1	2	3		
McDonald, Sarah			3		
Spiva, John	1	3	4		
McAuley, Murdock	1	3	2		
McLaine, Hector	1	1	3		
Cole, John	3	3	3		
Upton, Richard	3		5		
McDonald, Donald	1	2	4		
Shuffil, John, Jr	1	5	1		
Shuffil, John, Sr	3	1	4		
Moore, James	1		1	1	
Martin, Allen	1	1	1		
McDonald, Kennith	1	3	5		
Merrett, James	2	4	6		
McLeod, Anna	2		1		
McIntosh, Peter	1	1	3		
Grimes, George	1	2	2		
Smith, John	1	2	2		
Smith, William	1	1	2		
Carpenter, Owen	3	3	4		
Campbell, Charles	1	1	2		
Martin, William	1	2	3		
Martin, Murdock	1	1	4		1
Morrison, Kennith	1				
Harwick, Jacob	1	2	2		
Campbell, Angus	1	2	4		
Campbell, Angus	1	2	3		
Kitchen, Kintchen	1	2	7		
Cox, George	1				
Seale, William, Jr	1		3		
Sheals, Benjamin	2	5	3		
Evans, John	2	3	3		
Medlin, Joel	3		1		
Medlin, Rebecca		1	1		
Magee, Joseph	1	3	5		7
Smith, Archd	4	3	6		
Carrol, John, Esqr	3	3	5		2
Patterson, Duncan	2	3	4		
Mathews, James	2		1		
Ragsdell, Benjn	1	4	2		
Ragsdell, John	4		2		
Lancaster, Hartwell	1	4	2		
Ragsdell, Richard	1	5	2		
Cole, Andrew	1	2	6		
Buie, Archd	1	2	2		
Price, Lewis	1	2	2		
Phillips, Burwell	1				
Phillips, Mark	1	2	2		
Moore, Onwin	1		1		
Phillips, Lewis	1	2	1		
Phillips, John	2	1	4		
Hood, Abraham	1	1	2		
Maulding, Richard	1		1		
Hews, Niel	1	3	3		
Doud, Cornelius	1		3		3
Medlin, John	2	4	3		
Davis Mathews	3		2		
Tyney, Priscilla			1	2	
Davis, James	1	1	2		
Alston, James	1				3
McLeod, Niel	3	1	1		
Monk, James	1	1	2		
Jackson, James	1	1	1		
Miles, Jesse	1		1		
Doud, Patrick	1				
Dalrymple, Archd	1	1	3		1

FAYETTE DISTRICT, MOORE COUNTY—Continued.

NAME OF HEAD OF FAMILY.	Free white males of 16 years and upward, including heads of families.	Free white males under 16 years.	Free white females, including heads of families.	All other free persons.	Slaves.
Gastor, Henry, Sr	2	1	1		14
Gastor, Henry, Jr	1	6	2		
Dalrymple, John	4		3		5
Davis, Arthur	1		2		
Seale, Charles	1	3	3		
Street, Richard	1	2	6		15
Rogers, John	2		3		
Petty, Theophilus	1				
Maples, James	1	3	3		
Edwards, Jacob	1	2	3		
Hancock, William	1		4		
Cameron, John (Taylor)	1	1	1		
Merrett, John	1				
Cheek, Randal	3		5		1
Magee, Joseph, Sr	1		2		
Holliman, Josiah	1	3	1		
Black, John	4	2	3		
Tison, Thomas	2	4	4		
McDonald, Norman	4				1
McDonald, Mary			1		
Sheals, Rueben	1	3	7		
Muse, Thomas	1		1		
Atkinson, Thomas	1				
Collins, Thomas, Sr	1		2		1
Watson, William	1	3			
Cole, Daniel	1	1	3		
Moore, David	1	1	1		
Blanchet, Robert	1	2	1		
Comer, Adam	2	4	5		
Murchison, Elizabeth			1		
Loving, Presley	1	2	4		
Gardner, William	2	2	5		
Gardner, Peter	1	2	4		
McBride, Alexr	1	1	6		
Mashburn, Samuel	1	2	4		
Campbell, Charles	2		2		
Love, John	2	2	5		
Shepherd, John, Sr	2		1		
Goings, William	1	4	5		
Campbell, Charles, Esqr	2	1	3		
Wicker, David	2	1	3		4
Baker, Archd	4	1	5		
Morgan, John	2	4	4		
Oates, Stephen	1	2	2		
Carraway, John	3	2	2		
McCallum, Duncan	1	1			
McDonald, Katy			2		
Buchan, John	1	4	3		1
Stubbs, John	1	1	1		
Dun, Joseph, Sr	1				6
Dun, Joseph, Jr	1	1	4		1
McRae, Mary		2	2		
Edwards, Joshua	1	3	3		
McKenzie, Margaret	1		1		
McDonald, Allen	2	3	2		
Buie, Duncan	2	5	3		
Maples, Thomas	1	2	1		1
Wilson, Moses	2		2		
Williamson, William	2	2	4		1
Williamson, John, Sr	1	2	3		
Smith, Stephen	1		2		
Smith, David	1		4		
Berryman, William	2	2	6		
Barret, Patience		1	4		
Cameron, John, Sr	2	3	6		6
Purnal, James	1				
Wadsworth, John	1				
Buie, Daniel	6		4		6
Wicker, David	3	1	5		5
Thomas, Thomas	1	5	2		
Sloan, Alexr	1	2	3		
Morris, Frederick	2	1	1		
Morris, Henry, Sr	1	3	1		
Morris, Peter	1	2	1		
Morris, Henry, Jr	1		1		
Morris, Mathew	1	1	1		
McRae, Duncan	1	1	2		
McFee, John	1	5	3		
Cameron, John	1	6	1		
Monk, Asbel	1				
Monro, Malcolm	1	2	1		2
McLeod, Niel	3	1	3		
Temple, Lewis	1	1	1		
McLaine, Daniel	1	1	4	1	
Maples, Josiah	2	2	3		
Overton, John (Bigg)	1	2	2		2
Maples, Marmaduke	1	2	1		
Buie, Duncan	1	2	2		5
Hayes, James	1	1	2		
Carrol, John	3	3	5		3
Hall, Ignatius	1	1	2		2
Mills, Joshua	1	1	2		
McLeod, Charles	1				
Campbell, Murdock	2				
Cole, Abraham	1	2	4		
Patterson, Daniel	1		2		2
Greenhill, Joseph	1	1	2		10
Gallemore, James	1	1	5		
Morrison, Norman	1	2	4		
Morrison, Alexr	2		2		
Morrison, Malcolm	2	1	3		
Monro, Alexr	1	2	3		
McLaine, Hector	1		2		
Melton, Anseel	2	1	4		
McLeod, Norman	1		2		
McLeod, Murdock	1		2		
McLeod, Daniel	2		1		
McLeod, Nancy			3	4	
McLaine, Norman	1	1	3		
Campbell, Daniel	3		7		
McAuley, Murdock	1				
McLeod, Kennith	1		1		
Ducksworth, Jesse	1		5		1
Myrick, Francis	1	2	2		
McDaniel, Daniel	3	1	2		
Harding, James	1	3	4		
Harding, Gabriel	1	2			2
Clark, Kennith	5		3		6
McDonald, Findley	1	4	3		
Ruebottom, Simon	1		2		
Ruebottom, Thomas	2		6		
Cagle, Jacob	1	3	3		2
Gilchrist, Malcolm	3		4		2
McLeod, Malcolm	2	1	3		
Elkings, Benjamin	1	7	1		
Elkings, James	1	1	5		
Teague, William (Black)	1	3	4		
Phillips, John	1	1	4		
Brewer, Lanier	2	4	4		
Davis, Robert	2				1
Morris, Stephen	1	1	1		
Thornton, James	1	1	1		
Teague, William (Preacher)	2	4	4		
Overton, Amos	1	3	4		
Rogers, Ruth	2		2		
Hancock, Elizabeth	1	3	1		
Magee, Joseph	1	1	4		5
Johnston, Hezekiah	1	3	3		
McRae, Duncan	1	1	2		
McInnis, Alexr	2	5	2		
McRae, Donald	1		2		
Buie, Duncan (Red)	2		6		
Boyd, Frances			2		
Carlisle, Thomas	1	1	1		
Whitford, William B	1	1	3		
Carlisle, Hosah	1	1	1		
Carlisle, Robert	1	2	4		
McAuley, Angus	1	2	4		
McKinnen, Norman	1	1	2		
McKinnen, John	1	4	2		
McInnis, Murdock	1				
Monro, Niel			2		
Blanchet, John, Sr	1	1	2		
Brewer, Ambrose	2	3	4		
Jones, Rebecca		3	2		
Oliver, Moses	1				
Moore, Edward, Jr	1			1	
Overton, John (Little)	2		3		1
Carlisle, Robert	1	1	6		
Kelley, Hugh	3	2	4		
Coupland, John	2		2		
Hayes, John	2	2	2		
Davidson, David	2	2	1		
Morgan, John, Jr	1		2		
Mattheson, Donald	1	3	3		
Sewell, Lewis, Jr	2	3	5		
Sewell, Lewis, Sr	1	1	3		
Newton, Nicholas	2	1	7		1
Runnals, Fanny		1	2		
Runnals, Sarah		3	3		
Jackson, Elijah	1	4	5		
Jackson, Elizabeth	1	1	3		
Mattheson, Niel	2	2	3		
Merritt, Mark	1				
Paine, William	1	1	2		
Furr, Joseph	1	4	3		
Graham, Benjamin	5	4	2		
Stephens, Benjamin, Sr	2		5		
Stephens, John, Jr	1	1	2		
McFarland, Dugal	1	1	2		
Kitchen, Mathew	2	1	3		
Buchannan, Margery	1		1		
Freeman, Rueben	1	2	2		
Hillyard, John	2	2	2		
McLaine, Niel, Sr			5		
Hewings, Cornelius	1	2	5		
Harding, Gabriel, Jr	1		3		
Bowzer, James		1	1	1	
Dunlap, John	1	4	6		
Purkins, Thomas H	2		2		24
Gilbert, Benjamin	1		2		
Gilbert, Libra		3	3		
Womble, Samuel	2	2	1		
Houghton, Littleton	1	1	1		
Buie, Archd	3	1	4		8
Fields, Susanah			1	2	
Mears, John	1		1	1	
Brooks, William	1	5	4		1
Street, Henry	1		1		
McDugal, Angus	1		1		
Buie, Malcolm (Juniper)	1	1	5		
Dey, Ann	2	2	4		
Buie, Duncan (Taylor)	1	6	3		
Honeycut, Robert	1	1	2		
Ducksworth, Joseph	1	1	4		1
McIntosh, Mary			1		
Newman, Sarah		1	1		
Wicker, Ann			1		
Collins, Henrietta			4		1
Darke, Samuel	3	2	3		
McNiel, John	3	2	5		11
Cox, John	1	3	7		
Billings, Jasper	1	1	1		
Barrett, Solomon	1	1	1		
Demby, Joshua	1	2	3		
Patterson, John	3		2		7
Patterson, Archd	1		2		
Patterson, Donald	1				
Johnston, Duncan	3	2	4		
Patterson, John	1	1	1		
Patterson, Archd	2		2		
McDuffee, Norman	2	3	1		
McLaine, Donald	1	1	5		
McLaine, John	1		3		
McArthur, John	1				2
McMillen, Flora			2		
Patterson, Duncan	1	3	2		
Clark, Katy	1	1	2		
McDonald, Hugh	1				
Cooper, Jesse	1	3	2		
McFarland, Bartley	1				
Temple, Dickson	1				
Wood, Thomas	1	2	3		
Stephens, Benjamin	1	1	3		
Blanchet, John, Jr	2	1	3		
Nelson, John	1	1	2		
Harding, William (Buck)	1	2	4		
Brewer, Drury	1	3	3		
Harding, William	1	4	4		
Davis, Sarah			1	2	3
Goldston, John	1		2		
Cheek, Philip	1				
Stinson, John	2	1	3		
Smith, James	1				
McDugal, Duncan	1	1	3		
Baker, Malcolm	1				
McIver, Daniel (B. Smith)	1		1		
McLaine, John (Gasters)	1	2	4		
Brewer, Nimrod	1	2	3		
Bird, Robert	1	2	3		
Read, William	1	3	4		
McDugal, John	2	2	3		
Baker, Mary			1		
Campbell, John	1				
Sellars, Malcolm	2		2		
Oliver, Aron	2		1		
Campbell, Daniel	1	2	4		
McKenzie, Daniel	1	2	1		
Ragsdell, Daniel	1				
Watson, John	1				
Jordan, Mead	1	1	2		
Smith, William	1	2	3		
Yarborough, Benjamin	1	1	1		
Craig, John	1				
Strauther, Laurence	1		2		
Keys, Moses	1				
McAuley, John	1		1		
Stutts, John	1		1		
McDuffee, Agnes		1	2		
Dun, Isaac	1	2	4		
McLeod, Malcolm	3	1	2		
Lax, Robert	1	1	2		
Morrison, Christian		1	1		
Gillies, Archd	1				
McLeod, Kennith	1	2	2		
McKenzie, Betsy			2		
Lunsford, Augustine	1				
McDonald, Donald	1		1		
Jones, Silvanus	1	3	5		
McIntosh, Duncan	1		2		
McLeod, Alexr	3	1	3		
Brazel, George	1	3	3		
Bulling, Thomas	1	2	3		
Minyard, John	1	3	3		
Hunsucker, John	1	2	2		
Morris, John	2				
Moore, Edward, Sr	2	1	2		
Cagle, William	1	1	2		

FAYETTE DISTRICT, RICHMOND COUNTY.

NAME OF HEAD OF FAMILY.	Free white males of 16 years and upward, including heads of families.	Free white males under 16 years.	Free white females, including heads of families.	All other free persons.	Slaves.
Chambers, Moses	1	1	3		4
James, Philip	1		2		1
Wall, John	2	2	4	3	12
Haley, Randal	2		1		
McRae, Duncan	1	4	4		
McRae, Murdock	2	1	3		
Dawkins, George	1	2	2		1
Haley, Silas	1	2	2		1
Haley, William	1	2	3	1	
Moorman, Andrew	1	1	5		
Adcock, Henry	1	3	5		
Collins, George					4
Terry, Mathew	1	3	2		
Clark, Nicholas	1	2	2		
Moorman, Thomas	1	2	3		
Terry, William	2	1	1		5
Terry, James, Jr	1		1		
Long, James	1		1		
Curry, Edward	1	4	3		
Webb, Robert	2	3	2		3
Dawkins, William	1	5	4		
Mathews, John	3	1	3		
Webb, William	1	1	2		
Webb, George	2	3	3		
McRae, Malcolm	3	2	2		
McRae, Donald	2	3	3		
McRae, Christopher	1	3	2		
McRae, Alexr	2	2	4		
Sarterfield, George	1	3	5	1	
McRae, Alexr	2	4	3		
McRae, Nelly	1	3	4		
McDonald, John	1	1	1		
McRae, John	1	2	1		
McRae, Christopher	2	4	2		
Stewart, Angus	1	2	4		
McInnis, John	1	5	3		
Moorman, Archelaus	1	2	4		
Moorman, John	2		4		
Hunter, William	1	1	3		
Terry, James	2	2	3		7
McAskill, Findley	2		7		
Chambers, Rachael		2	3		
Perkins, Jacob	2	4	3		
Bounds, John	2	1	2		1
Cole, John	1		2		2
Usher, Thomas	1		2		
Williamson, Isaac	2	2	1		
Robinson, William	2		1		6
Crouch, John	2	1	4		
Crouch, Sarah		1	3		
Jowers, George	1				
George, Thomas	3	1	6		
Jowers, Thomas	1	4	1		
Jowers, John	1	4	3		
Covington, John	1	3	4		
Cottingham, Elisha	2	1	4		
McKenzie, Kennith	1				
McKenzie, Flora			2		
McDaniel, Daniel	3		3		1
McDaniel, William	1	1	4		3
Castle, Hawkins	2	1	4		
Willoughby, Edward	1	4	1		
Wilkerson, John	1	1	3		
Powell, Nathl	1	2	1		
Burt, Isbal	1		5		3
Ussery, Richard	1	2	2		
Elkings, Nathl	1	1	1		
Bennet, Peter	1		1		
Jackson, Daniel					8
James, Philip	1		1		
Harrington, Nath'	2	2	7		
Williams, Thomas P.	1	3	3		
Mathews, John	2	2	3		
Cole, John, Sr	5	2	2		12
Cole, John, Jr	1		1	1	1
Greer, George	2		4		
Riggell, Mark	1		2		7
Bond, Ailce	1		2		
McMillen, Dugal	2	2	3		
McMillen, John	1	1	1		
McMillen, Angus	1	2	2		
Gillies, John	2	3	1		
Meacham, John	2	3	2		
Robinson, Charles	3		1		12
Tarbutton, Joseph	2	2	6	1	
Tippet, Erastus	1	5	4		
Gad, Joseph, Jr	1	3	5		
Gad, Joseph, Sr	1		1		
Bounds, Jesse	3	5	3		
Stealy, Lovick	1				
Webb, Henry	1				
Slaughter, Walter	1	5	3		4
Bolding, Rachael	1	2	3		3
Robinson, Charles, Jr	1	2	3		3
Graham, William	2	2	6		
Covington, Samuel	1	1	5		
Graham, John	1	2	3		

NAME OF HEAD OF FAMILY.	Free white males of 16 years and upward, including heads of families.	Free white males under 16 years.	Free white females, including heads of families.	All other free persons.	Slaves.
Jones, John, Jr	1		2		10
Blewit, Thomas	2	1	1		10
Williams, Edward	2	3	4		7
Bowen, Alexr	1		1		
Williams, William	1	2	1		
Martin, Alexr	2	1	2		
McNiel, Hector	2		2		2
McNiel, Laughlan	1		2		
Bostick, John	1		2		
Bostick, Ezra	1				
Sutton, Jeffrey	1		1		
Permar, John	1	1	1		
Tarbutton, Mary	1				
Williamson, Shadrack	1				
James, Enoch	1				
Wall, William	2	1	1		7
Covington, Henry	2		5		3
Covington, John, Jr	1		1		
McDonald, Donald	1	2	3		
McDonald, John	1		1		
Campbell, Richard	1	2	2		
Gibson, Nelson	3	3	4		3
Gibson, Thomas, Jr	1		2		1
Cole, Stephen	1	4	2		3
O'Bryan, Dennis	1				
O'Bryan, Laurence	2	1	3		
Gibson, James	1	2	4		1
Curry, Angus	2		3		
Curry, Daniel	1	1	3		
Martin, Daniel	1	3	3		
McKay, John	1	3	3		
Nicholson, Roger	2	1	2		
Jones, John, Sr	3	3	4	1	
Jones, William	1	3	1		
Smiley, James	1	3	3		
Watson, Alexr	1		2		
Blew, Dugal	1	2	2		
Williams, Benja	1	2	2		
Slaughter, Owen, Sr	1		2		
Slaughter, Zeblon	1		2		
Powell, Benja	1	2	5		5
Willoughby, Edward	1	4	1		
Wilkerson, Samuel	1	3	3		
Phillips, Thomas	1	3	3		
Ezell, Gilliam	1	1	2		
McAskill, Kennith	1				
McAskill, Allen	1	3	3		
McIntosh, Sweny	1	4	4		3
McNair, John	1	2	3		
McAskill, Findley	1	1	2		
Strickland, Mathew	2		2		
Dawkins, John, Jr	1		2		
Dawkins, John, Sr	1	1	4		
Sprawls, Solomon	2	6	2		
Snead, David	1	1	2		1
Wilson, Robert	1	4	5		1
McRae, Duncan	1		3		
Smith, James	1	1	2		
Thomas, William	1	1	4		
Shaw, Rodorick	1	2	2		
Smith, John	1	5	6		
Campbell, James, Jr	1		3		
Campbell, James, Sr	1	3	3		
Ages, Noah	1	1	2		
McAskill, Christian	2		8		
Gun, Alexr	1				2
Ewing, John	3		2		
Beachum, Sarah		1	1		
Allred, Phineas	1	4	1		
McKay, William	2	2	1		1
Allred, Johnathan	1	1	8		
Allred, Solomon	3	2	4		
Covington, John, Sr	2	5	4		7
Burt, John	1	1	2		
Baldwin, Jesse	2		2		
Watson, James	3	1	4		
Strickland, Lott	1	2	2		
McLeod, Niel	1		2		
Cole, George	1	3	2		
Martin, Murdock	1		2		
Hunter, William, Sr	2		6		2
McDowell, John	3		2		1
Hines, Joseph	1	3	4		
Bostick, James	4	3	5		5
Usher, Samuel	1				
Price, Darcas		1	4		
New, William	1	3	1		3
May, Abner	1				
Moorman, Zachariah	3	2	7		
Harrington, Henry W.	2	3	3		60
Snead, William	1	1	2		
Thomas, simon	1	1	3		
Crawford, William	1				
Thomas, William, Sr	2	2	2		
Rowe, Susanah	1	2	2		
McRae, Alexr	1	2	2		
Snead, Israel	2	2	2		1

NAME OF HEAD OF FAMILY.	Free white males of 16 years and upward, including heads of families.	Free white males under 16 years.	Free white females, including heads of families.	All other free persons.	Slaves.
Howard, John	1	3	1		7
Mangrum, Jacob	2	2	4		1
O'Bryen, Tillotson	1	1	3		
Gullet, George	1	2	3		
Smith, James	1	3	2		9
Slaughter, George	2	2	3		
Morehead, Joseph	3		4		9
Chun, Silvester	1	2	5		1
Smith, Sarah, Sr	3		3		4
Hought, James	1				8
Mask, William	2	4	4		1
McInnis, Nancy	1	1	3		
Patterson, Alexr	1		4		
Freeman, Archd	1	1	4		
Woodel, William	2	4	3		
McDaniel, James	1	2	4		
Powell, William	1				
Ayer, Hartwell	1	2	4		8
Newberry, Jonathan	1	2	4		
Pankey, John	4	4	4		
Long, Mary	1		3		
Cole, James	1	2	1		3
Rye, Dunn	1	2	5		
Deerman, Solomon	1	2	5		2
Handly, William	2	4	3		
McLeod, Norman	1				
McRae, Alexr	1	2	5		
Rye, Solomon	1	3	3		
Mask, John	2	4	5		1
McDonald, Malcolm	1		1		
McDonald, John	1		2		
Stanford, Samuel	1		1		
Crowson, John	1	3	3		
McKellar, Niel	1	1	2		
McFarland, John	2	2	4		
McNair, Edward	2		3		
McNair, Archd	1		1		
McNair, Niel	1		3		
McDonald, John	1		4		
Nicholson, Peter	1	2	2		
Freeman, Sarah			1		
Husbands, John	2	4	4		1
James, John, Jr	2	4	2		
James, Philip, Jr	1		1		
Ingram, Benjamin	1	1	5		
Shelton, Micajah	1		2		
Robinson, Charles, Jr	1				3
Nicholson, Rory	3	1	3		
Williams, Josiah	1		1		
Curry, Duncan	3		2		
Yates, Isaac	1	2	6		
Brigman, Isaac	2	2	6		
McQuig, Duncan	1		1		
McLeod, Norman	1	1	1		
Love, William	1	4	2		14
McDowel, William	1		3		1
Pursley, Charles	1	1	3		
Webb, John Turner	1	1	1		
Everat, Laurence	1	3	1		2
McRae, Farquhard	3		1		
Robertson, James	1				
Campbell, John	2	1	2		
McLeod, Rorey	3		1		
Morrison, John	3		2		
Thomas, Stephen	1	1	3		
Snead, Solomon	1	2	2		2
Smith, William	2	3	4		
Long, Benjamin	1		1		
Snead, Solomon	1	1	3		
Coward, Joel	1	4	1		
James, Jeminy	1		2		
Pettit, Mark	1	1	3		
Strong, John	1	1	2		2
Dixon, Richard	2		4		
Jernigan, William	1	5	3		
Webb, William	2	3	5		
Covington, Mathew	1	1	1		
McColl, Paul	1		1		
Cameron, Duncan	1	2	4		
Collins, Elisha	1	1	2		
Hines, Absalom	1		4		
McQuig, Malcom	1	2	3		
Gunn, George	1	3	1		
McColl, Duncan	1				
Snead, Daniel	1	1	4		
Adams, Richard	1	1	3		4
Snead, John	1	1	3		11
Slaughter, Owen, Jr	1	2	3		
Watkins, William	1	4	2		1
Stealy, John	1	5	3		
Dawkins, Samuel	2	2	4		
McColl, John	1				
McCormick, Hugh	1	1	3		
McColl, Dugal	1				
McColl, Duncan	1	1	3		
McColl, Donald	1				

FAYETTE DISTRICT, RICHMOND COUNTY—Continued.

NAME OF HEAD OF FAMILY.	Free white males of 16 years and upward, including heads of families.	Free white males under 16 years.	Free white females, including heads of families.	All other free persons.	Slaves.
McColl, Hugh	1				
McNair, Gilbert	1	1	5		1
Findley, Duncan	3	4	2		
Cole, Peter	1		1		
Webb, John	1	2	2		
Everat, Thomas	1	3	5		
McPherson, William	1	1	2		
McDonald, Donald	1		1		
McDonald, Angus	2	1	3		
Watkins, Israel	2	1	3		1
Webb, George	1	3	3		
Bolten, Benja	1	1	2		
Pemberton, John	1	2	1		4
Hunter, James	1		4		
McNair, Niel	2		2		
Smith, Daniel	3	3	5		
Husbands, William	1		3		
Mims, Thomas	2	1	7		
Haley, Isam	3	3	3	1	
Ingram, Edwin	1	1	3		2
James, John, Sr	1		3		7
Skipper, Benjamin	2		3		
Bounds, William	1		1		
Rye, Robert	1	3	2		
McAskill, Daniel	1				
McInnis, Katy			1		
McFarland, Duncan	5	4	6		6
Long, John	2	3	2		
Fairley, Archd	1	6	2		2
McKinnen, Flora	2	1	2		
McNair, Malcolm	1	2	2		
Rogers, William	1	3	4		
Snead, Philemon	1		3		
Melson, Robert	2	1	5		
Herbert, Charles	1	2	4		
Thomas, Daniel	2	4	4		
Covington, Benjamin	1	4	6		5
Denson, John	1	1	2		
Denson, Thomas	1		2		
Cameron, Daniel	1		4		
Gibson, Thomas, Sr	2	5	4		5
Brock, Valentine	1		2		
Watkins, John	1	4	6		1
Watkins, David	1		3		
Allman, Edward	2		3		
Spiva, Jonas	1	3	1		
Burnes, William	1	2	3		
McCormick, Hugh	2		3		
Davis, Isaac	1		1		
Hannigan, Derby	1		1		12
Dixon, Archd	1		1		
Dixon, John	1	2	2		
Hall, John	1	3	4		
Oliver, John	1	5	2		
Leviner, John	2	3	3		
Lasseter, Micajah	2	2	6		
Mays, Mathew	1				
Strickland, Archd	1		2		
Hill, Richard	3	1	5		
Deerman, Thomas	1	2	4		
Bell, Zachariah	3	2	1		
Ezell, John	1	2	4		2
Collins, Elisha	1	1	2		
Collins, George	1	2	1		
Brazell, Nathan	1	2	4		
Peaton, Peter	1	4	1		
Adcock, Thomas	1	1	2		
Martin, John	1		2		
Johnston, Archd	1		1		
McDaniel, Daniel	3	1	5		
Johnston, Lazarus	1	3	1		
Henery, Thomas	1	3	3		
Gladis, Richard	3	3	3		
Collins, Charles	1	1	1		
McRae, Christo	3	3	2		
Pettis, Mack	1		3		
Goodson, Arthur	1		2		
Powell, Richard	1	3	4		
McRae, John	1		2		
Powell, John	1	2	2		
Pitcock, Stephen, Sr	1	3	3		
Rye, Absalom	1	3	5		
Newberry, William, Sr	2		1		
Coleman, John	2	1	2		7
Clements, John	1	1	2		
Pickett, William, Sr	1		1		6
Pickett, James, Jr	1		2		12
Strauther, Nancy		3	2		9
Spead, John	1	2	4		13
Watkins, Thomas	1	3	5		1
Watkins, Keziah	2	1	4		3
Buford, Daniel	1	2	1		
Wright, Jonathan	1	2			
Allman, Edward	1		3		
McKinnen, John	1	1	3		
Buchannan, William	2	1	6		
McLaine, John	1	2	3		

NAME OF HEAD OF FAMILY.	Free white males of 16 years and upward, including heads of families.	Free white males under 16 years.	Free white females, including heads of families.	All other free persons.	Slaves.
Hadly, William	1	2	1		
McLeod, Alexr	2	2	1		
McLeod, James					
Stone, Nicholas	1	3	3		5
Cotter, Hannah		2	4		
Johnston, William	1	6	2		
Crew, Joseph	1				
Tolson, William	2	1	6		
Bass, Alexr	1	4	2		
Hooks, Daniel	2	4	2		
Goodwin, Lewis	3		3		
Barnet, Carter	1	1	1		
Mathews, Charles	1	1	2		
Johnston, Thomas	1	3	4		
Marlow, Thomas	2	2	5		
McLaughlan, Daniel	4	4	4		2
McAllester, John	1	1	4		
Cole, Francis	1	1	4		
Stealy, Isaiah	1				
Cottingham, William	1	2	6		
Cottingham, Charles	1		1		
Rogers, Sarah		1	4		
Curry, Duncan	4	1	2		
McDuffee, John	2	3	5		
McAskill, Malcolm	1	2	5		
McAskill, John	1				
McDuffee, Angus	1		5		
McDuffee, Murdock	1				
Honeycut, Bolling	1	1	6		
Crawford, Rebecca	1	4	2		12
Phillips, Lamuel	1				
Everat, Benjamin	1	3	2		
Bennet, William	1	1	2		
Massey, Elias	1	1	1		
Chambley, Clayborne	1				
Kennelly, Rueben	1				
Coleman, James	1	1	2		2
Campbell, Archd	2	1	5		
McLeod, Archd	1	1	2		
McLerran, Hugh	4				
Murdock, John	1	1	1		2
Lewis, Zachariah	1	1	3		
Curry, Duncan	2		1		
Doud, John	3	1	3		
McKay, Archd	2	3	3		
Brigman, Isaac	3	1	4		
Luvinor, John					8
Lasseter, Micajah	3	1	4		
Shaw, Angus	1	1	5		
Monro, John	1	3	1		1
Carter, George	1				
McLennan, Daniel	1	2	4		1
Ferguson, John	1		1		
McDugal, Niel	1				
Keachey, James	1	5	3		
Keachey, John	1	2	2		1
Keachy, John	1	1	1		2
Johnston, William	2	2	4		
McInnis, John	1	1	2		
Black, John	1		2		
McDugal, Duncan	1	1	4		
Blew, Dugal	1	3	2		
Blew, Mary	1		5		
McNair, Margaret		1	2		
Graham, John	4		3		
Shaw, Murdock	1	5	2		
McDonald, Niel	4	2	2		
Chavers, Richard					5
Chavers, John					7
McAuley, Malcolm	1	2	4		
Overstreet, Silas	1	1	8		
Strickland, Mathew	1	2	4		
Strickland, Joseph			5		
Brigman, Ashur		2	3		
Norton, James, Sr	1	3	3		
Norton, Isam	1	1	1		
McLaughlan, Daniel	2				
Smith, Easter					2
Johnston, Winifred	2	2	3		
Norton, James, Jr	1	5	3		
Norton, William	1	4	2		
Pate, Stephen	1	1	2		1
Patterson, James	2	2	5		
Dunoho, Charles	1	2	2		
Hathcock, Thomas	1	2	3		
Wallis, Charity			2		
Wallis, Patty			1		
Rachael, Starling	1	1	3		
Butler, Edward	1	3	4		
Rachael, William	1	3	5		
Buie, John	1	3	3		
Chavers, Susana				3	
McDermad, John	2	1	5		
McAskill, John	1		3		
McNair, John (Hatter)	1		3		
McNair, Niel, Jr	1	1	2		
Snead, Hendley	1	1	4		3

NAME OF HEAD OF FAMILY.	Free white males of 16 years and upward, including heads of families.	Free white males under 16 years.	Free white females, including heads of families.	All other free persons.	Slaves.
Ferguson, Aphia		2	3		1
Graham, Dugal	2	1	4		
Watson, James	1		2		
Morrison, Norman	2	1	5		
McPherson, Edward	2	2	4		
McNair, Daniel	1	2	1		1
McIver, Margaret	1	4	2		
Blew, Mary		1	5		
McRainey, Allen	1	2	2		
McNair, Margaret		1	2		
McLaine, Catharine		1	5		
McFarland, Niel	1	1	4		
McLeod, Aphia		3	2		
Murchison, Flora			3		
McDermad, Daniel	1		2		
Shaw, Norman	1	1	2		
St Clair, Nancy	1		2		
Allen, James	1				
Green, Nicholas	1	1	1		1
McInnis, Findley	2	2	3		
McFarland, Peter	1	2	2		
Morrison, Angus	3	2	2		
McAskill, Daniel	1		2		
Campbell, Daniel	1	1	4		
McNair, John (S. Master)	1	1	1		
McLeod, Norman	1	1	3		
McLeod, Alexr	3	3	2		
McLerran, John, Sr	4	5	5		
McLerran, Laughlan	3		1		
McLerran, Duncan, Sr	3	6	4		
McLerran, Hugh, Sr	1	1	4		
Buchannan, John	1		1		
McKenzie, Duncan	1	1	1		
McLerran, Daniel	4		3		
McLerran, Hugh, Jr	1	3	2		
McMillen, Archd	3	2	6		
McLerran, Hugh	4		1		
Dove, John	3	1	3		
McLerran, Duncan, Jr	3	4	3		
McGill, Angus	2	2	5		
McGill, Allen	1	1	4		
Smith, John	1		2		
Smith, Daniel	1	2	2		
Smith, Archd	2		2		
McDaniel, Alexr	1	2	1		
McNair, Roger	3		2		
McDonald, Niel	4	2	4		
Shaw, Murdock	2	4	2		
Shaw, Daniel	2	3	3		
Shaw, Angus	1		3		
McAllum, Duncan	2		1		
Oxendine, Henry					5
Covington, William	1	5	1		
Purmair, John	1	1	1		
McQuig, Peter	1	1	1		
Boyakin, Samuel	1	1	1		
Ferguson, John	2		1		2
Thompson, Hugh	1	2	1		
Dees, James	5	2	3		
McMillen, Alexr	1	2	1		
McCarne, Daniel	3	1	3		
McInnis, Malcolm	2	1	1		
Curry, Angus	2	2	4		
Thompson, Hugh	2	3	2		
Duglas, Daniel	2	1	6		
McRae, John	2	1	5		
Carmichael, Archd	1	2	2		
Carmichael, Dugal	1	1	4		1
McLeod, Norman	1	1	3		1
McAskill, Allen	2	1	4		
McKay, Archd	2	3	3		
Smith, Allen	1	2	2		
McRae, William	1	2	2		
McAllester, Angus	2	1	3		1
McIntire, John		3	4		
McIntire, Mary		3	4		
McBride, Duncan	1	4	3		
Henderson, Archd	3	8	3		
McFarland, Duncan	1	1	1		
Grimes, George	1	4	3		
McNair, Edward	1		1		
McNair, Roger	3		2		
Fairley, John	2		1		
Fairley, Alexr	1				2
Carmichael, Hugh	1	2	1		1
Brown, Samuel	1	1	1		
Smith, Niel	1		1		
McAskill, Daniel	2	5	5		
Carmichael, Dugal	1	4	2		
Dees, William	1	4	2		
McNair, John	1	1	1		
Murphy, John	1	2	2		
McCasell, Daniel	1	3	3		
McLaurence, Hugh	1	2	5		
Campbell, Angus	2	1	3		
McCalman, John	1	5	3		2
Carmichael, Daniel	1	5	5		

FAYETTE DISTRICT, RICHMOND COUNTY—Continued.

NAME OF HEAD OF FAMILY.	Free white males of 16 years and upward, including heads of families.	Free white males under 16 years.	Free white females, including heads of families.	All other free persons.	Slaves.
Martin, John	1	3	1		
McKinnen, Daniel	1	1	4		
McLerran, John	2	4	5		
McDonald, Alexr	1	2	1		
Crowson, Sarah	2		1		
Briggs, Catharine		1	2		
Gladdis, Richard	2	4	3		
Gordon, Alexr	1	4	3		
McKay, Daniel	1	1	4		
Shaw, Donald	1	4	4		
Sellars, Sampson	1	3	3		
McKay, Alexr	1	2	3		
Grimes, Edward	1	4	4		
Grimes, Levi	1	1	1		
Shaw, Angus	1	1	4		
Boyakin, Mathew	2	3	3	4	
Spiva, Moses	1	1	3		
McAuley, Evan	2	1			
Chears, Nathl	1	5	5		
Campbell, Angus	1	1	4		
McKinnen, Daniel	1	1	4		
Gillies, Daniel	1	4	2		
Dees, Benjs, Sr	3	4	4		
Steen, James	1	4	4		
Gardner, Elias	1		2		
Tucker, John	1	2	1		
Grimes, George, Sr	1	2	4		
Wright, William	1	1	2		
Stewart, Hardy	1	1	2		
Webb, John, Sr	1	2	1		
Pankey, William	1	1	2		
Watson, Mathew	1	1	4	4	
McColl, Duncan	1	1	5		
Bowen, William	3		2		
McFarland, Dugal	1		2	3	
Smith, Archd	2		2		
Watson, Alexr	1	5	2		
Smith, Daniel	1	2	5		
Campbell, Daniel	1				
Millsap, Mathew	2	2	2		
Jernigan, David	2		2		
Morris, Valentine		1	7		
Stringfellow, Robert	1	1	1		
Stringfellow, William	3		3	3	
Gordon, Thomas	1	1	1	1	
Beasley, Daniel	1		3		
Jones, John, Jr	1		2		
Elkings, Richard	1	3	2		
Turnage, Luke	1	2	6	1	
Grimes, William	3	2	6		
Steen, James	1	2	3		
Mask, Dudley	1	3	2	10	
Stringfellow, Henry	1	1	3		
Mask, Pleasant M	2		3	5	
Phillips, Solomon	1	3	3	4	
Jones, Brice	1		2	2	
Stainbeck, Thomas	1	3	5	7	
Davis, Jonathan	1				
Rogers, James	1				
McColl, Daniel	1	3	2		
McLennen, John	1				
Walker, Thomas	1	3	1	3	
Blackwell, John	1	3	5		
Parker, Benajah	2	1	3		
Whitlow, Henry	1				
Bennett, John	1	4	1		
Henry, Isam	1	1	1		
McRae, Donald	1	3	3		
McRae, John	1	2	1		
Smith, Malcolm	1	4	5	1	
Clements, John	1	1	2		
Shepherd, John	1				
Shepherd, Jane			2		
Barnes, John	1	2	2		
Lampley, Jacob	4		3		
Allman, William	1	2	5		
Campbell, William	1	3			
Allman, John	1				
McInnis, Murdock	1	2	4		
Thompson, Thomas	1		5		
Merrett, Stephen	1	2	2		
Hall, Joel, Sr	1	2	1		
Hall, Isaac	1		3		
Hall, Jacob					
Hall, Joel, Jr	1	1	2		
Shaw, Norman	1	1	2		
Hall, Sarah			4		
Hall, John	2	2	4		
Green, Nicholas	1	1	1		1
Jenkins, John	2	2	4		
Bugget, John	1		1		
Slay, Nathan	1	1	2		
Slay, Thomas	1		2		
Usher, James	1		1		
Phillips, James	1	1	3		
McRae, Duncan	1	1	2		
Sumerall, Moses	1	2	2		
Williamson, Starling	2	3	3		
Thomas, William	2	3	3		
Pate, Samuel	1	3	3		1
McLaine, Charles	1	2	3		1
Pate, Thoroughgood	1	1	4		
Yates, Abraham	1		1		
Thornton, John	1		7		
Bower, Alexr	1		1		
Barlow, James	1		2		
Brown, William	1	1	2		
McColl, Donald	1	2	5		
McLeod, Rodorick	1	1	1		
McRae, Daniel	1	1	2		
Campbell, John	1		3		
Burnes, Davis	2	1	5		
Hall, Joseph	1	1	2		
Hall, Joseph, Sr	1		1		
Griffin, Joseph	1		1		
Turner, Moses				7	1
Izard, William	1		3		
McGuire, William	2	1	2		
Newberry, William	3				
Weeks, Shubel	1				
Spurling, John	4	4	5		
McDonald, John	1		4		
McDonald, Zachariah	2	3	5		1
McInnis, John	2	2	3		
Gillies, John	2	3	1		
McPherson, William	1	1	2		
Adams, William	1				
Brown, Thomas	2	2	1		
Gibson, Amey		3	1		
McColl, Alexr	1				
Johnston, Robert	1	1	2		
Hull, Joseph	1				
McGahee, Margaret	1		1		
Beasley, James		2	5		2
Moore, Jethro	1		2		
Dumas, Benjamin	3	3	4		21
Dumas, Andrew	1		5		1
Pitcock, Stephin	1		1		
Dumas, Thomas	1	3	1		4
Chears, Samuel	1	1	1		
Wilkerson, Samuel	1	3	4		
Alsobrook, Jesse	1	3	3		
Roberson, John	1	3	4		2
Hicks, Adrey	2	3	3		
Dumas Jeremiah	1		1		1
Rogers, Sarah		1	2		
Balding, Jonathan	1		1		
Watts, Peter, Sr	1		3		
Watts, Peter, Jr	1	2	3		
Watts, William	1		2		
Dumas, Susanah		3	1		1
Huchings James	1				
Thomison, Arnold	1	1	1		1
Cameron, Hugh	1	3	4		
Jordan River	1	1	3		
Strickland, Isaac	1	1	2		
Burnes, Darius	1	2	2		
Brown, Edmund	1	3	5		
Campbell Dugal	1	3	4		
Curry, Daniel	1	3	5		
Carmichael, Daniel	2		3		
Clark, Henry	1		6		
Cason, John	1	1	1		6
Crouch, James	1				
Cockraham, Thomas	1	1	5		
Bagget, Shadrack	2	1	3		
Bagget, James, Sr	1		3		
Bagget, James, Jr	1	4	1		
Bounds, George	1	2	6		
Brown, Daniel	2		2		
Bennet, Richard	1		4		
Douglas, John	2	4	3		
Dees, Gabriel	1				
Dorkery, Thomas	1	2	3		9
Ezell, William	1	1	5		
Graham, Archd	8		3		1
Greer, James	1		1		
Hall, William, Sr	1	1	4		
Hurley, Moses	1	3	1		
Henry, Isam	1		1		
Jones, Lurana	1	2	1		
Johnston, Thomas	1		4		
Johnston, John	1	3	3		
Johnston, Robert	1	2	3		
Johnston, William	1				
Jowers, William	1				
McKinnen, John	1	3	5		
McKinnen, Laughlan	2		5		1
McKay, William	2	1	2		
Martin, Niel	1		2		
McIntire, Daniel	1	2	4		
McPherson, Daniel	1		2		
Hall, William, Jr	1		1		
Morrison, Anguish	3	2	3		
McNiel, Archd	1				
McCarn, Archd	1		3		
McCarn, Daniel	1	2	4		
McLerran, Duncan	1		3		
McKay, Daniel	1	1	4		
McLerran, Duncan, Jr	1				
McNiel, Hector	1	1	2		2
Odom, Richard	2		2		
Watson, Mathew	1				
Woodel, Mathew	1				
Williamson, Starling	1	4	3		
Walters, John, Sr	1	2	5		
Mixon, Francis	1	1	2		1
Mooreman, William	1				
McQueen, Malcolm	1	2	4		
McKay, Duncan	1	1	4		
McAuley, Rovey	2				
Morrison, John	1		1		
Snead, Ann			2		
Skipper, Barnabas	4	1	1		
Lasseter, Joseph	2	1	5		
McKay, Christian			3		
McRae, Farquhard	1	2	3		
Bethune, Peter	1	3	1		
Miles, William	1	3	4		
Strickland, Jesse	1				
Shepherd, Bird	1	2	3		
Stewart, Thomas					1
Bolton, William	1	3	4		
Bennet, Peter	1	1	1		
Lyon, John	1				
McLeod, Ann			1		
McColl, Daniel, Jr	1	1	2		
McInnis, Duncan	1				
McColl, Daniel, Sr	2				
Morehead, Turner	1				
McColl, Duncan	1	2	3		
McRae, Duncan	1	1	4		
McRae, John	1		3		
Norman, Henry	1	1	3		
Stephens, Hardy	1				
Sarterfield, William	1	1	3		
Bounds, Stephen	1				
Bennet, Letitia			3		
Curry, Katy		2	3		
Thomas, Lewis	1	3	8		
Womble, James	1				
McKinnen, Hugh	1	1	3		
Pearce, Rebecca		2	4		
Johnston, Moses	2	1			
Lipscomb, Anderson (of Virginia)					6
Yates, James	1	2	6		
Blackwell, John	2	2	4		
Howard, Hiram	1		2		

FAYETTE DISTRICT, ROBESON COUNTY.

NAME OF HEAD OF FAMILY.	Free white males of 16 years and upward, including heads of families.	Free white males under 16 years.	Free white females, including heads of families.	All other free persons.	Slaves.
Chisolm, John	1	3	1		
Lamon, John	3	1	2		
McMillen, Daniel	1		3		
Lamon, Kenneth	1	1	2		
McKenzie, Gilbert	1	2	5		
McDonald, John	1	1	3		
McMillen, William	3	4	5		
Blew, John	1		5		
Thompson, Nepsy	2		5		
Patterson, Malcolm	1		3		
McMillen, John	1	3	3		
McAlpin, Alexr	1	4	3		
Taggy, Betsey			3		
Little, Archd	1	3	4		
Smith, James	1	2	5		
Gilchrist, John	2	4	4		4
Little, Robert	1		1		
McKenzie, Kenneth	1	3	4		
Councill, Charles	1	5	3		
Councill, John	1	1	5		5
Sims, Robert	2	1	1		
Stogner, John	1	1	3		2
McKinley, Daniel	1	1	4		
Mercer, Henry	2	1	2		1

FAYETTE DISTRICT, ROBESON COUNTY—Continued.

NAME OF HEAD OF FAMILY.	Free white males of 16 years and upward, including heads of families.	Free white males under 16 years.	Free white females, including heads of families.	All other free persons.	Slaves.
Mercer, Peter	1	1	3		
McNair, Duncan	1	3	1		1
McMillen, Archd	1	2	2		
Brice, Duncan	2	1	2		1
McDonald, Margaret		2	1		
Eikner, George	1	1	1		
Kennedy, Isaac	2	2	5		2
Powell, Ambrose	3	3	4		1
Crawford, Peter	1	1	3		
McSwaine, Roger	1		5		
Moore, William	3	1	8	1	1
Crawford, Duncan	1	3	2		
Stephens, James	1	1	3		
Williams, John	1	2	3		
Upton, Robert	2		5		
Musslewhight, Jesse	1	1	6		
Moss, Nancy		1	2		
Johnston, John	1	2	4		1
Baxley, William	2	6	5		
Smith, John	1	2	6		
Baxley, Job	1	2	1		
Powell, Lewis	1	3	5		
Powell, Joseph	1		2		
Powell, Katy			2		
Musslewhite, Leonard	1	1	3		
Baxley, Edmund	2	2	5		
Musslewhite, Nathan	1	1	6		
Musslewhite, Mary			4		3
Musslewhite, Thomas	1	3	1		
Hodge, Joseph	1	3	6		
Pintleton, Hiram	1	1	3		
Herring, Mary			3		
Hammonds, John				9	
Harrell, Jesse	2	2	3		1
Calvin, Francis	1	1	3		
Sizemore, Henry	1		5		
Colly, Thomas	1		3		
Humphrey, Lucy	3	1	2	1	
Acock, William	2		2		
Edwards, James	1	2	1		
Humphrey, William	1		4		1
Drury, Edy		2	5		
Jackson, John	1		2		
Lee, John, Sr	1		3		
Rozier, John	1		2		
Rozier, Briton	1	1	2		
Barlow, Mash	1	1	3		
Bullard, Elizabeth	2		4		
Jackson, Thomas	1		2		
Spears, Harris	2	2	3		1
Edwards, Frebe	1	1	2		
Sea, Nancy			4		
Musslewhite, Milby	1	4	3		
Ellis, William	1	1	3		
Thomas, Lewis	3		2		
Casa, Charity			2		2
Blount, Samuel	1	1	1		
Clyborne, John	1	1	1		1
Farro, Joshua	1	4	4		
Willis, George. Jr	1		1		
Baker, Sion	1	1	2		
Humphrey, John	1	1	2		
Evers, Betty			3		
Willis, George, Sr	3	2	2		7
Willis, Robert	1	1	2		
Willis, Agerton	1		1		2
Willis, Simon	1		1		
Miller, John	1		1		
Odom, William	3		2		1
Watson, Charles	2	4	3		
Thompson, William (B. Swamp)	1	6	1	1	5
Lockileer, Randal				10	
Kersey, America			3		
Lockileer, John			1		
Cade, John	2	2	3	5	17
Facundus, Abraham	1				
Kennedy, William	1	1	3	1	1
Cade, Stephen	1	2	3	1	3
Smith, Samuel (of Nuse)					13
Thompson, Niel	1	2	4		
McCormick, John	1	3	8		1
Murphy, Edward	3	2	3		
McAllester, Malcolm	1				
Powell, Elizabeth		3	1		
Hunt, Ferebe			2		
Brasswell, Arthur	2	1	4	1	2
Brown, Solomon	2	3	5		
Pittman, Nathan	5	3	2		
Pittman, Newett	2		1	1	
Brasswell, David	1		3		
Hunt, Alexr	1	3	2		
Chavers, Ishmael				10	
Taylor, William	1	2	2		
Barnes, Josiah	1	2	5		7
Hedgepath, Charity		1	4		1
Hedgepath, Peter	1		1		

NAME OF HEAD OF FAMILY.	Free white males of 16 years and upward, including heads of families.	Free white males under 16 years.	Free white females, including heads of families.	All other free persons.	Slaves.
Barnes, Abraham	1		4	6	8
Barnes, Elias	1	2	4	6	8
Smith, Benjamin	1		1		
Rhodes, Jacob	1		2		2
Willis, John	5	2	4	1	14
Moore, William (L. Town)	3		2		4
Hall, Enoch	2	2	4		1
Lewis, David	3	6	7		
McMillen, Neven	2	2	3		
Ferguson, John	1		1		
Ferguson, James	3		2		
McGill, Niel	2	3	4		
Love, Alexr	2	2	1		
Johnston, Angus	1		1		
Gillies, Niel	2	1	2		
McFater, Donald	1	2	2		
Jones, Zachariah	1	1	6		
Patterson, Alexr	1		3		
McBride, Archd	2	3	4		
Hall, Instance	1	2	3		
Hall, Lewis	2	3	2		
McGill, Roger	1	1	1		1
Curry, John	1		2		
Murphy, Niel	1	3	5		
Duncan, James	3	1	5		
Brown, Hugh	1	2	1		2
Clark, Nathan	1	2	2		
Hall, Lewis, Jr	1	5	3		
Hodges, Jesse	1		2		
Wilkerson, Angus	4	2	5		
Curry, Raynald	2		4		
Smith, Archd, Jr	2	3	4		
Murphy, Archd	2	3	4		
McNiel, William	2		3		1
Watson, Jennett, Sr	1		3		
Watson, Jennett, Jr			3		
Lamon, Malcolm	1	1	1		
McLaughlan, John	3	1	4		
McMillen, Daniel	2	2	4		
Ferguson, John	2	2	2		
Ferguson, James, Jr	1		3		1
Wilkerson, Duncan	1	3	2		
Fairley, Robert	1		1		
McEachran, Patrick	3	2	4		2
Watson, John	1	2	3		
Watson, James	2	1	5		
McPherson, Randal	1		1		
Hews, Duncan	1		1		
Smith, James	1		2		5
McMillen, Archd	1	1	3		4
McLeod, Alexr	1		6		
Wilkerson, Robert	1		2		
McArthur, Alexr	1	3	5		
McFaul, Mary	2		4		3
Patterson, John	1	2	4		
McLaine, Niel	1		3		
Crawford, Niel	3				
Boyd, James	1	2	4		
McLaine, John	1	1	4		
Gillies, Angus	3	2	5		
McNiel, Malcolm	2				
Colbraith, Angus	1	1	3		
Bird, Benjamin	1	2	6		
Teaster, Nathl	4	1	2		
Tutor, Dread					3
McNiel, Tarquil	2	1	3		9
Fennell, Ephraim	2	3	4		
Colley, George	2		5		
Hall, Isaac	2	1			
Shaw, Malcolm	1		1		
Gillies, Daniel	1		3		
Brown, Niel	2	5	2		2
Morrison, Daniel	1	1	5		
Morrison, Norman	1	1	5		
Grice, Robert	1	2	5		
Strickland, Abraham	1	2	5		
McNiel, Hector	1	2	4		
McRainey, John	2		6		
McLaine, Hector	1	3	3		
McRainey, Daniel	1	2	5		
McNiel, Danold	3	3	3		
McBride, John	2		5		
McBride, Archd	1				
Lockileer, John			4		
McAlpin, Malcolm	1	6	3		
Bussell, William					5
Johnston, Emanuel	1				
Kersey, James	1				
McFater, Christian		2	3		
McArthur, John	2	2	5		1
Lockileer, Joseph				6	
Lockileer, Jacob				6	
Lockileer, Robert				9	
Lockileer, William				11	
McNiel, John	1	2	6		
Ard, Thomas	1	3	4		6

NAME OF HEAD OF FAMILY.	Free white males of 16 years and upward, including heads of families.	Free white males under 16 years.	Free white females, including heads of families.	All other free persons.	Slaves.
Fort, James	1				6
Smith, Patrick	1	2	2		
McNiel, Niel	1	2	1		
McBride, Duncan	1	1	1		
Lockileer, Malcolm				6	
Brooks, Betty				4	
Baker, Niel	1	1	8		
Kersey, Redding	1				
Monro, Malcolm	3	2	3		
McMillen, John	1	6	3		1
McLaughlan, Daniel	1	2	3		
Oxendine, John				1	
Strickland, Aron	3	2	2		
Overstreet, Ferebe	2	3	2		
Ray, Angus	3		1		
Oxendine, Charles				1	2
Campbell, Hugh	2		1	2	2
Henderson John	1		1		
Henderson Alexr					
McLeod, Malcolm	1	2	1		
McEachran, John	2	3	4		
Campbell, Catharine	2		3		4
Wilkes, Francis	1	5	5		
McLaughlin, Duncan	1				
McFaul, Daniel	1	2	2		2
Campbell, John	1		3		4
McSwaine, Donald	1		1		
Douglas, Donald	3	2	1		
McBride, Angus	1				
McMillen, Duncan	1				
Wilkerson, Archd	1				
Smith, Daniel	1				
McDugal, Archd	1		5		
Gilchrist, William	1		3		
Ferguson, Angus	1		3		
Wilkes, John	1		3		
Campbell, Robert	1				
Gillies, John	1		2		
Wilkerson, Edward	1		1		
Coward, John	1				
Murphy, Duncan	1				
Lockileer, Samuel				1	
Johnston, Isaac				1	5
Valentine, Charles				5	
McPherson, Duncan	1				
McLarty, Niel	2	1	2		
Brown, Niel, Esqr	1	1	7		2
Harrell, Jesse	1	3	3		1
Harreil, Elisha	1	2	4		5
Braveboy, Lydia				7	
Jackson, Thomas	3		2		
Fort, Joseph	1				4
Oquin, Tarler	3	5	2		
Oquin, John	1		4		
Best, Bryant	1	2	4		
Best, Patience			4		
Buie, John (Farmer)	1	3	4		1
McDugal, Alexr	2	1	2		
Best, John	1	2	2		
Oquin, Charity	1	2	2	1	
Baker, Sion	1	1	2		
McNabb, James	2	4	4		
McKeller, Peter	1	2	5		
McNiel, Godfrey	4	5	4		
Spear, Harris	2	2	3		1
Jenkins, Benja	1		2		
Jenkins, Lewis	3	1	3		
Powell, Ambrose	1	3	2	5	
Powell, William	1	1	3		
Little, Archd	1		3		
Edwards, Ferebe		2	2		
Crawford, Duncan	1		3		
McDuffee, Duncan	1	2	4		
McDuffee, Archd	1	2	2		
Carlisle, Saunders	2	2	4		
Hammonds, Jacob				4	
Campbell, Donald	3	3	4		3
Patterson, Donald	1	1	3		1
Fort, John	1	1	1		10
Black, James	1	2	5		
Black, Mary					
Black, Angus	1	2	5		
McCorvey, Niel	4		5		
Buie, Niel	2	1	4		7
Tarver, Jacob, Sr	2	4	3		1
Edwards, James		4	2		
McDonald, Aphia	2	3	2		
Buchannan, Peter	2	3			
Oquin, Ezekiel	1				
Smith, Archd	1	3	4		1
McKay, Thomas	1		4		
Powell, Charles	5	4	4		1
Biggs, James, Sr	3	2	4		
Little, John	3	2	4		3
Grimes, Duncan	1	2	3		
Scott, John				1	
Newberry, Joseph	1	2	2		

FAYETTE DISTRICT, ROBESON COUNTY—Continued.

NAME OF HEAD OF FAMILY.	Free white males of 16 years and upward, including heads of families.	Free white males under 16 years.	Free white females, including heads of families.	All other free persons.	Slaves.
Crawford, Peter	1	1	3		
Brown, William	1	2	5		
McSwaine, Rodorick	2		6		
McSwaine, Angus	1		2		
McSwaine, Donald	1	1	3		
Little, Alex	3		3		
McLaughlan, Dugal	1	2	6		
Biggs, Samuel	1		2		
Revil, Burwell				1	
Humphrey, John	1	1	2		
Moore, James	1	1			
Ford, John	1		1		3
Buie, John (S. Master)	1	4	7		
McEachran, Robert	3	1	9		
Brown, Angus	3		1		1
Pitman, Hannah	1		1		
Oxendine, Charles				11	
Lowry, James				6	3
Kelly, Duncan	2	1	2		
Ray, Angus	4	5	2		
McGill, Archd	1	2	3		
Alford, Sion	1		4		4
Sellars, Archd	1	2	4		2
Brown, Angus	2	3	4		
Houston, Daniel	1	5	1		1
Strickland, Joseph	2		1		
Sled, John	1	1	2		
Smith, Angus	2	2	2		
Chavers, Richard				3	
Smith, Archd	1	2	2		
Pitman, Elizabeth	1	2	1		
Carrol, Thomas	2	1	4		
McNiel, Daniel	1	1	3		
Wilkerson, William, Jr	1	1	2		
McInnis, Donald	1	2	3		
Wilkerson, William, Sr	1		2		
Martin, Niel	1		1		
McClendon, James	2	1	3		
Moore, John	3	2	6		
Paul, Abraham	3	2	2		
Dees, Arthur	4	1	4		2
Turner, Aron	1	3	3		
McArthur, Peter	3		6		5
Paul, William	1	1	1		
McLaine, John	3	1	2		
McFarland, Daniel	1	1	3		2
McNair, Roger	2	1	2		
Atkinson, Molly			2	2	
Nicholson, Susanah	1		3		
McLaine, Niel	2	1	3		
McTyer, Robert	1	2	2		2
McKinven, John	1		3		
McLaine, Daniel, Jr	1				
Alford, Jacob	3	2	6	1	7
Alford, James	1	1	2		1
Little, Alex	1	2	4		
Hall, Susanah	1	4	2		
McKenzie, Kenneth	1	1	1		
Bridgers, Sampson	1		2		1
Parker, William	1		2		
McEachran, Duncan	2	2	6		
Fiveash, Elias	1		3		
Price, Lydia	1	2	4		
McLaine, Archd	2	1	4		
McLeod, Alex	1				
McKinnin, John	1		3		
Stewart, John	1	2	2		
McLeod, Norman	1	2	2		
McLaine, Hugh	1	1	4		
Traweek, Othinel	2	4	2		3
Ramsey, Niel	2	1	3		
McLaine, John	2		3		
Clark, John	1	1	2		
Grimes, Dugal	1		4		
Cameron, Aphia	1	4	4		
McCremon, Archd	1				
McCremon, Donald	1	1	4		
McLaine, Malcolm	1		5		
Watson, John	1	3	3		
McNair, Edward	1	1	1		
McKay, Donald	1	5	4		
McGirth, John	1		1		
Dannelly, John	1	5	3		
McGirth, Archd	1	2	5		
McCormick, Duncan	1	1	4		1
McQueen, Niel	1				
McMillen, James	1	1	4		
Carrel, Jesse	1		1		
McInnis, Molly			3		
Stewart, John	2		5		
McQueen, James	3	3	8		
McAllum, Ever	2	4	4		
McRae, Christo	1	2	3		
McRae, Donald	1	1			
McRae, Philip	1	3	4		
McIntire, John	3	2	4		
McRae, Mary		2	5		
McColl, John		3	1		
Henderson, Archd	2	3	3		
Fiveash, Demcy	1	3	3		
Fiveash, John	1	3	1		
Little, Niel	1		3		2
Thompson, Trimmigen		4	1		
Campbell, Kennith	2		2		
McNiel, John	1	1	2		2
McCormick, Archd	1	2	3		
McCormick, Gilbert	1	2	6		
McLaine, Daniel, Sr	1		2		
Little, Robert	1		2		
McClendon, Duncan	1		2		
Smith, Samuel	1	2	2		
Oquin, Tarler	1	3	7		
Thompson, Charles	2		1		7
Creel, Lazarus	2		2		
Jones, Ephraim	1	3	4		
Jones, Richard		1	1	3	
Bullard, James	1	5	4		
OHerne, Elizabeth		1	4		
Coleman, William	1		1		
Bullard, John	1	2	1	1	
Teddus, John	2		2		
Evans, Richard				4	
Grice, Mary	2	2	4		
Strickland, William	1	1	2		
Thompson, Henry	1	3			5
Wilkins, William	2		2		
Martin, Sarah		2	3		
Odom, James	1	1	3		1
Barfield, Sarah		2	2		
Star, Joseph	1	2	2		
Harding, Betty		1	2		
Rush, William	1	3	2		
Powell, Ann	2	2	3		
Odom, Jacob	2	1	3		
Lucas, Charles	2		1		
Hunt, James				4	
Layton, Henry	1			1	
Thompson, John	1	2	2		2
Hunt, William	2	1	2		
Drake, Britton	1	1	2		1
Kitchen, Joseph	1	1	5	1	
Thompson, George	1		1		
Atkins, Silas	1		2	2	8
Townsend, Thomas	1		4		
Thompson, William (H. Swamp)	1	4	2		4
Gaddy, Lucy	2		3		
Ward, Alley	1		2		
Thompson, Lamuel	1	1	1		
Murphy, Edward	2	3	3		1
Stableton, Alex					7
Bridgers, Samuel, Jr	1	1	2		2
Hunt, Alex	1	3	2		
Hunt, Richard	1	1	2		
Willis, Simon	1				
Ransome, Simon				6	
Moseley, Reddick	1				
Bird, John	1				
Hunt, Lewis				3	
Bridgers, Samuel, Sr	1		3		
Pitman, James	1				
Pitman, Isam	2		1		
Lowe, John	1		1		
Lowe, Daniel	1		2		
Lamb, Abraham	1		2		
Moore, James, Jr	1		3		
Rackley, John	1	1	1		
Moore, James, Sr	3	1	3		
Rowland, James	1	5	3		
Clyburn, William	2	2	6		
Bird, Isaac	3	1	6		
Britt, Samuel	1				
Britt, Lamuel	1	2	6		
Powell, Nicholas	1	3	1		1
Pitman, Joel	3	3	3		
Phillips, James	1	4	3		
Rowland, Elizabeth	2	1	4		
Rogers, James	2	4	3		
Hill, Slaughter	1	4	3		
Barfield, Charles	3	2	7		
Hill, Thomas	1		2		
Taylor, James	1	2	3		
Mitchell, Nazara	1	1	1		
Taylor, Teacle	1	1	2		
Allen, Nancy	2	2	3		
Hill, Nancy	2		2		
Lee, Stephen	1		1		
Barnes, Michael	2	2	5		
Powell, Duglas	1	4	3		
Edwards, Charles	1	1	5		
Flowers, Simon	1	1	1		1
Collins, James	1	1	2		
Davis, Thomas	1	3	4		6
Price, John	1	3	1		
Taylor, Willis	1		4		
Horn, Delilah	1	1	4		
Barnes, Josiah, Jr	1		3		1
Lee, Jesse, Jr	1	2	4		2
Lee, Joseph	1		4		
Pitman, Rachael	2	2	6		
Lamb, Campbell	1	4	1		
Rackley, Frederick	1	5	1		
Pope, Zedekiah	1	1	2		
Purvis, Henry	1	2	2		
Wright, Absalom	1		2		
Taylor, Jonathan	2		2		
Inman, Hardy, Sr	3	3	2		
Pitman, Isam, Jr	1	1	1		
Tholer, William	3	4	4		
Ivey, Adam	2	3	7		2
Stephens, William	1	3	3		
Lamb, Meady	1	2	6		
Atkinson, Joseph	3	1	3		
Atkinson, Samuel	1	3	5		
Pope, Henry	2	3	4		16
Pope, Jesse	1		2		
Bullock, Charles	3	5	1		
Pitman, Isam, Sr	2		1		
Bird, Isaac	3		6		
Wilcox, David	1	1	4		
Barfield, David	1	1	4		
Barfield, Sarah		1	2		
Maning, Hillery	1		2		
Hill, Moses	1	1	2		
Lee, Jesse, Sr	1	1	4		2
Cox, Simon	1	4	5		
Cox, John	1	2	2		
Lambs, Kinchen	1	5			
Whitley, Solomon	1	1	4		
Pitman, James, Jr	1	1	2		
Sutton, Jesse	1				
Atkinson, Howell	2		6		
Rowland, John	2	3	4		
Lamb, Arthur	2		5		9
Lamb, Barnaby	1		1		
Clyburn, Joshua	1	2	4		
Jones, Mathew	1	2	5		
Pitman, Hardy	1	2	1		
Atkinson, Jesse	1	2	3		
Perry, Philip	1	2	2		
Pitman, Thomas	1	3	8		1
Kersey, Solomon	2				
Drinkwater, Daniel	1	2	2		
Porter, Samuel	1	1	4		
Wingate, Cornelius	1	3	3		10
Holt, Francis	2	2	6		
James, Solomon				1	9
Rackley, Joseph	1	3	2		
Whitley, Solomon	1		4		
Jernigan, Capt Jesse	2	6	3		10
Stewart, Elizabeth		1	3		1
Ivey, Francis	2	3	5		
Williamson, Ellindor	1		1		
Grimsley, George	2	3	2		
Stephens, Moab	1	4	4		2
Lewis, Richard	1		4		
Lewis, James	1	2	4		
Edwards, Samuel	3	2	3		
Flowers, Mary	2	1	3		
Kennedy, Samuel, Jr	1		1		1
Kennedy, Samuel, Sr	1		2		4
Grantham, Nathan	1	1	2		
Page, Joseph	1	2	3		1
Ammon, Joshua	1	1	2		
Miller, George	1	3	3		1
Hill, William	1	1			
Grantham, James, Sr	1		2		
Grantham, James, Jr	1		2		
Page, Solomon	1				
Pate, Bennet	2		2		
Johnston, Absalom	2	2	4		
Horn, Ephraim	1	2	2		
Ashley, William	1		1		2
Barnes, Britton	2	3	7		1
Sealey, Tobias	2	3	4		
Grantham, Edward	1	1	2		
Grantham, Josiah	1	1	1		
Thompson, Reuben	1				
Fields, John	1		3		
Brumble, Elizabeth	1	1	2		
Lamb, William	1	1	2		
Ivey, Edey	1		4		
Harding, Solomon				6	
Branch, Randal				11	
Warwick, Moses	1	2	1		
Flowers, William	1	1	2		
Britt, John	1		2		
Cox, Gilbert				6	8
Hawthorn, Kedar	1	1	2		3
Inman, Hardy, Jr	1	1	2		2
Britt, Benjamin	2	2	5		

FAYETTE DISTRICT, ROBESON COUNTY—Continued.

NAME OF HEAD OF FAMILY.	Free white males of 16 years and upward, including heads of families.	Free white males under 16 years.	Free white females, including heads of families.	All other free persons.	Slaves.
Britt, William	1		1		
Ganey, Micajah	1		2		3
Mixon, Francis	1	1	2		
Barnes, William	2	5	3		1
Flowers, John	1		1		1
Barrett, John F	2	1	3		
Flowers, Edward	2		4		1
Little, John	1	1	1		
Ward, William	2		2		
Starling, William	1		2		
Lee, Everat	1				
Murphy William	1				
Lee, Lucy	2	1	2		
Long, Henry	1		1		
Bullard, Priscilla	1	2	4		
Ivey, Luke	1				
Phillips, Jesse	1		2		
Starling, John	1	1	2		1
Lamb, James	1		2		
Ingram, Jacob	2	2	3		
Grantham, Richard, Sr	2	1	4		
Watson, Tabitha		4	2		
Grantham, Moses	1	1	4		
Grantham, Richard, Jr	1		3		
Warren, John	1	1	4		
Legget, Wright	1	1	2		1
Barfield, Willis	1	6	1		
Bennet, William	1	1	1		
Hayle, Joseph	1	3	4		
Pitman, Thomas (Jernigans)	2	3	5		
Griffen, Andrew	1	1	3		
Hooks, Sarah		1	5		
Jones, Frederick	1		2		
Blount, Philip	3	2	5		
Hailes, Robert	2	1	1	2	
Oliver, William	3		3		
Glear, Stephen	1		3		2
Pitman, Sion	1	1	2		
Russell, James	1		4		
Irvin, Betty				2	
Travers, Patrick	1	3	2		7
Townsend, William	1	2	4		1
Coupland, James	1		1		
Coupland, John	3		3		
Thomas, Lewis	3	2	2		
Cobb, Exum	1				
Newsom, Ethelred				3	
Cumbo, John				3	
Cumbo, Cannon				11	1
Cumbo, Nathl				4	
Cumbo, Gilbert				1	
Blount, Jacob	1	3	4		1
Bryan, James	1		1		
Pate, Charles	1	2	3		1
Blount, Thomas	1		4		
Barker, Charles	2	3	1		1
Ezell, George	3		4		
Ivey, Thomas	4	2	5		
Butcher, Thomas	1	1	3		
Howell, Ralph	2	1	3		
Skeater, Joseph	1		5		
Russell, Nelly	1	2	2		
Williams, Joseph	2	4	3		
Revil, Edmund				9	
Williams, George	1	2	2		
Roberds, Ishmael				10	
Bagget, John	2	3	6		
Little, Sarah	3	2	2		
Gilbert, William	2		2		
Storm, John	1	4	3		
Bird, John	2	2	4		1
Wood, Joseph	2	2	4		11
Regan, John	3	1	3		13
Regan, Ralph	3	1	6		4
Rozier, Rueben, Sr	2	1	3		
Carter, Emanuel				5	
Regan, Anna			2	4	
Thomas, Richard	1	2	6		
Powers, Samuel	1	4	3		
Mathews, Thomas	1		2		
Bodiford, James	1	1	1		
Bird, William	2	1	4		
Smith, John, Sr	4		3		2
Kinlaw, Benjamin	1	1	4		
Regan, Richard	1	1	5		7
Kellyhan, Martin	1		1		
Anderson, Joseph	1		2		1
McRainey, Donald	1	1	3		

NAME OF HEAD OF FAMILY.	Free white males of 16 years and upward, including heads of families.	Free white males under 16 years.	Free white females, including heads of families.	All other free persons.	Slaves.
Lee, Shadrack	2	1	4		
Regan, Daniel	1	1	4		
McNair, Robert	1	1	4		
McAlpin, Malcolm	1	1	4		1
Taylor, Henry	2	1	6		
Glover, William	1	1	4		
Moss, Allen	1				
Powers, John	3		4		
Taylor, Patty		1	3		
Taylor, Ann	2	1	1		
Drury, Nancy			2		
Terrell, Philemon	2	5	4		
Terrell, Richmond	1	4	2		
Mercer, Christe	1		4		
Mercer, Solomon	1		4		
Cook, John	1	3	3		
Taylor, Mills	1	2	1		
Cook, William	1	1	4		
Kersey, William				4	
Taylor, Blake	1		2		
Howell, Ralph	1	2	3		
Mills, Anthony	1	2	4		1
Rozier, Reuben, Jr	1	2	2		
Pearce, Arthur	1	2	2		3
Ivey, Isam	2	3	4		
Ivey, Austin	1		1		
Niel, David	1				
Hawthorne, William	1		2		1
Bryan, Thomas	1	1	1		
Hawthorne, John	2	2	3		9
Kersey, Peter					7
Bryan, Isaac	1	2	2		
Freeman, Benjamin	2	3	4		
Kinlaw, Thomas	5	2	3		
Kersey, Betty					3
Stewart, John (Capt)	1	1	1		
Curry, Alexr	3	1	3		
Johnston, Alexr	2	2	4		
Brown, Hugh	2	1	3		6
Buie, Archd	1	2	2		1
McSwaine, Christian		1	2		
Godfrey, William	1		2		
Craft, James	2	2	3		
McMillen, Malcolm	1		1		
Buie, Archd (Capt)	1	1	2		
McLeod, Murdock	1	1	2		
McSwaine, Angus	1	1	2		
McLaine, Donald	1		2		
McSwaine, John	3	1	2		
Callyhan, Cornelius	1	3	1		
Councill, Mathew	3	2	7		
McLaine, Archd	1	2	3		1
Stewart, John, Sr	2		2		1
McGugan, Malcolm	1		1		
McSwaine, Alexr	1				
McDermad, Farquhard	1		3		
McPhail, John	1	4	1		
Patterson, Alexr	1	2	1		1
Smith, Peter	1		2		
Monro, Lewis	2	2	7		
McLaughlan, John	1	1	2		
Morrison, Norman	1	1	4		
Huneycut, Frederick	2	1	2		
Monro, Collin	2	3	2		
McMillen, Malcolm	1		1		
McMillen, John	1		1		
Malloy, John, Jr	1	3	2		
Smith, Niel	1	3	5		1
McMillen, John, Sr	2		4		
McMillen, Niel	2	5	4		
Patterson, Angus	2		2		
Barlow, Ralph	1	1	2		
Barlow, John	1		2		
Puff, Andrew	2	1	6		
Wilkerson, Richard	3	5	4		
Henderson, Duncan	1	2	3		
Kelly, Peter	1				4
McNiel, James	4		5		8
Stewart, John (L. Land)	1	1	1		
Mathews, John	1	3	2		
Murphy, John	3	1	3		
McFaul, John	1	2	3		1
McIntagart, Daniel	1	2	3		
Mathews, Daniel	1	4	7		
Stewart, John	1	2	3		
Oxendine, Benjamin					1
Patterson, John	1	2	2		
McGugan, Hugh	1		1		

NAME OF HEAD OF FAMILY.	Free white males of 16 years and upward, including heads of families.	Free white males under 16 years.	Free white females, including heads of families.	All other free persons.	Slaves.
Mason, Moses	1				21
McPherson, Daniel	1		4		
Dorman, Elizabeth		1	1		
Witherow, Malcolm	1		1		
McNiel, Niel	1	2	2		
McKay, Christe	2	6	4		
McLeod, Murdock	1		4		
Shaw, Donald	1	1	3		
McKinnen, Donald	1		2		
Shaw, Malcolm	2		1		1
Morrison, Murdock	1	2	3		
McNiel, Hector	1	2			1
McNiel, Archd	1	1	4		1
McMillen, Duncan	1	2	7		
Strickland, Abraham	2	2	4		
Brassell, William	1		2		
McEachran, Archd	1		3		
McDonald, John	1		6		
McLaine, John	2	1	2		
McArthur, John	1	4	2		1
Jernigan, Jesse	1	4	2		6
McMillen, Daniel	1	3	1		
McMillen, Niel	1	3	3		
McSwaine, Malcolm	1		1		
McInnis, Niel	1		2		
McInnis, John	2	3	2		
McInnis, Daniel	1	3	1		
Curry, Laughlan	1	2	2		
Craig, Alexr	2		1		
Curry, Malcolm	1	4	6		
McAllum, Duncan	2	4	4		
Ferguson, Anguish	1		2		
Teaster, Samuel	1				
McMillen, John	1	3	3		
McGeshy, Alexr	1		2		
Cameron, John	1	2	7		
Watson, James	2	1	5		
Wilkerson, Edward	1	2	1		
McNair, Daniel	1	2	2		
Wilkerson, Daniel	1		1		
Wilkerson, Niel	1	2	4		
Morrison, Murdock	1		3		
McKinnen, John	1		2		
McRae, Alexr, Jr	1	3	3		
McRae, Alexr, Sr	1	2	3		
Ferguson, Niel	1	1	3		
McDugal, Archd	1		5		
Buie, John	1	4	7		
Kelley, Duncan	2	1	2		
Stone, James	1		3		
Johnston, John	3	3	3		2
McKeathen, Daniel	3	3	3		
McKinnen, Duncan	1		5		
Smith, Samuel	1	1	3		
McLeod, Alexr	1		5		
Beaton, David	1	3	3		
Kelly, Daniel	1	3	3		
Ray, Laughlan	4	1	2		
McGill, Angus	2	1	3		
Morrison, John	1		4		
Thompson, Malcolm	1	2	4		
Buie, Duncan	3	1	2		1
McMillen, Archd	1	1	2		
Black, Archd	1	1	4		1
Black, James	1	1	2		
McDonald, Daniel	2	2	2		
Callihan, Bryant	2		1		
Campbell, Duncan	4		1		
Powers, William	1		2		
McEachran, Daniel	3	2	3		2
McLaughlan, Robert	1		2		
Gilchrist, William	1	3	2		
Campbell, Daniel	4	2	4		3
Laman, Kenzie	1	1	2		
McLeod, Alexr	1		4		
McDaniel, Daniel	1	1	3		
Buie, Malcolm	3		1		
Sinclair, Colin	1	2	4		
McNiel, Archd	1				
McEachran, Archd, Jr	1				
McCollum, Duncan, Jr	1	2	1		
Pledger, Joseph	1		1		
Pitman, Moses	1	1	1		
Walker, Charles	1	3	3		
Baker, James	4	1	2		
Griffin, James	2		1		1
McDonald, Angus	1		3		
McMillen, Niel	2	4	4		

FAYETTE DISTRICT, SAMPSON COUNTY.

NAME OF HEAD OF FAMILY.	Free white males of 16 years and upward, including heads of families.	Free white males under 16 years.	Free white females, including heads of families.	All other free persons.	Slaves.
Blocker, William	2	5	3		1
Sessoms, Solomon	1	2	5		
Faircloth, Samuel	1	1	3		
Sessoms, Isaac	2	2	2		
Faircloth, Benjamin	3	4	4		
Lucas, Lewis	1	3	3		
Harwood, John	2	4	3		
Faircloth, Hardy	1	5	1		
Fisher, Southy	2	3	2		3
Emanuel, Ephraim				3	3
Spiller, James	1		4	1	32
James, David	3	4	5		
Bryan, Bartrum	1	1	2		
Stanly, John, Sr	2	2	7		8
Stanly, Leven	2	6	6		
Stanly, Stephen	2	1	4		
Stanly, John, Jr	3	2	6		
Powers, Jesse	2	3	2		
Underwood, Thomas	2	2	4		
Cook, John	1	2	4		
Carrol, James	3	1	7		1
Wister, John	2	1	3		6
Clark, David	3	1	3		2
Kelley, Joseph	6		4		
Williford, William	2	3	4		
Bracher, John	2		2		
Dean, Jeremiah	1	1	3		
Bracher, Christopher	1	1	2		
Vick, Nathan, Sr	1		4		
Vick, Nathan, Jr	1		5		
Williford, Sion	1	1	2		
Brewer, James	3	4	3		
Mason, Mathew	1	1	6		3
Hollingsworth, James	2	4	4		
Gregory, Thomas	1	2	3		
Hines, Solomon	2		2		
Crumpler, John	1	3	4		10
Fisher, Bailey	1	2	2		1
Newman, Sarah	1		5		
Emanuel, Jesse				6	
Hayle, Joshua	1	2	4		
Purgen, Mathew	1	1	6		1
Fields, George	1	1	5		
Hall, John	3	3	3		
Bullard, Thomas	1	1	3		
Hall, Josiah	1	1	1		
Kelley, Jacob	1	2	2		
Herring, Martha	1	2	4		6
McIlewinnen, John	2	2	5		3
Bryan, David	1		3		
Bradshaw, Thomas	2	1	2		
Bradshaw, Ephraim	1	1	2		
Bradshaw, Jesse	1		3		
Stephens, Barnaby	1	1	5		6
McClendon, James	1	1	1		1
Sewell, Thomas	1		3		33
Oates, Jesse	1	4	3		8
Oates, Jethro	1	1	1		2
Oates, Artesha		1	2		11
Stephens, Mildred	2	1	3		10
Ratley, Joshua	2	2	3		
Ratley, Jesse	1		1		
Butler, Jesse	2	5	2		
Ryal, Wright	1		2		2
Ryal, John	2	1	1		
Williamson, Benjamin	3	1	2		
Pugh, Shadrack	2	2	3		7
Ammonds, Joshua	1	1	1		
Treadwell, John	2	1	3		20
Herring, Richard	4		3		12
Boon, William	3		4		
Hawes, Ezekel	1			1	
Dodd, David	2	3	3		6
Fort, John	3	1	4	1	
Coggen, Thomas	1				3
Bell, Orson	1	2	1		
Cook, John	1	3	4		
McClam, Solomon	1	4	4		
Bell, Benjamin	1				1
Register, Thomas	2		5		2
Register, John	1	2	3		
Ratley, Jeremiah	1		1		
Hay, Peter	1	3	1		
Boon, Stephen	1	4	5		
Lee, Henry	1	2	4		
Pope, Thomas	3	5	7		
Butler, James	2	3	6		3
Mathews, Rice	1	3	4		1
Mobley, Biggers	2	1	3		1
Robinson, William	1	1	1		
Merritt, Absalom	2	2	3		
Wootten, William, Sr	3	1	3		
Wootten, William, Jr	1		4		
Faircloth, John	1	3	4		
Wootten, Jesse	1		2		
Howard, James	3	3	6		
Register, John	1	1	1		

NAME OF HEAD OF FAMILY.	Free white males of 16 years and upward, including heads of families.	Free white males under 16 years.	Free white females, including heads of families.	All other free persons.	Slaves.
Ryal, Thomas	1		3		
Lockerman, Jacob	1		2		
Stephens, Micajah	1	1	2		2
Wiggins, William	2	5	2		
Wiggins, Thomas	1		2		8
Robinson, Thomas	1	1	2		6
Hatcher, Timothy	1	1	2		3
Johnston, Joshua	1	2	2		
Robinson, James	1				10
Robinson, William, Jr	1				9
Rainer, David	1	3	3		
Ward, Jesse	1	1	5		
Ratliff, Samuel	2	1	2		1
Hill, Jean	1	2	4		
Key, Robert	2	4	5		
McClendon, Jesse	1				
Key, Charles	1	3	6		
Joyner, Benjamin	4		4		1
Lynch, Nathaniel	1	1	4		
Elmore, Thavis	2	2	4		
Daniel, Isaac	2	1	6		
Pipkin, Ashu	1	1	5		
Westbrook, William	1	2	3		1
Mainer, Josiah	2	2	4		
Wilson, Elisha Moore	3	3	6		4
Fraser, David	1		2		
Wiggins, William	2		3		
McClan, William	1	3	9		
Wiggins, George	1	2	2		
Slokum, Joseph	2	1	3		3
Roach, John	1				2
Sutton, Thomas	1	5	3		6
Smith, Noah	1	2	3		
Murphrey, Charles	1	4	7		
Strickland, Samuel, Jr	1	3	3		
Strickland, Thomas	3	2	5		
Hodgson, James	1		3		
Ryal, Marmaduke	2				
Peterson, Nathan	1	2	3		1
Peterson, Thomas	1		1		
Peterson, Cassaann		1	1		
Bryan, Kedar	3	3	4		34
Merrett, Robert	2	1	6		5
Parker, Jonathan	1	2	5		3
Register, Thomas	1	3	4		
Marsh, Thomas	1	3	4		
Edwards, William	1		3		
Sykes, Needham	2	1	3	1	
Starling, Smiley	1	2	3		
Fowler, Richard	2	1	4		
McLeod, Daniel	1	1	3		
Daughtry, Benjamin	2	3	5		
Fowler, William	1	1	4		
Fowler, Daniel	1	3	1		
Scarbrough, Benjamin	2	1	2		
Blackburn, William	2	3	3		
Kinsey, Absalom	3	3	3		
Peterson, Aron	1	5	1		
Peterson, Moses	1	4	2		
Kinsey, Daniel	1	1	2		
Van, John	1		2		
Whitney, Josiah	1	2	1		
Nealy, Andrew	1	3	5		6
Bryant, Sarah	2		1		1
Gauff, Thomas	1	2	6		
Carrol, Demcy	1				
Oquin, Alexander	1	1	4		
Carrol, Stephen	1	1	4		1
Kennedy, Patrick	1	3	4		
Williams, Alexander	2	3	4		
Jackson, William	3	2	4		
Register, Benjamin	1	1	1		
Crumpler, Jacob	1	3	4		5
Tew, Philip	1	2	1		
Webb, James	2	3	2		
Starling, Seth	2	2	6		
Fields, John	1		3		
Kean, William	1	1	4		
Runnals, Mathew	1	1	2		
McLeod, John	1		2		
Tew, Jeremiah	1	3	6		
Carrol, Alexander	1	2	2		
Cooper, Coor	2		2		
Coor, Daniel	1	3	3		
Jones, Nathan	1	1	3		6
Butler, Charles	2		4		
Emanuel, Nicholas				5	
Carrol, Jesse	3	4	4		5
Goodman, Jacob	1		1		
Tatum, Laban	1	1	3		3
Sessions, Richard	2	7	6		14
Averatt, William	2	1	1		
Tatum, Joshua	1	2	4		1
Rich, Lott	1		3		
Ryal, William	2		3		
Ryal, Ormond	1	6	2		

NAME OF HEAD OF FAMILY.	Free white males of 16 years and upward, including heads of families.	Free white males under 16 years.	Free white females, including heads of families.	All other free persons.	Slaves.
Williamson, Stephen	1		2		
Harding, David	1	4	5		
Odom, William	2	2	1		2
Daniel, Elias	1		1		
Odom, Alexander	1	3	3		
Harris, Benjamin	1	2	1		
Odom, Abraham	2	3	4		
Bell, Samuel	1				10
Williams, Jacob	1	1	5		
Harding, Benjamin	1	2	2		
Harding, Abraham	1	2	2		
Mainer, Benjamin	1	2	4		
Wright, John	1		2		3
Downing, Nancy		2	3		
Nelms, Edmund	1	1	2		
Pope, West	3		2		
Colbraith, Daniel	1	1	2		1
Ammon, Thomas	1		1		
Strickland, William	5	3	3		
Holder, George	1	2	2		
Robinson, William	1				7
Tayloe, Leban	1		1		1
Tayloe, Jonathan	1	1	4		4
Herrick, Jesse	1	1	4		
Cook, James	3		1		
Register, Benjamin	1	2	2		
Jones, Henry	2	1	5		
Murrell, Merrett	1		1		
Tatum, Jesse	1	1	1		
Herring, Jacob	1		1		
Morgan, Edward	2	2	1		
Packer, Joseph	2	1	3		
Roberson, James	1				9
Cole, William	1	1	4		1
Hobbs, George	1	1	2		
Hobbs, Simon	1	2	4		2
Watson, Ezekiel	1	4	5		
Cameron, Isaac	1	1	4		
Scott, Joseph	1		2		5
Drew, Josiah	1	1	3		3
Peacock, Abraham	1	2	5		
Hargrove, Arthur	2	1	4		
McLeod, Niel	3	4	5		
Emanuel, John				5	
Smith, William	1		1		
Page, Thomas	3	2	4		
Garner, Thomas	1	1	4		
Oates, Samuel	1	2	3		
Williams, Joseph	1	2	2		3
Atwell, John	1	2	2		1
Oates, James	1	2	2		3
Butler, Jethro	1	1	5		
Hillburn, Vaughn	4	5	5		
Magee, Solomon	2		3		
Boyakin, Smithick	1	1	1		
Drew, John	1	1	3		14
Godwin, Jacob	4	1	5		
Godwin, Mary		1	1		
Magee, Philip	1		1		
Magee, John	2		5		4
Runnals, Amos	4	4	5		
Lockerman, Jacob	1	3	2		
Runnals, Mathew	1	1	2		
Holley, John	2	3	3		
Dean, Richard	2	3	4		
Magee, Robert	1	2	3	1	
Magee, John	1	2	2		
Ammon, Howell	2		2		
Ammon, Vaughn	2	3	4		
Daughtry, Joshua	1		2		6
Holmes, Hardy	2		2		14
Ship, Ephraim	1	2	4		3
Terry, David				4	
Ryal, William	1		2		
Salmon, Richard	3	3	5		
King, Stephen	2	5	3		13
Carr, Jonathan	4	3	5		2
Hargrove, John	1		1		
Smith, John	1	1	5		5
Herring, Joseph	1	1	1		3
Wootten, Thomas	1		1		
Ryal, Owen	2	4	1		5
Scarbrough, Michael	1	1	4		
Cameron, Daniel			4		
Epperson, Mary			4		
Fryer, Jonathan	2	4	5	1	9
Gregory, Lott	1	4	4		3
Lee, William	2	2	4		3
Bell, Arch	1				
Cameron, Philip	1	1	2		
Atwell, Benjamin	2	2	2		
Daughtry, Abraham	1	1	2		
Snell, Charles	1		1		6
Hargrove, Moses	1	1	3		
Tew, John	1	1	2		
Wilkins, James	1	1	2		
Cook, Shadrack	1		3		

FAYETTE DISTRICT, SAMPSON COUNTY—Continued.

NAME OF HEAD OF FAMILY.	Free white males of 16 years and upward, including heads of families.	Free white males under 16 years.	Free white females, including heads of families.	All other free persons.	Slaves.
Gavin, Samuel	1	1	2		2
Jernigan, Jesse	1	5	1		2
Fraser, Thomas	1		3		
Nolley, Josiah	1	2	4		
Turbevill, Joseph	2	2	4		3
Brady, John	1				
Hobbs, William	1	5	3		
Blackwell, William	1	1	2		
Chesnut, David	1		4		
Carrol, John, Sr	2	3	5		
Van, William	2	2	5		1
Scott, Joseph	1	3	4		3
Thornton, Thomas, Jr	1	2	3		1
Herring, Uzzill	1	5	1		
Lee, Isaac	1	1	7		
King, Michael	2	2	7		10
Cook, Lazarus	1	3	1		
Enzor, Sommers	1	1	3		
Merrett, Nothiel	1		4		2
Merrett, Frederick	1	1	4		1
Merrett, Jacob	1	1	2		
Merrett, Theophilus	1	2	4		
Merrett, David	1		2		
Lee, Noah	1	3	6		
Gavin, Lewis	1	2	1		1
Hollingsworth, Henry	1	2	4		
Merrett, Philip	1	2	4		
Chesnut, Alexander	1		1		
Tyler, Owen	1	4	1		
Bennett, John	1	4	4		
Carr, Thomas	1	8	3		2
Gavin, Charles	1	2	2		
Boyakin, John	1				
Morgan, Hamlin	1				
Turlington, Southy	4		2		
Sykes, Cornelus	1	1	3		
Jacobs, Abraham				3	
Cooper, John	1	3	5		
Carter, Moses				9	
Conner, Ishmael	1				3
White, George	1	1	5		1
White, Luke	2	1	3		8
Register, Joseph	1	3	3		
Register, Josiah	1	1	2		
Boykin, Bijus	1	2	2		2
Scott, Nehemiah	1	1	2		19
Boyt, John	1	1	3		
Carr, Patrick	1		3		
Parker, Nicholas	1		1		2
Young, Dobbs	1		6		
Oquin, Patrick	1		10		
Taylor, Henry	1		1		
Benton, Josias	4		3		
Airs, Thomas	1	1	3		
Johnston, Peregrine	2	1	3		
Givin, Josiah	1		2		
Strickland, Holly	1	1	2		
Strickland, William	2		3		
Strickland, John	1		2		
Williams, John	3	1	3		6
Jordan, William	1	1	5		
Jordan, Philip	2	2	3		
Butler, Robert	3	1	5		1
Hall, Armager	1	2	2		
Hall, William	1		4		
Gilbert, James	1	1	5		
Chesnut, Joshua	1		5		1
Chesnut, John, Sr	1	6	4		
Lasseter, George	2	1	6		
Murphy, William	1	2	4		1
Whitley, Elijah	1		4		
Fort, John	2	1	7		10
Turner, John	1		1		
Carter, Henry					8
Thompson, William	1	1	1		8
Faison, Frances			4		1
Holmes, Gabriel	1		2		15
Holmes, Owen	1	2	2		13
Scott, Nehemiah	1		2		4
Chesnut, Alexr, Jr	1		2		
Register, Joseph	1		2		
Butler, Isaac	1		2		
Van, King	1	3	4		
Stephens, Hardy	1	2	2		3
Sykes, Joshua, Jr	1		2		
Sykes, Joshua, Sr	2	1	5		
King, Henry	2				4
Butler, Stephen	1				
Butler, Jacob	1				1
Holland, Thomas	1		4		
Wiggs, Henry	1	3	3		
Blount, William	1	2	3		
Stephens, John	1	1	2		2
Hay, Charles	1	1	3		
Spiva, William	1	3	2		
Parker, William	1	3	1		2
Ward, John	1	2			
Cook, Cornelius	1	2	4		
Runnals, Dredrill	1	1	3		
Magee, Jacob	1	1	3		21
Chesnut, Jacob	3	1	7		8
Darden, Jesse	3	3	4		5
Tew, Jean	1	3	4		
Tew, Marmaduke	1	4	3		
Blew, Duncan	1		3		
Register, Shadrack	1	1	1		
Tucker, William	1	3	1		11
Baine, George	1	3	2		
Samford, William	1		2		
Bryant, Sarah	2		1		1
Blackmon, James	2	1	1		4
Flowers, John				1	
Fellow, William	1	2	3		20
Clinton, Richard	2	3	3		37
Murray, Leonard	1	2	4		
Pride, Josiah	1		2		
Bell, Robert	2		6		11
Bell, Felix	1				1
Bell, Micajah	1				1
Ryal, Isam	1	1	2		
Ryal, Thomas	1		3		
Turner, Myal	1	1	5		
Scarbrough, John	1	2	3		
Brewer, Henry	1	2	1		1
Peterson, William	1	3	3		
Williamson, Joseph	1		1		
Magee, Solomon	1		1		
Bell, Jesse	3	3	6		1
Kelley, James	2	4	4		
Butler, William, Jr	1		3		
Butler, Robert, Jr	1	1	3		1
Carrol, Demey	2		3		
Ryal, Willis	1	1	3		
Wiggins, Elihu	1	3	5		
Butler, William, Sr	2	3	4		
Williamson, William	2	2	5		
Hunnicut, William	1	2	5		
Dollar, William	1	3	4		
Williams, William	1	4	4		6
Bramble, William	1	5	4		
Lee, Joseph	1	1	4		
Williams, Rachael	1		1		
Williamson, William, Jr	2	1	2		
Jones, Benjamin	1	3	2		
Stewart, James	2	3	2		
Peterson, Malcolm	1	2	5		1
Jackson, George	1	5	3		
Wrench, John	1	1	2		
Maxwell, Thomas	1	4	2		1
Mathews, Frederick	1	2	6		
Lockerman, James	3	3	3		
Porter, Absalom	1	2	5		
Revil, Nathaniel					13
Crumpler, Mathew	2	1	6		
Bass, William	2	3	4		
Godwin, James	3	4	4		
Godwin, Aron	1		2		
McQueen, Norman	1	1	3		
McQueen, John	1	2	4		
Godwin, Richard	3	4	4		
Godwin, Rachael	2	2	1		
Holden, Ann	1	1	8		
Godwin Nathan	1	4	6		
Watson, John	1	1	2		
Godwin, Solomon	1	1	2		
Bullard, Thomas	1		3		
Holley, Ozburn	1		3		
Holley, Edward	1		2		
McDaniel, Malcolm	1		3		
Bagley, Elizabeth			2		
Smith, James	1	2	2		
Jackson, Lewis	2	5	3		
Dean, Farmer	1	2	1		
Williford, Micajah	1	3	1		
Goodman, John	1		4		
Bass, Burwell	1		6		
Hartley, James	1	2			
Bass, Elizabeth	1		6		
Carraway, Bedreddon	3	3			6
House, John	3		1		6
Dudley, Daniel	1	3	3		
Bass, Richard	1	3	6		
Holden, William	1	1	3		
Maclemore, West	1	2	4		
Creach, Simon	1	4	3		1
Dormon, John	1		1		
Jackson, Richard	1	1	1		
Warwick, Benjamin	2	5	2		
Wadkins, Isaac	1	1	1		
Odom, Demcy	1	1			
Odom, Jacob	1				
Williams, Joel	1	1	4		
Laighton, James	1		1		
Starling, John	1	2	2		
Strickland, Samuel, Sr	1	1	2		
Smith, Howell	1	5	1		
Ganey, Jacob	1		4		
Ganey, Edmund	1		1		
Thornton, John	2	4	3		
Grantham, David	1	3	2		
Smith, William	2		4		
Lee, William	1				
Salkeld, Isaac	1		1		
Wilson, Thomas	1	3	3		
Mihaynes, William	1	2	2		
Ingram, Pherebee	1	2	2		9
Jones, Charles	2	1	3		
Ganey, William	1		5		1
Wagers, Dawson	1	3	2		
Holley, John	1	2	6		
Blackmon, Esther	2	2	2		1
Ganey, Bartholomew	4		3		7
Barks, Joseph	1	3	6		
Lee, Peter	4	1	4		6
Lee, Jesse	2	1	2		3
Daniel, Jacob	1		3		
Joyner, James	1	1	3		
Bray, Benjamin	1	1	4		
Bray, Peter	1		1		
Ball, William	2				3
Ganey, Reddick	3	1	3		
Haynes, Joseph	3	1	6		
Godwin, William	1	6	4		
Peters, Ann	2	2	3		
Vick, Robert	2	1	4		3
Lee, Sampson	2	3	4		1
Holley, James	1		5		
Smith, Noah	1	2	3		
Williamson, William, Jr	1	3	4		
Blackmon, Josiah	4	1	4		9
Lee, Westbrook	1	2	4		
Thornton, Nathaniel	1	4	4		4
Thornton, Thomas, Sr	2		2		8
Lee, Bud	1				
Wood, Furnifold	1	2	2		3
Blackmon, Joab	1	1	4		
Colbraith, Niel	1	7	4		1
Autry, Theophilus	1		3		
Sutton, Christe	1	3	4		
Wood, Francis	1	1	2		
Jones, John Moss	1	1	6		
Porter, John	2	1	2		
Faircloth, Samuel	1	1	4		
Williams, Robert	1	4	4		5
Autry, Cornelius	1	1	1		
Hall, Moses	1		2		
Butler, John	2	3	5		
Daniel, John	1	4	1		
Autry, Rachael	3	1	2		
Johnston, John	1	3	4		
Carter, Josiah	1	2	3		
Sessums, Nicholas	1	1	2		
Sessums, Richard	1	2	2		
Grice, James	1	1	4		
Lucas, Lewis	1	3	3		2
Natt (Old)				2	
Owens, William	1	2	2		2
Wiggens, John	2	1	4		
Ryal, Young	1	3	4		4
Campbell, Alexr	1	2	2		
McKinnen, Murdock	2	4	5		
Moore, Sarah	1	1	4		
Jackston, Nathan	1		5		
Daniel, Elias	1		1		
Porter, Samuel	2	3	6		
Dees, Hardy	2	1	4		
Williams, Timothy	3		4		
Gibbs, Sarah	2		4		
Williams, Nathan	1		1		
Williams, Rueben	1	1	1		
Williams, Isaac	3	5	6		2
Williams, Joseph	1	6	5		1
House, George	1	1			
Williams, Henry	2	4	3		2
Brown, Arthur	1		4		
Brown, Therod	1	1	2		
Smith, Luke	1				
Drew, Judith	1	2			1
Chesnut, Alexr	1				
Runnals, Frances			4		
Houston, Peter	2		4		
Rich, Joseph	1		4		
Rich, Joshua	1		4		
Bracker, Christopher	1	1	4		
Wright, William	1		4		
Wright, Robert	1		1		3
Hair, John	1		2		
Bullard, Jeremiah	2		2		1
Edge, Elliott	1	2	2		
Adom, John	1		4		
Nance, Wynn	1	1	2		3

FAYETTE DISTRICT, SAMPSON COUNTY—Continued.

NAME OF HEAD OF FAMILY.	Free white males of 16 years and upward, including heads of families.	Free white males under 16 years.	Free white females, including heads of families.	All other free persons.	Slaves.
Walker, Baker	1		5		
Chesnut, Jacob	1	1	2		
Williamson, William, Sr	6	1	4		
Pope, Jeremiah	1	5	3		
Moore, Lewis	1				8
Moore, Ann	1	1	4		17
Moore, Ezekiel	1	1	1		5
Myhand, Silas	1		5		1
Pope, Jacob	1		3		
Magee, Willis	1		1		
Magee, Philip	1	1	3		
Pope, Harris	1		4		
Chesnut, Charles	2		5		
Jackson, John, Jr	1	2	3		
Creeck, Simon	1	4	3		1
Jackson, John, Sr	1		2		
Jackson, Richard	1	1	1		
Snell, Mary	2	2	3		13
Snell, John	1				5
Drew, William	1		2		
Bird, Edward	3	2	5		9
King, Michael, Jr	1				1
Izard, Henry	1	2	1		
Poitivint, Isaac	2	1	3		6
Goodman, Jacob, Sr	1		3		
Goodman, Jacob, Jr	1		1		
Lee, Edward	1				
Bryant, John	1	2	3		1
Register, John, Sr	1	2	4		
Cason, Charity	3		4		1
Hollingsworth, Zebulon	1		3		
Holmes, Lewis	1	1	2		7
Brewington, Amey				4	
Williams, Crecy				3	
Williams, Hannah			2		
Faison, James	1	4	3		5
Faison, Elisha	1	1	1		1
Gregory, Lott	2	3	3		3
Fisher, Elijah	2	2	4		1
Maclemore, Drury	1		5		
Johnston, Loasbe	1	3	3		
Ivey, Curtis	1	2	3		5
Williams, Daniel	1	3	3		11
Thompson, James	1	3	5		5
Ivey, Thomas	3		4		12
Stewart, Dugal	2		2		
Porter, Tully	1				4
Crumpler, Rayford	1				
King, William	1	2	5	1	31
Gilmour, Sophia		1	2		2
Hair, William	4	4	3		
Parker, Lessum	1	1	1		2
Holley, Sherod	1	1	2		
McPhail, Alexr	1		1		2
Vick, Cooper	1	3	2		
Kean, John	2	1	4		
Jones, Shadrack	3	2	6		
Oquin, Josiah	1		2		
McPhail, Alexr	4		2		
Cullee, Polly	1		2		
Fowler, John	3	3	3		
Fowler, Joseph	1	3	4		
Simmons, Jeremiah, Sr	4	1	3		
Simmons, Jeremiah, Jr	1		4		
Herringdine, James	1	1	4	1	
Simmons, John	2	1	4		
Morgan, John	1		7		
Morgan, Frederick	1		1		
Barnes, Eliazer	1	1	1		
Young, John Sampson	1		3		
Merril, Henry	2		3		
Watkins, David	1	2			
Martin, Paul	2	2	7		
Hutson, Miles	1		3		
Young, Winifred			4		
Willams, Joseph				4	
Jacobs, Thomas				7	
Ireland, Amey				5	
Davis, Fanny		2	3		
Whitley, William	1		1		
Mainor, Jack				1	
Hobbs, Henry	1	1	2		
Hobbs, John	1	1	1		
Bird, Edward, Jr	1	1	1		2
Lee, Christopher	1		4		
Burnet, Catharine		1	1		
Brewington, Ann				3	
Thomas, Luke	1	1	4		1
Justice, John	1	1	3		
Darden, Mary	1		3		
Darden, William	1	1	1		4
Blackman, Stephen	1	1	3		2
McClendon, Simon	1	1	2		10
Sutton, Thomas	1	4	2	1	5
Dunn, Jacob	1	2	2		
Faison, Fanny	3	1	2		1
McCullen, John, Sr	2		2		

NAME OF HEAD OF FAMILY.	Free white males of 16 years and upward, including heads of families.	Free white males under 16 years.	Free white females, including heads of families.	All other free persons.	Slaves.
McCullen, John, Jr	1	1	2		
Pipkin, Ashur	1	1	4		1
Livingston, John	1	5	3		1
McCullen, Lewis	1	1	1		
Williamson, George	1		1		1
Stephens, Bernard	1	1	5		7
McClendon, James	1	1	3		1
Bell, Benjamin	2	1	3		
Hill, Francis	6	1	3		4
West, William	1	2	3		1
Jackson, Archd	1	4	3		
Darden, William	2	1	3		4
Coley, William	1	5	2		
Hodges, Joseph, Sr	1		1		
Hodges, Joseph, Jr	1	2	1		
Hicks, Thomas	2	1	1		16
Murphy, Miles	2	2	3		2
Murphy, Richard	1	3	2		
Pope, Blackburn	1	1	1		
Pope, Jeremiah	2	2	4		
Murphy, Michael	2	3	4		
Wiggs, John	2	2	4		
Howard, Minron	1	1	1		1
Emanuel, Levi					5
Daniel, Jacob	1		2		
King, Mike	2				3
Magee, Jacob	1	3	5		
Wright, Lesee					1
Smith, Mary		1	1		
Jones, Rebecca		1	2		
Harris, Rebecca		1	2		
Harris, John	2	1	2		
Dyer, Samuel	1				1
Roach, Sarah					1
Wiggins, Patty					5
Clewis, Molly					3
Wiggins, Mary					6
Waldon, Jack					1
Coggin, Ruth				1	
Jones, Martha				2	
Cloeraly				4	
Fields, Samuel	1				
Womble, Suky			1	2	
Bayles, Jude			1	3	
Joyner, Isam	1		1	1	
Hatcher, Anna			1	1	
Godwin, Priscilla			1	1	
Williams, Anna				3	
Cobb, Becky					3
Hammonds, Miles					1
Dawson, Gilbert				1	
Taylor, George	1				
Gilbert, John	1				
Segars, John			1	4	
Strickland, Alexr	1	2	2		
Sullivant, Robert	2	1	3		
Williams, Benjamin	1				
Williams, John	1				
Stanley, Elizabeth			1	1	
Duae, William	1				
Duae, Robert	1				
Goodman, Sylvia			1	3	
Caruthers, Nancy			1	2	
Page, Thomas, Jr	1			1	
Waring, Jacob				1	2
Elliott, Elias	1	1	2		
Davis, Solomon	1	1	3		
Price, Richard	1	2	3		
Sessions, Richard	1	2	3		
Sessions, Nicholas	1	1	1		
Davis, Henry	1	1	3		
Davis, Jesse	1	1	2		
Davis, John	1		2		
Owens, Mary		1	2		7
Edge, Elliott	1	1	2		
Hair, Jacob	1		1		
Hair, William	1	1	3		
Hair, Thomas	1	2	5		
Whitley, Amey		1	2		
Perkins, Samuel	1	1	2		
Smith, William	1	1	1		
Morgan, Frederick	1		1		
Bell, Polly			1	2	
Williams, Christian		2	2		
Owens, Thomas	1	1	2		1
Bullock, Benjamin	2	2	2		
Parker, Lewis	1		1		
Clinton, Thomas	1	1	2		4
Easom, John	1	2	3		1
Ward, Betty		1	2		
Ward, Jane			1		
Price, Josiah	1		2		
Hargrove, Bray			1		
Hargrove, John	1				
Whitfield, William	1	1	1		3
Clark, James	1	1	1		4
Williams, John	1	1	2		

NAME OF HEAD OF FAMILY.	Free white males of 16 years and upward, including heads of families.	Free white males under 16 years.	Free white females, including heads of families.	All other free persons.	Slaves.
Clark, Nathan	1	2	3		1
Powell, Restore		1	1		4
Holland, Henry	1	2	3		
Snell, Stephen	1	1	3		
Griggs, John	1	1			
Harris, John	1	1	3		
Brooks, John	1	2	4		
Ryal, John	1	2	1		3
Powell, Jacob	1	1	3		
Cooper, Fleet	1	3	4		1
Cooper, William	2	3	3		
Futch, Martin	1	1	2		
Jenkins, John	1		2		
Jenkins, Thomas	1		2		
Hatcher, Bedy			2		
Nelms, Lewis	1		3		
Nelms, George	1	3	3		
Hudson, Job	1	1	1		
Mote, Jethro	2	4	5		
Hudson, Joseph	1	2	2		
Hudson, Lewis	1	2	5		
Elkins, Charity					
Van, Needham	1				
Tyler, Needham	1		2	3	
Berbage, Joseph	1	1	2		
Morriss, Elisha	1		1		
Long, George	1	2	1		
Hainey, Penny			2		
Hudson, Rachael			2		
Downing, Anna		2	3		
Pridgen, Jane			1		
Butler, Peggy			1		
Mathews, Mary	4	1	2		16
Bardin, Ephraim	1		1		
Pope, Robert	2		4		
Roberts, Solomon	1	2	4		
Cook, Elizabeth			1		
Bagget, Elizabeth			1		
Stringfield, William	1	2	4		
Bell, Hesekiah	1	2	1		1
Sellers, Jacob	4	2	4		
Sellers, Isam	1	4	3		1
Rees, William	1		4		1
Green, Rueben	1	3	4		
Bell, Mary	1	1	2		1
Van, Elizabeth			1		
Sellers, Joseph	1	1	3		
Sellers, Jacob, Jr	1	1	2		
Blantham, Joshua	1				
Van, Stephen	1	2	4		
Clary, James	1				
Merritt, David	1		3		
Cook, Ann			1		
Rowel, Benjamin	1	3	4		
Register, Judith		1	5		
Benton, Matthias	3	1	2		
Rowell, Sabra			2		
Chesnut, Mourning		1	2		
Chesnut, Solomon	1				
Rowell, Lucrece					
Merrett, Frederick	1	1	4		1
Merrett, Jacob	1	1	2		20
Bell, George	1		1		
Johnson, William		2	4		
Merrett, Solomon	1				
Johnston, Joel	1	4	3		
Johnston, Jesse	1	3	3		
Fryer, Jennett	2	2	3		2
Goodwin, Willis	1	3	3		
Watkins, Lewis	1				
Hollingsworth, Henry	1	1	1		
Chesnut, Needham	1	1	1		
Chesnut, David	1	2	2		
Jones, Levi	1				
Van, Kedar	1		1		
Benton, Anna			1		
Carrol, Elizabeth		1	2		
Merritt, Levi	1	1	1		
Merrett, Nathaniel	1				
Chesnut, Elizabeth		1	3		
Sutton, Elizabeth		1	3		
Packer, Mary		1	3		
Waters, Mary		1	2		
Jones, Moses	1		1		
Jones, Augustine	1		1		
Houston, James	1				
Williams, Bersheba		1	2		
Williams, Rachael		3	2		
Burks, Esther		1	2		
Carrol, Elisha	1	2	4		
Baine, Mary			2		
Kelly, Mary			2		
Green, Rachael				6	
Clenny, James		3	4		
Vick, Nathan	2		3		
Smith, James	1	1			

FAYETTE DISTRICT, SAMPSON COUNTY—Continued.

NAME OF HEAD OF FAMILY.	Free white males of 16 years and upward, including heads of families.	Free white males under 16 years.	Free white females, including heads of families.	All other free persons.	Slaves.
Starling, Robert	1	1	3		
Dean, William	1	2	4		
McClendon, Samford	1		1		
Buchannan, James	3		2		1
Williams, Isaac, Jr	1	2	3		
Williams, Arthur	1		3		
Williams, Brigget			2		
Bray, Bryant	1	1	2		
McClendon, Thomas	1				
Rhodes, William	1				
McClendon, Jesse	1				
Gaven, Charles	1	2	2		
Jones, Moses, Jr	1				
Hatcher, Hancock	1	1	5		
Godwin, Sally			1		
Godwin, Mary		1	2		
Wages, Submit			2		
Gainey, John	1				
Williams, Catharine		1	3		4
Chesnut, Shade	1	1	3		
McPhail, Dugal	1				
Williams, Johanna			2		
Gibbs, Thomas	1		1		
Sessums, Isaac	1		1		
Dudley, Rachael		1	1		
Lee, Joan			1		
Carraway, Archd	1		1		
Orion, Peter	1		2		
Hair, Joel	1		2		
Cason, Hillery	1		1		
Snell, Sarah	1	3	1		10
Wiggs, Lydia		1	1		
Atkinson, Thomas	1				
Chesnut, Arthur			1		
Turner, William	1	5	2		1
Livingston, John	1	1	1		1
Person, Jonathan	1		3		
Hall, Bickley	2	1	3		
McMoore, Elias	1		3		
Autry, Drury	1		3		
Autry, John	2	1	3		
Autry, Isam	1	2	5		
Bullock, Benjamin, Jr	1		1		
Dees, Sampson	1	3	2		1
Dees, William	1		4		
Parker, John	3	1	2		2
Faircloth, John	1	2	4		
Love, Murdock	1	2	5		
Taylor, Samuel	2	4	4		
Jones, Rachael	1	1	3		
Brady, John	1				1
Ryal, Penelope					
Dudley, Levi	2	3	7		
Gilbert, John	1	3	4		
Strickland, Alexr	1	2	2		
Sullivant, Aggy	2	2	1		
Strickland, Harmon	1		1		
Hall, Lazarus	1	3	4		
Hall, Mary	1		3		
Hall, Barnabas	1	2	2		
Sessoms, Isaac	1	2	1		

HALIFAX DISTRICT, EDGECOMBE COUNTY.

NAME OF HEAD OF FAMILY.	Free white males of 16 years and upward, including heads of families.	Free white males under 16 years.	Free white females, including heads of families.	All other free persons.	Slaves.
Cullin, Andrew	1	1	1		7
Battle, Jethro	2	2	5		20
Deaver, Thomas	1				
Battle, Elisha, Senr	2	2	3		22
Hilliard, Jeremiah	1	2	2		19
Ing, Christopher	2	3	4		8
Johnston, Jesse	1	2	6		12
Battle, John	2	2	2		16
Sumner, Joseph	1	4	2		16
Sumner, John	3	2	5		14
Battle, Jacob	1	1	4		24
Mainer, Aaron	3	2	3		3
Porter, Thomas	1	2	6		7
Stallings, James	1	1	3		
Philips, Hartwell	2	1	4		14
Odom, Richard	1	2	4		7
Price, Jesse	1	2	4		
Horn, Abishai	2	2	4		5
Philips, Joseph	1		4		9
Stallings, Willis	1	3	7		
Gray, William	4				18
Battle, Demsey	1	1	2		15
Battle, Elisha, Jr	1	5	3		10
Ross, Daniel	1	1	3		5
Pitt, Arthur	1				
Philips, Benjamin	1				10
Barnes, Williamson	1	2	4		
Sherwood, Robert	1		4		1
Faulk, William	1	1	4		
Murfree, Josiah	2	2	5		12
Pitman, Thomas	1				
Bryant, Smith	3	3	3		5
Britain, Bryant	1	1	3		9
Garner, Absalom	1	3	2		9
Deloach, Samuel, Jr	1		5		3
Knight, Peter	2	2	4		11
Bradley, Richard	1	2	9		
Bradley, Stephen	1	5	3		
Mials, Nasworthy	1	1	5		4
Elenor, Thomas	1	2	4		
O'Neal, Isom	2	1	3		
Vann, Elisha	1	1	4		
Bracewell, William, Senr	2		1		4
Williams, Thomas	1	6	4		1
Fort, John	1	1	1		2
Bracewell, William, Junr	2	3	4		
Hardy, Michael	1				
Horn, William, Junr	1		4		11
Fort, Elizabeth	1		5		9
Cavenah, Mary			1		
Bracewell, James	1				4
Bracewell, Abner	1				1
Bayley, Harrison	1	4	4		
Waller, Sterling	1	3	3		2
Patterson, George	1	1	6		1
Casna, Lewin	1	1	1		
Killibrew, Joshua	3	2	3		7
Griffin, William	5	2	5		
Fountain, James	1				
Griffin, John	2		2		
Watkins, John		2	3		2
Horn, William, Senr	1		6		
Tye, William			2		1
Williams, Margaret			2	1	
Horn, Joel	1	3	3		10
Robertson, Abner	1				
Woodman, Job	1				
Archer, William	1		2		
Vann, Edward	1	1	1		
Bloodworth, Thomas	2	6	4		
Blount, Thomas	3	1	4		27
Gerard, Charles	2		6		27
Jones, Hardiman	3	2	2		1
Killibrew, Kinchen	1	4	5		1
Greer, Andrew	1				4
Putow, William	1				
Sugg, Noah	2	2	2		22
Barrow, Moses	1	2	2		4
Ross, John	3		4		2
Smith, Lawrance	2	3	2		2
Jones, John	1	1	1		
Hodges, Joseph	1		1		
Coleman, Dolly		1	2		
Lyons, Henry	2	1			1
Coleman, Jesse	1				
Thompson, Archibald	1	4	4		2
Nowell, Isham	1				
Bilberry, Nathaniel	1	4	2		11
Bell, William	3	2			3
Stephens, John					9
Pender, John	1	3	3		
Dickenson, Thomas	1		2		
Fort, Jacob	1	3	3		
Dancy, William	2	2	2		22
De Loach, Jesse	1	1	3		8
Killibrew, Glidewell	1		3		2
Cohon, Simon	1		2		4
Cahoon, John	1	1	1		
Proctor, Aaron	1	2	5		
White, Jacob	1	3	5		
Stanley, William	1	4	4		
Vickers, Ralph	1	1	4		1
Drahon, James	3	3	3		
Hargrove, Unity		2	7		
Jones, Patience			4		
Williams, Benjamin	3	1	3		
White, Benjamin	1		1		
White, Mary			2		
Jordan, Thomas	1	5	5		3
Thomas, Jacob	2	2	1		3
Deloach, Samuel, Jr	3	3	2		10
Brake, Jacob	2		4		
Kurl, Willis	1	2	2		2
Wester, Fugham	1	4	1		
Robbins, William	2	4	4		
Molley, Jacob	1	2	3		
Burden, Joseph	1	1	2		12
Gad, William	1	4	3		
Holland, Jacob	1	5	3		
Horn, Jacob	1	4	6		4
Ricks, Isaac	1	3	1		
Coleman, Moses	1		1		
Holliman, Jediah	1		1		
Proctor, Moses	1	2	3		2
Brake, Nathan	1		1		
Wester, Elizabeth		1	2		
White, George	1		2		
Brake, Benjamin	2	2	4		
Eastwood, James	1		3		
Bates, Fredrick	1		2		
Cahoon William	4	2	2		19
Proctor, Ann	2		3		
Barrett, Thomas	1	2	3		
Griffin, Willis	1	1	3		
Jordan, Gray	1		1		
Gay, Mary	1	3	2		
Masengill, George	2	1	2		
Dowberry, Elizabeth	2		1		
Williams, Unity	2		3		
Bridges, Briton	2	2			13
Horn, Elijah	2	7	3		2
Misser, Thomas	1	3	1		8
Bloodworth, William	1	4	6		5
Proctor, Stephen	1	1	1		5
Bloodworth, Henry	1	3	5		
Bracewell, James			2		
Coleman, Hardy	1	2	3		
Gray, Jesse	2	2	2		
Sanders, William	1		2		3
Williams, Joseph	1	2	5		
Brake, Jacob, Sr	3	1	4		
Strother, Richard	1	3	4		3
Stephens, Peter	1	3	4		
Morris, John	2	2	3		
Thomas, James	1	3	2		
Proctor, Jane			2		
Long, James	1	3	2		
Waller, Lucy		1	5		
Ruffin, Samuel	2	2	3		2
Ruffin, Benjamin	2	2	2		
Littleton, Southern	1		1		
Harrell, Edmund	1		2		
Cannada, James	1		2		
Howell, Nathaniel	1	1	4		
Bracewell, Lamon	1	2	3		
Lane, Sarah	1		3		4
Artist, Lauer				5	
Seawell, John	1				
Thomas, Theophilus	3	5	5		21
Ruffin, Lamon	2				12
Ruffin, Bartholomew	1				
De Loach, Ruffin	1	2	3		9
Parnald, John	1		2		
Thorn, Benjamin	1	2	4		
Merritt, James	3	2	4		2
Tisdall, Rehizon	2	1	3		12
Bracewell, Benjamin	4	1	3		4
Cahoon, Joel	1	2	2		1
Gardner, Mary	1	2	4		1
Pitman, Mary	1		4		
Moore, Moses	2	3	3		
Weaver, Benjamin	1	5	4		
Boyt, Jacob	1	3	4		
Weaver, Benjamin	1	1	3		
Lancaster, Benjamin, Jr	1	4	4		1
Dixon, William	2	1	2		2
Boyt, Thomas	1	1	2		
Lancaster, Benjamin, Senr	2		2		2
Dehoiety, James	3		2		
Griffin, Lucy	3		2		2
Dehoiety, Abner	1				
Richards, John	2		4		
Bailey, Samuel	1	1	4		
Gay, Henry	3	4	3		
Healy, William	1		1		
Dawtridge, Benjamin	1		1		
Dawtridge, William	2	1	4		
Pitman, Jesse, Jr	1				
Watkins, Henry	1		2		
Lancaster, Robert	1		2		
Weaver, Absala		3	2		
Murray, Charity	3	3	5		
Weaver, Mary	2	2	3		
Lancaster, Henry	1	2	6		
Lancaster, Hartwell	1		3		
Lancaster, Robert, Jr	1	2	3		
Brand, Thomas	1	3	2		
Willifield, Benjamin	3	5	3		
Pitman, Jesse	1	2	4		
Williams, Drury	1		2		
Cobb, Edward	1	4	7		
Williams, Jesse	1		3		

HALIFAX DISTRICT, EDGECOMBE COUNTY—Continued.

Name of Head of Family	Free white males of 16 years and upward, including heads of families	Free white males under 16 years	Free white females, including heads of families	All other free persons	Slaves
Wilder, Michael	1		2		
Winstead, Peter	1		2		
Robbins, John	1	1	3		15
Brand, Benjamin	2				
Solomon, Isham	1	1	2		
Bryant, Gail	1	1	1		
Brand, William	1	3	2		
Williford, Jacob	1	4	1		
Williford, Thomas	1		2		
Story, Daniel	1		2		
Pitman, Edward, Jr	1	2	5		
Gay, William	1		1		
Todd, Hardy	1		1		
Coppage, Augustine	2	2	2		
Allen, Hardy	1	3	3		3
Pitman, Edward, Senr	1		2		
Granton, Jesse	2	2	6		
Pitman, Jesse	1	5	3		
Jackson, Edward	1		2		
Stone, John	1	3	4		1
Winstead, Joseph	1	1	2		
Winstead, Richard	1	2	7		
Dixon, Coffield	1	1	2		
Flowers, Hardiman	1	1	5		8
Robbins, Jacob	5	3	3		
Proctor, Sampson	1	3	3		
Watkins, Stephen	1	4	5		
Spicer, James	1	2	2		
Horn, Michael	2	3	5		4
Barnes, Sarah			2		
Pitman, John	1		2		
Price, Joseph	1	1	2		
Horn, Ann		2	4		1
Pittman, Jethro	1	2	5		
Pitman, Ann		1	5		
Adams, Briton	1	2	3		
Rose, Amos	1		3		
Trevathan, Sion	1		2		
Trevathan, Fredrick	1		2		4
Deloach, William, Jr	2	1	3		9
Elenor, William	1	4	5		3
Pitman, Joseph	1	2	2		
Williams, John	1				2
Skinner, Samuel	1	2	2		1
Williams, Henry	1		2		5
Emson, William	2	4	3		
Hynes, Isom	1	3	2		3
Fountaine, Mary		2	2		
Randolph, Giles	2	2	2		
Bridges, Drury	1		1		1
Spicer, William, Jr	2	1	3		
Anderson, Elizabeth			2		
Ricks, James	2	3	2		16
Ingles, John	1		4		9
O'Bryan, Francis			2		1
O'Bryan, Lawrance	2	3	4		14
Garner, Samuel	1		1		
Humphrey, Isham	1	5	2		
Ford, William	1				2
Batts, Joseph	1	3	3		1
Clements, William	2		2		9
Toole, Gareldus	1				26
McDade, Willis	2	1	6		
Woodard, Daniel	2	1	3		
Wimberly, George	1		2		17
Moore, Elijah	1	3	4		
Dilyard, Barnaba	1	1	1		2
Wimberly, Joseph	2	1	5		21
Gilbert, Nathan	1				
Williams, Matthew	1				
Dickenson, Jacob	1	3	4		20
Dilyard, Mary	1		2		
Dilyard, Matthew	1				
Hart, Priscilla			5		17
Hodges, Thomas	1	4	4		22
Savage, Loveless	3		1		4
Fort, Josiah	1	4	5		35
Fort, Elias	1	1	2		7
Fort, William	2	2	2		17
Ing, Sarah			2		
Odom, Absalom	2	4	3		
Odom, John	1				
Odom, Dempsey	1		2	1	
Odom, Jacob	1		4		
Odom, Aaron, Senr	4		1		
Pitt, James	3				7
Perry, Alse			3		
House, John	2	3	5		1
Trevathan, Robert, Senr	3		2		
Trevathan, Robert, Junr	1	2	1		
Rose, Robert	3	3	3		
House, Jacob	3	1	3		1
Etherege, Caleb	1	2	6		
Thompson, Robert	3	2	2		
Brown, Jesse	2	3	4		

Name of Head of Family	Free white males of 16 years and upward, including heads of families	Free white males under 16 years	Free white females, including heads of families	All other free persons	Slaves
Brown, Samuel	1	2	1		
Brown, James	1			1	8
Boykin, John	1	3	2		
Carlisle, Coleman	2		3		
Coleman, Robert	1	1	4		
Dilyard, Mary	2		3		
Evans, Abraham	1	2	2		8
Lynch, William	1	4	4		
Langley, William	1		2		4
Pitman, Abner	1	1	3		5
Pope, Benjamin	1				
Pritchett, William	1	1	2		2
Pope, Josiah	1	1	6		2
Philips, Etheldrid	1	2	5		11
Price, Elijah	1	3	4		
Rose, William	1		4		
Stallings, Simon	3	3	2		
Stallings, Elisha	1	3	5		2
Thorn, William	1	1	4		
Taylor, David	1	4	2		
Trevathan, William	1				
Teat, William	1	4	2		2
Whitley, Jonas	1	1	3		
Wiggins, Hardy	1	2	3		
Woodward, Noah	2		3		2
Pender, Wright	1				
Soary, Malakiah	1	1	4		
Rodgers, Robert	1		4		
Adams, William	1		1		1
Adams, James	1	2	3		5
Ayrs, Thomas	1	2	1		
Adams, Hopewell	2		3		2
Anderson, Henry	1	2	2		
Bonner, John	2	2	2		2
Ballard, Benjamin	1	2	3		
Billups, John	1	3	2		
Booth, James	1	2	4		14
Bell, John	1	1	1		8
Brown, John	2	2	1		
Cherry, Levi	1	2	7		1
Cherry, Robert	1				
Cherry, William	1		2		
Cromwell, Alexander	2	1	2		1
Cherry, Wright	1	1	1		
Cherry, Wily	1				
Cromwell, Thomas	1	4	3		1
Cobb, Edward	1	2	5		
Cobb, James	2	3	2		
Cherry, William	1		2		
Duggin, William	3	1	6		
Davis, Joseph	1	1	2		4
Dawson, John	1	1	1		20
Flood, Enoch	1	1	4		
Gaddy, Lucy			2		
Godfrey, Sarah		1	1		
Hawkins, Stephen	1		2		
Hacket, Michael	1	1	3		
Hines, John	1	1	2		
Henly, Jesse	1				
Hicks, James	1		1		
Hyman, John	1		3		1
Hardy, Robert, Sr	3		2		1
Hall, John	1		2		14
Hardy, Allen	2	2	3		
Hardy, Joseph	1	2	5		
Hodge, Miles	2	3	3		
Hodge, Abraham	1	4	4		
Hardy, Robert, Junr	2		4		
Hopkins, Elizabeth			3		
Hall, Edward	2	3	3		86
Jenkins, Thomas	1		2		
Jones, James	1	2	2		2
Johnston, Thomas	1		1		
Keal, Hardy	1	1	2		
Key, William	1	1	3		2
Knight, Jesse	1	2	5		
Knox, Robert	2		2		
Little, Exum	1				
Lawrence, John	1		2		
Little, John	1	1	2		5
Little, William	1		5		1
Lawrance, Solomon	2	2	4		
Lawrance, Elizabeth	2	4	6		2
Little, Gray	1		2		
Little, Jacob	1		2		5
Lawrance, Thomas	1	1	5		
Lawrance, Jesse	1		2		
Lawrance, James	1	2	1		
Lewis, Amos	1	1	5		
Lewis, Thomas	1	4	5		
Lees, Stephen	3	1	4		
Mitchell, Thomas					10
Morgan, Joseph	1		2		10
Manning, Benjamin	1		2		
Mayo, Judith	2	2	4		3
Mayo, David	1	1	4		
Newsom, Joseph	1	2	2		1

Name of Head of Family	Free white males of 16 years and upward, including heads of families	Free white males under 16 years	Free white females, including heads of families	All other free persons	Slaves
Newson, Hannah			5		
Newsom, Thomas	1		5		
Piper, Solomon, Jr	1	2	3		
Piper, Abraham	1	2	1		
Pippen, John	2		3		1
Pippen, Joseph, Jr	1	1	3		
Pippen, Benjamin	1	1	6		3
Pippen, Joseph, Senr	1	1	5		3
Pippen, Joseph	1		5		12
Pippen, Solomon, Senr	1	3	4		2
Pippen, Noah	1		3		
Reiner, Samuel	1	2	3		
Rogers, William	1	1	3		
Sharp, Joshua	3		9		
Scott, Israel				7	
Smith, Reuben	1	2	2	7	7
Scott, Isham				7	
Sharp, John	1		4		
Sessums, Solomon	1	4	3		12
Thigpen, Etheldred	1	1	1		
Thigpen, James	3		4		2
Taylor, John	1	5	2		
Thigpen, Jonathan	1				
Walker, Solomon		1	4		8
White, John	2	1	5		1
Wood, Ann	1		4		
Wiggins, William	2	2	2		
Walker, Thomas	1		1		
Summerlin, Thomas	2	3	5		
Hodge, Mary			2		
Knight, Walker	1	1	2		1
Bell, Frederick	1	5	1		7
Price, William	1	2	2		
Dozier, Peter	1				
Tool, Elizabeth		1	4		21
Kent, Thomas	1		1		
Armstrong, Joseph	1		1		
Bracewell, Jacob	1		1		3
Bracewell, Solomon, Senr	3	2	5		16
Bracewell, Solomon, Junr	1				
Burt, John	2	1	3		5
Bracewell, Unity		1	4		2
Bracewell, James	1	1			
Brown, Tarlton			2		3
Brown, Reuben	2	3	3		1
Clarke, Edmund	1	2	2		3
Davis, Joseph	1	2	2		3
Dickenson, Jane		1	2		
Dilyard, John	1	1	2		
Griffis, John	1	2	7		
Griffis, Demsey	1	1	2		
Griffis, Francis	1	1	2		
Griffin, Edward				1	
Harrell, Simon	2	6	3		6
Howell, Joseph	1	1	3		8
Haywood, Sherwood	2		2		16
Irwin, Lewis	8				36
Jewell, Thomas	3	1	2		8
Irwin, Henry					12
Lodge, Lewis, Senr	1	1	1		
Lodge, Josiah	1		3		
Lodge, Lewis	2	3	4		
Leigh, John	4				27
Mace, John	1	1	3		
Mitchell, John	1		1		2
Pass, Samuel	1		2		4
Permenter, James	2	4	5		7
Petaway, Micajah	1		1		3
Pope, Philip	2	1	3		
Pitt, Joseph	1	1	1		4
Pender, Josiah	1		1		2
Parker, John	2		3		4
Penn, William	1		3		10
Sarsnett, Richard, Senr	3	2	2		3
Sarsnett, Richd	1		1		1
Sherrod, John	1	2	2		13
Sugg, Mary	2		2		13
Southerland, John, Jr	2		3		5
Sherrod, John	1	2	3		2
Southerland, John	1	1	2		12
Waller, James	1		3		11
Watkinson, Michael	2	2	3		
Wiggins, Matthew	1			4	
Wilson, John	2	1	1		17
Griffin, Michael	1				8
Wilson, William	1	2	4		7
Woodward, Thomas	1	2	1		2
Wogan, Henry	1				
Teat, James	1	2	2		
Taylor, John	1	1	5		
Allin, Roda	2	3	6		1
Boazman, Britain	2		2		
Boazman, James	2	1	2		
Clark, Richard	2	4	3		
Dunn, John, Junr	1				
Dunn, John	3	2	3		
Davis, Emry	3	2	3		1

HALIFAX DISTRICT, EDGECOMBE COUNTY—Continued.

NAME OF HEAD OF FAMILY.	Free white males of 16 years and upward, including heads of families.	Free white males under 16 years.	Free white females, including heads of families.	All other free persons.	Slaves.
Dunn, Nicholson	1	2	3		
Dunn, Stephen	1	4	3		
Forehand, David	2		2		2
Griffin, Frederick	1	1	2		
Guin, Daniel	1	3	3		
Griffin, James	1	3	2		
Holliman, Isham	1	1	4		5
Hanberry, Elizabeth			6		
Hall, John	1	3	3		
Holliman, Jesse	1	3	3		
Hanberry, Samuel	1	3	3		
Kelley, William	1				
Langley, Isaac	1	2	1		
Mace, Equilla	2	1	3		
Nasworthy, Samuel	1	1	4		
Nasworthy, Elizabeth		1	4		5
Permenter, Nathaniel	1	4	4		2
Pitt, Joseph	1		2		1
Pitt, Robert	3	2	3		3
Pitt, Henry	1	4	3		
Proctor, John	1	1	2		
Peal, John	1	4	7		
Pitt, Thomas	1	1	1		
Ruffin, John	3	5	3		
Stringer, Josiah	1	4	3		
Stringer, Charles	1	6	5		
Small, Benjamin	1		3		
Stringer, John	4	2	3		
Surgernor, John	1	3	5		2
Scarborough, Samuel	1	3	2		
Taylor, Perigrine	1		2		
Thornton, Robert	1	1	3		1
Ward, Solomon	1	2	4		
Waller, Benjamin		1	5		4
Ruth, William	2		3		4
Bullock, Martha		1	3		
Ruffin, Hannah		1	3		
Edwards, Titus	1	1	1		
Allen, Nathan	1	1	4		
Andrson, George	1	1	2		
Anderson, James	1		1		
Atkinson, Josiah	1	1	1		
Atkinson, Mary		2	1		
Anderson, Mourning	3	1	5		
Brake, William	1	2	3		
Barns, Elizabeth			1		2
Bryant, Arthur	1	4	4		
Broadribb, Thomas	1				
Bridgers, William	1		3		
Dawterry, William	1				
Gray, Charles	2		3		26
Manning, Timothy	2		1		1
Williams, Benjamin	1	3	3		
Arrington, Benjamin	3	2	2		10
Arnold, Edward	2	2	1		
Arrington, John	2				3
Allen, Gabriel	1	3	6		7
Davis, Henry	1		1		
Blackburn, Benjamin	1	3	1		
Bolton, Richard	2	2	8		
Belsher, Bevilla	1	1	3		12
Brownrigg, George	1	1	2		17
Cartright, Hezekiah	2	1	5		7
Causey, Philip	2		3		
Causey, Philip, Junr	1	3	2		
Crairy, Hugh	1	4	6		1
Corbitt, John	1	1	5		
Crairy, Owin	4	5	5		5
Cartright, Thomas	1	2	3		2
Chitty, John	3	3	4		
Crairy, Huk, Junr	1				
Defnal, William	1				
Drake, William	1				2
Drake, Sarah			1		3
Downing, Matthew	1	4	2		
Drake, Jesse	1	2	2		
Downing, Judith	1	2	5		
Drake, David	1	2	7		2
Edwards, Nathan	2		3		2
Edwards, Simon	1	3	1		
Edwards, John	1		3		
Ellis, John	1	1	5		19
Edwards, Edmund	1		2		1
Flemming, William	1	2	2		
Flemming, Sarah	1	2	2		
Flemming, Charles	1	1	1		
Holland, Henry	3	2	5		7
Hines, Richard	1				3
Hicks, John	1			4	
Harris, George	1	1	4		5
Hearn, James	1			4	
Hines, Jesse	1		3		9
Hearn, Amos	1	1	3		
Holland, Daniel	2			6	
Hearn, William	2	1	5		
Holland, James	1	3	2		
Hines, Henry	2	4	2		14

NAME OF HEAD OF FAMILY.	Free white males of 16 years and upward, including heads of families.	Free white males under 16 years.	Free white females, including heads of families.	All other free persons.	Slaves.
Hines, Peter	1	3	4		13
Johnston, Mary			2		2
Johnston, Esther	1	1	4		12
Johnston, Amos	5	4	5		16
Kearney, Thomas	1	1	4		
Lane, James	1		2		5
Lester, Moses	1	1	4		
Mareley, Benjamin	3	1	4		
Matthews, Samuel	1		4		
Nowell, Enos	2	2	3		
Novel, Hardy	2	2	1	1	
Quin, William	2	2	3		
Spell, John	1	2	3		5
Summelin, Flowers	2	1	3		
Spell, Lewis	1	1	2		13
Southerlin, Daniel	2	1	3		8
Summerlin, Henry	1	2	3		
Stokes, Demsey	1		5		2
Shirley, Richard	1	5	1		
Taylor, Teagle	2	6	5		1
Thirston, William	1	1	1		
Walker, Daniel	3	1	1		
Wootten, Joel	1	3	4		
Wootten, James	1	1	3		1
Taylor, William	2	2	2		
Andrew, Joseph	1	1	4		
Andrew, Solomon	4				
Barnes, James	2	2	1		
Barnes, Benjamin	1	1	2		
Brinkley, Abraham	1	1	2		
Balsom, Sarah			2	1	
Brinkley, Aaron	2	1	4		
Boazman, Jesse	1	1	4		
Corbitt, William	1		2		
Corbitt, Elias	1		1		
Wilson, William (Guardof A. J. Haywood)					27
Causey, Ezekiel	1	2	2		
Cearney, John	1		2		
Copeland, Thomas	1	2	3		
Cearney, Thomas	3	2	4		
Cone, John	1		3		1
Cox, Moses	1		5		
Colwell, John	1	1	2		5
Davis, Nathan	1	3	3		
Dunford, William	4	2	2		
Doxey, Jeremiah	1	2	2		2
Drake, Sarah			1		3
Ellis, Reubin	1	1	2		
Drake, Henry	1	2	1		
Forehand, Solomon	2	4	6		3
Gardner, Joseph	1	4	3		
Gardner, Jonathan	1	4	2		3
Gay, Zerobabel	1		1		
Godwin, Mary					
Gay, Henry	2		7		
Gay, John	1		1		
Hadcock, Shadrach	1		1		
Jones, Ambrose	1	1	1		
Jones, Mary		1	3		
Kellibrew, Caleb	1	2	3		2
King, Henry	1	1	2		
Langley, Shadrack	1	1	2		
Langley, Hezekiah	1		4		
Lester, Moses	1	1	4		
Lee, Jesse	1		1		
Langley, Isaiah	1		2		
Langley, Josiah	1	1	1		
Lewis, Nathan	1	4	4		
Maund, Lott	1				
Marchment, Charles		4	2		2
Maund, Mary		2	4		
Mayo, Samuel	1	3	4		
Mittur, Thomas	1				
Nettle, John	1	3	5		3
Owen, Andrew	1				
Owen, William, Jr	1	2	2		
Owen, John, Senr	2	1	2		
Owen, William	1	1	1		
Owen, John, Junr	1				
Owen, Elizabeth			1		
Owen, Selah		1	1		
Owen, Moses	2	1	2		4
Perry, John	1	2	3		8
Permenter, Wright	1	3	4		
Philips, Solomon	3	4			2
Ruffin, Joseph	2			5	2
Russel, Sarah			3		
Robertson, Archelas	2	2	3		
Quin, Amos	1	1	2		
Rasbury, Jesse	1				
Stokes, William	1	1	4		1
Stokes, Demsey	1		5		2
Summerlin, Edward	1	2	8		
Stokes, David	1	2	3		2
Skinner, Demsey	2	3	4		
Summerlin, Hardy	1	2	4		

NAME OF HEAD OF FAMILY.	Free white males of 16 years and upward, including heads of families.	Free white males under 16 years.	Free white females, including heads of families.	All other free persons.	Slaves.
Scarbrough, James	2	5	6		5
Skinner, John	1				
Storey, James	1	2	3		
Summerlin, Nancy	2		1		
Taylor, Samuel	1	1	4		2
Thorn, Hardy	1				5
Taylor, William	1				
Tarlton, Josiah	1	1	1		
Wootten, Amos	3	4	5		
Wootten, Joshua	1	1	1		
Wootten, William	1		1		
Cearney, Thomas	2	3	3		
Whealer, Henry	1				
Amason, William	2				1
Amason, Abraham	1	2	2		
Amason, Jesse	1	1	2		
Atkinson, Sarah		1	1		
Amason, Benjamin	1	1	4		1
Amason, Eli	1				2
Amason, Benjamin, Junr		2	1		1
Amason, John	2	1	2		
Amason, Uriah	2	4	2		
Amason, Josiah, Jr	1		1		
Barnes, Absalom	1	2	4		
Bruin, George	4	1	4		
Barefeild, Mills	1	2	3		
Barns, Archelaus	2	2	5		2
Barns, Aziel	2	1	3		
Baggett, Blake	3	3	6		
Barnes, Ephraim	4	3	3		
Baggett, Nathan	1	2	5		
Barns, Jacob	2	2	3		2
Baggett, Joel	1	2	4		
Bartle, John	1	2	2		
Barns, Nathan	1				1
Bentley, Joshua	1	1	5		7
Bullock, John	2	2	2		
Barefield, Daniel	2	2	4		6
Bandy, Lewis	1	1	4		
Boltin, Isaac	1	1	1		4
Brantley, Malachi	1	2	4		
Boltin, Luke	1				4
Corbitt, John	1	2	2		
Chester, John	1	2	4		
Cox, Joseph	2	4	4		
Chittin, Thomas	1	3	4		
Chittin, Winifred		2	3		
Cato, Stephen	2	2	4		
Daniel, William	1	3	2		
Davis, Thomas	2	2	4		
Daniel, Asa	2	2	4		
Daniel, David	1	1	1		1
Daniel, Joseph		3	1		1
Dickenson, William	2		5		8
Daniel, Rebeccah	1	2	7		
Daniel, Josiah	1	1	4		
Daniel, William	1	2	6		
Barnes, Selah	1	2	2		
Daniel, Levi	1		1		
Davis, John	2		2		5
Davis, James	1	3	2		
Daniel, Nathan	1	1	6		
Daniel, Lemuel	1	1	3		1
Eason, Robert	2		4		
Ellis, William	1	1	2		3
Eason, Isaac	1		9		2
Eason, Shadrack	1	4	5		5
Eason, Abner	1	2	2		5
Gay, William	1	2	2		1
Gay, Richard	1	3	5		
Grice, Jesse	1	2	3		
Gay, John	2		6		
Gay, James	1		2		
Nowell, Patience		2	3		
Galloway, Richard	1	2	1		
Harrod, Wilson	1	2	1		
Joyce, William	1	4	2		
Johnston, James	1	3	3		
Johnston, Joshua	3	2	5		
Johnston, Daniel	1				
Johnston, Benjamin	1	1	3		
Lewellin, Edmund	1	1	2		
Mayo, Cyprian	2	2	4		
Mayo, Edward	2	2	2		
Mairs, William	1	1	1		
Mayo, John	2	3	2		
Mayo, Joseph	2		3		
Mason, John	1		5		9
Moore, Samuel	1				
Norwood, John	1	2	4		5
Parish, Henry	1	1	5		
Poole, Robert	3	4	1		4
Potter, John	1		3		
Prescoat, Benjamin	1		4		
Robertson, Henry	1	2	4		
Robertson, William	1	2	2		

HALIFAX DISTRICT, EDGECOMBE COUNTY—Continued.

NAME OF HEAD OF FAMILY.	Free white males of 16 years and upward, including heads of families.	Free white males under 16 years.	Free white females, including heads of families.	All other free persons.	Slaves.
Rogers, Trusse	3	2	6		
Rogers, Daniel	2	1	4		
Reason, William	1	1	5		
Reason, John	1	3	4		
Rogers, Jesse	1		4		
Stuckey, Edmund	3	3	4		3
Singleton, William	1	2	2		
Simms, Simon	1	1	5		2
Shepherd, Thomas	1		2		
Bateman, Thomas	3	2	2		
Stanton, James	4	1	3		24
Tart, Catherine			2		6
Tart, Millicent			1		3
Thigpen, Gilead	3	1	3		3
Thigpen, Cyprian	1	2	5		
Wells, Thomas	2	1	4		
Ward, Messer	2	2	4		
Whitley, William	1		6		
Wells, Leonard	1	3	6		
Whitley, George	1	3	5		
Winslow, Joseph	2	2	6		
Woodard, Elisha, Jr	1	3	4		2
Winslow, Thomas	2	2	3		
Lewellin, Thomas	1	2	2		
Ward, Daniel	1	1	4		
Bateman, Phebe		2	2		
Woodard, Elisha	2	2	1		1
Daniel, Milissent	2	2	2		
Amason, Josiah	2	1	2		
Walster, Henry	1				
Amason, James	2	2	4		
Cato, William	1	2	4		
Barnet, Lamon	1	2	3		
Runnels, Lamon	2	4	2		
Smock, John	2	2	2		
Robison, Patience	2	1	3		
Barnes, Joseph	2	3	5		5
Brooks, Elizabeth			1		
Blackburn, William	1		1		1
Barnes, Demsey	3	2	6		2
Bateman, Claburn	1	3	5		
Barnes, Jesse	1	1	1		1
Barefoot, Jeptha	4		1		
Barefoot, Jeptha, Junr	1	1	1		
Barefoot, William	1	1	2		
Barefoot, Noah	1		2		
Coleman, Robert	1		4		
Coleman, Charles	1	4	3		7
Cahoon, John	1	2	1		
Doudy, John	2	2	7		
Dixon, Thomas	1	2	3		5
Dew, John	1	3	2		6
Dixon, Nicholas	1	3	4		
Dew, Arthur	2	2	2		16
Deloach, John	1	3	2		5
Izzell, George	1	2	3		
Izzel, Jesse	1	1	2		
Izzel, Timothy	1	1	1		
Farmer, Benjamin	1	4	4		2
Farmer, Joseph	1	2	8		2
Forehand, Solomon	1	6	6		3
Farmer, Isaac	1	4	6		3
Farmer, Jesse	1	1	1		6
Farmer, Samuel	1	3	3		
Hall, Joseph	1	4	3		
Hedgpith, John	3		3		
Jordan, Cornelius	1	2	1		1
Jordan, Cornelius, Jun	1	4	1		
Johnston, Nathan	1	2	5		
Jordan, Joshua	3	3	4		4
Joiner, Cardy	1	1	2		
Joiner, Charles	1		3		
Murborn, John, Jur	1	2	2		
Morris, John	2	2	7		
Morris, Thomas	1	1	1		
Morris, Joshua	1	1	3		
Morris, William	1	1	3		
Murborn, John	2	3	2		
Marry, John	2		1		
Robbins, Roland	1	5	3		
Robbins, Sarah	1		4		
Robbins, William	1	3	2		
Roundtree, John	1		2		2
Robertson, Hardy	2		1		6
Robertson, Ezzel	2		2		6
Roundtree, Francis	1				
Roundtree, Moses	1	2	4		
Sanders, Thomas	3	1	3		
Sims, Benjamin	1	3	4		11
Stokes, William	1	1	4		1
Simms, Joseph	5		3		27
Sims, Jesse	1	2	2		
Winburn, Joseph	1		1		
Walten, John	1	4	3		19
White, John	1	4	1		1
White, Joshua	1		1		1
Whitehead, James	1	2	2		2

NAME OF HEAD OF FAMILY.	Free white males of 16 years and upward, including heads of families.	Free white males under 16 years.	Free white females, including heads of families.	All other free persons.	Slaves.
White, William	2	2	4		1
White, John	1	2	1		
Wood, Daniel	2	2	2		
White, Luke	1	3	2		
White, Daniel	1	4	3		
Whitehead, William	1		2		7
Askew, Josiah	3	3	2		2
Askew, Uriah	1				
Barren, Barnaba	1	1	3		7
Barren, James	1	4	4		4
Barnes, James	1	4	5		4
Bell, John	1	1	1		
Brasier, John	2	4	2		1
Barnes, Jethro	1	4	4		
Barnes, William	1		2		
Barnes, Stephen	2		1		
Batts, William	2	4	2		
Barnes, Briton	1	4	4		
Barnes, Abraham	2		2		
Brown, William	1	1	3		
Cahoon, Joseph	1				
Cahoon, John	1	2	1		
Ellis, Dehorty	1	1	2		
Ellis, Jacob	1		1		
Ellis, William	1	4	1		7
Edwards, Thomas	1	1	6		
Farmer, Joseph	1	2	2		
Farmer, Joshua	1	1	3		
Farmer, Thomas	1		1		1
Gill, Taylor	1	2	2		14
Gay, Henry	2		1		
Gardner, Martin	2	6	4		
Hickman, Nathaniel	2		2		6
Haynes, John	1		3		
Hall, David	1	1	4		
Hickman, William	1	3	3		4
Jordan, Joseph	1	1	2		
Mills, Naman	1	4	3		
Matthews, Gilbert	1	1	1		
Muburn, Eady	1	3	3		5
Parrish, Selathiel	1		4		
Page, Thomas	1	2	2		
Pitman, Samuel	1	2	1		
Page, Jacob	2	4	6		
Permenter, John	2	3	2		9
Powell, Daniel	1	2	8		
Permenter, Margarett	1	1	3		2
Pendor, Joseph	1	3	6		17
Page, John	1		2		
Rogers, William	1		2		
Rogers, William, Jun	1	2	2		
Solomon, William	1	1	5		
Sanders, Christian			1		3
Sherrod, Joseph	1	3	2		
Tart, Nathan	1	1	1		18
Thorn, Nicholas	1		3		4
Todd, Hardy, Junr	1				
Todd, Lewis	1		3		1
Thorn, Martin	3		2		
Taylor, Emanuel	1	2	3		
Thomas, Mary	1		2		8
White, William	2	2	3		
Williford, Hartwell	1	1	7		
Wiggins, Noah	1	1	2		2
Williams, John	1		2		5
Webb, Richard	1	2	6		
Williford, John	1	2	2		
Webb, John	1	3	2	1	
Thomas, Jonathan	1		1	2	
Lewellin, Alexander	3	3	2		
Hales, John	1	1	2		
Baker, Blake	3		2		16
Belhul, William	1				
Batts, William	4		2		
Batts, Field	1				
Broadstreet, Charles	1		2		
McCain, Ann		1	2		
Donaldson, Robert	1				
Goodwin, Tabitha	3		6		7
Gardner, Mary	1		3		1
Howerton, Thomas	1	2	5		
Howell, Esther	1		3		6
Jones, Frederick	1				
Knight, James	2	1	3		11
Kelley, Sarah			4		1
Spiers, Wright	1		2		
Schink, John	2				4
Matthews, William	1		2		
Ross, Joseph	6		2		2
Tolestone, Mary	1	2	3		
Thigpen, Nathan	1		4		
Norris, John	2	1	6		
Pope, Jonathan	1	4	4		
pitman, Mary	1	1	4		
pender, David	1	1	5		9
Weaks, John	1	2	3		
Webb, John	1	3	2	1	

NAME OF HEAD OF FAMILY.	Free white males of 16 years and upward, including heads of families.	Free white males under 16 years.	Free white females, including heads of families.	All other free persons.	Slaves.
Frier, Mary		2	2		
Harrison, Mary Ann	1		4		15
Smock, John	1	1	1		
Runnels, Thomas	1	3	2		
Coleman, Stephen	1		2		2
Coleman, Aaron	2		3		8
price, Samuel	1	2	4		
Coker, Brumbly	1	3	3		
Lewis, Exum	3	3	3		15
Lynch, George	1	4	6		11
Lewis, Figuret	1	1	3		12
Cooper, David	1		4		
Cooper, Martha	2	1	4		
Freeman, John	1		2		
Carlile, Ann			3		
Adams, Briton	2	3	4		
Alsobrook, Joseph	2	3	3		
Atkins, John	1	2	5		
Bradley, Samuel	1	4	3		3
Bradley, William	1	2	3		
Boykin, James	1	2	2		
Brantley, Amos	1	2	3		3
Benton, Abselom	3	3	2		40
Coker, Elizabeth	1	2	3		
Cherry, James	1	2	3		
Coleman, Josiah	1	3	4		
Coker, James, Junr	1	2	2		
Cofield, David	2				16
Coker, James	2		3		3
Coker, William	2	2	4		
Coffield, Benjamin	2	3	3	2	8
Cooper, Malakiah	2	2	3		
Colten, William	3	2	5		3
Coker, Richard	2	2	4		
Dixon, William	2	2	2		
McDaniel, Daniel	1	2	5		4
Daniel, John	1	3	3		
Thomas, Drahon	1	2	9		
McDaniel, Campbell	1	2	2		
Durley, Horatio	1		2		6
Dixon, John	1	2	3		
Dixon, John, Junr	1	1	2		
Deal, Adam	1	3	4		
Exum, John	1	1	2		2
Edwards, John	1	1	5		3
Edwards, Joseph	1	2	3		2
Exum, John, Junr	1	2	2		
Exum, Barnaba	1	2	3		2
Edwards, Benjamin	1	2	3		2
Exum, William	1		1		20
Exum, Etheldred	1				3
Exum, Rachael			1	2	
Exum, Susannah		2	2		2
Etheridge, George	1	2	4		
Fort, John	1		2		5
Flanagan, John	2	5	4		
Fort, William, Senr	4		1		6
Foreman, Isaac	2	3	4		
Foreman, George	1	2	4		3
Floara, Lazarus	1	2	4		
George, John	1		2		2
George, Michael	1	1	3		
Goodman, John	2	4	5		15
George, Thomas	1		1		
Hammons, Shadrack				8	
Hammons, Jordan				4	
Harris, Nathan	2	2	2		14
Hare, William	3	5	3		
Hare, Nicholas	1	1	3		
Hancock, Randolph	2		3		4
Howard, John	1	2	2		2
Hails, John	1	3	3		
Kinchin, Matthw	2	4	2		23
Howell, Nathaniel	2	1	2		
Hamilton, Andrew	1	2	3		3
Ing, Joseph	1	1	7		2
Jackson, Frederick	1				
Knight, Spier	1	4	2		
Landingham, Thomas	1	6	4		
Morgan, Isaac	1	2	2		
Morris, Hadley	3	3	2		
Manning, William, Senr	2	3	7		
Nelson, James	2	1	3		
Williams, Elizabeth	2	1	3		12
Nicholson, Malakiah	2	3	4		4
Nicholson, John	4	3	10		25
Pitman, Elijah	3	3	4		12
Powell, William	1	3	4		10
Parker, Francis	2	5	5		4
pyland, John	1	3	2		2
Penny, Malikiah	1		2		
pitman, William	2	2	3		
Pace, John	1	2	2		
Philips, Arthur	2	2	3		15
Price, Samuel	2	2	4		
Pace, Stephen	1	2	4		

HALIFAX DISTRICT, EDGECOMBE COUNTY—Continued.

NAME OF HEAD OF FAMILY.	Free white males of 16 years and upward, including heads of families.	Free white males under 16 years.	Free white females, including heads of families.	All other free persons.	Slaves.
Penny, John	1				
Powell, Moses	1	2	3		
Smith, Reddick	1	5	3		
Spier, Philip	2	2	2		
Spier, Christian	4	1	6		5
Lynch, Wright	1	2	2		
Watkins, Daniel	1	2	2		
Williams, John	1		4		2
Williams, Matthew	1	1	4		6
Wiggins, John	2	1	3		12
Watkins, Josiah	1	2	2		
Vann, William	1	3	2		
Vick, Josiah	1	3	3		
Murphree, David	1	3	2		
Cherry, Lemuel	2	2	4		
Perry, Ann		2	4		
Banks, Thomas	2	2	3		
Pace, John	2				5
perrit, Ann		1	3		
Anderson, William	1	3	3		
Barlow, Sarah			3	3	3
Bryant, George	1		1	1	
Bell, William	1	1	4		9
Bryant, Billey	1	1	5		
Bradley, Burwell	2	4	3	1	2
Bradley, Joseph	1		1		
Bell, Whitmil	2	1	1		
Bellamy, John	1	1	1		8
Bell, Bythael	1	2	3		14
Bracewell, Isaac	1	2	4		1
Bashford, Alexander	2	1	4		
Bryant, Evan	1				3
Colten, Samuel	3	5	1		
Colten, George	1				1
Cooper, Josiah	1	1	3		
Cooper, John	1	2	4		
Hall, David	1	1	4		
Ginn, Elisha	1	1	1		
Carlile, William	1	3	6		
Cofield, Thomas	1	2	3		6
Dilyard, Nicholas	2	3	4		
Dorman, John	2	1	4		2
Dancey, Archebald	2	1	6		8
Dorman, Mary	1		2	5	
McDowell, John	1	3	4		
Douge, Peter	1	2	5		
Dicken, Ephraim	2				6
Dilyard, James	2	1	1	1	
Foxall, Thomas	1		2		11
Foxall, John	1	1	2		
Foxall, Thomas, Junr	2	1	1		8
Fountain, John	2	2	6	1	
Faithful, William	1	2	4		
Fountain, Henry	2	3	5		
Harrison, Henry	1		4		6
Harper, Robert	1	3	2		5
Howell, Henry	2	2	3		
Howard, Jesse	1	2	3		
Jelks, Lemuel	2	2	3		9
Lackey, John	2		3	2	15
Meals, Jethro	1		2		

NAME OF HEAD OF FAMILY.	Free white males of 16 years and upward, including heads of families.	Free white males under 16 years.	Free white females, including heads of families.	All other free persons.	Slaves.
May, Hardy	2	3	4		
Moore, Elizabeth	1	3	4		2
Oneal, Edmund	1	1	3		
Oneal, Lamentation	1	3	6		
Proctor, Jacob	2		2		6
Price, William	1	2	3		
Philips, Henry			1		1
Price, James	1	2	2		
Price, John	1		2		
Philips, Sarah	1	2	3		16
Perritt, Solomon	1	3	3		2
Perritt, Ann		1	2		2
Rollings, William	2				
Stogdale, Matthew	1		4		14
Savage, Absolam	2	2	4		2
Sessums, Jacob	2	3	5		23
Soary, Malakiah	1	1	3		
Sessums, Amos	1	3	3		
Sessums, Elizabeth	2	2	4		
Stogdale, Dennis	1				1
Sebral, Joshua	1	1	3	2	
Webb, John	1		2		
Williams, Uriah	2	1	2		3
Anderson, James	1		1		
Braddy, Joseph	1	1	5		6
Braddy, Job	1		3		
Beavours, Aziel	1	1	2		
Bilberry, Donel	2	2	6		
Biggs, Bathia	1	2	5		5
Bridgers, Nathan	4	2	2		
Blackburn, William	1	3	3		
Bell, Joshua	2	2	1		14
Batts, Benjamin	1	1	1		1
Bryant, John	2	2	4		
Bryant, Jesse	1		2		
Batts, James	2	3	5		2
Clerk, Jesse	1		4		
Carlile, John	1	1	4		
Calf, Lewis	2	3	5		
Champaign, Jesse	1		4		
Carlile, Robert	1	1	3		
Carliles, Clark	1	1	2		
Champion, Willis	1				
Wombel, John					1
Cook, William	1	1	3		1
Dorman, Delilah	1		2		1
Dicken, Benjamin	3	1	6		7
Dicken, Edmund	1	2	2		
Davis, John	1	2	2		
Davis, John, Junr	1	1	1		
Edwards, Micajah	1		5		1
Freeman, William	1	2	4		
Garrett, Thomas	1	1	4		
Glover, Parsons	2		3		
Howard, Hardy	1	2	2		
Hodges, Willis	1	1	5		
Harris, Thomas	1	4	4		2
Hudnal, Robert	1	4	6		2
Haynes, Francis	1	1	3		1
Haynes, William	2	1	5		2

NAME OF HEAD OF FAMILY.	Free white males of 16 years and upward, including heads of families.	Free white males under 16 years.	Free white females, including heads of families.	All other free persons.	Slaves.
Howard, James	1	1	2		
Hackney, William	3	3	9		5
Howard, John	1	2	2		
Howard, Willis	1	1	4		6
Hudnal, Willis	1	4	2		6
Hudnal, John	1				
Hart, Benjamin	3	2	3		1
Irwin, James	1	2	3		2
Jackson, James	1	3	4		
Jones, Lazarus	1	1	2		
Key, Henry	1	3	3		
Lawrance, John	1	4	4		9
Loyd, Rederick	1	2	2		1
Northern, William, Junr	1	1	3		2
Northern, William, Senr	1	1	3		2
Pope, Atkins	1		2		
Parker, Caden	2	4	3		1
Pope, Jesse	1	1	3		
Pippen, Joseph	1	3	1		
Portice, Robert				1	
Parker, Jonas	1	3	3		7
Rhodes, Joseph	1	3	4		
Scutchion, Mary		1	4		6
Soary, Andrew	1	2	4		
Savage, Frederick	1	1	1		
Swails, John	2	1	4		4
Savage, Gerrod	1	1	1		
Swails, Joseph	1	1	2		15
Swails, Mary	1	1	2		4
Spinks, Presly	2	3	6		4
Tharp, Solomon	1		1		7
Terry, Thomas	1	3	2		1
Weathers, Howel	1		5		
Weaks, Sarah	1		1		2
Webb, Patience	1	2	2		
Wells, Willibe	1		1		
Weaks, James	2	3	5		2
Kitchen, Booze	1	3	2		3
Champion, Benjamin	1	3	2		8
Howard, Mary		1	3		4
Weaver, Asiel	1	2	3		
Scutcheon, Samuel	2	2	3		2
Owen, John	1	1	3		
Kitchen, Jethro	1	1			
Bell, Joshua, Junr	1		2		
Bell, Write	1		1		1
Weaks, Archelaus	1	2	3		
Alsobrook, Pethena			3		
Shuffell, William	1	2	3		
Fitzgerrald, George	3	2	6		2
Dancy, Edwin	2	1	3		13
Smith, Ann			2	3	
Flanagin, Mary			2		
Coleman, Aaron	2		1		9
Coleman, Stephen	1		4		2
Davidson, David	1	1	5		
Biggs, Tully	1	1	1		

HALIFAX DISTRICT, FRANKLIN COUNTY.

NAME OF HEAD OF FAMILY.	Free white males of 16 years and upward, including heads of families.	Free white males under 16 years.	Free white females, including heads of families.	All other free persons.	Slaves.
Arrendel, Thomas	1		1		6
Arrendel, Thos, Jr	1	4	5		3
Alfred, Hinchin	1	1	5		
Alfred, John	3	5	5		2
Alfred, Ansel	3	6	4		
Ally, Roser	1	1	2		
Asene, Charles	1	3	5		
Asene, William	1	5	3		
Adams, Jesse	1	2	5		7
Alfred, Lodwick	3		2		6
Allen, James	1				
Anders, William	2	1	1		16
Arrendel, Bridges	2	1	5		6
Alfred, Job	1				6
Alfred, Lucy		2	4		
Amos, John	1	1	2		
Andrews, John	1	2	3		
Andrews, Abram	1	2	2		9
Andrews, Green	1	5	2		14
Andrews, Evan	1		3		
Andrews, Gray	3	2	4		16
Anders, Atherton	1	1	3		
Allen, William	1	3	2		3
Anderson, Churchville	1	3	2		
Atkins, Rhoda	12	1			3
Andrews, John	1	2	3		
Arrendal, James	1	1	2		
Alfred, James	1	1	5		1
Andrews, Peter	4	3	4		3
Bell, Robert	1	1	4		12

NAME OF HEAD OF FAMILY.	Free white males of 16 years and upward, including heads of families.	Free white males under 16 years.	Free white females, including heads of families.	All other free persons.	Slaves.
Brooks, Christopher	1	3	5		5
Brickell, William	3	4	2		21
Bridges, Wm	2		1		1
Boon, Raiford	1	3	1		1
Boon, Phillip	1	1	3		
Bass, Jacob	3	1	3		10
Bass, Jacob, Jr	1		4		3
Bass, Theophilus	1	4	6		5
Babb, Moses	2	1	2		10
Boon, John	2	4	6		4
Bowls, Benjamin	1	2	2		
Barrow, James	1	3	6		5
Bird, Jesse	2	2	6		8
Bird, Enos	1	6	2		7
Brickell, Thomas	1	3			7
Bird, Jesse (for Needman Bird's orphans)	2	2	5		8
Barker, James	1		2		4
Bridges, Lewis	1	3	3		
Baker, James	1		2		6
Bradford, Thomas	1	1	3		7
Bridges, Doral	1	1	1		
Bowers, Giles	4	1	4		9
Bowers, Jesse	1	6	3		
Bridges, Joseph	1	2	4		
Betts, Wyatt	1	3	2		
Betts, James	1	2			3
Bradway, Eliza			1	4	
Battle, Micajah	1		1	1	
Battle, John	2	1			

NAME OF HEAD OF FAMILY.	Free white males of 16 years and upward, including heads of families.	Free white males under 16 years.	Free white females, including heads of families.	All other free persons.	Slaves.
Brown, Thomas	2	5	3		
Bowden, William	1		4		1
Babb, John	1	1	2		
Babb, Thomas	1		3		
Babb, William	1	2	3		
Boon, James	1	1	5		2
Bachelor, Solomon	2	3	5		
Bowden, John	1	3	4		
Butler, Robert	3		1		
Bledso, Aaron	1	2	1		
Barnes, John	1				
Brantley, Joseph	1	3	4		
Bass, Riddick	1	1	2		3
Bledso, Rush	1	2	4		4
Bibba, Absolem					4
Bibba, William					4
Bragg, Benj	1	1	2		
Bell, Lucy		1	4		6
Barnes, Grace		3	3		1
Burnett, David	2	5	4		1
Bowden, Elias	1	1	4		
Bobbit, William	1	4	2		1
Bobbit, Wm	1	1	2		
Bobbit, Turner	1	1	1		2
Bobbit, John	2		1		12
Brown, William	1		1		
Bradley, Frank	1	1	3		
Baker, Henry	1	3	5		12
Brownin, William	1	1	1		
Butler, Gwynn	1				

HALIFAX DISTRICT, FRANKLIN COUNTY—Continued.

NAME OF HEAD OF FAMILY.	Free white males of 16 years and upward, including heads of families.	Free white males under 16 years.	Free white females, including heads of families.	All other free persons.	Slaves.
Bridges, Lewis	1	3	2		
Bevin, Thomas	1	1	2		
Bridges, Thomas	1		3		
Babb, John	1	1	2		
Beck, Joseph	1	4	3		
Bridges, Aaron	1		1		
Barns, Laburn	2	4	4		
Cooley, Edward	1	4	3		1
Cooley, John	2	2	5		
Chieves, Thomas	1	2	1		
Cook, Allen	1		2		
Crabb, Jarratt	1		1		
Crabb, John	1		1		
Crabb, Ozborne	2		2		1
Crabb, John	2		3		
Carloss, Cole	1	2	3		
Clapton, Richard	4	2	6		18
Cook, Charles	2	3	7		
Cooper, Howell	2	2	1		
Carr, Moses	1	3	6		
Collier, Doctor	2	7	3		
Cook, John	1		2		
Cary, Elisha	1	1	2		
Cook, Thomas	2	2	2		11
Carr, Eliaz	1	2	3		
Carr, Robt	3	3	5		6
Cooper, Robert	1				
Crowder, Ruth			2		5
Cunningham, Geo	1	2	3		
Chieves, John	1	4	5		5
Cook, Jacob	2	4	3		
Clifton, Thomas	3		2		
Clifton, Nathan	1				
Carpenter, John	1	2	2		
Cook, John	2	2	5		3
Campbell, Martin	1	2	4		
Catlet, Laborne	1	1	1		
Cook, William	1	3	8		
Clapton, David	1				
Cook, William	2	2	8		3
Cole, Charles	1	1	6		
Clifton, John	1	1	3		
Conyers, Ephraim	1	1	3	1	2
Cooper, William	1	1	6	1	7
Cook, Thomas	1	2	3		11
Conyers, Richard	1				6
Christmas, William	1		5		11
Conyers, Joel	1				1
Carr, John	3	2	5		
Craig, Roger	1	3	3		
Crowder, William	1	1	3		
Crowder, Absolem	1	1	2		
Collins, James	2	5	1		
Cook, Benjamin	1	1	7	1	1
Collins, William	1	3	3		
Coppage, William	1		1		
Collins, James	1	5	2		
Carlilse, Edward	1		1		6
Carlile, James	1	2	5		4
Croctor, Jacob	2	4	2		
Conyers, William	1		1		6
Curry, Thompson	2	2	7		
Colbert, Thomas	1				
Conyers, Ross	1		2		
Cook, Blanton	1		3		
Cook, Shemuel	1		3		3
Carroll, John	1	2	2		
Cruzier, John	1	1	1		
Carter, Thomas	1	3	4		
Davis, Micajah	1	1	2		
Dixon, Eliza	2	1	8		
Deviny, Jenkins	1	3	9		9
Davis, Archibd	1		2		17
Davis, Federick	1	3	4		
Dukes, Saml	2	6	2		
Drake, Ely	1	3	4		
Davis, Ransom	2	2	3		
Denby, James	2	3	3		11
Denby, Elijah	1	2	3		6
Dowdy, William	1	1	1		
Daniel, Charles	2	5	5		
Dent, Michael	1	3	5		
Denson, John	2	1	1		
Davis, William	4	1	2		1
Driver, Charles	1	4	4		
Driver, Shaw	2	5			
Dunn, John	1		1		8
Dunn, William	1	2	2		4
Denton, Jesse	1	2	2		
Denson, William	1	2	3		
Denson, Witson	2	2	5		3
Denson, Edward	2	2	2		
Drake, James	3	3	4		2
Davis, Richard	1		2	3	
Dunstall, William					
Dorsey, Solomon	2	4	1		
Dorsey, William					
Debord, James	2	4	5		
Duke, Sally		2	1		
Dent, John	2	1	7		
Dorman, Michael	1	3	3		
Dent, Michael	1	3	5		
Drury, Harry	1	1	2		
Edwards, Daniel	1	4	5		1
Eaves, Benjamin	2		2		
Everitt, Judathan	1	3	5		2
English, Nathan	1		2		2
Edwards, William	1	2	4		
Eagerton, Hanah	1	3	4		
Ely, Josiah	3	1	5		12
Edwards, John	1	1	4		
Ely, Ely	3	3	4		8
Elliott, William	2	1	2		
Elly, Gately	1	2	2		
Fletcher, Joseph	2	4	2		
Floyd, Shadrack	2	2	6		
Fuller, Mesheck	1	3	2		
Fuller, Arthur	1	1	5		
Fitts, Jordan	1				
Finch, Edward	1	2	4		5
Frazier, Alexander	2		3		5
Foster, John	4	1	3		9
Fawn, William	2	1	2		5
Finch, Henry	1	2	2	1	
Fuller, Littleton	1	2	3		1
Fuller, Ezekiel	2	1	3		
Ferrel, John	1		5		12
Freeman, Joseph	2	5	2		1
Ferrell, Martha		2	5		7
Ferrell, William	1	2	1		2
Freeman, William	1	4	3		2
Freeman, Henry	1	2	2		
Freeman, Daniel	1	2	2		
Ferrell, Ancil	1	2	3		1
Freeman, Edward	1		4		7
Farmer, John	1	1	2		
Freeman, Rowland	1				
Green, John	1		5		7
Gill, Joseph	1	3	2		10
Glenn, Giddeon	2		1		10
Glenn, James	2	5	3		10
Gupten, Stephen	3	5	4		
Goodwin, Peter	1	3	6		5
Gant, Charles	1	5	1		6
Griggs, James	1	1	4		
Gosset, Nicholas	1	2	4		
Gupten, Abner	1				
Gibbs, Raborn	2	2	2		2
Gupten, James	2	2	6		
Gibbs, John	3	2	3		3
Goodwin, Willie	1	1			
Greggs, Thomas	1		1		1
Gossett, Joseph	1		1		
Green, John, Jr	1		5		7
Gay, Elias	1	1	3		
Gay, John	1	3	3		
Gay, Thomas	1	3	2		3
Griffin, Jesse	1	2	2		1
Goodlowe, Garratt	1	2	3		10
Gilliam, Marcus	1	2	4		
Greaves, Martha	1		2		2
Gilliam, Nathl	1	3	2		
Goodwin, Young	2	1	3		9
Gilliam, Ephraim	1	2	1		1
Green, William	3	1	3		35
Gordan, Isaac	1	4	3		
Gray, James	1	1	5		38
Green, Obed	1	1	4		5
Gant, James	3				
Goodwin, Nancy	1	1	3		6
Hammond, Jesse	2	2	4		1
Hammond, John	1		1		
Hubbard, John	1	4			
Harriss, Daniel	1		1		
Harriss, Brittin	4	1	1		8
Harriss, Howell	1	3	3		2
Hunt, Henry	1	2	5	1	1
Hubbard, John	1	3	3		
Hill, Thomas	1	2	3		
Hill, Richard, Jr	1	1	4		3
Hamm, Jesse	1		3		
Hamm, Elisha	1	1	6		
Harrisson, William	1	1	3		
Hilsmon, Hines	1	1	3		1
Hunt, Shadrack	1	2	3		
Hill, Henry	3	2	4		28
Hunt, James	4	1	4		1
Hill, Jordan	2		2		7
Hall, Thomas	1		1		4
Hunt, Henry	1	2	5		2
Hornsby, James	1	2	3		
Harriss, Harrisson	1	1	1		
High, Robert	2	4	3		4
Huckaby, James	2	2	4		8
Hendley, John	1	1	3		
Hester, James	2	3	5		28
Hicks, John	1		3		3
House, Thomas	1	1	1		7
Hill, Bennett	2	3	3	1	15
Huckaby, James	2	2	8		11
Hays, Hugh	1	2	2		35
Hightower, Rober	2	5	7		24
Hall, Durham	2	1	5		7
Hill, Thomas	1	1	7		37
Hill, Mary	1	4	3		45
Hill, Robert	1	1	1		46
Higgs, Zebulen	1		6		
Harriss, Exum	1		1		
Hogg, Charles	1	4	2		
Hogg, John	2	1	6		
Harriss, Benja	1	2	1		1
Hartfield, Jacob	2		3		26
Hogwood, Henry	3	1	3		
Howell, Margret		2	4		
Hammond, Robt	2	2	2		
Hamm, Richard	1		3		1
Hayse, Thomas	1	4	1		
Hill, Richard	1	3	3		
Hall, Jonathan	1				2
Hall, John	1		1	1	
House, Isaac	1	2	1		15
Huckaby, James	1	2	2		
House, William	1		5		7
Hight, Harbert	3	3	6		2
Hight, John	1	2	2		
Hencock, John	1	1	3		1
Hight, John, Sen	1		1		10
Hight, William	1	2	4		
Huks, Miles	1	3	2		6
Hight, Robert	2	3	4	1	3
Hencock, Saml	1	2	4		
Harvey, James	4	2			4
Hayse, James	1	1	1		
Haswell, Thomas	1	1			
House, Edmund	1		1		3
House, William	1		5		7
House, John	1		1		4
Hill, Green	2	2	5		14
Hunt, John	2	2	4		22
Haynes, William	1	2	4		
Jackson, Josiah	2	1	4		2
Jackson, Julius	2	3	2		7
Jones, Fredk	2	5	2		
Johnson, Moses	1	5	5		
Joiner, Moses	1	2	2		
Johnson, Charles	1		2		
Jarrall, John	1	2	3		
Jarrall, Nathan	1	2	4		
Jordan, John	3	2	4		8
Journagan, David	1		1		
Jones, Joshua	1	4	4		3
Jones, Jacob	3		2		16
Jones, Counsil	1	2	2		9
Jackson, John	1	3	2		1
Ivey, Charles	4		6		7
Jones, Leullen	2	1	1		18
Johnson, Dempsey	1	1	1		3
Johnson, Jacob	1				
Jones, William	1				
Jones, John	1	2	4		
Ingram, Thomas	2		3		
Jones, John	1	2	7		
Jones, William	1	1	1		
Jones, Richard	2	3	3		
Jones, Joseph	1	2	6		6
Johnson, John	1	3	4		12
Jones, Drury	1	4	5	3	9
Jeffreys, Simon	1	5	5	1	51
Jeffrey, Orsborn	1		2	2	69
Jeffreys, David	1	3	5		35
Jones, James	1				5
Jones, Saml	1		1		6
Jones, James	1		1		
Johnson, Benj	1	4	3		
Johnson, Nedon	1	2	2		
Jones, Roger	2	2	6		19
Jones, Daniel	2	2	5		19
Jarral, Nathl	2	2	4		4
Jones, John	1		1		4
Johnson, William	1	1	4		15
Jones, Armistead W	1	1	4		11
Jones, Betty	1		4		5
Jackson, Eliz		1	3		
Judd, William	1				
Kirny, Shemuel	2	3	4		20
Kimbell, Arch	1	1	4		2
Kimbell, Peter	1	3	3		1
Kilby, Exper	2		2		
Kilby, John	1	1	2		11
Kitchen, Jesse	1	2	4		
Lindsey, Saml	1	1	3		

HALIFAX DISTRICT, FRANKLIN COUNTY—Continued.

NAME OF HEAD OF FAMILY.	Free white males of 16 years and upward, including heads of families.	Free white males under 16 years.	Free white females, including heads of families.	All other free persons.	Slaves.
Lancaster, William	1	1	3		5
Lennard, Jones	2	2			4
Lennard, William	1	4	3		2
Liles, Jackson	1				
Liles, Mark	1	3	1		
Loyd, Thomas	1	2	2		
Loyd, Stephen	1	1	2		
Lambert, William	1	4	2		
Lambert, William S	2	1	2		
Lunsford, Seeman	1	3	5		
Long, Gabriel	1	2	4		25
Lewis, Sherode	1	2	2		
Leeman, Joseph	3	1	6		
Lashley, Howell	1	1	2		2
Liles, Charles	1	3	5		
Lemmons, John	2	2	6		
Lindsey, Betty	1	2	2		
Langley, Amy	1	1	1		
Melton, Robert	2	6	4		
Mitchell, William	1	1	1		
Meishaw, William	1	4	3		
Meishaw, John	1	3	2		
Mitchell, John	5	1	1		
Mitchell, John	1		1		
Murphy, William	1	2	8		
Morriss, William	1	3	5		
May, Thomas	1	2	2		1
Miller, George	4	3	5		
Morgan, Josiah	1		1		
Morgan, Benj	2	1	5		2
Morgan, Robert	1	2	1		
Miller, James	2	1	2		
Moody, John	1	1	4		8
Moody, Joel	1	1	1		
Milner, Jocobine	2	2	6		9
Mabry, David	1	2	5		5
Massey, Pettipol	2	3	7		
Medlong, James	1	1	2		
Mullens, Mary	2	5	4		
McMullens, Nathan	2	1	4		
Mitchell, John	2	6	1		2
Mullens, James	1	1	1		
Myrick, John	4	1	6		6
Murphy, Nicholas	1	3	6		4
Medlong, Matt^w	1	2	4		
McKinnish, William	2			3	
Medlong, Bradley	1		3		
Martin, John, Sen	1	1	2		
Martin, William	1	3	1		
Massey, Ezekiah	1	4	3		
Massey, Rich^d	2	5	4		2
Mabry, Jesse	2	2	6		6
Mabry, John	1		4		4
McLemore, Young	2		2		22
McLemore, Young	1				3
Meton, John	2	3	5		
Martin, John	1	2	2		
McLemore, Robert	1				4
Moses, Abram	1	3	7		
Morgan, Rubin	1		4		
Murphy, James	1	2	8		
May, Benj	1	2	2		
Madlesly, William	1	2	3		
May, William	1	1	2	1	1
May, Reubin	1		2		
May, Berry	1		1		
Miller, Thomas	2	3	4		
Moregraves, John	1		1		
Murry, Titus	1	1	2		5
Merrit, John	1	3	4		
Murry, James, Jr	1	1	2		1
Mabrey, Seth	1	1	4		20
Murry, James	3		1		15
Macon, Hannah	1	1	6		1
Medlong, Nancy		3			
Mabley, Benjamin					2
Medlong, Joseph	1	3	3		
Murphry, Arthur	1	1	1		
Murphry, James	3		3		1
Myrick, Mary		2	3		
Medlong, William	1		2		
May, Rubin	1		1		
Morgan, Nathan	1	2	2		
Matthew, Ford					2
Mitchell, Thomas	1	1	1		5
Nicholson, James	1	3	4		
Norwood, John	2	2	6		24
Nash, Joseph	2	1	2		
Nelms, Presley	2	3	3		25
Nunnery, Peter	1				
Norriss, Robert	1				
Norriss, John	1				
Norriss, Joseph	1		5	1	2
Nowland, Geo	1	3	2		3
Norwood, Jno, Jr	1	3	4		2
Norwel, James	2	3	3		6
Nowland, Danl	1	1	5		

NAME OF HEAD OF FAMILY.	Free white males of 16 years and upward, including heads of families.	Free white males under 16 years.	Free white females, including heads of families.	All other free persons.	Slaves.
Nowland, Budd	1	1	2		
Normon, William	1	1	2		1
Overton, Aaron	2	3	4		
Ownby, Thomas	2		5	1	4
Oden, Theo	1	3	2		
Ostwalt, Henry	1	2	3		
Privell, Thomas	4	3	5		
Pendergrass, Jesse	1	2	2		
Person, William	1				
Perry, James	1		1		
Perry, Burwell	1		1	3	3
Perry, Jeremiah	2	1	7		5
Perry, Jeremiah	1	1	1		3
Parish, Henry	1	1	2		1
Polliam, John	2	4	4		
Perry, John, Senr	1	2	1		22
Primm, John	1	3	5		
Parham, John	1				
Parker, John	2	2	1		
Pinnell, John	3	3	4		3
Person, Francis	1				5
Parker, John	3				7
Perry, Joshua	1	1	1		17
Perry, William	2	3			15
Perry, Joshua	1				
Perry, Ephraim	2		2		
Perry, Drury	2	2	5		4
Perry, Jeremiah	1	1	3		3
Perry, John	1		3		1
Paschal, Isaih	1	3	5		
Prarie, Lucres	2	2			
Pippin, John	1	3	4		
Perry, Ephraim	2		2		
Plummer, William	1	2	2		23
Pace, Geo	1	1	1		
Pace, Jeremiah	7		1		
Pippin, Isaac	2	2	5		
Parish, William	1		2		
Parish, Edmund	2	4	2		
Parish, Edm^d	1	4	4		
Pierce, John	2				
Pierce, Mildred		1	5		
Pippin, Thomas	1	2	3		
Pierce, Stephen	1	3	5		
Pierce, James	1		4		1
Pierce, Stephen	1	4	3		
Pierce, Amey	1	1	2		
Pierce, John	1				
Pace, William	1	6	1		
Powell, Sion	1	1	3		
Pace, John	2	1	2		1
Park, John	2	7	1		1
Perry, Burrell	1	3	3		3
Pace, William	1		8		6
Perry, William	1	7	5		5
Patterson, Filmore	1	2	1		1
Parish, Tho	1	2	7		
Perry, Nathl	1	3	1		1
Parish, Joel	1	2	5		5
Perry, Benj^a	2				19
Porch, James	1	1	3		
Porch, W^m	1		1		
Parker, Cornelius	1	1	2		
Perry, Simon	2	2	2		
Porch, John	1				
Primm, James	1	1	2		
Primm, Kitchin	1	2	2		5
Pasmour, W^m	1	1	2		3
Polland, Mary		1	2		
Partrick, Street	1	1	3		
Partrick, Spencer	1	2	3		
Pippin, Rich^d	1	2	2		
Perry, Priscilla		5	3		6
Powell, Enoch	1	3	1		
Perry, Mary		2	4		
Peterson, Salley		2	7		
Pumphry, Sylvanes	2	3	3		4
Portiss, John	1	4	3		1
Powell, Nathan	1				
Powell, Amos	1				1
Perry, Burwell	3		4		22
Rowe, Matthew	1	1	2		
Ransom, John	1	2	3		
Rainwabe, Gilliam	1	1	2		2
Richards, Benj	2	3	2		1
Read, Geo	1				3
Richard, William	1	2			10
Ratley, Macajah	1		3		
Rowland, Willie	1		2		
Ransom, Ruben	2	1	6		4
Rowland, William	1	2	4		1
Ragsdale, Baebe	1	2	4		
Rackley, Joshua	1	3	4		
Rush, Absolem	1	3	2	1	1
Rush, Benj^a	2				15
Rogers, Joseph	2	1	1		
Richards, Jesse	2		3		

NAME OF HEAD OF FAMILY.	Free white males of 16 years and upward, including heads of families.	Free white males under 16 years.	Free white females, including heads of families.	All other free persons.	Slaves.
Reaves, William	1	3	1		1
Ross, John	1	2	5		1
Richards, John	2	4	4		3
Richards, Geo	3		2		6
Richards, William	1	1	1		3
Robertson, Willoby	1				1
Ross, James	1	2	6		5
Richards, Joshua	1	3	4		
Ransom, William	1	3	1		9
Rush, Benj	1				
Richards, Major	1	1	6		8
Railey, Andrew	2	1	6		
Railey, Morriss	1		1		4
Rogers, Rubin	2	1	4		
Reed, Fred^k				4	
Rogers, Ruben S	1	1	3		
Rogers, Thomas	1		1		
Reeves, Richard	1	3	4		
Roods, John	1	1	4		
Roberts, Saml	1	3	4		
Rackley, John	1	5	2		
Rackley, Robt	1	2	6		6
Richardson, W^m	1	1	1		7
Ransom, Amey	1	1	1		7
Ross, Williamson	1	4	3		
Rose, William	1	3	4		8
Rose, Thomas	1	1	2		
Ricks, William	1	5	4		
Rossen, Daniel	1	2	3		1
Rackley, Matt^w	1	1	1		
Rogers, Jacob	1	1	2		4
Row, Matt^w	1	1	2		
Row, Patty	1		2		
Stephens, John	1	2	4		5
Stallions, Moses	1	1	1		5
Stallions, James	1	2	1		2
Stallions, John	1	1	2		2
Stiles, William	1	3	3		
Stephens, Jeremiah	2	1			11
Stallions, Wright	1		3		4
Sullivent, Cornelius	2		2		2
Solomons, James	1	3	5		3
Smart, Peter	1	1	1		7
Segars, David	1	3	11		6
Savage, Randolph	2	1	8		
Smart, Denton	1	2	3		
Smart, Stephen	1	2	3		1
Sandlen, John	1		1		
Sandlen, Eliza	1		3		
Smith, James	1	3	4		3
Self, Job	2	3	2		
Sandlen, James	1	3	1		
Stallions, Elias	1	1	2		9
Stallions, Rubin	1	4	5		2
Stallions, Josiah	1	2	4		4
Simmons, Mary	4	2	2		2
Simmons, Tho	1	1	1		
Simmons, Henry	1	3	4		1
Simmons, William		2	4		6
Smith, Fred^k	2	2	6		
Strickland, Jacob	2	1	2		1
Strickland, Obed	2	1	2		
Strickland, Abel	1	3	1		
Scrug, William	1	5	4		
Solomon, William	3	5	5		3
Solomon, Goodwin	1		3		
Shelton, James	1		5		
Sebrell, David	1				
Sumner, McKinne	1				
Stanton, William	1				
Sowell, Benj	4	3	1		20
Sanders, Vincent	2	1	2		3
Sanders, Kirby	2	1	4		5
Smith, John	1	2	4		5
Sanders, William	2	2	5		
Smith, Richard	1	3	4		
Strother, Christo	1		3		12
Sanders, John	2	2	4		
Swanson, Rich^d	1	2	3		5
Scarbrough, Edwd	1	2	2		
Striplen, John	3	1	2		
Sherod, Thomas	3	1	6		9
Sledge, Isham	1	3			7
Seawell, Lucey	1		3		8
Seawell, Tho	1	1	2		7
Stone, Jonathan	1	3	5		1
Smith, James, Sen	1		3		8
Smith, John	1				8
Smith, Joseph	1		1		3
Smith, John	1	1			3
Stone, John	1				3
Stone, William	1	2	4		3
Seawell, Joseph	1	3			21
Smith, William	1	3	5		4
Smith, William	3		5		4
Strickland, Matt^w	1	1	1		
Smith, Claborn	1	2	2		

HALIFAX DISTRICT, FRANKLIN COUNTY—Continued.

NAME OF HEAD OF FAMILY.	Free white males of 16 years and upward, including heads of families.	Free white males under 16 years.	Free white females, including heads of families.	All other free persons.	Slaves.
Sanders, Archur	1	1	2		
Sanders, Mary		4	3		
Stokes, Clary			2		
Smith, Patty	1		2		2
Seary, James	2	4	4		
Scarbrough, Peter	1	2	4		
Tharp, John	1	3	4		2
Taylor, Cornelius	1		1		
Taylor, Etheldred	1				5
Thomas, Eleza	1	2	2		1
Thomas, Anatha	1	3	1		1
Tharranton, Thomas	1	3	3		
Tharranton, Enoch	1	1	3		3
Thomas, Nathan	2		5		4
Tharranton, John	2	2	3		
Tant, Sion	1	10	3		
Tant, William	1	3	3		
Tant, Willis	1	2	5		1
Tharp, Timothy	1		2		
Thomas, John	1	1	2		
Tabb, Dianah			2		28
Tabb, Sally			1		28
Terrell, Joseph	4	4	5		16
Timberlake, Frank	1	3	3		1
Thomas, Benj	1		3		
Thomas, Benj	1	3	2		1
Thomas, William	2	3	2		17
Thomas, Carter	1	3	4		8
Taylor, Frances	2	2	3		34
Carter, Thomas	1	1	2		
Upchurch, Benj	1	2	5		1
Upchurch, Richd	1	4	1		
Upchurch, Richd, Jr	1	1	1		
Upchurch, Moses	1	3	4		
Upchurch, James	1	1	2		1
Woodliff, John	1	1	2		
Woodliff, Phillip	1	1	1		
Woodliff, Tho	3	1	2		
Wright, Griffin	1	2	7		17
White, Mark	2		5		8
White, Eliz			4	4	
Wiggin, Archer	1	3	1		
Wiggins, Sampson	2		4		
Willet, Dempsey	1	1	1		
Woodward, William	1	2	2		
Wood, William	1	4	4		1
Whittacar, Robt	1				2
Wilhite, Phillip	1	2	5		6
Wilhite, John	1				1
Wood, Brittin	1	4	3		1
William, Benj	2	1	3	3	6
William, John	1	3	5		4
Weathers, Jesse	2	3	5		12
Weathers, Mary			2		1
Wright, John	1	1	3		3
Wright, Jephtha	1		2		1
Wrenn, Elias	1		4		1
Wright, Benjn	1	1	1		1
Winters, John	2	3	4		1
Williams, Floyd J	1	3	4		
Wheler, John	1	2	3		
Williams, Huckman	1	2	3		
Wheelor, Joseph, Jr	2	1	3		
William, Harriss	1	1	1		
Wray, Thomas	1	2	2		
Wheelor, Joseph	1	2	4		
Walker, Amos	1	2	3		
Williams, Leeman	2	3	5		5
Williams, Floyd	1	2	6		
Williams, John	1	2	4		
Winston, John	1	5	1		7
Winston, Isaac	1	1	6		5
Winston, Anthony	1	2	4		
Winston, Nathan	1	1	2		
Winston, William		3	1		3
Winston, George	1				3
Williams, Richd	3		2		3
White, Gardner	2	3	3		
Wright, Benj					
Winston, Moses	1		2		5
Warmouth, John	3	3	8		7
Williams, Elisha	1	3	4		13
Walker, James	1	2	7		5
White, Berry S	2	3	7		7
Watkins, John	3		1		11
Wood, James	1		3		2
Watkins, John	1	2	1		11
West, Samson	1				
Wells, Frances	2	2	4		2
Wister, Daniel	1	4	1		1
Wells, John	2		1		
Whelar, William	1	1	2		
Wister, Benj	2	4	2		8
Webb, Richd	1	1	7		
Williams, Saml	1		2		2
Webb, Jacob	1		2		3
Webb, Jesse	1	3	2		2
Webb, William	2		3		2
Wrenn, Geo	2	1	7		1
Webb, Ried	1	2	3		
West, Jesse	1	1	2		
Whelar, William	1	1	2		
Winters, Barnett	1	1	2		
Welden, Pines	1	4	2		
Walker, William	1	1			
Williams, James	2	4	3		
Wilhite, William	1	3	2		4
West, Henry	1	1	3		
Webb, John	1	1	7		2
Webb, Lewis	2	2	1		2
Williamson, Green	1				5
Wynne, Charles		4	5		
Welton, Agness		1	2		
Wynne, K. Wyne	1	1	1		10
Waddell, Jacob	1	5	2		1
Wynne, John	1		1		1
Wilhite, Lewis	1	2	3		
Wilhite, Ambrose	1	1	3		
Vickory, Hezekiah	1				
Vinson, David	2				3
Verrell, William	1	2	3		14
Vincent, Ezekiel	1	2	3		
Young, James	2	2	1		
Young, Stephen	2				
Young, Mary	1	2	4		
Young, Demetrius	1	1	1		
Young, James	2	2	2		2
Yarbrough, Henry	2	5	3		14
Young, John	2		3		7
Yarbro, Micajah	2	2	4		
Williford, Esabell	1		4		
Edwards, John	1	3	3		
Wray, James	2		1		
Davis, John	1	1	6		

HALIFAX DISTRICT, HALIFAX COUNTY.

NAME OF HEAD OF FAMILY.	Free white males of 16 years and upward, including heads of families.	Free white males under 16 years.	Free white females, including heads of families.	All other free persons.	Slaves.
Crawford, Thomas	3	2	7		31
Carstaphin, James	1	3	4		16
Sexton, John	1	4	3		9
Nunnery, Anderson	1	1	1		
Iles, William	1	2	1		
Seat, Joseph	2	4	2		
Daniel, Lewis	2	3	4		8
Portin, William	1	2	2		
Smith, Isham	1	2			1
Corbin, Mathuel	1	2	5		
Hoalt, Thomas	1	2	2		1
Powers, William	1	2	2		
Crawley, David	2	4	1		10
Corbin, William	1	3	5		6
Nevill, William	1	1	2		1
Nevill, Benjamin	1	2	2		1
Allanack, John	1		3		6
Hoalt, Thomas	2		2		11
Cox, William	1				
Read, William	1	1	3		1
Hoalt, James	1	2	3		
Green, George	1	3	4		1
Smith, Thomas, Senr	1		3		5
Burt, John	1	3	3	1	4
Winter, Joseph	2		4		
Harlow, Thomas	1	2	3		
Martin, Patrick	1		1		20
Read, Moses	2		5		1
Nevill, John	1				
Burt, William, Senr	1	1	8		12
Kearney, Thomas	1		3		32
Daniel, Archibald	1				
Daniel, William	3	2	3		12
Daniel, Willie	1				
Iles, John	2	3	7	1	3
Knight, Meradith	1		2		1
Davison, James	1	1	3		
Sullivant, William	2		2		8
Sullivant, Jesse	1	1	2		1
Thompson, John	1		2		
Coan, Winifred	1	1	3		
Burt, William	2	3	4		
Dickens, John	1				
Read, Jesse	2	7	3		11
Daverson, Jesse	3	2	3		1
Heath, William	1	1	2		1
Brewer, Moses	1	2			
Smith, Miles	1	5	4		2
Smith, Thomas	1		1		1
Horton, Samuel	1		4		1
Jones, Francis	1	2	9		12
Nevill, Benjamin	1	2	2		1
Jones, Henry	2		4		
Scott, Abraham					6
Green, Daniel	2		2		
Daniel, Sterling	2	2	6		1
Hawkins, Thomas	3		1	1	10
Scott, James				5	
Cullum, Peter	3		3		1
Carter, Charles				5	
Carter, Randol					1
Carter, Frederick					1
Carstaphin, Robert	2	4	4		6
Knight, Ephraim	2	3	2	4	8
Dillard, Joel	1	1	5		7
Garland, Jonathan	1	2	3		
Qualls, Peter	5	3	4	2	18
Scott, Abraham					1
Brownlow, James	2		1	1	17
Marshall, Alexander	1		3		
Weldon, Daniel	2				6
Grinstead, William	1	5	2		4
Wood, John	2		2		
Medlin, John	1		1		6
Duffey, Samuel	1	1	4		5
Powell, John	1	2	2		
Taylor, Jeremiah	1		1		
Powell, Benjamin	1	1	5		
Solomon, John	3	1	4		
Pugh, David	2	2	2		1
Hethcock, Isham			1	5	
Downs, William	1	1	3		1
Mitchel, Gabriel	2	1	3		6
Matthews, John	1	2	4		1
Tabb, James	1				39
Corlew, Sarah	1	2	7		
Lausate, John	2		3		8
Parsons, William	1	2			23
Mitchel, Abraham	2		5		5
Parsons, Joshua	1				19
Hawkins, Solomon					14
Dempsey, Thorough-good					8
Turner, Lucy	1	2	4		16
Moss, Mary		1	2		2
Gray, John	1	1	5		
Manday, Sarah		1	4		
Munford, Jeoffry					
Mumford, Thomas					
Moreland, Barrot	2	3	3		
Harper, Isaac	1	5	6		4
Whitfield, William	2	5	5		3
Edmundson, William	1	1	5		1
Mason, Turner	1	2	1		3
Turner, James	1	1	2		4
Perry, James	1	1	4		1
Jones, James					
Waddle, Nowell	1	3	4		
Harper, Ambrose	1		3		6
Jones, Joshua	2	3	4	1	
Harper, Henry	2	1	6		
Mumford, John	1				
Stafford, David	1	1	2		
Hethcock, Frederick					7
Francis, Richard					
Demsey, James					3
Hawkins, Jeffrey					
Jones, Brackett	1	1	1		
Hethcock, Ptolemy					5
Hethcock, William					5
Perry, Joseph	1	3	5		1
Spiers, Joseph	1	1	1		1
Wood, William					
Batley, Moses	1	4	1		
Mumford, William	1	1	2		
Edmundson, Thomas	1				
Edmundson, Elizabeth		1	4		
Vaughan, William	1	3	1	1	3
Harper, Jett	1				
Harper, Vincent	1	2	1		3
Mumford, Richard	4	2	3		
Brasington, Samuel	2	1	1		3
Tabb, Thomas	2		1		54
Scott, Emanuel				7	
Moreland, Edward	1	1	2		2
Elbuk, Montfort	1	1	6		8
Ryanes, John, Senr	1	3	4		
Pugh, Eaton	2	4	5		35
Ballard, Walter	2	2	2		13
Johnston, Abraham	4	5	2		3
Carter, Jacob	1	1	1		

HALIFAX DISTRICT, HALIFAX COUNTY—Continued.

NAME OF HEAD OF FAMILY.	Free white males of 16 years and upward, including heads of families.	Free white males under 16 years.	Free white females, including heads of families.	All other free persons.	Slaves.
Carter, James	1	1	5		1
Handstred, Henry	1	2	1		
Coley, Charles	1	1	3		
Coley, Jeffry	2	1	2		
Mallard, John	1	2	1		
Carter, Robert	1	6	4		
Carter, William	2	1	4		11
Thompson, John	1	1	3		
Lee, Frederick	2	2	3		
Lee, Daniel	1				
Coley, William	1	2	1		
Morris, Philip	2	1	3		1
Coley, James	1	1	5		
Taylor, Nathaniel	1				
Carter, Joseph	1	4	2		
Yarborough, Charles	2	3	1		2
Pike, William	1	1	3		
Story, John	2				
Morris, William	1	1	4		1
Elms, Edward	1	2	5		
Sledge, Archibald	2	3	6		8
Adkins, Thomas, Jun	1				
Adkins, Thomas	1	2	4		
Allen, Taylor	1				1
Carter, Charles	1	5	6		
Sledge, John	2	2	5		10
Meloney, James	1	3			
Pike, William	3		2		1
Sledge, Mins	1				9
Clarke, Eldred	1	2	3		
Williams, Augustin	1	1	3		
Jinkins, William	2	3	5		6
Tony, John				7	4
Bradley, Benjamin	3		1		
Pike, Joseph	1				
Jones, William	1	1	2		
Rickman, Nathan	2		2		
Coley, David	1	1	2		
Smith, William	1	1	5		
Smith, Sarah			2		
Rickman, Mark	1	1	2		2
Price, William	2	2	2	10	5
Shine, James	2	2	6		1
Mallard, Joseph	1		1		
Dewberry, William	1	1	1		
Carter, Jesse	1	4	3		
Woodard, David	1		2		
Willis, Augustine	1		2		24
Parson, Benjamin	2	2	5		2
Baker, James	3	2	6		5
Smith, John	2	1	1		3
Newsome, Gillum	1	1	3		7
Johnston, William	1	2	4		3
Eaves, Mark	1	5	2		5
Hall, Theodorick	1	2	2	2	6
Southall, Furnith	1	1	3		1
Thompson, William	1		4		
Coley, Levi	1	2	2		
Willis, Lewis	2	4	5		15
Mallory, Francis	1	1	5		13
Groves, Thomas	1	4	5		3
Perry, Haleard	2	1	1		
Vike, George	1		2		
Marlow, John	1	2	3		
Ellis, John	1	1	5		4
Ellis, Mary			2		
Turner, James	1	2	2		5
Ingram, Ezediah	1				
Marshall, Thomas	1		2		4
Haws, Henry	2	3	6		9
Southall, Hoalman	1		2		13
Hamblin, Wood	1				78
Carter, Benjamin	1	1	4		
Carter, James	1		2		
Smith, Howell	1		4		
Malory, William	1				
Hamblin, Martha			2		5
Smith, Richard	1				16
Justiss, John	3	5	5		16
Southerland, John	3		7		
Grimmer, Thomas	1	2	4		
Southerland, William	4	2	2		
Grimmer, William, Jun	1		4		
Rogers, William	1	3	4		
Edwards, John	2		5		22
Manning, Joshua	1	3	3		
Pope, Elijah	1	3	5		1
Whitehead, William	2	3	2		12
Harrison, William	1				6
Brinson, Asehel	1	2	1		14
Barnes, Bartley	2		4		8
Champion, William	2		4		4
Edwards, Jesse	1	1	4		2
Whitehead, William	1				1
Edwards, John	2	2	4		
Dawson, Solomon	1	1	6		6
Smith, Drew	1	1	2		26

NAME OF HEAD OF FAMILY.	Free white males of 16 years and upward, including heads of families.	Free white males under 16 years.	Free white females, including heads of families.	All other free persons.	Slaves.
Williams, John	1	2	3		4
Bishop, Mercus	2	2	3		3
Bell, Shadrack	1		1		12
Bell, Elisha	1	2	3		12
Brewer, Jesse	1	2	2		1
Harrison, Jesse	1	1	3		
Lankford, William	1	2	1		1
Whitaker, Lunsford					7
Smith, Arthur	2	1	3		20
Barns, Matthew	2		3		1
Daffin, George	1	1	4		8
Fort, Willis	1	1	2		4
Pulley, Benjamin	1	2	4		1
Merritt, Drury	2	1	5		1
Bailey, William	2	4	1		10
Dickson, Josiah	1	3	4		3
Josey, Robert	2		1		3
Cooper, Thomas	1		3		25
Shield, Thomas	2	1	2		5
Baker, Jordan	2	2			
Mangram, Henry	1		1		
Pulley, Wasdon	1	1	3		
Jones, John					6
Vaughan, William	1	5	3		10
Merritt, Thomas	1	1	6		7
Gammon, James	1	2	2		
Whitehead, Susannah	1		1		2
Smith, James	2	1	3		57
Bell, John	1		2		6
Whitaker, Edward	2				
Jones, Joshua	1		3		
Poire, Francis	2	1	3		4
Barker, Joshua	1	2	5		
Jones, Elizabeth		2	4		
Whitehead, William	1	2	1		
Grimmer, John	1	2	4		
Davis, Thomas	1	2	3		37
Grimmer, William	1	1	1		
Pulley, John	1	1	4		
Ditto for Robt. Ricks	2	3	6	1	28
Rutland, Shadrack (for Rockets)					
Moore, John	1		5		10
Vinson, Thomas	1	1	5		
Tadlock, Thomas	2	4	5		
Tadlock, James	1				
Kendall, William	1		1		
Webb, George	1		2		
Tune, John	1	3	2	1	
Turner, Peter	1	1			9
Ditto for William Turner, decead			1	2	1
Turner, John	1	1	2	2	1
Hill, William	1	2	4		1
Kendal, James	1	1	1		
Mitchell, John	2	3	5		2
Dillard, William	2	1	5		3
Overstreet, Henry	2	2	4	1	13
Carson, John	2	2	2	6	3
Lowe, Thomas	2	1	4		3
Dillard, Owin	1		2		5
Branch, William Grog	1	2	4		5
Duncan, George, Senr	2		4		3
Lewis, Warner				3	1
Lewis, Morgan				4	
Lewis, Charles				6	
Motley, Henry	1		1		3
Wiggins, William	1	3	1		
Poredice, William	1	4	7	1	1
Jones, Robert	2	1	4	1	
West, George	1	2	4		5
Denton, John	1	2	1		2
Matthws, Moses	1	3	6		1
Heptenstal, James	1	1	2		
Elliot, Elisha	1	4	2		
Goodwin, Jane		2	3		11
Haywood, Egbert	2	1	2		17
Haywood, John	1	2	2		22
Elbuk, Joseph, Senr	1				36
Rawlins, Rodham	1	2	4		14
Pullin, William	1		4		
Burgess, Lovatt	1	3	4		40
Doggett, Jeremiah	1	3	2		13
Gaskins, John, Junr	1	1	4		
Philips, John	1				1
Rollins, Samuel		3	4		
Hill, Abraham	1	2	3		
West, William	1	2	2		
Merritt, Thomas	1		1		
Hanks, Luke	1		2		
Swett, Abreham					5
Merritt, Frederick	1	2	4		
Merritt, Shadrack	1	1	6		5
Duncan, William	2	2	4		
Gallidge, William	1	1	5		
Duncan, Zachariah	1		2		

NAME OF HEAD OF FAMILY.	Free white males of 16 years and upward, including heads of families.	Free white males under 16 years.	Free white females, including heads of families.	All other free persons.	Slaves.
Sturges, William	1	1	7		
Merritt, Shadrack	2	3	4		
Megee, William				9	
Crowell, Benjamin	1	3	2		10
Knight, Robert	1	4	2		
Merritt, John	1	5	2		
Knight, John	1	2	3		1
Pearce, Mary	2	1	1		7
Elbuk, William	1				12
Joiner, Benjamin	1		3		4
Merritt, William, Junr	1	1			
Merritt, William, Sen	2	3	2		
Morgan, Peter	1	1	2		8
Gaskins, John, Senr	2	1	3		
Crowell, Edward, Junr	1		2		7
Tillery, Eppy	3	3	6		
Taylor, John	1	3	1		
Turner, Winifred			1		1
Martin, James (Estate of)	2	3	8		25
Turner, Edwin	1	1	6		9
Rudd, William				8	
Branch, William, Senr	1	1	3		16
Pearce, Benjamin	2	4	5		7
Branch, William, Jua	1	1	3		12
Flewellin, James	1	4	3		11
Crowell, Edward, Senr	2		3		21
Clayton, John	1	4	2		9
Ditto for Jno Dickins					5
Lewis, John				1	4
Landman, William	1		3		
Smith, John	2	1	3		
Baker, James	1		2		2
Batchelor, William	1	2	3		
Butt, Jesse	1	2	5		
Bradford, Henry	1	3	3		10
Branch, John	9	3	5	1	28
Banks, William	1	2	2		
Butt, Moses	3	3	6		17
Bradley, Samuel	1	2	6		1
Carlile, Nathaniel	1	1	6		
Counsil, Mary	1		3		
Crowell, Samuel	1	3	3		15
Chrisam, William	1	2	3		1
Cooper, John, Sen	3		2		4
Curlins, Thomas	1	2			
Cooper, Iles	1		2		
Daniel, Ambrose	3	3	5		
Daniel, Randol	4	4	4		7
Drummond, Thomas	3	4	2		
Drake, Tristram, Sen	4	1	2		1
Everitt, Jesse	3		3		11
Edwards, Joseph, Senr	1	1	1		
Edwards, Ransome	1	1	2		
Grizell, Willie	1	3	2		
Hill, William	2		2		4
Harrington, Lewrancy			2		6
Hynes, Thomas	2	1	8		3
Robert, John	1		2		
Hataway, William	1		2		
Harper, James	1	1	2		
Herbert, William	2	1	1		
Ives, Dinah	1	1	2		
Izzard, Thomas	1	1	3		
Jones, John	3	2	7		30
Ditto for Benja Rosser					
Moran, William	3	2	8		
Lock, James	1		2		1
Long, Littleton	1	1	2		
Lorton, Thomas	1	3	5		
Moran, Samuel	1	3			
Moran, John	1		2		
Morris, Griffin	3		2		
Morris, Hezekiah	1		3		
Morris, Holloway	1	1	1		3
Morris, Hercules	1	1	2		6
Mann, Frederick	1	1	2		
Morris, Jesse	1	4	3		
Marshall, John, Senr	2	1	4		17
Nichols, Luke	1		2		
Nichols, James	3	1	3		
Nichols, Thomas	1		3		
Perkins, William, Jnr	1		3		
Perkins, Henry, Jun	2	5	6		2
Parker, Charles	1	1	5		
Read, John	1	2	6		2
Reed, William	2	3	3		
Taylor, John	2	1	3		2
Troughton, Swan	1	1	4		
Turner, Solomon	1	2	4		
Swett, George				3	
Suit, Richard	1	1	2		
Sullivant, Drury	1	1	2		2
Shelton, Ruth	1		2		6
Scoles, William	1				

HALIFAX DISTRICT, HALIFAX COUNTY—Continued.

NAME OF HEAD OF FAMILY.	Free white males of 16 years and upward, including heads of families.	Free white males under 16 years.	Free white females, including heads of families.	All other free persons.	Slaves.
Scott, Exum				9	
Wheales, Nordy	1	5	4		
Wilsey, William	1				
Wootten, William	1	3	4		14
Ditto for W. Bradford		1	1		9
Warren, Thomas	4	4	5		
Woolsey, Joel	1	2	2		4
Walker, Joel	1	1	2		6
Whealles, Joseph	1	1	2		
Willey, John	1		2		
White, Adam	1	5	2		
White, Joshua	2	1	3		2
Whitaker, Matthew	2		2		46
Ditto for Israel West					
Whitaker, Matthew (for Jno Brinkly's estate)		3	4		4
Hill, William	1		2		18
Alston, Joseph, Jno	2				11
Alston, Gideon	2	1	3		17
Angel, George	2	1	3		5
Angel, John	1	2	1		
Archer, John				9	
Burt, John	1	1	1		1
Bruce, William	1	2	5		
Burt, Richard	1		1		37
Burt, Elizabeth	1	3	3		10
Burt, Joseph	1		3		3
Bull, Thomas	2	1	5		2
Bull, Randolph	2	1	4		1
Brinkley, Abraham			2		4
Brinkley, William, Senr	3		2		9
Brinkley, William	1	2	1		7
Brinkley, Ely	1				
Brinkley, Judith	1		8		8
Brinkley, Jerry	1				
Broom, Burrell	2	5	2		
Broom, John	1	1	1		
Butt, Aby	1	1	5		
Bosedale, Robert	1		5		
Cleavis, John	3	3	3		1
Cavinah, Thomas	1	1	3		5
Conner, James	3	1	7		
Conner, William	1				8
Davis, Isham	1	6	6		6
Ditto for Hopkins's Orphans			8		
Doles, Jesse	2	1	5		3
Daniel, Elizabeth	1	1	7		9
Daniel, West	1	2	1		2
Davis, Merritt	3	1	4		4
Daniel, Buckner	1	2	4		1
Flewellin, Richard, Junr	2	2	3		
Flewellin, Abner	3	1	3		
Flewellin, Taylor	1	2	3		9
Fuqua, William	1	2	2		6
Fruar, Robert	1	1	2		33
Ganes, Moses	2	1	3		8
Gilbert, Matthew	1	6	3		4
Gilbert, James	1	1	3		
Gilbert, William	1	1	2		
Hart, Sinah			4		2
Harvey, Thomas, Senr	2	3	7		22
Hervey, William, Senr	1	3	3		1
Hervey, William	1	3	1		1
Hervey, John	1	4			1
Hervey, Thomas	1		3		1
Hall, Mary			3		5
Hawkins, Samuel				1	1
Humphris, Elijah	2		5		12
Hall, Robert	1	2	3		
Higgs, Samuel	2	3	4		
Jordan, William	2	4	4		
Jordan, Joseph	1	2	5		
Johnston, Jacob	2	1	2		3
Jordan, Edward	1	3	5		12
Kirk, Isaac	2	3	5		12
Kelley, William	1	1	2		
Long, John	1	3	5		
Lee, John	2	3	6	1	
Lee, Green	2				
Lock, Josiah	2		2		
Matthews, Richard	3	6	3		6
Matthews, Samuel	1	5	3		2
Matthews, Jerry	2	3	5		7
Moore, George	1	1	3		
Marshall, Stephen	1				
Matthews, James	3	3	4		12
McLilley, William	1	2	3		
Pritchett, Christopher	2	3	4		5
Ditto for Tho. William's Orphans			1		1
Powers, John	2	3	5		9
Porter, Samuel	1	3	4		6
Perkins, Thomas	3		2		
Perkins, William	1		1		
Perman, William	1	3	3		2
Rogers, Shadrack	1	2	2		1
Rogers, Thomas	2	2	4		1
Richardson, Benjamin					12
Richardson, William					7
Rams, Robert	1		2		3
Rosser, Isham	1	3	2		
Stephens, John	3		5		
Sullivant, Jerry	1	5	6		2
Smith, Samuel	2	1	2		8
Sullivant, John	2	3	4		
Sullivant, Christian	1		2		1
Vincent, Philip	1	3	4		2
Wright, Sterling	1	6	2		
Williams, Joseph John	1	2	4		66
Williams, James	2				27
Williams, Thomas	1		1		
Williams, Samuel	1	2	5		
Williams, Wood	1	1	3		1
Worley, John	1	2	4		
Worley, Lovick	1	1	2		1
Winter, Moses	1	1	4		
Weaver, James					4
Williams, Elisha	1	5	3		1
Edwards, Peter	1	1	4		5
Rose, Thomas	1				
Perkins, William, Senr	2	2	6		1
Lee, Jesse	1		1		1
Patrick, John	1		2		3
Malton, Samuel	2	1	3		
Morris, Dunston	1	3	3		
Sikes, James	1				
Mehoney, William	2	4	3		6
Parker, William	3	1	3		6
Smith, Zachariah	2	1	2		
Adams, Philip	1	1	2		2
Sikes, Joel	4	2	2		
Harris, Asey	1		2		
Miles, Thomas	2		3		
Williams, Francis	1	3	2		7
Green, Robert	2	3	3		4
Green, John	2	3	4		
Hardy, David	1	3	3	2	6
Blanton, Charles	1		2		2
Green, Berry	1	2	6		3
Dickens, William	1	2	4		
Brown, William	1		2		
Gammon, Jesse	1	2	1		
Grissam, Oliver	1	3	3		3
Good, Edward	3	2	5		
Dawson, Larkin	1	1	2		3
Mehoney, John	1	1	5		
Morris, George	1	2	2		
Carter, Molton	1	2	4		
Wright, James	1	2	3		3
Roper, John	1		4		3
Wilson, Joshua	1	1	2		2
Johnston, Lewis	1	2	2		
Moody, Burrell	1	2	4		1
Dameron, Tignal	1	2	4		
Harvil, Starling	1	2	3		16
Harris, Roe	1	2	3		
Tucker, Gray	1		1		1
Johnston, Abraham	3	3	2		1
Brown, Jesse	3	4	5		
King, Burrel	1	1	3		2
Williams, George	1	2	4		
Gill, James	1	1	2		
Bobbit, Sherret	1	3	1		
Allen, John	1				
Harris, Warner	3		8		12
A'len, William	3	3	1		
Williams, Samuel	1	2	4		
Sikes, Joshua	1	3	4		1
Jackson, Edward	2		2		6
McDougal, Samuel	2				7
Dennison, John	1				
Mehoney, William	1		2		5
Colley, John	2		2		2
Brown, John	2	3	4		
Yerby, Henry	1	2	4		
Stephens, Richard	1	1	2		
Stephens, Lewis	1	2	2		
Dickens, Thomas	1		2		
Megriggo, Anthony	1		3		4
Green, Jesse	1		1		
Newsome, Jacob	1	1	2		7
Alston, Joseph Jno	1				60
Mallory, John	1	3	3		3
Alston, Willis	2	5	5		40
Morris, George	1	2	2		
Morris, William	2	2	1		20
Lindsey, John	1	1	5		26
Harper, John	1	2	3		
Williams, William	2	3	6	3	
Carney, Richard, Junr	2	5	6		11
Carney, Stephen	1		2		24
Carney, Richard, Senr	2		5		27
Spane, Little Berry	1	2	1		2
Joiner, Theophilus	3	1	2		4
Daffin, John	1	2	3		5
Harden, James	1		1		3
Watson, Samuel	3	2	2		2
Homes, Willis	2	2			1
Howell, Matthew	1	1	1		
Moore, John	2	1	2		2
Mann, Absalom	2	2	6		9
Linton, Samuel	1	1	4		
Vaughan, Lemaston	1				5
Joyner, John	1		4		4
Corbin, Charnel	1	1	2		
Lane Gisburn	1	2	2		1
Buck, John	1	2	2		6
Langford, John	1	2	2		1
Harmon, John	1			4	
Brasill, Benjamin	1				50
Seat, Isham		2	4		
Lanturn, Joseph	1			6	
Lucas, Farnith	1		3		
Flood, Benjamin	1	1	3		
Epps, Thomas	1	3	1		3
Armstrong, John	1	1	1		
Pope, John	4				9
Pope, William	1				
Spellings, Frederick	1	2	1		
Qualls, Henry	1				
Flood, Jesse	1	3	2		
Dwyer, Patrick	1				11
Mason, Thomas	1				13
Fort, Micajah	2	1			4
Fort, Allen	1	1			3
Brantley, James	1	2	3		9
Harden, William	2	1	3		1
Onions, George	2	2	1		1
King, William	1		1		
Goodwin, Jesse	1				10
Lane, David	5		2		15
Shelton, Burrel	1	1	2		12
Lassiter, Jethro	4	4	2	2	51
Jallipp, Joseph	1		3		
Duke, Millia				1	1
Hardin, William, Jun	1				2
Fort, Elias	2	3	2		2
King, Edward	2	3	4		4
King, John	2				
Skinner, Thomas	1		4		
Pulley, James	1	2	3		
Steward, Joseph	1	1	3		
Hendley, James	1	1	3		
Langford, Zachariah	1	2	4		3
Pearce, William	2		5		4
Whitaker, Thomas	1	1	3		1
Fort, Sugar	1		2		19
Joiner, Henry	3	3	5		19
Lane, Levi	2		5		32
Joyner, Bridgman	2				16
Barnes, James	2		2		19
Ricks, Isaac	2	3	4		27
Qualls, Peter	7	2	5		24
Topp, George				4	
Sikes, Dempsey	1		1		1
Barker, Joshua	1	3	1		
Jackson, William & Edmund	2				
Undrew, Demsey	1	2	4		
Kelley, William	1	1	1		
Alsobrook, Edward	1	2	4		2
Emry, Edward	2	1	4		
Brantley, Lewis	2				1
Cotten, William	1	1	1		7
Sessums, Elinore			2		
Dew, Thomas	1		2		9
Biggs, Azeriah	1	1	2		
Biggs, Robert	1	2	4		
Drew, Joshua	4	4	4		
Alsobrook, Howell	5	4	4		
Wilkings, Elijah	2	2	5		1
High, Thomas	1	5	4		
Bynam, William	1	1	5		
Turner, William	1		1		
Bradley, Micajah	1				
Martin, John	1		1		1
Hogan, Lemuel	1				
Cain, Joseph	1		1		
Drew, John	1				17
Young, Marmeduke	1	4	4		21
Turner, Sarah			2		5
Fillips, John	1		2		
Spear, William	1	2	5		
Spear, William Exum	1	1	2		
Jackson, William	1		2		
Jones, James				3	
Alsobrook, Claburn	1	2	1		1

HALIFAX DISTRICT, HALIFAX COUNTY—Continued.

NAME OF HEAD OF FAMILY.	Free white males of 16 years and upward, including heads of families.	Free white males under 16 years.	Free white females, including heads of families.	All other free persons.	Slaves.
Taylor, Thomas	1	1	7		
Bynam, James	1		2		
Haynie, William	1	1	2		
Haynes, Thomas	1	1	2		
Harriss, Elij	2	6	3		19
McCombs, Alexander	1	2	2		
Norfleet, Marmaduke	1	1	5		59
Alsobrook, John	1	3	3		5
Alsobrook, Thomas	3		2		1
Drew, Thomas	3	1	3		
Hobgood, Lemuel	1		7		
Hobgood, Elijah	1	1	2		
Wall, Francis	1		1		
Good, Elizabeth	2		3		
O'Daniel, Jacob	1				
Cain, James	2	4	6		6
Killebrew, Wiggan	1	2	2		
Powell, James	1	3	4		1
Alsobrook, Samuel	1	3	2		
Brazwell, Drury	1	1	2		
Bass, Solomon	1	3	2		1
Whitehead, Benjamin	2	4	5		3
Slaughter, James	4	1	7		20
Alsobrook, Drew	3		2		9
Spear, Nathan	1	1	6		
Hill, Isham	1	2	7		
High, Luke	1	1	1		
Haynie, Benjamin	2	3	5		
Dicken, Lewis	1				1
Dicken, Benjamin, Senr	2	1	4		16
Rawls, Philip	2	3	4		
Hodges, Robert	1	1	2		1
Alsobrook, James	1	2	3		2
Hodges, James	2	1	4		1
Simmons, James	2	1	3		1
Hodges, David	1	1	3		1
Murrell, George	1				
Banks, Thomas	1				
Hail, Ogburn	1				
Dicken, Benjamin, Junr	1				3
Cotten, Young	1				
Alsobrook, William	2	1	4		6
Ford, Elias	2	4	2		24
Merritt, James	2				
Ford, Turner	1	1	1		1
Raifield, Babel	1	2			
Murry, Mark					9
Cotten, Theophilus	1	5	3		4
Cochran, Robert	1	4	3		1
Gayner, Samuel	1	2	4		4
Mellen, Ely	4	1	1		
Mullen, Robert	1	1	2		
Bradley, Thomas	1	4	3		
Haynie, Lewis	1	1	3		
Alsobrook, David	3	3	4		1
Carter, Benjamin	1	1	2		3
Bell, George	2	1	6		6
Lain, Cardy	1		2		
Bell, Benjamin	1	2	3		
Bell, Lemuel	1	1	3		3
Strickland, John	1				
Pernal, John	2	4	6		2
Ditto for Andrew Mead					18
Hail, Williamson	2	1	5		2
Ubanks, George	1	1	4		7
Jones, Briton	1		2		1
Hail, Aris	1		2		
Dewberry, William	2	3	1		
Hail, Jonathan	1	7	2		1
Dicken, William	3	7	3		
Hunt, Howell	1	4	3		
Hargrove, Sarah	2		4		9
Barrott, Priscilla	2	1	3		3
Hail, Jesse	1	1	2		
Stafford, Joshua	1	2	3		
Cullum, William	1				
Wood, John	1	1	2		2
Dicken, Bennet	1	1	1		
Crosslin, Edward	1				
Browning, Levy	1	3	2		
Cullum, William, Senr	2	1	3		
Cullum, Jeremiah	1		3		
Dewberry, Daniel	1	1	1		
Peobles, Drury	2	6	1		
Hargroves, John	6	3	5		13
Crawley, Daniel	1	2	4		
Harriss, Abner	1	2	6		5
Thompson, John	1				
Williams, Thomas	1	2	3		1
Bagby, Davis	3		6		4
Gillum, William	1	3	3		
Smith, Zacheus					8
Bagby, William	1	1	3		
Killingsworth, Mark	1	2	2		
Hawkins, Henry				3	
Killingsworth Matthew	1	3	4		

NAME OF HEAD OF FAMILY.	Free white males of 16 years and upward, including heads of families.	Free white males under 16 years.	Free white females, including heads of families.	All other free persons.	Slaves.
Bloss, Henry	2	1	4		1
Waddle, C.	1	4	2		
Dicken, Joseph	2	1	2		
Powess, Henry	1	2	1		
Smith, Josiah	1	1	3		1
Myrick, Ann					
Hawkins, Joseph				9	
Harriss, Robert	1	2	6		
Gardner, Josiah	1	2	2		1
Sherman, Matthew	1				
Roan, Jesse	1				
Corlew, Philip	3	2	5		1
Smith, Priscilla		2	2		
Corlew, John	2	1	4		
Potts, Mary Ann	1	1	2		
Killingsworth, William	1	1	5		
Richards, Richard	2		3		7
Harriss, Isaac	3	2	4	3	9
Crawley, Alice		1	1		1
Hargrove, Dudley	1		2		
Vinson, Benjamin	1	2	2		
Roan, John	1	2	3		
Smith, Sarah	2				1
Long, Elizabeth	1	1	4		2
Crabb, Susannah		3	3		
Evans, Mary	1		4		1
Hawkins, Isham	2	2	3		6
Edmunds, William	1	2	2		
Bumpass, John	1				
Bishop, James	3				9
Edmonds, Elizabeth	1	1	4		9
Alston, Joseph John (for W. Alston Esta)	1	2	1		
Alston, Willis, Jun	2	2	4		34
Stigall, Samuel	1		3		
Eubanks, Joseph, Sen	1		2		4
Thompson, Richard	1	4	5		
Harper, Jacob	1	3	4		
Vinson, Willis	1	1	4		
Ashe, Charles				11	
Killingsworth, John	1				
Hyde, Hartwell	2	1	7		9
Hide, Henry	1	5	3		21
Zoliofer, George	1	4	3		28
Lewis, Nicholas	1	5	2		
Pettypool, Henry	1	1	3		
Smith, William	3		2		1
Purnal, Charles	1				
Axum, Mary	1	1	1		
Griffis, Samuel	1				
Ashe, John Baptist	3	1	4	2	63
Aaron, Isaac	1	3	2		
Aaron, William	1	1	1		
Aron, George	1				
Aaron, Amey	1		3		1
Barnes, Thadeus	1				
O'Neill, Thomas	1				
Bond, Hance	5	1	3	1	9
Berryman, John	1			2 3	13
Barksdale, Benjamin	1				
Barber, Joshua	1	1	2		
Barksdale, Daniel	1				
Coleman, George	3	2	6	1	
Cotten, Robert	4	1	3	1	15
Ditto Exr of J. Bass	1	2	4	2	8
Cole, Joshua	1	2	4		26
Davis, Goodorum	2		1	1	14
Davie, William R.	1	2	2		36
Elbeck, Elizabeth			2		6
Eaton, John	1	1	3		12
Easley, Benjamin	1				
Elbeck, Dorothy			2		6
Elbeck, Mary			2		4
Elbeck, Penelope			1		
Fenner, Robert	1	1	4		31
Fawcett, James	1	2	4		
Gray, James	2				10
Gerrard, Thomas	2	1			5
Gilchrist, Martha		1	1		13
Gilmour, Charles (Admr of Wm Hendrie)					24
Gilmour, John & Charles	3		1		36
Gilchrist, John		1	2		1
Geddy, John	2		6		22
Gilmour, William	3	3	1		32
Gilmour, Charles, Junr	2	2	2		4
Garrigus, Matthew	1	5	1		
Green, John				16	
Greene, William					1
Pasteur, Thomas	1		4	1	
Hall, Robert	2	2	3	2	11
Harveey, John	1	1	3		40
Housin, Ann			2		1
Hannon, John	3	2	2		4
Hunter, Charles	1		2	1	
Hogg, Elizabeth		1	1		16

NAME OF HEAD OF FAMILY.	Free white males of 16 years and upward, including heads of families.	Free white males under 16 years.	Free white females, including heads of families.	All other free persons.	Slaves.
Hail, Lewis	1				
Housin, John	1				
Hendry, Michael	4	1	2		8
Harrison, Collier	1				52
Jones, Willie	2	2	6		120
Ditto for Jarrott Wallace					17
Isbell, Peter	1	1	2	1	1
Johnston, Jacob	1				
Jamica, Henry	1		1		
Kinchen, John	2	2	1		32
Kay, John	3				13
Kelley, William	1		4		
Kelley, John	1	3	4		
Lowe, William	2	1	3		9
Lowe, James	1	2	1		5
Long, Nicholas, Senr	5	2	8		89
Long, Nicholas, Junr	2	3	4		33
Long, Lunsford	1				1
Lyon, Richard	1				
Lynes, David	1				
Muir, William	5	1			9
Morgan, John	1	3	3		2
Miller, Christopher	1	2	2		
Ring, John	2	1	2		1
Morgan, George	1				
McCulloch, Alexander	1				60
McCulloch, Benjamin	3	6	11	9	40
Marsham, Samuel	1				
McDaniel, Patrick	1	2	2		2
Montfort, Joseph	1				2
McClanahan, John	1				4
Murry, Frances				6	
Pasteur, Charles	1	1	5		33
Perkins, William	1			2	17
Powers, Robert	1		5	2	
Pasteur, James	1		2		27
Ponns, John	3		2	5	13
Ponton, Mungo	1		2		3
Philips, Thomas	1		1		
Rymes, Jesse	1				
Roberts, Francis	1	1	2		1
Richardson, William				6	
Smith, Martin	1	1	2		
Sheeter, Josiah	1	1	2		
Suttles, Matthew	1				1
Smith, Major	1	1	2		
Tillery, John	2				4
Watson, John	2	2	2	1	4
Watson, William	1	1	1		
Williamson, George	1	2			10
Warren, Samuel	1				
Yarborough, John	6	1	2		
Young, George	1	1	3		4
Morgan, John					16
Drew, John					
Pulley, David	3	3	5		3
Russell, Richard	2	3	3		6
Dancey, John	2	1	2		9
Brantley, Robert	3		1		11
Powell, Benjamin		2	3		13
Carter, Joseph	2	1	2		22
Pitman, Elisha	2	4	5		11
Bird, Peter	1	1	3	1	3
Fort, Willie	1		3		7
Champion, John	1	1	1		9
Sands, Barham	2	2	2		12
Merritt, William	1	1	4		4
Wootten, John	2	1	3		2
Spier, Samuel	1	3	2		1
Spier, Ann		4	1		3
Brantley, William	3	1	6		1
Whitehead, Arthur	2	5	3		3
Lewis, Lewis	2	3	4		2
Bird, Allin	1	1	2		4
Applewhite, Henry	1	1	1		1
Applewhite, Thomas	4		2		
Knight, Moore	1		1		7
Dancey, Edwin	1	2	1		10
Ward, Robert	1	1	7		4
Pitman, Arthur	1	4	2		6
Jones, Jarvis	1	2	6		
Noblin, William	1	2	3		6
Ward, James	1	4	4		3
Jones, James, & Kindred Spier	2	4			12
Bass, Isaac	1		2		4
Barrow, Robert	1				9
Smith, Richard	1				1
Whitaker, Richard, Senr	2		3		17
Whitaker, Cary	2	2	1		25
Whitaker, Richard, Jun	2		4		6
Kindred, Knight	1	1	3		4
Barrow, Olive	1	2	3		45
Lain, Elizabeth	3	1	3		20
Pitman, Samuel	4	1	2		12
Haynes, Lucy	1				4

HALIFAX DISTRICT, HALIFAX COUNTY—Continued.

NAME OF HEAD OF FAMILY.	Free white males of 16 years and upward, including heads of families.	Free white males under 16 years.	Free white females, including heads of families.	All other free persons.	Slaves.
Cherry, Samuel	1	2	4		1
Foot, John	2	4			15
Hillman, Jesse	1				
Wyatt, Jesse	2	1	3		1
West, Arthur, Junr	1	4	2		6
Whitaker, John	3	5	4		28
Ditto for Wilson Carter	1				4
Howell, Thomas	2	1	3		7
Jackson, William, Senr	3	2	3		11
Jackson, William, Junr					
Jackson, Matthew					
Foreman, Samuel	2	3	4		5
Wyatt, James	1		4		
Simmons, Zadock	1		1		
Kirkley, George	1	1	2		
Pass, William	2				3
Hill, William	1	1	2		13
Whitmill, Thomas	2	3	2		18
Henderson, William	2	1	1		26
Smith, Ann	2	1	2		40
Bell, Marmaduke	1		1		8
Joyner, Joel	3		5		12
Harris, Norfleet	1	1	1		28
Hodge, Henry	1	5	2		6
Naron, Jesse	1	3	6		
Joiner, Ely	1	1	1		4
Young, Thomas	1	3	5		7
Sills, Benjamin	1	3	3		1
Sills, Isham	3	3	2		
Tippet, Erasmus	1	3	2		5
Myham, James	1	4	2		3
Atkertson, William	1	2	2		5
Joyner, Blount	1		1		11
Barber, Joshua	1	2			4
Doles, John	1	1	3		
Parks, John	1	1	2		1
Gayner, Thomas	1		3		3
Foreman, Benjamin	3	2	5		12
Young, Dolphin	1	4	5		12
Williams, John	1		3		5
James, Benjamin				6	
Winburn, Thomas				3	
Wiggins, William, Senr	2	1	1		9
Stamper, Robert	1	2	3		1
Wiggins, William	1	2	1		
Hunter, Henry	1	2	4		7
Young, Francis	1	1	2		10
Land, Sarah			4		3
Adams, John	1	1	4		3
Bryant, William	1	3	3		11
Baylis, John	1	2	1		4
Drew, John	4	4	3		99
Myham, John	1	1	2		2
Barrow, Millia		1	6		13
Bishop, John	3	1	4		1
Baylis, Britain	1		1		2
Maclemore, Howell	2	1	3		1
Boykin, William	1		1		42
Binston, Jacob		1	2		1
Dukes, Josiah	1	2	2		5
Garner, Ann			1		4
Griffin, Priscilla			6		5
Griffin, Michael	1				
Griffin, Brinkley	1				
Bryant, Lewis	1		3		
Bayliss, Amey	1		3		1
Armstead, Robert	1		3		5
Hines, Dempsey	1	1	1		
Cotten, Joab	2	3	5		25
Dawson, John	2	3	1		61
Jones, Phill				7	
Fair, Bythel	2	1	6		
Jones, James				4	
Davis, Thomas	1	1	3		
James, Elisha				6	
Nelms, Jeremiah	2	1	4		22
Moore, David	3	2	1		12
Sturdevent, Jesse	3	7	4		3
Sturdevent, Charles	1		4		
Tucker, William	2	2	6		
Christie, Jesse	2	3	4		
Sampson, Stephen	1		1	3	
Garner, Vallentine	2		9		
Judge, James	2	3	2		6
West, William	2	1	3		10
Heath, Richard	3	1	7		10
Hadley, Joshua	1	2	4		4
Hadley, Martha	1	2	6	1	5
Hadley, Ambrose	1	1	3		4
Coffield, Grissum	1	4	5		1
Butt, Joshua	4	1	3	1	
Sikes, William	1	1	3		
Thrower, Baxter	2	5	2		6
Davis, John	1	2	4		2
Pullin, William	2	5			6
Dean, Isaac	4	1	3		3

NAME OF HEAD OF FAMILY.	Free white males of 16 years and upward, including heads of families.	Free white males under 16 years.	Free white females, including heads of families.	All other free persons.	Slaves.
Passmore, Mary		1	4		
Leath, William	1				
Williams, Howell	1	1	3		1
Nicholson, Joseph	2	3	2		16
Hill, Sarah	1		2		18
Heath, Adam	2	2	6		13
Jones, Henry	2	2	5		15
Davis, William	1	2	2		3
Berryman, Balaam	1		2		8
Powell, Nathaniel	1	3	2		11
Parram, William	1				1
Hynes, Benjamin	1	2	3		5
Flewellin, James	1	1	4		13
Harden, Thomas	1				
Flewellin, Shadrach	1				
Flewellin, Elizabeth			3		9
Wright, John	2	4	2		16
Sikes, Willouchby	2	2	4		
Johnson, Josiah	2	1	1		3
Heath, William	2	1	1		8
Cox, William	1	1	1		1
Nelms, Meredith	1	1	4		
Bustion, Martha	1	2	4		16
Barksdale, William	1		1	2	12
Pitts, Ann		3	5		8
Long, Ann		3	2		18
Wood, Aron					
Ballard, Deverix	1	1	3		1
Brady, James	1	3	2		9
Wright, Roderick	2	1	4		
Pitts, Elizabeth	2	1	4		7
Wright, Joseph	1				
Lowe, William		1	2		2
Brady, Brasil	1	2	5		
Parrum, Rebeccah			5		6
Heath, John	1				
Heath, James	1	1	4		1
Williams, Joseph	1	3	3		
Matthews, Thomas	1	3	6		
Moore, Reubin	1	2	3		
Williams, Ely	2	1	6		3
Etheridge, William	2	1	3		
Cleveland, James	1	1	4		
Nicholson, Lemuel	1		3		5
Pace, Thomas	2	2	3		26
Ward, Benjamin	1	2	2		9
Williams, John	3		8		32
Ward, Joseph	1		3		1
Rhodes, David	1	2	1		
Anderson, Charles	1	3	4		2
Pitts, Henry	2	1	3		8
Williams, Jesse	1	2	1		12
Moore, James	1	3	1		7
Thrower, Mason	2	1	3		16
Davis, John (Exr of A. Davis, Deceasd)	2	1	5		9
Pitts, Mark	1				1
Etheridge, Calib	4		2		5
Williams, Daniel	1	1	2		1
Murden, John	2	2	5		10
Hopkins, Joshua	2				8
Robertson, Mary	1	1	2		1
Harrison, Elisha	1	1	3		
Whitehead, Lazarus	1	1	2		
Lowe, William	2		3		
Murden, Edward & Jeremiah	2				12
Drake, Thomas	3	1	2		
Scoles, Peter		1	6		
Etheridge, Caleb	4		2		6
Nicholson, Lemuel	1		3		9
Moore, Charles	2	1	3		15
Harwell, Gardner	1	3	1		24
Simmons, John					
Powell, Ptolemy	3	2	2		3
Hockaday, James	1	1	1		5
Norwood, Samuel	1	1			9
Spann, Willis	1	2	2		6
Taylor, Mary	1		4		4
Turner, James	2	1	2		7
Scott, John				5	
Good, William	1	3	3		1
Smith, Moses	2	3	2		6
Smith, William	2	1	2		2
Kelley, Thomas	1	1	4		1
Downs, William	3	1	4		
Martin, William	3	4	4		7
Hockaday, William	1		2		1
Narsworthy, John	2		3		3
Sikes, Jacob	1	2	1		
Heath, James	1	1	1		2
Glover, Nathaniel	1	1	1		2
Norwood, Richard	1		3		7
Arnold, David	1		2	1	4
Rose, Elisha	2	1	2		8
Simms, Zachariah	2	1	6		1
Hammell, Jenny	2	5	5		1

NAME OF HEAD OF FAMILY.	Free white males of 16 years and upward, including heads of families.	Free white males under 16 years.	Free white females, including heads of families.	All other free persons.	Slaves.
Easley, James	1	4	1		12
Simmons, John (for David Short)	2	2	4		16
Roan, Lewis	3	3	5		1
Gill, Philip	3		5		
Powell, George	1	1	3		
Bumpass, Samuel	1	2	2		
Jones, Thomas	1	1	1		
Sikes, James	1	1	2		
Hockaday, Warwick	1	3	2		
Jones, John, Junr	1	1	6		
Martin, Jesse	1	1	3		
Sikes, Joab	1	2	2		
McCrawley, John	1	1	4		
Edmundson, Bryant	1	3	3		
Smith, Uriah	2	2	3		1
Shaw, James	2	1	1		
Allen, James	1			3	1
Powell, William, Sen	1	3	5		7
Adams, Benjamin	1				
Walker, Solomon	1	1	2		
Shaw, John, Thomas, & Sarah	5	6	6		10
Smith, John	1		2		2
Spann, Richard	1		1		2
Rose, Wormley	1	1	2		5
Mills, Benjamin	1	1	2		1
Rose, William	1	2	3		6
Powell, William	2	2	4		10
Green, Benjamin	1	2	4		
Green, Hannah	1	1	2		
Pearson, George	3	1	3		
Kelley, William	1	1	2		
Winter, Joseph	1	1	2	2	
Smith, Peter, Junr	1	2	3		
Jones, John, Senr	1	2	4		
Powell, William	1	1	1		6
Davis, Owen	1	1	2		
Spann, Frederick	1	1	3		6
Brasington, Joseph	1	1	1		5
Yarborough, George	1	5	3		5
Smith, Peter, Senr	2		1		12
Ivey, Robert	1	2	2		3
Adams, James	1	1	8		
Powell, Zachariah	1	2	4		3
Shaw, Elizabeth	1	3	5		
Taylor, Richard	2	2	4		7
Dulley, James	1	3	4		
Powell, William, Junr	1	2	3		1
Siris, John	1		2		
Banks, Thomas	1	2	3		
Lewis, Cullin	1		2		
Porter, Benjamin	1	3	2		
Vinson, Hannah			4		
Yarborough, Richard	1	1	6		
McCalley, Joseph	1		4		
Axum, Mary	1	2	1		
Vinson, Charles	1	3	2		
Green, William	1	1	3		
Sarasho, Robert	1	1	2	1	1
Bogas, Ann	1	1	3		
Mattox, Samuel	2	2	3		
Hilton, John	1	1	4		
Hilton, William	1	1	1		
Hilton, Willis	1	2	5		
Edwards, Anthony	1	1	6		
Williams, Sarah			3		1
Wells, Mistress		1	4		
West, Dorothy			2	3	
Abbinatha, Abby	1	1	3		
Pulley, David, Senr	1	1	3		
Pulley, David, Junr	1	1	2		
Scurlock, Thomas	1				13
Scurlock, George	1		1		2
Lewis, John	1		1		
Williams, William	1	3	5		
Harris, Willie	1		2		
Edmonds, Martha				5	
Rock, John	2	1	3		
Young, Reubin	1		1		
Harrison, John	1	1	2		
Sledge, Hartwell	1	1	1		1
Bowler, Elizabeth		2	2		
Bowler, Sarah	1	1	2		
Carter, Jacob	1	1	3		
Armstead, Henry	1	2	1		
Stephens, Jones	2		5		
Winters, James	3	3	4	1	2
Burt, John	3	1	4		18
Cobb, Patsy			1		5
Fawcett, Mary	1	2	4		
Hogg, Rebeccah	2	2	4		
Sanders, Sarah	2	2	7		
Parker, Nancy			2		
Parker, Joshua	1		2		
Garland, Jonathan	1	1	6		
Davis, Nancy		2	1		1

HALIFAX DISTRICT, HALIFAX COUNTY—Continued.

NAME OF HEAD OF FAMILY.	Free white males of 16 years and upward, including heads of families.	Free white males under 16 years.	Free white females, including heads of families.	All other free persons.	Slaves.
Ray, William	1		2	1	3
Noble, Francis	1			1	
Herriman, Joseph				1	
Ring, John	2	1	2	1	
Burt, Stephen	1				1
Kelley, James	1	2	3		
Kelley, William	1		1		
Royall, John	1	2	2		
Bird, Polly				4	1
Bird, Peggy				3	
Bird, Richard				2	
Leach, Mary			3		
Smith, Mistress	1		3		
Harry, Nancy				2	
Coleman, Sarah			1		
Dennick, Peter	1	1	2		
Yarborough, William	1				
Scott, John				7	
Eilbeck, John	1	1	1	1	2
Navill, Thomas	5		1		8
Southall, Farnith	1		2		18
Warbutton, John	1				
Carstaphin, John	1				
Fountain, Jacob	1				
Cotten, Young	1				
Ellis, William	1				
Pope, Joseph	1				
Pope, Benjamin	1				
Hinesley, Joel	1				
Hinesley, John	1				
Cook, Francis	1				
Gain, John	1				
Clarke, Thomas	1				
Pattypool, William	1				
Garlock, George	1				
Markham, John	1				
Brickle, William	1				
Conner, William	1				
Brooks, John	1				
Chambers, David	2		2		1
Griffis, Daniel	1	2	1		
Dawson, John	1	2	3		
Smawley, Nancy			3		
Harrison, Joseph	1		3		
Harden, Richard	1	2	4		
Nairn, Sarah		1	1		
Churchwill, John	1				
Churchwill, William	1				
Peare, Jones	1				
Harrison, Gidion	1				
Landifor, Robert	1				
Broose, Abner	1				
Southintine, Nancy			2		
Doles, Sarah	1		3		1
Brasill, James	4	1	4		
Andrews, Sarah		1	4		
Gardner, Thomas	1	1	6		
Packer, Matthew	1		3		
Wall, Francis	1		1		
Cain, Jeremiah	1	2	4		
Jackson, Jesse	1	1	2		
Joyner, Jonathan	1	2	4		12
Dwyer, John	1		2		5
Jones, Thomas	2	1	2		
Blackmore, Absalom	2	1	2		
Edmunds, John	1				
Jackson, William	1	1	2		
Vance, John	1	1	1		1
Brown, Arthur	1				5
Morgan, James	1	1	5		
Pitman, John	2	1	3		9
Hyatt, David	2	2	4		
Whitehead, Callin	1	1	2		
Bynum, William, Senr	2		1	2	2
Edwards, Benjamin	1	2	2		2
Pass, Hunt	1				
Crab, Benjamin	1	3	3		
Bird, Charity			2		2
Pitman, Lilah			3		
Pilant, John	1	2	2		
Hammons, Anthoney				4	
Ford, Issabella	2	2	3		7
West, Arthur, Senr	1				5
Pass, Nelson	1				
Lowry, John	1	3	2		3
Brantley, Samuel	1		2		
Waller, Mary		1	3		
Cobb, Simon	1		1		
Vick, Mary		1	5		
Alsobrook, Martha	1		1		
Cain, Jeremiah	1	2	4		
Cain, Thomas	2	1	2		
Merritt, Sarah	1	1	5		13
Vorden, Christian	1		3		
Drew, Solomon	1	1	3		
Brassill, James	5	1	4		
Morgan, Mary		3	1		
Ross, Jacob	1	1	2		
Brantley, Martha			2		1
Adkinson, Thomas	1	2	2		
Turner, Jesse	1	4	4		7
Hobgood, Francis	1		3		1
Turner, Solomon	2		3		3
Joiner, Ely	1	1	1		4
Taylor, Harris	1	4	1		
Alsobrook, James	1	2	2		
Haynes, Xpher	1	3	1		
McMullin, Ely	4	1	1		
Haynie, Catherine	1	3	3		
Hobbs, Drury	1		1	6	
Hogan, Lemuel	1	4	6		59
Hill, Simon	1		1		13
Peete, Samuel	1				
Walker, John	1				
King, William	1				
McClanahan, William	1				
Stafford, Sterling	1				
Moore, John	1				
Fields, Henry	1				
Daley, John	1			1	
Printon, Tapley	1				
Ives, Thomas	1				
Magee, William	1				
Mosely, George	1				
Dundelow, Henry	1				
Horton, John	1				
Elliott, Leroy	1		2		
Lucas, Francis	1				
Wood, Horton	1				
Coon, William	1				
Tuttle, Jeremiah	1				
McCartie, John	1				
Sterling, Jesse	1				
Johnston, James	1				
Lisiver, Thomas	1				
Willkings, Robert	1				
Hoalt, Michael	1				
Tuttle, Peter	1				
Boyd, John	1				
Hays, Adam	1				
Durden, Daniel	1				
Dew, John	1				
West, William	1			1	
Kelley, Archibald	1				
Hall, Randol	1				
Jinkins, Joseph	1				
Blakey, Morris	1				
Reed, John	1				
Moore, John	1				
French, John	1				
Cartist, John	1				
Thompson, Adam	1				
Robertson, Nathaniel	1				
Pride, Halcot	4	1	2		54
Short, William	3	4	3		
Kindall, Ann	1	2	3		
Sweett, George				4	

HALIFAX DISTRICT, MARTIN COUNTY.

NAME OF HEAD OF FAMILY.	Free white males of 16 years and upward, including heads of families.	Free white males under 16 years.	Free white females, including heads of families.	All other free persons.	Slaves.
Moore, Maurice	1	2	3		7
Hardison, John	1	3	2		
Mizell, James	2	4	2		
Ross, Martin	1	4	3		12
Hardison, James	1	1	1		2
Hardison, Joshua	2	1	3		6
Clarke, Henry	1	1	2		
Moore, Winifred	2	1			1
Claghorn, Haws	1	1	3		
Claghorn, Benjamin	1		2		
Claghorn, Shubal	1	2	3		
Parsons, Levi	1	1	2		
Bonner, George	1		1		2
Smithwick, John	2		3		8
Carmer, James	1	2	1		
Mizell, John	2		4		1
Mizell, Lukeson William	1				9
Smith, John	2	2	3		8
Warbutton, Francis		1	2		2
Smithy, John			2		
Stewart, John	22	3	5	4	33
Hardison, William	2	2	3		1
Cooper, Edward	1		2		1
Simpson, Archibald	1	2	2		
Griffin, David	1	2	1		
Mizell, Edward	2	3	4		3
Morris, Esther		1	2		
Gray, Lovick	1		2		
Simmons, Edward	1	1	5		
Harriss, Josiah	1	2	4		
Morriss, Rebeccah		2	1		
Ange, Abigail			2		
Melone, Michael	1		2		
Vernatson, Mary	2	1	3		
Hardison, Richard	2		4		3
Hardison, Thomas	1	1	4	7	
Collins, John	2	7	2		2
Weatherton, Joseph	2	1	4		1
Sparkman, Thomas	1	1	3		
Taylor, Richard	1		2		1
Phagan, Stephen	2		3		1
Moss, William	1		4		
Buttery, John	1	4	3		
Hootten, Charles	1	2	5		5
Hootten, William, Senr					13
Hooten, Henry	1	2	3		1
Hooten, William	1		1		12
Seals, Hannah	1		6		
Milliner, Thomas	1		2		
Watson, Addison	1	1	2		
Phelps, John	1		3		
Watson, Mary	1	1	2		
Rolock, John	1		2		13
Ward, Francis	1		4		32
Karkect, William	2		3		1
Everitt, Nathaniel	3	1	4		10
Hinson, Mary			1		
Olivent, Henry	1	1	2		
Shields, William	1		3		
Demerritt, Aaron	1		4		
Crowley, Sarah			7		
Cooper, Henry	1	2	4		
Cooper, Lauton	1	2	3		1
Cooper, Griffin	1	2	1		
Raye, Samuel	2	1	4		4
Williams, John	1	1	2		
Mizell, James, Senr	4				
Amis, Edward	1	1	1		
Mizell, Hardy	1		2		
Hassell, Caswell	2		3		
Smith, John, Senr	2		4		
Brown, David	1	1	1		1
Holloway, John	1	2	5		
Holloway, Thomas	1		3		
Flood, James	1		2		
Smith, William	1	2	3		
Everitt, Nathaniel	1	1	3		
Cooper, Edward, Junr	1	1	3		
Amis, Thomas	1		2		
Hinson, William	1		3		
Moss, Sarah		1	2		
Hardison, David	1	1	3		
Buttery, Silvanus	2	2	4		
Middleton, John	1	1	3		7
Browney, Thomas	1	2	3		
Vernation, Charles	1	2	2		
Nearn, Drury	1	1	2		
Browney, John	1	1	4		
Ange, Francis	2	2	2		
Adams, William	1	2	4		
Gierkey, Jeremiah	3		5		
Garrett, James	1	1	3		
Bingall, Nancy			3		3
Stubbs, Tames	1	2	3		
Petty, Thomas	1		1		
Alexander, Gideon	3	1	2		
Alexander, Simeon	1		2		
Leggett, Mary			2		1
Soans, John	3				
Sawyer, James	1	2	2		
Leggett, David	1	3	2		
Caraway, Anne	1	2	2		2
Eason, Mary		1	5		5
Smithwick, Edmund	2	4	5		11
Smithwick, Samuel	5	2	4	2	31
Ross, William	1	3	4		5
Duggan, William	1	3	4		2
Duggan, Aaron	1	2	4		2
Swain, James	2	2	2		1
Holloway, Hardy	4	1	1		
Holloway, Jesse	1	1	2		
Reddick, Christian	1	1	3		
Reddick, Elizabeth	3	3	1		6

HALIFAX DISTRICT, MARTIN COUNTY—Continued.

NAME OF HEAD OF FAMILY.	Free white males of 16 years and upward, including heads of families.	Free white males under 16 years.	Free white females, including heads of families.	All other free persons.	Slaves.
Ellis, Michael	2		2		
Reddick, John	1	2	4		
Jones, Soloman	2	4	3		
Caraway, Jonathan	1				1
Maddocks, William	1	2	3		
Carroway, David	1	1	2		
Swain, Elizabeth	1	1	3		1
Swain, William	1		2		1
Bennett, John	1	1	2		
Flood, William, Senr	1	1	4		
Condau, William	1	3	4		
Garrott, James	1	1	2		2
Godward, George	3		2		
Mizell, Luke	1	1	4		
Gardner, Samuel, Senr	1	2	2		
Brown, Thomas	2		4		1
Gardner, John	1		1		
Gardner, James	1		1		
Gardner, Samuel	2	2	3		
Gardner, Thomas	1	4	1		
Hardison, John	1	1	1		4
Mizell, Mary	1		3		1
Mizell, James	3				
Manning, John	1		2		
Robason, Joshua	1				
Daniel, James	1		2		2
Daniel, William	1	1	7		
Robason, Daniel	1	1	2		
Woollard, Richard	1	2	5		
Woollard, Benjamin	2	3	3		
Robason, James	1	2	11	1	
Coovey, John	5	1	3		
Reddick, David	1	3	6		
Binnitt, William	3	2	5		7
Binnitt, Thomas, Senr	2		2		4
Binnitt, Thomas, Junr	2	1	6		
Reddick, Whitmill	2	2	1		3
Stallings, Hardy	2	2	6		
Ring, Robert	2			2	
Moore, Levi	1	2	5		1
Robason, John, Senr	4	1	2		
Robason, James	2	3	8		1
Smithwick, Simon	1		1		
Perry, Jacob	1		1		
Reddick, Mills	1	2	1		
Smithwick, John, Junr	1	1	3		
Perry, William	1	2	5		
Robason, David	2	3	5		2
Smithwick, Luke	1	1	2		2
Lanier, Robert	1	3	4		2
Peele, John	1	3	2		1
Reddick, Josiah	1	1	1		1
Woollard, John	1		1		
Perry, Sarah	1		3		7
Lilly, Timothy	3		2		
Robason, John	4	1	1		
Robason, James	1	2	2		
Rogers, David	4	2	5		
Smithwick, Edward	2	3	4		13
Smithwick, Edward Junr	1	3	1		1
Toyce, Jacob	2	4	2		
Swain, John	1	1	2		
Sparkman, William	1		1		
Campbell, James	4		3		
Lilley, Kadar	1	1	4		
Lilley, Josiah	1	4	3		
Smithwick, John, Senr	2		3		9
Robason, John	1		2		
Smithwick, William	1	1	2		3
Griffin, John, Junr	3	3	5		
Griffin, Martin	1	5	4		
Griffin, Edward	1	2	2		1
Griffin, Elizabeth		1	2		
Robeson, William, Senr	5		2		1
Robason, David	1	2	3		1
Gardner, Isaac	3	3	3		
Smith, Josiah	2	1	3		
Cushion, Isaac	2		1		
Peele, James	3		1		
Bachus, John	2	3	3		
Eason, Mills	1	2	3		
Gayner, Samuel	1	3	1		
Mizell, William	2	2	1		7
Mizell, John	1		3		
Lanier, William	1	2	3		2
Mizell, James	2	2	3		1
Swinson, Levi	1				4
Hooks, Charles	2	1	3		
Bennett, James	2	4	3		6
Lilley, Joseph	1	2	6		
Biggs, Cadar	2	3	3		
Lanier, John	1	1	5		7
Mitchell, Burrell	1	2	2		
Harrison, James	1		2		
Stallions, Joel	1	2	2		6
Chapple, Malachiah	1		4		2

NAME OF HEAD OF FAMILY.	Free white males of 16 years and upward, including heads of families.	Free white males under 16 years.	Free white females, including heads of families.	All other free persons.	Slaves.
Hollowell, Levi	3		3		
Waters, William	1		2		
Ashur, Jesse	2				
Jinkins, Osborn	1	2	1		
Jinkins, Winburn	1	3	2		
Parker, James	2		8		
Bryant, Joseph	3	3	6		22
Burroughs, Benjamin	1	2	9		8
Davis, William	1	2	3		5
Conroy, John	1		2		
Griffin, John	1	3	2		
Kelley, Auterson	1				
Smith, John	1		1		
Hyman, Thomas	1		1		
Haughton, William	1		1		
Cherry, Jeremiah	1	1	1		1
Jinkins, William	1		3		
Nicholson, John	1	4	1		1
Cherry, Job	3		3		3
Barnes, Allen	3				1
Burroughs, Anthony				1	
Cotanche, Willie				1	
Magruda, Nathaniel	1				
Burroughs, William	1				
Yellowby, Edward	1				
Pierce, John	1				
Prentice, Thomas Henry	1			1	
Foreman, Thomas	1				
Fisher, James	1		1		
Parker, John	1		1		
Lane, Joseph	1				
Detor, William	1		1	1	
Simmons, James	1	2	3		
Sowell, Hillery	1				
Canaday, Benjamin	1	3	3		
Martin, Sarah		3	3		
Hunter, Thomas	23	3	3		44
Hunter, Mary		1	2		10
Hunter, Henry, Senr	1				10
Hunter, Henry	2	3	3		14
Dashwood, John	1				
Barnes, Sarah		1	4		
Virgin, James	1		2		
Virgin, Samuel	2	1	4		
Mitchell, Suckey		2	1		
Summers, John	1	2	4		
Osbern, Rainny		2	4		
Anderson, Francis	1	1	2		
Anderson, Alexander	1		1		
Gayner, Elizabeth		1	3		
Gilbert, Nicholas	1		2		
Wilson, James Lewis	1	1	2		
Biggs, William	1	1	3		3
Powers, James	1		4		1
McKinzie, William	2		2	3	8
Watts, John	2	2	2	1	2
Morriss, Mrs		3	2		
Martin, William	1	2	1		
Gilbert, William	2		1	3	
Lawrance, George	1		2		
Jackson, Chloe				1	3
Price, Thomas	1	1	2	1	1
Garlinton, William	1	2	3		
Pulley, William	1	1	4		6
Collins, Margaret			2		7
Biggs, Joseph	1		2		2
Travis, Amos	1	1	1		1
Wheatley, Benjamin	2	1	4		5
Nicholson, Thomas	1		4		
Slade, William, Esqr	3	1	1		28
Slade, William	1	1	1		1
Cherry, Jesse	1		1		
Day, John	2		2	1	
Holloday, Miles	1				
Beach, Thomas, Senr	1		3	1	
Webb, Jiles	1	2	2		
Boaman, Thomas	1		1		
Garganus, Lamuel	1	4	1		
Basley, William	2	1	3		2
Ward, Spellar	4				
Wyatt, William	1	2	1		
Ward, William	1		2		
Ward, John	1	2	6	1	
Suvanner, Henry	2		2		2
Williams, Samuel	2	1	5		
Swanner, William	1	1	1		
Mitchell, Jesse	1	2	2		
Fowler, George	1		4		
Williams, Dixon	1	1	4		
Brewer, Robert	3	2	6		
Bond, William	1	1	1		
Hooks, William	1		1		
O'farrell, John	1		4		
Leigh, John	1	3	1		
Jenkins, John	1	1	1		
Kelley, Timothy	1	2	2		
Nowell, Emelia	1	3	1		

NAME OF HEAD OF FAMILY.	Free white males of 16 years and upward, including heads of families.	Free white males under 16 years.	Free white females, including heads of families.	All other free persons.	Slaves.
Sowell, Chloe			1	2	
Saunders, Zelpah			1	3	
Ward, Nancy			1	2	
Stallings, Job	1	4	3		4
Warren, Mary	2	1	6		
Warren, Joseph, Senr	1		1		
Hogan, Amey				3	
Turner, Penny				2	
Yarrell, Matthew	1	3	3		6
Pearce, William	2	1	4		3
Turlinton, William	2	1	3		
Brogdon, David	1		4		
Bowers, Silas	1				
Lanfesty, Elias	1				
Brontley, Matthew	1	2	4		
Anderson, Andrew	1	4	2		
Page, Absalom	1				
Page, William	1	2	3		
Page, John	1	1	4		
Whiters, Hillery	1	2	1		
Price, William	1	1	4		
Bilch, William	1	1	3		2
Matthews, Luke	1	1	3		
Balentine, Nehemiah	1	1	4		
Bryant, John	1	1	2		
Manning, Malachi	1	4	2		
Page, Ann		2	2		
Cobb, Sarah		1	1		
Edmundson, Joseph		1	3		
Brewer, Edmund	1		2		
Brewer, James	1		5		
Cogbern, Daniel	1	1	4		
Pinkett, Zackariah	1		2		
Harwood, William	1	2	3		
Coburn, George	3	1	5		2
Knowell, David	1		2		
Andrews, Warren	1		1		1
Collins, Jethro	1		1		
Ellison, William	1		1		
Glesson, James	1				
Joice, Caleb	2		3		
Bonner, Stalleton	1	2	2		1
Ross, Thomas	1	2	2		1
Cone, Levi	1		2		
Brown, Alexander	2	1	4		
Ross, Joseph	1		3		
Cobern, Abner	1	1	3		4
Joice, Martin	1	3	3		
Spivy, Nathaniel	1	3	3		
Manning, William	1	1	1		
Ross, Hugh	2	1	2		3
Nowels, James	1		1		
Brewer, Mary		1	2		
Ellison, Martha			1		
Brewer, Sarah			1		
Kelley, William	2	2	1		
Brewer, Mary			1		
Roebuck, Rolley	1		2		
Rogers, Sterling	1		4		
Haze, Martha			1		
Glisson, Isaac					
Whitfield, John	1	1	4		
Cobb, David	1		2		
Taylor, Sampson	1	2	3		
Taylor, Samuel	1	1	1		
Ballentine, Edward	1	1	3		1
Carder, James	1		1		
Cobern, James		1			
Ross, Martha		3	2		
Cobern, Francis	3	2	3		2
Cobern, John	2		3		
Cobern, John, Junr	1	1	4		
Cobb, John	4	1	1		
Cobb, Nicholas	1		1		
Whitfield, William	1	1	6		
Philips, Alexander	1		2		
Moore, William	1	1	3		
Smith, Malakiah	1	2	4		4
Nowell, Josiah	1		4		
Cobern, Andrew	1		2		
Manning, John	1	2	3		1
Carter, George	1		1		
Cobern, Griffin	1				
Ross, James	1		3		
Edmundson, James	3		3		
Drake, John	2	2	1		
Joyce, Elizabeth			1		4
Edmondson, Nathan	1	1	2		
Powell, John	1	1	3		2
Downing, James	2	3	5		2
Ives, James	1	3	3		1
Little, Micajah	1	4	6		
Southerland, James	3	3	2		1
Edmondson, John	1	4	2		
Rhoads, Benjamin	1	1	2		
Rhoads, Benjamin, Senr	2	1	4		
Awins, John			5		2

HALIFAX DISTRICT, MARTIN COUNTY—Continued.

NAME OF HEAD OF FAMILY.	Free white males of 16 years and upward, including heads of families.	Free white males under 16 years.	Free white females, including heads of families.	All other free persons.	Slaves.
Cogbern, George	1	3	4		3
Savage, Briton	1		2		2
Rainer, William	1	2	1		
Hill, Nathan	1	2	5		
Collins, Shadrach	1	2	2		
Savage, Warren & Carter	2	1	4		13
Savage, Robert	1		2		
Savage, Sterling	1	3	2		3
Jackston, George	1	1	1		
Knight, Richard	1	4	3		
Gayter, Samuel	1	1	3		
Howard, Wilson	1	1	2		1
Garrot, John	1	3	3		
Staton, Nehemiah	1	1	5		
Kent, Thomas	1	1	1		
Edmondson, Thomas	1	2	2		2
Barefield, Charles	2	3	4		1
Hyman, William	1	1	3		
Hill, Isaac, & E. Wallace	1	7	7		10
Rayner, Thomas	2		2		
Davidson, David	1	1	4		1
Jones, Frederick	1	2	2		4
Jones, William	2		1		3
Edmundson, William	1	1	4		
Wiggins, Mary		1	2		
Killingsworth, Patrick	1	2	3		
Johnston, Sarah			3		
Jones, John	1	1	5		7
Staton, Arthur	1	1	5		3
Grimes, Thomas	5	2	6		9
Staton, Jesse	4	1	2		1
Staton, Ezekiel	2	2	5		7
Staton, Zadock	2	1	1		
Everitt, James	1	3	6		1
Solomon, Barnes	1	1	3		1
Raynor, John	1	3	2		
Barefield, John	4	1	2		
Jones, John, Senr	1	1	3		10
Howell, Jethro	2	4	4		15
Mays, Natha	3	3	4		15
Jackson, Edward	3	3	6		
Lewillin, John	1	2	3		20
Taylor, Thomas	1		1		
Pervice, Lewis	1	3			
Jackson, Mary			1		1
Wallace, William	1	6	3		6
Taylor, Richard	1	1	7		
Cross, Thomas	1		1		
Deal, James	1	2	2		
Crisp, Benjamin	1	1	4		1
Crisp, Ezekiel	2	2	1		
Bullock, Josiah	1		3		
Crisp, Samuel	1	7	2		2
Crisp, Jesse	2	1	3		
Crisp, Francis		1	1		8
Mayo, Micajah	1		2		6
Manning, Marcus	2	1	4		2
Fillpott, Feroby	1	2	6		
Manning, William	1		2		
Scott, Jehu	1		1		
Scott, Luke	1	1	2		
Harrell, Samuel	2		6		
Freeman, Moses	1	3	5		3
Cross, John	1	2	4		
Cross, James	1	3	1		
Harrill, Ephraim	1		2		
Best, Thomas	2	3	3		14
Miller, Stephen	1	1	5		
Leggitt, Noel	1	1	1		
Staton, Kasiah			2		
Council, Charles	2	1	2		5
Council, John	1		1		
Harris, Richard	2	3	4		
Taylor, John, Junr	1		2		
Taylor, John	1	2	4		2
Taylor, Joseph	1		2		
Taylor, David	1	2	2		2
Taylor, John	4		2		6
Taylor, Richard	1	2	5		
White, Frederick	1		2		
Price, John	2	4	4		1
Pennywell, Thomas	1		2		8
Joyner, Thomas	2	1	8		
Edmundson, James	2	2	4		
Purvice, William	1	3	5		1
Griffin, John	1				14
Hoard, Micajah	1	3	2		
Church, William	1	2	2		
Ellison, Jesse	1	3	5		
Vance, Elijah	1	1	3		
White, James	1	2	3		
Banks, John	1	2	3		
Lawrance, Williamson	1	4	3		10
Hansill, John	1	3	4		2
Everitt, John, Junr	1				
Ballard, James	1	1	3		3
Carter, Michael	2	4	1		13
Andrews, Etheldred	1	1	5		13
Ballard, Silas	1	2	2		10
Griffin, William	1		2		15
Whorton, Elisha	1	1	3		
Stricklin, Jacob	2	4	2		
Barden, Asa	1				7
Boyt, Solomon	1	3	7		
Sherrod, Robert	1	4	5		9
Sherrod, John	1				1
Griffin, Micajah	1				
Wills, Edward	1				
Griffin, Epenetus	2		4		3
Johnston, Jesse	2	2	4		
Ellis, William	2		5		1
Boyt, Isaac	1	1	3		
Cooper, David	1	4	5		
Price, Elias	1	2	3		
Wheatley, John	1	5	2		1
Whorton, David	1	3	1		
Hansill, William	1		2		
Johnston, Robert	3		1		2
Chance, Jacob	1	2	2		
Carter, Reddick	1				
Everitt, William, Senr	3	1	2		
Carter, Micajah	1				
Griffin, Benjamin	1	1	4		
Wharton, John	1	2	6		
Clarke, Nathan	1				
Sherrod, Randol	1				1
Hyman, John	1				
Butler, Simon	1	1	2		8
Pearse, Jesse	1	3	3		9
Ward, Timothy	1	1	1		6
Barden, William	1				5
Bennett, John	1	2	3		11
Bennett, Robert	1	2	2		
Little, James	1	2	2		3
Spiller, Thomas	1	1		2	7
Sherrod, Lewis	1		1		5
Everitt, William	1	1			8
Hyman, Eleazer	1	2	5		4
Vance, John	1	1	2		
Vance, David	1	2	3		
Drake, John	1	2	1		
Hyman, William	2	1	5		5
Fortune, William				1	
James, Benjamin					4
Stricklin, John	1	1	1		
Drake, Jonas	1				
Price, Lewis	1	1	2		
Davis, Thomas	2		3		
Everitt, John	1				22
Outerbridge, William	1		2		8
Outerbridge, John	1	1			3
Outerbridge, Burrel	1				
Cooper, Stancell	1				
Callend, John	1				
Good, John	1				
Hundley, Humphry	1	3	2		
Wood, Jonas	1	1	1		1
Rooks, Charity		1	2		
Cooper, Mourning	2	1	3		
Clifton, Elizabeth			2		
Vance, John, Senr	1	2	2		
Cogburn, Jesse	1	1			
Council, Rachael	2		4	1	
Marshall, Nancy		1	2		
Chiff, Chloe	3		4		
Glisson, Ann			1		
Barden, Elizabeth			2		2
Mitchell, Sarah		2	1		
Jack, Buttlers				2	
Fortune, Hannah				2	10
Megaskey, Mrs	2	2	4		
Pearce, Chloe	1		3		
Frizell, Daniel	1		3		
Braveboy, John & mother				1	7
Day, William	1		2		
Rogers, Rebeccah		1	2		
Butler, Mrs		4	3		
Williams, William	2	4	3		94
Kindday, David	1	1	2		2
Carnal, Thomas	1	2	3		17
Andrews, Thomas	1	3	2		8
Weatherly, John	1		3		2
Harrill, Hesther	2		3		2
Jones, Dickey	1		4		
Brown, Reubin	1		3		1
Bryant, Lewis	1	4	2		2
Harrill, Joel	1	1	2		
Pearce, Andrew	1				
Baggett, Thomas	1				
Hyman, Thomas	1	3	4		
Weatherly, William	1	2	2		
Bernitt, John	1	3	3		9
Regerson, Daniel	1		4		
O'Cain, William	1	1	3		
Culpepper, Jeremiah	2				
Hyman, Hugh	1	1	2		1
O'Cain, John	1				
Brown, Jacob	1		4		2
Boyt, Thomas	1	1	2		1
Bland, William	1	3	5		
Medford, James	1	4	4		
Parker, Jacob	3	3	5		
Savage, Carter	1				
Price, William	1		4		1
Hyman, John	1	2	4		4
Byrnett, Matthew	2	1	6		4
Ballard, Jesse	1		4		
Price, William	1	1	1		1
Long, Equilla	1	3	2		1
Price, John	1				1
Cherry, Jonathan	2	2	5		
Bernett, James	2	4	4		
Hynes, Christopher	3	2	4		
Guy, William	2		2		10
Hynes, John	1		3		
Lynch, Henry	1	3	2		
Parker, John	1	2	3		
Ballard, Elisha	1	1	2		7
Forrest, George	1		4		4
Strawbridge, Elijah	1	4	3		10
Bernitt, Ephraim	1		5		
Pitman, Edward	1				
Cross, Stephen	1	1	4		
Hatson, Thomas	2	2	4		5
Moore, Hodges	3		4		30
Collins, Timothy	1	2	4		3
Savage, Thomas	1		3		
Weatherly, Thomas	1	1	3		7
Wiggins, Lemuel	2	4	3		24
Howell, James	1	2	4		3
Etheringane, George	1	2	2		5
Harrell, Lott	3	2	6		14
Stafford, John				5	
Bland, Thomas	1	1	3		
Brewer, Thomas	1	3	5		2
Watson, William, Junr	1		2		
Johnson, Joshua	1		3		
Harrell, Hezekiah	1	2	2		
Pierce, Thomas	1		3		2
Bryan, Hardy	1	3	4		1
Bryan, Needham	2	3	1		5
Belflower, William	1				
Bryan, Elias	2		3		7
Jackson, Gibson	1		3		
Williams, Samuel	1	5	7		104
Baggett, Thomas	2		2		
Watts, Lewis	1	3	1		
Bryan, Robert	2	2	3		2
Spivy, George	1	1	1		1
Lee, Mason	1				3
Archer, Zachariah			1	6	
Rawls, Silas	1		1		
Taylor, John	1	2	4		26
Whitney, Samuel	1				1
Taylor, Joshua	1	7	4		21
Mitchell, William	1				
Medfort, John	1	5	1		
Mitchell, James	1				
Kiff, James	1	1	4		
Culpepper, Jane		1	1		1
Pierce, Lovick	1	2	3		
Brown, James	2	4	5		5
Wiggins, John	1		2		4
Thompson, William	1		3		1
King, Michael	4		1		15
Brown, Abner	1	3	3		3
Kent, John	1	2	1		
Wiggins, Blake	2	6	3		43
Hill, Whitmill	34	4	6		140
Maning, Thomas	2	2	3	1	2
Reading, Joseph	2	2	3		6
Kent, William	1	1	1		
Vance, David	2	1	5		
Bates, Isra	1				
Parker, William	1	1	1		9
Singclair, Benjamin	1		1		
Short, William	2	1	2		
McDaniel, James				6	
Benbory, Miles	1		2		1
Cooper, Joseph	2	3	6		
Cross, John	1		4		
Cross, William	1	1	3		
Weathersley, Lucy		1	2		
Boothe, Elizabeth			3		
Jones, Richard				5	
Jackson, Mary		3	3		
Robason, Hardy	1				
Foster, William	1		2		
Watson, William, Senr	2		3		

HALIFAX DISTRICT, MARTIN COUNTY—Continued.

NAME OF HEAD OF FAMILY.	Free white males of 16 years and upward, including heads of families.	Free white males under 16 years.	Free white females, including heads of families.	All other free persons.	Slaves.
Jackson, James	1				
Medford, Henry	1	2	1		
Griffin, Matthew	1	2	4		
Ballard, Nancy			2		
Ballard, Betsey		1	2		
Watson, Jacob	1	1	1		
Watson, Thomas, Junr	1		1		
Lynch, Jesse	1		5		
Dickson, Thomas	1		2		
Glisson, Mary	1	2	3		
Harrell, Mourning		3	2		
Murray, Mark				9	
Mitchell, Isaac	1	4	1		
Hynes, Joseph	1		2		
Baggett, Thomas	1				
Waldon, Mary				3	
Belflower, Ann	1	3	2		
Anthony, John	1		2		33
Ross, John	2	1	5		6
Ross, James	1	2	1		
Rawls, James	1		2		1
Burrice, David	1		2		
Ross, Martin	1	2	1		
Rogers, Levy	1	2	4		
Ross, John, Junr	1	1	2		
Collins, John	3	3	5		2
Ross, William	1	1	3		
Britt, Joel	1		6		
Roebuck, George	1	2	3		
Barnhill, James	2	3	4		
Moore, Joseph, Junr	1	4	5		
Moore, Moses	1	3	1		2
Moore, Joseph	1		3		
Moore, John	1	1	1		
Carter, Benjamin	2	3	2		1
Bonner, Mary			2		2
Bonner, Stapleton	2	2	1		
Anderson, Ann	1	1	3		3
Morriss, Jacob	2	2	5		
Moon, Priscilla	1	3	1		
Cone, William	2	4	4		
Cone, Neal	1		7		
Cone, Levi	1		3		1
Brogdone, James	2	1	5		
Barnihill, Daniel	1	1	2		
Ballard, Sarah	1		6		5
Currell, Elizabeth	1	5	2		7
Ballard, Silas	1	1	3		2
Cooper, Jesse	2		3		
Cone, Jesse	1	2	1		1
Jones, Darling	3		2		
Norfleet, Sarah	1	1	1		
Wheatley, Hardy	2	2	6		
Qualls, Judith	1		6		
Beach, Thomas	1	5	3		1
Haselip, Southy	1	3	1		
Cherry, Joab	2	2	5		
Western, Jeremiah	1	1	2		
Harrill, John	2	1	2		
Cherry, Harrill	1	1	2		
Price, Elijah			2	7	5
Kenaday, John	2	2	6		1
Haselip, Frederick	1		3		
Lilley, Zachariah	2		2		
Hedgpith, Josiah	1	2	3		
Leggett, Samuel	1	2	3		
Hagges, Dorcas			1	4	
Mobley, William	1		4		
Williams, John	1				
Mobley, Edward					1
Price, John	1		2		5
Hurst, William	1	1	1		
Collins, James	1				1
Collins, John	2	3	4		2
Keneday, Isaac	1		1		
Rawls, Jesse	1	3	4		
Wynne, John	1	1	1		4
Bland, John	1		3		
Rawls, William	2	3	4		
Rawls, Joshua	1	3	3		
Everitt, Joshua	1		1		6
Leggett, Benjamin	3		3		
Leggett, Hezekiah	1	3	3		
Bullock, Obadiah	1	2	3		
Woollard, Jesse	1	1	1		
Wynne, Watkin W	3	3	4		8
Holloway, Thomas	2	3	7		7
Leggett, John	2	4	5		
Ward, William	2		2		
Mitchell, Jesse	1	2	1		
Biggs, Joshua	1	2	2		1
Ward, Henry	1		2		
Beach, Thomas	1		4		
Hodges, Francis	1	2	4		
Robason, Henry	3	3	2		9
Rolls, William	2	3	4		
Rolls, Jesse	1	3	4		
Rolls, Joshua	1	3	3		
Mizell, William	2				
Cherry, Jesse	2	5	5		6
Cherry, Joel	1	3	4		1
Cherry, James	2		1		
Cherry, Jonathan	1		1		
Hisk, William	1	3	2		
Bird, Edward	2	3	3		2

HALIFAX DISTRICT, NASH COUNTY.

NAME OF HEAD OF FAMILY.	Free white males of 16 years and upward, including heads of families.	Free white males under 16 years.	Free white females, including heads of families.	All other free persons.	Slaves.
Arranton, Arthur	1	3	5		13
Arranton, John	1				4
Arranton, Peter	1	2	1		5
Arranton, William	2	1	3		16
Arranton, Peter	1	2	4		5
Arranton, Joseph	1	3	3		10
Arranton, Joseph, Jr	3	2	3		10
Atkins, Newell	3	3	3		
Atkinson, James	1	2	4		4
Atkinson, Tho	1	3	4		
Atkinson, Henry	4	5	3		14
Allen, Thomas	1	3	3		
Allen, Arthur	1				
Andrews, Joseph	2		6		
Andrews, Wm	1		4		13
Avon, William	2	4	4	1	12
Blanton, Richard	1	4	2		1
Butts, Redford	1	1	2		
Battle, John	2		2		18
Battle, William	2	4	1		19
Boothe, Andrew	1	3	1		1
Bell, Green	1	4	5	2	
Bell, Benjamin	1	1	3		
Blount, John	1		3		4
Baggel, Nicholas	1	1	3		1
Bridges, Benja	2	1	4		4
Boyd, James	1	3	4		
Biggel, David	1	3	5		
Barrow, Barnaby	2	6	5		5
Brown, James	2	2	4		
Brown, Mary	3	1	4		
Burge, Jeremiah	1	4	1		2
Bryant, Benj	1	3	2		1
Brown, James, Jr	1				12
Boothe, ——					
Bond, John	1	2	7		13
Butler, Christopher	2		2		
Bryant, Wm	1		4		4
Ballard, Peter	1	1	2		5
Ballard, Edward	3	1	6		
Bunn, Henry	1		2		4
Brewer, Hardy	2	1	3		3
Brantly, John	1	2	5		
Baker, William	3	1	6		
Baker, Allen	1		2		
Baker, William	1	1	3		1
Baker, John	1	2	4		1
Baker, James	2	2	1		
Bone, John	1	6	4		
Brantley, Jacob	3	3	4		
Boddy, William	1	1	5		21
Boon, Benjamin	1	6	5		2
Braswill, William	1	1	4		
Braswel, Jacob	1	2	3		1
Braswell, Robt	1		1		3
Bridges, William	2	5	4		8
Bunton, Jeremiah	1				
Battle, James	1	1	5		13
Bass, Abram	1	2	4		12
Bass, Jesse	2		1		2
Boddy, William (for M. Thomas)					56
Bass, Isaac	3	3	4		9
Bass, John	1				
Bass, Sion	1	3	5		4
Brasswell, Jacob	4		4		13
Boddy, Nathan	4		2		40
Braswell, Saml	2	1	6		4
Braswell, Micajah	2	2			
Braswell, Dempsey	1	2	4		7
Beckwith, Tho	4	2	3		7
Beckwith, Amos	2	4	5		5
Barrot, John	2	5	7		
Barrott, Nathan	1	3	3		1
Barnes, James	1	2	4		1
Bone, John	1	6	4		
Brantley, Jacob	3	3	4		
Boddy, Wm	1				
Bunn, Redmon	2	1	3		4
Bunn, Benj	1	3	4		4
Bunn, Joel	1				
Bunn, Burwell			1		7
Bunn, Benj	1	3	3		7
Bunn, Benj., Sen	3	1	6		29
Barns, Benj	2	2	6		1
Barnes, John	1	1	2		
Barns, William	1	3	6		2
Barns, Jacob	2	3	2		
Boykin, Hardy	3	2	5		
Blankenship, Jas	2	2	4		
Brown, Edmund	1				
Barns, Joseph	1		1		
Boykin, Drury	3	4	4		
Bail, William	1	1	2		
Bottoms, William	1		4		
Boykin, Drury, Jr	1	4	4		
Ballard, William	2	3	4		
Bowls, John	2	3	1		
Burge, Burwell	1	4	4		1
Bachelor, Joseph	1	4	2		
Belile, Barnaby	1	1	1		
Bunten, William	1	5	2		
Bryant, Saml	2	6	1		19
Bachelor, Stephen	2		2		
Bachelor, Saml	2	4	4		
Braswell, William	1	3	4		1
Bryant, William	1	3	4		
Braswell, Benj	1	3	2		
Barnes, Benjamin	1	2	2		
Barns, John	2	2	6		1
Britten, Charles	1		1		
Barnes, Henry	1	3	5		
Bass, Jethro	2		2		5
Bachelor, James	1		3		4
Burge, Richard	2	1	1		9
Bruce, James	1	1	1		
Bryant, William	1		3		4
Basset, David	3	2	3		
Bail, Jordan	1	1	1		
Blackwell, Ferreby			2	2	
Bass, Charely			1	2	
Biggs, Efferd				3	
Bryant, Betty			1	4	
Bachelor, Daniel	1	1	1		
Barnes, John	2	1	5		5
Brantley, Lewis	1	3	3		
Bachelor, John	1		2		
Bachelor, Wm	1	1	2		
Bedgood, John	2	3	4		
Butts, Jacob	1				
Bass, Jesse	2				4
Bryant, William	1		1	1	4
Bryant, Benj	1	3	1		2
Bottons, Sami	2	2	4		
Barnes, Basset	1		1		
Benton, Agness		1	4		
Bass, Jethro	2	3	2		
Barrot, Reddeck	1		1		
Beckwith, Burwell	1		1		
Barrow, John	2	2	2		
Bottons, Saml	1		2		
Boddy, George	1		2		5
Benton, Ann	1	1	5		
Brantley, Sarah	1	1	5		
Bedgood, Jemima		1	1		
Cooper, Edward	1		2		
Cooper, Edward, Jr	2	2			6
Connel, Davis	4	3	5		2
Cox, John	1	3	4		1
Cooper, Penelope	1	2	5		2
Cain, James	1	3	4		20
Carter, Thomas	2	3	5		
Carter, Solomon	2	4	6	6	
Carter, Saml	1	1	1		
Chapman, John	2	1	6		1
Collins, Jesse	2	1	1	4	1
Collins, Abehue	1	2	1		
Chapman, William	1	1	4		1
Carigus, Job	1	1	2		
Carpenter, Tho	1	1	2		1
Carpenter, Tho., Jr	1				
Cone, Joshua	1	3	6		
Cone, James	1	3	5		
Cooper, Marcome	3	3	4		4
Currel, Lewis	1		7		4
Currel, Wilson	1	2	7		1
Clench, John	1	4	4		18
Currel, John	1	3	4		

HALIFAX DISTRICT, NASH COUNTY—Continued.

NAME OF HEAD OF FAMILY.	Free white males of 16 years and upward, including heads of families.	Free white males under 16 years.	Free white females, including heads of families.	All other free persons.	Slaves.
Currel, Joseph	1	4	2		4
Cross, Stephen	2	2	3		
Cobb, Benjamin	1	2	4		6
Carter, Charles	2	3	3	1	
Carter, Jacob	1	2	2		
Cochrell, John	1	2	2		
Cochrell, Jacob	1	2	2		
Coleson, Chester	1		2		
Carter, Toby	1				
Carter, Thomas	2	3	6		2
Coleman, Robert	1		1		8
Carter, Reese	1				7
Coleman, Theophilus	2		2		
Crowell, Martha	1	1	6	4	
Carter, William	4	7	3		
Cockrell, William	1	5	5		4
Curll, Matthew	2		3		
Cain, Currell	1	2	3		
Carter, Jacob	1	3	5		2
Creekman, Robert	1	2	5	12	2
Culpepper, James	2	2	4		
Culpepper, Christopher	1				1
Culpepper, James, Jr	1	3	3		3
Culpepper, Jeremiah	1	1	1		
Colley, Solomon	2		4		
Creekman, Volintine	1	1	2		
Cone, Jesse	1		7		
Cone, John	1	2	3		
Cone, James	1	3	5		
Cith, Iasabel		1	3		
Carter, Charles	2	2	4		1
Carter, Mary	1	2	4		
Council, Michael	1	1	4		
Cook, Patience		1	2		
Council, Mike	1		2		
Coleson, Jonas	1	1	2		
Cooper, John	2	1	5		3
Churchill, James	1	1	5		
Cobb, Nathan	2	1	3		24
Cooper, Benjamin	1	2	2		9
Dorch, Lewis	1	3	4		
Dozier, John	1		1		
Davis, John	3	3	4		
Drury, Henry	1	3	7		
Denson, Jethro	1	4	5		
Drake, Thomas	1	1	3		2
Davis, Abell	1		1		
Davis, Enoch	1				2
Drake, James	3	1	3		22
Devaughan, Saml	1	4	6		
Dyson, Mary		1	4		
Durley, Arthur	2	4	3		
Dudley, Elizabeth		1	2		
Dudley, John	1				
Dance, Etheldrede	1	2			2
Daughtridge, Benjn	1	1	3		
Denson, John	1	2	1		
Denson, Joseph	1	2	5		
Druett, James	1	1	1	1	
Drake, Edmond	4		7	1	13
Drake, Matthew	2	2	8		16
Drake, William	3	4	4		17
David, Donald	1	4	5		4
Daniel, Federick	1	5	2		
Drake, Hynes	1	2	3		1
Dawson, Dempsey	1		4		
Dew, John	1				8
Dew, Duncan	1		1		20
Dickerson, William	1	3	6		
Driver, John	1	3	6		
Dunn, Richard	2		2		
Deens, Willis	1	2	4		
Deens, Mary	1	4	4		
Deens, Sherrod	1	4	3		
Deens, Thomas	3		5		8
Deens, Richard	2		2		
Denson, Benjamin	1	2	2		
Denson, Jesse	1	1	2		
Denson, John	1	3	4		
Deens, Henry	1	4	3		
Den, William	1	1	1		8
Driver, Mary			4		
Dawson, Dempsey	1	4	5		
Driver, William	1	4	6		
Drake, Delilah	2	1	4		
Dozier, William	3	1	4	9	
Evans, William	2	2	3	4	1
Evans, Burrell	1				1
Eason, Samuel	2		2		
Eason, Elizabeth		1	4		
Eason, William	1		3		
Eason, Samuel	1	2	3		
Evans, John	1	6	3		
Evans, Sherrod	1				
Evans, David	1	3	5		1
Edmundson, Ambrose	1	1	4		
Howell, Ellen	1	1	6		4
Exum, Joseph	1	3	5		5

NAME OF HEAD OF FAMILY.	Free white males of 16 years and upward, including heads of families.	Free white males under 16 years.	Free white females, including heads of families.	All other free persons.	Slaves.
Exum, John	1		3		4
Edward, Solomon	1	2	7		1
Eatman, Noel	2		6		
Eatman, John	2	5	4		8
Etheridge, Jeremiah	5		8	3	3
Etheridge, Peter	1	3	4		
Evans, Thomas	2	3	1		
Eden, Richard	1		3		
Evans, Samuel	1	1	5		
Freeman, Henry	1	3	6		3
Fore, William	1	3	1		1
Finch, Isham	2	1	3		
Floyd, Pinnuel	1		3		5
Floyd, Benjamin	1	1	3		
Flowers, Henry	3	1	4	6	6
Flowers, John	1	4	5		
Flowers, Benjamin	1	5	3		3
Flowers, John (S. of H.)	1	2	3		2
Flowers, William	1		5		
Floyd, Thomas	1	1	4		2
Finch, Isrom	2	1	4		
Finch, Allen	1	1	4		
Flowers, Martha	1		2		
Griffin, Hardy	2	1	4		8
Green, James	1		2		5
Green, Nathan	1	1	2		
Gardener, Pryer	1	2	5		4
Goodwyn, John	1				1
Gardener, Wm	1		3		1
Gardener, George	1	2	6		6
Gardener, James	1	2	8		
Goodwin, James	1		8		
Gains, James	2	5	3		
Gray, Edward	2	2	3		8
Gandy, Amos	1	1	2		1
Gray, John	1	4	5		3
Griffin, Pierce	1	2	2		3
Griffin, Micajah	1		4		
Griffin, Matthw	2	3	5		
Griffin, Archibald	1				2
Griffin, Thomas	1		3		
Glanding, Major	1	1	3		
Griggett, George	1	2	2		
Griggett, William	2	1	2		
Griggett, Horrod	1		2		
Griggett, Ellick	1				4
Gracie, Theophilus	2		8		8
Glover, Thomas	1	2	5		
Gay, John	1	4	4		3
Glover, Elizabeth	2	1	4		1
Grimm, George	1	2	3		
Griffin, James	1	3	2		
Goodson, Betty		1	3		
Griffin, Ann	1	1	3		
Harrison, John	1	4	4		12
Harrison, John, Jr	1				3
Hayes, Joseph	2	4	5		20
Horn, Henry	1	2	4		3
Harris, Thomas	1		2		6
Hopkins, Peter	4	5	6		9
Hicks, Solomon	1	1	3		
Hall, William	1	2	3		1
Halton, Thomas	1		3		
Harper, Benjamin	1	1	3		1
Horn, Elisha	1	1	1		5
Hollon, Daniel	2	2	3		
Hunt, David	1		5		
Hunt, Christn	1	3	3		
Hamilton, Thomas	1				7
Hilliard, James	2	5	4		84
Horn, Edward	1	2	4		4
Harris, Harday	2	1			22
Hynes, Lewis	2		1		4
Hunter, Priscilla		2	3		5
Hunter, Drury	1	1	2		2
Horn, Jacob	1	1	3		2
Harris, Randolph	1	4	6		7
Harrell, John	1		3		1
Hamilton, Francis	1	2	5		
Horn, Josiah	1	1	3		5
Hynes, Federick	1	1	3		10
Hart, Thomas	1	2	1		
Hart, Thomas	1		2		4
Hunt, Jesse	1		4		6
Horn, Joshua	1	3	2		
Horn, Michael	1	2	4		5
Horn, Wilson	1		3		
Horn, Thomas	1	3	5		4
Harrison, Jethro	2	5	3		3
Horn, William	1		4		
Hitchpeth, Jesse	1		1		
Horn, Richard	1		3		
Horn, Jordan	1		3		
Henry, William	2	3	6		
Hill, Zion	1	2	5		
Hobbs, Herbert	1	2	5		3
Harris, William	1	2	1		
Harris, Wm	1	2	5		

NAME OF HEAD OF FAMILY.	Free white males of 16 years and upward, including heads of families.	Free white males under 16 years.	Free white females, including heads of families.	All other free persons.	Slaves.
Hammon, William	2	1	2		3
Harris, John	2	2	1		
Hithford, James	4		5		1
Hale, Polly			4		
Howlings, Charles	1	2	7		
How, William	1	3	3		
How, John	1	1	8		
Hight, Joseph	1				
Horn, Jeremiah	1	3	2		2
Hicks, Ciety	1		2		
Harrison, Hanah		1	3		
Hethpeth, Abram	1	1	3		
Hendrick, Wm	2	2	5		
Horn, Patience	1	2	3	1	
Hunt, Judah		1	3		
Hight, Daniel	2				
Henry, Isaac	1				
Jones, John	2	2	6		6
Jackson, Wm	1	1	4		
Johnson, Andrew	1	1	3		
Jones, Fedrick	2	2	3		
Joiner, Nathaniel	2	2	3		
Joiner, James	1	3	6		1
Joiner, Jacob	1	5	3		
Joiner, Lewis	1	3	3		1
Joiner, Burwell	1	2	3		1
Joiner, John	2		1		
Joiner, John, Jr	1				
Joiner, Jesse	1	1	3		
Joiner, Nathl	1	1	5		
Joiner, William	1		1		
Joiner, Jordan	1	1	1		2
Jackson, George	2	1	1		11
Joiner, Celia		1	4		2
Joiner, Joseph	1	3	2		
Johnson, Josiah	3	2	3		
Jones, John	2	2	7		5
Jones, Nusom	1	2	3		1
Johnson, William	1	2	4		
Jones, Brittin	1	1	2		
Jelks, Etheldridge	3	1	3		
Jones, John	2	3	6		14
Jolley, James	2	2	6		
Jones, Barnaby	4				
Joiner, Solomon	1	4	2		
Johnson, Andrew	1	1	3		
Joiner, Cordie	1	3	3		8
Joiner, Drury	1		1		3
Jones, Cooper	2	4	3		
Joiner, Cornelius	1		1		
Jenkins, Jesse	1				5
King, Thomas	1	2	4		
Kith, James	1				
Keachen, William			2		2
Kent, Jesse	2	4	1		4
Knight, Kinsman	2	2			
King, Julian	1				5
Kent, Jesse, Jr	3	3	1		
Ketchen, Jesse	2		4		
Kinton, Charles	1	3	3		4
Lewis, William	3	1	3		
Lassitor, Tobias	5	5	3		
Lassitor, James	1	3	2		
Lassitor, Arthur	1	3	3		
Lee, Charles	2	3	3		
Letbetter, Rowland	1	2	4		
Lewis, Mayor	1	2	3		
Letbetter, John	2	3	3		
Locus, Frank				8	
Locus, James				6	
Lee, James	1	4	6		7
Laurance, Jesse	3		4		
Lassau, James	1	2	4		
Lemmons, Duncan	2	3	5	6	40
Lemmons, John	1				4
Lemmons, Archd	1				15
Locus, Barnaby				8	
Locus, Abner	1		1		
Locus, John				6	
Locus, Arthur				7	
Locus, Frank				8	
Lewis, Nathl	2	1	6		
Lee, Jonathan	1	2	5		8
Lampkin, Lewis	1	2	2		
Lewis, Henry	1	4	3		
Lain, Jonathan	1		4		
Locus, George				5	
Lain, Elizabeth	2	1	5		
Lindsey, William	1	5	1		
Letbetter, Holding	1	2	2		
Letbetter, John	2	3	3		
Langley, Nathan	1	1	1		
Lindsey, Billy	1	1	1		
Lee, James	1		4	3	5
Lindsey, Sion	1	1	4		
Laurance, Betty			4		
Mason, Henry	4	4	4		
Mason, Ralph	2	5	6		

HALIFAX DISTRICT, NASH COUNTY—Continued.

NAME OF HEAD OF FAMILY.	Free white males of 16 years and upward, including heads of families.	Free white males under 16 years.	Free white females, including heads of families.	All other free persons.	Slaves.
Mason, Foster	1	4	3		1
Mason, Mark	1	1	3		1
Mason, William	1		2		
Matthews, Benj	1	3	4		1
Matthews, Joel	1		3		
Musten, Joseph	1	1	3		
Musten, John	3	4	5		
Mann, Thomas	2	1			36
Mitchell, Sam'l	2	3	5		
Mason, Mark	2		3		7
Mossly, David	1		1		
Mossly, Joseph	2	3	5		
Medleng, Shadh	2	4	4		
Morgan, John	2	2	6		
Medleng, Bryant	2	3	5		
Morgan, Hardy	1	2	3		
Morgan, William	1				
Moore, William	1				
Moore, Wade	1	1	1		
Matthews, William	1		3		
Milton, Zach	1		2		
Milton, John	2	5	1		
Milton, Josiah	1	2	3		
Mannen, Matt'w	1		1		
Mannen, Margret	1		7		14
Masengail, James	1		2		
Masengail, Walker	2		3		
Masengail, Joseph	1		4		
Masengail, James	1	3	6		
Masengail, Henry	4	2	2		
Moses, Smith	1	3	4		
Mann, Denton	1		4		14
Mearns, William S	1				14
Morriss, Thomas	1	4	5		
Mannen, Sam'l	2	1	3		
Merril, William	1		3		4
Morriss, Mitchel	1	2	5		
Merril, Benjamin	1		4		5
Merril, William	1		3		8
Mannen, Thomas	1	2	5		
Milton, John	1	1	6		
Moonahow, John	2	2	6		
Morriss, James	1	4	2		3
Moonahow, Tho	1	3	5		
Mannen, William	1	2	2		
Moore, James	1	2	4		3
Moore, Edward	1				4
Mannen, Benj'a	1	2	3		
Mannen, Willoby	1		5		7
Morriss, William	1	1	3		
Mannen, Matt'w	1				
Mitchell, John	1				1
Masengail, Eliz		1	3		
Mitchell, Mary			4		
Masengail, Nancey			4		
Mannen, Lucy		2	5		
Mannen, Margret		1	7		
Nicholson, Joseph	1	1	3		11
Norriss, James	1	5	5		7
Navin, William	1		4		
Navin, John	2	3	4		
Nash, Joseph	1	2	2		1
Newton, Benj	2		5		
Nicholas, Job	1	2	5		
Nicholas, Jeremiah	2	4	4		
Nicholas, Jeremiah, Jr	1		3		
Nicholas, John	1	4	5		
Nicholas, Edward	2		4		8
Night, Sarah	1	2	4		
Nolleyboy, Sally		1	1		
Owens, John	1		4		
Owens, Daniel	5	2	3		3
Owins, Elias	1	2	3		
Oneal, Arthur	3	2	6		
Otham, Willis	1	1	5		
Owens, Mary		3	3		
Powell, Willoby	1	3	5		12
Powell, Dan'l	1	1	1		4
Portes, John	2	2	4		
Powell, John	3	1			
Powell, Allanson	1		4		
Powell, Nathan	1	1	1		10
Pritchet, John	1	2	4	6	6
Perry, William	1	4	3		
Parish, John	1	4	3		
Parker, William	1				4
Pace, George	1	2	4		
Pucket, Abraham	1	1	1		
Pridgen, David	2	1	4		5
Pridgen, Eliz. Allen			1		5
Pridgen, M. Mannen		1			7
Pridgen, Drury	1		4		
Pollon, John	1	5	5		1
Pridgen, Hardy	1	3	3		1
Pasmour, John	1	2	3		
Powell, Jesse	2	4	5		8
Pitts, John	1	1	8		10

NAME OF HEAD OF FAMILY.	Free white males of 16 years and upward, including heads of families.	Free white males under 16 years.	Free white females, including heads of families.	All other free persons.	Slaves.
Parker, William	3		5		
Parker, Francis	1	1	1		13
Parker, Ann		1	1		1
Pope, John					3
Pope, Dempsey	1	2	4		
Pope, Elisha	2	3	4		
Pope, Micajah	1	3	4		
Parker, Gabriel	1	1	2		
Phillips, Jethro	1		4		9
Phillips, Ephraim	1	3	4		4
Phillips, William	1	1	1		1
Phillips, Josiah	2	1	3		7
Poland, William	1	2	3		
Parker, Aarn	1	3	4		
Parker, John	1	3	4		
Parker, John, Jr	2	3	6		
Pughe, William	4				
Parker, Eliz'a		3	1		4
Pope, Barnaby	1		3		9
Pridgen, Jesse	1	3	5		4
Pierce, Eliz'a			2		
Pursell, Eliz'a	2	3	4		
Parrott, Joseph	2	3	4		
Pierce, Joshua	2		3		1
Pace, W'm	4				
Parker, Mary		2	6		
Pellepet, Phillip	1	3	6		
Rose, Frances	2	1	5		
Robertson, John	1		2		1
Rose, William	1	2	4		6
Robertson, Peter	1	1	1		
Rutherford, James	2		2		1
Rutherford, Robert	1		1		
Rutherford, James, Jr	1		1		
Reed, John	1	3	4		3
Richardson, Thomas	1		2		2
Rose, Burwell	2	2	4		
Rackley, Parsons	1	2	2		
Rean, Howell	1	6	2		
Rose, Burwell, Jr	2	2	2		
Rose, John	1	4	2		
Rowe, William	1	3	3	4	4
Revell, Micajah					12
Revell, Elijah					12
Russ, Randolph	1	2	5		
Ricks, Mary			2		3
Richardson, William	2	3	2		
Richardson, W'm, Jr	3	3	2		
Rogers, Jacob	1	1	2		
Rogers, Robert	3	1	6		1
Ricks, Abram	1	3	4		
Ricks, Joel	1	2	3		
Ricks, Jacob	1	2	5		
Ricks, W'm	1		5		
Ricks, Sarah		1	4		
Ridley, Thomas			2		
Rackley, Parsons	1	2	5	3	2
Rackley, Matt'w	1	1	1		
Rackley, Frank	1	2	1		
Ricks, Priscilla			1		
Ricks, William, Jr	1	5	4		
Rossin, Daniel	1	2	4		1
Rackley, Matt'w	1	1	1		
Rogers, Jacob	1	1	2		4
Sandiford, William	3	2	7		1
Smelly, John	1	2	4		
Scruize, Henry	3	2	5		1
Statter, James	1	3	4		1
Smith, Samuel	1	2	4		
Strickland, Henry	2		2		4
Strickland, Hardy	1		2		8
Strickland, Nash	1	3	3	2	2
Strickland, Matt'w	1	1	1		
Strickland, Laz'a	4	1	1		
Strickland, Harmon	3		5		
Smith, Clayton		2	3		
Sutton, Thomas	1	4	4		
Strickland, Mark	1	4	6		17
Stallions, Moses	1	3	1		
Strickland, Tho	1	1	2		
Strickland, Joseph	1	2	4		
Strickland, Lazarus	1	1	2		
Strickland, John	4	1	2		
Strickland, Simon	1	3	2		
Smith, Peter	1	3	3		
Scott, Absolem				8	
Savage, Moses	1	1		4	
Savage, Drury	1	1	2		4
Sikes, Phillip	1	1	5		
Stephens, Joshua	1	2	3		
Sutton, George	1		1		
Sanders, John	1	6	3		
Sanders, Cornelius	1		1		
Sanders, Thomas, Jr	1	1	4		
Sanders, Thomas	1	1	3		
Seary, Aquilla	1		5		
Sanders, John	1	1	1		1

NAME OF HEAD OF FAMILY.	Free white males of 16 years and upward, including heads of families.	Free white males under 16 years.	Free white females, including heads of families.	All other free persons.	Slaves.
Sullivent, Owen	2		2		
Sossberry, Sam'l	2		5		
Skinner, Emanuel	2	2	5		1
Skinner, William	1	1	1		4
Strickland, David	3	2	5		
Strickland, Henry	2	2	5		5
Sanders, Henry	2	2	4		5
Sketo, William	1	1	6		1
Solomons, Lazarus	1	2	5		
Selah, Joseph	2	1	6		
Smith, Benjamin	1	3	3		28
Selah, Joseph, Jr	1	3	6		
Sheppard, John	3	1	1		
Sellers, John	1	5	1	3	3
Sherod, Jordan	1	2	5		
Strickland, Joseph	1	1	1		
Smith, Babson	1				
Sellers, John	1	5	1		5
Sellers, Arthur	1	1	2		
Smith, Peter	1	2	5		
Strickland, Matt'w	1	1	2		
Smith, Clayton	1		2		3
Stallions, Moses	1	1	3		
Skinner, Samuel	3	1	3		1
Selah, Drury	1	1	1		
Sellers, William	2		6		
Smith, Jesse	1		2		
Turner, James	2	3	3		
Taylor, James	2				1
Taylor, John	1		2		1
Taylor, Burwell				6	
Taylor, James'a	3	1	6		
Taylor, Sam'l	1	1	4		1
Taylor, William	1				
Taylor, Benj., Jr	1				3
Taylor, Demsey	1	2	2		
Tann, Benjamin				5	
Taylor, John	2	2	5		4
Tucker, Benjamin	1	3	4		4
Tucker, Jacob	1	2	5		
Tucker, Daniel	1	1	4		
Tucker, Benj	4	3	5		
Tucker, Thomas	1	2	2		
Tucker, James	1	3	6		
Tucker, James, Jr	1	3	5		
Tucker, Sarah			6	2	6
Taylor, Daniel	3	5	4		
Taylor, Drury	1	1	5		3
Taylor, Christopher	1	1	5		3
Taylor, Wilson	1	2	4		5
Tyce, Thomas	1	2	2		
Taylor, Reuben	2	3	5		15
Taylor, Milles	1	5	2		1
Thomas, Alexander	1				
Turner, William	1		5		
Turner, John	1	5	3		
Thomas, Jacob	1		4		
Thomas, Jesse	4	1	6		
Thomas, Jethro	1	2	4		1
Turlington, Elizabeth	1	2	3		
Tucker, Reubin	1				
Tucker, Jacob	2		7		
Underwood, Sam'l	3	2	4		3
Underwood, Jacob	3	1	4		3
Underwood, Howell	1	1	2		1
Vick, Robert	1	1	2		
Vick, Robert, Jr	1	2	4		
Vick, Joseph	2	5	5		
Vick, Jordan	2	3	5		
Vaughan, Dempsey	1	2	2		
Vaughan, Stephen	1		4		
Vester, William	2		4		
Vester, William, Jr	1	3			
Vaughan, Ephraim	1	3	5		
Viverett, Thomas	5	3	5		15
Vick, John	2	3	3		
Vick, Lewis	1	2	4		1
Vick, Wilson	3	1	4		1
Vick, Henry	1	1	4		1
Vick, Nathan	1	2	3		
Vick, William	2				4
Vick, Robert	2	1	1		
Vester, Ciely	1	3	2		
Vick, Richard	2		2		
Vaughan, Fred'k	2	3	2		
Wester, Hardy	1		2		2
Whitehead, Tho	1	3	3		9
Whitehead, Benj	1	3	4		9
Wright, William	3	4	5		21
Whitley, Solomon	2	1	8		
Whelas, William	3	2	5		1
Whelas, Mildred			2		
Ward, Francis	1		3		
Whitehead, Rachel			2		
Whitehead, Lazarus	1	1	2		10
Whitehead, Charles	1	1	1		3
Warburton, John	1				

HALIFAX DISTRICT, NASH COUNTY—Continued.

Name of head of family.	Free white males of 16 years and upward, including heads of families.	Free white males under 16 years.	Free white females, including heads of families.	All other free persons.	Slaves.
Williams, Benjamin	1	2	3		
Whitehead, Lazarus	3		1	7	20
Wenburn, Abram	1	2	5		
Wenburn, Josiah	1	2	4		
West, Arthur	2	1	2		
Wyatt, Dempsey	2	2	6		
West, Nathan	1	2	3		
West, Dempsey	1	1	4		
West, William	1	1	3		
Woodward, Jesse	1	5	3		5
Whelas, Jacob	1		3		8
Williams, Joel	1	5	3		
Williams, Rowland	1	1	4		10
White, Allen	1				
Williams, Benjamin	1	1	4		8
Whitfield, John	3	3	4		
Warren, Mary	1	2	3		
Williams, Philander	2	1	4		8
Whitby, Mary		2	2		
Williams, Drury	1	3	1		5
Woodward, Thomas	1	3	2		
Williams, Elkany	1	3	5		
Wright, Joseph	1				1
Williamson, Joseph	1	1	5		1
Willis, John	1		1		
Wright, Saml	2	2	1		
Winstead, Peter	1	3	4		4
Williamson, Wm	1	4	4		1
Williamson, Jonas	1	5	4		15
Williams, Nathan	1	1			2
Willson, Edward	1	2	4		
Wilson, Edward	1	3	5		
Wilson, John	2	1	2		2
Wilkins, John	2	1	4		2
Whitehead, Arthur	2		1		
Whitehead, Bennet	1				
Williams, James	1	2	5		11
Whitley, Thomas	1		2		
Watkins, Henry	2	1	5		
Whitfield, Thomas	2	2	3		4
Whitfield, Solo	2	1	8		
Whitfield, Willis	1	1	1		2
Willis, William	1	1	2		
White, Joseph	1	1	3		10
Wister, Elias	1	2	4		
Whitty, Jonas	1	1	1		
Webb, Stephen	1	4	3		
Walker, Green	2		4		
Walker, Joell	2	1	4		
Woodward, David	1		1		1
Williams, James	1	2	2		1
Watkins, James	1	1	2		
Williams, Burwell	3	3	7		2
Winston, William	1	2	3		5
Whitehead, Nathan	2	1	3		
Woodward, Aaron	1	3	2		
Williams, William	1	3	6	3	
Whitfield, Ruben	2	2	4		
Wills, Joshua	1				1
Wills, Absolem	1				
Wister, Samuel	1	1	8		4
Whitten, John	1	1	4		1
Whitfield, Benjn	1	1	2		2
Whitehouse, John	1		1		
Whitfield, Wm	1	2	5		
William, Charles	1	3	5		
Walker, William	1	3	3		
Walder, Robert	1				
Warren, John	1	2	1		
Wilder, Moses	1		3		
Williams, Edmund	2	2	4		
Willson, John	1	1	3		2
Walker, James	1	1	3		
Walker, Amos	1	3	3		
Wilder, Elenor		3	1		
Wilder, Robert	1	1	1		3
Whitfield, Benj	3	3	3	6	3
White, Joseph	1		3		
Whitehead, Henry	1	1	3		11
Wills, Elisha	2	1	1		
Wadkins, James	1		1		
Whitehead, Arthur	2		1		
West, Sarah		1	3		
Winstead, Joseph	1	1	2		
Whitfield, Nancy	1		6		
Whitehead, Mattw	1		2		11
Wiggins, James	1				
Woodward, James	3	1	4		1
Woodward, David	1		1		
Woodward, Aron	1	3			
Woodward, Nancy		2	2		
Whitfield, Mattw	1		1		
Whitehead, Tho	1	1	1		
Webb, William	1		2		
White, Olive			1		
Wall, Mark	1	3	2		
Whitby, Sion	1		1		
Williams, James	1		1		1
Willis, Stephen	2	2	2		
Young, Stephen	2	4	4		
York, Edward	1	1	2		3

HALIFAX DISTRICT, NORTHAMPTON COUNTY.

Name of head of family.	Free white males of 16 years and upward, including heads of families.	Free white males under 16 years.	Free white females, including heads of families.	All other free persons.	Slaves.
Edwards, Benjamin	1	2	2		25
Eaton, Thomas	1		2		51
Clanton, Mark	2		2		12
Jones, Captn William	2	5	5		22
Jones, William	1	1	6		8
King, Henry	1	2	3		3
Clemmons, William	1	2	5		10
Eaton, William A	1		1		38
Lashley, Howell	1	2	4		8
Gold, John	1		2		3
Patterson, John	1				5
Brock, Uriah	1	2	3		
Skinner, William	1	1	1		1
Cawthorn, William	1		6		1
Rook, John	1	3	2		17
Scott, Saul				1	
Scott, Sterling				6	
Scott, Stephen				5	
Peters, Gilliam	1		2		
Gilliam, Burwell	2	1	6		7
Goldson, John	1	2	3		4
Norwood, George	1	2	6		2
Jones, Lewis	2	1	5		21
Johnston, Benjamin	1	2	2		8
Day, Lewis	1	2	3		2
Dubry, Joshua	2	1	4		
Moody, Benjamin	2	1	7		11
King, John	2		3		3
Jones, Richard	1		3		13
Day, Thomas	1				
Woodson, Booker	3		1		38
Day, Edmund	1		2		
Ticker, Anthony	2	3	3		13
Brooker, John	1	2			1
Squire, Roger	1	2	3		
Fulks, William	2	7	5		6
Moody, Surrell	3	2	4		4
Rook, Benjamin	1	1	1		5
Crow, Robert	1	1	1		2
Harris, Edward				10	
Williamson, Benjamin	2		7		54
Jenkins, Thomas	2	5	7		29
Suite, Samuel	1	4	1		1
Smalley, John	1	1	4		2
Scott, Randol				7	
Tuter, Robert	1	2	5		
Gilliam, Wyatt	1	1	3		
Ingram, William	1		3		
Groves, Ezekial				6	
Rook, Martin	1				2
Parish, Peter	1	2	2		
White, Joshua	1	1	1		
Parish, Obed	1		3		
Brown, Robert				7	
Putney, Richard	4		1		17
Scott, Mason	2				1
Moody, Burwell	1	3	2		1
Tucker, Curle	1	3	3		4
Jones, Mary		1	4		
Thrift, Nathaniel	1	1	4		7
Jackson, Benjamin	1	1	2		1
Etter, John	1	1	1		1
Woodard, Simon	1		2		
Rook, Sarah	2		2		2
Carter, Sewil	1	1	1		
Haynes, Eaton	2		2		50
Smith, Benjamin	1	1	3		1
Lockhart, Samuel	1	3	5		26
Lucy, Burwell	1		2		
Wilkins, Sarah		1	3		
Roy, James	1		1		1
Archer, Thomas	5		5		
Love, Elizabeth		3	4		1
Glover, William	1		2		1
Hattaway, John	1			1	
Kemp, William	1	2	2		
Wornum, Elizabeth		1	2		1
Love, William	1		1		
Scott, David				8	
Harris, Nathan	1	4	2		2
Harris, Nathl	1	1	4		
Harris, Simon	2	3	1		6
Moody, Gilliam	1	3	2		4
Serrett, Thomas	1				
Rosser, Kinchen	1	1	2		3
Hudson, Thomas	1				8
Peebles, Seth	1		1		10
Horton, James	1		3		2
Love, Alexander	1		2		3
Narsworthy, William	2	2	4		
Horton, William	3	2	5		6
McDaniel, Jno	1		1		
Walthorpe, Michael	2	1	2		
Key, Matthew	1	4	1		
Collier, Also	1	2	3		4
Moughan, Peyton	1	2	1		4
Melone, Robert	2	2	3		3
Thompson, Charles	2	2	3		1
Weaver, Peter	1	2	6		14
Johnston, Isham	3	4	3		5
Land, Lemon			1	6	
Collier, Jesse	1	4	3		
Melone, Charles	3		2		1
Collier, Joseph	1	2	3		
Glover, Jones	1	3	2		3
Brewer, George	2		1		2
Moughan, Thomas	1		1		
Edwards, Isaac	3	2	4		
Moughan, William	3	6	5		2
Collier, William	1	2	1		
Turner, Capt. Jno					7
Morgan, William				3	
Hudson, Edward	1	2			9
Crews, James	1	4	1		
Gary, John	1		2		3
Horton, Jesse	2				
Glover, Benjamin	1		2		3
Mitchell, William	1	1	5		
Crittenden, Robert	1		2		20
Barker, Nathan	1		6		1
Ladd, Thomas	1		1		
Norwood, Nathaniel	1	6	4		20
Mitchell, Jesse	1	1	1		16
Wornum, Samuel	3	4	2		3
Hodges, Thomas	2	4	3		
Poythress, Odam				9	
Weaver, Henry, Senr	1	1	5		11
Capell, Edward	2	4	4		8
Collier, Frederick	1		4		
Meacham, Henry, Senr	1	1	3		
Morgan, John				4	
McGregor, John	1	1	4		9
Mitchell, William, junr	1				5
McGregor, William	1	3	3		2
Harden, John	3	4	2		6
Jean, William	2	1	1		4
Crew, Andrew	1	3	2		
Benford, John	1		3		1
Lee, Drury	2	1	2		1
Poythress, Hardimon				5	
Stafford, Cuthbert	1	1	2		2
Williams, Mark	1	3	2	1	1
Dancy, Francis	2	5	4		37
Rives, John	1	3	6		25
Johnston, Thomas	1				
Morgan, Mark				7	
Justis, Mark	1	1	4		
Brown, Jno				5	
Agers, Frances		2	2		
Sandifer, John	1	2	1		2
Hayle, Jonas	3	1	2		12
Hines, Kinchen	1		3		10
McDougall, James	2				1
Carr, Benjamin	1				2
Carr, William	1				
Barrett, Thomas	3		1		17
Barrett, Thomas, junr	1	1	1		14
Crump, Josias	2	1	3		32
Ellis, Robert, jr	1	1	3		
Smelley, Rhody		2	2		
Sills, Gray	1		1		10
Prince, John	2		1		
Peebles, Benjamin	1	3	2		
Peterson, Kinchen	1		1		7
Epps, William	1	2	5		2
Capel, Ann	2	4	3		3
Taylor, Christopher	1	3	3		
Vinson, James	1	1	3		9
Tarver, Benjamin	1	2	2		3
Penticost James	1	1	1		18
Peterson, John	2	3	1		26

HALIFAX DISTRICT, NORTHAMPTON COUNTY—Continued.

NAME OF HEAD OF FAMILY.	Free white males of 16 years and upward, including heads of families.	Free white males under 16 years.	Free white females, including heads of families.	All other free persons.	Slaves.
Stanton, Frederick	1		3		9
Roberson, Wyatt	1	3	4	1	
Roberson, John	1		1		
Mitchell, John	2	1	6		
Armstrong, Adam	1	1	2		
Gee, William	1	1	1		2
Williams, William	1	1	3		
Reams, William	1		1		
Collins, James	1		2		2
Moore, John	1		3		5
Stokes, John	2	3	5		
Smith, Arthur	1		4	1	
Moore, Anthony	1	1	4		11
Gee, John	1		1		4
Hayle, James	1	3	2		7
Gee, Charles	2		2		
Thompson, Charles	1	1	2		3
Thompson, William, junr	1	2	4		
Thompson, William	1	1			9
Thompson, William	1				
Gee, Joseph	1				1
Walden, Drury				8	
Ellis, William	1	1	5		
Ellis, Robert	3	2	1		8
Thompson, Henry	1	1	1		
Dobey, Nathl	1	2	5		5
Peebles, Howell	1		1		4
Wren, Alexander	1	2	2		
Medling, Richard	1				
Pace, William	2		2		11
Thompson, John	1				
Richards, William	2	2	2		9
Tarver, Mary	1	3	1		
Ellis, Drury	1				
Glover, Amey	2		2		
McGregor, Flower	1				2
Williams, Buckner	1	2	3		4
Medling, Michael	1		2		
Williams, Charles	1	3	2		
Metton, John	2		4		19
Jeter, Andrew	1	3	3		9
Ellis, John	1	1	3		
Faison, Henry	1	1	2		1
Short, James	1				5
Floyd, Morris, Senr	1		1		4
Binford, John M	2	3	3		19
Patterson, John	1		3		3
Patterson, Joseph	1	3	5		1
Patterson, William, jr	1	4	5		
Patterson, Jonathan	2		2	1	5
Patterson, David	1	2			
Patterson, William	3		3		
Patterson, Joseph, jr	1		4		
Patterson, Benjamin	1	2	2		1
Patterson, William	1	3	4		
Merrymoon, David	3	3	4	1	
Merrymoon, Francis	1	3	2		
Merrymoon, John	1	1	1		
Merrymoon, Peter	2	1	6		
Merrymoon, Robert	1	2	3		
Merrymoon, Kiziah			2		5
Reams, Margaret		2	5		
Reams, Willm, junr	1	1	2		
Binford, James	2		3		32
Peebles, Robert	2		4		8
Short, David	1		1		16
Short, John	2		1		23
Robirson, Nathaniel	1		1		2
Step, James	2	2	6		4
Edlow, David	1		2		
Webb, Cordall	1	1	3		1
Amis, William	4	3	4		74
Dupree, Jesse	1	3	2		9
Wilkinson, John	1				
Hicks, Thomas	1	1	2		
Roper, Ann		2	3		
Parker, Thomas	2				25
Emery, Balaam	1	2	1		
Coaker, Benjamin	3	4	1	1	
Richards, John	1	4	1		6
Epps, John	1	4	2		
Smith, Leonard	3	1	5		1
Simms, David	1		2		
Floyd, Morris, junr	1	2	2		
Floyd, Buckner	1	3	2		
Thompson, Henry, Senr	2	1	4		
Hathcock, Newmon				4	
Brady, John	2	3	3		
Wall, Robert	2	3	2		
Reams, John	1		1		
Moore, Richard	1		1		2
Rhymes, John	1		2		1
Hart, Hardy	2	1	2		8
Dupree, Thomas	1	1	6		13
Jordan, Benjamin	1	3	4		13
Jordan, Arthur	1		1		10
Smith, William	1		1		8
Hailey, Holliday	2	4	4		28
Tooke, John	4	6	2		4
Evans, John	2	2	2		
Smith, Joel	1	2	4		
Smith, Lewis	1		2		11
Jordan, George	2		2		17
Finnie, Robert	2	3	1		5
Grigory, Arthur	1				7
Grigory, Charles	3	1	5		11
Jordan, Batt	1		3		10
Bass, Samuel	2		2	1	3
Wall, John	2	1	2		4
Hart, Henry	1	2	3		12
Streater, Edward	1	4	1	1	2
Hollimon, Exum	2		2		11
Boyakin, Burwell	1	2	2		11
Ward, James	2	2	4		8
Pollard, Josiah	1				
Roberts, Jonathan					5
Roberts, William					1
Scott, Isaac					9
Dupree, Cordall	1		4		2
Smith, Littleberry	1		1		6
Tabon, Nathan					3
Anderson, Jeremiah					7
Spivey, Benjamin	2	2	3		1
Jordan, John	1				5
Howell, Henry, Jr	1	1	3		2
Roberts, Elias					4
Lewis, William	1	2	3		1
Howell, John	1				5
Howell, Henry	1	1	2		5
Spence, Joseph	1	2	1		
Munger, Henry	1	1	3		3
Stephens, Henry	3		2		
Boyakin, Sterling	2		1		4
Tabon, Allen					7
Roberts, James, Jr					7
Finnie, John	1	3	5	1	1
Hayley, William	1				
Warwick, Benjamin	1		1		1
Tabon, Isaac					3
Boyakin, Jesse	1		3		11
Doles, Francis	1		2		1
Grayham, George	1	1	3		
Peebles, Henry	1	4	3		5
Brown, Benjamin	2	3	6		8
Smith, Nancy			1		3
Chapman, Harrisson	1		2		
Bass, Matthew	1				
Boyakin, Robert	2	2	5		7
Homes, Henry	1				
Forster, Christopher	2	2	1		3
Sexton, Mark	1	1	3		
Roberts, John					8
Artis, Abraham					2
Jordan, Over	1		2		
Cumbo, Cannon					5
Stewart, Peter				2	5
Longbottom, Saml	1				
Clarke, Leonard	1	4	1		2
Clarke, James	1				
Boyakin, John	2	2	4		16
Wood, Hathorn	1				
Homes, Zebulon	1	1	3		
Clarke, Sarah	2		4		16
Cook, Giles	3	6	2		
Lewelling, Lyson	1		4		
Roberts, James				4	2
Kay, John	1	1	1		2
Scott, Hardy				8	
Jordan, Thomas	1	5	2		5
Brantley, Etheldred	1				4
Nicholas, William	2	1	1		
Sauls, Brittain	3	2	2		1
Campbell, James	2	6	3		3
Peterson, William	1	1	2		20
Bryan, John M	2		3		34
Goodrich, James	1		3		5
Bryant, Saml	1		1		26
Gumbs, Nathan	2		1		1
Gumbs, Abraham	2	1	4		1
Thompson, John	1				
Pace, Solomon	1		2		8
Pace, William	1				11
Bell, James	3				6
Jones, Frederick	1	2	8		
Parker, Samuel	2	2	3		2
Grant, Richard	2	3	3		
Griffin, Arthur	2	4	3		
Flanner, William	1		1		
Young, Thomas	1	2	1		
Taylor, Dempsey	2	3	7		11
King, Thos (Ovr for Pollock)	1				42
Grant, Absolom	1		1		
Cobb, Henry	1				
Goodwyn, Joseph	1	1	1		
Lewis, John	1	1	1		
Hays, John	3		1		
Winborne, Jesse	1				
Guthridge, Mrs.		1	4		
Daughtrey, Elisha	2	4	2		1
Boon, James	2				
Howell, Dempsey	2				13
Bell, Samuel	2	1	2		5
James, Jesse				9	
James, Jeremiah				3	
Jones, Servant	1	2	3		3
James, David				3	2
Goodson, Mandew	1	2	2		
Revil, Lazerous	1	1	1		
Winborne, Elias	1				
Bridgers, Willis	1				1
Nichols, John	1		1		4
Brazil, George	1	2	3		
Vaughan, John	1	1	1		
Duke, Sherrard	1				
Dales, John	1				
Alphan, James	1	2	4		
Bridgers, John	1	2	3		7
Sherrard, John	1	1	1		3
Griggs, John	1	1			
Winborne, John	1	2	4		1
Lewis, Eliphas	1	1	4		
Bedingfield, Sarah		2	3	1	1
Summersett, Joseph	1	1			3
Winborne, James	5	1	4		4
Grant, William	1	2	3		11
Durden, Carr	1		6		
Powell, Jesse	1	1	2		
Nelson, James	1	2	3		
Walden, John				7	1
Grant, Port	2	3	6		
Sherrard, Patience	3		4		
Branch, Burwell	1		1		6
Hays, Solomon	1	4	3		6
Boon, Thomas	3	1			16
Boon, William	1	3	5		1
Leeke, Higlow	2				
Boon, Nicholas	1		2		3
Allen, Harris	1	1	2		
Hays, Elijah	1		1		
Allen, Richard	1	2	1		2
Brewer, William	1	1	3		
Hays, Elias	1	3	5		
Dempsey, Rachel	1	4	5		1
Wilkinson, James	1		1		
Atherton, Elizabeth		1	3		28
Jones, Harwood	1				37
Jones, John	1	1	1		36
Dancy, John	1	2	1		11
Webb, Jno Thos.	1	2	3		2
Prichard, Swan	1	3	2		4
Buffelow, Matthew	1	1	4		1
Burke, John	1		1		
Vasser, James	1	3	1		3
Webb, Jesse	3	6	2		
Moore, Anthony, Jr	1	1	2		3
Tarver, Benjamin	1	1	2		3
Spivy, Brittain	3	3	4		
Tarver, Frederick, Jr	1				
Warbritton, William	1		4		9
Tarver, Frederick	1	1	3		1
Tarver, Lucy	2	1	3		3
Webb, Hill	1				
Lewis, James	1	3	1		3
Tarver, Samuel	2		2		5
Vasser, Joseph	2		4		9
Burke, William	2		2		6
Dancy, James	1				6
Dancy, Benjamin	1				11
Acols, John	1		1		
Wilkinson, John	1		1		
Smith, Etheldred	1	3	3		
Dancy, Sarah					5
Harrisson, Isham	3	2	5		22
Norton, Willie	1	2	1		
Thrift, Jenny			1	3	
Jubalough				2	
Wheeler, John	2	2	3		6
Underwood. Jesse	2	1	3		
Garriss, John	2	1	5	1	
Johnston, Silas	1	2	1		
Deloatch, Francis	1	3	3		10
Davis, Thomas	2		4		
Barkley, Rhodes	1	3	4		4
Bartley, Saml	1		1		
Daughtrey, Lawrence	1				8
Sumner, Richard	1	3	5		7
Underwood, Jesse	2				
Davis, John	1	4	4		
Davis, Arthur	1		2		

HALIFAX DISTRICT, NORTHAMPTON COUNTY—Continued.

NAME OF HEAD OF FAMILY.	Free white males of 16 years and upward, including heads of families.	Free white males under 16 years.	Free white females, including heads of families.	All other free persons.	Slaves.
Davis, Edward	1				
Copland, William	1	1	2		
Bridges, William	1	4	2		2
Edwards, John	1		2		1
Bridgers, Joseph	2		2		
Wade, Elisha	1		2		
Johnston, Joseph	1	1	3		4
Bridges, Benjamin	1		3		1
Sikes, Brittain	1	2	1		2
Parkes, Robert	1	5	6		
Warren, Henry	1	1	2		
Martin, John	3	1	4		
Robinson, Thomas	2		4		
Powell, Hardy	1	4	7		
Allen, John	2		2		7
Allen, Jesse	2	1	3		
Gay, Elisha	1	1	4		
Jones, Isham	1	1	1		
Newsom, Booth				3	
Johnston, John	1	3	1		
Gay, Solomon	1	3	1		
Garriss, James	1		1		
Gay, Prudence			4		1
Gay, Jonathan	1	3	3		1
Boon, Joseph	1	3	2	1	3
Jones, Sarah		2	4		
Edwards, John	1	5	3		
Taylor, John	1	1	4		
Sikes, Thomas	1	1	5		7
Parkes, Andrew	2		4		
Parkes, James	1	6	4		1
Parkes, William	1	2	1		
Pope, Joel	1	1	2		
Parker, John	2	1	2	1	
Rose, James	1	2	3	1	
Parker, Aron	1		4		
Taylor, Joseph	1	6	4		
Sumner, Isaac	1		1		1
Lassiter, Willie	1		1		1
Jackson, Daniel	1		2		6
Deloatch, Michail	1	1	8	4	
Bridgers, John	2	1	3	1	
Underwood, John	1				
Jackson, Edmund	1				
Edwards, Isaac	1	2	2		
Grizzard, Jeremiah	1	2	3		2
Brittle, Jese	1	3	3		
Murrill, Mark	1	1	4		
Cobb, William	1		5		
Suiter, Henry	1	3	4		4
Doles, Thomas	1		2		
Morgan, Timothy	1	3	5		1
Westbrook, Thomas	3	1	6		
Morgan, Arnold	1	4	3	1	
Maddra, Nathaniel	2	2	1		
Newsom, Moses				14	
Cook, John	1	2	2		3
Ingram, John	1	2			
Nicholas, Edmund	1		3		
Lawrey, Henry	2	2	5		8
Newsom, Amos				6	
Newsom, Nath¹				3	
Hathcock, John				4	
Tann, Drury				4	
Byrd, Arthur				5	
Artice, George				3	
Newsom, James				11	
Allen, Arthur				9	
Banks, Silas				3	
Demory, Daniel				10	
Conner, Benjamin	1		1		
Joyner, Jesse	1	2	3		8
Williams, Thomas	1	2	5		8
Joyner, Giles	1	3	3	1	4
Strickland, William	1	1	2		
Nicholas, Elemelitch	1		2		1
Boon, Jesse	1	4	5		7
Deberry, Absalom	1	3	3		8
Deberry, Drury	2				15
Joyner, Thomas	2	1	4		11
Roper, James	1	1	2		
Howell, Benjamin	1	1	4	1	3
Haynes, Bythal	1	2	1		
Davis, John	1		1		6
Brittle, Sarah		2	1		3
Monger, William	3		5		
Monger, Samuel	1	1	3		13
Taylor, Ann	1		3		15
Hart, Eliza		1	2		19
Broom, Hailey	1	4	4	1	6
Williams, Mary		1	2		3
Armistead, Anthony			4		10
Joyner, Abraham	1		1		6
Dawson, Solomon	2				5
Deloach, Solomon	2	2	3		6
Inmon, Judith	1	1	3		
Sawrey, John	1		1		2

NAME OF HEAD OF FAMILY.	Free white males of 16 years and upward, including heads of families.	Free white males under 16 years.	Free white females, including heads of families.	All other free persons.	Slaves.
Vaughan, James	2	2	5		16
Faison, William	1		2		2
Doles, Henry	1	1	2		2
Smith, Solomon	1		5		
Turner, Martha	1				22
Turner, Edmund					11
Branch, Benjamin	2		3		31
White, Davis	1		2		4
Brittle, Mary	1		2		1
Westbrook, Benjamin	1	1	2		
Coaker, Henry	1		2		6
Penrice, Joseph	1	4	2	1	9
Deberry, Benjamin	1	2	4		13
Jones, John	1	2	2		
Pope, Jonathan	2	4	3		2
Cary, Elphinston	1	1	2		
Harty, Sam¹	1	2	2		
Pierce, Jacob	1	2	4		
Drake, Jordan	1		2		
Hill, Spencer	2	3	2		
Lane, William	1	1	3		2
Stancil, Nathan	1		4	1	2
Davis, Josiah	1	4	1		1
Stephenson, Abram	2	4	3		4
Stephenson, Arthur	1		2		6
Burn, Owen	1	1	1		4
Boon, Benjamin	1	1	5		3
Stancil, John	1	3	3		1
Brittain, Jesse	1	5	4		
Luten, Giles	2	1	5	1	3
Gay, Elisha	2	1	3		
Wall, Abram	2	3	7		
Deberry, Henry	1	1			36
Daughtrey, James	1	2	2		
Allen, William	1	3	2		1
Pierce, Elisha	3	5	3		
Wood, John	1	2	6		10
Parker, David	1	1	2		
Tanner, Benjamin	2	1	4		
Powell, Jacob	2		5		7
Bennett, William	1	2	3		15
Johnston, Elijah	1	2	3		7
Stephenson, William	1		4		
Bennett, Bowen	1		1		4
MacCone, Jesse	1		1		
Clifton, Cloyed	1	2	5	1	1
Watkins, John	2	1	3		7
Smith, Joseph	1	2	2		1
Burn, William	3		1		
Daughtrey, Mandew.	3		3		1
Boon, Jacob	1	1	1		4
Boon, Jacob, jr	1	2			
Faison, Elias	1		2		3
Faison, Harwood	2	2	5		9
Underwood, John	1	4	3		
Lumley, Abraham	1		4		
Burn, Etheldred	1		2		1
Wall, Elizabeth			2		
Griffin, James	1		3		
Bridgers, William	1	2	2		25
Baum, John	1	3	4		
Pedan, William	2	2	5		
Dawson, Henry	2	1	2		23
Combs, Robert	1	1	3		1
Peele, John	3		4	8	
Hilliard, John	2	3	2		22
Narsworthy, John	1	1	1		1
Lawrence, Robert	1	4	5		17
Lawrence, John	2	5	8		27
Narsworthy, George	1	1	3		5
Narsworthy, Henry	1		5		
Dickinson, Eliza			1		9
Wood, Joseph	3	1	7		30
Wood, Henry A	1	3	1		17
Baggett, Josiah	1	1	1		1
Cotton, James, jr	5	1	2		32
Abington, Hardimon	1	2	4		17
Randolf, William	1		1		6
M°Donald, Isaac	1	2		3	12
Veal, John	1	1			23
Cotton, James			2		19
Peele, Edmund	1		5	3	
Randolph, Giles	3	2	4		14
Knox, John	2	4	1		
Temples, Solomon	4		1		
Horn, William	1	1	3		8
Horn, James	1	1	3		
White, John	3		1		9
Rutland, Thomas	1	2	1		2
Bittle, William	1				5
Peele, Thomas	1	1	4		4
Bittle, Jeremiah	1				
Daughtrey, Jesse	1	3	4		4
Cartright, William	1		3		
Outland, Jeremiah	1	4	2		
M°Donald, Peter	1	3			
Rutland, Reddick	1				4

NAME OF HEAD OF FAMILY.	Free white males of 16 years and upward, including heads of families.	Free white males under 16 years.	Free white females, including heads of families.	All other free persons.	Slaves.
Maddra, James	1	4	3		8
Hobday, Robert	2	4	4		5
Marshall, Isaac	1				1
Boddie, Willie	1	1	3		12
Lawrence, Robert, jr	1		2		
Garrott, Dan¹	1		3		2
Jordan, Benjamin	1	2	3		2
Bryan, Jane			4		
Sharrock, George	2				1
Ricks, Jacob	1				
Hiott, Elisha	1		2		
Daughtrey, Jesse, jr	1		2		
Bryan, Allen	1	4	1		1
Daughtrey, Henry	1		1		
Sherrard, Henry	1	2	2		
Daughtrey, Enos	1	1	2	1	2
Lamberson, James	1	3	4		1
Hall, Moses	1	1	1		
Hall, John	1				
Rutland, Blake	1	4	1		
Rutland, Charity			1		4
Outland, Josiah	2	3	4		4
Bass, Jethro				8	3
Bryan, Clarky	1	3	3		
Pinner, Joseph	1				
Lawrence, Elias	1		4		3
Burges, Robert	1	3	4		1
Josey, John	2	1	2		2
Bass, Council				7	2
Dortch, Isaac	1				21
Bryan, Jason	1	1	1		
Lightfoot, William	1	3	4		6
Temples, Daniel	1		3		
Carter, Brittain	2		4		
Temples, Jacob	1	1	4		
Temples, Thomas	1				
Bryan, James	1	2	3		2
Harpe, Alse		2	3		
Rich, John	1	1	3		
Roads, William	1		4		
Chase, John	1	1	4		
Baum, Adam	1		5		
Daughtrey, Eliza	1	2	1		5
Rawley, Jacob	1	1	1		
West, James	1				
Nichols, Bethias		1	3		
Mitchiner, John	1	1	5		
Jordan, Rich⁴	1				
Nichols, Lemuel	1	1	2		
Glisten, Thomas	1				
Bruce, Moses	1				
Vinson, Abner	2		3		
Tutrill, Arthur	2	1	2		
Darden, Abraham	1				19
Lawrence, Lemuel	2	2	4		
Powell, Exum	1	1	1		
Ozborne, Sarah	1		1		2
Pipkin, Stewart	1		2		9
Fawn, John	1	1	1		13
Futrill, Martha	1		1		6
Futrill, William	1		1		1
Powell, Willie	1		1		
Futrill, Sampson	1	1	1		1
Futrill, Sandras	3	3	4		
Parker, Sam¹	2		3		
Maggett, William	1		2		5
Jenkins, Winborne, jr	1		1		8
Futrill, Henry	1	1	2		1
Odam, James	3		3		
Futrill, John	1	1	2		3
Futrill, Ephraim	1	3	2		7
Jenkins, Winborne	2	2	1	2	7
Nelson, Abraham	2	4	5		
Blanchard, Ephraim	2	4	3		1
Powell, Mattᵂ	2	4	3		10
Johnston, Barnabas	2		5		6
Johnston, Barnabas, jr	1	4	1		
Fuller, Robert				4	
Lassiter, Joseph, jr	1		1		1
Lassiter, Mary			5		6
Lassiter, Joseph	2	4	6		3
Vinson, James	2	1	5		10
Roberts, Esther			5		
Cryer, Sam			5		8
Washington, Nicholson	2	6	1		7
Boon, Thomas	2	4	3		
Vinson, James, jr	2	2	2		
Conner, Burwell	1		2		
Parker, Charity	1	1	5		
Futrill, John, jr	1	1	3	1	1
Revil, Michael	1		3		
Futrill, David	1	2	4		4
Futrill, Thomas	2	1	6		3
Benthalt, Joseph			2		6
Benthalt, William	1	1	2		
Bowers, Thomas	1	1	2		

HALIFAX DISTRICT, NORTHAMPTON COUNTY—Continued.

NAME OF HEAD OF FAMILY.	Free white males of 16 years and upward, including heads of families.	Free white males under 16 years.	Free white females, including heads of families.	All other free persons.	Slaves.	NAME OF HEAD OF FAMILY.	Free white males of 16 years and upward, including heads of families.	Free white males under 16 years.	Free white females, including heads of families.	All other free persons.	Slaves.	NAME OF HEAD OF FAMILY.	Free white males of 16 years and upward, including heads of families.	Free white males under 16 years.	Free white females, including heads of families.	All other free persons.	Slaves.
Futrill, Benjamin	1					Stoke, William	1		3		2	Spraberry, Archd	1	2	2		
Long, Brittain	1		2		7	Washington, James	3				2	Griggs, Patience		2	4		
Bagby, Robert	1	6	3			Liles, Benjamin	3	4	6		2	Fulgham, Michael	2	3	4		16
Futrill, Dempsey, jr	1		4			Warren, Eliza	1	3	2		2	Prichard, Mary	1		3		3
Futrill, David, Jr	1	1	1			McLain, Lachlan	2				1	Revil, Humphrey	2	1	1		
Sherrard, Joel	1	2	1	1		Clarke, Hannah		2	2		1	Barnes, Zachariah	1	1	2		
Futrill, Dempsey	1	2	5		7	Gatts, John	1		2			Moose, John, jr	1		3		4
Smith, Jacob					4	Sherrod, Arthur	1		2	1	7	Vinson, Henry	1				1
Lassiter, Shadrack	1	2	4		1	Sherrod, Benjamin	1		2			Hill, Herman			1		2
Futrill, John	1	4	4		5	Woodard, Micajah	2	3	2			Hatton, Francis	1		2		4
Hall, William	1	1	3		10	Fly, William	1	3	5			King, Sarah			1		4
Oliver, John	1	4	3			Fly, Elisha	4	2	4			Williams, Eliza			1		1
Manly, Littleton				5		Barnes, Jane	1				2	Tucker, Drury	1				
Wood, Wynn	1		2			Butler, Kader	1	1	2			Moore, John	1				5
Bullock, James	1		1	1		Odam, Josiah	1		1			Owen, Thos	1				
Hollowell, Saml	2		3			Hogan, James	1	2	2			Hogwood, Jno	1				
Johnston, Darden	1	2	4		3	Murrill, Winborne	1	1	2		1	Hays, Saml	1		1		
Thompson, Hudson	1		3		3	Futrall, Stephen	1					Hathcock, Reubin	1	1	1		
Allen, Jeremiah	1		3			Barnes, Thomas	1	1	3			Wells, Ann				6	
Hawley, Benjamin				3		Coan, Thomas	1		1			Jenkins, Reubin	1		2		1
Sherrard, James	1		4			Woodard, Brittain	2		1			Underwood, John	1				
Manly, William				4		Maddra, William	1	2	2		2	Sikes, Jethro	1	1	3		
Lassiter, James	3	1	2			Maddra, Randolph	1	2	5		2	Mann, Theodorick	2		6	2	8
Fennell, Ann	1		4		4	Tyner, William	1		4			Dupree, Thos	1		1		
Shuffield, Ephraim	3	1	1		4	Tallow, Absalom	3	2	3			Parker, Mills	2	3	2		
Williams, Arthur	3	1	4	1	1	Tyner, Mary			4			Smith, Joseph	1	1	4		
Mabrey, Francis	3		1			Taylor, Sarah			3			Fiveash, Jas	2	5	2		
Rogers, Sarah	1		2		4	Strickland, Mary	1	1	5			Pope, Jonathan	2	4	3		3
Griffin, Robert	1	1	3		1	Strickland, John	1					Powell, John	1	2	1		
Clifton, Susannah	1		3		1	Strickland, Joseph	1		2			Hogwood, Hancil	1				
Mann, William	1	3	1			Slade, John	2					Hogwood, Howell	1				
Futrill, Joel	2	1	5	1	1	Brown, Warren	1		1			Owen, David	1				
Mann, Richard	1	2	6			Warren, Benjamin	1		4			Rowalton, Elias	1				
Lassiter, Jesse	1	1	4			Murrill, Patience			1			King, Benj., Junr	1				
Futrill, Etheldred	1	5	2		1	Strickland, Olive		1	1			Ellis, Batt	1	2	2		
Nelson, Jno	1	1	1			Johnston, Jno, jr	1	1	1		4	Collier, Joshua	2	1	2		2
Nelson, Jonas	1		1			Smith, Nathaniel	1					Daniel, James	1		2		
Parker, Richard	1	1	1			Woodard, Joseph	2		4			Sturdivant, James	1		2		2
Woodard, Oliver	2	2	1		6	Johnston, Joseph	1	1	6		4	Garner, William	2	2	3		6
Benns, Mourning	1		2		15	Strickland, Joseph	2	1	3			Smith, Lawrence	2		2		30
Crocker, Samuel	1	1	1			Burn, Jacob	2		1		3	Short, William	1		3		8
Simons, Sarah		2	2			Saunders, Thomas	1		4			Doby, Jarrot				7	
Darden, Reddrick	1	2	1		4	Luter, Hardy	1	4	4		1	Davis, Etheldred, jr	2	2	3		25
Woodard, Thomas	2	3	4	1		Smith, Jesse	2	2	2			Skinner, Kindred	1		7		
Woodard, Mary		2	1			Morgan, Sampson	1	2	5			Strickland, Drury	1	1	3		1
Coleson, James	1	2	2			Mungis, John	1	1	5			Seat, James	3	1	4		3
Smith, Robert	1	1	1			Newsom, Nelson	1					Davis, Edward, jr	1	2	2		
Futrill, Lawrence	1		1			Massingale, Abraham	1	1	7		1	Webb, Joseph	1	2	3		
Thomson, Etheldred	3	1	3		5	Phillips, Mark	1	1	4			Ricks, Dempsey	1	2	2		
Powell, Elizabeth			1	2		Parker, William	1	2	3			Parker, Saml	1		3		
Barker, River	1		2		5	Meacham, Henry, junr	1		5		2	Daughtrey, Lewis	1	3	4		
Cook, Christopher	1	1	3			Norwood, William	3	3	6		17	Dickinson, David	1	1	1		23
Rogers, Benjamin	1					Millikin, James	1	3	3			Phillips, Mark	1	1	4		
Warren, Joshua	2				1	Webb, Joseph	1		4			Howell, Ason				6	
Strickland, Benjamin	1	3	2			Seat, Gerrard	1	2	4			Clade, John	1	4	6		9
Tyner, John	4	2	3		12	Newsom, James	1	1	1			Gay, Henry	2	4	2		
Fly, Elisha, jr	1	1	1		1	Bradley, James	1				3	Stephenson, Silas	1	1	1		
Liles, Jesse	2	1	1		3	Smith, John	1	2	2		4	Mann, Richard	1	2	6		
Boon, John	2	3	5		10	Young, Gerrard	1		2			Dupree, Thomas	1		1		
Tyner, Nicholas	1	2	2		9	Powell, William	1		2			Cornet, Byrd	1		2		
Long, Joice	2	1	4		11	Crump, Richd	1		1		8	Drake, Jordan	1		2		
Sherrod, Mary			2		9	Webb, Mary		3	2		2	Smith, Joseph	1	1	4		
Warren, Robert	2		3	1	2	Gee, James T	1	1	2		12	Massingale, Abraham	1	1	7		1
Gray, Hannah		2	4			Jones, Robert	2				29	Boon, Jacob	1	2	6		
Murrill, Benjamin	1		1		5	Hart, Warren	2	3	2		4	Mann, Nathan	1		3		
Fly, John	2	2	4			Snipes, John	2					Edwards, Martha	2	6	1		3
Boon, Thomas	1		1		3	Tarver, Billison	1	3	7			Duberry, Solo	1		6		3
Judkins, Joel	1	2			1	Tarver, James	1	1	6		3	Horn, William	1		6		18
Judkins, James	1	2	3	1	1	Rowell, William	1		4		5	Hart, Thomas	1	1	1		12
Gardner, Nathan	2	1	3	1	2	Vaughan, Fredk	1		4			Rutland, Wilson	1	1	2		
Rodgers, Joseph	1	2	2		2	Hill, Henry	1	2	3		3	Cotton, Roderick	1				5
Edmunds, Howell	2		1		25	Wheeler, Henry	1	2	1			Poysland, Sabestian	1				29
Futrill, Jos	1	1	3			Hart, Jno	2	4	2		12	Rutland, Sion	1				
Figures, Mattw	2				8	Jones, William	1	2	1			Moore, Duke	1		1		
Mosson, Richd	1		1		3	Barnes, Moses	1	2	2			Ricks, William	1	2	2		4
Figures, Batt	1	3			4	Wilkinson, James	1		1			Sumner, Sarah	1	1	4		4
Coakley, Benjamin	2	1	4		15	Seat, John, jr	1				2	Odam, Josiah	2	3	6		
Hotfield, Benja	2		6	3		Wheeler, Boon	1	1	2			Benn, George	1		5		4
Hotfield, John	1	1				Gay, Henry	1	4	2			Brown, William	1	1	5		
Skinner, James	1				1	Chappell, Mary	1		3			Fennell, Jno	1		4		
Judkins, Carolus	1		3			Massey, John	1	1	1		1	Futrill, Nathan	1		1		
Riggen, Jonathan	1		2			Tarver, Andrew	2				3	Mann, Nathan	1		1		
Odam, Willie	1	1	1			Snipes, Robert	3		3		4	Lawrence, Elisha	1	1	2		
Figg, Joseph	1		1			Thompson, Henry	1	2	1			Parker, Lemuel	1	1	2		3
Horn, William	1		2			Carr, Jno	1					Parker, Susannah		1	3		2
Lowerby, Henry	2		2		11	Edwards, Isaac	1	2	2			Davis, James	1	2	3		3
Atkinson, William	1		2			Revil, Mattw	1	1	1			Rodgers, Joseph	2	3	3		
Jenkins, Dew	1	1	7			Smith, Jos	1					Deloatch, Thos	1		1		
Faircloth, Newsom	1	1	2			Seat, Jno, Senr	3	1	1			Stewart, Rebecca			3		
Boon, William	1	1	3		1	Luter, John	1					Odam, Jacob	2	2	3		
Franklin, William	1		4			Mac Dowell, James	2	1	3		2	Parker, Jos	1		1		
Powell, Thomas	3					Harris, Thomas	4		1		14	Benthall, Laban	1	1	2	8	1
Stephenson, Abraham	2		4		21	Sparks, William	1	1	1			Manuel, Christo					
Ramsey, Henry	2	1	2	1	12	Coats, John	1	1	3			Johnston, Joseph	1	1	6		4
Edmunds, Nicholas	1				8	Boon, Lewis	1	3	3			Fryer, William	1		2		
Cobb, Absalom	2		1		10	Prichard, Presley	1					Tadlock, Thos	1	1	2		3
Daughtrey, Jeremiah	2		4		13	Elren, John	1	1	2		1						

HALIFAX DISTRICT, NORTHAMPTON COUNTY—Continued.

Column headers for each block: Name of head of family | Free white males of 16 years and upward, including heads of families | Free white males under 16 years | Free white females, including heads of families | All other free persons | Slaves

Name of head of family	FWM 16+	FWM <16	FW females	Other free	Slaves
Sikes, Gethro	1	1	3		3
Boon, Jos	1	3	3		3
Clall, Abram	2	3	7		
Lassiter, Shad	1	3	1		1
Odam, Moses	1		3		8
Rogers, Abram	1	3	5		
Fetts, Archibald	1	1	2	1	
Medling, Mich¹, Jr	1		2		10
Norfleet, Marma	1				6
Bryan, Sarah		2	1		10
Parker, Jeremiah	1		2	1	1
Parker, Amos	1	1	5		
Scott, Stephen	1	2	1		7
Bass, Dempsey	1				
Peete, Mary			3		11
Bryan, Thomas	1		3		11
Ogborne, Charles	1	1	1		11
Winborne, Bryan	3		4		8
Dupree, John	1	2	7		
Flanner, Wᵐ, Jr	1				
Winborne, Will	2		3		4
Boon, James	1				
Howell, Elisha	1				
Howell, Will	2	1			

Name of head of family	FWM 16+	FWM <16	FW females	Other free	Slaves
Murfree, Margaret			1		
Byrd, Phil				5	
Walden, Michael				5	
Winborne, Will, jr	1				1
Allen, Will	1				
Duke, Sherrard	1				
Volentine, Nath¹	2		1		
Sharp, James	1		2		
Griffin, Mattʷ	1	2	4		7
Parker, Joseph	3		3		
Winborne, Dempsey	1				
Goodwyn, Pitt	1				
Taylor, Sylvia	1	1	1		1
Bittle, Eliza		3	4		5
Luten, Henry	1	2	5		
Parker, James	1	1	1		
Parker, Jacob	3	5	4		
Brewer, Jnᵒ	1	2	4		3
Moore, Will	1				
Gibbs, Thoˢ	1	1			1
Ezell, Isaac	1	3	2		
Pace, Hardy	2	2	3		29
Ricks, Betty			2		1
Branch, Mary		3	2		23

Name of head of family	FWM 16+	FWM <16	FW females	Other free	Slaves
Dawson, John					18
McLellen, Phillip	1	2	3		28
Whitaker, Richᵈ	1		3		6
Roe, Salley			4		
Sikes, Charity		1	3		
Atheridge, Anne		3	2		4
Sikes, Milly		1	1		
Godwin, Josiah	1				
Morgan, Humphrey	1	2	6		
Hays, Elijah	1	3			
Stewart, Christo				3	
Mitchell, Joyce				2	
Chace, Jnᵒ	1	1	3		
Byrd, Ruth					5
Cobb, Martha			2		
Cuningham, Charity					2
Plumbly, Obediah					7
Mitchell, George	1		2		
Daughtrey, Mʳˢ		3	3		
Branch, Benjamin	1		1	1	
Byrd, Nathan					8
Dales, William				10	
Jones, Allen, Esqʳ	10	5	13		177

HALIFAX DISTRICT, WARREN COUNTY.

Name of head of family	FWM 16+	FWM <16	FW females	Other free	Slaves
Alston, James	1	3	4		31
Armistead, William	1	2	2		5
Alexander, John	1				12
Allen, Jones R	1		1		
Allen, George	1	1	4		
Allen, William	1	1	3		1
Archur, William	1		6		
Allen, George, Senr	1		2		
Adams, John	1		2		12
Anders, William	2	4	4		7
Anderson, Daniel	5	4	2		7
Allen, John	1	5	4		7
Arnold, Solomon	2	3	6		1
Allen, Vinson	1		2		4
Allen, Charles	1	3	1		
Allen, George	1	2	2		3
Allen, James	1	1	1	1	
Allen, Charles, Sen	1	4	4		8
Arranton, James	1	2	5		4
Alston, Henry	2	2	4		41
Alston, Sam¹	1				31
Acock, John	2	3	4		
Alston, William	1	8	3		105
Phillip, A. G	2		5		42
Alston, Thomas W	2	2	2		39
Acree, Isaac	3		3		7
Allen, William	1				
Aslen, Lawrence	1	3	3		
Ballard, Jesse	1	1	2		
Balthrop, Augustin	2	1	5		10
Bell, Amey		2	6		
Bell, Mary	3	1	4		
Brown, James	1		2		
Bell, Thomas	1	1	3		
Bell, Charles	1	3	5	1	
Baxter, John	1	2	4		
Balthrop, William	1	4	4		
Baxter, James	1	2	4		
Brown, John	1	6	6		8
Baxter, John	1		2		
Bell, John	1	2	1		
Bobbet, Joshua	1	1	1		2
Blanchet, Henry	1	1	1		
Brown, Jeremiah	2		3		10
Barrow, Daniel	2		4		13
Bartholomew, John	1	3	2		10
Bilbro, Berry	1	1	5		
Blanchard, Sam¹	1	2	3		
Burford, Phillip	2				21
Burchet, William	1	2	3		6
Burford, Phillip	2	3	4		3
Bush, Jeremiah	1	2	5		6
Biard, Anthony	2	3	5		
Butrel, Thomas	1	1	2		1
Ballard, William	3	3	5		
Beasley, William	1		2		
Bobbet, Stephen	1	5	3		4
Barrow, William	2	2	2		10
Burrow, Thomas	1	1	1		2
Bartholomew, Lewis	1				
Bobbet, John	1		2		2
Bobbet, Drury	1	1	3		9
Basford, Patty	1	3	2		
Bartholomew, Charles	2	1	3		
Bobbet, Randolph	1	2	1		
Bobbet, John	1	1	1		8
Bennet, Joseph	1	1	4		3
Ballard, William	1		2		5

Name of head of family	FWM 16+	FWM <16	FW females	Other free	Slaves
Brown, James	1	1	2		
Blanch, Hezᵏ	2	2	2		2
Bradley, James	1	2	2		5
Bobbit, Miles	2	1	6		
Bobbit, Lewis	1	4	4		1
Brehon, G. James	3		2		16
Berry, William	1		4		
Boothe, Geo	1	3	4		
Berry, William	4	1	3		1
Burchet, Isaac	1		2		
Boothe, Eppa	1		1		
Boothe, John	1				
Bell, John	1	2	3		
Bullock, Len H	1	2	3		51
Buckham, James	2	5	7		
Bowdown, John	1	1	7		9
Bukham, William	2		6		
Bennet, Reuben	1	1	3		
Beckham, Solomon	1	1	2		
Beckham, Jesse	1	2	3		4
Beckham, Stephen	2	4	4		
Ball, Daniel	1	1	2		1
Ball, James	1	3	3		
Beckham, William	1	2	2		
Beckham, Phillip	1	3	9		1
Brown, Archᵈ	1	2	3		
Beckham, Benj	1	1	3		
Ballard, Lewis	1				
Beckham, Simon	1	5	1		1
Beckham, William	3	1	2		2
Bennet, Reuben, Jr	4		2		
Basket, Pleasant	4		4		8
Brogdon, William	2		3		
Bagby, William	2		2		20
Brown, John	1	4	8		9
Burt, William	2	2	3		20
Blanch, Tho	2	3	5		1
Beasley, Pitts	1	2	4		10
Betty, George	3	4	3		
Brewer, Hezekiah	1	2	6		
Bennet, Moses	1	1	2		
Blanchard, Thomas	2	5	2		
Blackburn, Elias	1	1	2		
Breedlove, John	1	3			7
Bennet, Nancey		1	1	1	
Bradley, William				3	3
Bennet, James	1	4	5		
Boswell, Ransom	1		1		10
Bartlet, Sam¹	1	2	2		1
Bell, Charles	1		1		
Bell, Jesse	4	1	5		1
Clanton, Ede	1	1	1		
Cyaras	1				
Colclough, Rice	1				2
Crain, Stephen	1	2	2		4
Capps, Henry	1	2	4		
Capps, John	1	2	6		1
Capps, Caleb	1	3	5		
Capps, Orasha	2	3	4		
Capps, Frances	1	2	1		6
Cyress, Fredᵏ	1		2		4
Capps, John	1		1		
Cocke, Joseph	1	3	1	1	35
Cheek, John	1		3		7
Cheek, William	2		2		18
Cheek, Randolph	1		2		4
Capps, Joshua	3	2	4		
Capps, Frances	1	1	4		

Name of head of family	FWM 16+	FWM <16	FW females	Other free	Slaves
Clark, William	2	6	4		
Cogwill, Isrom	3	2	4		
Cogwill, James	1	2	2		1
Chism, Benjamin	1				
Christmas, William	1		1		4
Clemmons, William	1		1		9
Clark, William	2	1	2		
Clark, John	1	6	4		
Cooper, William	2	2	3		3
Corsey, William	1	2	3		
Cauthron, William	1	3	2		1
Cole, Rhoda	1	2	3		1
Carten, Job	1	2	1		4
Cauthron, John	1	1	4		10
Cauthron, James	1	2	4		3
Clark, Lenn	1	1	1		
Christmas, Tho	2	1	5		23
Clark, Thomas	2		3		1
Capps, Hillery	1	1	2		
Clanton, Dudley	1				8
Clanton, Francis	3	1	2		16
Cheatham, James	1	4	2		8
Coleman, Sam¹	1	1	2		
Carrol, Thomas	1	4	6		6
Connell, Avery	1		1		
Croctor, Robert	1		3		
Cimp, William	1	1	2		
Colemon, Peter	2	1	2		5
Crutchfield, Sam¹	2	4	2		
Caller, James	1	1	1		13
Calvany, James	2		1		
Caller, Robert	2		1		36
Clack, John	1				
Clack, Sterling	1	2	3		
Cox, Peter	1		3		16
Crysick, Jemina	1	3	8		1
Christmas, Henry	2				4
Christmas, William	1		1		9
Christian, Giddion	2	1	2		8
Cannon, James	1	3	1		2
Coleman, Edward	2	2	2		1
Colelough, John	2	3	6		12
Clayborn, John	1	3	3		2
Colelough, Rice	1				2
Durham, John	1	1	7		4
Dunn, James	1	1	1		4
Duke, William	1		1		4
Davis, Jonathan	1	6	1		16
Duke, Simon	1	1	4		1
Dye, Martin	1	4	2		6
Duke, William	1	1	1		3
Daniel, Peter	1		4		2
Davis, Joshua	2	4	4		17
Dent, Susanah			2		4
Dent, William	2	2	2		
Dent, Isabell			2		
Davis, John	2	4	3		
Darden, James	1	3	2		8
Dorson, Henry	1	1	2		1
Dowden, John	1	3	3		2
Davis, Thomas	1	6	2		
Duke, Hardy	1	2	1		
Duke, Ransom	1		1		2
Duke, Repps	1				2
Duke, John	1	4	6		11
Duke, Isham	1	1	1		1
Davis, John	1	4	3		
Duke, Matthew	1	4	3		5

HALIFAX DISTRICT, WARREN COUNTY—Continued.

NAME OF HEAD OF FAMILY.	Free white males of 16 years and upward, including heads of families.	Free white males under 16 years.	Free white females, including heads of families.	All other free persons.	Slaves.
Davis, Mattw	1	3	9		10
Duke, William	2	4	2		53
Daniel, Sarah	2		4		16
Duke, Green	3	2	6		45
Daniel, John W	2		3		11
Drury, Charles	2	1	2		
Duncan, Blanch	1	2	3		
Duke, Saml	1		1		
Daniel, John	1	1	3		3
Daniel, Ruben	1	1	4		4
Duke, Burwell	1	4	8		4
Duke, Harrold	1	2	2		
Duke, Brittin	1	4	4		13
Dewilen, James	2		8		8
Davis, Peter	2	3	4		9
Davis, Burwill	1	1	2		1
Davis, Jiles	1	2	3		2
Davis, Saml	1	2	3		8
Elliott, William	1	2	4		
Evans, James				9	
Estes, John	3	3	4	1	
Emmerson, Catron	1	1	1		3
Eaton, Thomas	1	1	3		138
Eagerton, Wilmot	1	3	3		3
Ellis, Edwd	2		4		
Ellis, Martha	1	3	4		2
Ellis, Bray	3	3	3		3
Ellis, John	2	5	3		6
Ellis, Richard	1	3	4		1
Ellis, John	1	1	2		
Ellis, William	2	2	5		1
Ellms, James	1	1	1		3
Ellenton, James	2	1	4		3
Ellenton, Dan'l	1	1	4		
Ellenton, John	1	5	6		9
Ellenton, William	2	2	5		1
Ellis, Ephraim	1	3	4		4
Ellis, William	1	1	5		
Evans, Isaac				9	
Finly, John	1	1	2		
Freeman, Arthur	2	1	3		2
Fain, William	1				
Fain, Joel	1				
Fogg, Joseph	1			6	
Freeman, Robert	1		1		22
Featherston, John	1	2	3		
Fool, Henry	2		4		6
Fool, William	1	1	3		3
Fills, Henry	2	1	3		16
Faulion, John	2	1	3		78
Fills, Nathan	2		2		
Fills, Hardy	1				
Fills, Isham	1	2	1		
Fills, Nathan	1	2	3		
Fills, John	1	2	3		
Fowler, Thomas	1		2		11
Fills, Cary	1	1	1		3
Forkner, William	2	1	1		8
Fills, Francis	2	3	6		
Flemming, John	1	2	3		
Flemming, Peter	3	1	5		
Flemming, William	1	2	3		
Flemming, Thos	1	5	1		
Fussell, Aaron	1	1	2		10
Forkner, Hardy	1		2		
Forkner, Moses	1	3	2		
Forkner, John	1	5	4		
Forkner, Emanul	2		2		
Fussell, John	1	1	1		
Fain, Ann		1	3		6
Glover, John	1	1	2		
Gressam, Oliver	1	2	4		5
Gill, John	1		1		
Goodwin, Jane		2	1		
Gardner, Mary			3		
Granshaw, William	1		1		
Green, Josiah	2	3	4		7
Gregory, James	1	4	1		
Garrot, Thomas	1	5	7		
Garrot, Matthew	1	3	9		4
Goodfrey, James	1	2	3		
Guthrie, William	1	2	3		5
Garrot, William	2	1	3		
Gray, Benj	1	3	4		
Green, Solomon	1	1	2		12
Green, Edmund	1		1		11
Galespe, Robert	1		3		
Green, Tho	4	1	2		13
Green, John	1				6
Granshaw, John	2	1	2		1
Garrald, John	1	3	5		
Glover, Henry	3	2	3		
Green, William	2	1	7		61
Gray, William	1	6	4		
Gardner, Tho	1	1	3		6
Gorden, James	1	2	2		7
Green, Josiah	1	3	4		8
Harriss, John					6
Hazard, John	1	2	2		
Harriss, Billy		3	3		3
Hilton, Dianah			2		
Howard, Thomas	1				
Hamer, Brittin J	1	2	3		4
Hevlin, Benjamin	1	2	3		
Haines, John	1	3	3		
Huddleston, Robt	1	1	4		1
Harton, Howell	1	5	4		1
Harton, John	1	1	4		
Hall, Thomas	1	2	2		
Hastings, James	1				
Harton, Tho	1	2	2		
Howard, Charles	1				
Huff, Tho	1				10
Hunter, James	1	1	1		6
Hunter, Isaac	2	2	4		33
Hicks, Charles	1	1	3		
Hastings, Jeremiah	3	1	3		
Hawks, Fredk	3	4	3		
Hasting, John	2	2	3		
Hicks, John	1	5	4		1
Hicks, Susanah		1	1		
Hawkins, Wyatt	2	2	3		5
Harriss, Jordan	2	1	7		6
Harriss, Bedford	1	1	1		
Hail, Dudley	1	2	3		5
Harriss, Rachael	1	1	3		5
Harriss, Howard	1	2	2		1
Hudson, John	1	1	3		
Holleman, William	1	4	3		2
Hazlewood, Warwick	2	1	3		1
Harriss, Edwin	1	4	2		
Holleman, Blake	1	1	2		
Harriss, Claborn	1	1	1		
Harriss, Joseph	2		5		
Hawkins, John, Sen	2		1		3
Harriss, Michael	2	1	2		
Harper, Joseph	2	2	5		16
Harriss, Simon	1	1	2		2
Harris, James	1	2	4		
Harriss, James	1	3	4		4
Harris, Robt	1	1	1		
Harris, Sterling	1	1	5		7
Harriss, James	1	2	5		7
Harris, Fredk	1				2
Harriss, Harbert	1	1	1		1
Hazlewood, Randolph	1	1	2		9
Harriss, Mattw	1		1		9
Harriss, Edmd	1	3	4		
Hamlet, Richard	1	2	5		
Harriss, Elisha	1	1	3		
Harriss, Catron	2	3	3		4
Hogwood, William	1	1	1		1
Harper, William	1	1	2		1
Hudson, Henry	1	3	4		
Harriss, Newel	2	3	5		10
Haynes, Harbert	1				138
Harriss, Nelson	1				
Haethcock, John	2	4	2		2
Hilliard, Thomas	1	1	4		4
Hammock, Charles	1		3		
House, James	2	5	3		5
Harrisson, William	1		4		1
Harriss, Ransom	1	3	2		1
House, Dudley	1	2	3		
House, William	3	2	1		16
Hawkins, Philemon, H. T.	1	3	3		10
Hawkins, Philemon, Esq.	1	6	5		62
Harris, Isham	3	2	4		11
Harriss, Nusom	1	3	2		
Harriss, James	1	2	4		
Hawkins, Phil., Jr	2			1	5
Hawkins, Phil., Sen., Esq.	2		1	1	54
Howard, William	1	4	2		
Hawkins, Benj	2				19
Jackson, Jeremiah	1				
Jones, Susanah					6
Israel, Nancy		2	2		
Jones, Joshua	2	3	7		1
Jones, Richard	1				
Jeffreys, Peyton	1				
Jones, Martha		1	3		
Jones, Robt	1	5	5		1
Jackson, Drury	2	4	2	1	3
Johnston, William E	2				44
Johnson, Terasha	1	2	3		3
Johnson, Michl	1	4	4		
Jenkins, Jesse	1	4	6		11
John, Saint William	1	1	2		5
Johnson, Benj	2	3	4		21
Jackson, Benj	1	3	4		5
Jordan, Marcillus	2	2	7		28
Jenkins, Jeremiah	1	4	3		7
Jones, Leonard	1	4	7		
Johnson, Phillip	1	4	5		
Ivey, Peter	1	1	1		1
Johnson, John	1				
Johnson, Hugh	2	1	2		20
Johnson, M. Duke	4	3	5	1	35
Johnson, Joseph	1				
James, Isaac	1	3	4		3
Jones, Peter	1				5
Jones, Sugars	1	2	3		12
Johnson, James	2	3	2		23
Jones, Edward	3	3	6		32
Jones, Robert	1	2	5		16
Judkins, Thomas	4	1	1		2
James, George	1	1	1		
James, Charles	1	1	1		2
Jones, John	2	3	7		2
Johnson, William	2	1	2		39
Kindruk, Isham	1	2	1		4
Kinnemon, Philemon	2	1	3		
Kelly, Thomas	1	3	4		
Kimbell, Nathl	1	4	4		
Kimbell, David	1	3	1		1
King, Geo	1	1	2		3
Key, Luck	2	2	5		
Kimbell, James	1	3	2		6
Kimbell, Ransom	2	2	2		5
Kimbell, Benj., Sen	2	1	2		8
Kicker, John	2		7		
Knight, William	1				
Kerny, James	2		3		31
King, Anthony	1	2	3		
King, Charles	1	2	2		1
King, David	2	2	2		
Kerny, Phillip	2	2	5		88
Kelly, Benj	1	2	3		1
Kimbell, Leonard	1	2	3		1
Kimbell, Spell	1	5	2		
Kimbell, Benj	2	1	2		8
Knowls, Butler	1				
Knowles, Laurance	1	3	3		2
Knowls, William	2	3	4		
Little, Susanah	1	3	3		
Lancaster, John	1	3	2		
Lindsey, Joseph	2		2		
Lindsey, Laborn	1	2	2		1
Lain, Jesse	1				
Lee, Joseph	2				2
Lashley, Howell	1	1	1		2
Laughter, John	1	2	5		3
Laughter, William	1		2		
Lanier, John	2	1	2		8
Lamkin, Leanah			6		
Lancaster, Lawrne	1				
Lancaster, Joel	1	5	6		
Lancaster, James	1	3	2		
Lancaster, Moses	1	3	3		
Mills, Daniel	1				
Marshall, Hezb	1	1	5		
McClannan, John	1				1
Mabry, John	1	1	5		
Malone, William	1				
Mealer, James	1	2	3		1
Mabry, Mattw	1	5	5		15
Moss, Wilkins	1	3	4		
Merret, Silvanis	1	3	5		
Meadows, Isham	3	7	2		
Moss, Richard	1	3	5		3
Myrick, Richard	1	2	2		5
Massey, Hezekiah	1	2	2		
Macon, G. Hunt	1	2	3		21
Mayfield, Tho	1	1	5		23
Mills, James	2		1		11
Maddra, William	2	6	1		
Morriss, William	1	2	2		
Morriss, Saml	1	3	5		1
Marshall, Stephen	1		3		2
Marshall, Saml	2	5	7		
Moore, Lewis	1	2	5		
Moody, Tho	2	2	2		15
Marshall, Richd	1	2	5		8
Musten, William	1	5	1		
Musten, Patty		5	1		
Mosely, James	2	1	2		8
Marshall, Isaac	3		2		
Malone, John	3	1	5		
Moore, Mark	1				5
Myrick, Mattw	1				20
Moore, Thomas	1				
Mabry, Dilk	1	2	5		1
Meadows, Isham	1	4			
Mabry, Benj	1	2	4		1
Myrick, Moses	2				19
Myrick, William	1	2	2		3
Maddra, Richard	2	2	2		2
Myrick, James	2	1	3		22

HALIFAX DISTRICT, WARREN COUNTY—Continued.

NAME OF HEAD OF FAMILY.	Free white males of 16 years and upward, including heads of families.	Free white males under 16 years.	Free white females, including heads of families.	All other free persons.	Slaves.
Moore, Higdon	1	2	3		
Montford, Henry	1	1	3	2	16
Mabry, Joshua	1		2		11
Mayfield, Abram	1		1		22
Marshall, Dixon	1	1	4		
Marks, William	1	5	3		
Mabry, Repps	1	2	3		5
Mayfield, John	2	5	4		5
Moss, William	1				
Moss, David	3	4	5		21
Mabry, Charles	1	4	2		2
Milam, Drury	1	1	2		
Mosely, John	2				11
May, Enoch	1		2	1	
Milam, Rowland	1	2	2	1	
Mitchell, James	1	1	6	5	
Mosely, Jesse	2	2	2		12
Miller, Mary			1		11
Myrick, Matthew	2	2	5		2
Malone, Miles	1				
Miller, Thomas	3	4	5		39
Milam, James	1	3	4	1	
Malone, John	1				
Murrah, Charles	1	3	4		
Hawkin, John	2	3	5		56
Mayfield, Edwd	1	1	2		3
Marshal, Tibatha	1	1	3		15
McLemore, Atkins	1		3		16
Munday, Edwd	1	1	2		
Morriss, Mary	2	1	4		12
Merret, James	1	3	3		
Moss, Benj	2		2		2
Macon, John	2	3	4		36
Macon, Nathl	1	1	2		20
Mannen, Saml	1	1	3		
Macon, Saml	1	1	3		4
Marshall, Mattw	1				6
Monger, Tabitha	3	3	2		
Muckleroyah, John	1		1		1
Marcus, William	1		1		
Mabry, Gray	1	2	3		15
Nichols, Alexander	1	3	4		
Neal, Ralph	3	2	2		14
Nichols, James	1	1	2		
Nichols, Urbane	1	2	4		4
Nichols, Archd	1		5		1
Nichols, Davis	2	1	2		16
Nichols, Brittin	2	1	3		12
Newman, Tho	1		1		
Newman, Tho., Sen	1				1
Newman, Avery	1	2	2		
Neal, Aron	1	2	2		
Neal, Jeremiah	1		1		2
Neal, Moses	1	1	2		
Normon, William	1		2		
Normon, Saml				2	
Narsworthy, Wm N	3	3	4		3
Nichols, George	1				
Nichols, Michl	2		1		7
Newell, John	3		3		9
Nichols, James	2	1	1		13
Narsworthy, James	1	2	2		
Neal, Ralph, Jr	1	2	5		
Normon, Thomas	3	1	3		
Newmon, Daniel	1		1		
Night, Betty			2		
Newell, William	1		1		4
Newell, John	1				2
Owens, James	1	1	2		39
Owens, John	1	1	1		
Pope, Umphrey	1	1	1		
Partrick, Rubin	1		3		
Patterson, John	1		1		
Parrish, Edwd	1	2	4		
Patterson, James	1	1	2		
Patterson, Geo	2	1	1		
Patterson, Calway	1				
Pryor, William	1	2	3		
Patterson, Lewis	1	3	2		
Price, William W	1	1	5		
Person, Thomas	3		1		58
Pegram, Edwd	1	4	3		
Pickrell, Walker	1		4		
Paschael, Saml	1	2	2		8
Partrick, Lewis	1	3	3		3
Pascheal, Tho	1	6	3		6
Partrick, John	1	2	3		3
Procter, Richd	2	1	4		5
Pattersen, Peterson	2		1		5
Powell, Honorius	1	2	1		3
Person, Jesse	2	4	5		9
Powell, Wm	3	1	2		22
Powell, James	1				5
Patterson, Isham	1	2	3		
Perry, Joshua	2		3		20
Perry, William	2	1	7		4
Parrott, Nathl	1	1	4		
Paschael, Dennis	3	5	5		
Paschael, James	3	5	5		
Paschael, Elisha	3	5	5		
Paschael, Anderson	1				
Pegram, Danl	2	2	4		1
Pegram, Geo	2	3	5		
Pegram, William	1	4	2		
Pryor, John	1		3		4
Pegram, Giddeon	1				
Paine, James	1	2	8		26
Peebles, Thomas	1				1
Peebles, Nathan	2				4
Pardiew, Joseph	1	1	1		
Pardiew, William	1	1	3		2
Pardiew, John	1	5	3		
Proctor, Micajah	1	1	3		
Park, Betty	2	2	7		69
Person, William	1	1	2		22
Patterson, Eliz			3		
Patterson, Patty		1	4		
Pardiew, Beverly	1	5	2		
Plummer, Kemp	1				38
Pardiew, Patram	1	4	1		
Petway, John	1	4	2		22
Riggan, William	1	4	2		
Ransome, James	1		2		24
Reed, Tho	3	1	4		3
Riggan, Joel	1	2	2		
Riggan, John	2	3	4		1
Robbins, William	1				
Richardson, Lawrne	1	1	2		4
Rose, Ann	1	3	3		
Russell, Ann	1	3	1		17
Russell, William	3	4	4		5
Raibon, George	1	2	2		
Robertson, Mima	1	1	1		5
Robertson, Christo	1		2		16
Robertson, Isham	1	2	4		10
Rowland, William	3	3	4		2
Riggan, William	1	1	2		
Robertson, William	2	1	7		4
Riggan, Francis	2		5		3
Reeves, Joshua	1	2	4		
Reeves, William	1	1	1		3
Reed, William	1		5		
Riggan, Charles	1	2	7		
Redwood, James	1		1		
Riggan, Mary		1	2		
Rice, John	1	4	1		
Robertson, Burwell	1	4	4		20
Roirce, William	2				1
Reed, Dempsey					8
Redford, John	1	2	2		
Reeves, Joel	2	3	6		12
Sledge, James	1	4	4		9
Senseng, John	1	4	4		1
Senseng, Peter	1		2		
Stephens, Joseph	1	3	4		4
Stokes, Saml	1	5	1		1
Sosebery, Benj	1	1	1		5
Stokely, Jehue	1	3	2		1
Stephenson, Saml	1	1	2		2
Scott, John	2		4		9
Stiles, James	1		2		
Sheren, Isham	1		2		
Shearin, Lewis	1	1	4		1
Sherin, Sterling	1	2	2		5
Sherin, Fredk	2	2	1		2
Story, William	2	1	3		
Sherin, John	2	3			
Shearin, Amey	2		3		13
Shell, Stephen	1	4	6		3
Shell, Stephen, Sen	1	2	5		9
Sledge, Joel	1				
Sledge, Daniel	2		2		19
Sims, Elisha	3	4	4	2	9
Smith, William	2	2	4		17
Sartin, John	1		4		4
Simms, Lennard	1	3	3		36
Simms, Thomas	2	1	8		6
Short, John	3	1	1		
Sartin, Tho	1	2	3		
Shearin, William	2		9		19
Simms, Thomas	1	3	3		1
Sumner, E. Thomas	1				15
Sanders, John	2	4	4		5
Smith, Frank	2	4	4		
Storey, John	1	3	4		
Smelty, John	1	1	1		6
Standback, Patty		3	6		
Sherin, Aaron	1	2	1		
Shearin, William	1	1	1		
Shearin, William	1	2	6		
Snow, Spencer	1	3	4		4
Shers, Isham	2	1	1		
Swinny, Tho	1	1	8		
Saml, Andrew	1	1	1		5
Shearin, Major	1	3	4		
Sturdevent, Henry	1	3	5		
Sturdevent, Randb	1	1	5		3
Sallmon, Jonathan	1	2	3		
Shearin, Fredk	1				1
Sutton, Richd	1	1	1		4
Sutton, William	1	1	1		1
Simms, Edwd	1	2	4		7
Shearin, Moses	1	3	4		2
Tucker, John	1	1	1		
Tucker, Claibon	1				
Tucker, Henry	1	2	3		
Tucker, Claiborn	1	1	4		
Tucker, John	1		4		1
Tucker, John, Jun	2		3		9
Twetty, Peter	1	3	4		
Turner, Edward	1	1	3		
Tucker, Henry	1				
Thornton, Francis	1			3	25
Thornton, Betty		3	4		
Thomas, William	1	3	4		1
Taylor, Howell	1				20
Tanner, John	1	3	1		25
Thompson, Drury	1	3	3		
Turner, John	2				39
Thompson, John	1		1		3
Taylor, Samuel	1	3	2		1
Tucker, Willis	3	2	3		
Tuttle, Jeremiah	1				
Thomas, David	1	2	2		
Tattey, Fredk	1	5	3		3
Towns, David	2	2	8		5
Thomas, Richd	1	3	5		4
Tunns, Richd	2	3	4		1
Thorn, Thomas	1		8		
Tunstall, Richd	1				
Thorn, Charles	1				4
Thorn, Presley	1	2	3		3
Turner, Tirasha	1	2	2		7
Tycer, Richd	1	3	4		
Turner, Stephen	2	3	3		11
Terry, Benjamin	1	2	6		
Turner, James	1				20
Thompson, James	1	1			8
Thompson, William	1	3	3		
Urlls, Obed	1	2	4		
Vaulx, Daniel	1	1	5		17
Vanlandingham, Dorson	2	4	4		1
Vaughan, Vincent	1	1	4		
Virser, Wm	1	3	5		1
Willson, Richard	1		4		
Wood, Bennet	2	1	5		1
Wilson, Thomas	1	1			
White, John	4	3	6		3
White, Admeral	1	2	2		
Wilson, Tho	5	1	1		
Walker, Partrick	2				1
Williams, Lewis	1	2	5		
Williams, Amey			3		4
Wortham, William	2				3
Williams, Duke	1	1	3		4
Williams, Wyatt	1	1	9		18
Williams, Benj	1	4	1		11
Weathers, John	1				1
Wynn, John	1	2	6		8
Ward, Gilbert	1		1		
Wood, Misell	1				
Wright, Brittin	1		4		
White, Cajabeth	2	1	8		3
Williams, William	2	1	4		3
Waller, Robt	1		3		15
Wilson, Daniel	1	5	4		4
Wilson, William	1		1		5
Wilson, Robert	1		1		
Williams, Unity		2	4		1
Wilson, John	1	3	4		
Walden, Eaton				3	
Williford, Saml	3	3	5		
Williams, Sarah			2		2
Webb, George	2	3	2		2
Williams, Henry	2				49
Ward, Elizabeth	1	1	4	1	40
Williams, Saml	1		2		15
Williams, William	1		3		42
Williams, Solo	2		4		25
Wilden, William	2		2		2
Williamson, Wm	3	2	4		6
Walker, William	3	2	4		2
Ward, Benjamin	1		1		8
Ward, John	1				6
Ward, Ann	1	3	4		8
West, William	1	2	2		
Williams, Simon	3	1	6		26
Williams, Parmenas	2	3	4		23
Wilson, Mary			4		
Williams, John	2	1	3		7
Williams, Francis	2	2	4		8
Williams, Ashkinar	2	4	4		

HALIFAX DISTRICT, WARREN COUNTY—Continued.

NAME OF HEAD OF FAMILY.	Free white males of 16 years and upward, including heads of families.	Free white males under 16 years.	Free white females, including heads of families.	All other free persons.	Slaves.	NAME OF HEAD OF FAMILY.	Free white males of 16 years and upward, including heads of families.	Free white males under 16 years.	Free white females, including heads of families.	All other free persons.	Slaves.	NAME OF HEAD OF FAMILY.	Free white males of 16 years and upward, including heads of families.	Free white males under 16 years.	Free white females, including heads of families.	All other free persons.	Slaves.
Wilson, Henry	1	5	3		2	White, James	3	7	3		7	Wamble, Josiah	1	1	5		5
Watkins, Richd	2		2		2	Walker, Samuel	3	3	2		5	Wilson, James	2	3	3		5
Wortham, John	1	4	3		18	Watkins, Henry	1					Williams, Thomas	1	3	2		
Weaver, William	1	1	5			Watkins, John	1		2		1	Wood, Elizabeth			3		1
Williams, John	1	1	3		2	Worsham, Ludson	2	1			6	Yarbrough, Wm	2	2	3		7

HILLSBOROUGH DISTRICT, CASWELL COUNTY.[1]

CASWELL DISTRICT.	CASWELL DISTRICT—con.	CASWELL DISTRICT—con.
Arnet, Joseph	Graham, William, Jun	Swift, Dichard
Allin, Davis Scarlett	Grant, John	Swan, Thomas
Allin, Jesse	Howard, Henry	Strader, Lewis
Alverson, James	Humphreys, George	Shelton, Benjamin
Avery, Isaac	Hardister, Benjamin	Sommers, James
Atkins, William, Jun	Holloway, Obediah	Strader, Henry
Arnett, Joseph	Huston, Christopher	Sawyer, Absalom
Arnett, Thomas	Ingram, Thomas	Sommers, Capt. John
Arnett, John	Ingram, Charlton	Stansbery, Samuel
Allin, Davis George	Ingram, James	Smith, Thomas
Alverson, Archibald	Johnston, Alexander	Sommers, George
Brockman, Major	James, Thomas	Smith, Peter
Beaver, William	King, Robert	Stubblefield, Wyatt
Beaver, Jerrimiah	Kannon, John	Tony, Arther
Bullock, John	Kinnon, William	Turner, Berryman
Bullock, Samuel	Kinnon, Joel	Tinnason, Ignatious
Bevil, Robert	Lyon, Robert, Sen	Terry, Olive
Brackin, Samuel	Lanman, James	Tarply, John
Baxter, Thomas	Lyon, Robert, Jun	Trigg, William
Baxter, William	Long, John	Tucker, Obediah
Beaver, Joel	Lyon, William	Underwood, John
Boggins, William	Lutteral, Jerrimiah	Ware, William, Jun
Bastin, Thomas	Morgan, William	Ware, Thomas
Baldwin, Henry	Martain, Bailey	Whalebone, Thomas
Boggus, Richard, Sen	Meddlebrooks, John	Whitten, William
Boggus, Richard, Jun	McWilliams, James	Whitton, Robert
Brown, James	Mullins, Thomas	Watlington, Armstead
Baldwin, John	Mills, Edward	Walker, James
Black, Sarah	McClarney, Henry	Womack, Abram
Burton, Jane	McClarney, Paul	Waters, Thomas
Chitton, John	Martin, Joseph	Ware, John
Chitton, James	Mayo, Robert	Ware, William, Sen
Coleman, Spillsby	Millar, James	Weatherford, William
Clarke, Soloman	McGonegal, Patrick	Waters, Ezekiel
Cobb, John	Middlebrook, John	Weatherford, Thomas
Chitton, Jacob	Miles, Abram	Whitton, George
Chitton, Able	Miles, Thomas	Whitton, Thomas
Cobb, Jesse	Moss, William	
Conaway, Thomas	McCollum, John	GLOUCESTER DISTRICT.
Coleman, John	Nunnald, Alie	
Curtice, Henry	Nuhols, John	Arnold, Richard
Chapman, James	Norton, William	Azwell, Pearce
Cooksey, Abednego	O'Neal, Thomas	Anthony, Elijah
Dalton, Isham	O'Neal, John	Allin, Clifton
Dickerson, Wier	O'Neal, Edward	Atkinson, John
Dixon, Henry	Parr, Capt. William	Atkinson, Joseph
Dixon, Charles	Parr, John	Anthony, Jonathan
Dixon, Martha	Perkins, Abram	Bruze, Robert
Dixon, Tillman	Perkins, Archebald	Bates, John
Durham, Isaac	Perkins, Jesse	Burton, Henry
Dickerson, Nathaniel	Payne, John	Bryant, James
Dinnis, John	Perkins, John	Brukur, William
Durham, John	Perkins, Martin	Butry, Abram
Dameron, Joseph	Pendergrast, David	Bruce, Robert, Sen
Dixon, Wynn	Perkins, James	Bullis, Samuel
Dixon, Roger	Page, William, Jun	Browning, Edmund
Elmore, William	Perkins, Jesse	Bruce, John
Embery, William	Price, John	Burton, James
Embery, Robert	Price, William	Bruce, Alexander
Elmore, Peter	Paul, Samuel	Barnwell, William
Ethel, Benjamin	Paul, James	Browning, George
Ewell, Jonathan	Page, Nathaniel	Barnett, John
Foster, John	Porter, Capt. Alexander	Bush, Joseph
Ferrill, John	Powel, James	Byrd, John
Ferrill, Henry	Page, William, Sen	Bruce, Robert, Jun
Ford, Lem	Powel, Margaret	Browning, Samuel
Greenhaugh, Jonathan	Quine, Benjamin	Barker, Susannah
Gossage, Daniel	Quine, William	Browning, Edmun, Jun
Gossage, Robert	Rion, Mitchel	Bruze, William
Gatewood, Dudly	Roland, Findel	Burford, Daniel
Grant, Neeley	Ransom, Benjamin	Burch, George
Gattis, Thomas	Roberts, Vinsent	Burch, Nicholas
Griffith, Hillard	Richardson, James	Cheatham, James
Gibson, John	Richardson, Thomas	Culberson, Joseph
Grant, James, Sen	Rowark, Timothy	Carrell, William
Grant, James, Jun	Rodgers, Ademiston	Currie, James, Jun
Graham, John	Rogon, Timothy	Currie, Hugh
Gibson, James	Richardson, Laurence	Culberson, Joseph
Gibson, Mary	Smith, Peter (R. H.)	Childes, Hezakiah
Gomer, John	Strader, Conrad	Cole, Thomas
Gomer, William	Sammons, Edward	Cook, Augustine
Graham, William, Sen	Sammons, John	Corder, Lewis

[1] Names taken from county tax lists.

HILLSBOROUGH DISTRICT, CASWELL COUNTY—Continued.

NAME OF HEAD OF FAMILY.	Free white males of 16 years and upward, including heads of families.	Free white males under 16 years.	Free white females, including heads of families.	All other free persons.	Slaves.
GLOUCESTER DISTRICT—continued.					
Currie, Mary					
Cooper, Henry					
Culberson, William					
Cochran, John, Sen					
Crisp, John					
Corder, John					
Colemand, James					
Currie, John					
Dickey, John, Sen					
Dickey, David					
Donaho, William					
Dollarhide, Ezekiel					
Devenport, Samuel					
Davis, Henry, Sen					
Enock, David					
Enock, Benjamin					
Enock, Andrew					
Evanse, Thomas					
Evanse, Samuel					
Evanse, Walter					
Evanse, Lewis					
Everet Samuel					
Evanse, Zachariah					
Ford, Calvan					
Ferrill, John					
Fullar, Henry, Sen					
Florance, Obediah					
Forrest, William					
Greer, Ann					
Gooch, William, Sen					
Gooch, David					
Gooch, William, Jun					
Graves, Thomas					
Graves, Soloman					
Graves, Bazillia					
Gollerher, William					
Graves, Azariah					
Hightower, John					
Hightower, Richard					
Harks, Abram					
Hopper, Harmon					
Hays, James					
Hughes, James					
Hearndon, Larkin					
Haralson, Forbis					
Haralson, Thomas					
Huston, George					
Hughes, William					
Johnston, Richard					
Jackson, Thomas					
Jones, William, Sen					
Jones, Thomas, Jun					
Jones, Thomas, Sen					
Jones, James					
Jones, David					
King, Nathaniel					
Kimbrough, Thomas					
King, Edward					
Kitchen, James					
Kindreck, Thomas					
Kimbrough, John, Sen					
Kimbrough, James					
Kimbrough, William					
Kilgore, Thomas					
Knight, Absolam					
Knight, James					
Kerr, John					
Langly, Thomas					
Langly, John					
Love, Samuel					
Leak, William					
Lea, Gabriel					
Lea, James					
Love, Jane					
Motheral, Samuel					
Moore, Robert					
McGilvery, Daniel					
Melton, Daniel					
Melton, James					
Moore, George					
Martin, Robert					
Melton, John					
McIntosh, Alexander					
Morton, Peyton					
Morton, Masheck					
Melton, Benjamin					
Murphey, Gabriel					
Murphey, John					
Murphey, Gabriel					
Martin, Richard					
Martin, Anthorite					
McKoy, Neill					
Mason, Elijah					
McMinimy, John					
McMinimy, Alexander					
GLOUCESTER DISTRICT—continued.					
McReynolds, Joseph					
McMullin, John					
McMullin, Henry					
Muzzle, William					
McIntosh, Nimrod					
Nowel, James					
Nowel, Edward					
Pleasant, Major					
Pleasant, John					
Pleasant, William					
Phelps, Thomas					
Pendergrast, James					
Payne, John					
Parks, Solomon					
Poe, Jonathon					
Poe, Rhodin					
Paine, John					
Pearce, Moses					
Richmon, James					
Richmond, John					
Ray, James					
Rhone, Thomas					
Richmond, William					
Richmond, Mathew					
Robertson, Mark					
Rosson, Abner					
Reid, James					
Reid, John					
Rowark, Elisha					
Rainey, Isaac					
Sargent, Thomas					
Shy, Samuel					
Shy, John					
Simmons, Thomas					
Smith, William					
Siddle, Job					
Siddle, John					
Slade, William					
Smithey, Elizabeth					
Scott, ——					
Smith, James					
Smith, Moses					
Turner, John					
Turner, Henry, Sen					
Turner, Henry, Jun					
Taylor, Charles					
Thornton, Joel					
Taylor, Joshua					
Turner, James					
Whitloe, Jordon					
Wallis, John					
Wallis, Elias					
Wiley, Thomas					
Wisdom, Larkin					
Whitloe, John					
Warrin, Samuel					
Warrin, William					
Waterfield, John					
Williamson, Henry					
Wisdom, Martha					
Wisdom, Abram					
Wall, Buckner					
Woods, John					
Watkins, William					
Wiley, Alexander					
Washburn, Elizabeth					
Wallis, James					
Wallis, Elizabeth					
Yancey, John					
Yellock, William					
Yancey, Ann					
Yancey, James					
Yates, Thomas					
Zachary, John					
NASH DISTRICT.					
Allin, Charles					
Allin, Drury					
Auston, Stephen					
Archdeacon, James					
Brooks, Arther					
Brooks, Robert					
Brooks, David					
Brooks, John					
Barnett, Andrew					
Boswell, James					
Bright, Robert					
Barnett, David					
Briggs, Isaac					
Bailey, Yancey					
Brown, William					
Bright, Isaac					
Barnett, John					
Burchet, Robert					
NASH DISTRICT—con.					
Buckhanon, Andrew					
Buckhanon, James					
Baird, John					
Bozwell, Benjamin					
Coleman, Richard					
Clayton, Thomas					
Clayton, John, Jun					
Cooper, John					
Denny, Lachareah					
Denny, Clairborne					
Denny, Benjamin					
Day, John					
Donalson, Robert					
Deshazo, Richard					
Dixon, Jacob					
Davey, James					
Davey, Robert					
Davey, William					
Davey, Gabrial, Esq					
Ellis, Nimrod					
Gwin, John					
Gunn, Thomas					
Guttery, Garrott					
Grun, Major					
Gunn, Daniel					
Gill, Robert					
Gunn, Mary					
Gregory, Abraham					
Glenn, Joseph					
Harrilson, Paul, Sen					
Haliberton, John					
Haliberton, Charles					
Haliberton, Thomas					
Harrison, Ellin					
Hix, Daniel					
Huston, James					
Hix, David					
Holiway, John					
Harris, John					
Harrison, Sarah					
Huston, William					
Hudgins, William					
Johnston, Joseph					
Johnston, John					
James, Stephen					
James, Sherwood					
Jones, Stephens					
James, John					
Layton, John					
Layton, James					
Lawson, John					
Lawson, Francis					
Lord, Lord					
McFarland, Margaret					
Moore, Seth					
Mitchel, Charles					
Mitchel, James					
Morris, Zachariah					
Mann, John					
Mann, Elizabeth					
McNeill, Henry					
Neill, John					
Newton, Henry					
Owen, Edward					
Pettypool, William					
Parrish, John					
Pitman, Joseph					
Pryor, J. Henry					
Ragon, Jessie					
Ragon, Nathan					
Ragon, Owen					
Rooks, Buckner					
Rodgers, Byrd					
Stone, Hezekiah					
Sheppard, William					
Street, Moses					
Sanders, Richard					
Self, Abraham					
Turner, John					
Tatom, Joseph					
Thaxton, William					
Vanhook, Isaac					
Vass, Phillip					
Walker, Burkley					
Walker, Jesse					
Walker, Moses					
Wray, James					
Wheeler, Samuel					
Wall, Byrd					
Wood, Isaac					
Winstead, William					
Winstead, Manley					
Wilkerson, John					
Willson, James					
Willson, James					

HILLSBOROUGH DISTRICT, CASWELL COUNTY—Continued.

NAME OF HEAD OF FAMILY.	Free white males of 16 years and upward, including heads of families.	Free white males under 16 years.	Free white females, including heads of families.	All other free persons.	Slaves.	NAME OF HEAD OF FAMILY.	Free white males of 16 years and upward, including heads of families.	Free white males under 16 years.	Free white females, including heads of families.	All other free persons.	Slaves.	NAME OF HEAD OF FAMILY.	Free white males of 16 years and upward, including heads of families.	Free white males under 16 years.	Free white females, including heads of families.	All other free persons.	Slaves.
NASH DISTRICT—con.						RICHMOND DISTRICT—continued.						RICHMOND DISTRICT—continued.					
Winstead, Samuel						Hightower, Epiphraditus						Ragsdale, John					
Winstead, Cotance						Henderson, Samuel						Ragsdale, Montgomery					
Woody, John						Horton, Rawley						Ragsdale, William					
Yarbrough, Samuel						Hariss, Matthew						Randolph, James, Jun					
Yarbrough, John						Haralson, Hearndon						Roberts, Thomas					
						Ingram, James						Ragsdale, Peter					
RICHMOND DISTRICT.						Ingram, Susannah						Regnolds, Elijah					
						Jare, Philip						Sanders, Richard					
Atkinson, Rodger and John Jones						James, Joshua						Strother, Peter					
Atkinson, Rodger						Jean, Jessie						Smith, Robert					
Adams, John						Johnston, John						Stephens, Thomas					
Atkins, Thomas						Johnston, Samuel						Stokes, Man					
Boulton, Charles						Johnston, John						Starkey, Jonathan					
Bennet, Thomas						Jones, William						Sanders, William					
Bennet, John						Jeffreys, Thomas						Sanders, Col. James					
Baxton, Peter						Kersey, John						Samuel, Benjamin					
Barnett, John						Kersey, Drury						Stansbury, Luke					
Belus, Isaac						Kersey, John						Shelton, John					
Bradley, Judth						Kersey, James						Stafford, John					
Bradley, James						Kersey, Samuel						Swan, Joseph					
Bradley, John						Kiles, James						Swann, Edward					
Boulton, Thomas						Kiles, Elizabeth						Samuel, Anne					
Boman, Royal						Keeling, William						Samuel, Anthony					
Barnett, John						Lewis, Charles						Stephens, William					
Lands, Weston						Lewis, John						Shelton, David					
Bradley, Thomas						Lewis, Robert						Sherman, William					
Burke, James						Lea, Alexander						Samuel, Archebald					
Boman, Robert						Lea, James						Stephens, Benjamin					
Burton, John						Lea, John						Sanders, Col. Adams					
Carney, Joshua						Lea, Capt. John						Stansbury, Aquilla					
Carmon, John						Lea, John						Sanders, Obediah					
Carriol, George						Law, John						Stafford, Labon					
Cox, Phillip						Long, Robert						Smith, Joseph					
Carter, Jessie						Lea, William (L. B.)						Slade, Thomas					
Comer, Nathaniel						Lea, Major						Stafford, Adams					
Carman, Caleb						Lewis, John (Att.)						Staphens, Charles					
Cochran, David						Long, James						Stephens, William					
Camron, John						Merrit, Benjamin						Sanders, James					
Climer, James						Merrit, Soloman						Shackleford, Yonous					
Conaldy, George						Moore, James						Shackleford, John					
Cooenton, Richard						Miles, Jacob						Samuel, Jeremiah					
Dix, John						McGinnis, James						Suite, Enos					
Dyer, Samuel						Moore, James						Sanders, William					
Dobbin, Samuel						Matlock, Nicholas						Tolbert, Joseph					
Dobbin, Richard						Murphy, Archibald						Thomas, Phillip					
Dobbin, Hughes						Morrow, William						Tarpley, James					
Dobbin, John						Miles, Jacob						Thomas, David					
Draper, William						Maden, Catharine						Travis, David					
Dameron, Joseph						Montgomery, James						Thomas, Rupert					
Donaho, Patrick						Montgomery, Michael						Thompson, Cuthburt					
Dameron, Joseph						Moore, William (Parson)						Taylor, Reubin					
Dollarhide, William						McDaniel, William						Tuning, Thomas					
Dollarson, Mary						Merrit, Daniel						Vanhook, Loyo					
Dunaway, Abram						Nowel, Ephraim						Wright, Caleb					
Dameron, Christerpher						Newberry, Joseph						Womble, Demsey					
Dollarson, Andrew						Oxford, Jonathan						Wilson, Johnston					
Dobbin, Catharine						Ponds, John						Willson, Thomas					
Donaho, Maj. Thomas						Pass, Hollaway						Willson, Robert					
Delone, Nicholas						Poteete, William						Willson, Maj. William					
Evanse, Elisha						Ponds, James						Williams, Jacob					
Escridge, George						Phelps, Mary						Wade, Edward					
Escridge, Richard						Phelps, Reubin						Willson, Capt. James					
Farley, Hesekiah						Pass, Nath., Jun						Willson, James					
Fowler, Israel						Pass, Nathaniel						Watson, Richard					
Farley, Stewart						Phelps, Thomas						Welch, Samuel					
Farley, George						Parker, William						Watlington, Paul					
Flin, John						Preston, David						Wright, Abram					
Ferry, John						Prowel, William						Warwick, John					
Farley, J. James						Peterson, William						Wright, Jacob					
Farley, James						Peterson, James						Wright, Zachariah					
Farley, Sarah						Pettet, John						Williamson, Pulliam					
Glaspy, Joseph						Pearson, Jacob						Yates, John					
Grimes, Travis						Parks, Col. Robert						Yates, William					
Gomer, Benjamin						Quawls, Abner											
Harrison, Thomas						Quine, Henry						ST. DAVIDS DISTRICT.					
Harrison, Ninian						Roper, James											
Harwell, William						Ralph, Lewis						Anglin, William					
Hipworth, John						Roper, William						Adcock, Edmund					
Holcomb, Will						Roberson, James						Anglin, William					
Holcomb, George, Jun						Roan, James						Anderson, John					
Harwell, Peyton						Roberts, Absolam						Brintle, William					
Harney, William						Randolph, William						Brinsfield, Thomas					
Hudson, Joshua						Ragsdale, William						Burton, David					
Hardiwell, John						Roberts, Thomas						Blackwell, Robert					
Horton, Townsin						Robertson, Samuel						Beaver, John					
Horto, George						Reed, William						Barton, James					
Harrison, Andrew						Ray, Francis						Buchannon, John					
Holt, Claiborne						Reid, John						Brothers, John					
Hall, John						Ray, Darling						Brown, Leonard					
Hubbard, Ralph						Reed, George						Brown, William					
Hinton, Christopher						Randolph, James						Barker, David					
Hall, Darias						Rainey, William						Barker, John					
Hodge, Hannah						Rainey, Wesarn Waters						Barton, Lewis					
												Brown William					
												Baldwin, John					

HILLSBOROUGH DISTRICT, CASWELL COUNTY—Continued.

NAME OF HEAD OF FAMILY.	Free white males of 16 years and upward, including heads of families.	Free white males under 16 years.	Free white females, including heads of families.	All other free persons.	Slaves.	NAME OF HEAD OF FAMILY.	Free white males of 16 years and upward, including heads of families.	Free white males under 16 years.	Free white females, including heads of families.	All other free persons.	Slaves.	NAME OF HEAD OF FAMILY.	Free white males of 16 years and upward, including heads of families.	Free white males under 16 years.	Free white females, including heads of families.	All other free persons.	Slaves.
ST. DAVIDS DISTRICT—continued.						ST. DAVIDS DISTRICT—continued.						ST. JAMES DISTRICT—continued.					
Ballard, Dudly						Poston, Jerre						Farmer, William					
Barton, John						Rice, Thomas						Glenn, Beverly					
Barker, George						Rice, William						Glenn, Susannah					
Boyd, Joshua						Rice, Nathan						Gray, Alexander					
Brooks, Jonathan						Rodgers, Armstead						Hicks, John					
Barker, Isreal						Rice, Hesekiah						Hicks, Robert					
Browning, James						Rice, Ipsan						Hester, Robert					
Brooks, Thomas						Roberts, Humphrey						Hicks, Daniel					
Browning, John						Rice, John						Hubbard, Joseph					
Brown, John						Rice, Jchn						Harst, John					
Brown, Jethro						Rice, Nathan						Hawkins, Ephram					
Brooks, Richard						Rice, H. William						Harrison, Benjamin					
Cash, Howel						Rice, John						Jones, Benjamin					
Cantril, Joseph						Rudd, John						Johnston, Joshua					
Cantril, William						Simpson, Richard						Jay, James					
Cobb, Samuel						Simpson, Mary						Jeffrey, Paul					
Cobb, Noah						Starkey, John						Jones, Richard					
Carmical, Dunevan						Swift, Anthony						Kennady, James					
Carter, William						Shannan, John						Lansford, Joseph					
Carter, Joseph						Slade, Thomas						Ledbetter, Daniel					
Dickens, Henry						Scott, Joseph						Ledbetter, Ed					
Dill, Richard						Swift, Thomas						Ledbetter, Joel					
Dill, John						Swift, William						Medearest, Abram					
Davis, Cornelius						Staey, Malon						Miller, John					
Duke, Samuel						Sawyear, John						Moore, Ann					
Davise, Henry, Jun						Scott, James						Mason, Thomas					
Dickins, James						Swift, John						Meadows, Daniel					
Dorris, William						Sims, George						Morrow, William					
Dabney, Cornelius						Spence, John						Moore, Charles					
Estic, Bartlett						Sykes, Jonas						Moore, Ephram					
Estic, Richard						Smith, Francis						Neely, Samiel					
Foste, Thomas						Smith, Richard						Nichols, Willis					
Fanning, Middleton						Taylor, James						Oakley, John					
French, Samuel						Tate, Ann						Oakley, Walter					
Gwin, Daniel						Williamson, Nathan						Prat, Agness					
Graves, Capt. John						Williams, Daniel						Paine, William					
Hirriss, Tyre						Williams, Elizabeth						Parks, Joseph					
Harriss, Simpson						Walker, William						Parker, Powel					
Hornbuckle, Thomas						Wilkerson, William						Parker, Richard					
Hows, John						Williams, Col. John						Parker, David					
Hews, David						Watlington, John						Paine, Robert, Esq					
Haggard, Edmund						Williams, Jerremiah						Robert, George					
Humphreys, Thomas						Windsor, Jon						Rodgers, Samuel					
Hornbuckle, Solomon						Wright, Pleasant						Rimmer, James					
Hensely, John						Willis, Henry						Roberts, John					
Hensely, William						Williamson, James						Roberts, Arther					
Hay, John						Walker, James						Roberts, Daniel					
Harrison, James						Williams, John						Roberts, Duke					
Herbin, John						Walker, James						Ren, Benjamin					
Herbin, William						Wright, William						Satterfield, Jesse					
Holderness, William						Williamson, Benj						Swaing, John, Sen					
Harding, Prestly												Satterfield, Bedwell					
Hart, Col. David						ST. JAMES DISTRICT.						Satterfield, John					
Hensely, David												Swaing, James					
Hensely, Maisfield						Allin, David						Sneed, Samuel					
Haggard, Richard						Ashley, Graves						Swaing, Levi					
Isuit, Mathew						Anderson, George						Satterfield, Isaac					
Isuit, Mary						Anderson, James						Sneed, John					
Johnston, James						Burton, Daniel						Satterfield, John, Jun					
Johnston, Lanslotte						Broadaway, John						Scroggin, John					
Jones, John						Blalock, Millington						Scroggin, Francis					
Jackson, George						Blalock, William						Taylor, Joseph					
Jackson, Solomon						Bumpass, John						Taylor, John					
Kean, John						Blalock, Will, Jun						Tapp, William					
King, Kuthburt						Bividin, John						Terry, Thomas					
Kidd, Benjamin						Blalock, Thomas						Wells, James					
Kerr, Alexander						Bowls, John						Williams, Bennett					
Kimbrough, Robert						Burch, Benjamin						Waller, John					
Larrimore, Thomas						Bumpass, John, Jun						Yarborough, William					
Leath, Charles						Clixby, John											
Leath, Freeman						Cate, John						ST. LAWRENCE DISTRICT.					
Lackey, John						Crews, Hardy											
Lenox, John						Coleman, Daniel						Atkinson, Daniel					
Lay, Martha						Cochran, James						Atkinson, John, Esq					
Lay, Peter						Cozzart, Peter						Allin, William					
Mitchel, William						Cate, Robert						Bostwick, Charles					
Mallery, John						Caughran, James						Blueford, ——					
Mahone, William						Clayton, Daniel						Bradsher, John					
McIntosh, William						Clayton, Daniel, Jun						Black, Thomas					
Mallary, John, Jun						Clarke, Nathaniel						Browning, Joshua					
Martin, Joseph						Clark, Drury						Barnett, John					
Mitchel, Robert						Commins, John						Black, George					
Moore, Samuel						Cash, Moses						Black, John					
McCauley, John						Clayton, Colaman						Barnett, Thomas					
Owen, William						Cozzart, John						Bradsher, Moses					
Ove, James						Dickins, Robert, Esq						Barnett, Thomas, Jun					
Oldham, Moses						Daniel, James						Barnett, Hugh, Sen					
Powel, Abner						Davis, Robert						Barnett, Joseph					
Pike, Lewis						Day, Isaac						Barnett, Hugh					
Payne, William						Day, Henry						Bostwick, Chestley					
Payne, Greenwood						Day, Francis						Barnett, Thomas, Sen					
Payner, David						Daniel, Mathew						Barnett, Hugh, Jun					
Penix, John						Eddy, Thomas						Ball, Jacob					
Pane, Joshua						Eastwood, Alexander						Barnett, William					
Pike, Lewis, Sen						Farmer, Casandra						Bell, James					
Pool, Mecajah						Farmer, Daniel											

HILLSBOROUGH DISTRICT, CASWELL COUNTY—Continued.

NAME OF HEAD OF FAMILY.	Free white males of 16 years and upward, including heads of families.	Free white males under 16 years.	Free white females, including heads of families.	All other free persons.	Slaves.	NAME OF HEAD OF FAMILY.	Free white males of 16 years and upward, including heads of families.	Free white males under 16 years.	Free white females, including heads of families.	All other free persons.	Slaves.	NAME OF HEAD OF FAMILY.	Free white males of 16 years and upward, including heads of families.	Free white males under 16 years.	Free white females, including heads of families.	All other free persons.	Slaves.
ST. LAWRENCE DISTRICT.						**ST. LAWRENCE DISTRICT—continued.**						**ST. LUKE'S DISTRICT.**					
Beedles, Joseph						Lewis, Elizabeth						Allin, Drury					
Barnett, Thomas, Esq.						McKnabb, Robert						Aldridge, Joseph					
Clay, Edward						Mitchell, Robert						Aldridge, Peter					
Carnel, Richard						McNeill, Ann						Burch, Phillip					
Carnel, Mary						Mitchel, David						Brown, John					
Clift, John						Melene, Halloy						Burch, Henry					
Chamber, James						Mitchel, John						Burch, Richard, Jun					
Carver, Josias						Mason, Patrick						Burch, Pemberton					
Chambers, John						Miles, Thomas						Burton, Benjamin					
Carver, Thomas						McNeill, Benjamin						Brown, William					
Chambers, William, Sen.						McFarland, Daniel						Bryan, William					
Chambers, William						Moore, Robert						Badget, Thomas					
Campbell, John						McGhee, Muntford						Burch, Richard, Sen					
Carver, William						Moore, Joseph						Bryant, James					
Carlton, John						Mitchel, Arther						Brown, Abram					
Dickson, Josias						McFarland, John						Brooks, Aaron					
Dickson, Michael, Jun.						McNeill, John						Byrd, Bayton					
Debose, Frederick						Morgan, William						Bryan, William, Sen.					
Duncan, Mary						Milam, Lewis						Burton, Richard					
Darbey, George						McKain, John						Cock, William					
Darbey, Daniel						Morrison, Alexander						Cate, Thomas					
Dueast, Isaiah						Mitchell, Joshua						Cooper, Martin					
Duest, Hezekiah						Newton, Reubin						Cannady, John					
Duty, George						Neeley, Thomas						Cooper, John					
Doll, Edward						Newton, John						Cate, Joshua					
Debse, Benjamin						Newton, Benjamin						Christenbury, John					
Douglass, John, Esq.						Owen, Richardson						Carney, Joseph					
Douglass, Thomas						Olliver, Douglass						Douglass, Benjamin					
Denwiddie, John						Olliver, Stephen						Davis, Aquila					
Ellis, George						Pitman, Mathew						Durham, Daniel					
Fullar, Catherine						Parrot, Reubin						Durham, Isaac					
Ferguson, Andrew						Perryman, John						Duly, William					
Farrar, William						Phelps, William						Ellison, Hezikiah					
Farrar, Henry						Parker, John						Eubank, George					
Foley, Mason						Patterson, James						Eubank, John, Sen					
Fulcher, William, Sen.						Price, Acque						Eubank, John					
Fulcher, Henry						Paschel, William						Farrar, Joseph					
Fulcher, William						Paschel, Thomas						Farmer, Joseph					
Fleps, John						Pinkerton, Ann						Farrar, John					
Farley, John						Pendergrass, Richard						Fisher, Risdorn					
Fullar, Peter						Roberson, James						Foshee, Charles					
Fullar, George						Reynolds, Hamelton						Farrer, Peter					
Fullar, John						Roberson, Thomas						Farmer, Thomas, Sen					
Fullar, James						Rodges, John						Farguhar, James					
Fullar, William						Roach, John						Fullar, Stephen					
Fullar, William, Sen.						Roberson, John						Farrar, John					
Gregory, James						Roberson, Joseph						Grayham, Alexander					
Gold, Joseph						Stuart, Stephen						Gately, Thomas					
Gold, Daniel						Scroggin, Nathan						Green, Lewis					
Golph, Thomas						Simmons, James						Gately, William					
Going, Gutridge						Sargent, William						Graves, Thomas					
Gregory, George						South, Benjamin						Green, Burwell					
Glaze, Samuel						Standfield, Harrison						Green, William					
Hix, Reubin						Standfield, John						Graves, Henry					
Hughes, Ann						Sargeant, Daniel						Gately, Joseph					
Hughes, James						Sargeant, Stephen						Gains, Edward					
Hamlet, Moore Thomas						Stokes, Sylvanus						Hall, John					
Harrys, James						Stuart, Agness						Hargiss, Abrim					
Hunt, William						Stewart, James						Hargiss, Richard					
Hemphill, Hugh						Southward, Robert						Hall, Phillip					
Howard, Henry						Southard, William						Hargiss, William					
Hopkins, William						Standfield, William						Hargiss, Thomas					
Horley, Joseph						Stuart, William						Hargiss, Shadrach					
Hamlett, James						Seymore, Robert						Holman, Chas					
Henley, Edmund						Tunks, William						Holman, Richard					
Haralson, Sarah						Tunks, Rachael						Hunt, Samuel					
Hall, George						Twiner, Abram						James, Francis					
Hamlin, William						Twiner, Joseph						Johnston, James					
Henley, D. James						Trotter, William						Jacob, Benjamin					
Hamlett, William, Jun.						Trickey, Giles						Jones, Drury					
Hatcher, Benjamin						Tunks, Aisley						Jones, Goodrich					
Irvine, William						Underascon, Stephen						Jacob, Richard					
Justice, John						Vanhook, Thomas						Jones, Clayton					
Johnston, Theodoruk						Vanhook, Robert						Joblin, Benjamin					
Jamison, William						Virmillion, Wilson						Lockheart, William					
Johnston, Benjamin						Vanhook, Lawrence						Lyon, Richard					
Johnston, John						Williamson, James						Lewis, Joseph					
Johnston, George						Warrin, John						Lyon, Peter					
Lea, Zachariah						White, Thomas						Lowther, William					
Lea, James						Whitehead, Samuel						Lyon, Henry					
Lea, Abner						Warrin, Hedgman						Lyon, Jane					
Lea, George						Warrin, John, Jun.						Messer, James					
Lea, John						Walters, Abraham						Malone, David					
Lea, Barnett						Warrin, Goodloe						McKissock, Thomas					
Lea, William						Warrin, Jeremiah						Moore, Abram					
Long, William						Williams, Tobias						McKissock, William					
Lewis, Edmund						Warrin, Robert						Malone, John					
Long, Reubin						Wood, John						Malone, Thomas					
Lea, Richard						Walters, Paul						McMurry, John					
Lea, William						Warrin, Samuel						Malone, George					
Long, Ambrose						Wood, Stephen						Minzy, Richard					
Long, John						Walters, Henry						McMurry, James					
Lea, Carter						Walters, John						Malone, Nathaniel					
Long, James						Warrin, William						Moore, Dempsey					
Long, James, Sen.						Warrin, Hackley						Mann, David					
Long, Benjamin						Williams, Thomas						Mitchell, David, Sen					

HILLSBOROUGH DISTRICT, CASWELL COUNTY—Continued.

ST. LUKE'S DISTRICT—continued.

NAME OF HEAD OF FAMILY.	Free white males of 16 years and upward, including heads of families.	Free white males under 16 years.	Free white females, including heads of families.	All other free persons.	Slaves.
McKee, William					
Mitchel, David, Esq					
McMurry, Samuel					
Pope, Joel					
Pogue, John					
Pryar, Charles					
Price, John					
Pogue, Joseph					
Ragsdale, Thomas					
Roberts, Shadrach					
Ragsdale, Benjamin					
Rankin, James					
Robertson, Charles					
Robertson, David					
Rose, Alexander					
Surrall, John					
Sykes, John					
Step, Elizabeth					
Sherman, John					
Step, Joshua					
Surratt, Joseph					
Simms, Buckner					
Tarpley, Hosea					
Trim, Henderson					
Trim, Charles					
Vanhook, Jacob					
Vanhook, Lucy					
Wright, Jarrot					
Willingham, John					
Woods, Samuel					
Wheely, John					
Wilkerson, Thomas					
Woods, Joseph					
Williamson, James					
Womack, John					
Watkins, Phillip					
Wilson, John					
Willson, Joseph					
Watson, Jesse					
Willson, Henry					
Waite, William					

HILLSBOROUGH DISTRICT, CHATHAM COUNTY.

NAME OF HEAD OF FAMILY.	Free white males of 16 years and upward, including heads of families.	Free white males under 16 years.	Free white females, including heads of families.	All other free persons.	Slaves.
Bland, James	1	5	2		
Bland, John	1		2		
Brinkly, Thos	1		1		
Brewer, Nathl	2	6			
Burchard, Jeddediah	2	1	5		
Brumbe, James	2		3		
Burns, William	1	2	2		2
Burchard, Josiah	1		1		
Clark, Wm	1	1	5		17
Copeland, James	2	3	6		
Copeland, Daniel	1	2	4		
Cumbo, Jacob	1	2	1		
Campbell, John	1	2	3		
Clark, Benjn	1	2	2		
Chamberlin, Elijah	1				4
Crain, Wm	1	2	2		6
Clark, Phebee		3	2		5
Copeland, James, Jr	1				
Dillard, George	2		6		
Drummer, Daniel	1				
Davis, Ellithan	3	1	4		3
Dismicks, George	2	3	3		6
Dillard, Willis	1		2		
Ferrell, Francis	1		4		1
Fasker, Joseph, Senr	1	1	3		4
Fasker, Wm	1	4	4		
Fasker, Joseph, Jur	3				
Fasker, Elijah	1	1	1		3
Fasker, John, Jur	2	5	6		
Fasker, John, Ser	2				
Fike, John	2	3	2		
Fike, Elijah	1	2	3		
Fasker, Wm	1	1	2		
Griffith, Roger	2	3	3		4
Gee, George	1		1		
George, Harris	1	4	3		
Gunter, Isham	2	2	4		
George, James	4	3	2		3
Guthrie, Saml	2	3	4	1	5
Harmon, John	1	1	1		
Hackney, Wm	1	2	6		
Henderson, Wm	1	1	2		
Howard, Wm	3		3		9
Harmon, Zachariah	3	3	10		11
Harrington, Phillimon	1	3	4		2
Hatley, John	1	2	3		
Howard, James	2		3		6
Herndon, Stephen	1	2	4		
Hamblet, Wm	1	2	7		3
Hoget, Willis	1	2	3		
Henderson, Lewis	1		1		
Harrington, Thos	1	2	4	1	
Kelley, Giles	1	3			
Lucus, George	2	2	3		68
Lucus, Wm	1		4		3
Mossey, James	3	3	5		4
Miliken, Quaintain	1				
Manley, Basil	1	1	1		6
Mckeever, James	1		1		
Mash, Robert	2	1	5		2
Mash, Wm	1	3	4		2
Morgan, Zachariah	1	1	2		
Morgan, Edmon	1	2	4		
Morgan, Joseph	1	2	3		1
Morgan, Charles	2	3	1		
Millihen, George	1	1	3		
Morphus, John	1		4		
Moyer, Peter	1				
Malton, John	1	1			3
Mott, Joseph	1		1		2
Mironey, Wm	1				
Mironey, Pilliph	2	2	1		1
Paterson, James	3	1	3		3
Poe, Simon	1	4	2		
Pettey, James	1	2	1		2
Poe, Reuben	1		2		
Pettey, John	2	4	5		2
Pettey, Rueben	3	3	4		
Pettey, Isaac	1	1	1		1
Paterson, Thos	1		1		5
Poe, Wm	1	2	4		
Pettey, Ambrews	4	3	5		2
Pettey, Wm	2	1	2		11
Rigbey, James	2	1	2		2
Robertson, Thos	2		1		5
Riddle, Ricd	1	2	3		
Riddle, Wm	1	2	3		3
Straughn, Stephen	1	3	3		
Sanders, George	1	1	1		
Stewart, James	2	2	3		
Straughn, Crispen	3		4		
Siurlock, Sarah	2	2	4		14
Sanders, Wm	1	3	2		
Stewart, Thos	1	1	1		
Stewart, Spencer	1		1		6
Sanders, John	1	1	3		
Straughn, Rud	1	2	1		
Steedmon, Nathan	1		1		10
Snorlock, James	1		1		6
Stewart, Elizabeth			1		3
Thomas, Even	4		6		
Thomson, Robert	1	3	4		3
West, Philliph	1				
West, Rud	1				
West, Thos	2	1	3		2
Ward, Henry	1	2	3		
Williams, John	2	1	5		6
Brown, John	1	3	3		
Stewart, Joseph	2		4		
Peake, Benjn	2	1	1		
Poe, Stephen	1		5		
Johnson, Robert	2	3	6		
Gunter, Wm	1	1	1		
Gunter, Thos	1	2	5		
Minter, Margret	2	2	6		
Crofford, John	1	1	2		
Straughn, Hosea	1		3		
Riley, John	1		3		
Riston, Ricd	3				
Brown, John	4	3	3		
Henson, Charles	2	2	2		
Green, Hubbard	1	3	1		
Atkins, Thos	6			1	2
——, Ambrous	2	5	1		1
McBune, Daniel	1	2	2		
Poe, Simon, Ser	2				3
Gorden, John	1	1	2		4
Bradsberrey	1				
Curtis, Charles	1				2
Higdon, Charles	1	1	1		
Higdon, Daniel	1		3		
Page, Nathl	3	2	4		1
Stewart, James, Jr	1				
Wilson, Joshua	1				
Burge, Robertson	1				
Abet, Wm	1	3	3		
Brown, Archebell	2	1	3		4
Bohannon, Robert	2	3	5		8
Brantley, John	1	3	3		5
Bushop, Benja	2		1		
Brewer, Thos	3	1	2		
Branch, Edmon	1	1	2		8
Brantley, Joseph	3	2	2		12
Collier, Henry	1	2	3		
Clark, Jesse	2	1			
Cark, Ricd	1		1		1
Drake, Ricd	1	1	1		
Drake, Wm	2	2	4		6
Evins, Thos	2	3	3		10
Goss, Joshua	1				2
Gresham, James	2	2	4		
Gross, Francis	1	4	2		
Holding, Joshua	1		2		
Hesther, Robert	1		1		
Harden, Nicholas	2	1	1		
Hesther, Beveley	1	1	1		
Holden, Elizabeth	1	1	4		
Johnson, Wm	2		1		
Johnson, Joseph	1	3	5		1
Johnson, Wm	1	4	3		
Jones, S. I	1	3	1		3
Julus, Coley	1		2		
Lasseter, Wm	2	2	2		2
Lasseter, Abner	1	1	5		
Leopard, Wm	1	2	4		
Minter, Morgan	2	3	6		7
Matthews, Isaac	2	3	5		7
Minter, John	2	1	3		10
Minter, Joseph	3	1	2		6
Parham, Francis	1		1		1
Partridge, Thos	2	4	3		7
Parish, David	1	4	8		
Pettishall, Wm	2	3	1		1
Pritchit, Edward	1		3		
Parham, Drury	2	1	2		5
Parham, Wm	1	1	3		1
Pool, James	2	3	7		
Riddle, John	1	2	4		3
Ramsey, Ambrous & John Ramsey	4		7		11
Stephens, Ricd	2	5	5		
Stephens, James	1	2	6		
Simons, Solomon	2	2	2		1
Stokes, Thos	1	3	1		27
Tomlinson, John	2		1		4
Tomlinson, Moses	1		1		
Taylor, Simon	2		5		
Tabour, Thos			1	3	
Wicker, Thos	2	5	3		1
Wicker, James	1		2		1
Wicker, Plesant	1	2	2		
Yarbrough, Elisha	1		2		4
Yarbrough, Nathan	1		1		
Yarbrough, Joseph	2	2	2		
Minter, Margret	2	2	5		
Poe, David	1	2	4		
Parham, John	1	1	1		
Harris, Wm	1	1	2		3
Wormack, John	3	3	5		8
Matlock, David	2	3	5		
Parker, Elizabeth		1	1		
Lassiter, James	1		3		1
Brooks, John	1	2	3		
Motley, Robert	2	1	4		1
Simpson, Sarah		3	1		
Minter, Wm	1	1	3		10
Chatman, John	2	2	7		5
Harden, Phillip	3	2	3		7
Gunter, Isham	1	1	4		
Ranes, James	1	2	1		
Drake, Ricd	1	1	1		1
Anderson, James	1		2		15
Andrews, John	1	2	4		
Adkinson, Benja	2	2	4		
Andrews, Ellizair	3	2	7		
Burns, Thos	1	1	1		6
Bryant, Thos	1	1	9		
Brown, John	2	2	6		
Barter, Wm	2	3	3		
Bryant, John	1		1		
Burns, James	1		2		
Barns, Seth	1		1		
Beal, Thos	1	2	3		1
Burns, John	1		1		1
Burns, John	1		2		
Barns, Jonathan	2		5		1
Barter, Moses	2	1	2		
Brown, Daniel	1	5	4		1

HILLSBOROUGH DISTRICT, CHATHAM COUNTY—Continued.

NAME OF HEAD OF FAMILY.	Free white males of 16 years and upward, including heads of families.	Free white males under 16 years.	Free white females, including heads of families.	All other free persons.	Slaves.
Bryant, Aron	3	2	3		
Beal, Benjn	1	1	3		
Barber, Rud	2	3	5		
Bryan, Obediah	2	3	5		
Bryan, Aquilla	1	3	2		
Beck, James	1	1	1		
Caps, Wm, Jur	1	4	2		
Clark, Robert	1		2		
Caps, William, Sr	1	4	2		
Clark, James	1	2	3		
Clark, Nathl	1	1	3		
Campbell, Nicholas	1	2	4		
Carrot, Starling	1	2	2		
Caps, Wm, Ser	2	1	7		
Caps, Oliver	2		6		
Dowdey, John	1		3		
Duncan, Wm, Ser	3	6	3		
Dowdy, William	1				
Dowdey, Rud	1				
Dowdey, Jesse	1		2		
Dowdey, Benjn	1		2		
Dowdey, Joseph	2	6	2		
Dackerly, John	1	3	2		
Dodson, Wm	1	1	4		
Dowd, Judith	4		3		
Dowdey, Daniel	2	3	4		
Dodson, George	1		3		
Elliot, John	2	2	2		
Elliot, Ebenezer	1				
Gober, William	1	1	2		
Galiway, Thos	1	2	4		
Gilmore, Saml	2	4	4		
Green, Wm	1	3	4		1
Griffin, Edward	1	3	4		
Hillard, Ezechail	1	5	1		
Harley, Amos	2	4	5		
Harley, John	1		1		
Hodge, Wm	3	3	6		
Higdon, Phillip	1		2		
Hart, John	1				
Hart, Wm	1	4	3		
Jeffres, Henry	1	2	3		
Jones, Edward	1	3	4		
Kendrick, Martin	2		7		1
Kendrick, Wm	1	1	3		2
Lawton, Joel	1	1	3		
Lea, Joseph	3	2	6		13
McKeever, Alexr, Sr	1	3	3		
McKeever, Alexr, Jur	1	1	2		
McKinnis, Miles	1	2	5		
McIntire, John	2	1	4		
May, Henry	1	4	5		3
Modglin, Straingmon	2	1	4		
McKeever, John, Ser	2	4	3		
May, Joseph	1				
Modglin, Trumon	1	1	3		
McKinsey, Cristain	1		2		
McDaniel, James	2	3	6		
Mongomery, John	1		6		18
McKeever, John, Jr	1	1	2		
Merack, Moses	1	1	3		2
McCollum, Malcom	2	1	2		
Nall, Rud	1		4		2
Nall, John	1		4		
Oaldhum, Rud	2	2	2		
Paterson, Charles	2	5	5		
Paterson, Gilbert	2	8	6		1
Pasiel, Wm	1		2		
Poplin, George	1		4		
Powell, Confert	1	1	1		1
Paterson, Joel	1	1	3		1
Riddle, Cato	1	2	3		
Rogers, Randolph	1				
Riddle, Julus	1	1	3		
Roberts, Wm	1	4	4		
Riddle, Thos	1	2	6		1
Parish, Self	1	3	5		6
Smith, Daniel	1	2	6		
Smith, James	1	2	3		
Shammell, Wm	1		2		
Smith, Abner	2	3	4		
Swanson, Richardson	1	5	1		
Tison, Ricd	1	2	2		
Tayler, Willington	2	1	6		
Thomson, John	3	1	6		5
Taylor, Phillip	1	2	3		36
Taylor, John	1				10
Taylor, James	1		1		18
Temple, Saml	1	1	2		
Tyrrell, Simon	1	2	5		6
Tilmon, Joshua	1	4	2		
Tregle, Griffin	1	1	1		1
Temples, Benjn	2	4	2		
Wheelus, Isaac	1		1		
Wilkins, Robert	1	2	1		2
Wilkins, John	2	2	3		7
Wade, Peter	1		3		1

NAME OF HEAD OF FAMILY.	Free white males of 16 years and upward, including heads of families.	Free white males under 16 years.	Free white females, including heads of families.	All other free persons.	Slaves.
Wilcox, John	1	4	3	1	11
White, Spierwood	1	2	3	1	
Wilkerson, Thos	1		2		
Williams, Jacob	1	2	1		
Caps, John	1		1		
Rivard, Lion	1		1		
May, Thos	1	2	3		
Caps, Jacob	1		1		
Hinson, Saml	1	6	3		
Molding, Claton	1		6		
Right, Joseph	1	1	2		
Kelley, James	1	2	2		
Kelley, Wm	1	2	2		
Linklear, John	1	2	2		
Weaver, Shaderick	1		3		
Lawton, Wm	1		1		
Morgan, Wm	1		2		1
Self, Bradley	1	4	2		
Barnes, Jeremiah	2	1	4		
Turner, Matter	1	2	4		
Dowdey, Wm	3	5	4		
Berry, Wm	1	1	3		
McKeever, Edward	2	1	4		
Upton, David	2	3	6		
Bulluck, Saml	1	3	7		
Bradley, Wm	1	3	2		
Bass, Moses	1		3		
Bass, Edward	1		3		
Bray, Edward, Ser	3	2	2		
Bray, Edward, Jr	1		2		
Branson, Joseph	1				
Berry, John	1	4	6		1
Jones, Burrough	1	1	1		
Branson, Levi	3	2	3		
Bushop, Wm	1	2	4		
Cashatt, John	1	2	5		
Caster, Saml	3		2		
Caster, John	1	4	2		
Chamness, Joshua	1	1	7		
Casthat, John	4	2	4		
Caster, Isaac	1	6	5		
Culberson, Andrew	3	1	7		
Cox, John	1	3	5		
Davis, John	2	1	6		
Doan, Thos	1	2	4		
Dowdey, Thos	2		3		
Doan, John	4	1	6		
Davis, Joseph	1	1	3		
Dickson, Thos	1	3	2		
Doan, Joseph	1	2	3		
Doan, Jacob	1	1	2		
Dickson, Benjamin	1		2		
Dickson, John	1	1	4		
Dickson, Solomon	1		2		
Esiry, Thos	1		1		
Fox, John	1		3		
Freeman, Robert	1		4		
Fox, David	2	3	5		
Fox, Nicholas	2	5	3		
Fills, Isham	1				
Hopkins, Wm	1	2	3		
Hobson, Stephon	5	3	2		
Hickman, Joseph	1	2	6		
Hobson, Charles	2	3	7		
Hornaday, Christopher	1	4	3		1
Hobson, Wm, Ser	2	1	5		
Hobson, Wm, Jr	1		2		
Howell, Robert	1		7		
Henshaw, Benjn	1	5	5		
Henshaw, Joseph	1	1	2		
Harper, Travis	1	1	1		3
Hornaday, John	1	3	3		
Johnson, Matha	1	2	1		
Johnson, Joseph	1	6	2		
Johnson, Joseph	1				
Johnson, David	1	2	5		
Jones, Henry	2	1	5		
Johnson, Jesse	3	4	3		
Jones, George	1	1	1		
Kemp, Joseph	1	4	4		
Kemp, Ricd	1	1	2		
Moon, John	2	4	4		
Moon, Jacob	1	1	5		
Moon, James	2	2	5		
Morley, Benjn	1	1	3		
Marshall, Wm	1	2	3		
McMarster, Wm	1	4	2		
McMaster, James	3		1		
McMaster, Jonathan	1	2	2		
Marley, John	1	2	4		
Marshall, Benjn	1	3	3		
Marley, Henry	1	3	3		
Murphy, Archabell	1	2	3		
Mosset, Adam	1	2	3		
Macklefield, Hugh	1	1	2		
Pew, Thos	1		1		
Pew, Jacob	1	1	2		

NAME OF HEAD OF FAMILY.	Free white males of 16 years and upward, including heads of families.	Free white males under 16 years.	Free white females, including heads of families.	All other free persons.	Slaves.
Peyot, John	1	5	3		
Pigmon, Lennord	2	2	3		
Ratliff, Amoss	1	1	2		
Ransey, Joel	1	3	2		
Remonton, John	1		1		
Ricard, David	1	1	2		
Ray, Thos	1	1	2		
Lamey, James	1	3	4		
Stewart, Henry	1	1	4		
Smith, John	1	5	4		
Stewart, John	1		3		
Tison, Wm	2	4	2		
Lamb, Josiah	1	1	2		
Toppin, Wm	1	1	3		
Terry, Thos	2	1	1		
Thomson, John	1	1	2		
Terry, James	1	2	3		
Thomas, Temple	1	2	3		
Ward, Thos	2	2	3		
Whitehead, Thos	1	3	5		
Williams, Ezikiel	1	3	2		
Whitehead, Joseph	1	3	6		
Whinarey, Robert	1	1	3		
Wiers, James	1	1	1		2
Youngblood, Jacob	1	1	1		
Vestill, Wm	1				
Vestill, Capt Wm	1		4		
Vestill, Wm, Jr	1				
Vestill, Thos	4	1	1		
Vestill, David	3	2	7		
Silor, Pever		2	2		
Johnson, James	3		3		
Hussey, Ann	1	4	2		
Hobson, Isaac	1		4		
Hackman, John	1	3	4		
Hobson, Joseph	1		1		
Silor, Elizabeth	2		5		
Howell, Robert, Jr	1	1	2		
Silor, Philliph	3	4	5		
McDaniel, Marey	1		4		
Stanton, Robert	1	1	4		
Berry, Henry	1		2		
Johnson, Isaac	1	2	3		
Jones, George	1	1	1		
Unstot, Catey			2		
Blalock, Julius	2	5	2		1
Branton, Thos	2	3	4		
Brewer, Henry	1	2	5		
Baker, John	1	6			1
Balding, Saml	1	1	5		2
Buckner, Jesse	1	5	4		
Balding, John, Sr	2	1	4		2
Berry, Isaac	1		2		
Clark, Robert	2	1	2		
Conklin, Daniel	1		1		
Clark, Yelikel	4	2	1		1
Cool, Joseph	1	3	4		
Cook, Abraham	1	1	5		2
Copeland, Rebeccah	2		4		
Crutchfield, Milley	3	1	5		15
Cook, Benjn	1	2	2		
Curle, Wm	2	3	6		
Crutchfield, Martin	1	4	4		1
Davis, Elnathan	3	3	3		2
Dickson, Solomon	1	4	3		
Duglas, Wm	1	2	4		4
Davis, James	1	1	2		
Fasker, Joseph	2		1		
Fasker, Elisha	2		2		1
Folden, Lewis	1	1	2		
Gillum, Wm	1	2	5		
Henderson, James	1	3	6		
Henderson, Isaac	2	2	5		
Hadley, Simon	1	3	2		
Holliday, Saml	1	2	6		
Hadley, Thos	1	3	2		
Henderson, John	1				
Jones, Charles	1		2		
Jones, Thos	2	4	4		
Jones, John	2	6	2		
Jones, John	2		5		
Kirk, George	2		2		5
Lukes, Wm	1	2	4		
Linsey, James	1	3	3		2
Lee, Isaac	1		3		
Linley, Wm	1	3	1		
Linley, Aron	1		3		
Linley, Owen	2	2	3		
Litterloth, Lewis H	2	4	2		6
Moutre, James, Ser	1	2	2		
Martin, Wm	3	2	3		8
Meeham, Joseph	2	3	4		
Martin, John	1		4		
Meekam, Wm	3	2	1		2
Meekam, John	1		3		
Manor, John	2	7	3		
Meekam, George	1		1		

HILLSBOROUGH DISTRICT, CHATHAM COUNTY—Continued.

NAME OF HEAD OF FAMILY.	Free white males of 16 years and upward, including heads of families.	Free white males under 16 years.	Free white females, including heads of families.	All other free persons.	Slaves.
McMatt, Wm, Ser	2	3	3		1
McPherson, Othniel	1		1		
McMatt, Wm	1	1	2		1
McCracken, Wm	1	2	1		
Mashburn, Matthew	1	4	3		
Moutre, James	1	1	2		1
Nicholason, Isaac	1	3	3		
Newland, John	1	4	2		
Pickins, William	1	2	5		
Price, Lenny	1		2		
Pourtis, James	1	2	3		
Person, George	2	1	2		
Pasmore, David	1		2	1	
Quackenbush, Peter	2	1	4		
Quackenbush, John	1	1	2		
Rogers, Josiah	3	2	2		
Richardson, Isaac	1	3	4		
Loan, Thos	3	3	5		
Sinkler, John	1	2	1	2	2
Spurling, Wm	1	1	5		1
Steal, Thos	1	2	6		
Sinkler, Mary	4	2	2		
Simons, James	1		6		
West, William	1	3	3		5
West, Ignatus	1	2	6		1
Wilkey, George	1	3	5		
Witsman, Cannord	1		2		
White, Simon	2	1	4		
West, Thos	2	2	4		3
West, Ignatus	1	1	6		
Smith, Buckner	1	3	1		
Simmons, Thos	1	1	2		
Balding, John	1		1		
Groves, Jacob	1		1		
West, Phillip	1				
Morphus, John	1	2	4		
Cook, Henry	2	4	2		3
Tison, Wm	1	4	1		
Alwater, Justis	2	2	2		
Binom, Luke	3	1	4		15
Brigah, Cannon	2	1	1		
Baley, James	1	2	4		
Brown, Abner	1	1	5		
Allen, Elijah	1				
Beaver, Rigston	2	1	7		
Brewer, Oliver	4		2		3
Burnet, Daniel	2	5	2		2
Brewer, Edward	1	2	2		
Blalock, George	3	2	5		
Binom, Tapley	1	4	1		1
Cate, Rud	1	3	6		
Crow, Stephen	1	4	2		1
Crow, Isaac	1	2	2		
Crow, James	1		2		
Caudle, Beckner	1	3	1		
Crow, John	1	4	4		
Crow, Wm	1	1	1		
Clay, Thos	2	1			2
Cobb, Robert	2		4		8
Edward, John	2	2	3		
Ellis, Jesse	1	4	6		
Edwards, Wm	1	3	3		1
Edwards, Robert	2	1	2		3
Edwards, Hugh	1		2		
Edwards, Edward	1	1	2		
Duglas, John	1		2		1
Danor, Marmaduck	1	1	1		
Fan, Jesse	3	3	5		
Hathcock, Hosea	1	4			
Hearn, Howell	1	1	3		
Hearndon, John	1	2	3		
Hatley, Rich	1	3	5		1
Hackney, Joseph	1	3	3		
Hood, Athur	2	3	3		
Gunter, James	2	3	3		
Glawson, Sarah	3	4	4		
Griffin, John	2	3	3		
Griffin, Wm	1	4	3		5
Jewell, Absalom	1	3	3		
Jolley, Jalf	1		1		
Justin, Wm	1				
Justin, John	5	2	3		12
Jolley, John	3	1	3		
Kirksey, James	1	2	1		
Kirksey, Gidian	2	1	1		1
Kirksey, Isaac	1		3		
Kirksey, Wm	1		2		3
Kirksey, Christopher	3	5	5		17
Lacey, Pillimon, Ser	1		4		4
Lacey, Pillimon, Jr	1	1	1		
Lassiter, Hezekiah	1	4	3		
Lassiter, Jacob	1	2	2		
Merack, Wm	1	6	4		3
Moutre, Joseph	1	2	3		
Man, Rowland	1	2	3		
Man, Thos	2	2	3		
Owen, Jacob	1		1		

NAME OF HEAD OF FAMILY.	Free white males of 16 years and upward, including heads of families.	Free white males under 16 years.	Free white females, including heads of families.	All other free persons.	Slaves.
Odam, Thos	1		1		3
Owin, Oliver	1	2	3		
Owin, Daniel	2		7		3
Powell, Thos	1	3	2		
Powell, Wm, Ser	1	3	1		
Powell, Wm, Jr	1		1		
Powell, James, Ser	2	2	2		
Pilkerton, Saml	1				
Powell, Nicholas	1	3	1		
Pilkerton, James	1				
Person, Lewis	1	3	2		
Poe, Robert	1		5		
Powell, James, Jur	3	2	3		
Poe, Terry	1				
Poe, James	1	1	4		
Pritchit, Thos	1	1	1		
Powell, Elizabeth	1		2		
Pilkerton, Wm	1	4	1		
Person, William	2		5		
Person, Surling	1	4	3		
Ramsey, Wm	1	1	3		3
Rosser, Josser	1		2		14
Rigdon, Beaver	2	1	2		
Smith, Isham	2	1	5		
Smith, Henry	2	3	3		
Smith, Isham	1	3	4		
Smith, Mark	1	1	1		
Snipes, John	1		3		
Snipes, Thos	1	4			4
Snipes, Thos	1	3	5		
Snipes, Wm	1	1	2		1
Smith, Absalom	1	4	2		
Stephens, John	2	5	3		
Smith, James	1	2	5		
Smith, Moses	1		6		
Straughn, Edmon	1	1	1		
Tatom, Edmond	2	1	2		4
Tatom, John	1	4	2		
Trip, John	3	2	4		
Smith, Wm	3	2	2		
Ward, Robert	1		5		
Wood, James	2	3	4		
Williams, David	1	6	3		
Brown, Thos	2		2		
Pilkerton, Anthony	1				
Kellum, Daniel	1				1
Smith, Frances	1				
Powell, George	1	5	1		
Powell, James	1		2		1
Bellary, John	1	1	4		
Owen, Wm	2	3	4		
Mosley, George	1	1	2		
Coal, Thos	1	3	4		
Halley, Wm	2	3	5		
Wood, Solomon	2	4	2		
Pritchit, Thos	1	1	2		
Smith, Wm	1				
Andrews, Thomas	1	2	2		
Adcock, Joshua	2		3		
Brown, Mordica	2	5	1		2
Brewer, John, Sr	1	3	6		
Bray, Henry	1		2		
Bray, Mathias	1	3	2		
Bray, James	1	1	2		
Bray, Wm	1		1		
Brooks, Mark	2	4	7		
Brewer, John, Jur	2	1	4		
Brewer, Amos	1	1	3		
Brewer, George	2	5	3		
Bradley, Lewis	2	5	3		
Baker, Humphrey	1	1	6		
Brooks, Isaac	2	1	5		12
Bayley, Henry	3	1	2		8
Bayley, Benjn	1	1	1		3
Brewer, Wm	1		6		
Brewer, Nicholas	2	7	4		
Bright, Simon	2	1	4		
Bray, John	1	2	3		
Campbell, Wm	1	5	2		
Carvins, Rich	1	1	4		
Cox, Solomon	3		4		
Cox, Saml	1	1	3		
Culberson, James	1	2	3		
Dulley, Thos	1	2	2		2
Dickson, Jesse	2	3	8		
Dickson, Joseph	1				
Dickson, Hannah	1	3	6		
Dickson, Saml	1	3	1		
Dickson, Zabulen	1				
Deaton, James	1	5	3		
Edwards, James	1	2	2		
Edwards, Joshua	3	2	1		
Elkins, Benjn	3	2	6		
Emberson, James	4		3		
Fismire, Martin	1		5		
Flemmings, John	1	1	4		
Flemmings, David	1	3	4		

NAME OF HEAD OF FAMILY.	Free white males of 16 years and upward, including heads of families.	Free white males under 16 years.	Free white females, including heads of families.	All other free persons.	Slaves.
Glass, Josiah	1				
Groves, Wm G	3	6	3		
Groves, Thos	1	2	4		
Glover, Thos	1	2	3		
Glass, Josiah	1		3		
Glass, Daniel	1	2	2		
Gass, Thos	1	2	5		
Gregory, Rich	2	2	4		
Gillerland, Joseph	2	2	3		
Ginn, William	1	1	3		
Headen, John	1		5		
Hadley, Mary	2	1	5		
Hadley, Joshua	1	2	1		
Hart, Heath	1	4	4		
Hobson, George, Jr	1	1	6		
Dickson, Nathan	1	3	2		
Hobson, James	1	2	6		
Hobson, George	1	2	1		
Hayes, Saml	1	2	2		
Hunter, Elisha	1	3	4		
Headen, Wm	2				
Hackny, Daniel	1	2	2		
Jones, Andrew	2	1	5		
Johnson, Benja	1	3	2		
Jones, Piebius	1		3		
Jeffers, Henry	1	2	3		
Jones, Rich	1	4	4		4
King, Robert	1		3		
Kelley, Wm	1	2	3		
Kirk, Joseph	1	2	4		
Lambert, John	1		3		1
Lambert, John, Ser	2		3		
Lambert, Joseph	1	2	1		
Moore, Thos	1	1	2		
McRay, Martin	1	2	1		
Moodey, Wm	3	2	7		1
McCaslin, Catey	1	1	3		
Moodey, Thos	1	1	3		
McCaslin, James	1	1	4		
McAmus, Eli	1	1	4		
McSwane, John	4	4	5		
McCaslin, James	1	1	1		
Martin, George	1	2	2		
McMannis, Laurance	3	2	3		
Asten, John	1	2	2		
Moyr, John	2		3		
Maffett, Hugh	5	3	3		
Martin, Zachariah	2		2		6
Moon, Thos	2	2	4		
Moon, James	2	3	3		
Martin, James	2	3	1	2	2
Nall, Martha	1		2		1
Philliphs, Dennis	1	2	2		
Philliphs, Wm	1	1	3		
Philliphs, Willis	1		3		
Philliphs, Lewis	1	2	4		
Philliphs, Joel	1	3	1		
Pervis, Robert	1	4	3		
Philliphs, Jeremiah	3	3	3		
Powers, John	2	2	2		2
Parrot, Joel	1	5	2		7
Raglin, Thomas	1		2		
Rhodes, Wm	1	1	4		
Ratliff, John, Jr	1	3	4		
Ratliff, John	1	1	3		
Ramsower, Michael	2		3		
Ramsower, Edward	1		5		
Smith, Coley	1	3	2		
Smith, Abraham	1	3	3		
Smith, Wm, Sr	1	3	4		
Sanders, Benja	1	1	2		
Smith, Ambrous	1	7	4		
Smith, David	1	1	2		
Stinson, Robert	1		4		
Stephens, Joseph	2	3	6		
Tucker, John	1	2	4		
Thomson, Saml	1	3	5		
Talley, John	1	3	4		
Tucker, Wm	1		7		3
Thomson, Balom	2	3	5		
Underwood, James	3	3	2		
Collins, Wm	1		2		5
Hinton, Sarah	1	2	6		
Venderver, John	2	1	5	1	2
Grainger, James	1	2	1		
Smith, Wm	1		5		
Jones, Reuben	1	1	1		
Brewer, Sampson	1	1	2		
Estrick, Willis	1	2	4		
Wilson, Wm	1	2	4		
Dickson, George	2	2	1		
Grainger, Thos	2		4		
Willit, James	1		2		
Willit, John	1	4	4		
Willit, Rich	1		2		
White, Phillip	2		4		
White, Catey	1		4		

HILLSBOROUGH DISTRICT, CHATHAM COUNTY—Continued.

NAME OF HEAD OF FAMILY.	Free white males of 16 years and upward, including heads of families.	Free white males under 16 years.	Free white females, including heads of families.	All other free persons.	Slaves.
Stinson, Aron	1	2	5		
Rogers, George	2	2	3		
Bradus, Owin	3	2	3		
Jones, Sam¹	4	1	1		
Philliphs, Mary		2	5		
Welch, John	1	1	3		
Murry, Jane		1	3		
Ratliff, Edom	1	1	2		
Henry, Micajah	1		2		
Winter, Sam¹	1	3	2		
Ward, Job, Sʳ	1	1	2		
Ward, Job, Jr	1	1	2		
White, Charles	3		3		
White, Stephen	1		1		
Brantley, Wᵐ	1	1	1		6
Wimberley, Jesse	1	1	3		
Smith, John	2		3		
Wilson, John	1		1		
Tigue, Isaac	1	3	2		
Hobson, Thoˢ	1		1		
Hadley, Jeremiah	1		2		
Adcock, Joshua	1	2	3		
Burnet, Wᵐ	1	1	2		
Dutey, Wᵐ	2	1	5		
Wilkerson, John	1		2		
Collins, Wᵐ	1	1	3		
Marcus, Job	2	1	3		
Gillum, John	2	3	4		
Burges, John	1		3		
Mirphit, James	1		3		
Welch, Walter	3	2	5		
Wilkerson, Robert	1	2	4		
Wilkerson, Ricᵈ	2	4	9		
Routh, Robert	2	5	3		
Linin, James	1	3	1		
McVay, Martin	1	2	1		
Wilson, Daniel	1	1	3		
Terrell, Solomon	1		1		
Wismiland, Shadrick	1	2	1		
Wismiland, Patey	1		3		
Moody, Wᵐ	1		1		
Smith, David	1		1		
Younger, John	1	2	2		
Class, Cloe			3		
Dredyard, John	1	2	5		
Harper, Sam¹	2	3	4		
Allen, Henry	2	2	8		
Brantley, John	1	2	8		8
Brooks, Thoˢ, Seʳ	1	1	1		5
Brooks, Thoˢ, Jʳ	2	1	10		6
Brantley, Wᵐ	2	2	6		10
Burk, Millinner	1	2	4		
Brantley, Mary		1	3		10
Byant, Wᵐ	1	3	6		
Beal, Daniel	1	2	2		
Brown, Thoˢ	1	3	2		
Boyds, John	1	1	4		
Bullard, James	1	3	3		
Bagley, Henry	1	1	3		
Brooks, Stephen	2	4	2		
Beal, John	1		3		
Blalock, David	1	2	4		
Brooks, Sam	1	5	6		4
Copeland, Nicholas	2	2	3		
Copeland, John	1	2	1		
Copeland, Ruth			3		
Cox, Presley	1	2	4		13
Coan, John	1	1	4		
Dark, Joseph	2	4	7		6
Dark, Sam¹	1	3	3		
Evens, Ruth	2	3	5		
Edwards, Wᵐ	2	1	3		9
Evens, Owen	1	1	1		
Fields, James	1	2	2		
Fields, James, Jr	1	3	2		
Fike, Elizabeth	1	3	2		
Green, Abell	2	5	3		
Glosston, Wᵐ	1	1	5		10
Ginn, Elizabeth		1	5		1
Gutree, Wᵐ	1	4	1		4
Harden, John	1				1
Hunter, Margret	1	2	5		7
Hunter, John	1	1	2		
Hill, Wᵐ	2	3	2		5
Harrington, Agnes			1		5
Hart, Thoˢ	1	2	4		
Hayes, Joseph	3	3	5		
Harris, Benjᵃ	3	4	4		14
Henson, Lezacus	1	4	6		
Howell, Samuel	2	5	3		2
Harrington, Whitmill	1	2	2		1
Hayes, Wᵐ	1	5	6		
Hart, John	1	1	2		
Howell, John	1	2	5		
Headen, Andrew	1	2	3		4
Jones, Matthew	4	3	3		42
Johnson, Lewis	1	2	8		
Kennon, Ruᵈ	1	4	5		25
Malane, John	3	1	4		22
Morphis, Joseph	1	2	3		
Matthews, Britain	1	2	1		1
MᶜDaniel, Arthur	1		5		
Minter, John	2	3	3		8
MᶜPherson, John	1	1	2		
MᶜGee, Micajah	1	1			4
May, Joseph	1	2	5		5
Pettey, Wᵐ	1	3	3		1
Peoples, Hugh	3	1	4		5
Roe, Solomon	2	2	5		4
Roser, John, Jr	1	3	6		
Roe, John, Sʳ	1		2		
Ramsey, Matthew	1	3	2		8
Robertson, Upshear	1				
Roper, John, Sʳ	1		3		
Todd, William	2		1		
Tomlinson, Riᵈ	2	1	5		2
Tomison, Ricᵈ	1	3	7		2
White, Philliph	2	2	2		
White, John	3	1	2		
White, Jacob	3	1	8		
Wilkins, Alexʳ	1	1	1		
Womble, John	1	1	3		
Right, Simon	3	1	5		
Webster, Ricᵈ	1	1	2		
Roper, Wᵐ	1				
Dark, Wᵐ	1	3	3		1
Jones, Edward	1	4	4		
Hart, Wᵐ	1		1		
Landom, Abner	1	2	2		1
Standley, Danny	1	2	4		
Riley, John	1		3		
Coley, Julus	1	2	1		
Underwood, Wᵐ	1		3		
Baker, Humphri	2	1	7		
Bennet, James	1	1	3		
Ausley, Willis	1		1		
Avin, John	1	1	8		5
Ausley, Jesse	1	1	4		1
Ausley, David	1	1	4		
Brinkley, Peter	2	3	4		
Butter, James	2	3	6		
Burt, Ricᵈ	2	3	4		5
Bohannon, Joseph	1	1	2		
Bohannon, Benjᵃ, Sʳ	1	2	4		14
Booker, James	1	1	8		8
Branton, Wᵐ	1	1	2		2
Booker, John	3	3	5		
Browdey, Dorcas	1	2	2		
Branton, Thoˢ	1	3	3		
Browder, John	1		5		3
Clark, Burges	1	2	4		
Casten, Seth	1	2	5		4
Chapman, Solomon	2	3	2		8
Chapman, Henry	2	4	3		
Chapman, David	2		5		6
Covenah, David	1		2		1
Copeland, Wᵐ, Sʳ	1		1		
Christain, John	1	3	4		
Crump, Joseph	1	3	2		2
Copeland, Ricᵈ	1		1		
Copeland, John	1	2	3		
Caudle, Isham	1	5	3		
Caudle, Bleaker	1		3		
Davis, Matthew	1	4	2		
Daniel, Isham	2		2		
Dillard, Elisha	1		2		
Davis, Wᵐ	1	1	3		
Darton, Benjᵃ	2		1		
Dillard, Wᵐ	1	3	4		4
Daniel, Jesse	1				
Dreshill, John	1				
Dillard, John	1	2	1		
Dillard, John	1	2	3		
Dillard, Zacharias	1	1	2		2
Elkins, Joshua	1	1	3		
Edwards, John	1		3		
Griffis, Thoˢ	1	5	3		10
Hamton, John	1				
Hales, Josiah	1		3		
Hutchins, Gabril	1	2	4		
Horn, James	1	2	3		
Hinsley, Benjᵃ	3		2		
Hinsley, Nath¹	1	3	5		
Hogan, Wᵐ	1	6	4		
Hudson, Wᵐ	1		2		
Hudson, Allen	1		1		
Haley, Robert	1		4		
Hamton, Moses	3		3		
June, Jesse	1	1	2		1
Jones, Lewis	3	5	4		
Jinks, Wᵐ	1	1	1		
Johnson, Wᵐ	1	1	2		
Linn, Elizabeth	1	1	4		1
Lankston, Jamˢ	2	1	2		
Marshall, Wᵐ	1				
Matthews, Laurance	3	4	3		
Moore, John	2	1	6		
Mason, Ricᵈ	2	3	2		
Mims, David	2	3	3		
Matthews, Clabon	2	5	4		
Moore, Wᵐ	1	2	2		
Nevin, John	4	4	3		
Richardson, John	1	1	3		2
Richardson, Thoˢ	2	4	1		7
Redding, Charles	1	2	3		3
Raglin, Wᵐ	1	2	2		7
Richardson, George	1				
Raglin, Sarah		1	3		17
Redding, Wᵐ	2		1		3
Raglin, Federick	1				2
Rolins, John	1	5	2		2
Singlton, John	2	2	6		
Sigirs, Joshua	1	4	3		
Stephens, Jarrot	1	1	2		
Tedder, John	1	1	9		
Upchurch, John	2	2	4		
Wilson, Blumore	1	3	3		
Wormack, Britain	2	3	6		
Williams, Burwell	2	1	7		20
Watson, Christopher	2		3		
Winnington, James	1		2		2
Wallace, Sherrod	1	3	3		
Wilson, Stephen	1	1	1		
Wilson, Michael	1	1	2		
Weaver, Isham	1	1	3		
Wilson, Wᵐ	1	3	2		
Wilson, Blumore	1	3	3		
Yarbrough, Lewis	1	2	5		
Bass, Aron	1		2		
Hicks, Thoˢ	1	3	3		
Philliphs, James	1	5	2		
Stephens, Lewis	1	1	3		
Wilson, Sam¹	1				
Bodling, John	1	1	1		
Lankston, James	1		1		
Willis, Arthur	1		1		
Jinkins, John	2	1	5		
Johnson, Isham	1	3	6		1
Hogan, John	1	2	2		
Christain, James	1				
Christain, Thoˢ	1				1
Ozborn, Stephen	1	2	2		
Caudle, Jesse	1	1	2		
Chapman, Tabithey			1		8
Cotten, Wᵐ	1		2		
Hatch, Alexʳ	1				
Warthen, James	1		4		
Whitehead, Arther	1	1	2		
Dosit, Clemment	1		2		
Chambs, Charity	1	3	5		
Tigue, David	1	3	2		1
Tigue, Edmond	1	3	1		
Stewart, Edward	1	2	2		
Reynolds, Florence	2		2		
Dosit, Francis	1	1	5		
Silley, Federick	1	1	2		
Tigue, Francis	1	1	3		
Allen, George	1				
Adwek, Henry	1		1		1
Rogers, Henry	1	1	1		
Dosia, John	1	1	2		
Webster, John	1	2	3		
Rosser, John	1				
May, John	1				
Tigue, Jacob	3	2	4		
Stewart, James	1	1	2		
Watson, James	1	3	2		
Hackney, Joseph	3		3		8
Page, John	1	3	6		
Webster, James	1	1	4		
MᶜDaniel, Jacob	2	1	1		12
Bridges, Joseph	3	1	1		
Hadley, Joshua	3	4	5		
Hall, John	1	4	3		
George, James	1	3	6		
Whitehead, John	2		6		
Johnson, Levi	2	2	4		1
Hart, Morgan	1		2		
MᶜKinsey, Peter	1	2	2		
Laurance, Patrick S.	2	3	2		7
Claton, Ricᵈ	2	2	2		
Stewart, Sam¹	4	1	2		5
Rogers, Stephen, Seʳ	2	3	5		
MᶜDaniel, Sam¹	1		7		9
Rogers, Stephen	1				
Foster, Thoˢ, Seʳ	1	1	2		
Foster, Thoˢ, Jʳ	1	2	3		
Craton, Thoˢ	1	3	2		
Piles, John	2	1	3		
Holliday, Thoˢ	1	1	5		
Adcock, Wᵐ	1	2	3		

HILLSBOROUGH DISTRICT, CHATHAM COUNTY—Continued.

NAME OF HEAD OF FAMILY.	Free white males of 16 years and upward, including heads of families.	Free white males under 16 years.	Free white females, including heads of families.	All other free persons.	Slaves.
Tigue, Wm	1	1	1		
Collins, Wm	1		1		
Rogers, Wm	1	1	3		
George, Wm, Jr	1				
George, Wm, Sr	2		5		
Tigue, Mayner	1	3	2		
Forrester, Nathl	2	2	5		
Dossit, Solomon	1		1		
Tison, Francis		1	1		
Tigue, Moses, Sr	1		1		1
Tigue, Moses, Jur	1	1	1		
Womley, John	2	2	3		
Curshalt, Jacob	1	2	5		
Hadley, Joseph	2	4	4		
Nobbit, Robert	1	2	1		
Nobbit, Wm	2	3	4		
McDaniel, John	1				
Greer, Charles	1	3	2		
Davis, Joseph	1	3	1		
Christain, Drewry	2	1	1		2
Gunter, Isham	2	2	4		
Williams, Wm	1	2	6		
Adams, Thos	2	2	1		
Akemon, Adam	1	2	4		3
Adams, Thos	1	5	4		
Bishop, Benja	1		1		4
Bullard, Thos	1	2	5		
Bell, Thos	2	3	2		5
Brinkley, Peter	2	1	4		
Blalock, Charles	1	1	2		1
Binom, Isaac	1	2	2		
Buzby, Jesse	2		2		1
Bishop, Ricd	1	3	4		1
Buzby, Phindul	1		1		
Buzby, Phindul	1	2	5		
Bilbary, Isham	1		2		
Barber, Gray	1	5	4		6
Boling, Wm	1	1	1		
Bishop, Henry	1	2	4		1
Buzby, Henry	1		2		9
Buzby, Isham	1	3	3		1
Buzby, Ephraim	1	3	3		2
Bilbary, Thos	1	1	2		
Binom, Wm	1	2	2		
Cain, Hardy	1	1	1		1
Cuddle, John	1		4		
Cypruss, Thos	2	1	3		
Coal, Wm	1	3	1		1
Cole, Thos	1	3	4		
Cosins, Thos	1		1		
Copeland, Josiah	2	1	3		
Carter, Benjamin	1	5	2		
Coker, Jacob	1	1	1		
Copeland, Josiah, Jr	1				
Copeland, Wm	1	2	2		
Cuddle, Benja	1	3	2		
Carter, Vincent	1	2	2		

NAME OF HEAD OF FAMILY.	Free white males of 16 years and upward, including heads of families.	Free white males under 16 years.	Free white females, including heads of families.	All other free persons.	Slaves.
Cain, Elisha	3	1	5		11
Dickson, James	1	2	2		
Durham, Charles	1		1		
Dodd, William	1	2	4		
Edwards, Hugh	1	2	5		
Foremon, Benjn	2		2		2
Freeman, Howell	1	4	3		
Flowers, Jacob	1	1	6		15
Goodin, Shadrick	1	1	3		2
Goodwin, Wm	1	5	2		
Gregory, Harden	1	2	2		
Gregory, Thos, Ser	1	1	5		
Gregory, Wm	1		4		
Gregory, Bray	1	2	3		
Gregory, Presley	2	1	2		4
George, Isaac	1	2	1		1
George, Joseph	1				
Goodwin, Gideon	4	2	4		17
Gregory, Jeremiah	1	1	2		
Gregory, John	1	3	3		
Golson, Charles	3	2	6		
Horsey, Isaac	3		2		
Hatley, John, Ser	5	2	2		8
Hatley, John	1	1	1		
Hatley, Hardy	1		1		
Hatley, Jacob	1		1		
Harrod, Malakiah	1		2		
Hathcock, Wm	1	3	3		
Hathcock, James	2	1	8		
Hudson, Ricd	3	2	5		
Hanes, Robert	2	2	6		
Harndon, John	1	2	4		5
Harrod, Absalom	1	1	3		4
Holland, James	1	3	2		
Johnson, Robert	1	3	5		
Jones, Arthur	2	1	2		
Jones, Tignal	1		7		
Jones, Francis	1	1	2		13
King, Wm	1		3		1
Kelley, Henry	2	2	5		
Kirby, James, Ser	2	2	6		4
Kirby, James, Jr	1	4	2		
Lankston, Wm	1	2	4		
Lassiter, Mary		2	1		
Lambeth, John	2				
Ledbetter, Colmon	1				
Ledbetter, John	1				
Ledbetter, Wm	3	2	4		
Lambeth, Wm	1	2	1		
Moore, James	1	5	2		3
Moodey, Joel	3	3	5		
Merrot, William	2	3	2		8
Mass, John	1	1	5		
Mitchel, Allen	1	2	3		
Null, Presley	1	1	1		6
Ohiley, William	1	1	2		1
Oaldham, John	2	2	4		1

NAME OF HEAD OF FAMILY.	Free white males of 16 years and upward, including heads of families.	Free white males under 16 years.	Free white females, including heads of families.	All other free persons.	Slaves.
Parker, Lewis	1	4	2		2
Pewet, Joel	2	4	3		7
Powell, Simon	1	2	2		
Pendergrass, John	1	1	2		
Pitts, Joseph	1	1	3		1
Pitts, John	1	4	5		1
Parker, Robert	1	2	4		
Quishingberry, John	1	4	2		3
Quishingberry, Nicholas	2		2		5
Ragons, Charles	1		3		
Rhodes, Elisha	1		3		
Rickmon, John	2	1	3		1
Ragons, Wm	1	4	4		
Rhodes, Wm	1	3	4		1
Rogers, Isham	1	4	4		
Rowland, Jesse	1	5	5		
Rigsbey, Luke	1	4	2		
Rowland, Jesse	1		1		
Rogers, Bias	2	1	7		
Sanders, Philliphs	2	4	2		
Sillers, James	3	1	4		
Sillers, David	1	2	4		
Sillers, Robert	1	2	3		1
Stone, Francis	1	2	4		
Stegall, Mosses	3	4	5		
Sillers, James	2	3	4		
Sillers, Isaac	1				
Suars, Barber	1		1		1
Smith, Solomon	1	5	5		
Smart, Laborn	1	2	3		
Tatom, Jesse	1	1	2		
Williams, Wm	1		2		1
Wood, John	1	3	4		
Wilson, Benja	1	1	2		
Wimberle, Jacob	2	1	1		
Wimberle, Lewis	2	2	4		
Wayster, Wm	1	3	3		
Underwood, Hamblet	2	1	4		
Yeals, William	1	1	2		
Bullard, James	2	3	4		
Medlen, John	1	3	2		
Smith, Elias	2		2		
Bilbury, Laurance	1		2		
Honey, Bias	1	1	3		
Jenkins, Saml	1	1	3		1
Mitchel, Reuben	1	1	2		
Harrod, Joseph	1	2	2		
Gregory, Thos	1	1	3		7
Hatthcock, John	2	3	4		
Pilint, Cary		2	5		
Straughn, Ricd	1	3	1		
Jones, Aquilla	1		2		
Ferrington, John	1	1	2		
Odam, Thos	1	3	2		
Brown, Thos	1		4		
Rigsbey, Luke	1	4	2		

HILLSBOROUGH DISTRICT, GRANVILLE COUNTY.[1]

ABRAHAM'S PLAINS DISTRICT.					
Smith, Samuel					
Smith, Samuel, Jun					
Downey, James					
Howard, John					
West, James					
Davis, Baxter					
Norman, George					
Leavel, Edward					
Pittard, John					
More, John					
Graves, Henry					
Williamson, Thomas					
Towns, Henry					
Hart, John					
Smith, John					
Frasyier, Arthur					
Mitchel, Jacob					
Montague, Henry					
Burrage, Edward					
Hunt, James					
Graves, Mary					
Chavis, James					
Fraisyier, Wm					
Owen, Frederick					
Owen, Wm. (son of James)					
Owen, John					
Siddler, Jesse					
Hester, Wm					
Raven, John					
Montague, Young					
Johnston, James					

ABRAHAM'S PLAINS DISTRICT—continued.					
Tindal, John					
Roberts, Willis					
Downey, James, Jun					
Raven, John, Jun					
Graves, Ralph					
Montague, Latteney					
Melone, Robert					
Allen, Capt. Grant					
Allen, Thomas					
Lewis, Howel, Jun., Esq.					
Lewis, Howel					
Knight, Jonathan, Esq.					
Butler, Anne					
Owen, Jacob					
Morgan, Elizabeth					
Hendrickson, Ezekiel					
Knight, John					
Knight, Wm					
Amis, Wm					
Smith, Anderson					
Williams, Thomas					
Crieth, Samuel					
Oliver (Widow)					
Stamper, John					
Burch, Nicholas					
Hawley, Nathan					
Mutter, Thos					
Love, Allen (Est. of)					
Crenshaw, Abram					
Oliver, Mary					
Yates, Lovit					

BEAVER DAM DISTRICT.					
Pope, John					
Pope, Osborn					
Pope, John, Jr					
Moore, Major					
Lyles, Wm					
Bailey, Jeremiah					
Bailey, John					
Mangum, Absolom					
Mangum, James					
Bradford, David, Jun					
Phillips, David					
Jones, Frances					
Jones, Samuel					
Hawley, Jacob					
Horn, Howel					
Lawrence, Wm					
Nance, Harrod					
Harris, Edward					
Buckhannon, Wm					
Tanner, Wm					
Nance, Richard					
Austine, Valentine					
Pascall, James					
Hooker, John					
Huscatt, Farthy					
Brown, John					
Champion, Charles					
Bradford, Richard					
Wilkerson, Wm					
Weaver, Wm					
Hays, Leonard					
Harris, Harrison					

[1] Names taken from county tax lists.

HILLSBOROUGH DISTRICT, GRANVILLE COUNTY—Continued.

NAME OF HEAD OF FAMILY.	Free white males of 16 years and upward, including heads of families.	Free white males under 16 years.	Free white females, including heads of families.	All other free persons.	Slaves.	NAME OF HEAD OF FAMILY.	Free white males of 16 years and upward, including heads of families.	Free white males under 16 years.	Free white females, including heads of families.	All other free persons.	Slaves.	NAME OF HEAD OF FAMILY.	Free white males of 16 years and upward, including heads of families.	Free white males under 16 years.	Free white females, including heads of families.	All other free persons.	Slaves.
BEAVER DAM DISTRICT—continued.						**DUTCH DISTRICT—**continued.						**EPPING FOREST DISTRICT—**continued.					
Glasgow, Richard						McLemoore, James						Kittrell, Samuel					
Hendley, Wm						Hall, Futril						Ragsdel, David					
Allen, Robert						Merreman, Malekiah						Harp, John					
Bradford, Philemon, Jr						Oakey, Joseph, Jun						Rowler, James					
Winningham, John						Beck, Frederick						York, Thomas					
Wright, Hannah						Culberhouse, Thomas W						Moore, Charles, Jnr					
Taylor, George						Tatom, John						Harp, Thomas					
Harp, Henry						Beck, William						Moore, Charles, Senr					
Bradford, David						Merreman, William						Evins, Burrel					
Bailey, Rich						Culberhouse, Jeremiah											
Mann, Arnold						Hoofman, Jacob						**FISHING CREEK DISTRICT.**					
Bradford, Philemon						Jenkins, Thomas											
Griffin, Lawrence						Adcocke, Bowling						Peace, John, Sen					
Heflin, John						Harrison, Saria						Peace, Joseph					
Hooker, John, Jun						Lawrence, Abraham						Brummit, Nimrod					
Hudson, Drury						Haskins, James						Hayslip, Laborn					
Cape, Williamson						Ogilvie, Harris						Smith, John, Jun					
Moore, John						Green, William						Williams, Walter					
Thomas, John						Bradley, James						Carden, James					
Heflin, Wm						Claxton, James						Moore, Joel					
Heflin, Fielding						Potter, Lewis						Inschore, Stephen					
Mills, Robert						Parker, Samuel						Lankfurd, John					
Bradford, Booker						Willard, Augustine E						Parish, Jesse					
Champion, Joseph						Withus, William						Petyfurd, William					
Holt, John						Ogilvie, Kimbro						Harp, Sampson					
Roberts, Thomas						Freeman, Gideon						Tyler, Bartlet					
Bradford, Ephraim						Jones, William, Jun						Walker, Wm					
Mitchel, Isom						Adcocke, John						Snellings, Barnet					
Champion, John, Jun						Wade, Anna						Chavons, Wm					
Mitchel, Jane						Bullock, Micajah, Esq						Thornton, Solomon					
Carrell, John						Tippett, John						Harp, Thos					
Tanner, Finnings						Harris, Samuel						Anderson, Jacob					
Weathers, James						Williams, John						Bass, Nathan					
Nicholson, George												Hays, Henry, Jun					
Whitfield, John						**EPPING FOREST DISTRICT.**						Cooper, John					
Anderson, Frank												Lankfurd, Barrish					
Clement, Simon						Fuller, Henry, Senr						Dickerson, John, Jr					
Cavenaugh, George						Roberts, William						Miner, Wm					
Harris, Christopher						McDaniel, James						Garrott, Jesse					
Bridgers, John						Hornsby, William						Earls, Jesse					
Harris, John						Thomason, Richard						Dickerson, William					
Peet, John						White, Valentine						Thomas, Christian					
Bridgers, Drury						Roberts, Isaac						Snellings, Ann					
Fullar, Capt. Jones						White, Thomas						Walker, Samuel, Sen					
Fullar, David						Finch, John, Jun						Cooper, Conealut					
Allen, Champion						Edwards, John						Bynum, Henry					
Goodloe, Robert						Fuller, Britton						Newby, Thomas, Sen					
Leathers, James						Johnson, Benjamin						Barr, James					
						Alley, Rosser						Inscor, Reuban, Sen					
DUTCH DISTRICT.						White, Mark						Inscor, Reuban, Jun					
						Finch, Williamson						Williams, Wm					
Hunt, William						Cook, William						Hunt, Wm					
Peck, John C						Floyd, Mosses						Hunt, Daniel					
Wilkerson, Wyatt						Rogers, William						Lankfurd, Henry					
Carver, Edmund						Lloyd, Isaiah						Parrish, Elijah					
Veasey, Elijah						Fowler, William						Cork, James					
Clements, Thomas						Laurance, John						Snelling, Hugh					
Fussel, Moses						Highfield, Hezekiah						Smith, John, Sen					
Walker, Nathaniel						Hickman, Corbin						Priddy, Wm					
Jones, Thomas						Roberson, Robert						Bass, Reubin					
Stew, Jacob						Kittrell, Jonathan, Jun						Peace, Jos., Sr					
Cooke, Richard S						Hunt, John						Smith, James					
Moore, George L						Fuller, Henry, Jun						Harp, John					
Cash, Joseph						Cook, Blanton						Fowler, James					
Turner, Charles						Smith, Thomas						York, Thomas					
Moore, Benjamin						Spears, Phillip						Moore, Charles, Sen					
Taggle, John						Spears, John						Harp, Thomas, Sen					
Bailey, John						Leeman, William						Dickerson, John					
Bailey, Stephen						Bobbit, William						Dickerson, John					
Walker, James						Ragsbill, Backster						Ball, Eligah					
Brasfield, Caleb						Rogers, Joseph						Evins, Buril					
Story, George						Roberson, Nicholas											
Cash, Peter						McDaniel, Joseph						**FORT CREEK DISTRICT.**					
Cash, James						Floyd, William											
Ornerry, Richard						Parrish, Brisse						White, Wm. (X Roads)					
Byart, Mary						Kittrell, Jonathan, Senr						Carter, Jesse					
Baxter, Joseph						Finch, John, Senr						Kittle, Christopher					
Bottoms, Thomas L						Harding, Sterling						Magehee, Benjn., Sen					
Jarret, John						Askyou, John						Magehee, Benjn					
Swinney, William						Crowder, Ueel						Peace, John, Jr					
Cozzort, Jesse						Tedder, James						Vincent, Alex					
Toller, John						Johnson, Joseph						Vincent, Jacob					
Wheeler, Benjamin						Higgs, Leonard						Rogers, Wilson					
Carnes, Joseph						Finch, George						Magehee, Josiah					
Farmer, John						Lock, William						Magehee, Jesse					
Emmery, Ephraim						Laurance, Deborah						Philips, Garland					
Brasfield, George						Cooper, Kannon						Priddey, Robert					
Brasfield, Elizabeth						Kittrell, Joshua						Magehee, Joseph					
Pizor, Matthew						Hester, Joseph						Simmons, John, Sen					
Swinney, Thomas						Fuller, Samuel						Bowers, Philemon					
Beck, Michael						Eaton, Chas. R						Rust, John, Sr					
Landish, Joseph						Hays, Sarah						Rust, George					
Tucker, Thomas												Rust, Samuel					
Tucker, Frederick																	

HILLSBOROUGH DISTRICT, GRANVILLE COUNTY—Continued.

NAME OF HEAD OF FAMILY.	Free white males of 16 years and upward, including heads of families.	Free white males under 16 years.	Free white females, including heads of families.	All other free persons.	Slaves.
FORT CREEK DISTRICT—continued.					
Evans, Morran					
Champion, John					
Bradford, Benjn					
Nailing, Wm					
Blackley, James					
Blackley, Charles					
Welch, John					
Magehee, Robert					
Williams, Jeremiah					
Rogers, John					
Mayfield, Valentine					
Jenkins, James					
Whitlar, Nicholas					
Priddey, George					
Priddey, Thomas					
Blackwell, James					
Magehee, Nathan					
White, George					
Carter, Thomas					
Carter, Alex					
Mayfield, Abe					
Champion, John, Sr					
Blalock, David					
Myars, Jacob					
White, John					
Taylor, Lewis					
Mills, Wm					
White, Coleman					
Jeffrys, Wm					
Huddleston, John					
Gillam, Harris					
Lewiston, James					
Knowland, Chs					
Jones, Abraham					
Gowin, Jenkin					
Simmons, James					
Homes, Sam'l					
Bradford, John					
Magehee, Nathan					
Knowland, Dan'l, Jr					
Vincent, Peter					
Vincent, Isaac					
Blalock, Jeremiah					
Jones, Jonathan					
Cooke, Claborn					
White, Searl					
Cooke, Shem, Sr					
Alison, Robert					
Norris, James					
Heflin, Chs					
Taylor, Edm					
GOSHEN DISTRICT.					
Weston, James					
Oliver, John					
Olliver, Peter					
Mitchel, Josiah					
Knott, John					
Pointer, Samuel					
Jordan, Robert					
Ligon, Thos					
Beezley, Stephen					
Parrish, John					
Barker, Ambrose, Esq					
Ragland, Stephen (Est. of)					
Loyd, William					
Hester, Robert					
Knott, David					
Pool, Thomas					
Douglass, Joseph					
Evans, John					
Chandler, James					
Wade, Robert					
Wright, Francis					
Chandler, Joseph					
Lassiter, William					
Bedford, James					
Daniel, Chesley					
Tack, John					
Sandford, Robert					
Ashman, Lewis					
Bennet, Capt. Peter					
Daniel, Martin					
Owen, John, Jun					
Williams, Gideon					
Edwards, Thomas					
Pettyford, Seth					
Blanks, Joseph					
Jones, Reuban					
Obrian, Patrick					
Harris, John					

NAME OF HEAD OF FAMILY.	Free white males of 16 years and upward, including heads of families.	Free white males under 16 years.	Free white females, including heads of families.	All other free persons.	Slaves.
GOSHEN DISTRICT—continued.					
Harris, Robert					
Glass, William					
Mitchel, James					
Webb, John					
Graves, Henry, Jun					
Milinder, William					
Wilkerson, David					
Duty, Richard					
Aplin, Thomas					
Bennet, Lewis					
Le May, Susannah (Est. of)					
Wilkerson, Francis					
Palmer, William					
Jones, Ambrose, Sen					
Harris, Charles					
Le May, Samuel					
Lewis, Nathaniel					
Kennon, John					
Winfrey, James					
Wade, Charles					
Owen, John, Sen					
Pettyford, John					
Saterwhite, Michael					
Owen, Thomas					
Grant, Thos					
Allen, Francis					
Lumsden, John					
Paterson, Andrew					
Person, Thomas, Esq					
HENDERSON DISTRICT.					
Williams, Jno., Esq					
Burton, Ro., Esq					
Sneed, Step'n					
Burdin, Jno					
Gilliam, Wm					
Stark, Jas					
Craft, Thos					
Jordan, Arth					
Cox, Charnich					
Gresham, Rich'd					
Gresham, Stephen					
Harrison, Isham					
Smith, Ransom					
Smith, Edm'd					
Morse, John					
Stringfellers, Rich'd					
Craft, John					
Daniel, Joseph					
Pollin, William					
Rainwater, John					
Morse, Reuben					
Christian, Gideon					
Crichter, Thomas					
Wiggins, Thomas					
King, George					
Wiggins, Fred					
Seears, Joseph					
Grisham, Henry					
Harris, John					
Gillpin, Henry					
Henderson, Ples't					
Weaver, Minor					
Roland, Thos					
Perdue, George					
Denton, Benj					
Brame, James					
Brame, Thos					
Reaves, Sam'l					
Brack, Sam'l					
Barnes, Mirim'c					
Hanks, William					
Mitchel, Major					
Morse, Phillis					
Williams, Sam'l					
Weaver, John					
Yancy, Sterling					
Weaver, Edw'd					
Bowden, Francis					
Mitchel, David					
Mitchel, Ely					
Mitchel, Phillis					
Henderson, Rich'd					
Satterwhite, Thos					
Kimboll, Bartho					
Reves, Samuel					
Temerson, Will					
Shullhines, John ?					
Macon, John					
Chadwick, John					
Brack, Samuel, Jun					

NAME OF HEAD OF FAMILY.	Free white males of 16 years and upward, including heads of families.	Free white males under 16 years.	Free white females, including heads of families.	All other free persons.	Slaves.
ISLAND CREEK DISTRICT.					
Jones, Vinkler					
Kelley, Thomas					
Terry, Roland					
Norwood, Benj'n					
Pitchford, Daniel					
Davis, Absolom					
Davis, Solomon					
Scott, John					
Smith, Joseph					
Cardwell, Thomas					
Smith, Lenard					
Byars, William					
Perry, Peter					
Park, William					
Grizel, Harley					
Hargrove, Richard					
Fleman, Henry					
Hanks, Arguile					
Mason, David					
Akin, James, Sen					
Strome, Bartholomew					
Lewis, James					
Johnson, Henry					
Collins, John					
Akin, James					
Terry, Stephen					
Glover, Cap'n Dan'l					
Glover, Joab					
Matthews, James					
Gober, Martha					
Collins, Thomas					
Norwood, Jordan					
Scurry, Benjn					
Satterwhite, James					
Norwood, Gillum					
Akin, James					
Davis, Auguston					
Akin, Joseph					
Laniere, Lewis					
Duncan, William					
Barnett, Jesse					
Akin, Isom					
Whitlow, Jordan					
Harris, Christopher					
Lyne, Henry					
Hencock, Benj'n					
Smith, Sam'l					
Driskel, Timothy					
Smith, Henry					
Johnson, John					
Smith, James					
Gooch, Gidion					
Redd, Field					
Gober, William					
Sneed, Sam'l					
Sneed, Dudley					
Taylor, John (Br. G.)					
Barnitt, John					
Kindrick, Thomas					
Summerhill, Charles					
Bridges, Joseph					
Robertson, Benj'n					
Chapman, George					
Moor, William					
Parrish, Humphry					
Williams, Daniel					
Hargrove, John					
Robertson, John					
Dotson, Charles					
Dotson, William, Jr					
Barnett, Sarah C					
Hyde, Robert					
Harper, Jesse (Estate of)					
Hammond, Joab					
Lewis, Frances					
Suite, Dent					
Bullock, William					
Taylor, John, Esq. (Estate of)					
Bullock, James					
Goldsmith, Thomas					
Taylor, Elizabeth					
Penn, John					
Marshal, William					
Patillo, Rev. Henry					
Akin, Isom					
Hargrove, Stephen					
Butler, Reubin					
Ruth, David					
Burroughs, James					
Johnson, Benj'n					
Terry, James					

HILLSBOROUGH DISTRICT, GRANVILLE COUNTY—Continued.

NAME OF HEAD OF FAMILY.	Free white males of 16 years and upward, including heads of families.	Free white males under 16 years.	Free white females, including heads of families.	All other free persons.	Slaves.
ISLAND CREEK DISTRICT—continued.					
Moor, William					
Hester, Zacheriah					
Gooch, Joseph					
Melton, Henry					
Burch, Nicholas					
Crawley, Robert					
Cocker, William					
Wilson, Henry					
Hester, Abraham					
Carter, Thomas, Jun					
Stubbs, William					
Lyne, James					
Lanier, Thomas					
Howel, John					
Dodson, William					
Robertson, Mary					
Sumervil, John					
Maron, Daniel					
KNAP OF LEEDS DISTRICT.					
Tims, Amos					
Green, Henry					
Addams, Samuel					
Walker, Mary					
Tatum, William					
Green, Joab					
Oakey, Micajah					
Ellis, Joseph					
Ferrybough, Jacob					
Mangum, Joseph					
Cozzart, Ben					
Cozzart, Jacob					
Eastwood, Israel					
Long, George					
Eastes, Silvanus					
Brissil, Francis					
Ford, Absalom					
Clement, Stephen					
Eastis, William					
Jones, Charles					
Jones, William (big)					
Clement, Obediah					
Rose, Frederick					
Wilburn, Zachariah					
Wright, William					
Patterson, David					
Wright, George					
Phillips, Bennett					
Bowlen, John, Sen					
Jones, Edward					
Arnold, William					
Perkerson, Joel					
Jonse, Moses					
Waller, Joseph					
Clement, Samuel					
Mangum, Howel					
Partic, Ben					
Borolen, Wm					
Cole, Wm					
Terry, Stephen					
Oakey, Joseph					
Harris, Claburn					
Ogilsvie, Smith					
Ogilsvie, Wm					
Bullock, Jeremiah					
Bullock, Joshua					
Mauier, Jno. Wm					
Cozzort, Ann					
Meadows, Jesse					
Hunt, James					
Jones, Brereton					
Tims, Hollis					
Eastis, Lodowick					
Adcock, Leonard					
Cozzort, David					
Veasey, Zebulon					
Partee, Charles					
Gafford, Reuben					
Hawkins, John					
Harris, Richard					
Parker, Amos					
Adcock, Edward					
Goss, Thomas					
Primrose, Wm					
Jackson, Samuel					
Chambless, Joel					
Bullock, Charles					
Hawkins, Matthew					
Waller, Zephaniah					
Pulliam, Barnett					
Gorch, Rowlen					
Knott, James					
Jones, Wm					
KNAP OF LEEDS DISTRICT—continued.					
Clement, John					
Webb, Wm					
Merrit, Stephen					
Green, Daniel					
Brayleton, Jacob					
OXFORD DISTRICT.					
Linsay, Sarah					
Sniper, Nathaniel					
Searcy, William Hargrove					
Johnston, Saml					
Frasier, Jeremiah					
Hicks, Thomas					
Howard, Allen					
Bussure, Francis					
Mitchell, Charles					
Upchurch, William					
Cothran, William					
Gray, Morton					
Walker, Solomon					
Walker, Samuel					
Hunt, John					
Hunt, Samuel					
Maloney, Wm					
Parker, Jeptha					
Beardon, Benja					
Parham, Wm					
Longmin, Wm					
Crews, Caleb					
Walker, John					
Miner, John					
Hopkins, George					
Howel, Thomas					
White, Phil., Jun					
Hester, Francis					
Butler, Isaac					
Towel, James					
Hilliard, James					
Hicks, Robert					
Hester, Zachariah					
Williams, Thos					
Butler, Thos					
Taylor, Joseph					
White, Phil., Sen					
Tally, Reuben					
White, Jonathan					
Tomason, Thos					
Harris, Charles					
Harris, Samuel (Virga)					
Rose, Thos					
Clay, Samuel					
Mathews, Littlebury					
Harris, Robert					
Sample, John					
Noland, Edward					
Harris, Sherward					
Parham, Thos					
Lock, Jona					
Pulliam, John					
Robards, John					
Taylor, Edward, Sen					
Boyd, John					
Hunt, George					
Bird, Robert					
Marshell, John					
Morris, John					
Hunt, George					
Critcher, James					
Locust, Valentine					
Taburn, Drury					
Mitchel, Arch'd					
Anderson, Lewis					
RAGLAND DISTRICT.					
Rice, Thos					
Jetter, Sam'l					
Ragland, Reuben					
Ragland, Amis					
Loyd, Edw					
Driskall, Dennis					
Willson, John					
Hicks, Harris					
Williams, Charles					
Parish, David					
Parish, Claborn					
Bell, Josa					
Bates, John					
Hicks, Bishop					
Lindsey, Elijah					
Fordwine, Lemuel					
Allen, Samuel					
Thomson, Thos					
RAGLAND DISTRICT—continued.					
Wright, John					
Plummer, Zephaniah					
Ragland, William					
Currin, Hugh					
Sears, John					
Kimball, Henry					
Bass, Ed					
Davis, Jos					
Davis, P					
Grisham, James					
Norman, Thos					
Parish, Charles					
Parrish, Wm., Sen					
Parrish, Wm., Jun					
Harris, Darnin					
Parris, Thos					
Bishop, Jas					
Williams, Nath'n					
Hays, Joshua					
Hicks, Wm., Jun					
Earles, John, Sen					
Pettyford, Drury					
Earls, John					
Crews, James					
Harris, George					
Taylor, Will'm					
Hicks, Thos					
Wicker, Thos					
Foups, Mat'w					
Crews, Thos					
Wilkins, Rich					
Crews, Gidion					
Alston, George					
Wasff, George					
Neister, Benj					
Rivis, Lan					
Wilkins, Thos					
——, Drury					
Ridley, Bromfield					
Brodie, John					
TABB'S CREEK DISTRICT.					
Shemwell, James					
Parrish, David					
Bristow, John					
Tatom, Barnard					
Hays, Theophilus					
Johnston, Wm., Sen					
Sute, John					
Johnson, Gideon					
Parham, Cannon					
Parham, Thomas, Sen					
Johnson, Noel					
Johnson, Thomas					
Lanford, Jesse					
Clark, Leonard					
Hays, Joshua					
Page, Lewis					
Hicks, Samuel					
Reaves, Hardy					
Reaves, William					
Hicks, William					
Reaves, Frederick					
Johnson, Jonathan					
Johnson, William, Jr					
Parham, Lewis					
Parham, Ephraim					
Dunkin, John					
Wright, William					
Hayes, Joseph					
Parham, Avery					
Parham, Thomas, Jun					
Morriss, Henry					
Biram, John					
Hutchinson, Joshua					
Hedgpeth, Carter					
Riggs, Zachariah					
Woodall, Absolam					
Bristow, James					
Parham, Isham					
Debruler, Micajah					
Allison, Robert					
Allison, John					
Bryant, Rowland					
Barton, William					
Mathis, William					
Fowler, Henry					
Parham, William					
Parham, John					
Whitlow, Nathan					
Hicks, David					
Bristow, Philemon					
Farer, Searcy					
Smith, Edward					

HILLSBOROUGH DISTRICT, GRANVILLE COUNTY—Continued.

NAME OF HEAD OF FAMILY.	Free white males of 16 years and upward, including heads of families.	Free white males under 16 years.	Free white females, including heads of families.	All other free persons.	Slaves.	NAME OF HEAD OF FAMILY.	Free white males of 16 years and upward, including heads of families.	Free white males under 16 years.	Free white females, including heads of families.	All other free persons.	Slaves.	NAME OF HEAD OF FAMILY.	Free white males of 16 years and upward, including heads of families.	Free white males under 16 years.	Free white females, including heads of families.	All other free persons.	Slaves.
TABB'S CREEK DISTRICT—continued.						**TAR RIVER DISTRICT**—continued.						**TAR RIVER DISTRICT**—continued.					
Parham, Isham, Jun						Hopgood, Hezekiah						Oakley, Thos					
Parham, John, Jun						Gunter, Jesse						Thorp, John, Sen					
Hopkins, Ann						Hester, Wm						Terry, James					
Jett, Stephen						Pettyford, George						Thorp, John, Jun					
Higgs, Zacharias						Frazer, Ephraim						Oakley, William					
						Badget, John						Slaughter, Jacob, Jr					
TAR RIVER DISTRICT.						Lumpkin, Anthony						Cragg, John, Jun					
						Harris, Anthony (son of Rich.)						Millener, James					
Slaughter, Jacob, Sen						Thomason, John						Gooch, Amos					
Slaughter, Jacob (Taylor)						Mathews, John						Shearman, Michael					
Dunkin, Geo						Goss, Shearmon						Fowler, Richard					
Roberts, James						Brinkley, James, Sr						Cragg, John, Senr					
Wood, John						Long, Charles						Russel, John					
Williams, Solomon						Johnson, Isham						Howard, Graves					
Obryan, Dennis						Clark, Nathan'l						Bass, Benj., Jun					
Badget, Wm						Cock, Wm						Bass, Benj., Sen					
Hill, John						Meadows, James						Putman, Benja					
Gooch, Danl						Meadows, Daniel						Gill, William, Esq					
Forsythe, James						Washington, John, Esq						Bruer, Amery					
Bass, Rich						Wells, Miles						Williams, Capt. John					
Dunkin, Harrison						Adcock, Robert						Brinkley, Richard					
Brinkley, Peter						Brinkley, James, Jun						Jones, John					
Meadows, Michael						Badget, Peter						Pulliam, Barnett					
Briggs, Richard						Philpot, Wm											

HILLSBOROUGH DISTRICT, ORANGE COUNTY.[1]

NAME OF HEAD OF FAMILY.	Free white males of 16 years and upward, including heads of families.	Free white males under 16 years.	Free white females, including heads of families.	All other free persons.	Slaves.	NAME OF HEAD OF FAMILY.	Free white males of 16 years and upward, including heads of families.	Free white males under 16 years.	Free white females, including heads of families.	All other free persons.	Slaves.	NAME OF HEAD OF FAMILY.	Free white males of 16 years and upward, including heads of families.	Free white males under 16 years.	Free white females, including heads of families.	All other free persons.	Slaves.
CASWELL DISTRICT.						**CASWELL DISTRICT**—continued.						**CASWELL DISTRICT**—continued.					
Hunter, Robt						Williams, Fred'k						Bradford, Joseph					
Russell, Alex'r						O'Daniel, Henry						Jones, Thos					
McDaniel, Eli						Carrigan, John						Jones, Francis					
Dill, Isaac						Shy, Jesse						Marshall, Jacob					
Bradshaw, Thos						Stroud, Wm						Murdock, Wm					
Pain, Joseph						Brewer, Henry						Morrow, Andrew					
Durham, John						Kirk, Lewis						Thompson, James					
Roach, James						Horton, Abraham						Harvey, Eli					
Thompson, John						Curtins, John						Pickett, Alex'r					
McVey, James						Austen, Wm						Pickett, John, Jr					
O'Daniel, John						Cate, Thos						Patton, Catherine					
Millison, John						McDaniel, John						McPherson, Wm					
Trip, John						Lashley, Barnet						Holladay, Wm					
Taylor, Hardiman						Edwards, Henry						Holladay, Robt					
Peacock, Samuel						Edwards, John, Sr						Wilson, Thos					
Carter, Wm						Cate, Thos., Jr						Andrews, Robt					
Moore, John						Kirk, Wm						Ray, Robt					
Moore, Rich'd						Christmas, Mary						Holladay, Henry					
Rhodes, John						Pratt, Janie						Thompson, James					
Harsey, Isaac						King, Thos						McDaniel, John					
Dale, Henry						Gibson, James						Stockard, James					
Crawford, James						Nichol, Benj						McDaniel, James					
Isel, Randall						Pickett, Henry						Newlin, John					
Pinnin, James						Holwood, Thos., Jr						Tagart, Isaac					
Moore, John						Moore, James						Rayson, John (of Robert)					
Mickle, Abraham						Holwood, Thos						Allen, James					
Willis, James						Roberts, James						Matthews, James					
Morrow, William						Ray, Wm						Newlin, James					
Cate, Robt						Thompson, Thos						Maris, George (Est. of)					
Durham, John						Thompson, James						Madden, George					
Sykes, Allen						Thompson, Wm						Woody, James, Jn					
Sykes, John						Thompson, Thos., Jr						Andrew, Wm					
Cate, Richard						Paid, John						Laughlin, Rich'd					
Cate, Thos						McMullin, Sam'l						Ray, Wm., Sr					
Cate, Joseph						Powall, John						Morrison, Rob't					
Cate, Robert						Clendening, Wm						Brooks, John					
Moore, William						Johnston, Geo						Powell, Jesse					
Davis, Benj						Johnston, James						Carter, John					
Durham, Matthew						Pain, James						Holladay, Henry, Jr					
Hunnecut, Robt						Smith, Reuben						Common, Wm					
Bates, James						Smith, David						Lindley, Mary					
Lashley, Thos						Smith, Wm						Dix, Zachariah					
Lindsay, John						Jones, Jonathan						Dix, Nathan					
Robinson, Athanarius						McCracken, Jeremiah						Andrew, Rob't, Jr					
Stalworth, Joseph						Kennedy, John						Woody, John					
Strader, John						Williams, Arthur						Woody, James					
Kelley, Chanler						Howard, Thos						Woody, Wm					
Durham, Thos						Jones, Aquilla						Grimes, John					
Leary, Benj						McDaniel, Daniel						Lowrey, James					
Kirk, James						Pugh, Daniel						Whitted, Thos					
Cate, John						McDaniel, James						Woody, Joseph					
Workman, John						Gordon, Wm						Way, Nathaniel					
Williams, Peter						Rainey, John						Patton, John					
Cate, Stephen						Thompson, John						Harvey, Nathan					
Millikan, Robt						Pickard, John						Shoridine, Geo					
Millikan, James						Pugh, John						Murray, John					
Ray, John						Trousdale, James						Cox, Moses					
Millikan, Charles						Trousdale, John						Paris, Wm					
Dixon, Benj						Ray, Wm						Wilkins, George					
Durham, Wm						Baker, Tobias						Mann, John					
Buckner, Wm						Lewis, Henry											

[1] Names taken from county tax lists.

HILLSBOROUGH DISTRICT, ORANGE COUNTY--Continued.

NAME OF HEAD OF FAMILY.	Free white males of 16 years and upward, including heads of families.	Free white males under 16 years.	Free white females, including heads of families.	All other free persons.	Slaves.	NAME OF HEAD OF FAMILY.	Free white males of 16 years and upward, including heads of families.	Free white males under 16 years.	Free white females, including heads of families.	All other free persons.	Slaves.	NAME OF HEAD OF FAMILY.	Free white males of 16 years and upward, including heads of families.	Free white males under 16 years.	Free white females, including heads of families.	All other free persons.	Slaves.
CASWELL DISTRICT—continued.						CHATHAM DISTRICT—continued.						HILLSBORO DISTRICT.					
Cate, Bernard						Straders, John						Cloud, Daniel					
Carters, Nathaniel						Straders, George						Allison, John					
Bradley, Enoch						Straders, Henry						Thompson, Sam					
Shy, John						Holston, Jacob						Neelson, Abraham					
Edwards, Melen						Cockledress, Michael						Turner, Edward					
Hackney, John						Haney, John						Ringstaff, Conrad					
Edwards, John						Crowden, Jeremiah						Clark, Wm					
Edwards, Rich'd (heirs of)						Garner, Lewis						Thompson, Albert					
Edwards, Sylvanus (heirs of)						Hatchett, Wm						Thompson, Benja					
Edwards, Wm (Estate of)						Garner, Parish						Hastings, James					
Christmas, Rich'd						Holt, John, Jr						Collins, Andrew					
Holmes, John						Coble, John						Thompson, James					
Armstrong, John						Holt, Jacob						Huntingdon, Roswell					
Morrison, Nathaniel						Holt, Israel						Palmer, Martin					
Roach, Lewis						Garrison, John						Hart, Stephen					
Partin, James						Sellers, Thos						Crabtree, Thomas					
Lindley, Jonathan						Holt, George						Jamison, Wm					
Lindley, Wm (Estate of)						Thomas, Edward						Collins, Eli					
						Harden, Nicholas						McCallum, Jonathan					
CHATHAM DISTRICT.						Given, Wm						Murdock, James					
Marley, Adam						Turner, Rob't						Hastings, Henry, Sr					
Marley, Samuel						Albright, Ludwick						Aston, Wm					
Stalcup, Wm						Albright, Geo						Aston, Sam'l					
Holt, George, Sr						Holt, Jeremiah						Watson, James					
Harden, John						Bowldin, Wm						Adams, John					
Campbell, George						Whitesill, Adam						Lamb, Benj					
Cook, Nehemiah						Robbs, Alex'r						Crabtree, James					
Gimlin, James						Albright, Philip						Bailey, Thos					
Williams, Wm						Suthard, John						Roberson, Michael					
Bowen, James						Jordan, Jonathan						Rountree, Thos					
Fawcett, Wm						McCracken, John						Woods, Sam'l					
Harvey, John						Huffine, Dan'l						Taylor, John					
O'Neal, Wm						Jeffers, Garner						Hall, Wm					
Morris, Joseph						Jeffers, Evan						Shannon, Wm					
Crickman, Timothy						Jeffers, John						McCaulis, Jane					
Morten, Jacob						Powell, John						Ray, James					
Sullivan, Dan'l						Powell, John, Jr						Roberson, Michael, Jr					
Smathers, Wm						Hatmaker, Malachi						Thompson, John					
Cook, Ephraim						Hatmaker, Malachi, Jr						Roberson, James					
Tate, Rob't						Coble, Philip						Tinnin, John					
Jackson, Wm						Lynbury, Jacob						Combs, Wm					
Tate, Zacheus						Crisman, Geo						Tarlton, James					
Charles, Michael						McClure, Henry						Breeze, John					
Burch, James						Holt, Michael						Johnston, Thos					
Judge, Bryant						Harden, John						Hall, Robt					
Barber, Allen						Holt, John						Whealey, Benj					
Nelvin, John						Albright, Jacob						McCulloch, John					
Martin, Henry						Holt, John, Sr						McCulloch, James					
Boyle, James, Jr						Holt, Christopher						McMahan, Dan'l					
Boyles, John						Albright, John						Anderson, John					
Boyles, James, Sr						Gant, John						McCaulis, John					
Boyles, John, Jr						Killin, John						Collins, Enoch					
Bracken, James						Hudson, Chamberlain						Ray, Robt					
Moore, Thos						Staves, John						Allison, David					
Boyles, Wm						Long, Casper						McBroom, Andrew					
Robertson, Hugh						Cook, John						Anderson, Jane					
Dinning, David						Cook, David						Allison, Elizabeth					
Dinning, David, Jr						Cook, Edward						Griffin, Andrew					
McCauley, Joseph						Cook, Archibald						Williams, David					
Smith, Sam'l						Osborn, James						Parks, Wm					
Smith, Mary						Hudson, John						Rountree, John					
Garrison, Jacob						James, Abner						Rountree, Charles					
Moore, Rob't						James, Solomon						Smith, Robt					
Bracken, Isaac						Philips, Jesse						Murdock, Agnes					
Simmons, Peter						Gant, John						Donaldson, James					
Bracken, Isaac, Sr						Gant, John, Sr						Clark, James (Hiss)					
Smith, Andrew						Dawley, John						Nichols, John					
Dinning, John						Pyles, James						Wilson, Robt					
Groin, Alex'r						Cook, John						Wilkison, James					
Moore, John						Stark, John						Carson, James					
Moore, James						McCulloch, Robt						Clark, Thos					
McLean, James						Garrison, Geo						Clark, Wm					
Robertson John						Tickel, Peter						Bane, Thos					
Sloss, John						Tickle, John						McKee, Alex'r					
Rainey, Wm						Huffman, Suffah						McCulloch, Robt					
Rainey, Benj						White, Henry						Crabtree, John					
Litt, James						Wallace, Miles						Anderson, Robt					
Wishart, Absolom						Brinkley, Peter						Turrentine, John					
Wishart, Elias						Brinkley, Peter, Jr						Wood, Wm. (Bl. Smith)					
Wishart, Jacob						Coble, Antony						Clark, Wm. (Eno)					
Mickle, Andrew						Pate, John						Clark, James (Estate of)					
Davis, Wm						Griffiths, Wm						Whitehead, Wm					
Browing, John						Melvin, Edmund						Jackson, Wm., Sr					
Garrison, Garret						Armstrong, John						Williams, Rich'd					
Smathers, Thos						Averett, Nathan						Ray, Charles					
Swathers, John						Campbell, Ezekiel						Johns, John					
Smathers, Alex'r						Bracken, Thomas						Waggoner, Catharine					
Gwin Edward						Murray, Jonathan						Miller, Jesse					
Bracken, Wm						Servir, Henry						Strayhorn, Gilbert					
Hurdle, Hardy						McCulloch, Thos						Hannah, David					
Jacobs, Henry						Tate, James						Clark, Wm. (L. R.)					
						Bewswick, Caleb						Woods, John, Sr					
						Love, Thomas						Niel, Robt					
						Dunnivan, John						Jackson, Isaac					
						Collins, John						Boreland, Alex'r					

HILLSBOROUGH DISTRICT, ORANGE COUNTY—Continued.

NAME OF HEAD OF FAMILY.	Free white males of 16 years and upward, including heads of families.	Free white males under 16 years.	Free white females, including heads of families.	All other free persons.	Slaves.	NAME OF HEAD OF FAMILY.	Free white males of 16 years and upward, including heads of families.	Free white males under 16 years.	Free white females, including heads of families.	All other free persons.	Slaves.	NAME OF HEAD OF FAMILY.	Free white males of 16 years and upward, including heads of families.	Free white males under 16 years.	Free white females, including heads of families.	All other free persons.	Slaves.
HILLSBORO DISTRICT— continued.						**HILLSBORO TOWN.**						**ORANGE DISTRICT—** continued.					
Clark, James (L. R.)						Allison, John						Murray, James					
Allison, John, Sr						Thompson, Henry						Estor, Samuel					
Allison, John, Jr						Stone, David						Patton, John					
Hammond, Edward						Stubbins, Joseph						Daly, Wm					
Nichols, Baldwin						Wilson, Isabel						Dorris, John					
Nichols, Jonathan, Sr						Hunter, James						Williams, Thos					
Gray, John						Kelly, Wm						Mebane, Sam'l					
Nichols, Jonathan, Jr						Finley, Hugh						McAdams, John					
Regan, Thos						Courtney, Wm						Trolinger, Henry					
Copeland, David						Brooks, Thos						Barnwell, James					
Wilson, James						McCauley, Wm						Hodge, Robt					
Wilson, John						McCauley, John						Murray, James					
Woods, Wm						Ferguson						Murray, John					
Jordan, Robt						McCollom, Harvey						Pinnix, Overton					
Andrews, James						Bevans, Thos						Crawford, Hugh					
Jordan, Enos						Newman, Wm						McAdams, Hugh					
Jackson, James						Harris, Starling						Giffy, William					
Mitchell, John						Moore, Joseph						Carswell, John					
Killin, Wm						Alves, Walter						Beasom, Jacob					
Fowler, Sam'l						Wilkerson, Vincent						Anderson, James					
Keiley, John (Eno)						Anderson, Kenneth						McAdams, James					
Riley, Jacob						Whitehead, Jehu						Stanford, William					
Allison, James						Heal, Joseph						Anderson, Alexander					
Davis, John						Phillips, James						Bradford, William					
Clark, James, Sr						Farmer, Thos						Pattison, William					
Clark, James, Jr						Whithead, Wm						Murray, James					
McKee, Wm						Brooks, Asa						Whitmore, Charles					
Bowls, Thos						Huskins, Geo						Whitmore, Jesse					
Bowls, Wm						Duncan, John						Long, Koonrad					
Wood, John (son of Hugh)						Keys, James H						Hodge, William					
Riley, John (L. R.)						Nichols, John						Hodge, Margaret					
Armstrong, Wm						Cain, Wm						Eccles, William					
Riley, Wm. (L. R.)						Taylor, John						King, Armore					
Faucett, James						Burke, Andrew						Lindsay, Ely					
Barlow, Benj						Ray, David						Lapsley, James					
Thompson, Sam'l						Childs, Francis						McCracken, Samuel					
Jordan, Thos						McQuister, William						Thomas, Jacob					
Berry, Robt, Jr						Sharp, Joseph						Elmore, Randall					
Jackson, Jacob						Croer, John						Blackard, William					
Cragston, George						Hooper, Wm						Paul, Elizabeth					
Chambers, Sam'l												Baker, Joseph					
Strayhorn, James						**ORANGE DISTRICT.**						Beason, Henry					
Harvey, Caleb												Justice, John					
Crabtree, Wm						Mebane, Wilson						Turner, James					
Burnside, Robt						Walker, John (Stiller)						Dorris, Robert					
Scarlett, John						Stradwick, William						Patton, Samuel					
Toulson, Thos						Nelson, Sam'l						Allen, James					
Faucett, David						Walker, John						Chance, William					
Barton, Thos						Walker, Wm						Elmore, John					
Fruit, Uriah						Walker, Peter						Elmore, Athy					
Faucett, Rich'd						Walker, Andrew						Tate, Joseph					
Berry, John						Bradford, David						Faucett, Robert					
Blake, Isham						Dobson, James						Daly, John					
Fade, Joseph						Boyd, George						Wason, Henry					
Holden, John						Douglas, David						Cantrill, Mary					
Holden, Thos						Thompson, Joseph						Allen, George					
Flinlain, John						Foust, George						Foster, Richard					
Campbell, Wm						Douglas, William						Hall, Isaac					
Faucett, Ralph						Bryan, James						Ball, Richard					
Carson, Alex'r						Pate, James (Carpenter)						Elmore, Peter					
Berry, Robt						Bird, Thos						Hall, Levy					
Baldridge, Dan'l						Fitch, William						Hall, James					
Hart, James, Jr						Bird, Emmon						Dickson, Joseph					
McVey, Patrick						Bird, Rich'd						Pinnin, Robt					
Hart, James, Sr						Fitch, Thomas						Pinnin, Carnes					
Hart, Thomas						Bradford, George						Newland, Eli					
Berry, Joshua						Mason, Henry						King, Edward					
Allison, Joseph						Hicks, Zebedy						Stalcup, Isaac					
Jackson, Wm						Griffin, John						Rony, James					
Ray, John						Whiteside, Sam'l						Wason, Daniel					
Thompson, Theophilus						Hamilton, Joseph						Martin, Obadiah					
Hastings, Wm						Rives, John						Rippy, Thos					
Hastings, Henry						Lynch, Jesse						Gott, Robt					
Armstrong, John						Hughes, John						Trousdale, John					
Armstrong, James						Lynch, Thos						McFarlan, Walker					
Armstrong, Martin						Scott, Mary						Hopkins, James					
Elliott, John						Forrest, John						Patton, Robt					
Faddis, John						Fulton, Jesse						Foust, Deborah					
Miller, James						Witty, Joshua						Beason, John					
Cooper, Wm						Nelson, John						Stanford, Chas					
Benton, Jesse						Fulton, Margaret						McAdams, Joseph					
Hart, Col. Thos						Wilson, Robt						Scott, Wm					
Baldridge, James						Carr, James						McEvoy, John					
Parks, John						Wilkerson, Francis						Millington, John					
Doherty, Antony						Bradford, Thomas						Eccles, John					
Doherty, James						Whitman, Nowell						Norvel, Wm					
Tapp, Abner						Tinnin, Robert						King, John					
Taylor, Fred'k						Lapsley, David						Gooch, Wm. G					
Pratt, James						Wilson, Edward						Pendergast, Luke					
McCool, Archibald						Rickett, Edward						McMusty, John					
Gitson, David						Redding, Thos						Dorris, William					
Morgan, Thos						Murray, Wm						Dorris, Isaac					
												Stewart, Robert					

HILLSBOROUGH DISTRICT, ORANGE COUNTY—Continued.

NAME OF HEAD OF FAMILY.	Free white males of 16 years and upward, including heads of families.	Free white males under 16 years.	Free white females, including heads of families.	All other free persons.	Slaves.
ORANGE DISTRICT— continued.					
Smith, Andrew					
Thomas, Hannah					
Dicky, Zechariah					
McMon, James					
Lindsay, Matthew					
Huggins, Jacob					
Stalcup, Tobias					
Smith, John					
McCracken, Thomas					
McClury, Andrew					
Fawsett, Robt					
Lynch, John					
Gant, William					
Stanford, John					
Hodge, Joseph					
Freeland, James					
Freeland, James, Jr					
Hawly, Daniel					
Murray, Walter					
Thomas, George					
Shaw, Samuel					
Lake, Jacob					
Lake, Rich'd					
Wilson, Charles					
Galbreath, John					
Lyons, Frances					
Davis, William					
Ross, James					
Stevens, Henry					
Stanford, Rich'd					
Allen, John					
Jefers, Jacob					
Gate, William					
Hastings, John					
Stevens, Benjamin					
Holloway, Martha					
Rippy, Mathew					
Pate, Thos					
Rainey, William					
Rippy, John					
Wrightsmon, Peter					
Thompson, Joseph					
Carroll, Robt					
Carroll, Henry					
McAdam, Sam'l					
Galbreath, Wm					
Dickson, Thos					
Dickson, Stuart					
Stanford, James					
Smith, William					
Forrest, James					
Chance, Zekiel					
Dicky, James					
Dickson, James					
Dickson, Robt					
Rony, Benj'n					
Fy, Larry					
Compton, Aquila					
White, David					
Huchison, James					
Ellis, Thos					
Holgan, Thos					
Phillips, David					
Kirkpatrick, Alex'r					
White, Stephen					
Hugh, Wm					
McCloskey, Ed					
Barnwell, Robt					
Sturges, John					
McCauley, And'w					
Mebane, Alex., Sr					
Mebane, David					
Smith, Wm					
McMon, Wm					
Ward, Sutton					
Minson, Rich'd					
Blair, John					
McCracken, Robt					
Collins, Brice					
Thomas, Abram					
Jones, Lewis					
Paul, John					
Ward, John					
Murdock, Andrew					
Mebane, Alex'r, Jr					
Shepperd, Wm					
ST. ASAPH'S DISTRICT.					
Harden, John					
Williams, John					
Roberson, James					
Roberson, Elijah					
Hunnicutt, Dempsey					
Hunnicutt, Lewis					

NAME OF HEAD OF FAMILY.	Free white males of 16 years and upward, including heads of families.	Free white males under 16 years.	Free white females, including heads of families.	All other free persons.	Slaves.
ST. ASAPH'S DISTRICT— continued.					
Bates, Ambrose					
Woolf, Wm					
Jones, Jacob, Jr					
Holt, James					
Woolf, Peter					
May, John					
Tinnin, James					
Wells, John					
Eulis, Philip					
Williams, Elizabeth					
Ward, Stephen					
Springer, George					
Sugars, John					
Nail, Wm					
Courtney, Daniel					
Pike, Samuel					
Graves, Jacob					
Pridle, George, Sr					
Foust, George					
Cuntz, John					
Paterson, James					
Smith, James					
Piles, Conrad, Sr					
Rogers, Wm					
Snothley, Philip					
Loy, George, Jr					
Pore, Peter					
Clap, John					
Diason, John					
Graves, John					
Lynn, James					
May, Daniel, Jr					
Homes, Rob't					
Homes, Joseph					
Ward, Wm					
Taylor, Jonathan					
Courtner, Peter					
Ware, John					
Kinrow, Henry					
Fourt, Daniel					
Shaddy, John					
Thomas, Abraham					
Fogleman, Katrina					
Fogleman, George					
Sharp, Aaron, Jr					
Sharp, G. (Estate of)					
Hiefman, John					
Hiefman, Jacob (Estate of)					
Troxler, Barney					
Peter, Conrad					
Troxler, Jacob					
Roberson, Thos					
Thompson, Anthony					
Houseman, Joseph					
Kime, Henry					
Alexander, James					
Alexander, John					
Henseroe, John					
Roberson, Nathaniel					
Wells, Nathan					
Albright, Joseph					
May, George					
Noe, Peter					
Albright, Ludwick					
Shofner, Frederick					
Rich, Thos					
Smith, Adam					
Fogleman, Malachi					
Garnet, Henry					
Moser, Philip					
Williams, Edward					
Williams, Joseph					
Moser, Michael					
Antony, Jacob					
Shofner, Michael					
Price, William					
Fogleman, Michael					
Moser, Jacob					
Shofner, George					
Courtner, Daniel					
Fogleman, John					
Stoner, Jeremiah					
Stoner, Peter					
Rich, Jacob					
Holt, Joshua					
Randolph, John					
Campbell, Nancy					
Calk, Henry					
Smith, Henry					
Eafler, John					
Patterson, Wm					
Coble, John					
Spoon, John					
Coble, Henry					

NAME OF HEAD OF FAMILY.	Free white males of 16 years and upward, including heads of families.	Free white males under 16 years.	Free white females, including heads of families.	All other free persons.	Slaves.
ST. ASAPH'S DISTRICT— continued.					
Spoon, Adam					
Coble, David					
Nankins, Mary					
Smith, Tobias					
Shofner, Martin					
Counselman, Jacob					
Coble, Christian					
Mason, Philip					
Sharp, John					
Albright, John (B. Creek)					
Noe, John					
Bullock, John					
Albright, Henry					
Albright, Jacob					
Asley, Philip					
Sharp, Poyston					
Shofner, Michael					
Moser, Nicholas					
Williams, Shafney					
Albright, Jacob, Sr					
Calk, Conrad					
Kimbrough, Fred'k					
Loy, John					
Patterson, John					
Loy, Henry					
Cook, Henry					
Sharp, Aaron					
May, Daniel, Sr					
Eaflet, David					
Neace, Martin					
Albright, John					
Kimbrough, Paul					
Homes, James					
Godfrey, James					
May, Ludwick					
Boggs, James					
Helton, Peter					
Hilton, Abraham					
Hilton, James					
Hilton, Peter, Sr					
Cloud, Samuel					
Whinery, Abraham					
Foust, Peter					
Clendennin, Joseph					
Neece, George					
Norman, Joseph					
Kimrow, George					
Holt, John					
Jackson, Colby					
Lynn, John					
Smith, Adam, Jr					
Gurbs, Nicholas					
Moyer, Philip					
Coble, Adam					
Smith, Adam (Red)					
Noe, Rosanna					
Springer, Uriah					
Darknet, Jacob					
Rinehart, David					
Esley, Malichi					
Brown, Wm					
Marshall, Wm					
Morrow, Wm					
Brown, Ebenezer					
Stout, Charles					
Stout, Peter					
Stout, Joseph					
Allen, John					
Freeman, Samuel					
Underwood, Alex'r					
Clark, John					
Hunnicutt, Moses					
Picket, Benj					
Picket, Joshua					
Dale, Isaac					
Freeman, Dan'l					
Beverly, Elijah					
Wells, Isaac					
Wells, Joseph					
Wells, Joseph, Jr					
Gifford, Levi					
Moser, Frederick					
Pike, John					
Wheeler, John					
Buckingham, Joseph					
Moser, Abraham					
Dronebarger, Ludwick					
Long, John					
Neal, James					
Holt, Nicholas					
Holt, Francis					
Dison, Wm					
Fogleman, Peter					
Noe, Joseph					

HILLSBOROUGH DISTRICT, ORANGE COUNTY—Continued.

NAME OF HEAD OF FAMILY.	Free white males of 16 years and upward, including heads of families.	Free white males under 16 years.	Free white females, including heads of families.	All other free persons.	Slaves.
ST. ASAPH'S DISTRICT—continued.					
Clap, Barney					
Aycock, Jesse					
Hornaday, Lewis					
Stoneman, James					
Perkins, Thos. H.					
ST. MARK'S DISTRICT.					
Sears, Rosey					
Stanford, Israel					
Horn, Thos.					
Lewis, Enoch					
Massey, Abraham					
Bennett, James					
Daniel, Christopher					
Green, John					
Marcom, Richard					
Huggins, James					
Davis, Rich'd					
Watson, Dan'l					
Holden, John					
Holden, Wm., Jr.					
Hurst, John					
Rhodes, John					
Castlebury, James					
Hayes, Leonard					
Bilbo, Joseph					
Hampton, Robt.					
Lord, Wm.					
Horn, Wm., Jr.					
Marcom, Thos.					
Burgess, Thomas					
Davis, James					
Dollar, James					
Horn, Joshua					
Edwards, Charles					
Duggen, Alexander					
Price, John					
Fennell, Joseph					
Watson, Daniel, Jr.					
Massey, Abner					
Booth, Joseph					
Booth, Daniel					
Daniel, Sam'l					
Hobson, Wm.					
Marcom, Wm.					
Vaughan, James					
Barber, John, Jr.					
Davis, John					
Hall, David					
Daniel, George					
Hutson, Wm., Jr.					
Grice, Edward, Jr.					
Price, Joseph					
Hinkley, David					
Riggen, Powell					
Daniel, John					
Collies, Charles					
Barbee, Christopher					
Herndon, Benj.					
Merritt, Sam'l					
Tudor, Harris					
Price, Thos.					
Hall, Thos.					
Price, James					
Rhodes, Wm., Jr.					
Horn, James					
Barbee, Mark					
Leigh, John					
Grice, Ezekiel					
Shepherd, William					
Price, Edward					
Moore, John					
Rhodes, Wm.					
Dezern, James					
Barbee, John, Sr					
Carlton, Leonard					
Couch, John					
Couch, Edward					
Paterson, John Barbee					
Price, Wm.					
Davis, Nicholas					
Hobson, Elizabeth					
Moreland, Francis					
Shepherd, Sam'l					
Horn, Wm.					
Daniel, Paterson					
Marcom, John					
Anderson, Abraham					
Turner, Wm.					
Holder, Wm.					
Couch, James					
Edwards, John					
Hall, John					
Couch, Thos.					

NAME OF HEAD OF FAMILY.	Free white males of 16 years and upward, including heads of families.	Free white males under 16 years.	Free white females, including heads of families.	All other free persons.	Slaves.
ST. MARK'S DISTRICT—continued.					
Pickett, Wm.					
Pickett, Wm., Jr.					
Picket, Henry					
Farmer, Othniel					
Surles, Francis					
Surles, Thos.					
Farm, Sarah					
Herndon, George					
Herndon, Jachariah					
Pool, Wm.					
Pool, Samuel					
Standifer, Joshua					
Surles, Ephraim					
Glenn, King					
Glenn, Wm.					
Glenn, Ezra					
Miles, David					
Lloyd, Thos.					
Green, Daniel					
Westmoreland, Reuben					
Mitcham, John					
Browning, Mark					
Fogarty, Cornalis					
Chandler, Dan'l					
McDaniel, Dan'l					
Leigh, Rich'd					
Allen, Joseph					
Burton, Wm.					
Andros, Richard					
Stringer, Leonard					
Daniel, Wm., Jr.					
Magee, Daniel					
Hudson, David					
Huggins, Moses					
House, Peter					
Gwinn, Thos.					
Daniel, Roger					
Rone, Charles					
Briant, John					
Barbee, Joseph					
Barbee, John, Jr.					
Allen, Jersey					
White, Joseph					
Peeler, Benj.					
Paterson, Mark					
Booth, Gray					
Deserne, Nathaniel					
Hurst, Joseph					
Hudson, Wm.					
Barbee, Christopher					
Campbell, Rob't.					
ST. MARY'S DISTRICT.					
Horton, Henry					
Harris, Edmund					
Tilley, Jahn, Sr.					
Ashley, James					
Moore, John, Sr.					
Moore, John, Jr.					
Woods, Edward					
Craig, Jonathan					
McFarlin, Thos.					
Pilley, Lazarus					
Carrington, Nathaniel					
Cates, Richard					
Cole, Sam'l					
Nutt, David					
Cates, Benjamin					
Cates, Matthias					
Smith, Stephen					
Hunt, Thos.					
Grimes, Barney					
Brinkley, Eli					
Horner, Geo. Jr					
Horner, Thos.					
Woods, Joseph (Eno.)					
Woods, Sampson					
Carrington, Geo					
Dorsett, Thos.					
Harris, Hugh					
McFarlin, Wm., Jr.					
Horner, Geo., Jr					
McFarlin, Keziah					
Walker, James, Jr.					
Ricketts, Anthony					
Chisenhuse, Reuben					
Mannin, Charles					
Riggs, Geo., Sr					
Nealy, John					
Montgomery, Wm., Sr.					
Britton, Joseph					
Clower, Wm.					
Horton, Thos.					
Moore, Henry					

NAME OF HEAD OF FAMILY.	Free white males of 16 years and upward, including heads of families.	Free white males under 16 years.	Free white females, including heads of families.	All other free persons.	Slaves.
ST. MARY'S DISTRICT—continued.					
Leathers, Moses					
Roberts, Charles					
Tilley, John, Jr.					
Mize, John					
Duke, Robt.					
Carrington, Ephraim					
Mangum, William					
Roberts, Abner					
Ray, James					
Mashburn, Josh, Sr.					
Mashburn, Elisha					
Peddegwin, Wm.					
Robinson, Wm.					
McMullen, Alex'r					
Garvard, John					
Glenn, Warham					
Allen, Samuel					
Collins, Wm.					
Harris, Archer					
Clower, Dan'l					
Parish, Allen					
Roberts, Jeremiah					
Moore, James					
Watson, James, Sr.					
Bobbit, Sihon					
Watson, John, Jr.					
Wilson, Samuel					
Pickle, Henry					
Cates, William					
Wilson, Thos.					
Cozart, Anthony					
Bagley, Henry					
Walker, James, Sr.					
Mashburn, James, Sr.					
Horton, Charles					
Davis, Abraham					
Wilburn, John					
Dunnegam, Wm., Sr.					
Woods, Joseph					
Woods, Eli					
Lynch, John					
Guess, George					
Warren, Josiah					
Cannaday, James					
Piper, John, Sr.					
Wallace, Wm.					
Woods, James					
Grisham, George					
Woods, Thos., Sr.					
Dollar, Jonathan					
Fulton, James					
Roads, Thos.					
Cates, Lazarus					
Roads, Aquilla					
Woods, Blayton					
Dorsett, Wm.					
Dunwoody, Henry					
Holloway, Rich'd					
Forester, Benj					
Sears, Elizabeth					
Clinton, Matthias					
Ragan, John					
Townsley, Joseph					
Johnston, Drury					
Chisenhall, John					
Forrest, Isaac					
Forrest, Edmond					
Hill, George					
Woods, Thos., Jr.					
Sutherland, Mordecai					
Curry, James					
May, Samuel					
Turner, Elias					
Bunch, Henry					
Whitacer, Abraham					
Dunning, Nicholas					
Cole, Levi					
May, John					
Curry, John					
Riley, James					
Curry, James					
Riley, Wm.					
Downs, Wm.					
Lewis, Thos.					
Leathers, Wm.					
Alston, James					
Forrest, Stephen					
Paterson, Andrew					
Forrest, Shadrack					
Roads, Wm.					
Lewis, Fielding					
Woods, Wm.					
Scarlett, John					
Cates, Rob't.					
Jolly James					

HILLSBOROUGH DISTRICT, ORANGE COUNTY—Continued.

NAME OF HEAD OF FAMILY.	Free white males of 16 years and upward, including heads of families.	Free white males under 16 years.	Free white females, including heads of families.	All other free persons.	Slaves.
ST. MARY'S DISTRICT—continued.					
Nevis, John					
Grisham, Rob't					
Harris, Richmond					
Forrest, Hezekiah					
Dorsett, Wm., Jr					
Laycock, Thos					
Chisenhall, Wm					
Ray, Wm., Sr					
Umstead, David					
Roberts, John					
Wilson, James					
Turrentine, Sam'l, Sr					
Turrentine, Sam'l, Jr					
Latta, John, Jr					
Hopkins, Wm					
Parker, Abraham					
Mize, Henry					
Graves, Rob't, Jr					
Robinson, Edw'd					
Mize, Zachariah					
Taylor, John					
Jamison, Wm					
Smallwood, Wm					
Roark, James					
Forsyth, Rob't					
Glenn, Jeremiah					
Gabley, Isham					
Wurtham, Edward					
Dunnagam, Sherrid					
Umstead, Richard					
Riggs, Sam'l					
Latta, John, Sr					
Riggs, John					
Laycock, Wm					
Burres, James					
Ware, Wm					
Britton, Benj					
Baldwin, John					
Piper, Sam'l					
Morgan, Thos					
Walker, Rob't					
Morgan, Wm					
Linch, Darling					
Latta, James, Sr					
Latta, Thos					
Latta, James, Jr					
Morris, Hugh					
Redding, Thos					
Hite, Joseph					
Woods, Hugh					
Cales, John					
Cain, James					
Scarlett, Stephen					
Popley, John					
Clenny, Sam'l					
Carrol, Stephen					
Dollar, Elijah					
Holloway, Thos					
Cole, John					
Burton, Cuthbud					
Belvin, William					
Newton, George					
Sutton, Thos					
Lewis, John					
Carroll, Benj					
Browning, Thos					
Clenny, Wm					
Cabe, Wm					
Roades, Richard					
Durring, James					
Horn, Thos					
Woods, John (Sheriff)					
Clarke, Wm					
Guess, Joseph					
Clements, Thos., Jr					
Clements, John					
Chisenhall, Sam'l					
Wilson, Stephen					
Carrington, John, Sr					
Dunnagan, Charles					
Tatom, Mourning					
Tatom, John					

NAME OF HEAD OF FAMILY.	Free white males of 16 years and upward, including heads of families.	Free white males under 16 years.	Free white females, including heads of families.	All other free persons.	Slaves.
ST. MARY'S DISTRICT—continued.					
Critchen, James					
Carrington, John, Jr					
Cain, John					
Bennehan, Richard					
Hurley, Wm					
Cain, Wm					
Riggs, James					
Jones, John					
Kilby, John					
Hunt, Henry					
Hunt, John					
Rhodes, Rich'd					
Riggs, James					
Allen, Jacob					
Walker, Wm					
Sears, Joseph					
Douglas, John					
Redman, John					
Way, Thos					
ST. THOMAS' DISTRICT.					
Andrews, William					
Pendergrass, William					
King, Wm					
Blackwood, James					
Owen, Peter					
Bradbury, John					
Partin, Leonard					
Blackwood, Wm					
Pendergrass, Job					
Fann, John					
Strayn, Alexander					
Price, John					
Johnston, Geo					
Burns, Wm					
Wilson, John					
Freeland, John					
Riggans, James					
King, Nathaniel					
Rodes, Alex'r					
Massie, Abijah					
Hogan, John					
Lloyd, Wm					
King, Chas					
Gaddice, James					
Gaddice, Sam'l					
Scott, John					
Lloyd, Stephen					
Connolly, John					
Lloyd, Fred'k					
Stephens, Dan'l					
Price, Archibald					
Howell, Benjamin					
Kirkland, Joseph					
Bevill, Zechariah					
Hogan, David					
Ivey, Henry					
Lloyd, Owen					
Caldwell, John					
Craig, James					
Lloyd, James					
Ivay, David					
Owen, John					
Moseley, Samuel					
Williss, Peter					
Yeargin, Benj					
Patterson, Mann (orphan)					
Patterson, Charles P. (orphan)					
Reeves, Rev. George					
King, John					
McCauley, Matthew					
Walter, John					
Burrow, John					
Piper, Alex'r					
Piper, Sam'l					
Piper, Abraham					
Moseley, John					
Rigsbee, William					
Sparrow, John					

NAME OF HEAD OF FAMILY.	Free white males of 16 years and upward, including heads of families.	Free white males under 16 years.	Free white females, including heads of families.	All other free persons.	Slaves.
ST. THOMAS' DISTRICT—continued.					
Colther, Hinson					
Colther, Matthew					
Howell, Edward					
Stroud, John					
Partin, Wm					
Conally, Thos					
Hastings, Joseph					
Pate, John					
Jones, Edmund					
Strain, John					
Thrift, Isham					
Wemes, John					
Willis, Wm					
Stroud, Anderson					
Mitchell, Andrew					
Weeks, Joseph					
Hunter, Samuel					
Hunter, Aaron					
Cheek, Masting					
Baker, Thomas					
Woohley, Wm					
Coruthers, Hugh					
Cheek, Robt					
Forsith, Wm					
Long, George					
Baker, John					
Mitchel, John					
King, Hannah					
Pettiford, Elias					
Stroud, Elizabeth					
Trotter, Robt					
Haywood, Jesse					
King, Thos					
Pendergrass, Thos					
Bynum, John					
Brewer, Sackfield					
Honeycutt, Wike					
Fannin, John					
Rigsbee, Jesse					
Gaddice, John					
Gaddice, Alex'r					
Hinshery, John					
Gaddice, John, Jr					
Brewer, Ezekiel					
Brewer, Thos					
Cooper, Mark					
Smith, James					
Morgan, Hardy					
Herndon, Comfort					
Willis, John					
Morris, Henry					
Morris, Rich'd					
Nevill, Jesse					
Caudle, David					
Cheek, James					
Allen, Abraham					
Craig, Samuel					
McCauley, Wm					
Craig, Ellinor					
Craig, John					
Strayhorn, John					
Hart, James					
Wilmoth, Thos					
Hobbs, Wm					
Couch, John					
Carroll, Michael					
Bowls, John					
Baker, James					
Clerk, Joseph					
Hastings, Joseph					
Baker, Robt					
Miller, Joseph					
Bolling, Baxter					
Hinkley, Ezekiel					
Strayhorn, Wm					
Craig, James, Sr					
Flowers, Jacob					
Morgan, John					
Hogan, Sarah					
Maron, Jacob					
King, Baxter					

HILLSBOROUGH DISTRICT, RANDOLPH COUNTY.

Name	Males 16+	Males <16	Females	Other free	Slaves	Name	Males 16+	Males <16	Females	Other free	Slaves	Name	Males 16+	Males <16	Females	Other free	Slaves
Alexander, James			1		3	Barton, Elizabeth	1	1	7			Barton, Elizabeth		2	3		8
Brown, Michael	4	1	4			Beason, William	1	1	8			Brown, Federick	1	2	1		
Brewer, John	2		2	1	1	Beason, Richard	1	4	6			Clou, Thomas	2	2	3		
Beason, Edward	1	2	4			Bond, John	1	5	3			Coble, Nicholas	2	2	5		
Brown, James	1	2	3			Beason, Benjamin	1	1	2			Chamness, Joseph	3	2	6		
Beason, Isaac	2	3	2			Barnett, Obed	1		3			Crawford, Eve		2	2		
Barton, John	1		2			Barnett, Uriah	1	2	3			Coble, John	2		2		1
Brown, Jacob	1		2			Buntin, Ebenezer	3		2			Coble, John, Jur	2	1	5		

HILLSBOROUGH DISTRICT, RANDOLPH COUNTY—Continued.

NAME OF HEAD OF FAMILY.	Free white males of 16 years and upward, including heads of families.	Free white males under 16 years.	Free white females, including heads of families.	All other free persons.	Slaves.
Caucey, Isaac	1	5	4		5
Davidson, James	2	5	2		
Dennis, John	1	1	2		
Dennis, Thomas	1	1	2		
Elliott, William	2		1		
Elliott, Israel	1	1	3		
Elliott, Obediah	1		4		
Elliott, Peter	1	1	1		
Elliott, John	1	2	1		
Elliott, Abraham, Jur	1	2	2		
Elliott, Samuel	1	1	3		
Elliott, Abraham	1	2	2		
Elliott, Joseph	1	2	4		
Elliott, Jacob	1	2	8		
Elliott, Abraham, Senr	3		2		
Erwin, William	3	4	4		
Field, William	2	1	5		
Ferguson, John	1		1		
Field, Roger	1		1		
Field, William, Senr	1		2		4
Field, William (of Robert)	1		5		1
Gearing, Simeon	1	1	1		
Hudson, John	1	3	4		
Hemphill, Samuel	2	5	2		
Henshaw, Jacob	2		2		
Henshaw, William	2	1	4		
Hall, Joseph	1		1		
Harmon, Leonard	3		3		
Hogget, Joseph	1	1	3		
Hogget, Stephen	1	2	2		
Haman, Ephraim	1	1	2		
Julon, Jesse	1	1	3		
Jackson, Joseph	1	3	4		
Jones, Silas	1	1	3		
Jones, Aquilla	1	2	3		
Jones, Thomas	2	5	3		1
Jenkins, John	1				
Jenkins, Thomas	3		8		
Kins, David	1	2	1		
Kirkmon, Elisha	1	3	6		
Lamb, Jacob	1	1	4		1
Love, John	1		1		
Lewis, David	3	3	5		
Lamb, Henry	1	2	3		
Lewis, Richard	1	4	2		
Lamb, John	2	1	3		
Lamb, Joseph	2	3	2		
Lewis, John, Ser	1		5		
Lewis, John	1	2	3		
Lamb, Benjamin	1	1	4		
Lamb, Nathan	1		2		
Lamb, William	1	3	2		
Morris, John	2	2	5		
McCollum, Stephen	1	1	1		
Macey, Joseph	3	1	5		
Mattuck, Samuel	1	2	4		
Mendenhall, Elisha	1	1	1		5
Morriss, Christian	1	1	3		
Morgan, Ezekiel	1		3		
Nashon, Christopher	3		3		
Osborn, Samuel	3	1	3		
Osborn, Matthew	2	1	4		
Osborn, David	1	2	1		
Osborn, William	1		2		
Person, William	2		3		
Phillips, Joel	1	3	2		
Powell, Elijah	1		2		
Pennington, Levi	1	5	2		
Pugh, Thomas	1	2	3		
Reynolds, David	1		3		
Robbins, Christopher	1	2	5		
Robbins, John	1	6	2		
Richardson, Peter	3	2	4		
Reynolds, Jaremiah	5	1	6		
Reynolds, William	1	4	2		
Swim, John	3	4	4		
Scarlett, John	1	3	2		
Staley, Coonrod	3	3	5		
Staley, Martin	4	4	3		
Smith, Federick	1	5	2		
Stanton, Samuel	2	5	4		
Suites, Jacob	1	1	1		
Tillery, George	2	2	3		
Vucory, Sampson	1	1	5		
Vucory, Christopher	2	5	3		2
Weathington, John	3	3	3		
Wood, John	1	2	3		
Webb, Joseph	1	3	2		
Wood, Clement	1	1	2		
Wood, Zebedee	1		2		
Wilson, Jessee	1	2	3		
Worth, Joseph	4		2		
Wilborn, John	1	3	5		2
Wood, Reuben	1	4	3		2
Wood, Zebedee, Esqr	2	2	4		
Wilson, William	1	3	5		
Underwood, Samuel	1	5	3		
Branson, Thomas	1		5		
Jones, Aquilla	1		2		
Lamb, Elizabeth	1	3	2		2
Dennis, Rachel	3		3		
Harmon, William	1	1	1		
Wood, John	1		1		
Beason, Benjamin	1		1		
Dennis, William	1		1		
Bartin, William	1	3	1		1
Garner, Perish	1		3		
Canine, David	1	1	3		
Field, William (of William)	1	1	2		
Alred, John, Senr	2	1	5		1
Alred, Elias	1	5	1		
Alred, John	1	1	3		
Alred, William	2	1	4		1
Alred, John (of William)	1		4		
Allin, Samuel	1	1	5		
Alred, James	1	1	8		
Alridge, Nathan	2	4	7		
Barker, Robert	1	2	7		
Barker, William	1		1		
Benson, Thomas	1	1	4		
Crabtree, John	1	6	2		
Cox, Amos	2	3	7		
Crabtree, James	2	1	4		3
Code, Timothey	2	2	1		
Code, William	1		1		
Cox, Isaac	1		1		
Cox, Thomas	1	2	4		
Cox, William	1	2	2		
Cox, Harmon	2	1	2		
Duncan, John	1	2	2		
Davis, Enuch	1		3		
Fruit, John	1	2	3		
Fruit, James	1	5	1		
Fagin, William	2	1	2		
Garner, Thomas	1		1		
Garner, Jessee	1	1	1		
Garner, Henry	1	3	3		3
Gaving, Hugh	1	1	3		
Grimes, John	1	2	1		
Hudson, Richard	2	2	4		
Hudson, John	1				
Henson, Joseph	2	2	5		
Henshaw, William	1	5	4		
Henshaw, Israel	1	2	4		
Henshaw, Thomas	1	4	2		
Henshaw, John	1				
Hardin, Mark	1	1	4		
Henshaw, William	1				
Henson, William	1	3	3		
Harper, John	1		4		
Hislop, James	1		1		
Juland, George	1	2	6		
Juland, Rainey	1	4	5		
Jones, John	1	1	1		
Lewis, Stephen	1	3	4		
Lane, Joseph	1	2	4		
Lamb, Cornelius	1	1	1		
Lane, Isaac	1	1	1		
Lane, Abraham	1				
Lane, John	1	3	6		4
McCollum, James	1	1	4		
Moser, Tobius	2	2	6		
McCollum, Isaac	1	1	3		
McClane, Robert	3	4	1		1
McKee, Sarah			1		
Odle, Nehemiah	1		4		
Pugh, James	2		2		
Reines, Robert	2	4	7		
Smith, William	1	1	1		
Swift, Thomas	1	1	3		
Swift, Thomas, Ser	2		4		
Swaford, William	2	5	4		
Swift, Elias	1	2	2		
Spoon, Christopher	1	3	2		
Scott, James	1				
Trogdon, Solomon	1				
Trogdon, John	1		2		
Trogdon, William	1	1	3		
Williams, Abraham	1		2		
Wilburn, John	1	4	5		
White, John	3	2	5		
Wilburn, Esther			2		8
Walker, Samuel	2	2	5		1
Walker, Samuel	1	3	3		
Wilburn, Elijah	1		1		
Walker, Robert	1	2	3		
York, Henry	1	1	3		
York, William	1	1	3		
York, Samuel	1		3		
York, Silvana	2	1	2		1
York, Semore	1	2	4		
York, Jeremiah	1	4	5		
Yates, William	1	4	3		
Arley, Henry	1		1		
Long, Solomon	2	2	2		
Haild, Jacob	1	1	2		
Hackeb, Robert	1	2	2		
Avret, John, Jur	1		1		
Rigbey, John	1				
Duffey, Ann			1		
Avret, John, Ser	1		1		
Duncan, John, Ser	1	3	5		
Alred, William	3	3	4		
Dafrin, John	1	1	4		
Alred, Margret	2	1	1		
Husbands, William	1		1		
York, Eli	1				
Underwood, Mary			2		3
Loller, Evan	1	2	1		
Hendrix, Edward	1	3	2		
Cox, Nathan	1		1		
Bradley, Ambrus	1	3	1		
Hamer, John	1		1		
Aldridge, Elizabeth	2	2	4		
Ammick, Nicholas	1		2		
Alred, Ezekiel	1	3	3		
Aldridge, John	1	3	1		
Alred, John	1	5	2		
Amick, John	1	5	1		
Alridge, Isaac	1	3	3		
Barker, John	2	2	4		
Borough, Dobson	4	4	4		14
Beck, Jethro	2	4	5		
Bane, James	3	2	3		
Brown, Adam	1	1	2		
Burgis, William	1		1		
Burgis, James	3	1	2		
Brown, Christopher	1	3	1		
Black, George	1	3	3		
Bradley, Laurance	2	2	1		
Blair, Hugh	1		3		
Bootrout, Joseph	2		2		
Bennett, Benjamin	1	4	2		2
Cruthers, John	1	1	7		
Chaplin, David	1		3		
Chambers, John	1	1	3		
Curtis, Samuel	1	1	8		
Cammell, Malcum	1	2	6		
Curtis, John	1		3		1
Cox, William	1		4		
Campbell, John	1	4	3		
Cloud, Joseph	2	4	4		
Canter, James	1				
Clap, John	1		3		
Campbell, Alexander	1	2	1		
Chaplin, David	1		1		
Dickson, William	2		1		
Evans, Solomon	2	2	4		
Frasher, Francis	1	3	1		
Frasher, Thomas	2	2	2		
Frasher, George	2	6	4		
Fox, Leonard	1	1	1		
Grandey, John	1		1		
Graig, Jacob	4	4	2		
Grimes, Richard	1	2	5		
Grimes, Richard, Ser	1	2			
Hayes, Edmond	1		2		
Hammilton, Thomas	1	3	5		
Husbands, John	1		1		
Hammon, Elisha	1	3	3		
Harvey, William	2	3	4		
Harriss, Evan	2	4	4		
Hancock, Joshua	1	2	2		
Hamer, John	1		1		
Holder, John	1	2	3		
Jones, Leonard	2	5	3		
Jones, Charles	3	4	4		
Johnston, Henry	1				
Kivet, Peter	3		1		2
Kivet, Peter, Jur	1	2	2		
Kivet, Henry	1	4	1		
Lineberry, Jacob	3	5	3		
Langley, Allen	1	2	2		
Loller, Elie	1	3	3		
McDaniel, Abraham	1	2	6		
McGown, William	1	3	1		
Loller, John	3	1	2		
McDaniel, Isaac	1	3	6		
McDaniel, Abraham	1	3	7		
McDaniel, John	1		1		
Marley, William	2	3	3		
McCollum, Jonathan	1	1	2		1
McMasters, Andrew	1		1		
McDaniel, Amos	2		4		
Morfet, Adam	2	2			
Morfet, James	1		1		5
Matthews, William	3	2	5		1
Neadham, Thomas	4		5		

HILLSBOROUGH DISTRICT, RANDOLPH COUNTY—Continued.

NAME OF HEAD OF FAMILY.	Free white males of 16 years and upward, including heads of families.	Free white males under 16 years.	Free white females, including heads of families.	All other free persons.	Slaves.
Nelson, Samuel	2		2		
Overby, John	2	2		1	1
Pugh, John	1	2	6		
Provo, Catharine	1	1	2		
Rustin, James	1	1	2		
Reines, George	3	5	2		
Ruth, Jacob	1	6	1		
Russell, George	1	5	3		
Ruth, James	1	1	4		
Reines, John	3		3		
Reines, Antoney	1	2	2		
Reines, Israel	2	1	5		
Reines, Robert	1	2	7		
Stout, Peter	1				
Scotton, John	1	4	3		
Souch, Jacob	1	1	1		
Staley, Christopher	1				
Staley, Jacob	1	1	4		
Stout, Samuel	3	5	6		
Sillars, Phillip	2		2		
Savage, William	1				
Savage, Thomas	1	2	2		
Sutton, Joseph	2	5	4		
Scotton, John E	1		1		
Stout, Samuel	1		1		
Wilson, William	2	3	4		
Wilson, John	1	3	3		
Williams, Benjamin	1	5	2		
Walker, John	2	2	6		
Ward, William	1	3	3		1
Williams, Daniel	1	1	4		
Warren, James	1				
Warren, Joseph	1	1	3		
Watson, Jacob	3	2	3		
Ward, Thomas	1	4	4		
White, Nicholas	2	4	1		
Worrell, William		1	2		
York, John	1	4	4		
York, Edmond	1	3	2		
York, Joseph	3	4	4		
York, Aaron	1	3	4		
York, John	2	2	5		
York, Subell	1	1	4		
Wood, Joseph	1		1		
McMasters, Solomon	1	1	1		
Rightsman, Mary	2	5	5		
Chambers, Edmond	1	4	7		
Frazer, John	1	1	1		
Nelson, Samuel	1		1		
Foust, Jacob	1	5	3		
Billinsley, Sarah			1		
York, Elliner			1		
Rustin, William	1				
Reines, Laurance	1	2	5		
Barker, Samuel	3	2	7		
Phillips, Edmond	1	1	1		
Davis, William	1	1	3		
Asbell, Emanuel	2	1	3		
Andrews, Charity	1	4	4		
Andrews, Adam	1	2			4
Asbell, William	1	2	3		
Argo, John	1	1	3		1
Argo, William	1	2	5		1
Andrews, David	1	4	3		
Bird, Richard	2	3	4		1
Bookout, Charles	1	1	2		
Bell, Linsey	2	2	5		
Bell, William	2				
Bland, Benjamin	1				
Bryan, William	1				
Bland, Moses	1		1		
Bland, William	3	2	4		
Bowdown, James	1	2	1		
Bowdown, William	1	3	2		5
Brewer, Howell	3		8		
Cost, Thomas	1	3	4		
Comer, Jessee	1	1	5		
Cox, Nicholas	1	1	3		
Craven, Peter	2		2		
Carnes, Mathias	1	1	1		
Cox, Samuel	3		4		
Cox, Henry	1	2	2		
Cost, Thomas, Jur	1	1	1		1
Car, Robert	1	3	6		
Car, Joseph	2	3	2	1	5
Dempsey, Luke	1	1	1		
Derbey, William	1	2	3		
Edwards, John	1	2	5		
George, Moses	1	4	1		
Garner, James	1	2	1		
Garner, John F	2	3	4		3
Garner, James	1	3	5		3
Hammilton, Matthew	1	4	4		
Hall, Thomas	1	2	2		
Hicks, Joseph	3	4	3		
Johnston, John	1	5	2		1
Lodermilk, Jacob	1	4	5		
Lawley, Christopher	1	3	3		
Lodermilk, John	1	1	2		
Laurance, William	1		3		
Latham, James	1	5	7		
Ledloe, James	1	5	6		6
Laurance, John	3	3	3		
Latham, Cornelius	1	2	5		1
Lawley, John	1	1	3		
Mullins, Nathaniel	1	2	2		
Moon, Joseph	1	6	2		
Moon, John	1	4	2		
Mullins, Jeremiah	2		2		
Mallett, William	1	2	2		
Macon, Gideon	1		2		
Needham, William	1	1	2		
Needham, John, Ser	2	4	5		8
Needham, John, Jur	1		1		
Needham, William	3	2	3		
Odle, Isaac	1		1		
Powers, Bradley	1	1	4		
Pearce, Windsor	2	1	4		
Rede, John	1	1	1		
Ruster, John	1	3	2		1
Rede, Arthur	2	1	5		
Ruth, Joseph	3	4	4		
Spinks, Lewis	3	2	5		
Spinks, Enuch	1	2	2		
Smith, Arthur	1	1	4		
Spinks, John	1	5	5		
Smitheman, William	1	3	4		
Smith, Fortunatus	1				
Searcey, William	1	2	5		
Reines, William	1	3	2		1
Stuart, Charles	2	2	1		7
White, James	1		4		4
Waddle, Edmond	4	4	5		22
Routh, John	1	2	2		
Pope, Richard	1				
Ruster, William, Jur	1				
Stephens, Robert	1				
Mafet, Robert	1		5		
Grove, Sarah		1	2		
Reins, Mary	1	3	2		
Harden, Robert	1	2	1		
Carrelton, George	1	2	2		
Hicks, Robert	1		1		
Lawley, Joseph	1		1		
Reins, Isaac	1				
Mallett, James	1		1		
Andrews, Michael	1		1		
Rede, Benjamin	1	2	5		
Rede, William	1		2		
Bowden, Travers	1		1		
Pitt, Jessee	1				
Bookout, Marmaduke	1	3	4		
Latham, John	2		1		
Spinks, Garrett	1		2		
Smith, William	1	1	1		
Garner, Bradley	1		3		
Putman, John	1	1	2		
Redfearn, Isaac	1	3	4		
Daten, James	1		1		
Daten, Matthew	1	1	1		
Coller, Nancey	1	2	2		
Call, William	1	2	1		
Grey, Charles	1	3	3		
Bookout, Joseph	1	2	1		
Norton, Sarah					3
Smith, Febey			4		
Lawley, Elisha	1	1	4		
Ruth, Jacob, Jur	2	5	3		
Call, Josana		1	1		
Johnston, Mornin	2	2	3		
Andrews, Ephraim	1	1	1		2
Avira, William	1	3	4		
Brown, Joseph	2	1	2		
Brown, James	2	3	5		2
Barker, Nicholas	1	2	3		
Brown, Daniel	2	1	1		
Brown, Samuel	1		1		
Brown, Henry	1	2	2		
Craven, Peter	2	4	2		
Car, Thomas	1	2	2		
Carr, Joshua	1	3	2		
Carr, Joseph	1	4	2		
Craven, Thomas	2	5	5		
Craven, John	1		3		
Chaney, Francis, Ser	1				
Chaney, John	1		1		
Cox, Thomas	2	1	4		
Cox, Charles	1	2	3		
Craven, Daniel	1	2	3		
Cox, Thomas	1	2	3		
Chaney, Francis	1	2	3		
Cox, John	1	3	3		
Craven, Joseph	1	3	3		
Carter, Edward	1	3	3		
Cox, John	4	1	3		
Cox, Benjamin	2	1	4		
Corner, Amos	1	2	3		
Corner, Robert	3	1	10		
Cox, Nathaniel	1	2	4		
Cox, Elie	1				
Craven, Henry	2		3		
Cox, Jeremiah	1	1	4		
Diffey, Moses	1	1	5		1
Diffey, John	1	2	1		
Duskin, Sarah	1		2		3
Edwards, Peter	1	3	5		1
Giles, Chrispen	2	4	7		
Hussey, Stephen	3	2	2		
Henson, Jessee	1		3		
Hendricks, Samul	2	1	5		
Hopkins, Josih	1	1	2		
Hopkins, Dennis	1	2	4		
Henshaw, Absolum	2		3		
Hodgins, Robert	2	2	5		
Harland, Stephen	1	1	5		
Hendricks, Joseph	1	1	1		
Hendricks, Tobias	1	2	2		
Jackson, Isaac	1		2		
Kenworthey, David	4	3	4		
Kayes, John	2	1	2		
Kain, Isaac	1		1		
Kenworthey, Joshua	3		4		
Ledmon, Stafford	1	2	5		
Litter, Menshaw	2	2	7		
Morfit, William	3	1	4		
Moser, Jacob	1	1	3		
Morfit, Charles	2	6	4		
Pickett, Jeremiah	1	3	4		
Ramsower, Henry	1	2	4		
Richards, Isaac	2	2	3		
Ratliff, Moses	3	2	2		5
Shaffer, Jacob	1		2		
Stroud, Abraham	2		4		
Scott, Daniel	1	2	3		
Stroud, Jessee	1		2		
Stroud, John	1	1	2		
Stamper, Jammes	2	1	6		
Stafford, Trice	1	1	4		
Snede, William	1	4	2		
Sell, Enos	1	1	2		
Trogdon, Samuel	1	5	3		
Winniyham, Richard	1	2	6		
Williams, Onean	1	2	2		
Right, Peter	1	1	2		
Wright, George	1		2		
Mafit, Samuel	1				
Gradey, Thomas	1	1	1		
Smith, William	1	6	3		
Harriss, William	2	5	4		
Lawley, Elisha	1				
Moon, John	1				
Pugh, Rachel		1	3		
Richards, William	1	2	3		
West, Isaac	1	3	6		
Moon, Daniel	1		1		
Cox, Benjamin	1	1	5		
Alred, Thomas	2		1		
Henshaw, Absalum	1	3	5		
Goodwin, James	1	3	3		
Cantrel, Charles	2	4	3		
Anstat, George	1	1	2		
Anstat, John	1		5		
Taylor, Florance	1	2	6		
Winneham, Grace		1	1		
Askins, Richard	1	3	3		
Graves, William	2		1		
Davis, William	3	3	4		
Philps, Jonathan	1	1	2		3
Hudson, Obediah	1	2	2		
Tucker, Sarah			2		
Mann, Malicah	1	4	3		
McCraney, Kason		2	1		
Buckhannon, William W	1				
Bowling, Benjamin	1	3	5		
Bean, Richard	2	6	5		
Bowling, William	2	2	5		
Branson, Thomas	1				
Branson, Henry	1	1	1		
Barnes, Burwell	1	1	3		
Coontz, Gasper	1	3			
Cole, Matthew	1		1		
Cole, Stephen	3	1	6		2
Cox, Caleb	1	2	2		
Cox, Richard	1	1	3		
Comer, John	1	3	1		
Dollihide, Asel	1		4		
Dollihide, Hezekiah	1	1	5		
Edwards, Morgan	1		2		
Edwards, Jonathan	1	2	2		
Graves, James	1	4	2		

HILLSBOROUGH DISTRICT, RANDOLPH COUNTY—Continued.

NAME OF HEAD OF FAMILY.	Free white males of 16 years and upward, including heads of families.	Free white males under 16 years.	Free white females, including heads of families.	All other free persons.	Slaves.
Graves, Samuel	1	2	2		1
Graves, Richard	1	1	2		
Harvey, William, Jur	1	4	3		1
Hudson, Joseph	1	4	2		
Hammon, John	2	1	1		
Hammon, Moses	2	2	6		
Hooker, Robert	1	3	4		
Hooker, Jacob	1	3	4		
Hobson, John	1	3	5		
Harvey, William	1		1		5
Harvey, Michael	1	2	1		
Johnston, John	1	2	2		
King, Thomas	1	4	2		
King, Peter	1	3	4		
King, Johnston, Ser	2	4	5		
King, Johnston, Jur	1	1	1		
King, William	3	1	4		1
Lewis, George	3	1	6		2
Luther, Christian	1	4	3		
Lotham, John	2	4	4		3
Graves, John	1	2	2		
Mills, Micajah	1	2	2		
Melson, Peter	1		1		
McGloughlin, Stephen	1				
Oscar, Jaremiah	1	1	3		
Page, Benjamin, Jur	1		4		
Page, Benjamin, Ser	1				
Prisnal, William	1	3	3		
Prisnal, Daniel	1	2	1		
Prisnal, Stephen	1	3	2		
Prisnal, James	2	2	2		
Rolins, David	1	1	2		
Rede, John	1	2	5		
Rede, Lamburd	1	2	3		
Richardson, John	1		3		
Rooks, Hardy	2	1	4		
Steed, John	1	5	5		
Scott, John	3	1	1		
Stanfield, John	1	3	4		
Smith, John	1	3	4		
Tucker, Nathaniel	1		1		
Tucker, George	1	1	1		
Tucker, John	1	1	5		
Tucker, George, Senr	3		8		
Tucker, William	2	6	3		
Wright, William	1	4	5		
Williams, William	1	5	2		
Williams, John	2	1	5		
Voncannon, William	1	2	3		
Voncannon, Peter	2	1	2		
Voncannon, Peter, Jur	1	1	2		
Williams, William	3	3	4		
Williams, John	2	3	5		
Williams, George	1		1		
Williams, David	1	3	6		
Winslow, Thomas	2	3	5		1
Williams, John	1	2	2		
Macey, Richard	1		2		
Crow, Nancey	1	1	3		
Prisnal, John	2	3	5		
Richardson, William	2	1	4		
Constant, William	3	3	5		
Little, Abraham	1	1	1		
Rede, William	1	2	5		
McGloughlin, Ann		3	4		
Hill, Thomas	1	1	3		1
Belford, Margaret			1		2
McGloughlin, John	1		1		
McGloughlin, Jacob	1	1	1		
Williams, Jonathan	2	2	6		
Underhill, John	2	3	4		
Hancock, Vachel	1	1	1		
Hancock, Sarah	1		2		
Carmon, John	1	3	1		
Harvey, John	1	3	1		
Luther, Michael	1	4	1		
Latham, William	1		1		
White, Joseph	1		3		
Millsaps, William	1		1		
Hamm, Nehemiah	1		3		
Keneday, Sarah			3		
Spencer, John	1				
Thompson, John	2				
Cranford, Samuel	3	1	2		
Thompson, Henry	2		1		
Savage, John	1	2	6		
Cox, Enoch	1		7		
Botsford, James	1	2	4		
Arnold, Jeremiah	1		1		
Arnold, Francis	2	3	4		2
Arnold, Fielding	1		1		
Been, John	1		2		
Bingam, Thomas	2	4	2		2
Bundey, Samuel	1	3	3		
Bundey, Christopher	1	2	3	1	1
Brookshear, Emanuel	2	3	5		1
Brookshear, Thomas	1	1	2		

NAME OF HEAD OF FAMILY.	Free white males of 16 years and upward, including heads of families.	Free white males under 16 years.	Free white females, including heads of families.	All other free persons.	Slaves.
Bailey, William	1	2	5	1	1
Chandler, William	1	1	3		1
Carter, William	1	1	6		
Carter, Finch	1	2	5		
Cranford, Elias	1		1		
Charles, Samuel	2	2	5		
Charles, Joseph	1				
Canady, Sherwood	1	1	3		
Cranford, William	2		3		
Fuller, Isham	1	3	4		2
Fuller, Britain	1		4		
Farmer, Federick	1		5		5
Farmer, Joseph	4	2	3		
Griffin, Lewis	1	2	3		
Hopkins, Charles	1		1		
Hill, Aaron	1	3	2		
Hamilton, Samuel	1	1	2		
Hardester, Thomas	1	4	3		
Hartgrove, George	1	3	3		
Hannah, William	1	1	4		
Hartgrove, Thomas	1				
Hamon, Joshua	1	1	1		
Hamon, Abraham	2		2		
Hill, Aaron	1	3	2		10
Hannah, Andrew	1	1	2		
Henley, Jessee	3	1	3		8
Jackson, Thomas	1	3	2		
Irwin, John	1	2	3		1
King Thomas	2	1	5		
Kean, Silas	1				
Kain, John	3	1	4		
Lindon, Henry	1	1	2		
Lasiter, Sarah	1		6		5
Lax, William	1	3	3		
Lassiter, Micajah	2	2	1		1
Lewis, Samuel	3	1	4		
Lacey, William	1	2	3		
Muckleroye, Andrew	1		3		3
Millsaps, Thomas	2	2	2		
McLemore, Sterling	1	3	3		
Orick, William	1	4	3		
Orick, John	2	2	6		
Patterson, Thomas	1		4		
Patterson, Alexr	3		1		
Rich, Samuel	2	4	5		
Randolph, Thomas	2		2		
Rogers, Randolph	1	2	1		
Robbins, Joseph	1	3	2		
Hannah, William	1	1	1		
Anderson, Thomas	1	2	3		
Steed, Nathaniel	2	4	3		8
Shaw, Guardner	2	5	1		
Stiles, John	1				
Trublood, William	1	1	3		1
Trustey, John	1	1	1		
Towery, George	2	1	7		
Wade, Joseph	3	1	6		
Webster, William	2	2	7		
Winslow, John	2	2	3		
Thornberry, Thomas	1		1		2
Chandler, Timothey	2	2	7		
Seal, Solomon	1	2	3		
Oruc, Samuel	1		1	1	
Andrews, Writter		5	2		
Bean, Richard	1	1	2		
Gowin, William	2	3	4		1
Thompson, Walter	1	1	3		
Hall, William	2	1	1		
Patterson, John	1	1	1		
Randol, James	1	2	3		
Hannock, Richard	1		5		1
Albertson, Arthur	1				
Anderson, John	1	1	1		
Abertson, Joshua	1	4	6		
Arnold, John	2	2	5		1
Bell, Franciss	3	1	2		
Bassell, Barneby	1	2	2		
Bailey, John	1	1	3		
Bibbins, Joseph	1	5	1		
Bass, Jordan	1	2	3		1
Bell, John	1	1			
Bickerdick, Richard	1	4	4		
Bell, Thomas	1	2	8		
Brookshear, William	1	2	4		
Bell, William	3	3	4		
Curtis, Benjamin	1	1	4		
Curtis, John	1	2	5		
Curtis, Joshua	1	1	1		
Caps, Dempsey	1		4		
Debenport, John	1	5	1		3
Elliott, Axum	1		2		
Elliott, Jacob	1		2		
Fouts, Elizabeth	1	3	2		
Fuller, Ezekiel	1		1		
Fouts, Jacob	1	2	3		
Fuller, Solomon	5	3	4		10
Gibson, Thomas	1	1	1		

NAME OF HEAD OF FAMILY.	Free white males of 16 years and upward, including heads of families.	Free white males under 16 years.	Free white females, including heads of families.	All other free persons.	Slaves.
Green, Benjamin	3	2	5		
Gaddis, Archebald	3	4	1		
Gibson, George	1	4	4		
Hoover, Andrew	1	3	4		
Hall, Benjamin	1	1	1		
Hanley, John	4	5	3		
Hoover, Jonas	1	4	5		
Harvey, Jessee	1		3		
Hunt, Tumius	1	1	5		
Hill, Seth	1		3		1
Hall, William	1	1	2		
Hicks, Willis	1	1	2		
Hill, William	5	5	3	5	
Harvey, Michael	3		5		
Jackson, Andrew	1	3	5		
Ivey, Benjamin	1	1	6		2
Jackson, James	1	2	2		
Jackson, Robert	3	1	4		
Jackson, William	1	4	4		
Kindley, Edward	1	1	4		
King, James	2	3	7		
Ledford, John	1	1	5		
Lamb, Reuben	2	1	4		
Luvallin, William	2	4	2		
Marteal, Benjamin	2	5	2		3
Miller, Haman	3	1	5		17
Most, John	2		5		
Miller, Jacob	1	3	5		2
Masieu, Lemuel	1		3		
Miller, Peter	1		3		1
Millsaps, Thomas	2	1	2		
Mitchelner, Valentine	2	3	4		
Millsaps, Robert	4	1	3		
Nance, Hudson	1				
Newbey, Jessee	1		1		
Newbey, Joseph	1		1		
Newbey, Samuel	1	3	5		
Nance, Thomas	2	1	3		1
Overman, Epharimin	1	3	2		
Overman, Zebulun	2	2	2		
Prikit, John	1		1		
Prevo, John	1		1		
Prevo, Alexr	1				
Pool, William	1	4	3		
Ray, Ann	1		1		2
Ratliff, Cornelius	1	1	4		1
Ridge, Godfrey	1	6	2		1
Roberts, James	1	2	5		8
Robbins, Joseph	1		1		
Russell, Jeffrey	1	2	3		1
Ratliff, Richard	2	1	2		
Roberts, Riland	1		1		1
Ridge, William	1	1	1		
Small, Benjamin	1				
Shine, Jacob	3	1	6		
Small, Obediah	1	2	2		
Smith, Phillip	1	4	2		
Turner, Ezekiel	1		1		
Thompson, John	1				
Thompson, Robert	2		1		
Thompson, William	1		2		
Warrell, Amos	1	3	3		4
Wilemon, Elias	2	4	2		
Waymire, Federick	3	2	4		
Wright, Philburt	2	4	4		
Ward, Timothey	2	1	3		
Wood, William	1	2	6		1
Yates, Peter	1		2		
Zink, George	2	3	7		
Sandifor, Robert	1	1	1		
Gibson, David	1		2		
Gibson, Gilbert	1	1	1		
Hill, Jessee	2	3	2		
Vinters, Pharow	4	3	5		
Brookshear, Morning	1				
Bayel, William	1	1	3		
Taylor, Solomon	1		2		
McLemore, Wright	1				
Low, William	1				
Williams, Vinun P	1	1	3		2
Arnold, Whitlock	1	1	1		
Smith, Peter	1		1		
Ledford, George	1		1		
Bevvins, Joseph, Jur	1		2		
Dunber, James	1	2	2		
Fuller, Mary		1	1	1	
Hobes, Elisha	2	3	5		
Albertson, John	2	4	2		
Hicks, Elizabeth	3		2		
Eades, George	1	3	3		
Lacey, Ann		1	2		
Gaddis, Susanna	1	1	2		
Roberts, Sarah			2		
Hinshavins, Robertson	1				
Draper, William	1	1	6		
Fuller, Britain, Ser	2	1	5		4
Wright, Philburt	1		2		

HILLSBOROUGH DISTRICT, RANDOLPH COUNTY—Continued.

NAME OF HEAD OF FAMILY.	Free white males of 16 years and upward, including heads of families.	Free white males under 16 years.	Free white females, including heads of families.	All other free persons.	Slaves.
Luvellin, Jonathan	1				
Farmer, John	1		2		
Alexander, William	1				
Alexander, William, Ser.	3	2	7		
Alexander, Stephen	4		3		
Allin, James	1	3	4		
Archer, William	1	3	3		
Burkit, Christian	1				
Bearley, Phillip	1	3	6		
Bradley, Joseph	1	1	3		
Beard, John	2	3	3		
Galleymore, William	1	3	3		
Beaverley, Isaac	1		1		
Brothers, Miles	1	3	1		
Cains, Joseph	1		1	1	1
Curtis, Joseph	1	4	3		
Curtis, James	1	3	4		
Curtis, Caleb	1	2	4		
Darnald, William	2	4	5		
Elder, John	1	4	2		
Everley, George	1		2		
Fouts, David	1	1	2		
Fouts, Michael	2		5		
Fouts, Andrew	1	4	5		
Fouts, Jacob	1	3	5		
Failow, Nathan	4	3	5		
Fouts, John	3		5		
Fouts, Lewis	1		3		
Fouts, John, Ser.	2	1	4		
Fincher, Benjamin	2	1	3		
Galleymore, John	1	1	3		
Gray, John	2	5	2		
Galleymore, John	2	1	2		
Hoover, Daniel	3	2	3		
Hodge, John	1	2	2		
Hamon, Cutlif	1	2	6		
Hamon, George	1	2	2		
Hammon, Matthew	1	2	5		
Hoover, David	1	1	1		
Hoover, Jacob	2	5	1		
Hoover, John	1	1	3		
Harper, Jeduthan	1	1	6		14
Jones, Thomas	1	1	4		
Justice, Joseph	1	3	4		
Garren, Jacob	1	3	4		
Garren, John	1	2	1		
Johnston, John	2		2		
King, William	1		2		
Lutford, John	1		4		
Merrill, Benjamin	1	3	5		1
Most, David	1		3		
Mineas, Benjamin	1	2	1		3
Merrill, John	1	4	3		
Meanes, Andrew	1	4	5		
Merrill, Daniel	1	1	4		2
Most, John	1	1	3		
Moon, Joseph	1	3	5		
Mullanin, Jonathan	2	2	6		
Newbey, William	2	3	4		1
Newbey, Federick	1				3
Newbey, Joshua	1		1		
Overman, Obediah	1	2	4		
Plummer, Phillimon	2	2	6		31
Park, Samuel	3	1	2		1
Reading, Joseph	1	3	3		
Snow, Isaac	1		1		
Summers, William	1	3	2		
Summers, Thomas	1	1	3		
Smith, John	1		2		
Stone, Connoway	1	2	4		
Snow, Ebenezer	1	3	2		
Sheppard, Peter	1	2	4		
Sheppard, Charles	1	3	1		2
Stuart, John	1		1		
Snow, Martha	1	2	2		
Stootmon, Jacob	5	1	4		
Wright, John	2	5	2		
Wright, Benjamin	1	3	6		
Woodward, Abraham	4	1	5		
Wright, James	1	2	1		
Whisenhunt, George M.	3	4	2		
Waymire, Randolph	1	6	1		
Varner, Jacob	1	2	1		
Wright, Joseph	1	4	2		
Ward, Benjamin	2	4	4		3
Muliner, Greenberry	1	1	1		
Humbrie, John	1		1		
Varner, John	1	3	2		
Yount, Jacob	1	2	3		
Bryan, John	3	2	5		
Hoover, Peter	1		1		
Bryan, Peter	2	2	3		
Blair, Enos	1	4	5		
Brown, John	1		3		
Bratton, Robert	3	3	4		
Clark, Joseph	1	1	6		
Clark, Samuel	1				
Clark, Samuel, Jur.	2	2	6		
Clark, Edward	2	1	6		
Clark, Baptist	1	3	7		
Coltrain, David	1	1	4		
Coltrain, William	3	2	4		
Carnes, Samuel	1				
Davis, James	1	1	5		
Davis, Job	1		3		
Wright, Amos	1	2	2		
Davis, Amos	1	2	3		
Davis, Jessee	1	5	3		
Elder, James	1		1		
Ellis, William	1				
Ellis, James, Ser.	1	3	3		
Frasher, William	1	3	2		
Frasher, John	3	2	2		
Frasher, Samuel	1				
Gosset, Elijah	1	2	3		
Gossett, William	4		2		
Grey, Robert	3	2	3		
Hilton, Samuel	1	2	1		
Henderson, John	1	5	2		
Hilton, John	1	2	2		1
Hoggot, Stephen	1	1	1		
Hoggot, Joseph	1				
Hoggot, John	3	1	3		
Hill, Thomas	1		2		
Hill, John	1	2			
Hoggot, Jessee	1				
Hoggot, Moses	1		2		
Hill, William	1	1	1		
Johnston, Joseph	1	2	2		
Johnston, John	1	3	2		
Kendal, Benjamin	2	3	2		
Kendal, William	1	2	1		
Kendal, John	1	1	4		
Loe, James	1	1	2		
Loe, Thomas	2		1		
Lemare, Osborn	1	2	3		
Leach, Hugh	2		3		
Loe, Thomas	1		4		
Leach, William	1	3	2		
Millican, William	1	6	1		
McFetrick, Matthew	3		3		
McDade, John	1	1	2		
McFetters, Andrew	1	1	1		
Morgan, David	1	1	3		
Morgan, Lewis	1	1	4		
Moore, George	1	1	2		
Milton, Samuel	2	4	4		
Millican, William, Sr.	1		1		
Moore, John	2	3	5		
Mullins, Charles	2	2	5		
Pindry, James	1	1	3		
Ruddock, John	3		3		
Rice, Caleb	1	2	4		
Ruth, Samuel	1	5	2		
Ruddock, Joseph	1		5		
Serjant, William	1	1	4		
Smith, David	1	4	3		
Smith, Alexander	1		9		1
Smith, Bryan	1	1	3		
Tomlinson, William	4	3	4		
Thompson, Andrew	3	2	3		
Thornberry, Martha			5		
Thornberry, George	1	1	3		
Thornberry, Edward	1		4		
White, Ralph	2	5	3		
White, Joseph	1		3		
White, Thomas	1	2	6		
White, John	1	1	4		
Viccory, John	3	2	6		
Viccory, Christopher	1	1	1		
Ward, James	1	3	3		
Branson, Daniel	1		2		
Lane, James	1	3	4		
Croket, Eliza		1	1		
Thornberry, William	1		4		
Thornberry, Ann	1		3		
Moore, Robert	2	1	1		
Coonrod, Peter	1				
Collet, James	3	1	3		7
White, William	2		4		
Gray, William	1	1	1		
Brown, Mary			2		
Hoggot, Phillip			3		
Jackson, Isaac	1	2	5		
Smith, David, Ser.	1	1	1		
Thomas, Esther			1		
Martin, Joseph	1				
Turner, Moses	1		1		
Nucols, Zachariah	1		1		
Anderson, Robert	1		1		3
Broil, Federick	3		3		
Buller, Thomas	1	6	2		3
Bell, William	1		2		16
Boid, William	1	2	4		1
Bridgegan, Edward	1				
Curtis, Thomas, Senr.	2	3	1		
Collier, John	1	2	7		
Clark, William	1	3	3		
Cantral, Joseph	1		7		
Clark, Young	1	1	3		
Clark, George	2	1	2		2
Curtis, Thomas, Jur	1	3	1		
Clark, John	2		2	1	2
Dougan, James	1	5	3		
Dougan, Robert	1	1	2		
Dougan, Thomas	1	1	5		7
Farlow, William	1	4	2		
Farlow, George	1	3	3		
Green, Joseph	3	1	5		
Hascot, Abraham	2		1		
Hudson, Lemuel	1				
Hascot, Joseph	1	3	5		1
Hopper, Archebald	1	2	2		
Hencock, Benjamin	3	3	4		
Hendley, John	1		3		2
Juland, Isaac	1	4			
Ledford, Federick	1		3		
Ledford, Peter	2	2	3		
Lytle, Thomas	1		1		7
Low, Samuel	3	2	7		
Millican, Benjamin	1	3	4		
Moore, Samuel	1	2	5		
Nixon, Phinehas	1	2	3		3
Pearce, Richard	1	4	4		9
Viccory, Luke		1	1		
Robbins, John	1	4	6		3
Rich, Joseph	1				
Robbins, William	3		8	1	9
Robbins, Moses	1	1	2		1
Rich, Benjamin	1	6	2		1
Rich, Peter	1	2	1		
Reading, Robert	1	3	3	1	
Roddey, Phillip	1	4	6		
Robbins, Isaac	3	3	5		
Rush, Mary	1		4		
Rich, John, Ser.	2	1	2		
Sharp, Michael	1	1	6		
Simmons, Job	2	4	4		
Shites, John	3		5		
Viccory, George	1	1	1		
Alexander, Samuel	1	2	4		
Woodward, William	1		2		
Webb, Jessee	3	2	1		
Watson, Daniel	1	2	2		
Yount, Henry	2	2	5		
Yount, George	2	1	7		
Rush, John	1		1		
Loe, Ralph	1	2	5		3
Rich, John, Jur.	1	3	3		
Morrow, James	3	2	1		
Miller, Richard	1	3	3		
Ledford, John	2		2		
Ledford, John, Ser.	1	1	2		
Lorhard, William	1	1	1		
Ledford, Federick	1		1		
Yount, John	1		1		
Robbins, James	3	2	2		
Sanders, Joseph	1	3	5		
Curtis, John	1	1	1		
Randals, John	1		1		
Robbins, Joshua	1		2		
Dicks, William	1		2	1	
Hoof, Jessee	1	1	1		
Laurance, James	1		2		
Kelley, James	1				
Dickey, William	2	6	3		
Karr, Nathaniel	1	1	4		
Dougan, John	1		5		

HILLSBOROUGH DISTRICT, WAKE COUNTY.

NAME OF HEAD OF FAMILY.	Free white males of 16 years and upward, including heads of families.	Free white males under 16 years.	Free white females, including heads of families.	All other free persons.	Slaves.
Sugg, Aron	2	1	3		4
Bawsom, Britain	1	1	2		
Booth, Batt	1	1	3		
Medlin, Benjn	1	4	3		
Barnabas, Lane	1	1	4		6
Vick, Burwell	2				6
Pinney, Charles	1	2	3		
Curtis, Chrstepher	2	2	2		7
Partin, Drewry	3	2	3		
Ferrell, Ephraim	1	3	7		
Buzby, Edmond	2	1			1
Hobson, Francis	1		3		12
Rogers, Green	1		5		
Pool, George	1	1	2		
Pool, Hardy	1	3	2		
Depray, Haley	1	3	3		
Gregory, Howell	1				
Hubbard, Henry	2	2	5		
Peters, James	1	2	4		15
Recraft, John	1	1	2		
Nicks, John	1	1	3		
Moore, John	1	4	2		
Parnold, John	1	3	6		
Pool, John	1	2	4		
Orr, John	1	3	3		
Kelley, John	1	2	4		2
Huckins, John	1				
Green, Jemiah	1	1	2		
Hindon, James	2	1	2		6
Powell, John	1	2	1		
Lane, James, Ser	3	1	5		11
Clifton, John	2	1	3		
Bracken, James	3		3		
Bowcom, John, Sr	2	2	3		
Butler, James	1		3		
Bowcom, John, Jer	1	2	5		
Hutchins, John, Sr	2		3		
Sugg, Joshua	3		4		10
Laurance, John	1	1	3		
Sugg, Joshua	1		1		
Pool, Lewis	2				4
Sugg, Mosses	1	2	2		4
Nordan, Melchazedick	2		2		
Sugg, Mark	2	1	5		
Powell, Moses	1	2	6		
Dushin, Michael	1	3	5		1
Jordan, Nicholas	1	2	3		
Barber, Plier	1	3	2		
Smith, Ricd A	2	3	5		
King, Ricd	1	2	5		13
Hunter, Reuben	3	2	7		
Powell, Robert	1	1	3		
Johnson, Robert	1	2	3		
Proctor, Reuben	2	2	5		
Hockaday, Saml	1		2		5
Buffelow, Steel	1	1	1		
Tarver, Saml	1				
Rycraft, Thos	1	1	2		
Simpkins, Thos	1	3	1		
Buzby, Thos, Jer	1	4	4		3
Hunter, Theops, Senr	3	1	3		47
Hunter, Theops, Junr	1				
Thomas, Thos	3	1	3		
Hornby, Wm	2	1	7		
Hutchins, Wm	1				
Sugg, Wm	1	2	4		
Tipper, Wm	1	2	2		
Studefent, Wm	1	1	4		4
Nutt, Wm	1	4	2		2
Atkins, Wm	1	2	3		2
Clifton, Wm	1		3		
Jones, Wm	1	2	7		
Hutchins, Thos	1	2	2		
Tedder, Solomon	1				
Hutchins, Moses	1		1		
Studefent, Hollum	2	2	5		8
Nordan, John	1				
Chambers, Josias	1				
Simpkins, Wm	1	1	1		
Mustin, Thos	1		3		1
Harrod, Benjn	1	7	3		1
Brown, Joseph	1				
Minten, David	1				
Jordan, Abner	1	2	5		
Smith, Needam	1	1	3		
Bawcom, Ricd	1		1		
Jordan, Amos	1	2	5		
Hiot, Asa	1	2	4		
Fowler, Bullard	4	2	4		9
Body, Bennet	1				10
Oneal, Benjn	2		3		
Robertson, Chritepher	1	1	2		2
Hobbs, David	1	1	1		
Martin, David	1	3	4		
Henley, Elmore	2	3	5		1
Earp, Edward	1	5	2		
Hocut, Edward	3	4	6		

NAME OF HEAD OF FAMILY.	Free white males of 16 years and upward, including heads of families.	Free white males under 16 years.	Free white females, including heads of families.	All other free persons.	Slaves.
Trawick, George	1	1	4		
Warren, George	1		2		3
Lassiter, Hardy	2	3	1		
Bedingfield, Henry	1	4	3		
Shaw, Hugh	3	1	2		1
Earp, Henry	1	3	4		
King, Henry	1	2	4		1
Robertson, Harbert	1		1		2
Burge, Henry	1		2		
Segar, John	2	3	2		3
Earp, John	1	1	5		
Brown, John	2	1	2		
Edins, John	1		3		
Traywick, John	1		1		
Parker, John	1	1	5		1
Duck, John	1	2	4		
Edwine, John	1	1	2		
Watkins, Joseph	1		3		2
Watson, James	1	3	4		
Tucker, Joseph	2	1	3		20
Gilbert, James	2	2	5		
Ward, John	1				
Adams, Joshua	1	3	1		
Nicols, Josiah	1	8	2		
Moneyham, Jacob	1	2	2		
Johnson, Julus	1		3		
Brown, John	1		1		
Coal, John	1	3	7		
Johnson, James	1	2	2		
Jordan, James	1	1	4		
Snipes, John	1	1	6		
Hinton, Kimbrough	2		1		29
Alford, Lodwick	2	3	4		24
Ward, Lyda	1	1	3		
Benton, Moses	1	3	3		1
Tucker, Pashell	1	2	3		2
Benton, Robert	1		3		
Rabon, Ricd	1	4	3		
Hillard, Rightman	1		3		
Traywich, Robert, Ser	3	4	6		
Traywich, Robert, Jr	1		5		
Horten, Saml	2	4	2		
Hood, Thos	1	2	2		
Coal, Thos	1				
Meals, Wm	2		2		6
Cogbill, Thos	2	1	1		7
Robertson, Thos	3	2	5		8
Barron, Thos	2	2	3		
Wilder, Wm, Jer	1	1	1		
Hocut, Wm	1	1	3		
Tucker, Wm	2	1	1		2
Hobbs, Wm	3		7		3
Earp, Wm	1		4		
Wilder, Wm, Ser	1	1	1		
Wilder, Willis	1	3	1		
Rabon, Wm	1		5		
Abot, Sarah			3		
Earp, Susanna		1			
Prator, Thos	1		1		
Curtiz, John	1		4		4
Lee, Ann		1	1		
Edwins, James	1	5	2		
Massey, Hezekiah	1		2		
Duck, Robert	2		2		
Hood, Jesse	1	3			
Bedingfield, Wm	1	3	4		
Austin, James	1		1		
Lassiter, Isaac	1		5		
Youngblood, Delilah	1	2	5		
Bell, Burwell	1	1	2		8
Horten, Amos	2	2	4		3
Carpenter, Benjamin	1	2	1		
Austin, Charles	1	2	3		1
Amos, Charels	1	5	3		
King, Drewry	1	1	1		
Jones, Drewry	1	2	2		
Bunch, David	1		2		
Horten, Drewry	1	2	6		
Peoples, Elisha	1	1	5		3
Redding, Francis	1	3	4		
King, Francis	1	2	3		
Redding, Francis	1	4	1		
Philliph, Francis	1	1	1		7
Bradley, G.	1				2
Hosel, Henry	1		3		3
Alford, Hudson	1	2	3		7
Througher, Henry	1	1	3		
Williams, Hubbard	1	8	5		
Temple, Henry	1			6	
Temple, Henry	1	2	3		
Peoples, Joseph	2	1	5		
Mitchel, John	2	3	3		2
Walker, John	2		3		
Harrison, John	2	1	3		
Kelley, John	2	1	2		
Redding, James	2	1	2		
Scarbrough, John	1	1	1		

NAME OF HEAD OF FAMILY.	Free white males of 16 years and upward, including heads of families.	Free white males under 16 years.	Free white females, including heads of families.	All other free persons.	Slaves.
Privet, James	1	2	1		
Boon, James	1				
Jones, James	4	4	4		5
Laurance, John, Ser	4		4		
Lassiter, Jonas	2	4	6		
Thrower, Jesse	1		3		
Wright, James	1	1	1		
Ellis, Jacob	3	5	4		
Lassiter, Jothram	2		3		15
Davis, Jane			1		
Laurance, John, Jr	1		2		
Robertson, John	2	1	3		3
Malaby, John	2	2	6		
Gay, James	1		2		
Hinton, John	3	2	3		40
Peoples, John	2		5		1
Lassiter, Luke	1	1	4		
Jordan, Liles	1		2		
Davis, Lewis	2	4	8		1
Robertson, Lott	1				
Hill, Nathl, Ser	2	2	2		1
Hill, Nathl, Jur	2	2	5		7
Verser, Nathan	1	2	2		1
Temple, Robert	3	2	2	8	9
House, Ransom	1	1	2		
Scarbrough, Saml	1		4		
Carpenter, Saml	2	3	5		1
Scarbrough, Saml, Jr	1	1	2		
Harris, Saml	2	1	5		9
Wall, Saml	1	5	8		
Davis, Thos	1	2	1		
Harris, Thos	1		2		
Robertson, James	1	1	3		1
Brown, Thos	1	4	6		
Musten, Thos	1	2	2		
Dookam, Wm	2	3	5		
Walker, Wm	2		5		3
Hill, Wm	1	2	2		
Ambrous, Wm, Ser	1	3	2		1
Jones, Wm	1				
Matthews, Wm	1	1	3		
Ambrous, Wm, Jer	2	3	7		2
Arnull, Wm	1	2	5		
Gilbert, Wm	1				
House, Wm	1	2	2		
Hinton, Wm	1				6
Jeffres, Wm	2	2	6		60
Davis, Amey		2	3		
Wright, John	1		5		
Jordan, Wm	1		1		
Ellis, Charles	1	1	2		
Bunch, Thos	1		2		
Waters, Thos	1		2		
Weathers, Elzabeth		1	4		
Bunn, John	1	3	5		
Gay, John	1		2		
Gay, C.	1		2		
Davis, Susanna			3		
Winters, Barney	1	1	2		
Wade, Andrew	1		3		
Horten, Ann	2	3	3		
Fowler, Ann		1	4	2	3
Wheeler, Benjn	1		2		
Massey, Burwell	1		1		
Carpenter, Burwell	1	1	5		
Beaver, Benjn	1	4	2		
Filps, Boling	1		2		11
Bunn, Benjn	2	4	3		
Upchurch, Charles	2	4	6		
Bunn, David	2	4	6		
Philgo, David	1	3	3		
Bagwell, David	1	2	2		
Ray, Daniel	1	3	4		
Horten, David	1	2	2		3
Strickland, Elsha	1	1	2		
Bagwell, Federick	1	1	4		
Strickland, Federick	3	4	6		
Massey, Federick	1	4	4		
Bell, George	1	4	3		4
Fowler, Godfrey	4	2	6		5
Fason, Henry	1	4	5		
Dunn, Hardmon	1	3	5		
Massey, Herze	2	1	5		
Pendergrass, John	3	3	5		
Bolton, James	2	2	2		
Privit, Isarel	3		6		23
Crudup, Josiah	3		4		
Bird, Joel	2	3	4		
Pace, James	2	3	4		
Wheeler, John	1	3	4		
Stricklung, Joseph	1		4		
Chambley, Isaac	3	3	4		2
Walker, John	3		3		
Merrit, John	1	1	3		
Wright, Joseph	1	2	4		16
Hammon, Jesse	1		3		
Earp, Joseph	1		6		

HILLSBOROUGH DISTRICT, WAKE COUNTY—Continued.

NAME OF HEAD OF FAMILY.	Free white males of 16 years and upward, including heads of families.	Free white males under 16 years.	Free white females, including heads of families.	All other free persons.	Slaves.
Perry, James	2	3	3		2
Privit, Jacob	1	2	1		1
Fowler, Joseph	1				
Burin, Jesse	1	1	2		
Morphus, James	1		2		
Rhodes, Jeremiah	1	3	1		
Lee, James B.	1	1	2		2
Strickland, Joseph	1		2		
Privit, John	2		2		
Strickland, Isaac	1		1		
Butler, James	1	1	3		2
Segraves, Jacob	1	2	1		
Jilks, Kinchen	1	4	4		8
Earp, Luke	1	3	5		
Strickland, Matthew	1	2	7		13
Bird, Mosses	1	3	3		
Upchurch, Nathan	1	2	2		
Perry, Nathan	1	2	2		
Strickland, Nathan	1	4	4		
Massey, Nathan	1	2	1		
Chambley, Robert	2	3	4		
Rhodes, Radoll	3		3		
Lumlin, Stephen	1	2	2		
Strickland, Sampson	1	2	2		
Hall, Solomon	1	2	7		
Strickland, Saml	1				
Bolton, Sherrod	1	1	2		
Pulley, Thos	1	5	3		
Merrit, Thos	1	1	3		
Lewis, Thos	1	2	4		
Wheeler, W^m	2	1	5		
Ray, W^m, Senr	2	3	6		1
Bunn, James	1	2	1		
Massey, W^m	1		5		
Bagwell, W^m	1	3	1		
Reynolds, W^m	4	3	6		
Alford, Warren	2	3	2	3	11
Barham, W^m	1	3	5		13
Broadwell, W^m	1	2	4		
Nordin, W^m	1	1	4		5
Privit, W^m, Se^r	1	3	3		
Privit, Miles	1	1	3		
Jarrot, Willie	1	2	3		
Privit, W^m, Je^r	1	1	2		
Ray, W^m, Je^r	1		2		
Merrit, W^m	2	2	1		4
Fowler, W^m	2	1	7	1	1
Bell, Zadock	1	2	5		6
Ferrell, Pall	1				
Strickland, W^m	2	4	5		
Wright, William	1				
Perry, Nathan	1	3	4		
Jordan, Dempsey	1		1		
Chamley, James	1	1	1		
Hill, Joseph	1	7	3		
Privit, Peter	1		5		
Newsom, James	1		1		15
Hogwood, George	1				
Martin, Abraham	2	3	3		13
Holding, Arther	1	1	1		
Wall, Arther	2	3	4		
High, Aborgill		1	2		
Smith, Benj^a	2	3	4		11
High, Alsey	1	3	3		12
Williams, Dudley	1	3	1		
Williams, David	1	2	3		
Grimes, Dawson	1	1	4		
Powell, Dempsey	3	2	5	1	20
Perry, Francis	4		5		15
Spane, Federick	1		3		18
Perry, Francis	1		3		2
Holding, Federick	2		6		
Fort, Federick	3	4	4		7
Martin, George	1	1	1		20
Grimes, George	1		2		1
Rives, Hannah		2	2		
Meekans, Henry	1	2	2		
Dean, Hardy	2	4	3		
Moring, Henry	1		1		2
Eazel, John	4		4		
Holding, John	2	4	4		
Fort, John	2	1	2		8
Harris, John	1	2	2		
Kemp, Jesse	1	1	2		
Wall, Jesse	1	1	3		2
Williams, John	1	1	3		
Fort, James	1		3		6
Marlow, John	1		1	4	
Moreholland, John	2	1	4		1
Kemp, John	3		3		
Roan, John	2	3	3		
Lewis, James	1	1	3		39
Pullen, John	4	2	2		10
Moore, John	1	2	2		
Rogers, Jacob	1				
Lowry, Matthew	1	4	3		1
Rogers, Michael	5	1	6		25
High, Mark	2	3	2		7
Walle, Robert	1	1	2		
Smith, Ric^d	1	2	5		
Harris, Reuben	1		6		
Dean, Ric^d	1	2	4		
Kemp, Ric^d	1	3	2		
Rice, Ric^d	1		1		
Thomson, Saml, S^r	2	1	6		3
Harris, Sherrod	2	3	2		
Thomson, Saml, J^r	1	1	1		
Tyrrell, Solomon	2	2	5		7
Holding, Saml, S^r	1		2		3
Holding, Saml, J^r	1	1	2		1
Spane, Thos, Se^r	1	3	4		
Williams, Thos	1	2	2		2
Boyakin, Thos	2		2		2
Young, Thos	3	2	4		4
Spane, Thos, J^r	2	4	6		4
Lee, W^m	2	5	4		6
Grimes, W^m	1	1	2		
Williams, W^m	2		2		2
Philliphs, W^m	1		3		7
Grimes, W^m, Se^r	1	2	3		
Young, W^m	1		2		4
Hockaday, W^m	1		2		2
Martin, W^m	3		6		15
Thomson, Zachariah	4	2	1		2
Bledsoe, W^m	1		1		
Rice, W^m	2	2	4		
Ray, Nathan	1	1	1		
Wall, Burwell	1				
Woodward, Dempsey	1	3	1		
Matthews, John	2	6	5		
Dryars, Thos	1	4	2		
Rogers, Etheldred	4	1	5		7
Rogers, Aron	1				
Holding, Matthew	2	5	2		11
Ferris, James	1		1		
Mobley, Alex^r	1				
Lowry, Arther	1	2	3		
Bruce, Arnell	1		5		1
Davis, Benj^a	3	1	2		
Pace, Buckner	3		4		10
Wallace, David	1				1
Daniel, David	1	2	8		2
Gill, David	1				
Paterson, Francis	4				
Allen, George	2	3	5		
Davis, Glaphzoa	2	1	6		8
Brasfield, George	2	2	2	1	1
Bodine, Grbell	2	1	5		
Russell, George					11
Kennerday, Hugh	1	1	1		
Kemp, Henry	3	3	1		
Mobley, Hammon	2	1	5		
Hall, Joel	1	3	2		
Joplin, James	1	2	2		3
Shaw, John B.	3	2	6		12
Weaver, James	1	5	3		
Wallace, John	1	1	7		9
Huskey, John	2	1	4		1
Ward, James	1	1	2		
Gill, Isaac	1				
Hill, Jacob	1	2	1		
Ferguson, Joel	1	4	4		
Kilgo, Isaac	1	1	5		
Pace, John	2				1
Lowry, Jesse	1	2	3		
Ray, Joseph	1	1	6		
Mickilroy, John	1	2	2		1
Ray, John	1	2	6		
Ray, Luke	2				5
Guttree, Lewry	2	2	3		
Joplin, Mark	1	3	4		
Mobley, Milley	1		2		2
Forrist, Martin	2				4
Stewart, Mary		1			
Mobley, Mordica	2		6		19
Fluellin, Obediah	1	4	2		
Bruce, Peter, Se^r	2	2	3		
Bruce, Peter E.	1	3	3		
Surtherland, Ranson	1	3	4		25
Vinson, Reuben	1	3	3		
Vinson, Saml	1	2	3		
Goodwin, Theop^s	1	4	3		
Barlow, Thos	1	2	2		1
Burnet, Thos	1	2	3		
Shaw, W^m	1	5	3		1
Hall, W^m	1	1	2		
Kennerday, Waystaff	1	7	3		
Rockill, W^m	1	3	6		
Barlow, W^m	1	4	3		
Embrew, W^m	2	4	3		
Weaver, W^m	2		6		
Hall, W^m		2	2		
Jones, W^m	2	2	3		
Vinson, W^m	1	1	2		
Kittle, W^m	2	2	8		
Ferris, Jesse	1		2		
Rice, Roger	1	1	2		
Riddish, John	1	3	2		
Vinson, Joseph	1	1	3		
Tyrrell, Jeptha	3	1	2		13
Bledsoe, W^m	1				
Kittle, Benj^a	1	2	2		
Elliot, James	1		4		
Jones, Francis					5
Russell, James					3
Locklear, Thos					13
Paterson, Smith	3		3		
Turner, Sarah		1	1		1
Spencehead, Alex^r	2	2	3		11
Belvin, Abraham	1		2		
Parram, Avera	1		3		
Bledsoe, Barnabas	2	2	7		2
Ward, Benj^a	1		2		
Briggs, Charles	1	1	1		10
Dilk, David	1	4	1		4
Burton, David H.	2	5	3		
Ragan, David	1		3		
Melone, David	1		3		3
Spears, Dempsey	3	1	2		2
Justice, David	1		3		4
Holderfield, Elizabeth	1	3	5		
Brasfield, Elijah	1		1		
Barker, Edmond	2	3	4		6
Brasfield, Elizabeth			2		
Rigsbey, Federick	1		4		
Wilson, George	1	2	3		1
Thomson, George	1	4	3		
Warren, Henry	1	2	4		7
Rives, Hardy	2	1	3		
Mosley, Henry	2	3	6		2
King, Henry	1	1	4		
Humphris, John (Virg^a)	1	3	5		1
Kuton, John	2	1	4		
Goodwin, Isham	2	3	7		
Williot, John	1		4		
Belvin, John	1	4	4		
Moore, James	2		3		
Diol, James	1	4	5		
Brasfield, Joseph	1	1	3	1	1
Golihon, Joseph	1		1	1	
Riley, John, Se^r	1	3	3		
Moore, James H.	1	1	6		
Ward, John	1	1	6		
Ellis, John					3
Rifley, John, Jr.	1		1		
Yergin, John	1	1	2		
Dennis, John	1	1	1		
Goodwin, John	1	1	1		
Ward, Joseph	1	1	4		
Bledsoe, Jacob	3	1	1		11
Holleway, John	3	1	2		10
Bledsoe, Isaac	1	3	4		
Bledsoe, Jacob, Jr.	2	1	3		2
Bodine, John	1				
Dilk, Joseph	1		1		
Kercum, James	2	3	7		3
Bledsoe, John	2	1	3		3
Bledsoe, Jacob	1	3	3		
Dobey, John	1	3	3		
Martin, John	1	2	4		3
Pope, Jesse	1	2	1		
Brevis, Job	1		1		
Cheavis, James	1	4	3		13
Gray, John	3	2	4		9
Canneday, Leannerday			1	2	
Bledsoe, Lewis	1	3	3	6	3
Barker, Lewis	3	2	6		7
Moore, Lewis	2	1	5	1	4
Pollard, Major	1		4		3
Marshall, Moses	1	3	1		
Evins, Morris	1	2	8		
Sexton, Obediah	1	4			
Belvin, Pricilla			1		3
Kilgo, Peter	1	4	3		
Rogers, Peleg	4	3	6		17
Allen, Runnell, S^r	3	1	3		3
Robertson, Ric^d	3	3			
Gradey, Robert	1	3	3		
Pollard, Ric^d	1		1		
Harrell, Robert	1	1	3		
Mossey, Ric^d	3		3		7
Gradey, Robert	3	4	4		
Holderfield, Ralph	1	1	2		
Philliph, Robert	1	2	5		
Evins, Reuben	1				
Allen, Runnell	2	4	2		1
Thomson, Swan	2	5	4		10
Jackson, Thos	1		3		11
Ship, Teller	2	1	1	1	
Goor, Thos	1	2	2		1

HILLSBOROUGH DISTRICT, WAKE COUNTY—Continued.

NAME OF HEAD OF FAMILY.	Free white males of 16 years and upward, including heads of families.	Free white males under 16 years.	Free white females, including heads of families.	All other free persons.	Slaves.
Warren, Wm	2	5	1		3
Dennis, Wm	1	2	4		
Holley, Wm	1		1		
Kelgo, Wm	2	1	2		9
Tate, Wm	1	3	7		1
Commons, Wm	2	2	4		5
Gibbs, Wm	1		4		
Ship, Wm	2	2	4		3
Griggs, Wm	2	1	5		
Brasfield, Wm	1		2		
Moore, Wm	1				
Wilson, Whitfield	1	1	1		
Allen, Young	1	4	1		2
Shaw, Zachariah	1	2	3		1
Beaver, Zachariah	1	1	4		
Barnes, Lulley		1	4		
Raba, Elsha	1	1	3		
Thomson, Wm	1		3		
Thomas, James	3		2		
Barker, Abner	1	2	1		
Jones, Thos	2		1		4
Pollard, Wm	2	3			
Bullard, Joseph	1	1	2		
Robertson, James	2	1	3		
Capman, Saml	1	4	3		
Beaver, Thos	1		4		
Reynold, John	1	2	4		2
Jackson, Wm	1	3	4		
Powell, Willis	2	2	2		
Daniel, Winifred		2	2		
Harrison, Mary	1	7	2		
Evins, Thos				6	
Snede, Robert	1	4	3		
Gradey, Dennis	2	1	8		12
Hayes, Jery	1	2	1		
Humphris, Thos	1	1	2		
Hartsfield, Andrew	2	3	4	1	5
Abbott, Abraham	1	1	5		
Jones, Albridgston	1	2	2		1
Sims, Adam	1	1	4		
Pulliam, Benja	2	2	7		5
Dunn, Boling	2		6		10
Card, Benson	1	3	4		
Sexton, Britain	1	1	1		
Campbell, Collin	1	1	3		3
Dunn, Drury	1	2	7		13
Lee, Daniel	1	2	3		
Spane, David	3	2	6		
Andrews David	2	2	5		7
Rains, Enuch	2	1	4		
Parsons, Ephraim	1				
Page, Edward	2	2	5		
Vandegriff, Garret	4	4	5	1	
Andrews, Henry	1		1		
Buffelow, Henry	1	3	5	1	
Moodey, Henry	1	2	5		
Ivey, Henry	2	2	6		
Sexton, Absalom	2	2	1		
Hunter, Jacob	2	1	6		7
Nutt, John	1	3	3		3
Butler, John	2	2	3		
Rich, Jacob	1	3	4	3	
Hindon, James	1				
Ragan, James	1	1	2		
Walker, Joseph	1	2	4		
Miller, John	1	2	2		
Andrews, Jesse	1	1	5		
Foster, John	1		2		
Little, John	1	1	1		
Harris, Jesse	1				
Spam, John	1	6	4		
Sims, Isham, Jur	1	2	3		
Fergoson, Isaac				6	
Stephens, Joseph	1	1	2		2
Brown, Joseph	1	2	3		
Allen, Joshua	3	3	3		
Sims, Isham, Sr	2		2		2
Sing, John	2	1	3		
Hindon, Isham	2		2		3
Tipper, John	1	3	3		
Proctor, John	1	1	5		
Sexton, John	2	2	6		2
Ragan, Joseph	1		2		
Hunter, Isaac, Ser	3	2	5		29
Gray, Joseph	1	4	2		
Profit, Larkin	2	2	3		
Sims, Murry	1		5		1
Wallis, Matthew	1	4	4		
Sims, Mark	1	2	3		
Rich, Mary	1		2		5
Ivey, Peter	2	2	3		2
Lee, Rowland	1	2	6		
Dodd, Ricd	1		2		
Flemming, Robert	2	1	2		5
Brewer, Rice	2	1	3		11
High, Saml	1	3	5		19
Cheavis, Thos	1	1	3		9
Newby, Thos	1	1	3		
Proctor, Thos	3	4	5		
Embrew, Thos	3	3	2		1
Collier, Thos	1	4	3		
Sims, Wm	3	3	7		8
Ragan, Willis	1	2	2		
Dawson, Wm	1		1	1	
Campbell, Mary			2		
Sexton, Peter	1	1	2		1
Campbell, Walter	1	3	6	1	
Spane, Thos	1		4		
Shorte, George	1		2		
Card, Benson	1	1	2		
Campbell, John	1	1	3		
King, Arthur	1	2	4		
Hartsfield, Andrew	1				2
Loyd, Ebenezer	1	1	5		
Stripten, Benja	1		2		
Jones, Burwell	1				
Ward, Benja	1		2		
Hicks, Benja	1				
Low, Cardrick	1	1	1		
Valentine, David	1	1	1		
Hunter, David	2				
Pride, Edward	1		5		14
Silvy, Edward	2	2	4		
Thomas, Francis	2		2		11
Jinks, George	2	1	2		
Thomas, Giles	2	2	5		2
Lane, Henry	2		4		14
Vinson, Hozias	2	2	2		
King, James	3	5	4		
Hartsfield, James	1	3	2		
Sigers, Josias	2		1		
Freman, John	2	2	8		
Terry, John	1	3	2		
Oliff, Jesse	1	1	2		
Freeman, John	2	2	2		
Keath, John	1	6	2		
Hartsfield, John	1	2	2		1
Jones, James	2	2	4		
Rigsby, James	1	2	2		
Morris, John	1	1	3		1
Wallace, John	1	2	2		
Dillard, Joseph	2	3	3		4
Rhodes, John	1	2	2		
Kimbrough, John	2		4		30
Lane, Joel	2	2	5		27
Lane, James	1	1	2		16
Dillard, Josiah	1				
Smith, James	1				
Bodine, John	1	2	2		
Smith, Joseph	2	3	2		
Hambey, Mary			2		
Freeman, Needham	1	1	4		
Hicks, Nathl	1	4	1		
——, Newmon	2		4		
Duffee, Patrick	1	2	6		
Holderfield, Ralph	1	1	2		
Holiway, Reuben	1		2	6	
Hamby, Saml	1	2			
King, Sampson	1	1	2		
Hambey, Stephen	1	4	2		
Cope, Thos	3	2	5		
House, Thos	2	3	7		
Dillard, Theops	1	1	3		2
Hunter, Theop, Jur	2	2	1		10
Holliman, Thos	2	3	5		
Jinks, Thos	1	3	3		
Smith, Thos	1		4		
Brazor, Wm	3	3	4		
Brewer, Wm	1	1	2		
Cooper, Wm	1	4	5		4
Wilmouth, Wm	1		1		
Smith, Wm	2	3	6		2
King, Vinson	1	2	2		
Loyd, Ebenezer	1	1	5		
Hucks, Stephen	2	2	3		
Watson, David	1		4		
Rigsbey, Archabell	1		3		
Page, Edward	2	2	4		
Humphris, Thos	1	1	2		
Simons, Wm	2		4		
Pinney, James	3				
Johnson, Aron	1	3	3		
Burges, Athel	3	4	5		
Bird, Bonner	1	2	4		
Lewis, Berry	1	4	2		
Hobson, Benjn	1		1		
Almon, Cannada	1	1	3		3
Roberts, Curtis	1	1	3		
Surls, Coventon	1	4	3		
Pealer, Christain	1	3	4		
Blake, Dempsey	1	1	4		7
Barnes, Drewry	1	2	2		
Hobson, Daniel	1	3	3		
Bradley, Dennis	2	2	1		
Roberts, Edmon	1	3	4		3
Sorrell, Edmond	1		4		6
Barber, Going	1	1	4		1
Herndon, George	1		1		
Wardroop, George	1		1		
Motley, Harrison	1				
Surls, Henry	1	3	2		
Hill, Henry	1	2	1		
Buzby, Henry	1	3	4		
Mondaris, John	2	3	5		14
Smith, Isaac	1	3	4		
Loalan, Jesse	2	1			1
Smith, John	1	1	3		
Gatling, Jesse	1	4	2		
Humphris, John	2	3	3		3
Roberts, James	1		1		
Rigsby, John	1		4		
Rigbey, James	1	3	2		
Johnson, Isarel	1	2	2		
Wood, Jacob	1		1		
Motley, John	2	3	4		8
Marr, John	1		1		
Linn, John	1	5	2		2
Roberts, John	1	5	7		
Weatherspoon, John	1	1	2		
Harrod, James	1	2	2		
Herndon, James	1	3	4		
Laskley, Joseph	1		2		
Barber, Joseph	2	5	5		1
George, Jesse	2	2	4		
Motley, John	1	1	5		
Harrod, John	1	3	5		
Wardrop, James	1				
Lumley, Jesse	1	1	3		
King, James	2	4	4		
Brown, James	1		3		
Sicars, John	1		2		
Smith, John	1		1		
Blake, James	1	3	4		
Harrod, Martin	1	1	2		
Jones, Mary	2	1	4		16
Roberts, Moses	3				
Johnson, Nathan	1		1		
Perry, Nicholas	1	3	2		2
Marr, Nimrod	1	1	3		
Herring, Owing	2	4	5		
Hobson, Reuben	1		2		
Blake, James	1	4	2		4
Marcom, Saml	1	1	2		
Bradley, Sampson	1				
King, Saml	1		4		
Low, Stephen	2	2	5		
George, Solomon	2	1	3		
Roberts, Thos	1	4	4		3
Johnson, Thos	1		1		
Rich, Timothy	3	1	1		1
Brown, Thos	1	3	4		
Murry, Thos	1	3	5		2
Morris, Thos	1	4	5		
Hobson, Thos	2		4		8
Jones, Tignal	2	2	3		39
Smith, Uriah	1	1	1		
Bodine, Vinson	1		2		
Buzby, Wm	1	1	3		
Mainyard, Wm	3	5	3		7
Sorrell, Wm	1	5	2		2
Weatherspoon, Wm	3	2	2		
Thorn, Wm	2	2	4		2
Yeats, Wm	1	3	7		
Harrod, Wm	2		3		
Hill, Wm	1	2			
Brown, Wm	1	2	3		
Ward, Wm	1	3	5		10
Hudgins, Wm	1				
King, Wm	1	4			
Hobson, Zachariah	1		1		
Smith, Zachariah	1	1	4		2
Laulin, Moses	1	1	1		
Smith, Wm	1	1	1		
Smith, Thos	1	4	4		
Smith, Thos	1	2	1		
Holderfield, Elizabeth	1	4	3		
Jenkins, Saml	1		5		
Sorrell, Thos	2	3	4		6
Burns, John	1				
Corn, Julus				3	
Roberts, Solomon	1		1		
Roberts, Aron	1		2		
Burges, Thos	1		1		
Petiford, Laurence				8	
Bodine, John	1	1	2		
Smith, Drewry	1		3		
King, James	1		3		
Morris, Thos	1	5	3		18
Cook, Arther	1		1		
Franks, Anthoney	1	2	3		
Sicars, Asa	1	1	3		

HILLSBOROUGH DISTRICT, WAKE COUNTY—Continued.

NAME OF HEAD OF FAMILY.	Free white males of 16 years and upward, including heads of families.	Free white males under 16 years.	Free white females, including heads of families.	All other free persons.	Slaves.
Proctor, Benjⁿ	1		4		
Whitehead, Burwell		2	3		
MᶜGee, Charles	1	1	1		2
Babb, Christopher	1	6	3		
Joiner, Drewry	1	1	2		
Darnull, David	1		4		3
Hudson, Drewry	1	2	1		
Brown, Drewry	1				
Wiggins, Elijah	1	4	2		
Moore, Field	1	2	3		
Cole, George	1		3		
Utley, Hezekiah	1	1	4		2
Edwards, John	1	2	3		
Bradford, John	3	3	3		3
Linn, James, Juʳ	3	2	2		10
Taylor, John	4	3	6		
Stinson, Jarrot	1	3	3		
Brown, Josiah	1	2	5		
Cohoon, Jeremiah	1	1	1		
Hudson, John	2	1	6		
Turner, Jasper	1				
Hudgins, John		1	1		
Hunter, Isaac, Juʳ	2	1	1		
Yeats, John	1	1	2		
Woodall, James	1	4	3		
Lane, Joseph, Jʳ	1	1	3		7
Landinham, James	1	3	4		
Pulliam, James, Jʳ	1	4			
Streeter, John	2				5
Lane, Joseph, Seʳ	2				6
Smith, Lewis	1				
Shorte, Lundmon	3	2	4		
Jones, Levy	2	1	2		
Lane, Martin	1		4		5
Muckleroy, Micajah	1	2	3		1
Jones, Nathˡ, Seʳ	2		5		17
Jones, Nathˡ (x Road)	2	3	6		16
Pulliam, Paterson	2	1	3		
Joiner, Patience		1	4		5
Jones, Philliph	1	3	4		
Hunter, Reuben, Jʳ	1	2	2		1
Rench, Rebecah	1	1	2		
Edwards, Rias	1	1	2		
Bukingham, Sion	1	1	2		
Shorte, Sion	2		1		
Simmons, Solomon	2	1	3		
Behaney, Simon	3	1	1		
Philliphs, Thoˢ	2	3	5		
Hudson, Thoˢ	1	1	1		
Lane, Wᵐ	2				4
Spights, Wᵐ	1	2	2		10
Brown, Wᵐ	1	5	4		
Utley, Wᵐ, Sʳ	1		1		7
Brown, Wiles	1		3		
Self, Willibey	3	2	4		
Corder, Wᵐ	1		2		
Cole, Shadrick	1		2		
Low, Cradrick	1	1	1		
Bledsoe, Abraham	1	1	4		
Hill, Ann		3	3		7
Piddy, Andrew, Jʳ	2	2	4		
Wood, Arther	1	1	2		
Oliff, Abell	1	2	3		
Beckworth, Boling	1	1	1		
Utley, Britain	2	1	3		1
Utley, Burwell	2	1	2		
Stephens, Carnaby	1	2	2		
Straight, David	2	2	5		
Barker, Daniel	1	1	2		
Barker, Drewry	1	1	2		
Oaks, Daniel	1	2	6		
Herring, Ephraim	1	2	1		
Lashley, Edmond	1	2	3		
Watson, Elijah	1	1	2		2
Talley, George	1	1	1		
William, George	1	3	4		
Sinters, Henry	1	3	2		
Wood, George	1				
Bowers, John	1	3	1		
Holliman, James	1	2	3		
Huckabee, James	2	1	3		1
Holland, James, Sʳ	2		1		
Wood, James	1				
Harrison, John	1		3		
Huckabee, John	2	1	2		6
Hill, Jacob	1	1	2		
Linn, James	1	1	3		
Laurance, Joseph	4		4		
Leavins, Jacob	2		5		3
Leavins, James	1		2		
Norris, John	2	3	5		
Olive, James	2	4	3		4
Oliff, John	1	3	3		2
Piddey, Jeremiah	2	3	2		
Stephens, James	1		1		
Thomas, Joseph	5	4	2		
Wood, Kenehin	1	2	1		
Barker, Lewis	1	1	3		
Lashley, Lewis	3	3	2		
Barker, Mark	1	2	3		
Bledsoe, Moses	1	2	2		
Hicks, Moses	2	1	4		
Wood, Moses	2		5		6
Dennis, Nathan	1	4	5		
Holland, Ricᵈ	2	3	3	1	
Leavins, Ricᵈ	1	2	2		
Leavins, Ritchmon	1		2		
Barker, Shaderick	1	2	5		
Holland, Sampson	1	5	3		
Hamblton, Stewart	1	3	4		
Olive, Southwood	1	2	4	1	
Rowland, Samˡ	1	2	2		
Wood, Sampson	2	3	4		
Holland, Thoˢ	1		3		
Hayes, Thoˢ	1	1	4		
Reddin, Thoˢ	1	4	5		
Barker, Wᵐ	2	2	4		5
Hayes, Thoˢ	3	3	5		19
Jennings, Wᵐ	1	5	2		
Oliff, Wᵐ	2	3	4		1
Segraves, Wᵐ	1	2	3		
Thrailkill, Wᵐ	3	3	4		
Sillers, John	2	1	5		
Wood, Burges	1	1	2		
Rogers, Stephen			3		
Brown, Robert	1	4	3		
Brown, Barnabas	1		3		
Crain, Henry	1		1		
Thomas, Michael	1				
Hamblton, Andrew	1	2	5		
Turner, Augustus B.	2	1	2		
Poe, Benjⁿ	1	2	4		
Noles, Benjⁿ	1				
Woodward, Corbell	2	1	2		1
Stinson, Clemment	1	1	2		
Segraves, Daniel	1				
Peters, Deal	1		3		
Wheeler, David	3	1	6		
Matthews, David	1	3	4		3
Smith, Ezackail	1	4	7		
Jones, Elkin	1	3	4		
Jones, Etheldred	1	4			5
Jackson, Federick	1				
Wheeler, Henry	1	2	2		
Johnson, Hardy	1		1		
Lilley, Hardy	1	3	4		
Thomas, Hillery					2
Moss, James	2	1	3		
Lewis, Jesse	2	5	2		
Strickland, John, Seʳ	1	1	5		
Thomas, Jonathan	1	2	2		
Stinson, John	1	2	3		
Franks, Joseph	1	1	2		
Strickland, John	1		5		
Richardson, John	1	2	4		
Hodges, John	1	2	2		
Segraves, Jacob	1	4	3		
Stinson, James	2				
Dilk, Joseph	1		1		
Jint, Jesse	1		6		
Jint, John	2	1	3		
Segraves, John, Sʳ	1	2	3		
Utley, John	2	2	5		1
Woodward, Jordan	1	1	2		2
Farrar, John	3	6	3		11
Utley, Jacob	2	3	4		10
Driver, John	1				
Jones, James	1		2		
Jones, Jesse	2	3	8		2
Dorman, Keziah	2	2	2		
Caudle, Lewis	2	2	2		
Jones, Lewis	4	2	4	1	1
Stinson, Lovit	1		2		
Messer, Lott	2	2	4		
Yarbrough, Meredith	1	2	2		
Harvell, Moses	1	1	1		
Macklin, Matthew					6
Rowland, Nathan	2		3		
Thomas, Nathan	2	1	5		
Powell, Nathan	1		2		
Woodward, Plesant	3	1	4		1
Woodward, Ricᵈ	2	2	4		1
Green, Silas	1	2	2		5
Driver, Thoˢ, Seʳ	1	2	4		
Jint, Thoˢ	1	2	6		
Wood, Obediah	1	4	4		
Driver, Thoˢ, Jʳ	1				
Macklin, Thoˢ					11
Turner, Titus	1				
Strickland, Wᵐ	1		2		
Rowland, Wᵐ	2	2	5		
Harvell, Wᵐ	3	3	3		1
Love, Wᵐ	2	2	1		
Williams, Wᵐ	1		1		1
Stewart, Wᵐ					11
Braswell, Valenitin	1		2		
Jones, Wᵐ	2	2	6		7
Jones, David	3	1	5		
Jones, John	3	4	4		
Watkins, Robert	1	1	2		1
Jackson, Peggey		2	2		
Beaney, Thoˢ	1	3	3		
Segraves, Wᵐ	2	2	3		
Ren, Joseph	1	2	1		
Matthews, Redmon	2		1		
Hogan, Abraham	1	2	4		4
Griffis, Allen	1	4	1		
Collins, Andrew	5	4			9
Myat, Alexʳ	1		1		2
Turner, Ann	2		5		18
Ogdon, Benjⁿ	1		3		
Myat, Britain	2		2		1
Garner, Book	1		4		
Britt, Benjⁿ	1				
Wade, Benjⁿ	1	3	1		
Mills, Bethiah	2		4		4
Sanders, Britain	1	1	2		16
Peoples, Drewry	1	2	2		
Utley, David	1	1	4		
Stephens, David	1	3	3		
Turner, David	1				4
Sanders, Ellick	4				5
Buzby, Federick	1	3	2		
Sanders, Hardy	2	1	4		14
Freeman, Henry	1				
Britt, Joseph, Seʳ	1	2	1		
Atkins, Isaac	1		3		
Hudson, Isaac	1	2	4	1	2
Britt, Joseph, Jʳ	1				
Lewis, John	1	4	7		
Buzby, James	1	5	3		
Lewis, James (B.)	1	3	1		
Rice, John	1	2	2		
Singlton, James	2	3	7		
Boyeworth, James	2	3	4		
Fisk, Joseph, Jʳ	1	1	2		
Buzby, John	1		1		
Copeland, Isaac					4
Myat, John, Seʳ	2	1	1		5
Utley, Isham	2	5	2		4
Liptrot, James	2	1	2		
Atkins, John	5		4		13
King, John	1	4	3		6
Whitaker, John	2	4	5		7
MᶜCullers, Matthew	2	2	3		14
Nall, Martin	1	2	1		1
Tedrick, Michael	1	2	2		
Myat, Mark	1	4	4		5
Myat, Matthew	1	4	4		1
Nall, Nathan	1	1	3		
Atkins, Nicholas	1				
Hillard, Phillip	1	2	2		
Penney, Penul	1	3	5		3
Pearson, Parish	1	2	3		1
Britt, Ryals	1				
Nall, Ricᵈ	1		1		3
Swanson, Ricᵈ	2	1	7		
Fitch, Roger	1				
Britt, Wᵐ	1				
Gawf, Starling	1	2	5		
Wright, Samˡ	3	1	3		
Parish, Sherrod	2	1	4		
Pearson, Samˡ	2	2	3		8
Parish, Thoˢ	1	1	2		
Turner, Simon	2				6
Hill, Theopˢ	1	1	3		
Smith, Turner	3	2	4		1
Cormack, Wᵐ	3	2	4		
Rand, Walter	1	1	2	1	6
Bridges, Wᵐ	2	3	7		1
Tomlinson, Wᵐ	1	1	2		
Rivers, Wᵐ	1		2		
Walton, Wᵐ	3	2	5		14
Pope, Wᵐ	2	3	6		
Stephen, Zaichariah		1	1		
Pau, Wᵐ	1	6	1		
MᶜGuffin, Elizabeth		2	1		
Page, Jesse	5	1	5		
Lankford, Stephen	1	1	2		
Myat, Wᵐ	1	4	2		
Lewis, James, Jʳ	1				
Williams, John, Jʳ	2	4	2		
Smith, Jonathan	2	2	6		23
Fowler, Asley	1				
Sweat, Allen	1				
Jones, Benjⁿ	1	3	2		
Allen, Bartlet	1	1	5	1	
Clark, Benjⁿ	1	2	4		
Dunston, Charles	1	2	6		
Ferrell, Christain		2	4		
Tabourn, Dempsey				5	

HILLSBOROUGH DISTRICT, WAKE COUNTY—Continued.

NAME OF HEAD OF FAMILY.	Free white males of 16 years and upward, including heads of families.	Free white males under 16 years.	Free white females, including heads of families.	All other free persons.	Slaves.
Brasfield, David	2	1	2		3
Parkinson, Drewry	1	3	3		
Tucker, Daniel	1	5	3		1
Tucker, Ethel	3		2		4
Chammill, Elisha	1		1		3
Siat, Emanuel	1	1	2		
Ruth, Elizabeth			3		
Gear, Federick	2	2	6		9
Campbell, Fanney		2	2		
Evins, Gilber	2	4	3		
Ruth, Georth	2	4	6		
Brogdon, George	3		2		
Shaw, Gabell	2	1	5		2
Ellis, Hicks	2	2	2		
Dockery, Haslin	1	1	1		
Bagley, Harmon	1		4		1
Fowler, Henry	1	2	3		
Tulley, Halack	1	4	3		
Morris, Hugh	2	2	5		
Allen, Jesse	1	1	1		
Thomas, John	1		5		
Nichols, Julus	1		1		
May, John	2	4	4		
Allen, John	2		2		
Colton, John F	1		1		
Nicks, Joseph	3	2	4		
Murry, James	1		2		
Corn, Justin				3	
Jordan, John	3		5		
Shammill, Jonathan	1	1	5	1	
Phillips, John	1	4	2		
Rogers, Job	1	1			2
Sherring, John	1	5	3		1
Shammill, Isaac	1	1	2		4
Rives, Jonathan	2	5	4		
Parkinson, Joel	1	3	4		
Smith, Joshua	1		6		
Dockary, John	2	1	2		
Hicks, Isaac	3	1	4		8
Alston, John	1	7	4	5	15
Little, Joseph	1	3	2		
Little, John	1	1	1		
Carter, Jesse	1	2	5		1
Scoggins, John	1	2	5		
Alley, Joseph	1	1	1		
Parker, James	1	2	1		1
Tabun, James				3	
Sandey, Jarred	1	3	2		3
Conyers, John	1		1		
Freeland, Isaac	1		1		
Watts, John	1	1	1		
Reynolds, Jethro	1	1	1		
Rice, Jessee	1		1	1	3
Allen, Kinsmon	1		1		
Ragan, Larkin	1	1	2		
Ferrell, Micajah	2	2	4		6
Reynolds, Michael	3	2	1		
Patterson, Mary	1	2	6		
Holloway, Major	1	5	4		2
Jordan, Margaret	1	4	5		
Cammall, Mary		4	3		
Tomson, Maton	1	2	3		
Dempsey, Micajah				2	
Pollard, Nancey		1	3		
Hudson, Peter	1	3	5		
Hedgepith, Peter				5	
Gouch, Pumphrey	2		2		
Corn, Robert				4	
Tomlinson, Richard	1		8		
Pollard, Richard	3	2	4		
Hall, Robert	1	2	3		
Wilkins, Richard	2	1	4		4
Standley, Richard	1	1	4		
Talley, Richard	1	2	2		3
Patishall, Richard	1		1		
Gooch, Roley	1	1	2		
Griggs, Rodeyan	1	1	2		2
Banks, Richard	4	1	2	2	12
Smith, Samuel	1	2	2		
Peck, Samuel	2		2		12
Jenkins, Samuel	1	2	4		
Pitchford, Samuel	2	4	2		3
Tarrey, Starling	1	2	2		
Campbell, Sarah		1	3		
Watts, Spiner	3		2		5
Alley, Samuel	1	4	3		1
Talley, Spencer	1		1		
Ross, John	1	2	3		
Noe, Thomas	1	4	3		
Tomlinson, Thomas	1	3	5		26
Pruit, Thomas	1		4		
Nicols, Thomas	2	3	4		
May, Thomas	1	2	2		
Dorus, Valentine				8	
Carpenter, William	1	2	4		
Rives, William, Jur	1	1	1		
Nicols, William, Jur	1		5		
Nichols, William, Ser	2	2	3		
Evans, William	2	6	5		
Burks, William	2	4	1		
Hodge, William	1	2	6		
Allin, William	1	2	4		
May, William	1		3		
Grant, William	1	1	4		
Jones, Willis	1		2		5
White, William	2	3	4		7
Bagwell, William	1				4
Watts, William	1	3	5		
Ferrell, William	3	3	6		
Little, William		1	2	2	
Rives, William	2	4	3		8
Sandey, William	1		1		
Daniel, Woodson	3	3	6		26
Ashley, William	2	2	3	2	3
Reynols, William	1	2	2		
Floyed, Amos	1	3	3		
Rowland, Federick	1	4	4		
Allen, Josiah	1				3
Griffis, John	3	2	2		
Ivey, Peter	2	1	3		6
Emborough, William	2	2	4		
Olive, James	2		1		3
Myatt, John, Jur	1	1	1		2
Buzby, William	2		4		
Hinton, James	1	4	2		36
Herrington, Samuel	1	1	8		
Burt, John	1	2	4		13

MORGAN DISTRICT, BURKE COUNTY.

NAME OF HEAD OF FAMILY.	Free white males of 16 years and upward, including heads of families.	Free white males under 16 years.	Free white females, including heads of families.	All other free persons.	Slaves.
FIRST COMPANY.					
Dobson, Jos., Jr	3	3	5		1
Young, Joshua	1	5	4		
Davidson, George	1	3	1		1
Wasburn, Matthew	1	1	1		
Bradshaw, Isaiah	1	1	2		
Stroud, Peter	1	5	2		3
Stroud, Peter, Jr	1		1		
Stroud, Jesse	1	3	1		
Washburn, David	2		6		
Washburn, Drury	1	1	2		
Patten, Wm	1		2		
Patten, Sam	1	3	2		
McWilliams, Jas	1	2	5		
McCracon, Quilla	1	2	5		1
Reed, Robt	1	4	3		1
Trammell, Jno	1	3	4		
Brown, Jos	4		5		
McDowell, Jas	1	2	2		2
Cathey, Wm	3	4	5		3
McClure, Andw	3	5	5		
Durr, Wm	3	2	4		3
Welsh, Thos	1	3	1		1
Hannah, Tho H	1		1		
Dickeson, Cathrn	1	1	5		
Melony, John	1		1		
McClure, Francis	3		4		
Jones, Jno	1	3	3		
Edenten, Rhoda	2	5	2		
Collet, Wm	1	2	2		
Bibo, Thos	1	1	3		
Burchfield, Mishh	1	1	4		5
McDowell, Jno	1	1	1		1
Carol, Sterling	1		1		
Carol, George	1	1	8		
McDowell, Jos, Jun	1	2	1		9
Carson, Jno	2	5	2		12
Welsh, Jno, Senr	3	3	5		
O'Neal, Wat	2	1	3		
Webster, Moses	1	2	4		
McPeters, Jonathan	1	1	2		
McPeters, Jos	1	3	5		
Plumley, Wm	3	1	3		
Trorps, Nicholas	3	3	3		
Shuke, Jacob	1	6	3		
Davidson, Jno	3	5	6		6
Neall, Wm	4	1	4		
Patten, Elijah	1	2	6		2
FIRST COMPANY—con.					
Hobs, Mary			2		
Mitchell, Pounce	1	2	2		
Inman, Saml	1	2	1		
Inman, Henry	1		1		
Plumly, Stephen	1	1	2		
Williams, Henry	1	1	3		
Stout, Saml	2	5	3		
Reid, Jno	1		3		
Neall, Jas	1	4	2		1
Wiggins, Abram	1	2	2		1
Brittain, Aron	1		2		
Brandon, Martin	2	4	7		
Cathey, George	2	3	4		5
Brown, Chas	1		3		
Cathey, Marget		1	4		
Neall, And'w	1	1	4		
Lewis, Wm	1	2	4		
Kelton, Wm	1	4	6		7
Flord, Abram	1	3	2		
McGonigle, Jno	1	1	3		
Posey, Francis	1	4	2		
Wilson, Thos	5		2		12
Hill, Robt	1	1	1		
Rus, Rose	1	3	5		
Davis, Ben	5	3	4		
Culberson, Davd	1	3	4		
Bright, Tobias	1	1	1		
Blakely, Robt	1	1	6		
Mashburn, David	1		2		
Jetton, Jno	1	1	4		2
Higgins, Wm	3	2	6		
Norton, Messer	1	3	5		
Templeton, Arche	4	2	4		
Martin, Jno	3	4	5		
Hix, James	1	1	2		
Atwater, Isaac	1				
Melony, Edwd	1	2	6		
Davidson, Ben	2	1	9		
McBride, David	1	2	1		
Glass, Thos	2		6		
Glass, Henry	1	2	1		
McGonigle, Wm	1	1	3		
Logan, Jane	2	1	3		
Kelly, Wm	3	5	3		
Bird, Ben, Sen	2		2		2
Bird, Ben, Jr	1	1	2		
Brevard, Zeb, Jr	1	2	3		
FIRST COMPANY—con.					
Hemphill, Thos	2	2	7		11
Adkins, Jno	3	2	6		
Ellison, Thos	1	1	5		
Ellison, Henry	1	4	1		
Hambrick, Robt	1	2	2		
Thompson, Zach	1		1		
Penhly, Jno	1	2	2		
Regan, Thos	2	4	4		
Vickry, Luke	1	1	3		
Ellison, Ben	2	2	3		
Young, Jane		2	5		
Wilson, Jno	1	1	1		
Smith, Jared	1		1		
Gunter, Agusta	1	1	1		
McClisky, Jno	1		1		
Kelly, Alex. Ham	1	2	2		
Oneal, Charles	1		1		
Rogers, Mourning	2	3	2		
Adams, George	1	1	2		
Givins, Wilm	1	2	4		
SECOND COMPANY.					
Conally, John	1	3	5		10
Shell, Jno	2	4	4		
Martin, Isaac	1	6	3		
Hashan, Abram	1	4	3		1
Dudly, Rebekah			3		
Martin, Marget		2	1		
Wagoner, Marget			1		
Francum, Wm	1	3	3		
Francum, Jno	1		1		
Martin, Tho	1	2	4		
Moore, James	2		5		
Conally, Wm	2	2	2		
Fleming, Abram	1	3	3		8
Winkler, Conrod	1	1	3		
Spencer, Jno, Sr	1	3	5		
Smith, Zadock	1	5	3		
Murray, Jno	1	2	4		
Murray, David	1	5	2		
Clarke, Ben	1		1		
Suttlemire, Jacob	1	3	4		
Bradshaw, Wm	1		7		
Boman, Edw'd	1		3		3
Boman, Gilbert	1	2	6		
Fips, Jno	1	3	7		

MORGAN DISTRICT, BURKE COUNTY—Continued.

NAME OF HEAD OF FAMILY.	Free white males of 16 years and upward, including heads of families.	Free white males under 16 years.	Free white females, including heads of families.	All other free persons.	Slaves.
SECOND COMPANY—con.					
Bellew, Jos	2		3		
Clarke, Beverly	1		3		
Bellew, Stephen	1	1	4		
Howk, George	2	2	6		
Tillotson, Ben	1	2	5		
Turner, Nathan	1	1	4		
Francum, Rebekah	1	1	1		
Conally, Jas	1	3	4		
Conally, Hugh	1	1	3		
Barnhart, Jno	1	2	3		
Dereberry, Jacob	1	4	3		
Derebery, Mich'l	1	3	4		
Pain, Wm	1	2	7		2
Perkins, Joshua	3	3	2		
Taylor, Wm	1		1		
Stoner, Henry	3	2	7		
Clarke, Wilm	1		4		
Grenstaff, Michl	1	1	4		
Whitehead, Mary			3		
Winkler, Thos, Sr	1	1	2		
Suttlenire, Adam	2	3	3		
Bellew, Willm	1	9	2		
Master, Henry	1	1	5		
Williams, Anne	1	1	2		
Baker, H. Barton	1	3	5		
Brown, Dan'l	1	2	4		
Berry, Joseph	2	3	6		
Berry, Jas	1	1	1		
Berry, Jno	1	1	4		
Berry, Lot	1	2	2		
Baldwin, Wm	1	4	4		
Giles, Saml	1	2	2		
Winkler, Joseph	1	1	2		
Wilson, Jno	1		2		
Smith, Thos	2	1	4		
Erwin, Agnes		1	1		
Martin, Jas	1	1	1		
Spencer, Jno, Jr	1		3		
King, Jas	1	1	3		
Mason, Robt	1	1	5		
Marole, Laurenc	1	1	3		
Pack, Elisa	2		2		
Hart, Michal	1	3	7		
Winkler, Thos, Jr	1	1	2		
Gibs, Jno	1	6	3		
Baker, James	1	1	4		
Boone, Sherwood	1	1	2		
Parmer, Jno	2		2		
Pruett, Jno	1	2	5		
Grider, Martin	1	1	6		
Williams, Leah	1	1	2		
Pruett, Henry	1		1		
Innes, James	3	2	2		
Bradsha, Josiah	1	3	3		
Grasty, Mary		1	2		
Morgan, George	1	5	2		
THIRD COMPANY.					
Baker, Davd	1	3	3		
Penland, Robt	1	4	6		1
Penland, George	3	2	5		
Hanson, Bartlet	3	4	3		6
White, Ben	2	3	3		
Antony, Paul, Sr	2	2	2		1
Baker, Jas	1				
Baxter, Jas	1	4	2		
Browning, Jno	3	4	5		
White, Thos, Jr	1	6	4		
Parks, Ben	1	4	4		3
Antony, Jacob, Sr	3		4		
White, Reuben	1	2	2		
Baker, Jno	1	2	3		
Mason, Elisa			4		
Beck, Jacob	3	6	5		
Rogers, Stephen	1	1	2		
Shefela, Philip	2		1		
Penland, Wm	5	2	3		1
Baker, Charles	1		2		
Prichard, Jas	1	2	7		
Fowler, Edwd	2	1	3		
Walker, Tho	1				
Medly, Jos	1	1	1		
White, Thos, Sr	1		2		5
Shell, Simon	1		1		
Shell, Fred	1	3	6		
Shell, Fred, Jr	2	1	2		
Shenite, James	1	1	2		
McDonell, Dav'd	1	1	3		
Mitchenor, Thos	1	3	2		1
McGahey, Jno	1	1	2		
Erwin, Arthur	3		2		9
Avery, Waight	1	1	6		24
Brown, Jno Colwill	1	3	5		7
Pruett, Jos	2	4	2		7

NAME OF HEAD OF FAMILY.	Free white males of 16 years and upward, including heads of families.	Free white males under 16 years.	Free white females, including heads of families.	All other free persons.	Slaves.
THIRD COMPANY—con.					
Mosely, George	1	2	5		2
Pincy, Stephen	1	2	5		
Wright, Dan	1		1		
Fox, Titus	1	2	3		
Scott, George	1		7	7	
Baker, Henry	1	3	4		6
Gyer, Jacob	2	3	4		
Cole, Alex	1	1	3		
Fox, Jno	1	3	2		
Wakefield, Henry	1	2	4		2
Simpson, Jno	1	2	3		
Harbison, Alex	3	3	3		
Stilwell, Jno	1	3	3		
Odel, Reuben	1	1	1		
Rose, Ben	1	1	2		
Penly, Joshua	1	3	4		
Parks, Thos	2	3	6		1
Alexander, Elisa	1		2		
Antony, Paul, Jr	1				
Brasfield, Jno	1	1	1		
Antony, Philip	1		4		
Trammell, Jno	2	1	2		
Painter, Jno	2	2	3		
Alexander, James	1	5	4		
Antony, Jacob, Jr	1		1		
Fox, Allen	1	2	2		
Branch, Saml	1	2	4		
Scott, Miriah	2	1	3		
Gilmore, Robt	1	2	2		
Parks, Larkin	1		2		
Phillips, Larasus	1	3	3		
Penly, Willm, Jr	3	1	1		
Penly, Wm, Senr	2	3	3		
Hall, John	2	2	2		
Burkes, Rollin	4	4	4		
Church, William	1	2	1		
Church, Thom	1	1	1		
Tramel, Big Denis	2	2	3		
Simpson, James	1	1	1		
Wakefield, John	1	4	4		
Scott, Wiley	1		6		
Piercy, Elisa	1	3	3		
Ustam, Wm	1	1	2		
Tramele, Little Denis	1	1	3		
Allen, Jumima		2	2		
Sherrill, Ute	1	4	4		
Wagley, Jno	2		4		
Duk, Jno	1	2	2		
FOURTH COMPANY.					
Forgayn, James	3	3	4		
Edmison, Jas	3	3	3		
Holinsworth, Sam	2	2	9		
Adams, Howell	1	1	2		
Hailey, Mark	1		5		
Raybon, Kizzi			1		
Conizo, Harison W	1	2	8		
Green, Wm	2	4	1		
Green, Elijah	2	2	5		
Morris, Wilm	2	4	3		1
Haily, Rd	2	3	4		
Williams, Thom	1	2	2		
Raybon, Hodge	1	2	1		1
Harris, Wooton	2	1	3		
Huggins, Luke	1	4	3		
Wadkins, Else		2	1		
Adams, Ben	1	1	3		1
Fleming, Jno	1	2	3		
Fleming, Peter	1	3	4		
Davis, Clem	1	4	1		
Fleming, Thom	1	3	4		
Pickeral, Ben	1	4	3		
Hailey, Wm	1	4	4		
Humphris, Jas	1		1		
Smith, Jno	1		1		
Goodbread, Philip	1	1	3		
Goodbread, Jos	1	2	2		
Huggins, Phillip	2		1		
Stoker, Jas	1	1	2		
Wheeler, Thos	1	4	1		
Janis, Thos	1		1		
Wallace, Jno	1	2	1		
Oaks, Joshua	1	2	3		
Bradsha, Obadiah	1	1	5		
Bryan, Thom	1		1		
Mendinall, Jesse	1	2	2		
Burgin, Ben	2	6	1		
Hamby, Wilm	3		2		
Cozby, John	1	2	5		
Nicols, Thos	1	3	6		
Portman, Wm	1		1		
Jax, Wm	1	1	2		
Wilson, James	1		2		
Noblet, Jno	1	2	2		

NAME OF HEAD OF FAMILY.	Free white males of 16 years and upward, including heads of families.	Free white males under 16 years.	Free white females, including heads of families.	All other free persons.	Slaves.
FOURTH COMPANY—con.					
Chafen, Jos, Jr	3		3		
Petillo, Jno, Sen	2		2		3
Hodge, Robt., Sr	1		6		
Porter, Wilm, Sr	2		4		
Haws, Jacob	2	3	1		
Horrill, James	1		1		3
Chafen, Mary			2		
Hughes, Sam	2		1		
Jackson, Edward	2	5	3		
Fikes, Elisha	1	1	1		
Litle, Thom	1	1	2		1
Petillo, Midleton	1	1	1		
Brown, Thos	2		3		
Cornpin, Ellis	1	1			
Ledford, Nicholas	1		3		
Porter, Wm, Jn	1	1	3		
Strain, Henry	1	4	1		
Elliot, James	1		3		
Chaffen, Elias	1		1		
Diment, Mary	2	2	2		
Keller, Jacob	1	2	3		
Hodge, Robt., Jn	1	2	1		
Wood, Jos	1		1		
Doaty, Jno	1	2	2		
Davis, Thom	1	2	1		
Engld, William	1	2	3		
Scolds, Joseph	1		2		
Wallace, Ben	1	4	4		
Beward, Zeb., Jn	1		2		
Julin, Ben	1	1	4		
Julin, William	1	2	6		
Penkly, Michal	1	1	1		
Redick, Cornelius	1				
Chaffen, Amos	1	3			
Gilliland, Jno	1	4	4		
Collins, Prudence					
FIFTH COMPANY.					
Kilpatrick, Robt	1	5	4		
Webb, Jas. Crit	4	2	1		
Murphey, Wilm	1	3	1		3
White, Joseph	1	2	4		7
Johnson, Wm	1	3	6		
Boone, Jesse	1	3	5		
Hankins, John	1	3	2		
Holliway, George	1	1	4		
Lovin, Wilm	1	1	4		
Hickman, George	3	4	5		1
Weakfield, Charles	4		3		3
Wakefield, Thom	1		3		
Ewings, Isaac	1		1		
Fletcher, Reubin	1	2	2		
Church, Jno	1	1	4		
James, Jos	1		2		
Williams, Wm	1	3	2		
Hite, Reid	2		5		7
Moore, Jas, Senr	2	2	4		
Moore, Jno	1	1	4		1
Adkins, Ben	1	5	3		
Eastress, Reubin	1	4	3		9
Harris, Lewis	2	5	4		
Haris, Edward	2		13		
Miller, George	1	1	3		
Waters, Deep	1		3		
Waters, Abram	1	3	5		
Coker, Leonard	1	1	1		
Coker, Charles, Sr	2		3		
Coker, Charles	1	2	2		
Coker, Wm	1	2	2		
Moore, Jesse, Sr	2		7		
Moore, Jesse	1		1		
Moore, Danl	1		4		2
Coffee, Reubin	1		3		1
Coffey, John	1	1	3		
Coffy, Jas	1	4	3		1
Holland, Jas	2		5		
Coker, Joseph	1		2		
Moorhead, Jas	2	2	3		
Whitlock, Matha	2	1	5		
Mullin, Dani	1		3		
Calleway, Ricd	1		1		1
Hicks, David	2	2	3		
Beard, Ezekiel	2	3	2		
Beard, Saml	3	2	4		
Ward, Byn	2	4	2		
Ward, Joshua	1	1	2		
Giddins, James	1	1	4		
Searsey, Robt	2	3	3		
Edmison, Wm	1	2	4		1
Hays, Thom	3	3	3		1
Hays, George	3	1	1		
Webb, Ben	1		2		
Webb, Jas., Jr	1		2		
Walker, Reynard	1	5	2		

MORGAN DISTRICT, BURKE COUNTY—Continued.

FIFTH COMPANY—con.

NAME OF HEAD OF FAMILY.	Free white males of 16 years and upward, including heads of families.	Free white males under 16 years.	Free white females, including heads of families.	All other free persons.	Slaves.
Boon, Jonathn	1	3	5		
Dowell, George	2	3	3		
Helle, Moses	2		4		
Anderson, Thos., Jr.	2	2	6		1
Powers, Jessey	1	1	5		
Powers, Thom.	2	1	2		
Rice, Jno.	3		2		
Smith, Nathan	1	1	2		
Medecarst, Rice	1	2	5		
Staff, Moses	1	3	3		
Neely, Jas.	1	4	6		
Wilson, Michal.	1	3	3		
Jenell, Wm. F.	1	3	7		
Wilson, James.	1		2		
James, Rollin.	1		6		
Renault, Wm.	1		1		
Hutchins, George.	1	3	3		
Eastriss, Leonard	1		2		
Wilson, Wm.	1	1	3		
Church, Thom., Sr.	2	1	4		
Snead, Jacob	3		8		
Carter, George	2	4	5		
Church, Robt.	1	2	1		
Eastriss, Laybon	2		2		
Brown, Jno.	1	3	3		
King, Baker	1	2	2		
Whittenton, Jno.	1	3	2		
Guin, Champion	1		1		
White, Wm, Senr.	5		2		12

SIXTH COMPANY.

NAME OF HEAD OF FAMILY.	Free white males of 16 years and upward, including heads of families.	Free white males under 16 years.	Free white females, including heads of families.	All other free persons.	Slaves.
Cowan, Joseph	2	1	3		
Reed, Jno.	1		3		
Wilson, Greenberry	1	1	4		3
Bars, Caleb	1	5	4		
Sellers, James	1	1	4		
Hall, Jno.	1	3	6		1
Wilkinson, Moses.	1		3		3
Sellers, Jno.	1	2	1		
Pearson, Michal	1		1		
O'Neal, Patrick, Jr.	1		1		
Dizard, Jno.	1	6	4		
Sellers, Robt., Sr.	1	2	3		
Sellers, Robt.	1		5		
Rutherford, Jas.	1	2	3		2
Dizard, Marget.	1		1		
Allen, Jno., Sr.	4	2	4		
Hytle, Hezekiah	2	2	6		1
Morrison, Wm.	5	1	4		
Andrews, Danl.	3	4	4		
Rutherford, Wm.	2		2		5
Rust, Enos	4	3	2		
Rust, Peter.	1	2	3		
Moore, Wm.	1	3	5		6
Gunter, Claybon	1	1	1		
Plumly, Aham	1	1	5		1
Devine, Jas.	1	1	2		
Denton, Elisa	2		4		
Carely, Jas.	1	1	2		
Carely, Henry	1	4	2		
Sullivan, Danl.	1		2		
Grant, Isaac	1		2		
O'Neal's, Patrick	2		3		
Montgomery, Jno.	2		2		
Montgomery, Jas.	1	3	4		5
Blag, Jas.	1		2		
Leatherwood, Edw'd	1	3	5		2
Montgomery, Bridgt.			2		2
Hunter, Andrew.	1		4		
Justice, Jos.	2	2	1		
Simmons, Rd.	1	2	1		
Gray, Lydia	2	1	3		5
Bradshaw, Field	1	4	3		2
Hytle, Edwd.	1	3			
Tenison, Jacob	1		1		
Chanler, Henry	1	4	3		
McDowell, Jno.	2	2	4		5
Montgomery, Robt.	2	4	5		7
Beall, Thos.	1	4	5		1
Hyett, Simon		1	3	1	
Ferrile, Isaac.		5	4	1	
Robison, Alex.	1		2		
Barchfld, Aberilla.	1	3	3		
Bellew, Robt.	3	1	5		
Rust, David	2	3	3		
Mays, Jno.	1	3	2		
Finley, Charles	1	6	3		
Rutherford, Jno.	2	2	3		2
Gardner, Wm.	2	3	7		3
Polk, Jno.	2	4	3		
Downing, Jno.	2		2		
Long, Alex	2		2		
McAdams, Jno.	3	3	4		
Jones, Ben.	1	3	2		
Worley, Frank	1	3	2		
Sumners, Jno.	1	5	2	4	

SIXTH COMPANY—con.

NAME OF HEAD OF FAMILY.	Free white males of 16 years and upward, including heads of families.	Free white males under 16 years.	Free white females, including heads of families.	All other free persons.	Slaves.
Wood, Saml.	3	3	6		
Reno, Jno.	1	2	5		
Morison, Wm, Jr.	1		4		
Jackson, Chaswl.	1	1	8		
Probit, Wm.	1		1		3
Patten, Elijah, Jr.	1	1	2		
Hemphill, Jas.	3	4	4		
Morison, Eliza.		1	6		
Lonels, Davd.	1		1		
Martin, Henry.	2	1	5		
Jewell, Jas.	2	1	3		
Corby, Wm.	3		4		
Hicks, Zacheus	1	1	2		
Greg, Wm.	1	3	2		
Elder, Andrew	1	2	1		
Woods, Andw.	2	1	5		
Patten, Robt.	1	1	3		
Patten, Frank	3	1	6		2
Cowan, Marget.	1		2		
Daniel, Jno.		1	5		
Blankenship, Lodo	2	4	3		
Hodge, Frank	1	1	2		
Hodge, George.	1	1	3		
Hall, Jno, Jr.	1		1		
Hall, Joshua	1	2	1		
Hughes, Andrew	1	1	4		
Baker, Bardel.	1		2		
McElwrath, David.	2	5	7		
Woods, Robt.	1		3		
Evits, George	1		3		
Hall, Naomi.		2	2		
Walker, Jno.	1	3	2		
Smith, Jno.	1	3	3		

SEVENTH COMPANY.

NAME OF HEAD OF FAMILY.	Free white males of 16 years and upward, including heads of families.	Free white males under 16 years.	Free white females, including heads of families.	All other free persons.	Slaves.
Coreponong, Albert	1	4	4		
Franklin, Jno., Sr.	2	1	6		
Antony, Martin	2	5	2		
Sansom, Micaja	1	2	4		
Fais, Edmund	1	3	5		
Littlejohn, Eli.	1	3	3		
McDowell, Col. Jos	2		5		10
McKinny, Henry.			1		2
Tomson, Jeremiah.	2	2	4		17
Erwin, Jno.	1	6	3		3
Maxwell, Jno.	2	1	2		
Lane, Jno.	1	2	2		
McGimsey, Jno.	2		1		3
Fleming, Robt.	1	2	8		
Wilsken, Thos.	1	1	6		9
Coffee, Ben.	1	3	2		
Murphey, Jas.	1	1	1		5
Harper, Jno.	1		3		
Harper, Jno., Jr.	2	3	3		
Erwin, Alex	1	3	7		11
Fonay, Jacob.	1		2		6
Kelly, Ben.	1	3	1		
Tummins, Saml.	1	2	2		
Isom, Christn.	2	3	3		
Case, Thos.	1		2		
Macay, Hugh.	1	2	2		
Fismire, Wm.	1	1	3		
Cook, Adam	2		3		
Maxwell, Isaac	1	2	2		
Dotson, Esau	1		2		
McKinny, Elisa	1		4		1
Bradford, Bennet	3	2	4		1
Carter, Wm.	1	1	2		
Husband, Elsa			1		
Turmire, Saml.	1		1		
Goble, Jno.	1		1		
Clarke, Nancy	2	4	5		
Clarke, Joana	1	3	3		
Clarke, Jno.	1		3		
Arney, Lorane	1		3		
Wagoner, Christi.	1	3	2		
Sutser, Adam	1	4	2		
Cook, George.	1		5		
Dobs, Chesly	2	4	4		
Winkler, Adam	1	1	3		
Winkler, Thos., Sr.	2		4		
Winkler, David.	1		2		
Winkler, Jersey Conrod.	1		4		
Winkler, Big Conrad	1	2	2		
Howk, Mich.	1	2	4		
Moody, Tho.	1	3	2		
Moody, Jas.	1	1	2		
Sweat, Gilbert.	1	1	2		
Sweat, Ephraim	1		2		
Hughes, Hana.		1	4		
Martin, Phillip	2		1		
Martin, George	1	2	2		
Little, Wm.	1	2	1		
Little, Jno.	1		1		
Day, Thos.	3		2		
Stallins, Abram	3		6		1

SEVENTH COMPANY—continued.

NAME OF HEAD OF FAMILY.	Free white males of 16 years and upward, including heads of families.	Free white males under 16 years.	Free white females, including heads of families.	All other free persons.	Slaves.
Stephens, Phil.	1	3	7		
Davis, Wm.	2	2	2		
Fiass, Jonathan	1	2	2		
Hobs, Nathan.	1	3	2		
Lane, Thos.	1	4	3		
Trible, Jno.	2		2		
McDowell, Charles.	1	2	5		10
Perkins, Elisha	2	2	2		9
Murphy, Silas	1	5	2		
Pilm, Wm.	2	1	3		
Lorance, Wm.	1		2		
Dinbery, Adam	1	3	5		
Husband, Veasy	1		2		
Tips, Jacob	1	4	2		
Franklin, John, Jr.	1	1	3		
Cragg, Thos.	1		2		
Crag, Saml.	1		2		
Harper, Meredith.	1	1	2		
Baldin, Jacob.	1	1	3		
Crawford, Tom.	1		1		
Gibson, David	1	2	4		
Gibson, William	1	3	2		
Gibson, Harmon.	1		1		
Cray, Joab.	2	1	2		
Stafford, Jno.	3	2	2		
Barns, Rd.	1	1	2		
Coffee, Cleveland.	1	2	4		
Crag, Christn.	1	3	2		
Hughes, Jno.	1	2	1		
Bolinger, Danl.	1	3	2		
Henery, John.	2		2		
Little, Marget.			2		
Jones, Ambrous.	1		1		
Crisp, Wm.	1		2		
Baldin, Jno., Senr.	1		4		
Landers, Jno.	1	1	4		
Prichard, Jas., Sr.	2	2	2		
Gilbert, Joshua.	1				

EIGHTH COMPANY.

NAME OF HEAD OF FAMILY.	Free white males of 16 years and upward, including heads of families.	Free white males under 16 years.	Free white females, including heads of families.	All other free persons.	Slaves.
Reid, Henry.	1	2	3		
Reid, James	1	1	3		
Mayberry, Lewis.	1	2	1		2
Barns, George.	1	1	6		
Gibson, Stephen		2	1		1
Rutor, Lewis	1	1	1		4
Bradburn, Thos.	1		2		
Warren, Rob.	2	3	6		
Warren, Wm.	1	3	1		
Pane, George.	3	1	2		
Reid, Wm.	1	4	3		
Steel, Andw.	3		2		3
Burgess, Matthew	1	5	3		
West, Alex.	1	4	4		
Scott, Thos.	1	4	5		
Emmit, Rd.	1	1	5		
Bradford, Jno.	1	2	2		
Green, Thos.	4	3	6		
Russell, Ried	1	1	2		
Crisp, Bray.	2	1	6		
West, Alex., Sr.	1	1	1		
Horse, Jno.	1	1	1		
Collier, Jas.	1		1		
Smith, Jno.	2	1	1		
Cox, Matthew	3		1		4
Roberts, Wm, Jun.	1		2		
Moon, Robt.	1		2		
Brown, George, Jr.	1	1	2		
Brown, Rd.	1	2	2		
Steel, Saml.	1		2		
Winkler, Jacob	5		1		
Tuttle, Amos.	2	2	2		
Sherril, Wm.	1	4	5		
Headley, Jno.	1	2	2		
Austin, Ben.	2		6		
Hunsucker, Abrm.	1	2	5		
Hunsucker, Abrm., Jr.	1		5		
Hunsucker, Jno.	1	2	4		
Pain, Barnet.	1	4	2		4
Fletcher, Jas.	1	2	3		
Medlock, Nicolas.	1		1		
Medlock, Nicols, Jr.	1	1	2		
Falls, John.	1	1	4		
Bains, John.	1	2	2		
Reid, Hugh.	1	6	2		
Banks, Elijah	3	4	7		
Fox, Hugh.	3	4	4		
Baker, Henry.	1	3	4		
Keller, Jacob.	1	3	3		
Keller, Martin.	1		4		
Price, Jno Yeats.	1		2		
White, Luke.	1	3	7		
Jones, Nicholas.	1	4	4		
Walker, Dailey.	1	2	5		
Teague, Edwd.	1	6	3		2
Teague, Jno.	1	4	3		

MORGAN DISTRICT, BURKE COUNTY—Continued.

EIGHTH COMPANY—con.

NAME OF HEAD OF FAMILY.	Free white males of 16 years and upward, including heads of families.	Free white males under 16 years.	Free white females, including heads of families.	All other free persons.	Slaves.
Hadly, Joshua	1				
Green, Elijah	1		4		
Roberts, Wm, Sr	2	1	6		
Keller, Christina	1	1	1		
Tenny, James	1	3	3		
Colwell, Wm	1	1	1		
Gibson, Jos	1	1	1		
Hooker, Jno	1		2		
Dockery, Wm	1	2	2		
Conrod, Jno	2	1	1		
Roberts, Jno	1	1	4		
Cuningham, Jas	1	5	2		
Dockery, Jas	1	2	4		
Steward, Saml	1		2		
Peniton, Absalom	1		2		
McErtin, Jno	1	3	4		
White, Jonas	1	1	2		
Hood, Jno	1	1	2		
Reed, Tho	2		3		
Brown, Absalom	1	3	2		
Pain, Danl	1	1	1		
Hephaer, Phillip	1		1		
Grenstaff, Isaac	2	2	4		
Gibson, Isom	1		2		
Parmes, John	2	1	2		
Fullerton, Wm	1		1		
Clarke, James	1	5	2		
Thomas, James	1	1	4		
Grenstaff, Jane		2	2		
Walker, Charles	1	1	5		2
Walker, Simon	1	3	4		
Medlock, John	2		3		
Austin, Ben, Sr	3	1	5		
Gibson, Major	2		3		
Spradling, Jesse	1	1	2		1
Gibson, Wilburn	1	1	2		
Scott, Jno	1		3		
Dockery, Jno	1	1	2		
Banell, Jonathan	2		2		
Yokely, Jno	1		2		
Fox, Jas	1	3	2		
Graham, Aha	1	1	2		
Prisly, Jas	1		4		
Steward, James	1		4		
Davis, Uriah	3	5	3		
Green, Elizabeth			1	5	
Price, Rd	1	4	3		
Prew, Phillip	2	3	4		
Dishazer, Eliza		2	2		
Irons, Wm	1	3	3		
Smith, Wm	1	1	3		
Troutman, Adam	1	2	7		
Cumming, Jno	2	1	3		
Allen, Jno	2	1	3		
Alexander, Wm	1		1		
Macay, Wm	1	1	2		
Matthewson, Alex	3	2	2		

NINTH COMPANY.

NAME OF HEAD OF FAMILY.	Free white males of 16 years and upward, including heads of families.	Free white males under 16 years.	Free white females, including heads of families.	All other free persons.	Slaves.
Thomson, Peter	3	4	4		1
Sumpter, Jas	1		3		
Bartley, Jno	1	4	4		
Hays, Jno	2	4	6		
Murray, Joshua	2	1	3		
Howk, Nicolas	1	4	4		
Tucker, George	1		2		
Baker, Joseph	2	1	3		
Moony, Wm	3		2		
McCrary, Jos	4	5	4		
Murray, Jno	1		1		
Murray, Jno, Jr	1	1	3		
Grider, Fred, Jr	1	5	3		
Grider, Fred, Sr	2		3		
Murry, Barbara		1	4		
Smith, Saml	1	3	2		
Prowell, Thos	1	1	2		
Angely, Peter	1	2	1		
Hartley, George	2	2	2		
Lathrum, Johnsn	1	1	3		
Fincannon, Jno	1	5	3		
Grider, Jno	1	4	2		
Grider, Jacob	1				
Smally, Abner	1	3	5		
Repeto, Wm	1	4	4		
Wilson, Ezekl	1		4		
Wood, Jno	1	7	4		
Garlin, Eliza			2		
Perlman, Wm	1	2	4		
Shoat, Saybort	1		3		
Gilmore, Eliza	1	1	2		
Green, Rd	1	4	6		
Abshire, Christn	1	4	3		
Swaringin, Saml	1		6		

NINTH COMPANY—con.

NAME OF HEAD OF FAMILY.	Free white males of 16 years and upward, including heads of families.	Free white males under 16 years.	Free white females, including heads of families.	All other free persons.	Slaves.
Stilwell, Jeremy	1		2		
Smith, Solomon	1	3	4		
Penly, Jas	1	1	1		
Wilson, Edward	2	1	1		
Hines, Jno	2	4	5		
Pots, James	1		3		1
Nailor, Jas	1		1		
Coffee, Jno	1	4	4		
Amons, Mark	1		3		
Allen, Micajah	1	1	1		
Tucker, George, Sen	1	1	1		
Ramsy, Saml	1	1	1		
Davis, Wm	2		2		
Thornton, Wm	1	1	3		
Allen, Jno	2	1	2		
Hottsdaw, Henry	4		4		
Owens, Edwd	1		3		
Mayson, Isaac	1	1	4		
Streeton, Hezekiah	1		3		
Hartley, Wm	1	1	3		
Hartley, Sarah	1	3	4		
Blair, Jno	1	3	2		1
Hons, James	1		2		
Onions, Saml	1	4	5		
Day, Jno	1	3	2		
Day, Nicholas	1	3	5		
Day, James	2	1	2		
Hicks, Willis	2		8		
Green, Jacob	1		1		
Wisdom, Jos	1	3	5		
Highsaw, Fred	2	2	3		
Streetton, Susana	1	2	5		
Harris, Jno	1	2	2		
Hammons, Elijah	1	2	3		
Randolph, Thom	2	1	3		
Herrin, Wm	1		3		
Blair, Colvard	1	1	2		2
Sumpter, Wm	3		2		
Sumpter, Thos	2		3		
Sotherd, Abram	1	2	2		1
Neely, Jas	1	1	1		
Allen, Jonathn	1		2		
Allen, Jonthn, Sr	1		1		
Dennis, Rd	1		2		
Crisp, Jno	2	5	4		
Crisp, Wm	1		2		
Ramsey, Richd	1	3	4		
Constable, Linsy	1	3	2		
Ramsy, Eliza			2		
Hott, Peter	1	4	5		2
Hott, Jacob	2		2		1
Reily, Aron	1	1	1		
Swaringin, Check	1	1	2		
Powell, Ambros	2	4	5		1
Powell, Elias	1	3	3		1
Townsend, Jno	4	1	2		6
Grissom, Wm	1	1	1		
McDaniel, Jno	1	3	3		
McDaniel, Saml	1		2		
Thrasher, Wm	1		3	4	
Wilson, Ginral	1	3	2		
Greenaway, Joseph	1		1		
Greenaway, Jos, Sr	2	1	3		
James, Thos	1		2		
James, Wm	1		1		
James, Mary			2		3
Taylor, Jno	4	1	3		
Miller, Robt, Jesse	1	2	2		
McDaniel, Tempe		1	4		
Smith, Sarah			2		
Swaringen, Saml	1		1		
Phillips, Isaac	1	2	2		
Powell, Thos	1	1	4		
Powell, Eljas	1		1		2
Cox, Isaac	2	2	4		
Long, Edward	1	4	3		
Easthman, Isaac	1	4	4		1
Notherly, Robt	2	5	2		
Powell, Elias, Sr	1		2		1
Powell, Lewis	1		1		

TENTH COMPANY.

NAME OF HEAD OF FAMILY.	Free white males of 16 years and upward, including heads of families.	Free white males under 16 years.	Free white females, including heads of families.	All other free persons.	Slaves.
Young, Joseph	1		2		
Demerlin, George	1	4	2		4
Wofford, Wm	2		4		
Bolin, Amy		1	4		
Holinsworth, Jacob	1	5	1		
Wofford, Jno	1	1	1		
Hopper, George	1	2	7		
Holinsworth, Saml	1		3		1
Nation, Jos	2	4	4		
Nation, Wm	2	1	4		
Hancock, Joel	1		2		

TENTH COMPANY—con.

NAME OF HEAD OF FAMILY.	Free white males of 16 years and upward, including heads of families.	Free white males under 16 years.	Free white females, including heads of families.	All other free persons.	Slaves.
Spoons, Wm	1		2		2
Hall, Jno	1	2	5		
Burleson, Agnes	1	1	2		
Phillips, Charles	1		1		
Vann, Jno	2	1	3		
Phillips, Wm	3	5	4		
Holefield, Danl	1		3		
Rose, Isaiah	2	2	4		
Bridges, Wm	1	1	3		
McFalls, Delila			3	1	
Hopper, Charls	2	4	5		
Carson, James	2	2	6		
Robison, Jno	1	3	3		
Bell, Marget			3		
Hensly, Ben	3	3	3		
Lee, James	1	3	3		
Johnson, Louisa	1		1		
McKinny, Wm	1	3	6		
McKinny, Thom	1		2		
Medlock, Rd	1	3	4		
Gouge, Jno	1	2	3		
Rose, Jno, Senr	1	2	3		
Rose, Jno, Junr	1		2		
Wilson, Jas	2	1	4		
Harden, Jno	2	2	4		
Morron, James	1	5	3		
Ainsworth, Jas	2	4	3		8
Moody, Wm	1	5	2		
Billins, Wm	1	2	4		
Forsythe, Jacob	1	1	3		
McFalls, Jno	1	1	1		
Brown, Danl	1	1	1		
Turner, Robt, Sr	1		1		
Turner, Robt	1		3		
Moore, Wm	1	3	3		
Wilson, Jno, Jr	1	2	2		
McCracon, David	2	1	7		
Wilson, Jno	3	2	4		
Night, Thos	3	3	2		
Night, Thos, Jr	1	1	4		
Deaton, Neathn	1		2		
Moore, Thos	1		1		
Wilson, Sam	1		1		
Wilson, George	2	2	7		
Young, Thom	2	1	2		2
Young, Joshua	1		1		
Kensy, Abigail		2	1		
Hull, Sally		1	1		
Devenport, Martin	3	4	3		4
Bright, Saml	1	2	2		
Wiseman, Wm	4	4	5		
Wiseman, Thos	2	1	3		
Jones, Jos	1	3	4		
Price, James	1		5		
Bright, Wm	1	1	2		
Hill, Wm	2	1	6		
Taylor, Jas	1	1	4		
Hill, Wm, Senr	2		1		
Beckerstaff, Thos	1	1	2		
Loller, John	1	2	2		
Mullins, Jno	1	3	3		
McFalls, Arthur	1	3	2	1	
Gillespy, Henry	3		2		

ELEVENTH COMPANY.

NAME OF HEAD OF FAMILY.	Free white males of 16 years and upward, including heads of families.	Free white males under 16 years.	Free white females, including heads of families.	All other free persons.	Slaves.
Vance, David	2	1	5		3
Deever, Wm	6		4		
Smith, Jo	2		6		
Smith, Nat	1	1	2		
Beefle, Jacob	1	1	2		
Dunsmore, Adam	2	2	2		
Gilbert, Jno	3	2	3		
Heatly, Henry	2	1	6		
Unfrin, Sam	3	1	6		
Rogers, David	1	4	3		
Cunnigan, Jas	1		6		1
Bartlet, Nathn	2	2	3		
Bartlet, Jno	3	1	5		
McAfee, Wm	2	3	1		
Young, Wm	2	1	1		
Patten, Matthew	1		3		
Moore, Jno	1		3		
Graham, Wm	3	1	4		
Lacky, Jno	1		5		
Summers, Jonson	2		1		
Davidson, James	2		6		3
Davidson, Saml	1		4		
McWhorter, Ben	1		1		1
Patten, Robt, Sad	1	2	5		2
Long, Wm	1	1	3		
Patten, Thos	3	1	3		
Cunigam, Hump	1		3		
Patten, Jas	1		5		

MORGAN DISTRICT, BURKE COUNTY—Continued.

NAME OF HEAD OF FAMILY.	Free white males of 16 years and upward, including heads of families.	Free white males under 16 years.	Free white females, including heads of families.	All other free persons.	Slaves.
ELEVENTH COMPANY—continued.					
Clemments, Jas.	1	1	3		
Alexander, Jno.	3		4		
Alexander, James	1	3	2		
Patten, Matthew, Sr.	3		2		1
Patten, Aron	1		3		
Patten, Matt., Jr.	1		1		
Davidson, Wm.	4	2	4		8
McMahan, Jas	3	1	2		
Smith, Jno.	1	1	1		
Davidson, Thos.	2		2		
Ritchy, James	1	2	4		1
McNabb, Jas	1	4	2		3
Jones, Wm.	2	1	3		
Rice, Joseph	1		3		
Cunigam, George	2	4	3		
Gudger, Ben	2		1		
Neall, Arche	2		4		
Forgay, Sam	1	2	4		4
Kow, Wm.	1		2		
Patten, Jno.	1	1	4		2
Ragsdil, Gabrl	1	2	1		3
Lee, Eloner			5		
West, Jno.	1	1	3		
Gudger, Wm.	1	2	6		1
Randolph, Jos.	1	1	4		
Phillips, Ezra	1	1	2		
Whitson, Wm.	1	5	2		2
Smith, Phil.	1	1	2		
Killian, Danl.	1	2	1		
Phillips, Jno.	1	2	1		
Boys, James	1	1	4		1
Ryant, Wm.	1	5	3		
Case, Abram	2	4	5		
Davis, Jno.	1		6		
Bufle, Jno.	1	1			
Ingrum, Wm.	1	1	6		
Jenkins, Thos.	2		4		
Jenkins, Jno.	1		2		
Ramsy, George	1	3	4		
Davis, Baxter	3	6	1		
Blevins, Jnothn	1	1	3		
Cravens, Jas.	2	3	2		
Gillahan, Jno.	1	1	3		
Gouge, Jones	2	2	4		
Kennedy, Connell	1	1	1		
Bufle, Adam	1		1		1
Roberts, Jno.	1	2	3		
Weaver, Jno.	1	1	3		1
Wagoner, Jacob	1	5	2		
Roberts, Wm.	2		4		
Bound, Jno.	1	3	2		
Brittain, Wm.	1	2	2		
Dillard, Jno.	1	3	5		
Gregory, Wm.	3	4	3		
Baily, Wm.	1		3		
Guin, Jake	1	1	2		
Stanfield, Jas	1	2	6		
Guin, Chas	1	1			3
Chambers, Jno.	2	2	2		
Gregory, Jno.	1		1		
TWELFTH COMPANY.					
Parmer, Edmund	1	3	4		
Edes, Chals.	2	1	3		
Ramsy, Jno.	1		1		
Bailey, Wm.	2		1		
Bradly, Jno.	1	1	3		
Boiler, Jacob, Sen.	5	1	3		
Killer, Jno.	1	2	5		
Treadaway, Aron	1	2	5		
Atkison, Henry	1	3	4		
Bounds, Jos.	1	3	1		
Keller, Nicolas	1	1	3		
Barnett, Tim	3	3	3		
Treadaway, Wm.	1	1	4		
Treadaway, Robt	1	1	3		
Finley, Wm.	1	1	1		
Tony, Jno.	3	3	3		
Lekins, Jno.	1		1		
Shoat, Christi.	1		1		1
Shoat, Moses	1	2	1		
Devus, Henry	2	5	3		
Shoat, Christi, Jr.	1		1		
Pyburn, Jacob	3	1	5		
Pialms, James	1	4	6		
Tinker, Jno.	2	5	5		
Forsythe, Jos.	1		1		
Chanler, Josha.	1	2	2		
Blacwell, Jno.	1	1	3		
Webb, Mendoth	3	4	5		5
Win, Martha			4		
Bound, Jas	1		2		
Shoat, Austin	1	6	2		
Rice, Wm.	1	3	2		
Elkins, Gabriel	2	1	2		2
Pialms, Wm.	1	4	3		1
Pialms, Edmund	1	4	3		1
TWELFTH COMPANY—continued.					
Street, Jno.	1	2	2		
Higins, Koland	1	3			
Bunis, Elijah	1	2	4		
Hensly, Henry	1	5	5		
Renfren, Jno.	1	2	8		
Hensly, Jno.	1		3		
Langford, James	1	1	2		
Edward, Wm.	1		2		
Hinton, David	1	1	2		
Stanton, Jno.	1	3	4		
Angling, Isaac	1	4	3		
Hoodenpye, Phil.	2	3	5		
Caleway, Charls	1	3	2		
Summers, Allen	1	2	1		
Phips, Hana			2		
Hinton, Wm.		1	1	2	4
Robison, Julius	1	4	4		
Marcum, Abner	1	5	4		
Williams, Phil	1	3	3		
Hamons, Obadiah	1		3		
Baker, Robt., Jr.	2		2		
Hensly, Jas.	1	2	4		
Ray, Thos	3	3	2		
Carrol, Jno.	1	2	4		
Hamons, Peter	1	3	2		
Bennett, Jas	2	1	3		
Hensly, Hirman	1	4	3		
Baker, George	1	3	4		
Edwards, Jno.	2	4	6		
Arrington, Jas	1	1	5		
Baker, Jno.	1	5	3		
Foster, Mark	1	3	5		
Foster, Mark, Jr.	2	1	4		
Hughes, Jno.	1	4	1		
Paterson, Jane		1	2		
Hughes, Peter	1	2	1		
Dyer, Lettice		2	2		
Haeworth, Austin	1	3	4		1
THIRTEENTH COMPANY.					
Galliard, Jno M.	1	1	6		
Eagan, Mary	2		2		
England, Danl	3	2	6		
England, Jo.	1	2	3		
Hilterbrand, Conrod	1	2			2
Bellen, George	1		2		
Bradburn, Jno.	1		1		
Mull, Peter	3	1	3		1
Morgan, Josep	4	2	3		
Welsh, Wm.	1	3	2		1
Direberry, Anne	2		1		
Duckworth, Jno.	1	2	4		
Walker, West	1		1		
Direberry, Andrew	1		1		
Largin, Thom	1	3	5		
Hartley, Jno.	2		2		
Lack, James	1	1	1		
Macky, John	3	2	5		
England, Jno., Sr.	2	2	7		
Hughes, Jno.	2	4	1		1
Macay, Saml.	2	1	6		
Tomson, David	2	2	3		
Beall, Danl.	2	1	5		3
Downs, Zach.	2		2		
Macay, Thos.	2		4		
Tate, Jno.	5		3		3
Nulin, Ben.	1	2	1		
May, Erasmus.	2		1		
Hensy, Patrick	1	1	1		3
Jucin, Jno.	2		1		
Duckworth, Wm.	2	1	1		
Wood, Henry	2	4	3		
Dobson, Joseph, Jr.	1		1		3
Priest, Jo.	1		1		
Downs, Zach., Jr	2	1	2		
Brittn, Phillip	1	1	5		
Cooper, Jno.	1	2	3		
Lyon, Leonard	1	3	5		1
West, Wm.	1	3	3		
Young, Elisa.			3		
Spears, Jno.	2	2	1		
James, Wm.	2		4		
Craige, Robt.	1	2	1		
Guin, Debo	2		2		
McDowell, Wm.	2	4	1		
Skevely, Jno Henry	3		1		
Tompson, Isaac	1	1	2		
Bailey, Alex.	2	3	1		1
Wood, Robt.	1	1	3		
Cumings, Alex.	1		2		
Kell, Thos.	1		1		2
Smith, Thom	1		1		
Greeneu, Jas.	1		2		24
Mackey, Jas.	1	1	1		
Worthy, Sally		1	3		
Sorrils, Walter	1	3	2		
Lowman, Lewis			2		
THIRTEENTH COMPANY—continued.					
Anderson, Martha		1	3		
Pearson, Jas.	1	1	2		
Boteat, Edwd.	1	2	1		
Hawkins, Joseph	1	1	3		
Kell, Robt.	1	3	6		
Walker, George.	3	2	6		
Walker, Reubin.	1	3	2		
Southorlin, Wm.	2	2	7		
Howard, Ruson	1	1	2		
England, Thos.	1		2		
Hawkins, Austin	1	2	3		
Boteat, Wm.	1	1	2		
Kell, Thos., Jr.	1	1	1		
Kell, Wm.	1		2		
Hufman, Sam	1	3	3		
McTagart, Jno.	5		3		
Brown, Saml	2	1	4		
Higden, Thos.	1	2	2		
Chapmn, Nicolas	1	2	2		
Southorlin, Tindel.	1		1		
Wise, Adam	1	1	4		
Dougherty, Ed.	1	2	6		
Hart, Josiah.	1	1	2		
Burns, Nicolas	1		1		
Burns, Phillip	1	1	3		
Roper, James.	1	2	1		
Craig, Jno.	1	2	1		
Brittu, Jumima	1	1	1		
Stilwell, Jacob	2	1	1		1
Box, Henry	1	3	4		
Morrow, Dan	3		3		
Ross, James	1	1	5		
England, Jno., Jr.	1	5	1		
Bortles, Christn	1	1	1		
Jeferis, Jno.		2	4		1
Gibs, Rd.	1	1	2		
White, Wm.	1	1	3		
Hawkins, Wm.	1	1	2		
Rogers, Stepen	1	1	1		
Carol, Danl.	1		1		
Smith, Adam	1	1	3		
Craig, Ruth	1	1	1		
Daily, George.	1	1	4		
Clarke, Eloner		2	2		
Sealy, George.	1	1	4		
Oxford, Jno.	1	1	1		
Oxford, Saml.	1		1		
Elmore, Sarah.		2	4		
Howard, Robt.	1	3	3		
Mouser, Rd.	1	1	3		
Miller, Henry	1	1	1		
Overwon, Adm., Jr.	1		1		
Walker, Thom., Jr.	1		1		
Walker, George.	1	2	2		
Hughey, Eliza.	1	1	2		
Hughey, Jos.	1		2		
Scott, George.	1	2	3		
Jones, Wm.	1	5	4		
McEntirs, Jas.	4	3	4		5
Gibs, Jno.	2	3	4		
Garison, Henry	2	2	1		
Erwin, Wm.	1	3	2		11
Hays, Jno.	1	1	7		
Orr, Wm.	2	1	5		
Layman, Stophl	1		2		
Adams, Mary.		2	1		
Smith, Jno.	3	3	4		1
Scott, Jos.	1	4	7		
Neall, Jno.	2	2	6		3
Bailey, Wm.	1	3	6		
McMurry, Saml	1	5	4		
Rucker, Jos.	3	5	2		
Pearson, Thos.	1		2		
Pearson, Christe.	1		2		
Hips, Jacob.	1	2	4		1
Gallion, Thos.	1	3	5		
Hips, George, Sr.	3	2	2		
Hips, George.	2		4		
Cammell, Jno.	1	1	2		
Anderson, Bartlet.	1		1		
Hartly, Jas.	1	1	1		
Templeton, Jas	2	2	3		
Scott, George.	2	2	3		
Direberry, Hana.	1	2	2		
Patten, Thos.	2	2	6		
Burgess, Jno.	2	3	2		
Pearson, Jno.	4	3	8		1
Burgess, Rd.	1	1	5		
Downs, Thos.	2	2	2		
Carswell, Jno.	2	2	2		
Good, Solomon	1	1	6		
Boteat, Jno., Sr.	3	2	3		
Boteat, Jno.	2		1		
Camil, Anguish	1	3	4		
Wrenshaw, Aham	2		3		
Gunter, Jno.	2	1	2		

MORGAN DISTRICT, LINCOLN COUNTY.

FIRST COMPANY / SECOND COMPANY

NAME OF HEAD OF FAMILY.	Free white males of 16 years and upward, including heads of families.	Free white males under 16 years.	Free white females, including heads of families.	All other free persons.	Slaves.
FIRST COMPANY.					
Sherrill, Moses	2	5	2		5
Sherrill, Adam	4	2	7		4
Litten, James	1	3	3		
White, Elias	1		3		
Ward, Catharine	4	3	3		
Robison, Isaac	2	6	3		2
Alexander, Jno	3	3	6		
Brevard, Jane			3		3
Bates, Wm	1	1	1		
Brown, Wm	1	1	3		
Fikes, Mal	2	1	4		
Robison, Rebekah	1		3		
Davis, Upshire	1	2	3		
Taylor, Ben	1	2	5		
Johnson, Francis	1	2	2		
Gordon, Jane	1		3		
Loller, Henry	1	3	4		
Rail, Belser	2	1	4		
Kennedy, Wm	1		4		
Whitworth, Fendal	2	3	1		
Lyons, Jno	2	6	1		
Lyons, Wm	1	1	2		
Perkins, Rich'd	3	1	5		
Bridges, Elisha	1	2	5		
Fish, Jno, Sen	1	1	3		
Fish, Jno, Jr	1	3	4		
Fish, Wm	1	3	5		
Hamilton, Arche	1	4	5		
Snider, Jno	3	1	2		
Perkins, Augutn	1	1	2		
Freeman, Aron	1	1	3		
Wilcocks, Dav	1	2	1		
Hubbard, Richd	1	4	3		
Neall, Elizabeth	3		4		
Hamilton, Alex	1				
Bridges, Wm	1	6	3		
Bridges, Marget			2		
West, Robt	3		4		
Brown, Amos	1	1	3		
McCormic, And'w	3	4	3		
Sherrill, Jos	4	2	5		
Sherrill, Jude	4	1	5		6
Lowrance, David	1	4	1		
Sherrill, Jacob, Jr	1	3	1		2
Lowrance, Danl	1	2	1		
Lowrance, Abrm	1	1	1		
Aidon, Saml	2		6		
Duncan, Peter	2	1	3		
Spilman, Nathan	3		5		1
Brown, John	3		5		
Bodine, John	2		1		
Williams, Edward	1	2	4		
Litton, Sarah	2		2		
Sherrill, Wilson	1	2	2		
Allen, George	1	2	2		
Witherspoon, Eliz	1	1	3		
Jones, Jas	1		2		
Hill, Henry	1	3	5		
Wilbrooks, Jno	1	1	2		
Perkins, Jno	5	1	3		12
McDonald, David	1	1	1		
Colwell, Danl	1	2	4		
Gant, Jno	1		1		
Harwell, Saml	1	4	3		6
Litten, Thom	1	3	2		
Neall, Wm	1	2	1		2
Henyeaul, Rowell	1	1	1		
Wilson, Jas	2	1	7		
West, Thom	1	4	6		
SECOND COMPANY.					
Wilson, Matthew	1	3	5		
McKessick, Danl	2	4	3		2
Summy, Frederick	1	1	5		
Patten, Jno	1	3	2		
Wilson, Jas., Sr	1	1	5		11
Wilson, Jas., Jr	1				7
Earwood, Jno	1		2		
Sumrow, Mich'l	1		4		
Holman, Antony	1	5	6		1
Antony, Paul	1		3		
Braniman, Chiste	1	1	3		
Blackburn, Robt	3	3	3		
Lengeyer, Henry	1	1	3		
Wilson, Wm	3		4		3
Gortner, Jacob	1	1	5		
Lochart, James	1	1	1		1
Earwood, Wm	2	2	5		
Tepong, Conrod	1		5		1
Martin, James	1		3		
Crismore, Henry	1		4		
Obrian, Patrick	1	2	4		
Gross, Henry	1	5	4		
Wilson, Joshua	1				

SECOND COMPANY—con. / THIRD COMPANY

NAME OF HEAD OF FAMILY.	Free white males of 16 years and upward, including heads of families.	Free white males under 16 years.	Free white females, including heads of families.	All other free persons.	Slaves.
SECOND COMPANY—con.					
Rudeel, Phil	1	2	4		
Ramsour, Henry	1	1	1		1
Cunrod, Rudolph	1	2	2		
Keiner, Jno	1	5	4		
Keiner, Martin	1	2	4		
Gross, Christn	3	3	4		
Laurence, George	1	1	9		
Pfifer, Jacob	2		6		
Hepiner, George		1	3		
Boyd, Jno	1	4	4		5
Byers, Jno	2	4	6		
Huyet, Lewis	1	2	1		
Earwood, Mary	1	3	3		
Stroap, Peter	1	1	1		
Cresemore, Jacob	1		1		
Kline, Valentine	2	2	5		
Killian, Adam	1	1	4		
Earwood, Thom	2	1	4		
Johnson, John	1	4	4		
Garner, Jno Burn	4	3	3		3
Padget, Ephraim	1	2	5		
Johnson, Lewis	1	2	2		
Coddle, Moses	1	1	2		
Miller, Jno	1		2		
Wason, Jno	1	4	6		
Lutes, George	1				
Reather, Conrod	1	2	1		
Sumron, Henry	2	2	2		1
Earnest, Danl	2	3	4		
Sumron, Henry, Sr	1		2		
Barns, Jno	1	1	4		
Crissell, Andw	3	3			
Cumins, Laurence	1		1		
Bysinger, Henry	1		3		
Snider, Wm	1	3	4		
Tropick, Adm	1	2	1		
Tropick, Jacob	1		3		
Martin, Jno	1	1	1		
Martin, Solomon	1		1		
Witheron, Jas	2	1	5		
Summy, Jacob	1	4	2		
Launce, George	2	1	4		
Wise, Frederick	3	1	2		1
Ashtruner, Arben	1		2		
Scott, James	3		2		
Antony, Phillip	1	1	1		
Brilhart, Jacob	1	2	3		
Lutes, Jacob	1				
Stocking, Andw	2	4	5		
Carpender, Henry	2	1	3		
Lear, Peter	1				
Clay, Nicolas	3		1		
Smith, Mary	1	4	6		
Coonrod, Peter	1		1		
Renabaugh, Adm	2		3		
Horse, Phillip	2	3			
Bandy, George	1	4	3		
THIRD COMPANY.					
Tipong, Elias	1	2	2		
Coons, Adam	1	2	2		
Killian, Saml	1	2	3		
Killian, Jno	1	3	1		
Killian, Jno, Sr	4	1	3		
Killian, Jacob	1	2	1		
Mouser, Fred	1	3	4		
Bowman, Danl	2	4	5		
Deetz, John	2	1	1		
Phillips, Peter	1	3	4		
Harbison, Wm	5	4	9		3
Bolinger, Henry	2	3	4		2
Steel, Joseph	1	1	3		6
Crismore, Jno	3		1		
Yount, Phillip	1	2	3		
Mehaffy, Joseph	1		3		
Shell, Henry	1	3	4		
Antony, Jno	2	6	3		
Ichard, Peter	2	2	6		
Ichard, Henry	2	2	4		
Ichard, Lowrance	2	2	2		
Fry, George	1	3	2		
Boovey, Matthias	2	2	2		
Kline, Michal	2	2	2		
Kiffian, Jno	3	1	2		
Cline, Jacob	1	2	3		
Vanhorn, Isaac	1	4	4		
Fry, Jacob	1	2	2		
Fisher, Thom	1	2	3		
Houk, Jno	1				
Sigman, Jno	3	1	5		
Sigman, Mary		3	4		
Minges, Conrod	3	2	3		1
Coons, Wm	1		2		
Setser, Jno	1	2	3		

THIRD COMPANY—con. / FOURTH COMPANY

NAME OF HEAD OF FAMILY.	Free white males of 16 years and upward, including heads of families.	Free white males under 16 years.	Free white females, including heads of families.	All other free persons.	Slaves.
THIRD COMPANY—con.					
Sigman, George	3	1	1		
Ring, Francis	1	3	3		
Bolinger, Mathias	1	1	3		
Bost, Jno	2		1		
Brown, Jas	1		1		
Fry, Phillip	1	3	4		
Probst, Henry	2	4	2		
Phry, Jacob	2	1			
Gyger, Phillip	1	3	4		
Menskinon, George	2	3	1		
Horse, Simon	1	1	1		
Reather, Wm	1	3	5		1
Star, Jacob	1	2	3		
Bost, Wm	2	1	4		
Reather, Adm	1	1	4		
Smire, Jno	1	3	1		
Sigman, Jno, Jr	1	2	1		1
Wagoner, Conrod	1	1	1		
Baker, Phillip	1		2		
Baker, Susana	1	3	2		
Keller, Michal	1	3	5		
White, Joshua	1		2		
Sherrill, Jacob	1	1	6		2
Farloe, Thom	1	2	3		
Perkins, Jesse	2		3		
Holman, Henry	2		4		1
Pain, Robert	1	1	7		1
Belchel, Jacob	1		3		
Bealy, Wm	1		3		
Heager, David	1	2	1		
Keller, Henry	1		2		
Hestle, Jacob	1	2	3		
Huyet, Jno	1	1	3		
Kasler, George	1	1	1		
Punch, Thos	1	5	2		
Harmon, Wm	2	1	2		
Reid, Jno	1	5	2		
Baxter, Jno	1	3	3		
Baker, Elias	1	2	4		
Sirone, Nicolas	1		5		
Sirone, Jno	1	2	4		
Deal, Jacob	2	2	4		
Kline, Jno	2	3	4		
Cline, Chiste	1	3	1		
Peirce, Charls	1				
Gorman, James	1		1		
Davis, Hugh	1				
Doron, Patrick	1				
Peirce, George	1				
Wagoner, Mary		1	1		
FOURTH COMPANY.					
Horton, Joseph	1	1	4		
Cotter, Jno	1		1		
Whitener, Henry, Sr	1		2		10
Robison, Jesse	1	1	5		2
Whitener, Danl	1	3	3		
Moyer, Jno	5	1	4		
Whitenr, Henry	1	3	5		
Wilfong, George, Sr	3		3		
Shell, Gasper	3	1	6		
Mull, Jno, Sr	3	1	3		
Wilson, Jno	1	3	3		1
Robison, David	1	3	4		3
Whitener, Phillip	1	3	3		
Dillinger, Jno	1	3	4		1
Janet, Saml	1		2		
Robison, Jno	1	1	3		6
Wilfong, George	2	2	1		1
Bradly, Jno	4	2	8		
Hutson, Danl	3	3	4		
Wilfong, Jno	1		2		
Hyde, Jno	4	1	4		
Johnson, Jos	2	2	5		
Johnson, Robt	1		1		
Shuford, Jacob	1		2		
Canot, Wm	2		1		
Shuford, Daniel	1	3	4		1
Haun, John, Sr	4		1		
Hoover, Thomas	1	5	5		1
Gross, John	1	6	3		
Speigle, Marton	3	3	1		
Whitsil, Jacob	2		7		1
Clay, Abram	1		3		
Ichard, George	1	2	4		
Sigman, George	1	2	5		
Fisher, Jno	1		4		
Colter, Martin	1		1		
Colter, Phillip	1	3	4		
Sigman, Barnet	1		4		
Johnson, Martha	3		2		
Staymy, Henry	1	2	2		
Miller, Jacob	1	1	2		3
Agle, Josia	1	1			

MORGAN DISTRICT, LINCOLN COUNTY—Continued.

FOURTH COMPANY—con.

NAME OF HEAD OF FAMILY.	Free white males of 16 years and upward, including heads of families.	Free white males under 16 years.	Free white females, including heads of families.	All other free persons.	Slaves.
Hoselbareer, Jno	2	2	6		
Whitener, Ben	2	2	5		
Whitener, Michal	1		1		
Wilson, Andrew	1	2	2		
Johnson, Elizabeth	1	3	2		
Shuford, David	2		2		1
Hampton, Jno	1	1	1		
Haun, Jno, Jr	2	4	5		
Haun, Joshua	1	2	4		
Haun, Peter	1		2		
Haun, Benedict	1	5	4		
Haun, Jacob	1		2		
Low, Thom	2		2		
Wilson, Thom	1		2		
Havner, Frederick	3	5	2		
Pilgrim, Rebekah	2	1	4		
Lynn, John	1	1	3		
Shoup, Peter	1	2	2		
Ward, Estis	4		1		
Hogshed, Waller	1	1	1		
Queen, Sam	1	1	2		
Milroy, Henry	1		2		
Moore, Jackson	1		1		
Miller, John	2	2	4		
Cook, Didrich	1	2	2		
Borland, John	1	1	5		
Robison, Jonathn	1	1	4		
Blanton, Zech	1	2	2		
Sharp, Thom	1		7		
Whitley, George	2	1	4		
Martin, Jacob	1	1	2		
Martin, Eliza	1	1	1		
Orr, Robt	2	2	6		
Orr, Jno	2		5		
Harris, Nathan	1		1		
Covey, Jno	2		5		
Covey, Jno, Sr	3	1	4		
Rinehart, Jacob	1		1		
Rinehart, Jacob, Jr	1	1	1		
Penugh, Jere	1	1	6		
Shugie, Saml	1	1	3		
Shugie, Michl	1	1	2		
Mull, Jno, Jr	1	1	4		1
Orr, Wm	2	1	5		
Tumbleson, Jas	2	5	6		
Martin, John	1	3	3		
Oliver, Thom	1	1	1		
Gullet, Jesse	1	3	1		
Weaver, Conrod	1	1	1		
Weaver, Catharine		1	4		
Hiltebrand, Henry	2	4	6		
Fry, Peter	1	3	4		
Fry, Nicolas	1	1	5		
Coulter, Martin	1	2	1		
Majoir, Jno	1		5		
Gortner, Jacob	1	3	4		
Goder, Catharin	4	3	2		
Ney, Chrste	2		2		
Gatner, Martin	1	1	2		
Collins, Jno	1	1	1		
Jarrett, Jno	1	1	1		
Yount, Jacob	1	3	3		
Baldasser, Andw	1	3	1		
Rider, Frederick	1	4	5		
Ashbraner, Henry	1	3	5		
Miller, Henry	1	3	4		
Baker, Peter	1	3	5		
Chester, David	1	1	2		
Smith, Danl	1	2	5		
Hart, Peter	1	2	2		
Gilbert, Michal	1	2	8		

FIFTH COMPANY.

NAME OF HEAD OF FAMILY.	Free white males of 16 years and upward, including heads of families.	Free white males under 16 years.	Free white females, including heads of families.	All other free persons.	Slaves.
Edwards, Griffa	1	2	4		
Bolick, Adam	1		4		
Sigman, Wm	1	3	2		
Erlinger, George	1	2	2		
Sigman, Balsar	1	2	3		
Grount, Peter	3	1	4		
Grount, Jno	1	1	1		
Burnfield, Jno	2	5	4		
Turr, Adam	1		2		
Sigman, Barnet	2		1		
Dawfey, Ben	1		1		
Sigman, John	1	2	3		
Dawfey, Bazil	1	2	3		
Dawfey, Jno	1		1		
Delph, Jacob	1	1	5		
Hessian, Arthur	1	2	4		
Frizzel, Wm	1	2	5		
Fulbright, Jno	2	2	2		
Fulbright, Wm	1		1		
Yount, Peter	1	3	3		
Yount, Abram	1	1	2		

FIFTH COMPANY—con.

NAME OF HEAD OF FAMILY.	Free white males of 16 years and upward, including heads of families.	Free white males under 16 years.	Free white females, including heads of families.	All other free persons.	Slaves.
Goforth, Geo	1	1	3		
Mass, Mathias	1		2		
Coon, John	1	2	3		
Syps, Abrm	1	1	1		
Sypes, Paul	2		2		
Woodring, Danl	1		3		
Sypes, Danl	1	3	4		
Williams, Griff	1	2	4		
Goodwin, Isaac	2	3	3		
Lowrance, Isaac	2	2	9		
Shuke, Jere	1		3		
Plunk, Peter	2	1	6		
Williams, Isaac	1	2	4		
Smith, George, Sr	3		6		
Smith, George	1	1	1		
Loutsiba, Mary		2	2		
Eher, Adam	2	1	3		
Sigman, Cloe	1		2		
Moses, Francis	1	1	2		
Moses, Jacob	1	4	3		
Johnson, Robert	1				
Frissell, W	2		5		
Cross, James	2	1	1		
Oliver, Jno	1	4	3		
Whitenberg, Wm	1	4	5		1
Eher, Martin	1	2	2		
Sigman, Barnet	1	2	3		
Crider, Cornelius	1	4	3		
Lucamore, Geo	1		1		
Killian, Jno	1	2	2		
Justice, Peter	1	3	2		
Hunsucker, Devt	3	3	8		
Bolock, Boston	1	4	4		
Bolick, Godfrey	2	3	4		
Grount, Peter	1	2	3		
Graff, Fred	3		1		
Phlps, Burgess	2	5	4		
Clubb, Saml	1	2	2		
Freflesstet, Fred	1	1	4		
Deil, Wm	2	4	4		
Deil, Peter	1	2	3		
Sloan, Wm	3	4	1		3
Stayway, Barnet	3		1		
Yount, George	1		4		
Drim, Phil	1	1	3		
Deil, Geo	1	2	5		
Treflestet, Mary	3		1		
Pope, Henry	2	2	5		
Fulbright, Jacob	1	6	4		
Harris, Rd	1	2	1		
Bolick, Gasper	1	1	4		
Bolick, Jacob	1	4	3		
Gobb, Jno	2	1	4		
Havner, Melcar	1		2		
Traflestet, Peter	1		1		
Null, Jno	1	2	2		
Orm, Jno	1	2	3		
Cowan, Jas	1	2	6		1
Keller, Michal	1	4	3		
Matthes, Jno	1	5	1		
Cillars, Conrod	1	1	3		
Festler, Peter	1	1	3		
Wineberger, Geo	2		2		
Bridges, David	1	2	8		
Owin, Thomas	1	1	3		
Baker, Phil	1		2		
Rosemond, Jacob	1	2	4		
Levaun, Isaac	1	3	4		
Ischour, Valentine	1	4	4		
Ischour, Jno	1	3	4		
Cross, Ben	1		2		
Graves, Phil	1		1		
Armstrong, Nat	1				
Jonas, Simon	1	2	2		2
Jonas, Jno	1		9		
Oxford, Sam	3	4	4		
Graves, Wm	1	4	4		

SIXTH COMPANY.

NAME OF HEAD OF FAMILY.	Free white males of 16 years and upward, including heads of families.	Free white males under 16 years.	Free white females, including heads of families.	All other free persons.	Slaves.
Moore, Jno	2	2	3		11
Mooney, Adam	1	3	1		
Eher, Peter	1	1	2		
Hostirle, Eve	2	1	2		2
Fulweder, Jno	1	1	3		1
Teeoybaugh, Phil	1	4	4		
Delinger, Henry	1	2	3		
Rinehast, Christe	2	4	4		11
Carpender, Henry	1		2		
Earn, Ben	3		3		
Morris, Jos	3		1		
Warlich, Lewis	2	1	1		
Friday, Jonas	1		1		3
Friday, Andw	1	1	1		
Hedirk, Andrew	2	1	2		4

SIXTH COMPANY—con.

NAME OF HEAD OF FAMILY.	Free white males of 16 years and upward, including heads of families.	Free white males under 16 years.	Free white females, including heads of families.	All other free persons.	Slaves.
Deter, Nicolas	1	1	2		
Roberts, Josh	1	1	4		
Logan, Drury	1	2	3		
Edwards, Wm	1	2	2		
Haynes, Leonard	1	3	4		
Cox, Paul	1		2		
Eaker, Christe	1		2		
Havner, Nick	1		2		
Money, Valentine	5	3	2		1
Rine, Jacob	1		3		
Hovis, Jno	1	2	1		
Hite, Henry	1	4	1		
Wallis, Jno	1		2		
Havner, Abram	1		6		
Havner, Jacob	1		2		
Eaton, Jno	1		2		
Simerman, David	2	1	1		2
Bonham, Abr	1	1	6		
Campbell, Jno	1	3	1		
Shull, Charles	1		1		
Rush, George	1	2	4		2
Givens, Saml	3	5	8		7
Dellinger, Mich	2	1	2		
Strudle, Martin	2	3	4		
Havner, Martin	1	1	1		
Lower, Jno	1	4	3		
Cook, Phillip	1	2	3		
Hoke, Henry	2	1	2		3
Barnett, Wm	1		2		
Crous, Jno	2	2	3		
Friday, Martin	1		2		2
Peiry, Jno	1		1		
Srum, Jno	1	1	1		
Aderholt, Fred	2	1	2		
Rudesel, Phil	1		3		
Ramsey, David	3	1	2		
Ramsey, Wm	4		2		
Ramsey, James	1		2		
Carpenter, Christe	2	2	3		3
Plunk, Jacob	1	1	5		
Plunk, Peter	1		2		
Eaker, Christe	2	1	2		
Seigal, Jno	4		5		
Mestellar, Peter	2	6	3		
Nerns, Ben	2		2		
Rinehot, Conrod	1	3	1		
Whiter, Rd	1	2	1		
Eaker, Michal	1		4		
McCalin, Wm	1				1
Havner, Fred	2	1	3		
Null, Phillip	2	1	7		1
Cox, John	2	1	2		
Sigman, Jno	1	2	3		1
Kline, Henry	1		3		1
Refe, Mich	1		1		
Nixon, Sam	2	1	2		
Probst, S	3	1	1		
McCasland, Robt	2		4		3
Srum, Nicholas	2	2	5		1
McLurg, Nathan	1	3	5		
Carpender, John	1		2		
Ramsour, Amie	2	2	4		6
Brilhart, Jacob	2	2	3		
Stotler, Conrod	1	1	5		
Turner, Andrew	1				3
Streeker, Danl	1		1		
Carpender, Jacob	1	3	1		4
Cox, Aron	1	1	1		
Cox, Morris	1	3	3		
Black, Elizabeth		1	3		1
Black, Ephrm	1		1		
Moore, Moses	1	2	2		
Sullivan, James	1	5	2		
Sullivan, Thom	1				
Barr, Jno	1	2	1		
Plaidluler, Michal	1		1		
Cox, Elisha	1				
Horse, Jno	1	2	4		
Buff, Michal	2	2	5		
Horse, Frank	2		2		
Antony, Phillip	2	2	2		
Horse, Christe	1	2	5		
Carpender, Jno, Jr	1	5	6		
Eaker, Peter	1		1		7
Baker, Joseph	1		7		
Englefinger, Chs	1		7		
Brown, Anne		2	3		
Moany, Jacob	1	3	7		
Cross, Jos	1	1	3		
Lee, Abrm	1	1	6		
Froniberger, Jno	1	2	2		
Froniberger, Wm	1	1	3		
Foster, Thom	2	4	5		
Hagar, Simon	2	2	4		
Roam, Jacob	1	2	3		

MORGAN DISTRICT, LINCOLN COUNTY—Continued.

SIXTH COMPANY—con.

NAME OF HEAD OF FAMILY.	Free white males of 16 years and upward, including heads of families.	Free white males under 16 years.	Free white females, including heads of families.	All other free persons.	Slaves.
Hamilton, Wm	1	1	2		
Rudul, Phil	1		2		
Gilbert, Conrod	1		3		
Rudul, Michal	1		2		
Simon, Isaiah	1	4	3		
Ramsom, Mary		3	1	1	
Ramsom, Jno	1		1	1	
Warlick, Catharin	2	3	5		
Baker, Jos, Jr	1	1	2		
Conally, Neal	2	1	3		
Carpenter, Christe, Jr	1	2	6		
Welsh, Wm	1		4		
Duncan, Elijah	1	1	5		
Carpender, Jacob	1		1		
Reynolds, Jno	1		4		
Cobb, Ambrous	1	2	4		
Reip, Adm	2	1	4		
Canuller, Phil, Jr	2		1		
Carpenter, Peter	4	5	2		
Havner, Eliz	1		2		
Havner, Fred	1		2		
Reynolds, Jno	1	1	5		2
Fulks, Charles	1	2	3		
Haun, Jacob	1	1	2		
Reynolds, Thos	1		2		
Norman, Fan	1	2	5		
Tanhesly, Wm	4		6		
Probst, Lewis	2	2	4		
Cox, Jno	1	1	2		
Cyzer, George	1	6	1		
Cyzer, Adam	1	2	4		
Parker, Christ	1	2	2		
Plunk, Jacob	1		1		
Carpenter, Peter	1		1		
Penugh, Philip	1	3	2		
Bullenger, Phil	1	3	4		
Sepah, Jacob	1				
Nisenger, Jos	1	1	3		
Baker, Abrm	1		4		
Myers, Peter	1		1		
Myers, Pet, Jr	1	1	1		
Jackson, Jno	3	2	2		
Reynolds, Rd	1		2		
Reynolds, Wm	1	1	1		
Reynolds, Jno	1	2	3		
Welsh, Thom	1	1	5		
Patterson, Geo	1	4	4		
Welsh, Nei	1	2	3		
Bently, Hana			4		1
Davis, Mish	1	4	4		
Reynolds, Perry	1		2		
Tucker, Sam	1	2	4		
McNemar, Fran	1	3	3		
Reynolds, Rd, Jr	1	1	1		
Reynolds, Sarah	1	3	3		1
Sepah, Christe	2	3	3		
Buff, Martin	2	2	2		
Bullinger, Jacob	2	2	1		1
Wallaw, Jacob	1	2	3		
Boyles, Charls	2		4		
Rigdon, Enoch	1	1	1		
Whisenhunt, Adm	1		1		
Reinhart, Jacob	1	2	3		
Bently, Danl	1	2	3		
Cook, Phil	1	2	3		
Newcastle, Robt	1	4	3		
Lownrats, Andw	1	3	2		
Whails, Sam	1	1	2		
Alexander, Jno	1		4		6
Barker, Christe		2	2		
Whishenhunt, Phil	1	1	2		
Carver, Christe	1	1	1		
Roany, Jno	2		2		
Bruksten, Robt	1	2	2		
Snider, Jno	1		4		
Stotler, Adm	2	1	1		
Trout, Henry	1	6	3		

SEVENTH COMPANY.

NAME OF HEAD OF FAMILY.	Free white males of 16 years and upward, including heads of families.	Free white males under 16 years.	Free white females, including heads of families.	All other free persons.	Slaves.
Huggins, John	4		2		2
Beard, Jas	2	4	5		6
Graham, Jas	1	2	7		
Veneble, Rd	3	5	3		1
Ferguson, Andw	3	3	2		
Blackwood, Sam	1	1	4		
Martin, James	2	1	8		2
Vernor, Wm	1	1	1		
Barber, Jno	1	2	8		3
Wilson, Jno	3	3	4		
Gilliland, Alex	2	4	5		4
Martin, Jno	1		1		5
Martin, Joseph	1	1	2		2
Witherspoon, Jas	3	3	6		1

SEVENTH COMPANY—continued.

NAME OF HEAD OF FAMILY.	Free white males of 16 years and upward, including heads of families.	Free white males under 16 years.	Free white females, including heads of families.	All other free persons.	Slaves.
Venable, Rd	1		1		6
White, Thom	1	2	1		
Dunwiddee, Jno	1		4		1
Lewis, Jno	1	2	6		2
Nance, Sherwood	1	2	3		
Mellon, Edward	4		2		
Robinson, Jno	1	2	3		1
Nill, Jas	1	1	2		1
Finly, Robt	3	2	2		
Martin, Robt	2				7
Neel, Jos	1	2	3		
Lewis, Isaac	4	3	3		
McClever, Jno	2	1	4		
Beard, Adam	1	2	7		3
Beard, Sr	3	2	1		1
Tiltman, Jno	2	3	3		
Berry, Jno	1	2	4		
Miller, Robt	1	2	3		
Gorden, Hugh	1		3		1
Neely, Jno	1		2		3
Gullick, Jno	1	2	3		4
Henry, Jas	1	2	4		
Henry, Wm, Senr	1		2		
Wason, Jas	3	1	2		
Barrett, Sam	1	2	6		
Wason, Henry	1	3	1		
Oats, Jn	1	7	2		
Craigs, Jno	1	1	2		
Ferguson, Robt	3	3	4		
Patrick, Andw	2	1	6		
Gullick, Jno	1	6	4		
Clarke, Antony	2	3	3		
Falls, James	1	2	1		1
Gingles, Sam	1	3	2		1
Reynolds, Wm	1	4	3		1
Groves, Wm	2	2	2		
Carson, Jno	1	1	1		
Carson, Andw	2	3	5		1
Buccannon, Thos	1	2	4		
Falls, Andw	2	4	2		9
Robison, Joab	4	5	4		
Robison, W	3			3	
McLean, Charles	2		1		4
Wilson, Jno	1		2		
McLean, Ephm	1	1	1		5
Ford, Jno	1				
Hudson, Thos	4		2		11
Hudson, Jr	1				
McNear, Jas	1	2	4		
Rankford, Moses	1	2	1		
Dickson, Jno	1		2		
Ford, Teddy	1	2	3		3
Ford, Nathan	3	3	1		8
Husan, Mason	1				
Husan, David	1				
Wilson, George	3	3	4		
Bell, Jno	1	1	3		
Egnen, Wm	2	1	2		
Price, Thos	5	4	4		7
Ford, Jno	1	3	4		
Ferguson, Jno	2	3	2		
Mondenall, Nathn	1	1	3		
Price, Wm	1	4	1		1
Denny, James	1	2	2		1
Henry, Jno	1	2	5		
Carson, Peter	2	1	2		
Rice, Wm	2	1	3		
Torence, Hugh	3	1	3		
Massey, Jno	1	1	3		
Massey, W	2		2		1
Daniel, Moses	1	4	3		
Berry, Wm	2	3	3		1
Berry, Robt	2		2		
Brison, W	1	1	3		
Paterson, Wilm	3		3		3
Robison, Alex	8		2		2
Glen, John	5	2	2		1
Grissom, Drewry	1	5	6		
Triplet, Joel	1		2		1
Henry, Wm	1	6	2		1
Beard, Jno, Jr	1	1	2		1

EIGHTH COMPANY.

NAME OF HEAD OF FAMILY.	Free white males of 16 years and upward, including heads of families.	Free white males under 16 years.	Free white females, including heads of families.	All other free persons.	Slaves.
Center, Stephen	1	4	1		
Hovis, George	3	3	4		
Best, Boston	3	3	1		1
Best, Jno	1		2		
Best, Jacob	1	1	1		
Gosnel, Charls	2		2		
Spencer, Nancy	3	1	2		
Spencer, Jno	1	1	2		
Gosnel, Peter	1	2	1		
Smith, Wm	1	1	5		

EIGHTH COMPANY—con.

NAME OF HEAD OF FAMILY.	Free white males of 16 years and upward, including heads of families.	Free white males under 16 years.	Free white females, including heads of families.	All other free persons.	Slaves.
Jenkins, Jno	1	2	4		
White, Sam	1	2	2		
McCartey, Cornl	2	1	3		
Wayett, Edwd	3	2	3		
Hoyl, Jno	4	5	5		2
Black, Robt	1				
Witheriss, Jas	1	1	2		
Jenkins, Jos	1	2	5		3
Rine, Phil	1	1	3		
Rine, Michl	1	1	3		
Hoyl, Michl	1	2	6		3
Wells, Jas	2	2	5		
Wells, Wm	1		1		
Jenkins, Jenk	2	2	3		
Jenkins, Edwd	2	4	2		
Jenkins, Jno, Jr	1	1	2		
Golden, Jas	1		3		
Siden, Thom	1	1	3		
Costner, Mary	2	1	5		
Parmer, Eliza	1	1	3		
Parmer, Jesse	1	2	3		
Holloway, Jos	1	3	5		
Wilson, Saml	4		3		
Paster, Christen	2	3	3		
Hislet, Ezekl	1	4	3		
Smith, Jos	1	4	5		
Bennet, Wm	2	1	3		
Massey, Dron	1		1		
Rodes, Jacob	1	3	3		
Rhodes, Peter	1	1	2		
Hufman, Jno	2	2	2		
Pack, Jno	1	1	1		
Fariss, Stephn	1	1	1		
Bud, Sarah		1	3		
Pinnor, Jno	2	4	5		
Wilson, Eliner	1	3	3		
Linsey, Sam	1		1		
Crago, Jno	1		2		
Knight, Sam	1	2	2		
Rhodes, George	1	1	1		
Glance, Cath	2		1		
Poston, Danl	1	1	2		
Potter, Wm	1		1		
Withers, Jno	1	3	2		
Suthard, Henry	2		3		
Withers, Elisha	1	3	2		
Posten, Eliz		2	2		
Withers, Jas	1	3	5		
Rine, Jacob	1	6	1		
Rine, Peter	1	4	4		
Hoyl, Andw	1	4	6		
Pearson, Geo	1	1	2		
Pearson, Geo, Jr	1				
Edwards, Mark	2		2		
Mason, Peter	1	3	2		
Dudrow, Jno	2	2	7		
Weyet, Jas	2	4	4		
Lineberger, Fred	2	1	2		
Kender, Conrod	5	2	9		
Hoyl, Martin	1	3	5		1
Rhodes, Jacob	1	4	4		
Hamontree, Wm	2	4	4		
Costner, Michl	2	1	2		1
Boyd, Wm	1	2	4		
Reasoner, Jno	1		2		
Collier, Francis	2		2		
Holland, Julius	1	1	2		
Hawkins, Sam	1	5	7		
Best, Peter	1	1	4		
Smith, Jno	2	4	5		
Smith, Peter	1	2	1		1
Rodes, Christe	2		1		
Rodes, Henry	1		2		
Linberger, Barb		2	2		
McFarlin, Jacob	1	3	4		
Lisly, John	1		1		
Shaler, Boston	1		1		
Hunter, Patty		3	1		
Costner, Jacob	1		1		2
Jones, Charles	1		7		
Gibson, Davd	1	4	6		
Hoyl, Peter	1	2	3		
Holland, Isaac	3	4	4		
Rosner, Jno	1	1	1		
McGill, Thos	3	3	7		1
Vandycke, Rd	3	5	4		
McCarver, Jno	1	2	2		
McCarver, Jas	4	2	5		
Spencer, Zack	1	1	2		
King, Wm	2	2	2		
Cobb, David	1		1		
Kikendal, Sam	1		1		1
Massey, Winney		2	4		2
Beats, Henry	1	2	5		

MORGAN DISTRICT, LINCOLN COUNTY—Continued.

NINTH COMPANY.

NAME OF HEAD OF FAMILY.	Free white males of 16 years and upward, including heads of families.	Free white males under 16 years.	Free white females, including heads of families.	All other free persons.	Slaves.
Shully, Jacob	3	2	7		
Lear, Conrod	1	2	2		
Baldridge, Alex	3		6		2
Sherman, Sam	1		3		
Reed, James	2	3	4		
Reed, Jno	3		4		1
Ruditul, Henry	1	1	4		1
Wells, Jno	1	3	2		2
Fengar, Peter	2	1	3		
Sicles, Jacob	2	1	4		
Adleman, Peter	3		3		
Davis, Jno	2	1	3		
Hinkle, Jacob	1	1	1		
Abernathy, Jno	1		5		1
Addleman, Jno	1	2	2		
Jones, Richd	4	1	4		2
Hansil, Wm	3		2	1	1
Collin, W		1	5		
Sicles, George	4	4	4		4
Baldridge, Jno	2	1	3		
Hoskins, Jno	2	1	7		7
Bradsha, Jonas	1	3	2		3
Morison, Wm	2	4	4		
Hager, Jane	1	4	4		
Womac, Abner	1	1	2		
Cooper, Mary	2	2	3		
Long, Sam	2	1	3		
Long, Reuben	1	4	1		
Cohnan, Jno	1	6	5		
Cherry, David	3	2	5		
Pucket, Ben	1	1	2		
Beaty, Marget	1	2	9		9
Fornsy, Peter	8	2	3		4
Beaty, Wm	2				3
Wilkeson, Jas	1	3	2		
Childers, Robt	1		3		
Johnson, Jas	1	4	4		8
Martin, Jos	1		3		
Nelson, Jno	2	2	2		16
Nelson, Alex	2				7
Givins, Wm	1		2		
Kinkaid, Wm	1	1	5		
McMin, Sam	1	1	6		
Nixon, Wm	2	1	4		1
Nixon, Jas	1		1		
Nixon, Jno	1	2	1		
Womac, Abrm	3		2		
Riggen, Chas	1	3	3		
Davis, Jno	1	1	2		
Huchison, Jonathn	1		1		
Black, Wm	1	3	3		
Long, Jno	2	2	5		7
Caruthers, Wm	2		3		
Caruthers, Robt	1	1	3		3
Beall, Rd	1	3	4		
Beall, Wm	1		1		
Cloniger, Phil	1		1		
Killian, Leond	2		1		1
Killian, David	1		1		
Brian, John	1		1		
Litle, James	3	3	5		
Beall, Jno	1		2		5
Rankin, Jos	1		1		
Lysle, Arche	3	4	3		
Hagar, Wm	3	3	4		1
Hagar, Jno	1	1	2		
Robinson, Jno	1		2		
Beall, Jno, Jr	1		1		
Beall, Wm	1		1		
Thompson, Wm	1		3		
Bradsha, Charles	1		1		2
Sicles, Jacob	2	2	4		
Kinkaid, Thom	2				
Hager, Simon	1	2	2		
Kinkaid, Jno	1	1	2		
Kinkaid, Jno, Sr	3		3		7
Luckey, Jas	2		2		
Bonner, Wm	1	2	4		
Edwards, Jno	4		1		
Woods, Mary			3		
Reeper, Thos	1	1	3		
Abernathy, B	1	2	3		1
Robison, W		1	2		
Forney, Jacob	1		1		5
Bogs, Jno	3		3		
Bogs, Aron	3		3		
Williamson, Robt	3		1		
Wells, Conrod	3		4		
Statia, Barnet	1	3	2		
Williams, Charles	1	2	5		2
Williams, David	1		2		
Williams, Joel	1	1	2		
Williams, Wm	1		3		
Nill, Lewis	1	3	3		2
Hariss, Arthur	1		1		3

NINTH COMPANY—con.

NAME OF HEAD OF FAMILY.	Free white males of 16 years and upward, including heads of families.	Free white males under 16 years.	Free white females, including heads of families.	All other free persons.	Slaves.
Nantz, Clemm	1	1	2		
Nantz, Wm	4		4		
Fight, Jno	1	4	2		
King, Ester			3		
Kinkaid, Robt	1	2	1		
Kinkaid, Jas	1		3		
Arnhart, Abrm	1				3
Airhart, Catharin		1	2		
Airhart, Phil	2	3	3		
Goldman, Jno	1	1	1		
Edwards, Lewis	1	2	2		
Asberry, Danl	1	1	2		
Maize, Wm	1	2	1		2
Slinkard, Henry	1	1	1		
Slinkard, Jno	1		2		
Club, Peter	1	1	2		
Spice, Amos	1		4		
Sherman, Sam	3		2		
Club, Gasper	2	3	2		
Surat, Leonas	1		3		
Taylor, Sam	1	1	2		
Master, Jno	1	2	1		
Abernathy, Tarnul	2	2	1		2
Fortner, Wm	1	1	4		
Rominger, Geo	1	1	2		
Rominger, Geo., Sr	2		2		
Abernathy, Jos	1		7		
Reel, Geo	1	1	3		
Devault, Mathias	1	4	4		
Bowers, Jno	1	2	2		
Flat, Jno	2				
Cristis, David	3	2	2		
Abernathy, David	1	2	3		2
Abernathy, Jno	1		6		1
Abernathy, Sarah	5		1		11
Connuller, Phillip	3	1	4		
Walker, Jno	1	3	4		
Link, Fred	1	2	3		
Williams, Rd	1	4	5		1
Gardner, Jere	1	2	5		2
Edwards, Lewis	2	2	2		
Walker, Ben	1	3	2		
Bishop, Wm	3		1		
Bishop, Beal	1	1	2		
Statia, Aron	1		2		
Link, Jacob	2		2		
Hill, Jno, Sr	1		5		5
Hill, Jno, Jr	1	1	1		1
Hill, Thos	1	1	3		1
Maxil, Wm	1		2		
Sanders, Thom	1		1		
Sanders, Lemuel	3	4	5		
Goodson, Matt	1	3	3		
Abernathy, Jas	1		4		
Davis, Jno, Jr	1		2		
Snider, Christn	1	3	3		
Orm, Jno Godfry	1	1	6		1
Johnson, Robt	2	3	5		
Slinkard, George	1	2	2		
Club, George	1		3		
Ridicil, Wltr	1		1		
Rudcil, Jacob	1		1		
Rudcill, Henry	1	1	1		1
Duncan, Abs	1	2	1		1
Parr, Jno	1		3		3
Biniham, Sam	1	2	5		10
Duncan, Jno	1	2	5		
Richards, Jno	1	2	2		
Abernathy, Dav, Sr	3	1	2		18
Abernathy, Robt	1	1	3		1
Abernathy, Charls	1	3	3		1
Sutton, Saml	1		2		
Myers, Elias	3	1	2		
Myers, Elias, Jr	1	2	4		
Dellinger, Geo	1	3	3		
Benham, Arthur	2	3	3		1
Clifton, David	1	2	3		
Clifton, Wm	1	4	4		
Shoup, Jacob	1		3		
Shoup, Adam	2	3	4		
Reis, Geo	1		1		
Master, Jacob	2	1	5		
Crites, Peter	2	3	4		
Willms, Charls, Sr	2		1		6
Dellinger, Wm	1	1	2		
Sadler, Henry	1	2	6		
Bradshaw, Jos	1		2		
Bradshaw, Jude			2		4
Cloniger, Adm	1	4	5		
Rominger, Geo	1	1	2		
Summet, Frank	1	5	4		
Sites, Peter	1	3	6		
Rine, Jacob	1		2		
Hovis, Jno	1	1	2		
Rhades, Fred	2	2	4		

NINTH COMPANY—con.

NAME OF HEAD OF FAMILY.	Free white males of 16 years and upward, including heads of families.	Free white males under 16 years.	Free white females, including heads of families.	All other free persons.	Slaves.
Abernathy, Wm	1	3	3		
Chapman, Hana		1	4		
Dellinger, Jacob	1		4		
Bomgarner, Peter	1	1	3		
Filker, Michal	1	1	1		
Bumgarner, Joel	1	2	2		
Crotz, Tilly	2	2	4		
Engle, Jno	1	9	1		
Hopper, Adm	1	1	15		
Reel, Geo	3	1	4		
Slinkard, Jacob	1		1		
Ashbean, Web	2	2	4		
Master, Michal	3		8		
Master, Jno	1	1	1		
Stoup, Jacob	3	2	2		
Stoup, Phillip	1	1	2		
Engle, Michl	1	6	4		
Eaker, Jos	1	3	2		
Butt, Michl	2	1	4		
Hufman, Jacob	2	1	5		
Goodson, Wm	1	3	3		
Kuler, David	1	4	2		
Parker, Jno	1	3	2		
Srum, Peter	1	2	1		
Finger, Jacob	1	5	1		

TENTH COMPANY.

NAME OF HEAD OF FAMILY.	Free white males of 16 years and upward, including heads of families.	Free white males under 16 years.	Free white females, including heads of families.	All other free persons.	Slaves.
Reid, Jno	1	1	3		
Goltny, Nathan	1	1	4		
Nox, Robt	1	2	6		1
Cunkleton, Jno	1		1		
Crunkleton, Jo	1	1	2		
Keince, Abrm	3		2		
Dillon, Jno	2	1	6		
McCorkle, Frank	2	3	4		10
Bohnger, Jno	1	5	5		
Long, Jno	1	2	2		
Riden, Jno	1	2	4		
Hutchison, David	2		2		
Jones, Jesse	1	2	4		
Richison, Jno	1		1		
Wiliford, Theo	1	2	2		
Givin, Geo	1		2		
Givin, Wm	2	1	2		
Brotherton, Mary		4	2		
Fisher, Eliz	3		2		
Cunnigan, Jno	2	1	3		
Lockman, Sarah	2		2		
Allen, Wm, Sr	2	2	5		
Thompson, Mary		1	4		
Lytle, Geo	2		4		
Rutherford, Henry	1	3	3		2
Loller, Isaac	2	3	6		
Kein, Abrm, Jr	3		2		
Perkins, R. Bigm	3	3	3		
Hunter, Rd	1	1	6		1
Gabrull, Jacob	1	1	1		
Wheeler, Jno	1	1	3		
Childers, Jno	1	1	2		
Lytle, Ellis	1	1	2		
Ballard, Jas	1	3	1		
Ballard, Lewis	1	1			
Ballard, Wiley	1		1		
Glen, Jno	1		1		
Newman, Michl	2		1		
Parks, Andw	1	1	3		
Wheeler, Thom	1	1	2		
Clark, Wm	2	1	2		
Thompson, Sam	2	3	4		
Bell, Thom	1	4	1		
Cornelius, Ben	1		2		
Cornelius, Wm	2	1	5		
Hill, Inez	2		3		
Stiles, Ben	2		1		
Perkins, Wm, Jr	1	1	2		
Perkins, Wm, Sr	1	1	1		1
Perkins, Ben	1	6	1		
Arrowwood, Jno	1	2	2		
Long, Danl	2	5	4		
Hughes, James	1	3			
Patten, Henry	2		2		
Alexander, Lidiz	3		5		
Gilliland, Thom	1	3	2		
Lee, Jas	1	1	2		
Pitts, Jas	1	1	4		1
Pettilo, Littletn	1	2	1		
Hawkins, Matt	1		1		
Hawkins, Jas	1		2		
Culdwell, Jas	2	3	2		
Rainey, Aron	1	2	2		
Harwell, Jackson	1	2	9		
Holdiman, Jacob	1	2	3		
Hilderman, Nick	1	2	3		
Allen, Jno	2		7		

MORGAN DISTRICT, LINCOLN COUNTY—Continued.

TENTH COMPANY—con.

NAME OF HEAD OF FAMILY	Free white males of 16 years and upward, including heads of families.	Free white males under 16 years.	Free white females, including heads of families.	All other free persons.	Slaves.
Petty, Reuben	2	2	2		
Parten, Ben	2	3	2		
Allen, Wm	1	2	5		
Allen, Jos	1	4	3		
McCabe, Jno	3	4	6		
Turbefield, Jno	3	2	6		3
Edwards, Jno	2	6	3		
Narwell, Sam	1		1		9
Narwell, Nasbit	2	2			5
Narwell, Francis	1		3	1	
Abernathy, Nartil	1	1	1		2
Abernathy, Robt	1	4	3		7
Stiles, Jno	1	5	4		
Brewer, Buckly	1	2	1		
Davis, Jno	1		1		
Slinkard, Jacob	1	1	2		
Hoot, Uley			6		
Jackson, Nathnl	1	3	5		
Sherrill, Elisha	1	3	3		
Sherrill, Agness			2	1	
Robison, Isaac	1	3	7		
Perkins, Adm	2		2		
Narwell, Ambros	1	1	3	2	
Berkly, Robt	1	2	4	1	
Lineberry, Peter	3	3	4		
Wagoner, Edmond	2	2	3		1
Arrowwood, Zach	2	1	3		
Killian, Mathias	1	3	4		
Cummins, Wm	1		3		
Hugins, Henry	1	1	1		
Richards, Jno	1	2	2		
Ninzy, Jos	2	3	5		
Lollar, Thom	1	3	2		
Lynch, Anne		2	2		
Cunigan, Frank	1	2	5		2
Fleming, Arche	1	3	6		
Fisher, Ezek	1	4	1		
Jones, Jemima		2	5		
Cloniger, Mich	1	2	3		
Wooten, Lucy		2	1		
Loften, Jas	1				
Sherrill, Josh	1	6	2		1
Holsclaw, Jas	1	3	3		
Chapman, Mary		2	4		
Kelly, Mary			3		

ELEVENTH COMPANY.

NAME OF HEAD OF FAMILY	M16+	M<16	Females	Other free	Slaves
McLean, Alex	4		2		5
Johnson, Robt	3	2	3		5
Rankin, Sam	4	4	4		
McGee, Thom	2		2		4
Spencer, Zach	1	1	3		
Clubb, David	1	2	1		
Leeper, Jno	1	2	2		3
Cathey, Geo	1	1	3		2
Moore, Alex	1	2	4		
Taylor, Andw	2	1	2		
McCombs, Robt	3	2	4		
Alexander, Robt	1	1	3		14
McKee, Jas	4	4	4		4
Smith, Bennet	1	1	2		
Dickson, Jas	1	2	3		2
Shannon, Robt	1	1	5		3
Shannon, Jas	1	2	3		
Graves, Jno	1	2	2		5
Dickson, Thom	1	5	1		
Martin, Sam	6	4	5		1
Tayton, Jno	2	1	5		1
Harbison, Jas	1	1	1		
Barry, Hugh	5		2		1
Ewing, George	1		4		
Colwell, Wm	1		3		
Ewing, Hugh	1	1	3		
Colwell, Sam	1	1	3		8
McKee, Jas	2	6	2		4
Lute, Peter	1	7	2		
Clinton, Jas	2	1	2		
Farris, Jas	1		2		
Davis, Fr	3		5		
McElvin, Jas	3		1		
Camell, Robt	1		2		9
Newton, Ben	1	2	6		
Armstrong, Robt	2				3
Leeper, Moses	2		3		
Cunigam, Jas	1		2		
Hanks, Rd	1	1	2		
McCombs, Robt	4	4	6		1
Rhine, Thom	1	3	5		6
Graham, Jas	3	1	1		
Dickson, Jo	4	2	2		14
Mayberry, Jno	1	6	2		
Rudirill, Wirey	2	2	3		
Cox, George	2	6	4		2

ELEVENTH COMPANY—continued.

NAME OF HEAD OF FAMILY	M16+	M<16	Females	Other free	Slaves
Scott, Abram	2	2	2		7
Hays, Moses	1		2		2
Beaty, Jas	2	4	4		1
Erwin, Isaac	1	2	3		
Alison, Antony	1	1	3		
Chitton, Wm	1	1	7		6
Armstrong, Matt	1	5	4		
Henry, Jos	3	1	3		
Henderson, Jas	3	3	3		2
Patterson, Jno	1	2	3		2
Gillispi, Jno	1	2	1		
Hanks, Jas	1	2	4		
Swanson, Jno	1	1	3		
Davis, Wm	2	1	4		7
Dobins, Alex	3	1	6		
Barnett, Sion	1	1	2		
Cumin, Matthew	1		2		
McLean, George	1	1	1		
Lovsay, Shadrach	1	1	1		
Lewis, Henry	2	3	2		
Abernathy, Robt	2		1		1
Abernathy (Widow)	2		1		9
Abernathy, Jas	1		4		
Abernathy, Smith	1	2	3		
Abernathy, Robt. Jr	1	6	2		13
Abernathy, Betty	1	2	3		10
Arnold, Michal	1	1	5		
Bradsha, Wm	1		3		9
Bradsha, Charles	1	2	3		
Beaty, Jos	1	1	1		
Bull, Edwd	2	2	4		
Bealk, Jno	2	3	4		
Cobb, Ambrous	1		1		6
Cobb, Joseph	1	2	1		
Cox, Vincen	1	3	7		
Dildenhart, Wm	2	2	2		2
Devenport, Geo	1				1
Davis, Joel	2			3	
Pharaoh, Nat	1	2	2		1
Pharaoh, Jno	1	4	2		1
Feathernh, W	1	2	5		7
Fete, Leonard	1	4	2		
Gillispi, W	3	1	3		
Gaskins, Francis	4		3		
Flinkall, Wd	2	3	9		
Hamilton, Alex	1	1	3		
Hamiller (Widow)	2	2	2		
Jenkins, Moses	1	1	3		
Moreland, Francis	1				4
Moore, Jno	1	1	2		1
Moore, Jno	1		5		
Moore, Wm	1	4	5		2
McCalley, Jno	1	5	3		3
McCalister, Jas	1	3	2		
McCalister (Widow)	2	3	5		
Moreland, Francis	1	1	1		3
Newton, Ebenezer	3		2		
Newton, Wm	1	4	2		
Oliver, Jas	1				
Phillips, David	2	4	5		
Rutledge, Jas	1	3	4		4
Starit, Wm	3	1	4		
Starit, Moses	1				
Venatey, Peter	1	4	4		
Williams, Moses	1	4	3		
West, Isaac	4	2	4		
West, Barny	1				
West, Stephen	1	1	1		
Wells, Burrell	1	2	4		3
Campbell, Mary		2	3		
Abernathy, Jno	1	5	4		1
Drake, Jno	1	1	4		
Fetherson, Jesse	2	3	2		10
Abernathy, David	1	4	4		1
Starit, Alex	1		2		
Dumport, Abram	1				5
McCarver, Jas	4	2	5		
Rutledge, Chas	1	1	2		
Bradsha, Seth	1	1	2		1

TWELFTH COMPANY.

NAME OF HEAD OF FAMILY	M16+	M<16	Females	Other free	Slaves
Whishenheatt, Geor	1	2	6		1
Ormon, Ben	1	3	5		1
Weer, Robt	1	5	4		
White, Jas	1	5	4		5
Oakly, Lebon	2		2		
Carruth, Jno	1	2	4		8
Whitler, Thom	3	1	3		6
Magnis, Wm	2		4		12
Ferguson, Jas	2	1	1		
Creator, Phineas	2	1	6		1
Long, Jno	3	2	5		7
Alexander, Jno	1		4		

TWELFTH COMPANY—continued.

NAME OF HEAD OF FAMILY	M16+	M<16	Females	Other free	Slaves
Asby, Sam	2	1	5		1
Dyer, Saml	2	2	4		1
Rutledge, Jno	2	3	3		
Pauley, Jas	3	1	2		
Titterburn, Jno	3	4	4		
Harmon, Henry	1	2	1		
McCurey, Abrm	1	2	4		
Parker, Thom	1	2	2		
Lidford, Wm	1	1	1		
Hinsly, Ben	1	3	1		
Cortney, Jas	1	3	1		
Childers, Wm	1	3	1		
Hope, Saml	1	3			
Snider, Barich	1		4		
Parker, Nicolas	1	2	6		
Ensloe, Jno	3		3		
Parker, Tho	3	1	5		
Parker, Esau	1	2	2		
Tucker, Jno	1	2	5		
McAfee, Jas	3	2	1		7
Oats, Wm	2	3	3		
McCallon, Jas	2	2	6		1
Collins, Danl	2		4		
Self, Wm	1	4	4		
Bandis, Marget	1	3	6		
Guttery, Frank	3	4	6		
Smith, Danl	3	4	6		
McDaniel, Jas	1	1	2		
Gabby, Robert	1	3	2		
Harmon, Peter	4	2	1		
Harmon, Jno	2	2	1		
Dickson, Jno	2	1	4		
Dickson, Thom	2	1			
Fauls, Jno	2	4	5		1
Elder, Wm	1		4		
Hogan, Patrick	1		4		
Harris, Wm	1	2	6		
Patterson, Geo	1	4			
Kughley, Sam	1		1		
Carpenter, Michl	1	1	2		
Smith, Jas	1	1	2		
Dunlap, Wm	4	2	3		
Thompson, Charles	1	1	4		
Hederick, Thom	1	1	4		
Carpenter, Jacob	1	2	4		
Crous, Peter	1	2	1		
Paterson, Arthur	4	1	2		
Patterson, Tho	1	1	4		
Patterson, Wm	1	1	3		1
Arthur, Jos	1		2		
Fullinberry, Jno	2		4		
Boman, Wm	1	1	1		
Whitworth, Wm	1	3	5		
Weere, Jno	2	1	5		
Babtist, Jno	1	1	4		
Shermsha, Jno	1		4		
Alexander, Jno	1		5		
Hamright, Jno	1	2	2		
Hare, Jas	1	2	1		
Numan, Jonathn	1		3		
Gladdin, Jos	1	4	3		
Cottins, Saml	1	3	5		1
Wells, Jno	2	4	4		
Hamilton, Jane	1		3		
Goforth, Eliz		2	3		
Eldus, Mary		1	3		
Arthur, Sam	2	2	3		
Hullit, Mary	1		3	5	
Gien, Robt	1	5	7		
Davis, Winny	1	1	3		
Newman, Tho	1	1	1		
Cronister, Adm	2		1		
Landers, Felix	1	3	4		
Fowler, Wm	2	1	8		
McEntire, Alex	1	3	2		
Collins, Abrm	2	1	2		1
Collins, Jacob	1	3	3		
Collins, Jas	3		2		
Hawkins, Jos	2	1	3		
Waterson, Jno	2	3	5		
Romine, Abel	1	1	1		
Neall, Adam	1	7	1		
Beaty, Deborah	1		2		
Spurling, Jno	1		2		
Bird, Mark	3	3			5
Miller, Thom	1	1	2		1
White, Wm	1	1	1		
Hope, Henry	1	2	4		
Edwards, Charls	1	1	2		
Parker, Humphry	1	3	2		
Graham, Arthur	3	1	5		22
Williams, Wm	1	1	3		
Taylor, Jno	1	1	4		

MORGAN DISTRICT, LINCOLN COUNTY—Continued.

NAME OF HEAD OF FAMILY.	Free white males of 16 years and upward, including heads of families.	Free white males under 16 years.	Free white females, including heads of families.	All other free persons.	Slaves.
TWELFTH COMPANY—continued.					
Erwin, Jas	1	1	1		1
Martin, Agness	1	1	3		1
Auston, Jas	1	2	5		1
Potts, Dav	2		1		
Melton, Elisha	1	1	1		
Green, Jos	1				
Ferguson, Robt	1	3	2		
TWELFTH COMPANY—continued.					
Wadle, Wm	1	1	2		
Woods, Jno	1	1	4		
Conner, Saml	2	6	3		
Mestellar, George	2	1	1		
Dicky, Alex	1	1	3		
Whiteside, Thom	1	1	1		
Whiteside, Jno	1	1	3		
TWELFTH COMPANY—continued.					
Graham, Jas	1	4	5		
Graham, Arche	1	1	3		5
Burgan, Jno	2		1		
Head, Rd	2	2	2		
Ferguson, Robt	1				
Murphey, Jno	1		2		

MORGAN DISTRICT, RUTHERFORD COUNTY.

NAME OF HEAD OF FAMILY.	Free white males of 16 years and upward, including heads of families.	Free white males under 16 years.	Free white females, including heads of families.	All other free persons.	Slaves.
FIRST COMPANY.					
Lewis, Rd	1	1	2		9
Adams, James	1		1		5
Lewis, Jno	1	2	1		4
Frisman, Milone	1	1	2		
Miller, Jno	1	1	3		7
Lewis, Charls	1	2	1		3
Holland, Jas	2	2	3		24
Kilpatrick, Hugh	1	2	5		
Kennedy, Jno	1	1	3		
Roland, Thos	2	1	7		2
Lewis, Henry	1				4
McFadden, Alex	1		3		4
Miller, Col. James	1	1	3		10
Scott, Jas	3	3	4		
Scott, Jno	3	2	7		9
McClure, Rd	3	3	3		
McClure, Jno	3		2		
Driskil, Jno	1	2	5		
Williams, Jno	2	3	5		
Driskil, Wm	1	4	4		
Harmon, Micajah	1	4	5		
Upkirch, Sherwood	1		1		
Price, Wm	1		1		
Miller, David	2		1		3
Grant, Wm	3	1	4		
Grant, Andw	1		2		
Dicky, Anthony	2	3	5		
Taylor, Robt	2		3		9
Macay, Alex	2		2		1
Macay, David	1		1		
Willis, Stephen	1		1		7
Tyrrill, Anne		1	3		2
McClure, Jno	1	3	1		1
Watson, Adam	2	1	2		
Taylor, Joshua	1	1	3		3
Dorton, Wm	1	2	2		
Swinny, Edwd	1				
Bradley, Jno	2		1		
Hutson, Moses	1	3	2		
Taylor, Wm E	1	1	1		
Tully, Michal	1	3	2		2
Corby, Wm	1		2		
Medcalf, Warner	1	2	2		
Kilpatrick, Jas	2		2		
Richardson, Chas	1	3	4		1
Wise, Ben	2		2		
Young, Mary		1	3		
Benson, Bethia	2	2	5		
Brummet, Thom	1	2	5		
Billen, Wm	1	2	7		6
Hughes, Jno	1	3	4		
Hider, Ben	2	3	8		4
Twittey, Wm	1	2	2		
Sweany, Danl	1		3		
Young, Jo., Sr	3		2		
Fleming, Jno	2	2	2		
Twitty, Russell	1		1		2
Miller, Jas., Jr	2	2	7		3
Person, Chas	1	2	4		
Lynch, Fred	1	2	3		1
Wherry, Jno	1	4	3		1
Jones, Berry	1	2	4		
Hannah, Jno	1	4	2		
Evans, Jno	1	2			
Macay, David	1		1		
Morriss, Jas	1	3	4		
Hampton, Andw	2	1	5		5
Donalson, Tho'	1		4		
Dicky, James	1	1	1		
Wherry, Thos	2	1	2		
Walker, Tho'	1		3		
Bradly, Patty	1	1	2		2
Griffn, Chism		2	4		
Taylor, Sarah		2	3		
Kilpatrick, Jas	3	2	3		
Dickey, David	1	5	4		3
SECOND COMPANY.					
Harvey, Danl	2		4		14
Earl, Jno	4	2	9		12
SECOND COMPANY—con.					
Music, George	2	1	3		
Jackson, Jas	1	3	4		
Young, Cap. Sam	1	4	4		
Still, Tho	2	4	3		
Snowden, Lovel	1	2			
Matthews, Aoquilla	1	3	4		
Hogan, Edwd	1		1		1
Brigs, Gray	1	1	1		2
Jones, Jno	1		2		
Trapp, Jno	1		3		
Clarey, Wm	1		3		
Snowden, Jas	1	2			
Hays, Saml	1		2		
Newell, Jno	2		2		
Harper, Matt	3	4	3		
Music, Joel	1	2	2		
Cummins, Jno	2	2	6		
Brown, Speller	1	4	6		
Pullum, Marget	1	1	4		2
Vaughn, Ben	1	2	2		
Armstrong, Wm	1	4	3		
Snowden, Anne	1	2	1		
Hughes, Jno	1		2		
Tacket, Wm	2	4	3		
McMullin, Robt	2	1	4		
Music, Abram, Sr	6	1	2		6
Armstrong, Jno	1	4	4		
Jordan, Reuben	1	1	2		30
Kirkpatrick, Wm	1		1		
Alsup, Wm	1	1	1		
Ussery, Rd	1	3	2		
French, Moses	1	3	3		
Blackwell, Jno	1	4	4		
Hamilton, Robt	3	3	2		
Owens, Jas	1	6	3		
Martin, Lewis	1	2	2		
Martin, Adam	1	2	4		
Burgess, Wm	1	2	3		
Jones, Zacheus	1		3		
Swadly, Mark	1		3		
Jones, James	1		4		
Horton, Wm	1	3	4		
Morrow, Patrick	1	2	6		
Vaughn, Jno	1	3	1		
Hunter, Tobias	1		2		
Young, Saml Jr	1		2		
Kennens, Jno	2	1	4		
French, Sarah	1	1	1		
Wood, Wm	1	1	2		
Blackwell, Joel	1		2		
Price, Jno	2	3	4		
Wilky, Davis	1	5	3		
Barns, Wm	1	4	5		
Dunkin, Wm	1	2	2		
Jenkins, Tabitha			2		
Dipriest, Christn	1	2	4		
Ridens, James	1	3	4		
Robison, Amos	1	4	3		
Blacwell, James	2	1	5		
Lyles, Tho'	1	1	3		
Hawkins, Wm	2	2	4		11
Cooper, Wm	1	2	6		
Bailey, Mary	1		2		
Vaughn, Wm	1		2		
Caziah, Jno	1	2	2		
Swafford, Jas	4	3	2		
Moore, Jos	1	1	4		
Carson, Roger	1	1	3		
Wilson, Anne	1	4			
Redman, Saml	1	3	2		
Moore, Jno	2		5		
Jenkins, Rd	1	4	2		
Green, Rd	1	2	2		
Capshan, Wm	1	4	4		
Hunter, Peter	1		2		
Trapp, Robt	1	1	2		
Sherwood, Wm	1				
Hays, Mary			3		
Still, Richd	1		2		
Barns, Wm	1				
Brigs, Mary		3	7		2
Glen Andw	3	2	3		
THIRD COMPANY.					
Ledbetter, George	1	3	5		14
Coon, Nicholas	1	3	1		
Strayson, Henry	1	4	1		
Ledbetter, Rd	1	3	4		16
Nanny, Rice	1	3	4		2
Bradly, G. Walter	1		1		3
Ownby, Jno	3	5	3		
Morris, Thom	1	5	5		
Goodbread, Jno	3	4	4		16
Byers, Jno	2	4	4		
Pots, Mary		2	4		
McDaniels, Alex	1	1	2		
Justice, Jared	1	1	1		
Jones, Ephraim	3				
Hill, Wm	3	1	3		
Crawford, Jno	1	3	6		
Grant, Alex	1	2	3		
Yancy, Wm	1	1	1		
Dobs, Foster	1	2	1		
Morriss, Tho', Jr	1				
Jones, Jno	1	3	1		
Boils, James	1	2	4		
Hampton, Ben	1		2		1
Reeves, George	2	3	4		
Hunes, Sarah		4	2		
Kelly, Henry	1	5	3		
Bagwell, Lunsford	1	1	4		
Nanney, Tho'	1	1	3		1
Elms, Jno	1		1		
McDaniel, Jno	1		2		
Thomas, Abigail	2		2		
Williams, Jones	2	1	1		3
Middleton, James	1	1	3		
Williams, Austin	1		1		
Harriss, Wm	1	2	4		3
McDaniel, Alex., Jr	1	2	1		
Durnell, Eliza	1	2	5		
Curtis, Jonathn	2	2	6		
Alford, Jno	4	3	5		
Cook, Ephrm	1	3	4		
Alford, Jno, Jr	1		1		
Jones, Stephen	1		1		
Dorton, Tho'	1		2		
Dorton, Davd, Sr	1		7		
Dorton, Davd, Jr	1	3	3		
Siree, Rd	1	3	2		
Hill, Jas	1	1	2		
Ownby, Jas	1	2	3		
Morgan, Permenter	1	6	3		
Hill, Robt	1	3	6		
Stringfield, Ezekil	1		4		
Kirkland, Jess	1	4	1		
Bradley, Richd	1	5	3		1
Kirkland, Jas	2	1	2		
FOURTH COMPANY.					
King, Sam	3	2	2		
Davenport, Jno	1	2	2		1
Briggs, Jessee	1	1	2		1
Whiteside, Jno	1	3	3		1
Medcalf, Anton	2	2	4		
Shateen, Joel	4	2	5		
Miller, Laurence	1	2	2		
McCasky, Tho'	1	1	3		
Morgan, Elias	1	1	5		2
Latter, Jas	4	3	6		
Doyle, Jas	1	5	3		2
Ballard, Saml	1		2		
Hunter, Saml	2	3	4		1
Corbo, Wm	3	3	1		
Reeves, David	1	5	6		6
Rite, Moses	2	3	5		
Hill, Ephrm	1		4		
Gray, Wm	1	2	5		
Beard, Jas	1	3	1		
Robinson, Vol	1	2	2		
Dills, Peter	1	2	4		
McCane, Jno	1	3	4		
Hanes, Wm	1	2	3		
Dorton, Jno	1	2	5		
Elliot, Wm	1	3	3		

MORGAN DISTRICT, RUTHERFORD COUNTY—Continued.

FOURTH COMPANY—con.

NAME OF HEAD OF FAMILY.	Free white males of 16 years and upward, including heads of families.	Free white males under 16 years.	Free white females, including heads of families.	All other free persons.	Slaves.
Sirce, Wm	1		1		
Smithers, Garnet	1		3		
Taylor, Celia		2	4		
Taylor, Charls	1		2		
Spive, Jonas	1	1	3		
Spive, Isaac	1	2	4		
Wright, Grunby	1	5	4		
Sims, Tho'	1	1	2		
Metcalf, Wm	1		3		
Stice, Phillip	1	1	3		
Gray, Agnes	1		1		
Hill, Jno	1		2		
Nettles, Wm	2	1	3		
Haslip, Thos	1	3	4		6
Simmons, Wm	1		2		
Porter, Jane	2	1	5		
Dorton, Davd	1	3	3		
Jones, Ben	1	3	2		
Elliot, Merrill	1	2	4		
Hart, Harde	1				
Sheldon, Jno	1	6	4		
Nettle, Shadrach	1	3	4		
Latten, Ben	1	2	3		
Bryan, Isaac	1	1	1		
Covinton, Josiah	1		3		
Henson, Wm	1	4	5		
Brown, Jno	3	2	4		
Russell, Mary	1		1		5
Underwood, Jno	1		1		

FIFTH COMPANY.

NAME OF HEAD OF FAMILY.	Free white males of 16 years and upward, including heads of families.	Free white males under 16 years.	Free white females, including heads of families.	All other free persons.	Slaves.
Wilson, Mumfort	1	3	4		4
Smith, Jno	3	1	2		
Whiteside, Jno	2	2	3		
Fariss, Wm	1	5	1		1
Ross, Sarah		1	4		
Singleton, Rd	2	3	4		1
Tracy, Nathan	1	4	5		
Stocton, Saml	2	1	2		
Street, Thos	2	2	6		
Barnett, Martn	1	2	3		
Forbes, Wm	2		4		
Streets, Simon	1		1		
Money, Jacob	1	1	2		
Money, David	1	1	1		
Goforth, Zac	1	3	1		
Vinzant, Jas	1		3		
Vinzant, Jared	1	2	3		
Munroe, Anne	2		2		2
Smith, Hugh	1	1	3		1
Smith, Robt	1	1	1		
Stocton, Thos	1		4		
Munroe, Arthur	1	4	4		
Osborn, Arthur	1	2	4		
Phillips, Jno	1	1	2		
Barnett, David	2	1	2		
Barnett, Wm, Jr	1	1	1		
Barnet, Biram	2		5		
Phillips, Tho'	1		1		
Sellers, Jno	1	2	3		
Morrow, James	2		2		
Morrow, Henry	1	2	3		
Barnhill, Jno	1		2		
Barnhill, Jas	2		4		
Jones, Jno	1		2		1
Millon, Danl	1	1	2		1
Hall, Jno	1	5	3		
Jones, Jno, Sr	2	5	7		1
Jones, Isaac	1	2	6		1
Jones, Robt	1	4	3		
Steward, Wm	1	3	2		
Milton, Eli	1	2	1		1
Smith, Wm	1	2	6		
Munroe, Wm	1	7	3		
Black, James	1	3	4		
Stocton, David	1	3	5		
Cole, David	2	4	4		
Grissom, Jos	2	4	5		
Whiteside, Eliza	1	1	1		
Goldsmith, Jno	1	4	2		
West, Jos	1	2	8		
Megee, Rebeca		3	4		1
Laferty, Sara	1		3		
Laferty, Alex	1		1		
Walker, Jas	1	1	3		
Brown, Abram	1	3	4		
Lacefield, Jno	1		3		
Lacefield, Ben	1	2	3		
Boothe, Mary		1	3		
Lacefield, Dan	1	3	3		
Simons, Nancy	1		3		
Simons, Moses	1	1	1		
Thompson, Jno	1	3	2		
Lacefield, Wm	1		1		

FIFTH COMPANY—con.

NAME OF HEAD OF FAMILY.	Free white males of 16 years and upward, including heads of families.	Free white males under 16 years.	Free white females, including heads of families.	All other free persons.	Slaves.
Royally, Tho'	1	2	1		
Short, Chas	1		2		
Holden, Wm	1	2	3		
Hill, Burrel	1		2		
Sparnach, Jas	1	3	3		
Condor, Claybon	1	3	5		
McCracon, Jno	1	2	4		
Sheppad, Martha	1	1	5		
Gutters, Wm	1	2	2		
Webb, Tho'	1	1	3		
Rogers, Wm	1				
Chitwood, Jas	3				
Phillips, George	2	1	4		
Blantn, Claybon	1		2		
Phillips, Wm	1		1		
Latimor, Cap. Jno	2	2	3		7
Carson, Walter	1	2	2		
Carson, Danl	1	2	2		
Chambers, Alex	1	1	1		
Chambers, Jno	1	3	4		
Chambers, David	1		3		
Miller, Jno	1		2		
Mitchell, Andw	1	2	6		
Mitchell, Wm	1		2		
Latimore, Frank	1		6		5
Latimore, Danl	1	2	5		
Stocton, Jno	1	3	3		
Whiteside, Thos	1	3	3		1
Price, Jno	1	4	5		
Wilson, Wm	5		5		
Clarke, Abram	1	1	2		
Clarke, Abrm., Sr	2	2	3		
Stocton, Newbery	1	1	1		
Stocton, Davis, Jr	1	1	3		
Short, Wm	1		1		
Stocton, Danl	1	1	1		
Cogsdill, Jno	1				

SIXTH COMPANY.

NAME OF HEAD OF FAMILY.	Free white males of 16 years and upward, including heads of families.	Free white males under 16 years.	Free white females, including heads of families.	All other free persons.	Slaves.
Wilson, Jno	1	1	3		2
Rollin, Charles	1	2	1		
Vinzant, Jacob	1	3	3		
Harden, David	1		3		2
Graham, Jno	1		4		11
Collins, Isaac	1	2	2		
Bradly, Joseph	1	5	2		
Wilson, Jonathn	1	3	3		
Allen, Rahel		3	5		
Koil, Sam	1		2		
Botton, Solomon	1	1	3		
McEntire, Wm	1	1	1		
Holman, Isaac	1	7	2		
Moode, Jas	1	3	5		
Mode, Jno	1	1	1		
Mode, Wm	1	4	4		
Moore, Francis	1	2	3		
Moore, George	1		2		
Camp, Danl	1	1	3		
Curlock, Henry	1	3	5		
Parmer, Saml	2	2	6		
Ross, James	2	2	4		
Conn, Wm	1	2	4		
Coils, Alex	1	3	3		
Jones, Wm	1		3		
Fortenberry, Isaas	1	1	4		
Crane, Mayfield	1		4		
Mitchell, Mary	1	1	2		
Blackburn, David	1		1		
Parker, Jno	1	1	1		
McEntire, Jas	1	2	2		
McEntire, Anne		2	2		
Parker, Andw	1	2	3		
Blackburn, Jas	1	5	5		
Singleton, Dan	1	3	4		
McMurray, Wm	1	3	5		1
Fouch, Jonathan	1	3	6		
Gregory, Jas	1		4		
Cornwell, Edwd	1	3	2		
Person, Jno	1	2	4		
Portman, Ben	1	7	4		
Ridly, Wm	1	5	2		
Thomson, Jno	2	1	2		
Tomason, David	1		4		
Rice, Ben	1	2	5		
Wilson, Jno	1	1	3		2
Lusk, Sarah		1	2		
Lomac, Throp	1	2	1		
Bridges, Wm	1		2		
Hamrie, Nathan	2	2	4		
Nicols, Frank	1		1		
McGuire, Jas	1	6	6		
Earls, Frjd	1	2	2		
Wilson, Jno, Jun	1	1	2		
Downy, Patrick	1	2	4		

SIXTH COMPANY—con.

NAME OF HEAD OF FAMILY.	Free white males of 16 years and upward, including heads of families.	Free white males under 16 years.	Free white females, including heads of families.	All other free persons.	Slaves.
Magnes, Peregreen	2		2		3
Roberts, Jno	1		2		
Harden, Thomas	1		2		
Harden, Robt	1		2		
Durham, Kellis	2	2	5		
Smith, Micajah	1		5		
Lequane, John	1		5		
Constant, Edward	1	3	6		
Hamrick, Enoch	1	1	4		
Beaty, Wallace	1	2	3		
Beaty, Francis	1		2		
McBrian, Wm	3	1	3		
Collins, Jno	1	5	3		
Smith, Wm	3	2	6		
Mason, Peter	1	1	3		
Harden, Ben	1	5	3		1
Roberts, Morriss	1	3	6		7
Harden, David, Jr	1	2	1		
Harden, Jo	1	2	2		
Harden, Jonathn	5	3	5		
Weaver, Ruth	2		1		
Kinkendal, Abram, Jr	1	2	4		7
Bridges, Jno	3	3	8		
Bridges, Wm	1		4		
Bridges, Jas	1		2		
Adams, Wm	1		2		
Hambrick, Jas	1	1	7		
Stice, Andw	1	1	1		
Adams, Ben	3	3	4		
Stice, Charls	2	2	6		
Blanton, Jno	1	3	4		5
Hambrick, Jermiah	2	1	3		
Hamrick, Henry	1		1		
Cain, Wm	1	2	4		
McSwane, Wm	1	2	5		
Harris, Jno	1	3	2		
Linsey, Mary	1	3	2		
Randolph, Silas	1		1		
Hambrick, Sam	3	4	5		
Briges, Jno	1	4	4		
Kemp, Joseph	4	3	7		3
Camp, Wm	3	4	4		
McFastin, Jno	1	3			
Hogan, Michal	1	1	4		
Coleson, Robt	1	1	3		
Brookfield, George	1		1		
Hambrick, Price	1	2	1		

SEVENTH COMPANY.

NAME OF HEAD OF FAMILY.	Free white males of 16 years and upward, including heads of families.	Free white males under 16 years.	Free white females, including heads of families.	All other free persons.	Slaves.
Walker, Thom	1	1	4		1
Prince, Jos	2	6	4		
Freeman, Ben	2	3	2		
Freeman, Jesse	1	1	1		
Prince, Jno	2	3	3		1
Holland, Jno	1	2	6		
Hughey, James	1	3	6		2
Burnett, Joseph	3		5		
Watson, Patrick	1	3	6		
Inlow, Agnes	3		6		
Pell, Jonathan	1		2		
Erwin, Jno	2	1	2		2
Reives, Isom	3	5	3		2
Tomvelin, Moses	1		2		
Evis, Bartlet	2	2	2		
Burnett, Jesse	3	1	4		
Capel, Thom	1		2		2
Morris, Micajah	1		2		
Patterson, Matthew	2		3		
Baker, Wm	2	3	7		1
Lewis, Abel	1	1	2		
Price, Thom	1		1		
Dougherty, Rd	2	1	3		
Robison, Thom	3	1	4		
Andrews, Saml	3	2	2		
Long, Wm	4		3		
Turner, Michal	1	3	5		
Shunk, Henry	1		1		
Long, Gloud	3	2	4		
Robison, Jno	1	2	2		
Wickle, Peter	3	6	3		
Davis, Goodman	1	1	1		
Smith, Lewis	1		2		
Scott, Jno	1	3	1		
McAdams, Jno	1		1		
Goforth, Jno	1	5	4		
Tomson, Jas	2	1	4		
Price, Adah	1		3		
Parks, James	2	2	5		
Donaldson, Sam	1		1		
Huddleston, Wm	5	1	6		1
Cartwright, Eliza		3	3		
Patterson, Jos	1	1	1		
Smart, Mary	1	1	8		
Davis, Thom	1	2	3		

MORGAN DISTRICT, RUTHERFORD COUNTY—Continued.

NAME OF HEAD OF FAMILY.	Free white males of 16 years and upward, including heads of families.	Free white males under 16 years.	Free white females, including heads of families.	All other free persons.	Slaves.
SEVENTH COMPANY—continued.					
Evis, Groves	1	1	1		1
Davis, Simon	1	2	3		
Patterson, Robt	1	2	3		
Parks, Robt	1	1	1		
McMurray, Sam	2	1	5		
Cole, Wm	3	3	5		
Huddlestone, James	1	3	3		1
Nix, Jno	1	2	3		
Witherow, Jas., Es	1	2	2		9
Witherow, Jno	1		2		9
Carson, Jno	1	1	1		
Milton, Reuben	1	5	7		2
Huddleston, Wm	4	1	4		
Milton, Jesse	1	3	3		1
Norrill, Sam	1	2	5		
Milton, John	1	3	5		
Milton, Ben	1	1	2		
Early, Thos	1	9	1		
Moore, Wm	1	1	2		
Barnett, David	1	3	3		
McGahey, Danl	1		3		
Harden, Wm	1		1		
Garison, Richd	1	3	3		
McGahey, Mary		2	5		
Horton, Taunson	1				
Sweasy, Richd		3	3		
Ross, James	3	6	4		
Welsh, Thom	1	3	2		
Welsh, James	2	1	5		
EIGHTH COMPANY.					
Melone, Robt	1	1	2		
Geir, David	1	1	9		
Gilhy, Robt	5	1	6		1
Bates, Jno	1	1	3		
Sorrils, Jno, Jr	1	1	3		
Sorrils, Jno	1	1	6		
Smith, Thom	2	1	1		
McFadden, Saml	2	4	4		
Newton, Robt	1	1	4		
Nix, Wm	2	3	4		
Cook, James	1	4	4		
Logan, Francis	3	3	2		
Hampton, Andw., Jr	2	1	1		
Johnson, Arthur	1	3	5		
Hunter, Joseph	1	4	4		
Black, Rachal	1	3	3		1
Kestor, James	1	4	2		
Flack, Jno	1	3	4		5
Beall, James	1	3	5		6
Harris, Jno	2	3	5		
Mitchell, George	1	2	3		
Porter, Col. Wm	2	4	4		
Mitchell, James	2	2	3		
Campbell, Robt	2	3	7		
Baldrige, Alex	1	1	3		
Coxey, Wm	1	1	6		
Marshall, Jno	1	1	2		
Coxey, Jno	1	3	3		
Guffy, Jno	4	2	4		
McMurray, Thos	2	2	3		
Reid, Saml	2	1	2		
Watson, Hugh	1		1		
McGahey, Alex	3	2	5		
Baldridge, Jno	1	2	4		
Jones, Jno W	1	2	5		
Largen, Jas	1	4	3		
Bates, George	2	1	3		
Wren, Sarah		2	6		
Hanes, Ephrm	1	2	2		
Cherry, Robt	1	3	3		
Moore, Rachal		2	3		3
Moore, Elisha	2	1	2		
Fauman, Dug	1		1		
Ransom, Ezart	1				
Tanner, Michal	1	1	3		
Panter, George	1	2	3		
Nix, Jno	1	2	3		
Harris, Lewis	1	2	4		
Calihan, Henry	1	5			
Goforth, Jno	1	6	4		
Ketto, Henry	1	1	1		
Johnson, Henry	2	1	3		
Johnson, Martha	2	1	3		
Mastril, John	1	1	2		
Williams, Wm	1	1	2		
Williams, Wm, Sr	1	3	1		
Hamton, Jonathan	1	4	4	2	2
Johnson, Nathnl	1	3	3		
Goforth, Andrew	1	3	5		
Watson, Wm	1	1	3		
Clements, Rachl	2	3	1		
Clements, Cornelius	1	2	2		
Watson, Eliza	1	1	4		
Smart, Wm	3	1	1		

NAME OF HEAD OF FAMILY.	Free white males of 16 years and upward, including heads of families.	Free white males under 16 years.	Free white females, including heads of families.	All other free persons.	Slaves.
EIGHTH COMPANY—con.					
Smart, Wm, Jr	2	1	6		1
Spratt, Tho	1	3	3		
Watson, Jno	1	1	2		
Huddleston, David	1	1	5		
Logan, Drury	1	3	3		
Flack, Wm	2		1		
Wray, Fanne	1	3	3		
Jones, Jno	1	1	4		
Fleming, George	1	4	4		
Baldrige, Tho	1	1	2		
Bowen, Jno	1	3	4		
NINTH COMPANY.					
Carpenter, Saml	1	1	5		1
Bedford, Jonas	2	2	1		
McDaniel, Charles	1	1	2		2
White, Jeremiah	4		1		
Moss, Henry	1	2	4		
Chitwood, James	1	5	2		
Gardner, Wm	1	1	3		
McMurray, Wm	1	1	3		1
White, Isaac	1	1	3		
Anderson, Jno	2		4		
Woodard, Peter	4	1	6		
Thompson, Nathan	1	1	3		
Black, Robt	1	3	5		
Black, Jno	1	3	5		
Hinton, Isaac	2	1	3		
Buccannon, Jas	3		2		
Hiltebrand, Jno	2	3	5		1
Wolbert, Christe	1	1	4		
Wolbert, Jno	1	3	1		
Brown, Mark	1	1	2		
Blanton, Claybon	1		2		
Higdon, Jno	2		2		
Craig, Jno	1	1	3		
Craig, Ruth	1	1	1		
Higdon, Mary		1	2		
Sisk, Robt	1	3	3		
Smally, Nancy		1	1		
Morgan, Eliz		1	2		
Bracket, Mary		1	3		
Willis, Henry	1	1	4		
Smith, Jno	1	3	3		
Invistor, Hugh	1	2	3		
Nunnery, Jno	1	1	1		
Wilson, James	1	1	3		
York, Wm	2		2		
McCurdy, Abram	1		5		2
Lewis, Herculus	1		2		
Willis, Joseph	1	3	2		
Downs, Ezekiel	1		3		
Mitchel, Andrew	2	2	7		
Castion, Wm	1	3	2		
Upton, Edwd	1	7	3		
Francis, Edwd	1	3	7		
Bracket, Ben	2	2	4		
Davis, Hezekiah	1	4	1		
Cline, David	1		3		
McGlamery, Jesse	1		1		
Johnson, Danl	1	3	6		
Beaver, Ben	2	5	2		
Hucaboy, Joshua	1	3	4		
Mooney, Daniel	1		2		
Willis, Wm	2	5	2		
Wortman, Danl	1	3	2		
Harris, David	1	2	4		
Peeler, Peter	1	1	2		
Robinson, David	1		1		
Roper, Rev. David	1	1	5		
Roper, Charles	1	2	5		
Roper, Merideth	3	1	4		
Roper, David, Jr	1	1	1		
Falkner, Wm	2	1	5		
Falkner, Wm, Jr	1	2	3		
Falkner, Ezekl	2		1		
Thompson, Nathan	1	1	3		
Queen, Wm	1	4	6		4
Gardner, James	1		3		
Carpender, Jos	1		3		
Young, Saml	1	1	2		
Bowan, Joseph	1	2	5		
Hogan, Shadrach	2	3	4		
Thomas, Aron	1	3	3		
Chapman, Eurith	1	2	3		
Silman, Jno	1	4	3		
Green, Jno	1	3	3		
Burlison, Thos	1	4	3		
Burlison, Jo	1		1		
White, James	1	1	3		
Morris, James	1		2		
Wilman, Wm	1	1	4		
Cogsdil, Fed	1	2	4		
Willis, Jno	2	1	2		
Ravin, Wm	1	2	2		

NAME OF HEAD OF FAMILY.	Free white males of 16 years and upward, including heads of families.	Free white males under 16 years.	Free white females, including heads of families.	All other free persons.	Slaves.
NINTH COMPANY—con.					
Crowder, Phillip	1	2	3		
Moss, James	2	1	4		
Martin, Jno	1	1	1		
Hamson, Tho	1	1	2		
Johnson, John	1	1	5		
Ore, Robt	2		1		
Ally, Shadrach	1	4	4		2
McEntire, Jno	1		2		
White, Elinor			4		
Wilkinson, Ben	1	4	4		
White, Austin	1	1	2		
White, Stephen	1		3		
McEntire, Allen	1	1	3		
Arington, Sarah			5		
Wells, Jno	2		1		
Nowlen, David	1	3	3		
TENTH COMPANY.					
Alexander, Elias	2	3	4		1
Tomason, Wm	1		2		
Tomason, Eliza	1	2	7		
Russell, Jno	1	5	4		
Pain, Eliza	1		1		
Wilmoth, Wm	1		1		
English, James	1		2		
Witherow, Wm	2	4	4		
Mullin, Charles	1	3	4		
Osborn, Michal	1	1	1		
Walker, Wm	1	1	2		2
Farmer, Nathan	1	4	4		
Walker, Jno	3		3		3
Berry, Willm	1	2	3		
Bedford, Raymd	1	1	2		
McKinny, Jno	3		2		1
Thompson, Gideon	1	4	4		
Swann, Saml	2		6		2
Lyles, Brittn	1	1	2		
Sutton, Jno	3	3	6		1
Hedlow, Andw	1	1	1		
Evis, Wm	2	3	6		
Settle, Bushrod	1	5	2		
Swan, Robt	1		3		
McClane, Jno	1	2	3		
Suttle, Isaac	2	2	4		
Berry, Mary	1	3	3		
Bias, Nathan	2	4	6		
Dobins, Wm	1	4	4		
Dobins, Jas	1	1	3		
Scrugs, Rd	2	3	4		
Davis, Jacob	1	3	5		
Womack, Louisa	2	4	1		
Robins, Wm	2	4	4		1
Scott, Moses	1	4	4		
McKinny, Henry	1	2	1		
Greenwood, Hugh	3	7	4		2
Maddin, Danl	3				
Sealor, George	2	1	3		
Wren, Shadrach	2		2		
Renols, Mary		2	4		
McLean, Jno, Sr	1	3	1		1
Tomason, Jno	1		2		
Tomison, Eliza	1	2	6		
Draper, James	1		2		
Shumake, Landy	1	2	2		
Morrow, Tho	1	1	4		
Roberts, Jno	1		1		
McKinny, James	1		2		
Dills, Henry	1	2	4		
Robins, Wm	2	3	2		
Davis, Abner	1	3	2		
Poore, Sarah		1	3		
Sutton, Martha			3		
Cargil, Jno	2	2	5		
Hall, Thom	2		3		
Gaddis, Mary	1		1		
Harris, Eliza	1	3	2		
Paterson, Hugh	1				1
Morrow, Jno	1	3	3		
Webb, David	1	4	6		
Bicas, Sarahan	2	1	4		
Phillips, James	1	4	5		
Wadkins, David	1	2	2		
Wadkins, Peter	4		3		
Blackwell, Joel	2	2	7		
Camp, Thom, Sr	3	3	3		
Blacwell, James	1		2		
Goode, Jos	1	2	3		5
Dobins, Wm	1		1		
Cocran, Minor	1	4	5		
Ashlock, Josiah	1	1	2		
Ashlock, Sarah	1	1	2		
Gill, Joseph	1		1		6
Goode, Richd	1	2	2		7
Goode, Thom	2	2	3		4
Hopson, Wm	1	4	2		10

NAME OF HEAD OF FAMILY.	Free white males of 16 years and upward, including heads of families.	Free white males under 16 years.	Free white females, including heads of families.	All other free persons.	Slaves.
TENTH COMPANY—con.					
McAdams, Tho'	2	1	..	..	..
Oldhane, Danl	1	4	5	..	..
Hinson, Phillip	1	5	4	..	..
Huddleston, Jno	1	2	4	1	..
Goode, Jno	1	..	1	..	5
Crawford, Saml	1	1	1	..	..
King, Priscilla	..	4	4	..	..
Johnson, Wm	2	1	2	..	7
ELEVENTH COMPANY.					
Harrod, Thom	1	4	9	..	..
Moore, George	4	1	2	..	9
Erwin, Robt	2	4	4	..	..
Moore, James	1	1	1	..	1
Jones, John	1	6	6	..	..
Green, Shad	1	..	1	..	..
Kemp, James	1	3	4	1	..
Rigs, Timothy	6	1	2	..	..
Holland, Wm	1	2	5	..	..
Hoskins, Robt	2	2	1	..	..
Webb, Wm	2	4	3	1	..
Bradlove, Charls	2	3	6	..	..
Davidson, Jas	1	3	2	..	..
Shipman, Danl	2	2	4	..	..
McDow, David	2	1	6	1	..
Lyles, Burges	1	2	5	..	..
Webb, Robt	1	3	5	..	..
Webb, Thom	1	4	3	..	..
Green, Wm	1	4	3	5	..
Kirkendal, Jno	1	1	5	..	..
Cooper, Alex	1	3	5	..	..
Hill, Abel	2	3	3	1	..
Collins, Wm	1	1	2	..	..
Webb, Danl	1	..	5	..	..
Hill, George	1	..	6	..	..
Cooper, Alex., Jr	1	3	4	..	..
Armstrong, Eliza	..	2	2	..	..
Hill, Jno	2	1	4	..	..
McNess, Jo	1	..	1	1	..
Bridges, Aron	3	3	5	..	..
Hern, Denis	4	3	3	..	..
Kemp, Thom	1	..	4	..	..
Ellis, James	3	2	5	..	..
Blanton, Reuben	4	2	5	2	..
Blanton, Burn	1	3	2	..	..
Graham, Jno	1	..	1	..	..
Williams, Britn	1	1	2	..	..
Williams, George	1	2	1	..	..
Bolin, Layney	1	..	1	..	..
Robison, Isaac	1	..	3	..	..
Brown, Jno W	1	..	2	..	..
Bridges, Tho'	1	..	2	..	..
Rucker, Wm	1	1	1	..	..
Turner, Sam	1	1	1	..	..
Turner, Sam, Jr	1	..	1	..	..
Bridges, Isaac	1	1	3	..	..
Williams, Ben	2	3	7	..	..
Blackburn, Sam	1	4	2	..	..
Tabor, James	4	4	4	..	..
Dicas, Edw'd	1	1	3	..	..
Leis, Jos	1	2	4	..	..
Warden, Danl	1	2	4	..	..
Beard, Jno, Sr	1	..	1	..	..
Beard, Jno	1	..	1	..	..
Humphris, Wm	1	4	3	..	..
Wilkins, Charles	2	4	3	..	5
Willis, Peter	1	1	3	1	..
Brock, Reuben	1	5	1	..	..
Walker, George	1	..	..	..	3
Horn, Lucy	..	2	2	..	..
Night, Wm	1	2	4	..	..
Dedham, Mark	1	2	3	..	..
Adams, Jere	1	4	4	..	..
Bailey, Wm	2	2	4	..	..
Johnson, Wm	1	5	2	..	..
Sanders, Patrick	1	2	3	..	..
Holland, Matt	1	3	3	..	..
Hall, Wm	1	2	3	..	..
Williams, Geo	1	2	1	..	..
Saterfield, Jas	2	3	7	..	..
Green, Henry, Sr	1	1	3	..	..
Green, H., Jr	1	1	3	..	..
Hawkins, Tho'	1	3	6	..	..
Dicas, Jno	1	4	2	..	..
Southerly, Jno	1	1	4	..	..
Murray, Tho'	1	1	10	..	..
Johnson, Jno	1	..	..	..	..
Sally, Eliza	..	2	4	..	..
Hose, Jno	1	1	4	..	..
Kikendall, Matt	1	1	4	..	..
Norman, Isaac	1	2	4	..	..
Smart, Jo	1	4	4	..	..
Collins, Wm	2	..	2	..	..

NAME OF HEAD OF FAMILY.	Free white males of 16 years and upward, including heads of families.	Free white males under 16 years.	Free white females, including heads of families.	All other free persons.	Slaves.
ELEVENTH COMPANY—continued.					
Smart, Jo, Sr	2	3	4	..	..
Jones, Jno	1	7	6	..	..
Green, Shad	1	1	1	..	..
Green, Shad, Sr	1	2	3	..	..
Landers, Henry	1	3	6	..	..
Saterfield, Wm	1	1	1	..	..
Stater, Jehu	1	2	1	..	..
Lee, Robt	1	4	5	..	..
Lee, Isaac	1	..	1	..	..
Rolins, Prudy	1	2	3	..	..
Wilson, Jno	1	..	2	..	..
Street, Antony	1	1	3	..	..
Street, Wm	1	1	3	..	..
Harrell, Housen	2	3	5	..	..
Franklin, Mary	4	1	3	..	..
Franklin, Jno	1	4	2	..	..
Crispan, Jacob	2	..	1	..	..
McMin, Robt	1	4	4	..	..
Shipman, Jacob	1	7	2	..	..
Shipman, Danl., Jr	1	3	4	..	..
Shipman, Dan, Sr	1	1	1	..	2
Sunderlin, Wm	1	..	1	..	..
Bridges, Moses	2	3	6	..	..
Clarke, Jesse	1	..	3	..	..
Armstrong, Martin	1	..	..	..	..
Davidson, Alex	2	4	5	..	5
Davison, Jno	1	1	2	..	..
Davison, Alex, Jr	1	2	2	..	..
Lumn, Sam	1	2	5	..	..
Gage, David	2	2	3	..	..
Hill, Jno	2	1	4	..	..
Wilson, Wm	1	5	3	..	..
Gage, Lucy	..	1	4	..	..
Gage, Jas	1	1	2	..	..
McKeine, Tho	1	3	4	..	..
McNess, Ben	1	5	3	..	1
McNess, Jno	1	4	2	..	..
Gage, Reuben	1	..	1	..	..
Sally, Wm	1	..	2	..	..
Walker, Jno	1	4	4	..	..
Gibs, Jesse	1	..	3	..	..
Gage, Danl	1	2	2	..	..
Tolly, Elias	1	2	4	..	..
Miller, Jacob	3	..	..	..	..
Shipman, Edwd	1	7	4	..	..
Webb, James	1	3	4	..	..
Brook, Wm	1	6	1	..	..
Gage, David	4	..	3	..	..
Davis, Vachal	1	..	3	..	..
Webb, Jno	1	3	4	..	..
Collins, Wm	1	2	2	..	..
Webb, Bess	1	..	4	..	..
Webb, Dan	1	..	5	..	..
Webb, Jacob	1	..	..	..	..
Ashworth, Jos	1	2	1	..	..
Cooper, Jno	1	1	1	..	..
Barkster, Wm	1	..	2	..	..
James, Mary	..	4	2	..	..
Hetherly, Sam	1	2	1	..	..
TWELFTH COMPANY.					
Young, Robt	3	2	3	..	3
Caruth, Revr. Robt	2	2	5	..	..
Yielding, Rd	1	..	2	..	..
Jeffery, James	2	..	2	..	..
Russell, Henry	2	..	1	..	3
Young, Jno	2	..	4	..	..
Garrett, Mary	2	2	5	..	..
Mills, Jesse	1	..	3	..	..
Wilson, Spencer	1	1	3	..	..
Young, Jno	2	1	2	..	..
McBriers, Sam	4	5	4	..	..
Fisher, Jno	1	4	3	..	..
Mills, Wm	1	2	6	..	8
Logan, Jas	1	..	6	..	..
Neville, Yelverton	1	..	2	..	..
Carter, Alex	2	2	3	..	..
Jones, Jno	1	1	1	..	..
Justice, Tho', Jr	1	..	2	..	..
McQuin, Mich'l	1	2	1	..	..
Taylor, Drury	1	1	5	..	..
Lanford, Jno	1	..	2	..	..
Foster, Jno	1	1	2	..	..
Sullins, Jno	2	2	3	..	1
Hobs, Jno	1	..	3	..	..
Twitty, Allen	1	1	2	..	1
Case, Tho'	1	2	2	..	..
Caruth, Robt. Ma	2	6	2	..	3
Brader, Robt	1	3	6	..	..
Terry, Eliza	..	3	4	..	..
Sullins, Rd	1	..	3	..	..
Butler, Jas	2	2	2	..	..
Jones, Freeman	1	1	2	..	..

NAME OF HEAD OF FAMILY.	Free white males of 16 years and upward, including heads of families.	Free white males under 16 years.	Free white females, including heads of families.	All other free persons.	Slaves.
TWELFTH COMPANY—continued.					
Waldrip, Jeconias	2	4	3	..	..
Hawkins, Michl	3	3	6	..	..
Butler, Mildred	..	..	3	..	..
Johnson, Ben	2	..	3	..	..
Cochran, Jas	..	2	1	..	..
Jenkins, Richd	1	3	2	..	..
Cochran, Tho	1	..	2	..	..
Brown, Dan	1	4	3	..	2
Lyles, Robt	1	..	4	..	..
Donnom, Henry	1	5	4	..	..
Harmen, Wm	1	4	4	..	..
Hays, Wm	1	3	1	..	..
Rose, Bazil	1	1	3	..	..
Wadlington, Tho'	1	2	6	..	11
Brown, Francis	1	2	2	..	..
Brimer, Wm	1	3	3	..	..
Williams, Jacob	1	..	3	..	..
Carrick, Jno	3	1	7	..	6
Cochran, Tho'	1	1	5	..	..
Turner, Jonathan	1	2	4	..	..
Taber, Jno	4	4	3	..	..
Waldrip, Ezekl	1	6	1	..	..
Green, George	1	1	3	..	..
Music, Abram, Jr	1	5	3	..	..
Music, Abrm, Sr	1	4	2	..	..
Music, Jonathan	1	1	6	..	1
Sanders, George, Jr	2	2	2	..	..
Sanders, George	1	2	3	..	..
Williams, Jos	1	4	1	..	..
Langford, Robt	1	1	1	..	..
Taylor Lewis	1	..	4	..	..
Langford, Jno, Jr	1	1	3	..	..
Witt, Jesse	1	..	2	..	..
Witt, Hezekiah	1	2	3	..	..
Shields, Jeremy	1	4	3	..	..
Sawyers, Charls	1	3	3	..	..
Hix, Wm	1	2	4	..	..
Covran, Jonathn	1	1	2	..	..
Larince, Jo	1	..	1	..	..
Weaver, Tho'	1	1	3	..	..
Bartlet, Jas	1	..	1	..	..
Justice, Tho', Sr	2	3	1	..	..
Conway, Jeremiah	1	1	3	..	..
Tumins, Eliza	1	1	5	..	..
Ducaren, Waitmn	1	6	3	..	..
Langford, Wm	1	1	3	..	..
Fariss, Mary	1	3	3	..	..
Morgan, Jno	1	2	3	..	..
Barkley, George	2	4	1	..	..
Thomson, Wm	1	2	1	..	..
Jackson, David, Jr	1	2	3	..	..
Jackson, D., Sr	4	..	4	..	..
Chapman, Job	1	..	2	..	..
Brimer, Jesse	1	..	2	..	..
Fisher, Jno	1	4	3	..	..
Grivat, Jno	1	..	2	..	..
Tunnill, Wm	2	3	6	..	..
Conard, James	3	3	6	..	..
Case, Jno	3	4	1	..	..
Hall, Tho'	1	..	..	..	..
Ellison, Jno	1	2	2	..	..
Edwards, Tho'	1	2	5	..	..
Jones, Jno B. C.	2	..	4	..	..
Laxon, James	2	..	5	..	..
Tabor, Jn, Jr	2	1	5	..	..
Justice, Amos	1	1	3	..	..
Carter, Lewis	1	1	3	..	..
Junun, Antoney	1	3	2	..	..
Cooper, Mary	..	..	2	..	..
Blend, Jno, Lewis	3	2	2	..	..
Kendel, Nancy	..	3	6	..	..
Meban, Martha	..	2	7	..	..
Butler, Jno	2	..	2	..	..
THIRTEENTH COMPANY.					
Gash, Martin	3	..	1	..	..
Randolph, Sam	1	1	5	..	..
Randolph, Sam., Jr	1	..	1	..	..
Smith, Danl	1	3	4	..	..
Foster, Wm	2	1	6	..	3
Chambers, Abigail	2	1	4	..	..
Hawkins, Ben	1	..	4	..	..
Hitown, Oldham	3	2	4	..	..
Holcom, Kinchin	3	1	4	..	..
Davidson, Wm	4	4	4	..	1
Hitown, Austin	1	4	4	..	..
Fugit, Randolph	2	4	5	..	..
Medlock, Jas	2	2	3	..	..
Barren, Wm	1	1	5	..	..
Ingrm, Mourning	1	1	2	..	..
Kizzia, Sandefer	2	2	2	..	..
Kizzia, Jno	2	1	5	..	..
Anditon, Tho'	2	1	5	..	..

MORGAN DISTRICT, RUTHERFORD COUNTY—Continued.

NAME OF HEAD OF FAMILY.	Free white males of 16 years and upward, including heads of families.	Free white males under 16 years.	Free white females, including heads of families.	All other free persons.	Slaves.
THIRTEENTH COMPANY—continued.					
Bradly, Jno	1				
Hill, Wm	1	1	1		
Hill, Rd	1	2	2		
Lee, Elijah	1		3		
Williams, Edwd	1	6	3		
Hargett, Thos	1		3		
Ashworth, Jno	1	1	5		3
Bridget, Jas	1		3		
Selser, Matthias	1	4	2		
Wood, Jas., Senr	3	3	3		
Wood, Jno	1		2		
Wood, Jas., Jr	1		2		
Miller, Laurence	1	2	2		
Nanny, Nancy	1	1	2		
Hinson, Jess	1	1	3		
Wason, Wm	2	3	3		
Hinson, Jno	1	1	3		
Duncan, David	1	1	1		
Gibson, Jno	1		1		
Parks, Jno	5	1	2		
Cooper, Adm	1				
Wallace, Jno	3		3		
Yardly, Ben	3	3	6		
Johnson, Edwd	1	2	2		
Thomas, Jno	1	5	2		
Thomas, Stephn	1		2		
Fletcher, Wm	3	4	2		1
Winson, Elijah	1	1	4		1
Reed, Harmon	1	1	2		
Roberts, Mark	1	1	5		
Cody, Tho'	4		2		
Edmison, Basdel	1	2	2		
Cody, Godfry	4		2		
Johnson, Jas, Jr	1		7		
Johnson, James	1	1	1		
Warren, Jas	1	3	4		
Green, Jas	1	1	2		
Haslip, Robt	1	1	3		
Lyda, Andw	1	6	2		

NAME OF HEAD OF FAMILY.	Free white males of 16 years and upward, including heads of families.	Free white males under 16 years.	Free white females, including heads of families.	All other free persons.	Slaves.
THIRTEENTH COMPANY—continued.					
Case, Tho'	1	1	1		
Slipp, Jas	2	4	3		
Shelton, Wm		1	2		
Shelton, George	1	1	2		
Gray, Jno	1				
FOURTEENTH COMPANY.					
Reed, Abram	1	2	3		
Stringfeild, Jas	4	1	2		
Brittain, Jas	1	2	4		
Boidstone, Jas	3		1		
Kikendal, Simon	1	1	1		
Medcalf, Jas	2		1		
Medcalf, Norris	1	2	2		
Miller, Andw	1	1	4		1
Stringfeild, Jno	2	1	1		
Boidstone, Sam	1	2	1		
Boidstone, Jas., Jr	1	2	3		
Arnold, Tho'	1		4		1
Osborn, Jeremiah	2	1	1		
Claypole, Jno	1	1	3		
Osborn, Jno	1	1	1		
Box, Jno	1	2	4		
Osborn, Jonathn	1	1	3		
Claypole, Jonathn	1		1		
Newport, Michl	3		2		
Woodphin, Tho'	1	2	2		
Wood, Jno	1	1	2		
Woodpin, Nicholas	2	1	6		
Wood, Henry	1		1		
Newport, Jno	1		1		
Abbs, Thom	1		4		
Gardner, Jacob	2	1	3		
Gray, Jas	1		3		
Ashbrooks, Moses	3	3	7		
Parks, George	2	2	5		
Sweiton, Robt	1		1		
Sweiton, Jno	1	1	4		

NAME OF HEAD OF FAMILY.	Free white males of 16 years and upward, including heads of families.	Free white males under 16 years.	Free white females, including heads of families.	All other free persons.	Slaves.
FOURTEENTH COMPANY—continued.					
Sweiton, Edwd	3	2	4		
Gage, Aron	1	2	2		
Burlison, Jno	1	1	2		
Meda, Abram	2	2	5		
Craford, Moses	1		2		
Craford, Jas	1		2		
Craford, Isaac	1		1		
Crawford, Thom	3	1	3		
James, James	5	2	2		
Graham, Thos	1		1		
Durham, Wm	2		2		
Weaver, Sam	3	1	2		
Reid, George	1	2	4		
English, Wm	2	5	4		
Steward, Jno	1	2	5		
Allen, Sam	1		6		
Denton, Sam	1		2		
Odel, Ben	2		1		
Odel, Jno	1		1		
May, Tho'	2	2	3		
English, Joshua	1	4	2		
Lamb, Jno	1	1	2		
Graham, Spencer	1	1	2		
English, Jas	2	2	1		
Denton, Jonas	2	1	2		
Shateen, Abram	1	1	2		
Shateen, Edwd	1		3		
Shipman, Edwd	3	5	4		
Susco, Jacob	1	2	2		
Susco, Jno	3		4		
Davidson, Jas	1	3	2		
English, Jos	2		1		5
Still, Booze	1		2		
Jones, Stephn	1	4	4		
Robinson, Jas	1	2	3		
Vane, Jos	2	1	5		1
Roberts, Obadiah	1	2	2		
Hix, Wm	1	2	3		
Cooral, Jonathan	1	1	3		

MORGAN DISTRICT, WILKES COUNTY.

NAME OF HEAD OF FAMILY.	Free white males of 16 years and upward, including heads of families.	Free white males under 16 years.	Free white females, including heads of families.	All other free persons.	Slaves.
FIRST COMPANY.					
Ferguson, Thom	1	2	4		
Coffey, Ben	1	4	5		
Hays, George	1	1	3		
Coffey, Jane			1		7
Coffey, Eli	1		2		
Mills, Eliz		2	2		
Richardson, James	2	2	2		
Richardson, Sam	1		2		
Walters, Jno	1	2	2		
Edmison, James	1	1	2		
Israel, Michal	1	4	2		4
Coffey, Reuben	1	1	4		
Israel, Johnson	1		2		
Cox, Airess	2		2		2
Israel, Solomon	1		1		
Israel, Jesse	1		2		
Pierce, Jno	1	4	2		
Jackson, James	1	3	2		
Coffey, Thom	4	5	4		
Allen, David	1	1	2		
Jones, Joshua	1	5	4		
Coffey, Jno	1	2	4		
Alloway, Abram	1	3	7		
Gillum, Paphrodite	1	1	5		
Eperson, Robert	2	1	6		
Gordon, Charles, Jr	1		1		5
Silory, Stephen	1		3		
Elston, David	1	7	1		
Elston, Ben	1		2		
Epperson, Jas	1		1		
Long, Sam	1	4	1		
Parr, Methias	1	2	4		
Long, Robt	1	1	6		
Baird, Andw	3		1		5
Jacobs, Dutty	1	1	3		
Childers, Jno	1	3	3		
Runion, Jno	1	2	5		
Fields, Thom	2	1	3		
Crumton, Hezekiah	1	1	1		
Caffinder, Stephen	3	2	3		
Mills, Hardy	1	2	1		
Yarnell, Danl	3	2	1		
Reed, Thom	1	3	4		
Durham, Marshal	1	2	4		
Yarnal, Joseph	1	1	3		
Humphress, Owen	3	3	4		
Ferguson, Jos	1	3	4		
Lunn, Jno	1		2		
Hulme, Wm	1		2		

NAME OF HEAD OF FAMILY.	Free white males of 16 years and upward, including heads of families.	Free white males under 16 years.	Free white females, including heads of families.	All other free persons.	Slaves.
FIRST COMPANY—con.					
Hulme, Eliz	1		2		
Hulme, Geo	1	2	3		
Stacey, Jno	2		5		
Ferguson, Wm	1		2		
Horton, Zeph	1	1	1		
Ferguson, Nicolas	1	1	4		
Ferguson, Jeremiah	1	1	1		
Moore, Jno	3	3	2		
Northern, Peggy		2	3		
Baird, Zeb	3	4	5		
Steep, Thom	1	2	1		4
Demass, Jas	2	3	3		2
Demass, Lewis	2	3	3		5
Jones, Ben	1	1	6		5
Jones, Morton	3	4	2		
Wood, Elias	1	3	3		
Cody, Pierce	1		2		
Barrett, David	1	1	5		
Lenoir, Wm, Es	1	3	3		12
Munson, Moses	3		3		
Tate, Andrew	2	3	6		1
Duley, Wm	1	2	3		2
Crisp, Chesly	1	2	2		
Merrit, George	2	2	4		
Lay, Thom	1	1	3		
Coffey, Ambrous	3		2		1
Lansdown, Wm	2	2	6		
Campbell, Peter	1		1		
Cotrel, Thom	2	2	3		
Curtis, Wm	1		1		
Curtis, Jno	1		2		
Curtis, Josh	2		8		
SECOND COMPANY.					
Gordon, Nathanl	1	3	2		3
Ussory, Thom	1	2	1		
Carter, Edwd	1	2	1		
Keeling, Leonard	1	4	3		
Holman, Danl., Es	2	3	4		
Colvert, Wm	1		5		
Vickers, Elijah	1	2	3		
Fletcher, Spencer	1	4	2		
Russell, Buckmn	1	2	5		
Williams, Jas., Sr	2		4		
Humphriss, Milley		1	5		
Dobson, Jno	1		1		
Souther, Mary	2	2	4		
Greenstreet, Betty		2	2		

NAME OF HEAD OF FAMILY.	Free white males of 16 years and upward, including heads of families.	Free white males under 16 years.	Free white females, including heads of families.	All other free persons.	Slaves.
SECOND COMPANY—con.					
Tindal, Saml	1	3	4		
Stanley, Lucy		2	5		
Stanly, Jno	1		2		
Young, James	1	1	5		
Young, Ephraim	1	2	1		
Martin, Zadock	2	6	1		
Martin, Ben	1		1		
Martin, Jas	1	2	1		
Anderson, Jno	1	2	3		
Smoot, Jas	1	1	3		
Anderson, Cornelius	1		5		
Anderson, Geo	1		2		
Anderson, Sam	1		2		
Fletcher, Wm	2	1	1		2
Shinn, Sam	2	1	7		
Parker, Henry	1				
Parker, John	1	3	2		
Johnson, Wm	1	5	4		
Shumate, John	1	1	2		
Parks, Anne	1	3	5		8
Reynolds, Jas	1		3		
Cargil, Wm	1	1	5		
Cunningham, Jno	1	5	3		2
Chandler, Timothy	1	3	4		
Chandler, Robt	1	1	2		2
Chandler, Josia	1	3	1		
Herrin, Wm	1	3	2		
Hariss, Bradock	1	1	2		
Harriss, Edward	1	4	6		
Chandler, Danl	1		2		
Porter, Joseph	2	2	4		
Cornwall, Elijah	1	1	3		
Curry, Wm, Sr	1		1		
Curry, Nathan	1	2	4		
Curry, Jno	1	3	5		
Curry, Wm	1	1	2		
Fletcher, James	1	3	1		
Childress, Miller	1	1	2		
Burke, Jno	1		1		
Chambers, Wm	1	4	1		
Hull, Danl	1	3	1		
Busby, Isaac	1		1		
Busby, Jno	1	1	1		
Russell, Hilloval	1	3	9		
Burke, Jno	1	4	3		
Profit, Jno	2	2	7		
Fletcher, Jas., Es	2		2		2
Wilson, Sam	1	1	2		
McDonol, Geo	1		1		

MORGAN DISTRICT, WILKES COUNTY—Continued.

NAME OF HEAD OF FAMILY.	Free white males of 16 years and upward, including heads of families.	Free white males under 16 years.	Free white females, including heads of families.	All other free persons.	Slaves.
SECOND COMPANY—con.					
Keeling, Calton	2	3	6		
Underwood, Lewis	1	2	2		
Gordon, Charls, Sr	1		1		14
Hopper, Jno	1	2	2		
Bruce, Robt	1	1	2		
Gordon, Chapman	1	1	3		4
Miller, Jno	1	4	5		
Tanner, Comfort	1	2	2		
Huckerson, David	1	4	3		2
Huckerson, Charles	3		1		
Roberts, Jno	1	2	4		
Gordon, George	1	2	6		17
Cross, Asel	1	1	4		
Ray, Eliz		1	2		
Wilky, Mourning		1	2		
Tomkins, Silas	1	4	4		
Miller, Leonard	1	4	3		
Davis, Wm	1	1	3		
Reynolds, Elisha	1	1	3		
Estridge, Jno	1	1	2		
Herndon, Jos	1	2	3		9
Reynolds, Frank	4	3	7		6
Henry, Jno	1	1	2		
Carter, Henry	1	4	6		
Cargil, Jno	2		4		4
Cargil, Jos	1	5	2		
Vennoy, Danl	1	2	2		1
THIRD COMPANY.					
Cleveland, Robt	4	4	6		10
Hamby, Wm	1	5	4		
Jones, Henry	2	4	3		
Holeman, Thom	1	4	3		
Bushop, Roger	3	2	3		2
Bunton, Nell	1	3	3		
Brown, John, Esq	3	5	6		22
Lovelace, John	3	3	5		
Profit, Sylvester	1	1	3		
Castle, Sam	2	1	4		
Proffitt, Jno	1	1	2		
Cordwell, Prin'	1	4	5		
Jackson, Wm	1	3	5		
Fairchild, Eben	1	2	4		
Case, Isaiah	1		3		
Lips, Jno	1	3	2		
Lips, Jno, Sr	1		2		
Walters, Walter	1		5		
McLeain, Jno	3	3	6		
Minton, Meredith	2	3	2		
Webb, Ussby		1	2		
Webb, Frank	1		2		
Webb, Cutt	1	2	2		
Webb, Jno	1		5		
Flanigin, Jno	1		3		
Regins, Peter	1	4	1		
Stonecypher, Jno H	2	1	3		
Bankes, Wm	1		1		
Tomkins, Jonathn	1		1		
West, Wm	1		1		
Story, Joshua	2	5	3		
Jackson, Jas	1	4	2		
Tomkins, Moses	1	1	2		
Adams, Wm	1		1		
Elmore, Thos	1		3		
Profitt, Wm	1	1	1		
Case, Aron	1		3		
Adams, Jane		4	2		
Gullit, Danl	1	5	5		
Henson, Jno	2	2	3		
Adams, Jno	2	1	6		
Adams, Wm	1	1	8		1
Bushop, Frank	1	2	3		
Sewill, Abrm	1	2	6		
Sevell, Dawson	1		4		
Yates, Wm	1	2	5		
Hendrin, Jonathn	1	2	1		
Hendrin, Jo	1	1	4		
Fairchild, Elijah	2		2		
Wilson, Mary		1	3		
Wall, Jonathn	1	3	3		
McNeel, George	3	3			
Bingham, Robt	1		3		
Smith, Ben	1	3	3		
Givin, Peter	1	1	2		
Francis, Matt	1		1		
Yates, Jno	1	4	3		
Pincen, Elias	1	1	1		
Francis, Wm	1		1		
Baker, Andw	2	2	2		
Roberts, Jas	1	1	4		
Church, Phil	1		2		
Church, Amos	1	1	3		
Andrews, Jas	2		1		
Church, Jno	1	2	2		
THIRD COMPANY—con.					
Vancey, Nath. (E.)	3	3	7		
Baker, Philip	1		4		
Reed, Thom	1	3	2		
Harmon, Jno	1	3	3		
Carter, Jos	1	3	2		
Crane, Phil	2	3	4		1
Crane, Polly			3		
Yates, Jno	1		2		
Lowe, Isaac	1		1		
Sharp (Free Negro)				1	
Roberts, Sarah	2	1	2		
Paslier, Isaac	2	2	7		
Sam (A free neg.)				1	
FOURTH COMPANY.					
McNeel, Wm	1	1	3		
Smith, Wm	1	6	2		
Smith, Jno	1	3	4		
Robins, Jno	3	1	7		11
Sertain, Jas	1	1	2		
Owin, David	1	4	2		2
Tyre, Jno	2	3	5		
Colvert, Wm	2	2	5		
Tyre, Wm	1	3	4		
Tyre, George	1	1	3		
Lorance, George	1	1	2		
Querry, Wm	1		2		
Sheppard, Robt	2	1	7		
Judd, Rollin (E.)	3		1		
Judd, Rob	1	2	2		
Judd, Natt	1	3	5		
Pinion, Ben	1	1	2		
Robins, Reuben	1	1	4		
Baker, Peter	1	2	5		
Certain, Lucy			2		
Denny, Elijah	2	2	2		
Copland, Joel	1	3	4		
Vannoy, Frank	2	2	7		
Absher, Wm	1	1	1		
Owen, Jno	1	3	5		
Owen, Thom	1	2	10		
Owin, Jno	3		1		
Owin, David, Jr	1		1		
Erwin, Frank	3	1	3		
Cash, Wm	1	4	3		
Sheppard, Jno	1	1	1		
Copland, Joel, Jr	1		4		
Sheppard, John	3	1	4		
Wallers, Robt	1	2	2		
Copland, Wm	1		4		
Qurry, Jno, Sr	1	1	5		
Kilby, Adam	1	3	6		
Wall, Jonathn	1	3	3		
Kilby, Michl	1	1	5		
Kilby, Wm	4	4	5		
Carter, Sam	1	3	5		
Hopper, Thom	1	1	1		
Hays, Jas	1	2	3		
Sheroon, Isaiah	1		3		
Hays, Robt	2		3		
Adam, Henry	1		3		
Adams, Sarah			3		
Adams, Peggy		1	3		
Tinsly, Isaac	1	2	2		
Wilson, Mary		1	4		
Hockins, Jno	2	1	4		
Yates, Jas	1	1	2		
Brown, Walter	4		5		
Smith, Oswall	1	1	3		
Smith, Humphry	1		1		
Boon, Hiram	1		1		
Smith, Jarvis	1	5	2		
Forester, Fieldin	1		1		
Wooton, Eliz		1	5		
Sebastin, Lewis	1	3	2		
Sebastin, Ben	1	3	5		
Dickson, Wm	1	2	3		
Barker, George	1	2	3		
Underwood, Wm	1	2	1		
Estridge, Jno	1		2		
Barker, Hezekia	2	6	2		
McGrady, Jacob	1	5	1		
Pon, Rd	1	3	1		
Grimes, Moses	1	3	3		
Forester, Jno	1	3	3		
Hall, Owen	2	3	4		
McDowell, Mike	1	4	2		
Hall, Robt	2	4	2		
Jennins, Luke	1	3	1		
Venoy, Andw	2	5	4		
Pumphy, Henry	1	3	2		
Vears, Wm	1	3	4		
Jennins, Jno	3		1		
Atkins, Silas	1	3	1		
FOURTH COMPANY—con.					
Hall, Jno	1	1	3		
Hall, Jesse	1	1	7		
Ray, Dicey		2	1		
Hall, Wm	1		3		
Rhodes, Sarah		1	3		
FIFTH COMPANY.					
Harvell, Isom	1	3	2		
Norman, Jas	2	6	4		
Lican, J. Goodin	1	2	4		
Bell, Even	1	3	2		1
Love, Jno	1	2	1		2
Crabtree, Ben	1		3		
Pale, Mary	1	3	4		
Sanders, Francis	1	4	2		
Howard, Jno	1	3	4		
Bussell, Presly	1	2	4		
Reeves, Isaac	2	2	4		
Reeves, James	1	1	3		
Lewis, Wm, Jr	1	3	4		
Reeves, Jno	1				
Chambers, Nathn	1	2	2		
Mayberry, Randol	1	1	3		
Young, Vachal	1	1	6		
Longbottom, Jos	1	1	1		
Lewis, Wm	2	2	5		
Hethmon, Jonath	3	2	4		4
Roberts, Ros	3	1	2		
Wilson, Jno	1	1	3		
Wilson, Mary	1	3	4		
Roberts, Jas	1		3		
Johnson, Charles	3	2	7		
Chambers, Wm	1	4	3		
Chambers, Jno	1	1	1		
Chambers, Drury	1	2	2		
Brown, Danl	1	1	2		
Baker, Baswell	1	2	1		
Welch, Wallar	1	3	1		
Brown, Rebekah	3	3	2		
Mundy, Christopher	1	1	3		
Garrison, Jas	1	5	4		
Hughlin, Jno	1		2		
Hughlin, Ambrous	1		1		
Dickins, Wm	1	3	5		
Hendron, Jno	1	1	2		
Fitspatrick, Thom	1	3	4		
Bales, Mary		1	1		
Hooper, Wm	1	1	1		
Cole, Jobe	1	2	3		
Comps, George	1	4	2		
Combs, John	1	1	7		
Combs, Thom	2		2		
Silcox, Sarah		1	1		
Lunceford, Jack	1	1	2		
Stanley, Thom	1		3		
Nance, Wm	1	2	6		
Mills, Wm	1		3		
Stanley, Eliz		5	3		
Roberts, Eliz		2	2		
Kelly, Ben	1	1	3		
Cooks, Eliz	1	5	5		
Grant, David	1				
Lunceford, Jno	1	2	3		
Crabtree, Sam	1	1	4		
Lunceford, Ben	1	5	2		
Lunceford, Elisha	1	2	3		
Lunceford, Elijah	1	1	1		
Hendron, Nimrod	1		2		
Hendron, Wm	2	4	1		
Mullis, Sarah	1	2	1		
Needson, Abel	1		2		
Taylor, Chas	1	2	5		
Rush, Danl	3	4	5		4
Mitchell, Wm	1	2	4		
Nicolson, Sam	2	4	4		
Jarvis, Jas	1	3	1		
Mise, Martha			2		
McBride, Jas	1	3	10		
Mehaffy, Thom	3		3		
Hays, Henry	1	3	4		
Wooton, Patty		1	1		
Watts, Jno	1	1	4		
SIXTH COMPANY.					
Johnson, Sam	1	2	3		5
Wheatly, George	1	1	5		
Stamper, Jonathan	2		2		1
Turner, Thom	1	2	2		
Turner, Edmund	1	2	2		
Turner, John	1	2	1		
Grimsly, Thom	1	1	3		
Buttery, Timothy	1		4		
Sparks, Jno	1	4	3		

MORGAN DISTRICT, WILKES COUNTY—Continued.

SIXTH COMPANY—con.

NAME OF HEAD OF FAMILY.	Free white males of 16 years and upward, including heads of families.	Free white males under 16 years.	Free white females, including heads of families.	All other free persons.	Slaves.
King, Robt	1	2	1		
Love, John	1		2		
Turner, Roger	1	2	3		
Richeson, Alex	1	3	3		
Lyon, Wm	1	4	4		
Stone, Cudy	1		2		
Sparks, Reuben	1	1	3		
Gambell, Jno	2	3	4		
Holbrooks, Jno	1	2	3		
Joines, Thom	1	1	7		
Morgan, Thom	1	2	3		
Rice, Wm	1	4	4		
Billins, Gasper	1		1		
Lewis, George	2	1	10		
Townson, John	1	3	2		
Hicks, Claybon	1	1	3		
Morgan, Thom	1	2	3		
Morgan, Wm	1	1	1		
Fugate, Esom	1	2	1		
Conaliy, Henry	1	5	4		
Botts, Joshua	2	2	2		
Craft, Chilus	1	1	2		
Adams, Jacob	1	4	4		
Lovelace, Arche	1	1	1		
Colwell, Seth	1	2	4		
Stamper, Joel	1	3	3		1
Clarke, David	1		1		
Mulky, Jno	1		1		
Gambell, Mary	1	1	2		7
Oscar, Dan	1	3	2		
Hammon, John	1	3	8		
Hammon, Ben	1		3		
Hammon, Wm	2	1	2		
Adams, Ben	1	1	5		
Alex, Willis	1	2	1		
Johnson, Thom	1	1	5		
Bowe, Edmund	1	2	5		
Webb, Jas	1	3	2		
Hously, Charity		4	2		
Warner, Winney	1		3		
Johnson, Wm, Esqr	1	3	2		
Johnson, Phillip	1	1	2		
Johnson, Rachal	2	2	3		
Thaxton, Jno	1		4		
Coddle, Stephn	1	1	4		
Coddle, Jas	2		2		
Holbrooks, Colby	1	1	1		
Holbrooks, Randel	1	5	3		
Medlin, Wm	4	1	3		
Medlin, Duk	2				
Lorance, Jas	1	1	1		
Lorance, Thom	2	1	2		
Cate, Charls	1	2	5		
Cate, Jno	1	2	2		
Fugot, Patia			2		
Adams, Jno	1	1	5		3
Ross, Emanuel	1		5		1
Scott, Wm	3	3	5		
Manard, Kit	1	3	3		
Lion, Wm	1		2		
Adams, John	1	2	1		
Boggers, Rd	1	6	2		
Hagins, Jno	1	1	1		
Wiatt, Abby		1	3		
Hariss, Susana			4		
Harriss, Wm	1	2	4		
Welsh, Thom			4		
Lyon, Jacob			4		
Holbrooks, Zach	1	2	1		
Holbrooks, Jno	1	2	1		
Holbrooks, Wm	1	2	2		
Hargis, Wm	2		1		
Reed, Jas	2		2		
Stamper, Jonath	2	4	4		
Billings, Thom	2		4		
Billings, Thom	1	2	2		
Prewitt, Jo	1	2	3		
Stones, Sam	1	2	2		
Minor, Jesse	1		2		
Manor, Gibson	1	2	5		
Manor, Jas	1	1	4		
Blackburn, Wm	1	1	3		
Manor, Drury	1		4		
Frazer, Micajah	1	3	4		
Cornelius, Wm	1	1	1		
Roberts, Edwd	1	2	3		
Hammon, Jas	1	1	3		
Sparks, Jno	1	4	3		
Scrutchfield, Art	1	2	3		
Hidden, Elisha	3	1	4		
Adams, Spencer	1	3	3		2
Hiddy, Gilbert	1				
Pruitt, Lus		1	2		
Bradberry, Wm	1	2	2		
Bradberry, Jas	2	3	3		
Donathn, Nelson	1	2	2		

SEVENTH COMPANY.

NAME OF HEAD OF FAMILY.	Free white males of 16 years and upward, including heads of families.	Free white males under 16 years.	Free white females, including heads of families.	All other free persons.	Slaves.
Gynn, Rd	1	1	1		11
Bucknall, Sam	3	2	4		1
Lewis, Jas. M	1	1	1		8
Loving, Gabriel	1	2	7		
Parkes, Ambrous	2		2		3
Parks, Reuben	1	1	1		1
Johnson, Rachl	1		2		2
Jonson, Jelfery	1	1	1		
Jonson, Ben	1		2		1
Johnson, Jno	1	3	5		
Johnson, George	1	3	6		
Johnson, Wm	1	1	1		
Denny, Edmund	2		2		1
Baltrep, Jno	2		2		
Parks, Ruben, Jr	2	4	5		
Wheatly, Geo., Sr	3	3	4		
Sloan, Wm	1	2	1		
Dotson, Patty		2	2		
Allen, Rich'd, Es	3	2	4		1
Allin, Jas	1	1	1		
Borot, Abigail		3	2		
Stubblefield, Thom	3	4	6		
Garison, Isaac	2		2		
Watts, Rd	1	2	5		
Gray, Jno	1	2	6		
Gooch, Jos	3	3	5		
Powe, Jno	2	1	2		
Kennedy, Aron	1		3		
Powe, Wm	1	2	3		
Phillips, Stephen	1	1	2		
Davis, Jas	1	3	5		
Davis, Wm	1	4	2		
Kilburn, Jno	1		1		
Kilborn, Isaac	2	2	2		
Mailia, Patric	1	6	4		
Reed, Sam	1	1	4		
Dolison, Wm	1		2		
Darnell, Nancy	3	4			
Darnell, Cornelius	1	2	2		
Carter, Simon	1	3	6		
Bonsil, Wm	1		1	1	
Wall, Jacob	2		1		
Parks, Geo	1	3	3		
Tolby, Wm	1	4	3		
Smith, Lucy		3	1		
Burke, Rd	1	2	2		
Ross, Thom	1	2	7		
Carrol, Jas	3		4		7
Parkes, Jno					7
Parks, Sam	1	3	4		1
Loving, Gabriel	1	2	4		
Gyn, Jos	2	1	1		3
Wall, Wm	1	2	4		
Younger, Jos	1	1	1		1
Major, Jno	2	4	8		6

EIGHTH COMPANY.

NAME OF HEAD OF FAMILY.	Free white males of 16 years and upward, including heads of families.	Free white males under 16 years.	Free white females, including heads of families.	All other free persons.	Slaves.
Greer, Ben, Esqr	3	6	1		
Council, Jesse	2	3	3		
Council, Jurdin	1				
Ingland, Aron	1	3	1		
Ingland, Ezek	1	1	1		
Moss, Jacob	1		2		
Moss, Jos	1		2		
Green, Rd	4	4	3		
Horton, Nat	1	2	1		
Chambers, Henry	2	1	4		
Ayr, Jas	1	2	3		
Ellison, Thom	1		1		
Murphy, Mary			3		
Colman, Sarah		2	3		
Miller, Wm	2	3	2		
Reece, Felle	1	5	4		
Brown, Jno	1	1	3		
Wood, Andw	1	1	5		
Stoncypher, Jo	1	3	2		
Egers, Danl	1	2	3		
Duncan, Josh	2	3	4		
Baker, Mary	1	2	3		
Cabel, Casper	1	4	2		
Tomkins, Jas	3	2	3		
Bailey, Ben	1	2	4		
Sewell, Jos	1	4	4		
Hampton, Thom	1	4	4		
Culberth, Ben	1	1	1		
Culberth, Dan	1	1	3		
Wilson, Sam	1	4	3		
Sheppard, Jas	1	2	1		2
Calliway, Jas	1		2		
Calliway, Elijah	1		2		
Judd, Robt	1				
Bloomer, Jeremiah	1	4	2		
Vannoy, Wm	1		2		
Calliway, Rd	1	1	2		1
Givin, Champn	1	1	2		

EIGHTH COMPANY—con.

NAME OF HEAD OF FAMILY.	Free white males of 16 years and upward, including heads of families.	Free white males under 16 years.	Free white females, including heads of families.	All other free persons.	Slaves.
Linvill, Thos	3	1	1		
Whitenton, Wm	2	3	5		
Estepp, Shad	2	2	5		
Whittenton, Jno	1		2		
Linvill, Thos	1	1	4		1
King, Baker	1	1	3		
Green, Jesse	2	5	2		
Hanis, Jno	1	1	3		
Beard, Ezekl	3	2	2		
Beard, Sam	4	1	1		
Hoselan, Jas	1	2	2		
Hicks, Sam	2	1	2		
Holselan, Jno	1		2		
Ward, Ben	2	4	3		1
Stephen, Lewis	1	1			5
Ward, Josh	1	2	2		
Smith, Bashiba	1	1	1		

NINTH COMPANY.

NAME OF HEAD OF FAMILY.	Free white males of 16 years and upward, including heads of families.	Free white males under 16 years.	Free white females, including heads of families.	All other free persons.	Slaves.
Witherspoon, David	3		1		10
Triplit, Danl	2	2	2		
Bailey, Edmund	2	1	5		
Bailey, Ansel	1		2		
Bradly, Jno	1	3	6		
Rucker, Colby	2		5		
Goodruch, Jno	1	5	3		
Tucker, Sam	2	2	5		1
Deir, Jno	1	3	3		
Isbell, Thom, Esqr	2	2	3		4
Ross, Jno	1		2		
Donathan, Jered	2	2	3		3
Roberts, Jno	1	1	3		1
Brown, Larcan	1		1		
Roberts, Jas	1	1	6		
Padjit, Jas	1	1	6		
Hodjins, Rd	1	1	1		
Cox, Thom	1	3	3		
Cox, David	1	3	2		
Ayrs, Robt	1		1		
Herrin, Edwd	2	1	2		
Witherspoon, Martha	2	4	5		5
Loyd, Jas	1	3	2		
Brumly, Jno	1	3	3		
Morris, Cloe		1	3		
Wallis, Jas	2		3		
Wisdom, Anne			2		6
Calton, Ambrous	1		2		
Calton, Lewis	1	3	2		
Levinston, Jno	1	2	5		
Tilley, Ben	1		1		
Walker, Sam	1	3	4		
Camel, Jno	1	1	6		
Nowland, Peter	1	1	2		2
Triplitt, Nelly	1	1	4		4
Brown, Jas	1	5	4		
Perkins, Tho'	1	6	1		
Holman, Thom, Jr	1	2	5		
Lemon, Jno	1		5		
Welch, Andw	1	2	3		
McGee, David	2	3	7		
Land, Thom	2		3		
Ellison, Hugh	1	1	4		
Ellison, Wm	2	4	4		3
Norris, Jno	1	4	4		
Noland, Hary	1	4	4		
Noland, Pierce	2	3	4		
Nowland, Phil	1	1	1		
Rash, Wm	1		2		
Swanson, Jno	1	1	7		
Allen, Ananias	1	3	4		
Roberts, Rd	1		2		
Semkins, Jarid	1		1		
Laxton, Levy	1	1	1		
Laxton, Sarah	1		1		
Kulp, Reuben	1	2	3		
Pierce, Francis	1		4		
Parr, Jno	2		3		
Davis, Philip	2		4		
Stanton, Thom	1	2	7		
Stanton, Rd	1	2	6		
Lewis, Jas	1	5	4		
Coffey, Nebu	2	5	2		1
Stanly, Reuben	3	1	5		
Coffey, Cleveland	2	3	5		16
Cook, Isaac	2	2	3		
Durham, Jno	2		3		
Calton, Tho'	1	3	5		
Lewis, Geo	1	1	1		
Barton, Jno, Sr	1	2	4		
Barton, Jno	1		1		
Land, Jonathn	1		2		
Woodard, Sam	1	3	1		
Mooney, Patrick	1	3	2		
Suther, Michal	1	3	2		
Welsh, Jno	1	3	6		

MORGAN DISTRICT, WILKES COUNTY—Continued.

NAME OF HEAD OF FAMILY.	Free white males of 16 years and upward, including heads of families.	Free white males under 16 years.	Free white females, including heads of families.	All other free persons.	Slaves.
NINTH COMPANY—con.					
Greyson, Ben	3	2	2		
Greyson, Jno	1		1		
Parker, Jno	2	2	3		
Ferguson, Jas	2	4	4		
Davis, Phil	1		2		
Roberts, Jo	1		1		
Tilly, Lazarus	1	1	2		
Tilly, Edmund	2	4	4		2
Elmore, Jas	1	2	3		
Holt, Nelly	1	1	5		
Killian, Henry	1		2		
Rash, Jos	1	3	4		
Anderson, Jno	2	1	4		
Kerby, Jno	1				
Kerby, Wm	1	5	6		
Devenport, Reuben	1	1	1		
Stanley, Eliz		2	3		
Isbell, Nancy			4		8
TENTH COMPANY.					
Nall, Jno	1	3	3		3
Gibson, Andw	1	3	6		
Stephens, Rd	1				
Sigler, Phil	1		2		1
Gibson, Jordan	1	3	1		
Collins, Hardy	1	1	4		
Williams, Jas	3	4	8		
Colwell, Jo	1	3	6		
Richison, Danl	4		3		
Mulky, Jas	1		1		
Johnson, Alex	1		1		
Cole, Lenvil	1	2	3		
Hardin, Henry	1	1	3		
Collins, Vol	1		2		
Collins, Ambrous	1	1	2		
Lewis, Gideon	1	2	1		
Evans, Theop	3	2	3		
Baker, Ab	1	4	3		
Collins, Geo	1	2	4		
Smith, Jonathan	1	3	6		
Lewis, Jas	1	3	4		
Lewis, Jas	1	2	1		
Gamble, Martin	1	3	1		1
Toliver, Jesse	1		2		
Killian, Shadrach	1				
Gibson, Joel	1	1	3		
Gibson, Arche	1	1	9		
Gibson, Ezekl	1		2		
Nicols, Jo	1	2	3		
Clarke, Wm	2		2		
Parker, David	1	2	1		
Cox, Jno	2		4		11
Weaver, Wm	1	2	3		
Stiddim, Sam	1	3	4		
McDonell, Moses	1	2	3		
Jones, Sam	1	1	3		
Bolin, Jesse	1	3	4		
Sinington, Wm	1	4	4		
Richeson, Jno	1		3		
Huff, Wm	3	2	6		
Seritch, Stephen	4	2	4		
Spencer, Wm	1	1	2		
Boyd, Wm	1	4	2		
Sutherton, Enas	1	2	3		
Weaver, Mark	1		2		
Piniton, Micajah	3	3	4		
Pinniton, Ben	1	2	5		
Piniton, Elijah	1	1	2		
Angel, Nick	3	2	2		
Bodge, Jas	1	2	3		
Baker, Thom	1	1	1		
Sheppard, Jas	1		2		
Sheppard, Wm	1		2		
Sheppard, Bety		2	3		
Ruckerson, Canada	1				
McMullin, Jno	1	3	1		
Toliver, Moses	1	4	3		
Toliver, Jno	1		3		
Toliver, Chs	1	2	3		
Toliver, Wm	1	4	2		
Fips, Sam	1	2	4		
Long, Jno	1	4	4		
Perry, Wm	3	1	5		
Collins, Martin	1	3	4		
Collins, David	3	2	6		
Moore, Andw	1		2		
Gipson, Dorothy	2	2	2		
Baldin, Elisha	2	4	4		
Holsey, Wm	1	1	3		
Sanders, Wm	2	3	6		
Scott, Wm	3	3	5		
Nall, Wm	2	1	2		5
Dickson, Tho'	3	3	2		
Bryan, Jno	2		1		
Edward, Young	1	4	3		
Supott, Adam	4		1		

NAME OF HEAD OF FAMILY.	Free white males of 16 years and upward, including heads of families.	Free white males under 16 years.	Free white females, including heads of families.	All other free persons.	Slaves.
ELEVENTH COMPANY.					
Thurston, Wm	4	5	1		6
Scisk, Thom	1	3	6		
Fox, James	2	3	2		
Baker, Anne		6	3		
Roberts, Wm	1		6		2
Oliver, Susana		3	5		
Filts, Wm	1		1		
Wilcox, Wm	3	4	3		1
Flits, Aron	2	2	3		
Cook, Abrm	2	5	2		1
Filts, Jno	1	1	1		
Good, Peter	1		4		
Lorance, Peter	1	1	1		
Brown, Wm, Sr	1		3		
Brown, Jas	2	1	8		
Brown, Ben	1		1		
Brown, Sam	1		1		
Brown, Wm	1	2	4		
Mathis, Slip	2	1	4		
Denny, Jesse	1		4		
Allen, Patty	2		5		
Denny, George	1	1	3		
Denny, Isley	1		3		
Denny, Jas	2	1	3		
Denny, Jas., Jr	1		3		
Samuel, Mordecai	1	2	1		
Jackson, Wm	1	3	3		
Bange, Thom	1	4	4		
Scisk, Live	1		2		
Smith, Nathan	1	6	4		
Scisk, Barneby	1		1		
Fox, Danl	1	2	1		
Sish, Timothy	1		2		
Wason, Arche	3	1	6		
Davis, Evin	1	3	4		
Lewis, Wm T., Es	1		3		5
Bange, David	1	1	3		
Boling, Abel	1		1		
Herndon, Ben., Es	4	1	6		22
Hill, Jno	1	1	1		
Coligan, Wm	1	4	2		
Upchurch, Sarah	2	1	4		
Gray, Jas	2		2		
Gray, George	1		2		
Martin, Jno	1	3	2		6
Martin, Isaac	1		1		7
Green, Thom	1	2	3		1
Bagby, Jno	1	1	2		1
Gray, Sam	1	1	6		
Martin, Robt	1	3	1		1
Reddin, Jno	1	1	4		
Martin, Henry	1	3	1		
Martin, Sarah	2		2		7
Sale, Leonard	1	2	6		
Sale, Thom	1		3		
Sale, Cornelius	2	3	6		2
Sale, Nancy	3		3		10
Kerby, Ben	1	6	2		
Grant, Jno	1	1	3		
Lycan, Hanel	1	2	2		
Armstrong, Nancy		1	2		
Turnbell, Jno	1	3	4		
Rose, Jno	1	2	7		
Rose, Sterling	1	1	5		
Rose, Ben	1	3	4		
Rose, Jno, Sr	1		1		
Camel, Theo	1				
Woodbant, Silers	1	2	2		
Walker, Howard	1	4	4		
Adams, Moses	2	6	5		
Adams, Zach	1	2	2		
Wigins, Abram	2		2		
Jones, Mary		1	2		
Wood, Allen	1		1		
Johnson, Jno	1		1		
Fife, Wm	1	2	5		
McDaniel, Wm	2		3		
McDaniel, Wm, Jr	1	2	3		
Newberry, Tho'	1	3	3		
Macay, Patrick	1	3	3		
Norton, Jno	1	1	4		
Rutledge, Wm	1	3	2		2
Rose, Opy			1		
Thurmond, Thom	1	5	3		11
Martin, Ben	2	2	6		13
TWELFTH COMPANY.					
Jones, Russel	3	4	5		5
Howard, Ben	2	2	6		13
Howard, Joshua	1		2		1
Bates, Mathias	1	1	1		
Beaver, Thom	1				
Williams, Enoch	1	3	1		
Triplitt, Mason	1	2	2		
Hagler, Jno, Jr	2	2	4		2
Lay, Jesse	3		9		

NAME OF HEAD OF FAMILY.	Free white males of 16 years and upward, including heads of families.	Free white males under 16 years.	Free white females, including heads of families.	All other free persons.	Slaves.
TWELFTH COMPANY—continued.					
Anderson, Thom	1	1	2		
Anderson, Thom, Sr	1		3		
Hogg, Wm	2	6	2		
Lay, Davis	1	4	7		
Lay, Thom, Sr	1	2	3		
Hall, Thom	1	1	4		
Lansdon, David	1		2		
Mill			1		2
Stanley, Nathanl	1	2	4		
Northern, Jno	4	1	3		
Stanbury, Moses	1	2	5		
Hagler, Abrm	1	2	1		
Sweeton, Dutton	1	1	4		
Tugman, Edmund	1		2		
Tugman, Thos	1	2	2		
Southerton, Danl	1	4	2		
Shearer, Jno	1		1		1
Shearer, Robt	1		2		
Hagler, Jacob	1	2	2		
Lnorce, Thom	1	2	2		1
Robins, Jno	1	2	4		4
Foster, Thom	1	5	2		
Triplet, Wm	1	4	1		
Ferguson, Thom	1	2	1		1
Triplite, Thom	1	1	1		
Williams, Elijah	1	1	5		
Forbes, David	2	1	3		
Vanderpool, Jno	2		3		
Forbes, Sam	1	1	3		
Kendle, Sarah	4		2		
Corban, Jno	1	2	3		
Pitton, Charity		2	2		
Keeling, Jane	1		2		
Steid, Thom	1	4	1		
Sweeton, Robt	1		2		
Dugger, Ben	1	3	6		
Burns, Saml	1		3		
Hodge, Thos	1	3	6		
Hall, Martin	1	2	3		
Stoddil, Edwd	1		3		
Duglass, James	1	1	3		
Vest, Wm	1	1	3		
Owen, Barnet	1	3	7		
Duncan, Ben	1	4	5		
Brown, Rd	1				4
Bahs, Nat	2	2	3		
Elliott, Elis		3	4		
Walters, Jno	1		3		
Ellison, Hezekia	1	3	3		
Ferguson, Jno	1	4	4		
Ferguson, Rd	1		1		
Brown, Wm	3	2	6		
Adams, Wm	1	4	2		
Farmer, Thos	2	7	2		
Hendrix, Darby	1	1	3		
Hendrix, Ben	3	2	4		
Walters, Moses	2	3	4		
Mullin, Wm	1	2	4		
Mullin, Caty	1	1	3		
THIRTEENTH COMPANY.					
Trible, Wm	1	3	6		
Pain, George	1	2	2		
Blackburn, Jas	1	2	2		
Jones, Peter	1	3	2		
Anderson, Geo	1		2		
Whithead, Jno	1	1	2		
Madalf, Jo	4	1	3		
Null, Jno	1	2	2		
Law, David	1	3	3		
Freeman, Peter	1	2	4		
Lowe, Thos	1	1	1		
Lowe, Sam	1		1		
Sanders, Anne		2	3		
Elmore, Geo	2		5		
Sanders, Jas	1	2	2		
Jones, Ezek	2	1	2		
Johnson, Ben	1		2		
Hamton, Nancy		2	2		
Hamton, Turner	1		2		
Landsdown, Jno	1	2	2		
Jones, Jno L	1	4	2		
Lowe, Mary	1	2	2		
Trible, Shad	1	2	2		
Hubbard, Ben	1	1	1		
Martin, Zac	1				
Wright, Solomon	1		1		
Hamton, Jacob	2		1		
Gray, Jno	2	3	5		
Lowe, Isaac	1	2	4		
Trible, Spil	3	7	4		
Mongomery, Eliz	1	1	2		
Greer, Josh	1	6	7		3
Trible, Joel	1	2	2		
Southerton, Dan	1	2	1		

MORGAN DISTRICT, WILKES COUNTY—Continued.

NAME OF HEAD OF FAMILY.	Free white males of 16 years and upward, including heads of families.	Free white males under 16 years.	Free white females, including heads of families.	All other free persons.	Slaves.
THIRTEENTH COMPANY—continued.					
Donathon, Frd	1				3
Walker, Isaac	1	4	2		3
Sloan, John	1		1		
Elledge, Isaac	2		1		
Elledge, Ben	2		2		
Greer, Jude		2	4		
Hamton, Reuben	1	2	1		
Hargram, Francis	2	3	4		4
Lowe, Wm	2	4	3		
Lowe, Rachel		2	1		
Morgan, Jno	1	1	1		
Hamton, Joel	1	2	3		
Dyer, Minoah	3		3		
Hall, Jesse	1	1	2		
Starkey, Jo	1	2	2		
Donathn, Hawkin	1	1	1		
Nicols, Jacob	3		3		1
Green, Anne	1		1		7
Mitchell, Rachel		2	4		1
Bryan, Anne	1		1		1
Bryan, Henry	1		1		
Bray, Patrick	1	1	2		
Chanler, Jno	1		1		
Donathan, Wm	1	1			4
Donathn, Ben	1		3		
Morgan, Jos., Sr	2		6		
Poor, Betty		2	4		
Pasons, Jno	1	1	4		
Boman, Isom	1	2	5		
McGill, Wm	1	3	5		
Hines, Jonathn	1	2	2		
Stewart, Jas., Sr	3	5	4		
McCinny, Sam	1	2	9		
Holton, Alex	2	3	4		
Moore, Andw	2	5	4		
Majors, Jno	1	4	4		
Gilbreath, Wm	1	4	2		
Gilbreath, Alex	1	2	4		
Gilbreath, Jno	2	3	4		
Freeman, Jas	1	1	4		
Livinston, Jno	1	2	4		
Norman, Isaac	3	1	2		
Smither, Gabl	1	3	5		
Barber, Nat	1		2		
Barber, Rd	1	1	1		
Parkes, Aron	1	3	6		1
Preston, Isaac	1	3	2		
Lowe, Caleb	1	4	4		
Isbel, Wm	1	1	2		1
Davis, Ephrm	1		2		
Petty, Wm	1	3	2		
Woodforth, Jos	2	5	6		6
Hamby, Jno	1	2	3		
Choat, Seybert	1	1	2		
Slaton, Ben	1	1	1		
Mongomery, Jno	1	3	4		
Laws, Wm	1	2	5		
Boman, Amy		1	4		
Ward, Sarah			3		
Foster, George	1	3	4		2
Branham, Ben	2		3		
Ward, Jno	1	2	3		
Paterson, Agnes	2	2	4		
Patterson, Jno	1		2		
Mitchell, Wm	1	3	3		
Stephens, Jno	1	1	2		
Hill, Jas	1	3	4		
Elledge, Jacob	3	4	3		
Parks, Aron	1	3	1		
Elledge, Jos	1		2		
Allen, Sam	3	1	4		
Thomas, Notly	1	3	3		
Keller, Jno	1				
Walker, Patty		2	3		
Gilbert, Gideon	5		3		
Sheppard, Thom	1	4	3		
Mays, Reuben	1	2	2		
Hays, Jesse	2	2	2		1
Williams, Jot	2	2	5		
Sanders, Julius	1		1		
Williams, Jno	1		2		
Jones, Geo	3	4	4		
West, Sam	1				
Chanler, Mary			1		
Chanler, Eliz			2		
Shoat, Saybon, Jr	1		3		
FOURTEENTH COMPANY.					
Williams, Jo	1	3	4		
Israel, Jos	1	1	7		
Roy, Jos	3	4	4		
Wilmouth, Ezekl	2		5		
Snow, Jacob	1	3	3		
Franklin, Jacob	1	3	2		

NAME OF HEAD OF FAMILY.	Free white males of 16 years and upward, including heads of families.	Free white males under 16 years.	Free white females, including heads of families.	All other free persons.	Slaves.
FOURTEENTH COMPANY—continued.					
Lewis, Elias	3		2		
Franklin, Jno	1	1	4		
Umfrey, Isaac T	1	1	3		
Wolf, Danl	1	2	3		
Watts, Wm	1		4		
McCartey, Jos	1		4		
Davis, Lewis	1	2	6		
Snows, Henry	1	4	6		
Jennins, John	1	2	3		
Snow, Obed	1	1	2		
Holbrooks, Robt	1	2	1		
Snow, Wm	1		2		
Kennedy, Wm	2	2	6		
Thomson, Jo	2	2	5		
Tomson, Jo., Jr	1		1		
Tomson, Jas	1		1		
Kennedy, Saml	1	3	4		
Bench, Danl	1	2	4		
Haris, Dabney	2	3	6		
Austin, David	1	5	2		
Robison, Jno	1	1	2		
Franklin, Jesse	1		2		5
Franklin, Shad	1	1	2		
Underwood, Thom	1		1		
Underwood, Jno	1	1	1		
Underwood, Jno, Jr	2	1	1		
Watson, Jno	1	3	2		
Kirby, Henry	1		3		
Kirby, Kit	1	2	1		
McCloud, Wm	1	3	5		
Underwood, Wm	1	2	2		1
Hutson, Jno	1	2	5		
Williams, Jno	1	1	3		
Dugless, Andw	1	2	5		
Cuningham, Wm	1	3	4		
Rama, Wm	4	1	5		
Rama, Jos	1	1	4		
Rama, Ben	1	2	4		
Arnol, Thom	1	2	4		
Gallion, Jacob	2	3	2		
Gallion, Sam	1		1		
James, Abram	3	4	6		
Douglas, Edwd	1	1	4		
James, Wm	1	1	1		
Eldridge, Wm	1	2			
Duglass, Thom	1		1		
Franklin, Bernard	2	1	5		12
Franklin, George	1	1	6		
Johnson, Robt	1	1	1		
Canterbury, Anne		3	1		
Scott, Jno	1	1	5		
Ross, Jno	1	3	1		
Isaacs, Rachel	1	2	2		
Kenedy, Mark	1		3		
FIFTEENTH COMPANY.					
Forester, Charles	1	4	5		
Barns, Reuben	1		3		
Sanders, Cornelius	2	4	3		
Barns, Solomon	4	2	6		
Scott, Thom	1	3	3		
Hood, Aron	1	1	2		
Philips, Wm, Jr	1	1	2		
Philips, Thos	1				
Philips, Wm	1	1	1		
Sanders, Shad	1		2		
Sanders, Wm	1	3	1		
Sanders, Wm, Jr	1		1		
Spradling, Jas	3		1		
Kirby, Wm	2	1	2		2
Kirby, Jno	1		2		
Scott, Rd	1		3		
Kirby, Jo	1	3	1		
Scott, Mary	1	2	1		1
Russell, Wm	1	6	4		
Monday, Wm	1	1	7		
Monday, Frank	1	1	3		
Monday, Tho	1		3		
Drew, Jesse	2	2	2		
Leech, Jno	2		1		
Chambers, Jno	1		1		
Chambers, Wm H	1	1	3		
Hatton, Chas	1		3		
Russell, Ben	1	2	3		
Hines, Eliz		1	6		
McGee, Jno	2	1	6		
Chambers, Jno	1	1	2		
Carson, Sam	1	4	4		
Sloan, Sam, Junyr	1	1	1		
McGee, Sally			2		
Boyd, Robt	2	2	1		
Boyd, Robt., Jr	1	2	2		
Boyd, Wm	1	3	1		
Boyd, Thom	1	1	3		

NAME OF HEAD OF FAMILY.	Free white males of 16 years and upward, including heads of families.	Free white males under 16 years.	Free white females, including heads of families.	All other free persons.	Slaves.
FIFTEENTH COMPANY—continued.					
Hereford, Henry	2	7	2		
Vinson, Danl	1	1	2		
Meadow, James	1	1	2		
Scott, Nathan	1	4	2		
Munday, Sam	1	3	1		
Barns, John	1	2	5		
Sloan, Sam	1	1	4		
Wilson, Sam	1	5	1		
Barns, John	2	4	4		
Barns, Edwd	1	1	1		
Elledge, Isaac	2	2	5		
Sloan, Patrick	3	2	6		
Spradin, Charles	1	2	5		
Jones, Jno M	1	2	3		
Jones, Jos	1	3	2		
Robnet, Jas	1		2		
Brown, Geor., Es	2	3	5		1
Adams, Thom	1	1	2		
Chapman, John	1	3	5		
Chapman, Enoch	1	2	4		
Sanders, Jno	1	2	3		
Spradling, James	1		3		
Spurlock, Wm	1		1		
Whitten, Wm	1	3	3		
Brown, Edwin	1	5	2		
SIXTEENTH COMPANY.					
Bunyard, Jas., Es	1	5	3		
Grimes, Boston	1	2	4		
Custard, Jno	1	1	2		
Writer, Elir	1		7		
Writer, Michal	1		1		
Kisler, Olivick	3		1		
Burket, Jos	1	1	4		
Dick, Jno	1	3	5		
Reid, Jno	2	3	5		
Burket, David	1	2			
Kisler, Jos	1	2	2		
Wade, Thom	1	3	3		
Grove, Danl	1	1	1		
Jones, John	1	4	2		
Fouts, David	1	4	5		
Shirror, Christom	1	3	1		
Yonce, Laurence	1	1	2		
Carver, Jno	1	2	7		
Landers, Jacob	1	1	3		
Shirron, Christi, Sr	1	2	7		
Bowers, Jno	1	2	2		
Marsh, Aron	1	3	4		
Beasly, David	1		1		
Carvender, Patrick	1				
Goodman, Peter	1		3		
Crapeal, Peter	1	4	4		
Baker, Jas	1	4	1		2
Baker, Morry	1	4	5		
Smith, Alex	2		3		
Coons, Jno	1	2	5		1
Bumganer, Dan	1	1	4		
Miller, Jno	1		2		
Sheets, Jno	1	1	1		
Ray, Jesse	1	3	2		
Smith, Moses	1	5	2		
Locard, Jno	1	1	4		
King, Frank	2	1	3		
King, Jos	1		2		
King, Edwd	2	4	4		
Lewis, Gideon	2	2	5		
Reid, Stephen	3	2	5		
Vanwinkle, Jas	2	2	3		
Piniton, Micajah	1	1	2		
Little, Charls	1	1	4		
Weaver, Isaac	1	5	1		
Holinsworth, Vineon	1	5	3		
Jones, Vineon	1	2	2		
Jones, John	1	1	5		
Davis, Wm	1	1	4		
Jones, Wm	1	3	1		
May, Jacob	1	2	2		
Hubbard, Jacob	5	6	4		
Henson, Jno	1	2	7		
Munker, Jno	2	3	1		
Henson, Jas	1	3	2		
Henson, Paul	1	3			
Henson, Paul, Sr	1		2		
May, Abram	2		1		
Smith, Thom	1	3	4		
Barrier, Geo	1	2	4		
Cafinder, Matt	1		2		
Smith, Wm	1	4	7		
Piniton, Rd	1	3	2		
Lewis, Jas	1	2	1		
Osborn, Solomon	1	2	2		
Smith, Rd	1	3	3		
Henson, Richd	1	3	2		

MORGAN DISTRICT, WILKES COUNTY—Continued.

Name of head of family.	Free white males of 16 years and upward, including heads of families.	Free white males under 16 years.	Free white females, including heads of families.	All other free persons.	Slaves.
SIXTEENTH COMPANY—continued.					
Smith, Randol	1	2	6		
Sweeton, Wm	1	1	2		
Jonson, Jno	1	2	3		
Flanery, Jno	1	3	4		
Elkins, Wm	1	2	5		
Nolan, Sheppe	1	1	1		
Tyre, Geo	2	1	3		
SIXTEENTH COMPANY—continued.					
Sweeton, Chas	1	1	2		
Mitchell, Henry	2	5	4		
Bumgarner, Michal	1		1		
Mock, Fred	1	4	4		
Ellis, Peter	2	2	5		
Fouts, Jno	1	3	5		
Sturdy, Dolly			1		3
SIXTEENTH COMPANY—continued.					
Black, Frederick	1	1	4		
Grove, Jacob	3	2	4		
Stockerd, Michl	1				
Sheets, Henry	1		3		
Williams, Owen		3	5		
Reed, Robt	1	1	4		

NEWBERN DISTRICT, BEAUFORT COUNTY.

Name of head of family.	Free white males of 16 years and upward, including heads of families.	Free white males under 16 years.	Free white females, including heads of families.	All other free persons.	Slaves.
Jones, Josiah	1				
Sparrow, Samuel	2	2	2		3
Watson, John	1	2	2		
Campin, Thomas	1	1	4		3
Jones, William	1		4		
Tingle, Israel	1	3	2		
Harrington, John	2	4	3		
Creakmond, Edmond	1	1	3		
Harris, Judith	1		4		
Brothers, Samuel, Senr	2	1	2		
Squires, Amos, Senr	1		3		
Brothers, Joseph	1	1	2		
Muckleroy, Adam	3		5		
Curtis, John, Senr	2		3		
Holton, David	1	1	3		
Holton, James	1	4	2		1
Tingle, David	1	1	1		
Johnston, Abram, Senr					5
Jones, James, Senr	2	3	2		
Jones, Josiah, Senr	3	3	2		4
Jackson, Anna	3		4		
Wise, Matilda	1		3		
Wise, Joseph	1	3	2		
Rigs, James	1	1	6		
Slade, Henry	1	1	3		1
Wise, Johannes	1	4	2		
Harris, William	1	5	5		
Dowdy, Thomas	1		2		
Baker, Nathan	1	1	4		
Riggs, John	2	3	1		
Linton, Lemuel	1	3	2		
Dowdy, James, junr	2	3	5		
Dowdy, James, Senr	1		1		
Mews, John	1	4	4		
Riggs, Jemima	1	1	1		
McKinsey, David	1		3		
Dowdy, Elijah	1		2		
Dowdy, Samuel	1				
Dowdy, William	1		3		
Everit, Henry	2	1	1	2	1
Jones, William, Senr	3	4	4		
Missick, Joseph	1	4	2		
Dowdy, John	2	2	5		
Baker, Henry	1		4		
Linton, Luke	1	5	4		
Linton, Daniel	1	2	3		
Slade, William	1	2	1		
Everit, Robert	2	4	4		
Everit, Hugh	1				
Campin, Joseph	1				3
Campin, Robert	1				3
Jasper, Jonathan	2	2	4		8
Pringle, James	1	4	4		
Everit, James	1		3		1
Rew, Mark	1		4		
Pate, Isaac	2		1		1
Equals, George	2	1	1		1
Hodge, John	1				
Hodge, Zear			1	4	
Harvey, Richard	1		2		
Harvey, James	1		2		
Jones, Robert	1				
Leath, Elizabeth			2		17
Watson, Burgase	1	2	3		
Fulsher, Perigaine	1	1	2		2
Everit, Thomas	1		3		
Johnston, Sarah			6		
Jones, David	1	1	1		
Jones, Francis	3		2		24
Curtis, Ann				6	
Dowdy, Samuel	1				
Deer, Ann		2	1		
Squires, Lydia			1		
Denny, Patsey		3	2		
Scarborough, Benjamin	1	1	4		
Rollins, John	1		3		7
Respess, Richard	1	3	3		8
Dunbar, James	1	1	2		4
Respess, John	2		1		2
Grigs, John	1	3			
Marshall, Thomas	2		1		1
Patter, Sarah		1	2		
Dixon, Thomas	1	2			
Moor, Samuel	1				2
Lee, Benjamin	1	3	1		
Lee, Shadrach	1	1	1		
Banks, Lilleston	1	3	1		
Williams, Thomas	2	1			
Gregory, Samuel	1		1		
Locker, Henry	1		1		
Harrington, Joseph	1		1		
Holton, Richard	1	2	4		
Camper, Joseph	1	1	1		4
Rowe, Kitley	1	1	3		
Bennett, Josiah	1		2		1
Martindale, Henry	2		3		
Young, William	2		3		
Davis, Thomas	1	1	2		3
Everage, Jonathan	1	1	1		
Silverthorn, Bustin	2	2	3		
Wiet, Nathaniel	2		1		
Respess, Thomas	2		2		76
Collins, Timothy	1	2	1		2
Bennett, Leah	2		1	1	3
Rolls, Sarah	1	1	2		
Prescoat, John	1	1	3		
Staplefoot, Keziah	1		4		2
Peede, Henry	2	2	3		
Lewis, John	1	3	2		
Lewis, Joseph	1		3		
Keel, Ruth	1		3		
Whitus, Badson	2	2	4		2
Wainwright, Kezy		2	4		
Smiddick, David	2	5	5		
Lambert, William	1		4		
Marshal, John	1		1		1
Keel, John	1		3		
Warren, Edward	1	1			
Adams, Peter	1		1		
Equals, Frederick	1	1	4		
Campain, James	1		2	1	2
Pritchard, Abram	1	1	1		6
Wood, John	1	1	4		
Bennett, John	1	1	1		
Taylor, Jacob	1	1	3		
Dazer, Josiah	1		4	2	2
Equals, William	1		4		
Robinson, Luke	1	3	6		16
Tripp, Dorcas			4		
Tetterton, William	3	2	3		
Purser, James	2	2	3		
Brady, Benjamin	2	3	3		3
Lee, William	1	1	1		
Clark, John	1	2	5		
Clark, William	1	3	2		
Mayo, Thomas	2		4		
Campaign, Mary		2	5	3	2
Mayo, Solomon	2	3	3		
Mixon, Zedekiah	1	2	4		
Slade, Henry	1		3		
Barnett, John	2		2		
Davis, Arthur	1	2	2		
Veal, David	1	1	3		1
Blount, Frederick	1	1	2		
Spring, Aaron	1	1	3		
Spring, Abram	1	1	3		
Tutterton, Kizzy					5
Pringle, Charles	1		4		
Harvey, James, junr	1		2		
Farris, William	2		5	1	7
Bond, John	1	3	3		7
Pritchard, Abram	1	4	3		
Bond, Robert	2	1	4		8
Wallace, John	1		4	3	4
White, Solomon	2	2	2		10
Hudson, John	2		2		1
Vowse, Thomas	1	2	1		
Pritchard, Philip	1	2	5		
Landing, Richard	1	1	6		
Harvey, Thomas	1		2		
Harvey, Richard	1		2		
Harvey, James, Senr	1		2		
Langley, Lee	1	3	3		
Pringle, George	1	1	5		
Purser, James, Senr	2	1	5		1
Purser, Robert	1	2	7		1
Gainer, Samuel	2	2	3		5
Purser, David, jur	1	1	3		1
Purser, David, Senr	1	1	2		
Cotanch, Malicah	1	2	3		
Broomfield, James	2	1	1		
Whitus, Simon, Senr	2		2		
Whitus, Simon, jur	1	2	2		
Capps, John	1	1	3		3
Whitus, Henry	1	3	1		
Purser, Elizabeth	1	1	2		
Hodge, Leah	1		1	4	
Turner, Rebecca			2		
Baker, John	1		1		
Jarrod, Forbes	3	1	1		8
Crawford, Charles	4		1		21
Bonner, Sarah			6		
Moor, William	1	1	1		4
Healy, Catharine				3	
Foster, Christopher	1	1	1		
Purnal, Zachariah	1		1		
Trippe, Robert	3	3	3		13
Pilly, John	1	4	4	1	1
Smith, Thomas	1	3	2		17
Adams, Isaac	1	1	1		
Orrils, William	1	1	4		
Robinson, Hannah			5		
Ackley, Mary		5	4		1
Dixon, James	2	4	2		
Griffith, Edward	1	1	3		17
Stilly, John	2	1	2		
Cox, Abram	2	3	3		
Dixon, Benjamin	1	6	5		
Daw, William	1	3	1		4
Bennet, John, Senr	1	1	4		
Futon, Thomas	2	1	4		
Rowe, Joshua	1		3		1
Dowtry, Elisha	1	4	3		6
Lyons, Joseph	2	1	2		
Sermon, Thomas	1				
Fulsher, Morning		1	2		11
Blango, Sarah					5
Blango, Dinah					6
Conner, Merion					3
Blango, Thomas					10
Lee, Mary			1		
Moor, Rachel					2
Harris, Stephen	2	1	2		
Jones, Thomas	2		1		1
Hollingsworth, Mary			4		3
Prescoat, Benjamin	2	1	5		
Hagins, Christopher	1		1		
Surls, Covinton	1	4	4		
Everit, Thomas	2	1	4		
Jones, Jesse	1	1	2		
Dowty, Elisha, junr	1	1	2		
Garrot, Benjamin	1	1	1		11
Hagins, Darby	1	2	1		
Miller, Daniel	2				5
Orrell, Asa	1		2		
Cox, Aaron	1	1	3		
Adams, Joshua	1	1	3		
Smith, Jarvis	1				
Evit, John	1	3	6		
Harrison, Jesse	1		6		
Satterthwaite, Jeremiah	1		3		
Orrill, Stephen	1	1	5		
Walker, Thomas	1	1	4		1
Gallaway, William	2	4	5		
Jones, Walter	1	2	3		
Wright, Stephen	1	1	1		9
Rowe, Robert	1	3	2		
Rowe, Jesse	1	1	3		
Hill, Joshua	1	1	4		1
Dunn, Francis	2	2	2		
Shute, Giles	1	3	6		
Thomason, Matthew	3	4	2		
Taylor, John	2	2	3		
Rowe Richard	1	2	7		
Hollywell, Irey	1				

NEWBERN DISTRICT, BEAUFORT COUNTY—Continued.

NAME OF HEAD OF FAMILY.	Free white males of 16 years and upward, including heads of families.	Free white males under 16 years.	Free white females, including heads of families.	All other free persons.	Slaves.	NAME OF HEAD OF FAMILY.	Free white males of 16 years and upward, including heads of families.	Free white males under 16 years.	Free white females, including heads of families.	All other free persons.	Slaves.	NAME OF HEAD OF FAMILY.	Free white males of 16 years and upward, including heads of families.	Free white males under 16 years.	Free white females, including heads of families.	All other free persons.	Slaves.
Hill, Lazarus	1	1	1			Priggin, William	1		3			McClanny, John	1	2	1		
Mall, Moses	1				9	Downs, William	1		2			Timmons, Thomas	1	1	2		
Wilkinson, Aaron	1				4	Edwards, Britton	1					Jones, James	1	3	1		
Whitus, Simon	1	3	3			Ginn, George	1	1	4			Reed, Joseph	1	1	1		
Gideons, Moses	1	1	1			Edwards, Emanuel	1		2			Whitacre, Abram	1	3	4		
Adams, Elizabeth	2	2	1		1	Palmer, George	1	2	2			Crawford, Elizabeth	1		2		
Pierce, Hezekiah	1		7		5	Denby, Samuel	2	2	2			Jones, John R	1	1	3		
Price, Shadrach	1		1			Bryan, Thomas	1	1	3			Lee, George	1		1		
Moor, John P.			5			Buck, William	1		2			White, Thomas	1				
Blango, Solomon				1		King, Harmon	1		2			Lee, Elizabeth			2		
Johnston, Joshua			6			Palmer, William	1					Lanier, Hoziah	1		3		2
Carroll, William			4			Stephen	1		1			Carrow, Lydia			3		
Keys, Milley			4			Gladson, Dempsey	1	1	2			Cole, Richard	1	1	3		
Rose, John	2	1	4		1	Gladson, John	1		4			Singleton, Bethier		1	3		
Smith, Dolly			2			Gladson, George	1		2			Swanner, Jesse	1	3	3		
Godley, John	1	5	3		4	Lanier, William	1	3	2		9	Holland, Philip	2	1	4		
Worsley, Thomas	2		4		3	Lathum, Agnes	2	2	4		10	Blount, John G.	6	4	7		74
Harding, Stephen	2	1	1			Hinton, Isaac	1	1	2		2	Blackledge, Richard	1		2		
Richards, Ralph	2		4			Nowis, Philip	1		2		4	Arnett, Silas W	1				1
Walls, Joseph	2		1			Little, Josiah	2	1	4			Parker, Catherine		1	5		
Godley, Nathan, Senr	5		2		12	Floyde, John	1	2	2			Ryan, Elizabeth			2	1	
Pierce, Lazarus	1	3	3		20	Jackson, Mary		3	3			Robinson, Thomas	1		2		
Laughinghouse, Thomas, Senr	2		2			Floyde, Griffith	1				4	Jerkins, Mary	1	2	3		
Morris, Elisha	1	3	2	1		Williams, Godfrey	1	2	2		2	Burr, William	2	1	2		
Holmes, John				6		Taylor, Lydia	1	2	2			Gardner, Letitia			3		
Bartlett, Thomas	3	1	2			Floyde, Simeon	1	1	3		9	Miller, Henry	1		1		
Hill, Harmond	2	3	2		10	Griffin, Amaziah	1	3	2		2	Bertie, Reuben	2				4
Edwards, James	2	1	3		1	Wilson, Seth	1	1			3	Hatridge, Robert	1				1
Edwards, Walker	1	3	4			Freeman, James	1		2		1	French, Daniel	1		1		1
Blount, Lewis	2	6	4	1	2	Crandol, James	1	2	2		3	Young, John	1	2	2		8
Blount, Nathan	1	4	6		11	White, Daniel	1	1	3		2	Mullen, Thomas	1	1	2		2
Keel, Nathan	1	1	1			Fowler, George	1		1			Carraway, Joseph	2	1	3		7
Blount, Reading	1	1	2		8	Williams, Thomas	1		1		3	Stewart, William	2	1	3		1
Knox, Frances	2	3	2			Lathum, John	1		2			Sims, Keziah		1	3		1
Summers, Rachel		1	2		3	Jackson, Josias	1	2	1			Hodge, Samuel	1	3	1		3
Richards, Elizabeth			1		4	Davis, William	1	2	3		3	Greenwood, Nathan	1	2	1		
Buck, Francis	2	3	3			McDonald, Randal	2	2	2		8	Nowland, Kitty			2		
Buck, Isaac, Senr	2	1	4			Lenier, Martha	1		2		8	Horn, George	1	1	4		6
Nobles, Isaac	2	1	1			Lanier, Robert	1				12	Osborn, John	1		2		1
Hardin, Israel	1	3	1		1	Jolly, Solomon	1	4	4		3	Howard, John	1		2		1
Owens, Stephen	1	2	4		4	Wilson, Seth	1	2			3	Cherry, Charles	3	3	4		3
Pattin, Ann		1	2		7	Williams, Thomas, Senr	1	1	4			Kennedy, John	4		2		30
Blount, Abigail		3	4		8	Williams, James	1	3	5			Floyde, Gresham	1	2	1		5
Dunbar, Robert	2	2	2		2	Wells, John	3	1	3			Floyde, Peter	1				4
Raifield, Isaac	1	3	4			Crawford, William	1		4		2	Floyde, Elizabeth	1				6
Buck, Edward	1	5	2		1	Short, Markum	1	2	7		1	Cooke, Charles	2		4		12
Taunt, Jesse	1		3			Gainer, Joseph	1	1	3		12	Kies, Nathaniel	2	2	3	2	6
Holmes, Edward				1		Little, Thomas	1	2	2		1	Pickett, Joseph	1	1	1		2
Edwards, Isaac, Senr	2	2	5			Brown, Ephraim	1	3	3			Groves, Daniel	2	2	2		5
Grey, James	1	2	3			Dean, Margaret		2	2			Baldwin, Ann	2	1	2		3
Bright, Elizabeth			1			White, John	3		3			Sheridan, Dennis	1				1
Wilkinson, John	1	2	1			Hull, Samuel	1	1	3			McDonald, Andrew	2		1		
Caffy, Abner	1		1			Davis, Benjamin	1	1	3			Lowry, John	1		3		
Smith, Joseph	1		1			Kiel, James	1	3	3			Clark, George	1	1	4		
Barnes, Jeremiah	1	1	3			Legget, Jeremiah	1	2	2			Howell, Elias	4	4	2		3
Blount, Thomas	1	2	2		3	Bowen, John	1	1	2			Fullington, Mary	1	1	2		1
Kinson, Anthony, Senr	1	1	2			Bowen, Richard	2	2	3			Story, Mary			3		
Buck, Isaac, junr	1		4			Spears, James	1	5	2			Rose, Mary			3		5
Slade, Major	2	4	4		6	Hodges, James	1	2	2		1	Congleton, John	2				4
Godley, Elias	1	3	2		3	Tetterton, Joseph	1	1	2			Congleton, Jane		2	3		2
Reed, Sarah			3			Pinkum, James	1	2	3			Hilliard, Gersham	1		2		5
Butler, William	1		3			Anderson, Joseph	1	3	1			Worden, John	2		2		2
Long, Nathan	1	1	3			Brown, Andrew	1	1	5			Pickett, Jane			1		2
Pierce, Joseph	1	2	6		8	Warren, William	1	1	3			Groves, William	1	3	2		12
Edwards, David	1	2	3			Jackson, Jemima	1	1	3			Parker, Green	1	2	2		1
Edwards, Isaac, junr	1	1	2			Brown, Eli	1		1			Jones, Roger	1		1		2
Richards, Thomas	1	2	5		1	Lee, James	1	3	2			Lewey, John	1		1		
Nobles, John	1		2			Cherry, Samuel	1	2	1		1	Duso, Leonard	1				8
Godley, Nathan	1	4	3		2	Cherry, John, Senr	3		2			Symons, Hannah			2		
Grice, Benjamin	1		5			Cherry, John, Junr	1		1		1	Melonay, Laughlin	3				2
Grice, Frederick	2		3		29	Beechum, John	1	1	3			Jones, David	1	1	2		5
Vines, Samuel	1		2		3	Merry, Ann	1	1	3			Shoemaker, David	1	1	3		1
Lewis, Jonathan	1	2	3			Ball, James	1		1			Eastwood, James	2		9		9
Laughinghouse, Andrew	1	1	3			Ball, Mary			2			Cassoe, Peter	3		2	1	4
Pierce, George	1	4	3		5	Hodge, Thomas	1	2	2			Peacock, Isaac	3		5		
Laughinghouse, John	1	4	2		1	Hodge, Moses	1	2	3			Hurton, William	1		2		
Grice, Reading	2		2		7	Brown, Jacob	1	1	3		1	White, Milly			2		
Creamer, James	1	3	2			Woollard, Absolam	1		2			Loomiss, Jonah					7
Smith, Thomas	1	2	3			Fowler, Esther			2			Harvey, Augustus	1	1	1		15
Wall, Joel	1		2		4	Tutterton, Sarah			1			Maxwell, James	1		1		3
Smith, Benjamin	1	1	3			Jackson, Kizzy		2	3			Potts, Ralph	1				9
Muckleroy, William	1	3	3			Straddle, Dorcas	1	1	3			Hawrahan, Walter	2	1			20
Kinion, Anthony	1		2			Barrot, Abigail			3			Nowis, Willowby	1		1		
Palmer, James	1	2	3			Hodges, Henry	1					Brown, Thomas	1				12
Lee, Timothy	1		3			Woollard, John, junr	1	3	3		4	Bonner, Henry	1		2		51
Blount, Bryan	1	3	3		13	Woollard, Samuel	2	3	3			Bonner, James, Senr	1	2	4		51
Blount, Reading	1	1	2		4	Woollard, Jeremiah	1	5	4			Bonner, Henry S	3	3	3		6
Edwards, Walker	1					Woollard, John, Senr	1	1	3			Owins, Brannock	2	1	2		2
Edwards, John	1		2			Woollard, Willowby	1		1			Roundtree, Cadir	2		1		
Edwards, William	1	1	2			Hayes, Alexander	2		3			Bonner, James, Junr	2				2
Pollard, Jacob	1		6			Sparkman, Jesse	1	2	2			Bonner, Joseph	1				4
Nelson, Nathan	2	2	3			Walker, Daniel	1	1	3			Hendrixson, Salathiel	1				
Aicklin, Joshua	2	1	5			Walker, Thomas	1		3			Horton, James	1				
Worsley, Joseph	1				1	Walker, William	1		2			Worsley, Thomas	1	3	2		7
Ottery, James	1	1	1			McKiel, Matthew	1	3	3			Lucus, Henry	2	2	2		11
						Singleton, William	1		2			Jones, William	1				4
						Ferrill, Leah		2	1			Hair, Mary	2	1	4		26

NEWBERN DISTRICT, BEAUFORT COUNTY—Continued.

NAME OF HEAD OF FAMILY.	Free white males of 16 years and upward, including heads of families.	Free white males under 16 years.	Free white females, including heads of families.	All other free persons.	Slaves.
Smaw, Henry	1	1	3		5
Alligood, John	1		2	1	1
Smaw, John	2	2	2		9
Beezley, Thomas, Senr	4	3	4		8
Ellison, Alley	4	8	2	4	30
Vines, Thompson	1	3	4		8
Campbell, James	1		1	1	
McKeel, Edmund	2	4	3		17
Jefferson, Obadiah	1	1	4		
Cutler, Robert	3	3	5		
Elliott, Peter	1	2	5		
Tancred, George	2		2		4
Cone, Dorcas			1		
Brady, Henry	1	1	4	1	
Langley, Stephen, Senr	2		2		
Jefferson, Ann		1	2		
Woollard, Michael	2	4	2		
Bryan, Mary			5		
Alligood, Jacob	1	3	5		1
Alligood, Francis	2	4	7		
Bainer, Richard, Senr	1		2		7
Bainer, John	2	1	6		5
Congleton, Thomas	1	2	3		
Congleton, James	3		2	1	
Woollard, Absalom	1	1	4		4
Chester, Martha		1	3		
Beaman, Mary			2		
Jefferson, Martha			3		
Elliot, William	1	2	5		
Ellis, Robert	1	1	1		
Brock, Elizabeth			2		
Sutton, Peter				1	
Pluto, William				2	
McKeel, James	1	4	6	1	4
Sivils, John	1		2		
Bright, Mary			2		
Smith, John	1		2		
Woollard, Elizabeth	1	4	2		
Brady, Rachel	1	2	3		
Eborn, Catherine		1	3		
Pilley, Thomas	3	2	3		2
Lewis, Archibald	1	1	2		
Hawkins, Abier			1	2	
Whitehead, Willis	1	1	1		1
Lewis, Abigail		1	3		
Bocks, John	1	2	1		2
Jones, Elizabeth			1	1	1
Cutler, Moses	2	1	5		
Cone, Stephen	1				
Hawkins, Major	1	3	4		
Cutler, Aaron	1		1		
Chancey, Samuel	2	2	2		7
Boyde, William	1	3	3		6
Cutler, John	2	2	4		2
Chester, Samuel	1				
Woollard, Covinton	1	1	3		
Woollard, Coleman	1		1		
Worsley, William	2		2	1	
Sulivan, Richard	1		1		
Boyde, Thomas	2		2		5
Brock, Lawson	1		1		
Perkins, James	1	1	1		
Langley, Stephen	1		3		
Barrow, Thomas	1	1	2		3
North, Edward	1	2	3		
Hawkins, Benjamin	1	3	3		
Burbage, John	1	1	2		
Little, Jesse	1	2	2	1	1
Putnall, Stephen	1	1	4		5
Tancred, John	1		1		
Groves, William	1				
Brewer, William	1	1	5		
Wallace, John	1	1	1		1
Woollard, William	1	2	2		
Congleton, William	1	1	2		
Campbell, William	1				
Lixton, William	1				
Woollard, Jasper	1		3		
Sears, Philip	1				
Bainer, Richard	1	3	1		3
Horn, Mary			2		
McKeel, Elizabeth			4		

NAME OF HEAD OF FAMILY.	Free white males of 16 years and upward, including heads of families.	Free white males under 16 years.	Free white females, including heads of families.	All other free persons.	Slaves.
Juley, Arcey					1
Perkins, William	1	1	3	1	1
Brown, William	3		3		16
Roulhac, P. G.	2	1	2		19
Alderson, Thomas	1	2	3		20
Lanier, John	1	4	6		15
Smallwood, Charles	1		2		2
Woodward, Isaiah	1		1		6
Martin, Lucy			1		
Willis, Samuel	1		3		10
McAbe, Ann		4	3		
Archibald, John	2	1	5		1
Alderson, Ann		2	4		2
Thomson, Margaret		1	2		
Stewart, Robert	1	3	2		
Langley, George	1	2	4		1
Conde, Mary	1	3	2		
Tunnell, William	1	2	1		
McAbe, James	1	1	2		
Smith, Mary			2		
Few, William	1		2		
Trotaban, Mary		1	3		
Horn, Susannah			2		
Rogers, Thomas	1		4		2
Freeman, Lucy		1	1		
Dowlin, Edward	1				
Gautier, Joseph	1	1	2		
Winley, Aaron	2		4		6
Swan, Arthur	1	2	1		9
Whitley, Arthur	1	1	2		
Whitley, Arthur, Senr	4	1	5	1	
Condre, Dennis	1	1	2		2
Hammon, Hewell	1	2	3		1
Walsh, William	1	2	4		
Archibald, James	2	2	3		7
Benton, Bailey	1	2	5		
Williams, Francis	1		2		
Mixon, Elijah	2	5	2		
Condre, John	3	4	6		
Winley, Israel	4	1	3		8
Adams, Henry	1	1	3		5
Adams, Abram	1		1	1	
Adams, James	1		1		4
Smith, James, Senr	1		3	1	
Smith, James, junr	1		3		1
Wood, John	1	3	3		1
Abell, Arthur	1	1	2		2
Hammond, Levi	1		5		
Adams, Josias	2	1	3		2
Barrow, William	1		2		5
James, William	1	1	1		
Smith, Jeremiah	1	2	3		
Brock, John	2	1	5		
Adams, Samuel	1		1	2	
Adams, Elijah	1		1		
Cordin, Thomas	2	1	3		11
Caloge, Peter	1				
Windbey, Moses	1	1	2		2
Fullerton, Andrew	1	1		1	1
Harvey, John	2	3	3		2
Archibald, Nathaniel	1	2	2		4
Clifford, William	2		2		2
Ormond, Wyriot	2				2
Williams, Thomas	1	1	2	2	
Liscomb, John	1	1	2		
Moignaw, J. L.	1	1	3		3
Price, William	2	1	4		3
Lathum, James	1		2		1
Hammond, John	1				
Horn, William				1	
Mason, Christopher	1	1	2		
Price, Enoch	2	1	2		2
Ross, Francis	1	2	4		
Foreman, Michael	1		2		1
Blount, Joshua	1				
Smith, Margaret		1	1		
Turner, John					3
Brayboy, John				1	6
Hammond, John	1		1		8
Jones, John	4	6	5		
Hammond, John B	2	1	2		1

NAME OF HEAD OF FAMILY.	Free white males of 16 years and upward, including heads of families.	Free white males under 16 years.	Free white females, including heads of families.	All other free persons.	Slaves.
Equals, Joseph					1
Hammond, Philip	1	1	1		1
Sanderlane, Mary		1	3		
Asbell, Whitnum	1		2		
Thomson, Elias	2		2		
Whitley, William	1	1	2		1
Lind, Dorcas			1		2
Cogdell, Richard	2	1	2		5
Thornton, William	1	1	2		
Smaw, Henry	2		2		14
Clifford, John	1				
Jackson, Eleazer	3	2	7		1
Kelly, Charles	1		1		
Hamilton, John	1	4	8		
Girkin, Benjamin	3		2		
Sinnett, Elizabeth	1	2	2		
Jones, Walter	1	2	3		
Waters, Amos	3	1	3		
Waters, John	1	1	5		
Garrott, John	2		4		
Squires, Appleton	1	2	6		
Vandannel, Edward	3	2	2		1
Ready, Peter	1	1	2		2
Risbey, Thomas	1		1		
Miller, Nathan	1	1	5		
Gergainus, Elizabeth	1		2		
Howren, John	1	1	3		
Garrett, Thomas	1	1	2		
Sulivan, Lambeth	1	2	4		
Martin, William	1	3	5		
Lilley, Joseph	1	2	3		
Martin, Elizabeth		1	2		
McDonough, John	1	1	3		
Ross, Benjamin	1	6	4		
Boyde, William, Esqr	3	1	5		15
Barrow, John	3	5	5		7
McDonough, Henry	1	2	2		1
Lathum, Phineas	1	3	2		
Moore, John	2	5	2		
Waters, Zachariah	1	2	3		
Waters, Jeremiah	1		4		
Waters, Winifred	1				
Lathum, Charles	1	3	3		1
Howrin, Redmond	1				
Boyde, Thomas	2	3	3		16
Boyde, William	1	2	2		3
Chester, Henry	1		5		
Harris, John	1	3	3		
Everit, John	1	1	3		
Bowen, John	1	4	3		1
Kelly, Labin	1	2	3		
Risbey, Thomas	1		2		
Donnell, Arthur	1		2		
Risbey, Robert	1				
Risbey, Langley	1		1		
Ross, Elijah	1	1	7		
Gailer, Benjamin	1	1	3		
Ready, Alexander	1	1	2		7
Donnell, John	1				
Donnell, Edward	1				
Stubbs, William	1	1	3		
Odin, Charles	1	2	1		5
Odin, Richard	1				2
Donnell, James	1		3		1
Garrott, Shadrach	1	1	2		
Waters, Jesse	1	2	2		
Waters, David	1	1	1		
Waters, Frederick	1				
Waters, William	1				
Kelly, Custis	1	2	4		
Girkin, Charles	1	2	2		
Jackson, Thomas	1	2	2		
Waters, Isaac	1	3	3		2
Waters, John	1	3	2		
Hamilton, Lazarus	1		1		
Wallace, Thomas	1	2	3		2
Jones, Jonathan	1				
Risbey, Richard	1				
Stilley, Michael	1	1	2		
Girkin, Jeremiah	2	1	3		
Jones, William	1				
Lathum, Noah	1	2	2		

NEWBERN DISTRICT, CARTERET COUNTY.

NAME OF HEAD OF FAMILY.	Free white males of 16 years and upward, including heads of families.	Free white males under 16 years.	Free white females, including heads of families.	All other free persons.	Slaves.
Hill, Isaac	1	5	2		36
Davis, Solomon W	4	3	4		10
Hunter, Lebbeus	2	1	3		7
Stephens, Asa	1		1	1	
Howard, William L	1	2	3		
West, George	1	3	4		
Picket, Oliver	3				
Brigs, John	1				
Hackell, Armstead	3		3		6

NAME OF HEAD OF FAMILY.	Free white males of 16 years and upward, including heads of families.	Free white males under 16 years.	Free white females, including heads of families.	All other free persons.	Slaves.
Ostean, John, Senr	1	1	4		
Osteen, John, junr	1	1	3		
Weeks, Theophilus	1	2	6		
Pounder, Richard	1	2	3		
Prescott, Willowby	1	2	5		
Lovick, John	2	2	6		1
Freshwater, Thomas	1	2	2		
Miller, John	1		5		
Weeks, Sarah			3		

NAME OF HEAD OF FAMILY.	Free white males of 16 years and upward, including heads of families.	Free white males under 16 years.	Free white females, including heads of families.	All other free persons.	Slaves.
Weeks, Edward	1	1	5		
Weeks, Levy	1	3	4		
Weeks, Robert	1				
Weeks, Stephen	1				
Sanders, William		2	4		
Stelly, Ephraim	2	2	1		
Green, Samuel	2	2	4		2
Osteen, William	1	3	2		
Smith, Richard	1	1	2		

NEWBERN DISTRICT, CARTERET COUNTY—Continued.

NAME OF HEAD OF FAMILY.	Free white males of 16 years and upward, including heads of families.	Free white males under 16 years.	Free white females, including heads of families.	All other free persons.	Slaves.
Easlick, Isaac	1	2	3		2
Wilson, Andrew	2	2	3		2
Weeks, Jabis, Senr	3		2		
Weeks, Jabis, junr	1	2	3		1
Meadows, Jacob	1	4	4		
Garvey, Thomas	1	1	1		
Brice, Ross	1		3		
Brice, James	1	1	4		1
Hatchell, Willis	1		5		1
Prescot, Aaron	2	1	1		
Smith, Jesse	1				
Hatchell, William	2	1	3		3
Prescot, Elizabeth			2		
Nelson, John	1	2	3		3
Jarman, Littleton	1	2	6		
Hatchell, Richard	1	1	4		
Hatchell, Henry	1	1	1		
Harrington, Philip	1	1			
Smith, Sarah			2		
Osteen, Samuel	2		2		
Osteen, David	1	3	2		
Ostean, Jesse	1		1		
Melson, Levin	1	1	1		
Thomson, Margaret			2		
Fearn, William	1	2	2		4
Hill, Joseph	1	2	1		22
Wiley, Sarah		2	4		
Taylor, Stephen	1		4		
Blackhouse, Allen	1				5
Philips, William	2	4	1		
Beechum, John	1	1	3		
Harris, Thomas	1	2	4		
Cowell, Butler	2	3	2		2
Culliner, William	1	1	3		
Harvey, Marcum	1	2	3		
Simson, Joshua	2	1	3		
Weeks, Abram	1				
Bourdin, William, junr	1				5
Hill, Isaac, Senr	2	1	3		10
Russell, David	2	3	6		4
Hall, Samuel, Senr	1		7		
Hall, Samuel, junr	1				
Hall, Nathaniel	1		2		
Hill, William	1		1		1
Rew, Southy	1		3		2
Taylor, Richard	1	1	1		
Lane, James	1	2	3		
Nicholson, Risder	1	1	4		
Sanders, Thomas	3	2	3		
Wallace, Reuben	1	1	1		4
Wallace, Asa	1				1
Marine, John	1	2	1		
Marine, William	1				
Taylor, Isaac	1	1	2		3
Joiner, Nathan	1		3		
Smith, Solomon	1				
Russel, William	1	3	1	1	2
Russel, Habacuck	1		1		
Brace, William	2	4	5		
Harris, Elizabeth			2		
Maginis, Jonas	1	1	3		
Bell, Winifred			2		
Black, Martin					2
Wilson, Thomas	1		3		
Sanders, Winnifred			3		
Bell, Newell	1	6	1		3
Bell, Abner	2	3	3		2
Bell, Newell, Senr	1	3	3		
Bell, Malicah	7	1	3		18
Peltier, Jeremiah	1	1	3		
Yates, Charles	1	2	4		
Hill, Thomas	1	1	3		
Ogilsby, Joseph	1	1	4		
Garner, William	1	4	3		1
Bell, Joseph, Senr	1	5	4		
Taylor, Levin	1	2	3		
Bell, Mary			2		1
Penevil, Price	1		2		
Temple, Thomas	3		4		
Ogilsby, Thomas	2	2	3		3
Freize, George	1	2	6		
Gardner, John	3	1	4		
Lewis, Mary	1		1		26
Simmons, William	1	3	4		1
Sanders, Samuel	3	3	4		4
Gardner, Francis, Senr	1	1	3		
Adams, Joseph	1	1	1		
Bell, Billet	2	1	1		1
Sanders, John	2	3	3		
Meadow, Joel	2		4		
Bell, Joseph	2	1	5		12
Harbert, Hilary	1		4		4
Harbert, William	1		2		
Sheppard, David	1				6
Sheppard, Jane		1	3		
Bell, George	1		3		
Adams, Nathan	1	1	3		1

NAME OF HEAD OF FAMILY.	Free white males of 16 years and upward, including heads of families.	Free white males under 16 years.	Free white females, including heads of families.	All other free persons.	Slaves.
Kennedy, Jacob	1	1	4		1
Quin, Abner	1	3	3		
Ogilsby, Gideon	2	3	2		
Sanders, Amos	1	1	1		
Yates, Bazel	1	1	3		
Brock, Elias	1	1	2		
Ogilsby, Benjamin	3	2	3		
Gardner, Francis, junr	1		4		
Meadow, Isaac	1		1		
Sanders, Philip	1				
Weeks, Seth	1		4		
Dill, George	1				
Dill, Edward	1	1	3		
Kennedy, Richard	1	2	6		3
Smith, John	1				
Kennedy, Gideon	1	2	4		
Smith, Archibald	1		3		
Ogilsby, John	1	1	2		
Stewart, Francis	1	1	5		
Kennedy, Thomas	2		3		1
McKean, John	2	4	3		
Hibs, John	1	2	3		
Sheppard, Absalom	1		3		7
Dennis, John	1				
Dennis, Elijah	1				
Dennis, James	1				
Stewart, John	1				
Culley, Thomas	3	3	3		8
Peppers, Elijah	2		2		
Weeks, Thomas	1	1	2		
Longness, Caleb	1		4		1
Reed, Robert	4	1	3		1
Willis, Benjamin	1	3	3		
Roberts, John	2	2	4		
Dill, John	1				
Sikes, Abram	2	1	3		
Osteen, Isaac	1				
Russel, William	1	1	3		
Taylor, Joshua	1	1	1		
Morton, Joseph	1				
Kennedy, Willit	1		3		
Phelps, Uriah	1				
Vincent, Jesse	1	1	3		
Bell, Joseph, junr	4		3	1	
Man, Leonard	1				
Mitts, Jacob	1	1	3		
Martin, John	1				
Longness, James	1				
Tolsin, William	1	1	6		
Martin, Absalom				9	
Carter, John				4	
Burgase, Caesar				4	
Williams, Ann	2	1	4		2
Dennis, William, Senr	3		2		23
Dennis, William, junr	1				7
Ogilsby, William	1				
Sammons, William	1	3	2		
Bell, John	2	2	2		
Adams, John	1		4		
Sanders, James	2	2	2		
Smith, Samuel	1	1	2		
Bell, Nathan	1	5	3		
Jenny				4	
Bell, Joseph, Senr	3				
Borden, William	4		3		43
Stanton, John	1	3	3		
Williams, William	4		4		
Bell, John	2	2	2		
Kennedy, Edward	1	3	2		
Kennedy, Willit	1		2		
Small, Benjamin	1	1	2		
Welch, James	1	1	2		
Cooke, Martin	1				
Samson (Old)				3	
Tigner, William	2	1	2		1
Riggs, Benjamin	1	1	3		
Hardister, Benjamin	2	2	3		1
Hardister, Joseph	1	2	3		2
Harris, Jesse	1	1	3		
Willis, Elisha	1				1
Dickernson, John, Senr	1		1		
Dickernson, John, junr	2		2		
Mills, John	1	2	2		
Piner, Joab	1		1		
Peter (Free)				5	
Carolina (Free)				7	
Fisher, William	3	1	5		10
Warner, Frederic	2	1			
Dickinson, James	1	2	3		
Potter, Joshua	1	1	2		
Jones, Rebecca	2	2	4		4
Eason, John, Senr	2	1	3		7
Eason, John, junr	1		4		2
Chadwick, Gear	1		4		
Singletary, John	1	1	2		4
Gibble, Diderick	2	1	4		6
Piner, Charles	1	1	2		

NAME OF HEAD OF FAMILY.	Free white males of 16 years and upward, including heads of families.	Free white males under 16 years.	Free white females, including heads of families.	All other free persons.	Slaves.
Rial, Joseph	1		2		
Kennedy, Martha	1	2	5		
Piner, Unice			4		
Piner, Reuben	1	1	2		
Owens, William	1		2		
Locker, Hugh	2	2	2		1
Toby, Senr (Free)				2	
Dinah (Free)				3	
Chadwick, Zaer	1	3	3		2
Hancock, Cromwell	1	1	2		
Jones, Edward	1	1	1		
Fisher, Elizabeth				3	
Bushnell, Ann M		1	2		
Hendrixson, Sorrowful		2	4		
Lewis, Ann		1	2		
Russel, Cevil	1	1	1		
Noah, Letitia		2	2		
Pasquinet, Ann			2		2
Fuller, Bersheba		2	3		
Lecraft, Benjamin	1	1	4		4
Rickets, John	1		2		
Fuller, Solomon	1	2	2		3
Jones, Rier	1	2	1		4
Pasquinet, Isaiah	1				2
Severin, John	1	1	2		1
Sheppard, John	1	1	5		
Leffuss, Samuel	2		3		
Leffuss, Asa	1		1		
Ellis, Delino	1	1	2		1
Wade, Robert	1	2	3		
Cannon, Mary	1		2		2
White, John	1		2		
Murray, John	1		1		
Warner, William	1				
Thomas, Samuel	1				
Upton, Mary			2		
Saviston, David	1	4	2		
Appleton, Elizabeth	1		2		4
Ward, Thomas	1	1	2		
Piver, Peter, Senr	1	1	6		
Piver, Peter, junr	1	1	2		
Piver, Johannis	1		1		
Luton, Adam	1		1		
Guthry, Jane	1	1	3		
Easlick, Francis	1	1	2		
Gorton, Bowan	1	2	3		
Wharton, Eben	1	1	1		
King, Joseph	1		2		1
Brag, Thomas	1		2		
Crandol, Elijah	1	1	2		
McDonald, Thomas	1	3	4		
Crief, John	1	1	4		
Harris, Georgeabrin	2	2	4		
Stanton, Benjamin	2	2	7		2
Mace, John	2	1	3		
Mace, James	1	2	1		
Small, Jonas	1	3	2		
Stanton, William	1	2	3		
Stanton, Owen	2	1	6		
Bundy, Josiah	1	2	2	1	
Wade, Royal	1	1	3		
Harris, Nehemiah	1	4	3		
Harris, Jesse	1	6	3		
Williston, Elisha	1		2	1	
Parisher, Samuel	1	2	3		
Gibbs, Nathan	1	1	2		
Helen, Isaac	2		3		2
Gibble, Frederic	2		5		2
Longness, Joshua	1	2	5		
Guthrey, Frederic	1	2	2		
Piver, Daniel	1	2	2		
Gabriel, Benjamin	1	2	6		
Gabriel, James	1	1	2		
Guthry, Charles	2	2	4		
Bell, James	2	2	5		
Hall, David	1	4	4		5
Moss, James	3	2	5		1
Piner, John	1	1	1		
Riggs, Isaac	1	2	1		
Moss, Joshua	3	1	3		
Dickinson, James	1	3	5		
Fodders, William	1		1		
Fodders, John, Senr	1		3		
Fodders, John, junr	1	1	4		
Davis, William	1		3		
Gillikin, Charles	2	3	2		
Pairtree, James	1	1	3		
Moss, Thoder	1	2	2		
Heller, Jonathan	1	1			
Piver, George	1		3		
Blackson, Severin	1		2		
Fulford, Stephen	1				
Moncrief, Caselton	1		1		
Fulford, Prudence		3	3		1
Simpson, Rhoster	5	2	5		3
Moss, Daniel	1		2		1
Rhease, Thomas	2	2	3	1	3

NEWBERN DISTRICT, CARTERET COUNTY—Continued.

NAME OF HEAD OF FAMILY.	Free white males of 16 years and upward, including heads of families.	Free white males under 16 years.	Free white females, including heads of families.	All other free persons.	Slaves.
Russel, John	1	1	4		
Brown, William T.	1		3		
Foreman, William	1	3	2		
Riggs, Jesse	1	2	2		
Pasquinet, John	1	2	4		
Pasquinet, James	2	2	5		1
Carter, George				10	
Fodders, William		1	4		
Williams, William	1		2		
Parrot, James	1		3		12
Conner, George	1				
Williams, Absalom	1	1	3		
Gardner, Samuel	1				
Wallace, James	1		1		2
Cheney, Benjamin	1		2		7
Cooper, David	1	3	3		4
Fuller, Nathaniel	1	2	5		14
Gibbs, Nathaniel	1	2	4		13
Smith, Samuel	1	1	1		1
Thomson, William	1		1		14
Thomas, John	1		2		
Garrett, Ebenezer	1	1	4		
Kennedy, Elizabeth		2	3		
Henry, Joel	1	1	1		8
Watson, George	1		5		3
Love, Fanny			3		
Cooper, Peter				2	
Braddock, Peter				8	
Stanton, Joe Pie				1	
Lewis, Rosannah			1		
Jerry				3	
Ocre				5	
Lewis, Jenny			2		
Samson, jun				1	
Merrill, Arthur	1				
Picket, Cull	1	2	2		1
Chadwick, Samuel	1		1		1
Harker, Zachariah	1	3	3		5
Harker, James	1		1	4	
Harker, Ebenezer	3		1		4
Sulivan, John	1	1	5		
Shaklefoot, James	3	1	5		2
Piner, Caleb	2		3		
Sharp, John	1	1	5		
Ellis, Freeman	2	1	5		
Brooks, John	1	3	3		
Fulford, James	1	2	1		1
Picket, Levy	1	1	2		3
Whitehouse, John	2		1		8
Whitehouse, Robert	2	2	4	1	
Gillikin, Jesse	2			4	
Gillikin, Benjamin	1	1	1		
Gillikin, George	1	1	2		
Gillikin, James	1		3		
Wade, Barney	1	1	4		
Field, Ann		1	3		
Hancock, Sarah		2	2		
White, Leah		1	4		
Lawrence, John	1	1	3		
Gillikin, Ellick	1	2	3		
Gillikin, Thomas	2	2	4		
Lawrence, Abigail	1	2	3		
Ward, David	1	1			12
Pinkum, Job	1	1	1		
Fulford, Stephen	1	3	7		5
Chadwick, James	1		3		2
Fulford, William	3	4	5		5
Pigot, Civil	2	3	3		5
Pinkum, Nathaniel	1	1	1		
Chadwick, Solomon	1	1	3		3
Rumley, Ann	1	5	2		
Arthur, Richard	1	3	3		
Arthur, Sarah			2		
Arthur, Seth	1		3	1	
Simson, Joshua	1	4	3		
Simson, Robert	1	3	4		
Luster, Abel	2		3		
Waid, Toder	1		4		
Dudley, John	1	4	1		
Bell, Ross	5		2		
Waid, Abram	3		1	4	2
Picket, Culpeper	1		2	1	
Hill, John	1		1		
Chadwick, Gear, Senᵗ	3	1	4		10
Chadwick, Thomas	1	1	1		10
Chadwick, John	1	2	1		1
Chadwick, Mary			1		1

NAME OF HEAD OF FAMILY.	Free white males of 16 years and upward, including heads of families.	Free white males under 16 years.	Free white females, including heads of families.	All other free persons.	Slaves.
Picket, William	1	2	3		
Harris, Thomas	2		2		
Carter, John				3	
Rial, Marmaduke	1	1	2		
Jones, Adir	1	3	4		3
Jones, Ambrose	1				5
Guthry, Stephen	1	1	3		
Guthry, Samuel	2	2	4		
Guthry, Levi	1	2	4		
Hancock, Elijah	1	1	4		
Hancock, Sarah	2		3		1
Harris, John	1	1	2		
Russel, Thomas	1	1	2		
Williston, Abner	1		3		
Sipon, David	2	2	1		
Evans, John	1	2	5		
Guthry, Solomon	1	3	5		
Williston, Andrew	1	3	3		
Williston, Josiah	1	4	4		4
Moor, Nathan	2	1	3		
Pool, Matthew	2	1	5		
Waid, Valentine	5	2	6		
Davis, Isaiah	1	2	5		1
Williston, Samuel	1		4		
Harkwell, Margaret	1		2		
Moor, Thomas	2	1	5		
Williston, George	1		3		
Williston, Daniel	1	1	4		
Williston, Sophira	1	1	4		
Waid, Isaac	1	2	4		
Waid, David	1	2	4		
Fulford, Joseph	1	1	2	1	6
Fulford, John	2	1	8	1	7
Stewart, Alexander	1	3	3		2
Bell, Mary	1	2	2		1
Cruthers, William	1	4	3		
Davis, Joseph	3		3		
Williston, Seth	1	3	3		
Williston, Thomas	1	2	2		
Bell, George	1	2	5		16
Cratch, Richard	1	5	3		2
Ripley, William	1	2	4		
Heady, Thomas	1	2	5		
Heady, Daniel	3	2	4		
Copes, Stephen	1	1	2		
Heady, John	1	1	2		
Lewis, Thomas	2	4	3		
Bloodgood, Isaac	2	1	4		
Colbert, Matthew	2		4		
Norwood, Ann					2
Hill, John	1	2	2		
Gillikin, Enoch	1		1		
Bell, Joseph	1	1	5		
Williston, Daniel	1	2	7		
Molbern, Samuel	1	2	1		
Howling, Christopher	1		4		
Howling, William	1		4		
Howling, Zepheniah	1	3	4		
Smith, Samuel	1	1	3		
Davis, William	1	1	3		
Davis, Benjamin	2	3	6		
Davis, Anthony	1		2		1
Lewis, Thomas	1		3		
Bell, Joseph	1	1	5		
Bell, Francis	1	2	4		
Nelson, Ananias	1		2		
Turner, Mary		2	3		
Morton, Ann W		1	5		
Davis, Nathan	4		1		8
Berry, Thomas	1		2		
Hill, John	1		3		
Dixon, James	2	2	2		
Roberts, John	1	2	2		
Lewis, William	1	3	3		
Huff, Richard	1	1	1		
Wallace, Robert	1	3	2		1
Willis, Joseph	1	3	4		
Robertson, William	1	1	4		
Gaskins, William	2	4	6		
Willis, Reuben	1	7	1		1
Rosemary, Joseph	1	1	1		1
Stiron, John	1		2		
Stiron, George	1	1	2		
Smith, Samuel	1	3	6		
Stiron, Samuel	2	2	5		
Stiron, John	3	2	1		
Willis, George	1	1	2		

NAME OF HEAD OF FAMILY.	Free white males of 16 years and upward, including heads of families.	Free white males under 16 years.	Free white females, including heads of families.	All other free persons.	Slaves.
Hill, Wise	1		1		
Mason, Joshua	2	3	5		
Bishop, Asa	3	1	5		5
Nelson, Mary			4		2
Hamilton, Robert	1	1	1		2
Hamilton, David	1		1		
Nelson, William	3	1	2		
Nelson, James	3		5		
Taylor, William	1	3	2		
Lewis, Thomas	1		3		
Gaskins, Joseph	1	7	3		3
Smith, Henry	1	1	6		
Henderson, Henry	1		5		
Barrington, John	1		5		
Salter, Richard	1	3	3		
Golding, Thomas, junᵗ	1	2	1		
Ireland, Catherine			1		
Golding, Thomas, Senᵗ	3	1	2		
Salter, Christopher	1	4	2		
Salter, Joseph	1	4	3		
Smith, Richard	1	2	4		
Salter, William	1	3	2		
Smith, William	2	2	5		
Huff, Richard, Senᵗ	2		4		
Huff, Henry	1		1		
Smith, Thomas	3		3		
Barrington, Isaac	1		3		
Smith, Samuel	1		3		
Robinson, Allen	3	3	3		
Price, Esther			1		
Morris, Moses	2	4	2		
Fulsher, Thomas, junᵗ	1	3	3		
Fulsher, William	1	3	2		
Fulsher, Thomas	2	2	2		
Harris, Daniel	1	2	2		
Baker, William	3	3	4		
Dannels, James	1	2	1		
Dannels, Elizabeth	1	1	2		
Ireland, David	1	2	5		
Dannels, Jacob	1	1	5		
Emery, Shadrach	1		2		
Gooding, Thomas	1	1	6		
Lupton, Christopher	2	4	3		
Philips, Manido	1	1	2		
Stiron, Samuel	2	1	5		
Stiron, Adonijah	2		1		
Stiron, Wallace	2	3	3		
Stiron, Richard	1	3	4		
Ireland, Daniel	1		3		
Tolsin, Thomas	2	3	4		
Dixon, Sylvanus	4	2	3		2
Stiron, George	1	2	5	1	
Casey, John	1	4	3		
Gaskin, John	2	2	8		3
Tolsin, Jesse	3		4		
Wallace, David, junᵗ	3	1	1	1	1
Wallace, Robert	2	1	3		3
Wallace, David, Senᵗ	2		3	1	16
Wallace, Joseph	1				1
Wallace, John	2				3
Williams, John	1	1	3		9
Gaskins, Adam	1	1	5		4
Salter, Henry	1		2		1
Scarborough, Thomas	1	2	1		
Scarborough, William	1	3	1		1
Gaskins, Thomas	1	1	6		3
Gaskins, John	1	2	4		1
Stiron, James	1	1	2		
Brag, Joseph	1	1	3		
Scott, James	1		2		2
Williams, John	1	1	2		1
Williams, Joseph	1		2		
Gaskins, Sarah			3		
Bragg, Jesse	1		4		
Howard, William, Senᵗ	2	1	2		
Howard, William, Jur	2		1		
Garrish, Henry	1		1		
Stiron, William	1	1	7		
Stiron, Mary			2		
Howard, Cornelius	1	2	2		4
Howard, George	2	2	3		4
Neale, Francis	1		1		
Neale, William	1	1	4		
Neale, John	1	1	6		
Jackson, Francis, junᵗ	1	1	2		
Jackson, Francis, Senᵗ	4	1	4		
Dannels, Thomas	1	2	2		

NEWBERN DISTRICT, CRAVEN COUNTY.

NAME OF HEAD OF FAMILY.	Free white males of 16 years and upward, including heads of families.	Free white males under 16 years.	Free white females, including heads of families.	All other free persons.	Slaves.
Crispin, Joseph	1	2			15
Kelly, Thomas	1	1	3		11
Stiron, Wallace	1		1		6
Franklin, Joseph	2	1	2		9
Hineman, Rachel			1		

NAME OF HEAD OF FAMILY.	Free white males of 16 years and upward, including heads of families.	Free white males under 16 years.	Free white females, including heads of families.	All other free persons.	Slaves.
Harrington, Charles	1	1	4		
Brotin, John	1		3		
Brown, Mary		1	1		
Justice, Sylvanus	1	2	3		
Hoover, Samuel, Senᵗ	2	2	1		

NAME OF HEAD OF FAMILY.	Free white males of 16 years and upward, including heads of families.	Free white males under 16 years.	Free white females, including heads of families.	All other free persons.	Slaves.
White, William	1	1	2		
Hollice, Isaac	2	2	4		1
Vendrick, Jesse	1	2	5		
Hoover, James	1	2	2		
Davis, William	2	2	4		

NEWBERN DISTRICT, CRAVEN COUNTY—Continued.

NAME OF HEAD OF FAMILY.	Free white males of 16 years and upward, including heads of families.	Free white males under 16 years.	Free white females, including heads of families.	All other free persons.	Slaves.
Jones, William	1	2	3		
Prescot, Frederic	3	3	1		
Hoover, Shadrach	6		6		
Hollice, William	3		3		
King, Thomas	1	1	3		
Broughton, Abel, Senr	1	2	2		
Broughton, Abel, junr	2	1	2		1
Atherby, Joseph	2	1	5		
Ackiss, Frances		1	1		
Wilson, James	1	1			
Harrington, James	1		2		
Franklin, Peter	1	1	2	3	8
Hudson, James	1		4		
Horseanes, Joseph	1		4		
Carpenter, George	1	1	2		2
Lawson, Samuel	1	3	3		
Stephens, Alexander	1		4		
Reed, Isaac	1		2	1	
Reed, James	1	2	3		
Vendrick, William	1		1		
Vendrick, Alice		1	4		5
Atherby, Isaac	2				1
West, Joseph	2	1	4		2
Perkins, Jonathan	1	2	3		7
Vendrick, Ann	1	1	5		
Bradley, Daniel	1	1			
Lewis, Nehemiah	1		4		
Riding, Benjamin	1	1	3		
Vendrick, Abram	1	2	2		
Franklin, Thomas	1	4	4		
Vendrick, Peter	1	1	3		
Vendrick, John	2	1	5		
Simpkins, Joseph, Senr	1	1	1		
Simpkins, Joseph, junr	1	1	1		1
Simpkins, Daniel	1	1	2		1
Ince, John	1				
Cox, William	1	1	5		
Hewkins, Hardy	1	1	1		1
Neale, Matthew	1	1	3		11
Hoover, Samuel, junr	2	1	4		
Hoover, Samuel, Senr	1		3		
Hollice, Hezekiah	1		1		
Whitly, William	1	3	3		
Neale, Barry	1				
Nichols, James	1	2	2		
Harper, Thomas	1		6		
Hoover, John	1	1	3		2
Miller, James	2		2		
Dixon, Joseph	1				
Hoover, Jacob	1		3		
Edgington, William	1	1	2		
Higgins, Cormick	1			2	
Hineman, Michael	3		1		7
Masters, Joseph	1	4	4	1	13
McLinn, Charles	3	2	4		63
James, Charles	2		2		5
Mason, Benjamin	1	3	4		4
Caraway, Francis	1	1	4		4
Young, Robert	1	1	5		12
Holley, James	1		1		
Ferguson, Mark	1				
Whitehouse, William	2	2	3		
Grover, George	1	1	2		3
Pitman, Thomas	3	2	4		
Culley, Francis	1	2	4		
Cummins, John	2	1	1		1
Parsons, Thomas	1		2		
Oliver, Samuel	1	5	4	1	
Ferguson, Slocum	1	2	5		1
Cummins, Benjamin	1	2	5		
Martin, John	1	2	3		
Northon, John	1	1	3		
Royal, Daniel	1	4	4		
Neale, Daniel	1				
Wallace, Richard M	1	2	3		3
Nelson, Thomas	1	5	1		8
Wallace, Benjamin	1	3	5		
Mason, Joseph	1	1	1		
Masters, Thomas	1	2	3		
Holley, Richard	1	1	2		
Harper, Robert	1				
Smith, Benjamin	1				
Smith, Humphrey	1	3	1		
Messick, Hopkins	1	2	2		
Bragg, William	1	2	5		
Hamilton, John, junr	1				
Hamilton, John, Senr	2	3	2		11
Sampson, Avin	1	2	1		
Allison, William	1	2	2		3
Wallace, Robert	3	4	3		
Pitman, Joseph	1				
Wilkinson, Richard	1	1	2		
Jones, James	1	1	3		2
Wright, John	1		2		
Nelson, J. S.	1				
Tigner, Thomas	1		4		
Whitus, Elias N	1		2		
Clark, Severin	1	1	3		2

NAME OF HEAD OF FAMILY.	Free white males of 16 years and upward, including heads of families.	Free white males under 16 years.	Free white females, including heads of families.	All other free persons.	Slaves.
Cook, Zaphirah	1	3	4		
Smith, Daniel	1	1	2		
Biggs, William, junr	1		3		
Biggs, William, Senr	1	1	3		
Boyd, William	1	1	1		
Carraway, Edward	1	3	1		2
Sparrow, Henry	1	2	2		4
Chance, Richard	1	2	1	1	
Smith, Joseph	1	1	1		
Whitus, Samuel	1		2		
Cutrall, John	1	1	2		2
Moss, Joseph	1				
Hamilton, Michael	1		1		
Godfrey, Sarah	1		3		
McHains, Stephen	3		4		
Wallace, Archibald	1		2		
Sparrow, Paul	1	3	5		9
Quinney, Stephen	1	1	2		
Gilbert, William	1		3		
Williams, Samuel	1	1	3		
Jones, John	1				
Whitus, Reuben	1				
Wallace, Benjamin, junr	1				
Cooke, Samuel	1	2	4		4
Houston, James	1				
Houston, Francis	1		4		4
Merona, J. O	1				
James, Isaac	1	1	1		
James, Richard	1	1	1		
Scapp, Israel	1		1		
Guard, Joshua	1	2	3		
West, Gabriel	1				
Jones, William	1				
Barnes, Thomas	1		3		
Ferguson, Adam	2	1	4		
Leverin, John	1				
Parsons, John	2		2	1	
James, Hovinton	1				
Burney, Joseph	1				
Day, John	1	3	3		
Walker, Samuel	1				
Cullen, Nehemiah	2		1		2
Jackson, Daniel	1				
Masters, Enoch	1	1	2		1
Pitman, Southy	1				
Summons, John	2	1	2		
Hamilton, James	1		1		
Wade, Richard	3	1	3	1	
Pitman, Obadiah	1		1		
Rew, Southy I	1		2		2
Bryan, Elizabeth	1		2		7
Wilkinson, David	4	2	2		1
Lovick, Richard, Senr	3	1	4		4
Carter, Abel					7
George, William					10
Mitchel, Benjamin					3
Simmons, Samuel				5	1
Godet, Peter					1
Gregory, John					2
Godet, John					2
Dukes, Peter	1	3	2		
Ostean, Reuben	1	1	2		
Parsons, Thomas	2		2		
Priestley, Amy		5	3		
Stanton, John	1		4		
Cottle, William	1	2	3		
Johnston, Henry	2	2	2		2
Hill, Peter	2	1	4		
Mason, John	1		5		
Freebody, John	4				4
Cooke, Thomas	1	1	2		5
Thomas, John	1	4	2		
Thomas, Abner	1				
Collins, Alice		1	3		3
Jones, Lovick	1	3	3		13
Benners, John	3	7	7		85
Carney, John	2	2	4		13
Pritchard, Edward	1		1		6
Dew, Joseph	1	2	8		
Howard, Horton	1	1			26
Jones, Roger, Senr	3	4	1		18
Chance, Esther			2		
Rothburn, Jacob	1		2		
Carter, Joshua					4
Wilson, Thomas	1				3
Neale, Elizabeth	1		4		1
Copes, Jacob					16
James, Charity		1	4		9
Jones, James, Senr	1	2	5		7
Wallace Stephen	2	3	2		1
Blair, Moses	1	1	3		
Dixon, George	2	1	3		
Pitman, James	1	1			
Finnikin, James	1		3		
Thomas	1		4		
Wallace, Robin, junr	1		5		
Thomas, Reuben	1	2	1		
Steward, Andrew	2	2	1		

NAME OF HEAD OF FAMILY.	Free white males of 16 years and upward, including heads of families.	Free white males under 16 years.	Free white females, including heads of families.	All other free persons.	Slaves.
Cummins, Lurenah			2		
Turner, Frederick	1	1	2		2
Samson, James	2	1	2		
Casey, Thomas	1	4	3		
Bragg, Solomon	1	2	3		1
Hall, Simon	2		5		4
Bragg, John	2	2	6		9
Godet, Ann			6		
Neale, Philip	1	2	3		6
Rew, Southy	3	4	4		13
Wilson, David	1	1	1		
Wilson, Ephraim	1		1		
Morris, Dinah		1	2		
Shapley, Mary		2	2		
Moor, Deborah				3	
Williams, John	1		1		
Crew, Thomas	1		2		2
Spaight, Richard D	1		3		71
Simpson, John	2				8
Frilick, Joseph	1				
Smith, Nathan	3		1	1	25
Lindsey, Elizabeth		1	4	1	2
Young, Richard	1				
Bartlett, William	1		1		
Ellis, Richard	1				6
Kennedy, John	1				6
Stephenson, James	1				
Tomlinson, Thomas	1		1		4
Donald, Robert	1		2		7
Simonton, Sarah		1	2		
Ellis, James	1		4		7
Scranton, John	1		4		5
McAuslan, Alexander	1		1		3
Macken, Henry	1		3		2
Jenkins, John	1	1			1
Pendleton, Sylvester, Senr	2		3	1	2
Ferrill, Elizabeth	1		2	1	1
McKinley, James	6				6
Tinker, Stephen	1	1	4		7
Forker, John	1		2		1
Good, William	1	1	1		10
Saunders, Mary	1	1	4	1	5
Smallwood, John	2	1	1		5
Davis, Thomas	1		2	1	
Moor, Dinah				3	
Mackey, Isaac	2		2	2	2
Inloes, Abram	1		1	1	1
Inloes, Anthony	4				
Low, William	1		3		
Ramsey, John	2	1	2		
Kellum, James	1				
Levingston, Henry	1	2	3		
Levingston, Samuel	1		1		
White, Cato				7	
Black, Letitia				3	
Barrington, James	2	2	4		
Ambrose, David	1	1	1		1
McQuin, Thomas	1	2	2		
Stringer, Doll				4	
Stringer, Thomas				2	
Kelly, Joseph				2	
Bryan, John C	1	2	4		8
Custis, Thomas	1	1	4		
Sealey, Martha			4		3
Hatfield, Robert	2		2		
Dunn, Samuel	2				4
Ventures, Michael	2				
Wade, Joseph	1		4		2
Taylor, Mary		1	2		
Smuch, William	1		3		
Pendleton, Sylvester, Junr	1	3	1		1
Potter, Edward	1		2	1	
Anthony, William	1	2	2		2
Gilespie, Lydia			2		1
St Leger, De	1		2		1
Goodhue, Samuel	1		4		1
Hill, Ann			3		
Little, James	2	2	3		2
West, Stephen	1	1	3		6
Gainer, William	1		3		1
Johnston, Francis	1	1	1		
Scarborough, Nathaniel					
Landmeyer, Frederick	3	1			2
Tisdale, Nathan	1		1		3
Harris, John			1	6	2
Gerock, Samuel	1	1	2		3
Morrison, John	3	2	2		7
Justice, Rebecca		1	2		11
Harriot, James	1	2	4		
Turner, Philip	1		3		7
Chapman, Samuel	1	1	3		3
Durand, Ann		2	4		11
Cheek, Thomas L	1	3	2		5
McAlpin, Margaret			3		1
Halling, Solomon	1		3		5
Trippe, William	3	2	3		1

NEWBERN DISTRICT, CRAVEN COUNTY—Continued.

NAME OF HEAD OF FAMILY.	Free white males of 16 years and upward, including heads of families.	Free white males under 16 years.	Free white females, including heads of families.	All other free persons.	Slaves.
Martin, Francis Xavier	2				
Chaponelle, Joseph	1			1	2
Stephens, Mary		2	2	1	1
Dugnie, Alexander	2	1	1		5
Purss, Henry	1		3		7
Ellis, George	1				
Thomson, Justice	1				
Carney, James	3	1	4	1	7
Johnston, William	1	2	2		6
Hunley, Richard	1		2		8
Mitchel, William	1		1	1	2
Hawley, William	3	1	2		7
Devereux, John	3		1		3
Hunt, Robert	1		2		2
Hardy, Margaret		2	2		2
Wining, John	1				
Creusy, Jonathan	1				
Urquhart, John	3	1	2		1
Tagert, Joseph	5				1
Kean, Edward	1				1
McMains, James	2	3	2		4
Parker, John	2	1	1		
Savano, Lewis	1		1	1	1
Graham, Robert	1		2		1
Terry, David	1		4		
Gooding, Samuel	1	1	1		
Brightman, James	1	1			2
Steele, Thomas	1		2		
Haslen, Elizabeth			4		17
Stewart, Alexander	1		1		2
Haslen, Thomas	2	1	1		9
Stringer, Minge				2	
Myers, Jacob	1			1	
Moor, Jenny				2	
McCafferty, James	2		3		6
Barrington, John	2	3	1	3	
Dudley, William	1		3	1	5
Bagnall, Benjamin	1		2		
Gibbs, William	1	1			4
Smith, John Frink	1	2	4		16
Guion, Isaac	2	2	5		7
Macgrath, John	1	2	3		1
Duffy, George	2		5		2
Henry, William	1	1	1		17
Haines, Henry Pendergras	1			1	1
Sears, Ann	1	1	3		
Cooke, Jacob	2	2	3		4
Gill, Catherine			6	1	3
Sitgreaves, John	1	1	1		23
Pasteur, Edward	1	1	3		9
Sitgreaves, John			3		2
Bryan, John	1		1		1
Conner, John	2			1	
Moor, Drucilla			1	1	1
Craddock, John	1	2	3		5
Rhodes, Malicah	1		1		
Tisdale, William	1	1	3		3
Powers, Jerry				5	
Fulford, Sarah			3		2
Coor, James	1		2		9
Slade, William	1	1	4		7
Dailey, Thomas	2		1		
Burney, Sarah		4	2		2
Cox, Thomas	2	1	2		11
Heath, Mary		1	4	1	10
Williams, John	1	1	2	1	3
Russel, Ann				1	1
McLure, William	1	2	1		27
Cole, Jane			1		
Coleman, Samuel	1		2		
Palmer, Philip	1	1	2		
Stanley, James	1	1	3		
Turner, Thomas	2	4	2		
Hiet, George	1		2		77
Lewis, William	1				
Williams, William	1				
Delonay, John	1		1		1
Woods, Benjamin	1				
Bryan, Jesse	1	3	5	1	20
Leech, Joseph	2		1		15
McDowal, James	2	2	2	1	
Witherspoon, David	1	1	6		113
Muckleroy, Thomas				3	
Edgar, William	1	2	1	2	
Teer, William	1	1	3		
Field, Rachel		3	1		
Alexander, Enoch	1	3	2		5
Hyde, Luther	1	1	4		1
Willis, Abel	1	1			
Thomson, James	2				
Hanson, William	1		1		
Stewart, James	1	1			11
Grim, Philip	1				
Allen, John				4	2
De Bretighe, Marquis	1		1		
Linn, Volant	2	1	3		
Henrion, Peter	3				2
Thomague, —	1				2
Rich, Rebecca	1	1	2		1
Dorsey, Walter	1		2	2	1
Shepard, William	1				4
Tomlinson, Elizabeth			1		
Manning, Pierce	1				1
Lawrence, William	1				
York, James				1	
Hurley, John	3	1	2		6
Poddy, Hannah			3		
Cupps, William			2		
Harvey, John					2
Forbes, Richard	1	1	2	1	6
Vultius, George	1		2		2
Chuyler, John	1				
Lawrence, John	2		3		4
Gaston, Margaret		1	3		30
Lewis, Abby				4	
Trigler, Richard	2	2	1		
Montague, Jane	1	1	4		
Marshall, Mary			3		2
Carthy, Daniel	1				1
Tinker, Edward	4	3	6	4	
Hobday, John	1	1	2		4
Clark, Joseph	1		3		9
Pudril, Richard	1		1		
Butler, Temperance	1		2		
Biggleston, Ann C			1		2
Webber, Ann	2	1	1		7
Mansfield, John	1	3	3		
Dowdin, William	2				
Oliver, Joseph	1	3	2		14
McAlep, Archibald	1				
Cain, Alexander					
Hart, Mary		2			3
Adams, Mary			3		4
Johnston, Esther	1	1	2		15
Ducksworth, Mary			1		
Hannis, William	1	1	4	1	7
Cohun, John	2	2	2		
Stephenson, Stephen	1	1	2		1
Fairfield, Reuben	3				
Lowthorp, Francis	6	1	3	1	11
Cogdell, Lydia			2		4
Vail, Sarah			3		22
Green, Margaret			2		1
Bruce, James	1	2	2		
Gooding, Nancy			1		
Calaven, Hannah			2		
Dick, Merion			2		
Buxton, Jarvis			3	2	2
Collins, Matthew	1	1	2		
Hudrell, Daniel			1		
Green, John	1	1	1		11
Paxton, William	2		1		4
Clements, Frederick	1		1		1
Tolman, Phobe			1		
Shute, Joseph	1	1	1		7
Pearson, Thomas Wheelwright	1				2
Tinker, Euphamy			3		1
Cook, Silas	1	2	1		1
Reading, Jeremiah	1		2		2
Cutting, Leonard	2	1	1		2
Sandy, James	1	3	5		2
Daves, John	1	1	4		23
Bowers, Saul				3	
Potter, Sarah			2		2
Wrinsford, Mary			3		1
Snead, Wilson	1	1	2		1
Barry, John	1				
Arnold, Margaret			1		
Ambrose, Nancy			1		
Cosway, Abigail		1	1		
Cutting, James	1				
Reed, Elizabeth		1	2		
Almond, John					3
Moore, William	1				3
Griffin, Moses			2		2
Dunn, William	3	3	2		2
Parsons, Jeremiah	2	3	3		4
Ives, William	1	1	3		
Dunn, Stephen	1	1	3		2
Ives, John	2	2	3		
Stephens, Matthew	1	3	3		
Row, Benjamin	1	3	3		3
Henry, David	1	3	3		
Taylor, John	1	1	2		
Anderson, William	1		2		5
Always, Obadiah	4	1	4	2	
Austin, Thomas	1	1	2		1
Bailey, John	1	1	2		4
Bishop, John	2		3		1
Bradshaw, Thomas	3	2	3		2
Booty, Nicholas	2		3		
Blanks, John	1	3	2		14
Binum, Arthur	1	1	3		
Dunn, John	1		1		
Davis, William	1		2		12
Davis, James	2		2		12
Ellis, Michael	1		2		
Evans, Thomas	1		1		4
Ervin, James	1				
Flibus, Archibald	1		3		1
Foye, Frederick	2	2	1		29
Fooks, John	1	3	1		1
Fooks, Joseph	1		1		
Foster, Bazel	1		3		
Foster, Philemon	1		2		
Fosque, Richard	1	1	2		
Fosque, Luke	1		2		
Fulsher, Levy	1	1	1		10
Holland, Joseph	1				
Givin, Rolin	1				
Knox, John	1		2		12
Holland, Philemon	1				
Holland, William	1				
Foster, William S.	1		1		10
Hampton, Thomas	1	3	2		
Hampton, William	1	1	3		1
Hancock, Roger	1			1	
Hancock, Evan	1			6	
Heath, John	2	1	1		
Ives, Hardy	1		5		
Ives, Thomas P	1	1	3		1
Jones, James	1				
Jones, Roger	1	2	1	1	5
Johnston, Robert	1	2	2		
Jones, Evan	1		2	1	6
Kincey, William	1	3	1		
Lovick, George	1		1		18
Lovick, Thomas	1		1	1	12
Murphy, Edward	1	2	3	1	
Morgan, Edward	2		1		
Merchant, Christopher	1	1	1		
Potter, James	1	1	1		2
Porter, Thomas	2		4		
Porter, John	1				
Parsons, Thomas	1		1		2
Physic, Peter	3	2	4		11
Moor, Margaret				5	
Smith, Richard	3	1	1		
Norwood, Fanny			1	2	
Smith, Thomas	1	2	4		
Smith, Malica	1	1	1		
Smith, Jesse	2		2		
Edmundson, Bryan	1				
Tolsin, John	1	2	3		
Tolsin, Benjamin	1		3		
Tolsin, Thomas	1		1		
Tolsin, George	1		2		
Tolsin, Benjamin	1		2		
Thomsin, Thomas	1	1	5	1	
Whitehead, John	1				
Whitehead, James	1	2	1		
Whitehead, George	1	2	2		
Williams, Richard	1	1	7		
Winn, William	1	1	4		6
Upton, Major	1		2		
Yates, John B	4	1	3		
Jones, Moses	1				
Collins, Shadrach	1				
Jones, Bartholomew	1		2		
Hancock, John	1		2		1
Boin, William	1	3	2		
Taylor, John	3	2	3		1
Brittain, Catherine			5		2
Turner, John	1		1		3
Sykes, Jacob	1	3	3		1
Cobin, Daniel	1				
Pitman, John	3	1	2		
Tooley, Adam	1		1	1	9
Henry, Stephen	1	1	1		
Caviner, Bryan	2				
Dunn, Elizabeth			1		2
Hickman, Richard	1	2	4		
Hickman, Thomas	1		2		1
Fisher, Elizabeth			3		
Caviner, Sarah			3		
Ogilsby, John	1		1		
Fosque, Elias			2	2	1
Chambers, Lavinia		1	2		
Reasonover, Elizabeth			1		
Carter, Isaac				5	
Perkins, Isaac				2	
Dove, William			2	9	
Perkins, George				4	
Dove, Pompey				1	
Dove, Nelly				2	
Heath, William	2	1	6		
Styron, Samuel	2	1	2		
Jones, Charles	2	4	3		2
Wolfe, Hannah			1		

NEWBERN DISTRICT, CRAVEN COUNTY—Continued.

NAME OF HEAD OF FAMILY.	Free white males of 16 years and upward, including heads of families.	Free white males under 16 years.	Free white females, including heads of families.	All other free persons.	Slaves.
Holton, Jesse	1	2	2	1	1
Moss, Joseph	1	1	1		
Hampton, Mary	1		3		
Givin, Henry	2		5		
Dowdy, Richard	1	2	6		
Rieves, Courtney	2	4	2		
Hall, Rachel			3		
Taylor, Absalom	1	1	3		
Singleton, Spyers	1	2	5		18
Lofton, Joseph	1		1		12
Bishop, James	1	1	5		
Bishop, Joseph	1	3	1		2
Jessup, Isaac				11	
Hamilton, James	3	1	3	1	3
Foster, John	2	2	4		
Davis, Thomas	1				
Jones, Lewis	1	3	3		10
Bryan, Edward	1		2		12
Dubberly, Saccor	2	1	3		5
Dubberly, John	1	2	4		
Anderson, Thomas	1		1		
Oliver, Solomon	2	1	5		
James, John	1		4		
James, Charles	1				
Dubberly, William	1	2	1		
Felingims, Robert	2	3	3		
Anderson, Jonas	1	4	3		
Roundtree, Moses	1	3	2		1
Atherby, John	3	4	6		
Green, Thomas	2		4		
Mitchel, Elizabeth	3	2	6		9
Anderson, John	2	1	2		
Phips, William	2	1	3		1
Marshal, Charles	1		7		8
King, Mary	1	4	3		2
Willis, Francis	1	3	2		
James, Sarah	1	3	2		
Anderson, Peter	4		2		
Murphy, William	4	1	6		5
Cannon, Edward	3	1	2		
Cooper, Martha		2	8		
Jarrel, William	1		2		
Smith, William	1		2		
Harris, Stephen	1	1	2		6
Smith, John	1	1	2		
Tootle, Phoebe	2		4		
West, John	1	1	2	1	10
Duncan, Thomas	1				
Morning, William H.	1		1		
Willis, John	1	1	1		2
Causway, Philip	2	1	1		1
Bull, Micaja	1		1		
Tyre, Jesse	1	1	6		
Tant, Thomas	1	1	2		
Chance, Moses	1				
Palmer, Jacob	1	2	1		
Philingim, Samuel	1	3	3		1
Mitchel, William	1	1	2		
Gwartney, John	1		1		
Cooper, James	1	4	1		
Lane, Isaac	1	1	1		
Philingim, John	3	4	3		1
Phips, Joseph	1	1	1		
Worth, Thomas	3	2	7		
Philips, Jacob	1	2	5		
Warren, Jacob	1	4	4		1
Hafford, Malicah	1	3	4		
James, Jeremiah	1	1	3		3
Palmer, Elijah	1	1	3		
Allen, John	1	1	3		27
Tyre, Major	1	1	1		
Gaskins, Harmon	2	4	3		
Taylor, Charles	1	5	4		
Taylor, Jesse	1				
Fillingim, Benjamin	1	1	5		
Charlton, George	2	1	4		
Averite, John	1	3	5		
Butler, Charles	1		4		
McIntosh, James	2		2		
Kemp, Isaac	1	2	2		
Anderson, Thomas	1	2	6		
Curtis, Thomas	1	1	3		3
Gatlin, Shadrach	1	2	3		
Butler, Arthur	1	2	4		
Allen, John	2	3	5		1
Charlton, William	1	1	3		
Jarrell, Lewis	1		3		
Smith, William	1				
Smith, James	1				
Cox, Joseph	1	3	1		
Green, Thomas	1	2	1		18
Herritage, William	1	4	2		28
Lovick, William	2				13
Hollaway, John	4	2	3		6
Johnston, William	1		1		
Lambert, Moses	2	1	5		1
Clements, Thomas	1	1	5		3
Swann, Evan	3		3		2
Green, John	1		3		7
Wise, Thomas	1		2		3
Heath, William	1				3
Lofton, Joseph	1	2	1		1
Lofton, Longford	1	2	2		
Lofton, Thomas	1	1	4		
Carman, William, Senr	2	1	1		3
Green, Furnifold, junr	1				12
Lane, Frederic	1	1	1		16
Prier, Samuel	1	1	2		
Gilstrap, Peter	2	1	6		
Mastin, Jeremiah	1				6
Gatlin, Thomas	3	5	4		11
Gooding, John	4	4	2		12
Slade, Ebenezer	2	3	4		2
Beesley, John	1	3	3		
Cormack, Lydia			2		
Slade, Mary		2	5		8
McKoye, Willis, Senr	3	1	3		
Beazley, Solomon	3	1	3		1
White, David	1		1		
McKoye, Edward	1				
McKoye, Willis, junr	1				
Miller, Mary	2	2	2		
Beezley, Elisha	1	1	2		
Fonvielle, Francis, Senr	2	5	1		14
Fonvielle, Francis, junr	1				
Anderson, Isaac	1	2	2		
Nucum, Edward	1		2		
Melonay, William	1	1	4		
Taylor, James	1	3	5		
White, Mary	2	1	4		
Atlin, Keziah		1	3		1
Green, Furnifold, Senr	1				12
Daly, John	1	1	3		34
Bryan, William	2		7		36
Bryan, Hardy	1		1		22
Allen, Jonathan	1		2		1
Butler, Moses	2	3	3		
Bryan, George	1	4	4		5
Buchanan, William	1	3	2		
Doherty, Daniel	1	2	2		2
Doherty, Robert	1	1	2		
Fannin, John	1	1	2		
Gilstrap, Richard	1	1	1		
Green, Leah			2		24
Hall, Joseph, Senr	2	1	2		1
Smith, John	2		4		
Hammons, Charles	3	1	4		
Hall, Thomas	1	4	2		
Hall, Joseph, junr	1		4		(*)
Hill, William	2	3	5		
Heath, Frederic	1	5	4		
Lane, Daniel	2	2	5		
McKoye, William	2	2	2		5
McKoye, Gideon	1	1	2		
Oliver, Thomas	1	2	2		5
Streets, Nathan	1	3	3		1
Taylor, Moses, Senr	3	3	3		
Taylor, Moses, junr	1		2		
Willis, Joel	1	3	2		
Wingit, Mary	2	3	5		
White, Benjamin, junr	1		3		
White, Whiche	1	3	5		
Roberts, Patience			4		
White, Agnes		1			
Sivils, John	1		4		
White, Benjamin, Senr	3	2	3		
Doherty, Mary		1	2		
Doherty, Ephraim	1	1	1		
Taylor, Susannah			1		
Spelman, Jenny					3
Newcombe, Jemima	2		4		
Fruit, William, Junr	1		2		
Darby, John	1				
Prevat, Thomas	1		1		
White, Vincent	1				
Hutchins, James	1	2	1		
Fruit, William, Senr	1	1			
Peete, Jesse	1		2		
Whitfield, Constance	1		3		25
Barney, Ashley	1	2	2		
Green, Elizabeth		3	2		
Cox, William	2	3	2		8
Smith, William	1	1	3		
Prior, Thomas	1		3		
Gardner, William	2	2	2		2
Lane, John	3	1	3		3
Heath, Thomas	4	1	6	1	
Randal, Nehemiah	1	4	4		
Pierce, Thomas, junr	1	2	2		
Pierce, Thomas, Senr	1	1	6		1
Doherty, Absalom	1	1	5		
Doherty, Richard	1	1	4		
Prescot, Austin	1		2		
Prescot, John	2	1	5		
Hawkins, Willowby	1	1	2		
West, Daniel	1	2	3		4
Cormack, John, Junr	1		2		
Fruit, Levy	1	2	5		
Jones, William	3	1	4		3
Jones, Thomas	3		1		
Carlton, Elizabeth	2	3	4		
Clark, William	1		3		
Kent, Levy	1		2		
West, William	2	2	3		
Russel, Malicah	1	2	3		3
West, Levy	1		1		1
Heath, James	1	1	2		
Heath, Christopher	1		3		3
Heath, Richard	1	1	2		
Doherty, William	1	1	2		
Heath, Stephen	2	4	2		
Heath, Rigdon	1		2		1
Moye, Elijah	1	1	3		
Griffin, William	1		3		
Lewis, Frederic	1	2	4		4
Tyre, Ann	1	1	1		
Prevat, Sarah	1	1	5		1
Smith, Sarah		2	2		
Carlton, Fereby		2	1		
Watson, Richard	1	2	4		
Watson, Neal, Senr	3		2		6
Rheam, Jacob	2	5	4		24
Watson, Neal, junr			3		
Kilpatrick, Wary	1	3	3		11
Watson, Benjamin	1	2	2		
Bryan, Isaac	2	6		1	18
Cox, Hezekiah	1		3		
Lane, William	1	2	2		
Lambert, Samuel	3	1	2		
Griffin, Benjamin	1	2	4		1
West, Elizabeth		3	3		
Prier, David	2		3	1	
Philips, Rose		1	1		
Bryan, David	2	4	4		
Cormack, John	1	3	2		
Heath, Henry	2	3	4		
Sherrod, Joseph	1		7		
Kent, Samuel	1	1	2		1
Kent, Margaret		1	1		8
Lofton, Shadrach	1	1	3		
Broadway, Jesse	1		3		
Williams, Tolbert	1	1	4		1
West, John	1	3	4		2
Tyre, Lewis	1	1	2		1
Heath, John	1	2	4		
Broadway, James	1		3		
Cormack, Joab	1	1	3		
Arnold, James	1				
Doherty, Daniel	1		1		5
Carlton, Richard	1		2		
Cox, John	2	1	1		10
Cox, Ann			2		1
West, John	1		2		1
Gibbs, Richard	3		2		
Heath, Henry	1				
Doherty, Owen	3	2	4		
Whittington, Solomon	1	1	4		
Heath, Reuben	1		1		
Wadsworth, Jonathan	1	2	3		2
Wadsworth, William	1		2		1
Mits, Frederic	1	3	3		4
Rogers, William	2	1	5		
Wise, John	1	2	6		
Cormack, Solomon	1		2		
Lambert, Ann			3		9
Morris, Thomas	1	2	4		
Jackson, Mary		1	3		
Gilstrap, James	1				
Ebins, Elizabeth		1	1		
Tyre, Thomas	1	1	3		1
Coleman, Thomas	2	2	4		7
Allen, Joseph	2	4	6		19
MacLevain, Francis			1		2
Fish, Thomas	3	3	7		9
Browning, Hannah			4		
Kennedy, John	2	1	4		
Davis, Brisgow	1		3		
Clark, Isaac	1	2	3		
Bentley, William	1	1	4		
Peters, Elizabeth	1	4	5		
Philips, Thomas, junr	1		3		8
Arthur, Lawson	1		3		
Blount, Reading	1		2		2
Sears, James	1	1	2		2
Davis, John	1	2	1		
Davis, Lawson	1	4	6		
Smith, John	1	1	4		
Philips, John	2	3	3		16
Wiggins, John	1	1	2		
Moor, William	1	1	3		1
Kittrell, Jethro	1				

* Illegible.

NEWBERN DISTRICT, CRAVEN COUNTY—Continued.

NAME OF HEAD OF FAMILY.	Free white males of 16 years and upward, including heads of families.	Free white males under 16 years.	Free white females, including heads of families.	All other free persons.	Slaves.
Kittrell, Joseph	1				
Harrison, Joseph	1	3	3		
Trife, Ebenezer	1	2	3		
Hardison, James	2	1	4		
Roundtree, William	1	3	2		1
Philip, Thomas, Senr	2	2	5		
Roundtree, Francis, Senr	2	1	1		1
Frizzell, Jonathan	1	1	7		11
Hutchins, Edward	1	1	3		1
Clark, Edward	2		2		
Coleman, James	1	2	2		1
Dotson, Benjamin	1				
King, Brittain	1	1	5		2
Jones, Walter	2	1	2		2
Spiva, Moses	1	5	4		
Holland, James	1				
Dwans, John	1	3	3		
Clark, David	1				
Jones, William	1	2	4		2
Jones, Thomas	1				6
Jordan, William	3	1	2		
Pool, James	1	3	1		
Philips, Richard	1	2	1		
Coker, Hardy	1	3	2		
Roundtree, Francis, junr	1				
Warnum, John	1	3	2		
Kitrell, Jonathan	1	3	7		
Williams, Ann		2	3		
Philps, James	1	3	2		
Moor, James	1	1	3		
Jones, Thomas	1				
Jones, Richard	1		1		2
Wheathington, Robert	2	5	4		2
Branton, Samuel	2	2	3		1
Wheathington, Ambrose	1				
Lines, William	1		2		1
Stanley, Ephraim	1		2		1
Bryan, John	1		1		14
Bryan, William	1	1	1		11
Lewis, Elisha	1	2	4		
Lewis, Mary	1		3		
Nelson, Rebecca	1		1		
Roach, Charles	3	3	3		8
Tire, John	1		5		
Mills, Anthony	1	1	3		
Pollard, Thomas	1	1	4		
Butler, John	1	4	4		
Ottison, Malicah	1		3		
Phillingim, Jarvis	1	2	3		1
Hartley, Joseph	2	2	3		2
Nelson, George	1	4	3		
Hill, John	1	2	5		3
Nelson, William	2		3		
Pierce, David	1	1	2		6
Bryan, Lewis	1		2		19
Nelson, John	3		1		
Harrington, Jonathan	1	2	4		
Nelson, Edward	1		3		1
Nelson, Levi	1	1	2		
Chapman, Jesse	1	2	3		2
Kennedy, William	1				
Ball, Elizabeth		2	4		2
Campbell, Joseph	3	2	3		2
James, Joseph	2	3	4		
Worsley, Stephen	3	3	3		5
Johnston, Charles	1	2	2		
Bond, John	2	1	3		
Allen, Walter	1	2	2		5
Williams, William	2		1		
Williams, Solomon	1				
Lancaster, Benjamin	2	2	3		
Chapman, Freelove					5
Laughinghouse, Rd Ripley	1	2	1		
Clark, James	1	4	4		1
Johnston, Frederic	1	1			5
Williams, John	1		2		
James, Jeremiah	1		2		
Pollard, Frederic	1	3	1		
Bryan, Darby	1		4		
Winnum, Stephen	1	1	2		
Tant, William	1		2		
King, Joel	3	1	7		
Hays, William	3	3	5		
Willis, Isaac	1		2		
Denmark, James	1		2		
Fornes, Thomas	1	1	2		2
Mills, John	1	1	3		
Chapman, Weeks	1	3	6		6
Mills, Anthony	4	2	6		
McKinney, Isaac	1		4		8
Warren, Horsington	1	3	3		
Taylor, John	1	2	3		
Williams, Benjamin	1	1	4		
Otterson, Caleb	2		4		
Pierce, Benjamin	1	1	2		4
Harris, John	3	1	3		11
Hays, William	1	1	2		
Arnold, Elizabeth			1		
Mitchel, Sarah			2	2	
Hagins, Frazer			2	1	
King, Mary			2		
Gatlin, James	1	2	3		13
Lewis, William	1		4		1
Spyers, John, Junr	1	1	2		
Spyers, John, Senr	1		2		
Warren, Jeremiah	3	1	4		
Hendrix, Nathan	1	4	2		
Lawley, William	1	2	5		
Bright, Stockl	1				13
Winnum, Sarah			3		
Bright, John		2	1		
Warren, Henry	1	2	3		
Wiggins, Samuel	2	2	4		1
McAfity, James	2	2	3		
Palmer, Joseph	2	3	6		24
Johnston, Jacob	4		4		12
Richardson, William	1		3		
Bryan, Danl	1				
Gatlen, Hardy	1		3		14
Arnold, Moses	1	4	2		4
Arnold, Aaron	1	1	2		54
Ives, James	1		2		
Willis, Neomy		2	3		1
Thomas, Evan	1	1	4		
Whitford, Thomas	1	2	5		1
Gatlin, John, Senr	1	3	5		
Asque, James	2		2		
Hypock, John, junr	1	1	1		
Evernton, John	1				
Evernton, Ezekiel	1		4	1	
Gatlin, John, junr	1				
Arthur, Joseph	1			3	
Evernton, William	1	2	1		
King, Harrington	1	1	6		
King, William	1				
Gaskins, John	1		2		
Hypock, Arthur	1				
Hypock, Peter	1	2	4		
Pierce, Mary	1	4	3		
Hill, Richard	1		2		1
Rowe, Elizabeth			2		
Rowe, John	1				
Rowe, Edmund	1				
Whitford, Richard	1	4	2		1
Stilly, Stephen	1				
Stilly, Ishmael	1	1	1		
Willis, Caleb	1	5	4		1
Willis, Richard	1	1	4		4
Willis, Joshua	1	3	7		
Hill, Francis	1				
Warren, Abram	1	1	2		1
Willis, James, Senr	1	1	4		5
Cuttrell, Amos	2	3	3		
Norton, Tomsey		2	3		
Hill, William	2	2	2		
Williams, Charles	1	1	3		8
Willis, James, junr	1	6	2		
Fruit, Henry	2	2	2		
Hellis, James	2	2	3		1
Rowe, James	1	3	5		
Parsons, Hilary	1	2	4		5
Wain, William	2		3		
Gatlen, William	2		4	2	2
Tingle, Solomon	2	1	2		
Barrington, Richard	1	1	3		
Gaskins, William	2	3	3		
Rowe, Thomas	1				4
Gaskins, Thomas	1		1		5
Willis, Joseph	1	4	1		1
Chandler, Henry R	1				
Surles, Ann			3		1
Gatlen, Pierce	1				
Morgan, John	1	1	5		
Whitford, David	3	1	3		
Arthur, William	1		1		
Rigby, Thomas			2		
Rigby, Hugh	3		2		
Stilly, Fountain	1	3	6		
Arthur, John	1	1			
King, Joseph	1	1	2		
Ipock, Jacob	2	2	3		
Kerman, Michael	2	1	2	1	8
Hall, David	1	1	3		
Dunn, Elizabeth		2	1		
Warrin, Abram, junr	1	1	5		1
Hall, Jane		1	2		
Willis, Samuel	2	2			7
Hypock, John, Senr	1	4	3		
Carney, Elizabeth	1	1	2		
Calaway, Mary		1	2		
Hypock, Samuel	1		2		
Gaskins, James	1		3		
Willis, Thomas	2	2	4		2
Willis, Ephraim	1	1	3		1
Thomas, John, Senr	2	2	1		
Sneed, Zadiac	1	2	3		
Thomas, John	1				
Rice, James	1		3		
Reel, Peter	1		1		
Reel, James	3	1	3		12
Harris, Sarah	1		2		
Surles, William	1	2	2		4
Gatlen, Joshua	1	1	3		
Pierce, Ephraim	1		2		3
Toler, Caleb	1	1	2		
Gaskins, Fisher	1	3	1		1
Toler, William	1				
Rowe, Joshua	1		6		
Pierce, James	1	1	1		4
Barrington, Isaac	1		3		3
Toler, James	1				
Dunn, John D	2	2	5		
Whitford, John	2	2	4		3
Bexley, Simon	3	1	4		5
Gaskins, Joseph	1	3	2		
Burch, John	2	2	2		
Smith, Samuel	4	2	1		22
Hill, Levi	1	1	2		1
Gallins, John	1	3	2		
Gatlen, Elizabeth	1		2		
Barnet, Mary			2		2
Clark, William	1	3	2		
Hill, Jane		1	2		
Werst, Daniel	2		6		3
Dixon, William	1	3	5		8
Dawson, Levi	1	2	8		13
Bedscot, John, Senr	1	1	2		4
Bedscot, John, junr	1	1	2		2
Edgington, William	1	1	2		
Lane, John	1	1	3		1
Brinson, Benjamin	1	2	1		1
Caton, Solomon	2	1			
Barnard, Jesse	1	1	2		3
Scot, John	2	2	5		
Daw, James	1		2		
Tingle, Hugh	1		3		
Caton, William	1	5			
Gatlin, William	1		2		1
Lee, John	1	1	2		
Rice, Evan	2		2		
Whitford, William	1	1	7		1
Holton, George	1	3	3		
Richmond, Jacob W	1				
West, David	1	2	3		
Cox, Hinson	3	2	2		
Tingle, Gideon	2		1		1
Brinson, Cason	1	5	2		
Caton, Moses	2	2			
Daw, William	1		2		
Gabriel, Nathaniel	2		2		
Price, James	2		6		
Bexley, William	1	1	2		
Tingle, James	1	1	2		
Holton, Thomas	1		3		
Cutrell, David	2		3		
Murphy, Sarah	1		3		
Purify, Thomas	2		3		2
Rice, John	1	1	2		
Smow, James	2	1	4		
Vendrick, James	2		3		
Daw, John	2		3		
Dixon, William	2	2	1		1
Holton, Barry	1				
Gardner, Francis	1				
Arnold, John	1		3		7
Caton, John	2	1	2		
Holton, Jesse	1	1	1		
Simkins, John	1		3		
Vendric, Rebecca			3		
Spikes, Thomas	1	1	5		8
Brinson, James	1		2		4
Tindon, Ruel	1	2	1		
Brinson, Joseph	1	1	4		1
Dixon, Elijah	1	2	2		
Harper, Abram	2	2	5		
Simkins, James	1	1	2		
Tire, William	1	2	4		3
West, Elizabeth			3		
Wells, Samuel	1	2	4		
Harris, Sarah	2	2	2		
Fell, John	3		1		1
Rumley, Mary		1	2		4
Vendrick, Francis		1	5		
Daw, John, Senr	1	1	2		
Jordan, Thomas	1		2		8
Hoover, William	2	1	3		
Gabriel, John	1	1	1		
Mecans, James	2				
Mott, Abram	1				

NEWBERN DISTRICT, CRAVEN COUNTY—Continued.

NAME OF HEAD OF FAMILY.	Free white males of 16 years and upward, including heads of families.	Free white males under 16 years.	Free white females, including heads of families.	All other free persons.	Slaves.
Baker, John	1		1		
Brinson, Matthew	2	2	2		
Brothers, Mary			4		
Banks, Peter	1	3	1		
Cuttrell, Rhodes	1	2	4		
Daw, John, junr	1				
Blakey, Lawrence	3	2	3		
Price, Lucretia	1	2	2		
Brinson, Daniel	1		1		1
Brinson, James	1	2	3		
Sparrow, Samuel	3	4	2		5
Hall, Thomas	1		1	1	
Bowdon, Avery	2	1	2		
Manley, James				1	
Gathen, David	2	1	3		
West, John	1	1	4		4
Spikes, William, Senr	2		1		9
Blakey, William	1				
Dilemar, Francis	1	3	3		5
Dilemar, Francis, Senr	1	2	2		8
Dilemar, Francis, junr	1	2	3		4
Bond, Francis	3	1	3		
Carraway, Nathan	2	4	4		2
Sparrow, Thomas	1	4	3		5
Dawson, John	1	1	1		11
Parish, John	1		2		
Hall, Oliver	1		3		5
Carraway, James	1		2		
Ives, Thomas	1	1	2		
Lewis, Mason	1		4		
Ives, William	1	4			
Parish, Zadiac	1		3		
Simmons, James	1	4	4		
Morris, Abram	1	1	2		
Simmons, William	1	3	4		
Clayton, William	2	3	4		
Good, Joseph	1	4	3	1	1
Moor, Jesse	2		2		8
Cary, Richard	1	1	3		
Cary, Nicholas	2	2	3		
Thomas, John	1	2	3		5
Creakman, Southy	1	1	5		
Fulsher, Ephraim	2	2	4	1	2
Carraway, William	2	1	1		3
Carraway, Joseph	2	2	3		7
Carraway, Thomas	1		2		2
Carraway, John	1	2	2		
Nelson, Joseph	1	2	2		10
Dilemar, Thomas	1	1	1		3
Biggs, John	2	1	5		4
Paul, Robert	1	1	1		
Green, Joseph	4	2	4		
Ballance, Benjamin	3	5	3	1	
Ballance, Joshua	2		1		
Lester, Jesse	2	1	1		3
Munford, Jesse	2	2	2		
Banks, John	1		7		
Shine, William	1	2	3		8
Wallace, William	3	4	2	1	1
Parish, George	2		5		
Fulsher, Joshua	1		3		16
Fulsher, Elizabeth			1	3	
Carter, Jenny				1	
Waw, Amos	1		3	1	5
Carraway, Sarah	2		2		
Clayton, Mary			2		
Good, Mary			1		2
Dawson, Elizabeth			4		5
Brothers, Robert	2		1		
Gilgo, Mary			2		
Owens, James	1	3	3		
Hudson, Sarah		1	2		
Miller, Enoch	1	1	2		
Holland, Spear	1	2	2		
Smith, William	1		3		1
Spelman, Asa				5	
Spelman, David			1	1	
Tolsin, Benjamin			2		3
Tilman, Henry	6	1	7		11
Fulsher, Jesse	1	3	4		10
Carruthers, Alexander	2				1
Brooks, William	1	1	1		
Lewis, Nathan	2	3	5		
Morris, Nathan	1	2	1		
Brothers, David	1		3		
York, Thomas	1		2		6
Clayton, Thomas	3	1	3		6
Squires, Amos	2	4	1		
Harris, William	1		1		

NAME OF HEAD OF FAMILY.	Free white males of 16 years and upward, including heads of families.	Free white males under 16 years.	Free white females, including heads of families.	All other free persons.	Slaves.
Riggs, Shadrack	1	2	4		
Lewis, Joseph	2	3	3		
Wright, John	1	2	3		
Lewis, Joshua	1	2	3		
Harris, James	1	1	2		
Lewis, John	1		2		
Lewis, Jacob	1	1	3		3
Tilman, John	1		2		
Riggs, David	1	2	3		
Bateman, Hopkins	1	3	4		3
Driggers, Johnston				4	
Martin, John	1		1	1	1
Wharton, James	2		1		7
Martin, David	1	1	2		
Lewis, Major	1	2	3		
Wilcox, John	1				
Harrison, Samuel	3		3		
Rice, Gideon	2	6	3		
Slobuck, Nathaniel	1	4	3		
Morris, Aaron	1		2		
Carruthers, Clayton	1		2		4
McOtler, Hezekiah	4	1	6		
Wharton, William	1	1	1		2
Pitman, Joseph	2	4	2		
Wharton, David	1		2		1
Veal, Elijah	1	1	4		
Phips, Nathan	1	4	4		
Brooks, Joseph	1	2	4		
Morris, Thomas	1		1		
Harper, Peter	1		2		
Brickhouse, Jedediah	1	1	3		
Ives, John	1	5	1		
Howard, Thomas	1				
Mews, Caleb	1		1		
Dilemar, Dempson	1	1	3		2
Fulsher, Cason	1	3	1		
Tingle, Joseph, Senr	3	1	3		5
Martin, Mary	1		2		
Willis, Jeremiah	1	3	6		
Mews, James	1	2	2		
Riggs, Mary	1		1		
Tingle, Joseph, junr	1	2	2		
Clark, John	1		1		
Kirk, Roger	1	1	2		
Hammontree, Griffin	2	3	1		
Carraway, Joshua	1	1	1		1
Muse, John	2	3	2		
Howering, Jesse	1	2	4		
Clark, John, Senr	3	4	2		
Simmons, Nathan	1		1		
Squires, Jeremiah	1		3		
Hewit, William	1				
Lindsey, Joshua, Senr				4	
Wheaton, John	1	3	4		
Sermons, Ephraim	1		2		
Willis, Thomas	1	1	3		
Holland, Martha			2		
Carruthers, John	2	2	1		9
Rigs, Miller	1	2	4		
Lewis, Jacob, Senr	1		2		
Wheelton, Levin	1	1	5		
Paul, John	2	3	2		
Brooks, Elizabeth	1		2		2
Wilcocks, James	2		2		
Morris, John	1	1	2	1	
Bond, Sarah			1	2	1
Macbay, Abel	1	1	4		
Paul, George	1		4		
Bryan, Needham	1	1	4		
Wilcox, William	1	2	2		1
Veal, Elizabeth		1	4		
Rice, Rebecca		1	5		
Rigs, Sarah		3	6		2
Roach, James	1		2		
Avery, John	1		6	1	
Hammontree, Hardy	1				
Johnston, Ann				2	
Lindsey, Mary				3	
Griggers, Elizabeth				5	
Tilman, John	2		6	1	12
Draper, Sarah			2		8
Harper, John	1		3		7
Lewis, David	1		3		
Williams, Thomas	1		1		28
Jones, Humphry	1	2	2		35
Fonvielle, John	1	2	3		22
McCrohon, Mary		1	3		16
Nixon, Richard	3		5		19
Neale, Abner	1	1	2		20

NAME OF HEAD OF FAMILY.	Free white males of 16 years and upward, including heads of families.	Free white males under 16 years.	Free white females, including heads of families.	All other free persons.	Slaves.
Blackledge, William	1		3		1
Cheney, Mary	1		3		2
Kennedy, George	1		1		2
Collier, Thomas	2	3	5		15
Saunders, Charles	2		7		4
Williams, Benjamin	1		1		92
Blount, Wilson	1	1	2		45
Pilchard, John	1		2		
Wilkes, Humphry	1		2		
Conner, Sarah			3		2
Jump, William	1	2	4	1	
Taylor, Abraham, Senr	2	2	1		
Williams, Benjamin, Senr	5	2	3		
Bradshaw, Mary			2		
Yates, Daniel	2	1	3		
Moor, John					12
Hunter, Catherine	1		2		
Stephenson, Silas S.	2	2	3		20
Herritage, John B	1				3
Pearson, John	3	1	2		
Bogue, Benijah	1		2		
Stanley, Wright	1	2	2		31
Carter, James	1	1	1	1	
Carter, Joseph	2	1	4	1	5
Carter, Elijah	2		1	1	2
Kelleham, Barsheba	1	2	2		
Black, Letitia			3		
Lewis, Jesse	1	3	3		4
Gooding, Bardin	1		3		
Bogue, Dixon	1		2		
Sevils, William	1	2	2		
Sevils, James	1		7		
Perkins, Edmund	1	4	2	1	9
Dickinson, Edmund	1		1		
Wheathrington, James	1	3	1		
Fonvielle, Richard	1				3
Tooley, William	1	1	1	1	6
Clark, John	2	3	2		13
Hilbert, Leonard	1	1	2		
Green, William	1	1	2		2
Stafford, Mary	1		2		
Lambert, John	1	1	5		1
Keef, Edmund	1	2	3		
Fonvielle, William B	2		2		11
Charlot, John	1	2	4		4
Green, Joseph	1	2	3		
Richardson, Andrew	2		1		3
Taylor, Abram, junr	1	2	6		
Bogey, Alexander	1		1		
Johnston, Richard	1				
Wilks, Matthew	1		1		
Smith, Arthur	1	1	7		1
Williams, Stephen	1		2		1
Harrison, James	1		1		
Grenade, Benjamin	1		2		2
Davis, Thomas	1	1	6		
Smith, John	1	1	2	1	1
McKubbins, Samuel	1				
Sanders, James	2	2	3		2
Fonvielle, Thomas G	1				5
Lane, George	1	2	1	1	5
Moor, John	1	1	1		5
Wheathrington, Thomas	1	1	2		
Barnet, Ashley	1	2	2		
Mitchell, Alexander	1	2	1		1
Moor, Jesse					3
Sanderson, Esther			1	2	
Ranson, Isaac					7
Moor, Simeon					11
Ranson, George					5
Moor, John					2
Brown, Samuel					4
Harris, Thomas					10
Moor, Abraham					1
Morgan, James					1
Spelman, Aaron					3
Mosley, Caty					1
Davis, Michael					3
Moor, Susannah					3
Dickinson, Levin	1		1		1
Copeland, Cato				2	
Jack (Old)				7	
Lewis, Thomas				7	
Wilson, Thomas	1		1		
Wilson, James	1	1	1		13
Stafford, Lodon	1				

NEWBERN DISTRICT, DOBBS COUNTY.

NAME OF HEAD OF FAMILY.	Free white males of 16 years and upward, including heads of families.	Free white males under 16 years.	Free white females, including heads of families.	All other free persons.	Slaves.
Edwards, Thomas	1				8
Holms, Moses	1	2	2		1
Barrow, Micajah	1		1		
Sheppard, Abram, Senr	3		1		18
Ward, Darling	3	5	2		3
Faircloth, William, Senr	4		4		15
Faircloth, William, Junr	1		3		1
Martin, William, Senr	1	1	1		
Wall, John	1	1	4		
Shepherd, William	1		4	4	5
Glasgow, James	5		5		50
Wright, James	1		3		
Holmes, James	1	1	4	1	2
Williams, John	1	1	3		4
Andrews, William	2	2	4		1
Holms, Jesse	2	2	5		
Holms, Timothy	1		3		4
Holms, John	3	1	4		
Downing, Elisha	1	3	1		
Downing, Joseph	1		3		3
Pope, Poole	1		7		
Aycock, William	1	2			
Cannon, James, Senr	3		3		
Cannon, James, junr	1	2	3		
Cannon, John	1	4	3		
Taylor, William	1	1	4		4
Taylor, John	1	1	3		1
Butcher, Thomas	4	5	6	1	
Price, John	1	5	1	1	
Edmondson, John	3	2	5		
Sheppard, John	1	1	1		9
Ruffin, Etheldred	1	5	3		19
Brown, Mary		3	2		7
Salls, James	2	3	2		
Price, Redick	1	2	1		1
Barrow, Harold	2	3	4		
Barrow, Sherrard	1	3	6	3	
Smith, David	1	2	2		
Barrow, Jeremiah	1	1	3		
Smith, Nicholas	1	2	6		
Smith, Mark	1	6	5		
Hinson, Jesse	1		1		
Hinson, William	1	1	1		
Hinson, Joseph	1		4		
Smith, Henry	1	3	4	1	
Jordan, Evan	1	2	4	4	
Jordan, Frederick	2	2	5		15
Smith, Richard	2	3	3		10
Smith, Thomas	1	2	2		2
Smith, Etheldred	1	1	1		2
Spann, John	2		4		2
Parker, John, Senr	1		4		
Parker, John, junr	1	1	1		
Taylor, Robert	1		2	1	
Smith, James	1		4		
Warters, William	2	4	5		
Barfield, Ane		2	3		
Henby, John	1	2	3		
Tiddor, George, Senr	2		2		
Tiddor, George, junr	1		1		
Tiddor, Thomas	1	2	4		
Brown, Samuel	1	2	2		
Glasgow, Mary		3	1		12
Reynolds, Mary		2	3		
Thornton, James	1	1	3		
Faircloth, Frederick	1		3		
Faircloth, Thomas	1	5	2		1
Sibert, John Dan	1		4		
Stephenson, Mary	1		2		
Long, Jesse	1	4	2		
Ward, Dierdamer		1	3		
Newby, Matthew	1				
McAlpin, Robert	1				
Brumley, Thomas	1	2	4		
Jordan, Thomas	2	5	5		2
Grainger, John	2		4		5
Harper, Francis, Senr	1		1		1
Harper, Francis, junr	1	3	2		1
Sheppard, Benjamin	8	12	19		71
Harrel, Benjamin	1	2	3		5
Pridgeon, Ruffin	1		4		
Tindale, Samuel	1		3		
Tindale, John	2	4	4		1
Best, Benjamin	5	1	2		18
Best, Henry	1		2		2
Wood, James	2	5	9		9
Garland, John	1	1	2		4
Garland, Josiah	1		1		3
Edwards, William	1	4	3		7
Harper, Blaney	1	1	3		4
Hall, Poole	2	1	1		
Hall, Dempsey	1		2		
Sugg, Absalom	4	2	3		
Sugg, John, Senr	2	1	3		5
Sugg, John, junr	1	1	1		2
Sugg, Josiah	1		1		2
Oliver, Anne			4		
McNeale, Isaac	1	1	3		
Dixon, Frederick	1		4		3
Dixon, Shadrack	1		1		1
Dixon, Murfree	2	1	5		1
Harper, William	1		1		3
Kilpatrick, William	3	1	2		2
Fitzpatrick, John	1	1	1		6
Moore, Samuel	3	3	2		1
Wilson, John	2		1		
Wilson, William	1	1	1		
Lassiter, Jesse	1		2	2	7
Caswell, Benjamin	2	2	2		4
Hooker, William	1		1		11
Hooker, Nathan	1	1	2		3
Hooker, Samuel	1		7		5
Haile, John	1		3		4
Cale, John	3	2	4		1
Hill, Robert	1	2	3		4
Hill, Michael	1		2		
Hill, Richard	1		2		
Aldridge, Jesse	1	1	4	1	
Aldridge, Drury	2		4		8
Whitley, Josiah	1	2	2		1
Whitley, William	1		1		
Rowe, Jesse	1		2		
Stanley, Isaac	3	2	4		7
Bright, Graves	1	1	1		7
Hill, Zilpha			3		
Hall, Celia			2		
Ludwell, Richard	2		1		
Freeman, John	3	2	7		3
Jones, John	1	3	2		
Jones, Frederick	2	1	3		
Jones, James	1		2		
Lassiter, Jacob, Senr	2				20
Lassiter, Jacob, junr	1		1		4
Pridgeon, Thomas	2	2	4		20
Edwards, Mary	1		2		13
Ward, David	1		1		
Johnston, James	1		2		
Ward, Daniel	1	1	2		
Ward, Thomas	1		2		
Edwards, Henry	1		2		3
Wade, James	2		2		12
Wade, Joseph	1		2		2
Reynolds, Christopher	1	5	4		
Morris, Charles	1		2		
Reeves, William	1		2		
Rieves, Joseph	1		2		
Combe, Ebenezer	1	1	2		1
Kenney, William	1		1		
Mitchell, William	1	4	4		
Kenney, Jane			3		
Madens, John	1		3		
Lane, Thomas	1	3	4		2
Kilpatrick, William	1		1		1
Davis, Icabod	1		6		
Davis, Lewis	1		1		7
Sugg, William	1	1	2		
Sugg, John	1	2	4		
Sugg, Michael	1	1	1		
Sugg, James	1		2		
Bailey, Lewis	1		1		4
Denny, Mary			5		
Denny, Abram	1		2		
White, John	1	1	1		
Bush, Abram	1		1		
Corwell, Spencer	3	1	4		6
Patrick, John	1				4
Harold, Ann			2		
Williams, Jonathan	1		3		
Broom, Mason	1	1	4		
Stewart, James	1	1	4		
Wilson, Acquiton	1	2	5		1
Lewis, Cadir	1	1	1		
Lewis, James	1	1	3		
Lewis, Stephen	1		2		
Harris, William	1		5		
Lohorn, Sarah			2		
Wosdon, Austin	1	1	3		2
Hinson, Elizabeth			5		
Mezings, Ann			3		5
Spright, Samuel	1	2	5		3
Elliott, Zachariah	1	1	2		2
Hart, Moses	1		2		
Hart, Zachariah	1	1	2		5
Pate, Joseph	2	4	4		3
Sparkman, John	2	4	4		
Scarborough, Nathan	1	2	2		
Ellis, Enos	1	2	2	2	
Matthews, Alexander	1	2	1		1
Williams, Jonas	1	4	2		8
Field, Moses	1		2		13
Shepherd, Abram	1	2	4		14
Brann, John B	3	4	5	1	12
Matthews, William	3	1	2		
Matthews, Richard	1	2	3		
Wilson, Mary	1	2	4		5
McCarthy, Timothy	2	1	4		
Carter, Jesse	2		1		1
Bryan, John	2		3		
Britt, Margaret	1		3		
Britt, William	1	1	1		
Hardy, Dorothy	1		2		4
Hollwell, Mary			1		1
Grimsley, John	2		3		4
Deale, William	2	2	4		
Smith, John	3		2		4
Morris, Charles	1		2		
Chalcraft, David	1	1	1		
Henby, Joseph	1	4	1		1
Rasberry, Francis	1	3	4		5
Williams, John	3	3	5		9
Jones, Jesse	2		3		8
Garner, Speedham	1	2	3		
Minshew, Isaac	1	2	5		1
Garner, Simeon	1		1		
Rasberry, John	3	1	3		8
Jordan, Richard	1		2		
Ellis, Hyperion	1		3		
Ellis, John	4		3		
Taylor, Robert	1	1	3		
Hallows, Josiah	1	3	4		
Taylor, Stephen	1	3	2		
Grear, John	1	4	3		
Grizzard, Lucy			4		
Minshew, Jacob	1		2		
Minshew, Keziah		2	1		4
Minshew, John	1	1	1		
Grizzard, Thomas	1	1	1		
Pipkin, Lewis	1	1	3		
Hart, William	1	1	5		
Pipkin, John	2	3	3		
Pipkin, Sarah			3		1
McKeel, John	1	1	1		
Moore, William	7		4		
Conner, Jonathan	2	4	3		
Williams, Willowby	1	1	1		8
Henby, James	3	3	2		
Spight, Stephen	2		3		
Spight, John	2	1	3		
Spight, John, junr	1		1		
Hall, Thomas	1	1	1		
Anneson, Abram	1		2		
Cuter, Stephen	1	2	1		
Hays, Isaac	1	3	5		
Butler, Elisha	1		4		1
Scarborough, Benjamin	2	3	5		
Riff, Daniel	3	3	4		
Sorrow, William	1		1		
Barrow, James	4	3	5		
Price, Nathan	1		2		
Price, Absalom	2		1		4
Hays, Mary		2	3		
Ellis, Edwin	4	1	2		13
Dannels, Delijah	1	4	4		1
Price, Thomas	1		2		
Moor, Britton	3		4		
Eason, Stephen	2	1	4		3
Beaman, Edmond	2		4		
Beaman, Jeremiah	1	3	2		
Mercer, Shadrach	1	4	4		
Paul, Jacob	2	3	4		
Minshew, Nathan	4	3	5		5
Sharp, Thomas	1	2	2		
Shacklefoot, John	1	2	1		
Spight, Alice	2	2	4		
Spight, William	2	5	6		
Hays, Ann	3		3		
Ward, John	1	1	3		19
Ward, Needham	1	1	2		5
Spight, Sarah			2		1
Lewis, John	1		1		
Ellis, Joseph	3	1	3		10
Davis, Joshua	1	3	2		7
Peal, David	2	2	2		3
Barzarum, Abier	1		5		
Walston, John	2		5		
Scarborough, Martha			3		
Walston, William	2	3	4		
Garris, John	1	1	2		
Barzarum, John	1	2	3		
Rasberry, Daniel	1		2		
Carter, William	2		3		1
Price, John	1	1	3		1
Thigpin, Margaret	2	1	2		
Walston, Philip	1	1	2		
Moor, William, junr	1	1	2		
Vicks, Robert	1	1	3		2
Price, Thomas	1		5		
Spight, William	2	2	2		23
Spight, Seth	1	3	3		11

NEWBERN DISTRICT, DOBBS COUNTY—Continued.

NAME OF HEAD OF FAMILY.	Free white males of 16 years and upward, including heads of families.	Free white males under 16 years.	Free white females, including heads of families.	All other free persons.	Slaves.
Barfield, William	2		2		
Barfield, Mills	2	3	5		
Barfield, John	2	2	3		
Barfield, James	3	3	6		
Hooke, Roger	2	3	2		
Hays, Susannah	3	3	3		
Shacklefoot, Willowby	1	2	3		
Ormond, William	2	3	3		12
Barfield, Thomas	1	1		1	
Murfree, William	1	1	4		4
Murfree, John	1	4	4	1	5
Murfree, Jethro	2	1	4		9
Young, James	1		5		
Jones, Joseph	1	1	4		
Wade, Samuel	1	3	3		
Sanderson, John	1		2		
Hicks, Jesse	1	1	4		
Grunsley, Sherod	1	1	2		
House, Joseph	1	1	3		3
Turnage, Luke	1	1	1		
Turnage, James	2	1	1		
Magee, Daniel	1		4		
Edwards, Benjamin	1	1	5		
Butts, Elizabeth	2	1	1		
Butts, George	1		1		
Butts, Aaron	1	1			
Butts, James	1		1		
Tunnage, Daniel	1	1	4		
Deale, Abel	2		1		
Tunnage, George	1	2	3		
Jones, David	1		5		
Mayers, Timothy	1	3	3		
Readick, William	3	2	4		
Deal, Thomas	1	2	5		
Mayers, Mark	4	1	2		
Goodson, William	1	2	3		
Mayers, James	1	1	3		
Mayers, John	1	4	3		
Tonnage, Jesse	1	2	2		
Chalcraft, Levi	1	2	5		
McGee, John	1		1		
Taylor, Hillary, Senr	3	2	4		
Taylor, Hilary, Junr	1		2		
Davis, Martin	1	1	3		
Davis, James, Senr	1	3	1		1
Davis, James	1	3	3		
Griffin, William	1	2	2		
Griffin, Drew	1	1	3		
Hooker, Hymerick	1	4	2		5
Jones, John	1	2	8		2
Holliday, Samuel	1	1	4		8
Jones, William, Senr	1	1	3		
Jones, Sylvanus	2	1	5		
Lassiter, Nathan	2	1	4		14
Jones, William	1	1	2		
Pope, John	1	4	5		15
Harper, John	1	2	3		1
Tindale, Joshua	1	2	1		
Barfield, James	1	3	3		
Bryant, Benjamin	1	1	4		9
Roberts, Roger	1	4	3		
Olds, Arthur	3	5	1		5
Readick, John	1	2	4		1
Hamilton, John	1		2		
Hort, Robin	1	4	4		18
Carr, Titus	2	3	4		29
Durdin, William	2	1	1	1	11
Tunnage, William	2	2	2		
Broom, Melius	1	4	6		4
Taylor, Henry	1		5		7
Taylor, John	1	2	2		
Rolls, Cornelius	1	2	2		
Spiva, Ephraim	1	1	1		
Spiva, Caleb	1	2	2		3
Hart, Lucretia	2	2	3		1
Smith, William	1	4	2		
Farris, William	2	1	5		5
Parrymore, Benjamin	1	1	2		
Dukes, John	1	3	3		
Hardison, James	2	1	4		
Van Pelt, Anthony	3	2	4		
Menter, James	1	6	2		
Butler, William	1	1	1		
Griffin, Joshua	1	3	3		
Coward, Edward	2	2	4		2
Coward, James	2	2	6		
Coward, Needham	1	5	5		1
Miller, George	2	1	6		
Miller, William	1				
Holliday, John	2				2
Jones, Daniel	1	1	2		
Ormond, William	1				
Musick, John	2		3		
McCoye, William	1				
Harrell, John	1				
Griffin, Benjamin	1				
Miller, John	1		1		

NAME OF HEAD OF FAMILY.	Free white males of 16 years and upward, including heads of families.	Free white males under 16 years.	Free white females, including heads of families.	All other free persons.	Slaves.
Jones, John	2	3	4	2	1
Vance, David	1	2	2		
Coward, John	1	1	5		2
Coward, Elisha	2	2	3		
Howard, Frederick	1		6		
Coward, James	1	2	2		
Coward, Ann			1	1	1
Philips, James	1	1	2		
Putnell, Stephen	1	1	2		
Kilpatrick, Israel	1		2		
Wade, John	1	2	4		
Moore, John	1	2	4		
Pate, John, junr	1	1	3		
Pate, John, Senr	2		2		3
Pate, Sarah		2	3		
Owens, Ann Pelia			2		
Pate, William, Senr	2	2	2		2
Pate, William, Junr	1	2	3		
Philips, Mark, junr	1	2	1		
Moseley, Elizabeth		2	3		8
Moseley, Tully	1	1	2		5
Patrick, Martha			2		5
Partridge, John	1	3	5		
Voss, Ephraim	1	2	4		
Parker, Joseph	1		2		
Withrington, Robert	1	2	3		2
Johnston, Isaiah	1	1	1		1
Bond, Isband	1		3		
Jones, William	1	1	2		2
Jones, John	1	2	3		1
Jones, John	1	1	1		3
Jones, Richard	1	4	7		
Harvey, Matthias	2	1	4		4
Philips, Mason	3	1	2		
Philips, Benjamin	1	1			
Voss, William	1	2	5		
Moore, Ephraim	1	1			
Fortner, William	1	2	2		
Sulivan, John	1		4		
Johnston, Mary	2		5		
Johnston, Elijah	1	4	2		1
Cole, Thomas	1	2	1		
Tull, Charles	1	2	3		4
Ward, Hugh	1	2	4		
Peters, William	1	2	4		
Britton, Joseph	1	1	6		4
Withrington, Willis	1	1	2		
Withrington, Nathan	1		2		6
Patrick, Manning	2	1	3		9
Smith, Isum	1	1	1		1
Pope, William	1	1	4		3
Dannel, Josiah	1		2		4
Bright, James	1	2	6		8
Bell, George	2	1	8		7
Ingram, Charles	2	1	4		
Williams, Job	1	4	3		
Baker, Elijah	1	2	2		2
Baker, Frederick	1	2	2		2
Adams, Willowby	1		1		
Powell, John	1		2		
Micks, Jacob	1		2		
Grant, Isaac	1		2		
Grant, Mary		3	2		
Fortner, James	3	1	4		2
Powell, Daniel	1	1	5		
Fortner, Emanuel	2	3	3		
Moore, William, Senr	2	2	3		
Moore, William, junr	1	3	6		
Moore, John	1	2	2		
Moore, Isaiah	1	5	3		
Moore, Ephraim	1		2		
Moore, Amaziah	1	3	2		
Taylor, Christopher	2		2		
Taylor, James	1		4		
Hamilton, John	1	4	2		
Hutchins, Elijah	1		4		
Hamilton, Sarah			4		
Budd, Thomas	3		1		
Smith, Job	1	2	2		
Jones, William	1	2	2		1
Withrington, Stephen	1	3	3		
Withrington, Daniel	1		2		
Dismal, John	1		2		
Philips, Thomas	2	1	2		
Dismal, Daniel	1		3		
Dismal, Jeremiah	1	5	2		
Ingram, James, Senr	2	1	5		
Ingram, James, junr	2	5	3		2
Jackson, Sarah			2		
Alexander, Frances		1	2		
Falconer, Olive	1	2	2		
Wootus, Merkland	1		1		
Wootus, John	2		2		
Bruton, Simon	2		2		1
Cunningham, Jester	1	2	3		
Withrington, Cleaverly	2	4	4		
Turner, Reuben	1		2		

NAME OF HEAD OF FAMILY.	Free white males of 16 years and upward, including heads of families.	Free white males under 16 years.	Free white females, including heads of families.	All other free persons.	Slaves.
Abbot, Elizabeth	1	3	3		6
Bond, William	1		2		6
Wilson, John	3	2	3		2
Collier, Mary	1		3		3
Withrington, William	1	2	3		
Griffin, Simon	1	1	6		
Ramsay, Thomas	2	1	4		
Moore, Thomas	1	1	4		
Philips, Mark, Senr	2	7	7		
Browning, George	1	4	4		
Croom, Joshua	1	2	2		9
Parrot, John, junr	1	4	2		
Parrot, John, Sen	3	1	4		3
Parrot, Jacob	2	2	3		4
Hartsfield, John, Senr	2		1	2	2
Hartsfield, David	1	1	2		
Hodges, John	1	1	3		
Hodges, Richard	2	2	5		
Creach, Benjamin	2	2	4		
Creach, Ezekiel	1	3	4		
Bird, Richard, Senr	1		1		2
Bird, Richard, junr	1		1		
Mewborn, Parrot	1		2		
Bird, Eleanor		1	3		1
Tull, John	1	3	3		15
Tull, William	1	1	5		5
Bright, Mary			3		8
Baker, Abram	2	2	4		9
Thomas, Ratio	1	3	5		
Williams, Joseph	1		1		
Arnet, Peter	1		1		
Hutchins, Miles	1	4	7		2
Hartsfield, Paul	2	1	3		4
Williams, Joseph	2	1	4		
Williams, Joshua	2	2	7		
Wilson, James	2		2		
Frizell, John	1		1		
Hill, Mary	1	2	3		
Birton, Benjamin	1		1		
Brown, Richard	1				
Brown, John	1	4	3		
Robinson, Benjamin	2	3	1		
Bush, Sanders	1	2	1		
Cox, John	2		1		
Scean, Elijah	1	1	3		
Freeman, John	1	2	2		
Tillman, John	1	2	2		
Sutton, William	1	1	1		
Hardy, Major	1	1	2		1
Kennedy, Mary		1	2		1
Lewis, Benjamin	1	1	3		
Kennedy, Walter	1		4		1
Kennedy, Ann	1		2		
Morris, Jonathan	1	1	3		2
Arundell, William	1	1	6		3
Pool, Aaron	1	3	3		
Pool, Joseph	1	1	3		
Caswell, James	1	1	2		
Caswell, Ann	1	1	2		3
Westbrooke, Moses	2	4	5		6
Wiggins, John	1	3	2		
Wiggins, Gersham	3		3		3
Hartsfield, John, junr	1	1	2		
Hartsfield, Shadrach	1		4		3
Pool, Josiah	1		1		
Pool, Samuel	1	2	5		
Lovick, Moses	3	2	3		
Bush, Abram	1				
Difnall, David	2	1	4		
Pool, William	1		3		
Dannels, Mary			2		
Iler, Nelly			2		
Thomson, John	1		2		
Smith, Elizabeth			3		
Smith, Joshua	1	1	3		
Smith, Nathan	1	2	1		
Smith, Jesse	1	1	1		
Iler, William, Senr	1		4		
Iler, William, junr	1	1	4		
McCoye, Ann			2		
Barwick, Margaret		2	3		
Wine, Claret	1		3		
Bars, John	2	1	8		5
Garret, Ann			5		
Harrison, Thomas	1	1	4		
Martin, William	1		4		
Templer, Rachel		2	2		
Paradise, John	1		4		
Arnett, John	1	1	3		2
Aldridge, John	1	1	2		
Aldridge, Jesse	1		2		
Aldridge, William, Senr	1	1	4		2
Taylor, Isaac	2		2		
Aldridge, William, Jur	1				2
Aldridge, Thomas	1		3		15
Hardy, Sarah	1	1	3		5
Croom, Hardy	1		1		17

NEWBERN DISTRICT, DOBBS COUNTY—Continued.

NAME OF HEAD OF FAMILY.	Free white males of 16 years and upward, including heads of families.	Free white males under 16 years.	Free white females, including heads of families.	All other free persons.	Slaves.
Farmer, Jesse	1		2		
Bird, Nathan	1	1	4		1
Bird, Richard	2	4	2		
Shine, Francis	1		4		1
Creach, John	1				
Caswell, Lany		1	3		1
Potts, Stringe	1	2	2		
Ingram, Isaac	1	2	4		
Linton, Tabitha			2		
Clark, John	1				
Freeman, Francis L	1	1	3		
Glover, Elizabeth			3		
Philips, Thomas	2	1	2		
Langston, Abram	2	2	6		
Christophers, Christopher	1	1			3
Smith, John	1	2	5		1
Grace, William	1		1		
Richardson, Richard	2	1	2		1
Lord, William	1				1
Tilman, Ann			2		
Totwine, Simon	2		1		7
Spencer, Elizabeth		1	1		2
Markland, Charles	1			1	
White, William	1		3		11
Hill, John	2	4	3		4
Bryn, Matthew	1				
Cobb, Jesse	1	3	4		42
Caswell, Winston	1	1	1		6
Caswell, Sarah	2	2	3		21
Crooms, William	1				23
Uzzell, Thomas	1	3	2		2
Sutton, Benjamin	1	3	6		
Stanley, Jonathan	1	3	2		
Hunter, Job	3	4	3		
Stanley, William	1	3	1		
Maxwell, Arthur	1	1	2		
Seamore, John	4	1	2		
Elmore, Francis	1	3	1		
Titterton, Isaac	1	2	1		
Henry, Robert	1		4		
Mitchel, Hardy	1		1		
Mitchel, Ezekiel	1	2	2		
Heron, John	1	4	5		7
Ellis, Jacob	1		4		
Waters, Sarah	1	2	2		3
Ellis, John	1		2		1
Scipper, Jacob	1	6	2		
Rouse, Jesse, jun^r	1		3		
Mezingo, Pierse	1	2	8		
Sutton, James	1				1
Sutton, John	2		2		2
Gray, John	1	3	5	1	
Stephens, Absalom	1	7	2		
Smith, Martin	1	3	2		
Elmore, Morgan	1		6		
Crooms, Major, Senr	1	1	1		14
Lassiter, Stephen	1		3		6
Hinson, Aaron	1	6	3		
Benton, Jonathan	1	3	3		
Heron, Elisha	1	3	2		1
Langley, Isaac	1	1	5		
Hardy, Samuel	2	2	4		20
Hardy, Benjamin	1		1		2
Rouse, Jesse, Senr	1	2	3		
Rouse, Simon	2	3	7		
Surles, Edward	3	2	2		
Potter, William	2	2	7		
Mosley, Matthew	1	4	2		11
Rouse, John, Senr	1	2	3		5
Rouse, John, jun^r	1	3	1		3
Woostin, John	2	3	1		
Hughes, Thomas	2	1	1		9
Waters, John	1	7	4		
Waters, Moses	2	3	6		
Waters, Abimelech	1	2	5		4
Waters, John	1	6	4		1
Bird, Joshua, Senr	3	4	3		
Bird, Joshua, jun^r	1		2		
Creel, Charles	1	2	3		
Lovit, Patience	2	4	1		
Dannel, James	1	1	2		
Lawson, John	3	1	3		10
Dannel, Owen	1		4		
Dannel, John	1	2	5		
Heron, Mitchel	1	3	5		8
Taylor, William	1	1	5		12
Taylor, Robert	2	4	6		3
Taylor, Daniel	1	3	6		3
Uzzell, Isum	4	1	2		14
Totwine, Simon	1		1		
Elmore, Randolph	1		1		
Creel, John	1		2		7
Creel, Thomas	1	3	4		
Creel, Nathan	1		4		
Creel, Willowby	1	1	4		
Totwine, Isaac	1				
Mezingo, Booth	1	4	2		
Elmore, William	1	3	3		
Tucker, William	2		1		
Tucker, John	1	1	5		
Field, Brittle	2	4	8		
Wilson, Thomas	2	1	1		
Wilson, Joseph	1	2	1		1
Hanks, Epaphroditus	1	3	1		
Hanks, Moot	1	2	4		
Aldridge, William	1	2	2		12
Aldridge, Thomas	1	1	2		2
Dawson, Thomas	1	6	1		2
Surles, Robert	1	2	1		
Gatlen, Lazarus	1	4	6		
Gatlen, Jesse	1		2		
Rouse, Solomon	1	1	3		
Whitman, Jeremiah	1	2	3		
Crooms, Isaac	1		5		32
Crooms, Richard	1	2	2		26
Martins, Higalty	1	1	5		1
Martin, John	1				
Tutterton, Sarah			5		
Whitfield, Bryan	4	4	4		58
Lovit, Edward	1	2	3		
Kennedy, Henry	1	3	2		
Smith, Booky	2		2		
Perdue, Dennis	2	1	3		1
Waters, Winifred			2		
Rouse, Joseph	1		1		2
Dawson, John	2				1
Joe				1	
Walker				1	
Whood, Robert	1				1
Lovit, David	1		2		
Creamer, George	1	2	3		
Ellis, Ebenezer	1	2	1		
Wilson, Obadiah	1		2		
Tucker, Delilah	1	2	3		
Cotton, Lucy		1	2		
Glohorn, Edmond	1				
Scipper, James	1	1	5		
Woodland, Robert	1		2		
Lovitt, Joseph	1		1		
Priest, David	1	2	1		
Crooms, Major, jur	1	5	4		13
Wilder, Ann		1	4		
Anders, Drury	1	2	5		
Burnet, William					5
Henry, Burrel	1	1	1		
Lawson, John	1		1		
Aldrigde, William, jur	1				
Westbrooke, Grey	1	2	2		5
Waters, John, Senr	1	1	2		
Hardy, John	2	3	5		
Smith, Martin	1	3	2		
Dawson, Joel	1		5		2
Goodman, Henry	1		1	2	8
Tetterton, Thomas	1		3		
Tetterton, John	1		2		
Pipkin, Jesse	1	4	3		6
Pipkin, John	1	2	1		1
Hines, Isaac	2	3	3		1
Bush, Beby	1	1	4		10
Benton, Francis	3	2	7		
Carter, Edward			1	8	20
Carter, John		2	3	1	2
Hunter, Thomas	2	2			
Waterman, William	1	2		1	1
Whitfield, James	1				9
Jones, Peter	1	4	2		
Smith, David	1	1	4		9
Davis, Windol	1	1	4		9
Davis, Cato	2		4		6
Whitfield, John	1	3	2		10
Grady, John	2	3	3		7
Smith, John	1	1	1		
Grady, William	1	2	1		2
Hines, Prudence	2		3		
Calley, Roger	1	6	2		4
Borin, William	1	2	4		
Pickle, Michael	1	3	3		
Spence, John	3		3		
Whitfield, Luke	1		2		8
Jones, Sukey			3		
Jones, Ezekiel	1	2	3		
Parker, Sarah			1		1
Thomas, John	1		1		
McMuller, Thomas	1	3	1		
Thomson, John	2	3	1		
Harper, John	1	1	4		
Johnston, Reuben	1				
Cox, John	2	1	2		
Jones, Jesse	1				2
Jackson, Jacob	2	4	2		1
Loiton, Leonard	2	2	6		
Delahunta, John	1	2	2		8
Jones, Frederic	1		2		9
Tilman, Joseph	3	3	3		7
Goodman, William	2	2	2		9
Jones, Thomas	1		4		
Burne, William	1		1		
Fisher, George	1				
Croom, Lott	1		1		8
Taylor, James	1	1	4		
Taylor, Isaac	1	3	5	5	7
Jones, Thomas	1				
Jones, John	2		7		
Gibbs, John	3	3	4		8
Goodman, Henry	1		2		9
Jackson, James	1		2		
Moye, Joseph	1	1	3		
Jump, John	1		2		
Wootin, Shadrach	2	6	3		6
McBearn, William	1	1	2		
Goodman, Timothy	1		2		6
Wright, Grove	1				
Wootin, William	1				
Law, Jonathan	1		1		
Williamson, Tully	1		1		
Easterling, William, Senr	2	1	6		
Ingram, Isaac	1	2	4		
Herritage, John	2		4		38
Spence, Charles	2		1		
Taylor, Joseph	1	2	2		9
Tilman, Mary		1	4		
Thomas, Jesse	1	3	4		
Cox, Harmon	4	1	4		
Cox, Tobias	1		3		7
Marklund, John	1				1
Lankston, Mace	1	1	6		
Edgley, John	1	1	3		
Wilson, James	1	3	3		
Coleman, Benj^a	3	2	5		25
Nunn, Francis	2	1	1		3
Nunn, William	1	1			
Nunn, Joshua	1	1	1		6
Lofton, Samuel	1	2	2		2
Nunn, Stephen	2		1		
Tardwel, Rebecca			3		
Lofton, Jeremiah	2	2	4		20
Mew, William	1	2	2		
Benson, William	1	2	6		1
Benson, Richard	1				
Heron, Nelly		3	4		
Griffin, Samuel	2		4		1
Parker, Lydia	4		2		
Griffin, Evan	1	3	5		
Griffin, James	1	2	3		
Griffin, Jacob, Senr	1		4		
Nobles, Philpenny	2	3	4		
Ivy, Robert	3	1	1		3
Trueit, Thomas	1				
Gray, Lodovick	2	2	3		
Gray, Nathan	1	1	2		
Miller, John	1				
Taylor, John	1	3	4		
Heron, Michael	1	1	2		1
Harper, Nathan	1	3	1		
Harper, Jesse	1	3	2		1
Goodman, James	1		4		
Gray, Billimillender	1		4		
Irvin, Edward	1	1	4		
Irvin, Francis	1	1	4		
Munn, Richard	3		4		
Carter, Margaret		2	4		
Hudler, John	1	2	2		
Harper, George	1	2	1		
Williams, W^m	2	3	3		
Howard, Barnet	1	2	4		
Williams, John	2	3	4		
Nobles, George	2	3	3		3
George, David	1	2			
Gray, Sylvanus	1		3		
Ventures, George	1	2	5		
Ivy, John	1	2	2		
Leary, Ciby	1	3	2		5
Barnet, Joshua	1		3		
Davis, James	1		4		
Brady, Stephen	1	1	4		
Garriss, John	1	1	5		
Jarmin, Joseph	2	2	4		4
Boyde, Applum	2	1	3		
Irvin, William	3	7	3		
Dotch, Walter	1	5	4		1
Mauldin, Tucker	1	1	4		2
Cooke, John	1	3	2		
Perry, John	1	2	2		
Dinkins, Joshua	1		3		
Williams, Edward	1	1	3		
Grey, Joseph	1		1		
Whaley, Ezekiel	1		3		
Mainer, Jacob	1		1		
Taylor, Jesse	1	1	2		
Taylor, William	1	1	2		

NEWBERN DISTRICT, DOBBS COUNTY—Continued.

NAME OF HEAD OF FAMILY.	Free white males of 16 years and upward, including heads of families.	Free white males under 16 years.	Free white females, including heads of families.	All other free persons.	Slaves.
Ratcliff, Aaron	1	1	2		
Jermin, William	1		2		1
Jermin, Thomas	1		1		
Hart, John	1		3		
Brown, James	1	3	2		1
Miller, Philip	1	2	4		2
Nobles, Richard	1		1		
Williams, Mark	1				
Blackman, Arthur	1	1	2		6
Mainor, Henry	1	2	4		
Ives, Job	1				
Barnet, Matthew	1				
Brown, Philip	1		2		
Howard, John	1		1		
Baker, Job	1	1	1		
White, Robert	4		2		17
Goodin, Moses	1	2	1		2
Goodin, Daniel	1	3	4		
McClain, Grace			1		3
Nots, Tabitha	1		2		
Davis, Mary			2		
Heron, Sarah			2		4
Sanders, Catherine	1		3		
Williams, Catherine			1		1
Howard, Penelope			3		3
Howard, Esther			2		
Benson, Joseph	1		2		
Stroud, Lapson	1	2	3		
Quiney, Ann			2		3
Taylor, Ann			2		3
Wilson, Thomas	1	1	1		1
Tootle, William	1	1	6		1
Tootle, John	1	1	4		
Tootle, Edward	1				
Lofton, Elkaner	3	2	1		11
Lofton, Francis	2	1	4		3
Prier, Ephraim	2	1	2		
Griffin, Jacob, junr	1	1	4		
Sheppard, John M	1	1			
Pierce, Lazarus	1	1	3		2
Taylor, William, Senr	1	1	8		
Ball, Moses	1	3	9		1
Ball, Elizabeth		2	3		

NEWBERN DISTRICT, HYDE COUNTY.

NAME OF HEAD OF FAMILY.	Free white males of 16 years and upward, including heads of families.	Free white males under 16 years.	Free white females, including heads of families.	All other free persons.	Slaves.
Sanders, Andrew	1		2		
Money, Charles	3	2	4		
Williams, Joseph	1		2		
Swindall, Wade	1		1		
Cutrall, Peter	2		2		
Carteret, Bazel	1	1	2		
Windley, Elijah	1		3		
Williams, George	1	2	7		
Porter, William	2				
Carpenter, James	1	1	1		
Cutrill, Jacob	3		1		
Davison, James	1	1	2		
Hopkins, George	1	2	2		
Swindall, Caleb, junr	1	1	1		
Davidson, William	1		2		
Cutrill, Joseph	1	3	2		
Dunbar, James	1	1	3		
Eastwood, Israel	1	1	7		
Williamson, Samuel	2	2	3		
Blake, Elizabeth			1		
Howard, William	3		2		2
Turner, John	1	1	2		
West, Samuel	1	1	2		
Brinn, Richard	2	1			5
Adams, William	2	4	3		5
Sanders, William	1	1	1		
Berry, James	1		3		
Hall, James	2	1	6		
Morris, David	1		1		
Dannels, Joab	2	4	3		
Sawyer, Zepheniah	3	3	6		
Swindall, Benjamin	1	1	3		
Davis, John	1	2	4		
Brin, Nicholas	1	1	2		
Mason, Thomas	1	1	3		
Swindal, Joseph	1		5		
Carpenter, John	1		4		
Sadler, Richard	1	2	4		
Sadler, Samuel	1	1	5		
Swindall, Zedekiah	1	1	2		
Swindall, Parky	1		1		
Swindall, Sarah		3	2		
Boomer, Nathan	2		1		
Swindall, Isaac	2	4	4		
Thornton, Thomas	1	2	4		
Lary, Lother	1	1	1		
Lary, Joseph	2		3		
Bridgeman, Thomas	2		4		
Mason, James	2	5	2		
McGown, Joseph	3	3	3		
Sadler, John	2	3	3		
Sermon, Joseph	1		3		
Bray, John	3	2	4		
Cutrill, David	1	1	2		
Rowe, Edward	1	2	5		
Turner, Benjamin	1		3	1	
Binston, Reuben	1		2		
Harris, Elisha	1	1	2		
Hodges, James	1	1	2		3
Carter, Peter	1	2	1		
Carter, David	1		3		
Carraway, William	1	2	6	1	
Green, David	1	2	4		
English, James	1		2		
Rowe, Mitchel	1	1	2		
English, Joseph	1		2		
English, Thomas	1		4		
McGown, William	1	2	3		
Binston, John	1	1	5		
Swindill, Caleb	2	1	1		
Harris, Jesse, Senr	1	4	3		
Swindill, Christopher	2	3	5		9
White, Caleb	2	2	5		
Tunnell, Warrington	1	2	2		
Watson, James	1	1	4		
Murray, Daniel	3	1	3		
White, Lydia	1	1	4		2
Sermon, Ann	1	1	1		
Sermon, Peter	1		3		
Carraway, John	2	3	3		
McCloud, Reuben	1	3	2		
Harris, Jesse	1	1	1		
Swindill, Joel	2	1	2		
Benson, Massey	1	2	4		
Gibbs, Cason	1	4	5		13
Jones, Abram	2	1	3		5
Dudley, George	1	1	3		2
Gibbs, Robert	1	2	5		4
Carter, George	1	3	4		
Peters, Michael	1	2	4		11
Kingsborough, Jabis	1				
Jennett, Robert	1	3	3		13
Jennett, Sarah			1		6
Jennett, James	1	3	3		
Gibbs, Benjamin, Senr	1	1	6		10
Henry, Robert	1	4	2		
Henry, Samuel	2	4	4		
Insley, John	4	1	5		1
Thornton, William	1		3		
Neale, William	1	1	3		
Boomer, William	1	1	4		
Neale, John	2		3		1
Migget, Neale	1		1		
Jones, Solomon	2	2	3		2
Mann, Thomas	1	2	2		7
Jones, Morris	1	2	3		4
Gibbs, Benjamin, junr	1	5	2		4
Cohun, William	1	3	3		5
Gibbs, William, junr	1	2	2		4
Gibbs, John, Senr	1	2	3		3
Gibbs, Joseph, junr	2	2	2		9
Brinson, John	2		5		
Walls, Joshua	3		2		
Spencer, Edward	2	3	3		22
Spencer, Elizabeth		1	3		8
Spencer, William, Senr	3	3	5		8
Gibbs, Robert, Senr	2	2	2		31
Gibbs, Joseph	1	1	4		7
Williamson, Henry	2	1	3		
Gibbs, Selby	1		5		8
Gibbs, Jeremiah	1	1	2		3
Gaskill, Jacob	1	4	3		4
Gibbs, Robert, junr	1		2		4
Selby, Burrage	1		1		
Selby, Hutchins	1		2		7
Spencer, Benjamin	1	3	5		1
Harris, Thomas	3	1	1		
Carew, Henry	1				
Spencer, Nathan	1	3	5		3
Gibbs, William	2	2	3		
Hopkins, William	1		1		
Swindall, Josiah	3		5		
Spencer, Tucker	1		1		
Spring, Samuel	1		4		15
Gibbs, Thomas	1	1	4		
Sermon, Job	1	1	3		
Harris, Stephen	1	1	3		
Swindall, Joshua	1	1	2	1	
Swindall, John	1	1	2		1
Cox, Jesse	1	2	2		
Neale, Benjamin	1	1	6		
Spencer, Nathan, junr	1	2	4		2
Gibbs, Benjamin	2	2	2		1
Clayton, Jemima		2	2		
Swindall, Solomon	1	3	1		
Neale, John	1		3		
Harris, William	2	3	3		
Jones, Henry	1	1	2		1
Jones, Rebecca			1		4
Western, James			3		4
Harris, Ezekial, Senr	3	2	3		
Selby, Samuel, junr	1	2	3		5
Selby, Samuel, Senr	1				4
Gibbs, Joseph, Senr	1		1		7
Gibbs, Jesse	1	1	2		2
Smith, William, Senr	3	3	3		
Harris, Ezekial, junr	1	2	3		2
Gibbs, Thomas	1	2	1		
Spencer, Richard	2	6	3		6
Kincey, Solomon	1	2			
Dier, Michael	1				
Neale, Ephraim	1	1	4		
Cutrill, Stephen	1				
Harbert, Ignatius	1	3	2		
Brooks, Thomas	1	2	3		1
Farrow, John	2	2	3		2
Caroon, Levi	1	2	2		
Swindall, Willis	1	1	2		
Sibley, Elizabeth	6	1	3		10
Spring, Abner	1	2	3		
Spencer, David	2	1	4		2
Gaskins, Jane	1	2	3		2
Gibbs, Henry	1	1	2		1
Gibbs, John	2	3	3		6
Carron, John	1	1	1		1
Boomer, Matthew	1				
Gibbs, Daniel	2	1	3		2
Spencer, Elizabeth			3		8
Reed, Ezekiel	1				
Henry, Robert	3	1	3		
Reed, Margaret	2	4	1		
Cutrill, John	1				
Cutrill, Charles	1	1	1		
Moor, John	1	1	2		
Isdall, George	1		2		
Selbey, Nathan	1	1	4		3
Spencer, Christopher	1	3	2		
Jones, Richard	1	2	5		
Coffee, Benjamin C	1	1	1		3
Cox, Winnifred	1		1		
Smith, Lucretia	1	1	4		1
Sanders, Elizabeth	1	4	3		8
Wormington, Mary			7		14
Mason, Caleb	1		2		
Wilson, Willis	1				3
Carron, Thomas	2	1	2		
Hopkins, Margaret	2		1		
Harris, William	2	1	3		
Watson, William	3	1	3		1
Duke, Francis	2	1	3		
Brooks, Stephen	2		4		4
Brooks, William	1	1	4		1
Brooks, Isaac	1	3	3		
Adams, Absalom	1	3	1		
Rascal, John	1		1		
Gibbs, Uriah	1		1		1
Hall, William	1		1		
Williams, Elizabeth	1	2	4		
Dixon, Elizabeth	1		4		4
Selbey, Samuel	1	2	1		
Spring, Aaron	1	2	4		2
Jones, Thomas	1		4		
Spencer, Thomas	2		3		
Brinn, John	2		3		
Evans, Caleb	1				
Swindall, Thomas	1		1		
Jones, David	1		1	1	5
Gaskell, Zerobabel	1	1	3		
Jarvis, Josiah	3	1	7		
Caffey, John	2		2		
Jarvis, Elizabeth	2	1	2		
Jarvis, Zachariah	1	1	3		
Jarvis, Foster	1		4		
Mason, Jeremiah	1		4		
Creedle, Francis	2	6	2		
Hudson, Abel	1	1	3		
Tooley, Abel	1		3		
Fodrea, Thomas	1	2	3		

NEWBERN DISTRICT, HYDE COUNTY—Continued.

NAME OF HEAD OF FAMILY.	Free white males of 16 years and upward, including heads of families.	Free white males under 16 years.	Free white females, including heads of families.	All other free persons.	Slaves.
Creedle, James	1	1	2		
Harris, Jesse, junr	1		2		
Tooley, Thomas, Senr	2	1	3		2
Tooley, Thomas, junr	1		2	1	
Tooley, Jacob	2	1	1		11
Esther, Dorcas	1	1	2		
Slade, Benjamin	1				
Slade, Furniford	1				
Richards, Adam	1	3	1		
Richards, Richard	1	1	2		
Bell, Watson	1	2	1		
Slade, Nathanl	1	2	3		
Fortescue, John	1	1	6		5
Alderson, Simon	1	1	4		6
Jewell, Ebenezer	1	2	2		
Banks, Ann	1		3		1
Banks, William	1	2	4		
Jewell, Mary		1	2		2
Slade, Ann	1	2	5		1
Whitehead, Kelan	1	4	2		
Fortescue, Moses	1	2	3		1
Slade, Ebenezer	1	2	1		1
Jasper, Elizabeth	1		2		15
Bell, Sena		1	4		
Slade, Ann			1		3
Fortescue, Simon	1				2
Tyson, Rebecca	2	2	4		10
Russel, Benjamin	1	2	5		9
Winfield, John	1				
Allen, Jesse	1	1	4		1
Allen, Josiah	1	1	2		
Allen, Jacob	1		3		
Allen, James	1	1			
Allen, Isaac	1	2	3		
Esther, James	1	2	7		
Thomas, Ross				1	
Booty, Richard	5		1		
Allen, Jeremiah	1	1	5		
McCarthy, Archibald	1	1	4		1
Fortescue, John	3		4		4
Morris, Francis	1	1	3		
Whitehead, Willis	1		1		
Allen, Raphael	1	3	3		
Allen, Hannah			2		1
Robinson, William	1	1	1		1
Huston, Hugh	1	1	2		7
Whitney, Sarah	2		2		23
Tyson, John	1	3	4		3
Buchum, William	3	4	3		
Satathwaight, Abram	1	1	1		2
Cleaves, James	2	1	4		5
Jordan, Richard	2	1	3		
Burgose, Malica	1	1	4		3
Ellis, Benjamin	5		3	1	
Swindall, Jacob	2	1	2		
Russel, John	1		2		5
Russel, William	2		8		3
Palmer, Samuel	2	1	3		2
Smith, Thomas	1	3	4		
Davis, Samuel	2	1	3		5
Parmerle, Benjamin	3	3	2		14
Brittal, James	4		2		8
Tooley, Henry	1		3		2
Hasseys, Thomas	1	1	2		2
Davis, David	1	1	1		2
Bernard, German	1		1		2
Alderson, John	1	2	5	1	10
Mallison, Francis	1		8		
Tooley, Nathan	2	3	4		3
Tooley, Levi	1	2	3		1
Jasper, James	1	1	2		7
Jasper, Selden	1		1		5
Henderson, Thomas	2	1	2		2
Dennison, George	1		3		2
Leary, Mary	1		3		
Seabrook, Daniel	2	1	1		
Campbell, John	2	5	1		
Fortescue, Richard	1	1	2		
Slade, John	1		3		1
Silverthorn, Robert	1		3		
Carter, Stephen	1	1	3		
Cutrill, Solomon	3	2	4		
Rew, Thomas	2	1	3		
Mason, Christopher	2	3	4		1
Grey, Elisha	1	3	2		
Richard, Mary	1	1	3		
Tooley, Cornelius	2		1		1
Jordan, John	1	2	1		21
Rew, Southy	1		2		
Mason, Samuel	1	1	4		4
Jasper, Richard	1	1	2		2
Mason, John, Senr	1		5		
Tooley, Richard	1	2	2		
Rew, Mary			4		
Mason, Thomas	2	1	2		
Rew, Southy, junr	1	2	1		

NAME OF HEAD OF FAMILY.	Free white males of 16 years and upward, including heads of families.	Free white males under 16 years.	Free white females, including heads of families.	All other free persons.	Slaves.
Mason, John, junr	1	1	2		
Tooley, Jeremiah	1	2	1		1
Silverthorn, John S	2			1	2
Bell, Joshua	2	2	4		7
Bell, Morris	3		1		2
Slade, Elijah	1	1	1		
Bell, Dixon	4		6		5
Cleaves, John	2	2	3		1
Esther, John	1		3		1
Wickerson, Shadrach	1				
Inloes James	1				
Bell, Jonathan	1				3
Bell, John	1		1		3
Esther, Thomas	1	4			6
Richard, Jacob	1		3		1
Powers, Elizabeth					3
Tooley, Rachel	3	1	3		
Bell, George	2	2	4		1
Bell, Lyttleton	1	3	4		
Bell, Jaconias	2		1		
Bell, Cornelius	1	1	4		
Rew, Reuben	1	2	2		1
Rew, Frederick	1	3	2		1
Clark, Thomas	1		3		
Kipps, Francis M	1				
Davis, John	1				
Davis, William, Senr	1		2		
Davis, William, Junr	1	1	2		
Warner, James	1	2	1		
Tooley, Rhodes		2	2		
Whitehead, Nathaniel	1		3		
Whitehead, John	2		1		
Lacy, Isaac	1	2	1		
Lacy, John	1	1	1		
Jasper, William R	4		4		8
Potter, John	2	1			7
Fortescue, Elijah	1		4		
Mason, Morris	1				
Richard, John	1	1	3		
Richard, Henry	1		2		
Tooley, Major	2	4	3		
White, Church	1				
Arthur, Wilson	1				
Lacy, Adam	1				
Richard, Thomas	1				
Esther, William	1				
Alberd, Richard	1		2		
Dixon, George	1	1	2		2
Boston					2
Pairtree, Noah	1	1	4		
Pairtree, Wilson	1	1	4		
Pairtree, Holmes, Senr	2	4	4		
Webster, John	1	1	3		4
Cording, William	1		3		
Jordan, Rothers	3		5		6
Spruell, Stephen	2	1	3		
Jordan, Abram	1	2	3		1
Seabrook, Daniel	1	1	1		
Wright, Sarah	1		5		
Wright, Thomas	4	2	3		
Moor, Henry	3	3			
Fair, John	2		5		
Capps, James	1	2	4		
Harrington, Charles	1	2	3		
Burgase, Sarah			3		
Chambers, John	3		2		3
Wilkins, Patrick	1	1	2		6
Foreman, Lazarus, Senr	1	2	7		5
Bailey, James	1	2	4		
Linton, John	1		4		3
Foreman, Benjamin	1		2		6
Wilkins, Thomas	2	1	4		6
Barrow, Elizabeth		4	2		4
Cordan, Sarah		2	1		
Eagleton, John	3	2	2		
Wilkins, Benjamin	1	1			5
Cordan, Benjamin	1		3		
Equals, Joseph	2		1		
Collins, Henry	1		2		
Harvey, John	2	2	3		1
Gergainus, Joel	2		4		
Capps, Richard	1	2	2	2	1
Capps, Marmaduke	1	1	1		2
Capps, Thomas	1		2		
Keach, Jasper	1	4			
Wilkinson, Abraham	1		3		1
Winfield, James	1		4		
Kepps, Seth	1	3	3		1
Bailey, Jesse N	1	2	2		2
Bailey, Joshua	1	2	3		
Daley, William	3		1		6
Winley, Thomas	1		1		
Ebern, Lyttleton	2		1		1
Foreman, Lazarus G	1	4	4		
Chambers, John	3		4	3	
Harvey, Nathan	2	2	4		

NAME OF HEAD OF FAMILY.	Free white males of 16 years and upward, including heads of families.	Free white males under 16 years.	Free white females, including heads of families.	All other free persons.	Slaves.
Bailey, Joshua	1		2		3
Bailey, David	2	1	3		
Foreman, Joshua	1	3	2		
Hardison, Charles	2		2		1
Hardison, Samuel	1		1		
Wright, John	1	1	2		
Eagleton, Noah	1		5		
Abrams, Robert	1		2		
Conner, Jacob	1	1	3	1	1
Booty, Rainal	1	2	3		
Hammon, Rose			4		
Bailey, William	1	1	2		
Bailey, Simon	1		1		1
Keach, Joseph	1	2	2		2
Fulsher, Joseph	1		3		2
Bailey, Samuel	1	1	5		
Hamilton, James	1	1	3		
Highth, Thomas	1	1	4		2
Webster, Richard	1				
Foreman, Uriah	1				
Wilkins, John	1		2		11
Simons, Gideon	1	3	2		
Selbey, Henry	1		2		
Harris, Gibson	1		1		1
Pairtree, Holmes, junr	1	1	1		
Pairtree, Major	1				
Slaughter, Richard	1			2	
Williams, Thomas	1				
Abrams, John	2	1	1		
Abrams, William	1	1	1		
Hardison, Isaac	1		3		
Mallison, Thomas	1	1	2		1
Mallison, John	1				
Elsbrey, Ormond	1	1	1		3
Jordan, Zachariah	1				1
Jordan, James	1				
Gordon, William	3		2		9
Harris, Ebenezer	1				
Martin, Hosiah	1	3	4		12
Adams, William	1				
Smith, Duncan	1	2	2		1
Harris, Sarah		1	3		6
Lathum, Jesse	1	1	3		8
Jordan, Abram	1	2	3		
Robins, James	1		4		(*)
Cordin, Thomas, junr	1	1	1		1
Selbey, Burridge H	1	2	4		8
Capps, Cason	2	3	2		
Barrow, George	2		1		11
Barrow, Zachariah	2		6		21
Hovey, Seth	1	1	3		5
Webster, James	1			3	1
Harvey, Wheriet	1				7
Foreman, Elizabeth		1	2		2
Thorogood, Esther		2	3		
Chance, Sarah				9	
Jordan, Thomas	1	1	1		9
Wilkinson, Elizabeth			2		9
Gailerd, Mary		3	4		1
Eborn, James	3	2	3		13
Flinn, Rebeccah		3	2		
Hobbs, Edward	1		2		
Gailard, Rosanna		1	2		
Winley, Thomas, Senr	2				
Sachwell, John	1	2	5		9
Scott, Henry, Senr	2	2	3		8
Gergainus, William, Senr	1		1		
Gergainus, William, Junr	1	2	4		
Lloyd, Susannah		6	3		
Lathum, Fennus	2	4			8
Eagleton, Mary					
Graidless, John	1				
Scot, Henry, junr	1		2		
Foreman, Rebecca			1		8
Eborn, John	2	2	4		17
Eborn, Rebecca	1		1		
Gergainus, Jesse	1	1	1		
Winley, Maple			1		4
Winley, Sarah		4	1		2
Gergainus, Lydia			3		
Eborn, Mary	2	1			5
Flinn, Benjamin	2	1	1		6
Winley, James	1				
Gailerd, Jeremiah	2		7		2
Manderwell, Samuel	2		3		
Eborn, Zenus	1	1	2		2
Wilkinson, Isaac	1		3		3
Wilkinson, Jacob	1	2	4		4
Barnett, Robert	1	2	5		
Flinn, Enoch	2				
Manderwell, Samuel, Junr	1		1		
Stow, Alexander	1	1	3		
Toppin, Thomas	2	1	2		2

* Illegible.

NEWBERN DISTRICT, HYDE COUNTY—Continued.

NAME OF HEAD OF FAMILY.	Free white males of 16 years and upward, including heads of families.	Free white males under 16 years.	Free white females, including heads of families.	All other free persons.	Slaves.
Philips, John	1	1	2		
Eborn, Jehu	1	2	1		3
Gergainus, Jonathan	2	1	6		
Durdin, Jacob	1		2		7
Gailard, James	1	4	5		2
Winley, Michael	1	1	3		1
Winley, Churchill	1		1		1
Smith, James	1	2	4		
Davenport, Joel	1	2	1		
Howard, William, Senr	2	1	4		
Davenport, George	2	3	4		
Ratcliff, James	1	1	1		
Eborn, William	1	3	2		2
Howard, William, junr	1		2		
Hollawell, Benjamin	1	1	1		
Bilberry, William	1	1	1		
Hollawell, Zadiac	1		1		
Spruell, Michael	1	1	2		
Gailerd, John	1		1		
Gailerd, William	1	1	1		
Hollawell, Margaret	1	1	3		7
Manderwell, John	1				
Eborn, Nathan	1		2		1
Winley, Levi	1	1	1		1
Eborn, Samuel	1	1			3
Simons, Elias	1				
Winley, James	1				
Jermin, Henry	1		3		
McSwain, Edward	1	1			1
Craig, James	1		1		2
McSwain, Zachariah	1	1	2		7
Harvey, Wherry	1	2	5		
Smith, Joseph	1	3	5		
Hollaway, William	1	2	2		1
Gaiber, Stephen	1	2	2		2
Ratcliff, James	1	3	1		
Blount, Reading	2				36
Galaway, Francis	1	1	1		
Gailard, Winfield	1				1
Satterthwaite, William	1	2	4		6
Clark, William	1	3	3		13
Clark, Henry	1		3		8
Arthur, John	1		1		
Winfield, John	2	1	5		10
Harvey, Richard, Senr	2		1		8
Winfield, Obadiah	1	1	2		
Davis, Samuel	1	3	3		1
McWilliams, John	2	1	3		4
Gergainus, Ellen	1	2	3		
Johnston, Jeremiah				5	
Davis, William	2	1	5		6
Paul, Jacob	4		4		
Bishop, William	1		5		
Smith, Stephen	2	2	2		
Winfield, Withy		1	3		3
Wilkinson, Abram	1	4	2		7
Arthur, Abram	1	2	6		1
Arthur, John	1		1		
Satterthwaite, Abram	2	3	2		
Banks, Dorcas			4		
Kimmey, Ann			3		
Adams, Mary		3	3		
Mason, Mary			2		
Smith, Solomon	2	2	3		
Chambers, James	2	1	2		
Maynard, William	1				
Smith, Thomas	1		2		
Elsbre, Ephraim	1				4
Winfield, Richard, junr	1	2	2		
Slade, William	1		2		
Rogers, Stephen	1		3		
Wilkinson, Frederic	1	3	2		
Wilkinson, Robert	1		2		
Wilson, John	1		2		
Bishop, George	1	1	2		
Slade, Major	1				
Harvey, Richard, Senr	1		5		
Winfield, Robert	1	1	2		1
Davis, John	1		2		
Davis, William	1		4		
Winfield, Bryan	1	1	2		3
Gallaway, Francis	1	1	1		
Banks, Charles	1				
Davenport, Edmond	1	1	2		
Satterthwaite, William, Senr	1	2	3		
Stilley, Ezekiel	1	3	2		
Wilkinson, Thomas	2				
Morris, William	1		2		
Rogers, Benjamin	1		2		
Wilkinson, John	1	2	3		
Banks, Moses	1	1	3		
Smith, James	1		4		
Jones, Christopher	1	1	2		
Ryan, William	1		1		
Satterthwaite, Samuel	1		1		
Harvey, David	1		2		1
Gergainus, Aaron	1	3	5		3
Wilkinson, James	1	2	5		3
Winfield, Richard, Senr	1		7		7
Satterthwaite, Jonathan	3	4	5		5
Winfield, Jesse	1		6		
Davis, John	1	5	2		
Grey, Jeptha	1		5		
Satterthwaite, Isaac	2	1	3		
Davis, John	1	3	2		
Bishop, John	1	1	2		
Johnston, David	1		1		
Slade, John	1				
Spady, Peter	1		2		
Winfield, Obadiah	1	1	2		
Stokesberry, John	1		1		
Brown, Nathan				1	

NEWBERN DISTRICT, JOHNSTON COUNTY.

NAME OF HEAD OF FAMILY.	Free white males of 16 years and upward, including heads of families.	Free white males under 16 years.	Free white females, including heads of families.	All other free persons.	Slaves.
Boon, Joseph, junr	3	3	3	3	24
Gurley, John	2		2		
Tiner, Nicholas	1		2		
Musslewhite, Leonard	1		1		
Capps, William	1		1		
Boon, Joseph, Senr	1		1	2	10
Raiford, Philip	1	4	4		11
Lynch, Elizabeth			1	1	1
Gurley, Mary, Senr			1	2	
Gurley, Ann	2	2	2		3
Bulls, Rachel	1		4		
Davis, Milly	1	2	3		
Hughes, John	3	3	4		
Gurley, Mary, junr	1	2	2		
Edwards, Elizabeth	1	1	2		
Brazil, Jacob	2	1	4		
Rains, Ann			1	1	1
Talton, William, Senr	2	1	2		
Oliver, John, Senr	2	1	2		
Woodall, John	4		3		
Burnet, Doll				5	
Bulls, William	2	2	4		2
Holt, James	1	3	1		
Whitley, Needham	1	3	2		10
Rains, Oliver	1	3	4		1
Pierce, Philip	1	2	4		2
Watkins, Jesse	2	3	5	1	
Hays, John	1	1	2		7
Davis, William	1	3	1		
Sims, Benjamin	1		2		
Gurley, Isum	1	3	2		
Wellings, Charles	2	1	3		
Talton, John	1		2		
Capps, William	1		2		1
Hays, Jesse	2	2	6		6
Howell, Elisha	1		3		
Wise, Thomas	1		3		
Capps, Matthew	1	1	2		
Bridges, Benjamin	1	4	2		2
Gurley, Joseph	1		1		
Oliver, Needham	1		1		
Pedin, William	1	1	1		
Stephens, Bethany	1	1	3	2	1
Stephens, Benjamin	1		2		2
Bulls, Barnaby	2	2	3		4
Bulls, Jethro	1		1		
Edwards, Jacob	1		1		
Barwick, John	1	3	1		
Gurley, Edward	3	3	3		
Pierce, Shadrach	1		1		
Massey, Ralph	1	1	2		
Whood, Charles	1		2		
Lynch, Cornelius	1	3	3		
Jernigan, Arthur	1	4	4		3
Hill, William	1	1	2		
Woodard, Benjamin	1	4	2		
Edwards, Joseph	3	2	4		1
Strickland, Benjamin	1	2	3		
Battin, Joshua	2	4	6		
Runnell, Michael	2	2	2		
Peedin, James	1	1	4		
Overbay, David	2		4		
Oliver, John, junr	1	2	3		
Oliver, Thomas	1		1		
Tiner, Benjamin	2	1	3		
Edwards, Micajah, junr	1	1	1		
Bassingale, George	1		2		
Stattons, Isaac	1				1
Edwards, William	1	1	2		1
Edwards, Benjamin	1				
Vincent, Levin	1	5	3		
Musslewhite, William	1	4	4		
Wilson, John	1	1	4		
Whurley, Winifred			1		
Sims, Patience	2	3	1	1	
Worrin, Elijah	2	1	4	1	4
Prance, Solomon	1	3	2		
Pervis, James	1	2	1		
Hughes, Josiah	1	1	1		
Rains, Ambrose	1	2	1		2
Brewer, David	1	2	3		
Brewer, Martha		3	2		
Edwards, Micajah, Senr	2	1	4		
Spencer, Jesse	1	2	2		
Holt, Etheldred	1	1	2		
Musselwhite, Uriah	1				
Brady, James	1				
Oliver, James			1		
Warrin, Elijah		2	3		7
Daughtry, Jacob	1	1	2		
Bryan, Lovit	1				20
Ingram, Joseph	1	3	2		12
Roberts, William, Junr	1	3	3		
Powell, Nathan	1		2		10
Howard, Thomas	1	2	1		
Strickland, David	1		3		
Strickland, Uriah	1		3		
Roberts, William	1	1	2		9
Warren, Richard	1		2		7
Bridges, Jane			2		10
Whitley, John	1	1			
Langford, James	1	1	2		
Gray, Thomas	3	4	5		26
Williams, John	1				4
Powell, Needham	1	2	1		7
Thomson, Nicholas	1	3	4		5
Farmer, William	1	4	3		10
Powell, Isaac	2	1	5		7
Guein, Thomas	1	3	4		5
Powell, Jeremiah	1				5
Dees, Daniel	3	2	1		7
Allen, John	2	2	4		15
Davis, Jacob	1	1	3		
Davis, Arthur	1	2	3		1
Creech, Joshua	2	6	2		
Collins, Deal	2	1	3		
Phillips, John	1	3	2		
Blackman, William	2	2	5		20
Wiggins, Willis	4		4		13
Camelion, Abram	6	4	2		22
Adkinson, Nathan	1	2	3		12
Adkinson, John	2		1		15
Stephens, William	1				
Jernigan, Jacob	2	2	3		13
Lyttleton, Charles	1		1		1
Craddock, Thomas	1	2	5		6
Jernigan, Lewis	3	1	5		6
Lyttleton, William	2		5		
Williams, Benjamin	1		4		
Pervis, Jesse	1	3	4		
Thomson, Elijah	1	3	2		1
Thomson, Jarret	1	3	4		1
Prance, John	1		1		
Adkins, Raimond	4	4	3		
Pilkington, Richard	4				
Burnet, Sander					12
Tiner, Jesse, junr	1	1	5		
Patterson, John H	1	4	3		
Strickland, Jeremiah	1		4		
Musselwhite, Drew	1	1	4		
Brady, William	1	5	4		
Lankford, James	1	1	2		
Tiner, Jesse, Senr	3	3	2		7
Parnal, Benjamin	1	5	2		
Piner, Thomas	1		1		
Harold, Samuel	2				5
Collins, George			4		
Adkins, Joseph	1	3	2		
Bailey, Margaret			4		
Davis, John	1	3	3		
Turley, Richard	1		7		
Warren, Isaiah	1	4	4	2	1
Isler, John	1		1		9
Crawford, Hardy	2	2	4		
Scott, Olive				8	
Armstrong, Clement	1	1	6		
Stephens, Rebecca			1		
Simpson, Thomas	2	2	2		
Mitchel, Henry	2				
Harold, Samuel	1				5
Credle, William	1	7	2		
Bryan, Benjamin	1				24

NEWBERN DISTRICT, JOHNSTON COUNTY—Continued.

NAME OF HEAD OF FAMILY.	Free white males of 16 years and upward, including heads of families.	Free white males under 16 years.	Free white females, including heads of families.	All other free persons.	Slaves.
Taylor, William	1	1	2		1
Duck, Jacob	1	1	6		3
Goodwin, Samuel	2	3	2		
Hinnant, William	2	1	7		2
Odum, John	3		3		11
Keen, Alice	2		3		
Saucer, William	1	2	5		
Brassil, Richard	1	2	4		1
Boyte, Sarah	3		3		
Watson, Elizabeth	2		2		
Watson, Mary		3	4		
Brown, William	4		3		
Langley, James	2	1	5		
Horn, William	1		2		
Durdin, Judith	2	2	2		
Pierce, Arthur	1	1	2		7
Brewer, Martha			2	1	
Garrell, John	2	1	2		
Godin, Thomas	2	4	4		
Wadkins, James	2	2	4		
Peacock, Uriah	1	2	2		
Peacock, Archibald	1		3		
Richardson, John	1	5	4		
Pierce, Sarah			2		6
Kirby, Jesse	2		3	1	
Neusum, Patience			3		4
Bailey, William	3	1	2		
Bailey, Micajah	1	2	2		
Brown, Jesse	1	2	1		
Brown, William	1		1		
Bateman, Jonathan	2	2	1		
Gulley, George	1	1	3		2
Bateman, William	1	1	3		
Boyekin, Judith		1	4		
Barnes, Archilaus	1		2		
Boyte, Thomas	1		4		
Bateman, Jesse	1	5	3		
Corbit, Joshua	1	2	3		
Cockroll, Thomas	3	4	5		
Folk, James	1		1		
Folk, Thomas	2	2	2		
Folk, John	1	1	3		
Folk, Henry	1				
Garrell, Isaac	1	1	3		
Grice, Lewis	1			1	1
Grice, Stephen	1				
Horn, Joel	1	1	6		
Hinniont, James	1	3	6	1	
Hollimon, John	1		4		
Horn, Caleb	1		1		
Johnston, William	1		3		
Kerby, James	1				
Keen, John	1	1	3		
Kerby, Absalom	2	1	2		
Pierce, Everit	1	1	4		11
Pierce, Theophilus	1	1	3		1
Pierce, Richard, junr	1	3	1		
Pierce, Simon	1	1	2		2
Pugh, Tignal	2				
Pierce, Ephraim	1		5	2	
Pierce, John	1	1	1	3	4
Rentfrow, Noel	1	4	4		
Register, Jesse	1	2	3		
Ramsay, Anderson	1	1	1		
Saucer, Arthur	1	1	3		
Saucer, Abel	1	1	2		
Smith, Nathan	2		1		
Spiva, Aaron, junr	1	3	3		
Saucer, Joseph	1		1		
Spiva, John	1	1	3		
Spiva, Aaron, Senr	1		2		
Thorn, John	1	3	5		
Talton, Hardy	1	2	2		
Woodard, Thomas	2	4	7	1	
Watson, Levin	1	3	3		
Watson, James	1		3		
Woodard, Luke	1	2	3		
Watson, Obadiah	1	1	2		
Williamson, Hardy	1				
Watson, Ephraim	1	2	2		
Wadkins, Kinchen	1		3		
Watson, Solomon	1		3		
Wilkinson, Alaenor	1		5		
Waddle, Edward	1	4	2		
Pierce, Jesse	2	4	4		4
Oneale, Patrick	1	1	6		
Neusum, Joel	1		1	2	
Sims, Shadrack	1		6	3	
Bass, John	1	4	3		
Hackney, William	1	3	1		13
Ponder, Thomas	1	2	3		4
Holder, Elizabeth	2	1	2		10
Broughton, Jesse	2		3		
Stancil, John, Senr	3	3	3		5
Johnston, Solomon	2	3	4		
Hocket, Sophia	2	1	3		
Oneales, Alice	1	2	3		1

NAME OF HEAD OF FAMILY.	Free white males of 16 years and upward, including heads of families.	Free white males under 16 years.	Free white females, including heads of families.	All other free persons.	Slaves.
Hinton, Mary	1	1	6		
Bailey, David	1	3	1		
Hollimon, Frederick	2		2		2
Richardson, William	2	4	2		6
Richardson, Applewhite	1	3	5		7
Holliman, William	4	1	6		1
Stephens, Ann		1	2		
Bailey, Tamsey		1	2		3
Price, John	1		6		
Bailey, William	1	4	6		
Crumple, Benjamin	2	1	4		
Gilmore, Harbert	1	1	2		1
Price, Dixon	1	1	4		
Onailes, Moses	1	4	4		
Price, Richard	2	2	4		
Jourdin, Henry	1	4	4		
Price, Etheldred	1	1	3		
Price, Rice, Senr	2	4	3		
Price, Nathan	1		6		
Woodard, Jethro	2	2	5		
Price, Micajah	2	2	3		
Oneales, Isum	1	4	1		1
Johnston, Arthur B	1		2		
Oneales, Zachariah	2	4	5		1
Bailey, Arthur	1		2		1
Pope, Arthur	2	3	5		
Johnston, Burrel	1	2	2		
Hinton, Jesse	1	2	1		
Parker, Matthew, Senr	3	3	4		
Holmes, Frederick	1	2	3		
Moore, Randal	1	3	1		
Thomas, John	1	1	2		
Wilkinson, Benjamin	1	3	3		
Eatman, Thomas	1	1	3		
Onailes, William, junr	3	3	3		2
Price, Rice, junr	1		1		
Bailey, Isum	1	1	1		
Price, James, junr	1	2	2		
Onailes, Samuel	1	2	2		
Naron, Acquilon	1		4		
Price, Simon	1	2	3		1
Pope, Richard	2		5		
Johnston, Lewis	1		1		
Cobb, John P	1	1	5		
Hall, Martin	1	3	2		
Duck, John	1	1	2		2
Boyekin, Francis	1	2	2		
Bailey, John	1		3		2
Joiner, Hardy	1	4	2		
Bailey, Judith		1	3		2
Joiner, Nathan	1	1	2		
Lyles, Lewis	4		2		
Crumpler, West	1	3	3		
Barber, John	1	1	2		
Barber, Henry	2	2	4		
Joiner, Thomas	1	2	2		
Starlin, William	3		7		
Stephens, William	1				
Strickland, Samuel	1			1	
Tolbert, Samuel	1	3	4		2
Onailes, Amos	1	1	2		1
Vincent, John	2	1	5		3
Godin, Edmond	3	1	2		
Hatcher, Mary			1		4
Wilkinson, Charles	3		2		
Onailes, William, Senr	1	4	2		
Parker, Gabriel	1		2		1
Gardner, Joseph	3	1	6		
Gardner, John	2	2	3		
Watson, Jesse	2	4	3		1
Watson, David	4	2	5		
Johnston, Sampson	2	7	6		
Batten, Nathan	2	7	8		
Hailes, John, Senr	2	1	5		7
Spicer, Joseph	2	3	5		
Parnal, Jeremiah	1	4	2		
Thomas, Elisha	2	2	4		15
Rairies, Anthony	1				
Walker, Major	1	1	1		
Eason, Moses, Senr	4	2	6		
Siercey, William	1				
Horn, Milley			4		
Adkinson, Milkey		2	4		
Pool, John	2	1	3		
Hill, Shadrach	1	3	1		
Smith, Samuel	2	4	7		53
Blurton, Edward	1	3	5		4
Hinnant, William	1	3	3		5
Moore, John	1	4	4		
Hearn, Mason	2	1	4		
Eason, Sanders	1	3	2		
Jones, Thomas	1	3	5		
Searcey, George	1	4	1		
Eason, Moses, junr	1	1	2		
Spicer, James	1	1	1		4
Hailes, Chapman	1	1	4		
Hill, Thomas	1	5	2		

NAME OF HEAD OF FAMILY.	Free white males of 16 years and upward, including heads of families.	Free white males under 16 years.	Free white females, including heads of families.	All other free persons.	Slaves.
Battin, John	2	1	4		
Walker, Jacob	1		1		
Smith, William	1		4		
Elvinton, Shadrach	1	3	2		2
Wilkinson, Charles, junr	1	1	4		
Elvinton, Gideon	2		4		1
Gardner, William	1	1	2		
Starling, Adam	2	4	7		
Monk, Willis	1		2		
Watson, Silas	1				
Hatcher, Benjamin	1	1	2		
Adkinson, Amos	1	2	3		
Cooper, George	1	2	5		2
Hailes, John	1	2	1		3
Watson, Jacob	1		1		
Bullard, James	1				
Johnston, James	1	4	1		
Lynch, Joshua	1	3	2		
Price, Jeremiah	1	3	3		
Watson, Ezekiel	2	3	4		
Adkinson, Micajah	1				
Hatcher, William	1	1	6		1
Parker, Hardy	1	3	3		2
Raines, Frederick	1	1	3		
Johnston, Robert	1		3		
Searcey, Daniel	2	3	3		
Price, Rice	1	1	3		
Spiva, William	1		1		
Onailes, Ross	1		1		
Stancil, John	1		1		1
Killingsworth, John	1	1	2		1
Stallens, Jacob	1	2	1		1
Jones, Ambrose	1	1	1		
Bankum, James	1	2	3		
Watson, Simon	1	1	1		
Sessions, Ferreley			1		
Oliver, William	1				
Wilkinson, Reuben	1	3	3		
Searcy, John	1	2	4		6
Shaw, James	2	2	5		1
Lee, John	3		2		6
Hinton, Malicah	1	3	3		17
Hinton, Sarah		1	1		4
Parry, Dempsey	1	2	5		
Gale, Patience		1	2		
Muniham, Judith		1	1		
Lee, William			3		
Woodard, Elizabeth	1	1	2		2
Brenan, Thomas	2		2		
Nowell, John	2	1	5		
Owtin, Jesse	4	1	1		4
Delk, Jacob	2	3	2		
Wimberly, Malicah	1	2	5		1
Green, Elizabeth		2	2		
High, Joseph	1	3	3		
Walker, Elijah	1	1	1		
Gulley, Robert	2		4		4
Green, Jesse	3	4	5		
Walls, William	2		1		
Taylor, Josiah	1	3	5		2
Irvin, Joseph	2		4		
Hill, Benjamin	2		3		
Holliman, Seth	1	1	4		
Snipes, John	1	1	2		
Walker, William	1	1	3		
Wilder, Samuel	2	4	7		3
Green, John	1	2	4		
Wall, Jesse	1	2	4		
Gulley, Meed	2	4	4		
Lee, Edward	1	2	1		
Killingsworth, Freeman	2	2	3		
Wilder, Matthew	2	3	5		2
Bryan, Lewis	3	2	5		
Langley, Miles	2	4	2		
Hinton, George	1				1
Watson, John	2	4	2		12
Brenan, William	1	3	3		
Wilder, William	2	1	2		
Williams, Harold	2	1	2		
Walls, John	2				
Newell, James	1	1	1		
Brenan, Joseph	1		2		
Killingsworth, Free-man, Jr					
Hailer, Henry	2	1	4		
Duck, Timothy	1	5	2		
Nelson, Wilson	1		3		
Hinton, William	2	1			10
Earpe, William	1	4	2		5
Welbern, Lewis	1				
Brenan, Cason	1				
Hinton, Isaac	1	1	4		13
Parcy, Reuben	1		1		
Lee, John	2	1	3		
King, Ilse	2	2	4		2
Earpe, William, jr	2	2	3		
Finch, Henry	2	2	3		

NEWBERN DISTRICT, JOHNSTON COUNTY—Continued.

NAME OF HEAD OF FAMILY.	Free white males of 16 years and upward, including heads of families.	Free white males under 16 years.	Free white females, including heads of families.	All other free persons.	Slaves.
Lysle, George	1		3		
Oneales, William	1		2		
Bryan, William	3	1	1		2
Reading, Francis	1	1	2		
Jones, Isaac	3	2	2		5
Chesser, Mary			4		
Rollins, Drury	1	1	3		
Rogers, Daniel	2	2	1		
Lockhart, James	2	4	3		11
Killingsworth, John	3	2	3		1
Turner, John	1	3	5		
Gulley, John	2	2	3		
Rivers, Richard	1	1	5		
Sauls, Abner	4		3		12
Philips, Benjamin	1				
Ferrill, Cornelius	1				
Dodd, John	1	4	5	1	
Carter, Evan	1	1	1		1
Ellis, John	1				
Bryan, Arthur	1	1			11
Gregory, Etheldred	3	3	1		8
Price, John	2		3		
Hinton, John	1	3	3		6
Averit, Daniel	1	5	2		3
Penny, Edward	2		3		
Price, Edward	1	1	2		2
Price, Thomas	1	4	2		
Hardcastle, James	1	4	1		1
Massey, Drury	1	4	3		1
Johnston, Sylvanus	1	2	3		
Penney, Caleb	2	2	5		3
Penney, Alexander	1		2		
Copeland, Charles	1	1	5		
Luper, William	2	2	7		
Rogers, Daniel	1				
Ferrill, Jacob	1	2	6		
Ferrill, Nicholas	1	3	2		
Gulley, John	1		5		
Carter, Matthew	2	4	3		8
Bendinfield, John	2	3	3		
Willowby, Solomon	1	1	4		4
Price, James	1		3		
Jordan, Abner	1	3	2		
Kelly, John	2	1	3		
Johnston, William	2	3	3		
Brite, John	1	3	4		
Lockhart, Stephen	1				
Johnston, Joel	1	1	1		
Snipes, William	2	2	2		
Stallions, Zadik	1	3	4		5
Smith, Benjamin	1	2	4		
Hinton, Hardy	1	2	1	1	
Copeland, William	1	1	2		
Prince, David	2	4	4		
Lockhart, Osborn	1				
Holt, Richard	3	2	4		
Smith, Jesse	1	2	3		
Harvey, Jane			1		
Kelly, Charles	1	3	5		
Duncan, John	1	1	4		
Bryan, Needham	1		2		6
Nordin, Thomas	1	1	2		
Franklin, William	1	5	3		
James, Thomas	1		1		2
Price, Rial	1		1		
Cheshire, John	1				
Cheshire, Zachariah	1				
Blurtin, Henry	2	2	2		1
Gurlin, Mary	1		2		
Sanders, Reuben	1		2		8
Smith, Margaret		1	2		
Johnston, Moses	2		4		1
Youngblood, Thomas	2	1	2		
Austin, John	2	3	4		
Stephenson, Solomon	2		4		
Messer, William	2		1		
Perry, Abram	2	3	3		
Fluellin, Sarah			4		
Johnston, Amos	3	1	2		
Barber, Plye	3		4		
Johnston, Martin	2	2	5		
Stephens, Edward	3	3	4		9
Johnston, Henry	2	2	3		5
Pate, Traverse	3	1	2		
Fish, Sarah		1	2		3
Leech, Thomas	2	1	5		7
Jones, Matthew	4	3	4		
McCuller, John	1	1	4		12
Johnston, Sarah	1	1	2		
Taylor, William	2	2	5		7
Gower, John	2	1	2		
Wood, John	2		2		
Smith, John	2	3	1		16
Blount, William	1	3	4		1
Smith, Etheldred	1		2		6
Carrol, John	1	3	4	1	
Lowell, Clayton	1		2		
Johnston, Isum	1	1	1		
Langdon, James	1	1	5		1
Lankford, Henry	1	1	1		
Alston, Asa	1	1	2		
Stephenson, John	1	2	4		
Whittington, Richard	1	5	4		
Gower, William	1	3	5		
Johnston, Starlin	3		3		
Johnston, Amos, jr	3		3		
Williams, John	1	2	4		1
Messer, John	1		4		
Flowers, Jacob	2	7	3		
Johnston, Simon	1	2	1		1
Sanders, William	1	1	3		3
Right, Josiah	1	2	2		
Young, John	1	3	4		
Coats, Solomon	1	1	3		
Parish, Jabis	1	3	7		
Carr, Samuel	2		1		
Wren, Martha			2		
Coats, William	1	1	7		
Carrol, William	1	1	3		
Johnston, Abel	1	4	4		
Smith, Benjamin	1	2	3		
Barber, George	1	2	1		
Johnston, Philip	2				
Stephens, William	1	1	2		3
Carrol, James	1				
Munihan, John	1				
Bryan, Clement	1				13
Ivy, David	2	4	3		
Jennings, Hezekiah	1				
Barnes, Mirac	1		3		14
Johnston, Isaac	1		1		
Coats, John	1		5		
Flowers, Needham	1		3		
Lowell, Mary			2		
Honeycutt, Drury	1	3	4		
Williams, Ephraim	1	2	3		
Powers, Jesse	1	2	3		
Thorpe, Thomas	1		6		7
Woodall, James	1		3		
Dodd, Robert	1	3	2		
Rials, William	1		1		
Stephens, Zachariah	1		1		
Utley, Allen	1	1	1	1	
Stephenson, James	1	1	5		9
Bryan, Blake	2	2	2		9
Eason, John	2	1	3	1	9
Pool, John	2	4	3		3
Norris, Noah	1		5		1
Youngblood, William	1		3		1
Dorham, William	1		2		1
Holston, Selathial	1	2	1		
Averite, Alexander	2	1	4		5
Adams, Howell	1	2	4		
Avery, Lewis	1	2	1		
Avery, Jacob	4	2	6		
Brite, Jesse	1	2	6		
Durham, Samuel	2	5	4		2
Dodd, William	3	4	5	1	3
Dodd, John	2	1	2		
Bell, David	1	7	4		12
Bridges, Young	2	1	1		1
Peoples, Abner	1	1	3	1	
Orr, Samuel	1	1	4		
Pool, William	1	2	3		2
Lassiter, Elizabeth	1		3		3
Rainwater, William	1	2	2		
Johnston, Obadiah	1	4	3	2	
McCullers, John	2	4	4		
Starboard, Solomon	1	1	3		
Smith, Nehemiah	1	1	2		1
Vincent, Drew	2	2	4		14
Whittington, Phady	1		3		
Hobby, William	1		3		
Rainwater, Moses, Sr	2	2	4		
Smith, John	1		2		1
Rails, Charles	1		1		
Whittington, Robert	1	3	4		
Norris, James	3		6		2
Thomlinson, Edmond	1		2		
Smith, Alexander	1		2		6
Kindal, Isaac	1	1	2		
Clark, Harris	1	1	2		2
Rosser, John	1	2	2		1
Peoples, Archibald	1		1		
Parish, Charles	1	1	4		
Shehorn, Henry	1		5		
Stallons, Ezekiel	1		1		
Roberts, Britton	1	1	4		
Bankum, Alexander	1		2		
Parsons, Harris	1		1		
Woodall, Absalom	1	2	2	1	5
Giles, William	2	1	4		
Avery, Thomas	1	1	4		
Staton, Bathier	2	1	2		
Rosser, James, Sen	2	5	4		3
Norris, Ann	1	1	5		
Sanders, Mary	1		2		19
Thomlinson, Thomas	1	2	4		6
Avery, William	3		5		11
Avery, Alexander, Sr	4	2	5		
Brady, John	1		2		2
Bryan, Hardy	1	6	2		14
Bryan, John	1		2		22
Hewit, Goldsmith	1				
Hundy, Matthias	1				
Gillis, Malcolm	1				
Hobby, Alexander	4	3	3		
Osborn, James	1				
Hobby, Lucy	1	1	2		
Wren, James	2		1		
Willowby, Richard	1	4	3		
Gale, Solomon	1	2	3		
Lohorn, Rebecca			2		
Oncale, Isum	1	1	2		
Bridges, Etheldred	2	1	1		
Powell, Stephen					11
Holland, William	1				
Vincent, Aaron	1	3	4		12
Vincent, Amelia			1		
Lynch, Martha			1		
Avery, Mary	1	1	4		
Bryan, Asa	1	2	3		1
Ottman, Thomas	2		3		
Barfoot, Noah, Senr	1		2	1	1
Jackson, John	1		2		
Blackman, John	3	3	7	1	
Lynch, Milberry		1	2		
Lynch, Sarah			2		
Williams, Miles	2		2		
Ivy, James	3	3	2		2
McClenny, James	1	4	1		
Bryan, Lewis	1		4		
Adkins, Moses	1		1		
Seats, Nathan	2		5		
Lee, Mary			3		6
Kean, George	1	5	1		
Johnston, Etheldred	1	3	3		
Blackman, Icabod	1	2	2		2
Langston, Joseph, Senr	1	1	1		
Lankston, Joseph, jr	1	1	2		
Williams, Nathan	2	1	2		41
Smith, Samuel	2	1	2		21
Baker, James	2	3	5		
Harold, Francis	1		1		
Harold, Edward	3	4	2		1
Ballanger, Mary			2		2
Webb, David	1	1	5		
Diamond, Margaret		2	3		
Diamond, Frances	1		4		
Barfoot, Noah, jr	1		3		
Morgan, John	2	1	3		
Johnston, Moses	1	3	6		1
Ballinger, John	1	1	1		
Collins, Andrew	1	1	1		1
Rhoads, John	3	4	4		
Ingram, Shadrach	1	3	8		4
Lee, William	2	2	6		
Harris, Sharrod	1		2		
Hobby, Reuben	2	4	5		
Flewellin, Archibald	1		2		
Lee, David, Senr	2	1	3		5
Blackman, Barzella	1	3	4		
Bryan, John	1	2	6		1
Blackman, John	1	3	7	1	
Blackman, Arthur	1		4		
Shepard, Valentine	1		2		
Bridges, Joseph	1	3	5		
Lee, Samuel	3	1	2		1
Lee, Cato	1	3	2		
Woodal, Jacob	2		2		
Lee, David, Junr	2	3	4		
Jones, William	1	2	3		
Proctor, John	1	2	2		
Barber, Reuben	1	1	1		
Woodall, Jacob	1	1	4		
Lee, Stephen	1	3	2		1
Brewer, Hubbard	1	1	2		
Baldwin, Samuel	1		4		1
Connolly, Michael	2		6		
Bryan, William	1	2	2		2
Lee, John	1	2	2		
Guein, John	1	2	2		10
Allen, Nathan	1	2	8		1
Ballinger, William	2	1	2		13
Fail, John	2	3	4		
Adams, Bryan	2		5		
Aithcock, Holiday					6
Harrell, Etheldred	1	2	5		
Sellers, Samson	1	3	1		
Farmer, Nicholas	1	3	4		4
Lee, James, junr	1	3	2		3

NEWBERN DISTRICT, JOHNSTON COUNTY—Continued.

NAME OF HEAD OF FAMILY.	Free white males of 16 years and upward, including heads of families.	Free white males under 16 years.	Free white females, including heads of families.	All other free persons.	Slaves.
Lee, Lemuel	1	3	5		
Johnston, Joshua	2	3	3		
Russels, Charles	2	2	2		
Lee, Jeremiah	1		1		4
Ingram, Isaac	1	3	2		
Hairgroves, William	2		3		
Dement, John	1		2		
Fail, Dixon	1	4	4		3
Eldridge, Samuel	1	1	2		6
Lee, James, Senr	1		4		2
Baker, Dempsey	3	2	6		
Rials, William	1	6	2		
Keen, George	1	6	1		
Ward, Elijah	1	3	2		
Adkinson, Thomas	1				
Smith, Abram	1	1	2		
Smith, John	1		1		
Attman, Joel	1				
Dees, Edmond	1		1		
Powell, William	1		1		
Billington, Ezekiel	2	3	1		
Smith, Isaac	1	2	2		
Mott, Benjamin	1	2	2		
Binum, Drury	1		2		
Harold, Theophilus	1				
McGlohon, William	1	2	3		
Brown, Richard	1	2	4		
Barnes, Abram	1		2		
Ellis, Elisha	1	2	2		
Moore, Thomas	1		3		
Collins, Thomas	1				
Lankston, Charity	1	3	3		
Ellis, Elijah	1				

NEWBERN DISTRICT, JONES COUNTY.

NAME OF HEAD OF FAMILY.	Free white males of 16 years and upward, including heads of families.	Free white males under 16 years.	Free white females, including heads of families.	All other free persons.	Slaves.
Hatch, Charles	1	2	1		9
Hatch, Mary		4	3		10
Bryan, James	1	1	1		11
Hatch, Samuel, Junr	1	2	3		27
Steel, Peter	2	1	5		
Steel, Benjamin	1	1	1		
Gregory, William	1		1		3
Simmons, Emanuel	3	1	1		12
Grimes, Robert	1	2	6		8
Grenade, Joseph	1	1	5		3
Simmons, Daniel	1	2	3		16
Whitly, Edward	1	6	5	1	3
Lipsey, William	2	3	3		1
Lipsey, Arthur	1	1	3		1
Hatch, John	1	2	2		20
Gregory, Matthew	2	1	3		6
Simmons, James	1				7
Simmons, Benjamin	1	1	1		10
Hatch, Joseph	1		2		6
Hatch, Durant	1	1	4		18
Ubank, John	1	4	6		
Hatch, Edmund	1	2	1		24
Lavender, Benjamin	1		4		6
Simmons, John	3		3		8
Simmons, George	1	1	2		6
Smith, Bazel	3	1	4	2	16
Johnston, Collinson	2	2	5		
Prentice, Solomon	1				
Reed, George	1		1	1	1
Kincey, Stephen	1				24
Gardner, William	1	2	4		1
Lee, Burton	3	2	5		
Phelps, Jacob	1		2		2
Ramsay, Esther			2		
Littleton, Thomas	1		1		
Waters, Margaret	1		1		
Duin, Sugar	1	2	5		1
Taylor, John	1	1	3		36
Sanderson, Elijah	1				46
Knight, Kadir	1	2	2		
Andrews, Ruth	1	2	4		
Sanderson, Shadrach	1		2		
Foscue, Frederic	1	1	2		25
Sanderson, Thomas	2	2	5		2
Brinkley, Comfort		1	2		
Sanderson, Jesse	2	1	2		2
Sanderson, John	1	2	3		1
Sanderson, James	1	2	3		
Griffin, William	2	3	3		
Grenade, John	3	1	4		3
Hall, John	1	2	3		
Smith, Peter	2	1	3		
Cohun, Dudley	1	1	5		
Sanderson, Levy	1	1	2		
Kincey, Joseph	1	1	5		
Mosley, John	1		3		
Dunn, William	1				
Andrews, Dorcas	1		2		
Hall, James	2				
Binum, Lewis	1		1		
Smith, Thomas	1				
Kincey, John	2	2	3		1
Hancock, James	1	5	3	3	2
Bumpus, Jabis	1		2		
Taylor, William	1	3	2		4
Lepsy, Timothy	1		1		4
Bray, Nicholas A	1		2		9
Market, John	1		1		
Market, Frederic	1				
Harrell, Enos	1		3		
Brocket, Benjamin	1	1	2		32
Lyttleton, John	1	4	2		
Lyttleton, Thomas, Senr	1		3		
Lee, Thomas	1	2	5		52
Wallace, Stephen	1	1	2		
Hatch, Samuel	1	3	4		7
Boyd, Coleman	1	2	5		
Mace, William	1		4		
Ross, Reuben	2	1	4		
Foye, James	1				31
George, William	1	4	1		1
Mundine, Francis	1	1	3		7
Jones, Brigger	1	2	2		7
Jones, John	1	2	4		
Jones, James	1	1	4		
Mundine, Benjamin	1				
Mundine, James	1				1
Reynolds, Ephraim	1	1	2		
Eubank, Elijah	1	2	4		
Gibson, Isaac	1	2	1		3
Yates, Stephen	1	2	2		
Barry, David	1	3	3		1
Watson, Moses	1	3	2		9
West, John	1	1			2
Mundine, John	1		1		9
Taylor, William	1				2
Morgan, John	2	4	4		
Taylor, James	1				4
Dolly, Esther			2		
Mundine, Kittrel	2	1	6		13
Kellum, William	1				
West, Andrew	1	1	4		
Dixon, Joel	1	2	3		
Dudley, Elijah	1	1	1		1
Collins, John	1	2	3		4
Meadows, Abraham	1	2	2		
Meadows, Thomas	1	3	2		
Meadows, Job, Junior	1	3	3		
Meadows, Job, Senior	3	2	4		
Houston, James	1	1	1		
Gray, William	1	2	3		
Starkey, Edward	2		1		61
Key, Jonathan	1	1	3		5
Meadows, Bartholomew	1	1	2		6
Frazer, Ellen		1	3		
Hay, Thomas	1	5	3		2
Howard, Titus	2	1	7		12
Arnold, Mablin	1		3		2
Collins, Joseph	1		1		
Stephenson, Samuel	1	1	2		
Tilman, John	2	3	3		
Tilman, Isaac	1		3		
Jones, Josiah	1	1	3		
Prescot, Mary	1		3		
Godwin, Joseph	1	2	4		
West, Eli	1	1	4		34
Herrington, James	1		1		
Dudley, Abraham	1	3	6		27
Dudley, Thomas	1	2	5		5
Modes, Thomas, Jur	1	1	3		
Modes, Thomas, Senr	1		2		
Watson, James	2	2	2		21
Dudley, Susannah	2		3		
Dudley, Stephen	2	2	7		16
Collins, Benjamin	1	2	1		6
Timmons, Mary			2		
Williamson, David	2	3	3		1
Jones, Richard	1	1	3		(*)
Watson, Jeremiah	2		2		(*)
Frazer, Micajah	2	2	4	7	21
Stephens, George	2	3	2		1
Bender, John	2	3	2		
Morris, John	1	1	1		
Watson, Jeremiah	1	4	4		9
Amyst, Vincent	1	5	4		
Amyst, Enoch	2		1		
Ventures, Mary	1	1	3		
Williamson, John	1		5		
Bradshaw, Samuel	2	2	2		
Wilcocks, Benjamin	1	3	3		
Mackay, Samuel	1		1		
Lipsey, Roscoe	3	1	4		
Stokes, Arthur	2	4	4		
McDonald, James	3	2	6		
Pybus, John	1		2		
Pybus, Mary		2	3		
Hicks, Alexander	1		3		2
Weeks, Dixon	1	1	3		
Pybus, James	1				
Ubank, George	1	6	3		
Morris, Thomas	1		5		2
Oliver, William	3	2	2		2
Williamson, Joseph	1		3		
Williamson, Richard	1	4	2		
Wood, Gasham	3	3	6		
Critchfield, Uribius	1	3	3		
Taylor, Cornelius	1				
Critchfield, Ann	1	1	2		
Goslin, John	2		7		1
Andrews, Adam	2	3	5		
Edwards, Robert	1	1	3		
Andrews, John, Senr	2	1	3		
Pollock, James	1	1	1		1
Harrison, John	1		2		
Critchfield, Philip	1	1	3		
Critchfield, Richard	1	2	1		
Bailey, J. Ag	1	2	1		
Thomas, Jesse	3		3		
Amyst, Shadrack	1				
McJay, James	1		1		
Simmons, Abram B	3	3	7		3
Hill, Mary		2	2		
Perry, Maxwell	1		2		
Perry, Robert	2		1		
Perry, Daniel, Junr	1	1	3		
Perry, William	1	1	1		
Harris, Zemeriah	1	1	2		
Pickeron, Benjamin	2	4	3		
Pickeron, Jemima		3	7		
Thornton, Thomas	1	1	4		
Busick, James	2	1	2		2
Harrison, Susannah		2	4		7
Perry, Daniel, Senr	3	2	1		7
Thornton, Thomas	1	1	3		
Busick, Michael	1		1		
Amyst, Daniel	1				
Witton, Thomas	1				
Conner, Abram				1	
Stokes, George	1				
Pritchard, William	1				
Slaughter, Sarah			2		
Mackay, Jane			1		
Williamson, Margaret	1		4		
Runnels, Penelope		1	2		7
Bradshaw, Reuben	1		1		
Green, Samuel	1	2	1		
Busick, William, Junr	1	3	2		
Sanders, Solomon	1		3		
Sanders, Southy	1		4		
Brown, James	1		3		
Busick, William	2		2		
Hill, Ann	1	1	2		
Clark, John	1		2		
Robinson, David				3	
Taylor, Edmond	1	3	2		
McDonald, John	2	4	3		1
Mallard, Adam	1	1	1		
Edwards, Rebecca	1	1	1		
Ross, Reuben	1		3		
Perry, John	3		4		
Small, Reuben	1	3	2		
Perry, William	1	1	1		
Jermis, William	1	2	4		2
Boxon, Adkin	1	5	3		
McKinsey, Alexander	3	2	2		3
Bryan, Lewis	2	5	2		24
Brown, John	2	1	3		2
Downs, Michael	2	1	2		4
Waring, Joseph	1		2		1
Allgood, Darcal	1	5	4		
Koonce, Daniel	1	5	2		
Green, James	2	4	3		8
Gilbert, John, Senior	1	2	2		1
Gilbert, Jesse	1	1	2		
Jones, Henry	2		1		
Stephenson, Matthew	2	2	3		

*Illegible.

NEWBERN DISTRICT, JONES COUNTY—Continued.

NAME OF HEAD OF FAMILY.	Free white males of 16 years and upward, including heads of families.	Free white males under 16 years.	Free white females, including heads of families.	All other free persons.	Slaves.
Miller, Mary	2	2	2		
Bryan, John	2		3	2	31
Bryan, Frederick	1		1		6
Murry, Tobias	1		1		
Gilbert, John, Senr	2	2	2		5
Tippet, John	2	1	1		1
Tippet, Joseph	1	1	3		
Blacksher, Agnes			3		2
Blacksher, Abram	2		4		
Bryan, William	1	1	3		10
Bryan, John Hill	1	2	3		14
Harrison, William	2	1	5		29
Gilbert, John, Junior	1	1	2		2
Hypock, Christopher	1	2	2		
Wade, Peter	1	1	1		
Bryan, Edward	1	2	2		18
Witton, Robert	1	1	2		3
Spencer, Benjamin	1		4		
Still, John	1	1	2		1
Lavender, John, Senr	1	2	3		2
Lavender, William	1	1	1		
Shine, John	1	3	5		8
Pitman, Ann	1		1		
Paradice, William	1	2	4		
Carlisle, Robert	1	2	1		
Johnston, John	1	3	4		
Tippet, William	1	2	3		
Potter, James	2	1	1		
Shine, Daniel	3		3		12
Tippet, James	1	5	1		
Pitman, Jeremiah	1	1	1		
Dulin, Thomas	2		3		
Turner, Smith	1	3	2		
Dulin, Rice	1	1	4		9
Blacksher, Edward	3	1			33
Messer, Noah	2		3		
Washburn, James	2	3	4		
Philyan, James	3	1	4		5
Whaley, John	2	2	3	2	
Randall, William	1		2		19
Stanley, Elizabeth	1	2	2		
Morris, William	2		2		
Sanders, Joseph	1	1	4		
Sanders, Benjamin	1	5	1		
Freeman, Jesse	1	1	2		
Westbrook, John	1		2		
Brown, Samuel	1		4		
Brown, William, Junr	1	1	3		
Brown, William, Senr	1	1	2		1
Freeman, John	1	1	2		
Sanders, John	2		5		
Sauls, John	1	4	7		1
Gooding, James	1	1	2		
Bowers, Giles	2		3		
Conner, John	1		2		
Miller, Tobias	1		2		
Farrow, Lurah	1	1	2		
Smith, Michael	1	1	3		3
Killegrove, Hinch	1	2	4		4
Frank, Edward	1		3		8
Frank, John	1	2	4		5
Sanders, John	2		5		
Kincey, William	1	2	4		4
Pollard, William	1		3		
Pollock, Jesse	1	1	2		
Brown, John	1		3		
Kincey, Elany		2	4		4
Winsit, Joseph	1	2	6		1
Dinkins, Joshua	1	1	4		
Price, John	2	1	3		1
Cocks, Andrew	1	1	6		4
Cocks, Charles	2		2		1
King, Samuel	1		2		
Cocks, Aaron	1	2	1		
Winsit, Robert	2	4	2		2
Brock, William	1	5	3		
Alfin, David	1	2	4		
Whitlidge, Ambrose	1	1	2		
Alfin, Thomas	1		2		
Baggs, Marianne			2		
Cox, Mary			2		
Rhodes, Jacob	1	2	3		1
Johnston, Jacob	3	4	5		13
Turner, Jacob	3	4	4		
Jarmin, John	1	3	3		1
Jelks, Richard	1		2		2
Pate, William	2	5	1		1
Stephens, William	1		3		
Simson, Peter	1	3	1		
Williams, Chap	1	1	1		2
Rhodes, James	2	1	3		
Alfin, William	1	1	4		
Jones, Frederic	1	1	2		1
Barnet, William	3	2	5		
Barnet, John	2	2	5		
Stewart, John	2	3	3		
Taylor, Jesse	1	1	1		

NAME OF HEAD OF FAMILY.	Free white males of 16 years and upward, including heads of families.	Free white males under 16 years.	Free white females, including heads of families.	All other free persons.	Slaves.
Jones, Hardy	2		2		5
Jones, William	2	2	2		9
Killegro, Mary		1	3		
Jones, James	1	3	4		2
Winsit, Hannah			3		4
Jermin, Rachel		1	4		4
Jermin, Hall	1	1	1		3
Simson, Peter	2	2	1		
Sanders, Moses	1	3	2		
Branson, Vincent	1		2		
Blacksher, Moses	1	3	3		
King, Samuel, Senr	2	1	6		
Moor, John	2	1	4		
Wamble, Nathan	2	1	2		
King, Charles	1	2	3		
King, Samuel, Junr	1	2	2		
Strickland, Harman	1	2	4		
Croft, Samuel C	2	1	6		
Brown, Edward	3	3	2		
Blacksher, Elis S	2		5		1
Blacksher, Jesse	1		2		
Brown, Howel	1	3	4		
King, John	1	3	6		
Kincey, Joseph	2	2	4		
Kincey, Edward	1	2	4		1
Kincey, Samuel	1	1	3		
Westbrook, James	1		2		
Lee, Jacob	2		5		13
Everit, Hannah		1	4		13
Fordom, Benjamin	2	1	7		
Davis, Benjamin	3	1	6		
Morgan, William	1	1	2		
Stanton, Benjamin	1	2	3		2
Packer, Holiday	2	2	2		
Pickeron, Aaron	2	2	5		
Westbrooke, Benjamin	2	4	1		
Ives, Isaac	1		1	1	
Morgan, Elisha					4
Jones, James					11
Jones, Hardy					5
Jones, Jacob					2
Connor, Mark					9
Connor, John					13
Stanley, James	3	1	7		1
Batts, William	1	1	2		
Atkinson, Elisha	2	3	2		
Blackman, Arthur	1	1	3		6
Quince, George, junr	1	5	6		7
Quince, John, Senr	1		3		9
Pritchard, Bazel	1		1		17
Pritchard, Clement	1				14
Brown, Richard	1	3	3		
Quilling, Daniel	1	2	2		
Quince, John, Junr	1	3	2		5
Bush, William	2	2	1	1	15
Gregory, Amy		1	2		5
Lavender, Samuel	1	1	6		1
Jermin, Robert	1	3	3		1
Khuince, Christopher	2	1	5		4
Perry, Adonijah	1	2	1		1
Williamson, Francis	2	1	1		
Small, Benjamin	2	2	3		
Stanley, Martin	1	2	5		
Little, John	2	1	4		
Stanley, Ann	2	1	7		
Stanley, Benjamin					
Stanley, William	1	1	3		
Pickeron, John	1		3		1
Hypock, Felton	2		3		
Khuince, George, Senior	1	3	4		
Khuince, Philip	1	1	3		3
Khuince, John, junr	1	2	2		
Pate, Philip	1	2	2		3
Khuince, George, junr	1		2		1
Hargate, Daniel	2	4	3		8
Maldin, Henry	1	1	2	1	1
Gergainus, Wiley	1	3	2		
Miller, Thomas	1	6	1		
Hall, Samuel	1	1	1		11
Dean, William	1	1	4		
Godwin, Aaron	2		1	1	
Gilbert, Joseph	1	2	1		1
Runnels, Richard	2	2	6		8
Cooms, Sarah		1	3		
Isler, John	2	3	3		47
Pate, Richard	2	4	3		
Asque, Benjamin	1	1	3		
Shute, Thomas	1	1	2		
Cox, Benjamin	1		2		
Mets, George	1	2	2		
Men, Philip	1	2	3		
Mets, William	1	2	3		
Moye, John	2	2	3		
Simmons, Daniel	1	2	1		11
Pierce, Seth	1	2	3		
Jones, William	1		1		
Sanders, John	1	2	3		

NAME OF HEAD OF FAMILY.	Free white males of 16 years and upward, including heads of families.	Free white males under 16 years.	Free white females, including heads of families.	All other free persons.	Slaves.
Huggins, Isaac	2	1	3		
Cox, Solomon	1		4		
Spikes, Simon	4	2	4		20
Becton, Michael	1	3	4		14
Becton, John	2	2	4		34
Becton, George	1	2	4		10
Asque, Thomas	2	2	7		
Bryan, Nathan	2	4	4		15
Jackson, John	2	2	4		
Delahunta, John, Senr	2		2		2
Delahunta, Thomas	1		1		1
Bailey, James	1	1	4		
Cox, John H	1	1	2		
Mets, George	1	3	3		
Truel, Joseph	1	1	2		
Taylor, John	1		1		
Cox, Abner	1	2	3		
Herbert, William	1		3		
Stanley, Benjamin	1	2	3		
Caviner, Sylvester	1	2	2		
Williams, Huggins	1	2	6		
Shetfer, John	1	4	6		1
Gilstrap, Idolet	3	2	5		
Fearn, Mary	1		7		
Antwince, Andrew	1	3	1		
Huggins, James	1		3		
Brice, Margaret	1		3		1
Williams, Benjamin	1	2	3		
Kelly, John	1	1	1		
Isler, William	1				6
Delahunta, Samuel	3	2	2		1
Bailey, Abram	1	1	3		
Taylor, Mary		2	1		
Runnels, Robin	1	1	2		
Scean, John	1	3	1		
Scean, Alexander	1	2	1		
Scean, Sarah	1		4		
Kent, Margaret		1	2		
Green, Stephen	1				
Jones, Mary			2		
Conolly, William	3	2	5		4
Cox, Marmaduke	1	2	6		
Macafee, John	1	1	4		
Gilstrap, Isaac	1	1	3		
Kellum, Elijah	1	1	4		
Gilstrap, Henry	1		3		
Allen, Thomas	1	1	3		
Green, William	1	2	3		
Swiley, Zeno	1	1	6		
Scean, Jesse	1		1		
Little, Abram	4	1	4		
Khuince, Jesse	1				
Macfashion, Daniel	2	3	2		
Hunter, Ezekiel	1				
Runnels, Sharp	1	3	4		1
Bratcher, James	1		1		
Normon, John	1	1	3		
Men, William	1		2		
Knox, William	1	3	2		
Fearn, Sarah			2		
Gilbert, Priscilla			2		
Hynes, Masten	1	3	1		
Stiller, Sarah			1		
Hargat, Peter	1	3	6		12
Brock, Joseph	3	2	5		10
White, Benjamin	1	2	2		7
McDonald, Reddick	1	2	6		
Morris, Philip	3	3	1		
Alcock, Richard Nelson	3	3	1		5
Alcock, Gatlin		2	3		
Shepherd, Rachel	2	1	2		5
Stephenson, Charles	2	3	2		1
Collins, Joshua	2	1	3		
Dunn, Thomas	2	1	3		
Foscue, Arthur	1	1	1		1
Alcock, Lemuel	1	1	1		
Bogue, Josiah	1	1	5		
Perisher, Josiah	1		3		
Bogue, Mark	1	1	3		
Stanton, Bindon	1	3	2		
Smith, Henry	1	1	3		1
Harrison, James	1	1	1		1
Tice, William	1	1	1		1
Harrison, Edward	1	1	1		
Merritt, Hezekiah	2	2	7		5
Gray, Cox	1		3		
Gray, Israel	1		2		1
Richards, John	1	1	5		
Chance, Oldfield	2	4	4		3
Smith, John	2	4	3		
Sheppard, Elijah	2	1	3		2
Gray, James	1	5	2		2
Roberts, Zachariah	1		2		
Johnston, Edmund	1	1	3		
Grenade, Jacob	1		3		
Harrison, Stephen	1		2		
Harrison, James, Senr	3	1	2		

NEWBERN DISTRICT, JONES COUNTY—Continued.

NAME OF HEAD OF FAMILY.	Free white males of 16 years and upward, including heads of families.	Free white males under 16 years.	Free white females, including heads of families.	All other free persons.	Slaves.
Grenade, William	1	2	3	....	1
Hackburn, Joseph	1	.....	2	....	4
Harrison, William	1	.....	.....	....	....
Simons, Felia	1	2	2	....	....
Yates, David	2	2	1	....	....
Baker, William	1	.....	2	....	....
Oram, William	1	4	1	....	3
Cornegie, Daniel	1	.....	.....	....	....
Grace, William	1	1	1	....	....
Gregory, John	1	1	1	....	4
Kernegy, John	3	1	5	....	10
Colbert, Tamer	1	3	6	....	....
Dollard, Jacob	1	.....	.....	....	....
Hudler, David	1	.....	.....	....	....
Frost, James	1	.....	.....	....	....
Andrews, Francis	1	.....	1	....	....
Hudley, Henry	1	.....	.....	....	....
Moze, George	1	.....	1	....	....
Moze, Isaac	1	.....	.....	....	....
Clifton, Ezekiel	3	1	6	....	3
Colway, John	1	.....	2	....	....
Tracky, John	1	.....	5	....	....
Mercer, Robert	4	2	4	....	....
Peters, John	1	1	3	....	....
Griffin, Richard	1	1	3	....	....
Hudley, Joseph	1	2	1	....	....
Moor, Levy	2	1	1	1	2
Hudler, John	1	.....	1	....	....
Nelson, Sarah	.....	.....	3	....	....
Gray, Gilbert	1	5	3	....	1
Sanderson, Benjamin	1	2	1	....	2
Andrews, John	2	2	7	....	4
Andrews, Daniel	1	1	3	....	....
Rickerson, Jesse	1	1	3	....	....
Murphy, John	1	2	2	....	....
Alcock, Gatsy	1	1	3	....	....
Mallard, Lawson	1	.....	4	....	1
Mallard, Daniel	3	.....	3	1	....
Foscue, Simon	1	2	3	....	14
Kennedy, Elizabeth	.....	.....	2	....	....
Mallard, John	2	3	6	....	....
Kornegay, Abram	1	1	.....	....	15
Burnet, John	1	2	3	....	1
Sanderson, Joseph	1	.....	7	....	14
Lambert, Aaron	1	5	4	....	1
Lambert, Abner	2	4	3	....	....
Mercer, Benjamin	1	.....	2	....	....
Harrison, Daniel	1	3	2	....	2
Stephenson, James	1	.....	2	....	....
Harrison, Joseph	1	1	1	....	4
Miller, Daniel	1	.....	3	....	2
Harget, Frederic	3	2	3	....	16
Jones, Henry	2	.....	1	....	....
Busick, James	2	1	2	....	2
Wamble, John	1	6	3	....	....

NEWBERN DISTRICT, PITT COUNTY.

NAME OF HEAD OF FAMILY.	Free white males of 16 years and upward, including heads of families.	Free white males under 16 years.	Free white females, including heads of families.	All other free persons.	Slaves.
Rix, Edmund	1	3	1	....	4
Hodges, Benjamin	1	1	4	1	5
Barrow, James	1	1	1	....	8
Cason, Hilary	6	3	2	....	7
Cucksaul, Abier	1	2	2	....	....
Whichard, Anthony	1	.....	3	....	....
Moore, John	1	.....	4	....	....
Carmean, James	1	.....	.....	....	....
Davis, Thomas	2	1	5	....	1
Moore, Obadiah	1	1	5	....	11
Fowler, Abram	1	1	1	....	....
Hodges, Robert	2	.....	1	....	17
Hodges, Henry	3	1	4	....	12
Hodges, Margaret	2	2	3	....	5
Hodges, Elizabeth	1	1	3	....	5
Smith, Elizabeth	1	.....	3	....	....
Jordan, John	5	4	3	....	15
Wallace, John	2	.....	2	....	3
Dudley, James, Senr	2	2	3	....	....
Guilford, Joseph, Senr	1	2	3	....	....
James, Thomas	2	2	5	....	....
Lloyd, Benjamin	1	2	2	....	....
Morris, Mary	1	.....	3	....	1
Griffin, John	1	.....	1	....	1
Congleton, William	1	2	3	....	....
Smith, David	3	2	5	....	21
Guilford, Joseph, Junr	1	3	2	....	1
Jones, John	2	4	4	....	4
Spear, John	1	3	4	....	....
Keel, Simon	1	.....	2	....	1
Keel, William	1	.....	1	....	....
Langley, William	1	.....	3	....	....
Biggs, John	1	1	4	....	....
Evans, Michael C	3	.....	3	....	4
Brinkley, John	3	.....	9	....	....
Hinton, Dempsey	2	1	2	....	8
White, Francis	1	1	1	....	1
Little, George	1	3	4	....	2
Little, James	1	.....	1	....	3
Little, Josiah	1	3	4	....	3
Piercy, John	2	.....	1	....	....
Langley, James	1	3	3	....	1
Hodges, William	1	2	3	....	9
Kingsall, John	2	1	3	....	....
Little, William	1	6	4	....	6
Smith, William	2	3	6	....	....
Hodges, Edmond	3	1	3	....	8
Spears, James	1	1	5	....	....
Nichols, Mary	.....	1	3	....	....
Dean, Anthony	1	1	2	....	....
Dean, Moses	1	1	3	....	....
James, Daniel	1	3	1	....	....
James, Thomas	1	1	1	....	....
James, John, Junr	1	2	2	....	....
Wallace, Richard	1	3	2	....	....
Wilson, William	1	1	2	....	....
Whitehead, John	1	4	2	....	4
Shepherd, Jordan	2	.....	5	....	15
Pinkett, William	2	.....	1	....	7
Patrick, Solomon	2	.....	2	....	3
Crandol, Christopher	1	1	3	....	....
Daniel, Joseph	1	.....	3	....	4
Whitehead, Charles	1	.....	.....	....	....
Griffin, James	1	3	2	....	....
Dudley, James, jun^r	1	2	4	....	1
Knox, Robert	1	.....	5	....	....
Whitacre, John	1	3	1	....	....
Harris, William	1	.....	.....	....	....
Ames, Thomas	1	2	2	....	....
Hewbanks, John	1	.....	.....	....	....
James, Joshua	2	2	5	....	....
M•Dugal, Ducan	1	1	5	....	....
Rodgers, Shadrach	1	1	1	....	....
Congleton, David	1	.....	1	....	....
Jolly, Jesse	1	1	1	....	....
Ivey, John	1	.....	2	....	....
Brown, Charles	1	3	5	....	....
Stewart, William S	1	.....	.....	1	16
Stewart, Alexander	1	1	.....	....	12
Stewart, James	1	.....	.....	....	20
Piercy, John, Junr	1	2	1	....	....
Spears, John	1	.....	1	....	54
Bryant, William	1	1	1	....	....
Ewell, James	1	.....	1	....	....
Bryerly, Abram	1	3	3	....	....
Parrymore, John	1	1	3	....	....
Pressey, William	1	.....	1	....	....
Davis, Daniel, Junr	1	.....	.....	....	....
Davis, Daniel, Senr	1	.....	3	....	....
James, John	3	2	3	....	....
Parrimore, Ezekiel	1	.....	.....	....	....
Albritton, James	3	2	1	....	8
Knox, Josiah	1	2	2	....	....
Barrow, Samuel	2	1	3	....	15
Barrow, James	1	1	1	....	9
Adams, Archibald	1	.....	.....	....	2
Jones, John	1	.....	3	....	5
James, Lemuel	1	.....	3	....	....
Leggett, Sarah	1	2	6	....	1
Harris, William, Senr	3	1	3	....	....
Salter, Clarissa	.....	.....	4	....	11
Nelmes, Thomas	1	3	2	....	1
Mooreing, William	1	1	4	....	3
Ewell, Catherine	.....	.....	2	....	....
Proctor, Abner	1	1	8	....	....
Dudley, Samuel	1	4	6	....	2
Albritton, James	1	1	4	....	4
Baldwin, William	1	1	7	....	1
Moore, Matthias	3	2	3	....	10
Moore, Jesse	1	.....	.....	....	1
Moore, Richard	1	4	1	....	3
Moore, Kennedy	1	1	2	....	1
Bryerly, William	2	1	5	....	....
Shivers, Ann	.....	1	1	....	....
Ewell, Elizabeth	.....	1	3	....	....
Barber, William	1	1	1	....	....
Barber, Charles	1	2	2	....	....
Harris, Major, Senr	1	2	3	....	....
Harris, William	1	1	1	....	....
Harris, Major, jun^r	1	.....	1	....	....
Spear, William	1	1	4	....	....
Harris, Jacob	1	.....	1	....	....
Robertson, James	2	3	5	....	....
Mooreing, William	1	1	3	....	3
Flake, Arthur	1	.....	1	....	....
Flake, John	3	.....	3	....	....
Tucker, Wright	1	1	2	....	1
Herrington, Henry	1	.....	.....	....	....
Herrington, Joshua	1	1	2	....	....
Barber, John, Junr	2	1	4	1	3
Barber, John, Senr	2	1	2	....	4
Tucker, Joshua	1	.....	.....	....	....
Hatten, John	1	4	2	....	2
James, William	1	.....	1	....	....
James, Matthew	1	1	3	....	1
Cason, John	1	4	4	....	12
Balderee, William	1	2	4	....	....
Perry, Shardach	1	3	3	3	1
Tucker, Kealy	1	3	4	....	....
Moze, Gardner	1	1	3	2	1
Daniel, Thomas	1	1	.....	....	2
Daniel, Lanier	1	.....	1	....	1
Daniel, Robert	2	1	1	....	15
Adams, Calston	1	3	3	....	5
Cason, Henry, Senr	2	.....	3	....	7
Shivers, Jesse	1	3	4	....	....
Cherry, Nathan	2	.....	3	....	1
Fleming, David	1	2	3	....	....
Cason, William	1	.....	.....	....	....
Little, Joseph	2	3	7	....	1
Cason, Joseph	1	.....	.....	....	....
Stokes, Sarah	1	.....	1	....	....
Halton, Robert	3	.....	1	2	1
Robertson, James	2	3	6	....	....
Norcutt, Nicholas	2	.....	1	....	2
Norcutt, William, Ju^r	1	.....	3	....	3
Norcutt, William, Senr	2	.....	1	....	2
Ewell, Solomon	1	.....	2	....	....
Ewell, John	1	.....	.....	....	....
Shivers, Jonas	2	3	2	....	....
McCoffee, James	1	.....	.....	....	....
Flake, Arthur, Senr	1	.....	2	....	....
Little, Jacob	1	.....	3	....	....
Cherry, John	1	1	3	....	....
Whicherel, John	1	2	2	....	....
Albritton, Adam	1	.....	.....	....	....
Proctor, Henry	1	1	2	....	....
Proctor, Nee	1	.....	3	....	....
Davis, Thomas	1	2	1	....	....
Braley, Solomon	1	1	2	....	....
McGowns, John	1	1	2	....	....
Fleming, John	1	1	4	....	....
Powell, Thomas	2	1	3	....	....
Bedford, Levin	1	.....	.....	....	....
Moore, Henry	2	.....	4	....	4
Porter, George	3	.....	1	....	4
Moore, Thomas	1	.....	2	....	1
Moore, Edward	3	.....	3	....	....
Nobles, Nathaniel	2	3	7	....	1
Moore, John	1	.....	4	....	....
Hysmith, John	1	.....	4	....	....
Barnhill, Henry	3	.....	1	....	....
Bowers, Benjamin, Senr	1	.....	1	....	10
Moore, Sarah	2	2	2	....	....
James, Henry	2	1	3	....	....
Mac Dearman, John	1	3	3	....	....
Whitacre, William	2	4	3	....	....
Clements, George	1	2	2	....	....
Knox, David	1	4	3	....	....
Ward, John, Senr	3	1	5	....	....
Jolly, Jesse	2	1	2	....	2
Anders, Edmond	2	2	3	....	11
Sessions, Walter	1	.....	3	....	....
Jolly, John	3	1	7	....	....
Levi, Alexander	1	1	1	....	....
James, Lance	2	.....	3	....	....
Hubanks, Richard	3	2	4	....	....
Gray, Joseph, Senr	2	.....	3	....	....
Keel, Ezekiel	1	2	3	....	....
Hubanks, Elizabeth	.....	2	1	....	....
Clements, William	3	4	5	....	1
Tarr, Nehemiah	1	2	2	....	....
Dannels, George	1	1	3	....	3
Cooper, William	1	1	2	....	....
Cooper, George	2	.....	1	....	....
Knox, William	1	.....	1	....	....
Knox, Archibald	1	2	1	....	....
Hewbanks, George	1	2	4	....	....
Moore, Caleb	1	1	3	....	....
Moore, Moses	1	2	3	....	....
Bullock, Edward	1	.....	1	....	....
Moore, Edmond	1	.....	1	....	1
Moore, Reading	1	1	2	....	....
Roye, Darling	1	.....	2	....	....
Collins, Josiah	1	.....	2	....	....
Harvey, Joshua	1	2	2	....	....

NEWBERN DISTRICT, PITT COUNTY—Continued.

NAME OF HEAD OF FAMILY.	Free white males of 16 years and upward, including heads of families.	Free white males under 16 years.	Free white females, including heads of families.	All other free persons.	Slaves.
Harvey, John	1	2	2		
Bowers, William	1	2	4		4
Moore, Jacob	1		1		
Bowers, Benjamin	1	3	4		
Grimmer, Robert	2	1	2		2
Mayo, Peter	1	3	3		4
Highsmith, John, junr	1				1
Barnhill, Hervey, junr	1	1	2		
Ward, James	1		1		
Everite, James	1	1	2		
Levi, Henry	1	2	1		
Chance, Thomas	2	1	5		
Ward, John, junr	1		1		
Everite, Simon	1	1	2		
Mobley, Eleazer	2	3	6		
Porter, Frederic	1	3	1		1
McDearman, Michael	1				
Barnhill, Jesse	1		1		
Taylor, James	1		2		
Gilbert, John	2	2	4		
Rollins, Charles	1	2	5		
Nobles, Drew	1		2		1
Highsmith, Jacob	1	1	3		
Knox, William, Senr	2	2	2		
Barnhill, William	1		1		
Ward, William	1	2	3		
Pilgreen, William				3	
Stancell, Noble	1				3
Kelly, Jeremiah	1		3		
Jolly, Peter	3	5	4		
Perkins, David	1	2	2		9
Dannels, Robert	2	1	1		10
James, Lemuel	1		3		
Cason, Henry	4		3		6
Congleton, William	2	2	4		
Lock, John	1		3		
Page, Joseph	3	1	6		
Manning, Reuben	3	3	7		6
Windom, John	3	1	3		
Thomas, Abel	1	3	5		1
Brown, Mourning			1		
Mayo, Mary			2		
Osborn, Luke	1	1	4		11
Stancill, Sarah	3	4	4		14
Jenkins, Henry	2	1	1		2
Williams, Robert	1	1	2		
Anders, Levi	2	2	5		9
Whitus, Badson	4	1	2		
Bowers, John	2	1	7		1
Rogers, Isaac	1	1	5		
Martin, Peter	1	3	5		
Gatlen, Edward	1	2	2		2
Keel, Rachel		2	4		
Hopkins, William	1	4	3		7
Cherry, Samuel	2	3	5		8
Luter, Matthew	2	2	5		4
Windall, Benjamin	2		5		
Bonner, William	3	3	4		13
Brown, Isaac	1	2	2		
Mayo, Peter	3	1	5		1
Mayo, William	1		3		4
Bullock, Drury	1	4	3		
Downs, Nehemiah	2	3	3		
Waldron, Charles	1	3	4		5
Windom, Green	2	3	3		
Mayo, Shadrack	1	1	5		
Windon, Solomon	2	3	5		
Coggin, William	1	2	5		
Meeks, Robert	1		4		
Nichols, Jane	1	2	3		
Taylor, John	2	3	6		
Taylor, William		1	1	2	
Taylor, Frances		2	1	3	
Lewis, Willis	1	1	3		
Wilkinson, William	1				2
Wilkinson, Benjamin, Senr	2	2	3		4
Cobb, James	1	4	5		
Wilkinson, Benjamin, junr	1				
Bryant, Frederick	1	5	2		8
Horeso, William	1	5	2		11
Cherry, Solomon	4		4		5
Summerland, James	1		4		
Etherage, Malicah	3	1	2		
Rogers, Isaac	2	1	5		
Anders, Whitten	1		2		
Batton, Thomas	1	3	3		
Ross, Thomas	1	1	1		
Whitus, Richard	1	1	4		
Whitus, Arthur	1	2	3		
Page, John	2		1		5
Buntin, Daniel	1	1	5		
Buntin, John	1		1		
Wilkinson, Joshua	1	2	4		4
Cearson, Thomas	1	4	2		4
Whitley, Samuel	2	5	5		8
Nichols, Elizabeth			3		
Carter, Robert	1	1	2		

NAME OF HEAD OF FAMILY.	Free white males of 16 years and upward, including heads of families.	Free white males under 16 years.	Free white females, including heads of families.	All other free persons.	Slaves.
Williams, George	1		1		
Buntin, Mary	1		2		
Williams, Margaret		3	2		
Whitus, Samuel	1	2	1		
Strawbridge, William	2	2	4		
Adkerson, Benjamin	4		2		23
Bryant, Nicholas	2		5		5
Evans, Moses	1	4	1		1
Evans, Ephraim	1	3	1		1
Evans, Amos	1				
Clark, Samuel	1	1	4		5
Harris, William	1	1	1		
Harris, George, Senr	3		5		
Harris, Hood	2	1	4		
Williams, George	1	2	1		
Williams, Harris	1	1	5		
Harris, Henry	1	1	3		
Mourning, John, junr	1		1		1
Mourning, John, Senr	2	1	4		14
Mourning, James	1				
Gwartney, Thomas	2	4	2		7
Sherod, William	1		3		14
Rieves, Peter	1		1		20
Brady, James	2	5	5		
Brady, Susannah	2		3		
Teale, Emanuel, Senr	2	2	3		1
Teal, Jacob	1	2	1		
Teal, Moses	1	1	3		1
Savage, Joseph	1				
Pollard, John, Senr	3	1	5		
Pollard, John, junr	1	2	3		1
Pollard, Everit	1	3	3		
Brown, Samuel	1	1	2		1
Brown, James	1		3		
Brown, James, junr	1	3	3		
Teal, Emanuel, junr	1	2	1		
Brown, Benjamin	1	1	4		1
Bryerly, Jacob	1				
Williams, Joel	1	2	4		1
Brierly, Joseph	1	2	5		1
Brierly, Isaac	1		1		
Brierly, Richard	2	4	3		
Teal, Lodovick	1		2		
Teal, Richard	1				
Adams, Levi	2	7	7		
Parrimore, Amos	1		1		
Mills, Henry	1		2		
Williams, John	1	3	2		
Little, Isaac	2		4		
Little, Pleasant	1	1	2		
Womble, Benjamin, junr	1	1	1		
Womble, Simon	1		2		
Stokes, James	1				
Pennington, William	1				
Brown, Sophira			2		1
Anderson, John	1	2	3		
May, John	1	2	5		
Teal, William	1	1	4		
Spain, William	1				
Robertson, Severin	2	4	8		
Anderson, William	2	1	3		1
Anderson, Lawrence	1	2	4		2
Bell, Benjamin	2	5	3		16
Spain, Fetherston	1	1	1		
Griffin, Samuel	1	1	1		
Griffin, Caleb	1				
Mayo, Jacob	1		3		
Mitchel, Thomas	1	1	4		
Fulford, Joseph	1				
Herrington, Isaac	1	1	2		
Lewis, Winnifred	1	2	1		
Avery, Bridget		1	2		
Wyett, Keziah		2	2		
Love, Thomas	1		2		
Robertson, William	1		7		
Venters, Lancaster	3	1	2		3
Spain, Augustus	1	2	4		
Spain, Drury	2	1	1		
Mayo, Nathan	2	2	3		
Meeks, James	1	2	5		
Harris, Ann	1		1		
Ewell, Elizabeth		1	3		
Teal, Bradbury	1	4	2		
Teal, William	1	1	3		
Ward, Isaac	1	1	2		
Lewis, Willis	1	1	3		
Ward, William	1	1	1		
Reeves, Richard	1	3	2		9
Hickman, Joseph	1		3		
Little, James	1	4	4		5
Stokes, Markus	3	1	2		12
Adkinson, Amos	2		5		14
Hathaway, Edmond	1		1		
Hathaway, David	3	1	2		11
Hathaway, Thomas, Senr	1		4		
Hall, Thomas	3	2	3		16
Perry, Sarah			5		
Hearn, Benjamin	1	1	3		3

NAME OF HEAD OF FAMILY.	Free white males of 16 years and upward, including heads of families.	Free white males under 16 years.	Free white females, including heads of families.	All other free persons.	Slaves.
Averit, David	1		1		
Summerland, Thomas	1		1		
Meeks, Uranah	1	3	3		
Church, Isaac	1	2	7		
Church, Cornelius	1	2	2		
Church, John	2	1	4		
Mayo, Richard	2		2		
Robinson, John	2	1	6		
Hall, Charles	1				2
Adkins, Allen	1		1		6
Mayo, John	3	2	2		
Cobb, David, Senr	2	2	5		2
Cobb, Keziah	1	3	2		
Whitley, Mary			2		11
Moseley, William	3	1	1		
Milbern, John	1	2	3		1
Drake, Elizabeth	1		3		
Clark, John	1	2	3		
Whitley, William	1	2	2		7
Lewis, Nathan	1	2	2		
Meeks, Francis, junr	1		1		
Right, Isaac	1	2	3		
Randal, Latimer	1				
Everit, David, junr	1	2	6		
Coggin, John	2	1	6		
Hix, David	1				
Rix, Lucy	1		1		4
Cobb, Edward	3	2	5		
Jones, Henry	1	3	4		14
Cobb, Briton	1	3	4		
Swearinggame, Mary			5		
Taylor, John	1	5	2		
Avery, James	1		3		
Asbel, Joseph	2	2	2		
Grimmon, Jacob	1		4		
Womble, Benjamin, Senr	2	4	3		
Dupree, Bird	2	2	2		20
Dupree, Starling	2	3	5		8
Williams, Roderick	1	2	6		
Dupree, Benjamin	2	2	4		11
Proctor, Richard	1		2		9
Williamson, Henry	1		1		6
Duffil, Thomas, Senr	2	1	4		
Wallace, Thomas, Senr	2	1	6		2
Williams, John, Senr	3		1		13
Williams, John, Junr	1	2	2		3
Williams, James	1	4	2		5
Johnston, James	2	3	5		4
Wootin, John	2	1	2		7
Allen, Richard, Senr	2		3		7
Trust, Samuel	2	1	2		1
Peal, James	3	2	5		
Harrill, Reuben	1		5		
Buxton, William	1		3		4
Ross, William	1	1	3		
Tyson, Thomas	2		2		8
Foreman, Jesse	1		5		1
Evans, George	1				6
Lester, Jeremiah	1	1	3		
Sturdivant, Henry	1	1	4		8
Williams, Robert	1		3		6
Sturdivant, Matthew	1	1	2		4
Sturdivant, Sarah		1	2		3
Moye, George	2	3	6		5
Lawrence, Josiah	1	1	2		9
Lawrence, Jesse	1				4
Foreman, John	1	2	2		12
Harris, Henry	2	3	2		4
Allen, Merryman	2	2	4		
Blann, John	1	1	3		
Browne, Arthur	1	1	2		1
Hathaway, Nathan	3	1	3		
Hathaway, James	1	1	4		
Harris, Richard	1	1	1		1
Sugg, Elizabeth	2		3		6
Eason, Ann		1	2	1	
Hathaway, Francis, Jur	2	1	9		
Trust, Joel	1	1	3		1
Bell, William	1		1		
King, John	3	2	2		2
Peedin, Patrick	1	1	5		4
Taunton, Henry	1	2	7		
Powers, David	2		5		
Powers, Ephraim	1	2	3		
Wadford, Joseph	2	4	3		
Moore, John	4	3	3		3
Williams, Edward	1		1		5
Williams, Abram	1	2	3		2
Philips, Mary		1	1		
Corbett, Merida	2	3	2		
Allen, Paul	1	1	4		4
Mourning, Christopher	1	2	2		4
Jordan, Richard	1	1	2		
Rogers, Absalom	1				
Spaniard, Pumbererer	1	1	2		
Cobb, James	2	2	6		
Rogers, Joseph	1	2	3		

NEWBERN DISTRICT, PITT COUNTY—Continued.

NAME OF HEAD OF FAMILY.	Free white males of 16 years and upward, including heads of families.	Free white males under 16 years.	Free white females, including heads of families.	All other free persons.	Slaves.
Hodges, Portlock	1	3	4		
Rogers, Drew	3	1	5		1
Cobb, Moses	1	1	2		
Harris, James	1		1		
Duffel, Thomas, junr	1	2	2		
Allen, Richard, junr	1		2		2
Anders, Catherine			3		
Peeples, Baldwin	1		2		
Bullock, Samuel	1		1		2
Dilde, Jesse	1	1	2		
Rigging, Darbey	1		1		
Pastern, Elizabeth	1	1	4		
Little, Noam	2		1		
Matthews, Joseph	1	1	3		
Tidder, Martha			1		
Williams, Josiah	1		2		2
Edwards, Elizabeth	1	2	4		
Lester, Jeremiah	1	2	3		1
Leggott, James	2	4	6		10
Barnes, Joshua	1		1		3
Francis, John	1		1		
Langley, Azaniah	2	1	4		
Page, William	3	2	3		1
Page, Joseph	1	3	2		
Turnage, Emanuel	1	1	2		1
Jolly, Jonathan	2	2	3		
Turnage, Abram	1		1		
Tyer, George	2		4		
Baker, Richard	2	1	3		
Jones, John	2	3	3		
May, Benjamin	1	2	8		29
Tyson, Job	1	3	3		9
Pope, John	1		3		6
Nicholas, Benjamin	1	1	1		
Joyner, Abraham	3	2	6		
Messer, John	1	4	1		
Baker, James	1	3	4		
Moore, John	1	3	2		
Baker, Asa	1		2		2
Flanagan, Edward	1	4	5		
Jordan, Jesse	1	5	7		
Dew, Arthur	1	2	3		
Forbes, Joseph	2	3	2		3
Forbes, Henry	1		2		
Johnston, William	2	1	3		
May, Benjamin	1		2		
Smithe, William	1	1	4		
Sulivan, Joseph	2				
Grizzard, Hardy	2	4	4		
Davis, Samuel, junr	1	1	5		
Scoggins, Jeremiah		1	2		
Davis, Samuel, Senr	3	1	6		1
Davis, Lewis, Senr	1	3	3		
Davis, Lewis, Jur	1	2	1		1
Moye, William	1		4		3
Easton, John	1		4		21
Tison, Bethany			2		5
Tison, Sabra			1	4	
Walston, Thomas	2		5		
Walston, George	1	1	5		
Moore, John	3				
Moore, Nathaniel	2	4	3		
Moore, William	2	1	9		
Moore, James	1	3	3		
Beazley, William	1	3	2		
Nicholas, Joel	1	2	1		
Dunning, Ezekiel	1	1	2		
Dunning, Jesse	3		3		
Lockhost, Merinah		1	4		
Bunday, Sabra		1	3		
Cartwright, Matthew	1	1	5		3
Alberson, Solomon	1	2	1		
Pipkin, Jesse	3		3		
Rogers, Drury	2	2	5		
Davis, Thomas	1	1	3		
Moze, Joel	1		1	1	5
Deberry, Lemuel	3	3	6		18
Ashen, David	1	1	2		
Bynum, Benja	1	3	1		5
Jordan, Benja	1	5	5		
Tyson, Frederick	1	5	4		
Senders, Abram	2				2
Wincles, William	1	4	1		
Oberry, Thomas	1				3
Smith, Stephen	3	1	2		
Ellis, Henry	4	6	6		12
Rix, Benjamin	1	3	3		
Lacy, Parker	1	3	1		
Joiner, Abram	1	4	3		
Joiner, Isaac	1		3		1
Goff, Henry	1	2	3		
Hort, Barrom	1	1	3		
Wallace, George	1		1		
Goff, Thomas	1		1	3	
Moore, Arthur	1		1		
Murray, Gardner	1		1		
Ivy, Samuel	1		5		
Narris, John, Senr	1	1	5		
Senders, Robert	1	2	2		2

NAME OF HEAD OF FAMILY.	Free white males of 16 years and upward, including heads of families.	Free white males under 16 years.	Free white females, including heads of families.	All other free persons.	Slaves.
Hervey, James	1	2	2		
Moye, George	1		1		5
Numans, John	1		2		6
Tison, Richard L.	1	1	1		1
Moye, Richard	1	3	3		3
Moore, Levi	1	3	2		4
Smith, Benjamin	1	3	3		
Allen, Charles	1	2	3		
Tyson, Joab	1		1		
Jones, Zadiac	1	3	3		
Baldwin, William	1	3	5		5
Moore, Elisha	1	2	5		
Tison, George, Senr	2	1	2		2
Tison, Cornelius	2		1		
Tyson, Icabod	1	4	2		2
Ryland, Benona	1		1		
Tyson, Cornelius	2		3		12
Forbes, Arthur	1		5		18
Moore, Jesse	2	3	6		13
Moore, John	1	1	2		1
Williams, John, Esqr	3	1			13
Joiner, Elizabeth		2	3		6
Bland, George	2		2		3
Barney, Lucy	1	1	1		2
Tison, Moses, junr	1	2	3		4
Joiner, Rebecca	1		2		
Coward, John	1	2	3		2
Tison, Edmond	2		1		
Moore, Arthur	1	2	6		
Bunday, Gideon	1	2	2		
Otterey, William	1	3	3		
Barrow, Benjamin	1	3	3		8
Ellis, John	1		4		3
Moye, George	1	2	5		
Dixon, Jeremiah	1	1	2		3
Ellis, Shadrack	1	2	2		
Forbes, Clement	1	5	4		5
Allen, Roger	2	3	5		
Allen, Peter	1	2	6		
Robeson, John	1	2	2		
Vines, John	1	2	6		5
Tison, Hezekiah	1		2		
Randolph, James	1	1	3		5
Tison, Henry	1	3	1		
Vines, Samuel		1			2
Moye, James	1		1		3
Tison, Moses, Senr	3	1	2		6
Allen, Zachariah	1	3	6		
Dilday, Charles	1	4	2		
Moor, Shadrach	3	3	3		
Forbes, John	2	1	1		9
Moore, Anna		3	3		
Norris, John	1				
Tison, George, junr	2		2		
Tison, Abraham	1	1	7		3
Tison, Moses	1	2	3		4
Bryant, John	1	4	3		
Rogers, Dewey	1		5		
Randolph, Jesse	1		2		4
Ewell, Stephen	1	1	2		
Smith, Lazarus	2	3	2		
Smith, William	1	1	2		
White, Richard	1	1	1		
Harris, Mary			1		
Lester, Martha		1	1		
Wiscaney, Elizabeth	1		1		
Coleman, Isaac	2		1		1
Sutton, Abimeleck	1		3		
Powell, John	1	3	4		
Granby, George	1	3	4		
Jenkins, Zadiac	1				
Harrington, Paul	2	2	5		
Slaughter, Elizabeth			1		1
White, Rachel	1	1	1		
Powell, James	1		2		
Barber, John	1	6	4		
Joiner, William	1		2		
Powell, Reuben, junr	2		3		4
Ringold, Sarah		3	2		6
Powell, John	1	2	3		
Blount, Isaac	1	3	3		
Blount, Benjamin	1	1	2		2
Roundtree, Jesse	1		2		2
McGlohon, Adams	1	2	3		
Jackson, John	2	3	1		4
Jackson, Joseph	1	4	4		3
Cannon, William	2		2		
Manning, Elijah	1	1			
Bell, Balaam	1		1		
Sutton, Solomon	3	3	3		
Garret, Thomas	2	1	1		
Sirman, Eli	1	1	1		
Dennis, Lucy	2	1	3		
Powell, Reuben, Sr	1		1		
Wingate, Jeremiah	1		2		
Williams, Willis	1	5	3		
Moss, Dempsey	1	2	4		
Hardy, Thomas	1		8		
Calcraft, Mary	1		1		

NAME OF HEAD OF FAMILY.	Free white males of 16 years and upward, including heads of families.	Free white males under 16 years.	Free white females, including heads of families.	All other free persons.	Slaves.
Mariner, John	1				
Banod, Boaz	1		2		
Peels, Josiah	1		1		
Peels, Reuben	1	2	4		
Bentley, Thomas	1	3	3		
Windom, Micajah	2	1	2		
Wilson, John	1		2		
Bentley, Tapley	1	1	1		
Braxton, James, junr	1	1	4		
Branton, William	1	1	2		
Bowden, May	1		2		
Hamilton, Lucius	1	4	3		
Wingate, Joel	1	1	1		1
Harris, Joseph	1	2	3		
Sutton, Jacob	1	2	1		
Dewe, John	1		1		
Trueluck, George	1		1		
Trippe, Caleb, junr	1		1		
Powell, James	1		2		
English, Samuel	1	4	3		
Smith, Edmond	1		2		
Smith, Joseph	2		2		
Jackson, Joseph, Senr	1		2		
Wingate, Isaac	1	1	1		1
Falconer, George	1	3	6		1
Surman, Thomas	2	1	5		
Turner, William, Senr	2	4	6		
Turner, William, jur	1	1	5		
Alaster, Jacob	1	1	5		
Slatter, John	2	2	3		
Trippe, Caleb	3	4	3		
Ringold, James	1	3	4		
Fulford, John	3	5	4		
Blackston, John	4		3		
Blackston, Thomas	1	5	4		
Blackston, James, Senr	2	3	4		
Deale, Paul	1	3	3		
Whitfield, William	2	3	5		1
Powell, Simpson	1	1	4		
Trizell, John	1	3	6		1
Kitrall, John	1	2	1		3
Blount, Jacob	1	2	1		12
Williams, Dennis	1	1	1		
Williams, Ephraim	1	1	3		
Manning, Samuel	2	1	5		
McGlohon, Jeremiah	1				
McGlohon, George	1		3		
Castle, John Innis	1	1			
Vincent, John	1		3		
Smith, Joseph	3		2		
Smith, Jesse	1	1	1		
Hardison, Joseph	1	1	4		
Hardison, Joshua	1	3	2		
Sirman, John	1	2	4		
McClain, Daniel	1	2	4		
Clark, Jethro	1	1	3		
Barber, Elizabeth		1	3		
Bowen, Abraham	1		3		
Holland, John	2	1	3		5
Johnston, Holland	2	1	2		10
Brooks, Stephen	6	2	3		31
Blackledge, Thomas	2		3		24
Wright, Josiah	1	3			2
Cambriling, Stephen	2	1	3		4
Bullard, Daniel	1	1	2		
Smith, Oliver	1		2		6
Blount, Benjamin	1		1		4
Patrick, Cornelius	2		3		1
Manning, Hilary	1	1	2		8
Wilcox, Stephen	1		2		
Moye, John	1	2	2		14
Green, George	1	1			
Easton, James	2		3		12
Simpson, John	2				10
Crawfort, Andrew	3		3		
Simpson, Elizabeth			3		30
Adams, Abram	3	5	6		5
McKean, Edy	1				
Hall, James	1	2	2		
Nobles, Winifred		2	3		2
Gwartney, William	1		3		7
Tyron, Elisabeth	1		3		
Blount, William	2	3	2		30
Simpson, Samuel	1		3		10
Hilling, William	1	3	5		5
Hardy, Abram	2	4	2		9
Smith, David	3	2	4		21
Tyron, William	1	1	5		
Badard, William	1		2		
English, Thomas	1	1	3		2
Richards, Solomon	1		1		
Cherry, Lemuel	1	5	5		2
Hannis, Jesse	2	3	4		2
Slatter, Sampson	1	1	7		
Slatter, Absalom	1				
Eastwood, William	1		6		1
King, John	1	2	3		1
Smith, Abner C.	1	1	1		

NEWBERN DISTRICT, PITT COUNTY—Continued.

NAME OF HEAD OF FAMILY.	Free white males of 16 years and upward, including heads of families.	Free white males under 16 years.	Free white females, including heads of families.	All other free persons.	Slaves.
Corry, Joseph	1		2		
Corry, Elizabeth		1	1	1	
Bell, Starkey	1	4	4		
Hardy, Elizabeth	1	2	4		21
Hardy, Robert	1				
Williams, George	3	1	1		3
Williams, David	1				
Williams, Simon	1				
Williams, Anne	2	2	1		
English, Peter	1				
Tyron, Noah	2	5	1		1
Nobles, Margaret			2		
Lasley, John	1	2	4		1
Harris, Elijah	1		2		
Scotfield, William	2	1	2		1
Patrick, Benjamin	1				
Tyron, Jonathan	2	1	8		
Balderee, Isaac	1		3		
Driding, John	1	1	2		
Gordon, Stewart	2	2	4		
Moye, John, Senr	1		1		1
McGowns, William	2	1	5		
McGowns, George, Senr	1	1	4		
Moss, Peter	2	4	3		
Leadom, Christopher	1		1		2
King, William	1	1	3		3
Moore, David	1		1		
Diggins, Joseph	1				
Phaling, Edward	1				
Barnhill, John	2				
Davis, John	2				
Kennedy, Bartholomew	1				
McNeale, Hopestill	2				
Cobb, William	1	2	4		2
Bullock, John	1	2	3		
Roads, William	1				
Everit, Reuben	1				
Blount, Benjamin H	1				
Moore, David	1		1		
Salter, Cloe			2		
Adams, Archibald	3	1	5		5
Cannon, Lewis	1	1	2		13
Brooks, James, Senr	2	1	5		6
Cannon, Henry	1	2	3		16
Cannon, Nathaniel	1	4	5		9
Moss, Michael	1	3	7		
Mills, Nasby, Senr	2	4	6		
Williams, George	2	1	1		3
Haddock, John	2	4	5		
Mills, John	2	3	5		
Mills, Isaac, Senr	3	1	6		
Stock, Isaac	1		6		8
Stock, John	2	5	5		9
Kite, Samuel	2	1	2		
Muckleroy, William	4		1		
Moss, Peter	2	4	3		
Cannon, William	2		2		
Moye, John, Senr	2		2		
Hancock, James	4	4	6		1
Deale, Abel, junr	1	1	4		
Cannon, Mary			1		7
Brooks, John	1	5	2		
Brooks, William, Junr	1	3	4		
Mills, Nesby, junr	1		1		
Hardy, Thomas, Senr	2	1	4		1
Moore, Newton	1	3	2		
Tucker, Readick	1				
Moye, Gideon	1	1			
Brooks, William, Senr	1	2	4		
Adams, William	1		2		1
Cox, Aaron	1		3		
Stocks, William	1	1	2		
Pettite, Gideon	1	2	3		
Mills, Isaac, junr	1		4		
Tootle, William	1	1	4		
Roach, James	1	1	3		
Haddock, Charles	1	1	3		
Deale, Abel, Senr	2	4	5		
Cox, Abram	1	3	2		
Stocks, Sarah	1	2	4		
Cannon, Thomas	1	5	4		2
Cannon, Furney	2				2
Tuten, John		2	5		
Wilson, Daniel	2		4		
Wilson, Willis	1	2	5		
Kite, Henry	1	1	3		
Kite, John	1	1	2		
Adams, William	1	2	3		
Carrill, Isaac	3	4	5		
Corben, Esther		1	2		
Haddock, William	1	4	5		3
Haddock, Admiral	1	2	5		
Simmons, Mary		2	3		
Mills, William, junr	1	4	3		2
Mills, William, Senr	1	2	3		
Putnall, Joshua	1	2	3		
Mills, Frederick	1	4	9		4
Slatter, Thomas	1	1	5		

NAME OF HEAD OF FAMILY.	Free white males of 16 years and upward, including heads of families.	Free white males under 16 years.	Free white females, including heads of families.	All other free persons.	Slaves.
Slatter, John, Senr	2	2	3		
Slatter, Samuel	1	1	1		
Curlee, John	1	2	3		
Randal, William	1	1	2		1
Deale, Thomas	1	4	1		
Brooks, Ephraim	1	3	3		
Smith, Joseph	1	4	5		
Dudley, Hannah			2		
Smith, William	1	2	3		
Smith, Charles	1	3	6		
Smith, Henry	1	4	3		
Smith, Francis	1	1	2		
Golding, Lemuel	1	2	3		
Wilson, William	1	4	4		1
Barber, Elizabeth		1	3		
Deale, Abel, junr	1	1	4		
Mills, Henry	1	2	4		
Buck, William	2	4	3		3
Armstrong, James	3	2	3		10
Salter, Ann, Senr	1	1	3		11
Salter, Ann, jur	1		4		22
Salter, John, Senr	1	3	3		8
Wade, Joseph	1		1		
Moore, James	1	2	1		
Hall, William	1	2	2		
Arnold, Elizabeth	2		3		
Jones, Thomas	2	1	2		15
Boyde, Robert, Senr	3	2	4		12
Boyde, Isaac	3		2		8
Watkins, Thomas	1	1	3		
Walkins, Janet		1	4		1
Mayo, John	2		2		
Mayo, Benjamin	1		1		
Ward, George	3		3	1	
Boyde, Joseph, Senr	3		4		4
Boyde, William	1	1	1		1
Boyde, Robert, junr	1	2	1		1
Taylor, Mary	1	1	3		1
Buck, Benjamin	3	4	3		2
Grimes, William	1	1	2		15
Buck, James	1	3	5		4
Dixon, Ann	2		3		7
Dixon, John	1		2		
Gorham, James	2	8	4		50
Noble, Levi	1	4	4		2
Nelson, Giles	1	2	2		
Nelson, James	1	2	3		
Nelson, Martin, Senr	2	3	5		5
Nelson, Martin, junr	1	1	1		1
Bates, James	3		2		
Tuten, Shadrach	2	3	8		1
Edwards, William	1	1	2		
Elks, William	1	1	2		5
Elks, Uriah	1		2		1
Robeson, Amy			1		1
Dixon, Edward	4		4		
Dixon, Abraham	1	2	3		
Dixon, William, Senr	3	3	3		
Dixon, Absalom	1	1	2		
Dixon, William, junr	1	1	3		
Albritton, Peter	4	1	1		4
Albritton, James	1	1	3		3
Albritton, William	1	1	3		
Kemp, Joshua	1	1	4		
Moore, Moses	2	1	6		10
Newman, James	1		2		
Moore, Jacob	1	1	1		
Brooks, Isaac	1	1	3		
Edwards, Daniel	2	1	3		
Whitfield, Alexander	1	1	2		
Edwards, Israel	1		5		
Nelson, Samuel	1	2	2		
Buck, John	1				10
Tildsley, Charles	1	3	3		
Tildsley, Thomas	1		1	1	
Nelson, John	2	2	3		
Rochel, Jacob V	1	2	2		2
Salter, John, junr	1		4		9
Watkins, Ann	2		4		9
Stewart, Elizabeth	1		2		
Angel, Sarah		1	2		
Moore, Obadiah	1	1	1		
Crafton, Ambrose	2		5		
Campbell, Archibald	2	3	5		
Fleming, George	1	2	6		
King, Priscilla		1	2		
Buck, James, Junr	1		3		
Stevens, William	1		1		
Brooks, John	1	1	1		
Buck, Appollos	1	2	2		
Albritton, Henry	1	3	2		
Savage, Joseph	1		2		
Arnold, William	1	5	2		
Tindale, John	1				
Judkins, Thomas	2		2		
Judkins, Charles	1		1		

NAME OF HEAD OF FAMILY.	Free white males of 16 years and upward, including heads of families.	Free white males under 16 years.	Free white females, including heads of families.	All other free persons.	Slaves.
Elks, Samuel	2	2	2		
Mills, Nasby	3	3	6		
Allen, Shadrach	2	2	4		15
Smith, Samuel	1	3	4		5
Avery, David	1		3		
Cadeaduff, Mary	2	2	3		
Blount, Sharp	2		1		47
Harvey, Ann			1		18
Mills, James	1	1	4		
Jarrell, Henry, Senr	2		1		6
Jarrell, Henry, junr	1	3	7		1
Murphy, Thomas	1	3	6		
Pugh, Hugh, Senr	1	1	1		26
Cabell, James	2	2	5		4
Pelt, Henry	3		3		
Ventis, Benjamin	1	1	2		
Sutton, David	5	3	4		
Gardner, Isaac	1	4	2		3
Gatlin, Stephen	1	1	1		3
Gatlin, Elizabeth	1		4		7
Gatlin, John	1	1	1		3
Gatlin, Levi	1	3	2		1
Pugh, Hugh, junr	1		2		12
Smith, Henry, junr	1	2	3		2
Smith, Henry, junr	1		2		5
Shipp, Mary	1		1		4
Shipp, William	1		1		
Clark, Osborn	1		1		
Burney, Simon	1	3	2		5
Wherry, William	1	2	4		12
Pollard, John	1	5	2		
Jarrell, Jacob	1	6	4		
Smith, Abram	1		4		
Smith, John	5	2	3		1
Browning, William	1	2	8		
Pugh, Stephen	1		1		7
Adams, Ezekiel	3	6	2		
Ventis, Patience	2		3		
Rice, John	1		2		
Cox, Aaron	3		2		
Nelson, Peter	1	3	5		
Hickman, Jacob	1		1		
Smith, Cannon	1	3	3		3
Roys, Charles	1		2		
Stafford, William	2		8		
Dunn, Walter	1	3	1		1
Kight, Samuel	1	5	6		
Pelt, John	1	2		1	
Gwartney, Benjamin	1	1	1		
Roys, Edward	1		1		1
Roys, Leaven	1	1	1		
Jarrel, Shadrach	1	6	1		1
Peters, Joseph	3	6	3		1
Patrick, Joel	2	1	5		2
Patrick, Micajah	1	1	2		
Coart, John	2		4		18
Forms, Ruth			2		
Dunn, Walter	1	3	2		2
Kennedy, David	1	1	2		
Kennedy, David, junr	1		2		1
Quinlow, Patrick	1		1		
Quinlow, Edward	1		1		
Gardner, Edward	2	2	2		5
Patrick, Micajah	1	1	2		
Browning, Peregrine	1	5	4		
Cannon, Radford	1	2	2		
Carmaday, Jonathan	1		3		
Wingat, John	1	2	1		4
Davenport, William	1	2	2		1
Branch, James	1	1	2		
Branch, Simon	1	3	1		
Cannon, Edward	3	2	2		2
Kite, Stephen	1	2	1		
Kite, David	1		1		
Cox, Daniel	1		1		
Stokes, John	1		1		
Stokes, James	1				
Conner, John	1				
Smith, Platt	1	3	1		
Peters, William	1	1	1		1
Everit, William	3	2	6		
Nichols, William	3	2	3		
Cobb, David, junr	1		1		
Tolsin, James	1				
Edwards, Britton	2	4	1		8
Alford, Jesse	1	1	1		
May, Allen	1				
Ayres, Thomas	1		1		
Thigpin, Dennis	1	2	1		
Hatway, John	2	2	1		
Hatway, Edmond, Junr	1		1		
Hatway, Francis	1	1	3		
Peebles, William	1	1	1		
Meeks, Matthew	1		2		
Lewis Joshua	1				

NEWBERN DISTRICT, WAYNE COUNTY.

NAME OF HEAD OF FAMILY.	Free white males of 16 years and upward, including heads of families.	Free white males under 16 years.	Free white females, including heads of families.	All other free persons.	Slaves.	NAME OF HEAD OF FAMILY.	Free white males of 16 years and upward, including heads of families.	Free white males under 16 years.	Free white females, including heads of families.	All other free persons.	Slaves.	NAME OF HEAD OF FAMILY.	Free white males of 16 years and upward, including heads of families.	Free white males under 16 years.	Free white females, including heads of families.	All other free persons.	Slaves.
Slocum, Ezekiel		1	2		1	Ingram, William	1	1	1			Scull, Alexander	1				
Whitfield, Needham	2	2	4		27	Rhodes, William	1		3		15	Brown, Khelan	1	1	3		
Whitfield, William, Sr	1		2		27	Wolfe, George	4		1		5	Harp, Richard	1	3	4		
Heron, William	2	3	2			Manley, James	3	2	2		8	Bizzell, John, junr	1	3	3		
Whitfield, William, Jr	2	3	3		36	Pipkin, Arthur	2	2	5			Pike, John	1	4	3		
Winkfield, Joseph	1				5	Pipkin, Philip	1	1	2			Quimby, Jonas	1	3	6		10
Casey, Micajah	1	4	4		1	Thomas, William	1	2	2			Moore, Luke	1	3	5		1
Heron, Samuel	1	4	4			Thomas, Thomas	3	1	5		2	Bass, Edward	1	4	3		16
Hines, Reuben	1	5	2			Odum, Jacob	2	3	2			Musgrove, John	1		1		
Carraway, John	1	2	3		1	Dennin, Robert	4	1	6			Musgrove, Joel	2	1	4		
Holmes, Charles	3	1	2		16	Howell, John	2	3	3			Shaw, Hugh	1	1	2		1
Heron, Jane	1	1	6		2	Cole, James	2	2	3			Pierce, Elizabeth			1		
Martin, Paul	1	2	4			Joiner, Joel	2	1	9			Benton, Charity			1		
Davis, Hugh	1	2	2			Vick, Benjamin	1		4			Hamm, Resters	1	1	3		1
Bass, Rice	1	3	1			Parker, Arthur	1	3	2			Mourning, Burrel	3	4	6		9
Bass, Aley, Senr	1	2	7			Rhodes, James	1	3	3			Mourning, William	2	1	5		
Lane, William	1	3	2			Raifield, Southy	1	3	2			Shadding, James	2	2	2		
Rieves, Jesse	1	1	1			Pipkins, Elisha	2	3	5		14	Grace, James	2	2	2		6
Rieves, William	2	2	4		4	Crawford, William	3	1	2			Lane, Isum, Senr	2	3	5		5
Gideons, John	1	2	3			Whood, Nathan	2	3	4			Taylor, William	1	5	10		2
Bass, Thomas	3	1	4		4	Pipkin, Luke	3	2	2		1	Howell, William, Junr	1		1		1
Jones, John	2	2	2			Pipkin, Jesse	1	3	3			Bell, William, junr	1	1	3		2
Rieves, John	1					Fulgum, Raiford	2	2	5		7	Bell, John	1	3	1		1
Carraway, Adam	1	2	5		12	Cogdell, David		4	5		21	Bell, William, Senr	1	1	2		1
Hines, Willis	1	1	1		1	Heron, Frederick	2				5	Howell, William, Senr	5	2	4		13
Hines, Owen	1				3	Buck, Caleb	3	2	3		1	Packer, Micajah	2	3	4		6
Griffin, Dempsey	3	2	4			Dannel, Hardy	1	1	1			Parker, Samuel	1	2	2		
Brown, John	1	2	3			Holliman, Jeremiah	1		1			Page, Ephraim	1	1	1		
Brow, Noah	1		2			Holliman, Ezekiel	1	3	3		1	Sauls, Raimond	1	4	3		1
Brown, Ann		1	3			Mayhon, Dixon	1	1	4			Warrick, Jacob	1	1	1		
Brown, Christopher	1		1			Carraway, Willis	1		6			Gardner, Olive			3		
Boyekin, Thomas	1	2	2		1	Carraway, Elijah	2		4		3	Wells, Micajah	1	3	3		
Langston, Isaac	1		1			Carraway, Thomas	1	1			12	Hanley, James	1	2	6		8
Bass, Joshua	1	1	4		1	Brown, Amy	1	3	1			Cato, George			1		7
Husk, Mary			2			Thomas, Solomon	1	2	3			Hollawell, Thomas	3	1	3		
Drew, George	2	1	7		2	Lloyd, John	1		3			Wosdon, Jonathan	1	2	6		12
Turner, Joseph	1	2	6		3	Holliman, Christopher	1	3	5			Flitcher, Sarah	1	3	3		
Bass, Alice, junr			3		24	Wallace, Aaron	1	1	3			Flitcher, Ralph	1	3	2		
Bass, Andrew	1	1	5			Barbary, William	2	2	5			Howell, Etheldred	1	1	5		10
Falconer, Robert	1	3	3			Dannels, Shadrach	1	3	3			Bell, James	1	1	5		
Edwards, John	2	3	5		1	Dannels, John	1	2	4			Malliby, William	1	1	6		
Edwards, David	1	1	2			Mayhon, William	1	3	3			Nixon, Henry	3	1	3		
Edwards, Sampson	1	2	1			Pipkin, Stephen	1	3	6			Nixon, John	2	2	4		
Newell, Peter	1		2			Rhodes, William, Jur	1	2	2		9	Outland, Thomas	2		2		7
Newell, John	2	2	8			Sharp, Groves	1	2	5		1	Britts, Henry	2	3	3		
Birquit, Moses	1	2	1			Bizzel, John, Senr	2		1		2	Hamm, William, Senr	1		3		9
Starling, Robert	1	2	1			Jourdin, William	2	1	3			Hamm, William, junr	2	3	6		
Starling, Abram, Jr	3	1	4			Bradbury, James	1		4		1	Lancaster, William	1	1	6		
Beard, John	3	3	3			McKinney, Mary	3	2	5		16	Gin, Hardy	1		2		
Everit, Amy	2		3		2	Cox, Micajah	1	5	3		1	Lane, Isum, junr	1	2	1		1
Norris, Jesse	1		1			Cox, Mary	2	2	3			Johnston, Henry	2	1	1		
Flowers, John	1	4	3		2	Kennedy, John	2	1	2			Mitchel, Isum	1	2	3		
Lane, William, Senr	1					Cox, Phoebe	2		3			Lanch, Linum	1		1		
Lane, Samuel	1	2	3			Cox, Smithson	1	1	2			Donnels, William	1	2	4		
Hill, John	1	1	2			Cox, Richard	1		3			Dannels, Margaret		2	2		
Taylor, Jonathan	2	1	4			Cox, Josiah	1	1	6		1	Packer, Marmaduke	1				
Jennett, Thomas	1	1	2			Grantum, Mary	1	2	2		1	Outland, Jonathan	2		1		1
Jernigan, David	3	1	3		26	Bennett, Sarah	2	3	2	1		Dawson, William	3	3	7		3
Frazer, George	3	1	5		4	Pellis, Dinah				2		Smith, Arthur	5	1	3		
Carraway, Elizabeth		1	3		5	Lee, Christopher	1		2			Peele, Willis	1	1			
Smith, John	1		2			Musgrove, Thomas	4	2	3			Smith, John	1		1		
McKinney, Richard	2	6	3	1	16	Musgrove, Moses	1	4	4			Ham, Henry	1	3	4		1
Linton, George	1		3			Grantum, Joel	1	2	3			Ham, Zachariah	1	2	1		
Frazer, James	1	1	1			Grantum, Jacob	1	1	3			Ham, Richard	1	5	1		
Neusam, David	1					Lohorn, James	1	2	2		2	Monday					4
Jennett, Joseph	1	3	4			Miles, James	1	2	3			Beamon, Uzias	1	1	3	1	
Starlin, Elijah	1		4			Salmon, Vincent	1		3			Luke				1	
Starlin, Abram, Senr	1	2	5			Wigs, Joel	1	1	2			Revil, Edmond	1				
Boyte, Stephen	1					Bizzel, William, Senr	1					Revil, Micajah	1				
Hudson, Ann			2			Bizzel, William, junr	1				1	Dawson, Isaac	1		2		
McCullen, Bryan	1	3	4		2	Grantum, Jesse	1	1	3			Hollawel, John	1	2	1		
Bradley, James	1	1	3			Grantum, James	1		4			Peacock, Peter	1	1	1		2
Bryan, William	2	3	5			Bizzel, Jesse	1		3			Wradford, William	3		1		6
Flowers, Simon	2	1	1			Pettite, David	1		2			Best, Robin	1				
Flowers, William	2	1	6			Dunn, Benjamin	1	4	5			Sherrod, Benjamin	1	1	3		2
Harrell, Samuel	2		3		2	Brogdon, Thomas	1		4			Parker, Isaac	1	2	4		
Martin, Aaron	3	4	3		2	Westbrooke, John	2	3	4			Fort, William	1		2		10
Flowers, Jacob	1	2	1		1	Flowers, Humphrey	1	1	3			Robinson, Thomas	1		2		
Harrell, Daniel	2	2	5			Dunn, Thomas	2	2	4			Radford, Noah	1	1	4		
Harrell, Hazel	1		1			Dinkins, James	2		2			Parsons, Solomon	2	3	3		4
Barfield, Blake	2	1	4		1	Westbrook, James	2	5	3		4	Bundy, Jane		1	2		
Killit, Sarah			1		1	Brogdon, John	1	2	6			Beaman, Francis	3		4		
Barfield, Solomon	1	1	3			Salmon, Zachariah	1		4			Beaman, James	2		1		
Wolfe, Charles, Senr	4	2	5			Linch, Bryant	1	2	2			Warwick, Wiat	1	4	2		
Adkinson, John	1		1		10	Dunn, Richard	2	3	3			Wilson, John	1	3	2		
Adkinson, Samuel	1	1	3			Grantum, Solomon	1		1			Wilson, Robert	1	1	2		
Goodman, William	1	3	5			Shaw, Joseph	1		2	1	1	Aicock, Simon	1	2	6		
Elmore, Reuben	1	2	2			Bizzell, Thomas	1	1	2		2	Beaman, David	1	1	2		
Crow, Sarah	2	1	1		4	Pipkin, Willis	3	5	3		6	Joiner, Matthew	1	1	6		
Crow, Isaac	1	3	1			Bizzell, David	1					Handley, John, junr	1	1	1		
Dannel, John	1	2	4			Strickland, John	1	1	1			Bundy, Mark	1	2	3		
Benson, Benjamin	1	4	5			Holmes, William	1	1	1			Williams, William	3	1	2	2	
Benson, John	1		1			Harper, John	2		2			Bundy, John	1	2	3		
Wolfe, Charles, junr	1		1			Sohorn, Benjamin	1	2	3			Burdin, John	2	2	1		1
Killit, John	1	2	3			Johnston, William	1		5			Bordin, Woodard	1				
Dannels, Alice	1	1	4		4	Hull, Nathaniel	1					Smith, Benjamin	1	2	1		
Odum, Jethro	1	1	4			Westbrooke, Burrel	2	2	4		9	Amey				4	

NEWBERN DISTRICT, WAYNE COUNTY—Continued.

NAME OF HEAD OF FAMILY.	Free white males of 16 years and upward, including heads of families.	Free white males under 16 years.	Free white females, including heads of families.	All other free persons.	Slaves.
Pate, Shadrack	1	3	1		
Bundy, William	1	3	2		
Coley, Gabriel	1	5	5		
Branch, Edy	1		2		
Combs, John	1		2		
Powel, Eli	2		2		
Fort, Benjamin	1	1	6	3	24
Sherrard, William	2				
Morris, Milley			1		
Bogue, Jesse	3	1	2		
Lancaster, Wright	2		1		
Lancaster, Levi	1	1	5		
Edmundson, James	1	5	5		19
Johnston, Abram	1	2	2		
Sherrord, John	2		3		16
Bryan, Willis	1	2	2		5
Bryan, Joel	2	1	1		
Perkins, Jeremiah	1	3	4		
Coleman, Elijah	1		1		
Parker, Isaac	1	2	1		
Sanders, Dicy		2	4		9
Sandiford, John	3		1		
Sandiford, James	1	1	3		
Bundy, Dempsey	1	4	3		
Hall, Caleb	1	1	2		
Elvinton, Noah	1		4		1
Johnston, Abram	1	2	2		
Brassil, Sampson	1	2	2		2
Elvinton, John	1		2		7
Brassil, Richard	1	2	3		1
Brassil, Shadrach	1	2	1		3
Brassil, Elizabeth		1	2		3
Sauls, John	1		3		3
Martin, William	1	3	2		
Lane, John	1				2
Sauls, Henry	1	1	3		
Sauls, Cord	1		2		
Elvinton, Hardy	1	5	2		2
Downing, George	1		4		
Hasty, William	1	1	3		
Hasty, Joseph	1		2		
Hasty, Edwin	1	1	1		
Hagins, Mary				1	
Stanton, John	2	2	7		7
Minshew, John	2	3	2		10
Bartlett, Samuel	2	4	7		
Bridger, James	2	2	3		
Deal, William	1	1	3		2
Sceater, John	2		1		
Hasty, John	1	1	3		
Outlaw, Cornelius	1	2	4		
Woodward, Isaac	2		1		19
Hollawell, Joseph	3	4	5		
Overman, John	3		2		
Morris, Zachariah, Sen.	1		1		
Cooke, Margaret		1	2		2
Cooke, Thomas	1	3	4		
Cooke, Arthur	1	1	4	1	
Cooke, Stephen	1	1	2		5
Stephenson, Lemuel	1		2		
Brassil, David	1				1
Blow, Priscilla	2	3	3		
Green, James	1		4		
Morris, Thomas	1		2		
Woodard, John	1	1	2		1
Morris, Zachariah, Junr.	1		1		1
Morris, Isaac	1	1	2		
Morris, Jeremiah	1		2		
Parker, Elisha	3	1	3		
Wootin, William	1		3		
Overman, Aaron	1	2	4		
Overman, Thomas	1	1	1		
Arnold, Benjamin	1	4	4		
Cooke, Jacob	1		2		3
Davis, Richard	1	1	1		
Morris, Benjamin	1	3	2	1	
Arnold, Joseph	1	2	3		
Bailey, Henry	1	1	3		
Talton, Josiah	1		3		
Davis, Huldy			3		
Davis, John		3	2		
Davis, Joshua	1	1	1		
Hollawell, Silas	3		4		
Pervis, John	1		2		
Lovin, William	1	1	2		
Lovin, Isum	1		2		
Nusum, David	2	3	5		
Alberson, Joseph	1		2		
Casey, Jeremiah	1	3	4		
Gilbert, Joel	1	2	4		
Nusum, William	2	3	4		1
Dodd, Aaron	1	4	3		
Brookins, Bridgman	3	1	5		
King, John	1	2	5		5
Peel, Jesse	2	3	1		
Dannels, Isaac	2	1	2		
Dannels, Ephraim	1	1	2		11
Merritt, Sarah			1		
Lovin, Reddick	1	2	1		
Parisher, James	1				
Rogers, Jonathan	1	1	2		3
Martin, Joseph	1	1	2		1
Ellis, John	1	1	3		
Downing, Mary			3		
Boswell, Simpson	2	2	2		
Brookins, Hannah		1	1		
Brookins, Absalom	1		1		
Peale, Pasco	1	1	5		
Nousum, Joel	3	2	3		
Peter				1	
Aicock, Jesse	2	4	2		3
Watkins, William	2	3	3	3	
Watkins, John	1	3	5		1
Maddocks, Robeson	1	2	2		1
Holland, James	2		1		
Holland, Elisha	2	1	1		
Tucker, Robert	1	2	5		
Smiddick, Samuel	2	2	2		
Pender, Hardy	3	4	3		
Peacock, Samuel, Senr.	1	2	3		4
Peacock, Samuel, junr.	3	3	2		
Sims, Robert	1	2	3	1	4
Love, Edmond	1	3	5		
Davis, Thomas	3	2	4		
Dickinson, David	1				
Sims, Abram	2		2		11
Cooke, Benjamin	1	3	3		1
Dannels, Isaac	1		1		
Chance, Stephen	1	2	2		
Dickinson, Shadrach	1	2	7		14
Dickinson, Joel	3	1	3		13
Dickinson, Daniel	2	6	1		3
Sims, Barnes	1	1	1		2
Tomberlinson, William	1	2	4	1	
Coleman, Elias	1	3	4		
Dickinson, Henry	1		2		
Dickinson, Jacob	1		1		
Dickinson, William	1				
Powell, Jacob			3		
Fooks, Solomon		3	1		
Sandiford, John	1	1	2		
Ferrill, William	1	3	1		
Pope, Henry	2	2	4		
Sulivan, Owen	1		2		
Simmons, Jesse	1	1	2		
Rose, Theophilus	1		2		
Evans, John	1	3	2	1	
Evans, Isum	3	2	2		
Evans, Joel	1	5	3		
Woodard, Joshua	1	3	4		
Dannels, Elias	1	2	3		
Hay, Reuben	2		4	1	
Love, George	1		2		1
Brookins, Thomas	1	1	1		1
Turner, Matthew	2		5		28
Whood, Edward		3	3		4
Whood, Edward, junr.	1	2	2		
Hilliard, Francis	1	1	1		
Hilliard, Francis, Senr.	3		3		
Fooks, William	1	2	3		1
Boswel, John	1	2	5		
Barnes, William	1		2		1
Boswel, Zadik	1	3	3		
Lucus, John	1	3	4		
Watson, Samuel	1	2	5		
Evans, David	2	4	5		
Spiva, Joab	3	1	5		
Rentfrow, Jacob	3		4		
Bass, Abram	1	1	2		
Ridgin, Frederick	1	2	4		
Ridgin, William	1				
Lamb, Merion		3	5		
Rogers, Jesse	1				
Roundtree, Francis	1				
Whood, William	4	3	6		
Barnes, Samuel	1	4	5		8
Barnes, Simon	2	3	4		6
Watson, Isum	2	2	3		4
Barnes, Jesse	2	2	2		9
Barnes, James	1	1	3		
Barnes, Jacob	1	1	2		
Whitley, Drury	1		3		
Whitley, Micajah	1	1	4		
Rose, Thomas	1		3		
Wiggins, Thomas	1	2	3		
Hatchel, Morris	1	6	3		
Horn, Thomas	1	3	7	1	
Horn, Henry	1	3	5		5
Horn, Jeremiah	1	2	2	2	
Cobb, James	3	2	1	2	14
Cobb, Patience	1	4	7		5
Cobb, Bridget		1	3		13
Barefoot, John	1		2		25
Lee, John	3	1	5		
Lee, Jonathan	1	1	1		
Arthurs, Sarah				2	
Lamb, Jacob, Senr.	2	2	2		2
Lamb, Hardy	1	3	4		
Lamb, Abram	1	3	4		
Lamb, Joshua	1		2		
Rentfrow, James	2	2	3		
Brown, Jesse	1		1		
Holland, John	1	4	3		1
Nichols, John M	1		3		
Ellis, Sampson	1	1	3		
Durdens, William	2		3		
Ellis, Josiah	1	1	2		
Ellis, Joel	3	2	3		
Lamb, Isaac	1		5		
Pearson, Christopher	2	4	6		
Cobb, Stephen	2				5
Cobb, Nathan	2	2	3	1	21
Horn, Damaris		1	1	2	1
Lamb, Reddick		1	2		
Lamb, Jacob, junr.	1	2	4		
Lucus, Joseph	1	2	4		
Simmons, Jesse	1	2	3		
Barnes, John	1		2		7
Peacock, Levi	1	3	3		1
Thomson, William	1	1	3		5
Powell, Peter	2	1	3		1
Powell, Enos	1		2		
Powell, William	1		3		
Sanders, William	1	4	3		
Price, Rice	1		4		
Copeland, Joshua	2	3	5		
Edgington, Joseph	1	1	3		
Edginton, Thomas	1	4	3		
Rogers, Willowby	1	4	1		
Peacock, Kate		1	1		
Mitchell, Reuben	1	3	2		
Biggs, Elijah	1	1	2		
Baggott, Every	1		5		
Boyd, Josiah	1	1	1		
Morrison, Alexander	1	2	2		
Sears, David	1	2	1		
Buntin, James	1	1	2		
Bradbury, George	2	1	4		
Howell, John	2	1	3		10
Hooks, William	2	3	5		14
Pike, Nathan	1	2	2		
Hall, Isaac	2	3	4		
Collier, Samuel	1	4	2		
Gibson, Charles	1	2	3		
Worrell, Richard	1	2	3		1
Worrell, Priscilla		1	1		
Worrell, Benjamin	2	1	4		
Worrell, William	3		5		
Cithum, Sabry		2	3		
Alford, Benjamin	1	2	3		
Afley, Daniel	1	4	6		
Howell, Joshua	3	1	2		5
Worrell, John	1	1	2		
Modlin, Edmond	3	2	4		
Langley, Oswell	1	2	4		
Price, Kinchin	1		1		
Howell, Admiral	1	2	1		3
Heron, John	1		1		3
Hanley, John	2		1		11
Applewight, John	2	1	1		4
Saint, Samuel	1		2		
Brown, Jesse	1	1	6		
Modlin, Thomas	1	2	5		
Scott, Thomas					
Worrell, Elizabeth					
Worrell, James	1	3	1		
Langley, Miles	1		1		
Tilton, Elizabeth	1	1	2		
Wilson, Henry	1	2	2		
Pate, James	1	3	4		1
Pate, Isum	1	3	2		
Pate, Elias	2		2		
Pate, Daniel	1	2	2		
Pate, Martha			1		
Thomson, Peter	1	2	1		
Thomson, Jethro	1		1		
Thomson, Zadik					1
Howell, Archilaus	4	4	2		1
Davis, James	3	1	4		2
Deanes, Dempsey	1		1		1
Deanes, James	1	2	1		
Boyekin, William	1		2		13
Thomson, Thomas	2	3	4		
Boyt, Joseph	1		3		
Boyt, Amos	1	4	2		
Boyt, Thomas	1	2	3		
Deanes, Elizabeth	1		6		
Alford, William	5	2	9		11
Rhodes, James	1				
Thomson, Rachel	1	1	1		2
Pope, Charles	2		4		1

NEWBERN DISTRICT, WAYNE COUNTY—Continued.

NAME OF HEAD OF FAMILY.	Free white males of 16 years and upward, including heads of families.	Free white males under 16 years.	Free white females, including heads of families.	All other free persons.	Slaves.
Pope, Winfield	2	1	4		
Pope, Hardy	1	2	2		
Pope, John	1		1		
Howell, Daniel	2	5	4		
Whitney, Ebenezer	1	3	2		
Peacock, John	1	4	4		1
Langley, Jacob	1	1	2		
Scott, Andrew	2	2	3		4
Hopton, Charles	2		2		10
Howell, William	2	1	4		
Howell, Noel	1	1	1		
Thompson, John	1	4	4		2
Vincent, Sarah	1	3	2		
Thomson, James	1	1	4		1
Lane, John Thomson	1	2	4		
Langston, Uriah	1	2	3		
Heron, John, Senr	3		6		20
Windum, Jesse	1	1	2		
Boyt, Shadrack	1	1	5		
Holleman, Silas	1	3	3		
Daughtery, Martha	1	1	4		
Hix, Micajah	1	2	1		
Musgrove, James	2	2	3	1	
Langston, Ann	1	2	4		
Ward, Sarah	1	2	1		12
Heron, George	1				3
Howell, Hopton	1				
Wilson, John	1	1	4		
Blanchet, James	1		1		
Humphries, John	1	1	2		
Jonerkin, Josiah	1	4	3		2
Jonerkin, David	3		2		6
Pope, Sarah		1	5		16
Jones, Elizabeth		2	4		1
Jones, Arthur	1	2	4	1	
Barnet, William	1	1	2		
Jones, James	1	1	1		
Jones, Sarah	1	1	5		
Ammons, Jesse	1	2	3	1	
Bicard, Edmond	2		3		
Waldin, Benjamin	2		3		
Waldin, Samuel	1		1		
Holland, Matthew	1		3		
Jonerkin, Miles	2	1	2		2
Jonerkin, George, Senr	2		4	1	
Coor, Thomas	3	2	2		
Howell, Benjamin	1	2	4		2
Howell, Rachel	2	1	1		2
Jonerkin, George, junr	2		4	1	
Robertson, John	1		2		
Alford, Theophilus	2	2	3	1	
Hetchpeth, Daniel	1	1	2		
Howell, Mills	1	1	4		
Hetchpeth, John	1	4	2		
Hetchpeth, Ezekiel	1	1	3		
Hines, Joshua	1		3		
Howell, Major	1	1	3		
Howell, Abram	1	5	2		
Jones, William	1	2	1		
Jonerkin, William	1	1	2		
Wise, Josiah	1	1	3		
Saucer, Ruth		1	5		8
Hooks, Robert	1	3	1		14
Saucer, Stephen	1	3	5		
Coorpender, John	1	2	3		11
Fellows, Robert	2	1	4		1
Wiggs, Jordan	2		2		
Corbitt, John	1	3	4		
Corbitt, Samuel	1	1	4		
Daughtery, Arthur	1		6		
Wiggs, Ralph	1	2	4		
Slaughter, Samuel	1	3	4		
Wiggs, John	2	3	6		4
Boyt, Edward	2		2		
Boyt, Benjamin	1	4	2		
Wiggs, Benjamin	2	3	6		
Fulgum, Miles	1	3	5		
Brewer, Moses	3	2	1		
Crawford, Lazarus	2	2	6		6
Page, John	1		3		6
Raiford, William	3	5	4		5
Davis, David	1		3		5
Boyt, Etheldred	1	3	6		2
Wiggs, William	1		3		
Crawford, Robert	2	4	8		4
Rogers, Isum	2	2	1		5
Hamilton, Aaron	1	1	3		
Shehorn, Joseph	1	1	5		
Saucer, John	1	3	2		
Gurley, Lewis	1	2	4		2
Howell, Ralph	1	1	1		
Pitman, Noah	1		1		6
Hines, Peter	1	1	3		
Coor, Thomas, Senr	3	5	5		7
Massey, William	1		3		
Wiggs, Henry	3	1	3		
Holland, John, Senr	1		2		
Holland, John, junr	1	2	2		
Howell, John	1	3	5		
Toler, Robert	2	2	7		5
Moore, John	2	2	1		
Toler, Nehemiah	1	3	5		1
Edginton, James	1	2	2		
Smith, John	1	2	2		7
Toler, John	1	2	2		6
Gurley, Joel	2	2	7		4
Wise, John	1	2	4		
Wise, Isaac	2	2	2		
Wise, James	1	3	3		1
Oliver, Henry	1	3	3		2
Tiner, William	2	1	6		
Coggell, Celia			2		8
Bass, Richard	2	1	1		28
Toler, Stephen	1		1		
Toler, Thomas, Senr	1				1
Blanchet, Jesse	1	1	2		1
Rogers, James	1	1	2		
Whurley, William	1	1	4		2
Massey, Pelick	1	2	2		
Baggot, Allen	1	3	2		3
Toler, John, junr	1	1	1		
Boyte, Josiah	1	1	1		
Tiner, James	1	2	4		
Gurley, George	1	1	2		
Bridges, John	2	3	5		
Lupsey, Bolin	1	1	2		
Jones, Willis	1	3	3		
Jones, Hardy	1	4	4		2
Howell, Arthur	1	2	1		
Potts, Daniel	1				
Linton, John	1				
Heron, Jesse	2	1	4		
Jernigan, Stephen	1	2	4		24
Green, Joseph	8	1	4		70
Daughtery, Lawrence	1	1	4		
Grooms, Jesse, Senr	1	1	5		4
Vincent, Benjamin	1	3	3		
Pope, Henry	1		5		2
Heron, David	1		3		16
Burn, James	4	2	7		
Heron, Bridget		1	3		6
Bradberry, Chambers	1	2	5		
Wests, John	2	2	3		
Grooms, Jesse, jr	1		2		
Grooms, Charles	1	2	3		2
Grooms, Daniel	1		2		
Rosser, Burrel	1		1		
West, Charles	1	1	2		4
Wallace, Mary			5		
Windom, Jesse	1	1	2		
Cummins, Elizabeth			2		
Edwards, Absalom	1	3	5		
Smith, John	1	2	2		
Douglass, Rhody		2	3		
Roberts, John		1	5		5
George, David	2	4	7		9
Thomson, Thomas	1	3	1		1
Langston, William	1	3	2		
Jones, Traverse	1		3		1
Williams, Absalom	2		2		7
Garland, John	1				8
Wood, William	3	3	2		
Smith, Benjamin, Senr	1	3	4		
Smith, Benjamin, jr	1	3	1		
Smith, William	1	1	2		
Williams, Arthur	1		1		
Smith, Josiah, Senr	1	4	3		
Smith, Josiah, junr	1		1		
Smith, John	2	2	2		
Smith, Drew	1		2		
Smith, John	2		4		8
Lohorn, Nathan	1	2	1		1
Lohorn, William	1	1	3		
Uzzell, Elisha, Sr	2	1	3		5
Uzzell, Elisha, Jur	1	1	3		
Grant, William	2	3	2		
Grant, Elisha	1	2	2		
Grant, Michael	1	2	2		
Anderson, John	1	1	1		
Ballard, Robert	2		2		
Anderson, Jesse	1	1	2		
Stuckley, James	2		3		
Colton, Ephraim	1	2	4		4
Wilson, William	1	1	3		
Smith, John	2		3		
Hart, Richard	2	1	6		
Davis, William	1	1	3		
Medlin, Nicholas	1	3	5		
Dannels, Nathaniel	2	3	5		
Hinson, James	3	3	5		
Hinson, Elijah	1	1	4		
Scrivins, James	1	1	3		1
Dawson, Patience	1	2	3		
Heron, Henry	1	1	2		
McArtney, Michael	1	2	1		
Bachelor, Unity		1	10		
Benton, Jemima	1	1	2		
Heron, Anthony	1	2	5		
Heron, Joel	1	1	3		7
Saucer, Benjamin	1	5	3		
Heron, Simon	1	2	6		
Hines, Hardy	1	2	2		
Heron, Jacob	2		4		
Keethly, John	2		1		6
Homes, John	1		2		2
Anderson, Mills	1	1	5		
Anderson, Thomas	1	1	2		
Heron, Michael	1	2	3		10
McKinney, William	1		2		8
McKinney, Barnaby	1		2		11
Whitfield, Lewis	1	1	2		32
Stanley, Moses	3	4	5		12
Ivy, John	2	3	4		
Forehand, William	1		3		
Henderson, Robert	1		4		
Surles, William, Senr	1		3		
Roach, Sarcenet	2	2	7		
Hanks, John	2	2	3		
Roach, Solomon	1	1	3		
Garris, Joshua, Senr	2	1	2		
Garris, Joshua, junr	1	1	2		
Burley, John	1	1	2		
Thomas, James	1	2	4		

SALISBURY DISTRICT, GUILFORD COUNTY.

NAME OF HEAD OF FAMILY.	Free white males of 16 years and upward, including heads of families.	Free white males under 16 years.	Free white females, including heads of families.	All other free persons.	Slaves.
Dent, William	2		3		7
Graham, William	1		1		2
Smith, Samuel	1		5		1
Nicholson, Elisha	1	1	2		
Wilson, Richd	2	1	3		
Benbow, Thomas	3	2	1		
Buchanan, James	1		3		
White, Benja	2	2	4		
Lambert, William	1		3		
Foster, John	1		2		
Foster, Saml	1	1	2		
Reed, William	2	4	3		
Johnstone, Andrew	1		3		
Touchstone, Jonas	1		3		
Dent, William, Junr	1	5	3		
McNary, Frances	1	3	2		1
Stuart, George	2		2		
Shaw, Patrick	4	1	4		
Moreland, William	2	5	4		14
Briges, William	1	2	3		
Laurence, Augustus	1	1	1		
Burney, Adam	1		1		
Massey, Joab	1	5	1		
Johnston, Benja	1	2	1		
Maxwell, Thomas	3	3	4		
Strickland, Jacob	3	3	6		9
Holen, Laban	5				
Wheler, Saml	1	2	1		
Fruer, Isaac	1	2	1		
Brown, John	1	3	6		
Hart, Henry	1	3	2		1
Winegarden, Joseph	1	1	3		
Cob, Henry	2	3			
Gardner, Caston	2		2		
Islig, Philip	1	2	2		
Shoemaker, Suzanah	2	3	5		2
Goodner, Mary		3	3		
Montgomery, Willm	1	1	3		
Canaday, Charles	1	2	7		
Sweet, John	3	2	6		
Doherty, John	3	1	5		
Finley, Michael	2	1	3		
Peyatt, James	2				
Coffield, John	1		1		
Findley, Josiah	1	2	3		
Kerr, Davd	1	3	2		
Lackey, Adam	1	1	4		4
Gawdy, William	5	1	1		
Stephens, Even	2	5	2		
Howlet, William	1	3	5		
Hunt, Thomas	1				

SALISBURY DISTRICT, GUILFORD COUNTY—Continued.

NAME OF HEAD OF FAMILY.	Free white males of 16 years and upward, including heads of families.	Free white males under 16 years.	Free white females, including heads of families.	All other free persons.	Slaves.	NAME OF HEAD OF FAMILY.	Free white males of 16 years and upward, including heads of families.	Free white males under 16 years.	Free white females, including heads of families.	All other free persons.	Slaves.	NAME OF HEAD OF FAMILY.	Free white males of 16 years and upward, including heads of families.	Free white males under 16 years.	Free white females, including heads of families.	All other free persons.	Slaves.
Hunt, Jacob	1	3	3			Endsly, Abraham	2	1	5			Stafford, William	1	4	3		
Night, Abel	2	2	6			Goff, Stephen	1	4	3			Braden, Alexander	2	1	2		
Hiatt, George	1		1			McCuiston, Walter	3	1	3			Underwood, Joshua	1	4	2		2
Stephens, Davd	1		3			Wilson, James	3		2		2	Saxton, Thomas	1		1		
Porter, James	3	1	2			Willis, Joel	1	1	3			Rumbly, Smith	1	2	1		
Cook, Abraham	4	1	2			Denney, James	1		1			Smith, William	4		1		
Weatherley, Jesse	4	2	5			Denney, William	2		4		1	Weatherly, William	1		1		
Thompson, John	2		1			Pierce, Robert	2	5	4			McCuestion, Moses	2	1	5		2
Thompson, Willm F	1	2	1			Hunt, Abner	2	2	6			Given, Robert	2		1		6
Learkin, John	1	4	3		1	Mendenhall, Richd	1	2	1			Weatherly, Abner	3		1		
Clement, Peter	2	3	8			Maxwell, Saml	2	3	5		2	Witt, Michal	1	1	10		
McBride, Isaiah	2	2	6		1	Peasly, Robert	2	4	5			Flack, Andw	5		3		1
Land, Reubin	2		2			Masey, Timothy	1		5			Mathews, William	1	3	3		
Cansbey, James	2		2			Widows, Isaac	4	1	3			McNight, William	2		3		
Holloday, John	1	2	5			Worth, Francis	2		3			Dawson, Elijah	2		1		
Tharp, Joseph	1		3			Gardner, Stephen	1	4	5			Cample, Thomas	1	2	1		
Masey, Nathl	3	1	3			Peasley, John	3	2	7		12	Caldwell, David	3	5	3		8
Clagg, William	1	1	1			Albright, William	1	1	3			Fulton, Samuel	2	5	2		
Murphey, Jonathan	1	2	2			McGrady, James	4	3	2			Coats, James	1		5		1
Dick, William	2		2			Jester, Nimrod	1	2	1			Casey, Samuel	1	1	3		
Rankin, Robt	2		2	2		Smith, Richd	1	2	3			Gardner, Isaac	1	4	2		
Dick, James	1	2	1	1		Masey, Thomas	1		2			Springer, Stephen	1	1	2		
Rankin, John	1	3	3	1		White, Isaac	2	1	5			Russel, William	1		2		
Hunt, William	1	2	2			Smith, Ralph	2	1	5			Werick, Martin	1	2	5		
Sisney, Joseph	1	2	3			Loakey, John	2	2	3			Morgan, Thomas	1		1		
Cain, Jerediah	1	4	4			Jones, Jesse	1	1	2			Ramsey, James	1	1	3		
Mongomery, William	2	3	4			Millis, James	1	1	1			Bell, James	3	1	8		
Wilson, James	1	3	6			Sherwood, Hugh	1	1	4			Shelkott, Kain	1	1	2		
Hiatt, William	2	2	5			Jones, Davd	1	1	4			Holland, John	1				
Hiatt, George	2		3			Ford, Henry	1	3	4			Werick, Jacob	2	3	4		
McClain, Moses	3	1	2			Scott, Absolem	1		2			Roberson, William	2	2	3		
Pegg, Martin	2		1			Philips, Ezekeal	1	1	1			Roberson, Abner	1		1		
Roberson, Jacob	1	5	4		1	Williams, Jesse	1	2	2			Roberson, Nicholas	1		3		
Hunt, Eleazor	1	4	1			Masey, Enoch	2	2	4			Hester, James	1		1		
Donnal, John	1	4	6		1	Hoggatt, Philip	1	1	4			Greeson, Jacob	1	1	1		
Donnal, Andw	1	3	3		1	Osburn, Saml	1	4	5			Jessop, Caleb	1	1	4		
Donnal, James	1	2	5			Sullaven, Flurance	3	2	2			Mills, Reuben, Junr	1	2	4		
Driskel, George	1	2	2			Osburn, Richd, Senr	1	1	2			Pegg, Valentine	3	3	5		
Unthank, Allen	1	4	4			Sullaven, Joel	1		1			Morrow, Robert	1	2	4		
Cuningham, James	3		1			Covey, George	1	1	3			Dean, Joshua	2	3	4		
Rogers, Jacob	1		1			Osment, John	1	1	4			Hodgson, Thomas	1	3	3		
Hiatt, Christopher, Junr	1	4	4			Valiant, Ansel	1		2			Baldwin, Danl	1	3	4		
Night, Thomas	5	2	9			Craner, Moses	1		1			McClaig, John	1	1	1		
Pegg, Isaac	1	1	1			Masey, Paul	1	2	7			Pullen, John	1		1		
Conner, James	1	2	5			Rankin, Robert, Jun	1	2	3			Allum, Saml	1		1		
Briket, Isarel	1	2	3			Miller, William	1		1			Wright, John	1				
Britton, James	2	2	6			Toney, Dennis	1	1	4			Wright, Frances	2		2		1
Wicker, William	1	1	2			Russel, Andrew	1	2	3			Warren, John	1	5	4		
Hardgrove, Frederik	1		1			Armfield, John	1	2	1			Covey, William	2	4	5		1
Brown, George L	2	1	2			Egle, William	1		2			Fields, Robert	1	1	1		
Brown, William	2	2	3			Holland, William	1	1	1			McGlamery, Edwd	1	1	6		2
Whicker, Thomas	1	1	1			Osburn, William	1	1	1			Peasley, William	5	1	2		
Brown, William	1	3	1			Sullaven, Wm	1	2	4			Blizard, Purnel	1	2	3		
Larkin, Saml	1	2	1			Jestor, Thomas	1	1	1			Bishop, Robert	4	2	4		
Carney, Arthur	1	1	2			McGrady, William	1		3			Stuart, Findlay	4		4		2
Gray, Isaac	1	1	2			Lester, Nathan	1		2			Wright, James	2		1		5
Gray, James	1	4	4			Sullaven, Flurance	1	1	1			Thomas, John	3	4	4		
Gray, William	4		2			Wheler, William	1	1	3		1	Mitchel, Saml	1				
Wolfenton, John	3	5	6			Gardner, Richd	2		5			Stack, Elisha	1		3		
Britton, Saml	1	3	5			Macy, David	1	3	2			Drury, Saml	1	4	1		
Bingerman, Thomas	2		4			Knott, James	1	2	7		3	Haskins, Moses	1	3	1		
Raper, William	3	1	1		1	Baldwin, Uriah	1	3	1			Hussey, Thomas	2	2	6		
Bingerman, John	1	3	3			Kenman, James	1	1	3			Tatom, Edward	1		1		3
Gray, William, Junr	1		3			Perkins, Isaac	1		2			Tatom, John	2	3	5		6
McNight, Robt	1	2	2			McClintock, John	1	1	1			Allum, Robert	2	1	3		
Russel, John	1	4	1			Poore, Jeremiah	1		1			Moore, Camm	1	3	3		1
Russel, Robert	1	3	4			Tatom, Edward	2	3	1		6	Cummins, Joseph	1	2	5		
Akin, William	2	1	6			Hunt, Atha	2		3			Burney, Robert	1	2	2		
Denney, George	1	5	3			Terrel, Micajah	1		2		2	Trotter, Benja	1		1		
Starratt, John	1	2	6			Dicks, Joshua	1		4			Hughey, James	1	2	4		
Starratt, James	1	1	1			Knott, James	1	2	4		1	Nix, Quinton	1		1		12
Mitchel, Adam	1		2		2	Poore, David	1	1	1			Cannaday, William	1	1	7		
Simmons, John	1		1			Thompson, Robert	1		6			McCaddin, Wm	1				
Stuart, John	1	1	5			Gray, Leven	1	2	1			Lownsburry, Wm	1	2	2		
Cross, Jonathan	5	2	3		7	Idelot, Benjamin	1	3	5			Trotter, Josiah	1	3	4		2
Tharp, William	1		4			Nix, George	1	3	4		11	Moore, Smith	2	2	5		7
Owen, Mathew	1	1	3			Nelson, Alexander	1	2	5			Moore, Mary	2		5		1
Jackson, Joseph	1	1	3			Mortemore, William	3		2			Alexander, George	1	5	3		
Climer, John	2	4	4			Hays, James	1	2	3		4	Doherty, Danl	2		3		
Tomlinson, James	1	1	1			Farguson, Alex	1	2	6			Gulbreath, Robt	1	3	4		
Cross, William	1	1	3			Idelot, Jedediah	1	1	1			Thompson, Benja	1	1	6		
Sisney, Stephen	1	1	2			Pope, George	1	6	2			Sullaven, Saml	1	3	3		
Downey, William	1	3	3			Peggot, Saml	1	3	3			Britton, Wm	3	1	3		1
Williams, William	1	3	3			Nelson, George	1	3	4			Donnal, Danl	3		3		3
Calhoon, Robert	1	1	3			Idelott, Rhody		3	4			Donnal, Robt	3		1		4
Persons, George	4	4	4			Perry, Richd	2	2	5			Evians, Warrenton	1	2	3		
Calhoon, James	2		3			Kirkpatrick, Hugh	1	1	1			Callaway, Obediah	1	1	3		
Green, Robert	2	1	3			Tharp, Laben	1	1	2			Dennis, William	1	2	4		
Arnet, Valentine	1	5	2			Stokes, Thomas	2	3	2			Callaway, Jonathan	1	2	3		
Williams, Leven	1	1	3			Wilcots, Thomas	1	2	1			Hannah, Roddy	1	4	1		
Wright, Willis	1		3			Everet, Saml	5		2			Hannah, Robert	1	5	2		8
Mendenhall, Aron	1	3	4			Maxwell, James	1	1	3			Doak, John	1		2		4
Waid, Thomas	2	4	4			Keene, Richd	1	2	3			Brown, Arther	1		2		
Armfield, William	3	2	3			Bell, Francis	1	2	6			Bliar, John	1	2	4		
Sisney, John	1	1	1			Tindle, Jeremiah	1	5	3			Coulk, Leven	1	3	4		2
Hunt, Isaiah	1	3	5			Dixson, John	1	2	3			Donnal, William	1	4	1		2
Stuart, John	1				2	McKamie, Nathl	1					Coulk, John	1	1	2		

SALISBURY DISTRICT, GUILFORD COUNTY—Continued.

NAME OF HEAD OF FAMILY.	Free white males of 16 years and upward, including heads of families.	Free white males under 16 years.	Free white females, including heads of families.	All other free persons.	Slaves.
Anderson, Robert	1		3		
Kerr, William	1	1	3		
Kerr, David, Senr	1		1		5
Doak, William	2	4	3		2
Ross, Reuben	1	4	3		
Hardin, Charles	2	2	4		
Barr, James	1	1	2		2
Macy, Mathew	1		3		
Russel, Timothy	2	3	3		
Leventon, John	2	4	5		1
Nilson, George	1	3	4		
Kimman, James	1	1	3		
Coine, Lias	1	1	5		
Fields, Jeremiah	4	2	6		1
James, John	1		1		
Loyd, Humphrey	3	3	5		
McClintock, John	4	1	2		7
Haskins, Joseph	1	2	4		1
White, Thomas	1	2	3		
Gamble, William	1	2	1		
Gamble, Andrew	1		3		
Brasel, Jacob	1	3	3		
Night, Jonathan	1	2	3		
Guite, William	2	2	5		
Sullaven, Andrew	1		2		
McCuiston, James	2				1
McAdaw, James	3		1		7
Loman, Adam	1		1		
McCuistion, Ann	1		1		
Shaw, Benjn	3	5	3		
Mullin, John	1		3		
Osborn, Joseph	3	1	2		
Shepard, Isrel	1		1		
Philips, Nancy		2	3		
Spruce, William	3	2	3		
Archer, Thomas	1	3	3		3
Rogers, William	1		1		
Archer, John	1		3		
Sampson, James				4	1
Britton, Benjn	2		2		1
McCain, Hanie	1	1	1		
McGlauheny, Wm	1				
Donnal, Latham	1		2		2
Perkins, John	1		4		
Perkins, Joseph	1	2	2		
Johnston, Joshua	1	2	5		
Johnston, James	1				
Johnston, Caleb	1		2		
McDowel, Joseph	1	2	3		1
Duck, Saml	3		2		
Johnston, Jere	1	2	3		
McAdow, James	1	2	3		1
Parker, Howel	1		2		
Parker, Jesse	2	1	6		
McGee, William	1				
Stone, Barton	1				
Merunnels, Benjn	1				
Dodson, Richd	1	2	2		
Hartgrove, Saml	2	6	5		
Peeples, Nathl	1	1	1		8
McGee, Andw	1	2			4
Dillon, Danl	1	3	4		
Chapple, Ambros	1	1	3		
Dillon, Isaac	1		2		
Hilton, Alex	1				
Hilton, James	2	1	4		
Farrington, Willm	1		2		
Perry, John	1	3	2		
Perry, Ebenezor	1	2	5		
Gilbert, William	1	3	2		2
Plafield, Willm	1				
Martin, Rhodeham	1	3	4		
Walker, John	2	3	3		
Gilbert, John	1		2		8
McMurry, John	1	1	1		1
Dillon, William	2	3	3		
Black, George	1		3		
Williams, Prudence	2		5		
Williams, Richard	1	3	2		
McCuistion, Thomas	1		2		
McMurry, James	1	3	6		
Billingsley, James	2	3	3		2
Rale, George	4		4		
Billingsley, Henry	1	1	3		
Harris, Hannah		3	7		
Hunt, Nathan	1				
Findley, Andw	2	1	8		
Smith, William	1	2	5		
Hiatt, Joseph	1				
Hiatt, John	4		3		
Hiatt, Even	2	4	4		
Hiatt, John, Junr	2	3	4		
Hiatt, Enos	1	1	4		
Hiatt, Isaac	2	4	6		
Brown, Thomas	1	4	2		
Coffin, Bathewel	1	3	3		
Edwards, Wm	1	3	3		

NAME OF HEAD OF FAMILY.	Free white males of 16 years and upward, including heads of families.	Free white males under 16 years.	Free white females, including heads of families.	All other free persons.	Slaves.
Erwin, Saml	1	3	3		
Erwin, James	1	2	2		
Erwin, Robert	1		1		
Nowland, Paul	1				
Lane, Danl	1	6	3		
Lane, William	1	5	5		
Stuart, Sampson	1	4	4		2
Armfield, William	1	2	3		
Ryann, Edwd	2	1	2		
Guin, John	1	2	4		
Thornbury, Joseph	1	5	1		
Mordack, John	1	1	2		
Lain, Mordica	1				
Lamb, Saml	1	2	4		
Wilson, Allin	1				
Brown, James	1		1		
Mongomery, James	1	2	5		
Macy, Matthew	1	1	5		
Fraisor, Isaac	1	1	4		
Osburn, William	1	4	2		
Gosset, Thomas	1	2	4		
Swain, Joseph	1	4	2		
Leonard, William	1	2	7		
Hodgings, William	1		2		
Osburn, Davd	1	1	2		
Clearwaters, Jacob	1	3	6		
Young, William	1	1	2		
McCrackin, Jane	1	1	6		
Edwards, James	1	2	2		
Hodgings, Heer	1		2		
Gamble, James	1		1		
Idilot, Obid	1	3	1		
Hodgings, Robert	5		6		
Hodgings, Richd	1		2		
Hogings, Jonathan	1	1	1		
Hodgings, David	1		2		
Higmut, John	1	2	3		
Richards, Annanias	1	1	1		
Hodgings, George	2	3	6		
Hubbard, John	1	1	5		
Dillon, Leven	1		1		
Sanders, James	1	2	2		
Ballard, William	3	1	6		
Osburn, John, Senr	4		3		
Osburn, John, Junr	1	2	5		
Coffin, Barnabas	2	2	5		
Coffin, Sermon	1	4	4		
Johnston, Margret	1	2	2		
Lowder, John	1	1	1		
Bruce, Edward	5	3	3		
Book, Thomas	1	6	4		
Jessop, Jacob	1	4	3		
Moon, Simon	2	3	5		
Moon, James	1		1		
Sesney, John	1	1	3		
Sesney, Stephen	1	1	3		
Forbus, John	4	2	4		
McMin, Danl	2	3	8		
Hacket, Oliver	1	5	1		
Hendrick, Henry	2	1	2		1
Causy, Nehemiah	1		4		
Kirkman, James	3		1		10
Cook, Jesse	1	1	2		
Mcimma, William	1		3		
Iddings, Joseph	1	4	3		
Howel, John	1	1	4		
Mountain, John	1	1	4		
Doake, Robert	2	4	6		5
Coffin, William	2		1		
Woodburn, Thomas		4	3		
Coffin, Peter	1	2			
Coffin, Peter, Senr	1		2		
Hilton, Peter	1	2	3		
Heath, Smith	1	4	1		
Hamilton, George	2		2		2
Harris, John	1	3	2		
Smith, Robert	1	3	5		3
Stanfield, William	4		4		
Charles, Leven	3	3	4		
Deay, Richd	1	2	4		
Martin, James	1	1	2		
Stuart, James	3	2	4		
Thornbury, Joseph, Senr	2	1	2		
Ham, Philip	3		2		
Way, Henry	1	4	2		
Gardner, William	1	2	7		
Bunker, Reuben	2	4	6		
Balwin, John	1		3		

NAME OF HEAD OF FAMILY.	Free white males of 16 years and upward, including heads of families.	Free white males under 16 years.	Free white females, including heads of families.	All other free persons.	Slaves.
Harris, Obediah	2	1	5		
Thornbury, Thos	1		3		
Thornbury, James	2	2	6		
Thornbury, Marthey		2	5		
Stanly, Micajah	3	3	4		
Stanly, William	2	1	5		
Hunt, Azor	2		2		
Burny, John	1		4		1
Donnal, William	1		1		1
Blear, James	1	1	1		
Stuart, James	1		1		
Crouch, Thomas	1	3	1		
Thompson, James	1		7		
Lovet, Joseph	1	2	3		
Stanly, Shadrack	2	3	5		
Evins, Jesse	1	3	2		
Jestor, Jacob	1		1		
Rice, William	1	1	1		
Hady, Saml	1	5	4		
McAdow, James	1	2	3		
McAdow, Davd	1	2	2		
Blear, Thomas	1	2	2		7
Gladson, Nathan	1	3	3		
Hunter, John	1	3	1		
Mabin, David	1		1		
Ballenger, John	2	4	6		
Craner, Thomas	1	3	3		
Jackson, Joseph	1	2	1		
Jackson, William	2		5		
Tharp, James	2	1	6		1
Hawrin, Windsmore	1	3	1		
Jackson, Willm, Junr	1	2	3		
Knolt, Justin	2	1	2		
Clark, Nathl	1	3	2		1
Dillon, Danl, Senr	1		1		
Donnal, Robert	1		2	4	
Allison, Alex	1	4	1		
Frazor, Solomon	2	1	1		
Dillon, Nathan	1	1	4	1	
Mulloy, Edward	1	4	2		
Bullock, Edwd	2	3	5		
Bell, Saml	4	4	6		
Slown, William	1				
Harvey, William	1		3		
Wilson, Michal	1				
Masey, George	1	1	3		
Moore, John	3	1	3		
Jean, Philip	1	2	1		4
Madaris, Charles	3	3	4		
Wright, Leven	1	4	2		
Bruce, Charles	3	1	6		10
Garrel, Ralph	2	2	6	1	5
Archer, James	1	1	4		5
Mitchel, Adam, Senr	1				5
Thompson, Saml	1	1	4		5
May, Martin	1	1	4		
Fisher, Danl	2	4	3		
Lomax, William	2	2	2		
Eliott, Moses	1	2	2		
Perdue, James	1	6	2		
Wiley, Davd	1	4	3		1
Wiley, Hugh	1	3	4		1
Donnel, George	1	2	2		3
Owens, Edward	1		2		
Rawly, Elisha	1	3	4		
Knuitt, Jacob	3	1	4		
Brawly, Prier	1	1	2		
Dun, Solomon	1		1		
Gibson, Jacob	1	2	1		
Dunn, Federick	1	2	9		
Stanly, Joseph	1	4	4		
Foster, James	2	2	1		
Brasher, Asa	3	4	4		7
Hayley, John	3	1	3		2
Parks, George	1	4	3		2
Erwin, Joseph	2	1	3		2
Gillaspie, John	2	1	2		7
Holland, Edward	3		2		
McCuestion, Thomas	1		3		
Lewis, Aron	1	1	3		1
Wilson, Andrew	1	5	2		2
Chambers, John	1		1		2
Jeans, Edward	1	5	5		1
Hill, Nathan	1	1	3		
Jean, William	1	1	3		2
Jean, Willm, Senr	2	1	1		3
Brown, Thomas	1		1		
McCain, Alexander	1				
Perry, Cornelias	1				
Millis, Edward	3	1	3		
McBride, John	1	1	2		
Hiatt, Ashor	1	1	1		
Smith, Henry	2		3		
Hiatt, Christopher	2	3	3		
Hamilton, John	1		4		6
McNary, Robert	1				
Hamilton, Thomas	1		1		

SALISBURY DISTRICT, GUILFORD COUNTY—Continued.

NAME OF HEAD OF FAMILY.	Free white males of 16 years and upward, including heads of families.	Free white males under 16 years.	Free white females, including heads of families.	All other free persons.	Slaves.
Hamilton, Hance	3	1	2	....	14
Stanley, Strangeman	3	1	4		
Dunlap, John	2	....	1		
Prichard, Alexander	1				
Bunch, William	1	2	5		
Dunlap, Robert	1	....	1		
Gorden, Moses	1	2	5		
Wheatly, Thomas	1	1	1		
Copper, James	2	3	4		
Fleming, John	2	....	3		
Smith, John	2	....	3		
Smith, John, Junr	1	1	2		
Shilcut, John	1	3	6		
Tate (Widow)	1	2	4	....	9
Underwood, Abraham	3	2	4		
Isely (Widow)	1	4	2	....	5
Dausen, Daniel	2	3	2	....	5
Gibson, Andrew	1	5	2	....	11
Elmore, John	1	3	2		
Tate, Zepheniah	1	2	8	....	11
Brumfield, Philip	1				
Isely, Christan	2	1	4		
Isely, Philip	1	....	2		
Isely, Elizabeth	....	4	3	1	
Loman, Adam	1	1	4		
Waggoner, Peter	1	....	2		
Whitsel, Ludwick	1	1	2		
Cook, Henry	1	2	2	....	26
Fall, Christian	3	3	6		
Shaver, William	2	2	3	....	1
Shaver, Jacob	1	....	2		
Shaver, William	1	....	2		
Loakey, William	1	3	5		
Sullinger, Peter	3			....	5
Dunlap, Robert	3	3	4		
Boon, John	1	3	4	....	4
Summers, Peter	1	2	3	....	1
Summers, Filty	1	....	4	....	1
Diclenger, John	4	1	6	....	1
McKamie, Robert	4	....	1	....	1
Woodside, John	1	....	1		
Ross, Henry	2	4	4		
McAdow, John	2	2	4	....	2
Gilchrust, John	3	2	4		
Gorsil, William	1				
Nicks, John	4	3	5	....	5
McClain, Joseph	2	3	2		
Alexander, Joseph	1	4	4	....	1
McCollister, James	1	3	2		
McClain, John	1	....	3		
Leak, William	1	1	2		
Gillaspie, Danl	3	4	4	....	6
Williams, Roland	1	....	1		
Williams, William	3	....	3		
Williams, Wm, Junr	1	....	2		
Hughs, Thomas	1	1	2		
Morgan, Lewis	1	2	4		
Harry, Even	1	....	2		
Cork, John	1	1	2		
Coffin, William	1	2	1	....	1
Wright, Isaac	2	3	3	....	7
Cannon, Minas	1	3	3		
McDauman, Michal	2	5	3		
Charles, Elisha	1	4	2		
Chipman, John	1	3	2		
Peeples, Hubbard	3	....	2		
Barham, Charles	2	3	3	....	4
McGibbony, Patrck	1	2	6	....	5
Dickson, William	1	2	5		
Knight, Archd	1	2	3		
Barrom, Newsom & John	2				
Dick, James	1	2	1	....	1
Hoskins, Arnol	1	3	3		
Landreth, Thomas	3	3	1		
Dicks, James	1	....	6		
Thompson, John	1	2	2		
Duck, Samuel	3	....	2		
Starbuck, William	1	2	7		
Parker, Jonathan	1	2	1		
Widdop, William	1	1	2		
Calhoon, Saml	1	....	1		
Calhoon, James	2	....	5		
Clark, Nathl	1	2	3	....	1
Stuart, Saml	1				
Shannon, William	2	....	2		
Stephenson, John	1	3	3		
Armfield, Nathan	1				
Sherwood, Danl	1	2	4		
Linthacum, Richd	1	1	1		
Swain, William	1	1	1		
Sherwood, Hungh	1				
Kirkman, Leven	1	2	3	....	1
Stanly, Saml	1	3	3		
Wheatly, James	2	5	4		
Madaris, Oliver	1	3	2		
Love, John	1	....	2	....	1

NAME OF HEAD OF FAMILY.	Free white males of 16 years and upward, including heads of families.	Free white males under 16 years.	Free white females, including heads of families.	All other free persons.	Slaves.
Coffin, Leve	1	....	4		
Stuart, George	1	3	4		
Young, Davd	1	3	3		
Mathews, Hugh	1	....	2		
Wiley, John	2	5	3		
Forbus (Widow)	2	....	3		
Mills, James	1	4	5		
Shear, Jacob	1	4	4		
Shear, Jacob, Senr	3	1	2		
Shaver, William	1	2	3	....	1
Isely, Christian	2	1	6		
Isely (Widow)	1	....	4		
Shaver, Frederick	1	4	1		
Whitemon, Mathias	1	1	3		
Low, David	2	3	4	....	4
Clapp, Jacob	4	2	4	....	3
Clapp, Tobias	1	....	2		
Wakes, Danl	1	2	5		
Fifer, Valentine	1	1	1		
Clapp, George	2	3	3	....	5
Clapp, Lodwick, Senr	2	2	3	....	1
Clapp, Jacob	1	....	3		
Clapp, Jacob	1	....	2		
Clapp, Lodwick, Junr	1	....	2		
Neace, George	3	3	5		
Albright, William	1	2	3		
Denney, William	3	3	5		
Allison, Saml	3	1	4		
Stuart, Findly	4	....	4	....	3
Causbey, James	2	....	4		
Dun, Shadrick	1	5	4		
Waggoner, Peter	1	....	4		
Waggoner, John	1	3	4		
White, Edward	1	4	7		
Isely, Balser	1	3	4		
Wiley, William	1	2	1	....	1
Wiley, Alexander	1			....	3
Forbus, George	1	4	5		
Ross, Reuben	1	5	3		
Tomb, John	2	5	4		
Buzard, David	1	....	4		
Tingle, George	2	5	11		
Paterson, Michal	1	4	2		
Coble, George	3	2	2		
McDill, Saml	1	1	7		
Causby, Hance	2	....	4		
McBride, John	2	....	5		
McBride, Jno, Senr	2	3	3		
Coble, Jacob	3	....	6		
Clap, Philip	2	....	2	....	5
Cooper, David	2	3	2	....	1
Coan, Elias	1	1	5		
Clark, Hance	2	....	5		
Coble, Nicholas	1	....	3		
Shatterlin, Michal	1	1	7		
Clapp, Valentine	1	1	3		
Prowel, Sampson	2	2	4		
Crowel, Mary		....	4		
Swing, Lodwick	2	1	2		
Swing, Mathias	1	3	3	....	1
Eamicks, Mathias	3	....	6		
Eamicks, Nicholas	1	1	2		
Coble, Anthony	2	....	4		
Coble, Samuel	1	2	3		
Coble, George, Junr	1	3	6		
Foust, Christian	2	2	4		
Heaga, Coonrod	2	....	2		
Low, Davd, Senr	1	3	4	....	1
Oneal, James	1	3	4		
Low, Peter	2	1	8		
Low, Thomas	1	1	3		
Low (Widow)		3	3		
Deveney, Samuel	1	3	7	....	2
Wilkerson, Thomas	1	....	3		
Walker, George	2	....	8		
Glass (Widow)		1	2		
Harman, Jacob	1	1	1		
Shatterlin, Andrew	1	....	5		
Glass, George	1	3	4		
Borow, Charles	4	3	3		
Coble, Peter	1	1	4		
Kime, Philip	1	1	1		
Camick, Philip	1	2	1		
Plunket, William	1	2	3		
Wing, John	1	1	3		
Cortner, Danl	1	2	3		
Smith, Peter	4	2	3		
Sullavent, Fletcher	3	4	5		
Evins, Davd	3	2	3		
Brown, Adam	1	....	4		
Walker, James	1	....	5		
Tingold, Peter	1	3	2		
Bennet, Elisha	1	1	4		
Shoe, Philip	1	4	4		
Whitsel, Adam	1	3	4		
Limebary, George	1	2	8		
Burrow, Philip	2	....	3		
Burrow, Starling	1	....	2		

NAME OF HEAD OF FAMILY.	Free white males of 16 years and upward, including heads of families.	Free white males under 16 years.	Free white females, including heads of families.	All other free persons.	Slaves.
Greenson, Isaiah	2	1	2		
Shockman, Christopher	1	2	1		
Low, Samuel	1	2	3	....	1
Burrow, Ishmal	1	1	1		
McClain, John, Senr	3	1	2		
McClain, Thomas	1	....	3		
McClain, Joseph	1	2	3		
McClain, John, Junr	1	3	4		
Greer, Mathew	2	....	3		
Greer, Thomas	1	....	3		
Smith, Thomas	1	2	3		
Lesly, Peter	1	2	2		
Holland (Widow)		2	3		
Barnhil, William	1	3	4		
Forbus, John	1	....	3		
Shaw, Hugh	4	1	3		
Morrow, Robert	1	2	5		
Jobb, John	4	5	4		
Cartright, Wm	3	4	2		
Wright, Willis	1	....	4		
Miner, Leven	1	1	3		
Dickson, Thomas				1	
Wright, Charles	1	....	1		
Mead, John	1	3	4		
Dwiggins, John	2	4	3	....	1
Thornbury, Edwd	1	2	5		
Cain, Danl	1	1	4		
Cusick, William	2	....	3	....	3
Anderson, John	3	1	4		
Garner, William	1	....	1		
Morgan, Thomas	1	....	3		
Warton, Watson	1	3	4	....	2
Shelly, James	1	3	3		
Rian, John	1	2	4	....	1
Lindsey, Robt	2	4	4	....	11
Whealer, James	1				
Findley, James	1	....	5		
Price, Zacariah	1	1	2		
Hamilton, Thomas	1	3	3	....	1
Burton, Richd, Senr	3	....	5	....	1
Heath, William	1	....	1		
Burton, Richd, Junr	1	....	1		
Simpson, Peter	1	1	1		
Heath, Jacob	1	1	1		
Boyd, James	1	3	3		
Houlton, Isaac	3	3	1		
Kersey, Eleazor	1	1	4		
Kersey, Thomas	1	1	4		
Ballard, Joseph	1	4	2		
Hiatt, Joseph	1	1	3		
Way, William	1	3	3		
McKeen, Alex	3	....	2		
Rittey, James	1	2	2		
Langril, Curtis	1	1	2		
Fitzgeral, Wm	1	1	2		
Coe, John	1	4	4		
Unthank, Joseph	1	4	4		
McCallock, Thos	2	1	1		
Clapp, Jacob	1	4	4		
McBride, John, Senr	2	....	5		
McBride, John	1	3	2	....	2
Donnal, Lathan	1	....	2		
Huston, Richd	2	....	1		
Evins, David	1	....	1		
Blisset, William	1	....	1		
Dewese, Ezekel	1	2	3		
Simpson, Nathl	2	3	3		
Simpson, Richd	1				
Carrel, Elizabeth		1	5		
Cuningham, John	1	1	2	....	3
Criswell, James	2	2	2	....	1
Maxwell, John	1	....	1		
Bussell, James	1	3	2	....	1
Minner, Leven	1	1	4		
Hardin, Thomas	1	....	4		
Weatherley, Jobb	1	1	5		
Barnhill, William	1	....	4		
Cartright, William	2	3	2		
Wheeler, Charles	1	....	2		
Kirkman, George	1	4	6	....	1
Mabin, John	1	....	2		
Kirkman, Levin	1	1			
Rankin, William	1	3	4		
Rankin, John	2	2	9		
Russell, Robert	1	3	4	....	2
Cummins, Robt	1	2	7		
Summers, Joseph	1	2	5		
Cummins, Thomas	2	....	6		
Fitchee, Saml	1	2	2		
Hopkins, Erle	1	3	4		
Hancok, Maiga	5	1	4		
Buckingham, Levi	1	....	4		
Williams, Celas	2	4	6		
Charlscroft, Thos	1	....	6		
Hilton, James	1	2	2		
Hilton, Peter	1	1	4		
Hilton, William	1	....	2		

SALISBURY DISTRICT, GUILFORD COUNTY—Continued.

NAME OF HEAD OF FAMILY.	Free white males of 16 years and upward, including heads of families.	Free white males under 16 years.	Free white females, including heads of families.	All other free persons.	Slaves.
Walker, James	1		6		
White, James	2	2	1		3
McMurry, John	3		2		
Scott, William	3	2	5		4
Henderson, Betty			1		
Ructman, Joseph	1	2	3		
Waddle, Davd	1	1	2		
Lamb, Simon	1	1	3		
Wilson, Michal	1	5	6		
Newman, John	1	2	3		
Lamb, Robt	1	1	3		
Linard, Joseph	1		2		
Davis, John	1	1	2		
Davis, Tristan	1	1	2		
Anderson, Thos	1	5	4		
Reeves, Thomas	1	2	1		
Wilson, John	1				
Stone, Salathial	1	3	5		
Wiley, Robert	1	2	6		
Davis, Epsebi	2	1			
Barr, James, Senr	2		1		4
Chambers, John	1		1	1	
Wright, Thomas	1	1	1	1	
Law, Andrew	3		3		
Simpson, Richard	3	1	4		
Simpson, Richd, Senr	1				
Reeves, William	1	3	5	1	
Lambert, Saml	1	2	2		
Jones, Isaac	1		4		
Jones, Isaac, Senr	1	1	2		
Linard, John	3	1	7		
Jester, Jacob	2	3	4		
Gray, Alexander	4		6		
Mendingall, George	2	5	5		
Hines, Saml	1		2		
Mabin, Davd	1		5		
Cannaday, John	5	2	3		
Wilson, George	3	4	4		
Simpson, Thomas	3	2	7		
Knight, Davd	1	3	2		
Taylor, John	1	1	2		
Mendingall, Mordica	1		2		
Charles, William	3	1	5		
Hoggat, Joseph	3	2	3		
Mendingall, Richd	1	2	1		
Harbin, Enoch	3	6	3		
Mendingall, Mordica, Senr	1	2	1		
Mendingall, Jesse	2	4	2		
Carsey, Jesse	1	2			
Mendingall, Seth	1	1	7		
Mendingall, John	1	2	1		
Mendingall, Moses, Senr	1	1	2		
Mendingall, Stephen, Senr	1		3		
Rix, James	2	3	5		
Mendingall, Benjn	3	1	4		
Mendingall, Moses, Junr	3		4		
Mendingall, Stephen	3	4	6		
Stephen (Negro)				11	
Lay, John	2	2	3		
Rice, William	1	1	1		
McGuire, John	1	1	4		
Leonard, George	1		2		
Dicks, Peter	1		3		
Beals, John	1	5	3		
Wilson, Abbigal	1		3		
Swain, Marthey			2		
Worth, Danl	2	2	4		
Stone, John	1	1	2		
Coffin, Aaron	1	2	4		
Osburn, Danl	2	3	3		
Swaim, William	3	2	5		
Swaim, Michal	1	4	6		
Coffin, Adam	1		2		
Armond, Jacob	1	1	6		
Osburn, Peter	1		2		
Edwards, Henry	1	1	5		
Wilson, George	1	1	3		
Wilson, Thomas	1		1		
Buller, Moses	2		4		
Worth, Jobb	1	1	2		
Hoggat, William	1	1	1		
Frazier, Isaac	1	2	4		
Macy, Henry	2	2	3		
Osburn, John	2		2		
Hodson, John	1	4	4		
Mash, William	1		4		
Scott, Thomas	1		1		
Barr, Davd, Junr	1	3	3		
Barr, Davd, Senr	1		1		
Hester, Francis					4
Bishop, Aron	1				
Smith, Henry	3	1	2		
Dennis, Mathias	1		2		
Tharp, Isaac	2				
Scott, Margret		2	5		
Barham, Hartwell	1	7	3		
Harris, Joel	1	4	3		3
Tharp, Laben	1	1	1		
Tharp, Joseph	1		2		
Cairy, Hezekiah	1		1		
Peeples, Drewry	1	1	3		3
Schrader, John I	1		2		
Hester, Robert	3	4	2		
Small, Knight	1		1		
Starbuck, Hezekiah	1	5	3		
Wheeler, John	3	1	5		
McCairny, Francis	1	3	2		
Hunt, William	1	3	2		
Coggeshall, Job	2		5		
Mendingall, Phinias	3		2		
Melrainy, Joseph	1	1	2		
Mendingall, John	3	1	3		
Stanford, John	1		1		
Gifford, Jonathan	2	1	5		
Beason, Isaac	4	1	3		
Tolbert, John	2	1	3		
Beason, Benjn	2	3	5		
Hains, Joshua	1	6	3		
Beason, Saml	3		3		
Beason, Edwd	1		1		
Beard, Richd	1				
Sanders, Joel	3	3	5		2
Sanders, David	1	2	3		
Hunt, John	1	4	1		
Sanders, John	2		2		
Mills, Reuben, Senr	1	2	4		
Johnston, Tarlton	2	2	9		
Whickershem, Jehu	1	3	4		
Gardner, Sylvenus	5	3	3		
Hayworth, Stephen	3		5		
Stuart, Jehu	1	2	4		
Mills, Joseph	3		4		
Mills, Amos	1	2	6		
Beard, William	2	2	3		
Huddleston, Seth	1	1	9		
Mendingall, James	1	2	2		
Mills, John	1		1		
Beard, Reuben	2	2	2		
Wheeler, Manlov	1	4	3		
Ball, Thomas	1	1	1		
Sanders, Marthey	1		6		2
Hoggat, Jonathan	1				
Crew, William	1				
Barr, Davd	1		2		1
Barr, James	1		3		4
Bellingsley, Brasel	1	1	1		
Reeves, Thomas	1	2	1		
Reeves, Jonathan	1				
Reeves, Jesse	1	2	1		
Hogans, John	1	1	5		
Dearens, John	1	2	3		3
Mileham, Saml	1	2	4		
Mileham, Welter	3	3	2		
Pealt, Jacob	1	1	2		1
Williamson, Lewis	1		1		
Callum, Henry	1	3	4		
Cannady, William	1	1	7		
Johnston, Andrew	1		1		
Barham, James	1	4	5		3
Williamson, Upton	3	4	3		1
Love, John	1		2		1
Tharp, James	1	2	6		1
Goslin, Wm	1		1		
McDannil, Isaah	2	4	4		
Coffin, Mathew	1	1	6		
Persons, Thos	2	2	4		
Thornbury, Joseph	1	3	8		
Carsey, Daniel	1	4	1		
Raduck, William	1	5	2		
Beall, Thadeous	1	4	6		12
Whitsel, Henry	2	2	3		
Cortner, George	2	3	4		

SALISBURY DISTRICT, IREDELL COUNTY.

NAME OF HEAD OF FAMILY.	Free white males of 16 years and upward, including heads of families.	Free white males under 16 years.	Free white females, including heads of families.	All other free persons.	Slaves.
Auton, Thomas	1	1	3		
Almery, Benjamin	1		3		1
Anderson, John	1		3		
Batey, Thomas	3	3	4		7
Brown, William	1	2	3		
Brevard, Benjamin	1		3		5
Baker, John	1	3	2		
Braley, Neil	2	5	4		1
Baird, Margret		2			
Biars, James	2	5	4	1	6
Baird, John	1	2	5		4
Biars, Joseph	1				21
Bowman, William	1	2	3		
Brown, Robert			4		
Brown, John	1	1	3		8
Bowman, James	3	4	2		
Brevard, Adam	1	2	3		5
Brevard, Robert	2		4		
Brevard, John	1	2	3		5
Brevard, Alexr	2	2	3		12
Cooke, John	3	1	8		11
Creswell, William	1		4		
Creswell, David	2		2		
Cupples, Elizabeth	3		2		
Cooke, Thomas, Senr	1		1		4
Cooke, Thomas, Junr	1	2	4		1
Carruth, John	2	3	3		1
Cooke, James	1		2		
Davidson, George	5		3	1	11
Davidson, William	1	2	4		3
Duncan, Thomas	3		4		
Durham, Joseph	1	2	4		
Dickey, John	2				3
Dickey, Samuel	1		2		5
Douney, Charles	1	1	3		
Gracey, Patrick	1	2	4		
Gracey, William	1	2	2		
Ewing, Nathaniel	1	3	4		6
Gray, Hugh	2	2	3		
Gray, Robert	4	1	2		
Gray, Thomas	1	1	1		1
Huston, James	1	3	5		2
Henderson, Mary	2	3	3		
Hains, James	1	2	3		2
Hains, John	1	2	3		
Huggins, Robert	1	1	6		4
Huggins, John	1	2	5		3
Hart, James	1		3		
Hughes, Alexander	2		2		2
Hughes, Thomas	1		2		
Hart, Mathew	1	1	1		1
Hughey, John	1	1	2		
Hains, Joseph	1	4	4		
Huggins, James	2	1	4		
Hughes, James	3	3	3		9
Hannah, Samuel	1	2	3		11
Kelton, Robert	1	1	2		
Kerr, Nathaniel	1		2		3
Kerr, Revd David	3	1	2		3
Kitchen, John	2		1		
Lindsay, John	1		2		
Lair, John	2		3		
Logan, George	1	2	2		
McCrery, Samuel	3	3	2		
McfeSion, Robert	4		1		
McConnell, John, Ser	1		1		8
McConnell, John, Jur	2	1	7		1
McEwin, John	1	3	4		
McEwin, Joseph	2	2	3		
Milholland, James	1	2	2		
Moore, Abraham	2	2	3		
Moore, Adam	2				
McEwin, James	1	1	3		
McGee, Patrick	1	1	3		
McKnight, Hugh	4	2	5		6
McKnight, James	3	3	5		2
McNeely, Robert	1	1	2		
McConnell, Benjamin	2		1		1
Moss, Benjamin	2	1	2		
Nelson, Joshua	1	4	4		4
Norad, John	2	2	4		
Osborn, Adlai	2	5	5		19
Porter, James	1	2	2		
Porter, John	1		6		
Porter, Robert	1	1	7		
Reese, William	1		2		
Rankin, Robert	1	3	6		1
Redman, John	1	2	2		
Scott, Robert	1	2	4		
Strain, Andrew	1	4	2		
Sloan, Robert	1	2	1		2
Thompson, John	3		3		6
Templeton, Robert	2	1	3		
Templeton (Widow)			3		
Templeton, George	1	2	4		
Templeton, Joseph	2	2	4		
Torrence, Hugh	4		3		5
Torrence, George	2	1	2		1
Thompson, Benjamin	1		1		

SALISBURY DISTRICT, IREDELL COUNTY—Continued.

NAME OF HEAD OF FAMILY.	Free white males of 16 years and upward, including heads of families.	Free white males under 16 years.	Free white females, including heads of families.	All other free persons.	Slaves.
White, Robert	3		1		
Wingfield, Thomas	1	1	7		
Work, Alexander	1		2		25
Work, John	2	4	5		10
Wilson, James	3		5		
White, Mary	1	2	3		3
Williamson, Richard	1	3	4		
Winslow, Moses	1		4		7
Walker, Robert	1	1	1		
Wallice, William	1	2	4		
Young, Alexr	1	1	4		
Young, James	1	2	2		
Andrew, James	1	3	4		
Anderson, James	1	3	6		
Allison, Theophilus	1	1	3		4
Armstrong, John	1	1	2		
Brown, William	5		2		
Barr (Widow)	1	2	3		2
Bell, Walter	2	2	6		
Berringer, John Henry	1		2		
Brown, Valentine	1	1	3		
Crawford, John Miller	1	2	3		
Clendennin, Mathew	2		3		1
Clayton, George	1	2	3		1
Cammins, Gasper	1		1		
Crawford, James	1	2	1		3
Clayton, Lambert	1	4	2		
Crawford, John	1	1	2		
Cavan (Widow)	3		3		
Cavan, John	1		3		
Cooke, Thomas	2	3	6		
Chambers, James	1	2	3		
Chambers, John	1	1	1		
Campbell, Allen	1	3	4		
Christey, Andrew	1	3	3		
Christey, Joseph	1	1	3		
Christey (Widow)	1		1		
Davidson, Joseph	1		2		2
Davidson, Alexander	1	3	5		
Duglas, Solomon	2	1	6		
Erwin, John	1	1	3		1
Erwin, William	1	2	1		
Erwin, Thomas	4	1	4		
Erwin, Abraham	2		6		1
Erwin, John, Ser	2	4	3		
Flemming, James	1	5	1		
Foley, Thomas	1	1	3		
Flemming, John	4	2	4		9
Flemming, Samuel	1	3	3		
Flemming, Samuel, Jur	1	2	4		
Gamble, Thomas	1	2	1		
Hibath, James	2		1		
Hendry, James	4	1	1		1
Herrald, John	1	3	4		
Huston, James	1		1		1
Huston, Samuel	1	3	5		
Henner, Levi	1	3	1		
Justice, Hance	2	1	2		
Kerr, James	1		2		6
Kerr, Andrew	1	3	5		2
Kerr, William	1	4	1		2
Kerr, William, Jur	2	2	1		
Knox, Mary	1		4		6
Knox, Joseph	1	4	4		
Koyle, William	1		3		
Kitchen, Stephen	1	2	2		
Knox, John	2	3	4		4
King, Thomas	1	2	5		4
Mclaud, William	1		4		
McCoy, (Widow)	1	1	2		
Lawrance, Adam	1	1	2		
McCoy, Aluxander	1		2		
McCoy, Daniel	1	1	2		
McDaniel (Widow)		2	2		
McKisick, Robert	3		2		
McCoy, George (S. M.)	1	1	2		
McCoy, Alexander	1	2	5		
Morton, John, Jur	1	1	1		1
McCoy, William	1	3	3		
Morton, John	2		4		
McLoud, William	2	1	2		
Mcbride, William	1	4	4		
McLoud, Anguish	1		3		
McCoy, Daniel, Jur	1		4		
Moore, Robert	2	2	7		
McClain, James	2	1	5		
Miller, John	1	3	3		
McEwen, James	2	3	5		1
Murdock, William	2	3	5		
McHenry, Isaac	1	1	1		2
Mares, William	1		3		
McCoy, Robert	2		3		
McCoy, Daniel (S. M.)	3		1		
McCoy, George	1	2	4		
McKinsey, Robert	1		4		
McRavey, John	1	3	2		
Moffet, William	1		2		

NAME OF HEAD OF FAMILY.	Free white males of 16 years and upward, including heads of families.	Free white males under 16 years.	Free white females, including heads of families.	All other free persons.	Slaves.
Nail, Andrew	1		1		5
Nail, Gilbraith	2	6	2		2
Nail, Samuel	1		2		
Nail, William	2	1	4		
Nail, Robert	1	1	3		
Nislett (Widow)		1	1		
Nail, James	2		1		
Nail, James, Jur	1		3		
Orbison, James	1	1	2		
Oliphant (Widow)	2	1	1		5
Olliphant, John	2	1	5		3
Orton, James	1	2	6		
Patterson, James	3				1
Phillips, Thomas	1	4	2		
Baker, Peter	2	2	4		
Pustle, Henry	2		4		
Patten, Robert	1	3	5		
Patten, John	1		2		
Ramsey, James	3	2	2		
Ramsey, David	1		3		
Ramsey, Robert	1		2		2
Ramsey, Andrew	1	2	2		1
Raynolds, William	1	1	4		
Scroggs, John	2		2		
Smith, Robert	1	3	2		
Simenton, Theophilus	1	2	1		1
Troutman (Widow)	1		2		
Thomas, James	1	1	3		
Torrence, James	1	3	1		
Troutman, Jacob	1		1		
Thompson, John	1	1	1		
Wetherspoone, John	2	1	3		
Walker, Arthur	4	2	4		1
Wetherspoon, William	1	1	2		
Wilson, John	1	2	4		
Samuel, Wilson	1	1	3		
Wilson, Samuel, Jur	1		3		
Young, William	2		3		1
Alexander, Gabriel	2	3	5		
Andrews, John	1	1	6		
Alexander, James	2	2	6		
Alexander, Ebenezer	1		3		2
Allen, Moses	3		6		
Adams, James	2	2	3		5
Black, David	2		3		
Brady, Archabald	1	2	4		
Boyd, Robert	1	3	4		
Davis, Patrick	1	1	5		
Erwin, William	1	1	2		1
Eslinger, Gasper	1	1	3		
Flemming, Peter	1	4	2		
Femster, William	2	2	3		3
Harris, Samuel	2	2	3		7
Guy, James	2	3	4		7
Hill, Abraham	1	1	4		
Hannon, William	1		1		
Hill, John	3	1	5		
Hill, Robert	1		1		
Hill, James	1		1		
Huston, James	2		2		
Hogland, Tunis	1		2		
Ireland, William	1	1	2		3
Ireland, John	2		2		2
Ireland, William, Jur	1		1		1
Johnston, Andrew	3	1	5		
Johnston, Adam	2	3	6		
Lewis, Richard	2		4		4
Landen, Robert	1	1	3		
Massey, Jacob	1		3		
Massey, Nicholas	1		3		2
Morrison, James	1	4	2		
Morris, Samuel	2	3	3		
McKee, John	2	1	3		
McClelland, William	2	3	3		5
McKnight, James	1	3	4		1
Morrison, James, Jun	1	5	3		1
Morrison, Andrew	3	2	6		5
McKnight, William	1	1	3		
Morrison, William	1	1	6		1
Milligan, Alexander	1		2		
McKnight, David	2	5	2		
Murdock, Robert	1	1	3		
Moore, Alexander	1	3	3		
Mcfarlin, James	4		4		
Moore, James	1		1		
Morrison, Thomas	1		4		4
Morrison, William (Miller)	4	3	5		1
Murphey, Samuel	1	3	4		
McClathey, John	1	1	1		
McAdoe, William	1		2		
McCulloch, James	2	2	2		1
McClathey, Hamilton	2		6		
McCollum, James	1	1	2		4
McClachey, John	1		2		1
Nesbitt, John	1		5		6
Olliphant, Mathew	3	1	5		

NAME OF HEAD OF FAMILY.	Free white males of 16 years and upward, including heads of families.	Free white males under 16 years.	Free white females, including heads of families.	All other free persons.	Slaves.
Purviance, David	1	1	2		
Reed, Abraham	1	2	4		
Potts, James, Jur	1		3		
Purviance, James	2	3	7		7
Potts, William, Jur	1	1	2		1
Potts, James, Senr	4		5		
Potts, William, Ser	2	3	3		3
Purviance, John, Ser	2	1	9		2
Rodman, Francis	1				
Roberts, Moses	1		3		
Ramsey, John	1	3	2		
Stephenson, Robert	3	2	6		
Stuart, John	3	5	4		
Scroggs, John	1	5	3		
Scroggs, David	1	1	2		
Stephenson, William, Ser	3	1	2		4
Stephenson, John, Jur	1	2	4		
Stephenson, James	1				
Scroggs, Jeremiah	1	1	3		
Stephen, William, Jur	1	1	3		1
Henry, Thomas	1		2		
Thomas, John	1	4	3		1
Thomas, Jacob	1	4	3		3
Thompson, John	2	4	2		
Wallis, John	4	2	4		1
Whealy, John	1				
Woodside, John	1		2		
White, Andrew	1	1	2		
Wetherspoone, Alexander	1	4	4		
Woodside, Hannah	2		3		
White, Samuel	1				
White, William	1		2		
Whealey, Joseph, Senr	1	1	10		
Waugh, William	2	2	4		
Watt, James	3		6		4
Watt, William	1	4	4		4
Whealey, Joseph, Jur	1	1	3		
William, Woodside	1	3			
Woodside, John	2	1	1		
Alexander, Allen	3	4	1		9
Alexander, William	2	3	5		
Barns, Elijah	1	5	3		
Campbell, Colin	1	4	1		3
Draxin, John	2	3	2		
Gordan, John	1				
Gordon, Gilbert	1	3	5		
Gordon, George	1		1		
Galleher, James	1	3	2		
Hood, Solomon	1	2	3		
Huston, Joseph	2	1	4		1
McCoy, Robert	1		1		
McCoy, Nail	1		3		
McCoy, Daniel	2	3	2		
Morrison, Murdock	2		2		
McCloud, William, Jur	1		1		
McClain, Donald	1	2	1		
McClain, John	1	2	3		
McIntosh, Anguish	1		3		
McCloud, Robert	1		3		
McIntosh, John	1		2		
McCoy, Alexander	1	3	4		
McIntosh, Alexander	1	3	4		
Milligan, James	1	1	1		
Milligan, Fergus	2	1	6		
McCloud, William	2		2		
McCoy, George	1		5		
McCoy, Alexander	1	2	3		
McKinsey, Kenith	1	2	4		
McDonald, Alexander	2		4		
McCoy, Thomas	1		2		
Rice, John	1	1	3		
Rounsevall, John	1	1	3		
Rector, Benjamin	1	2	3		
Ramsey, John	1	2	2		
Stuart, James, Ser	2	2	7		6
Snodey, Samuel	1		1		
Wallace, Robert	2	2	3		2
Wallace, John	1	4	3		
McIntosh, George	2	2			
Matison, George	1				
McCaskey, Daniel	4		4		
McCoy, James	1		1		
McCoy, William	1	1			
McCoy, George	1	2	4		
McKinsey, Kenith	1				
McKinsey, George	1				
Arington, John	1	2	3		
Black, John	1	1	2		
Black, Gavin	1	3	3		
Buteram, William	1	3	3		
Bogle, Samuel	1	3	5		
Barnes, James	1	2	2		
Brown, Isach	1	1	5		
Baker, Howell	4	3	5		
Bentley, Benjamin	4		4		
Bell, William	2	1	4		

SALISBURY DISTRICT, IREDELL COUNTY—Continued.

NAME OF HEAD OF FAMILY.	Free white males of 16 years and upward, including heads of families.	Free white males under 16 years.	Free white females, including heads of families.	All other free persons.	Slaves.	NAME OF HEAD OF FAMILY.	Free white males of 16 years and upward, including heads of families.	Free white males under 16 years.	Free white females, including heads of families.	All other free persons.	Slaves.	NAME OF HEAD OF FAMILY.	Free white males of 16 years and upward, including heads of families.	Free white males under 16 years.	Free white females, including heads of families.	All other free persons.	Slaves.
Barkley, James	2	2	5			Matison, George	1	3	4			Reed, John, Jur	1		1		1
Baker, Isaac	1	1	1			Marlow, Mark						Reed, Abner	1		1		
Bogle, Robert	1	1	3		2	Marlow, James	1	2	2			Stuart, James	4	3	4		1
Baker, Howell	1	4	4		1	Mules, George	1	1	1			Scott, James	4	1	1		
Couden, William	1		1			Owens, Barsheba	1		1		1	Summers, William	1	1	1		9
Caeton, Peter	1	5	4			Weslock, James	1		1			Sutfin, Jacob	1	1	2		
Carson, Robert, Jur	1	1	3			Pickett, Henry	1	3	3			Sharpe, John	2	2	3		5
Caeton, William	3	1	2			Roberts, John	1	2	3			Sharpe, James	2	2	7		11
Cooke, Richard	1		1		6	Roberts, Humphrey	1	5	3			Sharpe, William	3	5	3		8
Cathey, James	1	1	5			Redman, Thomas	2	3	4			Shelley, Richard			3		
Carson, Robert, Senr	1					Simenton, Adam	3		5			Swingford, Elijah	1	1	3		
Davis, James	1	2	4			Speaks, Luke	1	2	3			Shelly, James	1		1		
Davis, Solomon	1	4	3			Speaks, Thomas	1	2	3			Shelly, Benjamin	1	1	2		
Davis, Joshua	1	1	3			Sanders, Aron	1	1	1			Swingford, James	2		2		
Durham, James	2	2	5			Sanders, Moses	1	4	4		5	Summers, Bazil	1	1	1		
Freemon, Aron	1	2	3			Shoemaker, John	2	3	3			Slavin, William	2	1	4		2
Fortune, Aron	1	5	4			Shoemaker, Tarlton	1	2	2			Simenton, John	1	1	3		
Griffith, John	1	1	2		1	Shoemaker, Randol	1	1	2			Grour, Tomlin	1				
Griffith, Robert	1		2			Thomas, Smith	1	3	3			Tomlin, John	1	1	1		
Griffith, Edward	1	4	1		5	Sanders, Jacob	1	2	2			Templeton, John	1	2	5		
Graham, John	2		2			Taylor, William	1	3	4			Templeton, Robert	1	1	1		
Hughes, William	1	5	1			Williams, James	2	2	4		1	Templeton, Thomas	1				
Harrison, Joseph	3	3	3			Williams, Samuel	1	4	3		6	Travis, Mary	2	1	4		
Harrison, Nathaniel	1					Williams, Phillip	1	2	5			Todd, Nathan	2	2	4		
Harrison, Jeremiah	1					Wots, Valentine	1		1			Tomlin, Humphry B	1	4	5		5
Hartness, Nathaniel	1	1	2			Andrew, Hugh	3	2	3		1	Wasson, James	1	3	3		
Hall, Adam	2	2	6			Andrew, John	1	2	2		5	Welch, John	1	1	3		2
Hogston, Archabeld	1	1	2			Black, William	1		1		2	Wiselock, James	1		1		
Kelley, Solomon	2	2	5			Brotherton, John	2	2	4			Wasson, Robert	1		1		
King, James	2	2	4		8	Bones, William	1	2	2			Wilson, Lewis	1		3		2
Lackey, William, Jur	1	3	2			Beaty, Thomas	1	2	2		2	Butten, John	5	3	2		
Lackey, Thomas	1	2	4			Beatey, James	1		2			Clampet, James	1	2	3		
Lackey, George	1	1	4			Burten, Edward	1	1	5			Carson, Andw	1	1	2		1
Lackey, William, Ser	1		3			Bailey, Thomas	1	2	3		5	Caiton, Stephen	3	2	4		
Lackey, George, Ser	2	1	2			Boone, Thomas	2	3	2			Duncan, Isaac	1	2	4		
Leach, William	1	1	2		2	Belt, Benjamin	1	1	2			Donaldson, William	2	2	4		
Montgomery, John	1		1			Bell, Thomas	2	1	5			Dyson, Barton	2	1	6		
Milsaps, Joseph	2		3			Boone, John	2	3	3			Erwin, Robert	1	4	3		
Meadows, Daniel	1	1	2			Boone, Hezekiah	1	1	1			Erwin, Samuel	1	2	2		
Meadows, Daniel, Jur	1	1	2			Cooper, John	1		1			Erwin, William	2		2		
Meadows, John	1	1	6			Callihan, James	1	1	2			Evans, James	1		2		
Milsaps, Thomas	1	2	3			Campbell, Collin	2		6			Evans, Zacheriah	1	2	2		1
McHenry, Archabeld	1	1	3			Callihan, John	1	2	6			Evans, Ann	1		6		
McEwin, Daniel	1	2	5			Curent, John	1	3	1			Gipson, James	1	1	1		
McHargue, William	1	4	1			Clegit, Henry	1	3	4			Gaither, Jeremiah	1				
Madows, John, Jur	1					Carney, David	1	1	2			Gaither, John	2	1	5		
McCurdey, John	1	2	7			Decker, George	1	3	2			Gaither, Burges	2		2		3
Madows, Randolph	1					Dobson, Benjamin	4	3	7			Holeman, Isaac	1	2	4		
McClelland, John	3		2		2	Dobbins, John	1				6	Holeman, James	1	1	2		1
Melsaps, William	1					Dobson, Robert	1		1			Hays, Solomon	2	3	1		
Nesbitt, John Maxwell	2	1	2			Allison, Wm	1	4	3			Huston, Christopher	2	3	4		6
Poin, Thomas	1	1	1			Ellis, Samuel	1		2			Jacobs, Zacheriah	1	3	3		
Patterson, James	1	2	1			Ellis, Joshua	1	8	5			Jacobs, Edward	1	2	3		
Queene, Francis	1	3	4			Ellis, Zepheniah	1	3	6			Lovlace, Charles	1	2	3		5
Robison, William	1		1			Ellis, Samuel	1	3	3			Mitchell, Andrew	1	2	5		9
Reavs, Henry	1	2	4			Grigory, James	1	3	4			Marlow, Thomas	3		1		7
Shaw, John	2	3	7			Greene, John	2		2			McCord, James	1	3	6		
Sloan, Archabeld	1		2			Greene, Isaac	1	3	2			Maddin, James	1		1		
Stephenson, James	2		2		2	Holms, Hubbart	1		2			Martin, William	1	1	3		20
Smith, John (Miller)	2	3	5			Holms, Francis	1	1	4			Nelson, Jeremiah	1	7	3		
Smith, John, Ser	3		3			Hardin, William	1		6		5	Nichols, Becket	1	1	4		
Stephenson, James, Jur	1	5	2		2	Hantsman, John	1		1			Patrick, Jeremiah	2	1	2		
Sharpe, Joseph	1	4	2		3	Hoy, Marcis	2		2		2	Pugh, John	1	3	2		
Taylor, Thomas	1	4	2			Holms, Robert	1	1	5			Riley, James	1		1		
Upchurch, George	1	4	2			Henry, David	1	3	4		1	Riers, David	1	1	4		
Willis, James	1	2	2			Holms, James	1	1	1			Read, James	1	2	1		2
Wableton, Joseph	1	1	4			Harris, Aron	1	2	2			Sergeler, Phillip	2		1		
Whitaker, Mark	2	2	4			Hardin, Jeane	2		5		5	Swann, Zepheniah	1		5		
Baker, Wonsley	1	2	1			Hendly, John	1		3			Smith, John	1	1	1		
Ball, Daniel	1	1	1			Kerney, David	1	2	2			Summers, Thomas	1	2	2		
Ball, William	1	2	1			King, John	2	3	7		2	Speaks, Charles	1	3	2		
Cast, James	1	3	5			King, Richard	1		2		6	Tucker, Rubey	1	6	2		
Cast, Elijah	1	1	1			Larde, John	1		2			Tagard, Andw	2	4	6		
Camp, John	1	4	1			Lochrey, William	1	2	2			Wooton, George	2	2	5		
Campbell, William	1	1	1			Lock, George, Jur	1	1	1			Willis, George	2	1	6		
Crabtree, Samuel	1	1	4			Lard, Nathaniel	1	2	2			Webb, Caleb	2	3	4		
Campbell, Elizabeth		1	2			Lock, George	2	2	3			Webb, George	1	2	3		
Campbell, Pennifull	1	1	1			McGuire, Thomas	2	5	7		1	Young, Thomas	2	3	2		13
Dumbush, John	1	2	2			McCrary, James	3	1	7			Young, William	2	3	1		1
Felps, John	2	2	2			McHarge, James	1	4	3			Archabeld, Thomas	1	3	7		3
Felps, William	1		2			Morris, Thomas	1	1	2			Archabeld, Mathew	2		4		
Fletcher, Reuben	1	3	3		2	McConnell, William	3	2	4			Armstrong, John	2		4		1
Gipson, James	1	1	2			McConnell, Alexander	1	3	2		1	Allen, Drury	1	3	8		
Gipson, Joseph	1	1	3			McConnell, John	1	2	4		1	Bell, Zadock	1		3		1
Hunt, John	3	1	4			Means, Alexander	1		2			Beggarly, Thomas	1		4		
Henderson, Samuel	2	4	4			Nichols, Jacob	3		2		12	Beggarly, David	2	2	3		
Hughes, John	1	3	4			Nichols, Joseph	2	3	2		1	Bell, David	2	4	3		1
Hughey, Lewis	1	1	4			Nichols, Joshua	1		1		1	Bell, Thomas	2		2		
Johnston, William	1	5	2			Nichols, John	1	1	1			Beggarly, Benja	1	1	4		1
Jolley, Charles	1		1			Praither, Bazil	3	4	4			Bowman, Hugh	2	1	3		1
Jolley, William	1	2	1			Peeler, Richard	2		3			Baird, Thomas	1	2	3		1
Lunsford, Normond	1	1	1			Peeler, Jeremiah	1		4			Bone, William	1	4	4		2
Luper, Daniel	1	2	2			Praither, William	1	2	2			Baird, David	1	2	4		
Morgan, Theophilus, Ser	1	2	2			Reed, John	4	1	4		1	Baird, William	1		1		7
Morgan, Martin	1	1	3			Kinsay, Rodger	1		2			Bowman, John	1		1		
Morgan, Reuben	1	2	3		2	Reaves, Edmond	2	3	3			Chambers, James	1		2		3
Morgan, Theophilus, Jur	1	2	3		1	Remington, Richard	1	2	3								

SALISBURY DISTRICT, IREDELL COUNTY—Continued.

NAME OF HEAD OF FAMILY.	Free white males of 16 years and upward, including heads of families	Free white males under 16 years	Free white females, including heads of families	All other free persons	Slaves
Caldwell, David	2	4	2		14
Caldwell, Andrew	1	1	1		1
Chambers, Arthur	2	5	3		1
Chambers, Henry	1	3	3		9
Erwin, Stephen	1	1	2		
Campbell, Mathew	2	1	2		
Erwin, James	1		5		
Allison, Adam	2	3	4		6
Allison (Widow)	1	1	3		2
Allison, Richard	1	2	3		5
Allison, Theophilus	1	2	2		4
Allison, Thomas	2	2	6		
Erwin, John	1	1	3		1
Erwin, William			3		
Freeland, Andrew			3		1
Ferril, John		1	5		
Gidions, Bosle		4	4		
Gordon, Robert		3	3		
Gaither, Nicholas		4	1		1
Gay, James	2	1	3		
Gipson, Margret	2	1	3		
Houpt (Widow)	1	3	2		
Hall, William	1		4		
Hogshead, David	4		7		
Hall, William, Jur	1		3		
Hair, Robert	1		3		
Hall, Rev'd Jas			4		9
Hall, Alexander			2		4
Hall, John			3		1
Hall, Thomas		3	7		5
Hall, James, Senr	1		2		
Hawill, Jerard	1	1	2		
Hall, Hugh	2	2	6		2
Hall, James, Jur	1	4	2		3
Hall, Andw	1		2		
Eston, Henry		1	4		
Hair, Daniel	5		2		
Kilpatrick, Joseph	2	4	4		
Kilpatrick, Andw	1	4	5		
Lesenbey, Joshua	1	2	1		1
Lesenbey, Henry	1	1	3		1
Love, Samuel	1	1	4		
Long, Samuel	2	2	2		
Lewis, Daniel	1	2	4		
Lesenbey, Thomas	1	2	5		
Mathews, Musentine	1	4	3		3
McKinzey, Andrew	3	1	5		
McKee, William	1	3	3		4
McWhorter, John	3		3		
Murdock, John	3	3	3		5
McGuire, Patrick	2	5	3		
Morrison, Andw	4	3	5		1
Murdock, James	1		3		2
McHenry, John	1	1	6		1
McClelland, John	1	3	4		1
Morrison, John	2	6	3		1
McKee, Alexander	1		1		1
Murdock, John, Jur	1		1		
Mathews, Robert	2	2	8		
Nesbitt, John	2	4	5		3
Perter, Thomas	2		8		1
Pithey, John H	1		1		
Baker, Jeremiah	1	1	3		
Rosbrough (Widow)	3	1	1		4
Roby (Widow)		5			
Robison, George			3		
Stuart, James	2		1		4
Steele, Nenien	2	5			1
Summers, John	1	3	3		4
Simenton, William	4	3	4		15
Scott, John	1	2	6		
Simenton, John	1	1	2		
Sloan, Fergus	2		3		3
Stephenson, Joseph	1	1	2		
Sawyers, Edward	1				
Sloan, Fergus, Jur	1		2		2
Thornton, Theophilus	1		3		
Tucker, David	1	3	6		
Taylor, James	1	1	5		
Vandever, Mathew	1	2	4		
Vickers, John	1	3	1		
Wasson, Joseph	2		1		
Wasson, Samuel	1	3	2		
Wilson, James	1	1	1		
Wilson, Thomas	1	1	1		1
Wilson, James, Jur	1		1		1
Watt, William	3		4		5
Wilson, John	3		3		1
Wilson, Alexander	1	1	1		1
Johnston, Francis	1		2		

SALISBURY DISTRICT, MECKLENBURG COUNTY.

NAME OF HEAD OF FAMILY.	Free white males of 16 years and upward, including heads of families	Free white males under 16 years	Free white females, including heads of families	All other free persons	Slaves
Allison, Robert	1	3	4		3
Allison, Archabeld	3	1	3		
Allison, David	1				
Alexander, Wm, Jr	2	1	3		
Alexander, Ezra, Senr	3	1	3		
Elga, Francis	1	2	1		
Allison, Joseph	1		3		
Allen, John	3	3	4		
Alexander, Able	2	2	2		
Alexander, Phenias	1	3	4		
Berryhill, Wm	1		4		1
Barnet, Robert, Jur	1	1	1		2
Bryan, Mathew	2	5	4		
Brown, Patrick	4		2		
Beaty, John, Jur	1	2	4		9
Beaty, John, Senr	2	3	5		
Baker, George	1	4	3		
Buam, James	1	2	2		
Brown, David	3	1	3		
Berryhill, John	3	3	3		
Clark, Jessey	2	3	2		2
Davis, George	1	2	2		
Cooper, Doctor	1	1	2		
Clarke, Robert R	1	3	3		
Clarke, William	3		3		3
Campbell, Robert	1	1	6		
Cathey, George, Senr	3	1	3		5
Cathey, Esther	2	3	5		
Cathey, Alexander	2	1	3		
Cummins, John	1		2		
Cooper, John	2		2		
Carson, John	1				
Castillo, Miles	1	2	4		
Carroll, Joseph	3	2	2		3
Cathren, Robert	1	4	5		
Corcham, William	1	3	3		
Clayton, James				1	
Carroll, James	1		2		
Cattor, George	1		1		
Currethers, Edmond	1	1	1		
Coreham, Robert	2	1	3		
Freemon, Michael	1		4		1
Freemon, David	3	2	5		
Freemon, Reuben	1		1		
Griffey, Aron	1		3		
Gibbeney, Nicholas	1	2	4		6
Greene, John	2	2	4		2
Graham, Majr Joseph	1	1	2		8
Graham, George	1	2	2		4
Graham, James				1	
Hucheson, John	1		1		
Hern, Jesse	1	3	4		
Hucheson, George	2	1	1		1
Hargrove, Thompson	1	2	5		
Hargrove, John	2	1	3		
Hunter, John, Ser	1	2	2		6
Hunter, Robert	1	3	2		3
Hogden, Nehemiah	1		2		
Haynes, David	3	2	3		2
Hepworth, John	1		5		
Hann, Margret & Son					2
Hanks, Thomas	1	1	1		
Isler, Nicholas	2	1	2		
Jackson, Shadrick	2	7	1		
Kirkes, Thomas	1	2	1		
Kerr (Widow)		1	3		1
Kithcart, John	1	2	1		
Love, John	2	1	2		
Love, Samuel	1		1		
McCord, John	4	1	4		1
McCord, Robert	2	1	4		
McClarey, Wm	2				
McDowell, John	1	3	4		5
McClarey, Michael	2	2	1		3
McDowell, Esther	1		3		
McKinley, William	1	4	7		
McKnight, Robert	1	1	8		
McKnight, James	1	1	1		
McNeely, James	1	4	3		
Moore, Joseph, Ser	3	1	5		
Montgomery, James	1	4	3		
McNeely, Andw	1		1		
McClure, John, Jur	4	1	2		
McClure (Widw)	1	1	2		
Cleffland (Widow)			4		
McKee, Andw			2		6
McKee, John	1	2	5		
McGee (Widow)	3	1	3		
McCormack, William	1	1	2		
Mariner, John	1		1		
McClure, Moses, Jur					1
McClure, Thomas, Jur	1		1		
McDonald, David					1
Nation, Thomas	1	3	4		
Null, James, Ser	1	2	6		
Nicholson, John, Senr	2	1	5		2
Nicholson, George	1		2		
Owens, James	1	4	5		
Van Pelt, Simon	2	5	5		
Pierson, Henry	3		4		
Parks, Hugh	1	2	4		2
Porter, John	1	3	4		
Plummer, Zepheniah	1		2		
Plummer, Thomas				1	
Reed, James, Senr	3	2	2		
Reed, James, Jur	1		2		
Reed, James (middee)	1	4	2		1
Reed, Robert	2	1	2		1
Reed, Thomas	1		2		
Reed, John	1	4	4		
Sloan, John	1	1	3		
Sloan, James	1	2	3		1
Sumter, John	2	1	1		5
Spratt, James	1	1	4		3
Stinson, John	1	3	2		2
Stinson, Michael	1			1	
Shields, David					1
Tagert, James	2		2		
Wilson, John	3	2	2		5
Walker, John	2	3	4		
Walker, William	1	2	4		
Wilkeson, George	1		2		
Verner, John	1		5		
Mcfalls, John				1	
Alexander, Judith	1	1	1		
Alexander, James	1		3		
Bigham, John	2	3	3		4
Bigham, James, Sr	1	1	3		
Bigham, Robert	1	1	2		
Bigham, Samuel, Sr	2		1		
Bigham, Samuel, Jur	1	4	4		
Bigham, William, Jur	1	2	4		
Bigham, James, Jur	2	2	2		
Bigham, Hugh	1		1		
Barnet, Robert, Senr	1	3	4		
Barnet, John, Ser	1		3		1
Barnet, John, Jur	1		3		
Blackwood, James	2	2	4		1
Brownfield, Robert	1		3		
Brownfield, William	1	3	3		
Brown, Richard				1	
Cathey, Andw	1		1		
Cathey, George	1		1		5
Carruthers, James	2	3	2		
Carruthers, Robert	1	2	5		1
Carruthers, John	1	3	2		
Calhoone, Charles	1	1	3		3
Calhoon, Samuel	1	3	5		9
Cheek, Silas	1				
Calhoon, George			1		
Davis, Walter	3	4	5		8
Davis, John L	3	1	2		
Dunn, William	1	2	4		
Darnell, William	1	3	5		
Darnell, Joseph	1	3	5		6
Dinkins, John	2	3	3		12
Ferguson, Thomas	1		1		1
Ferguson, William	1				
Gilmore, William	1		3		
Gilmore, Margret	1	2	3		
Gillan, John	1		3		
Greer, Thomas	2	2	3		5
Greer, James	2	2	3		2
Herron, Andw	2		2		
Hart, James			2		
Hart, Joseph	1	1	1		
Hart, David	1	2	3		
Harris, Hugh	1	2	3		
Herron, Hugh	1	2	3		5
Herren, Allen	1	2	3		
Herron, Samuel				1	1
Erwin, Robert	2	2	6		3
Knox, James	1		1		
Knox, Samuel, Jur	1		2		2
Knox, Mathew	2		3		5
Knox, Samuel, Senr	3		3		9
Knox, John	1		2		2
Kindrick, John	1	3	2		2
Kindrick, William	2		5		12
McClarey, Robert	2		5		6
McCormick, Robert			4		6
McCrum, Rachel		3	3		1
McKee, Robert	3	3	6		1

SALISBURY DISTRICT, MECKLENBURG COUNTY—Continued.

NAME OF HEAD OF FAMILY.	Free white males of 16 years and upward, including heads of families.	Free white males under 16 years.	Free white females, including heads of families.	All other free persons.	Slaves.
McKee, James	1	3	2		8
McGill, Thomas				1	
McKee (Widow)	1	4	7		
Maxwell (Widow)	2	4	4		1
Null (Widow)	1	1	4		3
Neely, John	2	3	7		6
Neely, Thomas, Jur	1	4	2		2
Null, James, Jur	1		2		1
Neely, Samuel	2		2		3
Neely, Moses	2	1	4		3
Nicholson, John, Jur				1	
Porter, William	1	4	5		4
Porter, Alexander	1	1	7		
Porter, Joseph	1	1	4		
Porter, Hugh	1	1	1		
Porter, James	1	2	4		4
Patterson, William	2	2	2		
Price, Isaac	4	4	3		7
Howe, Joseph				1	
Price, John	2	1	3		13
Reed, Joseph	1		2		
Ramey, Thomas	1		4		
Robison, Richard	1		2		1
Robison, David	1	2	1		
Robison, Mathew	1	4	5		
Ramey, William	1		2		
Ramey, William, Senr	2	1	2		
Smart, George	2		1		4
Smart, Littleberry	1				2
Smart, Elijah	2	1	2		
Smart, Francis	2	1	2		9
Swann, Joseph	1	4	3		
Speers, James	1	3	6		
Scott, James	1	1	4		
Shepperd, William				1	
Thomas, Benja	2		2		9
Taylor, John	2	4	2		4
Vance, David	3	3	3		
Whitsitt, John	2	4	3		2
West, Martin	1	5	2		
Walker, John	1	2	4		
Wilson, Robert	6		2		
Wilson, Zachias	2		4		
Wilson, Isaac	1	1			2
Wilson, William	1	1	1		
Wilson, Joseph	1	3	3		
Wilson, James	1				
Withers, Reuben	2	1	5		4
Yurce, Francis	1	3	2		
Alexander, Isaac, Esqr	1				1
Bigham, John	1	5	2		
Barnhart, Henry	1	2	3		
Cook, Isaac	2	2	3		8
Cooper, Joseph				1	
Emerson, Henry	1	1	1		
Elliott, Samuel	2	3	4		1
Elliott, Thomas	3		2		2
Henderson, Dor Thomas	1	1	6		2
Hutcheson, William	2	4	2		3
Isham, John	1		3		
Holt, William			1		
Kennaday, James	2	1	4		
Kennaday, Esther	3		1		1
Kennaday, Samuel				1	
Lefeever, Joseph	2		2		
Luckey, William	1	3	3		1
Mason, Richard	2	4	2		5
McCombs, Samuel	1	1	1		3
McCulloch, William	2				1
McClary (Widow)	1	1	2		
Martin, Thomas	1	2	1		
McNabb, Duncan	1	1	3		
McKee, David	2	5	3		3
Martin, Ephraim	1	1	2		
Cliver, George	1	2	3		
Polk, William	1		1		21
Polk, Thomas	5		4		47
Polk, Charles	2	2	1		9
Pattison, William	2	1	3		5
Riley, John	1	3	4		
Rice, George	1	1	3		
Robison, John	1	1	6		
Stuart (Widow)			2		
Springs, John	3	3	5		50
Wisehart, Joseph	1		2		1
Wright, William				1	
Alexander, Darkus	3	1	3		8
Alexander, Wm, Ser	3		2		11
Alexander, Ezekiel, Senr	3	2	6		
Alexander, David	1				
Alexander, Ezekel, Jur	1		1		
Alexander, Daniel	1	2	2		
Alexander, Elijah	1	2	2		
Alexander, Elias, Jur	1	1	2		
Alexander, Capt Thomas	1	3	6		
Alexander, Dor James	1		1		1
Alexander, John	1		4		

NAME OF HEAD OF FAMILY.	Free white males of 16 years and upward, including heads of families.	Free white males under 16 years.	Free white females, including heads of families.	All other free persons.	Slaves.
Alexander, Capt (B) William	2	4	2		9
Alexander, Charles	1	4	3		
Alexander, Benjamin	2		1		
Alexander, George, Jur	1	1	1		
Allen, Agnes		1	2		6
Allen, George, Senr			1		1
Alexander, Ezekieh, Esqr	4	2	3		3
Alexander, Capt Andrew	2				9
Bailey, Richard	1	3	3		
Batey, Samuel	1	3	4		4
Barlow, Amrose	1	2	4		
Braley, Thos C.				1	
Batey, William	1	1	1		
Balch, Thomas	1	3	3		
Campbell, Alexander	1	1	2		2
Carney, Patrick				1	
Davis, Samuel	1		1		4
Fipps (Widow)			7		
Daker, Christopher	3	2	4		
Goforth, William	2	2	6		
Graham, Samuel	1				1
Gipson (Widow)	2	2	4		
Houston, Henry	1		2		1
Henderson, Cairns	3		1		1
Houston, William	2	2	2		
Henderson, Andrew	1	1	3		
Johnston, William	3	3	5		2
Johnston, David	1	1	3		
Kennaday, David	2		2		
Kewer, Henry	1	2	2		
Lemons, Robert	1	3	2		
Luckey, Robert	1	3	3		
Mitchell, John	1		1		
McGee, John	2	2	1		
Mitchell, Robert	3		3		2
McCulloch (Widow)		1	2		
McGintey, Alexander	1		1		2
Montgomery, John	1		2		
Montgomery, Robert	1	3	5		
McClure, Thos Senr	2	1	1		
McKee, Wm, Junr	1		1		1
McDowell, Archabeld				1	
Miller, Samuel				1	
Neely, Hugh	2	3	3		
Neely, Thomas				1	
McCall, James	2	2	4		
Orr, Nathan, Senr	3	1	6		
Orr, Wm	1	1	7		9
Orr, James (Jockey)	1	4	3		6
Orr, Nathan, Jur	1	3	1		1
Orr, James (white)	1	2	2		
Parks, John, Senr	3	3	4		3
Parks, David	4	2	3		4
Parks, John, Junr	1		2		3
Parks, Samuel	1	1	2		
Reed, George	1	4	2		
Richey, David	2	1	5		
Richey, John	1		3		
Ross, George	2		3		
Robison, John	1	1	2		
Robison, Robert, Senr	1		3		
Robison, Robert, Jur	1	2	7		
Robison, Moses	1		1		
Robison, David	3	1	1		
Robison, James, Senr	1		1		2
Robison, Wm & Richard	2		3		
Rogers, David	1		2		
Shields, William	1		3		
Stuart, David	1	3	4		
Strachback, Daniel	1		1		
Sample, Samuel	2	1	3		
Starling, James				1	
Tasey, Alexander	1	1	2		
Wise, Thomas	2	2	5		
Wallace, Ezekel					4
Wallace, Mathew	1	1	2		
Wallace, William	1	1	3		1
Wallace, George	1	1	3		
Wallace, Alexander	3		1		
Wiley, William	3		3		2
Wiley, John	1	4	3		
Williamson, Benjamin	1	1	3		
Watson, William	1	1	4		
Wiley, Joseph	1		1		
Alexander, Col George	3	1	5		11
Archabeld, Rev. Robert	1	1	3		4
Alexander, Abraham	1	1	2		
Alexander, William	2	3	5		1
Alexander, Moses	3	7	2		1
Alexander, Benjamin, Jur	2	2	5		
Alexander, Moses, Jur	1				
Alexander, Andw	1	3			6

NAME OF HEAD OF FAMILY.	Free white males of 16 years and upward, including heads of families.	Free white males under 16 years.	Free white females, including heads of families.	All other free persons.	Slaves.
Alexander, Hezekiah	1		2		1
Alexander, Abijah	2	1	5		
Bouchfriend, George	1		2		
Brown, James	1	2	3		1
Black, William	2	1	3		7
Buckhanon, Robert	3	2	4		
Cowden (Widow)	1		2		
Caldwell, Charles	1		1		2
Caldwell, Capt David	1				
Craighead, Robert	2	4	3		4
Clark, Eliner	1		1		
Doherty, James	2	3	1		1
Edmiston, John	1	2	4		
Giles, Edward, Esqr	4	2	4		
Gardner, James	1	1	6		2
Gilmore (Widow)	1	3	3		2
Gilmore, Nathaniel	2	1	5		
Gardner, William	2	2	4		
Gardner, John	1	1	2		
Galliway, Thomas	1	5	2		
Garrison, David	1	3	5		
Giles, Nathaniel	1	1	3		
Hunter, Henry	2	7	3		2
Hunter, John	1		3		1
Hope, Robert	3	5	4		6
Irwin, Robert	1	2	2		1
Kelugh, Samuel	2	3	4		3
Meek, Adam	2		2		
Meek, Moses	1	2	5		
McClain, Joseph	2				
McCandeless, John	1	1	2		3
McCay, Michael	1		3		
McCallister, John	1	2	4		
Meek, Robert	1	1	1		
Newman, John	1	3	3		
Query, Alexander	3	2	4		
Reed, John	1	3	4		
Robison, Alexander	2		2		
Russell, James	1	1	3		
Pickens, William	1				2
Smith, Col Robert	1	1	3		15
Sharpe, Ezekel	2		7		3
Smith, James	1	1	2		
Sloan, John	1	2	2		
Sloan, James, Senr	1	1	3		
Sloan, James, Jur	1	1	2		
Sloan, Thomas	1	2	2		
Simmons, William	1	2	4		
Shelby, Evan	1	1	6		4
Strain, Dor Wm	1				
Simmons, Thomas	1	3	5		
Wallace, James	2		3		6
Wilson, Zachias, Senr	1	1	1		
Wallace, John	1	2	1		1
Woods, John	1		2		
Young, Joseph	2		7		5
Young, William	1	3	8		2
Montgomery, David	1	3	3		
Winings, Peteter	1	1	2		1
Alexander, John Mn, Esqr	3		1		16
Alexander, William, Senr	3	1	3		
Atkins, Samuel	1	2	5		
Alexander, Ezekel	1	3	4		2
Abernathey, Miles	1	2	4		
Aldridg, Isham	1				
Aldridg, William	1	3	2		
Bradshaw, Josiah	2	1	5		1
Beach, Justice	2	3	4		
Blackwood, William	1	2	5		2
Bradley (Widow)	1	1	4		
Blackwood, Thomas	1		3		1
Cannon, John	1	3	1		
Clark, James	1				
Cannon, Margret	1	1	2		2
Cannon, Joseph	1	1	5		
Cannon, James, Senr	1	1	1		
Crocket, Robert	2		7		
Dunn, Andrew, Senr	2		2		2
Dunn, Robert	1	1	2		
Dunn, James	1		2		
Dunn, John	1		1		
Doherty (Widow)	1		4		2
Davidson, John (Mercht)	2	1	3		9
Ewart, Joseph	2	3	4		
Elliot, George	3	3	3		3
Elliot, William				1	
Frazer, Joseph	1	4	3		
Frazer, Samuel	1		2		
Frazer, James	1				
Ferrill, John	1		1		
Ferrill, Gabriel	1	2	1		
Flenniker, Charles	1		2		
Gailbraith, Martha	1	3	2		
Garrison, John	1	1	2		1
Gibson, John	1	3	4		2
Henderson (Widow)			2	4	

SALISBURY DISTRICT, MECKLENBURG COUNTY—Continued.

NAME OF HEAD OF FAMILY.	Free white males of 16 years and upward, including heads of families.	Free white males under 16 years.	Free white females, including heads of families.	All other free persons.	Slaves.
Henry, James	1	4	3		
Hudson, Richard	1	2	5		
Hammond, Mathias	1	1	4		
Hipp, Stephen	2	1	3		
Hipp, Valentine	1	2	1		
Jimeson, Robert	1	1	2		
Johnston, Nathaniel	1	3	5		
Jemison, Arthur	1	4	4		
Jemison, Thomas	1		2		
Erwin, Edward	1	1	5		
Johnston, Isaac	1	4	4		1
Johnston, John	1	2	4		1
Kerr, Joseph	1	2	6		
Knox, Capt James	2	1	3		15
Kerr, Robert	1	3	4		
Kerr (Widw)	1	2	3		3
Lewing, William	3	1	5		
Lewing, Andrew	1		4		
Lather, Robert				1	
Long, Capt John	3	2	3		1
McClennahan, Reuben	1	2	2		
McClure, Capt Mathew	3		2		6
McIntire, James	1		2		1
McCoy, Beaty	4	5	3		5
Moore, Joseph	2	3	5		2
McClure, John, Junr	1	2	4		
McCracken, James	2	2	7		
Maxwell, Ann	1		4		
Montieth, Jane	3		4		2
Montieth, Nathaniel	1				
Moore, James	1	3	6		
McClure, William	3	2	3		
Moore (Widow)	2		3		3
Mullen, Harris	1	1	3		
McGinn (Widow)	3		2		
McClure, Moses (Thos Son)	1	2	3		
Moffitt, William	1		1		
Nation, John	2	2	6		
Nighten, John	1	1	3		
Patten, Charles	2		1		1
Parker, Isaiah	1	4	6		
Peoples, John	1	2	1		
Robison, Mathew	1	2	3		
Robison, George	1	1	2		
Robison, Alexander	1	2	2		
Russell, David	1	2	6		3
Ramsey, William	2	3	4		
Raphil, John	1	1	2		
Stephenson, Richard	3		1		
Sharpe, James	1	1	1		3
Sharpe, John	5	3	2		1
Steele, Peter	1	1	2		
Sample (Widow)	1	1	6		
Sullivan, Patrick	1	1	3		1
Sullivan, Jeremiah	1		1		
Thompson, John	1	1	6		
Thompson, Gideion	2		2		2
Thompson (Widow)	4	1	3		
Todd, William	3		4		
Todd, Adam	1	2	1		
Todd, Joseph	2		2		1
Todd, John	2	1	6		
Williams, Billy	1	2	2		
Woods, Robert	1	2	3		
Woods, Mathew	2	1	1		
Watkins, James	1	2	2		
Alexander, Amos	1	4	3		6
Alexander, Moses	2		1		
Alexander, Aron	2	3	4		1
Alexander, David	5		4		2
Alexander, Daniel	1	1	2		
Alexander, Joel	1		1		
Alexander, Isaac				1	
Bryson, Hugh	2	4	4		
Bell, John	1				
Black, Thomas	1	4	5		
Berry, Capt Richard	4		6		
Bailey, Francis	1	1	5		2
Blythe, Samuel		2		1	1
Blythe, Richard	1		2		
Bell, Walter	1				
Brodinax, John	1	3	3		16
Currey, James	1	3	4		
Caldwell, William	1	4	2		4
Cathey, Capt Archabeld	1	1	3		11
Cochran, Benjamin	1		1		
Conner, James	3				4
Cooke, James	2	5	4		6
Carson, Jane			2		
Conner, William	1	2	1		
Doherty, David	2	1	5		
Davidson, Thomas	1				
Davidson, Samuel	1	2	1		
Davidson, Majr John	2	2	6		26
Duck, John	1	1	3		
Duck, Simon	1	2	3		

NAME OF HEAD OF FAMILY.	Free white males of 16 years and upward, including heads of families.	Free white males under 16 years.	Free white females, including heads of families.	All other free persons.	Slaves.
Duck, George	1	4	2		
Duck, Abel	1	2	3		
Duck, Absalom	1	3	1		
Duck, George, Jur					1
Davis, David	1	1	5		
Davis, Daniel	1				
Evitts, William	2	1	3		
Forsyth, Robert	3	3	4		
Gillaspie, Joseph	3		2		1
Gillaspie, James	1	2	2		2
Gilmore, Patrick	1	7	1		
Givvins, John, Senr	2		2		
Givvins, John, Junr	1	2	2		
Givvins, Edward	2				11
Givvins, Jno Ruther	1	4	3		
Garrison, Samuel	1	1	2		4
Graham, William	3	7	1		4
Harper, William	1	2	3		3
Henderson, John	1	1	1		3
Henderson, John, Jur	1	1	6		
Henderson, William, Senr	2	2	2		3
Henderson, William, Jur	2	4	4		6
Hill, William	1	4	6		
Hansill, John	1	3	2		
Hampton, Patrick	3	1	4		9
Henry, Capt Henry	2	4	6		
Harris, Majr Thos	2		5		7
Hunt, Turner	1	1	6		15
Hunneycut, Howell	1	1	1		
Hamilton, William					1
Jetton (Widow)			1		1
Jetton, Lewis	1	4	5		3
Johnston, John	3	4	1		
Irwin, Samuel	1	1	1		1
Kelly, Thomas					1
Knox, Allison	2		6		
Latta, Joseph	1	1	5		
Lucas, Hugh	1	3	5		
Lowrance, Michael	1	1	2		
Jetton, Abraham	1	1	1		2
Morrow, John	2	2	2		
Morrow, Robert	1	2	3		
Morrow, John, Jur	1	2	2		
Maxwell, James	1	4	2		
Maxwell, Benjamin	2	1	3		
McDugal, Thomas	1				
McCorkle, Thomas	2		2		6
Meek, James, Esqr	1		3		
Meek, James, Jur	1	1	2		
Montieth, Henry	2		2		
Montieth, Samuel	1	1	4		
Martin, Thomas	1	1	2		
McNair, James	1	2	2		
Osborn, John	1		4		
peele, James, Ser	2	1	1		5
peele, James, Jur	1	1	2		
Potts, Robert	1	5	3		10
Potts, Jonathan	2	1	7		1
price, James	1	3	5		
price, John	1		4		
price, Robert	1		1		
Sloan, David	1	4	2		
Sloan, John	1	1	3		
Clark, Benjamin	1	1	4		
Hutchison, David	1	1	2		
Shelds, Robert	1		1		
Clark, Joseph	1		2		
Wilson, Samuel, Senr	1	1	3		
Sloan, Robert	2		2		
Stanford, Samuel	2	1	4		
Stanford, Isaac	1		1		
Smith, David	1				5
Smith, James					1
Torrence, Hugh	1	1	5		12
Tucker, William	2	1	1		
Taylor, Elijah	1	3	3		
Wilson, David	1	4	2		1
Wilson, Benja	1	1	2		3
Wilson, Samuel, Jur	1				9
Wilson, John	1				1
Wilson, Joseph	1				
Wise, John	2	4	4		
Wise, William	1				
Walls, Abin				1	
McCong, Thomas	1				
Wilie, John	1		4		
Wilie, William	1	2	3		
Wilson, William	1				
Waddle, William	1	3	4		1
Wilson (Widow)	1	1	2		
Williams, Jas L.				1	
Emmerson, James	1	1	4		4
Christenberry, Nicholas	2	1	3		
Christenberry, Moses	1		1		
Wilson, John, Junr	1				
Andrews, Moses	1	1	2		

NAME OF HEAD OF FAMILY.	Free white males of 16 years and upward, including heads of families.	Free white males under 16 years.	Free white females, including heads of families.	All other free persons.	Slaves.
Andrews, Robert	2	2	7		
Anderson, Robert	2		5		
Alexander, Capt Stephen	2	1	7		2
Alexander, Josiah	1	3	2		2
Brown, Benja	2	2	3		1
Brown, Samuel	1	2	2		
Bradford, Mary	2	1	3		
Benson, Thomas	1	2	2		
Benson, Robert	1		2		
Bell, James	2	2	2		
Bradford, James				1	
Bowman, Samuel	1	1	5		3
Bartley, Daniel	1	1	6		
Carrigan, James	2		4		2
Cooper, John	1	2	2		
Copeland, Dennis	1	2	3		
Casey, Mary	1		1		
Carruthers, John	3	3	3		
Davis, Isaac	1		2		
Davis, John, Senr	2		3		
Davis, David	1		2		
Flemming, Mitchell	1	2	2		
Farr, Margt	2		2		6
Gilleland, John	2		4		
Gilmore, Archabeld	1	1	1		
Gillaspie, James	1	1	4		
Houstin, John	1	3	4		1
Houstin, Capt Archabeld	2		1		3
Houstin, David	1		2		2
Hamilton, Hugh	1	1	2		
Harris, Robert, Esqr	2	1	4		11
Henderson, John	2		2		
Harris, Oliver	1		2		1
Harris, Robert	1	1	6		1
Harris, James	2	1	4		1
Irwin, Thomas	1	2	3		
Lewis, Benjamin	1	2	1		4
Moffit, Martha	3		3		2
McCulloch, John	1	2	6		
Morton, Samuel	4		1		
Martin, Robert	2	1	3		
McCown, Margt		1	3		1
McCabb, James	1	3	3		1
Null, John	1	1	1		
Null, James	2	4	6		
Pruie, Reese	1		1		13
Penney, John	2	1	2		
Penney, William	1	3	4		
Pickens, Capt Samuel	1	4	4		5
Ross, William	1	4	3		
Ross, Joseph	1	2	2		2
Ross, George	1	2	1		
Stevenson, Jas	1	2	5		
Steele, John	1		2		2
Templeton, David	1	4	3		2
Tanner, James	1	3	3		
Wells, William	1	2	1		
Wilson, John	1	1	5		
Allison, John, Esqr	3	1	3		5
Armstrong, John	1		1		
Armstrong, John, Jur				1	
Alexander, Francis	1	1	2		
Baker, John	1	5	4		3
Berry, George	1		2		
Baker, Christopher	2	3	3		3
Baker, Joshua	1	1	3		
Biggers, Robert	1		2		
Barns, William	1	5	4		
Booker, Joseph	1	2	5		
Campbell, Thomas	1		4		
Carruthers, Andw	3	1	8		1
Creaton, James	1		1		1
Cannon, James	1		1		3
Doherty, James			1		
Frazer, William	1	3	6		
Glover, Ezekel	1		2		
Glover, John	1			1	
Glover, William	1		1		
Gaseway, John	1	4	2		
Houston, Capt William	2	2	3		4
Holbrook, John	2		4		
Holbrooks, Caleb	1	2	5		
Holbrooks, William	1	3	1		
Houston, David	1	1	2		
Hall, Morgan	1	1	3		
Hosey, Jonathan	1		3		
Holbrook, Vaitch	1	2			
Kyles, James	1		2		
Lock, Francis	1	2	4		5
Lingo, Daniel	1	1	4		
McClartey, Archabeld	1		4		
McClartey, Alexander	2	1	4		
Means, John	3	2	2		4
Martin, James	2	3	2		
Martin (Widow)	1		2		
Morrison, William	1	1	3		1

SALISBURY DISTRICT, MECKLENBURG COUNTY—Continued.

NAME OF HEAD OF FAMILY.	Free white males of 16 years and upward, including heads of families.	Free white males under 16 years.	Free white females, including heads of families.	All other free persons.	Slaves.
McCray, William	1	2	5		1
Martin, Richard	1	4	5		
McKinley, David	1	2	3		
McKinley, John	2	1	2		
Murphey, John	1	1	5		
McRea, Arthur	1		3		
Martin, William	1	2	2		
Phifer, Col Caleb	1	1	6		19
Phifer, Capt Martin	1	2	4		16
Patton, Benjamin	2		2		
Patton, Samuel	2		3		
Patton, Joseph	1	3	1		
Patterson, Samuel	5	2	3		
Patterson, Alexander	2		4		3
Patterson, Robert	1	1	1		1
Phifer, Henry	1		2		
Pasinger, Thomas	1	2	2		1
Reese, Solomon	1		4		
Rogers, Joseph	1	3	4		3
Rogers, Moses	1	1	3		
Rogers, Thomas	1	2	1		
Rogers, James, Junr	1		2		
Rogers, Seth	1	3	1		
Ross, Francis	2	5	2		
Russell, David	1	2	1		1
Rogers, John	1	1	1		
Scannell, John	1		1		
Scales, John					1
Skitleton (Widow)	1	2	4		
Taylor, John	1	3	2		
Wallace, Ludwick	1	1	9		
Wallace, Jediah	1	1	1		
Wallace, John	1		1		
Wodington, John	1	1	2		
Goodman, Jacob	1	2	4		
Blackwelder, Charles	1	2	3		
Blackwelder, John	1	1	6		
Black, Thomas	1	2	2		
Bawyers, Adam	2		3		
Bryance, Henry, Senr	1				
Bryance, Henry, Junr	1		3		
Bryance, William	1	2	2		
Barnhart, Mathias	1	2	1		
Barnhart, George	1		2		
Barbrick, Leonard	1	1	5		
Barnhart, Christian	1		1		
Barnhart, Christian, Junr	1	1	3		
Blackwelder, Jno Adam	1		1		
Coleman, Mark	1	6	5		
Cerlaugh, George	1	1	4		
Campbell, James	1	1	5		
Cook, Nicholas	3		2		
Chamberlain, John	1	1	7		
Clerice, George	1	2	2		
Corzine, George, Senr	3	1	5		
Corzine, Levil	1	3	4		
Corzine, Nicholas	1	1	4		
Corzine, George, Jur	1	2	4		
Corzine, Samuel	1	1	3		
Caster, John	1		2		
Kerlock, Fredrick	1		1		
Cook, Nicholas, Jur	1	1	1		
Deaton, Mathew	1		2		
Eagley, Phillip	1	2	3		
Farr, Walter	2	5	4		1
Farr, John	1	5	6		
Ferguson (Widow)			2		5
Furr, Henry	1	1	3		
Faggenwinter, Christian	1		1		
Goodnight, Christian	1	4	6		
Groner, Jacob	3	1	2		
Gonder, George	2	4	4		
Haddock, James	1	1	2		
Hadley, Joshua	3	1	4		
Hartman, George	1	1	6		
Hobley, John	1	3	2		
Townsand, Dudley	1	2	2		
Townsand, George	1	4	3		
Long, John	1	1	5		
Lewis, Jacob	1	2	5		
Lewis, Christor	2		1		
Lewis (Widow)	1	1	6		
Mitchell, Mathias, Senr	2	2	4		
Miller, William	2	1	4		
Minster, Frederick	2	2	3		
Misenhimer, Jacob	1	3	4		
Mock, Thomas	2	2	3		
Masters, George	2	3	1		1
Morgadine, John	1	1	1		
Mitchell, Jacob	1		1		
Mitchell, Mathias, Junr	1	1	2		
Moyer, Elias	1	2	4		
Murph, Jacob	1	2	3		
Nichler, John	3	4	4		
Phifer, Martin, Senr	2		1		14

NAME OF HEAD OF FAMILY.	Free white males of 16 years and upward, including heads of families.	Free white males under 16 years.	Free white females, including heads of families.	All other free persons.	Slaves.
Phifer, Jacob	2	1	2		
Plott, George	3	3	3		
Phifer, George	1	1	2		
Rogers, George	2	1	6		
Russell, James	2		5		7
Russell, Robert	1	3	3		7
Russell, John	1	3	5		
Rogers, Nat	1		3		
Shinn, Capt Joseph	3	3	5		6
Shinn, Benjamin	1	5	5		1
Shive, Phillip	1	2	3		
Smith, John	1	2	1		1
Shaver, John	2	6	4		
Scott, James	1	5	4		
Siminer, John	1		1		6
Shelhoas, John	1		2		
Shank, Manas	1	4	1		
Tedford, James					1
Slowgh, Martin	1	3	3		
Voyls, William	2	5	2		
Voyls, James	1	3	2		
Walter, Paul	1	2	3		
Walter, Nicholas	1		3		
Winesaugh, Michael	1		1		3
Winesaugh, Michael, Junr	1	4	3		
Wiley, John	2	1	1		
White, William	1	2	3		1
Young, John	1		3		
Young, Martin	1	1	3		
Yewman, John	1		2		
Townsand, Henry	1	2	1		
Townsand, William	1	1	4		
McGraw, William	1	1	1		
Bless (Widow)	2	2	3		
Boger, Daniel	1	2	3		
Boger, Peter	1	2	5		
Best, John	1	1	2		
Bussard, John	2		2		1
Berger, John	1	3	3		
Beck, Fredrick	1	3	8		
Baringer, Mathias	3	3	6		2
Cottiser, Henry	1		1		
Cruse, Andrew	1	1	1		
Cruse, Adam	1	1	2		
Clonts, Jeremiah	1	3	2		
Clonts, George	1	1	3		
Closian, Jacob	2		3		
Christman, George	1	1	2		
Caple, Peter	2	1	2		
Culp, John	2	2	4		
Cox, Moses	1		2		
Cox, John	1		3		
Cox, William	1		1		
Coble, Peter	1		4		
Dolin, Henry	1	2	3		
Dry, Martin	2	2	2		
Evalt, Michael	1	4	2		
Adelman, George	1		1		
Evalt, Jacob	2	2	2		
Easenhart, George	2	1	3		
Fesperman, Fredrick	1		4		
Fesperman, Michael	1	4	5		
Festerman, Henry	1		1		
Festerman, John	1	1	2		
Goodman, George	1		4		
Goodman, Michael	1		1		
Goodman, Elizabeth	2		2		
Gregory, Christian	1	3	3		
Goodman, Christopher	2	2	2		
Goodman, Michael, Jur	1		4		
Goodman, Christopher, Jur	1	2	4		
Hese, Conrad	1	3	5		
Herron, Elijah	2	3	3		1
Herron, Jesse	1	3	6		3
Harris, Ephraim D	2	1	6		
Juke, John	1	3	5		
Creps, Tobias	1		3		
Creps, Phillip	1	2	4		1
Lippard, Jacob	3	4	5		5
Lippard, William	1	2	2		
Long, Henry	3	2	4		
Lingie, Jacob	1		4		
Lingie, Conrad	1		4		
Lingie, Casper	1	2	3		
Misenhimer, John	1	1	5		
Moyer, Adam	2		1		
Misenhimer, Abraham	2	1	5		
McMahan, James	1	3	4		
Minsinger, William	1	1	3		
Netterhever, Paul				1	
Ovenshine, Rinholt	1	1	2		
Ovenshine, Christian	2	1	3		
Aurey, Martin	1		2		
Pence, Jacob	1	2	6		
Props, Henry	1	3	1		1

NAME OF HEAD OF FAMILY.	Free white males of 16 years and upward, including heads of families.	Free white males under 16 years.	Free white females, including heads of families.	All other free persons.	Slaves.
Perry, Jacob	3		1		
Brineger, Erasmus	2	1	1		
Slaugh, Jacob	1	2	4		
Seferit, Barnhart	1		4		
Seferit, Charles	2		4		
Semions, John	1	1	6		
Stierwalt, Adam	1	1	1		
Speck (Widow)	3		3		
Sides, Michael	1	4	5		
Isenhaker, Nicholas				1	
Rigey, George	2		2		
Richey, Jacob	2		3		
Richey, Henry	1	5	2		
Rogers, Benjamin	1	3	4		
Wolf, Phillip	3	5	3		
Wisel, Michael	2	1	3		
Walker, Fredrick	1	1	2		
Foil, George	3	2	1		
Goodman, Jacob	1	2	4		
Rosberry, Benjamin	1	3	2		
Clemments, Samuel				1	
Allen, Thomas	2	1	2		
Christman, George	1	1	1		
Hartis, John	2	2	4		
Ashley, John	1	2	4		
Brown, William	1	3	3		
Cresco, William	1	3	3		
Barringer, Paul	1	4	4		13
Barenhart, Charles	3	5	4		
Bost, George	2	3	1		
Bost, Jacob	1	1	5		
Blackwelder, Caleb	1	1	4		
Blackwelder, Isaac	1	4	2		
Bost, Elias	1	3	3		
Bostion, Jonas	1		5		
Blaster, Abraham	2		1		
Barringer, John	1	5	4		2
Blackwelder, Martin	1	1	1		
Blackwelder, Jacob	1	1	1		
Bever, Daniel	1	2	1		
Caigle, Charles	2	3	5		
Casey, Jacob	1	1	3		
Carriger, George	1	3	4		
Carriger, Andrew	1	3	3		
Carriger, Phillip, Senr	1	2	2		
Carriger, Phillip, Junr	2		1		
Coile, John	1	2	3		
Clots, Tobias	1		2		
Croul, Peter	1		2		
Cline, Michael	1		5		
Coan, Lewis	1		3		
Caigle, Charles, Junr	1		1		
Dry, Charles	1	2	3		
Dry, Owen	1	3	3		
Dry, Phillip	1		1		
Dove, Caleb	1	1	4		
Gruff, William	1		2		
Eafrit, Jacob	1	1	2		
Clain, George	1		2		
Furr, John	2	6	2		3
Furr, Paul	1	3	4		1
Fogleman, Melcher	3	2	3		
Fisher, Lewis	1		4		
Fink, David	1	2	2		
Faggett, Jacob	2	2	3		
Foil, John	1		4		
Folk, William	1		1		
Fink, George	1		1		
Fruseland, George	1	1	3		
Faggott, Valentine	1		1		
Briges, James	4	1	4		
Hagler, John	2	3	6		
Hartwick, Conrad	1	3	2		
Hardman, George	1		2		
House, John	2	2	1		
House, Elias	2		2		
Hagler, Jacob	1	4	4		
Huber, Jacob	1	3	4		
Hardwick, George	1		3		
Hennager, Michael	1		3		
Hise, George	1	2	5		
Hurlaugher, Christor	3		3		
Hargey, Martin	1	3	3		
Hoan, Henry	1		5		
Hineman, William	1	1	1		
House (Widow)			6		
Hartsel, John	2	2	4		
Jarret, Daniel	3	2	5		
Little, James	1	1	1		
Honeycut, Thomas	2	1	1		
Kerlock, Fredrick	2		1		
Kerlock, George	1	1	4		
Krepps, John	1	3	2		
Little, Daniel	1	2	4		
Kneese, John	2		2		
Lidaker, Conrad	1		2		
Linker, Henry	1	2	2		

SALISBURY DISTRICT, MECKLENBURG COUNTY—Continued.

NAME OF HEAD OF FAMILY.	Free white males of 16 years and upward, including heads of families.	Free white males under 16 years.	Free white females, including heads of families.	All other free persons.	Slaves.
Loften, Isaac	1	3	2		1
Lidaker, Phillip	2	2	5		1
Lierly, Christopher	1		3		
Lype, Jonas	1		5		
Lype, Godfryt, Senr				1	
Lype, Godfryt, Junr	1	1	1		
Lierly, Zamah	1	3	1		
Mathews, Andrew	1	4	3		
McGraw, James	3	4			
Moyer, Mathias	1		2		
Melcher, John	3	1	6		
Misenhimer, George	1	2	3		
Misenhimer, Peter	1	2	3		
Miller, Jacob	1	3	3		
Neusman, Revd Mr	1	2	4		
Oudy, Conrad	1	4	3		
Ourey, George	1	3	3		
Ourey, Godfryt	1		1		
Ourey, Barenhard	1	1	3		
Price, Henry	1		4		
Pliler, Fredrick	1	2	2		
Pliler, Henry	1		5		
Starns (Widow)		2	3		
Quilman, Peter	1	2	2		
Rape, Agustian	1	2	2		
Reed, John	1	3	3		
Ridenaur, Nicholas	1	3	7		
Redland, Geo M	2		8		
Rinhart (Widow)		2	2		
Rigsbey, Thomas	1	3	3		
Sell, Phillip	2	1	2		
Smith, George	1		2		
Smith, Henry	2	2	3		
Stough, Andw	1	1	1		
Sides, Andw	4		4		
Sides, Henry	1	1	1		
Smith, Henry	2	2	3		
Starns, Conrad	1	3	5		
Stucker, Daniel	1	1	2		
Sides, Christian	1		1		
Sell, Peter	1		3		
Starns, Charles	1	1	1		
Tucker, George, Sr	3	3	5		
Tucker, George, Jur	1	1	3		
Teem, Jacob	2		1		
Teem, Adam	1	4	2		
Voyls, Thomas	2	2	3		
Wilhelm, George	1	4	6		
Witenhouse, Martin			2	1	
Wiser, Phillip, Jur	1		2		
Wiser, Phillip, Senr	3		1		
Wagginor, William	1	5	2		
Weaver, Jacob	1	1	1		
Weaver, Henry	1	3	4		
Weaver, Peter	1		2		
Walker, Michael	1		10		
Walker, Adam	2	1	2		
Cook, Jacob	1	3	3		
Suther, David	1		2		
Suther, John	1	3	2		
Miller, George	1	2	2		
Winchester, William	2	2	4		
Caigle, John	2	3	6		
Winchester, Dugles	2	3	2		
Andrews, William	1		2		
Armstrong (Widow)	1	1	4		
Alexander, William S	1	3	2		4
Allen, Alexander, Jur	1	4	2		
Allen, Alexr, Senr	1	3	2		
Burns, James	2	1	6		
Bradshaw, James	2	4	6		
Biggers, Joseph	3	1	5		
Bean, Robert	3	4	1		
Black, James	2		2		
Black, Wm	1	3	2		
Black, John	1		2		
McClain, Allen	2		4		
Carruthers, Hugh	1	3	2		
Carruthers, James	1	1	4		
Colland, William	3		1		2
Crumel, James	1	2	2		
Crumell, John	2	2	5		
Coldwell, Daniel	1	4	1		
Coldwell, Robt	1		2		
Cochran, Benja	1	4	2		
Cochran, Robert	1	2	6		
Campbell, Andw	1	2	2		
Cochran, Wm	2		2		
Cochran, Paul	2	4	1		
Cochran, John	1	2	1		1
Corruthers, Robert	3	3	6		
Davis, Robt	1	6	5		
Dunn, Simon				1	
Davis, Thomas	2	4	4		
Davis, Andrew	3		6		
Davis, William	1			1	3
Ferguson, Alexander	1	4	2		3

NAME OF HEAD OF FAMILY.	Free white males of 16 years and upward, including heads of families.	Free white males under 16 years.	Free white females, including heads of families.	All other free persons.	Slaves.
Harris, William, Jur	1	4	1		1
Hays, Patrick	1	2	5		1
Harris, John	1	1	2		1
Harris, Capt James	6		4		6
Harris, Robert, Junr		2	4		
Harris, Samuel	2	1	6		11
Harris, William, Senr	1	3	5		2
Gingles, John	1		1		
Harris, Capt Robert	1		1		8
Howell, Joseph	3	3	2		3
Howell, John	1		2		
Kirkpatrick, Valentine	1	3	3		
Kimmins, Hugh	1	2	5		
Kimmins, Alexander	1			1	
McClelland, Rebeca	1	1	3		
McCinley, David	1		7		
McCinley, Charles	1	3	2		
McKentire, Capt William	2	4	3		
McMurray, Francis	1		1		
McMurray, Robert	1		6		3
McCahern (Widow)			6		
Mcfadian, Thomas	1	1	1		
Morrison, James	3	2	2		2
Morgan, Enoch	1	2	1		
McCammon, Charles	2				
Morrison, Robert	4	1	5		
Morrison, William	2	1	3		1
Morris, Griffin	1	4	5		
McClelland, John	1	3			
Mash, Ebenezer	2				
McGinnis, Charles	3		3		
McCurdey, Capt Archabeld	1	4	5		6
Maxwell, James	2	4	2		
Newill, Francis	1	1	4		
Newill, William	3		3		
Newill, David	1		3		
Plunket, James, Senr	1		1		6
Plunket, James, Junr	1	4	1		
Purviance, David	3	1	4		1
Purviance, Joseph	1	1	2		
Purviance, James	1	4	1		1
Purviance, John	1	1	3		
Russell, James	1		2		3
Ross, William	2	2	5		3
Ross, James	1				1
Scott, James	2		2		
Scott, Alexander	1	2	4		
Simons, John	1	5	2		
Stuart, Samuel	1	3	5		
Spears, William	4	2	4		
Stafford, James, Senr	2				1
Stafford, James, Junr	1	4	3		
Scott, William, Esqr	3		2		1
Stuart, William	1	2	4		
Stuart (Widow)			4		
Taylor, William	1	2	3		
Taylor, David	1		1		
Wite, John	2	4	3		2
White, Thomas	1	3	2		
White, William	1	3	6		
Wiley, Oliver	1	4	6		4
Widington, Samuel	1	1	2		
Wallace, Aron	1		2		
White, Archabeld	3	1	2		
White, David	2	2	3		4
White, James	1		2		
Watson, Thomas	4	2	3		
White, Joseph	1		3		
Wallace, Moses	1		2		
Dorton, Charles	1	6	4		
Davis, George	1	6	4		1
Morgan, Robert	1		4		
Stuart, John	1		2		
Harris, Samuel, Junr	1		2		1
Welch, Joseph	1	1	4		
Eager, Adam	2	1	3		3
Eager, Hugh	1	2	4		5
Alexander, Col Adam	3	1	3		
Alexander, Evan	1				
Bean, William	3	1	4		
Bugg, William	1	2	3		
Bean, Daniel	1	1	2		
Barnhill, Robert	1	1	2		
Bailey, Joseph	1	3	2		
Brandon, John	1	4	1		
Brown, James	1		1		
Bryan, Kiah	1		1		
Cuthbertson, John	1	1	3		
Crowle, Samuel	2	2	3		
Cuthbertson, David	1		2		
Crowle, Samuel, Junr	1	1	2		
Carruthers, John	1		2		7
Clay, Isham	1		3		
College, Henry	1		2		
Freemon (Widow)		3	4		
Dickson, James	1	1	2		

NAME OF HEAD OF FAMILY.	Free white males of 16 years and upward, including heads of families.	Free white males under 16 years.	Free white females, including heads of families.	All other free persons.	Slaves.
Davis, James	1	3	2		
Freeman, Allen, Junr	1		2		
Freemon, Allen, Senr	1	3	3		12
Freemon, Gidion	1	1	4		1
Flaugh, David	2	3	5		
Ford (Widow)	1	1	4		
Freemon, William	1		4		
Freemon, Elyburn	1		2		
Garmon, Michael	1	1	7		9
Garmon (Widow)	1	1	1		8
Guiliams, Travis	1		3		
Harkey (Widow)	1		3		
Hall, James	1	2	3		
Harbison, William	1	1	2		
Hall, Thomas	1	3	4		
Harris, Majr James	4		4		13
Hall, John	1	3	3		
Johnston, William	1	2	2		
Johnston (Widow)	1	2	2		
Kiser, Fredrick	1	3	3		
Kiser, George	1	4	2		
Kyger, George A	1	2	2		
Long, James	1		2		
Mulls, John	1	1	2		
McMurray, James	1	4	5		1
Miney, Martin	1	3	2		
McCracken, John	3	3	4		
McClartey, Alexr	1		2		
Murphey, John	2	1	5		2
McCoy, John	1	1	5		2
Miller, Phillip	1		2		
Mitchell, William	1		2		
McGuist, John	2	4	3		
Masser, George	1	1	1		
McGehey, Amos	1		1		
Nelson, John	1	1	2		
McCummons, John	2	3	4		1
Pickens, William	1	2	2		
Pyron, William	2	2	5		
Powell, David	1	2	2		
Pyron. John	1	2	2		
Powell, John	3		2		
Polk, William, Jur	1	4	2		2
Polk, William, Senr	1	1	1		2
Polk, Capt Charles	2	3	3		4
Powell, Abel	1		2		
Purser, John	2	2	5		
Polk, John, Junr	1	1	3		
Polk, Thomas, Junr	1	1	2		
Rabb, Capt William	2	4	3		3
Rogers, James	3		3		5
Rogers, Hugh	1	1	3		2
Ramsay, William	1	3	6		
Rodgers, Joseph	1	1	7		
Simpson, William	1	3	2		
Snell, Francis	1	3	4		
Smith, Thomas	1		1		
Smith, William	1		1		
Shelley, Capt Thomas	1	1	3		6
Stansill, John	1	2	2		
Smith, Samuel, Senr	2	1	2		4
Self, Jacob	2	3	2		
Smith, Samuel, Junr	1		1		
Smith, Saml (son of Saml)			1		
Talley, Priar	1		3		
Townsand, William	1	1	2		
Warden, Samuel	1	2	2		
Witherford, Wilka	3	3	3		
Witherford, William	1	1	3		
Wise, Benjamin	1			1	
Watts, Andrew	2		2		
Reed, John	1	3	2		
Tetter, George	2	3	2		
Crawford, John	1		1		
Miller (Widow)	1		6		
Miller, Mathew	1	2	3		
Miller (Widow) Senr			1		1
Clay, James	1	4	1		
Caegle, Henry	1	4	5		
Blair, William	3	3	5		
Buckhannon, Samuel	3	2	6		2
Black, John	1	1	2		2
Black, Ezekel	1		2		
Black, Samuel	1		1		1
Black, William, Sr	2		2		
Carragan, Thomas	1		1		
Charles, Henry	1		1		
Crum, Conrad	1	1	4		
Contz, Lewis	1	2	3		
Donaldson, John	1	2	5		
Ford, Zeblin	1		1		
Fisher, George	2		1		7
Ford, John, Esqr	1		2		
Glass, Robert	1		1		
Glass, Francis	1	2	1		5
Grubble, Thomas	1	4	5		

SALISBURY DISTRICT, MECKLENBURG COUNTY—Continued.

NAME OF HEAD OF FAMILY.	Free white males of 16 years and upward, including heads of families.	Free white males under 16 years.	Free white females, including heads of families.	All other free persons.	Slaves.
Gonder, Lewis	2				
Hood, Tunis, Senr	1				7
Hood, Capt Tunis	1	4	4		4
Hood, Reuben	1	2	3		
Harrisson, Nehemiah	1	3	5		2
Hartwick, Conrad	1		2		
Harkey, John, Senr	2	1	2		
Hartis, Lewis	1	2	4		
Irwin, William, Senr	3		3		
Irwin, Thomas	1	1	2		
Kenneday, William	1	3	2		
Kidwell, William	1	2	5		
Leagh, Henry	1		6		
Lippe, Leonard	1	1	2		
Laigh, Jacob	1	1	4		
Lemmonds, John	2	3	3		
McFersion, John				1	
McIntire, William	1		4		
McGinnis, Peter	3	1	3		
Morris, William	3	3	3	1	
Montgomery, John	1	3	3		
McCall, William	1	3	2		
Moore, Hugh	2	4	4		
McCombs, James	2		5		5
Miller, Abraham	3	1	1		
McCollum, Malcom	1	3	2		
McCraven, John, Jur	1		3		
McGintey, James	1	2	4		
Moore, Andw	1	2	3		
Moore, David, Jur	1	1	4		
Nail, John	1	2	4		
Orr, James (whistling)	2	5	3		
Orr, James	1	2	3		
Phillips, Adam	1	1	1		
Query, William, Senr	1		1		
Quary, John	3		1		
Quary, William, Jur	1	2	4		
Ray, Isaac	1	1	5		
Routh, Edward	1		1		
Stansill, Jesse	1		4		
Stansill, John	1	1	2		
Shaver, Fredrick	2	5	4	1	
Stuart, Mathew	2	1	2		
Stevens, Emmanuel	1	4	3		
Stains, James				1	
Stilwell, Jesse	1		3		
Walker, William	2		2		
Wilson, James	3	1	4		
Wilson, Thomas	1	4	3		
Walker, Capt Archabeld	2	1	1		
Walker, Mathew, Senr	1	2			
Vance, Andw	1		6		
Irwin, William, Jur	1	1	1		
Ormond, James	1	1	2		
Carrigan, William				1	
Walker, Moses	1		1		
Wilson, Thomas, Senr	1		1		
Coul, James				1	
Vance, Valentine	1		1		
Culbertson, William	2	3	5		
Darbey, Charles	1		1		
Dunn, James	2	1	2		
Dunn, Andrew	1	2	6		
Demsey, John	1	1	6		
Duglass, James, Esqr	1	3	3		1
Dunbarr, Nathaniel				1	
Craig, John	1		2		
Elkins, Shadrick	1	1	3		
Eakins, John	1		4		
Bradshaw, Samuel	1		2		
Bradshaw (Widow)	1	2	1		
Crye, William	1	3	2		
Appleton, William	2	2	2		
Adams, Charles	3	2	5		
Blythe, James	1	6	3		
Basdill, Reuben	1	3	3		3
Barnet, Robert	1	3	3		
Bonds, George	2	3	2		
Bickett (Widow)	3		3		
Crye, John	3	1	2		
Craige, Moses	2	2	4		
Cochran, Thomas, Senr	2	2	1		1
Cochran, Thomas, Junr	1	5	7		
Crye, James	3		2		
Courtney, William	2		1		
Cochran, John	1		3		
Chainey, William	1	4	2		
Fincher, James	1	4	2		
Fincher, Richard	1	2	4		
Finley, James	1		2		
Fincher, Jonathan	2	3	6		
Fowler, John	2	1	2		
Forsythe, Hugh	1	2	3		
Finley, William				1	
Finley, Charles				1	
Forbers, Hugh	1		3		
Givvins, William	1	1	4		
Gibbens, John	1	4	2		
Givvins, Samuel	1	2	1		
Gray, Jacob	3	1	1		
Gray, Sherrod	1	2	2		2
Gordin, John	3	2	3		
Gillaspie, Jacob	1		1		
Hargitt, James	1	1	1		
Hellums, George	1	3	3		
Hellums, John	1	2	4		
Hellums, George, Senr	1		1		1
Houston, Hugh	3		1		4
Hargitt, Henry	1		2		
Helms, Jacob	1	1	4		
Houston, William, Senr	1		3		1
Houston, William, Junr	1		3		1
Howey, George	1	2	2		
Howard, William	1	1	3		
Helms, Tilmon	1	2	2		
Hargitt, Henry, Junr	1	6	2		
Hise, Leonard	1	3	3		
Howey, William	2	1	1		1
Henninger, Dennis	2	3	6		
Howey, John	1		3		5
Houston, James	3	1	2		5
Heggins (Widow)	2	1	2		4
Harris, John	1		5		
Hellums, Isaac	1		2		
Izel, Fredrick	2	1	3		
Queban, John	1		2		
King, Robert	1	3	2		
Lawson, John	1		2		
Lewis, William	1	2	4		
Lewis, Martha	1		3		1
Lewis, James	1	5	3		
Lawson, Moses	1		1		
Leggit, Esther	2	3	4		2
Lawson, Thomas	2		2		
Leggit, William	2	2	2		1
Linn (Widow)	2	1	3		
McNeely, John	2				1
McCall, Francis	1		3		
McCorkle, John	1	1	3		
McCallum, John	1		1		
McCablum, Thomas	1	1	2		
McCain, Hance	1		2		
McWhorter, Aron	2	1	4		
McCauslin, James	1		3		
Mcquistion, Joseph	1		4		
Morrison, Dr William	1		1		2
McCrorey, Hugh	1	1	2		
McCain, John	1			1	
Newton, Robert	1	2	5		
Orr, George	1	1	5		1
Osborn, William	3	1	7		
Ormond, James	1	2	2		
Orr, David	1	4	4		
Osborn (Widow)	2	1	4		
Ormond, Jacob	1	2	4		1
Porter, William	1		1		
Paxton, Moses	1	2	2		
Potts, John	1	1	5		3
Potts, William	1	1	3		14
Porter, Capt Robert	2	3	5		
Richardson, Edward	3	2	4		
Rape, Peter	1	1	2		
Ramsay, Robert	1	3	3		
Rich, James	1	2	2		
Rape, Henry	1	1	2		
Rederick, Shadrick	1	2	2		
Redford, John	4	2	4		
Rogers, John, Senr	1		2		
Ramsay, Alexander	1	1	1		
Rich, John, Junr	1		1		
Shepperd, John	1	1	2		
Shepperd, James	1	1	3		
Shepperd, Edward	1	2	1		
Secrist, Michael	1	2	3		2
Secrist, John	1		3		
Rich, James, Senr	2	3	5		
Stuart, Joseph	1	1	2		
Storey, James	4	1	3		1
Secrist, Jacob	2	4	2		
Stevenson, James	1	4	4		
Thompson, Elijah	3	1	4		
Tanner, Thomas	1	1	4		
Thompson, John	1	2	5		
Spratt, Andw	1	5	5		
Williamson, James	1	1	2		
White, Thomas	1	1	2		
West, Benjamin	1	2	3		
Yarbrough, Joshua	3	3	1		
Uans, Robert	1		6		
Avent, James	1	1	6		5
Abbott (Widow)			4		
Allen, Andw	1	3	2		
Allen, Thomas				1	
Blue, Stephen	1	2	3		
Broom, John	3		2		
Belk, John, Esqr	1		1		8
Belk, Darling	1	3	2		
Cairns, Alexander	1	4	5		3
Coak, Robert	1		2		
Coak, Charles	1		6		3
Cairns, Daniel	2	1	4		
Davis, James	1	2	6		1
Dosber, James	2		5		
Davis, Capt Robert	2	3	6		4
Findly, John	1		1		
Forster, Capt Joseph	1		1		4
Fisher, Paul	1		1		
Fisher, William	1	1	2		
Fisher, John	1	2	2		
Fisher, Charles	1		4		
Fisher, Fredrick	1	2	2		
Gantt, William	1		1		
Gillaspie, Andw	1		1		
Gantt, Thomas	1		5		
McCain, William	1	1	4		
Yerbey, Avent	1	3	2		
McCammon, John	3	3	5		
McCorkle, Archabeld	1		1		
McWhorter, James	1	1	2		
Odum, May	1		2		
Orr (Widow)			3	7	
Potts, Joshua	1	1	1		
Rogers, Hugh	1	5	3		
Rogers, Mathew	1	3	4		
Ramsay, John	1	3	2		
Rogers, John	1	3	2		
Rowan, Henry	1		2		
Faggett, Moses	1	2	4		1
Rogers, William	2	4	3		
Starns, Fredrick	1		3		
Starns, David	1	3	1		
Stevenson, John	1	4	3		1
Sibley, John	1	2	3		
Shannon, James	1	1	1		
Titus, Dennis	1	1	7		
Thompson, Alexander	1		5		
Thompson, Obediah	1	1	5		
Vinan, Thomas	1	5	3		
Vinan, William	1		3		
Gillaspie, Charles	1	1	1		
Haggins, John	1	1	1		
Gillaspie, John	1	4	4		
Kendrick, Philand	1		3		
Hughey, John	1		6		
Lathlin, Samuel	1		2		
Lathlin, John	1		2		
Lasley, James	1	2	3		1
Lackey, Robert	1		2		
Lackey, Thomas	1	3	3		1
Lesley (Widow)	2	1	1		
Lanley, George	1	2	4		1
McWhorter, John	1		1		
Myars, Hermon	1	1	2		
McElroy, John	4	2	2		
McElroy, James	1	3	3		1
McWhorter, Moses	1	2	5		
McCorkle, James	1	4	2		
McWhorter, George	3		2		
McCorkle, Owen	1		2		
McCain, Andw	1		1		
Meller, Buie	1	3	4		
McCain, John	1	1	4		
McCain, Hugh	3	1			3
McCain, Thomas, Junr	1	3	1		
Vinen, Drury	1	5	3		4
Washam, Jeremiah	2	1	1		
Walker, Capt Andw	2	1	6		3
Williams, John	1		2		
Wahaub, James	3	2	3		9
Williams, Ishmael	1	2	2		
Walker, John	3		1		
Walker, Thomas	1		1		
Griffin, Richard	1	3	1		
Redick, Barnabas	1	4	1		
Oats, Michel	1	1	3		
Bruster, James	2	2	3		5
Barnet, Hugh	3	1	5		
Black, James	2	3	5		
Black, William, Junr	1		3		
Batey, Walter	2	1	5		2
Chambers, James	1		2		
Crocket, Archabeld	4	1	5		2
Coningham, Roger	2	1	2		
Currey, James	1	4	3		
Dawns, Henry	2				3
Dawns, Samuel	1		2		1
Dawns, Thomas	1	1	1		
Donaldson, Robert	1	2	1		
Greer, John	1	2	3		
Guire, John	1	1	3		

SALISBURY DISTRICT, MECKLENBURG COUNTY—Continued.

NAME OF HEAD OF FAMILY.	Free white males of 16 years and upward, including heads of families.	Free white males under 16 years.	Free white females, including heads of families.	All other free persons.	Slaves.
Hoge, Francis	2		4		
Harkness, George	1	3	6		
Hadden, George	1	2	1		
Hodge, John	1	1	2		
Housten, David	1		1	1	
Harrison, Isaiah	1	3	3		2
John, Daniel	1	1	3	1	
McSparren, James	1		1		
Means, William	1	3	5		1
McKee, William	1	3	2		6
Miller, John	1	2	2		
McCauley, Daniel	1		3		
McKee, Alexander	1	3	4		
Moore, Phillip	2	1	4		
Montgomery, George	1	4	1		
Moore, David, Senr	4	4	6		1
Miller, George	1		2		
McGoughen, James				1	
Morrison, Alexander	2		2	1	
Mathews, William, Esqr	1	3	1	1	
Null, Jesse	1	1	1		1
Null, Andw	1		2		
Osborn, Robert	1	2	2		
Osborn, Alexander	1	1	3		
Ormond, Adam	1		1	1	
Osborn Able	1		1		
Parks, Moses	3	3	3		
Patson, Simon	2		3		
Potter, Gordon	3	3	4		
Patterson, John				1	
Ray, Andrew, Senr	2	2	4		
Reed, James	1	2	4		
Ray, John	1	1	1		
Reed, Joseph	2	3	2		2
Robison, John	1	5	3		2
Ray, David	1	3	4		
Robison, Thomas	1	2	5		
Stuart, William	2		2		
Slitt, William	2	5	2		

NAME OF HEAD OF FAMILY.	Free white males of 16 years and upward, including heads of families.	Free white males under 16 years.	Free white females, including heads of families.	All other free persons.	Slaves.
Simeson, Capt John	1	1	1		
Shanks, James	1	1	6		4
Sharpe, John	1	2	2		
Stevenson, John				1	
Stuart, John	2	3	4		
Springs, John, Senr	1		2		2
Stevenson, David				1	
Tawns, Elijha	2		2		
Wyatt, Sylvester	1	2	2		
Wylie, James	1		2		1
Vaich, William	1	4	3		
McBoyd, Patrick	1	2	3		
Smith, John	1	2	2		1
Gailbraith, Robert	2		5		
Rendricks, William	1		2		1
Cleymon, Simon	1	1	4		
Cleymon, Richard	1		6		
Alexander, Capt Charles	3	1	4		6
Alexander, Abner	1	1	3		
Alexander, George	1	1	2		
Alexander, Levine	3		2		
Alexander, Samuel	2		2		
Bigham (Widow)	3		2		
Bays, James	3	2	3		
Benham, Daniel	1	3	4		1
Brown, James	2	1	1		
Brown, William	1	2	6		
Barnett, John	1	1	3		
Baxter, James	1		4		1
Cuningham, William	1	2	3		
Cuningham, Nathaniel	1	1	2		1
Cook, Joseph	1		5		2
Dermond, James	1	2	3		
Esselman, James	1	2	2		
Flemmekan, David	1	8	3		
Graham, William	1		2		
Gaston, Thomas	1	2			
Hays, Robert	2	1	4		
Kirkpatrick, John	3		3		3
Knox, David				1	

NAME OF HEAD OF FAMILY.	Free white males of 16 years and upward, including heads of families.	Free white males under 16 years.	Free white females, including heads of families.	All other free persons.	Slaves.
Erwin, Christor	1		6		3
McCulloch, John	5	2	4		3
Menson, William	1		3		
Mulwee, John	2	2	6		
Merchant, William	1	2	7		
Osborn, Capt James	1	4	6		
Osborn, John	2	2	2		
Phillips, Robert	1	1	2		3
Page, Nicholas				1	
Rogers, John	1	3	2		
Reed (Widow)	2	2	5		
Sturgeon, John	2	2	2		
Smith, John	1	1	3		
King, John	2	3	4		
Sharpe, Edward, Senr	1		2		
Swann, John	4		2		1
Sharpe, James	2	2	5		
Sharpe, Edward, Junr	1		2		
Walker, Robert	1	1	2		
Weeks, Phillip	2		3		
Wilson, William, Esqr	2	2	3		1
Wilson, Robert	1	2	2		
Wilson, John	1	2	2		
Washingtown, John				1	
Wetherspoon, William	1	1	1		
Walker, John	1	1	1		
Yandell, James	1	3	4		
Yandel, William	4	4	7		
Yandel, Andrew	1	4	3		
Jinkins, John	3	2	3		
Smith, James	1	3	3		
Robison (Widow)		3	4		
Lindsey, Walter	1		3		
Wilson (Widow)	1		2		4
Alexander, Eli	1	2	3		1
Wallace, George	1		3		
Wallace, Mathew	1	2	2		
Wallace, William	1	2	3		
Miller (Widow)	1		1		

SALISBURY DISTRICT, MONTGOMERY COUNTY.

NAME OF HEAD OF FAMILY.	Free white males of 16 years and upward, including heads of families.	Free white males under 16 years.	Free white females, including heads of families.	All other free persons.	Slaves.
Earles, William	4	3	5		1
Frazier, William	3	1	2		
Frazier, Henry	1				
Frazier, William	2	3	1		
Fowler, David	1		1		
Faircloth, Mary			5		4
Frazier, John	1	2	3		
Frazier, Alexander	2	4	3		
Fry, James	2		7		
Fridle, Gasper	1	1	3		
Fry, Thomas	1		3		
Freeman, Hartwell	2	3	5		1
Fisher, Littleton	1	1	2		
Fox, Lawrance	1	2	3		
Fox, Gates	1		3		
Fincher, Benjamin	1	2	3		
Fletcher, James	2	3	3		2
Fisher, George	1		1	1	
Forrist, Abraham	3	1	5		18
Forrist, Nathan	1	1	1		1
Gowers, Thomas	1	1	5		
Gowers, Mathew	1	2	2		
Gibson, James	1		4		
Gibson, William	2	1	2		
Grifith, Isham	1				
Gross, Solomon	2		1		
Garratt, Presley	1		2		
Green, Richard	2	2	5		
Gibbs, William	1				
Gillam, Jordan	1	3	2		
Gorden, Alexander	1		5		
Garratt, William	1				
Golahorn, Asa	1	1	5		
Gain, Thomas	1	2	5		
Green, Richard	3	3	3		
Gray, James	3	2	1		1
Gilbart, John	2	1	3		
Gray, David	2	3	3		
Gusley, James	1	3	3		
Gilbart, Jesse	1				
Gilbart, John	1				
Gilbart, Nathan	1		1		
Green, Nathum	1		1		
Gurly, James	1	1	3		
Harris, Joshua	2	2	7		8
Hogan, Zakeriah	2	2	7		
Horn, Nathan	1	2	3		4
Harriss, Arthur	1	1	3		4
Haygood, Bird	1	5	4		
Haygood, Griffin	1	2	4		
Hill, John	2	2	2		

NAME OF HEAD OF FAMILY.	Free white males of 16 years and upward, including heads of families.	Free white males under 16 years.	Free white females, including heads of families.	All other free persons.	Slaves.
Harriss, John	2	1	3		
Henry, Benjamin	2	2	5		
Hix, Littleberry	1	2	3		
Haygood, Elizabeth	1		1		
Hix, Daniel	2		2		
Hix, Robert	1	1	1		
Hix, William	1		1		
Hays, Saley		1	2		
Heldness, Reuban	1	2	5		
Haltom, Joseph	1		3		
Heltom, Spencer	1		3		
Hurt, Jesse	1	1	2		
Harrison, Andrew	1		3		
Howard, John	1	1	2		
Harril, Mathew	1	2	3		3
Haltom, William	1	1	3		2
Humble, Jacob	2	3	3		1
Hurt, Joseph	2		3		
Humble, John	1		3		
Hardin, John	1	2	3		
Humble, Henry	1	1	1		5
Hix, John	1	1	2		
Hix, Demcy	1	2	2		
Hearn, Thomas	1	1	1		1
Harris, Jesse	3		5		6
Hearn, Ebenazer	1	1	4		4
Harris, James	2	6	4		4
Hendcock, Samuel	2	4	3		9
Hearn, Pernal	2	3	5		
Harris, Arthur	1	1	4		9
Harris, Brantly	1	3	3		
Harris, Atheldred	1	3	1		2
Hearn, Stephen	1	3	4		
Hall, William	1	3	7		
Harris, West, Junr	2	4	4		7
Harris, West, Senr	2		3		13
Harris, Turner	3	3	5		1
Hurley, Joshua	1	1	3		
Harris, James	1	2	3		2
Handcock, Martin	2		5		
Hurley, Joseph	1	2	3		
Harris, John, Senr	2	2	3		
Hall, Joseph	1	4	1		1
Hopkins, Benjamin	1	3	2		
Hambleton, Walter	1	1	2		
Harris, Wilby	1	1	3		
Hopkins, Richard	1	2	1		
Hall, Anthony	1				
Hopkins, John	2	3	5		
Huckoby, Thomas	1	4	4		
Harris, Rowland	1	3	1		3

NAME OF HEAD OF FAMILY.	Free white males of 16 years and upward, including heads of families.	Free white males under 16 years.	Free white females, including heads of families.	All other free persons.	Slaves.
Hearn, James	1	5	2		
Hamblett, John	1		2		
Hatchcock, Banjimen	1	2	5		
Howal, James	1		8		
Hamblett, Peter	1	1	4		
Horton, William	1	3	5		
Hosty, James	2	2	4		
Holland, Anthony	2		3		
Hearn, Fenlary		1	3		
Handcossle, William	1		4		
Hopkins, Alexander	1				
Jordan, John	1	1	4		
Jordan, Francis	3	1	5		
Jones, Jesse	2		2		6
Jinnings, John	1		2		3
Jordan, John	1				
Jackson, Henry	1	4	6		
Jinkins, Thomas	1	2	5		
Steel, Robert J	2	1	8		1
Jordan, William	3	3	3		
Jordan, Ruban	1		4		
Jones, Thomas	1	2	2		
Jones, Charles	1	4	3		5
Johnston, William	3	3	5		16
Irby, James	1	4	3		
Johnston, Thomas	2	1	7		9
Irby, William	2	1	2		4
Johnston, James	1		1		
Johnston, James, Junr	1		1		
Johnston, William	1		2		
Jordan, John	1				
Kimbrough, John	1	4	2		5
Kelly, Thomas	1				
Kelly, Samuel	2	2	5		1
Keller, George	1	2	4		
Keller, Jacob	1	2	2		
Keller, Thomas	1	1	1		
Key, Eligah	1		2		
Kirk, George	1	2	2		9
Kirk, Thomas	1	3	3		15
Kindal, William	1	3	1		5
Kirk, John	1	2	2		1
Kindal, Samuel	1		2		
Lucas, Thomas	1	4	5		
Leverett, Robert	1	2	2		
Leverett, Richard	1	2	4		1
Leverett, William	1		4		
Lethercut, William	2	2	5		
Lesrand, William	2	1	1		14
Langin, William	1	2	2		
Lilly, Elizabeth	1	1	1		6

SALISBURY DISTRICT, MONTGOMERY COUNTY—Continued.

NAME OF HEAD OF FAMILY.	Free white males of 16 years and upward, including heads of families.	Free white males under 16 years.	Free white females, including heads of families.	All other free persons.	Slaves.
Lightfoot, John	1	4	4		1
Lilly, Edmond	1				5
Loe, James	1		3		
Lunsford, Auguston	1	1	1		
Lunsford, James	1	3	4		
Landron, Timothy	2		1		
Lomsey, Thomas	1	1	4		
Loftin, William	2	3	5		10
Leathers, James	2	2	4		
Loftin, Moses	2	1	7		6
Lynch, Phillip	1		2		
Lilly, John	1	5	2		6
Lee, John	1	3	5		
Lilly, Edmond	1	1	1		28
Aldred, Mary		2	1		
Allen, Joseph	3		2		
Armstrong, Isaac	3	2	5		2
Andress, John, Junr	1	2	6		
Andress, John, Senr	1	2	1		
Andress, David	1	2	1		
Allen, Reuban	1	1	2		
Allen, John	1		4		
Ashford, William	2	3	4		1
Archen, George	2	4	4		
Atkins, James	2	4	7		4
Arnold, Peter	1	1	1		
Atkins, John	1	3	5		4
Almond, Richard	1	4	4		
Austin, Bryant	1	1	3		
Aldman, Nathan	1		1		
Aldman, Thomas	1	1	2		
Aidman, Edmond	1		5		
Avitt, Elijah	1				
Allen, John	3	3	1		1
Allen, William	1	3	3		
Atkins, Hezekiah	1				
Arldurth, Reuban	1	1	5		
Bruton, William	1	2	2		
Baton, Peter	1		2		
Bruton, George	1	1	4		
Blake, Randle	1		4		
Beard, Alexander	4	6	1		10
Blake, Thomas	1	5	2		1
Boyd, John	2	2	2		
Barlow, William	1	1	1		
Bolin, John	1	4	1		
Bolin, Jessee	1		2		
Bowlin, John	2		1		5
Bray, Peter	1	2	5		
Butler, John	1	3	2		
Butler, Joshua	1	1	5		1
Butler, Elias	1	3	2		1
Butler, Thomas	1	2	3		
Benton, Job	1	2	4		
Bowling, William					
Ballard, John	2	2	6		
Belinsly, Sias	2	6	4		
Berry, Enoch	1		1		1
Avit, James	1	3	1		
Buckler, John	1		1		
Barlow, William	1	1	1		
Bennett, Mark	1	2	1		
Bennett, Solomon	1	1	5		
Barman, John	1	1	5		
Bell, Joseph	1	1	4		
Bean, Walter	1	3	3		
Bond, Elisabeth	3	1	5		4
Bennett, Drury	1	2	2		
Benton, Joseph	1	3	3		
Bell, Richard	1		2		1
Bell, David	1		2		
Bell, John	1		3		
Bell, Benjamin	1	3	3		
Barnet, William	1	2	1		1
Bolland, Walter	1		2		
Boyd, Samuel	3	2	3		
Boycom, Nicholas	1	1	3		
Burns, Samson	1				
Bankston, Andrew	1	3	3		1
Brooks, John	3	2	4		8
Brookes, William	3	2	4		6
Burlison, David	2	2	5		
Burrows, Solomon	1	3	3		
Burnett, Elijah	1				
Burlison, Isaac	1	2	3		
Brown, Isaac	2	6	4		
Barnet, Elijah	3		2		
Barnet, John	1				
Patton, Daniel	1	2	7		
Allen, Isaac	4	4	3		
Chiles, Thomas, Jur	1		3		11
Chambers, Edward	3		4		2
Cox, Robert	2	4	2		
Chisom, Maliom	4	1	2		
Chambers, Edward	1	2	4		
Chambers, John	1		3		
Carpenter, Jonethan	1	1	2		

NAME OF HEAD OF FAMILY.	Free white males of 16 years and upward, including heads of families.	Free white males under 16 years.	Free white females, including heads of families.	All other free persons.	Slaves.
Cotton, Thomas	1	2	1		1
Cotton, James	1		1		1
Chiles, Thomas, Senr	2		1		10
Choppel, Christopher	2	3	5		2
Cathole, Josiah	1		3		1
Clark, George	4		7		
Carpenter, Soloman	1				
Cockran, Abraham	1	1	2		2
Downs, Richard	1	3	4		
Delamp, Joseph	1	1	3		
Deaton, Joseph	1	3	3		
Connel, Francis	1	1	3		
Cannon, Laurana		2	4		
Cammel, John	1	3	1		
Cockran, Jacob	1	5	3		
Carpenter, Temple	1				
Camel, John	1	3	2		
Clark, Evan	3		2		4
Carpenter, Owen	2	2	1		
Chance, Daniel	1	1	2		
Chisom, Alexander	1		2		
Cheek, Randle	1	3	2		
Caudle, David	1	2	2		
Crosswell, Nimrod	1	1	4		
Christian, Nicholas	3	2	4		2
Christian, John	1		1		2
Couples, Ama	1		2		7
Crump, John	1	6	3		5
Clemmons, Thomson	1	5	4		
Clifton, William	1	2	3		5
Coltharp, Henry	1		4		2
Crump, James	1	1	6		12
Clifton, Pricilia		4	5		1
Coggin, Simon	1	2	1		
Curtis, Moses	1	4			
Curtis, Russell	1				
Cranford, Lenord	1	6	6		
Case, James	1	4	4		1
Carnes, Joseph	1	4	1		
Carrill, William	1	4	2		
Carrill, Jane			3		
Carnes, Edward	2	1	2		
Cranford, William	1	2	2		
Cato, Daniel	1	4	2		4
Carter, Ephraim	1	1	4		
Carter, Charles	1				
Carter, Samuel	2	1	9		
Carter, Joshua	2	2	4		3
Cox, William	2	3	1		
Cumins, Banjemin	2	2	4		
Calloway, Isaac	1	4	5		
Carter, Samuel	1	1	2		
Cox, James	1				
Cooper, Isaac	1	2	3		
Carpenter, Jonathan	3	2	5		
Cretentor, William	2	1	2		
Cooper, James	1	1	3		
Coley, George	1	1	5		
Cose, Valentine	1	3	4		
Coley, William	1	1	1		
Cooper, Joseph	1	2	2		
Couples, William	1	2	2		4
Cheek, Siles	1		2		
Carter, Jacob	3	3	3		
Codee, Richard	1		1		
Cooper, John	3	2	3		
Coley, Joyce	2		2		
Cato, Judith	1		2		
Codee, Richard	1		1		
Casle, George	1	3	3		
Clanton, Reuben	1				
Dafford, Rhody	1	1	3		
Deberry, Henry	1	4	5		2
Dumas, David, Senr	1	5	2		15
Dumas, David, Junr	1		1		3
Davison, Josiah	1	2	5		
Davis, Robert	1	4	4		1
Dennis, Aandrew	1	1	6		
Davis, John	1	4	4		
Dennis, Nathaniel	1	6	4		
Dunn, Barnaba					13
Davis, John	1	5	4		
Davison, George	3	3	4		14
Durham, Thomas	1	4	4		2
Davis, Gabriel	1	4	4		
Daniel, Barton	1	1	5		
Davis, Isaac	1				
Dotson, Hightower	1	1	8		
Davis, Nathaniel	1				
Duke, James	1		3		
Denson, Edmond	2	2	4		
Durgin, William	1	1	1		3
Davis, Abraham	1	2	2		
Edins, William	1		5		
Edwards, Nathaniel	2	5	1		1
Lee, James	1		1		
Lee, William	2	1	3		

NAME OF HEAD OF FAMILY.	Free white males of 16 years and upward, including heads of families.	Free white males under 16 years.	Free white females, including heads of families.	All other free persons.	Slaves.
Lathran, William	1	1	4		
Lee, Sarah		2	6		1
Lesby, Christopher	1	1	3		
Lewis, Charles	1	2	1		
McClain, Duncan	1	1	1		2
Munroe, Cathrine	1		2		2
Martain, John	1	4	3		
Macafee, Malcom	1		4		
Mask, William	3	2	3		10
Mathews, Daniel	1	5	1		
Mecauly, John	2	4	5		
Mecoskell, John	1	4	1		
McCloud, Duncan	1		3		
Mecoskill, William	3	3	3		
McClannon, Alexander	1	1	3		1
McCloud, Norman	3	1	4		
Megill, Hactor	1	3	2		
McCoskill, Mary	1	1	5		
McClannon, Edward	1	2	3		
McCloud, Elizabeth	1	2	3		
Mein, Donold	1	5	2		
McCinnan, Christopher	1	2	1		
Meckintush, Swain	1	3	4		
Murkinson, Donold	3				
Morgan, Thomas	1	4	4		1
Menosko, Jeremiah	1	3	5	1	
McCaskill, Hurdly	1				
McClandon, Isbal		2	4		
McDuffe, Donold	1	4	2		
McDonnold, Allen	1		3		
Munn, James	4	2	4		
Morton, William F	1		2		
Mathews, Martha	1				2
McCloud, Norman	1	1	4		
Moore, Micajah	2	4	3		
McCloud, Mary	1	1	3		
Mumford, Henry	2	1	1		4
McCloud, Christian	2	2	3		
McCallum, Edward	2	3	4		
McCallum, John	1	1	2		
Monroe, Daniel	2	1	1		4
McKinnon, Alexander	1	3	1		
Morris, Mary	1	2	2		
Minard, Thomas	2		3		
Morris, Thomas	1	1	4		
More, John	1	1	5		
McDonald, James	3	1	1		10
More, Jesse	2	2	7		
More, Thomas	3	3	3		
McClay, Colin	1	5	3		1
Mason, Thomas	1	3	4		2
Megginson, Thomas	1	3	4		6
McClendon, Jesse	2	5	3		8
Morris, John	2		6		
Morris, Haton	2	2	4		
More, Nathan	2	1	2		
Morris, Thomas	1	2	3		
More, Thomas	1	2	2		
McKeshon, Nehemiah	2	4	3		5
Morris, Haton, Senr	1		4		
More, James	1	1	2		
McCray, Alexander	1		2		
More, Morris	1		1		
Mercer, Christopher	2	2	2		
Morton, George	2	3			
Mabry, Phillip	1		1		
More, William	1	5	4		1
McClemore, John	1	3	3		
Morgan, Garrat	1	3	1		4
Morgan, William	1	1	1		1
Monday, Mary	2		3		
Monday, William	1		3		
McClemore, Stamley	1	3	3		
Morris, William	1	1	2		
Morris, William, Senr	1	1	2		
Morris, John	1	1	1		
Morris, John, Senr	2	4	3		
Morris, John, Junr	3		4		
Miller, Conrodhush	1	1	2		
Mabry, Sarah	1	3	4		1
McClisten, Daniel	1	2	3		
Moss, Robert	1	5	6		9
Merienan, Nicholas	1		3		
Megrigler, William	1	2	3		4
Morris, John	1				
Megrigler, Bartlett	1	1	2		
Meniman, Charles	2		3		
Miller, John	1	1	3		
Megche, Charles	1	1	3		
Megche, William	1	2	4		
McClendon, Thomas	1	4	2		
Mothary, William	1	3	4		
Mariman, Abraham	2	1	1		
Mariman, Isham	1	1	2		
Motley, Thomas	1	3	1		
Morgan, Jonathan	1	1	2		
Miller, William	2	1	5		

SALISBURY DISTRICT, MONTGOMERY COUNTY—Continued.

NAME OF HEAD OF FAMILY.	Free white males of 16 years and upward, including heads of families.	Free white males under 16 years.	Free white females, including heads of families.	All other free persons.	Slaves.
McKentire, William	1		1		
Mainer, John	1	2	1		
Mathews, Anthony	3	5	6		
McKentire, William, Ser	1		1		
Meriman, Stephen	1		2		
Morgan, William	1	1	7		
Chub, John					1
Nickols, Edmond	1	3	3		
Nickols, Joseph	1	2	3		
Nickols, Edmond, Senr	1		2		
Nickols, William	1	3	1		
Nickols, John	2	2	4		
Nesbit, Jane			2	2	22
Noble, David	1	5	3		
Noble, Samson	1		3		
Noble, William	2	1			
Noble, Mary				6	
Naran, Sarah	1	2	1		7
Ozier, William	3		2		
Orie, Samuel	1		1		
Obrian, James	2	3	5		
Onsby, Walter	1	4	4		
Pemberton, Stith	1	1	4		3
Persons, John	1	2	4		
Persons, Joseph	1	1	2		1
Persons, Samuel	2		5		
Pemberton, Richard	1				5
Poore, David	4	4	2		5
Pierce, Sion	2	1	3		
Pritchard, Cary	2	4	3		4
Pitcock, Stephen	1				
Pritchard, Thomas	2		2		
Pierce, Gadwell	1	6	2		
Pennington, Neddy	1				
Pennington, Nelson	1				
Parker, Howel	1	3	4		3
Pennington, David	3	3	8		9
Palmore, John	3	3	4		
Pennington, Kinchin	1		4		
Pistole, Charles	1	1			
Pool, Sanders	1	2	1		
Pool, Alexander	2	4	3		
Philips, James	3	2	3		
Pistole, Charles	2	1	3		2
Pilcher, Robert	1	2	2		
Polland, Thomas	1	3	3		
Poplin, John	1	3	6		
Philips, William	1	3	3		
Pierce, Philip	1	1	2		
Poplin, Richard	1		1		
Queen, Henson	2	2	3		1
Lusk, William	3	3	5		10
Raynolds, Anderson	2		2		
Robertson, Cornelius	3	1	3		13
Robertson, Charles	1				3
Robertson, John	1	4	4		1
Randled, John	2		4		8
Right, Edward	1	3	3		
Randle, Johnson	1	4	1		
Randle, Benajah	1	1	5		
Raiford, Mathew	1	3	4		1
Raiford, James	1		2		2
Russell, Mathew				3	
Randle, Colby	2	3	5		2
Raynolds, James	2	4	3		
Redwine, Michael	1		2		
Russel, John	1	4	2		
Redwine, Jacob	1	2	7		
Russel, William	1	3	4		
Russel, Tames	1	3	1		
Russel, Thomas	1		1		1
Reaves, Josias	1		1		
Reaves, Samuel	1	3	4		
Russel, Lenard	1		2		
Redwine, Fredrick	1	1	1		
Reaves, William	1		1		
Rowland, Thomas	1	3	2		
Robins, John	2	1	5		2
Rowland, Hosea	1	2	3		
Rumage, George	1	2	3		
Rumage, George	1		1		
Rice, William	1	5	4		
Randle, William	2	3	2		16
Randle, Edmond	1	3	5		
Randle, John	2	2	7		8
Rogers, James	2	1	4		
Rogers, Fredrick	1				
Ransby, Isaac	2	2	4		
Rowland, Agustine	2		1		
Roberson, Tyry	1	3	5		1
Randle, Peter	2	3	4		14
Randle, Paton	1		3		4
Roland, Sherwood	1	4	6		
Loland, Isaac	1	3	1		
Roland, Ausburn	1				
Rusby, Unslis		1	2		
Martin, John	1		1		
Sanders, Joshua	1	4	1		
Spencer, William	2	2	5		6
Spencer, Johnson	1		1		
Simons, John	1	5	1		
Smith, Alexander	1	1	2		
Simons, Benjamin	1		1		
Smith, John	1	1	2		
Smith, Joseph	1	2	4		
Swon, John	2	3	6		1
Sumner, Benjamin	1	1	5		3
Smith, John	1	1	3		
Story, James	2	2	2		
Singleton, Edmund	1	3	2		
Singleton, Robert	1				
Stringfallow, William	2	1	2		
Singleton, Robert	2	3	3		
Simmons, Elizabeth			2		2
Simmons, Jesse	1		1		
Sawel, John	1	2	3		
Smith, Nathan	2	3	6		
Sawel, John, Senr	1	1	2		
Smith, Isham	1	2	6		
Suggs, Jasse	1	1	2		
Sanders, Aaron	1		1		
Stogner, George	1	2	2		
Smith, John	1		2		
Scarber, John	2	2	3		7
Stephens, Henry	1	1	4		
Stephens, James	1	5	4		
Suggs, Harbert	1		4		
Stephens, John	1	2	1		
Spirey, Charles	1	1	4		1
Stephens, Francis	1	1	3		
Stephens, Robert	1		3		
Stavy, Joseph	2	2	4		
Smith, James	1	2	3		1
Scarber, James	1	4	2		
Shephard, John	1	3	3		
Suggs, Thomas	1	3	2		
Stagner, John	1	2	1		
Stagner, Benjamin	1	4	3		
Sanders, James	3	2	2		
Sanders, Joshua	1	3	2		
Sanders, Jeffrey	1		4		
Steed, Moses	2	3	5		5
Sanders, Jacob	1	4	3		
Stewart, William	1	1	4		
Sanders, James	1	4	2		
Stewart, John	1	1	4		
Suggs, John	1	3	3		
Suggs, George	2	1	2		
Seratt, Joseph	1	1	1		
Seratt, Joseph, Senr	1	1	1		
Sworngance, John	1	4	4		
Suggs, John Henry	2	2	3		
Suggs, Thomas	1		2		
Stokes, Robert	3	4	6		3
Simpson, Thomas	2	1	2		
Shankle, Jacob	1	3	2		
Smith, Richard	1				
Shankle, George	2		1		4
Shankle, John	1	3	4		
Smith, John	2	1	6		11
Styles, William	1		4		
Suggs, William	1	3	3		
Smith, Joseph	1		3		
Smith, John	1		5		8
Stokes, Young	2	3	1		
Self, Spencer	2	5	3		
Self, Francis	1		6		
Stokes, William	1	1	2		
Self, Isaac	1	1	4		
Smith, Asa	1	1	2		
Shankle, Valentine	1	1	1		
Smith, William	1	1	5		
Smith, Josep	1		5		
Shinpock, Lawrance	1	1	2		
Smith, Sherwood	1	1	2		
Self, Presley	1	2	3		
Still, Banjamin	1		2		
Turner, James	2	2	2		25
Travers, Charles	3	2	1		3
Touchstone, Stephen	2	1	2		
Trent, William	1	3	3		7
Thomas, John	3	7	5		1
Touchstone, Caleb	2	2	5		1
Thorn, Robert	3		2		
Turner, Susanah			1	2	
Taylor, George	1	1	2		
Turner, Brehabuck			1		4
Tedder, Benjemin	1		3		1
Tilman, Richard	1	2	4		3
Thomson, John	1	2	4		
Thompson, Elisha	1	4	4		
Tucker, George	1	2	7		
Taylor, John	1	1	3		1
Taylor, Cannon	1	1	3		
Thompson, Walter	2	1	3		
Thompson, John	1	3	2		
Tredwell, Stephen	3	3	4		
Tankisby, John	1		5		
Tindle, James	3	4	5		24
Truct, Parnel			3		
Tindle, Richard	1		2		3
Telby, Thornton	1		1		
Telby, Henry	1	3	5		
Taylor, Edmond	1	6	5		
Taylor, Hudson	1	1	5		3
Taylor, William	1	2	5		
Turner, James	3	1	8		
Turner, Thomas	1	1	2		
Thomison, Richard	2	2	4		
Tresby, David	1	2	1		
Tresby, Sarah			1	6	
Taylor, Robert	1	2	2		
Tredwell, Samuel	1		2		
Usseroy, Wilcon	1	1	6		
Usseroy, Thomas	1	5	7		4
Usseroy, Peter	1	2	3		
Usseroy, John	1		2		
Usseroy, Joshua	1	2	3		
Usseroy, David	1	1	4		
Usseroy, Elijah	1		3		
Usseroy, John	1		7		
Upenurch, Thomas	1	3	5		
Vickry, Joseph	1	2	4		
Vanhooser, Valentine	3	3	3		
Vanhooser, John	1		1		
Vandike, Thomas	1	1	6		
Walice, Jesse	1		3		
Ward, Thomas, Senr	2	1	2		
Williams, Thomas	2	1	11		
Williams, Solomon	1	1	10		
Wilson, Martha	1		2		5
Williams, Stephen	1		3		
Williams, Isham	3	2	4		2
Williams, James	2	2	4		1
Williams, Roger	1	3	3		
Williams, Seth	3	5	1		3
Wilson, Joseph	1		2		
Williams, Samuel	4	4	4		
Ware, Thomas	1	2	6		4
Watts, Peter	1	2	2		
Williams, Amos	1	2	2		
Williams, Benjamin	1		2		
Wolby, William	1	4	2		1
Williams, William	1		2		9
Williams, Thomas	1	2	6		2
Brooks, Jacob West	1	3	4		
Wester, Axem	1	2	6		
Wallis, William	1				
Ward, Philip	1	3	4		
Wall, John	1	6	3		
Weaver, Michael	1	5	2		
Wardrupt, Edward	2	4	4		
Whitby, George	2	4	3		
Whitby, Exedus	2	1	2		
Wimberly, Moses	1		3		
Whitby, George	1	3	3		2
Weaver, William	1	2	3		
Yeoman, Stokes	2	3	2		
Young, James	2	2	4		
Yarborough, John					

SALISBURY DISTRICT, ROCKINGHAM COUNTY.

NAME OF HEAD OF FAMILY.	Free white males of 16 years and upward, including heads of families.	Free white males under 16 years.	Free white females, including heads of families.	All other free persons.	Slaves.
Stublefield, Richard	6		4		5
Bethel, Samuel	1	3	4		
Lewis, Peter	1	3	2		
Mullin, Thomas	3		2		3
Mullin, William	1		1		
Adair, Stephen	2	2	3		
McClain, Joseph	1	3	2		
Hainey, Reuben	1		1		
Samuel, Andrew		2	3		
Dixon, Berry	2	3	1		
Harris, Robert	1	3	3		
Bentin, David	1	2	3		
Humphris, John	1		2	2	1
Johnston, Henry	1	3	5		
Owen, Joseph	1	1	1		

SALISBURY DISTRICT, ROCKINGHAM COUNTY—Continued.

NAME OF HEAD OF FAMILY.	Free white males of 16 years and upward, including heads of families.	Free white males under 16 years.	Free white females, including heads of families.	All other free persons.	Slaves.	NAME OF HEAD OF FAMILY.	Free white males of 16 years and upward, including heads of families.	Free white males under 16 years.	Free white females, including heads of families.	All other free persons.	Slaves.	NAME OF HEAD OF FAMILY.	Free white males of 16 years and upward, including heads of families.	Free white males under 16 years.	Free white females, including heads of families.	All other free persons.	Slaves.
Burton, John	1	1	1			Norman, Courtney	1	1	9			Walker, John	1	1	4		
Caldwell, William	1	6	1		2	Curry, Ezekiel	1		1			Covington, Mary		1	3		
Hainey, Spencer	1		2			Roberts, Elizabeth		1	7		3	Moceat, Matthias	1	2	5		
McClain, Thomas	1		1			Lefew, Stephen	2	6	2			Brown, John	1		2		
Watt, Samuel	3	5	3		8	Lefew, Mary		3	1			Brown, Hubbard	1		1		
McCallum, Jas	1	3	8			Lord, James	1	3	4			Williams, David	1	4	5		
Horseford, John	1	4	4			Burril, John	1	1	4			Shelton, John	1	2	3		
Jones, Ezekiel	1	2	4			McBride, Francis	2	2	4			Knight, Robert	1	2	3		
Dean, James	2	2	1		8	McBride, Isaiah	1	3	2			Stone, Burgis	1	1	2		
Loftis, William	1	3	4			Moore, John	1	6	3			Short, Moses, Senr	3	1	2		1
Dean, Elisha	1	2	2		1	Dobbins, James	3	1	4			Warner, John	1	2	5		
Dean, Charles	1	1	2			Lanier, Sampson	1	2	2		4	Simpson, Thomas	1	2	3		
Dean, Charles, Jur	2		2			Paris, Samuel	3	3	2			McCarty, Timothy	1	1	3		
McCallister, William	1	3	2			King, Thomas	2	4	4			Campbell, Rebecca	1	1	1		
Carrot, Henry	2	4	4			Frost, James	1	6	3			Massy, Machner	1	1	1		
Watt, John	1	1	2			Daily, Patrick	1	1	3			Murphy, Archibald	1	1	3		
Mills, Mathew	2	5	4		13	Jones, Benjamin	1	4	2			Mack, John	2	4	3		
Chandlor, John	1	3	4			Ditto for Iron Works	2				35	Mack, James	1	2	1		
Marr, Richard		3	4		23	Hayes, James	1		3		3	Wilson, Aquilla	3	3	2		5
Challis, John	2	2	2		7	Purtle, John	3	4	1			Wilson, James	2	2	6		2
Thrasher, Pleasant	1	1	3			Hunter, John	2		6		9	Wilson, Thomas	2		4		4
Hoverton, Obediah	1		1			Peeples, Burwell	1	2	3		3	Murphy, Miles	4	5	7		
Knight, John	1	1	2			Mobley, William	2	2	6			Murphy, William	1		3		
Russil, William	1	2	3			Elliott, William	2	1	2			Fitzgerald, James	1	4	5		2
Smith, Drewry	1	1	2			Lyrus, Jas, Sen	1	2	5			Brim, Richins	1	2	1		
Pipkin, Isaac	1					Walker, David	1	1	4		4	Cantril, Charles	1	2	2		
Davis, John	2		2			Sanders, Jas, Jur	2		3			Brim, Keziah		3			
Newcomb, Joseph	1	3	1			French, Mason						Compton, Ebenezer	1		1		
McCubbin, Jas	1	2	1			Fits, Conny		2	5			Nighton, William	1	3	2		
McCubbin, John	1	1	4			Martin, Spencer	1		3			Smith, William	1	3	4		
Smith, John, Jur	1		4			Overton, Moses	1	4	1			Challis, Martha	1		3		10
Aldedair, Alexander	1		4			Brown, Margaret	3	1	1			Ward, William	2	1	5		
Smith, Samuel	1	3	2		1	Allen, John	1	4	1			Bents, Abraham	2	3	3		
Wright, John	1	2	3			Grogan, Henry	2	3	6			Garrison, Aron	1	1	3		
Harris, William	1	4	1			Terry, Peter	2	1	7		7	Huckman, William	1	2	6		
Smith, John	2		2		4	Herring, Saml	1	1	5		1	Adcock, Edward	1	3	4		
Wright, Francis	1	4	3			Hendricks, Abraham	1	1	2			Wilson, Andrew	1	1	5		2
Cantril, Aron	1	1	5			Williams, Robt	1	1	7			Humphries, John	2		2		
Porter, Lawrence	1	2	5			Stublefield, Richd	6		2		2	Wilson, William	1	5	2		1
Sparks, Thomas	1		2			Amberson, Mathew	3		6			Wilson, William, Jur	1	1	2		
McCubbin, Nicholas	1	6	3		4	Conner, John	2		2			Williams, James	1		2		2
Dill, John	4	3	2			Conner, Thomas	1		3			Taylor, James	1		3		4
Allen, Thomas	1	3	3			Wall, Peter	1	1	2			Adams, Thomas	1	1	4		
Hopkins, Jonathan	1	2	3			Wall, David, Sen	1	1	2		1	Wiseman, Martin	1	5	3		
Bishop, Joseph	1		4			Grady, Reuben	1	3	2			Wiseman, Henry	1	1	1		
Moore, William	1		2			King, Wiat	1		1			Burk, John	2	1	1		
Ratchford, Luke	1		2			Carter, Thomas	1	2	8			Burk, Henson	1	1	2		
Williams, Nathaniel	3	1	6		13	Guttery, Thos	2	5	4		1	Jackson, John	1		2		
Reagon, John	1		2		1	Hinton, Jesse	1		2			Roberson, William	3	1	2		
Hornbuckle, William	1	3	6		1	Larkin, Thos	1	1	3			Wilson, James	3		1		
Barnet, David	1		3			Bernard, Thos	1	4	4			Roberson, William, Jur	3		2		
Lowe, Thomas	2	1	4		2	Chance, Thomas	1	2	1			Vandegrift, Christo	3	1	4		1
Ewes, William	1	1	4			Curry, John, Senr	3		2			Traynum, William	1	1	3		
Lowe, Nancy			3		1	Jones, William, Senr	2	1	5			Walker, Robert	1	1	2		
Martin, Andrew		1	2			Walker, William, Jur	1					Dodd, John	1		2		
Todd, William	2	4	3		2	Loftis, William, Sen	1	3	2			Curtier, Peter	1	1	2		
Miller, William	1	2	3			Taylor, Hartford	1		1			Howel, John	2	3	4		
Lowe, John	1	2	7		6	Akins, John	1	1	3			Witty, Elijah	1	3	3		
Procter, William	1	1	3			Thomas, George	1		3			Tharp, William	1		6		
Patrick, Hugh	1	1	4			Prewit, Joshua	1	1	3			Cunningham, Jno, Jur	1		1		
Patrick, Mary	3		4		2	North, Thomas	1		3			Stockard, John	3	5	4		
Gray, Thomas	1		1			Cornelious, George	2		3			Heath, John	1		4		
Appleton, Jas	2	2	3		2	Bellingsly, Henry	2	2	3			Young, Samuel	2	4	3		2
Patrick, Jas	1	1	2			Wall, Rebecca	3	1	1			Kirkpatrick, Sarah	1	1	3		1
Moore, Samuel	1		2			Lord, Aaron, Senr	1		3			King, Levi	1		4		
Hanby, David	1	3	2		12	Dollerhide, Aquilla	1	1	3			Peeples Lewis	1		4		4
Nelson, Levina		2	6		6	Jones, William (R. S.)	2	2	4			Brown, George	1	1	2		
Johnston, Jos Pair	1	4	5			Conn, John	1	2	2			McPeck, William	1	1	1		
Brown, Samuel	1	1	3			Wallace, William	1	3	3			Lemore, Thomas	2		3		
Russel, William	1		5			Nickles, Jas, Senr	3	5	2		1	Blagg, William	1	1	3		
Vaughan, David	1		2		4	Jones, John	1		3			Bennet, Joseph	1	4	4		
Cockran, Wm	2		1		1	Fleming, Robert	1	5	2			Moore, Thomas	2	4	5		
Hubbard, William						Bethel, Duncan	2	1	1			Knight, Thomas	1		7		
Hubbard, William	1	3	4			Dimond, Stewart	1	1				Lovel, William	1		1		
Martin, Andw	1	2	2			Philips, Joseph	1		3			Lovel, Syrus	1		2		
Hall, Andrew	1	2	5			Carman, Hezekiah	2		1			Toney, Sherwood	1	3	2		
Matear, Jas	2					Spencer, Benjamin	1	4	4		2	Traynum, Reuben	1	1	4		
Roberson, Andrew	1	2	3			Spencer, Thomas	1		3		1	Simmons, Isham	1	4	5		
Wardlow, John	2		3			Hodge, Francis	1	2	2			Spencer, Abraham	2	3	2		1
Blockus, John	2		2			Donaky, Jas	3		4			Simmons, John	1	4	5		
Stratton, William	1					Garner, Joseph	1	2	2		2	Armstrong, John	1		1		
Hopper, Thomas	1	2	2			Linder, John	1	4	5		3	Patterson, William	2	1	5		
Thomas, Lewis	1	3	4			Mabry, Cornelius	2	1	2			Thompson, Edward	1	1	2		
Key, Thomas	4	1	6		4	Sealy, John	2	3	3		4	Patterson, Francis	1		1		
Martin, John	1	2	3			Glenn, John	2	2	4			Farley, Benjamin	1	2	2		
Mitchel, Levin	2	1	2			Todd, William, Senr	2	4	4		3	Akin, Jas	1	2	3		
Moore, Benjamin	1	5	3		2	Walker, Elmore	2	2	2			Leachman, John	1		3		2
Jones, William	1	3	3			Walker, Jesse	1	1	1			Stephens, William	2	4	5		3
Curry, John	1	1	2			Scurry, Susannah	1	2	6			Toney, Charles	1	2	3		
Seales, David	1	2	2			Lewis, Shadrack	1	3	4			Nichol, Thomas	1		6		
Denny, Joseph	1		2			Deatherege, Elizabeth	2	1	2		2	Howerton, John	1	1	6		
Denny, Walter	1		2			Joyce, Robert	1		6		1	Norris, Ann			3		
Harris, Robert	1	3	3			Morton, Jehu	2	2	6		1	Pritchet, William	1	1	3		
Mount, Thomas	1	1	3			Nelson, Robert	2	1	4			Parrott, Abner	1	4	5		21
Vincent, Moses	2	2	3		6	Nelson, Samuel	1		4			Connelly, William	3	2	2		
Burton, Robert	1	2	3			Main, Henry		1	4			Jones, William, Senr (H.)	3	1	5		
Morgan, Orson	1	2	3									Mussely, Peter	1	1	6		

SALISBURY DISTRICT, ROCKINGHAM COUNTY—Continued.

NAME OF HEAD OF FAMILY.	Free white males of 16 years and upward, including heads of families.	Free white males under 16 years.	Free white females, including heads of families.	All other free persons.	Slaves.	NAME OF HEAD OF FAMILY.	Free white males of 16 years and upward, including heads of families.	Free white males under 16 years.	Free white females, including heads of families.	All other free persons.	Slaves.	NAME OF HEAD OF FAMILY.	Free white males of 16 years and upward, including heads of families.	Free white males under 16 years.	Free white females, including heads of families.	All other free persons.	Slaves.
Jones, William, Jur	1	3	3			Bartie, George	1	3	4			Lacy, Martha	2	1	3		18
Denny, Walter, Jur	3		2			Barns, James	2	3	4			Menzin, John	1	3	6		11
Norris, William	1	3	4			Periman, Joseph	1	1	2			Clark, Joseph	1		1		3
Curry, Ezekiel	3	2	6			Baker, William	1	3	2			Peay, George, Sen	6		1		7
Cox, Joseph	1	1	1			Smith, Saml	1	2	2			Clark, William, Ju	3		3		4
Brannock, Henry	1	1	2		1	Brown, Saml	1	3	3			Rose, Philip	5	3	5		4
Wright, Ann	2		5			Grogan, Bartholomew	1	3	3			Gibson, John	1		1		
Waford, John	2	3	6			Moxley, Nathl	3	2	5			Bradberry, William	1	2	2		
Cox, Jas	1	2	1			Pratt, Thomas	1	3	4			Cunningham, Joseph	3		3		
Cox, Joseph, Senr	2	2	4			Pratt, John	1	3	3			Haynes, John	2	3	5		
Buckanon, Wm	2	4	4			Fanning, William	1		1			McDaniel, Jas S	1	1	3		2
Gill, William	2	3	4			Allen, Wm Hunt	2	3	4		7	Medlock, John	1	1	3		
Mason, William	1		5			Cooper, William	2	1	1			Hayes, Henry	1		1		
Bean, John	1	1	3			Kennon, William	1		2			Hodge, Sarah	1		2		
Conner, Andrew	3	1	1			Gains, Robert	2	2	3		4	Walker, Elmore	1	1	1		
Philips, Abraham	1	2	3		3	Gilleland, Robert	1	3	5			Garrison, Samuel	1		1		
Nance, Peter	1	1	5			Whitworth, Jacob	2		3			Dines, William	1		1		
Mullin, Patrick	1		1			Whitworth, Isaac, Jur	1		1			Cunningham, Wm	1		2		
Sheppard, John	1	2	5			Bailey, Robert	1	2	4			Spurier, Theophilus	1		1		
Carner, John D	1		1			Gates, Philip	2	2	5			Short, Samuel, Sen	1	3	4		
Gorman, Joseph	1	1	1			Burns, John	1	3	3			Lancir, Nathl	1	5	4		
Purnel, Samuel	2	2	4			Mathews, William	1		2			Jones, William	1	2	5		
Case, William	1	3	2			Poindexter, David	1		3		1	Short, Oldham	1	4	2		
Webster, Solomon	2	3	5			Fore, Francis	1	1	9		2	Bradley, John	1				8
King, Thomas, Senr	3	2	2			Stephens (Widow)			3			Peeples, Henry	1	1	3		3
Young, William	2	3	4			Stephens, William	1	2	3			Peggs, Mathew	1	1	1		
McCollister, Sutton	1	1	2			Cotteril, Edward	2	5	1			Jones, John	1	1	4		
Gray, Thomas, Jur	1		1			Alexander, Daniel	1	2	4			Moore, Thos	1	6	4		
Crowel, Zenas	1	2	3			Grogan, Thomas	1	1	2			Gwin, Hugh	2	3	4		
Tatom, Nathl	3	2	2		6	Harris, John	3	2	5			Brasher, Zaza	1	4	3		
Conger, Benjamin	1	2	2			Grogan, Mary		2	2			Brown, Robert	1		3		
Harris, George	1	2	4			Alexander, Alexander	1		4			Allen, Aron	1	3	2		
Cunningham, John	1	1	2			Sams, Joseph	1	2	4			Philips, Jacob	1		2		
Duncan, Peter	1	2	4			Oliver, Williams	1	1	1			Moore, David	1	2	2		
Linder, Joseph	1	2	1			Watson, David	1	4	7			Lovuss, Michael	3	2	3		
Falling, Agnis	1	2	3			Fields, Mary	1		1			Short, Moses	1	1	1		1
Harrison, William	2	5	3			Fields, Nelson	1		1			Simpson, Nathl	1		1		
Purtle, George	1	1	2			Pratt, Jas	1	3	4			Boyd, Andw	1		2		
Kirkman, Thomas	1	1	1			Dearing, William	1	1	3		3	Williams, William	1	5	5		
Jones, David	2	4	3			Parker, Elisha	1	3	3			Lewis, Shadrack	1	3	3		
West, Charles	1	3	2			Hardin, William	1	1	1			Owen, John	2	2	1		2
Scott, Thomas	1		2			Warren, Robert	2	4	5			McKinney, John	2	1	4		1
Reesers, Leven	1	2	3			Settle, Benjamin	1		2		1	Akin, James	1	2	5		
Lowe, Thomas (T. C.)	1	3	4			Yell, Moses	1	2	2		5	Murphy, John	1	2	1		
Lowe, Isaac, Senr	1		2			Hallums, John	1	5	3		2	Hand, Christo	1	4	2		
Lowe, Isaac	1	2	3			Odell, John	2	1	6			Patterson, William	2	1	5		
Edmondson, John	1	2	2			Thrasher, Richard	1		2		1	Lillard, Moses	2	5	2		
Pearson, John	1	2	3			McCollom, William	1	1	3			Yeoman, Drewry	4		3		18
Hodge, Sarah	1		3			Prichard, Rachael	2	1	4		3	Mackie, John	1	2	4		
Allison, John	1	3	5			Pearson, Sullivan	1	2	6			Hopper, Joseph	3	1	7		
Fields, Ansil	2	3	4			McCalib, Jas	1	2	1			Cantril, Jacob	2	4	3		
Gowing, Jas	1	3	3			Hallums, George	1	1	1			Oneal, Peter	4	5	5		11
Colson, George	2	4	4			Terrant, Henry	1		3			Walker, Alexander	1	1	5		
Pratt, Richard	1		2		1	Barton, John	1	1	1			Lynch, Hugh	1	2	6		
Wright, William	1	2	7			Dudley, Christo	2	1	4			Barr, Robert	1	3	3		
Bowers, Henry	1	4	4			Williams, James	1		2			Martin, John	1	4	4		
Watson, William	1		3			Williams, Edward	1	4	3			Martin, Walter	1		1		2
Smith, Polly		2	1			Brown, Samuel	1	1	3			Spout, William	3	1	3		
Barns, Terbefield	2	4	3		1	Simmons, John	1	4	4			Hill, John	3	2	3		
Grogan, Francis	3					McCarrol, John	2	2	7			Dilworth, George	1	1	2		
Thompson, John	1	2	5			Morris, Nancy		2	1			Boyd, William	1	2	3		
Fleming, William	2	3	3		2	McCarrol, James	1		2			Walker, William	1	2	4		1
Strange, Jas	1	2	5			Forkner, Thos	1	1	4			Walker, Joel	1	2	2		
Farguson, John	1	6	5			Tyler, Reuben	1		1			Scurry (Widow)	1	2	5		1
Reagan, James	2	2	2		3	Chambers, Thomas	1		2			Walker, Allen	1	1	2		
Wright, Prudence		2	3			Brown, Joshua	1	1	2			Roach, James	1	2	4		
Timmons, Nathl	1	2	1			Martin, Andrew	1	1	1			Barnet, Jacob	2		7		
Vernon, Richard	2	1	1			Walker, William, Jur	1		3			Stanford, John	2	1	5		
Axton, Robert	2	5	4			Thrasher, John	1	1	3			Coffer, Joshua	2		2		24
Irion, Henry	1	2	3			Short, Samuel	1	3	4			Henderson, Samuel	1	2	6		10
Smith, Zachariah	1	5	3			Thrasher, John	1	1	3			Dodd, Allen	3		6		1
Reed, John	1	4	2			Kelly, Jas	1	5	1			Thomas, Michael	1	2	6		1
Smith, Drewry	3	3	7			Oakley, Richard	1	3	3			Odell, Joseph	3	5	7		
Russil, Enoch	1	1	5			Seales, Henry	2	3	5		13	Pain, Thomas	1	3	4		
Brooks, Humphry	1	2	2			McBride, John	1		2			Sutherland, William	1	1	3		3
Smith, Fanny	1	1	2			Young, John	4	2	4			McElroy, Jas	1	1	3		
Smith, Thomas, Senr	1	1	4			Massey, Thomas	1	3	6		9	Wardlow, Patrick	1	1	3		
Motby, William	1	1	2			Moceat, John	1	4	6			Dunlap, Henry	3	5	3		
Hunter, George	1		1			Oakley, Jas	1	3	2			Caffey, Michael	1	2	3		
Hunter, Peter	1	1	1			Adkinson, John	1		4			McElroy, Wm	1	1	1		
Roach, William	1	1	2			Williams, John	1		1			McElroy, Agnis			2		
Shropshire, Winkfield	4		1			Hamlin, George	1	3	1			Sheppard, John	1	2	2		
Perry, Thomas	1	2	7			Haynes, Daniel	1	3	2			Richardson, Edward	2	1	2		
Frost, Jonas	2	2	3		2	Barnet, Elisha	1	1	3			McCallister, Ezekeil	1		1		
Russil, Richard	3	3	2			Winchester, Coleman	1		3			Bright, James	1	2	3		
Haynes, Daniel	2	3	3			Barnet, Luke	2	3	2			Covington, John	1		3		
Led, Aron, Jur	1	3	2			Blear, John	1		1			Brigs, Elisha	1	1	2		
Haynes, Elijah	1	1	1			Kinman, George	1	4	3			Thrasher, Joseph Cloud	2	2	2		5
McCollister, John	1	2	2			Winchester, John	1		1			Hendricks, Henry	3		2		
Geiren, Nathan	2	5	2			Duncan, Peter	2		1			Chisolm, John	1	2	2		2
McElroy, Jas, Jur	1	1	1			Winchester, John, Senr	2		1			Williams, Drewry	1	3	3		7
Blackburn, John	1	5	4			Adkinson, John	1		1			Roland, George	3	1	2		
Patrick, Jas	2	1	2		1	Cunningham, John	1	1	2			Hill, Walter	1	2	2		
Wright, Jas	2	3	2			Herron, John	1		1			Langham, Jas	1	1	7		
Haynes, Jonathan	2	3	4			Hardiman, Thomas	3	2			7	Hodge, John C	1		1		
Morris, Nancy		2	1			Walker, William, Jur	1	1	3			Brown, Alexander	1	1	1		1
Russil, James	1	2	2			Lacy, Bats Cock	1				7	Williams, Edward	1	3	2		
Lord, Andrew	1	2	4			Philips, Thomas	1	2	2		1	Strong, John	3		3		

SALISBURY DISTRICT, ROCKINGHAM COUNTY—Continued.

NAME OF HEAD OF FAMILY.	Free white males of 16 years and upward, including heads of families.	Free white males under 16 years.	Free white females, including heads of families.	All other free persons.	Slaves.
Richer, Jas	1	1	1		
Deaver, Mary		3	1		
Strong, Mary		4	6		
McAllister, Jesse	1	1	1		
Vanlandingham, Richd	1	3	3		
Tate, Adam	2		1		11
Cox, John	1		3		2
Adkins, Daniel	1	1	6		
May, Peter	1	3	1		7
Larimore, Nicholas	4	3	5		
Grady, William	1	1	5		
Prichard, John	1	1	3		
Walker, Elmore	2	2	3		
Gustrer, Absalom	1		3		
Haggard, Benjamin	1		1		
Young, Samuel	1	2	5		
Wall, John	1	2	5		3
Reed, Hugh	1	5	3		
Hill, Saml	1		3		
Corry, Saml	1				
Dilworth, Thomas	1	1	2		
Dilworth, John	3	4	3		
Philips, Joseph	1		3		
Scarboro, Jas	1	2	1		
Smith, Edward	1				
Dilworth, Benjamin	2	6	3		
Allen, Joseph	3		1		
Jones, Edward	1	4	4		
Allen, Daniel	1	5	5		1
Johnston, Gideon, Jur	4		8		2
Massy, Mackness	1	1	3		
Johnston, William	2	2	4		1
Fields, John	2	3	4		1
Wray, Jas	2	3	4		
Walker, David, Sen	1	1	3		4
Abbott, John	1	2	5		
Hayes, James, Senr	4	2	7		1
Bailey, Thomas	2	1	1		
Martin, Robert	1				2
Henderson, Thomas	4	3	4		14
Calhoon, James	1	2	5		
Whitworth, John	1	4	2		
Whitworth, Isaac	1	1	4	1	
Bevers, Abigail	1	1	2	1	
Overton, Ann Booker	3	3	3		7
Lemmon, John	3	2	5		7
Fields, William	1		2		
French, William	2		1		
Barker, Leonard	1	2	4		1
McClellan, William	1	3	3		
Barker, Mary		2	4		
Holderness, Jas	2		1		5
Linder, Nathl	1		5		
Allison, John	2	1	4		1
Hosford, John	1	4	4		
Nance, William	1	4	4		
Williams, David	1	4	5		
May, John	1	3	1		8
Odeneal, John	1	1	6		7
Hardin, Henry	1	1	4		3
Oliver, John	1	2	3		
Thrasher, Ruth			1		
Newcom, Joseph	1	2	2		
Bishop, Joseph	1		4		
Thacher, Nathan	1		3		
Larimer, Philip	2	1	3		
Williams, Aron	1		2		10
Roberts, Naman	1	1	2		5
Rhodes, Hezekiah	2	2	2		3
Richey, John	1	3	3		
Fowler, William	1	2	3		
Norris, John	1	1	4		
Johnston, John	1	1	2		4
Hardin, Thomas	3		4		7
Allen, Benjamin	1		4		
Allen, John	2	1	4		
Small, Robert	1	6	1		1
Henderson, Richard	2	4	5		
Henderson, Jno	1	1	1		
Trolender, Michael	4	2	4		
Trolender, Adam	1	1	1		
Jones, John	1	1	1		

NAME OF HEAD OF FAMILY.	Free white males of 16 years and upward, including heads of families.	Free white males under 16 years.	Free white females, including heads of families.	All other free persons.	Slaves.
Lovel, David	2	1	2		
Lovel, David, Ju	1	2	5		
Lovel, Zachariah	1				
Lovel, William	1				
Lovel, Syrus	1				
Cummins, John	2		5		2
Cummins, Robert	1	1	2		
Jones, David	1	1	2		
Rhodes, Jas	1	1	2		
Lemmons, Alexander	1	2	2		
Winston, William	2	2	3		
Triplit, Catharine	1		2		
Conner, Jas	2		1		
Jennings, William	1	2	1	1	1
McClellan, Robert	1		4		
Martin, Govr Alexander	3	1	2		47
Allen, Valentine	3	1	1		28
Wall, David, Jur	1	1	3		
Chadwell, John	2	4	8		9
Irish, Philip Jacob	4	2	5		5
Peay, George, Jur	1	2	2		3
Gunn, Elisha	1	2	3		
Jenkins, William	1	4	1		
Wright, William	1		2		
Corry, Robert	1	1	2		1
Vermillon, Guy	1	1	2		
Cobbler, Thomas	1	1	2		
Asten, William	1		1		11
Odell, Lewis	1	1	4		
Bloyd, John	1	3	4		
Norman, Cortney	1	1	10		
Sanders, Robert	4	1	3		
Price, John	1		2		
Coleman, Robert	1	5	5		8
Harris, Nathl	4	2	5		10
Leak, John	3	1	6		4
Scales, Joseph	1		4		7
Clifton, Nancy	1				
Scales, Nathl	2	2	5		16
Scales, Mary	1				2
Davis, John	1	3	5		
Compton, Ebenezer	1				
Cobler, Harvey	1	3	2		
Strong, Sneed	1		4		
Roberts, Syrus L.	1	2	3		3
Cook, Benjamin	1	1	3		10
Burch, Wm S.	1		1		2
Smith, Joshua	3	2	4		3
Peggs, Mathew	1	3	3		
Gentry, Watson	1	2	4		9
Joyce, James	1	3	4		7
Whitworth, Jno	9	2	3		8
Sanders, James, Senr	2	3	6		
Harrison, William	1		5		
Harrison, Nathl	3	1	3		
Odell, William	1	4	6		
McReynolds, Thomas	2	3	3		10
Pounds, Thomas	2	2	6		
Wall, Daniel	1		5		
Dabney, John	1	3	5		9
Sims, Edward	1	2	2		
Suttle, Josiah	2		1		6
Lemmons, William	3	4	2		
Settle, David	1	1	2		2
Flack, Jas	1	1	5		
Mabry, Cornelious	1	3	2		
Work, Henry (&c.)	1	2	5		6
Taylor, Jas (for self & Farleys Estate)	2		4		32
Peay, William	3	2	13		
Gallaway, Robert	3				3
May, William	1				
Seales, Thomas	2	1	5		
Sharp, Richard	2	3	3		2
Smith, William	1		1		
Seales, John	2	2	1		3
Rogers, Samuel	3	3	4	4	4
Sharp, Saml	1		1		
Vernon, Mary		1	4		
Morgan, Milley		2	2		
Oliver, Jas	1	2	2		
Bundrant, Richard	2	2	3		

NAME OF HEAD OF FAMILY.	Free white males of 16 years and upward, including heads of families.	Free white males under 16 years.	Free white females, including heads of families.	All other free persons.	Slaves.
Camplin, Jacob	1		3		
Crawford, Adam	1		3		1
McClaran, Alexander	1	3	3		3
Smothers, Elizabeth		1	1		
Lister, Biddy		1	1		
Rickles, John	1	1	1		
Odell, Uriah	1	5	4		
Chandlor, Joseph	1	5	4		
Gibson, Elizabeth	1	3	4		
Shropshire, Winkfield	2	2	1		
Garrott, Henry	1	4	1		
Chandlor, Joseph	1		3		4
Hill, John	1	1	2		2
Hill, Elizabeth	1	2	5		13
Joyce, Elijah	1	4	5		8
Joyce, Robert	1		1		2
Colson, Henry	1	2	3		
Joyce, John	3	4	5		2
Deatherigs, George	2	1	3		2
Oliver, Martha	1	4	5		
Bethel, William	1	3	4		5
Martin, Walter	1				
Boak, Robert	2	1	3		
George, Mathew	2		1		
Granger, John	1	2	3		
Williams, Allen	2	1	5		
Young, John	2	1	5		
Herdson, Robert	2	3	3		
Lovel, David	1	2	5		
McCulloch, Joseph	1	1	1		
Crump, William	1		3		4
Joyce, John (P.)	1	2	3		7
Jones, John	1	1	5		
Irwin, George	1	4	2		
Walker, Jas	3		2		5
Joyce, Thomas	3	4	6		4
Gordon, Charles	1		2		
Gordon, Mary	1		3		
Scales, James	1	1	4		11
Philips, John	1	1	5		
Gann, John	1		3		
Vaughn, John	1	4	2		
Sharp, James	2	1	2		2
Sharp, Catharine			1		2
Hunter, James	3	3	4		11
Dalton, Charlotte	3	2	6		9
Burton, Edward	1				
Glenn, John, Jur	1				
Davis, John	2	3	5	4	3
Glenn, William	1		2		1
Shropshire, Dr John	1	4	4		
Osten, Richard	1	3	4		
Curtin, Joshua	1	3	5		
Curtin, Reuben	1	3	2		4
Colley, Maynard	2	2	4		
Cruak, Richard	1	1	2		4
Roberson, James	3	2	5		
Martin, James	3	2	4		
Walker, James	2	2	4		
Roland, George	2	3	4		
Grear, Ananias	2	4	3		
Stewart, John	1		1		2
Stewart, Jas	1	3	2		
Bundrant, Richd	2	3	4		
Childers, Stephen	2		2		
Brim, Joseph	2	1	2		7
Scales, Absalom	2	1	2		
Garne, Thomas	1	2	4		
Philips, Irby	1		2		
Syrus, James	1	2	4		
Means, Robert	1	3	4		
Philips, John	1	1	5		
Pratt, Thomas	1	3	5		
Sharp, Samuel	1		1		
Sharp, Catharine	1		1		2
Dalton, Saml	2		1		17
Gallaway, Charles	6	1	5		14
Gallaway, Robert	2		2		12
French, William, Ju	2	1	1		
Main, Henry	1	1	4		

SALISBURY DISTRICT, ROWAN COUNTY.

NAME OF HEAD OF FAMILY.	Free white males of 16 years and upward, including heads of families.	Free white males under 16 years.	Free white females, including heads of families.	All other free persons.	Slaves.
Dickey, James	5	1	2	1	
Niblock, George	2	4	3		
Steller, Richard Graham	2	3	2		3
Graham, James	1	2	1		6
Graham, John, Senr	1	5	4		2
Carrigan, John	1	2	2		3
Kerr, John	1				
Young, Samuel	4	1		1	11
Young, Samuel	1	1	3		1
Erwin, Christopher	3	3	4		8

NAME OF HEAD OF FAMILY.	Free white males of 16 years and upward, including heads of families.	Free white males under 16 years.	Free white females, including heads of families.	All other free persons.	Slaves.
Cowin, Isaac	1	3	2		1
Lowrey, William	1	1	2		2
Anderson, Isaac	2	4	5	1	8
Graham, Richard	1	1	5		4
Gray, James	2	2	3		
Cowin, William	1	3	1		
Wilkinson, Samuel	1	1	3		
Foy, William	1		1		
Hemphill, William	1		1		3
Luckey, Richard	1		3		

NAME OF HEAD OF FAMILY.	Free white males of 16 years and upward, including heads of families.	Free white males under 16 years.	Free white females, including heads of families.	All other free persons.	Slaves.
Hughell, Thomas	1	3	4		
Porter, Robert	4	2	5		
Steele, James	1	1	2		
Byers, William	2	3	5		
Trott, James	3	3	2		2
Barkley, John	1	3	3		
Kerr, James	1				
Armstrong, Able	1	2	4	1	2
Ensley, Alexr	1		1	1	
McCracken, Samuel	1		1		

SALISBURY DISTRICT, ROWAN COUNTY—Continued.

NAME OF HEAD OF FAMILY.	Free white males of 16 years and upward, including heads of families.	Free white males under 16 years.	Free white females, including heads of families.	All other free persons.	Slaves.
Morrison, David	1	2	3		
Love, Robert	1	1	6		
Smith, Samuel	1		1		
Cannaday, John	1	2	4		
Graham, Jean		3	1		2
Hall, Joseph		1	2		
Garwood, Joseph	1	1	4		
Johnston, William	2	4	3	1	5
Lowrey, John	1	2	2		
Lowrey, James	1				
Brandon, Benjamin	1	1	2		1
Brandon, Robert	1	1	1		5
Johnston, Elizabeth			1		
Brandon, William	1		1	1	2
Hughey, Jacob	1	1	4		
Hughey, Henry, Ser	1				6
Hughey, Henry, Jur	1	3	4		
Hall, Walter	3	1	1	1	
Brown, William	1	3	1	1	
Cowin, Henry	5	1	3		
Hall, George	1	1	1		1
Steele, Nemin	1	2	2	2	1
Morgan, John	1	1	6		
Tate, John	1		1		
Graham, Elizabeth			3		2
Graham, Agness			1		4
Steele Robert	2		3		
Brandon, John	1		1	1	2
Luckey, Samuel	5		2		2
Bunten, Robert	1	2	3	1	1
Short, Peter	1	2	4	1	2
Clarke, Thomas	1	1	2		
Clarke, John	1				
Hughey, Robert	1	2	1		
Renshaw, William	1	1	2		
Smith, William	1	1	2		
Lewrance, John	2	2	3	1	1
Fitzpatrick, James	3	1	1		
Fitzpatrick, John	1		3		
Bailey, William, Ser	1	4	3		
Smith, Samuel	1		2		
Horton, John	2	2	3		
Horton, Joseph	1	3	3		
Law, William	2	3	4		
Steele, Samuel	1	1	3		
Salisbury, John	2	2	4		
Parker, Robert	1	2	3		
Dickey, Thomas	1	3	5		6
Dickey, Jcel	1				
Campbell, Joseph	3	2	4		3
Cooke, John	1		1	1	
Holdman, John	1	2	1		
Parker, Thomas	3	4	3		
Patrick, Jeremiah	1	2	1		
Johnston, Henry	1	3	4		
Steeleman, William	1	1	2		2
Steeleman, George	1	1	4		
Bedwell, Elijah	1	2	5		
Herin, Shadrick	1	1	2		
Speaks, Richard	2	3	4		
Hendricks, David	1	2	2		
Stogdale, Sarah	1		3		
Stogdale, Vachel	1	1	1		
Beach, Aquillah	1	2	4		
Parson, John	1	1	1		
Renolds, Henry	1	2	1		
Patrick, William	3		2		
Stogdale, Zebediah	1	3	4		
Madden, Jonathan	1	4	3		
West, Isaac	1	1	3		
West, Hezekiah	1		2		
West, Elizabeth	1	2	2		
Roach, Thomas	1	1	2		
Stogdale, Thomas	1	2	1		
Blackwood, John	2	3	6		
Holms, Robert	1	2	5		
Brooks, Robert	1	4	3		
Stogdale, Warnel	1		3		
Patrick, Hezekiah	1	1	1		
Beal, Joseph	1	2	5		
Renolds, Richard	1	2	1		
Busey, Mathew	1	3	5		
Speaks, Martin	1	3	3		
Hadox, William	1	1	3		
Manon, Christopher	2	1	5		6
Pinchback, John		1	4		
Garther, Lydia			1		
Bucey, Samuel	1		1		
Speaks, Charles	1	4	3		
Whitaker, Thomas	1	4	5		
Casey, Samuel	2	2	2		
Trevit, John	1				
Wilkins, George	2	2	5		
Wilkins, Abraham	1		1		
Whitley, Ebenezer	2	1	3		
Owen, Lawrance	2	4	3	1	
Cherry, Benja	1	1	10		

NAME OF HEAD OF FAMILY.	Free white males of 16 years and upward, including heads of families.	Free white males under 16 years.	Free white females, including heads of families.	All other free persons.	Slaves.
Brewer, William	2	2	4		
Bryan, John	1		1		
Bryan, James	1		1		
Little, John	2	2	5		
Luckey, Robert	1	2	2		
Boone, Benjamin	1	3	3		
Bryan, Samuel	1	3	5		
Boone, John	1	1	4	1	3
Leach, James	1	3	4	1	
Leach, Richard	1	2	5		
Welman, Thomas	1	1	1		
Pennery, Thomas	1	3	4		
Watkins, John	1	1	2		
Huff, Valentine	3		2		1
Helper, Jacob	3	1	4		
Black, James	1				6
Jones, Isaac	1	2	3	3	
Cain, Thomas	1	2	4		
Holdman, William	1	4	5		
Jones, Solomon	2		8		
Seny, Owen	1	3	2		1
Bartey, Thomas	1	2	2		
Edwards, Enoch	2	2	6		
Holeman, Isaac	2	2	2		4
Beamon, John	2	5	4	1	1
Bucy, John	1		1		
Clark, William	1	1	3		
Beck, Sam'l Elija	1	3	3		
Eaton, Isaac	4	4	6		
English, Alexander	1	2	1		1
Wolket, Barney	1	1	2		
Clifford, Jacob	1	1	6		
Brown, William	1		2		
Hall, Abm	1	1	1		
Cherry, Peterson	1	1	1		
Whitehead, Lazarus	1	2	4	1	1
Glascock, Peter	3	4	5		
Brooks, George	2	5	3		
Luckey, Samuel, Ser	1	1	3		2
Luckey, Samuel, Jr	1	2	2		1
Andrew, James	2	1	5	1	3
Guffey, Henry	3		4		
Erwin, John	2	3	5		
Morrow, John	3	3	4		
Lovlace, Elias	1	2	6		
Bean, Thomas	2	2	6		1
Prather, Thomas	2	2	6		2
Summers, William	2	3	3		
Freeman, Moses	1				
Ratlage, James	1	1	4		3
Teneson, Thomas	1	2	4		
Ratledge, Daniel	1	2	2		
Miller, Henry	1	2	2		1
Hudson, Isaac	1	1	1		
Hudson, Daniel	1	1	1		
Hudson, Absalom	2		1		
Brown, Bazill	1	3	4		
Howell, Joseph	1	2	3		
Brandon, John	1		3	1	1
Hurley, James	1	1	3		
Nichols, William	1	1	2		
Brandon, Christopher	2		5		1
Renshaw, Thomas	1	3	2		
Davis, John	1	1	2		
Evans, John	1	2	2		
Stanley, Thomas	1	2	2		
Hardin, Alexr	1	3	4		
Brandon, Abraham	2	3	4		1
Taylor, William	2		2		
Veach, Richard	2		3	1	
Brandon, Mary				4	
Maguire, John	1	2	4		1
Bell, William	1	2	4		2
Neely, Richard	4	1	2		1
Sharbert, Samuel	3	2	6		
Davis, Sarah	1	2	1		
Smith, Jonathan	1	4	2		
Bailey, William	1				1
Harper, William	1		3		
Hudson, John	1	2	4	1	
Mott, Simmons	1	2	3		
Lard, John	1	2	3		
Howard, William	3	3	5		1
Hurley, Nehemiah	1	2	3		
Robison, Joseph	1	3	2		
Tegart, Andrew	1	3	5	1	
Webb, Daniel	1	5	2	1	2
Teneson, Abraham	3	2	3		4
Maguire, James	1	2	4		
McMurrey, James	1	3	2		
Hughes, John	2	2	2		
Coleman, Peter	1	2	4		
Garther, Bazil	3	2	2	1	4
Garther, Benjamin	1	5	6	2	2
Eckles, John	1		1	2	1
Johnston, Jacob	1	2	4		
Jams, Vachel	1				1

NAME OF HEAD OF FAMILY.	Free white males of 16 years and upward, including heads of families.	Free white males under 16 years.	Free white females, including heads of families.	All other free persons.	Slaves.
Jams, Beal	1		1		
Nichols, John	2	1	2		5
Clifford, John	1	1	5		
Eaton, Ebenezer	1	4	2		
Johnston, John	2	4	4		
Smith, James	1		1		
Eaton, Daniel	1		2		
Ellis, Evan	5		3		
Smith, Joseph	3		1		
Stockdale, Elizabeth			2		
Ellis, John	5	2	4	1	1
Holderfield, Valentine	2	1	4		
Call, Daniel	1		1		
Stockdale, Masheck	1		1		
Glascock, Spencer	2	2	2		10
Hendren, Oliver	1	1	2		1
Hendron, John	1	1			2
Dulin, Phillip	2	2	3		2
Harris, Isaac	1	1	1		
Williams, George	1	5	2		
Williams, Benjamin	2		2		
James, James	2		2		
Hays, Samuel	1		1		
Welman, Jeremiah	1	5	2		
Welman, John	1		2		
Dedmond, Edmond	2		2		
Noland, Ledston	1	4	6		
Allen, John	3		2		
Noland, James	2	2	4		
Penenton, Charles	1	1	3		
Thompson, Thomas	1	3	3		
Noland, Stephen	2	2	4		
Turley, Benjamin	1	2	1		
Whitaker, William, Ser	2	1	7		
Whitaker, John	1	4	1		
Whitaker, Wm, Jur	1	1	3		
Biles, John	1		1		
McMahan, Samuel	2		4		
McMahan, James	3		2		
Penington, James	1		3		
Shaw, Michael	1	1	1		
Williams, Simon	1	3	6	1	
Etcherson, Walter	1		4		
Glascock, Harmon	2	1	7		1
Keffer, Frederick	1	2	2		
Johnston, David	2	3	4	1	
Call, Henry	1	2	3		
Lane, Gallent	1	3	4		
Dial, Joseph	1	4	1		
Humphrey, John	2		1		1
Etcherson, Henry	1		2		
Baker, George	2		2		
Eaton, George	2		2		
Jones, David	3	5	3		
Noland, Daniel	1		3		
Johnston, Majr John	3	1	5		6
Williamson, Francis	1		1		
Rich, Henry	1	1	1	1	
Read, James	1	2	6	2	
Hall, George	1		2	2	
Hall, Samuel	1		1		
Deaver, Samuel	2	1	1		
Boland, James	1		3		
Venable, Sarah	1		7		
Alexander, John	1	1	3		
Wood, Cornelius	1	1	4		
Ralisbeck, Henry	2	1	5		
McKnight, Lidia	2	1	4		
Hughes, Jeremiah	1		5		
Sain, John	1		4		
Mills, David	1		2		
Mills, William	1	1	3		
Easburne, John	1	1	2		
Malon, Jeremiah	1	4	4		
Graham, Edward	1		4		
Rector, Jessey	1	1	5		
Ball, John	1		2	1	
Adams, Abraham	3		2		5
Call, John	1	4	5		
Frost, Ebenezer	3	5	4		
Hunter, Margret		2	4		
Sites, Jacob	1	2	2	1	
Peck, Ludwick	1		4		
Manas, Sephes	1	4	2		
Wells, Thomas	1	3	5		
Hunter, Charles	1	3	3		
Howard, Cornelius	4	3	4		
Garner, Henry	2	1	3		
Rupert, Peter	1	1	3		
Howard, Christopher	4	4	8		
Hanley, Christopher	2	3	6	1	
Stuart, Edward	1		1		
King, Jeremiah	1	1	3		
Stinnet, William	1	1	3		
Kenatzer, Catherina	1	1	3		
Stinnet, John	1	1	3		
Williams, Elizabeth			3		

SALISBURY DISTRICT, ROWAN COUNTY—Continued.

NAME OF HEAD OF FAMILY.	Free white males of 16 years and upward, including heads of families.	Free white males under 16 years.	Free white females, including heads of families.	All other free persons.	Slaves.
Henkle, Benjamin	2	3	7		
Williams, Edward	2	1	5		
Forster, James	1	5	3		2
Harper, William	1		3		
Hawkins, Abraham	2	1	4		
Forster, Hezekiah	1	2	2		
Forster, Robert	1	2	2		
Evans, David	3	3	5		
Hurley, Moses	1	3	1		
Ford, Ralph	1	1	3		
Aniwood, James	1		5		
Brenneger, Adam	1	3	3		
Bracken, Thomas	1		1		
Bryan, Joseph, Jur	1	1	3		1
Bryan, Joseph, Ser	2		2		4
Moler, John	2	2	1		
Gentle, George	1	1	4		
Higden, Joseph	1	3	2		
Dowell, John	1	4	5		1
Felps, James	1	2	2		
Hardisty, Henry	1	1	3		
McDaniel, Allin	1	3	3		
Berryman, Benja	1	4	5		2
Pain, Richard	1	3	2		
Shecks, Christian	2	1	2		
Smith, Michael	1		2		
White, William	2		4		3
Cooper, Phillip	1	1	5		
Snow, William	3		3		
Lafey, James	2		4		
Carender, Ezekiel	2	3	2		
Harper, Zepheniah	1	3	3		
Obriant, John	1		1		
Dowell, Phillip	1	2	2		
Robison, Demsellah		1	3		
Dowell, Peter, Ser	1		1		5
Tennesy, Abraham	1	1	5		
Dowell, Peter, Jur	1		2		3
Dowell, William	1	3	5		1
Sparks, Jonas	2	3	3		
Wiatt, John	1	1	4		
Bryan, Francis	1		2		
Gilpin, Benjamin	1	1	1		
Felps, Samuel	1		2		
Felps, Sarah	1	2	3		
Sidden, John	1	1	3		
Felps, Thomas	1		3		
Sheets, Jacob	1	2	3		
Blackheart, Willibee	1		3		
Caiton, Charles	3	1	4		
Caiton, George	1	1	1		
Hill, Jacob	1		1		
Tinneson, Thomas	1		3		
Martin, Asa	1	3	3		
Speaks, Ann		2	3		
Harris, Zepheniah	2	1	4		
Harper, William	1		5		1
Sparks, David	1	2	1		
Sparks, William	1	2	3		
Enochs, Mary	3		3		
Moler, Henry	1	1	3		
Rumbly, Edger		1	2		
Wesh, John	1		3		
Smith, Michael	2		4		1
Oirel, Daniel	1	1	3		
Adams, Ephriaim	1	1	2		2
Sidden, Joseph	2		1		
Holden, Edmond	1	1	2		
Enochs, Enoch	1	1	1		
Speeks, Adam	1	2	3		
Penn, Richard	1	3	3		
Hendricks, Abraham	1		2		
Wetty, Jacob	3	1	3		
Hendricks, John	1	1	3		
Watkins, David	2	4	3		2
Hendricks, Frederick	1	2	2		
Black, Jacob	1	1	2		
Black, Frederick	1	1	4		
Enochs, Isaac	2	4	9		1
Enochs, Gabriel	3	3	6		
Bryan, Samuel	1	2	6	1	1
West, Thomas	1		4		
Job, Thomas	2		1		
Sheets, Martin	2	1	7		
Crankfield, Lewis	2	3	3		
Karns, Alexander	1		5		
Dial, Robert	1		2		
Hutson, Thomas	1	1	1		
Williams, Joseph	2	1	6		
Hendricks, James	1	3	3		
Bryan, William	1	1	1		
Wearen, Conrad	1	3	3		
Dagley, James	1	3	2		
Dalley, Lawrence	1		2		
Maxwell, Thomas	3		1		
Renshaw, Joseph	3	3	6		
Renshaw, Elijah	1	3	4		

NAME OF HEAD OF FAMILY.	Free white males of 16 years and upward, including heads of families.	Free white males under 16 years.	Free white females, including heads of families.	All other free persons.	Slaves.
Renshaw, Abraham	1		1		
Warren, James	1		1		
Roland, Joseph	2	1	5	1	
Roland, John	2	3	4		
Hendricks, Phillip	1	2	2		
Hendricks, John	1	1	3		
Lewis, Daniel, Sr	2		4		
Lewis, Daniel, Jur	1		2		
Roland, Gasper	1		3		
Person, Stephen	1	2	2		
Beam, Michael	1		2		
Welch, Thomas	1	1	2		8
Welch, Jean	1	3	2		
Johour, James	1		2		
Doyale, Gregory	1	2	1		
Ridle, James	1	2	2		
Doyale, Samuel	2	3	1		
Spilman, George	2		1		
Sims, Elizabeth	1		2		
Beaman, Abraham	3	1	2		1
Beam, Jacob	1		2		
Wilcoxon, William	3	2	2		2
Wilcoxon, John, Ser	1		2		
Wilcoxon, John, Jur	1	4	6		
Nalson, Elizabeth		1	6		
Miller, Rachel			2		
McDaniel, James	1		3		
Hall, William	1	3	3		4
Keller, Jacob	1	4	5		
Wattar, William	1	1	6		
Dutero, Bolser	1	2	3		
Hinkle, Henry	1	1	3		
Nail, Caleb	2		1		
Sain, Casper	2	2	2		
Sprigg, Reason	2	1	2		
Nelson, William	2	3	4		
Donner, George	1		5		
Stokes, Elizabeth		1	1	1	9
Neat, Rudolph, Senr	1		4		1
Neat, Rudolph, Jur	1	2	4		
Tatom, Jean	1	3	4		
Tatom, Laurance	1		6		
Buckner, John	1	1	2		
Lastep, Samuel	1	6	4		
March, John	1	3	6		
March, George	1	4	5		
Henline, Jacob	1		5		
Banks, John	1	3	5		
Buckner, David	1		2		
Hendricks, Isaac	1	2	3		
Defi, James	2		4		
Wallis, Samuel	1	1	1		
Roberts, Carnie	1	1	1		
Johnston, Joseph	1	2	2		
Allin, John	2	1	3		
Bracken, Samuel	1		2		
Bracken, Samuel	1		2		
McCulloch, James	1		2		1
Bird, Thomas	1	2	4		
White, Thomas	1		4		
Dobbin, Samuel	1		3		
Bailey, Samuel	2	4	3		31
Hails, Mary		1	1		
Mock, Andrew	2	1	6		1
Kenatzer, Jacob	1		2		
Booe, Jacob	1	2	3	2	
Booe, George	1	1	1		
Bartlison, William	1		4		
Coone, Jacob	2	1	3		
Nail, John	2	3	5		
Bartlison, Zacriah	1	3	4		1
Langford, John	1	1	2		
Trout, Jacob	1	2	5		
Forster, Lucy	2		3		5
Foster, Robert	2	1	6		3
Giles, William	1		1		28
Rogers, Richard	1	3	3		
Owens, Elijah	1	1	3		
Owens, John	1	1	1		
Owens, Normon	1		1		
Roberts, Lazarus	1		1		
Walker, William	1		4		
Wood, John	1	3	4		
Potts, Jeremiah	1	2	3		
Buckner, Henry	2	3	2		1
Johnston, William	1	2	4		2
Dedmon, Ezekel	1	1	2		
Dedmon, Sarah	2		6		
Hudson, Peter	2		3		
Johnston, Joseph	1		3		
Smart, Thomas	1		1		
Bailey, John	1	2	1		2
Arriwood, Ann		2	1		
Williams, Charles	1		3		
Srock, Henry	1	3	5		
Marshal, Humphry	2	1	4		
Williams, George	2	5	1		7

NAME OF HEAD OF FAMILY.	Free white males of 16 years and upward, including heads of families.	Free white males under 16 years.	Free white females, including heads of families.	All other free persons.	Slaves.
Linster, Moses	2	4	6		8
Howell, John	1	1	3		2
Andrew, Joseph	1	2	2		
Williams, James	2		4		1
Daniel, Josiah		2	4		
Click, Nicholas	1	4	4		
Person, Richmond	1	5		5	101
Person, John	1	5	2		6
King, William	1	3	6		
Isbale, John	1	1	2		
Gentle, George	1	3	3		
Little, Jacob	2	2	4		
Koon, John	1	3	4		
Jones, Benja	1		2		
Harry, Isaac	1	1	2		
Barlow, John	1		2		
Williams, George	1	3	2		
Haggins, William	1	1	2		
Graham, Edward	1	1	3		
Adams, Abraham	1		1		
Adams, Isaac	3	2	1		
Williams, Ralph	1		2		
Adams, Silvenus	1		1		
Philips, John	2	2	5		
Brothers, Robert	2	1	3		
Thomas, John	1		3		
Clifton, Thomas	1	1	2		
Etchison, James	3		1		
Etchison, Edmond	1	2	6		
Wesh, Jeremiah	1		1		
Cummins, Thomas	1	3	4		
Bridgfarmer, Martin	2	1	3		
Mock, Henry	1	1	1		
Mock, Peter, Ser	1	1	2		
Mock, Peter, Jur	2	1	3		
Harris, Joseph	1		2		
Harris, John	1	4	2		
Martin, Allin	1	1	2		
Walker, Burch	1		1		
Mock, John	1		3	1	
Little, Lewis	1	1	3		
Stonestreet, Edward	2	2	4		1
Harben, Edwd Villers	2		2	1	4
Bryan, Sarah	2	2	3		1
Shepperd, Nathen	1	4	7		5
Harben, Reason	1	3	2		
Literal, Richard	1	1	4		
Adams, Elisha	1	4	3		
Bailey, Henry	1	1	2		1
Easters, Thomas	2	6	6		4
McCathe, Ebednego	2	1	3		
McBryan, John	1	2	5		
Spilmon, Harmon	2		1		
Johnston, Robert	1	5	5		
Jinkins, Rodrick	2		2	1	
Phillips, Elijah	2	1	4		
Cowman, Thomas	1		2		
Phillips, John	2	1	5		
Phillips, Mary			1		
Updegrove, Isaac	1	1	3		
Hunt, Charles	4	4	6		
Dagley, Jonathan	1	2	2		
Hoges, William	1		1		
Easteb, Thomas	3	2	4		
Howell, Stephen	1	3	3	1	
Horn, Thos, Jur	1	3	2		
Humphreys, John	1	1	1		
Tuches, Tobias	1		2		1
Brian, Samuel	1		2		
Wilsen, James	1		3		
Deposter, John	1	4	2		3
Chafin, Nathen	1	1	6		11
Griffith, William	1	2	1		
Eaton, Peter	1		7		5
Horn, Thomas, Sr	1		7		
Eaton, Thomas	1	7	6		5
Wilson, Michael	1	1	1		
McCartey, Zacheriah	1	3	4		
Hunt, Margret	3		4	5	
Keen, Nicholas	1		3	2	
Griffin, Ezekel	1	2	2		
Haiden, Unity	1		2		11
Haiden, Dugles	1	2	1		9
McDermon, Michael	1	1	4		
Smith, Obediah	2	3	6		5
Butler, William	1	5	1		1
Cornwell, Elijah	1	1	4		
Adams, Jacob	1		2		
Buck, Charles	1	3	4		
Bennet, Jacob	1	1	1		
Braley, William	1		1		
Braley, John	1		1		
Braley, John, Jur	1	2	1		4
Braley, Walter	1	2	1		
Bradley, Josiah	1		1		
Braley, John, Sr	2	1	2		6
Backley, Samuel	3		2		
Baker, Harate	1	1	5		

SALISBURY DISTRICT, ROWAN COUNTY—Continued.

NAME OF HEAD OF FAMILY.	Free white males of 16 years and upward, including heads of families.	Free white males under 16 years.	Free white females, including heads of families.	All other free persons.	Slaves.
Batey, Charles	1	1	2		
Coleman, Phillip	1	2	4		
Kennaday, Andrew	2		6		
Cochran, Robert	4	2	3		
Donaldson, Alexr	3	2	4		
Flemming, Allison	1		3		1
Grove, Abraham	1	2	5		
Goose, George	3	1	2		
Graham, John	1	1	2		
Graham, Garret	3		2		
Hart, William	1	2	3		3
Holland, Zacheriah	1	4	3		
Hobbis, John	1	3	1		
Hart, William, Jur	3	1	3		1
Hart, James	2		3		
Jemeson, William	3		3		
Kerr, David	2		4	1	6
Laser, John	1	4	5		
Mellen, Charles	2	2			
McRea, Thos	2		1		
McClain, John	1	1	2		
McKnight, William	3		3		1
McClain, William	2	2	5		2
McGlaughlin, James	1	2	1		
Parks, John	1		4		3
Slaugh, Phillip	1	2	4		
Swann, Thomas	2	4	7		
Thompson, William	1		3		3
Tolbert, Samuel	1	2	3		
Voras, Aron	1	1	2		
Woods, David	2	2	4		2
Wodside, Archabeld	1	2	4		
Woods, Mathew	2	2	4		2
Burket, James	1		1		
Burket, Elazarus	1	3	4		
Bradford, Richard	1	2	3		
Baget, John	1		1		
Bradey, Joseph	1	1	2		
Briggs, Nathan	1	2	2		
Baget, William	2	4	3		
Briggs, James	1	3	4		
Black, Mathew	1	2	5		
Black, John	1	2	2		
Caps, Thomas	1	3	3		
Cole, William	3	1	5		10
Coggin, Burrel	1	2	3		
Crook, John		1	3		2
Coggin, John	1	2			
Cox, David	2	1	1		1
Codey, James	2	2	5		
Cotten, Alexander	1				
Cameron, John	1		1	1	
Cameron, Absalom	1	3	2		
Cotten, Abner	2	3	4		1
Cole, Stephen	1	1	1		
Davis, Henry	1				
Davis (Widow)	2	2	4		
Davis, Benjamin	2	5	5		1
Davis, John	1				
Daniel, James	2	4	3	1	9
Davis, Edward	1	2	2		
Davis, Hardy	1	2	4		
Devenport, Agustian	4	3	7		
Eps, Plesent	1	3	4		
Ellis, John	3	1	2	1	
Ellis, James	1	1	1		
Fry, Daniel	1		2		
Fry, Joseph	1	1	2		
Fisher, Michael	1	2	3		1
Giles, Richard	1	1	2		
Golsby, Wade	1	2	1		
Gainer, John	1	2	2		
Grist, William	3	2	6		
Giles, Absalom	1	1	2		
Gess, Jacob	1	1	2		
Golsbey, Drury	1	1	1		
Gillim, Conrad	1	1	3		
Henly, William	2	1	4		
Hoges, Joseph	1	2	3		
Harris, Jesse, Ser	2	1	2		1
Harris, Jesse, Jur	1	2	3		1
Johnston, John (B. D.)	1	4	5		
Johnston, John	1	2	4		
Jones, Else	1	2	3		
Kinney, William	1	5	4		
Lofland, Daniel	1	2	7		
Lofland, Richard	1	4	4		
Loften, Lewis	1	3	5		8
Lenair, Clemment, Jur	1	1	1		
Lenair, Clement, Sr	3	5	2		3
Low, Frederick	2	1	6		
Lofland, John	1	3	4		
Ledwell, William	1	2	4		
Mills, Jonathan	1	3	7		
Mash, Joseph	1	2	3		
Mills, George	2	4	6		
Morgan, James	1	1	2		
Morris, John	1		3		

NAME OF HEAD OF FAMILY.	Free white males of 16 years and upward, including heads of families.	Free white males under 16 years.	Free white females, including heads of families.	All other free persons.	Slaves.
Maraum, Sarah			2		
Newson, Lewis	1	3	4		
Parks, Charles	3	3	6		
Parks, Timothy	2	3	5		
Parks, Ebenezer	2	6	3		
Parks, Allen	2	3	4		
Parks, John	1		4		3
Penney, William	1		4		4
Peeler, Anthony	1	4	4		
Quick, Tunis	1	3	5		
Quick, Benjamin	1	1	2		
Riley, Ann	2	2	1		
Riley, James	1		2		3
Reed, John	1	2	3		
Roberts, Samuel, Jur	1		2		
Russell, Nathan	1	2	3		
Runyen, Joseph	1	1	3		
Runyen, Phineas	3	4	3		
Riley, George	1				
Runyen, Befford	1	1	3		
Roe, John	1	3	3		
Stevens, Martha		3	5		
Sarrat, Thomas	3	2	5		
Seeret, Simon	2	3	4		
Stokes, Christopher	1	2	2		3
Smith, James	1	1	3		
Smith, Alexander	1	1	4		
Silvers, William	2	1	2		4
Skeans, Mathew	3	2	4		4
Shipton, Robert	1	3	4		
Stilwell, David	1	3	6		
Serrat, Allen	2	4	6		
Stilwell, John	1				
Thompson, William	1	7	5		
Tenpenney, Nathaniel	1	2	5		
Vonner, John	1	2	3		
Vonner, Henry	1	1	3		
Wallis, William	1	1	2		
Wyatt, John	2	3	5		
Wyatt, Nathan	2	3	3		
Ward, John	1	1	4		
Ward, James Jordon	1				
Williams, Thomas	2		4		
Wyatt, John, Jur	1		1		
Yont, John	2	2	9		
Daywalt, Beck	1	1	1		
Buckhart, John	1	1	1		
Boss, Phillip	2	1	4		
Beger, Henry	1	1	3		
Buckhart, Daniel	1	2	3		
Billing, Dr John	2		5		2
Belling, Frederick	1				
Belling, Bessima	1				
Belling, John, Jur	1		3		
Beck, John	1	4	3		
Buckhart, George	2	6	4		
Buckhart, George, Jur	1	1	2		
Blaze, George	1	1	2		
Bierly, David	1	1	4		
Bierly, Martin	3	3	4		
Bierly, Jacob	2	4	5		
Brooks, Humphry			5		15
Brookshire, Manering	1				
Billings, David	1				
Billings, Henry	1				
Conger, Jonathen	2		5		
Cross, Jacob	2		5		
Cross, Peter	1		3		
Cross, Jacob, Jur	1	3	5		
Claver, Frederick	1	1	1		
Claver, John	3		4		
Kimball, Caleb	1	2	3		
Crotts, Jacob	1	3	6		
Carn, Phillip	1	2	3		
Carn, Leonard	1	2	6		
Christopher, Thomas	1	3	1		
Charles, George	1	1	2		
Capely, John	1				
Carn, Peter	1	2	3		
Derr, Melcher	1	3	3		
Duice, Thomas	1	1	4		
Davis, Merick	3	2	2		
Elston, William	2	2	2		
Floyd, John	1	2	2		
Frank, William	1	1	6	2	
Feazer, George	1	3	3		3
Frank, John	1	1	3		
Frank, Martin	1	2	2		
Fry, Henry	1	3	3		
Floyd, Francis	1	1	6		
Gallimore, James	1	2	3		
Gallimore, John	1	2	1		
Gallimore, William	1	1	2		
Gibbens, Peter A	2	3	2		
Garner, Phillip	2	2	5		
Goss, Ephraim	3	1	7		
Goss, Frederick	3	4	5		1
Goss, Frederick, Jur	1	1	2		

NAME OF HEAD OF FAMILY.	Free white males of 16 years and upward, including heads of families.	Free white males under 16 years.	Free white females, including heads of families.	All other free persons.	Slaves.
Huffman, Daniel	2	3	4		
Hedrick, Francis	1	6	3		
Homes, Reuben	1	1	4		1
Hinkle, Jacob	1				
Hedrick, Peter	4	3	4		
Hinkle, George	1				
Hlshouser, Michael	1	2	1		2
Holliway, William	1	1	4		
Jackson, Thomas	1	1	2		
Jones, John	1				
Lain, William	1	1	4		
Lucy, Frederick	1	2	3		
Lucy, John	1	1	2		
Lucy, Michael	1				
Lockebey, Henry	1	3	4		
Merrill, Samuel	1	2	3		1
Merrill, Elijah	1	1	1		3
Michael, Barnet	1		3		
Myars, Michael	1	3	3		
Miller, Frederick	1				
Miller, George	1		1		8
Marbrough, Leonard	1	3	5		
Miller, John	1		5	1	
McKaren, Michael	1	5	5		
Merrill, William	1	2	5		2
Madewell, John	1	3	2		
Madewell, James	1		2		
Martin, George	1		2		
Miller, Jacob	1	1	3		1
Miller, David	1		1		
Notheren, Samuel	1	1	1		
Notheren, Joseph	2	2	3		
Owen, James	2	1	4		8
Owen, Richard	1	1	3		
Owen, William	1				
Owen, Benjamin	1	1	1		
Owen, Ambrose	2	1	2		1
Owen, Henry	1				
Tisinger, Adam	1	2	2		
Rich, John	2	2	5		
Rickard, John	1	4	5		
Rickard, Leonard	2	1	2		
Rickard, Casper	2				
Roblin, Lewis	1		1		
Rickard, Jacob	1				
Rider, Adam	1	2	3		
Rich, Thomas	1		1		
Shepperd, John, Jur	1		1		
Sumey, Peter	2	5	1		
Sims, John	1	1	1		
Shepperd, John	3	2	5		
Sumey, Michael	2	1	4		
Smith, Lucy	2		1		
Smith, Leonard	1	3	5		
Senoner, Benjamin	1	2	4		
Smith, Peter	1		3		1
Smith, Casper	1	2	1		
Smith, Margret	1	1	2		4
Smith, David	1	2	4		3
Strange, William	1	2	6		3
Smith, Frederick	1	1	4		
Smith, John	1	1	1		
Shults, George	2	3	4		
Thomas, Jessey	1				
Thomas, Elisha	1	2	2		
Wolf, Jacob	1				
Wortman, Henry	3	2	5		
Womack, Archabeld	1		2		
Wolf, Michael	1	1	3		
Womack, Abraham	5	1	1		
Womack, Richard	1	1	4		
Welch, Mathew	1	2	2		
Womack, Richard	1	1	4		
Wyman, Henry	1	2	5		
Young, Jacob	1	2	2		
Young, Frederick	1				
Young, Francis	1	3	3		
Avery, John	3	3	2		1
Adinger, Christopher	2	3	6		
Blessing, Jacob	1				
Berger, Charles	1	1	1		
Buck, Daniel	1	3	5		
Berger, George	1	3	2		
Clotfalder, George	1	4	6		
Clotfalder, John	1	4	6		
Coonse, John	3	3	5		
Conrad, Adam	3	2	4		
Clotfalder, Felix	2	1	2		
Cook, John	1	3	4		
Conrad, Henry	1	1	2		
Clotfalder, Peter	1		1		
Derr, Henry	1	3	5		
Day, Michael	1	2	2		
Day, Valentine	2		2		
Easter, Peter	1		3		
Easter, Michael	1	3	1		
Everhart, Peter	1	3	3		
Everhart, Chetian	1				
Eller, George	1	1	4		

SALISBURY DISTRICT, ROWAN COUNTY—Continued.

NAME OF HEAD OF FAMILY.	Free white males of 16 years and upward, including heads of families.	Free white males under 16 years.	Free white females, including heads of families.	All other free persons.	Slaves.
Frits, George	1	3	5		
Freidle, John	1		4		
Grub, Conrad	1	3	2		
Grub, George	2	2	4		
Grimes, John	2		3		
Grimes, Christian	1		3		
Grimes, Charles	1	2	2		
Hesley, Jacob, Jur	1		1		
Harmon, Adam	1	2	2		1
Hesely, Jacob	2	2	2		
Hamm, Melcher	2		2		
Hamm, Jacob	3		2		
Hagey, George	2	4	5		
Hedrick, Adam	3	4	3		
Hagey, Henry	3	2	6		
Hoppis, Henry	1		4		
Knipe, Christian	1	2	4		
Kain, Peter	3		3		
Lenard, Phillip	2	1	4		2
Livengood, Christian	4		5		
Lowrey, Lucy		3	4		
Livengood, Henry	1		2		
Lenard, Jacob	1	1	4		1
Lenard, Michael	1	4	4		
Lenard, Valentine	3	4	3		
Lopp, John, Sr	3	2	5		4
Lopp, John, Jur	1		1		
Lopp, Jacob	1	1	5		
Myars, Christian	1				
Michel, Barney	2	2	5		
Myars, Peter	1	4	1		
Myars, Michael	1	2	5		
Magines, Alexander	1	4	3		1
Myars, David	1	4	1		
Michel, Peter	1		2		
Myars, Peter	1	2	1		
Michel, Nicholas	1	2	2		
Nifong, George	1	2	4		
Pew, Reuben	2	2	1		
Picket, Ralph	3		4		
Parnell, Edward	1	4	2		
Rake, Frederick	1	3	5		
Repperd, Melcher	1		1		
Sappenfield, John	1	1	2		
Sauer, John	1		2		
Sauer, Phillip	1		3		
Shofe, Henry	2	2	5		
Slagle, Charles	1		6		
Slagle, Frederick	1				
Sappenfield, Michael	1	2	2		
Sink, Michael	1	3	2		
Sink, John	2	4	5		
Sink, Phillip	1	2	3		1
Spraker, George	1	3	1		
Shofe, Henry, Jur	1	4	1		
Snider, Jacob	2		2		
Snider, George	1	1	1		
Unger, Laurence	1				
Weaver, George	1		5		
Weavil, Stephen	2	3	5		
Wacley, Peter	1	2	2		
Wagginor, Joseph	2	1	2		4
Wagginor, Daniel	3	1	4		17
Wagginor, Jacob	2	3	6		7
Wagginor, Mary		1	1		
Yonce, William	1	4	4		
Yokley, Hugh	1	2	2		1
Yonce, Rudolph	1	3	5		
Blaze, Lewis	2		1		
Blaze, John	2	3	1		
Beck, Phillip	1	1	1		
Blaze, Daywalt	1		2		
Beard, Michael	1	3	3		1
Coningham, Joseph	3	3	5		
Coningham, William	1		1		
Cummins, Samuel	2	3	1	1	4
Coyl, Patrick	1	2	2		
Coningham, Hugh, Jur	1		2		
Cope, Jacob	1				
Dancy, John	2		1		
Davis, Joseph	1	1	3		
Dancy, William	1	1	2		
Dancy, John, Jur	1	2	3		
Agers, Landrine	1	1	5		1
Greene, John	1	1	2		
Huff, Jacob	1		1		
Hollis, John	2	3	6		
Hunt, Daniel	2	1	4		
Hunt, Gasham	1	4	3		
Harper, Thomas	2		3		
Hannah, Joseph	3	2	4		
Harper, Samuel	1		4		
Hilton, Beachem	3	2	5		
Hunt, Jonathan	1	2	2		
Helmstatler, Peter	1		3		
Helmstatler, Adam	1		2		
Hunt, John	2	4	4		

NAME OF HEAD OF FAMILY.	Free white males of 16 years and upward, including heads of families.	Free white males under 16 years.	Free white females, including heads of families.	All other free persons.	Slaves.
Hollis, William	1	1	1		
Lanning, Joseph	2		5		
Lanning, John	1	3	2		
Loyd, John	1	2	4		
McCrary, Boyd	2	6	4		
McCrary, Hugh	1	1	3		
McCrary, John	1	1	4		
Morefield, John B	1	4	4		
Milsaps, William	1	2	2		2
Michel, Frederick	1	2	2		
McCrary (Widow)			3		5
Kelly, William	1		1		
Owen, John					
Owen, Samuel	1				
Owen, Robert	1	2	3		
Parks, Joseph	2		2		
Reed, Eldad	3	2	4		
Reed, George	1	1	3		
Rushen, Arnold	1	1	3		
Silvers, John	1	2	3		
Tracey, Michael	1	2	1		
Thompson, George	1				
Whitaker, Joshua	3	1	3		
Wilson, John	1	5	3		
Winkler, Henry	2	3	1		
Winkler, Lewis	1		1		
Wiseman, William	1	4	4		
Wallen, Carhart	1	4	3		
Whitaker, Peter	1	5	5		
Wilson, Richard	2	3	3		
Wilson, Boyd	1		2		
Whitaker, John	1		1		
Wilson, Charles	1		3		
Yarbrough, Alexander	4		2		
Yarbrough, Henry	1		2		
Arenhart, Killian	1	1	2		
Arenhart, George	2	4	3		
Arenhart, Phillip	1	3	2		1
Arenhart, John	2	3	1		
Bird, Valentine	1		3		
Beam, Jacob	2	3	5		
Bullen, George	3	2	5		3
Brougher, Jacob	2		3		
Basinger, John	1	2	3		
Bradey, John	1	2	5		
Parks, Noah	2	4	5		
Bullen, Phillip	1	3	5		
Brooner, Henry	1	1	4		1
Basinger, Jacob	1		3		
Krite, Michael	1	4	2		
Koble, Adam	2	1	5		
Cason, Samuel	1	2	1		
Davis, Richard	2	4	1		
Derr, Valentine	2		1		
Dillo, Michael	1	2	4		
Derr, George	1	2	3		
Draxler, Peter	1	1	5		
Davis, Solomon	1	1	2		
Frick, Jacob	1	2	1		
Frick, Henry	2	4	2		
Frock, Conrad	1	2	3		
Fisher (Widow)	1	1	2		5
Fulwider, Henry	2	2	4	1	2
Fenil, Frederick	1	2	5		
Frick, Mathias	1				
Gatts, Joseph	2	3	1		
Crison, Nicholas	2	1	5		
Hollar, John	1	2	3		
Hess, John	4	2	5		
Hartline, George	2		2		
Huffman, Francis	1	3	2		
Holshouser, Jacob	1	1	3		
Hartline, Peter	1		3		
Hess, John, Jur	1		1		
Jarret, Phillip	3		1		
Kelley, William	1		1		
Kyger, Conrad	1	4	4		
Caylor, Lewis	1	2	5		
Kenup, William	1	2	2		
Klots, David	1	2	6		
Klingleman, Alexander	3	4	4		
Kyger, Christian	2		1		
Lembley, Phillip	1		3		
Lembley, John	1		2		
Lambley, Joseph	1	1			
Lentz, Henry	1	1	5		
Messemer, John	1	2	3		
Morgan, Nathan	1	4	2		
Miller, Peter	1		3		
Moyer, Semion	4		3		
Morgan, Hugh	2	2	3		
Miller, Christian	1	3	2		
Miller, Michael	1	4	4		
Messer, Serget	1	1	3		
Miller, Jacob	1		3		
Miller, George	2		1		
Parker, Richard	1	1	4		2

NAME OF HEAD OF FAMILY.	Free white males of 16 years and upward, including heads of families.	Free white males under 16 years.	Free white females, including heads of families.	All other free persons.	Slaves.
Pool, Jacob	2	1	4		
Pool, David	2	3	4		
Pitman, Michael	1	5	4		
Reedwine, John	1	4	4		
Rough, John	1	1	3		
Reed, John	2	1	1		
Reed, Madad	3		2		
Shooeman, Christian	1	3	4		
Smethers, William	2	2	5		
Shueman, George	1	3	4		
Stoner, Michael	1		5		
Shuman, John	1	1	9		
Walker, William	1		7		
Woliever, Joseph	1	1	2		
Walker, Leonard	2	4	3		
Youst, Jacob	1	1	5		
Anderson, John	1	2	4		
Albright, Frederick	2	2	3		
Benson, Leven	2		5		1
Brummel, Jacob, Jur	1	2	2		
Bodenhimer, John	2	3	4		
Bodenhimer, Peter	1		1		
Bodenhimer, Christian	1		2		
Brummel, Jacob	1	1	3		
Beene, Nicholas	1	1	1		
Burke, Edward	1	1	5		
Bodenhimer, Charity	2		1		
Billingsly, Ruth	1	1	6		
Connely, William	1	2	2		
Cormon, Joseph	1	1	1		
Coppis, Peter	1		2		
Credlespaugh, Thomas	1		2		
Chadewick, Joshua	1		4		
Chainey, John	2	2	3		
Covey, Noble	1	2	4		
Credlespaugh, William	1		2		
Craver, Phillip	3	2	3		
Clinard, Jacob	2	2	5		
Conrad, Peter	1				
Craver, Michael	1	1	1		
Cooper, James	1	3	3		
Dills, William	2		4		
Dial, Shadrick	1		6		
Davis, Hannah			3		
Davis, Jacob	2	3	4		
Davis, Henry, Jur	1	1	2		
Davis, Jacob, Jur	1	1	2		
Davis, John	1	2	3		
Davis, Samuel	1	1	2		1
Davis, William	2	2	3		
Davis, James	1	1	2		
Davis, Henry	2		4		
Danil, Peter	2	1	3		
Danil, Paul	1		1		
Danil, Lyon	1	1	2		
Derr, Andrew	3	1	3		
Danil, Randal	2	2	7		6
Evans, James	2		5		
Ensley, David	1	1	4		
Fox, John	4	3	7		
Fleshman, Ferdinand	1		1		
Grove, John	1	2	7		
Grimes, Jacob	1	2	6		
Howard, Stephen	1		2		
Hinkle, John, Jur	1		2		
Howard, Mikajah	4	3	4		
Harris, John	1	2	4		
Howard, John	1	2	1		
Hinkle, Nathan	1	1	3		1
Hinkle, Anthony	1	1	3		
Hinkle, Wendle	1	2	4		1
Harmon, Adam	2		7		
Houk, Jacob	1	1	2		
Hinkle, Casper	2	2	4		
Heneger, Conrad	1	5	4		
Harron, Richard	2				
Hinkle, John	1	2	1		
Harmon, Valentine	1		1		
Johnston, Archabeld	1	2	3		
Idle, George	3	2	3		
Idle, Elizabeth	2	1	2		
Jones, Ebenezer	1	4	1		1
Jones, Isaac	1	2	3		
Jones, Joseph	1	3	5		
Kestler, Jacob	3	2	3		
Klinart, Phillip	2		1		4
Kimbrough, Thomas	1	1	5		2
Klinart, Peter	1	1	5		
Klinart, Daniel	1		2		
Kamp, Abraham	1	1	2		
Ledford, William	2	1	1		11
Ledford, Thomas	1	2	5		2
Lewis, Walter	1		1		
Lewis, Thomas	1		1		
Livengood, Hartman	5		5		
Long, Thomas	2	4	4		
Long, Jacob	2	3	5		

SALISBURY DISTRICT, ROWAN COUNTY—Continued.

NAME OF HEAD OF FAMILY.	Free white males of 16 years and upward, including heads of families.	Free white males under 16 years.	Free white females, including heads of families.	All other free persons.	Slaves.
Ledford, John	1	2	4		5
Lechner, Michael	1				
Long, Felix	2		1		
Miller, Fredrick, Jur.	1	1	1		
McCurrey, John	1	1	2		
Moore, Nathaniel	2	1	3		
Mock, Phillip	6	4	5		
Manlove, William	3		2		
Moore, Joseph	1	1	5		
Monrow, John	2	4	3		2
Molrainey, Joseph	1	1	6		
Motzinger, Daniel	1	2	3		
Motzinger, Felix	2	3	3		
Mauk, Daywalt	1	2	3	3	2
Miller, Fredrick (Sadler)	2		5		11
Miller, Fredrick, Sr.	1	1	2		
Motzinger, Jacob	1	2	4		
Motzinger, Elizabeth		3	1		
Odle, John	2	1	2		
Osborn, Stephen	1	4	1		
Osborn, Nathaniel	1	2	3		
Pain, Barnabas	2	2	5		
Pain, James	1	1	4	1	1
Parsons, Robert	1				
Pope, Nathan	1		1		
Perkins, Thomas	1	2	2		
Perkins, Moses	1	1	3		
Passons, William	2	2	3		
Ross, Jean		3	4		
Russem, William	1	3	6		
Rosax, William	2	3	4		
Reese, Enoch	1	1	3		
Robison, Hugh	2	2	4		
Raper, Jacob	1		4		
Richards, Ulerigh	1	2	3		
Richards, Catherina		1	4		
Rosenbam, Alexander	2	2	3		
Ripple, Henry	1	3	3		
Salisbury, John	2	2	5		
Smith, William	2	3	6		
Sapp, Nowell	1	1	2	1	
Smith, Isaac	1	2	6		
Smith, Josiah	1	2	1		
Spurgin, Jean	1	2	3		
Simmons, William	1	1	2		1
Spurgin, William	2	1	6		
Sercker, John	3		3		
Stanley, William	2		1		
Sitzloch, Airhart	5	1	5		
Stanley, Joseph	2		3		
Tharpe, Thos.	2	3	1		
Tharpe, James	1	1	2		
Teague, Moses, Jur.	1		2		
Teague, Isaac	1	3	6		
Teague, Abraham	3	4	3		
Teague, Jacob	1		2		
Teague, Mathias	1	1	3		
Tice, Jacob	1	3	5		
Turner, Adam	1	4	2		
Teague, Moses	2	1	5		3
Vitteto, Stephen	1		2		
Vail, Joseph	1		1		
Wilborn, Isaac, Jur.	1	1	1		
Wilborn, William	1	2	3		
Wilborn, James	2	3	4		
Willborn, William, Sr.	1	3	2		
Wilborn, Isaac	1	1	1		
Waitman, George	2		4		
Wire, Barnabas	3		5		
Wilson, Christena	2	1	4		
Wilson, Jacob	1	4	1		
Watson, William	1	3	4		
Wire, William	1	5	1		
Wilborn, Isaac, Sr.	4	2	5		
Wilson, Judith	1	4	5		
Wilborn, Gidion	1	1	1		
Albright, Peter	1	1	6		
Albright, John	1	1	4		
Albright, Jacob	1	2	2		
Albright, Christian	1	2	5		
Beasley, William	1	1	3		
Boston, Andw.	2	2	3		
Baighel, Andw.	1		3		
Bever, Nicholas	3	2	3		
Bever, Henry	2	1	8		
Boston, Phillip	1	2	3		
Boston, Mathias	1	3	2		
Baker, Jacob	1	2	2		
Boston, Stofel	1	1	3		
Bace, Henry	2	1	6		
Campbell, John, Jur.	1	6	1		
Campbell, John	1	1	1		4
Freeze, Jacob	3	1	4		
Freeze, John	1	2	3		
Freeze, Peter, Jur.	1	1	2		
Freeze, Peter, Senr.	2	4	5		
Ferrill, John	1		1		
Gibson, George	1	3	2		2
Gibson, James	1	4	3		2
Gilbraith, Thomas	1		2		
Gougher, Henry	1	2	2		
Gibson, William	2		1		
Galliher, Hugh	1	3	6		
Graham, John	4	2	4		5
Goose, John	3	1	3		
Graham, Richard	3		5		7
Hough, Henry	1	1	5		
Hough, David	2	2	4		
Hays, Andrew	1		1		
Hileman, John	2	1	3		
Kertner, William	1	1	3		
Ketner, Peter	1		2		
Kenneday, Alexander	2	1	1		5
Long, Fredrick	1	1	2		
Laymon, Fredrick	1	4	5		
Linch, John	1	2	4		
McClennahan, Andrew	3	5	4		
Miller, David	3	3	3		
Miller, William	1	3	3		
McFersion, Joseph	1		2		
McCulloch, James	3	2	6		9
Nixon, William	2		3		
Plink, John	2		2		
Penney, Alexander	2	1	2		1
Penney, James	1				2
Ross, Joseph	1		1		
Reed, John	1	2	5		
Rutherford, Griffith	4	1	3		8
Ross, John	1	2	4		
Sewill, Joseph	1		1	1	
Sigler, Fredrick	2	2	4		
Sloop, Conrad	1	2	6		
Sewill, Elizabeth		3	3		1
Savits, George, Jur.	1		3	1	7
Savits, George, Senr.	1		2	1	
Smith, Everhart	2	3	4		
Smith, Tobias	1				
Upright, Samuel	1	3	1		
Crider, Jacob	1	3	5		
Woods, William	1	4	2		
Correll, Jacob	1	1	4		
Dule, Jacob	1	2	2		
Craglo, William	1	1	1		
Anderson, William	3	3	3		
Alexander, William	2	1	4		9
Albright, Michael	1	3	4		
Atwood, James	1				1
Brandon, Mathew	1	2	5		4
Brandon, Elizabeth		2	2		4
Brandon, William	1	1	7		4
Boston, Mathias, Sr.	1		1		
Blue, John	4		1		
Boston, Jacob	1	2	2		3
Brandon, John	1	3	4		9
Boston, Andw.	1	1	4		
Brougher, John	1	3	2		
Bellah, Moses	2				4
Bellah, Samuel	1	6	2		
Brown, Timothey	3	2	6		
Boston, Jonas	2		3		
Bird, John	2	1	12		
Cathey, William	2	3	2		6
Cathey, John	2	3	5		5
Cathey, Jean		2	3		4
Correll, John	1	5	2		
Cooper, Samuel	1	2	1		
Cooper, Thomas	3	1	1		
Cooper, William	1	1	4		
Dobbins, David	1	2	2		1
Dunnevan, Mathew	1	1	1		
Eagle, George	1	1	4		
Frazer, John	1	1	3		
Finten, John	1		1		
Graham, Fergus	1	1	6		
Hill, Thomas	2		2		
Hill, Abraham	4	1	3		
Hays, Joseph	3		2		
Hays, John	1				
Hays, David	1	1	2		
Hartman, Michael	1	3	5		
Johnston, Nathaniel	2	2	2		2
Letaker, John	1	3	2		
Lock, Mathew	3	2	2		27
Lock, Richard	1	1	1		3
Lock, Mathew, Jur.	1	3	2		1
Lock, John	1		1		8
Lock, Alexander	1	3	2		2
Lock, Francis	3	1	2		14
Lamb, James	1	3	1		
Lamb, John	1	4	2		
Laughren, Lawrence	3	1	3		
Meanes, Frederick	1	1	1		
May, John	1				
Mahon, Dennis	1	6	4		
Marshall, Thomas	1				
McFeeters, Daniel	3		2		1
McConnell, Daniel	2	1	4		
Martin, Martin	1				
Phillips, John	2	4	4		
Phillips, Reuben	1	2	7		
Plummér, William	1		1		
Robison, Benjamin		1	2		1
Robison, Moses	1		1		
Rian, William	1				
Sawyers, Joseph	1	3	2		1
Stuart, Robert	3	2	1		
Stuart, John	1		2		
Smith, John	2	4	4		2
Savets, Henry	1	1	2		3
Stiller, Peter	1	2	1		
Sever, Fredrick	1		4		
Wallace, John	1	3	4		
Woods, Robert	1				
Amborn, William	1		5		
Akle, John	1	2	2	1	1
Aplin, Lewis	1	1	5		
Akle, Henry	2	2	2		2
Brown, Michael, Jur.	1	1	4		
Boyer, Jacob	1		1		
Bedwell, Caleb	2	2	4		
Barier, Catherina		2	5		
Butner, Sarah		2	4		
Bumgardner, Leonard	1	2	4		
Benket, John	2	2	4		
Brindle, John, Jur.	1	1	1		
Bolevar, Thomas	1		4		
Brookshier, Jesse	1	2	5		
Bolevar, Stark	1	4	3		5
Butner, William	1				
Brindle, John	2	4	6		1
Boyer, Henry	3	2	6		
Kimoroe, Leonard	1	2	3		
Cooper, Thomas	1	2	1		
Cresey, Nicholas	1		1		
Cox, James	1	4	1		
Cressema, Conrad	1	2	2		
Davis, David	1	2	1		2
Donner, Jacob	1		1		
Douthet, Thomas	1	2	4		
Douthet, William	3	5	3	2	5
Douthet, Jacob	1	1	2	1	6
Douthet, Abraham	1	2	2		
Davis, John	1	4	3		
Davis, James	2	4	3		
Dunnahoe, Ann		1	2		1
Elrod, Adam	3	1	9		1
Elrod, John	1	1	3		
Elrod, Christopher	1	3	2		
Elrod, Abraham	1	1	1		
Ellis, Stephen	2	5	2		
Ellis, William	1	2	3		
Felps, John	2	2	2		
Felps, Thomas	2	4	2		7
Fletcher, Mary	2		2		
Felps, Avengton	1	2	2		
Fry, Valentine	1				3
Fry, Peter	3	1	3		
Fry, Christian	1		3		
Fry, John	1	3	3		
Folts, John	1		4		
Fletcher, James, Jr.	1	1	2		
Folts, Fredrick	1		3		
Fry, George	2	2	4		
Farley, Archabeld	1		2		
Farley, Stephen	1		2		
Farley, Francis	2		6		
Griffith, Andrew	3	1	5		1
Griggs, Minus	1	5	4		
George, Andw.	1	3	3		
Gallion, Thomas	1	2	3		
Greenwood, Joseph	1	3	5		
Hall, William	1				
House, Archabeld	1	3	2		
Harrald, Hugh	1	1	3		
Hains, Phillip	1	5	1	1	
Hawkins, Henry	1	2	1		
Huffman, Jacob	1	1	2		
Hartman, Jacob	1	2	1		
Haye, Lazarus	1	1	1		
Hampton, Ephraim	3	5	7		7
Hopper, Thomas, Sr.	1		2		
Hopper, Charles	1	2	2		
Hoozer, Jacob	1		1		
Hickman, William	1		1		
Hopper, Thomas, Jur.	1		1		
Hill, James	1	5	3		
Hallin, William	1	3	2		
Hartman, Adam	2		3		
Hartman, James	1	1	2		
Hartman, Mary	1		4		

SALISBURY DISTRICT, ROWAN COUNTY—Continued.

NAME OF HEAD OF FAMILY.	Free white males of 16 years and upward, including heads of families.	Free white males under 16 years.	Free white females, including heads of families.	All other free persons.	Slaves.
Harington, Jonathan	1	2	4		
James, Nicholas	1	3	2		
Jarvis, Elijah	1	1	3		
Johnston, James	1	2	3	1	
Jarvis, Zadock	1	3	4		
Jarvis, James	1		2		
Koons, George	1	1	1		1
Kent, John	1	1	2		
Kent, James	1				
Kehely, Christopher	1	2	3		
Knows, Joseph	1	2	6		
Latherman, Jonas	1	1	2		1
Link, William	1	3	4		
Lynn, Alexander	1	1	2		
Latherman, John	1	4	1		
McKnight, George, Jur	1	2	1		
Miller, John	1	2	3		
Miller, Valentine	1	2	3		
Markland, Jonathan	1	1	2		
Miller, Michael	1	3	3		
Miller, Nicholas	1	2	1		
Monrow, Thomas	1		2		5
McKnight, Roger	1	1	1		
Miller, Mary	2	1	1		
Michael, William	1	4	3		
Milligan, Lewis	1	4	1		
McKnight, George	3	1	4		3
Miller, Henry	1	3	4		
Matherly, John	1	2	5		
Miller, Martin	1	4	1		
Mock, Jacob	1	2	4		
Murrey, John	1	3	1		
Nock, George	1		3		
Pain, Zacheriah	1	5	7		
Perryman, Isaac	2	3	5		
Petrey, Adam	1	2	6		
Peck, Samuel	1		4		
Peck, Nathan	1	1	3		
Pelley, James	2	1	4		3
Pool, William	3	1	4		
Jacobs, John	1	3	6		
Pool, William, Jur	1	1	1		
Pickel, Fredrick	2	3	3		1
Petrey, Henry	2	3	2		
Riddle, John	1		1		
Richardson, Robison	1	2	2		
Riddle, Stephen	2	1	5		4
Rys, John	1	1	7		
Spaugh, Joseph	1		1		
Stuart, Daniel	1		1		
Stuart, John, Jur	1		2		
Shoars, John	1	2	4		
Stuart, John, Ser	1	3	2		
Sluder, Henry	1		2	2	
Sluder, Isaac	1	2	2		
Simermon, Christian, Jur	1		1		
Spaugh, Adam	1		2		
Starr, Gasper	3	2	6		4
Simmermon, John	1		1		
Deele, Henry	1	4	5		
Taylor, Isaac	1	1	2		
Taylor, Rachell	1	3	3		
Tish, Henry	3	2	2		
Turnage, Michael	1		4		
Vanuver, Cornelius	1	3	5		
Vanuver, Cornelius, Jur	1	2	2		
Walk, Martin	2	5	7		
Wood, Vinsen	1		2		
Waitman, Adam	4	1	4		
Wells, Thomas	1	1	1		
White, David	1	1	2		
Wilkison, William	2	3	7		2
Warner, William	2		4		
Wasner, Mathias	1		2		
Wesner, Jacob, Jur	1	2	1		
Williams, Francis	1	1	4		2
Welch, Samuel	2	3	1		
Welch, John	1	2	3		
Winskot, John	2	4	4		
White, James	1		3		
White, Isaac	1	2	2		
Wosley, William	1	4	1		
Wood, Thomas	1	1	1		1
Wilson, James	1	1	2		
Weaver, Jacob	2	2	2		
Wilson, Robert	1		4		1
Olngs, Thomas	1	3	3		
Jones, Michael	1	2	1		
Johnston, James	2	2	2		
Cross, Asel	3	2	5		
Michael, Barney	1	1	1		
Helsley, Jacob	1	5	4		
Hartman, Mary		1	2		
Fisher, Michael	1		2		
Elrod, Samuel	1	2	1		
Elrod, Peter	1	1	3		

NAME OF HEAD OF FAMILY.	Free white males of 16 years and upward, including heads of families.	Free white males under 16 years.	Free white females, including heads of families.	All other free persons.	Slaves.
Elrod, Jeremiah	1	1	3		
Creaseman, Adam	2	2	5		
Shull, Joseph	1	3	3		
Stuart, Josiah	1		3		
Stuart, Joseph	1		3		
Hickman, John	2	3	3		
Huffman, Jacob	1	6	4		
Ruckman, Josiah	1	1	5		
Morris, John	1	3	2		
Simerman, Christian, Sr	1	2	5		
Simerman, John, Sr	1	2	1		
Michel, William, Jur	1	2	1		
Aldridg, William	3	1	2		
Atkison, James	1	2	3		2
Bates, William	1	1	1		
Baxter, Charles	2	1	7		
Borders, John	3	2	6		
Barkhiser (Widow)		2	2		
Barns, Richard	1	5	3		
Boothe, John	2		5		
Chainey, Judith		1	6		1
Chambers, Mary		2	2		
Cline, Simpson	1	1	2		
Cline, Peter	1	4	2		
Croswell, Andrew	1	1	3		
Croswell, Elener			1		
Club, Jean		2	2		
Croswell, Thomas	2		3		
Chainey, James	1	1	3		
Chapman, William	1	2	3		1
Champaign, William	1	2	2		
Dotey, Moses			3		
Davis, John	1	3	4		
Jones, Wise		2	4		
Earnest, George	4	3	1		
Earnest, Henry	1	1	3		
Fisher, Michael	1		2		
Farley, Stuart	1	2	2		
Farley, Daniel	1		1		1
freemon, Agnes		2	4		
German, Thomas	1	1	1		
Greer, John	1	4	2		
Gobble, John	1	4	3		
Gobble, Jacob	1				
Fitzgerrald, Garret	2	3	2		
Goss, Margaret	1				2
Gardnor, David	1	2	1		
Harrell, Hugh	1	3	2		
Helsley, Michael	1	4	3		
Harmon, Phillip	1	3	5		
Harrawood, Zaniah	1	1	2		
Hartley, Labon	1		5		
Hartley, Benja	1	2	2		
Hill, Isaac	1	2	3		
Hise, George	1	1	4		
Hicks, Thomas	1	1	2		
Jinnings, Robert	1	2	2		
James, Peter	1	3	4		
Jinnings, William	1	2	3		
Jinnings, John	1		3		
Latherman, Christian	1	3	5		
Latherman, Daniel	1				
Lynn, William F	1	2	4		
Leach, Richard	2	1	3		
Lyons, William	1	1	3		
Lee, Andw	1	2	3		
Long, Alexander	3	3	2		26
Loyd, John	1	2	4		
McKatee, Edmond	3	2	1		
Moore, William	1	1	6		
Metsler, John	1	1	1		
Morris, John	1	2	3		
Myrick, John	1	2	2	1	
Michael, Christian	2	4	3		
Morainey, Joseph	1	1	2		
Nicholson, Lucy	1	3	3		
Patterson, James	2	4	3		
Beck, Jacob	3	3	6		1
Beck, George	1	2	2		
Pain, Joshua	1		2		
Beck, Phillip	2	5	3		
Pain, Charles	1		1		
Pain, Enoch	1	2	1		
Parreck, Thomas	1	1	1		
Reed, Avington	2	5	4		
Simpson, Ross	1	2	1		
Reess, John	1	2	2		
Ridgway, Phillip	4	4	9		1
Rinkard, George	1	5	3		
Roberts, Henry	1		6		
Reed, George	2	2	3		
Robertson, John	1		3		
Stallings, Jacob	1	1	4	1	1
Stanfild, Thomas	1	2	3		
Simpson, Benjamin	2	4	6		
Swisgood, Phillip	1		4	1	

NAME OF HEAD OF FAMILY.	Free white males of 16 years and upward, including heads of families.	Free white males under 16 years.	Free white females, including heads of families.	All other free persons.	Slaves.
Swisgood, Adam	1	2	3		
Slagle, Peter	1				
Smith, Landers	1	1	3		
Smith, Nathan	3	1	4		
Smith, Jacob	3		2		
Stuart, William	1	1	4		
Zevely, Henry	1	4	4		
Trentham, Jeptha	2	1	3		
Young, Michael	1	2	5		
Vaun, Fredrick	1	1	4	1	
Wotton, William	1	5	2		
Wood, Archabeld	1	1	2		
Werlau, Elizabeth	3		4		
Williams, James	2		4		1
Wood, Daniel	2	1	2		1
Wood, Joshua	1	2	1		
Wood, Jarret	1	6	4		
Walsor, Martin	1	1	3		
Walsor, Fredrick	2	1	2		
Williams, Ezekel	2		3		
Williams, Henry	1		1		
Watkins, Ambrose	1	2	2		
Winkler, Adam	1	2	4		
Wood, Mary			1		
Wood, Isham	3	4	2		
Wood, William	1	1	4		
Watkins, David	1	1	3		
Wood, Elizabeth, Jur	1	2	1		
Wood, William, Ser	1	1	1		
Wood, James	1		3		
Winkler, Francis	1	5	5		
Anderson, Thomas	1	2	2		
Allemang, Fredrick	3	1	1		
Allemang, Daniel	1		3	3	
Atkeson, James	1	2	2		2
Allison, Andw	1	1	3		3
Brandon, John	1		1		
Beard, Christina			3		2
Betts, Andrew	3	2	2		1
Beroth, Henry	1	2	3		
Biles, Joseph	2	1	8		2
Biles, Thomas	1	4	2		
Biles, Jonathan	3		5		
Biles, John	1				
Bues, John	2	1	2		8
Brinkle, Nicholas	2	2	2		
Beard, John	3		1		1
Blake, John	2	1	7		6
Brown, Peter	1	1	5		4
Bream, Conrad	2	2	2		7
Brown, John	1	3	3		
Beard, Lewis	1	1	5		5
Belfore, Elizabeth		1	2		3
Busley, John	2		4		
Coyl, George	1				
Coughenam, Christian	1		3		
Cowin, David	1	2	4		
Coughenam, Jacob	1	3	4		
Erwin, John	2		1		
Crosser, Leonard	2	1	2		
Cross, John	3	5	3		
Casey, William	1		2		
Clary, John	1	5	4		1
Clary, Daniel	2	5	6		11
Carson, Henry	1	1	4		1
Chambers, Maxwell	4	4	3	1	35
Carson, John	2		6		1
Carson, Hugh	1				
Carson, William	2				5
Carson, James	1				1
Craige, James	1	3	2		13
Cross, Henry	1	1	1		
Craige, Mary		2	3		
Cotten, Isaac	1				
Dunn, Silas	1	1	2		
Dickson, Richard	1	1	1		
Dunn, Charles	1				
Dayton, Samuel	1		2		1
Easton, Zadock	1	1	3		
Ellis, Radford	1	2	3		4
Furr, Tobias	2		1		
Frazer, James	1		2		2
Frohook, Thomas	1				52
Frohook, Isham	1				
Frazer, Peter	1				
Ford, Wiatt	1	2	2		
Fisher, John	1		2		
Gay, Robert	1	2	4		
Gardner, Robert	1	2	2		1
Gardner, John, Jur	1	2	2		
Gardner, James	1				
Gardner, John, Ser	1				
Giles, Henry	1	1	3		7
Horah (Widow)			2		
Howard, Gidion	1	1	3		
Hamton, William	1				
Hoover, George	1	1	3		2

SALISBURY DISTRICT, ROWAN COUNTY—Continued,

NAME OF HEAD OF FAMILY.	Free white males of 16 years and upward, including heads of families.	Free white males under 16 years.	Free white females, including heads of families.	All other free persons.	Slaves.
Holland, Richard	1		4		
Hulin, Arther	1	6	2		
Hunt, Charles	4		2	1	6
Hendricks, Daniel	1	4	6		
Hughes, Joseph	5	3	4		20
Horah, Hugh	1		3		2
Jacobs, Abraham	4	2	4		
Kinder, George	1		1		
Leaf, John	1		2		
Harris, Charles	3		1	5	
Lauman, George	1		3		1
Moore, Samuel	1	1			
Moore, Audlen	1	1	2		
Moore, John	2	1	6		
Macay, Spence	1	1	4		19
Murr, George	1		3		
Montfort, Absalom				1	
Mealy, Owen	2		1		2
Miller, Casper	3	1	5		
Mull, John	2	3	2		
Miller, David	1	1	1		
Newman, Anthony	3	3	4		22
Pinkstone, William	2		2		
Patton, John		2	3		1
Pinkstone, Thomas	1	3	3		
Pasinger, Martin	2	2	1		
Pinkstone, Mashick	1				2
Rice, Isham	2	4	3		
Robison, Joseph	1	1	1		
Swink, George	1				
Steele, John	2		5		16
Strain, William	1				
Shrode, Christian	1	3	3		
Shuls, Jacob	1				
Swink, Leonard	1	2	3		
Swink, John, Jur	1				
Swink, Henry	2	2	2		
Story, Benjamin	1	2	2		
Silverthorne, George	1	3	4		
Swink, John, Ser	1	1	3		
Stocke, Charles	1		1		2
Shrode, Adam	1		2		
Shafer, John	2	2	3		
Stokes, Montfort	1		1		15
Taylor, Absalom	1	2	3		3
Trotter, Richard	1	1	1		7
Troy, Jean		2	4		7
Turner, Benjamin	1	3	1		
Torrence, Albert	1				1
Townsly, James	2		1		
Troy, Michael	2	4	3		2
Veal, Edward	1		2		
Vickers, William	1		2		
Vickers, Thos	2	1	2		
Utzman, Jacob	2	3	3		2
Woodson, David	2	2	4		2
Williams, Thos	4	2	4		
Wood, Charles	1	5	2		
Yarbrough, Edward	1	1	2		3
Young, Henry	1	3	2		3
Adler, Francis	2		3		
Aginder, Henry, Senr	1				
Aginder, Henry, Jur	1	3	5		
Adams, John					
Aginder, David	1	1	3		
Arenhart, Henry	4		4		
Arenhart, Jacob	1		2		
Arenhart, Abraham	1		1		
Biven, Randal	1		2		
Brown, Phillip, Jur	3	1	1		
Brown, Andrew	1	4	3		
Brown, Abraham	2	3	1		
Brown, David	1	2	3		
Brooner, George	1		2	5	
Brown, Jacob	6	1	3		
Butner, Harmon	1		1		
Butner, David	3	2	3	1	
Bartley, John	1		1		
Brooner, John	1	2	1		
Brown, Phillip	2	3	4		
Brown, Michael	5		2		15
Biven, Corbin	1	1	2		
Beard, Valentine	1	1	4		3
Basinger, George	1	2	4		
Biven, Leonard	1	2	5		4
Crider, Michael	1	1	1		
Coldiron, George	2	1	5		
Coble, Peter	1		2		
Coldiron, Conrad	1	3	2		
Crider, Christian	2		3		
Crider, Barnet					
Crider, Leonard	1	2	4		
Doremire Andrew	1		4		
Dahenhart, Henry	1		2		
Eller, John (son of Chs)	1		1		
Eary, John	1	1	1		
Eary, Abraham	1	3	2		

NAME OF HEAD OF FAMILY.	Free white males of 16 years and upward, including heads of families.	Free white males under 16 years.	Free white females, including heads of families.	All other free persons.	Slaves.
Eller, Christian	3	1	4		
Eller, Melcher	1	4	2		
Eller, Henry	1	2	3		
Eller, John	1	2	3		
Eller, John Milker	1	3	2		
Eary, Zachriah	1		4		
Eller, Jacob	1	1	1		
Eller, Fredk	1		2		
Eller, Jno (son of Melcher)	1		2		
Fisher, Fredrick	3	1	4		13
Fite, Peter	4		5		
Fraley, Henry	1		2		
Fraley, George	2	4	4		
Fite, Conrad	1		2		
Fraley, Jacob	1	4	1		
Fredrick, Christian	1	2	1		
Folts, Peter	1		1		
Fisher, Jacob	2				
Faust, Peter	2	1	4	1	
Fults, Henry	1		2		
Getchey, John	1	3	7		
Getchey, Fredrick	1	1	1		
Grub, Elizabeth	1	1	5		
Hartman, John	1				
Hendricks, Daniel	1	4	5		
Holobaugh, George	1	2	3		
Hendricks, Peter	1	1	4		
Hill, John	3	3	2		
Hildebrand, John	1	2	2		
Caren, Adam	1	1	3		
Kesler, John	1	2	2		
Karen, John	2	2	6		
Coble, John	1	2	1		
Karen, Conrad	3	2	5		
Kroul, William	1	2	4		
Krotser, Phillip	2	1	3		
Kobble, Peter, Senr	1	1	4		1
Kobble, Peter, Jur	1		3		
Kobble, Michael	1		2		
Kroul, Peter	1		2		
Lance, John, Ser	1	3	4		
Lance, Peter	1	3	5		
Lance, Benjamin	1		3		
Moyer, Henry	1				
Marbery, Francis	4	3	2		6
McCann, John	1		2		
Popst, Henry	1		2		
Rusher, Jacob	1	2	2		
Ribley, Martin	2	1	6		
Swink, Michael	1	1	2		3
Slighter, Henry	1				
Smith, George	1				
Sasaman, Henry	1	2	1	1	
Shriver, John	1	4	2		
Shooman, George	1				
Smithell, Joseph	1	1	3		
Truse, Adam	1	2	3		
Truse, Michael	1	2	4		
Wervel, Jacob	2	2	3		
Walton, Richard	5	1	2		
Waller, Elizabeth	1	2	2		
Wise (Widow)	1	2	2		
Weighant, John	1	2	3		
Williams, John	1	3	2		
Wetheraw, Aywalt	2	2	4		
West, William	2	2	2		
Biles, Charles	1	3	2		3
Biles, John	1	7	3		
Burris, Jonathan	5	2	5		5
Culbertson, John	2	4	6		
Clary, Conner	1	2	1		
Cotten (Widow)		1			
Cowen. Phebey					5
Duglass, Mary			2		
Eanis, William	1		3		
Ghean, James, Ser	4		6		
Ghean, James, Jur	1		2		
Ghean, Thomas	2		2		
Hightower, Messenger		1	3		
Hunter, John	1		1	1	
Heathman, James	1	3	4		
Howard, John	2	3	4		1
Hains, Ralph	1	2	3		
Howard, Mathew	1	4	3		
Jones, James	1	4	3		
Kenhard, James, Ser	4	3	3		
Kerr, Stephen	1	2	1		2
Kinkade, John	1		3		
Lowrey, John	2	1	2		
Leach, Benjamin	1	3	3		
Lewis, Peter, Ser	1	1	3		
Lewis, Peter, Jur	1	1	1		
Lewis, Samuel	1	1	4		
Link, Jacob	3	1	8		
McCrakin, James	1	2	6		
Montgomery, John	1	3	1		2

NAME OF HEAD OF FAMILY.	Free white males of 16 years and upward, including heads of families.	Free white males under 16 years.	Free white females, including heads of families.	All other free persons.	Slaves.
Marlin, James	2	2	2		
Marlin, John	1	1	2		
Marlin, Thomas	1	2	3		
Marlin, Jas, Esqr	4	1	3		
Marlin, John, Jur	1	1	1		
McCoy, William	1	2	1		
Pinkstone, Peter	2	1	3		
Palmer, Edmond	3	1	3		
Raimond, Wm	1	3	2		
Robley, John	1		1		
Robison, Richard	3		1		1
Rainey, William	1				
Robison, Henry, Jr	1				
Robison, Henry	1		4		5
Robison, Hugh	1				
Robison, George	1	1	4	1	
Robison, Henry, Esqr	4		6		
Robison, William	1	1	2		
Reary, George	2	2	1		
Smith, Martha			3		
Spring, Albert	1	3	5		
Sanders, Robert	1	2	3		
Tomison, George	2	3	1		3
Todd, John, Jur	1	2	4		1
Tomison, Richard	1	3	2		
Trott, Henry	3	3	4	1	
Todd, John	1		1		
Todd, James	1	2	2		
Turner, William	1	3	5		
Williamson, William	3	3	5		2
Wallace, Samuel	1	1	6		
Wilson, Samuel, Sr	2		4		
Wilson, Samuel, Jur	3		2		
Wilson, William	1	3	1		
Abbott, Benjamin	1	2	3		2
Bartley, Robert	3		3		
Blair, James	3	4	4		1
Beard, Hannah	1	3	3		
Barkley, David	1				
Bowen, Joseph	2	1	4		
Band, Brezilla	1	2	3		
Barkley, Samuel	1	1	2		
Cathey, Richard	1	1	6		2
Carson, Thomas	1	3	4		11
Cox, John	2		3		
Cox, Charles	1	2	5		
Clemmens, Henry	2	3	7		
Coningham, George	2	1	6		
Conger, John	2	3	6		
Conger, Jonathan, Jr	1	1	1		
Davis, Conrad	3	1	1		
Daily, William	1	3	4		
Dusenbery, Samuel	2	2	2		
Elston, Jonathan	2	2	2		
Ellis, Thomas	3	3	2		9
Elliot, John	1	2	2		
Elliot, William	1	1	6		
Ford, John	2		2		1
Gadbery, Nathaniel	1	4	4		
Giles, John	1	3	4		
Greene, Jeremiah	1	5	2		
Haiden, Joseph	1		3		2
Hudgins, William	2		2		14
Hunt, Gasham	2	2	4		
Hunt, Able	1	2	2		
Lewis, Abraham	1	3	5		
Lynn, Isarel	1	1	1	1	
McCartney, Lewis	1	3	4		1
McCartney, Thomas	2	3	4		
Mills, Samuel	1	4	4		
McKee, Robert	1		2		3
Merrill, Andrew	2	3	5		
Morlin, Vinsent	1		2		
Merrill, Jonathan	1	1	2		
Moore, William, Ser	3	2	5		8
Macay, James	4		3		
Moore, William, Jur	2	1	3		1
McKee, Robert, Jur	1		1		1
Maguire, Zebilla		4	1		
McKee, Dorsay	1		3		
Maguire, Daniel	2	1	3		
Owen, Raph	1	1	3		2
Patton, John (O. R.)	2	1	3		
pippinger, Abraham	1	1	2		
Pew, Joseph	1	1	1		
Quick, Richard	1				
Williams, Reese	1	2	2		
Rounseval, David	1	1	3		
Ross, John	1	2	2		
Rodsmith, Paul	2	1	2		
Rats, Godferry	2	2	4		3
Richardson, Charles	1	2	4		
Smith, Thomas	2	4	2		
Smith, Andrew	1				
Smith, Joseph	2	1			
Sloan, John, Ser	1	1	3		1
Sloan, John, Jur	1	1	4		5

SALISBURY DISTRICT, ROWAN COUNTY—Continued.

NAME OF HEAD OF FAMILY.	Free white males of 16 years and upward, including heads of families.	Free white males under 16 years.	Free white females, including heads of families.	All other free persons.	Slaves.
Smith, Benjamin	1	1	3		1
Smith, George	2		1		1
Smith, Barbara	1		2		6
Scrivner, James	1	3	6		
Stoner, John Abm	1	2	1		
Simpson, Robert	2		1		
Smith, Cornelius	2	2	3		
Scudder, Mathias	1		5		
Scudder, Abner	1	1	1		
Scudder, Isaac	1	1	1		
Smith, Clara	2		2		1
Strange, Owen	1	1	2		
Todd, Caleb, Senr	3	1	4		
Todd, Thomas	1	3	3		
Todd, Peter	1	3	4		
Todd, Benja, Jur	1	3	3		
Todd, William	1	1	3		
Todd, Joseph	1	3	2		
Todd, Benja, Ser	2	2			
Todd, Caleb, Jur	1	1	3		
Tensey, John	1		1		
Willis, Thomas, Senr	1		1		
Wiseman, Jacob	2	3	2		
Warford, Joseph	2	1	3		
Wilson, John	2		1		1
Wiseman, Isaac	1	2	3		
Wilson, John, Jur	1	2	3		
Willis, Thomas, Jur	1	3	2		
Willis, George	1	5	3		
Wiseman, Jacob, Jur	1		1		
Wiseman, James	1	1	3		
Aldeman, Peter, Jur	1	4	2		
Aldeman, Peter	1		2		
Overkersh, Francis	1	3	3		
Overkersh, George	1	2	1		
Overkarsh, Jacob	1		1		
Berger, George H.	2	2	6		3
Bullen, John	3	3	2		
Bever, Peter	4	5	3		
Brown, Thomas	1	3	5		
Baringer, Peter	3	1	3		
Berger, John	1	1	1		
Casper, Henry	1	2	2		
Cummins (Widow)		1	1		
Corl, Peter	1	2	4		
Correll, Adam	1	1	4		
Cruse, Phillip	1	1	5		
Casper, John	1	1	5		
Casper, Adam	1		3		
Crouel, George	2	3	5		
Deele, Youst	1		4		
Deele, Peter	1				
Dillo, Jacob	1				
Dillo, Michael	1	1	4		
Akle, John	1	1	5		
Fisher, John	1	1	2		
Freeze, Jacob	3	1	4		
Fisher, Jacob	1	2	4		
Garner, Mathias	1	3	6		
Helms, George	1		2		
Hofner, Martin	1	4	1		
Hampton, John	3	2	4		
Hornbarier, Valentine	4	1	3		
Hampton, William	3	1	4		
Hofner, George	1		1		
Hiley, Michael	1	4	1		
Josey, John	4	1	3		
Klotts, Jacob	1		2		
Klotts, Wendle	1	1	2		
Klotts, Jacob, Jur	1				
Klotts, Leonard	1		2		
Koone, Anthony	1	2	6		
Kenup, John	1	2	4		
Kaster, Jacob	1	2	4		
Kenup, Jacob	1	2	2		
Klotts (Widow)	1	2	1		
Lance, David	2	1	2		
Lance, Peter	1		3		
Lierly, Peter	1	1	2		
Lierly, Jacob	1	2	2		
Lance, Bostion	2	2	4		
Lance, Bostion, Jur	1		2		
Lingle, Anthony	1	1			
Lenard, Henry	1		5		
Lynn, Robert	1	4	1		
Lingle, Francis	1	4	2		
Miller, Nicholas	2	2	2		
Miller, Fredrick	1	5	2	1	
Morer, Fredrick	2	1	4		
Miller, Wendle	2	4	4		
Messemer, Peter	2		2		
Miller, Martin	3	1	6		
Miller, Daniel	1	4	1		
Mourer, Rudy	2	4	2		
Miller, Phillip	2	4	2		
Morer, Jacob	1				

NAME OF HEAD OF FAMILY.	Free white males of 16 years and upward, including heads of families.	Free white males under 16 years.	Free white females, including heads of families.	All other free persons.	Slaves.
Pool, John	1	4	3		
Peeler, Michael	2	2	4		
Phillips, Jessey	1		1		
Poules, Adam	1	2	2		
Randleman, John	3	3	4		2
Rimer, Nicholas	3	4	4		
Roseman, George	1	4	3		
Rebley, Peter	1		3		
Siffard (Widow)	1	1	3		
Shuppin, Nicholas	2	2	2		
Siffard, Leonard	1	7	2		
Stierwalt, John	3	2	2		
Stierwalt, Fredrick	1		2		
Troutman, Peter, Jur	1	2	2		
Troutman, Peter	2		1		
Troutman, Adam	3	1	6		
Troutman, Melcher	2	5	3		
Wensel (Widow)		3	4		
Walker, Henry	1	1	2		
Youst, Phillip	1	4	6		
Byrns, Charles (B. O.)	3	1	2		
Byrns, Thomas	2	2	2		
Bodenhimer, William	4	2	3		
Bettis, William	2	3	4		
Bowers, Jacob	1	3	5		
Butrem, William	1	3	6		
Blessing, John	1		1		
Benblossom, Jacob	1	2	1		
Benblosom, Abraham	1	2	2		
Barkshier, Henry	2	3	3		
Bowers, Adam	1	2	2		
Black, Jacob	2	2	6		
Bierly, Jacob	2		2		
Brown, James	1	3	5		
Benton, Isaac	2	5	5		
Bradburn, John	1	2	1		
Bowers, George	2		1		
Bringle, Casper	2	3	5		
Byrel, Martin	3	6	4		
Boen, John	1		1		
Benson, Reuben	1	1	2		
Crum, Godferry	1	1	3		
Cooper, Job	1		3		
Cooper, Charles	1		1		
Cooper, Jonathen	1	2	4		
Clotfalder, George	1		1		
Clotfalder, Rudolph	2	3	4		
Crum, Christian	1		1		
Cobble, Jacob	1	4	4		
Delap, Daniel	1	4	3		
Delp, Peter	2	4	6		
Highat, John	1	3	5		
Embler, William	3	2	5		
Eller, Leonard	1	3	4		
Ledford, Obediah	1		3		
Frisbey, Abraham	3	5	4		
Fox, Thomas	1	5	3		
Fouts, Nicholas	3		2		
Fouts, Peter	1		2		
Fouts, John	1		3		
Ferguson, William	1		1		
Tenneson, James	1		2		
Garren, Andrew	1	5	2		
Gordon, James	1	2	3		
Garren, James	1	1	6		
Grimes, George	1	3	3		
Gillim, Jesse	1		1		
Gillim, James	1	4	2		
Gillim, Drury	1		3		
Pigen, Samuel	1		3		
Henson, Samuel	2	2	6		
Haun, Fredrick	3		4		
Helms, John	1	3	1		
Hilton, Thomas	1	1	3		
Hichcock, Isaac	2	1	3		
Hilton, Jonathan	1	2	3		
Hughes, James	2	2	6		
Heplor, Christopher	2	3	2		
Herner, Christian	1	3	2		
Hucheson, Thomas	1	1	2		
Hilton, James	1	1	5		
Jones, Thomas	1	1	8		
Isaacks, John	1				
Kiddle, Elenor		2	1		
Kenoy, Phillip	1	2	5		
Kenut, William	1	2	5		
Krudle, John	1		3		
Pendrey, George	2		3		
Luckebey, John, Jur	1	1	2		
Luckebey, David	1	1	2		
Lusk, William	1	2	1		
Lusk, Hugh	1		1		
Luvin, John	1	3	1		
Lusk, Samuel	1		1		
Stiff, Moses	1	5	3		

NAME OF HEAD OF FAMILY.	Free white males of 16 years and upward, including heads of families.	Free white males under 16 years.	Free white females, including heads of families.	All other free persons.	Slaves.
Secrist, Fredrick	3	1	5		
Miller, John	1		2		
McCrary, William	1	5	7		
Morris, Isaac	1		1		
Morgan, James	2	1	2		
Mings, Joseph	1				
Morgan, James, Jur	1		3		
Manering, Andrew	1	3	2		
Miars, David	1	1	3		
Miars, John	1	2	4		
Miars, George	1	1	3		
Miars, Jacob	1	1	5		
Miars, Christian	1	3	2		
Miller, Fredrick	1	1	1		
Morris, William	1				
Odle, Isaac	1	1	2		
Owens, Andw	2	3	1		
Pair, Arthur	1	2	4		
Plummer, John	1		2		
Roberts, John	1	6	3		
Ring, Michael	1		2		
Reggins, James	1	3	2		
Ring, Martin	2	2	4		
Rimer, David	1	1	3		
Ragan, Eli	1	2	3		
Rodes, Mary	2	2	2		
Snider, Jacob	3		2		
Sears, Christian	3	2	8		
Seacrist, Jacob	1	1	2		
Shuler, Peter	1		2		
Shuler, Michael	2	4	3		
Shults, Mark	1	1	1		
Shutz, Andrew	1		2		
Seeley, Joseph	1	2	2		
Snider, George	1	2	1		
Summers, Thomas	2	3	5		
Sayrs, Richard	1				12
Spoolman, Fredrick	1	1	4		
Sears, John	1	4	3		
Sacrist, George	1	3	1		
Tacker, James	1	2	3		
Tharpe, John	1	2	3		
Tacker, Seaborn	4		4		
Tacker, Robert	2	1	3		
Tumbleson, Saml	2	2	4		1
Tumbleson, Josiah	2	2	3		
Wortman, Peter	1	1	1		
Wright, Richard	1	2	5		
Wright, Evan	1		2		
Wright, Phillimon	2	1	5		
Williams, Joshua	1		1		
Wakasor, Jacob	2	2	3		
Wright, William	1	1	2		
Williams, Postem	1				
Waller, Benja	2		3	1	4
Wright, Easaw	1	1	2		
Veach, John	1	2	4		2
Shuts, Mark, Sr	1	3	5		
Yokley, William	1				
Yarbrough, Joab	1	2	4		
Tacker, James	1	2	2		
Andrew, James	3	2	8		1
Bartley, James	1	1	2		
Barr, Hugh	1				4
Barr, Patrick	1	4	3		1
Barr, John	2	2	3		2
Barkley, Henry	2		1		2
Bunten, John	1	1	2		6
Cowen, Thomas	1	3	8		
Cowen, William	1	2	3		
Cowen, John	1	1	4		1
Crawford, David	1	2	4		2
Cowen, David	1		1		
Cook, Alexr	2	1	3		1
Erwin, Joseph	1		2		3
Erwin, William	1	2	3		2
Forster, David	1	2	5		2
Forster, Robert	1	4	6		
Forster, John	1	2	4	1	3
Gillaspie, Thomas	1	1	4		3
Harvey, John	1		2		3
Huston, Thomas	2	4	2		
Hartsaugh, Paul	1	5	2		
Huston, James	1		2		
Huston (Widow)	1		2		
Kestler, George	1	4	3		
Kilpatrick, John	3		4		1
Kerr, Margret	2		2		
Kerr, John	1	1	3	1	
Knox, Benjn	3		3		1
Kerr, James	3	1	5		
Lowrance, Josiah	1	1	5		
Lowrance, Ann	1				
Lowrance, Andrew	1	3	3		
Lowrance, Abraham	1		1		1
Moffit, William	1	1	1		

SALISBURY DISTRICT, ROWAN COUNTY—Continued.

Name of head of family.	Free white males of 16 years and upward, including heads of families.	Free white males under 16 years.	Free white females, including heads of families.	All other free persons.	Slaves.
McCorkle, Alexander, Sr	2				6
McCorkle, John	2		2		
McCorkle, Alexander, Jur	1	2	3		
McClain, John	1	2	3		
McKrakin, John	3	5	3		
Gillaspie, Thomas, Sr	4		1		7
Gillaspie, David	1		1		1
Gillaspie, Richard	1		6		8
Gillaspie, Thomas, Jur	1	2	3		4
Wasson, John	3	1	3		1
Philwoward, Nicholas	1		1	1	
Price, Charles	1	1	3		
Patterson, James	1		1	1	
Patton, John	1				
Yarwood, Benjamin	1		1		
Rutledg, John	2		4		
Auton, Richard	1	3	5		
Bell, Thomas	3	1	2		
Bell, William	1		6		
Bowman, William	4		4		2
Baxter, Daniel	2	2	7		
Brandon, James	1	1	7		9
Baringer, Jacob	1	1	2		
Cathey, Jean			1		
Carson, Thomas	1	1	2		2
Cowin, William, Senr	3	4	3		1
Cowin, William, Jur	1	1	2		
Cowin, Benjamin	1	3	6		5
Cadihan, James	1	2	2		1
Dobbins, Alexander, Sr	5	1	5		5
Dobbins, Hugh	1	3	3		
Devenport, William	1	3	6		
Dobbins, Alex, Jur	1		2		
Dobbins, John, Jur	1				
Dobbins, John	1		4		
Forster, Joseph	1	4	3		1
Fisher, James	1	2	4		
Fergison, Andrew	2	1	1		
Gellihan, Abraham	2	1	3		4
Gillaspie, George	3	3	4		4
Haggins, John	1		5		10
Hamilton (Widow)			2		
Jinkins, Hugh	3	1	3		3
Jinkins, Samuel	1	1	4		
Kerr, Joseph	1	2	2		5
Kerr, Samuel	2		1		6
Lock, Mathew	1	3	5	1	2
McCorkle, Samuel	1	1	4		6
McNeely, John, Senr	3		2		
McNeely, John, Junr	1	3	5	1	2
McNeely, James	1	1	2		
McConnahey, Sampson	2	1	1		
McNeely, David	3	3	3		
McGlochland, John	1	2	1		
McGlochland, Samuel	1	1	15		
McCollum, Andw	1		5		
McConnahey, Joseph	2		2		2
McConnahey, James	1				1
McConnahey, Hugh	1				
McBroom, James	1	4	2		
McNeely, Archabeld	4	3	7		
Miller, Samuel	3	4	4		2
Miller, Jean	1		4		2
Mathewson, Daniel	1		2		
Nevins, William	1	1	5		
Steele, Martin	1	1	1		
Sillimon, John	2	5	1		
Skiles, John	2		4		3
Stuart, Mathew	1	2	4		
Sloan, Joseph	2	1	4		
Thompson, Thomas	2	2	6		7
Thompson, Joseph	1	3	6		3
Tygart, John	2	4	6		
Nesbitt, William	1	1	2		13
Job, Samuel	2	1	5		
Cox, Edward	1	2	7		
King, Jeremiah	1	1	3		
Morris, Benjamin	1	2	1		

SALISBURY DISTRICT, STOKES COUNTY.

Name of head of family.	Free white males of 16 years and upward, including heads of families.	Free white males under 16 years.	Free white females, including heads of families.	All other free persons.	Slaves.
Deatherage, George	2	4	1		5
Tilly, Lazarus	2	1	7		4
Simmons, Jesse	3	1	4		
Fenley, James	2	2	3		
Tilly, Edmund	2	4	2		1
Tilly, David	1	1	1		
Cox, Joshua	2	3	3		6
Nelson, Joshua	2	6	6		2
Sprouse, David	1	1	2		
Bohannan, James	2	2	4		1
Hickman, Edwin	1	1	1		
Hickman, William	1	1	1		
Cloud, Joseph	2	2	6		1
Edgmond, Samuel	1		3		1
Lawson, John	1	3	1		
Davison, David	1	3	3		
Sherry, William	1	3	4		
Wilson, John	1		3		
Faukner, Jonas	1		2		
Cloud, William	2	5	4		
Bohannan, Philemon	1		1	1	
Lawson, John	1	2	1		
Collins, Jeremiah	1	3	4		
Mitchel, Ralph	1	1	4		
Collins, Roger	1	1	4		
Fields, Davis	1	1	4		
Gains, James	2	3	7		3
Pruitt, Peter	1	1	4		
Bailey, William	1	1	4		
Urillis, Moses	1	1	2		
Beasley, Richard	2	2	4		
Collins, Watson	1	4	2		
Hall, Randoph	1	2	4		
Fields, Lansford	1	1	7		
Beasley, William	1	1	3		
McHone, Arche	1	3	4		
Fly, John	1	1	3		
Burge, Allen	1		1		
Lawson, Patmon	1	1	5		
Shelton, Mary	2	1	4		1
Ship, Josias	2		2		2
Isbel, Hickman	1				
Garner, John	1		2		
Coomer, William	1		2		
Bullin, Isaac	1	2	1		
Lawson, David	3		8		
Bridgman, William	2	1	3		
Coomer, Richard	1	3	3		
Ship, Josias	1	2	2		1
Fields, John	1		3		
Fields, Davis	2		4		
Holt, Fetherston	1	2	4		
Harris, Mathew	2	2	6		
Deatherage, John	3		1		3
Moore, Mathew	6	3	4		15
Goans, Joseph	1	3	3		2
Isbel, Jason	1	2	4		5
Pierce, Jacob	1	1			
Nudson, Peter	1		6		
Childress, David	1	1	3		
Isbel, Thomas	1		3		
Gains, Thomas	1	5	3		3
Floyd, Caleb	1	3	3		
Smith, John	1		2		
Carroll, Benjamin	1		1		
Baker, Sylvester	1	4	4		
Skeef, William	2	1	4		
Jessop, Joseph	2	3	3		
Jessop, William	2	4	4		
Jessop, Timothy	2	2	5		1
Bailey, David	1	3	4		
Jessop, Thomas	1	4	5		
Clark, James	1	1	5		
Lawson, John	1	1	4		
Lawson, Jonas	2	3	3		
Langford, William	1	2	4		
Harris, Mathew	1	2	3		
Bailey, David	1	3	2		
Lyon, James	1				8
Cook, James	2	2			4
Harriss, John	1		3		
Grig, Moses	2	4	5		
Jessop, Joseph	1		1		
Horton, Daniel	1	3	3		
Garrott, Welcom	1	5	4		
Stevens, William	3		4		
Bates, William	1	4	3		
Hancock, John	1		3		
Miller, Randolph	1	5	3		
Wordly, Henry	2	1	3		
Jackson, John	4	2	4		
Bellow, Peter	2	3	4		
Harold, Jonathan	1	2	6		
Southerlin, Daniel	1		3		
Gibson, John	1	2	3		
Cooper, Thomas	1	3	5		
Gibson, Valentine	2	1	3		
White, William	1	3	3		
Gibson, Garrott	1	2	4		
Sumner, Caleb	2	2	4		
Carson, John	1	2	3		
Sumner, Thomas	1	5	4		
Gibson, Archelus	2	1	2		
Nunn, Richard	2	1	2		
Nunn, William	1	3	1		
Bartlett, William	1		1		
Riddle, Tyre	1	1	1		
Watson, Alex	1	2	2		
Jackson, Samuel	1	2	2		
Harison, Jonathan	2	4	2		
Easley, Joseph	1	2	3		
Price, Elisha	1	2	8		
Wordly, Jacob	1	1	1		
Ballard, German	1				
Ballard, Byrum	1		1		
Beasley, Richard	1	1	2		
Lockhart, Thomas	1	2	2		
Cox, Richard	2	2	8		3
King, Peter	2	3	4		
Gibson, James	1	5	4		
Beasley, Robert	1		2		
Ship, Thomas	1	2	2		5
Shinalt, John	1	2	4		
Blanchett, Peter	1		1		
Martin, John	1	1	3		
Burrus, William	1	1	2		
Hort, Joseph	1	2	5		
King, Benajah	3	2	3		
Stevens, William	2	2	7		
Sizemore, George	1	1			
Harold, Elisha	1	1	1		
Gordan, John	1		1		
Shelton, John	3	3	8		
Fields, Josias	1		1		1
Witt, Ann		3	3		
Love, Thomas	1	1	3		
Harold, John	1		4		
Freeman, James	1	5	3		
Eaton, Christopher	1	2	2		
Bails, William	2	3	3		
Cantwell, John	1	2	3		
Deatherage, William	1	2	4		
Goodman, Ansylem	1	2	4		
Harold, Richard	1	3	4		
Low, Thomas	1	2	3		
Harold, Jacob	1				
Landers, Moses	1	2	3		
Roark, Timothy	1		1		
Safford, Richard	1	3	1		
Mcginnis, Michael	1	2	4		
Parker, Jeff	1	1	3		
Price, Charles	1		1		
Scott, George	1	1	2		
Lanes, Thomas	1	2	2		
Rabe, Jacob	1				
Ransom, Joseph	1	3	1		
Teage, John	1		3		
Hunter, John	3	1	3		
Hunter, David	1				
Jackson, John	1	2	5		
Ballard, Archelus	1		1		
Bates, William	1	4	4		
Oglesby, Asea	1	2	2		
Bond, Samuel	1	3	5		
Horton, Margaret		2	3		
Jessop, Joseph	1		1		1
Jackson, Samuel	4	1	7		
Mcarter, Aaron	1		3		
Martin, George	1		3		
Isbel, Richard	1	2	3		
Cardwell, Thomas	1	2	3		8
Ketchum, Joel	1	2	2		
Lester, Archebald	1	3	4		
Mullens, William	2		4		
Hickman, Edwin	1	2	4		
Lawson, Mirymon	1	1	1		
Johnson, Thomas	1	3	4		
Ballard, Thomas	2	3	4		
Burge, Alex	2	2	7		1
Beasley, Benjamin	1				
Angill, Charles	1	3	5		1
Angill, Laurance	1	2	1		
Angill, James	1	1	1		
Atwood, William	1	2	2		
Bradley, George	1	2	1		1
Bair, Patrick	1	3	3		
Bair, John	1		4		
Brooks, William	1	4	4		
Crump, Robert	3	4	5		1
Cliburn, Thomas	1	5	3		
Dunlap, John	2	1	2		
Dunlap, James	1	1	4		7
Dearing, Anthony	2	1	2		
Flint, Roderick	1	2	2		
Grinder, Joshua	1	2	3		

SALISBURY DISTRICT, STOKES COUNTY—Continued.

NAME OF HEAD OF FAMILY.	Free white males of 16 years and upward, including heads of families.	Free white males under 16 years.	Free white females, including heads of families.	All other free persons.	Slaves.
Grinder, Mary	1		3		
George, Jesse	2	4	6		
Guin, Alman	1	1	3		10
Hazle, Moses	3	1	4		
Hazle, Robert	1	4	3		
Hazle, Kindler	1		3		
Harston, Peter	3	1	3		58
Kimmins, William	1	3	3		
Vest, Charles	2	2	2		
Briggs, Robert	1	3	3		
Hess, Jacob	1	1	3		
Corder, Joseph	1	4	2		
Gymon, Isaac	1	3	6		
Martin, John	1	3	1		
Hillsebeck, Jacob	1	2	4		
Flint, Leonard	1	3	4		
Flinn, Thomas	1	2	1		
Armstrong, John	1	1	4		16
Carr, John	1	2	5		
Burch, William	1	4	4		
Randalman, John	1	1	2		2
Kerby, Edmund	3	2	4		
Lester, Jesse	2	1	5		8
Martin, Valentine	2	3	4		
Hughlitt, William	1	1	5		2
Thomlinson, Alex	1	2	1		
Franklin, Malekiah	1	2	1		
Waller, Jacob	1	2	1		
Waller, Sarah	2		4		
Franklin, John	2	1	2		
Bostick, Absalem	3	1	4		21
Legrand, Abraham	1	2	2		
Ladd, Noble	1	4	3		1
Ladd, William	1	1	1		3
Lewis, William	2	4	5		
Lewis, James	1		3		
Ladd, Joseph	1	1	4		2
Moore, James	1		1		
Majors, John	2		4		
Majors, Robert	1	2	2		
Morgan, John	1	5	5		
Morgan, Valentine	1		6		
Newcam, Thomas	2	5	3		
Roberts, Bob	1	4	1		
Read, Joseph	2	4	3		
Ray, George	2	1	5		
Syrus, Jesse	1	5	2		
Southern, William	2		3		
Southern, Rubin	1	4	4		
Southern, Ford	1		1		
Southern, Boas	1	1	2		
Smith, Lemuel	1	2	4		14
Southerlin, Jesse	2	3	6		
Childress, Mathew	1	1	3		
Scott, John	3	4	5		
Franklin, Walter	1	1	1		
Spanehaur, Henry	1	2	6		
Arnal, Henry	1	3	6		
Short, James	1	2	4		
Hunter, Thomas	1	1	1		
Hunter, David	1	1	1		
Hunter, Benjamin	1		1		
Gatewood, Gabriel	1	1	4		
Doss, Mathew	1	3	6		2
Overby, Freeman	1	1	2		
Stone, John	1	2	1		
Craiger, George	1	2	4		
Edwards, Edward	1	4	2		
Fulk, Adam	1	7	1		
Fiskus, Adam	1	2	4		
Arnal, Henry	2		5		
Boyls, William	1	3	4		
Boyls, William	2	1	2		
Speace, John	1	3	1		
Thomson, James	1		1		
Terrill, Hary	4	3	3		27
Taylor, Richard	1	3	6		
Vernon, Jonathan	1	2	4		
Vernon, Jonathan	2		1		
Vaughn, Joseph	1	3	6		
Webster, John	1	3	5		
Warnock, Samuel	2				
Warnock, Mathew	1				
Ward, John	1	3	4		
Walker, William	1	8			1
Wiljohn, Abraham	1	2	1		
Nelson, Joseph	2		1		
Nelson, Alex	1	1	2		8
Angill, Sabour	1				
Wilson, Richard	2	1	6		
Ladd, Judath			3		2
Syrus, Alec	1	1	3		
Banks, Samuel	1	1	3		
Langham, James	1	1	7		
Chrissolm, John	1	2	2		2
Reighly, Charles	1		5		
Darnal, Joseph	1	1	5		
Gordan, John	1		2		
Childress, Armajah	1	7	5		
Tate, Arthur	1	2	2		
Oliver, Ahijah	2	5	4		
Venable, William	1	2	3		
Hampton, John	1	1	1		
Boyls, John	1	1	1		
Boatright, Daniel	2	2	5		5
Christman, George	1	1	4		
Horne, Jesse	1	1	2		
Carr, John	1	2	2		
Edwards, Abel	1		2		
Spanehaur, Jacob	1	6	6		
Kerby, Jesse	1	1	1		
Brown, Samuel	1		3		1
Vest, Samuel	1	2	3		
Sprinkle, George	2	3	7		1
Shifford, Jacob	2	5	3		
Curry, Malcom	1		2		
East, Thomas	1	2	2		8
Armstrong, Martin	3	2	3		10
Martin, Job	3	3	5		1
Pettitt, George	1	2	1		
Poindexter, Thomas	2	1	5		13
Reynolds, Justice	1	3	2		
Kelly, John	1		4		
East, Joseph	2	1	6		
Wright, Hezekiah	1		1		
Connel, John	1		2		
Wright, Elizabeth		1	2		
Fearer, Christian	1	4	2		
East, Isham	2	4	1		1
East, William	4	1	6		
Johnson, David	1	1	4		
Fitzpatrick, John	1	1	5		
Venable, John	1	2	3		
Vest, Isham	1		1		
Prater, William	1	2	2		1
Quiller, James	1	2	3		
Steele, William	1	3	3		
Arny, Henry	1	3	7		
Arnold, William	1	4	4		
Briggs, John	1		2		
Dillard, James	1	1	2		
Martin, William	2	2	5		9
Ridle, John	1	2	4		
Hutcherson, Richard	1	4	6		
Cox, Isham	2	1	1		1
Elliott, Charles	2	5	6		1
Gibson, John	1	5	2		
Ridle, Randolph	1	3	3		
Woode, Robert	1	4	3		
Newman, Payton	1	1	3		
Johns, Arther	1	4	3		
Tilly, Bennett	1	3	1		
Dean, Mathew	1		5		
Calahan, Josias	1	1	2		
Calahan, William	2	1	3		
Woode, Richard	1	3	4		
Hutcherson, Daniel	2		1		2
Nelson, Jacob	1	4	4		
Gains, Robert	2		6		4
Sergant, John	4		1		
Joyce, Alex	3	1	5		3
Smith, William	1		1		
Banister, Nancy		4	3		
Childress, Abraham	1	1	4		
Davis, Sarah	1	3	3		
Eavans, Elijah	1	1	3		
Eaton, Christian	1	1	3		
Eads, Thomas	1	3	4		
Flinn, Leoflin	1	4	5		
Franklin, Owen	1				
Hunter, John	1				
London, William	1	4	4		
Melton, John	1	1	3		
Menakey, Joseph	1		2		
Melton, David	1				
Philips, Richard	1	2	2		
Philips, John	1	2	2		
Ransom, Joseph	1	3	4		
Duncan, Thomas	2	2	8		
Nichols, John	2	4	4		
Ward, William	1	2	4		
Kerns, William	1		1		
Kerns, James	1	2	1		
Kerns, Hubbard	1		1		
Steward, Charles	1	5	4		
Meridith, James	4	1	5		
Newman, John	2	5	2		
Joyce, Isaac	1	3	2		2
Gill, William	1	2	2		
Gill, Thomas	1		4		
Whitlock, James	1	3	3		
Gill, Young	1		3		
Radford, William	1	2	5		
Shelton, John	1		2		
Hutcherson, Daniel	1		3		
Hutcherson, William	1	7	2		
Brown, John	1		1		
Linkhorn, John	1	1	4		
Gillaton, Nicholas	1	1	3		
Young, James	3	3	5		
Musick, Elexious	1	3	7		
Leysle, Alex	1	4	4		
Gibson, John	1		1		
Wilkins, John	1	3	5		
Shelton, John	1		2		1
Shelton, William	1	4	2		
Shelton, Daniel	1	2	2		
Watkins, Zewel	1	1	4		
Read, Joseph	2	3	5		
Hail, John	2	5	2		
Joyce, George	1	3	2		
Robison, John	2	1	6		
Manu-l, Phyle	3	4	4		
Watkins, Thomas	1		3		
Hunter, Mathew	1	3	4		
Banks, John	1		3		
Davis, William	2	1	3		1
Mayab, John	1	2	1		
Mayab, John	3	1	3		
Childress, Mary	1		2		1
Beasley, Charles	1	1	3		1
Childress, William	1	1	1		1
Walker, James	1	3	1		4
Farmer, John	3	1	2		5
Chandler, William	2		3		
Hawkins, Benjamin	1	3	5		
Hawkins, Benjamin	2	1	3		
Dodson, Rubin	5	2	3		
Southern, William	1		3		1
Hammet, Robert	1	1	2		
Whaler, Richard	1		2		
Shelton, Sarah		3	3		
Cameron, Jarne	1	1	2		
Certain, Levi	1		1		
Duncan, James	1	3	6		
Millwoode, James	1	3	4		
Whitlock, Charles	4		3		
Martin, James	2	2	4		15
Neal, Thomas	2	5	3		
Nelson, William	1	4	7		
Nelson, John	1	1	2		
Nelson, William	1		3		
Perker, Charles	1		1		
Hughs, John	1	2	3		6
Lovin, Thomas	2	3	4		
Hughs, Archelus	1		1		2
Vanters, John	1	4	4		
Easley, John	2	3	3		
Aynett, Sam	2		1		
Hawkins, William	1	1	3		3
Taylor, Joseph	1	1	3		
Mayab, Robert	6	1	1		
Welch, Joseph	1		2		
Austen, Nathaniel	1	1	3		
Dolton, David	3	2	2		14
Tilly, Hary	1	6	4		
Webb, William	2	1	6		4
Hilton, John	1	3	9		
Musick, George	1		2		
Oliver, Gilson	1	2	4		
Angill, Elizabeth		1	3		
Asbury, Calup	1		3		
Cox, Mildred		1	5		7
Foster, Joel	1	1	3		
Holt, William	1	3	5		
Holt, Ambrose	3	2	3		
Richeson, Benjamin	1		1		
Vernon, James	3	2	6		
Lane, James	1	4	4		
Pafford, William	1	2	5		
Dickerson, William	2	1	5		
Baker, Henry	1	2	3		
Warden, William	2	2	2		
Pruitt, Micajah	1	1	4		
Mesinger, Coonrod	1		2		
Hedgspeth, William	1	2	2		
Rennolds, John	1		2		
Smith, Martha	1	3	6		
Okey, Nathan	1		2		
Hart, John	2	2	3		3
Davison, John	2	2	2		
Davison, Richard	1		2		
Fulton, Francis	1		1		
Davis, James	3		6		5
Mannan, John	1	1	3		
Duggans, John	1		2		
Huckby, Robert	1	2	2		
Bailey, Edward	1		1		
Nixon, Absalem	1	2	4		
Fearell, John	1	1	1		
Stanley, Jesse	1	1	4		

SALISBURY DISTRICT, STOKES COUNTY—Continued.

NAME OF HEAD OF FAMILY.	Free white males of 16 years and upward, including heads of families.	Free white males under 16 years.	Free white females, including heads of families.	All other free persons.	Slaves.
Boales, John	1	2	5		2
Rutledge, Johnson	1	3	2		
Clayton, Jesse	1		2		1
Bayse, Nathaniel	2	1	4		
Boales, Alex	2	3	2		
Spears, William	1		1		
Spears, Joseph	1	1	3		
Carter, Edward	2	2	4		
Mirritt, Thomas	1		1		
Brown, Jahue	3	2	3		
Cook, William	2		6		
Davis, John	1	2	3		
Mcinley, John	1	2	1		
Branum, Benjamin	2	4	6		
Sizemore, Newman	1	2	1		
Moore, Alex	4		3		
Fancher, Richard	1	2	2		
Bennett, Benjamin	2	5	3		
Ward, Elizabeth	1	1	5		
Barns, Sarah		3	3		
Mitchel, Adam	3	3	4		
Clayton, Stephen	1		3		1
Clayton, Stephen	1		2		
Cummins, Stephen	1	2	3		
McMillon, Andrew	2		1		
Blackbern, Younger	1	3	5		1
Heath, Richard	1		3		2
Childress, William	2	1	5		5
Childress, William	1		1		
Cook, Thomas	3		4		
Coffey, James	3		4		
Boales, James	1	4	3		
Vest, William	1	2	4		
Fitzpatrick, Sam	2	2	5		
Fulton, Robert	1		1		
Southerlin, Philip	2	4	3		
Fox, Samuel	1	4	1		
Merrett, John	1	2	3		
Wadkins, Henry	4	1	5		
Ward, James	1		8		
Halbert, Joel	1	3	3		1
Hover, Gasper	2	2	2		
Davis, Margan	2	3	4		
Hill, Mathew	4	1	3		
George, Travis	1		1		1
Duggans, Sarah			5		
Bailey, John	1	2	4		
Boales, William	1	3	2		
Branum, Malekia	1	4	3		
Clayton, William	1	1	2		
Brown, John	1	1	1		
Rhedick, Hardy	2	4	6		
Messor, Christian	1	4	5		
Jones, Samuel	1		2		
Moore, John	1	1	1		
Sizemore, William	1	2	4		
Sizemore, Elizabeth	1		2		
Eavans, John	1	2	1		
Martin, Mathew	1		2		
Moore, David	1	2	3		
Gallaway, John	1		5		
Mcanally, Jesse	3	3	5		
Campell, William	2	2	6		2
Mcanally, John	1	4	3		
Hampton, Thomas	3	1	7		
Eason, Joseph	2	6	3		
Wilson, Philip	1	4	4		1
Smith, John	4	3	2		
Smith, Philip	1	2	2		
Smith, Daniel	1		2		
Fergason, Stephen	2		2		
Fergason, Rebecca	2		4		
Branum, John	1	6	6		
Davis, Daniel	2	1	3		
Dodson, Nancy		2	2		
Heath, William	1	1	2		
Martin, Moses	1	2	4		
Mellon, William	1				
Rutledge, William	1	3	4		
Smith, Meridith	1	2	4		
Mcanally, Charles	3	1	3		5
Moore, James	1	2	4		
Burnes, Tarence	1	2	1		
Cook, Abel	1				
Kizor, John	1	3	2		
Sulavan, George	1	1	3		
Cooley, John	1	5	3		
Cooley, Edward	1	2	1		
Cooley, Joseph	1		1		
Hill, Robert	2	3	4		4
Linn, John	1				
Cook, John	1		1		
Banner, Joseph	2	1	5		5
Martin, Abraham	2		2		12
Young, Benjamin	1	1	3		
Banner, David	2	1	8		2
Wells, John	2	3			

NAME OF HEAD OF FAMILY.	Free white males of 16 years and upward, including heads of families.	Free white males under 16 years.	Free white females, including heads of families.	All other free persons.	Slaves.
Samwell, Edmund	1	2	2		4
Ham, Mordicai	1	1	5		
Mathews, James	1	1	2		10
James, Wm	1		4		
Prat, Thomas	1		1		
Morriss, Thomas	1	1	2		
Flint, John	1	3	8		
Hampton, Samuel	1	2	1		5
James, David	1	2	6		
Flint, Thomas	1	5	4		7
Hill, Jesse	2	2	3		5
Petree, Jacob	1		3		
Flint, Richard	2		4		7
Hampton, James	1		1		2
Peniker, William	1	1	4		
Peniker, Peter	1		2		
Peniker, Mathias	1	2	2		
Smith, Peter	1	4	4		
Zygar, Leonard	1	1	3		
Halbert, John	3	4	3		3
Goode, George	1		2		
Young, Nathaniel	1	1	1		
James, William	2		2		3
Waggoner, Joseph	2		4		1
Morriss, John	1	2	4		
Fry, Henry	1	4	4		3
Adams, John	1		4		
Clayton, John	1	3	4		6
Denton, Arther	2	4	4		
Day, James	1	3	3		
Goode, Richard	2	2	4		8
Martin, Robert	1		2		
Moriss, Hammond	1	1	1		
Ray, Andrew	1	1	2		
Ring, Martin	1		3		
Sims, Pariss	1	2	3		
Ham, John	1	2	2		
Ham, Joseph	4		1		
Ham, Thomas	1	3	1		
Fountain, Stephen	1	1	5		
Merritt, William	1	3	2		
Ring, Thomas	1	2	5		
Eavans, Thomas	1		3		
Branson, John	4		2		
Davis, Letitia	2	2	5		
Gazaway, Thomas	1	3	4		
Branum, Barny	1	2	2		
Winston, Joseph	2	5	2		18
Banner, Ephraim	2	4	3		4
Mcknown, James	1		1		
Rutledge, William	1	3	3		
George, Rubin	3	5	4		
Waggoner, Samuel	1		2		1
Heath, Johnson	1	1	6		
Mounts, Jacob	1	2	3		
Petree, Jacob	1	1	2		
Merritt, Edward	3		1		
Cox, Joseph	1	2	1		
Fry, Michael	1	2	7		2
Fry, Valentine	2	7	2		
Waggoner, Gabriel	1	2	5		1
Waggoner, William	2	3	6		1
Follis, William	1	3	3		
Goode, Thomas	1	2	4		
Adams, George	1	2	2		
King, Henry	2	2	6		
Gibson, William	2	3	3		
Ring, John	2	3	5		
Ring, James	1		5		
Davis, William	1	2	5		
Raper, Thomas	1		4		
Davis, George	1	2	3		
Smith, Lias	1		4		
Petree, Doherty		5	3		
Morriss, Hammond	2	1	1		1
Morriss, William	1	2	4		
Samwell, Percilla	4		4		
Vittatoe, Thomas	1	2	1		
Wells, Anthoy	1		1		
Welch, Dosha	1	2	2		
Woolf, Gottleib	1	2	4		
Pinkston, Peter	3		4		
Young, Benjamin	1	2	3		
Young, William	1	1	4		
Young, Joshua	1		3		
Young, Samuel	1	1	2		
Goode, Richard	1		2		8
Martin, William	1	4	2		
Banner, Benjamin	1	5	3		6
Blackbern, Elizabeth	2		2		2
Ray, Usly	1		1		1
Wolf, Calup	1	2	4		
Adams, John	1	1	3		
Hartgrove, Howel	1	2	1		
Tutle, Peter	2	1	1		
Appleton, John	1	3	7		1
Adams, William	1	2	4		

NAME OF HEAD OF FAMILY.	Free white males of 16 years and upward, including heads of families.	Free white males under 16 years.	Free white females, including heads of families.	All other free persons.	Slaves.
Earnest, Gottleib	1	4	1		
Bynum, Gray	2	2	4		8
Rutledge, William	2	2	1		
Eavans, Daniel	1	1	1		
Eavans, Edward	1	1	5		
Clark, Samuel	2		3		
Southerlin, Charles	1		1		
Hall, John	1	2	4		
Fergason, John	1				
Tanner, James	2	4	4		
Heath, Thomas	3		1		
Cook, William	1	1	3		
Tutle, John	1	2	3		
Garison, Isaac	1	3	5		
Blackbern, John	1	4	4		3
Bolcem, Thomas	1		1		1
Branson, Zakariah	1		1		
Blackbern, William	1				5
Clark, Francis	1		2		
Davis, David	1				
Day, Thomas	1	2	4		
Davis, Charles	1	2	6		
Ham, Thomas	1	3	1		
Hampton, Henry	1	2	5		5
Holebrook, John	1	5	4		
Owens, Thomas	1	1	4		
Watson, Joel	1	1	2		
Watson, William	1	1			
Sell, Jonathan	2	1	4		
Mills, Aaron	1	5	4		
Sanders, John	1	4	4		
Sell, Thomas	1	1	2		
Melton, Jesse	1	2	3		
Campell, Arche	1	2	4		
Ralph, Isaac	1	2	3		
Close, John	1	1	1		
Robbins, Daniel	1	1	3		
Dobson, William	3	3	2		
Crew, David	1	2	6		
Sanders, Jesse	1	2	4		
Graham, Thomas	2	3	4		1
Walker, William	1	1	4		1
Sapp, John	2		1		
Sapp, Benjamin	1		2		
Jones, Richard	3	1	2		
Boyd, Phenehas	1	1	2		
Smith, Thomson	1	4	5		
Swallow, John	1	6	2		
Wright, William	1	4	5		
Jones, Cadwallader	2	1	3		
Jones, Quiller	1	2	2		
Mendenall, Joseph	2	1	4		
Willitts, Henry	2	1	9		
Cooper, Michael	1	2	2		
Macy, Gayer	1	1	4		
Jones, Philip	1		2		
Nations, John	2	2	5		
Nations, Christopher	1	1	1		
Jones, Robert	1	2	4		
Johnson, Ashly	1	1	2		
Paterson, Joseph	1				
Perry, James	1	1	1		
Vanhoy, John	2	6	3		
Beasley, William	1	2	2		
Culver, John	1	2	2		
Fore, Peter	3	5	2		5
Fulp, Peter	1	2	4		
Fair, Michael	1	2	2		1
Fair, John	1	1	4		
Fulp, Michael	1	4	5		
Hutchings, John	2	1	10		2
Ludwick, Daniel	1				1
Lane, William	1		1		
Leverton, John	1		1		
Linville, David	1	1	3		
Lowry, James	1	1	5		
Ludwick, Peter	2	3	3		
Linvill, Aaron	2	2	5		2
Linvill, Mary		3	4		
Snipes, Mathew	1	1	3		
Sapp, Jesse	1		3		1
Wadkins, James	1	2	6		
Jones, Benjamin	1		1		
Swim, William	3	5	6		
Coffin, Seth	2	2	2		
Barnhard, Francis	2	5	5		
Swain, Judath		2	2		
Hester, John	1	2	4		
Green, William	1	2	3		
Mealup, Andrew	2	2	5		
Mcphesson, Joseph	1	4	6		
Teague, John	2	2	7		3
Willis, Garvis	1	2	5		
Paterson, Simmons	1	4	2		
Paterson, Joseph	2	3	3		
Stogdan, Daniel	3	1	2		1

SALISBURY DISTRICT, STOKES COUNTY—Continued.

NAME OF HEAD OF FAMILY.	Free white males of 16 years and upward, including heads of families.	Free white males under 16 years.	Free white females, including heads of families.	All other free persons.	Slaves.
Story, Calup	1	2	2		
Bowman, Edmund	3	2	1		
Thomason, John	2	2	7		5
Walker, David	1	3	2		
Smith, Moses	2	2	3		
Lundy, Richard	1	3	3		
Ladd, Constant	1	1	3		7
Majors, Alexander	1	1	2		
Mcalup, Hugh	1		1		
Brooks, David	2		4		1
Elmore, Thomas	3	2	5		
Drawn, Jacob	1	4	2		
Idle, Jacob	2	1	4		
Willert, George	1	3	8		
Elmore, Austan	1		2		
Watson, Claburn	1	2	2		
Paterson, Jurdan	1		2		
Pique, Nathan	2	2	6		
Estes, Lyddle	1		2		
Pitts, Samuel	1	3	4		
Pitts, John	1		1		
Pitts, Andrew	1	1	2		
Brooks, John	1	1	1		
Stogdan, Joseph	1	2	2		
Roose, Aaron	1	1	2		
Pitts, Martha	3	2	3		
Clampett, Richard	1	2	2		
Shields, Abel	1	2	6		
Frazer, William	1		1		
Green, Thomas	1	2	1		
Wortman, William	1	2	5		
Mills, Jacob	3	1	2		
Swim, John	1	1	1		
Fields, Robert	1	2	1		
Vance, Alee	1	1	3		
Williams, Owan	2	4	1		
Jurdan, John	2		2		
Thomason, George	1		1		
Tucker, Thomas	1	4	3		
Folger, Lathem	2	1	6		
Long, Israel	2	2	3		
Barnhard, Trustam	3	2	5		
Brown, James	2	3	5		
Coffin, Libni	2	2	6		
Hasket, John	1	1	2		
Huff, Daniel	2				
Mills, Thomas	1	2	4		
Marshal, Thomas	1	3	3		
Love, James	1	1	7		7
Hester, William	1		1		
Howel, William	2	1	4		
Lowry, John	1	1	4		
Long, Charles	1		2		
Clasby, George	1		2		
Hinshaw, John	1	4	2		
Waisnar, Micajah	1	2	1		
Scooley, Samuel	1	5	3		
Bratin, William	1	1	2		
Johnson, Thomas	2	1	3		
Green, Thomas	2	1	3		2
Piper, James	1				
Cummins, Asea	1		1		
Dillard, Katy			2		
Mastin, John	1		2		
Adamson, Jesse	1	4	3		
Adamson, Enos	1	2	3		
Starbrick, Paul	3	5	4		
Beason, Richard	1	3	3		
Whicker, James	1	3	3		
Mcinsy, William	2		1		
Davis, Samson	1	1	3		
Garland, James	1		1		
Suns, Casander		1	1		
Knight, John	1	1	2		
Whicker, William	1	2	2		
Quillin, John	1	2	2		
Robison, Andrew	1	3	4		
Shaw, Ralph	1	1	5		
Towmey, Patrick	1	3	4		
Watson, William	1	1			
Ward, Leavan	1	3	5		
Mcown, Sarah	1		4		
Long, John	1		1		
Crew, Thomas	1		1		
Tatem, Barny	1	3	3		
Anthony, William	1		3		
Angill, John	1	4	4		
Aynett, Andrew	1	4	4		
Anderson, Daniel	3		6		
Allday, Seth	1		1		
Brim, John	1	5	5		
Bennett, Jesse	1	1			
Burns, James	1		2		
Barrow, Moses	1	1	2		
Cook, Henry	2	4	4		3
Cook, Stephen	1				
Billeton, Alexander	2		4		

NAME OF HEAD OF FAMILY.	Free white males of 16 years and upward, including heads of families.	Free white males under 16 years.	Free white females, including heads of families.	All other free persons.	Slaves.
Cline, Stoful	1	1	1		
Doubt, John	2	5	3		
Fortney, Henry	1		1		
Fokel, Samuel	1	1	3		
Huff, Daniel	2		2		
Hartgrove, James	2	2	3		
Hoegest, John	1	4	3		
Reigh, John	1				
Rasel, John	1		2		
Smith, Robert	1	1	1		11
Segier, George	1	2	4		
Seinard, Samuel	1	1	1		
Shamell, John	1	4	2		
Marshal, Frederick W	1		3		
Benzun, Christian	1		3		
Kohler, John	1	1	2		
Usley, Sarah			1		
Koster, Adam	1				
Snepf, Daniel	1				
Holland, John	1	3	1		
Schulz, Samuel	2		1		
Cummins, John	2	3	3		5
Crew, David	1	1	2		
Clifton, Elizabeth			2		
Clasby, Charles	1		3		
Dwigings, John	2	3	3		
Elmore, Joel	1		2		
Easter, John	1	2	3		
Endsley, Hugh	1				
Freeman, John	1	1	1		
Gamell, John	3	1	4		
Holebrook, James	1	2	4		1
Herron, Delany	2	2	2		
Hoole, John	1				
Jones, Aquilla	2	1	3		
Jones, William	1		1		
Jones, Gabriel	1	2	3		
Jones, Joshua	1	4	4		
Johnson, Robert	4	2	4		
Johnson, James	1	1	1		
Johnson, Henry	1	3	3		
Knott, William	1				
Ledford, Nicholas	1	1	2		
Love, James	1		2		
Christ, Rudoph	3	3	3		
Hauser, Hannah			3		
Holder, Charles	1		3		
Hester, Abraham	1		3		
Curling, Samuel	1		2		
Meinung, Ludwick	1	1	5		
Kushke, John	1		1		
Yerrell, Peter	2	2	3		1
Christman, Daniel	1	1	4		
Lick, Martin	3	1	2		
Rights, John	1	4	3		
Vogler, Philip	1		3		
Micksch, Mathew	1	1	3		
Kramch, Samuel	2				
Vogler, Christopher	1				
Herbst, John H	4		2		2
Stolz, Samuel	2				
Merkle, Christopher	1				
Paterson, Nitts	3				
Landman, John	4				
Reigh, Christopher	2				
Buttner, John F	2				
Lawton, John	1				
Linvill, Richard	2	2	3		2
Linvill, Moses	1				
Low, John	1	1	4		
Miller, Jacob	1	1	2		
Mills, Asea	1				
Meningall, Mordecai	1	1	6		
Mcalup, Hugh	1	2	3		
Meridith, James	3	2	4		
Nelson, Isaac	1				
Perkins, Joseph	1	1	1		
Perry, William	1	1	1		
Paterson, Turner	1				
Palmore, John	1	2	2		
Quillin, Teague	1	2	3		
Shields, Rubin	1	2	5		
Sanders, Naman	1	5	2		
Stokely, Sturd	1				
Styers, Samuel	1	1	3		
Sapp, Robert	1	3	2		
Stiles, John	1				
Wilburn, Martha			3		
Bartley, Edward	2	1	3		
Kraus, John	2	1			
Schnepf, Jeremias	2				
Schmidt, George	2		1		
Schroser, Charles	3	1			
Hanke, John	5				
Triebit, Christian	1				
Bagge, Traugott	1	2	2		
Meyer, Jacob	1		2		

NAME OF HEAD OF FAMILY.	Free white males of 16 years and upward, including heads of families.	Free white males under 16 years.	Free white females, including heads of families.	All other free persons.	Slaves.
Blum, Jacob	2	2	2		5
Loech, Abraham	2		2		
Kaske, Renatus	1		1		
Transu, Philip	2		3		
Bewighouse, George	1		3		
Praezel, Mary			3		
Schober, Gottleib	4	2	3		
Nissen, Salome		2	4		
Buttner, Sarah			1		
Aust, Mary			2		
Green, Ann			8		
Colver, Elizabeth			6		
Quest, Ann			3		
Ebert, John	1	1	5		
Blum, Henry	1	4	1		
Steiner, Jacob	2	1	2		
Beroth, Jacob	2	2	5		
Schulz, Gottfrey	1	3	1		1
Reigh, Mathew	1				
Hauser, Abraham	1	1	2		
Spach, Gottlieb	1	2	2		
Baumgerten, John	1				
Claus, Philip	1	1	4		
Sam (free negro)				6	
Scott (free negro)				3	
Earnst, Jacob	1		3		
Krouse, Gottlieb	2	2	1		2
Stehr, Henry	1	1	2		
Micky, John	1	1	3		1
Kinast, Christopher	1		2		4
Wageman, John	1	2	2		1
Renner, Hans	2				
Shope, John	2	2	2		
Christman, Balthaser	1	1	2		
Esterline, Mathew	1	1	2		1
Stauber, Christian	1		2		
Schmidt, Christopher	1				
Hillsebeck, Jacob	1		3		
Pfaff, Peter	1		1		
Kruger, Henry	1		2		
Pfaff, Isaac	2		3		
Kraus, John	1	3	7		
Folk, Johanes	1	1	2		
Stols, Jacob	1	1	2		
Pfaff, Samuel	2		2		
Binkele, Peter	3		2		
Feisser, Peter	2	5	4		
Spanehaur, Henry	2	3	5		
Binkele, Jacob	1		1		
Miller, Johanes	2	2	3		
Philips, Richard	1		1		
Miller, Jacob	2				1
Clayton, Briton	1	5	3		7
Brinkele, Peter	1	2	4		
Shouse, Henry	3	1	2		
Spanehaur, John	2	1	1		
Billetor, Alexander	2		4		
Binkele, Jacob	1	1	1		
Loggins, Majors	1		3		
Steiner, Abraham	2		1		1
Kapp, Jacob	3	1	3		
Shelhorne, John	1	2	4		
Ranke, John	2		3		
Brising, Andrew	1	2	3		
Limeback, Lewis	1	2	3		
Holder, George	2		1		
Akkerman, Barbara			1		
Wernley, Henry	1	1	1		
Aust, George	3		1		
Hauser, George	3	1	4		8
Hauser, Peter	3	2	3		
Strooper, Samuel	2		4		
Lash, Christian	1		2		1
Coonrod, John	1	3	1		
Buttner, Adam	2	1	1		
Hauser, Michael	2		1		
Shore, Henry	2		3		
Hauser, Peter	2	2	6		1
Hauser, George	2	2	1		2
Hauser, Joseph	2		2		1
Lash, Jacob	1	1			
Beck, Valentine	1		3		
Stults, Abraham	1	1	1		
Binkele, Frederick	1		1		
Cornelus, West	3	1	5		
Fiskus, Fredrick	2	2	4		
Teague, Michael	1	2	2		
Binkele, Peter	1		3		
Shore, Henry	2		5		
Shouse, Daniel	1	3	3		
Spanehaur, Michael	2	1	3		
Strube, Adam	1		2		
Shore, Jacob	1	1	2		
Boose, George	1		2		
Clayton, Charles	1	3	3		1
Shouse, Philip	1		3		
Shouse, Frederick	3	1	1		

SALISBURY DISTRICT, STOKES COUNTY—Continued.

NAME OF HEAD OF FAMILY.	Free white males of 16 years and upward, including heads of families.	Free white males under 16 years.	Free white females, including heads of families.	All other free persons.	Slaves.
Smith, Christian	1	2	2		
Giles, John	1	1	2		1
Woolf, Lewis	1	1	5		
Martin, Moses	2	3	3		
Lucas, Thomas	1	1	2		
Stanton, Christopher	2	1	7		
Markland, Robert	1	1	1		1
Grabs, William	3		2		1
Seids, Michael	1		4		
Ranke, Michael	3		9		1
Cramer, Gottlieb	2	2	1		
Transu, Philip	3	2	2		
Berod, John	2		2		
Opitts, John	1	2	2		
Schnert, Samuel	1		2		
Transu, Philip	2		2		
Stols, Gasper	1	2	4		
Folk, Andrew	1		3		
Hauser, Christian	1		1		
Coonrod, Christian	2	2	4		
Limeback, Benjn	3	1	10		
Miller, Jacob	3		1		1
Hauser, Martin	2	1	2		
Hauser, Martin	1		2		
Politshek, Joseph	4	1	4		
Limeback, Abraham	4	3	5		
Saler, John	1	3	5		
Hillsebeck, Frederick	2		4		
Kreiger, Jacob	1	3	3		
Miller, Joseph	2	3	4		
Dobb, David	3	1	3		
Davis, Josse	1	4	4		
Padgett, John	2		3		
Markland, Joseph	1		2		1
Taylor, Josias	2	2	4		
Westmoreland, Alex	2	4	3		
Gordan, William	1	4	4		
Chitty, Benjamin	1	2	3		
Chitty, John	1				
Hill, Isaac	1	1	4		
Slator, Henry	2	2	5		1
Null, John	2	4	3		
Stults, Philip	2	3	2		
Hollowman, William	3	5	3		
Ruck, Christopher	1	7	5		
Williams, Reason	1	2	4		
Lasmutt, Elias	1		1		
Pedycort, Thomas	1		1		
Blake, Jacob	1				
Craig, William	1				
Andrews, David	1	4	4		
Mayse, Henry	2	1	3		1
Pedycort, Basil	2	2	3		
Cooper, John	2	1	6		
Williams, William	2	1	4		
Padgett, Thomas	1	1	4		
Markland, Mathew	2		2		
Padgett, Benjamin	1	2	2		
Markland, Mathew	1	3	1		
Blake, John	1	2	5		
Spears, William	1	2	2		
Hill, Joshua	1		1		
Boger, John	1				
Olspough, Henry	1		4		
Pedycort, William B	1	3	2		1
Pedycort, John	1		2		
Hamilton, Oratis	1	2	5		
Martin, James	1	1	7		1
Crook, William	1		1		4
Bennet, Richard	1	2	4		7
Hillsebeck, Frederick	1		3		
Binkele, John	4	4	4		2
Lynch, John	3		2		9
Woolf, Adam	3	1	1		4
Moser, Peter	1	5	2		
Busy, Charles	1	1	6		
Shadock, John	1		1		
Yeats, William	1	1	2		
Ridge, Thomas	1	2	4		
Lynch, John	1		1		1
Mathews, Rubin	1	1	4		
Green, Peter	1		1		
Rominger, Michael	1	2	6		
Read, John	1	1	2		
Kersner, Anthony	3		7		
Hines, Jacob	1				
Miller, Jacob	1	1	2		1
Schruzfeser, Henry	1				
Kimble, Henry	1	1	2		
Snyder, Martin	1		2		
Alverd, William	1	4	6		1
Albert, Martin	1	4	5		
Weaver, Christian	1	2	1		
Fansler, Sovene	1	1	2		
Shadock, William	1		1		
Forester, James	1				
Stults, Adam	1		3		
Limeback, Ann	2	3	4		
Holder, George	1	3	4		
Deits, Jacob	1		1		
Watson, James	1	1	2		
Huffman, George	3		3		
James, John	3	3	3		6
Bitting, Anthony	3	2	3		4
Miller, John	2	2	3		
Billetor, Zebdiah	1	2	1		
Fiddler, Gottfry	1	2	4		
Miller, Frederick	2	2	4		
McBride, John	1	4	5		
Hasket, John	3	4	4		
Bolingjack, John	2	1	2		
Holder, Herny	1	5	1		
Fields, William	1		2		
Hall, Joseph	1	3	5		
Forester, John	1	1	1		
Murphy, Stephen	1	1	3		
Carver, George	1		4		
Krouse, John	1	1	4		
Shamlin, William	3	1	3		
Tull, Nicholas	5	1	2		
Fishell, John	1	1	2		
Fults, Peter	1	2	5		
Brady, Charles	1	1	3		
Windle, Henry	1	1	1		
Woolf, Larance	1	2	2		
Weisner, John	1	1	2		
Green, Philip	1	3	3		
Trewett, John	1	2	3		1
Tull, Frederick	1		1		
Thomson, Jonathan	1				
Snyder, Philip	1	2	3		
Seward, Samuel	1	1	1		
Steward, David	2		3		5
Stulz, Henry	1	2	4		
Snyder, Philip	2	3	4		
Smith, Daniel	2	3	4		
Stevens, William	1	1	1		
Spach, John	1	1	2		
Spach, Jacob	1				
Spach, Adam	1	3	4		
Seaner, Peter	1	4	2		
Shutt, Jacob	2	3	2		
Black, Andrew	1	1	5		
Hauser, Martin	1	1	1		
Lyon, John	1	3	5		
Curd, James	2	2	1		
Kitner, Francis	3	2	3		1
Carver, Christian	1	3	1		
Steward, Samuel	1		2		
Steward, Rubin	1	1	2		
Runyan, Adam	1	1	2		
Purdon, John	2	7	3		
Fair, Elizabeth	1		3		
Davis, Jonathan	1		1		
Jones, Jehue	1				
Fogler, Samuel	1	1	3		
Adaman, Thomas	2	1	2		
Black, Jacob	1		1		
Logans, John	1	3	5		
Philips, Joseph	3	2	6		
Robison, Jacob	1		2		
Gentry, Lucy			2		
Tull, William	1	2	4		
Grace, Allen	1	2	3		
Hauser, Martin	2	1	2		
Snyder, David	1	2	5		
Snyder, Henry	1	2	5		
Sitz, Michael	3	1	3		
Shoarwood, Thomas	2		2		
Snyder, Cornelus	1	4	2		
Riech, Mathew	1		2		
Robison, William	1	2	3		
Read, Jacob	2	5	2		
Rominger, Michael	2	1	3		
Rominger, Jacob	2	3	5		
Rodrick, Valentine	1	3	2		
Rodrick, Philip	3	6	2		
Rotrock, Peter	2	2	7		
Philpott, William	2	2	2		
Pickel, John	1	2	4		
Philips, John	1	4	4		
Nathing, Mathias	1	3	1		
Null, Michael	1		1		
Null, Jacob	3		3		
Miller, Joseph	2	3	1		
Miller, Monis	1	2	1		
Mock, Henry	2	2	1		
Miller, Henry	1	4	2		
Miller, Stephen	1		1		
Limeback, Joseph	1	1	6		
Leonard, Abner	1	1	1		
Lash, Nathaniel	1		1		3
Loghanhore, George	1		4		
Loghanhore, Jacob	1	4	1		
Lanouse, John	2	2	5		
Krouse, Henry	1		2		
Krouse, Andrew	1				
Krouse, John	2	3	4		
Krouse, Windle	3	1	4		
Garner, Francis	2	5	3		
Kichnast, Christopher	1		2		4
Kleinart, Laurance	1		1	3	1
Kelly, Benjamin	1	2	1		
Kerby, Samuel	1		4		3
Kerby, Pleasant	1				
James, Ebenezer	2	3	3		1
Harvey, William	3	2	6		
Huffines, Daniel	1	2	5		
Harvey, John	1	1	2		1
Holder, Joseph	4		2		
Fesler, Andrew	2	4	3		
Fentor, Baston	1		1		
Fentor, Christian	1				
Fokel, Samuel	1	1	3		
Fisher, George	1	4	2		
Fogler, Michael	1	2	4		
Fiddler, Peter	2	2	4		
Faw, Jacob	3	1	2		
Engrim, David	1	1	1		
Elrod, Adam	1		2		
Elrod, Jeremiah	1	1	3		
Elrod, Robert	1	2	3		
Douthard, Isaac	1	2	2		
Dull, Nicholas	4	1	2		
Cinsil, Frederick	2		2		
Crator, Jacob	1		4		
Croom, John	2	1	3		
Bonn, Jacob	1		1		
Boger, Henry	1		3		
Burton, Henry	1	3	1		
Billetor, Edward	3	3	1		
Bruner, Daniel	1	3	5		
Stevens, John	2	1	2		
Seward, Samuel	1		5		
Hauser, Jacob	3	5	3		
Hines, Jacob	1	2	3		
Hill, John	3	2	3		
Hancock, William	1				
Hill, Thomas	1	1	1		
Hartman, John	1	3	2		
Hines, John	1	2	4		
Hines, Christopher	1		2		
Hines, John	2	1	6		
Hanke, John	5				
Higher, Rody	2	4	6		
Humel, Christian	1	1	5		
Grace, James	2	2			
Gentry, Claburn	1	1	3		
Garner, George	1				
Geiger, Adam	2	4	4		
Glenn, Thomson	1	1	3		3
Glenn, Jeremiah	2				1
Gault, David	1	2	4		
Green, Coonrod	1	2	4		
Fishell, Adam	1	4	2		
Brooks, Mathew	3	4	5		
Bolingjack, Joseph	3	1	4		
Binkele, Joseph	1		1		
Duggans, Agnus		1	3		
Cyrus, Nimrod	1		3		
Wauters, John	1	2	4		

SALISBURY DISTRICT, SURRY COUNTY.

NAME OF HEAD OF FAMILY.	Free white males of 16 years and upward, including heads of families.	Free white males under 16 years.	Free white females, including heads of families.	All other free persons.	Slaves.
Adams, Patrick	1	3	5		
Alberty, Frederick	1	2	1		
Ballard, Thomas	1	2	4		
Brock, Sherod	1	2	5		
Brannum, John	1	4	4		
Barras, Martin	1	2	4		1
Bean, William	1		2		
Barker, William	1	2	3		
Cockram, Moses	3	2	4		1
Chamberlin, Thomas	1	4	3		9
Clarke, John	1	2	2		
Carty, John	1	3	3		
Craigg, Edward	1	2	2		
Barrs, Leonard	1				
Brock, Alexander	1	1	2		

SALISBURY DISTRICT, SURRY COUNTY—Continued.

NAME OF HEAD OF FAMILY.	Free white males of 16 years and upward, including heads of families.	Free white males under 16 years.	Free white females, including heads of families.	All other free persons.	Slaves.
Cadle, Thomas	1	1	1		6
McAffee, William	3	4	5		
Norman, Henry	1	3	4		
Norman, Thomas	1	1	2		
Norman, William	1	2	4		
Oglesby, Micajah	2	1	2		5
Phillips, Ephraim	1		1		
Phillips, Cornelius	1				
Phillips, Robert	1		1		
Douglas, John	1	3	1		
Sisk, Timothy	1	1	4		
Pritchett, Phillip	2	2	2		
Pigg, William	1		2		
Porter, Joseph	1	5	3		
Rion, Derby	1	5	4	1	
Riggs, David	2	5	6		
Riggs, Samuel	3		1		
Riggs, Zadock	1	4	3		
Rainwater, James	1	2	4		
Ramey, Joseph	2	2	8		
Raybourn, Thomas	1	2	3		
Rayborn, Silvanus	1	1	3		
Ross, Thomas, Junr	1	1	3		
Davis, William	2	3	5		
Davis, Jonathan	1		2		
Doan, John	1	2	4		
Dean, Job	1				
Edwards, Gideon	1	2	2		19
Fruman, Aaron	1	4	4		2
Fletcher, John	3		5		
Gentry, Joseph	2	1	4		3
Gentry, Shelton	1	2	3		
Galaspy, Elijah	1	2	5		1
Holt, John	2		2		
Hughs, John	1	2	3		8
Hill, Thomas	1	4	1		
Hill, William	4		5		
Hill, James	1	1	1		
Hill, John	1		2		
Hodges, Edmund	3	3	2		
Hudson, William	1		4		
Hodge, Bartholomew	1	1	4		
Hodge, Ambrose	1		3		
Hodge, William	1		2		
Riggs, Hiram	1	3	3		
Rutu, Isham	1	2	4		
Ross, Thomas	1		5		
Stewart, Hambleton	1	2	3		
Senter, Zachariah	1	1	2		
Stottz, John	1	2	2		
Scott, Benjamin	1	2	4		
Stewart, James	1		3		
Sims, Mathew	1	2	5		
Stewart, William	2	4	1		
Stewart, Nathaniel	1	5	3		
Tucker, James	3		2	1	
Tucker, William	1	2	3		
Tucker, Garner	1	1	4	1	
Taylor, Edward	1		1		
Tallifarro, John	1		6	3	
Talifarro, Charles	1				
William, Moses	1	3	2		
Straughn, Larkin	1	2	4		
Snead, Benjamin	1	2	4		
Williams, John	1	3			
Cohone, William	1		3		
Hall, Hudson	2		2		
Hudson, Sterling	1	2	2		
Hayes, John	2	2	5		
Jervis, Eliphalett	1	4	4		
Kirby, Joseph	1		2		
Kirby, Philip	1	2			
Kirby, Josiah	1		3		
Kirby, Henry	2	2	4		
Keith, William	1		2		
Lanthrop, John	2	2	4		
McCloud, Wm	1	3	5		
Standfield, Thomas	1	1	1		
Love, Steven	1		4		
Laffoon, Stephen	1	3	2		
Laufield, Joseph	1	2	6		
McCarow, Archer	2	2	5		5
Munkur, William	2	4	5		
Mackey, Joseph	2	2	5		5
Murphy, Richard	1		2		4
Moore, Samuel	1	1	2		1
Murphy, Joseph	1	1	1		
Cohone, Wm, Junr	1	1	1		
Haddock, Henry	1		2		
Clifton, Job	1	1	2		
Frewett, Jesse	1	1	2		
Ross, Patrick	1	1	1		
Bridgman, Matthew	1		3		
Ferguson, Robt	3	1	3		
Porter, Dudley	1		2		
Pettijohn, Job	1		3		
Ashley, William	1	4	4		

NAME OF HEAD OF FAMILY.	Free white males of 16 years and upward, including heads of families.	Free white males under 16 years.	Free white females, including heads of families.	All other free persons.	Slaves.
Blackman, John	1	1	5		
Hicks, Thomas	8		2		
Gray, Biddicks	1	3	1		
Shote, Edward	1		4		
Martin, Thomas	2	1	4		
Cornelius, Andrew	1	3	1		
Ballinger, John	1		2		
Vestal, Daniel					
Lindville, Andrew	2	1	4		
Rutledge, Mary	2	2	4		
Adams, Moses	1	1	1		
Vestal, James	3	2	2		
Finney, Joseph	1	1	3		
York, James	2	3	4		
Barnes, John	1		2		
Reynolds, Sophia	1	2	1		
Willard, Augustin	1	4	2		
Hoott, Jacob, Junr	1		1		
Woolfe, James	1	3	2		
Franklin, John	1	1	4		
Hannah, John Doak	1		3		2
Benson, Benjamin	1	2	6	1	
Lawrence, James	1	1	4	3	
McLarver, Joshua	1	1	2		
Jinkins, John	5	1	5	4	
Harris, Moses	1	2	1		
Chamberling, Charles	2	2	1		
Lawrence, Randolph	1		2		
Dollasson, Jane		1	3		
Reed, George	1	1	6		
Harris, Nathaniel	2	1	3		
Puckett, Thomas	2	2	1		
Puckett, Richard	1	1	2		
Puckett, Benja	1	1	1		
Creed, John	1				8
Humphries, Samuel	1	2	2		
Brison, Alexander	1	2	1		
Stow, William	2		1		
Sheppard, Jacob	2	1	5		
Filer, Ruth	1	2	4		
Finn, Daniel	2	4	5		
Bridgman, Solomon	1		1		
Maine, Presley	1		2		
Askew, James	1	1	3		
Appeson, William	1	6	1		1
Pettite, Thomas	1	4	3		
Badgett, James	1	3	3		7
Brown, Josiah	1	3	2		
Brown, James	1	1	4		
Brown, Samuel	1		1		
Brown, Jesse	1		1		
Brown, John	1				
Bevenders, John	1		2		
Hargrave, James	1	4	1		
Kerr, Alexander	2	2	4		
Chanley, John	1	3	2		
Cockburn, Henry	1	4	2		
Childress, Thomas	1	1	3		
Carson, James	1	1	2		
Carson, Thomas	1				
Cox, Isaiah	1	2	3		1
Kerr, John	2	2	5		
Dooling, John	2	2	4		2
Dooling, John, Junr	1		2		
Dooling, William	2		2		2
Poindexter, David	1	1	2		
Davis, George	1	2	3		
Devenport, William	2	3	5		
England, Joseph	3	3	9		
England, William	1		3		
England, Samuel	1				
Hynn, Jacob	1	1	2		
Hynn, William	1	2	3		
Hynn, George	1	2	2		
Hynn, Hezekiah	1	4	3		
Floyd, Thomas	2	1	3		
Pu, James	1	1	1		
Garrett, Blunt	3	2	4		
Grayham, James	2	4	5		
Gentry, Samuel	2	5	3		1
Gentry, Atha	1	2	3		
Halcomb, Lawrence	1	5	5		
Huchins, Nicholas	2	3	3		2
Hammons, James	1	1	4		
Huchins, Strangman	1		2		2
Hugguman, Joseph	1		6		
Harvey, John	1	1	5		
Head, William	1	3	5		
Hutchins, John	2	3	3		
Johnson, Archibald	1		2		
Lakey, Francis	3		1		
Longino, John	1		2		
Longino, Thomas	1	2	2		
Laws, Moses	1	1	1		
Logan, James	1		2		1
Logan, John	1				
Longino, John Thos	2	3	6		7

NAME OF HEAD OF FAMILY.	Free white males of 16 years and upward, including heads of families.	Free white males under 16 years.	Free white females, including heads of families.	All other free persons.	Slaves.
Logan, Patrick	1	2	6		
McDaniel, William	1	2	6		
Matthew, James	1	6	3		
Matthis, Aaron	1		6		
Matthis, Matthew	1	4	4		
Martin, William	1	1	5		
Miller, John	1		3		
Finney, Joseph	1	1	3		
Moore, William	3		3		
Morphew, James	1	5	3		
Nerdicke, Adin	1		2		
Pollock, Joseph	1		2		
Passwaters, Samuel	1	3	4		
Price, John	1	3	5		
Phillips, Solomon	1	1	2		1
Phillips, William	3	4	3		
Martin, John	1		3		
Robinson, John	1				
Renolds, Ezekiel	1	1	5		
Roch, John	1	1	2		1
Ridins, John	1	3	5		
Reach, William	1	5	1		
Robinson, William	1	1	5		
Scudder, Moses	1	1	1		
Stow, Abram	1	2	2		
Scott, Daniel	2	3	4		
Spur, Levi	1		8		
Spur, Leven	3	1	6		
Spur, Joshua	3	1	3		
Spur, Andrew	2	1	4		
Spur, Shadrack	1	1	2		
Spur, Aaron, Junr	1		2		
Scott, James	1	3	4		
Standley, Archilaus	2		2		
Standley, Jesse	1		3		
Smith, George	1	3	6		
Scott, Jesse	1		7		
Savage, Leven	2	4	3		
Thompson, Frederick	1	3	3		
Taylour, Matthew	1	2	4		
Vandever, Charles	2	1	3		1
Vandever, George	1		3		
Vaughn, Abram	1		1		
Williams, John	2	3	3		1
Wheatherford, John	1	1	3		
Williams, Thomas	1	4	2		2
Wood, Obediah	1	1	2		
Spur, John	1	1	1		
Spur, William	1		1		
Allen, John	1		4	5	4
Brooks, George	2	6	3		
Brown, Thomas	2	2	2		
Bruce, John	2	3	5		3
Baker, Moses	1	3	5		
Brown, John	1	1	1		
Brown, William	1		5		
Brown, Joseph	1	2	2		
Brown, Joshua	1	2	2		
Bates, George	1	1	1		
Burns, Patrick	1		2		
Carter, John	1	3	3		2
Crochett, Samuel	1	1	7		
Orison, Abram	1	1			8
Creson, Joshua	1	3	5		2
Clarke, Robert	1		4		
Cambell, James	1		1		
Coe, John	1	3	7		7
Colverd, John B	2	1	5		
Colverd, William	1				
Douglas, Alexander	2		5		
Danner, Frederick	1	4	2		
Dinkins, Stephen	1	2	5		
Donnalay, John	1		4		
Dicke, Stephen	1	2	4		
Douden, Zephaniah	1		4		
Daniel, James	1	2	4		
Dennis, John	1	1	2		
Edleman, Margarate	1	1	1		
Enjard, Silas	1	2	4		
Garner, Whiatt	2	2	4		
Grose, Simon, Junr	2	3	8		
Grose, Devall	1	4	4		
Grose, William	2		6		
Grose, John	1	6	1		
Grose, Simon	1	1	1		
Gutry, Charles	1		3		
Gibbons, Winnifred			3		
Spur, Richard	1		2		
Spur, Henry	2	3	4	2	13
Spear, Jacob, Junr	1	2	2		
Spur, John, Junr	1	4	1		
Spur, Andrew, Junr	1	1	1		
Stielman, Matthias	1				
Shore, Frederick	2		2		
Skidmore, John	1	3	3		
Shermer, Peter	1	3	1		
Steelman, Charles	1	2	3	4	2

SALISBURY DISTRICT, SURRY COUNTY—Continued.

NAME OF HEAD OF FAMILY.	Free white males of 16 years and upward, including heads of families.	Free white males under 16 years.	Free white females, including heads of families.	All other free persons.	Slaves.
Skidmore, Abram	1		4		
Steelman, John	1	2	3		
Soter, John	1	2	5		
Sweat, William	2	4	3		2
Summers, Manning	2		4		
Steward, David	1	2	3		
Spoon, Adam	1	3	10		
Standfield, John	2	2	3		
Thornton, William	1	4	5		2
Turner, Rodah	2	1	3		
Thompson, Catharine	1	2	4		1
Hiet, Joseph, Junr	1		3		
Horton, John	2		2		
Harrel, William	1	2	3		
Horn, Nicolas	1		2		2
Hill, William	3	3	5		
Holtsclaw, Josep	1		3		
Gibbons, James	1	5	1		
Hudspith, Thomas	1	2	1		1
Hudspith, George	1	2	3		
Hudspith, Jiles	2		3		14
Hudspith, Charles	1	1	2		2
Hudspith, Benja	1	2	2		
Haggins, William	1	4	4		
Hudspith, Joseph	1	2	2		
Head, George	1	1	3		
Halliman, Mark	1		1		1
Hawell, David	1	1	2		3
Halke, James	1		3		
Howard, Phillip	3	3	3		
Hootts, Jacob	3	5	3		
Hootts, John	1	1	2		
Humphries, John, Junr	1	1	1		
Humphries, John	2		3		
Hawell, James	2		2		
Humphries, Samuel	1		1		
Hawell, David	2	1	2		1
Joiner, John	5	3	3		3
Kimbrough, George	2	2	1		5
Kimbrough, Ormond	3				4
Kitchen, John, Junr	1	1	1		
Kitchen, John	2		4		
Harber, Adonajah	4	2	7		19
Herd, John	3	2	2		1
Holder, James	1	2	2		
Harper, Martha		1	3		
Hiett, George	1				
Jackson, Reuben	1	3	6		
Jackson, Curtis	1	2	7		
Jessop, Jacob	1	1	2		
Lockheart, Robert	1		2		
Hill, Bartlett	1		1		
Critchfield, Joshua	3	1	3		
Jones, Isaac	1				
Jackson, John	1	1	2		
Jackson, Joseph	2		4		
Isan, Nathaniel	1	2	2		
Kirby, Joel	4	2	7		
Kirby, Richard	3	3	4		5
Lovell, Edward	2	2	3		4
Love, William	1	3	3		
Lisby, Aaron	1	4	4		
Lane, John	1	2	1		
Linvill, Moses	2	5	5		
Lane, William	2	1	5		
Louder, John	1				
Pinnions, Thomas	3	2	4		
Thomson, John	1	1	3		
King, Mason	1	3	2		
Lash, George	3	2	5		
Mosby, Samuel	1	3	6		15
Marsh, John, Junr	1	1	1		
Marsh, John	2		2		
McCallum, John	1		3		
McCallum, Thomas	1	1	3		
McCallum, James	1		3		
Martin, James	2	3	4		
Mayes, William	2	1	5		7
Miller, John	2	1	2		
Murphy, Joseph	1	2	4		
Poindexter, Francis	3		4		
Pilcher, Daniel	1		3		
Pilcher, James	3	1	3		
Prough, Christian	1		1		
Rineger, George	2	2	2		
Rineger, George, Junr	1		2		
Richards, Leonard	1	2	6		
Rutledge, Joseph	2	3	3		
Reavis, James	1	2	2		
Rogers, Hezekiel	1				
Stockdell, Thomas	1	1	4		
Spur, William	1	2	3		
Spear, Benjamin	1	2	6		
Thompson, Samuel	2	4	1		
Langley, John	1	1	4		
McKinney, James	1	7	2		
Morton, Richard	1	2	1		
Morton, Patrick	1		5		
Morton, James	1				
Meeks, William	2		2		
Powell, William	1		3		
Pinson, Richard	1	5	3		
Pinson, Reuben	2	2	5		
Parker, Samuel	2	1	4		
Reter, James	1	1	2		
Reter, Aaron	1	1	1		
Reynolds, William	1	6	1		
Scott, Arthur	1	4	3		
Studdard, William	2	1	2		
Summers, Boster	2	1	4		
Stephens, John	2	3	4		
Stone, Enoch	1	3	2		
Smallwood, John	1	1	2		
Stone, John	3	1	3		1
Simmons, Peter	4		2		6
Simmons, Charles	1	2	2		
Sheppard, Jacob	2	2	5		8
Stone, William	3	3	4		
Tansey, William	1	1	5		
Tilley, John	2	3	2		
Vanderpool, Abram	1	3	3		
Watkins, George	1	2	6		
Whitehead, Robert	1	2	2		
Wheeler, Benjamin	1		6		
Watkins, Joseph	1	2	5		
Waldrop, Joseph	1	1	4		
Langford, Mary		2	3		
Simmons, Rial	1	2	3		
Chandler, Daniel	1	4	6		
Austill, Major	1		1		
Allen, Thomas	1	4	5		
Austill, Isaac	3	2	4		
Baldwin, Zenus	3	2	8		
Blackledge, Acabud	2	2	4		
Blackmon, Solomon	1				
Binge, Obediah	2	3	3		
Cobb, Clisby	3	2	6		
Cochram, Samuel	1		4		
Coock, William, Junr	1	4	3		
Crawley, Samuel	1	1	1		
Carter, Samuel	2	2	5		2
Cochram, William	1	3	4		
Cook, William H	2	2	1		
Collins, Obediah	1	3	3		
Cochram, Humphrey	1	2	5		
Downey, Samuel	1	2	3		
Whinrey, John	1	1	4		
Johnson, John	2		1		
Turner, Ezekiel	1		1		
Rose, John	1				
Jervis, John	1	5	4		
Adams, Moses	1		1		
Ashley, Joseph	1	4	7		
Ballard, Iram	2	1			
Bales, John Bostor	1	1	3		
Bales, Jacob	3		5		
Ballard, Jerman	1				
Ball, Thomas	1		1		5
Bohannan, William	3		1		
Barrow, John	1	3	2		
Brown, George	1	1	1		
Brown, Randolph	1	2	5		
Reynolds, Nathaniel	1	1	3		
Bohannan, Elliott	3	2	4		
Bursham, John	2	2	4		
Carr, Benjamin	1	2	2		
Curry, Joseph	1	2	5		
Cooper, Samuel	1		1		
Carn, Russel	1	1	5		
Cooper, Jonathan	1				
Critchfield, John	1		2		
Coleman, William	1		4		
Dunningham, Thos	2		10		
Downey, Abram	1	4	4		
Downey, Peter	1		2		1
Etheridge, Abner	1	2	1		
Fillden, John	3		2		2
Faircloth, Thomas	1		3		
Fariner, Nathan	2	2	3		
Greenwood, Samuel	2	4	5		1
Hide, Stephen	2	5	5		
Hill, John	1	2	5		
Hudgins, John	1	1	1		
Hurst, George	1	2	3		
Hide, James	1				
Ginnings, James	1	2	1		
Johnson, John, Junr	1	2	5		
Cadle, Thomas	1	1	1		
Daniel, James	1	2	3		
Jervis, Jabez	2				
Jervis, William	1				
Jervis, Stephen	3		1		
Jones, James, senr	1	1	1		1
Johnson, Isaac	1				
Anderson, James	4	5	3	1	
Jervis, Keziah	1	2	6		
Jiles, Samuel	1	3	2		
Keaton, Francis	1				
Meredith, William	3	3	6		2
Dunningham, Thomas, Junr	1	1	3		
Dudley, Charles	2		2		
Denney, Hezekiah	1	4	6		
Denney, William	2	2	5		
Donaly, John	1	1	3		
Dunningham, John	2	2	1		
Hiett, William	4	4	3		
Dunningham, James	1				
Dunningham, Jesse	1				
Evans, Daniel	1	3	2		
Early, Jeremiah	6				
Freeman, William	4	2	3		3
Gunston, James	1		3		
Haines, Jonathan	1		1		6
Hiett, Benjamin	1	2	1		
Hiett, John	1	3	1		
Hiett, Joseph	5	2	4		
Reavis, Joseph	1	1	3		1
Ryley, Gerard	1	2	2		
Riley, Jeremiah	1	1	1		6
Reavis, John	1	2	1		
Roark, John	1		1		
Rutor, John	2		2		
Reavis, Jesse	2		2		
Roton, Jacob	1		1		
Roark, John, Junr	1	1	1		
Russell, Charles	1	2	3		
Marsh, William	2	3	2		
Moseley, West	1	3	2		
Moore, Moses	1	1	1		
Marsh, John, Junr	1		1		
Marsh, Minor	2	3	2		
Marsh, John	3	3	3		
Meredith, John	1	4	6		
Meredith, Samuel	1	2	2		
Monaham, Shadrack	1	2	4		
McMickle, John	2	2	5		
Meredeth, Daniel	1	1	2		1
Martin, Andrew	3	1	2		
Pace, Sarah			2		
Pettite, Rachel	3	1	4		
Richards, John	1		3		
Richards, William	1	1	2		
Robertson, John	1	2	4		
Suedder, John	1	3	1		
Shores, John	1		3		10
Sutton, John	1	2	2		
Spur, Aaron	1	1	4		
Shores, Reuben, Junr	1	1	8		4
Sugart, John	2	1	2		
Sugart, Zachariah	3	1	4		
Thompson, George	1	3	4		
Whitlock, William	1	3			
Halcomb, Drury	1				
Phillips, Jonathan	1		2		4
Reavis, James	1		1		4
Masters, William	1		1		
Miller, Christian	1		1		
Debord, George	2		6		
Debord, Jacob	1	1	2		
Grace, George	1				
Chappel, James	1	1	1		
Hudspith, Mary		1	1		
Spurling, Zachariah	1	4	7		
Sparks, Matthew	1	3	4		
Stubbs, Isaac	1	1	2		
Scofield, Joseph	1		2		
Swim, Moses	1	3	3		
Shaw, James	1	2	2		
Stephens, John	1	3	3		
Standley, John	1	1	1		
Stephens, Edward	1	3	4		
Smith, Bennett	1	3	2		
Sanders, James	2	2	2		9
Talberd, Joshua	1	1	3		
Vestal, Thomas	1		4		
Whitfield, William	1		1		
Waggoner, Henry	3	2	7		
Waddle, Noil	1	2	4		
Wheatherman, Christian	2	4	5		
Wright, Thomas	1	3	4		
Whalen, John	1	1	1		
Wooldridge, Edward	1				3
Whootton, Richard	1	4	5		
Wiggfield, Benjamin	1		5		
Whitehead, Ann	4		2		
Williams, John	1		5		6
Whiles, Thomas	1	2	3		1
Whiles, Thomas, Junr	1		3		
Whiles, John	1	4	1		

SALISBURY DISTRICT, SURRY COUNTY—Continued.

NAME OF HEAD OF FAMILY.	Free white males of 16 years and upward, including heads of families.	Free white males under 16 years.	Free white females, including heads of families.	All other free persons.	Slaves.	NAME OF HEAD OF FAMILY.	Free white males of 16 years and upward, including heads of families.	Free white males under 16 years.	Free white females, including heads of families.	All other free persons.	Slaves.	NAME OF HEAD OF FAMILY.	Free white males of 16 years and upward, including heads of families.	Free white males under 16 years.	Free white females, including heads of families.	All other free persons.	Slaves.
Whiles, Luke	1		2			Halcomb, John	1	2	6	3		Brown, Thomas	1	1	2		
Windsor, Isaac	1	2	3			Halcomb, May	1	2	1			Barrett, Joseph	2		3		
Wilson, Alexander	1	1	6			Hudspeth, John	1	3	3			Bowen, Thomas	2		2		
Wright, Ann	1	3	6			Hudspeth, Airs	1	3	6			Meriam, Bartholomew	1	2	4		
Wright, John	1					Hough, Daniel	3	2	7			Meriam, John	1		8		
Wilson, Samuel	1		1			Inkshaw, Joseph	1	2	5			Manis, Henry	2		6		
Whiles, Pinson	1	1	2			Hall, William	1		5			Oversby, William	1		4		
Wagoner, Adam	1					Hagin, Peter	1	2	1			Parnell, Joshua	1		5		
Weatherman, Christa	1	1	2			Hadley, Simon, Junr	1		4			Pace, Edmund	1	1	3		
Wood, Stephen	2	1	7			Halcomb, Thomas	2	3	1			Ray, Benjamin	1	1	3		
Zachary, William	1	4	2			Hadley, Thomas	1		6			Summers, John	2	3	3		
Colton, John	4	1	3			Hobson, Stephen	1	2	1			Critchfield, Joshua	2	1	3		
Bitticks, Francis	1	3	3			Hutchings, Thomas	1	1	3			Smith, Edward	1	2	1		
Pilcher, Phebe	1		2			Hutchings, Benja	2	6	4		4	Silvie, William	1	3	5		
Philips, Mark	2	1	2			Inshaw, Thomas	1	1	1			Summers, Johnson	1		1		
Inshaw, Jacob	1	4	1			Hadley, Simon	1	3	4			Wheeluss, Lewis	1		4		
Hoppes, John	1		4			Hudspith, Airs, Junr	1	1	4		3	Whitaker, William	1	5	3		
Husband, Robert	2	2	6			Halcomb, Grimes	2	4	2			Whootton, Thomas	1		1		
Hoppes, Daniel	1	1	2			Harding, William	2	2	4			Whootton, Thos, Junr	1	1	1		
Johnson, Isaac	2	2	5		4	Halcomb, George	2	2	4			Weaver, William	3		2		
Jacks, Thomas	1		1			Petty, Ransdall	1	1	1			Weaver, Thomas	1	1	3		
Jacks, Richard	2	3	7			Poe, William	1	3	5			Wheeluss, Reuben	1	1	2		1
Johnson, Elisha	1		3			Parson, Richard	2	1	2			Watson, John	2	1	3		
Jones, James	3	1	3			Petty, William	2	3	3		1	Whitacker, Jonathan	1	3	2		
Jeffrey, William	1		4			Penright, John	2		4			Walker, Joseph	1		1		
Johnson, John	4	1	4			Rutledge, William	1		3			Wright, James	1		1		
Johnson, Benja	1	2	1			Roton, Josiah	1	2	2		1	York, James	1		5		
Kell, John	1		1			Riley, Edward	1	1	3		3	Jones, Samuel	1		1		
Keys, Joseph	2		2	1		Riley, James	1		3		4	Melton, Richard	2	4	1		
Kell, John, Junr	1		1			Reese, Abram	2	6	4			Brown, John	1	4	6		
Lackham, Robert	1	1	2			Reynolds, Jonas	1	2	3			Bailie, James	1	1	6		
Lacham, Aaron	1	1	1			Revis, John	1	1	3			Blacklock, Richard	1	2	4		
Long, Frederick	1	5	4			Ray, William	1		1			Brown, Christian	2		3		
Lacham, Alexander	1	1	1			Roton, David	1		3			Burnsides, James	1	1	5		
Liverton, Daniel	1		3		1	Roton, James	1	4	5			Brown, Richard	1	1	4		
Moore, George	1	2	2			Riley, Nincan	1		1			Brown, William	1	3	3		
Miller, Jacob	1	3	6			Riley, Nincan, Junr	1		1			Bills, Gersham	1	1	1		
Messick, Richard	1		2			Forester, James	1		4			Bond, Stephen	1	4	8		
McLemore, Wright	1					Freeman, Jacob	1	3	1			Biddicks, John	1	1	4		
Masters, Nicholas	1		2			Freeman, Samuel	1	2	3		5	Blackman, Jeremiah	1	1	5		
Masters, James	1					Freeman, Joshua	1	1	5		8	Brown, Jacob	1	3	3		
Ayers, Samuel	1					Fanning, Thomas	1	1	3			Bramblet, Ambrose	1	4	3		2
Lambert, Sterling	1		4			Greenly, James	2	3	4			Clinton, Edward	2	3	4		1
Thomas, George	1	1	1			Green, George	1	4	5			Colton, Elijah	1	5	1		
Hains, Elis	2	1	5			Hammons, Ambrose	1	1	6			Colton, Lindsey	1	2	1		
Debord, John	3	6	3			Howard, Jane	1		4			Carpenter, Matthias	1	3	3		
Elsbery, William	1		1			Horn, Richard	1	2	7		2	Callaway, Samuel	1	3	3		
Ayers, Eliue	1	1	2			Haggard, Samuel	3	3	7		1	Copeland, John	2	4	3		
Ayers, Thomas	3		7			Hicks, Nathaniel	1	1	5			Castevin, John	1	2	3		
Adkins, William	1	1	1			Haggard, John	1					Coleman, Charles	1				
Allen, Isaac	1	1	2	1		Harrison, William	1	1	2			Chappel, Ambrose	1	2	3		
Ayers, Nathaniel	1		5			Hughs, Thomas	2		1			Clanton, Thomas	1	2	1		3
Ayers, Moses	3	6	8			Hammons, John	1	4	4			Clanton, Benjamin	4	1	3		
Bills, William	1	1	2			Holyfield, Valentine	1	2	4			Keer, William	1	3	3		
Broughton, Job	1	3	1			Henderson, George	1		4			Davis, Andrew	2	3	5		
Bills, Daniel	1	3	1			Hopperoumes, John	1	2	3			Dillard, John	1	4	3		
Bray, Little Barry	1	7	4			Horn, John	3		3			Debord, Isaac	1		2		
Colman, William	1		3			Hatton, John	1	4	2			Hall, Joshua	1	2	2		
Colman, Isaac	2	2	2			Johnson, William	2	5	3			Bray, Hannon	5	1	5		
Conner, John	1	1	2			Jones, John	1	3	4			Burch, John	2	1	2		3
Davis, Isham	1	1	4			Johnson, Jeffrey	2	2	3			Burch, William	1	2	4		1
Durham, James	1	1	3			Johnson, Moses	1	2	5			Burch, Thomas C	1		2		
Denney, Samuel	1	1	1			Johnson, Joseph	1	4	6			Critchfield, William	1		5		
Ayers, John	2	1	2			Kelley, Barnabas	1					Blackburn, Susanna		2	3		
Anderson, George	1	1	3			Knight, Reuben	1		6			Bledsoe, Benjamin	3	2	5		
Devern, Frederick	2	4	4			Knight, William	1	4	3			Bray, Stogner	1	1	2		
Messick, George	1	2	2	1		London, Amos	2	1	2			Burch, Thomas	1		4		
Martin, John	1	1	4			Lay, Charles	1	3	1			Biddicks, John	1	2	6		
Marshal, William	1		1			Lucas, John	1	1	2			Cook, William	3		5		10
Marshal, Joseph	1		1			Lucas, William	1	1	3			Critchfield, Nathl	1	1	3		
Marshal, John	1	2	1			Mears, Thomas	2		1			Critchfield, Wm	1		5		
Meirs, Peter	2		4			Mears, Moses	4	3	2		1	Cockran, David	1	1	1		
Marshal, Ruanah	1	2	2			Vindever, John	1	2	4			Crawley, Thomas	1	1	1		
Moore, John	2	3	7			Vindever, Charles	1	2	4			Bledsoe, Learking	1	1	2		
Mannering, Jordan	1	3	6			Woolridge, William	1	2	5		2	Allen, John	1	1	2		
Mannering, Andrew	1	1	2			Wall, William	1	3	4			Owens, George	1	3	3		
McLemore, Ephraim	1	3	5			Winston, John	2	2	1		4	Davis, William	1	3	3		
McHand, Matthew	2	2	4	1		Whoshon, Philip	1	1	1			Critchfield, John	1	1	3		
Maxfield, Sidney	1					Whoshon, Leonard	1	3	6			Cooper, James	4	2	2		
Mackey, John	1	2	3			Wells, James	2	1	4			Coons, Francis	3	2	5		
Murphy, James	1		1			Wright, William	1	3	3			Emanuel, Isaac	1				
Mehaffey, Thos	1	4	5			Witasker, Johnson	1	1	2			Fretwell, William	1				
Mires, Joseph	1	4	5			Welch, David	2	2	1			Todd, James	1	2	5		
Sprinkle, Peter	4	2	3			Williams, Joseph	2	6	2		20	Davis, Gabriel	1	2	2		
Masters, William	1		1			Shelton, Jeremiah	2	1	3			Dobbins, Jacob	2	3	6		
Moler, Valentine	1	3	4			Spear, Thomas	1	4	4			Davis, William	1	2	3		
Noblett, John	1	3	3			Robinson, William	1	2				Dibord, Reuben	1	3	1		
Parker, Jonathan	2	3	6			Adam, William, Junr	1					Day, William	1	5	3		
Petty, Zachariah	1	1	5			Aldridge, Joseph	2		2			Elsberry, Isaac	1	5	3		
Patterson, Greenbery	4	4	4			Anthony, David	1	1	4			Elsbery, John	1	3	1		
Pettijohn, Henry	1	2	3			Aldridge, Nathl	1		2			Elmore, Abijah	3	4	1		
Pettijohn, Job	3	1	2			Andersons, John N	1	2	4			Eastwood, Joseph	1		1		
Dunningham, Joseph	1	1	4			Adams, William	2	1	5			Elsbery, Jacob	1	2	2		
Evans, James	1	1	2			Adams, Jonathan	1	1	2			Elliott, Lewis	2	2	3		6
Edward, Andrew	1	3	3			Alnutt, William	1	4	4			Elliott, William	2	2	6		1
Hoppes, George	1	4	4			Arnold, Samuel	2	4	4		3	Elis, William	1	4	3		
Hoppes, George, senr	1	2	1			Aldridge, Joshua	1					Everton Thomas	1	2	5		

SALISBURY DISTRICT, SURRY COUNTY—Continued.

NAME OF HEAD OF FAMILY.	Free white males of 16 years and upward, including heads of families.	Free white males under 16 years.	Free white females, including heads of families.	All other free persons.	Slaves.
Fender, Nimrod	1	1	1		
Fender, Gabriel	1		1		
Felton, Amoriah	1	2	5		
Fender, Christian	1	3	3		
Farris, James	1	2	2		
Frazier, Robert	1	3	2		2
Frazier, William	1	2	4		
Gentry, Nicholas	2		2		
Gentry, Richard	4		2		
Gentry, Allen	1	3	5		
Gallion, Thomas	1	3	2		1
Gallion, Jacob	1	2	2		
Garner, John	3	3	4		
Garner, William	1		3		
Garrish, Benjamin	1	1	3		
Gentry, Richard, Junr	2	1	3		
Hambrick, Henry	1	4	1		
Hill, Joseph	3	1	5		
Hurt, John	6	2	4		
Harvil, David	1	7	3		
Harris, John	1	1	8		4
Edwards, James	1		1		
Downey, James	1		2		2
Gordon, Thomas	1	5	2		
Johnson, Charles	1	4	2		
Kirby, Francis	1	2	7	1	1
Lewis, Joel	1	2	2		18
Lewis, William Terrel	3	2	6		58
Moore, Aaron	1	1	3		
Morris, Nathl	3	3	3		
Morris, James, Junr	1		4		
Morris, Nathl, Junr	1				
Martin, Obediah	1		4		5
Martin, Salathiel	1	4	2		3
McBride, William	1	4	4		
McBride, Minassith	2		6		
McLaine, William	1		2		
McLaine, Laughly	2		2		
Morris, Daniel, Junr	1	1	2		
Morris, Daniel	2	1	2		
Burris, William	5	4	7		1
Bledsoe, Moses	2	1	7		
Blanchett, Joel	1		3		
Bruce, William	1	2	3		1
Brison, James	3	6	4		
Burras, John	1	2	1		1
Burras, Jacob	1	1	4		1
Burch, William	1	1	2		
Baker, Obediah	4	2	5		
Bryant, Thomas	1		3		
Cadle, Benjamin	2		3		
Cox, John	1	5	2		
Crud, Matthew	2		2		1
Crud, Bartlett	1	1	2		
Cook, William	5	2	7		
Crud, Bennet	4	2	4		
Clarke, David	1				
Crud, Colsby	1				
Doak, Alexander	1	1	4		
Davis, John	2		2		
Davis, Matthew	3	2	5		1
Dickerson, James	2	1	5		5
Davis, John	3		4		6
Conrod, Elrod	1	2	4		12
Fleming, John	4	5	6		12
Faulkner, William	2	6	3		5
Griffith, Edward	1	2	3		
Griffith, Benjamin	1	4	1		4
Morrisson, William	1				
Parsons, John	1	4	3		
Parsons, James	1	2	3		
Phipps, Matthew	1	2	2		
Phillips, Abner	2	3	3		
Pipes, John	3	1	6		
Wray, Zachariah	2	4	5		
Roberds, Oliver	3	3	9		
Sparks, William, Junr	2	1	5		
Sparks, George	1	1	1		
Sparks, Joseph	1	4	4		
Spence, Thomas	2	1	1		
Suthard, Isaac	1	1	7		
Suthard, Henry	1	4	5		
Sparks, Thomas	1	1	2		
Sparks, William	1	1	2		
Spence, John	1	1	2		
Spence, David	1	2	3		
Salle, Peter	2	4	5		
Shores, Reuben	1	1	2		4
Swim, Michael	1	1	4		
Sisk, James	1	2	3		
Spurling, Zachariah	2	1	2		
Sisk, Thomas	1		2		
Swim, John	1		2		
Sisk, John	1		1		
Gittins, John	3	2	3		
Gittins, Richard	1		3		6
Golden, William	1	4	2		4
Griffith, Daniel	1		1		
Green, Thomas	2	3	4		1
Harris, Robert, Junr	1	1	2		
Harris, Tyre	1	2	2		
Hooper, Richard	3	4	6		11
Hill, Richard	3	2	3		
Harris, Robert	1				
Holder, Joseph	4	2	5		
Holder, John	1	4	2		
Hampton, Collins	4		5		
Harvey, Joseph	1	2	3		
Humphries, Benja	3			1	
Hannah, John	3	2	5		
Herren, Henry	1	1	6		
Harris, Jonathan	1	1	4		
Holder, Solomon	1		1		
Laurence, Claibourn	1	1	3		1
McCraw, Francis	1		3		
Humphries, David	1		2		3
Hammock, Robert	1	2	3		
Hammons, John	3	1	5		5
Hammons, William	1	2	3		
Harris, Robert	2	2	3		9
Hicks, John	2	3	1		
Jones, Levi	2	1	5		
Shores, Simon	2	1	5		3
Snow, Frost	2	8	2		
Van vinkle, Abram	1	2	3		1
Wilbourn, Richard	4		3		1
Woodruff, Gideon	1	3	2		
Woodroff, Moses	3		2		
Turner, Thomas	1		1		
Morrisson, James	2		4		
McKinney, Matthew	1	2	2		
Findley, James	3	1	3		3
Cochran, David	1	1	1		
Cooper, Nathaniel	1		3		
Bench, Christ	1	2	2		
Johnson, John	1	5	4		
Benson, Benjamin	1	2	6		1
Ahart, Michael	2	6			
Aplin, Joel	1		4		
Aplin, Thomas	1		1		2
Armstrong, William	1	1	3		4
Armstrong, Hugh	2	1	3		9
Adams, James	1				
Ballard, Thomas	1	3	5		
Brison, John, Junr	1	2	5		2
Burris, Thomas	2	2	4		8
Blackwell, David	1	1	3		12
Brison, John	1		5		
Keith, Cornelius	3	3	4		
McCarver, John	1	2	1		
Morris, Daniel	1		4		
McKenney, Jesse	1		2		
McKenney, John	1		4		
McGee, Drury	1	1	3		
Spur, John	1	1	3		
McCraw, William	2	1	4		4
McCraw, Benjamin	1	3	4		
McKenny, John, Junr	1	2	2		7
McCraw, Jacob	1	5	2		
Parkes, James	1	2	3		
Birke, John	1		3		
Patterson, Thomas	1	1	5		
Rowles, Christopher	1	3	4		
Roberts, James	1		4		
Rosinover, Joseph	4		1		4
Robertson, William	1				
Roberds, John	4	2	6		4
Ross, William	1	2	8		
Ramsey, William	2		7		
Ross, Charles	1	1	3		
McCarver, Joshua	1	1	2		
Steward, John	1	1	1		
Spain, Benjamin	2	1	5		
Smallwood, Elijah	1	1	3		
Studdyman, John	1	3	3		
Snow, Frost, Junr	1	3	1		
Smith, William	1	3	4		
Frost, Snow	3	3	6		10
Steward, Edward	1				
Smith, Stephen	1	3	5		1
Smith, Charles	2		5		9
Nap, Justus	1				
Brown, Samuel	1	6	2		
Guinn, Nathl	1				
Muckleyea, Hugh	1	1	2		
Wittaker, Mary		1	3		
Chambling, William	2	3	4		
Sessions, Isaac	1				

WILMINGTON DISTRICT, BLADEN COUNTY.

NAME OF HEAD OF FAMILY.	Free white males of 16 years and upward, including heads of families.	Free white males under 16 years.	Free white females, including heads of families.	All other free persons.	Slaves.
Watson, William J	1		3		19
Singletary, Joseph	3		3	1	12
McCree, Mrs. Margiret	1	1	1		16
Nance, Daniel	3		2		7
Handen, Josiah	1	3	3		8
Handin, Lydia			2		
Hill, Phillip	2	1	2		1
Bryant, William	2	4	2		1
Ashford, Street	3	2	1		6
Butlar, Henry	1				
Colvete, Henry	1				1
Lennon, John	1		4		7
Kemp, Joseph	3	1	2		3
Lemmon, Anguish	1	1	3		
Fetzrandolf, Benja	2	1	5		10
Shaw, Neal	4	3	1		10
Harvey, John	1				
Harvey, Travis	1				
McCree, Samuel	2	2	3		1
Jones, Isaac	1	2	2		5
Moess, Elisha	1				
Hayns, Elizabeth		2	6		12
Guthre, William	1		2		
Owen, Thomas, Esq	1	2	3		37
McConkey, Robert	1	2	3		6
Elkins, John	1	1			
Redding, Rehun	1		2		1
Bradley, James	5	1	3		20
White, David	4	2	6		4
Elkins, Saml, Junr	1		1		
Gaylor, James	1	5	2		
Alston, Peter	2	5	3		11
Sanderson, William	1		1		2
Bryant, John	1		3		2
Odair, Frances		1	3		1
Morehead, James	1	2	4		26
White, John	6	1	4		14
Elkins, Samuel	1	5	1		1
Elkins, Evan	1		1		
McClennan, Thomas	2	4	3		2
Pointer, Argulus	2	2	4		1
Ervan, James	1		2		
Noles, George	1	2	4		
Cake, Phillip	1	2	5		
Hesters, John	1	2	5		
Baker, Samuel	2		3		
White, Mathew Rowan	1		4		
Salter, Richard	1	2	2		
Plummer, Aron	1	4	2		
Singletary, William	1	1	3		2
Wair, George	1		2		
Chessur, William	1	1	2		
Chessur, Richard	1	3	1	1	5
McMillin, John	3		1		
Shaw, Anguish	2	1	4		
Singletary, Josiah	1	2	2		3
Hesters, Jesper	1	2	2		
Hesters, Tho	1		4		
Hesters, Joseph	1	1	2		
Guyton, James	2	2	1		
Dowlas, William	1	3	4		
Evers, James	1	2	4		
Russ, Will, Senr	2	4	5		
Russ, Will, Junr	1	4	1		1
Fason, James	1	1	3		
Bryan, Stephen	2	1	1		
Chesshar, Randolph	1	1	1		
Whetty, Joseph	1	4	4		
Wiley, Will	1		3		
Harisson, Mrs. Margerit			3		
Turner, Samuel	1				3
Hesters, William	1	2	4		3
Smith, Lucy	2	3	3		3
Singletary, Mary	1	2	2		
Morris, Thomas	1	1	3		
Bryant, Pheliman	1	3	3		
Gaylor, James	1	2	2		
Guyton, Priscilla	1	2	1		
Clifton, Boasman	1				
McDonald, George					
Olifant, Jesse A	1	5	3		1
Rowan, Pollice	1	2	3		3
Raford, Robt	2				
Fosters, Margarit	1		1		
White, Hannah		1	5		
Ellis, John	1	1			
Hilliard, John	1		5		

WILMINGTON DISTRICT, BLADEN COUNTY—Continued.

NAME OF HEAD OF FAMILY.	Free white males of 16 years and upward, including heads of families.	Free white males under 16 years.	Free white females, including heads of families.	All other free persons.	Slaves.
Curray, Samuel	1		1		
Allen, Tobitha		1	3		
Months, Mathew	1	3	3		
Hesters, Stephen	3	4	5		
Russ, Mary		1	2		
Stevens, Isoom	1	1	2		
Wisher, Elizabeth	1	2	2		5
Russ, John	1		3		
Carter, John	1	2	4		
Gray, William	1	2	12		
Bryant, Stephen, Jur	1		2		
Green, Betty			1	3	2
Russ, James	1	2	6		
Taylor, George	1		2		
Ervan, Jarod	1				6
Latestead, Erick, Esq.	1		1		16
Singletary, Whamon	1	2			1
Spears, Robert	1				6
Robinson, Batrum	2	2	3		24
White, Mary		3	1		4
Lock, John	1	2	5		2
Lock, Joseph	1	1			10
Stanton, John	2	1	2		5
Purdy, James	1	2	4		28
McCree, William	1	2	4		1
Plummer, Zackeriah	1				1
Johnston, Rachel		1	2		
Cain, Joseph, Esquire	1		1		9
Serwin, Thomas	1	1	4		
Walker, John	1	1	2		
Counsel, Mrs. Mary		2	4		17
Singletary, John	2	1	2		8
Wilkins, John	1	3	1		11
Millar, Frederick	2	1	3		6
Wood, Lucy		1	3		
Evans, Elizabeth	2		1		
Stone, David	1	2	3		
Lock, Thomas	2		5		5
Wills, Daniel	1	4	2		1
Gause, Nedam	1		1		11
Wills, Jacob	1		2		7
Plummer, Jeremiah	1		4		
Moore, John	3	1	5		1
Singletary, Richard	2	1	4		5
Singletary, James	1	4	3		1
Yancey, Charles	1	4	1		
Jones, Edward	2		4		6
Plummer, John	1	3	1		
Plummer, Moses	2	1	3		
Rogeson, Elizabeth			2		7
Singletary, James, Jur.	1	2	4		2
Singletary, Joseph	1		3		2
Butlar, Joseph	1	1	3		2
Oveler, Amelia			2		9
Ellis, James	1	3	4		4
Storm, Mary			2		
Gales, Mary			4		
Gales, Jane			2		
Gales, John	1	3	4		
Langdel, Benja	1	3	1		
Cain, John	2	4	3		6
Parnel, John	1	3	3		
Counsil, Robt	1	2	2		3
Bennet, John	1	1	2		
Cain, Samuel	2		2		13
Robinson, Jonathan	2		1		
Cain, Mrs. Olive	1		2		4
Cain, James	1	3	5		5
Messer, Mary			4		
Landzdel, John	1	1	4		
Avery, Thomas	2		1		
Pricket, Josiah	1		2		
Pricket, Eley		1	2		
Brown, Tho	1	1	3		
Brown, John	1				
Gibbs, John	1	1	2		7
Wilkerson, William	1	1	7		1
Powell, Isaac	1	1	2		2
Powell, Elizabeth			4		
Powell, Barney	1	2	2		1
White, William	1		3		1
Chanchey, Keziah	2		4		
White, Mary		1	4		6
King, Duncan	5	4	4		
Begford, Jeremiah	2	2	5		
Smith, Eley	1	1	2	1	
Counsil, James	2		3		
Smith, Anne		2	2		5
Brown, Gerorge	1	1	3		
Linnen, Dennis	1	3	2		7
Griffin, Joseph	1				
Buzby, Ezekel	2		5		1
Jones, Augustus	1		1		
Hodges, James	1	1	5		
Camble, John	1	2	3		
McMillin, Dugal	2	1	5		1
McKee, George	3		2		
Camble, James	1	3	1		2
Camble, James	2		1		
McColom, Daniel	1	4	6		
Taylor, Daniel	1	3	2		
Blew, John	1	2	5		
Lemmon, Duncan	2	2	3		
McKay, John	1		3		
Kelley, Archabald	3		3		1
Camble, Archabald	1		3		
Taylor, Daniel	1		3		
McCown, Robert	1	4	2		
McCown, William	1	3	1		
McCown, Mathew	2		2		
Lesley, Joseph	2		4		
Kelley, Methew	2	4	5		22
Kelley, John	1	1	2		3
Adams, Benja	1	3	1		
Bradley, Mary	1	3	2		
Munk, Jacob	1	1	2		3
Turner, Lazarus	1	1	1		
Luois, Aron	1	2	2		
Turner, Ester	2	4	5		
Bryant, John	1	1	3		
Fitzgarald, Thomas	1	1	3		2
Lewis, Josiah	2	1	7		
Simpson, Tho., Senr	1		2		5
Simpson, Tho., Junr	1		4		1
Simpson, Edward	1		1		5
Lewis, Richard M	1		3		7
Shipman, James	1	3	4		4
Lee, Jacob	1		4		1
Hawkins, Gideon	2	1	3		
Lee, Joshua	4	2	4		3
Lewis, Moses	1		3		
Robinson, John	1	3	2		
Wiggins, Joseph	2	3	8		
Hardcastle, William	1		2		
Browden, Thomas	1	5	5		
Brown, William	4	3	5		
Stevens, Eley	1	2	2		2
Ellis, William	1	3	2		
Ferrel, William	1	2	3		
Ferrel, Cornelus			1		
Taylor, Philip	2		3		
Hays, Joshua	1		5		4
Burney, William	1		4		5
Chan, Moran		4	2		
Wiggens, Isoom	1				
McNeal, William	2		3		14
Pockerpine, John	1	2	2		11
Begford, William	1	1	2		3
Lewis, Josiah	1	1	4		3
Mooney, John	1		4		
McKethen, John	1	1	2		
McColskee, Neal	2		3		6
McKay, John	1	3	4		
McClaren, John	2		4		2
Shaw, Archabald	1		2		
Shaw, Macum	1		3		4
McNaughton, Charles	3		3		
Chesnut, Arthur	1		3		
Folks, William	1	3	4		
Folks, Joney		1	1		
Mills, Roley	2	2	2		
Baldwin, John	1	2	4		
Green, Simon	1		5		
Stricklen, David	2		5		
Bright, James	2	3	2		
Folks, Josiah	1		2		
Folks, John	1	1	2		
Melican, Andrew	1	1	1		
Wall, Edward	2		2		
Paget, James	3	2	4		
Johnston, Thomas	2	1	1		
Johnston, William	1	2	1		
Carterite, Richard	1	1	2		
Carterite, John	1	1	1		
Williams, Joshua	3		4		
Smith, Sol	1	1	4		
Hardewick, Lenville	2		3		
Sanders, Thomas	2		3		
Flen, James	1	1	2		
Adkins, John	1	1	1		
Best, John	1	1	1		1
Bright, Simon	2	1	3		
Powers, Joseph	2	2	3		
Powers, Charles	1	2	2		
Register, William	3	4	4		
McColski, James	1		4		1
Lawson, Francis	2	2	4		
Parker, Ezekeil	2	3	6		
Powell, Thomas	1	2	4		
Spivey, Edmond	1	2	3		
Risen, James	1	4	4		
Camble, Elexander	3	2	3		
Shaw, John	1	2	3		
Talom, Richard	1		5		
Sebbet, William	1	1	3		
Wells, Joel	1	2	4		
Godden, Stephen	1	2	2		
Williamson, Lewis	2	5	3		
Hilbourn, Hamilton	2	2	2		
Nobles, Joseph	3	7	2		
Hill, Mekijah	3	1	6		
Flowers, Indignation	2	2	6		4
Flowers, Goldsbury	1		1		2
Stevens, Abraham	1	2	3		
Powell, Absolom	1	4	3		3
Sanderson, Thomas	1	2	2		
Wilson, John	1	1	2		
Nobles, Tenesser	1	1	1		
Branton, Mathew	1	1	2		
Peters, William	1		2		
Niles, Coalman	2	1	2		1
Niles, Averit	1	1	3		
Godden, Pearce	1	1	4		
Herring, Priscilla			2		
Hays, Mary			1		
Yales, John, Esq	2	1	4		4
Coalsman, John	2		5		
Coalsman, Moses	3	2	4		
Eason, Benja	1	3	6		
Hollyman, Saml	1	1	4		
Folks, Richard	1	1	6		1
Gibbs, Heman	1	1	3		
Pope, Saml	1	2	2		
Hall, Burrel	1	3	3		1
Gobson, Charles	2				2
Rols, Marmaduke	1	1	2		
Hollyman, James	1	4	3		
Coalsman, Theophelas	1	1	2		
Pate, Samuel	2	2	3		
Summerset, Frances		3	4		
Tyler, Moran	1	2	4		
Stricklen, Philip	1	1	2		
Coalsman, John	1		2		
Godden, Alexander	1	1	4		
Barfield, Stephen	1				6
Folks, William	1	2	3		
Folks, Wright	2	1	4		
Folks, Simon	1	3	4		
Folks, Philip	1	2	5		
Tyler, Moses	1	1	2		
Riggen, John	2		2		
Simons, John	1	2	3		
Smith, Simon	1	2	3		
Wilson, Edward	3		6		
Green, John	1	2	5		2
Yeates, Luke	1	1	3		
Runnels, Ann	2	1	3		3
Wadkins, Mathew	1		7		1
Cannon, Archabald	3	3	4		
Stricklen, Mary		1	4		
Loften, Mark	1		3		
Loften, Frederick	2	1	1		
Hays, Sothy	3		5		4
Clark, George	3	1	6		
Mems, Thomas	1	2	4		4
Winget, John	1	1	2		6
Winget, Walter	1	1	3		2
Robbins, Jethro	1	1	5		
Wilson, Edward	1	1	1	1	
Young, John	1	1	3		1
Desin, Leonard	1	1	1		
Fling, Elizabeth		1	3		2
Fling, Mary			4		
Hodge, Robert	1				
Bozzell, Elizabeth	2	2	4		
Bozzell, Tho.	1	1	3		
Sessions, Thomas	4	4	2		7
Bozzell, William	1	1	2		
Mooney, John	1	2	2		
Hardwick, Allen	1	2	4		
Bright, Simon, Jur	1	1	3		
Folks, John	1		2		
Chairday, James	1	2	6		20
Hairgroves, Briton	1		1		8
Column, Richard	1	1	1		
Busley, Robert	1	1	4		
Clark, David	2	1	1		
Hobbs, Isaac	1		3		
Pitman, Moses	2	1	3		2
Richardson, Thomas	3		3		2
Baldwin, William	1	2	3		4
Green, Calop	1		2		
Baldwin, John	1		1		27
Baldwin, Charles	1	1	4		10
Green, William	1		3		1
Green, Robert	1		2		
Pope, Briton	1	1	1		3
Edwards, Newet	1	1	3		
Sols, Abraham	1		2		
Swendel, Samuel	2	2	2		
Warren, Archabald	4	1	3		11

WILMINGTON DISTRICT, BLADEN COUNTY—Continued.

NAME OF HEAD OF FAMILY.	Free white males of 16 years and upward, including heads of families.	Free white males under 16 years.	Free white females, including heads of families.	All other free persons.	Slaves.
Lewis Hanson	2	4	5		2
Ellis, John	1	1	7		2
Hobbs, Joseph	1		1		
Ellis, James	1	2	4		7
Folks, John	1	1	3		1
Bryan, William	3	2	3		4
Folks, Jacob	2		2		
Door, John	1	2	2		4
Jones, Thomas	1		2		
Fetchet, Christian	1		1		
Shipman, Daniel	3		2		19
Baldwin, Warren	1	1	4		
Broom, Elps	2	2	6		2
Simpson, Scarimore	1	1	2		
Stubs, George	1	1	2		
Folks, James	1	1	3		
Baldwin, Joseph	1	5	4		7
Wilson, James	1		2		2
Lewis, James	1	3	3		
Simpson, Simon	2	1	1		
Simpson, Jacob	1		4		
Stubs, Richard	1	3	3		
Stubs, John	1	1	1		3
Lambert, Richard	1	2	5		1
Simpson, Robert	2		4		
Clark, John	1	5	3		3
Simpson, John	2	2	4		
Ray, Jemina	2		2		
Baldwin, Anne		2	4		
Holms, Edmund	2				10
Johnston, Hugh	1	3	3		15
Bryant, Will, Junr	1		4		3
McCalop, Catherine		2	2		
McMullen, Runnel	1	3	2		
Robeson, Charles	1	3	4		
Richardson, Robert	2		1		
Haddesk, Drury	1	1	3		
Parker, William	1	3	3		
Edwards, Charles	1	2	3		
Richardson, John	1		1		
Council, David	2	1	3		
Murrel, Zachariah	1	4	2		
Peebody, John	2	1	3		
Green, James	2				
Banefoot, James	1	1	5		
Mems, David	1	1	4		10
Carman, Samuel	1	3	3		
Mems, James	1	2	2		2
Mems, Shadarach	1	1	2		
Mems, Volentine	1		1		1
Port, Peter	1	1	4		2
Penny, Thomas	1	3	3		
Runnels, Demsey	1	2	2		1
Runnels, Richard	1	1	2		
Runnels, Richard	1		1		
Lamberson, John	1		2		
Lamberson, Courtney			3		3
Smith, John	1	1	4		
Lamb, John	1	2	5		3
Chansey, Demsey	1		1		
Whitehead, Jacob	1		2		
Davis, Thomas	1				
Runnels, Elijah	1	1	2		3
Wolf, Isaac	1		2		
Hairgroves, Burrel	1	1	5		
Murrel, Barnabas	1		1		
Morrison, Mrs. Margret	1	2	2		20
Dupree, James	5				22
Brown, Richard	1				2
Smith, Thomas	2	1	3		20
Singletary, Mary			2		4
Brown, John	1		2		5
Egleson, James	1				4
Doway, James	1	1	1		5
Taylor, Harbot	1	3	1		
Davis, Turner	1				20
Davis, Ezekiel	3	1	4		4
Murrel, Barney	2	2	2		3
Clayton, Benom	1	1	5		
Smith, William	1	1	1		4
Smith, William	1	1	4		4
Smith, Simon	1	1	4		
McViker, John	2		2		
McKethen, Duncan	1		2		1
McFater, Daniel	1		3		
McKethen, Daniel	2	1	4		

NAME OF HEAD OF FAMILY.	Free white males of 16 years and upward, including heads of families.	Free white males under 16 years.	Free white females, including heads of families.	All other free persons.	Slaves.
Baine, Donald	1		1		13
Malsby, Anthoney	1		2		2
Blew, Dugal	3		1		
Downey, Daniel	3	1	4		
McEwen, Daniel	1	2	2		
McMillen, John	3		2		1
Meshaw, Peter	3		3		
McKay, John	2	2	3		15
Malsby, James	1	1	2		2
Davis, William	1	3	2		3
McKethen, Archabald	2	1	1		
Darrow, John	2	1	3		
Camble, John	1		6		
Malsby, James	1	2	2		2
Kellyham, Pearce	1	1	2		
Camble, Neal	1	1	1		
Kellyham, Cornelias	1	1	2		
Cousnel, Robert	1	1	2		4
Landzdel, Benja	1	3	1		
Millar, Ralph	1	2	7		14
Lock, Benja	1		3		7
Spendlove, Jenot	3	1	2		78
Daniel, Margaret		1	4		35
Johnston, Robert	1		2		
Holmes, Moses	5	1	3		
Lucus, George (of Chatam)					20
How, Arthur	1	2	1		50
Grange, John	2	1	5		18
Perry, John	1	3	4		
Brown, Thomas, Esq	1	3	4		30
Oliphant, Uphemia		5	2		2
Dewry, Uphemia	1		3		12
O'Neal, Charles	1	5	2		
Dafford, Jeremiah	1	2	2		
Lucus, Elizabeth		3	1		12
Willis, Ann			2		2
Jones, William	2				7
Pointer, John	1	4	4		
Pemberton, Margaret	1	1	1		8
Pemberton, John	1	1	1		
Singletary, Richard	2				4
Slingsby, Arabellah		1	3		
Taylor, John	1	3	4		
Seamore, Sarah			1		
Gantur, Joseph R	3				30
Due, Seth	1	4	5		
Johnston, Robert	1		2		
Ray, Jane	3	1	3		
Mulford, Ephram	3	5	9		15
Thomas, George	1	2	4		5
Lock, Mary	3		3		11
Salter, James	1		1		8
Lock, Agnis		3	2		5
Russ, Joseph	2		6		
Loyd, David	2	2	5		4
Thomas, John	1	2	2		1
Gavan, John	1	3	4		
Davis, Joseph	1	3	2		1
White, Will	1	1	4		3
Parnell, Elizabeth			2		
Singletary, John	1		1		1
Taylor, Sarah			4		
Statter, William	3	1	4		30
Parker, John	1	2	3		
Wilson, George	1		1		
Yerby, Henry	1	1	3		
Sutton, Beman	1	1	2		
Sutton, Beman	2		6		11
Larkins, James	3	5	7		11
Anderson, Catherine	4	1	4	1	12
Andres, John	3		2		21
Sikes, John	3	2	4		
Prigion, Peter	3		4		
Baity, William	2	2	2		21
Prigion, Mathew	3	1	2		
McMasters, Felex	2		3		1
McCalister, Hutor	1	1	2		
Strayhorn, Alexand	1	1	3		5
Coock, Daniel	1	3	4		
Henry, James	1	1	3		
Dane, Jeremiah	1	2	5		
Prigion, John	1		4		
Ennis, William	2	1	2		4
Cain, James	1	3	1		

NAME OF HEAD OF FAMILY.	Free white males of 16 years and upward, including heads of families.	Free white males under 16 years.	Free white females, including heads of families.	All other free persons.	Slaves.
Johnston, Samuel	1	1	4		
Johnston, Charles	1				
Averit, William	1	1	5		1
Sikes, Isarel	1		2		
Sikes, Jonathan	1	2	2		
Singletary, Richard	1	1	3		1
Cathwell, John	1		2		1
Bedson, Thomas	2	1	7		
Melom, John	1	1	2		
Parker, John	1	3	3		
Simmons, Jeremiah	1	2	3		
Clark, Hardy	1	1	3		
Davis, Henry	1		3		
Smith, Thomas	1	2	4		
Edge, John	1	2	4		
Edge, William	1		4		
Sellars, John	1	4	4		
Cain, John	1	1	5		
Gardens, James	4	3	2		
Bosman, Samuel	3	3	4		
Witherby, Kade	2	3	3		13
Cashwell, Thomas	1	5	5		
McClain, Peter	1		6		
Sellars, Duncan	1		4		
Clark, Henry	1	2	3		
Carr, James	1		3		
Curray, Edward	1	5	3		
Smith, William	1	4	3		
Davis, John	2	2	5		
Sessions, Saml	1	3	3		
Jones, Ezekiah	1	3	3		
Sessions, Culmore	1		2		
Daniel, Archabald	1	2	5		
Grim, William	1	1	3		
McColm, Rachel		1	3		
Davis, Balster	5		4		
Suggs, Will	1	1	4		
Sugs, Aligood	1	2	3		
West, James	1	4	6		
Cashwell, James	1		4		
Davis, Samson	3	3	3		
Thomas, Micheal	2	2	5		
Simmons, Sandrs	1		5		
Smith, John	2		3		
Cain, Neal	1		3		
Cain, Samuel	1	1	1		
Smith, William	1	2	4		
Valentine, Hardy	1		1		
Maclemore, Drury	3		2		
Bryant, Nedam	1	3	10		
Bryant, Bartum	1		2		1
Roan, Saml	1	3	5		
Bryant, David	1		3		
Edge, John	1	1	1		
Morehead, William	1	3	1		
Sikes, James	1		1		
Meloins, Daniel	1		1		
Sessions, Mary			3	4	
Avery, John	1	2	2		
Blackwell, Jesse	3	4	3		
Melvin, George	1	1	2		
Feston, Stephen	1		2		
McGee, James	1		3		
Carrol, John	1		1		
Carrol, Thomas, Junr	2	2	4		
Carrol, Thomas	1		2		
Picket, Gideon	1	1	1		
Hale, Nathan	4	4	4		
Bryant, Barney	4		1		
Edwards, Cloe			4		
Reaves, Edward	2	5	5		
Marafield, Daniel	1	1	3		
Devam, John, Senr	1	1	3		29
Devam, John, Junr	1	2	2		11
Brym, Mathew	1		1		14
Davis, Francis	1	2	5		7
Robinson, Peter	1	2	3		12
Blanks, John					8
West, Will					
Cavers, John					3
Cavers, Rasmus					4
Cavers, Gilley					3
Moon, James					7
Demery, John					6
Cavers, Mary					9
Melchel, William					6
					4

WILMINGTON DISTRICT, BRUNSWICK COUNTY.

NAME OF HEAD OF FAMILY.	Free white males of 16 years and upward, including heads of families.	Free white males under 16 years.	Free white females, including heads of families.	All other free persons.	Slaves.
Neal, Thomas	1	2		1	20
Vernon, Elinor		1	3		13
Rundleson, Archibald	1	3	1		3
Betts, William	2	3	2		5
Richardson, Elizabeth		2	2		2

NAME OF HEAD OF FAMILY.	Free white males of 16 years and upward, including heads of families.	Free white males under 16 years.	Free white females, including heads of families.	All other free persons.	Slaves.
Watters, Sarah		1	3		26
Vines, Samuel	1	2	4		
Turner, Amy			2		12
Graves, Benjamin	1		5		
Holms, Moses	3	1	1		1

NAME OF HEAD OF FAMILY.	Free white males of 16 years and upward, including heads of families.	Free white males under 16 years.	Free white females, including heads of families.	All other free persons.	Slaves.
Hall, John, Esq	2	1	4		43
Grange, John	2		3		39
Taylor, Solomon	1	3	3		
Keator, Sarah		1	3		
Boon, John	1	3	5		

WILMINGTON DISTRICT, BRUNSWICK COUNTY—Continued.

NAME OF HEAD OF FAMILY.	Free white males of 16 years and upward, including heads of families.	Free white males under 16 years.	Free white females, including heads of families.	All other free persons.	Slaves.
Freeman, James	2		7		1
Curray, Daniel	2		2		
Cain, Allen, Junr	1				8
Roots, John	1	2	6		16
Smith, James	1	1	4		
Keater, Nehemiah	1		2		1
Keater, William	1				
Norris, Thomas	1		2		
Morris, Robert	1				
Morris, Thomas	1	1	3		
Jeanots, Benjamin	1		1		
Jeanots, Winey			2		
Jeanots, John	1		1		
Pounds, John, Senr	1				
Pounds, John, Junr	1		2		
Pounds, Isaac	1		2		
Skipper, John	1		3		
Skipper, Moses	1	3	2		
Skipper, Abraham	1	2	3		
Flours, James	3		2		20
Rowan, John	1		2		21
Allen, Drury	2		2		12
Newell, Thomas	2		4		
Liles, Benjamin	1	2	5		
Clark, Thomas	1		1		56
Mills, Jane		1	3		3
Skipper, James	1		2		
Wheeler, William	1		2		
Heghemeth, John	3		3		
Potter, James	1	3	3		
Potter, Mills	1	3	1		2
Leonard, Samuel	2	1	2		2
Carrol, John	1	1	3		
Simpson, Elisha	1	3	4		
Leonard, Henry	1	1	3		
Sparksman, William	1		1		
Williams, Margaret	2		2		
Barrow, Huzzy	1		3		
Mills, Benjamin	1	1	3		9
Leonard, Elinor	3	1	5		10
Gause, Benjamin	1	2	3		4
Aderson, John	3		7		2
Mills, William	1	2	1		
Sulivan, Edward	1	3	2		4
Holms, John	1				
Sillars, James	2	5	3		
Potter, Miles	1				
Harris, Richard	1	3	2		
Sparksman, Levi	1	3	1		1
Sparksman, Richard	1		1		
Johnson, John	1	2	1		
Young, William	1				
Holms, Joseph	1				
Hays, John	1	3	4		
Taylor, John William	1				
Robbins, Benjamin	1	1	1		
Robbins, Arthur	3	2	3		
McMurray, William	1	1	2		
Greer, John	1	2	3		
Moore, Mary		3	3		5
Bell, James, Senr	1		2		9
Daniel, Stephen	2	3	3		8
Woodside, Robert	1	1	5		1
Grissel, Reauben	1		2		
Gause, Charles	1	1	4		15
Swain, David	1		1		1
Bell, James, Junr	1	2	4		3
Folks, Shadrick	1	2	3		
Wescut, John	1	1	1		
Galloway, Nathaniel	1	1	1		
Umphry, Joseph	1		2		3
Galloway, Sarah		2	3		1
Long, Henry	1	2	3		1
Cains, John	1	1	5		9
Goodman, Henry	1	4	1		
Sellars, Siman	1	1	2		1
How, Sarah		2	2		20
Goodman, William	2	1	3		3
Bell, Samuel	1	2	2		
Gibberd, Rebeca	1	2	4		
Felps, Martha		1	1		1
Wescut, Jeremiah	2	1	1		
Price, Solomon	1	1	3		
Sellars, Mathew	2	1	5		2
Hammer, Solomon	1		1		
Bell, Nathaniel	1	1	2		
Beesley, Oxford	1		2		1
Morgan, William	1	2	2		
Alexander, James	1	2	3		
Sparksman, William	1		4		
Williams, Benjamin	1	2	3		
McDugal, Runnel	2	1	3		
Bennet, Daniel	1		3		
Swain, Joseph	2		3		2
Dozur, Richard	1	3	3		
Boatright, William	1		1		
Gibbs, William	1	1	1		1
Goodman, William	1				1
Parker, William	1	2	3		11
Clemmings, Timothy	1		2		5
Chains, James	1	1	2		3
Rooks, John	1		1		
Balloon, Daniel	1	1	4		16
Bell, Robert	1		6		23
Russ, Thomas	3	3	4		8
Holdan, Sarah	1	1	3		
Swain, Levi	1	2	2		
Swain, James	1	2	3		
Gause, Susanna	1	1	2		19
Hewit, Philip	1	4	4		
Hewit, William	1	2	1		
Hewit, Ebenezar	1	2	2		
Clark, Jonah	1	3	2		5
Clark, Henry	1		1		8
Hewit, Joseph, Senr	2	1			1
Hewit, Joseph, Junr	1		1		1
Sharp, William	1		1		
Holden, Job	1	2	3		
Holden, James	1				
Holden, Famus					
Hines, Betsey			4		
Singletary, Benjn	2		1		
Willis, Henry	1	1	1		
Hewit, Ezekiah	3		2		
Hewit, Robert	1		1		
Hewit, Samuel	1		1		
Gause, Bryant	1		3		18
Stanley, Thomas	1	4	2		
Stanley, Samuel	1	2	3		1
Tharp, Charles	1		5		
Hewit, Reuben	1		2		
Robinson, John	1	3	3		
Hewit, David	1	3	3		
Dudley, Jeremiah	1	1	1		3
Ivey, Lewis	1	1	6		
Jones, William	1		1		
Holden, Benjamin	1		3		
Hawkins, Dennis	1	2	3		46
Daniel, Robert	1	2	3		14
Tharp, Samuel	2	1	3		
Smith, Jeremiah	2		1		1
Gause, John	1	1	1		7
Fosters, Electus Medus	1	3	1		15
Sulivan, Martha	2	3	2		2
Craig, Benjamin	1	3	3		
Craig, Lewis	1	2	3		
Jones, James	1	2	3		
McCree, Griffeth	2	1	2		8
McKensee, George	1	1	3		30
Clark, James	1	2	2		19
Drew, John	1	2	1		
Gause, Nedam	2	4	1		5
Goodman, Henry	1	2			
Franks, Sarah			1		18
Roberts, Patty	1	2	1		16
Gause, William	2	3	3		37
Clark, Henry	3		3		19
Taylor, Mary			2		3
Corneers, John	1		4		
Wills, Henry	1		2		
Sillars, Mathew	1	2	2		
Sillars, Elisha	1	3	1		
Malsby, Samuel	1	3	2		
Quince, Richard	1		2		40
Weathers, Thomas	1		3		23
Lord, William	1	1	3		15
Rulks, Samuel	3	1	3		6
McAlester, Archibald	1				70
McAlester, James	1				13
Wear, George	1				21
Davis, Thomas	3	1	3		35
Supper, Isaac	1	2			
Supper, Clemon	1	2	3		
Elkson, Samuel	2		2		
Elkson, Benjamin	2		6		
Supper, Jesse	1	1	1		
Rutterland, Reddon	2				2
McKethern, Gillard	1	1	2		
Howard, George	1	1	6		
Ward, John	3	2	4		
Hickman, Thomas	1	1	1		
Hickman, Samuel	1		2		
Runneles, William	1	2	3		3
Solio, Silvenus	1		1		
Mansfield, William	2	2	3		
Sellars, James	1	3	1		
Little, Thomas	3				
Bennet, Joseph	1	1	2		
Bousman, Etherland	1	2	3		
Hill, Joel	1	2	3		
Hill, Ezekel	1	3	4		
Colbert, James	1		2		2
Conniel, Redy	1		1		
Newel, Peter	1	1	4		
Aderson, James	1	1	4		2
Taylor, Benjamin	2	2	7		
Gressel, William	1	3	5		12
Taylor, Benjamin	1		2		
Hargroves, Samuel	1	1	5		
Wengate, William	1	1	4		7
Simmons, Benjamin	1	3	1		
Simmons, John	1	1	3		
Russ, John	2	3	1		1
Floyd, Morris	1	2	4		
Sellars, William	1	3	4		
Sellars, Jordan	1		2		
Floyd, Bits	1	1	2		
Roach, James	1		4		
Ward, Milly	3	3	7		
Dugger, John	1	4	2		
Edwards, Thomas	1	4	4		
Stevens, Mekajah	1		1		
Soles, Timothy	1		2		
Soles, Nathaniel	1	1	2		
Goodman, Luke	1	1	2		
Soles, Joseph	2	1	7		
Imrit, Elnis	1	1	4		
Carter, William	1				
Alford, Amy	1	2	3		
Moony, William	1		8		7
Beck, John	1	2	4		
Reaves, Solomon	1	5	3		
Hickman, Samuel	1	1	3		
Sugs, Ezekel	2	2	3		
Gooden, Jonas	3		2		
Arnold, Elinor		1	3		
Simmons, Ann	2	2	2		
Simmons, John	1		2		
Norris, Frederick	1		2		
Norris, William	1		2		
Norris, Jerutia			2		
Benson, Nathan	1	1	2		
Marlow, Nathan	1	1	5		
Simmons, Thomas	3	1	3		
Sims, William	1	3	3		
Duncan, Elias	1	3	3		
Mooney, John	2	3	2		3
Stevens, Alexander	1	1	6		3
Counsel, Hardy	1	1	3		
Simmons, John	1				
Smith, Simon	1	2	2		
Clark, Benjamin, Jur	1	3	1		
Hardy, Andrew	1	1	2		
Soles, Mackinne	1	3	1		
Powel, Abraham	1	3	2		
Powel, Jacob	1		2		
Cox, John	1	2	3		2
Connel, Edward	2	1	3		4
Williams, Benjamin	1	1	2		
Soles, Benjamin	1		2		
Williams, Moses	1	1	2		
Mills, John	1	2	3		
Grissel, William	1	2	2		17
Simmons, Moses	1	2	4		1
Russ, Francis	1	2	2		
Simmons, Isaac	1	2	1		5
Stevens, Joshua	1	2	2		
Abbot, William	2		1		
Canniday, John	1		7		
Gore, Jonathan	1	3	5		
Wingate, Sarah	1		1		7
Stevens, Mathew	2	2	4		
Rhoads, John	1		3		
Reaves, Mark	1	2	1		
Rhoads, Mary	1		1		
Rogers, John	1	1	7		
Smith, James	1	1	3		2
Thomas, John	3	3	2		
Lay, John	2	3	2		
Gore, James	1	1			
Ellis, Mary	1	1			
Smith, John	1		3		
Cox, Elijah	3	2	5		
McKeather, Alexander	1	2	1		
Cox, Elisha	2	1	2		
Norris, Thomas	1		2		
Smithart, John	1	3	3		
Jordan, Thomas	1		2		
Smith, John	3	3	3		2
Simmons, Benjamin	1	1	1		
Simmons, John	1	1	1		
Sellars, Mathew	1		2		
Cleus, George	1	1	3		
Outlaw, Palatiah	1	1	2		
Benton, Hardey	1	2	4		
Benton, Joab	1	3	2		
Lay, Joseph	1		2		
Stanley, Hugh	1		3		
Mooney, Thomas	1	2	3		
Stanley, Nedam	1	2	3		
Beasant, Abraham	1	2	3		4

WILMINGTON DISTRICT, BRUNSWICK COUNTY—Continued.

NAME OF HEAD OF FAMILY.	Free white males of 16 years and upward, including heads of families.	Free white males under 16 years.	Free white females, including heads of families.	All other free persons.	Slaves.	NAME OF HEAD OF FAMILY.	Free white males of 16 years and upward, including heads of families.	Free white males under 16 years.	Free white females, including heads of families.	All other free persons.	Slaves.	NAME OF HEAD OF FAMILY.	Free white males of 16 years and upward, including heads of families.	Free white males under 16 years.	Free white females, including heads of families.	All other free persons.	Slaves.
Stanley, Margret		5	2		2	Alston, Francis	2	2	2		60	Dry, William	1				2
Minks, Lucretia		5	2			Howel, James	1					Ward, Frederick	2				6
Murrel, William	1	1	3			Egle, Joseph	1	3	1		29	Smith, Benjamin, Esq.		2	14	2	221
Gore, William, Esq.	1	3	2		2	Moore, Alfred					48	Richards, Nicholas	1	3	1		
Deupree, Lewis, Esq.	1	2	2		34	Flanican, William	1		5								

WILMINGTON DISTRICT, DUPLIN COUNTY.

NAME OF HEAD OF FAMILY.	Free white males of 16 years and upward, including heads of families.	Free white males under 16 years.	Free white females, including heads of families.	All other free persons.	Slaves.	NAME OF HEAD OF FAMILY.	Free white males of 16 years and upward, including heads of families.	Free white males under 16 years.	Free white females, including heads of families.	All other free persons.	Slaves.	NAME OF HEAD OF FAMILY.	Free white males of 16 years and upward, including heads of families.	Free white males under 16 years.	Free white females, including heads of families.	All other free persons.	Slaves.
Rutledge, Thomas, Esq.	3	1	2		9	Grady, Frederick	1	6	5		2	Gauff, Samuel	1		1		
Pearsell, James, Esq.	1	2	4		15	Grady, James	1					Garrin, Bedford	1	1	3		
Beck, William, Esq.	1	3	6		12	Wester, Rheuben	1	1	1			Sulivan, William	2	4	2		6
Hurst, William Broad..	1	2	1			Sholders, Moses	2		2			Linear, James	3	1	5		
Beck, Elizabeth			2		10	Merritt, William	1	5	7			Williams, Labin	2	2	2		
Glisson, Daniel, Esq.	3	2	3		7	Picket, Solomon	1	1	4		1	Connor, Dennis	4	3	6		3
Kornagy, George	3	2	2		12	Hollard, James	1	3	5			Bryan, Auston	1		2		7
Herring, Steven	3	2	2		13	Sholders, William	1	2	1			Garisson, Adonazab.	1	4	1		
Herring, Samuel	1	1	2		1	Glisson, John	1	4	2			Rodes, Benjamin	2		5		7
Stevens, William	2	6	5		6	Smith, George	1	5	3		1	Turlington, John	1	2	4		
Phillips, Samuel	1		2			Gulley, William	2	2	6		1	Branch, Archibald	1	3	1		
Stevens, Loammy	1		2		7	Worsley, John	1		2		4	Brown, Jacob	2	4	4		6
Dickson, Monice	3	1	3			Whitehead, John	2	4	2			Daniel, William	1		2		2
Kinard, Nathaniel	1	1	1			Westbrook, Demsey	1	1	3			Bray, Joseph	1		1		
O'Daniel, Alexander			3		2	Taylor, Jacob	1	4	5			Bray, Joseph, Junr	1	2	5		
Whitfield, Joseph	1		1		2	Houston, Edward	1	4	1		6	Money, Wumlark	2	4	2		7
Carr, Archibald	1	3	4		2	Sutwan, John	2	4	5			Boney, John	1		1		2
King, Charles	2		4		8	Sanders, Alexander	1	1	5			Boney, Daniel	1	2	4		1
Southerland, William	1	3	1		1	Jurnigan, Elisha	2	2	2		1	Dickson, Joseph, Esq.	2	6	3		13
Lowell, Samuel	1	4	3			Richards, John	3					Savage, William	1	1	2		
Blizzard, Hezekiah	1		5			Hodgeson, Aron	2	2	3			Savage, Jacob	1		1		
Cox, John	1	2	3			Keeley, Jonathan	1	2	6			Tearley, Jacob	1	4	1		
Smith, Joseph	1	1	1		3	Lenear, Benjamin	1	2	3			Bearfield, Stephen	2		2		6
Waller, Alexander	1	2	3			Hodgeson, Joseph	1		2			Woodward, John	2		6		2
Moshburn, Benja	2		3			Best, Benjamin	1	1	1			Wilson, Alexander	1		3		1
Federick, Andrew	1	3	2			Best, John, Junr	1	3	2			Bradley, John	2	4	4		
Pearsall, Edward	1		3		7	Best, John, Senr	2	3	1			Midleton, James	1	1	9		5
Armstrong, John	1	7	4			Best, Abraham	1	1	1			Ward, Charles, Esq.	1		2		12
Johnson, Benja	1	1	1		1	Williams, John	2	1	3			Houston, Samuel, Esq.	2	1	4		18
Thomas, Lewis	2	1	3		16	Mumford, Zedekiah	1		4			Blount, Benjamin	2	1	3		
Carrell, Hardy	1	1	3			Strowd, Arthur	1	1	1			Dickson, Alexander	1				7
Johnston, Thomas	4	5	2			Smith, Lewis	3	2	2		1	Woodward, John	1				
Morris, James	2	1	1		16	Parker, John	2	3	3			Woodward, Elisha	1	2	3		
Houston, William Ann.	1		3			Gibbons, George	1	2	4			Murrah, Adam	2	1	4		
Middleton, James, Senr	2	1	5		12	Housman, John	1	5	2			Harris, Jesse	1	4	1		
Brown, Charles	1	1	2		6	Branch, Archibald	1	3	1			Everit, John	1	3	1		
Patterson, James	1	1	1			Gufford, Andrew	2		3		7	Rutledge, Thomas	1				1
Murrow, James	2	2	3		1	Heath, James	1	2	5		1	Blount, Warren	1	5	2		1
Pearsall, Jeremiah	1	2	2		4	Heath, Thomas	1	5	3			Bunting, David	2		2		7
Southerland, John	1	1	2			Grimes, Sampson	1	2	3		2	Wright, Thomas	2		2		1
Cooper, John	1	1	2			Getstrap, Benjamin	1	1	2			Bostick, Charles	2	2	5		1
Hunter, William	1	6	2		3	Taylor, Samuel	1	1	2			Gulley, Nathan	1				
Pelcher, Richard	1	1	3			Midleton, Isaac	1	1	1		2	Millard, Joseph	1	1	4		
Waller, Nathan	1		2		1	Bearfield, Frederick	2		4		6	Gauff, Charles	1	1	3		
Hooks, Charles	1	1	1		1	Beck, William	1		2		2	Millard, George	2		2		
Quinn, David	1		4		1	Swinson, John A	1					Burton, Watson	2		1		
Williams, Joseph	2		1		1	Duncan, Edmund	1	1	2		1	Strickland, Absolam	1	4	2		
Barfield, Lewis	2	3	7		2	Bryan, John	1	2	3			Stone, John	1	1	2		
Hooks, Hillery	1	3	3			Boyt, William	2	2	3			Taylor, Elizabeth			2		
Sanderland, Samuel	1	1	3			Rodgers, James	2	1	2			Outlaw, Martha		2	6		
Johnston, Joseph	4	3	4			Motlen, Abraham	1	2	2		7	Ward, Philip	2	3	8		
Rigsby, William	2	3	3		2	Williamson, James, Senr	2	1	4			Motten, Michial	2	1	6		11
Thomas, Philip	1					Outlaw, James	2	5	5		8	Herring, Stephen	3	1	5		14
Linear, John	6	1	6		1	Grady, William	3	2	5		4	McCollah, John	1	1	2		
Garison, Thomas	2	1	2		3	Roberts, Richard	2	1	2			Peacock, Theophilas	1		1		
Newton, Patrick	2	3	4		8	James, Thomas, Esq	3	1	5		21	Joiner, James	1	4	2		
Stoks, William	2	4	4			Allen, Lewis	1	2	5			Marsey, Berthea		2	3		
Brook, Joseph	1	2	9			Millar, Robert	1		2			Jernigan, Jane	1		3		3
Sunderland, Nicholas	2	1	4		1	Gore, John	1	5	7			James, James	2	1	7		17
Oliver, Francis	1	3	5		3	Midleton, James	1	2	3			Glisson, Michial	1	1	1		
Sulivan, Samuel	1	3	3			Rogers, Pelick	1	1	3			Hill, Thomas	2	2	3		24
Murdock, David	4	3	6		13	Midleton, Stephen	1	2	4			Boyt, Arthur	1	1	3		
Wilkinson, William	2	1	1		10	Rogers, Job	1		1			Carr, John	1	1	1		1
Hines, Lewis	1	2	2		1	Delaney, Benjamin	1	3	3			Boyt, Ephram	1	3	3		
Jones, Elisha	1	1	3			Carr, William	1	2	3		3	Matchett, John	1	3	4		7
Houston, Henry	2	2	7			Beaman, Francis	2	4	4			Gray, William M	1		2		
Millar, Anthony	1	1	4		2	Cramtop, Thomas	1	1	3			Haycraft, John	1	1	2		
Wilkinson, William	1	1	1		4	Thalley, Andrew	1	3	4		1	Gray, Nathan	1	1	2		
Guy, William	3	3	4		4	Wills, Jacob	1	3	3		11	Chambers, John	3	2	4		5
Reardon, James	1	2	2			Southerland, Robert	1	3	5		1	Rhodes, John	1	2	1		
Wright, James	1	3	2		7	Wills, Jacob, Senr	1	1	3		3	Stone, David	1	1	2		6
Gillispie, James, Esq.	3	1	6		30	Rogers, Samuel	2				3	Carlton, John	2	1	2		
Maxwell, James	3	3	2			Herring, Stephen	1	1	4		6	Carlton, Thomas	2	2	3		2
Beck, John	1	2	2		13	Johnston, John	3		2			Stone, Robert	2	2	1		3
Orsburn, Joseph	2	1	2			Herring, Benjamin	1	3	3		1	Strafford, Josiah	1	2	4		
Rouse, Andrew	2	3	1			Carter, Silus	1	4	3			Dobbson, Mary			3		
Williams, Theophilas, Esq.	1	2	5		7	Korneagy, William	3	3	3		4	Robert, William	1	2	1		
Hooks, Thomas, Esq.	1	3	4		16	Worley, Loftus	1	3	4			Taylor, Jacob	1	3	2		
Beorn, Joseph	3	1	4			Worley, Ann	1	1	1			Forehead, James	1	3	2		
Wright, John	3		2		9	Millar, Charles	1	1	2		1	Benton, Joshua	3	2	4		
Beorn, William	1	2	4			Neal, John	2				1	Glisson, Jacob	2	1	1		
Sutwan, Humphrey	1					Swenson, Theophilus	1	3	4			Brock, Jesse	1	5	2		
Evers, John	1	1	2			Alberson, Samuel	3	1	5		5	Brock, Benjamin	1	2	1		
Grady, Alexander	2	3	6		6	Herring, Arthur	1	2	1			Becks, Seven	1	1	1		
Dawson, Isaac	1	3	6		2							Carter, Edward	1	1	2		
												Carter, Solomon	1	1	1		3

WILMINGTON DISTRICT, DUPLIN COUNTY—Continued.

NAME OF HEAD OF FAMILY.	Free white males of 16 years and upward, including heads of families.	Free white males under 16 years.	Free white females, including heads of families.	All other free persons.	Slaves.
Blizzard, Hezzekiah		1	1		
Carter, David	1	4	1		
Deaver, Rheuben	1				
Sumerland, Mary			2		
Jones, Anthony	1				
Snipes, Benjamin	1	2	6		
Pepkin, Lewis	2	2	3		1
Carter, Man	1		1		
Mainer, John	2	1	2		
Flemming, Alexander	1		1		1
Branch, Jesse	2	2	3		
Sumerland, Jacob	5	4	3		
Thomson, Isaac	1				
Moody, James	1	2	1		
Bowan, Elijah	1	4	1		
Gray, Eloderick	1	1	3		
Herring, Isaac	1	3	4		
Johnston, Henry	1		1		
Garione, Likes	1				
Thompson, John	1	1	1		
Thompson, Elizabeth	2	1	2		
Carlton, David	1	1	3		
Brock, Bizon	1	1	3		
Carter, Walker			1		
Thompson, Bersheba			2		
Ellison, Jesse	1	3	5		
Ward, Mathew	1				
Smith, George	3	3	5		
Smith, Frederick	1	5	2		
Moore, William	1	3	2		
Strond, Ludson	1	1	3		
Herring, James	1	4	2		7
Ray, William	1	1	3		
Mainer, Mary		2	2		
Mathews, James	2	3	4		
Dawson, James	1				
Duff, William	4		4		
Fussell, Elizabeth	1	3	4		
Rivenback, Simon	1	5	3		
Smith, Stephen	1	2	3		
Whetfield, William	1	1	3		4
Slocum, Samuel	1		2		1
Pickett, James	2	3	5		1
Pickett, Henry	1	1	2		
Fleming, John	1	1	2		
Beaman, Abraham	2	3	2		
Aron, John	1	1	2		
Federick, William	1	4	4		4
Parker, John	2	2	2		
Alberson, William	2		2		2
Gufford, Stephen	1		1		
Rhodes, Joseph T., Esq.	1		2		8
Casson, Ame	2	2	2		
Fooley, Flood	1	2	3		
McIntire, James	2	1	2		13
Hunter, Priscilla		3	5		4
Gaylor, George	1		2		
Walkins, Leban	4	4	2		9
Martin, Christopher	2	1	4		
Rutley, John	2		3		2
Winders, John	1		5		
Rogers, John, Senr	5	1	4		
Blanchard, Jediah	1	1	2		
Parker, Daniel	1	3	4		
Rogers, John	1	2	5		
Spince, Timothy	2	1	3		
Salmon, William	1		3		
Wilkins, Michial	1	2	3		1
Stokes, Rading	2		2		2
Taylor, John	1	1	4		
Deaver, John	2	3	1		
Taylor, Demsey	1	1	5		
Bowdin, Samuel	1	3	2		
Parker, Peter	1		2		
Bennet, Thomas	2	3	3		1
Durell, John	1	3	4		
Sauser, Joel	1	2	3		
Vick, Joseph	1	1	2		
Korneagy, John	1	2	1		1
Jones, Lewis	1	1	3		
Jones, Anthony	2	2	2		
Tanner, Samuel	1	1	5		
Sevinson, Jesse	1	4	2		
Ward, Andrew	1		3		
Herring, Lewis	1	2	2		1
Vick, John	1	1	2		
Parker, Jonathan	1	4	3		
Wilkerson, William	1	3	4		
Sollus, James	2	1	2		
Chaimbers, Joshua	2	2	4		
Wilkins, John	1		2		
Killbrue, Buckner	1	2	2		5
Bennett, William	1		2		
Bennett, Samuel	1		2		
Taylor, Elef			3		
Harris, Edward	1	1	1		
Taylor, Catharine	1	1	3		8

NAME OF HEAD OF FAMILY.	Free white males of 16 years and upward, including heads of families.	Free white males under 16 years.	Free white females, including heads of families.	All other free persons.	Slaves.
Bowden, Baker	1	2	2		
Walkins, Peter	1	1	1		1
Tunnage, Ezekiel	1		1		1
Duncan, William	2	4	4		3
Millard, Zedekiah	1		2		
Gancy, Mathew	1	3	4		
Duncan, Edmand	2		3		
Duncan, Isaac	1		2		
Johnston, Reubin	4	3	6		
Hicks, Daniel	1	6	4		19
Reaves, Hardy	2	3	5		
Reaves, Adam	1		4		
Rogers, Mark	1	2	3		2
Ratleff, Samuel	1	5	1		
McCann, Hugh	1	3	5		
McCann, William	1		1		
Gilman, John	1				
Federick, Felen	1	4	3		
Chason, Richard	1		2		
Floyd, James	1	3	2		
James, Isaac	1		2		
Murrow, Daniel	1	1	2		1
Bowser, Luke	1	1	2		
Hall, William	3		2		
Coock, Daniel	1		4		
Allen, Ezekiel	1	4	6		
Allen, William	3	6	2		
Jones, Henry	1	3	2		
Jorge, Jesse	1	3	3		
Parker, Hardy	1	1	2		
Bowser, Emanuel	1	1	2		
Fussell, Benjamin	1	1	1		
Bryan, Nicholas	1	1	1		
Cummings, Thomas	2	5	4		
Hedgeman, Lewis	1		2		
Cook, John	1	3	3		1
Cook, Mary	1		2		2
Bryan, Walter	2				
Boney, John	1	4	4		
Knowls, James	2	4	3		
Blanton, John	4	3	4		
Williams, Joseph	1		1		4
Williams, Aron	1	1	2		2
Newton, Lewis	1		3		
Green, John	1	3	6		
Bowan, Elisha	1	1	4		
Cook, Thomas	1	4	1		
Knowls, John	1	2	3		
Green, Thomas	1		3		
Newton, Isaac	1	2	5		
Edwards, Nathan	1		3		
Waters, John	1	3	3		
Brown, Aron	1	2	1		
Alderman, David	1	3	9		
Wallice, Robert	1	1	7		
Wills, Federick	3	2	5		1
Tucker, David	1	3	3		
Wood, Simon	1	1	5		
Mathews, Jacob	1	2	5		
Smith, James	2	3	1		
Davis, David	1		4		
Thompson, Benjamin	1	4	2		
Duff, John	1		2		
Ezzell, Michial	2		2		1
Ezzell, Reuben	1		3		
Ezzell, Benjamin	1	1	1		
Revenback, Simon	1	3	4		
Young, John	2		2		
Brown, John	1	1	2		
Williams, Joseph	2	1	5		4
Hall, David	1		4		
Mathews, Ezekiel	1	1	2		
Green, Lott	1	1	6		
Wilson, John	1	1	2		
Blake, Joshua	1	1	1		
Mathews, John	1	1	2		1
Wilson, Joseph	2		3		3
Roney, Hugh	1				
Shuffield, Amos	1	1	4		
Merett, Charles	1		2		
Mathews, Arthur	1	2	1		
Williams, Stephen	3		4		
Knowls, Robert	1	3	2		
Williams, Byrd	1	1	3		1
Coock, Nathan	1	2	3		
Williams, John	2	3	1		
Williams, Federick	1	6	4		2
Holiway, Taylor	1		2		
Gauff, John, Senr	1	2	4		2
Singleton, David	1	3	3		
James, Elias	2	4	3		
Ensor, Ambrose	1		5		
Murphry, William	2	4	5		7
Bowan, Dann	2	2	4		
Cook, John	2	3	3		
Blanton, James	2	3	1		
Daniel, John	1	2	6		

NAME OF HEAD OF FAMILY.	Free white males of 16 years and upward, including heads of families.	Free white males under 16 years.	Free white females, including heads of families.	All other free persons.	Slaves.
Holms, Hardy	1	1	3		
Holms, Key	2	3	6		
Daniel, Aron	1	2	2		
Burnham, William	3	6	2	1	2
Hunt, John	2	1	2		10
Kennard, Michial	5	3	3		5
Dickson, Moses	2	2	2		
Taylor, William	1		1		
Bradley, Thomas	1	2	1		
Ward, Luke	3		4		3
Harris, William	3	3	6		
Duncan, Edmand	2		3		
Bezzell, Lewis	2	2	5		
Gauff, John	1		3		5
Bezzell, William	3		4		2
Bezzell, Arthur	1	1	1		
Cherry, Willis	1	3	4		4
Duncan, Isaac	1		2		3
Byrd, Robert	6		3		
Ward, William	2	3	6		
Henes, William	2	5	3		
Bezzell, James	2	2	3		3
Flowers, Thomas	2	2	3		1
Penelton, Noah	2	3	6		
Underhill, William	2	3	6		
Beck, Stephen	1		4		1
Reaves, Hardy	4	4	5		
Quinn, James	1		2		
Grimes, Joseph	1	1	1		
Cooper, Benjamin	1		3		1
Farrior, John	1	4	3	1	4
Burgel, Edmand	1		1		
Millard, Jacob	3		1		
McCollah, Thomas	1	3	1		
Daniel, Jeptha	1	1	2		
Jones, Stephen	1	1	1		
Cannon, David	2	4	5		
Odum, George Jurnigan	1	6	4		2
Winders, John	2		4		9
Grimes, James	1	6	2		
Kenan, Michael I	2	5	3		21
Ward, William	1	2	2		5
Guy, Lemuel	2	3	4		
Beesley, Auston	1	2	2		
Guy, James	1	2	3		
Jones, Abe	3		5		
Wood, Peter	2	1	6		
Coventon, Levan	1	1	2		
Connerley, Cullen	2	2	6		3
Cook, John, Senr	1	2	2		1
Brown, Jesse	1	1	4		2
Harrel, Kedar	1	4	2		
Evans, James	2	4	5		1
Caniday, Joseph	1	1	4		
Williams, Jacob	1		3		3
Adams, Robert	1	2	2		
Ward, John	5		1		2
Hawkins, Uzzell	1	2	2		
Stuckey, Lewes	1				
Carter, Zack	1	1	5		
Branch, William	1	3	3		
Newton, James	1	2			
Mobley, Burwell	2	2			
Ivey, John	1		1		8
Linear, Benjamin	2		1		
Linear, Jesse	1	3	2		2
Murrow, James	1	2	2		
Wood, John	2		3		
Halso, John	1	2	3		
Sirews, Joseph	1	5	2		
Woodward, Elisha	2	2	2		1
Murrow, James	2	2	1		5
McGee, John	2	3	2		2
Land, Benatus	1	1	7		
Ward, Samuel	1	1	1		1
Castul, Lydia	1	4	3		
Hancock, Stephen	1		3		1
Farrior, William	1		6		4
Ellis, James	1	2	4		
Hines, Daniel	1	2	3		
Flowers, William	1	2	4		
Fountain, Nathan	1		4		
Myrell, Jo	1				
Hall, William	1	6	2		11
Bachelor, Mary	1	1	3		
Lenear, John	1		2		
Cannon, Abraham	1				
Dobbson, Mary			3		
Haws, James	1	1	3		
Shelton, Thomas	1	1	3		
Shuffield, Elizabeth		6	3		
Johnston, Amus	2	1	3		8
Mashbourn, Christopher	1	1	6		
Shoulders, Lewis	1	1	1		
Sanders, Ezekiel	1				
Baker, Isaac	1		2		

WILMINGTON DISTRICT, DUPLIN COUNTY—Continued.

NAME OF HEAD OF FAMILY.	Free white males of 16 years and upward, including heads of families.	Free white males under 16 years.	Free white females, including heads of families.	All other free persons.	Slaves.
Harp, William	2		2		
Garisson, Epharam	1	2	2		
Rains, Daniel	1	3	2		
Quinn, Calop	1		4		
Simpson, Enoch	1		1		
Winders, James	1	1	6		1
Millar, Heck	1		3		
Pu, Jonathan	1	1	2		
Craford, John	1	3	5		
Halso, Stephen	2	2	4		
Lenear, Jesse	1		4		
Brinson, Henry	1	4	3		
Holingsworth, William	1	1	2		1
Andrews, Abraham	1	2	4		3
Wallace, James	1	4	3		
Collings, William	1	4	3		
Wallace, Jacob	1	1	2		
Tuelling, Robert	3		3		2
Newkirk, Henry	1	2	3		1
James, William	5		3		2
Bryan, Timothy	1	2	3		
Poweil, Brittian	1	2	4		
Meritt, Robert	1	3	4		
Sutton, Elius	2	1	1		
Powell, Hardy	1		4		
Bland, Mary	1		5		
Wills, William	2	1	3		
Willise, Jonathan	1		3		
Gitstraf, Harly	1		3		
Stallings, Shadock	2	2	4		6
Cook, James	1	1	2		
Hall, Isaac	1				
Filman, William	1	4	5		
Hennesey, David	1		2		
Beven, Joseph	1	2	4		
Leigh, Josiah	1	4	4		
Bland, William	1		2		
Stallings, Meshack	1	4	7		1
Hill, Mary			6		
Blanton, Joshua	1	1	2		
Harwell, William	2	4	5		
Coock, John	1	1	2		
Rawlings, John	1	1	5		
Newton, Abraham	2	3	5		
Newton, Jacob	1				
Rogers, Reuben	1		1		
Sweetman, William	1	1	1		
Mathews, John	1		4		
Dickson, Barbara	3	2	5		21
Martin, Paul	1	3	3		
Ward, Joseph	1	2	6		
Jones, Mary		1	7		
Walker, David	1		3		
Taylor, Thomas	2		3		
Bradley, Richard	1	3	1		
Shuffield, Ephram	1	1	2		
Serews, Joseph	1		3		
Spence, Isaac	1	1	2		
Bowden, Nicholas	3	2	1		
Korneagy, George	1		5		1
Branch, Dred	1	1	1		
Korneagy, Jacob	2	4	3		19
Durele, Roby	1		3		
Chandlor, Sarah			4		
Peas, Jonathan	1	1	2		
Rogers, William	1				
Cannon, Mary		1	3		3
Dickson, William	3	2	6		31
Dickson, James	4	3	6		3
Millar, Anthony	1	1	4		2
Southerland, Daniel	2	4	3		1
Norment, Thomas	2	1	2		43
Hill, John	2	3			26
Page, Silus	1		2		
Gibbs, John	5	1	6		4
Simplor, Christopher	1				
Walker, John	2	4	3		
Olat, Adam	2	1	2		
Stocks, Henry	2	1	2		
Newell, Joshua	2	1	2		
Pheps, Thomas	2	1	3		
Cooper, Richard	1	2	2		
Rouse, George	2	4	1		
Allen, Henry	2	3	1		
Jones, Samuel	1	2	1		
Pearce, Mikajah	1	1	3		
Southerland, Phil	2		3		
McGees, William	3	1	8		
McCann, William	3		3		5
Sanderland, Samuel	3		3		
Rigsby, John	1	1	2		
Grimes, Charles	1	2	1	1	
Cooper, George	1	2	6		6
Carr, James	1		2		6
Stuckey, John	2	2	5		7
Wetts, Joseph	1		1		7
Johnston, John	1	1	1		3
Odaniel, Owen	1	1	3		7
Moore, Auston	2	2	1		
Gauff, William	1	2	3		2
Williams, David	1		1		2
Facon, Susanna	2	2	5		8
Blanchard, Uriah	4	2	3		1
Best, William	1	5	3		4
Dickson, Edward	2	2	6		12
James, Charles	1		2		
Mares, Richard	1	1	3		2
Waller, John	2	2	5		1
Waller, Nathaniel	1	1	1		
Streets, Mary		3	3		
Cox, Moses			5		
Edwards, Mathew	1		6		9
Williams, Christan	1	2	3		
Umphreys, John	1	2	4		
Williams, Syvea		1	1		
Houston, Edward	1	3	1		6
Housten, Doctr William	1				10
Smith, Joseph	1		2		3
Millar, George	2		2		14
Housten, Griffeth	1	2	5		
Jones, Jesse	1	1	2		
Serews, Joseph	1				
Hubbard, James	1				6
Smith, Ivey	2	1	2		
Southerland, John	3	2	2		
Lowell, Shadrach	1	2	4		
Toomer, Thomas	1	1	3		
Fountain, Henry	1		2		
Manner, Lydia	1	1	3		1
Cottle, Robert	2	3	2		
Parker, Amiss	2	3	7		
Pickett, Margaret	2	1	2		
Batts, Sarah	2	2	3		2
Paget, Joab	2	4	3		
Paget, James	1		2		
Paget, Cornelar	1	1	2		
Thigpen, Joab	1	4	5		
Pickett, James	2	1	2		3
Thomas, William	4	3	2		5
Parker, Abigal		2	3		
Parker, John	2	1	3		
Thomas, Isaac	1	1	4		3
Williams, Stephen	1		4		
Williams, Jeremiah	1	1	2		2
Williams, Jacob	2		3		6
Henderson, Anne		2	2		
Hubbard, William	1	1	3		8
Moresey, George, Esq	6	3	3		35
Teachey, Daniel	2		1		17
Tonans, Thomas	4	2	6		10
Kenan, James	3	2	6		37
Young, Peter	1	2	2		
Hodgeson, Joseph	1		2		
Ostean, Calop	1	2	2		
Balley, John	1	1	2		
Pickett, William	2	1	1		3
Pickett, William, Senr	1		1		2
Meaks, Reuben	1	2	6		
Sholders, Thomas	2		1		
Burton, William	1	5	1		1
Evans, James	1	5	4		
Lenear, Benjamin	1	1	4		
Cool, Robert	1	2	1		
Batchelor, William	2	1	2		
Jones, Edward	3		2		
Martindal, Stephen	1	4	4		
Martindal, Samuel	1	2	4		
Whaley, Francis	1		4		
Medford, Jeptha	2	4	6		
Thigpin, John	1	5	4		
Thomas, John	1	1	2		
Bracher, Edward	1		2		1
Whaley, James	1	5	5		
Whaley, Samuel	2	3	5		
Whaley, William	2	3	7		
Millar, Stephen	2		1		4
Chambers, James	2	3	4		5
Bass, Jerediah	1		1		

WILMINGTON DISTRICT, NEW HANOVER COUNTY.

NAME OF HEAD OF FAMILY.	Free white males of 16 years and upward, including heads of families.	Free white males under 16 years.	Free white females, including heads of families.	All other free persons.	Slaves.
Long, William	1	5	1		1
Carr, Daniel	2		2		1
Treadaway, Moses	1	1	7		2
Jones, Isabella			2		2
Taylor, Henry	1	2	4		3
Herring, Joshua	1	2	1		9
Holley, Henry	1	2	4		
Snell, Samuel	1		2		
White, John	1	3	3		3
Portervin, Samuel	1				2
Larkins, Roger	1	1	4		2
Boyling, John	1				
Busley, Abraham	3	2	4		1
Richards, Nicholas	1	3	2		
Molpass, John	2	1	7		
Parker, Hardy	2	3	5		
Stanley, James	1	2	1		1
Stanley, James, Senr	4		2		5
Eakins, Joseph	1		4		
Murphey, Fenla	3	1	4		
Sloan, William	2	5	5		1
Bannerman, George	1	1	2		3
Bennerman, Elizabeth	1	1	4		1
Loban, Micheal	3		2		
Dowd, John	1	3	4		
Lewis, John	1	1	1		
Wood, Willis	1	1	3		
Spearman, Edward	3		2		12
Bourdiant, Isaac	1	2	2		
Fellows, John	2	1	3		15
Busley, Thomas	1	1	2		
Moore, Pettigrew	2	4	5		9
Deburgue, Isaac	1	1	1		
Hale, Mathew	1	4	2		
Corbet, Thomas	3	1	3		16
Rettor, Moses	1	3	7		
Rossor, John	2	2	3		
Mason, Richard	1	2	4		
Malpass, Hardy	1	4	1		3
Evans, Edward	1		2		1
Rogers, Thomas	1	1	2		5
Taylor, John	2	1	5		
Sellars, John	1	2	4		2
Larkins, Samuel	1	1	2		3
Carr, Mary			4		
Lee, James	1	2	1		2
Burns, Bartholemew	2	3	5		1
Devane, William	1	1	2		8
Devane, Thomas	1	1	4		18
Devane, Thomas	1	2	3		28
Lamb, William	1	4	1		4
Bond, Scruting	1				
Bowden, John	1	1	4		
Corbet, John	1		3		
Lamb, Isaac	1	2	2		1
Savage, Arthur	1	1	4		
Rivenbark, John	3	2	5		
Devane, George	2	1	4		6
Button, Henry	1	1	3		
Porbus, James	1	1	4		
Pigford, William	3	4	5		
Collins, John	1		3		
Larkins, Benjamin	1		3		4
Geddans, Thomas	2	1	5		
Wright, James	2	2	3		3
Marshall, John	2	3	6		
Rooks, Jesse	1	3	4		1
Smith, James	2	1	3		
Kernear, James	1		3		5
Moore, Jacob	1	2	2		
Moore, Moses	1		4		
Malpass, James	1		3		
Herring, Bright	1	3	1		6
Corbet, Thomas	1	3	3		1
Baker, Arthur	1	4	2		
Jones, John	2	1	8		2
Johnston, Jesse	1	3	2		
Harper, James	2	1	1		13
James, John, Junr	1		1		
Larkins, James	1	2	3		10
Scull, John G., Esq	1	1	5	1	8
Colide, John	1				15
McKensie, John	1		1		
Oliver, John	1	1	4		10
Taylor, William	2	4	4		2
Morgan, Abel	1		1		7
Morgan, Daniel	1		2		1
Prigeon, William	2	1	3		
Lee, Solomon	1	4	7		1
Plair, Thomas	2	2	5		4
Wright, James	3		4		4
Wright, John	3	1	3		
Moore, James	1	2	3		1

WILMINGTON DISTRICT, NEW HANOVER COUNTY—Continued.

NAME OF HEAD OF FAMILY.	Free white males of 16 years and upward, including heads of families.	Free white males under 16 years.	Free white females, including heads of families.	All other free persons.	Slaves.
Ramsey, Thomas	1	3	5		1
Savage, Francis	1	1	3		
Lewis, Thomas	1	2	7		16
Anderson, Elizabeth	1		4	3	
Herring, Mary			2		4
Wilson, James	2	3	7		
Ennis, Daniel	1	3	1		
Walters, William	3	5	6		7
Rogers, James	1		2		4
Shaw, Mary	4		2		
Henry, Mary	1	1	3		
Simpson, Federick	2	5	3		14
Simpson, Charles	1	2	3		11
Grau, William	1	1	2		
Herring, Samuel	2	3	4		
Prooby, Richard	1		3		
McGuilford, James	2		2		12
Strong, David	1	1	6		8
Howard, Paramas	1				4
Bourdeaut, Daniel	1	3	3		5
Buxon, Bryan	5		3		
Lewis, Penelope	1	3	2		
Fennel, Morrice	1	2	4	1	3
Newton, Samuel	1		1	1	1
Jones, David, Senr	2	5	5	2	12
Harvey, John	1	2	3		1
Brook, Lewis	1	2	4		4
Decoine, Edward	1				
Jones, Mrs. Sarah	2	1	4		55
Williams, John Pugh, Esq	1		4		39
Ashe, Samuel, Junr	2				20
Row, John	1				3
Herring, Samuel	1	3	2		
Ramsey, William	2	1	6		
Ashford, John Stone-street	1	1	4		
McGowen, George	1				7
Hale, David	1	2	1		
Johnston, Mathew	2	1	2	1	
Bird, Agnis	1		4		
Hamilton, Malakiah	1	1	1		
English, Margaret		1	4		
Orgood, Priscilla			4		
Bloodworth, Thomas	3	3	3		8
Wilson, Timothy	1	2	8		1
Leddon, Benjamin	1	2	2		7
Bloodworth, Timothy	2	1	5		9
Bloodworth, John	1	2	4		4
Jones, David	1	2	1		15
Corbet, Daniel	1		1		
Blake, Henry	2		1	1	
Croom, Jesse	2	3	3		
Fullard, Plen	1	1	2		2
Blake, John	1		1		
Fullard, Barney	2	1	4		
Norvet, Solomon	2		2		
Stone, Allen	1		1		1
Wills, Marten	1	2	3		10
Williams, David	1	1	1		3
Highsmith, Solomon	4		4		1
Evans, Thomas	1	2	6		
Powell, Jacob	4	1	5		
Newkirk, Abraham	3	1	3		5
Highsmith, David	4		4		1
Herring, Enoch	1	2	2		
Fennell, Nicholas	1	1	3		6
Fennell, Nicholas	1	2	3	1	
Johnston, Jacob	1	1	1		
Portervim, Peter	1				4
Rackford, Patrick	1				
Highsmith, Daniel	1	2	3		
Page, Thomas	1				
Newton, Ann	3	1	6		
Powell, Elisha	1		1		
Bland, William	2		3		
Alderman, Daniel	1	3	5		
Herrington, William	1	3	2		
Penny, Joshua	2	2			
Beardeaux, John	1	2	3	1	
Bourdeaux, Isreal	1	2	2		
Turner, Nedam	1	1	2		
Woodside, Thomas	1		4		
Larkins, William	2				12
Stokely, John	2	4	4		
Lamb, Gibbs	1	1	3		1
Lamb, Thomas	1	3	4		4
Jones, Federick, Esq	1		3		77
Johnston, Thomas	1	2	3	.3	
Ward, Mary Ann		1	3		5
Larkins, John	2	2	5		5
Portervine, Jann		2	4		7
Kernier, John	1				
Moore, John	2		3		42
Moore, James	1		1		16
Smith, James	1	2	1	2	
Moseley, William	1		2		16
Lambert, Elizabeth		2	4		2
Leguiwl, Mathew	1	4	3		5
Moore, George, Esq.			3		34
Macnaughton, Archd	4				4
Johnston, Mathew	1	2	2		5
Heartwell, Daniel	1				
Cook, William	1	2	5		1
Furgus, John	5		2		33
Joslin, Amasiah	2	2	3		6
Machain, John	1		1		
Reardan, Dennis	1				
Wills, Robert	2	2	1		3
Talfair, John	4	2	4		9
Springs, Sedgewick	1	1	1		3
Claypoole, William	1		2		4
Walker, John	4	1	3		61
Cunningham, Thomas	2				9
McNeal, Daniel	1	3	1		2
Wilkins, Mar R	1	2	1		2
Wright, Thomas	1	1	1		31
London, Samuel	5	2	3		8
Nicles, John	2	1	5		16
Quigley, Easter		1	1		
Huntington, Jonathan	1			1	2
Martin, John	1	1	1		8
Johnston, Betty			2	3	
Lefong, Mary					2
Harisson, Joseph	1		3		
Black, Sarah		1	2		
White, Darios			3		
Plain, Nancy		1	1		
Rooks, Henry	1		3		4
Rundle, Richard	4	1	3		4
Bemes, Patty		1	1		
Ceater, Sarah			2		
Lard, Elizabeth			1		
Potts, Joshua	2		2		6
Hoskins, Henry	1	1	1		4
Duffey, Daniel	1		2		
Millar, James	1	1	2		
Maxwell, Peter	1		2		18
Wooton, Nathan		4	4	1	1
Wooton, Thomas	2		3		
Blakely, John	2				2
Wooten, Robert	1	1	2		6
Dodge, Joseph	1	1	2		
Camble, John	2		1		3
Watson, Richard	1		2		5
Tompkins, Jonathan	2				
Golden, Thomas	2				
Johnston, John	3		2		2
Meaks, Mary	8	1	3		6
Routledge, William	1		3	1	2
Erutson, Severin	2				1
Hooper, George	3		2		14
Jones, Edward	1	1	2		2
Maclain, Thomas	1				10
Styles, Joseph	2				
McCollah, George	2	2	3		1
Levi, Jacob	2				
Nicles, Calop	2				
Levi, Eleager	3	1	4		3
Bransby, John	1		1		
Younger, Thomas	1	1	2		2
Jennings, Jonathan	2		2		5
Bradley, John	2		3		5
Maclilling, John	2				3
Lord, John	1		3		10
White, James	2	1	2		2
Henderson, John	1		7		2
Davis, Mrs. Hariot		1	1		3
Davis, Roger	1				
Read, James	2				32
Toomer, Henry	1	2	3		51
Mabron, Arthur	1		4		8
Mabron, William	1				14
Mabron, Mary			2		25
Mabron, Samuel	1	3	1		30
Dorsey, Sal	1	2			11
Cropton, Charles	1	1	2		1
Cunnings, Henry	1	1	1		
Patterson, Elizabeth		1			
Welch, Margaret		1	4		
Stevens, James McCoy	2				6
Davis, Joseph	1		2		1
Carpinter, Peter	1		1		13
Furgesson, Daniel	2	1	1		2
Mooran, James	1		3		6
Bowdish, Else	3		2		
London, John	1				8
How, Robert	1				6
Tucker, Henry	1	1	1		4
Rundelson, Margaret			2		1
Burnard, Isaac	2		3	1	3
Herring, Mrs. Else			1		12
Darlington, Meredith	1		1		
Harris, Peter	2		2		1
Keenan, Mecheal	6		4		3
Plair, Comfort			2		4
Dunlap, Elizabeth			1		
Martelhaney, John	4	1	2		2
Glisser, Abraham	2	1	2		4
James, David	3	1	2		4
Germillion, Henry	1	1	3		1
Allger, James	1		1		1
Cooper, Nathan	1	2	1		
Jecoks, Charles	2		1		13
Blith, George	1		3		3
Balloat, Cesar A.	1		3		17
Dry, Mrs. Mary Jane			1		4
Camble, Mrs. Sarah			1		1
Fryat, Mrs. Sarah		1	3		3
Ward, Anthony			1		1
Geckee, James	1		2		12
Hostler, Mrs. Mary	1		2		35
Everet, Elizabeth		1	1		
McCloud, Daniel	3	1	1		
Herbe, Henry D	1				1
Nutt, William	1		1		2
Nutt, John	1	2	3		3
Camble, Hugh	1	1	1		5
Murprey, John	3		3		
Swann, Mrs. Lameret		1	3		8
Myter, John	1		1		
Gordon, William	1	1	1		1
Beeryman, Robert	1	1	2		1
Halsey, Henry	2	2	1		1
Ross, Wity	1				44
Hanson, Mary			2		2
Cathorda, John	2		2		2
Nance, Samuel		1	2		3
Robenson, Sarah	1	2	2		
Moon, Thomas	1	1	2		14
Davis, William	1		2		
Moon, Mrs. Sarah			2		76
Duncan, Joseph	2				
Brice, Francis			2		5
Major, John	2		2	1	4
Millar, Mary			1		2
Huske, John	3			1	7
Hooper, William	1				10
Flemming, James	2	2	6		47
Mackenzie, John	1	1	2		31
Mackenzie, Mrs. Catharine				1	16
Simpson, Mrs. Ann		1	5		4
Mallet, Peter	1	1	5		105
Burguin, John	4	1	1		81
Walker, James	1		3		96
Qunce, Mrs. Ann			1		21
James, John	2	3	2		26
Barrow, Josiah	1		3		
Walters, Henry	2		2		27
Bloodworth, David	2	2	7		2
Quince, Richard	1				5
Duront, Amond I	1		1		14
Hill, William H	2		2		45
Hill, John	1	2	1		52
Hill, Nathan	1		2		25
Scott, Robert	1	2	2		16
Waddle, Hugh	1		2		85
How, Jane	2		4		24
Wheton, Daniel	1		2		1
Lestor, Robert	1		1		1
Downing, James	2	1	2		4
Vann, William	1		3		
Grout, Daniel	1				
Ervan, John	1		4		9
Ervan, Jane			1		12
Bunting, Samuel	1	5	2		9
Meris, Jane		1	1		18
Waddle, John	1		2		70
Moseley, Samson	1		2		64
Ervan, James	1	2	2		3
Ramsey, James	1				
Beaufort, Frederick	1	1	4		4
Hill, Henry	1	3	2		34
Sampson, Michael	1		2		5
Martin, Clem	2		3		
Fish, Stephen	1		2		
Frances, Anthony	1		2		
Wiggon, John	1	1	1		
Moore, James	1		2		7
Erle, James	1		1		
Shadwick, Joseph	1	5	1		
Toomer, Anthony	1	1	1		11
Jones, Thomas	1		1		7
Swann, John	1	2	2		56
Jones, Federick	2		2		23
Green, William	1		3		31
Mallett, Daniel	1		2		45
Cracke, Thomas	2	1	3		26
Huffum, Richard	2	2	3		1

WILMINGTON DISTRICT, NEW HANOVER COUNTY—Continued.

NAME OF HEAD OF FAMILY.	Free white males of 16 years and upward, including heads of families.	Free white males under 16 years.	Free white females, including heads of families.	All other free persons.	Slaves.
Johnston, Jesse	1	3	4		
Rollens, James	4		2		
Cowen, John	1	1	9		
Bowden, Martha	1	3	3		
Rivenbark, Philip	4	1	7		1
Millar, John	1	1	4		7
Strudwick, Samuel					45
Millar, Bushrod	2				
Parish, Mary	2	1	3		13
Millar, Richard	2				
Lewis, Jacob	1		2		
Henry, William	1	2	2		1
Curray, John	1		1		1
Jones, William	1		4		9
Osbourn, William	1				4
McAllester, Charles	1		2		
Evans, William	2	3	4		21
Green, David	3		3		14
Howard, Nathan	1	1	1		
Howard, Ezekiah	1	3	5		
Henry, Catharine	1		1		2
Cowen, Magnus	1	7	3		1
Huzzey, John	1	4			
Robinson, William	2		5		3
McCalop, Archibald	2	1	2		
Busley, Solomon	2	2	4		2
Cook, Robert	1	2	2		
Sharpless, William	1	3	2		10
Cogdale, Charles	1	3	2		
Devane, Thomas	1	1	4		24
Robinson, Benjamin	1	4	4		34
Devane, James	1	3	3		10
Sulivan, John	1	3	1		
Felyau, Stephen	2		1		1
Felyau, John	1	1	3		
Doty, James	1	1	3		2
Murray, Thomas	1	4	3		1
Calender, Thomas	1	2	3		8
Kingburg, Henry	1		1		
Smith, Nathan	2				
Oldfield, Nathan	1				1
Allen, John	2		1		10
Ashe, Samuel	1		1		40
Sellars, John	1	1	4		2
Sloan, William	1	5	5		
Camble, Alexander	1	1	1		
Walker, James	1		1		
Wood, Willis	1	1	3		
Evans, David	2	2	2		
Squires, Thomas	1		1		
New, William	1	2	2		
Hanchey, Martin	1	1	5		
Armstrong, Thomas	1	2	1		
Ramsey, David	1				
Shadwick, James	2		2		1
Turner, David	1		3		
Tyler, Nicholas	1	1	1		
Jeneft, James	1		2		1
Hines, John	1	1	4		
Collins, John	1	2	3		
Messer, Swan	3	2	5		
Night, Miler	1	2	3		
Hews, Thomas	3				
Carter, Ann			3		
St. George, Elisha	1	2	1		11
Nedes, Cathrine		2	2		3
Walls, Joseph	1	2	2		
Perkins, David	4	1	3		2
Green, Rebecca	1	1	2		
Wood, Edward			1		
Bishop, James	1				
Bowan, Mary			1		
Bowan, Elisha	1	1	3		
Fuch, John	1		2		
Hambleton, James	1		1		
Barwick, White	1		2		
Barwick, Drucilla	1		2		
Nicles, Robert	1	1	1		
Messet, Aron	2	2	6		
Edens, John	2	1	6		3
Nixon, Robert	2	1	7		27
Nixon, Nicholas	1	1	1		10
Towning, James	1	1	3		1

NAME OF HEAD OF FAMILY.	Free white males of 16 years and upward, including heads of families.	Free white males under 16 years.	Free white females, including heads of families.	All other free persons.	Slaves.
Collings, Joseph	2		2		
Edens, Jacob	1		2		
Balston, Peter	3	2	3		1
Blak, John Flemming	1	1	1		
Howard, Christopher	1	2	2		2
Townley, William	1	3	2		
Turnigan, Alexander	1	3	1		
Nixon, Thomas	1	4	3		10
Coston, Isaac	1		4		
Howard, James	2	1	7		7
Coston, John, Senr	1		4		
Coston, John, Junr	1		1		
Hedgman, George	1	1	2		
Smith, James	2		1		
Byard, Ann			1		
Bishop, Thomas	1	2	2		7
McClammy, Luke	2	2	5		9
McClammy, Mark	1	2	5		11
Nioles, John	1		2		
Adkinson, Daniel	4	2	4		3
Sadbury, Stokley	5	1	5		
Barlow, Thomas	2	2	4		2
Camble, John A	1	2	6		36
Doty, Edward	1				31
Read, Arthur	1	2	3		
Cowen, Thomas	1	1	1		1
Merrick, George	1				87
Fewell, Thomas	2		3		
Routledge, Ester					
Ashe, Samuel, Esquire	3	1	2		62
Harp, Mrs		3	2		
Stevens, Zelphia		1	3		
Williams, Henry	2	3	5		4
Craft, Charles	1	2	2		1
Garrell, William	1		4		
Bloodworth, Rebeca		1	5		17
Garrell, Jacob	1		3		
Alexander, Benjamin	1	2	2		
Mathews, John	1	2	3		
Pickett, Thomas	3	2	3		2
Nicles, William	3	1	4		2
Jones, Mrs. Monice			3		17
Henry, Jane			2		
McCollah, Alexander	1		2		8
Henry, James	1		3		
Celson, Daniel	1	1	1		
Beauford, Yarington	2				
Simpson, William	1		1		4
Mott, Benjamin	2	4	4		9
Messam, Patsey	1	1	3		
Young, Catharine		1	2		4
Nicles, John	1		3		
Riley, John	1		2		
McKinney, Charles	1		1		
Logan, George	6	1	3		9
Holden, John	1				
Russell, Edwar	1	2	5		
Wane, John	2	2	4		
Hewlet, Jeremiah	1	1	3		1
Wilson, John	1	1	2		1
Chester, Nixon	1		2		4
Surs, John	1	1	4		
Rebenson, Thomas	4	2	6		
Steremeri, George	2	2	2		
Pervines, Elinor			2		2
Johnston, William	1		2		
Hunt, John	1		2		
Henderson, Daniel	1	2	2		
Solders, Ephram	1	1	3		
Simmons, Thomas	1	2	2		7
Deal, Adam	1	4	6		
Venters, James	1	2	3		2
James, Sarah	1	1	5		
James, Isaac	2	2	5		
James, Thomas	1	1	1		
Deal, Isaac	1		2		
Scarborough, Thomas	1		1		
Sutten, Joshua	2	2	5		13
Shepherd, Jacob	1	2	2		
Rochel, Etherington	1	2	6		
Rochel, Amos	1	4	5		
Burton, Thomas	2	1	2		12
Henderson, John	1	2	4		

NAME OF HEAD OF FAMILY.	Free white males of 16 years and upward, including heads of families.	Free white males under 16 years.	Free white females, including heads of families.	All other free persons.	Slaves.
Howard, John	1	1	2		22
Livington, George	1	1	3		13
Blanks, William	2	2	4		
Shadwick, Benja	1	2	2		
Shadwick, Minite	1	2	3		
Morris, John	2	4	2		
Looper, Thomas	1		2		4
Rouse, Sander	2	2	5		4
Sell, Oswell	1	2	3		7
Smith, Peter	2	1	5		
Howard, Thomas	1		4		5
Cook, Archabald	2	2	5		
Hazzell, Sophia			1		14
Roach, William	2		1	1	2
Jones, John	2	1	2		
Little, Robert	1				
Adkins, Jesse	1	2	2		
Newton, Edward	1	4	3		
Henry, Francis	1	2	1		
Hines, Lewis	3	4	6		
Canble, Edward	1				
Millinder, Mrs			2		
Robinson, Calop	1		2		
Cutter, William	1		2		5
Henry, Robert	1	6	3		
Murpry, Robert	1		3		4
Henry, William	1		1		1
Pages				5	2
Hannah				1	1
Hesse				1	3
Johnston, Abram				4	
Martin, John				6	
Martin, Robert				4	
Jacob, John				9	
Freeman, William				2	
Jacobs, Mathew				2	
Jacobs, Primus				1	
Jacobs, Zachariah				4	6
Jacobs, Mathew				8	
Benson, James	1		1		
Wilson, Ambrose	2		4		
Kelley, William	1		1		
Murpry, Hugh	1	1	4		4
Russ, Thomas, Senr	2	2	5		6
Russ, Thomas, Junr	1	2	1		
Berry, Elizabeth		1	3		
Singlary, Mary	1	2	2		
Benson, Elizabeth	3	2	3		
Davis, Ezekiah	1				21
Fogetu, Edmand	1				7
Singlary, Brate	2	3	2		6
Struley, William	1	3	2		
Huffum, Patty	2		7		2
Russ, Eley	1	2	2		
Satter, Richard	1	2	3		8
Lock, Unus			1		
Lock, Isaac	1	1	1		1
Larkins, John	1		1		
Burdaux, Peter	1	3	4		
Edwell, Benja	1	3	3		
Daves, John	1	3	5		
Parker, William	2		4		1
Andrews, John, Junr	1	6	1		
Meridith, Nathan	2	4	6		
Smith, Drury	1	1	2		
Henry, Alexander	1	1	3		1
Robinson, John	1	2	2		
Smith, Benja	1	2	2		
McMellens, Robert	1	1	5		
Sutten, John	1	1	1		1
Smith, James	1	2	4		
Maclemon, William	1		1		
Camon, Lucrescia	1	2	2		
Crumertree, William	3	2	8		5
Barry, William	1	1	2		
Stewart, Duncan, Esq	3		6		30
Sekes, Josiah	4	2	8		
Sekes, John	1		1		
Row, Frederick	1				
Fisher, Thomas	1	3	3		
Sutten, William	1	3	3		

WILMINGTON DISTRICT, ONSLOW COUNTY.

NAME OF HEAD OF FAMILY.	Free white males of 16 years and upward, including heads of families.	Free white males under 16 years.	Free white females, including heads of families.	All other free persons.	Slaves.
Shaw, William	1	1	2		7
Barono, Arthur	5	5	5		
Williams, Ann Mary	1		3		16
Williams, Obed	1		2		5
Shackelford, George	1	2	2		12
Sumner, Francis	1		2		
Askew, Nathan	1	3	3	1	
Williams, James	1		3		8

NAME OF HEAD OF FAMILY.	Free white males of 16 years and upward, including heads of families.	Free white males under 16 years.	Free white females, including heads of families.	All other free persons.	Slaves.
Wood, Jacob	1	1	1		3
Sanders, Robert	1	1	3		3
Battle, Ephram	2	4	4		17
Snead, Robert W., Esq.	2				24
German, Lawrence	1	3	4		
Wood, Jesse	3	1	3		11
Hufman, Christopher	1	3	3		
Elles, John	1	1	1		1

NAME OF HEAD OF FAMILY.	Free white males of 16 years and upward, including heads of families.	Free white males under 16 years.	Free white females, including heads of families.	All other free persons.	Slaves.
Lillebridge, Joseph	1		5		13
Barrow, Zachariah	1	1	5		6
Barrow, Abraham	1	1	2		3
Barrow, Abraham, Senr	2	1	4		5
Pitman, Jordan	1		3		
Bell, William	1				
Shaw, Stephen	1		1		
Mills, James	1	1	3		

WILMINGTON DISTRICT, ONSLOW COUNTY—Continued.

NAME OF HEAD OF FAMILY.	Free white males of 16 years and upward, including heads of families.	Free white males under 16 years.	Free white females, including heads of families.	All other free persons.	Slaves.
Mills, Joshua	1	4	2		
Mills, William	1	5	2		
Mills, George	1		3		5
White, Edward	1	1	3		
Wiley, Hardy	1	1	4		
White, George	1	3	3		
Thigpin, Jonas	1		2		
Thigpin, Joshua	1	2	2		
Wiley, Hardy	1	3	2		
Dudley, Christopher, Esq.	1	3	1		17
Dudley, Rebecca		2	2		17
Roan, William	1				
Snead, Robert, Senr	2	1	2		11
Waldron, Mary	1	2	4		4
Waldron, William	2	3	3		
Barono, James	1	2	2		
Gland, Thomas	2	2	4		
Parker, John	2	6	2		
Hufman, Jacob	1		3		
Sumner, Phibia			2		
Pennywell, John	1		2		
Ramsey, Jeremiah	1		2		
Ramsey, David	2	1	2		
Mills, Sarah	1		2		
Laws, Wilson	1		1		
Shingleton, Polly	2		2		
Umphrys, Mary		1	2		
Shingleton, Lurana		1	1		
Umphrys, Eustace	2	1	2		
Umphrys, Eustace, Junr	1	2	3		
Umphrys, Josiah	1	1	4		
Umphrys, Francis	1		2		
Umphrys, Jacob	2		2		
Parker, Thomas	1	3	1		
Mashbourn, James	1		2		
Rose, Betty			3		
Langston, James	1	1	3		
Foster, William	1	5	3		
Brown, Demsey	1	2	2		
Cox, Aron	2	5	5		
Cox, Jesse	1		1		
Cox, Charles	1	3	5		
German, Susanna		3	1		
Shackleford, Elizabeth	1	1	3		
Gland, John	1	3	2		
Parker, Francis	1		5		
Britton, Benjamin	1	2	1		
Ward, Patty	3	1	1		
Horn, Thomas	1	3	2		
Petuway, Peton	1	1	1		3
Turner, Mabry	1		1		7
Averet, John	1	2	4		2
Williams, Benjamin	1		1		
Wilder, Jonathan	1		1		2
Yates, Benjamin	1	3	4		
Williams, Samuel	1	3	4		
Averet, Jenken	1	2	1		12
Brady, Samuel			2		4
Smith, John	1		4		
Young, Edward	2	2	2		13
Williams, Jesse	2	3	3		13
Grant, Rubean, Esq.	2	1	5		32
Grant, Bazel	1	1	2		6
Horn, Henry	1	2	3		
Grant, Alexander	1	2	3		4
Greer, John	1	2	5		
Mumford, James	1	1	4		32
Brady, Joshua	1				4
Williams, Benjamin	2		2		7
House, Mary	2		2		8
Davis, Jeremiah	1	1	3		7
Murrel, William	1	5	4		8
Ballard, James	1		2		1
Ballard, Joshua	1		1		
Ballard, Joshua, Junr	2		2		
Umphrys, David	1	3	3		7
Oliver, Benjamin	1		2		10
Hopkins, Neal	1	2	2		5
Seles, John, Senr	2	1	5		
Henderson, Thomas	1	4	2		2
Williams, Uzzey	2	2	8		18
Yates, Daniel	2	3	4		27
Averet, Arthur	2	2	3		2
Gregory, Hardy	1	2	3		17
Mumford, Lewis	1	2	2		17
Wilder, Joel	1	1	7		1
Wilder, Hopkins	1	1	1		2
Williams, Thomas	2	4	4		7
Jones, John	2	4	4		7
Baezdon, Jesse	1	3	3		
Williams, Nathan	1	1	3		
King, James	1		1		1
Jones, William	2	3	3		4
Barber, Thomas	2	1	2		
Manor, Henry	1	4	2		
Manor, Jacob	1	1	1		

NAME OF HEAD OF FAMILY.	Free white males of 16 years and upward, including heads of families.	Free white males under 16 years.	Free white females, including heads of families.	All other free persons.	Slaves.
Stiles, John, Junr	1		1		
King, William	2	5	1		
Daves, Mathew	1	2	1		
Brown, Jacob	2	3	3		
Hall, Mary		1	4		
Gurganus, Nicholas	2	1	7		2
King, John	1	1	4		1
Feutral, Moore	1	2	1		
Nixon, Robert, Senr	2		3		6
Fields, Zachariah	1	2	3		
Cox, William	2	4	1		
Barfield, Moses	2		4		1
Barfield, Aron	1	3	1		
Screws, Joseph	3	2	9		
Jordon, John	1	1	2		
Bachelor, Lydia			2		
Manor, Elizabeth	1	2	1		
Calvert, Ruth		1	2		
Brown, Nancy			2		
Mashbourn, Mary	2	1	2		
Daves, Aron	2	3	5		
Rainor, Molley	1	1	5		
Fox, Moses	1	1	1		2
Cummings, Susannah		1	2		
File, James	2	3	5		2
Dunn, James	1	1	8		1
Jones, John	1	2	3		
Brenson, John	1	1	1		
Bond, John	1	3	2		
Mason, Richard	1	2	1		1
Cason, James	1				
Jones, Benjamin	1				
Turner, James	2	2	2		3
Shepherd, Sipian	1	1	2		
Evans, John	1	1	2		
Evans, Samuel	1		2		
Shepherd, Stephen	1		1		
Hall, Benjamin	1		1		4
Bryan, Jonathan	1	4	4		2
Heidelburg, Catharine	1	1	3		3
Heidelburg, John	1	1	2		1
Dickson, Jonathan	3	2	3		
Burnson, Adam	1	4	2		
Mabees, Charles	1	1	2		
Bennett, William	3				1
Mashbourn, Joseph	1	1	6		7
Dunn, Drury	1	1	1	1	
Brinson, George	2				5
Shepherd, Daniel	1		4		3
Love, Amos	1	2	7		9
Rhodes, Woodhouse	2	3	3		19
Hatch, John	1	2	2		10
Rundles, William	1	4	4		
Gurganus, Zachariah	1	2	3		4
Hadnot, Lebins	1	1	2		2
Whitehead, Ebenezar	1	2	3		
Lee, David	1	3	5		
Ennet, John	1				
Haney, Priscilla		1	4		
Fisher, John	1	3	4		
Aman, Jacob	1	1	3	1	1
Grant, John	1	1	4		
Wadkins, John	1	2	2		
Smith, John	1				
Jenkings, Liuis, Junr	1	2	3		
Wilson, James	1		4		
Wood, Mark	1	1	3		
Kemmy, Thomas	2	2	3		
Green, Benjamin	1	3	1		1
Sanders, Elizabeth		3	2		
Loyed, Thomas, Junr	1	3	1		1
Dunn, Henry	1		3		1
Miles, Sarah			1		
Umphrys, William	1	1	4		
Simpson, Richard	2	1	3		7
Wheler, William	1	1	2		6
Mellon, Jonathan	1		1		
Ellis, Ely	1		1		
Butler, Jesse	1		5		
Butler, Robert	1		5		
Pescot, William	1		3		
Pitts, Thomas	1		1		1
Lee, Charles	1		1		
Butler, John	1		4		
Ward, Solomon	1	4	3		9
Jarrott, Isaac	1	1	2		10
Lairy, Darby	2	3	4		
Murray, Nathan	1	2	3		
Jenkings, William	1		2		1
Jenkings, George	1		2		2
Craft, Charles	1		1		9
Orrel, John	5	1	2		
Brinson, John	2		3		
Thomas, Richard	2		3		4
Fullar, John	1	2	3		
Haus, Joseph	1	1	1		
Whitus, Thomas	1				

NAME OF HEAD OF FAMILY	Free white males of 16 years and upward, including heads of families.	Free white males under 16 years.	Free white females, including heads of families.	All other free persons.	Slaves.
Parish, Stephen	1		2		
Williams, Stephen	1	2	1		3
Whitus, Mary	3		3		6
Flay, Thomas, Junr	2	4	3		12
Landing, Stephen	1	1	3		
Johnston, Isaac	1	1	3		
Pollock, William	1	2	1		
Roach, John	1		1		
Grissom, John	2	3	4		2
Wilson, James	1		3		
Fullard, Thomas	1	4	3		
Thomson, Margaret			4		
Thomson, Thomas	1				
Hall, Edmund	1		2		
Penalton, Mrs			4		
Butt, John	1		4		4
Mannon, Lydia	1	1	3		1
Fullard, Mary			3		
Gibson, John	1		1		
Thompson, James	1		2		
Thompson, Enoch	1	2	1		
Meirrah, Hannah		1	2		
Mills, David	1	2	5		
Spicer, Elzey	1	1	3		24
Gill, Benjamin	1		2		
Gun, Alexander	2	2	2		
Perry, Thomas	1	1	2		
Burnet, John	1	1	4		
Averet, John	1		1		
King, Priscilla	1		2		13
German, Moses	2	3	4		
Malsby, Thomas	1		2	2	
Edins, James	1	1	3		
Walton, James	1	2	1		
Hobs, Simon	2	1	1		
Henderson, Nancy			3		
Howard, Thomas	1	3	4		18
Barber, Richard	1		1		
Fengsenger, William	1		2		
Edins, Thomas	1	2	4		
Harrison, John	1	2	5		
Hatch, Asa	1		1		24
Avert, Benjamin	3	2	3		1
Goodeem, Abner	2	2	4		
Ennet, Joseph	3	1	2		5
Norman, Elijah	1	2	3		
Camble, Sarah	1		2		2
Hardeson, Gabriel	2	1	2		
Hardeson, Jesse	1		2		
Devawl, George	1	3	3		
Rhodes, Solomon, Senr	1	1	3		
Rhodes, Solomon, Junr	1		2		
King, John	1	1	1		2
Busby, Benjamin	2	1	3		
Spicer, John, Esq.	2	5	3		22
King, Benjamin	1	2	1		5
Williams, Robert	1	3			2
Read, William	1	3	2		
Russel, Linton	1	2	1		
Caston, Thomas	1		2	1	
Jones, Peter	1	2	2		
Harris, David	1	1	3		
Lain, James	1	2	3		
Adamson, George	1	1	3		1
Fumviel, Jeremiah	2	3	1		30
Wilkins, John	1	1	3		3
Fumveil, Lucy	2		2		15
Hunt, Onsipharus	2	2	5		
Hardison, Charles	1	4	3		
Singluf, Aron	1	1	1		1
Hall, Winey		1	3		1
Dickson, John	2	3	2		
Hobs, James	1		2		
Jenkings, Joshua	1	1	1		
Collear, John	1		2		3
Hansley, John	3	3	2		3
Austin, Francis	1	3	2		
Brice, Cornelias	1	1	3		
Cranford, Mary			3		
Hansley, William	1	2	1		4
York, John	3		1		5
Ennet, Nathaniel	1	3	1		
Curtis, George	1	2	2		
Williams, Richard	1		4		
Parker, Ann		2	2		
Rows, Dedemiah	1		1		1
Ketchum, Jonathan	1	1	2	2	2
Badock, Jonathan	1		2		
Owens, Whitton	1		2		
Wills, William	1	1	3		
Hawkins, Stephen	1	1	4		1
Hawkins, Ezeriah	1	4	4		1
Hawkins, William	2	2	4		2
Burne, Francis	1		3		5
Taylor, Isaac	2	1	2		
Milton, Joseph	2	4	4		

WILMINGTON DISTRICT, ONSLOW COUNTY—Continued.

NAME OF HEAD OF FAMILY.	Free white males of 16 years and upward, including heads of families.	Free white males under 16 years.	Free white females, including heads of families.	All other free persons.	Slaves.
Hawkins, John	1	1	2		
Perry, William	2		3		1
Cullay, Edward	1	1	2		
Gray, Sarah		1	3		
Scott, Lucin	3	1			
Price, Benjamin	1	1	2		
Howard, William	2	1	3		1
Rows, Martha			2		
Spooner, Susanna		2	5		
Smith, Calop	2		3		
Smith, William	1		4		
Sanders, John	2	1	4		5
Scott, Lurina			3		
Hazzard, George	1	2	3		6
Rows, Elizabeth		1	2		
Cranford, James	3				
Lain, James	2	1	2		
Clark, William	2		1		
Burns, Federick	3	3	4		8
Gregory, Jesse	4	2	4		
Williams, Benjamin	3	3	4		9
Murrell, John	1		1		
Dudley, Edward	1		2		4
Godfree, William	1	3	1		2
Lyster, Banister	2	1	4		6
Hicks, Lewis	1		1		3
Noble, Samuel	3	2	2		7
Orrel, James	1		2		1
Johnston, Thomas, Junr	1	1	2		
Eagerston, John	2	1			1
Edmandson, James	1	1	5		
Johnston, John	2	1			1
Fair, Richard	1	3	6		5
Willey, Alexander	2	1	2		
Murrell, Kemp	1	3	2		1
Murrell, William	1	1	2		
Johnston, Thomas, Senr	2	4	4		9
Loyed, William	1	3	4		
Godfrey, Enoch	1	2	5		1
Ward, Richard	1		3		
Godfrey, Francis	1		2		
Orrell, Thomas	1	2	1		1
Edmandeon, William	1	1	3		
Hammond, Edward	3	4	3		8
Jarman, Thomas	1		4		
Willey, John	1		3		3
Howard, Edmand	1	3	3		
Godfree, Francis	1		1		
Thompson, Charles	1	2	5		5
Weeks, John	1	1	3		
Bryant, Thomas	2		3		1
Eagerton, William	2	3	5		
Hazelip, Abner	1	1	3		
Marshall, Joseph	1	1	3		
Littleton, Lurry, Junr	1	3	2		
Littleton, Lurry, Senr	3		3		
Taylor, William Wilkins	1	3	2		7
Marshall, Pernal	1		2		
Huggans, Francis		2	2		
Huggins, Jacob	1		1		
Eagerton, James	1	1	2		5
West, Mary	1	2	2		
Hicks, Solomon	1	2	4		
Ball, Nancy	2	1	2		
Marshall, Umphry	1	2	2		
Row, James	1	1	1		
Farnell, Benjamin	1	2	1		2
Farnell, Mikajah	1	1	1		5
Morton, William	1		1		
Heart, Absolom	1		1		
Simons, Nancy			2		3
Simmons, Benjamin	1	1	3		
Farnell, Elizabeth	1		1		2
Ward, Joseph	1		3		
Dudley, Stephen	1	1	2		
Roberts, Holster	2	3	3		30
Newton, Elijah	1	3	2		4
Newton, Mn		1	3		
Ball, James	1		2		
Barns, Ezikiah	1	1	4		
Milton, Edward	1	1	6		
Yewell, William	5	1	4		1
Milton, Benjamin	1	2	2		
Milton, James	3	4	4		
Edwards, Henry		2	2		3
Todd, John	1	3	1		
Todd, Aron	1		2		
Todd, Moses	1		3		
Erixson, Jonathan	1	1	1		
Yewell, John	2	2			
Jarrott, John, Junr	1	1	5		
Erixson, Samuel	1		1		
Farrow, Benjamin	1	4	2		
Collens, Richard, Senr	4	1	2		
Thomas, Betsey			2		
Collens, Richard, Junr	1		6		

NAME OF HEAD OF FAMILY.	Free white males of 16 years and upward, including heads of families.	Free white males under 16 years.	Free white females, including heads of families.	All other free persons.	Slaves.
Taylor, John	1	2	3		
Heart, John	1	2	2		
Hicks, Robert	1	2	2		3
Hadnot, Aldridge	2	1	1		15
Pearson, Thomas	1	1	2		2
Pearson, John	1	1	5		1
Edge, John	1	3	4		
Hadnot, Stephen	1	2	3		
Robenson, Mr	1	2	3		
Hancock, Enoch	3	1	3		2
Snead Thomas	1	1			
Cary, Nathan	1	1	3		1
Mumford, William	1	4	3		16
Weeks, John	3	3	3		
Venturs, Arthur	2	3	4		
Erexon, Andrew	1	2	2		
Jarrott, John	1		1		
Craeg, Elias	1	3	1		
Hancock, Nathaniel	3	2	4		1
Howard, Josiah	1		5		19
Simmons, Henry	1		5		
Mitchell, George, Esq	3	7	3		29
Gibbs, William	1		1		2
Cary, Miles	1				
Ward, David	1	2	7		15
Ward, Cari	1	1	4		22
Delany, Thomas	1	5	3		4
Ward, Benjamin	1	1	1		4
Ward, Edward, Esq	1	1	1		30
Fumviel, Brice	1		2		8
Felyau, James	1	1	4		4
Davis, James	1	1	3		3
Ross, David	1	2	2		
Wilson, Josiah	1	4	5		
Wilson, James	3	4	3		
Nixon, Charles	1	3	4		3
Hadnot, Joseph	1	1	2		
Strange, James	1		3		
Ryals, Nancy		1	2		
Tow, Abigail		2	5		
Burns, Otway	2	1	5		4
Jones, Kibby	1		3		17
Pastures, John	1	1	3		
Burnett, Abraham	1	2	5		7
Jones, Hull	1	4	3		7
Marcy, Edward	1		2		3
Mumford, Jehue	1		2		1
Fulcher, Benjamin	1	3	1		6
Sanders, Jesse	1	1	4		3
Mumford, Leark		3	1		7
Woodman, John	2		3		
Newtout, Elizabeth			3		
Whaley, Eogdal	1	1	2		
Conneway, John	2		3		1
Hewitt, John	2	1	2		1
Moss, John	2	2	5		
Rodgers, Daniel	1		3		
Wire, Thomas	1	1	3		
Wren, Catherine			1		5
Sharard, Amy		1	2		
Bell, George	1	1	2		
Farior, Benjamin	1		2		
Trott, Richard	1	1	2		
Dodd, George	1	1	2		
Burnett, John	1	3	1		1
Lovett, John	1	1	1		7
Snead, John	1	1	3		
Gibson, Richard		1	6		3
Newbowl, Levi	1	2	6		1
Martek, John	1		1		4
Burnett, Isaac	1		1		2
Newbowl, Sarah		1	3		
Taylor, Moses	1	2	5		
Truman, Patience	2	3	5		1
Arnold, Peter	4	1	1		
Starkey, John	2	1	5		50
Hicks, David			6		
Horton, Abraham			3		
Dudley, Betsey	2		2		1
Hewbanks, John	1		1		
Hewbanks, Elijah	1		4		4
Hewbanks, Thomas	3	1	6		4
Hewbanks, Ezekiel	1	1	1		
Simpson, Adra	2		2		
Bedale, Elijah	2		3		
Trott, Adam	1	3	1		
Trott, John	1	2	1		
Tolman, John	1				
Starkey, Elizabeth		2	3		35
Fields, Samuel	4		6		
Fields, Jacob	2	2	4		5
Fields, James	2		2		2
Fields, Moses	1		2		1
Keys, Joseph	1	2	1		6
Smith, Calop	3	3	11		
Sparman, George	1	2	2		10
Gibson, Thomas	3	3	3		

NAME OF HEAD OF FAMILY.	Free white males of 16 years and upward, including heads of families.	Free white males under 16 years.	Free white females, including heads of families.	All other free persons.	Slaves.
Gibson, Abraham	1		2		5
Perry, Waxwell	1		2		
Owens, Edmund	2				1
Williams, Stephen	1		3		
Wood, James	2	1	5		
Gibson, Archibald					8
Jones, William	1		1		8
Marshall, Leark		1	1		
Newton, Daniel	1		5		3
Willey, Susanna	2	1	5		
Godley, John	1	1	2		2
Willey, John Alexr	1		2		7
Chalcraft, Isaac	1		2		5
Cray, Joseph Scott, Esq	1	1	2		30
Chalcraft, Stephen	1	3	2		2
Chalcraft, Anthony	1	1	3		9
Johnson, Rachel			2		
French, James	1				
West, Levi	1	1	3		
Hawkins, Obediah	1		1		
Melton, Mary Ann	2	2	2		
Eagerton, James	1	2	2		5
Eagerton, Charles	1		4		4
Hawkins, White Huck	1				
Averit, John	1				
Godley, Ann		1	3		
Linger, Elizabeth		1	3		
Hall, Doratha		3	2		13
Brinson, Mathew	1	1	3		
Serews, William	1	1	1		
Burton, Charles	1	1	1		
Shepherd, Benjamin	1	1	1		
Walton, James	1	1	3		
Garnton, Daniel	1	1	3		
Aman, Philip	1	5	6		
Brinson, Gause	1	4	1		4
Pitman, Arthur	1	1	2		
Fisher, John	1	3	3		
Cray, William	1	3	3		13
Fair, John	1	2	2		
Lee, Rachael		1	4		3
Walker, Samuel	1		2		6
Ambruse, Daniel		3	4		5
Farnell, Thomas	3		1		3
Marshall, Jonathan	1	1	2		
Marshall, Isaac	1				
Marshall, John	1				
Morton, Peter	3	2	3		7
Morton, Richard	1		1		
Wood, Penelope	3		3		
McKenney, John	4	2	5		
Morton, Joseph	2	1	3		
Morton, Joseph	2		3		
Askins, William	3	2	4		
Melton, Richard	1	1	3		
Yates, James	2	2	3		
Chambers, Sarah	3	1	3		
Gairy, George	1	3	1		
Wood, Frederick	1	1	2		
Bowen, John	1	4	2		
Bowen, Joshua	1	1	2		
Jackson, Bazzell	1				
Wood, Joseph	1				
Carver, Henry	1	1	1		
Smublage, John	1	1	7		
Strange, Seth	2	3	3		
Kelly, Betsy		2	2		
Williams, William	1	3	4		
Teachy, John	1	2	3		
Williams, Stephen	1	4	2		
Skipper, Nathan	1	2	5		
Brown, Stephen	1	2	5		
Skipper, Joseph	1	4	2		
Baizdon, Patience			1		
Baizdon, Josiah	1	4	6		
Sumner, Mathew	1	1	1		
Petteway, Amy			1		
Cermott, Alexander				1	
Mason, Abraham	3	2	5		2
Boardsman, Jonathan	2	1	3		1
Adams, Penelope			1		
Hopson, Horatia	1		5		
Adkinson, Harisson	1	2	3		
Bennet, James	1	1	5		
Pierce, Benjamin	1		3		
Weeks, Cornelas	2	3	1	1	1
Mason, William	1		2		
Wright, Elizabeth			2		
Scott, Adam	2		3		2
MCollah, John	1	1	3	1	5
Murray, James	1		2		
Dudley, Thomas	3	1			9
Javanson, Andrew	1	1	1		4
Pitts, Mary			1		8
Parks, William	1		2		9
Nalms, Martha	1	1	1	4	9
Swift, Epram	3		4		

WILMINGTON DISTRICT, ONSLOW COUNTY—Continued.

NAME OF HEAD OF FAMILY.	Free white males of 16 years and upward, including heads of families.	Free white males under 16 years.	Free white females, including heads of families.	All other free persons.	Slaves.
Hott, Elizabeth	1		1		5
Gabriel, Nathaniel	1	1	3		
Bell, Eden	3	2	2		
Villard, Gabriel	1				1
Newbowl, John	1	1	4		
Hellen, William	2		2		1
Noble, William	1		1		
Hewit, Polley		1	3		
Newbowl, Polley			1		
Pew, Robert	1	1	2		
Gibson, Thomas	2	6	3		
Pitts, Rigdon	1	1	2		9
Taylor, Moses	1	2	5		
Gillet, John	1				
Chancy, Abel	2	3	4		
Loyd, Peggy		2	2		
Cummings, Sarah			1		
Jones, Ezekiah	1	2	4		
Row, Christopher	1	1	1		
Ward, John	3	3	3		
Rigs, John	1	4	3		
Burk, Rebeca			4		
Morris, Thomas	2		2		
Tewday, Jesse	1		3		
Chelley, Joseph	1		2		
Thomson, John	1	3	4		2
Wood, James	1	1	2		
Baety, Mrs	2	1	3		
Shaw, Francis	1	1	2		
Williams, John	1	2	2		
Simmons, Daniel	1	1	2		
Williams, Jacob	1				4
Baety, Benjamin	1		3		
Knights, Mr	1	4	4		7
Gage, Robert	1	1	6		
Gellet, Phillana		4	3		5
James, Thomas	1	2	3		
Gibson, William	2	4	3		
Smith, Thomas	2	1	3		3
Venters, Malaka	1		3		
Venters, Francis	1	2	3		
Morris, Sylvia			1	1	
Justice, Laban	1	3	4		
Perry, John	1	1	4		
Walton, Thomas	2	2	2		
Sinclair, Robert	1		2		
Coston, Francis	2		1		
Walton, John	1	1	5		
Howard, John	3		2		
Coston, John	1	4	3		
Hunt, Nesse	2	2	5		
King, Elizabeth			3		8
Fulward, Andrew	3		1		3
Hammons, Martha	1	2	4		
Hanket, John	1	1	4		
Hibs, Wilkin	1	2	3		4
Mitchel, Barsheba			5		
Caroch, John Henry	1	2	1		
Scott, Obed	1	2	2		
Ward, Edward	1		3		4
Heart, Absolom	1		2		
Howard, William	1	4	2		
Colomn, George	1	4	3		
Colomn, William	1	3	2		
Edwards, Josiah	1	3	5		8
Dewral, Mary			2		
Proctor, Shadarick	1	3	3		
Gerganus, Jesse	2	3	7		
Shepherd, Wiliby	1		1		
Hecks, John	1	4	1		7
Murray, Jonathan	2	1	3		7
Landing, James	1	1	3		
Landing, William	4	1	3		
Haws, John, Senr	1	1	2		1
Gurganus, Barbary	1	2	3		
Loyed, Thomas	1		2		
Heidleburg, Samuel	1	1	1		2
Loyed, Susanna	1		3		
Loyed, Daniel	1		1		
Shepherd, John, Senr	1	2	3		4
Shepherd, George, Junr	4	4	3		5
Shepherd, John, Junr	1	1	1		1
Shepherd, Smith	1	1	2		
Loyed, Nancy			2		
Thomson, Mary	2		2		
Thomson, Absolom	1		2		
Johnson, Sarah			5		
Haws, John, Junr	1		1		
Giddins, Abraham	1	1	4		1
Boardsman, Jonathan	1	1	3		5
Aman, John	1	2	4		
Hedgepeth, Dude	1	1	2		
Bell, William	1				
Ross, Rheuben	1	1	4		
Farrah, Benjamin	1	2	1		
Clark, John	2		1		1
Britton, John	1		1		
Bender, Daniel	1	1	3		15
Askins, Joseph	1	4	1		
Costen, Robert	1	2	2		
Venters, Mrs			5		
Howard, William	2	2	5		
Clark, Rheuben	1				
Jemboy				1	6
Dry, Virgil				1	5
Freeman, Samuel				8	
Freeman, Roger				7	
Perry, Colop				4	
Perry, Charles				11	
Davis, Deck				7	
Milley				4	
Sweet, James				6	
Hays, Jacob				6	
Cumbo, Rheuben				4	
Cumbo, Stephen				4	
Cumbo, Solomon				6	
Jones, Stephen				5	

INDEX.[1]

[1] No attempt has been made in this publication to correct mistakes in spelling made by the assistant marshals, and the names have been reproduced as they appear upon the census schedules.

Mabry, Sarah, 165.
McAamd, Joseph, 31.
McAbe, Ann, 127.
McAbe, James, 127.
McAdam, Sam'l, 95.
McAdams, Hugh, 94.
McAdams, James, 94.
McAdams, John, 94.
McAdams, Jno, 108.
McAdams, Jno, 117.
McAdams, Joseph, 94.
McAdams, Tho', 119.
McAdaw, James, 153.
McAdoe, William, 156.
McAdow, Davd, 153.
McAdow, James, 153.
McAdow, James, 153.
McAdow, John, 154.
McAfee, Jas., 115.
Macafee, John, 144.
Macafee Malcom, 165.
McAfee, Wm., 109.
McAffee, William, 183.
McAfity, James, 133.
McAlep, Archibald, 131.
McAlester, Archibald, 189.
McAlester, James, 189.
McAllester, Alexr, 39.
McAllester, Angus, 46.
McAllester, Charles, 194.
McAllester, Coll., 39.
McAllester, John, 46.
McAllester, Malcolm, 48.
McAllister, Alexr, 39.
McAllister, Ann, 39.
McAllister, Jesse, 169.
McAllum, Duncan, 40.
McAllum, Duncan, 46.
McAllum, Duncan, 50.
McAllum, Ever, 49.
McAlpin, Alexr, 47.
McAlpin, Angus, 40.
McAlpin, John, 40.
McAlpin, Malcolm, 48.
McAlpin, Margaret, 130.
McAlpin, Niel, 40.
McAlpin, Niel, 50.
McAlpin, Robert, 135.
Mcalup, Hugh, 181.
Mcalup, Hugh, 181.
McAmus, Eli, 86.
Mcanally, Charles, 180.
Mcanally, Jesse, 180.
Mcanally, John, 180.
Mcarter, Aaron, 178.
McArthur, Alexr, 42.
McArthur, Alexr, 48.
McArthur, Daniel, 39.
McArthur, James, 40.
McArthur, John, 44.
McArthur, John, 48.
McArthur, John, 50.
McArthur, Peter, 39.
McArthur, Peter, 42.
McArthur, Peter, 49.
McArtney, Michael, 151.
McAskill, Allen, 45.
McAskill, Allen, 46.
McAskill, Christian, 45.
McAskill, Daniel, 35.
McAskill, Daniel, 46.
McAskiell, Daniel, 46.
McAskiell, Daniel, 46.
McAskill, Findley, 45.
M Askill, Findley, 45.
McAskill, John, 46.
McAskill, John, 46.
McAskill, Kennith, 45.
McAskill, Malcolm, 46.
McAuley, Angus, 44.
McAuley, Auley, 40.
McAuley, Evan, 47.
McAuley, James, 40.
McAuley, John, 44.
McAuley, John, Sr, 43.
McAuley, Malcolm, 46.
McAuley, Murdock, 40.
McAuley, Murdock, 43.
McAuley, Murdock, 44.
McAuley, Rovey, 47.
McAuley, William, 43.
McAuslan, Alexander, 130.
McAuslan, Duncan, 42.
Macay, Alex., 116.
Macay, David, 116.
Macay, Davd, 116.
Macay, Hugh, 108.
Macay, James, 176.
Macay, Patrick, 123.
Macay, Saml., 110.
Macay, Spence, 176.
Macay, Thos, 110.
Macay, Wm, 109.
Macbay, Abel, 134.
McBearn, William, 137.
McBoyd, Patrick, 164.
McBrian, Wm, 117.
McBride, Alexr, 44.
McBride, Angus, 48.
McBride, Archd, 42.
McBride, Archd, 48.
McBride, Archd, 48.
McBride, David, 106.
McBride, Duncan, 46.
McBride, Duncan, 48.
McBride, Elisha, 17.
McBride, Francis, 167.
McBride, Isaiah, 152.
McBride, Isaiah, 167.
McBride, Jas., 121.
McBride, John, 48.
McBride, John, 153.
McBride, John, 154.
McBride, John, 154.
McBride, John, 168.
McBride, John, 182.
McBride, Jno, Senr, 154.
McBride, John, Senr, 154.
McBride, Minassith, 186.
Mcbride, William, 156.
McBride, William, 186.
McBriers, Sam., 119.
McBroom, Andrew, 93.
McBroom, James, 178.
McBryan, John, 171.
McBune, Daniel, 84.
McCabb, James, 160.
McCabben, Mightry, 163.
McCabe, Jno, 115.
McCaddin, Wm, 152.
McCafferty, James, 131.
McCahern (Widow), 162.
McCain, Alexander, 153.
McCain, Andw, 163.
McCain, Ann, 57.
McCain, Hance, 163.
McCain, Hanie, 153.
McCain, Hugh, 163.
McCain, John, 163.
McCain, John, 163.
McCain, Thomas, Junr, 163.
McCain, William, 163.
McCairny, Francis, 155.
McCalib, Jas, 168.
McCalin, Wm, 112.
McCalister, Hutor, 188.
McCalister, Jas., 115.
McCalister (Widow), 115.
McCall, Archd, 42.
McCall, Francis, 163.
McCall, James, 159.
McCall, William, 163.
McCaller, Archd, 40.
McCalley, Jno, 115.
McCalley, Joseph, 65.
McCallister, Ezekeil, 168.
McCallister, John, 159.
McCallister, Robert, 34.
McCallister, William, 167.
McCallock, Thos, 154.
McCallon, Jas., 115.
McCallum, Duncan, 44.
McCallum, Edward, 165.
McCallum, Jas, 167.
McCallum, James, 184.
McCallum, John, 163.
McCallum, John, 165.
McCallum, John, 184.
McCallum, Jonathan, 93.
McCallum, Thomas, 163.
McCallum, Thomas, 184.
McCalman, John, 46.
McCalop, Archibald, 194.
McCalop, Catherine, 188.
McCammon, Charles, 162.
McCammon, John, 163.
McCandeless, John, 159.
McCane, Jno, 116.
McCann, Hugh, 191.
McCann, John, 176.
McCann, William, 191.
McCann, William, 192.
McCants, William, 42.
McCarn, Archd, 47.
McCarn, Daniel, 47.
McCarne, Daniel, 46.
McCarow, Archer, 183.
McCarrol, James, 168.
McCarrol, John, 168.
McCartey, Cornl., 113.
McCartey, Jos, 124.
McCartey, Zacheriah, 171.
McCarthy, Archibald, 139.
McCarthy, Timothy, 135.
McCartie, John, 66.
McCartney, Lewis, 176.
McCartney, Thomas, 176.
McCarty, Timothy, 167.
McCarver, Jas., 113.
McCarver, Jas., 115.
McCarver, Jno, 113.
McCarver, John, 186.
McCarver, Joshua, 186.
McCasell, Daniel, 46.
McCaskey, Daniel, 156.
McCaskill, Angus, 43.
McCaskill, Hurdly, 165.
McCasky, Thos, 116.
McCasland, Robt., 112.
McCaslin, Catey, 86.
McCaslin, James, 86.
McCaslin, James, 86.
McCate, ——, 14.
McCathe, Ebednego, 171.
McCauley, And'w, 95.
McCauley, Daniel, 164.
McCauley, John, 82.
McCauley, John, 94.
McCauley, Joseph, 93.
McCauley, Matthew, 97.
McCauley, Wm., 94.
McCauley, Wm., 97.
McCaulis, Jane, 93.
McCaulis, John, 93.
McCauslin, James, 163.
McCay, Michael, 159.
McCinley, Charles, 162.
McCinley, David, 162.
McCinnan, Christopher, 165.
McCinny, Sam., 124.
McClachey, John, 156.
McClaig, John, 152.
McClain, Allen, 162.
McClain, Daniel, 147.
McClain, Donald, 156.
McClain, Duncan, 165.
McClain, Grace, 138.
McClain, James, 156.
McClain, John, 154.
McClain, John, 156.
McClain, John, 172.
McClain, John, 178.
McClain, John, Junr, 154.
McClain, John, Senr, 154.
McClain, Joseph, 154.
McClain, Joseph, 154.
McClain, Joseph, 159.
McClain, Joseph, 166.
McClain, Moses, 152.
McClain, Peter, 188.
McClain, Thomas, 154.
McClain, Thomas, 167.
McClain, William, 172.
McClam, Solomon, 51.
McClammy, Luke, 194.
McClammy, Mark, 194.
McClan, William, 51.
McClanahan, John, 64.
McClanahan, Mary, 31.
McClanahan, William, 66.
McClandon, Isbal, 165.
McClane, Jno, 118.
McClane, Robert, 98.
McClannan, James, 21.
McClannan, John, 21.
McClannen, John, 77.
McClannon, Alexander, 165.
McClannon, Edward, 165.
McClanny, John, 126.
McClaran, Alexander, 169.
McClaren, John, 187.
McClarey, Michael, 158.
McClarey, Robert, 158.
McClarey, Wm, 158.
McClarney, Henry, 79.
McClarney, Paul, 79.
McClartey, Alexander, 160.
McClartey, Alexr, 162.
McClartey, Archabeld, 160.
McClary, Keziah, 32.
McClary (Widow), 159.
McClathey, Hamilton, 156.
McClathey, John, 156.
McClay, Colin, 165.
McClease, John, 33.
McClellan, Robert, 169.
McClellan, William, 169.
McClelland, John, 157.
McClelland, John, 158.
McClelland, John, 162.
McClelland, Rebeca, 162.
McClelland, William, 156.
McClemore, John, 165.
McClemore, Stamley, 165.
McClendon, Benjamin, 35.
McClendon, Dennis, 36.
McClendon, Dennis, Sr, 37.
McClendon, Duncan, 49.
McClendon, Ezekiel, 35.
McClendon, Frederick, 37.
McClendon, James, 49.
McClendon, James, 51.
McClendon, James, 53.
McClendon, Jesse, 51.
McClendon, Jesse, 54.
McClendon, Jesse, 165.
McClendon, Samford, 54.
McClendon, Simon, 53.
McClendon, Thomas, 54.
McClendon, Thomas, 165.
McClennahan, Andrew, 174.
McClennahan, Reuben, 160.
McClennan, Thomas, 186.
McClenny, James, 31.
McClenny, James, 142.
McClenny, Ruth, 18.
McClever, Jno, 113.
McClintock, John, 152.
McClintock, John, 153.
McClisky, Jno, 106.
McClisten, Daniel, 165.
McClone, Hepsiber, 14.
McCloskey, Ed., 95.
McCloud, Christian, 165.
McCloud, Daniel, 193.
McCloud, Duncan, 165.
McCloud, Elizabeth, 165.
McCloud, Mary, 165.
McCloud, Norman, 165.
McCloud, Norman, 165.
McCloud, Reuben, 138.
McCloud, Robert, 156.
McCloud, Wm, 124.
McCloud, William, 156.
McCloud, Wm, 183.
McCloud, William, Jur, 156.
McClure, Andw, 106.
McClure, Francis, 106.
McClure, Henry, 93.
McClure, Jno, 116.
McClure, Jno, 116.
McClure, John, Jur, 158.
McClure, John, Junr, 160.
McClure, Capt Mathew, 160.
McClure, Moses, Jur, 158.
McClure, Moses (Thos Son), 160.
McClure, Rd., 116.
McClure, Thomas, Jur, 158.
McClure, Thos, Senr, 159.
McClure (Widw), 158.
McClure, William, 160.
McClury, Andrew, 95.
McCoffee, James, 145.
McColl, Alexr, 47.
McColl, Daniel, 40.
McColl, Daniel, 47.
McColl, Daniel, Jr, 47.
McColl, Daniel, Sr, 47.
McColl, Donald, 45.
McColl, Donald, 47.
McColl, Dugal, 40.
McColl, Dugal, 45.
McColl, Duncan, 45.
McColl, Duncan, 47.
McColl, Duncan, 45.
McColl, Duncan, 47.
McColl, Hugh, 42.
McColl, Hugh, 46.
McColl, John, 45.
McColl, John, 49.
McColl, Niel, 40.
McColl, Paul, 45.
McCollah, Alexander, 194.
McCollah, George, 193.
McCollah, John, 190.
M'Collah, John, 196.
McCollah, Thomas, 191.
McCollister, James, 154.
McCollister, John, 168.
McCollister, Sutton, 168.
McCollom, Harvey, 94.
McCollom, William, 168.
McCollum, Andw, 178.
McCollum, Duncan, Jr, 50.
McCollum, Isaac, 98.
McCollum, James, 98.
McCollum, James, 156.
McCollum, John, 79.
McCollum, Jonathan, 98.
McCollum, Malcom, 85.
McCollum, Malcom, 163.
McCollum, Stephen, 98.
McColm, Rachel, 188.
McColom, Daniel, 187.
McColskee, Neal, 187.
McColski, James, 187.
McCombs, Alexander, 64.
McCombs, James, 163.
McCombs, Robt., 115.
McCombs, Robt., 115.
McCombs, Samuel, 159.
MacCone, Jesse, 74.
McCong, Thomas, 160.
McConkey, Robert, 186.
McConnahey, Hugh, 178.
McConnahey, James, 178.
McConnahey, Joseph, 178.
McConnahey, Sampson, 178.
McConnell, Alexander, 157.
McConnell, Benjamin, 155.
McConnell, Daniel, 174.
McConnell, John, 157.
McConnell, John, Jur, 155.
McConnell, John, Ser, 155.
McConnell, William, 157.
McCool, Archibald, 94.
McCord, James, 157.
McCord, John, 158.
McCord, Robert, 158.
McCorkle, Alexander, Jur, 178.
McCorkle, Alexander, Sr, 178.
McCorkle, Archabeld, 163.
McCorkle, Frank, 114.
McCorkle, James, 163.
McCorkle, John, 163.
McCorkle, John, 178.
McCorkle, Owen, 163.
McCorkle, Samuel, 178.
McCorkle, Thomas, 160.
McCormack, William, 158.
McCormic, And'w, 111.
McCormick, Archd, 49.
McCormick, Duncan, 49.
McCormick, Gilbert, 49.
McCormick, Hugh, 45.
McCormick, Hugh, 46.
McCormick, John, 48.
McCormick, Robert, 158.
McCorvey, Niel, 48.
McCoskill, Mary, 165.
McCown, Margt, 160.
McCown, Mathew, 187.
McCown, Robert, 187.
McCown, William, 187.
McCoy, Alexander, 156.
McCoy, Alexander, 156.
McCoy, Alexander, 156.
McCoy, Alexander, 156.
McCoy, Beaty, 160.
McCoy, Bridget, 16.
McCoy, Daniel, 156.
McCoy, Daniel, 156.
McCoy, Daniel, Jur, 156.
McCoy, Daniel (S. M.), 156.
McCoy, George, 156.
McCoy, George, 156.
McCoy, George, 156.
McCoy, George (S. M.), 156.
McCoy, James, 16.
McCoy, James, 156.
McCoy, Joel, 16.
McCoy, John, 16.
McCoy, John, 21.
McCoy, John, 162.
McCoy, Joshua, 16.
McCoy, Kesiah, 16.
McCoy, Malachi, 16.
McCoy, Malachi, 28.
McCoy, Mary, 16.
McCoy, Nail, 156.
McCoy, Nancy, 16.
McCoy, Nathan, 16.
McCoy, Robert, 156.
McCoy, Robert, 156.
McCoy, Thomas, 156.
McCoy (Widow), 156.
McCoy, William, 16.
McCoy, William, 21.
McCoy, William, 156.
McCoy, William, 156.
McCoy, William, 176.
McCoye, Ann, 136.
McCoye, William, 136.
McCracken, James, 160.
McCracken, Jeremiah, 92.
McCracken, John, 93.
McCracken, John, 162.
McCracken, Robt., 95.
McCracken, Samuel, 94.
McCracken, Samuel, 169.
McCracken, Thomas, 95.
McCracken, Wm, 86.
McCrackin, Jane, 153.
McCracon, David, 109.
McCracon, Jno, 117.
McCracon, Quilla, 106.
McCrakin, James, 176.
McCraney, Kason, 99.
McCrary, Boyd, 173.
McCrary, Hugh, 173.
McCrary, James, 157.
McCrary, John, 173.
McCrary, Jos, 109.
McCrary (Widow), 173.
McCrary, William, 177.
McCraven, John, Jur, 163.
McCraw, Benjamin, 186.
McCraw, Francis, 186.
McCraw, Jacob, 186.
McCraw, William, 186.
McCrawley, John, 65.
McCray, Alexander, 165.
McCray, William, 161.
McCree, Griffeth, 189.
McCree, Mrs. Margiret, 186.
McCree, Samuel, 186.
McCree, William, 187.
McCreman, Peter, 40.
McCremon, Archd, 49.
McCremon, Donald, 49.
McCremon, Malcolm, 43.
McCremon, Norman, 43.
McCremon, Sarah, 40.
McCrery, Samuel, 155.
McCrohon, Mary, 134.
McCrorey, Hugh, 163.
McCrum, Rachel, 158.
McCubbin, Jas, 167.
McCubbin, John, 167.
McCubbin, Nicholas, 167.
McCuestion, Moses, 152.
McCuestion, Thomas, 153.
McCuistion, Ann, 153.
McCuistion, Thomas, 153.
McCuiston, James, 153.
McCuiston, Walter, 152.
McCullen, Bryan, 149.
McCullen, John, Jr, 53.
McCullen, John, Sr, 53.
McCullen, Lewis, 53.
McCuller, John, 142.
McCullers, John, 142.
McCullers, Matthew, 105.
McCulloch, Alexander, 64.
McCulloch, Benjamin, 64.
McCulloch, James, 93.
McCulloch, James, 156.
McCulloch, James, 171.
McCulloch, James, 174.
McCulloch, John, 93.
McCulloch, John, 160.
McCulloch, John, 164.
McCulloch, Joseph, 169.
McCulloch, Robt., 93.
McCulloch, Robt., 93.

Rice, Roger, 103.
Rice, Thomas, 82.
Rice, Thos., 91.
Rice, Thomas, 153.
Rice, William, 14.
Rice, William, 82.
Rice, Wm, 103.
Rice, Wm, 110.
Rice, Wm, 113.
Rice, Wm, 122.
Rice, William, 153.
Rice, William, 155.
Rice, William, 166.
Rich, Benjamin, 101.
Rich, Henry, 170.
Rich, Jacob, 95.
Rich, Jacob, 104.
Rich, James, 163.
Rich, James, Senr, 163.
Rich, John, 74.
Rich, John, 172.
Rich, John, Jr, 101.
Rich, John, Junr, 163.
Rich, John, Ser, 101.
Rich, Joseph, 52.
Rich, Joseph, 101.
Rich, Joshua, 52.
Rich, Lott, 51.
Rich, Mary, 104.
Rich, Peter, 101.
Rich, Rebecca, 131.
Rich, Samuel, 100.
Rich, Thos., 95.
Rich, Thomas, 172.
Rich, Timothey, 104.
Richard, Henry, 139.
Richard, Jacob, 139.
Richard, John, 139.
Richard, Mary, 139.
Richard, Thomas, 139.
Richard, William, 60.
Richards, Adam, 139.
Richards, Annanias, 153.
Richards, Benj., 60.
Richards, Catherina, 174.
Richards, Elizabeth, 126.
Richards, Geo., 60.
Richards, Isaac, 99.
Richards, Jesse, 60.
Richards, John, 54.
Richards, John, 60.
Richards, John, 73.
Richards, Jno, 114.
Richards, Jno, 115.
Richards, John, 144.
Richards, John, 184.
Richards, John, 190.
Richards, Joshua, 60.
Richards, Leonard, 184.
Richards, Major, 60.
Richards, Morris, 40.
Richards, Morriss, 42.
Richards, Nicholas, 190.
Richards, Nicholas, 192.
Richards, Ralph, 126.
Richards, Richard, 64.
Richards, Richard, 139.
Richards, Solomon, 147.
Richards, Thomas, 126.
Richards, Ulerigh, 174.
Richards, William, 31.
Richards, William, 60.
Richards, William, 73.
Richards, William, 99.
Richards, William, 184.
Richardson, Andrew, 134.
Richardson, Applewhite, 141.
Richardson, Benjamin, 63.
Richardson, Chas., 116.
Richardson, Charles, 176.
Richardson, Daniel, 29.
Richardson, Edward, 163.
Richardson, Edward, 168.
Richardson, Elizabeth, 188.
Richardson, George, 87.
Richardson, Hugh, 17.
Richardson, Isaac, 86.
Richardson, James, 79.
Richardson, James, 120.
Richardson, John, 29.
Richardson, John, 87.
Richardson, John, 100.
Richardson, John, 105.
Richardson, John, 188.
Richardson, John, 141.
Richardson, Joseph, Esqr, 29.
Richardson, Labias, 29.
Richardson, Laurence, 79.
Richardson, Lawrne, 78.
Richardson, Peter, 98.
Richardson, Richard, 29.
Richardson, Richard, 137.
Richardson, Robert, 188.
Richardson, Robison, 175.
Richardson, Sam., 120.
Richardson, Sarah, 16.
Richardson, Stephen, 29.
Richardson, Thomas, 29.
Richardson, Thomas, 71.
Richardson, Thomas, 79.
Richardson, Thos, 87.
Richardson, Thomas, 187.
Richardson, William, 29.
Richardson, Wm, 60.
Richardson, William, 63.
Richardson, William, 64.
Richardson, William, 71.
Richardson, William, 100.
Richardson, William, 133.
Richardson, William, 141.
Richardson, Wm, Jr, 71.
Richason, Hannah, 32.
Richer, Jas, 169.
Richeson, Alex., 122.
Richeson, Benjamin, 179.
Richeson, David, 43.
Richeson, Drury, 42.
Richeson, John, 37.
Richeson, Jno, 123.
Richeson, Stephen, 43.
Richeson, William, 35.
Richeson, William, 42.
Richey, David, 159.
Richey, Henry, 161.
Richey, Jacob, 161.
Richey, John, 42.
Richey, John, 159.
Richey, John, 169.
Richison, Danl., 123.
Richison, Jno, 114.
Richmon, James, 80.
Richmond, Jacob W., 133.
Richmond, John, 80.
Richmond, Mathew, 80.
Richmond, William, 80.
Rickard, Casper, 172.
Rickard, Jacob, 172.
Rickard, John, 172.
Rickard, Leonard, 172.
Rickerson, Jesse, 145.
Rickets, John, 128.
Rickett, Edward, 94.
Ricketts, Anthony, 96.
Ricketts, John, 35.
Ricketts, John, 37.
Ricketts, Moses, 37.
Ricketts, William, 36.
Rickles, John, 169.
Rickman, Mark, 62.
Rickman, Nathan, 62.
Rickmon, John, 88.
Ricks, Abram, 71.
Ricks, Betty, 76.
Ricks, Dempsey, 75.
Ricks, Isaac, 54.
Ricks, Isaac, 63.
Ricks, Jacob, 71.
Ricks, Jacob, 74.
Ricks, James, 55.
Ricks, Joel, 71.
Ricks, Mary, 71.
Ricks, Priscilla, 71.
Ricks, Robt. *See* Pulley, William, for Robt. Ricks, 62.
Ricks, Sarah, 71.
Ricks, William, 60.
Ricks, Wm, 71.
Ricks, William, 75.
Ricks, William, Jr, 71.
Riddick, Abraham, 22.
Riddick, Christopher, 23.
Riddick, Jobe, 23.
Riddick, John, 23.
Riddick, Joseph, 23.
Riddick, Leah, 24.
Riddick, Micajah, Junr, 24.
Riddick, Micajah, Senr, 24.
Riddick, Nathaniel, 24.
Riddick, Robert, 24.
Riddick, Ruben, 24.
Riddish, John, 103.
Ridditt, Constant, 14.
Ridditt, Job, 14.
Ridditt, Lodwick, 14.
Riddle, Cato, 85.
Riddle, James, 43.
Riddle, John, 84.
Riddle, John, 175.
Riddle, Julus, 85.
Riddle, Ricd, 84.
Riddle, Stephen, 175.
Riddle, Thos, 85.
Riddle, Tyre, 178.
Riddle, Wm, 84.
Riden, Jno, 114.
Ridenaur, Nicholas, 162.
Ridens, James, 116.
Rider, Adam 172.
Rider, Frederick, 112.
Rider, Nancey, 26.
Ridge, Godfrey, 100.
Ridge, Thomas, 182.
Ridge William, 100.
Ridgin, Frederick, 150.
Ridgin, William, 150.
Ridgway, Phillip, 175.
Ridicil, Witr, 114.
Riding, Benjamin, 130.
Ridins, John, 183.
Ridle, James, 171.
Ridle, John, 179.
Ridle, Randolph, 179.
Ridley, Bromfield, 91.
Ridley, Thomas, 71.
Ridley, Timothy, 26.
Ridly, Wm, 117.
Riech, Mathew, 182.
Riers, David 157.
Rieves, Courtney, 132.
Rieves, Jesse, 149.
Rieves, John, 149.
Rieves, Joseph, 135.
Rieves, Peter, 146.
Rieves, William, 149.
Riff, Daniel, 135.
Rifle, Elizabeth, 16.
Rifle, Rebecca, 16.
Rigbey, James, 84.
Rigbey, James, 104.
Rigbey, John, 98.
Rigby, Hugh, 133.
Rigby, Thomas, 133.
Rigdon, Beaver, 86.
Rigdon, Enoch, 113.
Rigey, George, 161.
Riggan, Charles, 78.
Riggan, Francis, 78.
Riggan, Jacob, 78.
Riggan, Joel, 78.
Riggan, John, 78.
Riggan, Mary, 78.
Riggan, William, 78.
Riggan, William, 78.
Riggans, James, 97.
Riggell, Mark, 45.
Riggen, Chas., 114.
Riggen, John, 187.
Riggen, Jonathan, 75.
Riggen, Powell, 96.
Rigging, Darbey, 147.
Rigging, Thomas, 14.
Riggins, Jemimiah, 32.
Riggs, Abraham, 17.
Riggs, Benjamin, 128.
Riggs, David, 17.
Riggs, David, 134.
Riggs, David, 183.
Riggs Geo., Sr., 96.
Riggs, Hiram, 183.
Riggs, Isaac, 16.
Riggs, Isaac, 17.
Riggs, Isaac, 128.
Riggs, Isaac, Junr, 16.
Riggs, James, 97.
Riggs, James, 97.
Riggs, Jemima, 125.
Riggs, Jesse, 129.
Riggs, John, 97.
Riggs, John, 125.
Riggs, Mary, 134.
Riggs, Noah, 16.
Riggs, Sam'l, 97.
Riggs, Samuel 183.
Riggs, Shadrack, 134.
Riggs, Zachariah, 91.
Riggs, Zadock, 183.
Right, Edward, 166.
Right, Isaac, 146.
Right, Joseph, 85.
Right, Josiah, 142.
Right, Peter, 99.
Right, Simon, 87.
Righton, William, 18.
Rights, John, 181.
Rightsman, Mary, 99.
Rigs, James, 125.
Rigs, John, 197.
Rigs, Miller, 134.
Rigs, Sarah, 134.
Rigs, Timothy, 119.
Rigsbee, Jesse, 97.
Rigsbee, William, 97.
Rigsbey, Archabell, 104.
Rigsbey, Federick, 103.
Rigsbey, Luke, 88.
Rigsbey, Luke, 88.
Rigsbey, Thomas, 162.
Rigsby, James, 104.
Rigsby, John, 104.
Rigsby, John, 192.
Rigsby, William, 190.
Riley, Ann, 172.
Riley, Edward, 185.
Riley, George, 172.
Riley, Jacob, 94.
Riley, James, 96.
Riley, James, 157.
Riley, James, 172.
Riley, James, 185.
Riley, Jeremiah, 184.
Riley, John, 84.
Riley, John, 87.
Riley, John, 159.
Riley, John, 194.
Riley, John, Ser, 103.
Riley, John (L. R.), 94.
Riley, Nincan, 185.
Riley, Nincan, Junr, 185.
Riley, William, 26.
Riley, William, 42.
Riley, Wm., 96.
Riley, Wm. (L. R.), 94.
Rilley, John, Jr., 103.
Rimer, David, 177.
Rimer, Nicholas, 177.
Rimmer, James, 82.
Rindal, Joseph, 26.
Rine, Jacob, 112.
Rine, Jacob, 113.
Rine, Jacob, 114.
Rine, Michl., 113.
Rine, Peter, 113.
Rine, Phil., 113.
Rineger, George, 184.
Rineger, George, Junr, 184.
Rinehart, David, 95.
Rinehart, Jacob, 112.
Rinehart, Jacob, Jr, 112.
Rinehast, Christe, 112.
Rinehot, Conrod, 112.
Ring, Francis, 111.
Ring, James, 180.
Ring, John, 64.
Ring, John, 66.
Ring, John, 180.
Ring, Martin, 177.
Ring, Martin, 180.
Ring, Michael, 177.
Ring, Robert, 67.
Ring, Thomas, 180.
Ringold, James, 147.
Ringold, Sarah, 147.
Ringstaff, Adam, 40.
Ringstaff, Conrad, 93.
Rinhart (Widow), 162.
Rinkard, George, 175.
Rion, Derby, 183.
Rion, Mitchel, 79.
Ripley, Ann, 29.
Ripley, William, 129.
Ripple, Henry, 174.
Rippy, John, 95.
Rippy, Mathew, 95.
Rippy, Thos., 94.
Risbey, Langley, 127.
Risbey, Richard, 127.
Risbey, Robert, 127.
Risbey, Thomas, 127.
Risbey, Thomas, 127.
Risen, James, 187.
Riston, Ricd, 84.
Ritcheson, Elizabeth, 40.
Ritchie, James, 41.
Ritchy, James, 110.
Rite, Moses, 116.
Ritter, Jesse, 43.
Ritter, John, 43.
Ritter, Thomas, 43.
Rittey, James, 154.
Rivard, Lion, 85.
Rivel, Matthew, 26.
Rivel, Silis, 26.
Rivenback, Simon, 191.
Rivenbark, John, 192.
Rivenbark, Philip, 194.
Rivers, Richard, 142.
Rivers, Wm, 105.
Rives, Hannah, 103.
Rives, Hardy, 103.
Rives, John, 72.
Rives, John, 94.
Rives, Jonathan, 106.
Rives, William, 106.
Rives, William, Jur, 106.
Rivets, Mary, 25.
Rivis, Lan., 91.
Rix, Benjamin, 147.
Rix, Edmund, 145.
Rix, James, 155.
Rix, Lucy, 146.
Roach, Charles, 133.
Roach, James, 92.
Roach, James, 134.
Roach, James, 148.
Roach, James, 168.
Roach, James, 189.
Roach, John, 51.
Roach, John, 83.
Roach, John, 195.
Roach, Lewis, 93.
Roach, Sarah, 53.
Roach, Sarcenet, 151.
Roach, Solomon, 151.
Roach, Thomas, 170.
Roach, William, 168.
Roach, William, 194.
Roades, Richard, 97.
Roads, Aquilla, 96.
Roads, Thos., 96.
Roads, William, 74.
Roads, Wm., 96.
Roads, William, 148.
Roam, Jacob, 112.
Roan, James, 81.
Roan, Jesse, 64.
Roan, John, 64.
Roan, John, 103.
Roan, Lewis, 65.
Roan, Saml, 188.
Roan, William, 195.
Roany, Jno, 113.
Roark, James, 97.
Roark, John, 184.
Roark, John, Junr, 184.
Roark, Timothy, 178.
Robards, John, 91.
Robason, Daniel, 67.
Robason, David, 67.
Robason, David, 67.
Robason, Hardy, 68.
Robason, Henry, 69.
Robason, James, 67.
Robason, James, 67.
Robason, James, 67.
Robason, John, 67.
Robason, John, 67.
Robason, John, Senr, 67.
Robason, Joshua, 67.
Robason, Peter, 34.
Robbins, Arthur, 189.
Robbins, Bashford, 22.
Robbins, Benjamin, 189.
Robbins, Christopher, 98.
Robbins, Daniel, 180.
Robbins, Isaac, 101.
Robbins, Jacob, 55.
Robbins, James, 101.
Robbins, Jethro, 187.
Robbins, John, 23.
Robbins, John, 36.
Robbins, John, 55.
Robbins, John, 98.
Robbins, John, 101.
Robbins, John, Junr, 23.
Robbins, Joseph, 100.
Robbins, Joseph, 100.
Robbins, Joshua, 101.
Robbins, Moses, 101.
Robbins, Roland, 57.
Robbins, Sarah, 57.
Robbins, William, 54.
Robbins, William, 57.
Robbins, William, 78.
Robbins, William, 101.
Robbs, Alex'r, 93.
Robenson, Mr, 196.
Robenson, Sarah, 193.
Roberds, Ishmael, 50.
Roberds, John, 186.
Roberds, Oliver, 186.
Roberds, William, 37.
Roberson, Abner, 152.
Roberson, Andrew, 167.
Roberson, David, 14.
Roberson, Edward, 40.
Roberson, Elijah, 95.
Roberson, Jacob, 152.
Roberson, James, 51.
Roberson, James, 81.
Roberson, James, 83.
Roberson, James, 93.
Roberson, James, 95.
Roberson, James, 169.
Roberson, John, 14.
Roberson, John, 40.
Roberson, John, 47.
Roberson, John, 73.
Roberson, John, 83.
Roberson, Joseph, 83.
Roberson, Mark, 40.
Roberson, Michael, 93.
Roberson, Michael, Jr., 93.
Roberson, Nathaniel, 95.
Roberson, Nicholas, 89.
Roberson, Nicholas, 152.
Roberson, Philip, 40.
Roberson, Robert, 89.
Roberson, Thomas, 83.
Roberson, Thos., 95.
Roberson, Tyry, 166.
Roberson, William, 152.
Roberson, William, 167.
Roberson, William, Jur, 167.
Roberson, Wyatt, 73.
Robert, George, 82.
Robert, John, 62.
Robert, William, 190.
Roberts, Abner, 96.
Roberts, Absolam, 81.
Roberts, Aron, 104.
Roberts, Arther, 82.
Roberts, Benjamin, 31.
Roberts, Bob, 179.
Roberts, Britton, 142.
Roberts, Carnie, 171.
Roberts, Charles, 18.
Roberts, Charles, 96.
Roberts, Curtis, 104.
Roberts, Daniel, 82.
Roberts, Duke, 82.
Roberts, Edmon, 104.
Roberts, Edwd., 122.
Roberts, Elias, 73.
Roberts, Eliz., 121.
Roberts, Elizabeth, 167.
Roberts, Esther, 74.
Roberts, Francis, 64.
Roberts, Henry, 175.
Roberts, Holster, 196.
Roberts, Humphrey, 82.
Roberts, Humphrey, 157.
Roberts, Isaac, 89.
Roberts, James, 73.
Roberts, James, 92.
Roberts, James, 92.
Roberts, James, 100.
Roberts, James, 104.
Roberts, Jas., 121.
Roberts, Jas., 121.
Roberts, Jas., 122.
Roberts, James, 186.
Roberts, James, Esqr, 18.
Roberts, James, Jr, 73.
Roberts, Jeremiah, 96.
Roberts, John, 23.

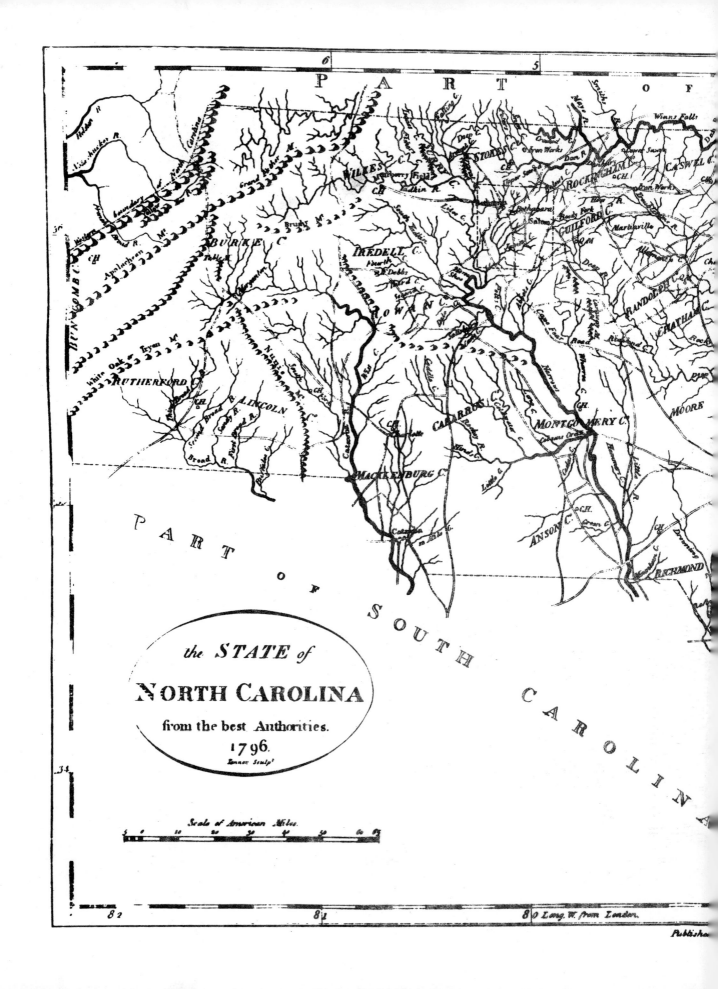

the STATE of
NORTH CAROLINA
from the best Authorities.
1796.
Tanner Sculp.